WILEY PLUS

www.wileyplus.com

WileyPLUS is a research-based online environment for effective teaching and learning.

WileyPLUS builds students' confidence because it takes the guesswork out of studying by providing students with a clear roadmap:

- what to do
- how to do it
- if they did it right

It offers interactive resources along with a complete digital textbook that help students learn more. With *WileyPLUS*, students take more initiative so you'll have greater impact on their achievement in the classroom and beyond.

SOCIAL PSYCHOLOGY

CATHERINE A. SANDERSON
AMHERST COLLEGE

SABA F. SAFDAR
UNIVERSITY OF GUELPH

John Wiley & Sons Canada, Ltd.

Library and Archives Canada Cataloguing in Publication

Sanderson, Catherine Ashley, 1968-
    Social psychology / Catherine A. Sanderson, Saba Safdar. — Canadian ed.
Includes bibliographical references and index.
ISBN 978-0-470-67809-1
    1. Social psychology.   I. Safdar, Saba F.   II. Title.
HM1033.S26 2011   302   C2011-904628-8

Production Credits
Acquisitions Editor: Rodney Burke
Vice President & Publisher: Veronica Visentin
Senior Marketing Manager: Patty Maher
Editorial Manager: Karen Staudinger
Production Manager: Tegan Wallace
Developmental Editor: Andrea Grzybowski
Media Editor: Channade Fenandoe
Editorial Assistant: Laura Hwee
Design: Adrian So
Typesetting: Thomson Digital
Cover Design: Maureen Eide
Cover Image: Brand New Images /Getty Images
Printing and binding: Quad

Printed and bound in the United States.
1 2 3 4 QD 15 14 13 12

WILEY
John Wiley & Sons Canada, Ltd.
6045 Freemont Blvd.
Mississauga, Ontario L5R 4J3

Visit our website at: www.wiley.ca

To Newsha, for being my jewel
and
Rees, for foolishly thinking I am one

ABOUT THE AUTHORS

CATHERINE A. SANDERSON is an Associate Professor of Psychology at Amherst College. She earned her A.B. at Stanford University and her M.S. and Ph.D. at Princeton University. While at Princeton, she received the Psychology Department's First Year Merit Prize, a National Science Foundation Fellowship, and a Dissertation Research Award from the American Psychological Association.

Professor Sanderson's research, which has received funding from the National Institute of Health, is based in social-personality psychology and specifically on issues within close relationships and health-related behaviour, such as the interaction of individuals in close relationships; individuals' accuracy in perceiving others' attitudes and behavior; and why individuals learn more when they receive personally-relevant or "matching" messages. Professor Sanderson is the author of *Slow and Steady Parenting: Active Child-Raising for the Long Haul* as well as a textbook entitled *Health Psychology*. She has served on the editorial boards for *Health Psychology*, the *Journal of Personality and Social Psychology*, and the *Journal of Research in Personality*. In addition, Professor Sanderson writes a "Body Talk" blog for *Psychology Today*.

· ·

SABA F. SAFDAR is an Iranian-born Canadian-educated Associate Professor in the Psychology Department at the University of Guelph in Ontario. She moved to Canada in the 1980s after the Islamic revolution in Iran. She completed her undergraduate honours degree at McMaster University in Hamilton and earned her MA and PhD at York University in Toronto.

Professor Safdar is the Director of the Centre for Cross-Cultural Research at the University of Guelph where she and her students conduct research that lies broadly within the area of cross-cultural psychology. Her research primarily examines the wide range of factors that could help to understand the adaptation processes of immigrants. She studies the influence of the psychological resilience of immigrants, of their beliefs and strategies, and of their ethnic and national identities on their adaptation in a new society. In addition to her research on immigration, she is interested in examining the academic, psychological, and social adaptation processes among international students. She currently studies the relation between the expression of identity and attitudes toward clothing (both ethnic and conventional fashion) among second generation immigrants in Canada.

With her Polish collaborators, Professor Safdar edited *Culture and Gender*, a book which examines the complex interplay of gender identity and psychological adaptation across culture. She is an active member of the International Association of Cross-Cultural Psychology (IACCP), the Canadian Psychological Association (CPA), and a fellow of the International Academy for Intercultural Research. She has served as Chair of the International and Cross-Cultural Section of the CPA (2006–2008). She is also a member of the editorial boards of the *International Journal of Cross-Cultural Psychology*, the *Journal of International and Intercultural Relations*, and the *Journal of Iranian Psychologists*.

PREFACE

THE PURPOSE OF THIS BOOK

Students vary considerably in their backgrounds, interests, experiences, and personal and professional aspirations. This book brings social psychology to all of these students—students who will continue their interest in social psychology in graduate programs; students who will become educators, business people, or health professionals; and students who take this course out of sheer curiosity about social psychology.

Through a combination of a lively and current introduction to social science research, a uniquely accessible approach to thinking scientifically, and online teaching and learning resources that immerse students in social psychology in the world today, this book will help you open students' minds to a world beyond their own experience so that they can better understand themselves and others. Our primary goal is to help students see the many intersections of social psychology in everyday life. An appreciation of the scientific processes behind these connections will enable them to develop the skills to become critical consumers of information in the world around them.

To reach every student, the writing about social psychology must be accessible, the research presented with clarity, and the content stimulating and comprehensive, but not overwhelming. This text is therefore written in a light and engaging style, to appeal to every student—non-majors and majors. Both classic and contemporary research is described in a clear and vivid way, with examples of research studies throughout specifically chosen to be interesting and relevant for the post-secondary student reader.

Students benefit as they see themselves reflected in the discussion of social psychology and are given the opportunity to connect to this discussion and see social psychology through the lens of their daily lives. In addition, the diversity of the student population is mirrored in the evolving and diverse views in the field of social psychology (which has growing research on culture, gender, and neuroscience). The role of culture in social behaviour is incorporated in every chapter of this book, reflecting the growth of research in this field and encouraging cultural awareness in students.

THE CANADIAN EDITION

Social Psychology, Canadian Edition has been updated to reflect the Canadian social psychology landscape. These updates include

- **Expanded coverage of intergroup relations.** Chapter 10, Intergroup Relations, is unique to the Canadian edition. It covers an area whose significance is increasingly recognized in North America and much of the content. The chapter reflects research conducted in Europe and other countries, such as Australia and was added to distinguish between the processes that happen within a group from those that happen between groups. It discusses early crowd theories and recent European research developments focused around social identity theory. In addition, there are sections on intergroup conflicts, strategies for resolving intergroup conflicts, and acculturation of immigrants.
- **Opening stories that reflect either Canadian or international events.** Each opening story was selected to highlight the relevance of a particular topic of social psychology in our social world. Relevant examples and images from arts, sports, and a variety of other current events were also used in each chapter.

- **References to roughly 100 Canadian researchers and studies.** This is an attempt to illustrate the rich and extensive social psychology research that is being conducted in Canada and to familiarize students with these studies.
- **Focus on Gender and Focus on Neuroscience sections updated** with additional and more recent material. New empirical evidence is included in the Research Focus on Gender sections to illustrate the roles of social and cultural factors on gender differences. Furthermore, the links between hormonal and brain activities and social psychological behaviours and attitudes are further developed using Canadian and international studies in the Research Focus on Neuroscience sections of each chapter.
- **Updated connections boxes** (Health, Law, Environment, Business, Education, and Media) in each chapter reflect Canadian, cross-cultural, or important research findings within these topics.
- **Expanded culture discussions.** In each chapter, the influence of culture on socio-psychological behaviour and attitudes has been explored more extensively. The focus has been broadened to include cross-cultural research that examines cultural differences in social behaviour and attitudes from different continents rather than specifically focused on North America.

FEATURES

Social Psychology, Canadian Edition helps students learn to think critically, to apply social psychology to everyday life, and to address the central role of diversity in the student population, the world at large, and even in the field of social psychology. It frames content coverage with five key ideas designed to get students actively participating in the study of social psychology.

- Think Critically
- Make Connections
- Understand the Big Picture
- A Picture Is Worth a Thousand Words
- Culture Matters

These ideas are carefully interwoven throughout the narrative and pedagogy. The Illustrated Book Tour on the following pages provides a guide to the innovative features contributing to Social Psychology's pedagogical plan.

THINK CRITICALLY

Social Psychology, Canadian Edition shows students the many ways that social psychology helps them to think about the world. It provides the tools they need to actively engage in critical thinking and analysis.

- A separate chapter on research methods describes the strengths and weaknesses of different methods, as well as strategies for increasing the validity of research studies.

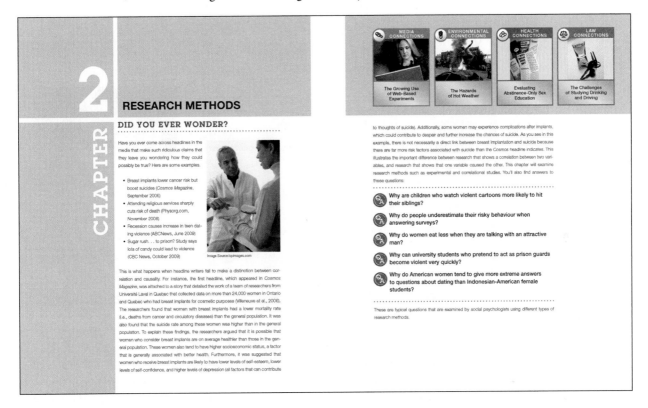

- **Questioning the Research** queries in each chapter prompt students to actively question the results and implications of particular research studies. For example, if you find that university students who come to a workshop entitled "stopping binge drinking" are shown to drink less than their peers, can you be sure that the workshop caused this change? Why or why not? These features encourage critical thinking and facilitate students' awareness of the many ways that social psychology helps them to think about the world.

Questioning the Research:

How can it be that people seem *more* attractive when they're with very attractive people when the contrast effect would lead us to the hypothesis that being with a highly attractive person would make the other person seem *less* attractive by comparison?

MAKE CONNECTIONS

Social Psychology, Canadian Edition helps students learn to apply social psychology to everyday life, and helps students make critical connections to real life as well as to their own lives. Students will be most willing to commit time and energy to a topic when they believe that it is relevant to their own life or to their future career. There is no better way to demonstrate relevance than to ground discussion in the real world.

- **Connections Boxes** apply topics in each chapter to the broader themes of health, law, environment, business, education, and media. These applications are uniquely integrated directly with the topics as they are discussed, instead of being grouped in chapters at the end of the book. This organization responds to the preference expressed by a vast majority of reviewers.

MEDIA CONNECTIONS

Does the Internet Facilitate Intimacy or Inhibit It?

With our increased reliance on the Internet for communication over the last 20 years, researchers have started examining how Internet use influences interpersonal relationships. One concern that has been expressed is that the Internet can discourage real (as opposed to virtual) relationships—people may be spending time online (e.g., "talking" in chat rooms, updating their status, sending emails, shopping) instead of spending time interacting with real people and thereby forming real relationships.

Does time on the Internet lead to gaining relationships? Not really. One survey found that only 22 percent of respondents (all of whom had been using the Internet for two or more years) had made a new friend online—and, as you might imagine, more than 22 percent of people make a new friend in real life during this amount of time. The Internet may also have different effects on different people. For example, some evidence suggests that greater Internet use is associated with positive outcomes, such as increased community involvement and decreased loneliness, for extroverts, but the reverse for introverts

© M4OS Photos / Alamy

(Kraut et al., 2002). Similarly, adolescents who are lonely and socially anxious are more likely to use the Internet to interact with strangers as opposed to close friends (Gross, Juvonen, & Gable, 2002). This means the Internet may be serving as a means to connect with those who are not part of one's daily life, which in turn could impair the formation of normal social relationships.

On the other hand, other research points to the value of the Internet in helping people meet and form relationships (Bargh, McKenna, & Fitzsimons, 2002; McKenna & Bargh, 1998, 2000; McKenna & Green, 2002). For example, McKenna and colleagues
(continued)

- **Rate Yourself Quizzes** in each chapter encourage students to become active participants in the material they are learning and see how their personal results or reactions to the material compare with those discussed in the text. They encourage the reader to make a connection to the topic and to increase awareness of their own thoughts and perceptions.

HOW STRONGLY DO YOU FEEL PASSIONATE LOVE?

The Passionate Love Scale

INSTRUCTIONS: *Rate each item on a scale of 1 (strongly disagree) to 6 (strongly agree).*

1. I sense my body responding when ____ touches me.
2. I would feel deep despair if _____ left me.
3. I possess a powerful attraction for _____ .
4. _____ always seems to be on my mind.
5. I eagerly look for signs indicating _____ 's desire for me.
6. I would rather be with _____ than anyone else.
7. I melt when looking deeply into _____ 's eyes.
8. No one else could love _____ like I do.
9. For me, _____ is the perfect romantic partner.
10. Sometimes I feel I can't control my thoughts; they are obsessively on _____ .

SCORING: Sum up your total score on these 10 items.

INTERPRETATION: This scale measures passionate love, meaning the cognitive, emotional, and behavioural reactions we have toward a person we love (Hatfield & Sprecher, 1986). Higher scores indicate more intense feelings, whereas lower scores indicate less intense feelings.

[RATE YOURSELF 1]

- **In the News** boxes throughout the book make the link between the real world and social psychology theory by highlighting news events that relate to concepts presented in the chapter.

IN THE NEWS

The Challenge of Attribution: On December 6, 1989, 25-year-old Marc Lépine shot 28 people, killing 14 women at the École Polytechnique in Montreal before killing himself. Lépine claimed that he was fighting feminism and that he specifically targeted women. Canadians have debated various interpretations of the events. Many have characterized the massacre as anti-feminist and as a representation of societal violence against women (situational interpretation), while others have pointed to the abuse he experienced in childhood and his mental state (personal interpretation).

THE CANADIAN PRESS/Shaney Komulainen

- **Take Action** queries at the end of each chapter ask students to take an active role in applying social psychology to their own lives.

Take Action!

1. Let's say your roommate is interested in dating a woman in his history class. What three things would you suggest to help him establish a relationship with her?

2. Your aunt and uncle have been married for 30 years. Based on your knowledge of triangular theory, what love components are likely to be highest in their relationship right now?

- **Who's Who in Contemporary Canadian Social Psychology Research** boxes briefly profile one Canadian researcher whose work is either featured or discussed in the chapter. The boxes enable students to become more familiar with the contemporary Canadian social psychology landscape by discussing the research interests and activities of each researcher and, where relevant, providing information about their research lab.

Who's Who in Contemporary Canadian Social Psychology Research

Steven J. Heine is a professor at the University of British Columbia. He received his BA from the University of Alberta and his master's and PhD from the University of British Columbia. In his research, Professor Heine examines psychological processes that are universal and those that are limited to certain cultural groups. He has specifically investigated similarities and differences between Japanese and North Americans on self-enhancing and self-improving motivations. Professor Heine has received many awards, including the Distinguished Scientist Early Career Award from the American Psychological Association in 2003 and the Early Career Award from the International Society of Self and Identity in 2002.

Courtesy Steven J. Heine

UNDERSTAND THE BIG PICTURE

To help students appreciate the connections between the broad range of topics covered throughout the book and understand how each topic contributes to the whole of social psychology, the first chapter describes three central themes of social psychology:

- The social world influences how we think about ourselves
- The social world influences our thoughts, attitudes, and behaviour
- Our attitudes and behaviour shape the social world around us

- **The Big Picture** summary table at the end of each chapter connects the specific material learned in each chapter to these key ideas in the course.

THE BIG PICTURE

LINKING ATTRACTION AND CLOSE RELATIONSHIPS

This chapter included many applications of the three "big ideas" studied in social psychology. The examples below should help you see the connection between interpersonal attraction and close relationships and these big ideas, and contribute to your understanding of the big picture of social psychology.

THEME	EXAMPLES
The social world influences how we think about ourselves.	• Thinking about a close relationship helps us cope with threatening information about ourselves. • Married couples feel happiest in their relationships when their partner sees them as they see themselves.
The social world influences our thoughts, attitudes, and behaviour.	• Attractive professors get higher teaching evaluations. • People in an inequitable marriage are more likely to leave for an alternative relationship.
Our attitudes and behaviour shape the social world around us.	• People with an anxious attachment style see negative behaviour as worse than do those with secure or avoidant attachment styles. In turn, they respond to negative behaviour by acting more negatively themselves, which leads to conflict. • People who are lonely engage in less self-disclosure, which in turn inhibits self-disclosure from their partner.

A PICTURE IS WORTH A THOUSAND WORDS

In *Social Psychology, Canadian Edition,* art is a true learning tool! This text features a completely unique new approach to research-based graphs throughout all chapters.

Graphs are annotated to help students interpret the key findings in the research and to help students understand the independent and dependent variables in the research studies through consistent reinforcement of these concepts.

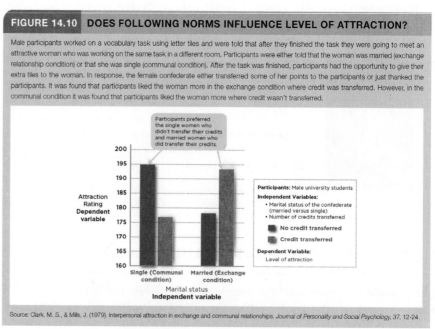

FIGURE 14.10   DOES FOLLOWING NORMS INFLUENCE LEVEL OF ATTRACTION?

Male participants worked on a vocabulary task using letter tiles and were told that after they finished the task they were going to meet an attractive woman who was working on the same task in a different room. Participants were either told that the woman was married (exchange relationship condition) or that she was single (communal condition). After the task was finished, participants had the opportunity to give their extra tiles to the woman. In response, the female confederate either transferred some of her points to the participants or just thanked the participants. It was found that participants liked the woman more in the exchange condition where credit was transferred. However, in the communal condition it was found that participants liked the woman more where credit wasn't transferred.

Participants preferred the single women who didn't transfer their credits and married woman who did transfer their credits.

Attraction Rating
Dependent variable

Marital status
Independent variable

Participants: Male university students
Independent Variables:
- Marital status of the confederate (married versus single)
- Number of credits transferred

No credit transferred
Credit transferred

Dependent Variable:
Level of attraction

Single (Communal condition)   Married (Exchange condition)

CULTURE MATTERS

Unlike some social psychology textbooks that discuss the relevance of culture in a separate chapter, *Social Psychology, Canadian Edition* examines the relation between cross-cultural psychology and social psychology in each chapter. This will allow students to see the powerful influence of culture in a wide range of topics within social psychology. Sections at the end of each chapter review chapter topics with a focus on how the findings and theories that have been presented might in fact differ in various cultures. These sections simultaneously review prior material from the chapter and engage students meaningfully with cultural issues. Through this consistent approach, students will better appreciate the role of culture in social behaviour. For example, students will learn that some expressions that are extremely popular in North American culture (e.g., "Be Yourself") might not work so well in countries that value connection and interdependence over individualism.

HOW DOES CULTURE INFLUENCE ATTRACTION AND CLOSE RELATIONSHIPS?

Think about your own friendships. Would you say you're more satisfied with your best friendship, or with your friendships in general? Research in social psychology suggests that your culture may influence your answer to this question. In one study, researchers examined friendships among both Arab (more collectivistic) and Jewish (more individualistic) grade four and five students in Israel (Scharf & Hertz-Lazarowitz, 2003). Arab students tended to have better quality peer relationships in general. In contrast, Jewish students tended to have better quality best-friend relationships. These findings make sense given the relative importance placed on connectedness and reciprocity in collectivistic cultures (and hence, strong social networks), as well as the relative importance placed on independence, autonomy, and personal relationships in individualistic ones. This study demonstrates that the predictors of friendship satisfaction are different for people in different cultures. This section will examine this and other ways in which culture impacts on people's views about attraction and close relationships, including their definition of beauty, the nature of love, and definitions of friendship.

FOCUS ON GENDER AND NEUROSCIENCE

- **Research Focus on Gender** sections examine a particular issue related to gender in depth. This information will help students understand how research in social psychology contributes to our understanding of gender differences and similarities.

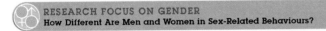

RESEARCH FOCUS ON GENDER
How Different Are Men and Women in Sex-Related Behaviours?

Although people in general show a preference for physically attractive dating partners, men and women differ in the extent to which they prefer attractive partners (Buss & Schmitt, 1993; Feingold, 1990, 1991; Fletcher, Tither, O'Loughlin, Friesen, & Overall, 2004). As you might expect, men place more importance on physical attractiveness in a dating partner than women do. One out of every three men advertising in personals requests an attractive partner, whereas only one in seven women make such a request (Koestner & Wheeler, 1988; Rajecki, Bledsoe, & Rasmussen, 1991). Similarly, women's ads tend to offer physical attractiveness (e.g., describe what they looked like), suggesting that they're aware of what men are hoping to find in a dating partner. Men also prefer partners who are younger than themselves (Buss, 1989; Rajecki et al., 1991). These preferences for a physically attractive partner are generally found in homosexual as well as heterosexual men (Bailey, Gaulin, Agyei, & Gladue, 1994; Kenrick, Keefe, Bryan, Barr, & Brown, 1995).

- **Research Focus on Neuroscience** sections examine specific neuroscience research studies in depth. This information will help students understand how the rapidly growing field of neuroscience contributes to our knowledge about social psychological theories in a way that is not currently seen in other books.

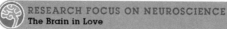

RESEARCH FOCUS ON NEUROSCIENCE
The Brain in Love

"Have you just fallen madly in love?" This question was posted on the psychology bulletin board on the SUNY Stony Brook campus in New York. Students who had fallen in love within the previous few months and had strong and vivid passionate feelings toward their beloved were invited to take part in the study. Dr. Helen Fisher (2004) was the researcher behind the study. She was interested in looking at the brains of those who were in love. After a screening process, 20 participants were selected to take part in the study. On the day of the experiment, participants were asked to bring a picture of their beloved and a picture of a neutral person. Each participant was then put in an fMRI machine that records blood flow in the brain and shows the brain cells that are active. The brain was scanned multiple times while the participant was looking at the picture of the beloved, than the picture of a neutral person, and counting backwards, as a distraction task between viewing the two photos. It was found that when participants were looking at the picture of their beloved, than the

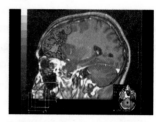

Photo Researchers
Brain scan showing emotional activity.

BRING SOCIAL PSYCHOLOGY TO LIFE

- **Research Connections** activities take students from passive observers to active participants in the process of "doing" social psychology and will help to ensure their mastery of core concepts and ideas. The online environment allows students the freedom to accomplish things they couldn't do otherwise, such as participating in research studies, testing research hypotheses, designing their own social psychology experiments, manipulating data, and analyzing their results.

RESEARCH CONNECTIONS

Participate in Research

Activity 1 Are Average Faces Most Attractive?: This chapter described how people see composite faces, meaning those that are made up of many different faces, as more attractive than single faces. Go online to look at different faces and rate how attractive you find each one—then find out whether you too see composite photographs as more attractive.

Activity 2 Testing the Triangular Theory of Love: This chapter examined the three distinct components of love, according to triangular theory. Go online to rate your feelings of intimacy, passion, and commitment to see what type of love you have in your current (or had in your most recent) relationship.

Activity 3 The Impact of Attachment Styles on Dating Patterns: This chapter described the impact of attachment styles on patterns of dating as well as interactions in romantic relationships. Go online to test your own attachment style and see how this style may influence your dating patterns and interactions.

Activity 4 Gender Differences in Jealousy: You learned in this chapter about the impact of gender on reactions to different types of infidelity. Go online to read about different types of infidelity, and then rate how upset you would be in each situation.

Activity 5 The Impact of Culture on Love: The final section of this chapter described how people from different cultures vary in how strongly they believe that love is an essential part of marriage. Go online to rate your agreement with the importance of love in marriage, and the absence of love in leading to divorce. Then see how other students rated their own agreement.

Test a Hypothesis

As you learned in this chapter, men and women tend to look for different characteristics in dating partners. To test whether this hypothesis is true, find personal ads for dating either online or in a local newspaper, and calculate the percentage of men and women who are looking for particular traits (such as attractiveness, wealth, or intelligence). Then, go online to report your findings to other students.

Design a Study

Go online to design your own study that will test factors that predict interpersonal attraction. You'll be able to choose the type of study you want to conduct (self-report, observational/naturalistic, or experimental), choose your own independent and dependent variables, and form your own hypothesis. Then you can share your findings with other students across the country!

ORGANIZATION AND PEDAGOGICAL PLAN

The book moves logically from beginning to end, starting with how we see ourselves and others, and then moving to address how we interact with others in group settings, including both positive and negative interactions. The chapters can be covered in any order, depending on the organization of a particular course.

We encourage readers to ask themselves these questions as they read each chapter, and chapters are organized to facilitate this:

- What does the research say about this topic?
- How can I think critically about the research?
- How does this concept relate to everyday life?
- How does culture influence this concept?

Each chapter follows a carefully developed pedagogical approach designed to help students master the material. Chapters are organized around five central topics, listed on the opening page of the chapter under the heading **What You'll Learn**, and each of these topics is introduced via a specific research study with compelling and highly relevant findings. **Did You Ever Wonder?** questions at the start of the chapter introduce these high-interest findings which are then described in detail in each of the five sections throughout the chapter. Then, at the end of each of these major sections comes a **Concepts in Context** summary table. These section summaries help students synthesize the material, but more importantly, understand its real-world applications. Finally, at the end of the chapter comes **What You've Learned**, a summary of the material in the chapter, organized around each of the five main chapter headings. The chapter concludes with **Review Questions**, **Take Action** activities and **Research Connections** activities, all organized around the five main chapter headings and designed to help students review and apply core concepts while, at the same time, allowing them to take the material further through real-world applications and opportunities to experience social psychological research firsthand.

STUDENT AND INSTRUCTOR SUPPORT

Social Psychology, Canadian Edition, is accompanied by a host of ancillary materials designed to facilitate a mastery of social psychology.

WILEYPLUS

WileyPLUS is an innovative, research-based online environment for effective teaching and learning.

WileyPLUS builds students' confidence because it takes the guesswork out of studying by providing students with a clear roadmap: what to do, how to do it, if they did it right. Students will take more initiative so you'll have greater impact on their achievement in the classroom and beyond.

RESEARCH CONNECTIONS ACTIVITIES

These interactive online activities (available in WileyPLUS) take students from passive observers to active participants in the process of "doing" social psychology and will help to ensure their mastery of core concepts and ideas. These online activities allow students to participate in research studies, test hypotheses, and design their own research studies.

VIDEOS (UPON ADOPTION)

Wiley partners with the Films for the Humanities to offer an outstanding selection of videos (including Roger Bingham's series on the brain). Perfect for introducing new topics, enlivening your classroom presentations, and stimulating student discussion.

INSTRUCTOR RESOURCE WEBSITE

This comprehensive website is uploaded with resources to help you prepare for class, enhance your lectures, and assess your students' progress. Ancillaries available include:

- test bank (available in Respondus format and in Word format)
- instructor's resource guide
- PowerPoint presentations
- clicker questions

ACKNOWLEDGEMENTS

A number of colleagues provided thoughtful comments and expert feedback that helped in the development of the Canadian edition. They are:

Heather Price, University of Regina

Donald Sharpe, University of Regina

Patrice Karn, University of Ottawa

Christine Lomore, St Francis Xavier

Rajiv Jhangiani, Capilano University

Jason Plaks, University of Toronto

Anne Wilson, Laurier

Leandre Fabrigar, Queen's University

Deborah Matheson, Vancouver Island University

Anne Wilson, Wilfrid Laurier University

Simon Sherry, Dalhousie University

Susan Boon, University of Calgary

Ken Fowler, Memorial University of Newfoundland

Theresa Bianco, Concordia University

Danu Stinson, University of Victoria

Kenneth Hart, University of Windsor

Rebecca Malhi University of Alberta

Rodney Schmaltz, Grant MacEwan University

Christopher Motz, Carleton University

Jennifer Ostovich, McMaster University

Nancy J. Smith, University of Calgary

Jessica Rourke, University of Victoria

Jennifer Stamp, Dalhousie University

Jill Esmonde, Georgian College

Valery Chirkov, University of Saskatchewan

Since the inception of this project in February 2009, I travelled a journey that was consuming, challenging, unfamiliar, and appealing. There are many people who contributed to the full circle of this journey. I would like to start by thanking the Acquisitions Editor of Wiley Canada, Rodney Burke, who called me in France while I was doing my sabbatical at the University of Bordeaux and invited me to adapt this textbook for Canadian students. I accepted the invitation because it came with a good degree of freedom: the chance to illustrate the scholarly works that are conducted in Canada and to introduce the tremendous research on social psychology that is conducted outside of North America. I am grateful for this opportunity. I would also like to thank all the staff at Wiley and particularly Andrea Grzybowski (Developmental Editor), for working tirelessly with me in every step of this journey. As well I'd like to thank copyeditor David Schwinghamer, proofreader Ruth Wilson, photo researcher Julie Pratt, and indexer Belle Wong. Their guidance, feedback, and assistance are much appreciated.

I would also like to thank my PhD student, Stryker Shay Calvez, for helping me find current material and particularly for his contribution to Chapter 10, Intergroup Relations, a new chapter added to the book. Thank you to several of my undergraduate students who reviewed the earlier drafts of the book and provided valuable feedback.

It may be a bit collectivistic (see chapters 2 and 3), but I would like to thank my daughter, Newsha, my parents, sisters, brother, niece, and nephews for taking an interest in my work.

Most importantly, I would like to thank my partner, my intellectual and emotional support, Dr. Rees Lewis. Thank you for listening to my thoughts, for reading my drafts, for helping me to make decisions, and for encouraging me to take this challenge. Thank you for winking smilingly every time I finished a draft of a chapter.

Saba Safdar, University of Guelph

BRIEF CONTENTS

CONTENTS

3 THE SELF: SELF-PERCEPTION AND SELF-PRESENTATION 62

6 ATTITUDE FORMATION AND CHANGE 178

11 STEREOTYPE, PREJUDICE, AND DISCRIMINATION
354

1

CHAPTER

INTRODUCING SOCIAL PSYCHOLOGY

DID YOU EVER WONDER?

Source: U.S. Department of Defense/photo by Tech. Sgt. Prentice Colter.

If you read a magazine or watch the news on television, you'll encounter varied acts of human behaviour. The following stories are example of some news that were widely reported in the past few years:

- Haiti was struck by a massive earthquake, and Canadians donated large sums of money to help survivors.
- Twenty imams had just issued a Fatwa declaring that any attack on Canada and the United States by a Muslim extremist would be an attack on all 10 million Muslims living in North America.
- Gunmen in an area of Angola plagued by separatist violence fired on a bus carrying Togo's national soccer team to an international soccer tournament, the African Cup of Nations, killing three people and wounding at least six, including two players.
- Malawi police arrested two Malawian men who had become the first gay couple to publicly marry in Malawi, a country where homosexuality is illegal.

HEALTH CONNECTIONS

Why University Students Don't Always Practise Safe Sex Although They Know They Should

These examples illustrate a range of human behaviours, from altruism to reasoning to aggression to love. But what do you really learn about the people in these media reports? How well do you understand what drives their behaviour? How accurately could you predict their behaviour in the future? This chapter will explore these questions, and others, to help us understand how we think about people in the social world and, in turn, the impact of the social world on our attitudes, thoughts, and behaviour. In addition, you'll find out . . .

 Why do university students often fail to ask questions during class?

 Why do soldiers sometimes mistreat prisoners?

 Why eating dinner as a family could be related to better grades among teenagers?

 Why should parents be more worried about car seats than kidnappers?

 Why do North Americans see themselves through their personal traits, while South Americans see themselves through their group memberships?

- What social psychology is
- How social psychology has evolved over time
- Whether social psychology is really just common sense
- How social psychology is connected to other fields
- How social psychology applies across cultures and subcultures

PREVIEW

The "Did You Ever Wonder . . . ?" questions all address real-world issues that are examined by social psychologists—and this book therefore explores these and other issues that relate to how people interact in the social world, influence it, and at the same time are influenced by it. This chapter first defines social psychology and the specific topics that are examined in this area, or sub-discipline, of psychology. Next, you'll learn about how social psychology has evolved over time, and how it connects to other disciplines. Finally, you'll learn about this field's reliance on foundation in the scientific method, and about the impact of culture on both theory and research in social psychology.

WHAT IS SOCIAL PSYCHOLOGY?

John Donne, the 16th century English poet, wrote:

"No man is an island, entire of itself;
every man is a piece of the continent, a part of the main . . ."
Donne, *No Man is an Island*

Four hundred years later, these words still ring true, though we might now say "person" or "human" rather than "man." Our lives are connected to each other by hundreds of threads, and our survival and well-being depend on these connections. Social psychology is about understanding our social connections to each other—how they influence and are influenced by what we think, feel, and do.

Social psychology is the scientific study of how people's thoughts, feelings, and behaviour are influenced by factors in the social world. Social psychologists study how people explain their own and other people's behaviour (e.g., attributions), how people influence others (e.g., persuasion), and how people connect with each other (e.g., attraction). A classic and widely used definition of social psychology was given by Gordon W. Allport in 1954: he defined it as "an attempt to understand and explain how the thought, feelings and behavior of individuals are influenced by the actual, imagined, or implied presence of other human beings" (p. 5).

There are many ways to try to understand and to present any phenomenon, whether through an artistic perspective, a documentary approach, folk wisdom, or a scientific inquiry. All capture different aspects of the topic. For example, Woody Allen, a contemporary American director, examines love, hate, and jealousy in interpersonal relationships in movies such as *Vicky Cristina Barcelona*. His approach, although valid and intelligent, lacks scientific value and method. It is one person's account and therefore reflects only one person's perspective, making it merely anecdotal. Similarly, the controversial American documentary filmmaker Michael Moore examines violence and marginalization in movies such as *Bowling for Columbine*. His movies, although powerful and informative, lack the objectivity and systematic observation that is required in scientific inquiry. Religious beliefs, in turn, offer explanations for many things (from how the universe was created to why a person suffers pain), but these are based on a doctrine which gives explanations that one must simply believe—they are not amenable to scientific tests or objective verification.

USING THE SCIENTIFIC METHOD

Social psychology provides an alternative perspective to these approaches to explaining a phenomenon by using scientific inquiry, which includes each of the following: a commitment to collecting accurate and error-free information; a commitment to objectivity and collecting data that are free of bias (and a commitment to verifying information empirically. To fulfill these commitments, social psychologists follow the **scientific method**, a research method for investigating phenomena, acquiring new knowledge, and evaluating and integrating previous knowledge. Social psychologists form an educated guess, called a **hypothesis**, about the relationship between events, and then examine the accuracy of this hypothesis by collecting data through observation and/or experimentation, to determine whether this hypothesis is supported by the data (i.e., whether the initial guess was a good one). You will read more about research methods in Chapter 2. Social psychology therefore uses the same approach to evaluate hypotheses as other scientific fields, such as biology, chemistry, and physics.

scientific method – a technique for investigating phenomena, acquiring new knowledge, and/or correcting previous knowledge

hypothesis – a testable prediction about the conditions under which an event will occur

This research process helps us find objective answers to questions about why people think, feel, and behave as they do.

In some cases, this research leads us to conclusions that are quite surprising. If, for example, I told you that competitors who receive a bronze medal (third place) are happier than those who receive a silver medal (second place), you might be quite puzzled. But this is exactly the finding of considerable research on errors we make in social cognition, as you'll learn in Chapter 5. Similarly, although we often assume that children from upper-class families face fewer problems than those from low-income backgrounds, some research suggests exactly the opposite: one study found that adolescents from high-income communities actually report significantly more anxiety and depression than those from inner-city, low-income communities (Luthar & Latendresse, 2005). Moreover, adolescents from high-income communities have also reported higher rates of substance abuse for alcohol and cigarettes, as well as marijuana and other illegal drugs. Using the scientific method is crucial as it allows researchers to test whether our beliefs are actually correct.

In other cases, this process of testing hypotheses simply leads researchers to accepting findings that one would expect to find true. For example, a widely accepted finding in **social psychology** is that men are more interested in casual sex than women are (you'll read more about this in Chapter 14). This is unsurprising as it conforms with socially recognized gender stereotypes (which are discussed in Chapter 11).

social psychology – A scientific study of the way in which a person's thoughts, feelings, and behaviours are influenced by the real, imagined, or implied presence of others.

Based on Gordon W. Allport's classic definition, we could now say that social psychology is a scientific study of the way in which a person's thoughts, feelings, and behaviours are influenced by the real, imagined, or implied presence of others. As an introduction to social psychology, this book will therefore focus on three distinct, but inter-related topics that social psychologists address:

- How we think about ourselves
- How we think, feel, and act in the social world
- How our attitudes and behaviour shape the social world (imagined or real)

These three topics are highlighted in The Big Picture table at the end of each chapter to help you see how each chapter's topics relate to these three broad themes and contribute to an understanding of the big picture of social psychology. Let's now examine each of these topics in turn.

HOW WE THINK ABOUT OURSELVES

self-perception – how we think about ourselves

Social psychology examines how we think about ourselves, or **self-perception**, and in particular, how our views of ourselves depend on our sociocultural environment. Many students arrive at university feeling rather good about themselves. They may have been one of the smartest, or most athletic, or most artistic members of their high school class. However, students quickly realize that in the university environment, the comparison group is different. Once you are surrounded by hundreds, or thousands, of people who themselves were the smartest, or most athletic, or most artistic, members of their own high school class, you may not feel quite as good about yourself as you did back in high school. Similarly, you may feel quite confident about your own appearance. But after skimming through a *Cosmopolitan* or *Maxim* magazine, you may feel rather insecure. These are just some of the ways in which factors in the social world influence how we think about ourselves.

Bonnie Kamin/PhotoEdit
How we see ourselves is often strongly influenced by the type of comparison we are making to other people.

Social psychology also examines **self-presentation**, or how we present our ideas about ourselves to others. We

self-presentation – how people work to convey certain images of themselves to others

use many strategies to convey impressions about ourselves to others—the car we drive, the clothes or jewellery we wear, even the model of our cell phone or size of our television. Even the casual references we make in conversations—about where we are going on vacation, parties we've attended, and items we've bought—convey information about our habits, interests, and resources.

HOW WE THINK, FEEL, AND ACT IN THE SOCIAL WORLD

social perception – how people form impressions of and make inferences about other people and events in the social world

Social psychology also examines how people form impressions and make inferences about other people and events in the social world, a process called **social perception**. We form these impressions easily and frequently—we decide why our favourite hockey team won the game, why a grade on a test was lower than we expected, and why our best friend's dating relationship probably won't last.

social cognition – how we think about the social world, and in particular how we select, interpret, and use information to make judgements about the world

A particular type of social perception, **social cognition**, describes how we think about people and the social world. In some cases, we see the world accurately. For example, you might assume that expensive restaurants serve better food than cheap restaurants—and this is a pretty good rule of thumb (or heuristic). But in other cases, we make errors in our judgements about people and events. For example, many people are more afraid of travel by airplane than by car. In reality, however, more people die each year in car accidents than airplane accidents, suggesting that our fear of air travel isn't well founded.

social influence – the impact of other people's attitudes and behaviours on our thoughts, feelings, and behaviour

Another central issue examined by social psychologists is **social influence**, meaning the impact of other people's attitudes and behaviour, or even their mere presence, on our thoughts, feelings, and behaviour. In some cases, social influence is quite direct: advertising messages are a good example of deliberate efforts to influence attitudes and behaviour. In other cases, however, social influence is very subtle. We are, for example, less likely to help a person in need if we are in a large group than if we are alone with the person, in part because we don't feel personally responsible for helping when there are others around us.

Social psychology examines not only the impact of people's attitudes and behaviour, but also the impact of a person's perception of other people's attitudes and behaviour. In other

words, people's thoughts, feelings, and behaviour are influenced not only by what other people think or do, but also by what they imagine other people think or do. Let's take an example that occurs frequently in university classes. Imagine that your professor finishes a section of the lecture and asks whether anyone has a question. You might have a question that you'd like to ask about the material that was just presented, but when you look around the room, you notice that no one else has a hand raised. You then decide not to ask your question, because you fear looking stupid for being the only person with a question. In this case, you assume that no other students have questions, and therefore believe that they must have understood all the material. This perception of their knowledge—whether it is accurate or not—influences your behaviour. Our beliefs about the social world can influence our attitudes and behaviour even when these beliefs are inaccurate, as the following Health Connections box shows.

HEALTH CONNECTIONS

Why University Students Don't Always Practise Safe Sex Although They Know They Should

To help you make connections between research in social psychology and real-world issues, in each chapter there are Connections boxes that show how principles in social psychology relate to education, law, health, business, the media, or the environment. In Chapter 6 you will read more about the link between attitudes and behaviour: although attitudes do help predict behaviour, they do not guarantee future actions. This is important when it comes to, for example, promoting healthy behaviour such as having protected sex. Intentions to use a condom do not always translate into actual condom use, and researchers have attempted to establish some of the reasons why. According to data produced in a study by Tara MacDonald of Queens University, and Michaela Hynie of York University (2008), a high proportion of young Canadian adults are aware of the possible negative consequences of having unprotected sex, including the risk of pregnancy or of contracting HIV and other sexually transmitted infections (STIs). However, in 2003, between 21.5 percent and 43.6 percent of 15- to 24-year-olds in Canada reported not using a condom the last time they had sexual intercourse. As young adults catch a disproportionate amount of STIs, including HIV, it is important to understand why knowledge of the potential negative consequences of unprotected sex often fails to lead to actual condom use among young people.

MacDonald & Hynie (2008) found a connection between ambivalence about sexual activity and failure to use a condom. Undergraduates were asked to predict whether they would have intercourse and use condoms in the next week. A week later, those same students reported their actual sexual and contraceptive behaviour. Among those who had intercourse and had intended to use condoms, actual condom use decreased as ambivalence toward sex increased. Researchers also found that whether or not intercourse was planned also influenced students' decisions: ambivalence was negatively associated with accuracy in planning sex, and unplanned sex was less likely to be protected. In another study, Hynie, MacDonald & Marques (2006) found that anticipated shame at having not used a condom was also a relevant

factor in the decision to practise unsafe sex (if you expect to feel bad about practising unsafe sex, you are less likely to do it). Self-esteem and mood (MacDonald & Martineau, 2002) and, alcohol use (MacDonald, Fong, Zanna & Martineau, 2000) are also factors.

Can anything be done to help translate intentions into behaviour? A study carried out in part by researchers from the University of Waterloo (Dal Cin, MacDonald, Fong, Zanna, & Elton-Marshall, 2006) suggests that strategies such as reminder cues can increase the effectiveness of health intervention programs. In this study, participants were shown a video documentary about young people with HIV/AIDS. One group of students was given a friendship band to remind them of the stories of the people in the documentary and were instructed to wear it until the follow-up session. Five to seven weeks later at the follow-up session, it was found that condom use when participants had last had sex was higher among those who had received a bracelet (55%) than among those who had just seen the video (27%) or among those who watched an unrelated video about drunk driving (36%). The authors also found that the bracelet remained effective even when participants were under the influence of alcohol.

Mike Watson Images

Social psychology also examines the impact of events (including thoughts, which are cognitive events) on our attitudes and behaviours. Have you ever noticed that when you are in a bad mood you are more likely to act rudely? Would you believe that just feeling really hot can lead you to behave more aggressively, or that smelling a cinnamon bun baking could lead you to be nicer to others? We'll examine these and other ways in which aspects of the social world influence how we feel, how we think, and even how we behave.

HOW OUR ATTITUDES AND BEHAVIOUR SHAPE THE SOCIAL WORLD

self-fulfilling prophecy – the process by which people's expectations about a person lead them to elicit behaviour that confirms these expectations

Finally, social psychology also examines how our attitudes and behaviour can shape the social world. In the process called **self-fulfilling prophecy**, people's expectations about someone else's traits influence how they act toward that person. In turn, these actions elicit the behaviour that is expected. The self-fulfilling prophecy therefore leads people to confirm whatever beliefs they have, and makes it very difficult for these beliefs to be disconfirmed.

[**CONCEPTS IN CONTEXT**]

WHAT IS SOCIAL PSYCHOLOGY?

THEME	EXAMPLE
How we think about ourselves	Mariam feels smarter when spending time with her high school friends than when spending time with her college friends.
How we think, feel, and act in the social world	Ahmad is very afraid of flying, even though his mother has assured him that flying is a safer way of travelling than driving.
How our attitudes and behaviour shape the social world	Katerina believes her new co-worker is aloof and distant. She therefore doesn't ask him to join the other staff members for their regular after-work happy hour on Fridays. Katerina then notices that he seems even more aloof and distant—thereby confirming her original opinion of him.

HOW HAS SOCIAL PSYCHOLOGY EVOLVED OVER TIME?

The field of social psychology is a relatively new one in the discipline of psychology. It was first established as a unique discipline only at the start of the 20th century, with the publication of the first textbook in social psychology, written by Floyd Allport (1924). Early research in social psychology was heavily influenced by three major factors: behaviourism, Gestalt psychology, and historical events. As such, social psychology is deeply rooted in the intellectual and cultural environment of North American and, to a lesser extent, European societies.

BEHAVIOURISM

behaviourism – a theory of learning that describes people's behaviour as acquired through conditioning

In the early 20th century, many psychologists believed that for psychology to be truly scientific, it should only focus on measurable phenomena. As thoughts and feelings are unobservable, and therefore (it was argued) unmeasurable, these psychologists focused on the impact of positive and negative events on behaviour. Known as **behaviourism**, this discipline described people's behaviour as being determined in a very straightforward way. Behaviour that was followed by a reward, it was argued, would continue, a process referred to as conditioning. Behaviour that was followed by punishment would not. This perspective was very influential in much of the early work on understanding animal behaviour. For example, using a reward to reinforce target behaviours, renowned American behaviourist B. F. Skinner trained pigeons to turn in a circle, nod, and "play" the piano.

The behaviourist approach is still influential in social psychology today. As you'll learn in Chapter 6, the social learning perspective describes how people form attitudes and behaviour through both receiving reinforcements for their own attitudes and behaviour and watching other people's attitudes and behaviour. Children who watch movies where people are smoking are more likely to form positive attitudes toward smoking (as you'll learn in Chapter 6), children whose parents show prejudice toward people form negative attitudes about others (as you'll learn in Chapter 11), and children who watch aggressive cartoons are more likely to behave aggressively (as you'll learn in Chapter 12).

Although the behaviourist approach clearly explains some behaviour, it ignores the role of people's thoughts, feelings, and attitudes, and therefore is too simplistic to explain other behaviour. Giving a child a reward for reading a book, for example, can actually backfire and reduce his or her interest in reading—because the child then sees reading as driven only by the prospect of a reward, and not as driven by the pure enjoyment of reading. This is one example of how people's interpretation of their behaviour matters, as you'll learn in Chapter 3.

GESTALT PSYCHOLOGY

In part due to the limitations inherent in the behaviourist approach, other psychologists in the early 1900s examined the influence of people's *perceptions* of objects and events in the world, not simply their objective appearance. This sub-discipline, called **Gestalt psychology**, emerged from Germany and means "whole form." Gestalt psychology emphasized the importance of looking at the whole object and how it appeared in people's minds, as opposed to looking at specific objective parts of the object. For example, in the classic *Dog Picture* shown in the photo here, people don't recognize the dog by individually identifying all of its parts (head, ears, nose, and so on). In fact, if you look at a small enough area of the picture and ignore the rest, it is very difficult to determine that these seemingly random marks are part of a dog. In contrast, when you look at the picture all together, you simply perceive the dog as a single object all at once.

Gestalt psychology was in sharp contrast to behaviourism as it focused on how people interpret their surroundings and the cognitive processing that was involved in people's interpretations. A key idea in Gestalt psychology is that we sometimes experience more than what is supplied by our sensory perception. For example, if we see a series of images in quick succession, we perceive a moving image, not a series of static ones. We also organize our perceptual experience. For instance, in Figure 1.1 (a), we see three horizontal lines of stars, rather than 14 vertical groups of three. In Figure 1.1 (b), we tend to perceive a diagonal line of Os in a field of Xs. We do this not only with diagrams but with all our sensory experience. Organizing our experience is how we make sense of our world.

Kurt Lewin, who is often considered the founder of modern social psychology (as well as the sub-disciplines of organizational and applied psychology), was trained in the Gestalt approach. Born into a Jewish family in Poland, Lewin served in the German army during World War I. Following a war injury, he

Gestalt psychology – a theory that proposes objects are viewed holistically

Melissa Kieselburg
This picture is a classic example of the Gestalt perspective: without having first seen the whole picture, it is virtually impossible to recognize the object by looking only at a specific part of the picture. When you look at the picture all together, it is quite easy to recognize that these individual pieces together form a picture of a dog.

FIGURE 1.1 EXAMPLES OF HOW OUR MIND ORGANIZES ITS EXPERIENCE

```
                                        OXXXXXXXXX
                                        XOXXXXXXXX
                                        XXOXXXXXXX
                                        XXXOXXXXXX
                                        XXXXOXXXXX
                                        XXXXXOXXXX
                      **************     XXXXXXOXXX
                                        XXXXXXXOXX
                      **************     XXXXXXXXOX
              (a)     **************  (b) XXXXXXXXXO
```

Kurt Lewin, a German-Jewish professor living in Germany in the 1930s, is often considered the founder of social psychology.

attended the University of Berlin and received a PhD in 1916. Lewin initially worked within the schools of behavioural psychology, and then in the Gestalt school of psychology, but his largely Jewish reading group was forced to disband when Hitler came into power in Germany in 1933. Lewin then moved to the United States, where his commitment to applying psychology to society's problems led to the development of the M.I.T. Research Center for Group Dynamics. Lewin had a keen sense of the importance of perception in determining attitudes and behaviour, and he offered one of the earliest theories in cognitive social psychology. His research focused on the role of social perception in influencing people's behaviour, the nature of group dynamics, and the factors contributing to stereotyping and prejudice (you'll learn more about his work on these topics in chapters 9 and 10).

HISTORICAL EVENTS

Historical events also influenced other young social psychologists. Muzafer Sherif grew up in Turkey and later moved to the United States to attend graduate school. After receiving a PhD in psychology in 1935 from Columbia University, he then returned to Turkey to teach at Ankara University. Sherif's outspoken opposition to the Nazi movement during World War II led to his imprisonment in a Turkish prison. Following complaints from his American colleagues, Sherif was released from prison after four months, and he was allowed to return to the United States. This personal experience with the dangerous powers of groups during times of war led him to carry out a series of studies on group influence, and in particular on how introducing tasks that required cooperation between groups could reduce intergroup conflict. You'll read about Sherif's work on group processes and group conflict in Chapter 10.

Similarly, Stanley Milgram, a social psychologist who began his work in the late 1960s, was deeply affected by the events of Nazi Germany. Although many people blamed these events on the "cruel and evil" German people, Milgram wondered whether the people themselves were less to blame for the atrocities of Nazi Germany than the situation. While a professor at Yale University, Milgram conducted a series of experiments demonstrating the powerful role of authority in leading to obedience. This research, which was greeted by much controversy when its results were first published, is one of the most famous studies in social psychology, and has been used to explain many real-world events, including mistreatment of prisoners during times of war. You'll read about Milgram's research on the power of authority in leading to obedience in Chapter 8.

Table 1.1	**Six Virtues and Their Component Character Strengths**
VIRTUE	**COMPONENT CHARACTER STRENGTHS**
Wisdom and knowledge	Creativity, curiosity, open-mindedness, love of learning, perspective
Courage	Bravery, persistence, integrity, vitality
Humanity	Love, kindness, social intelligence
Justice	Citizenship, fairness, leadership
Temperance	Forgiveness, humility, prudence, self-regulation
Transcendence	Appreciation of beauty and excellence, gratitude, hope, humour, spirituality

Source: Peterson, C., & Seligman, M. (2004). *Character strengths and virtues: A handbook and classification*. Washington, DC, New York, NY: American Psychological Association.

In part because early theory and research in social psychology was sparked by truly horrific events, such as the Holocaust, much of the early work in social psychology focused on explaining behaviour that might be regarded as problematic, such as aggression, stereotyping and prejudice, and misplaced obedience to authority. However, research in social psychology has also increasingly focused on positive behaviour, such as altruism, attraction, and leadership. In fact, **positive psychology**, which is a new sub-discipline within social psychology, was established in 1998 to focus specifically on people's virtues and strengths (Peterson & Seligman, 2004). The roots of positive psychology are in humanistic psychology, which has a focus on individual potential and fulfilment. Positive psychology is not about finding what is wrong with an individual or treating mental illness, but rather aims to improve and fulfill normal people's lives. Martin Seligman and Milhaly Csikszentmihalyi are two prominent researchers in this sub-discipline. These researchers argue that psychology should be about human strength as well as weakness, building strength in the lives of normal people and nurturing talent. As shown in Table 1.1 researchers in this field examine the traits that are associated with life satisfaction and are predictors of healthy human functioning. Researchers then design interventions to improve well-being.

positive psychology – a recent branch of psychology that studies individuals' strengths and virtues

Social psychologists continue to be interested in examining, and solving, real-world issues, including decreasing prejudice and discrimination, helping communities regulate the use of natural resources, and improving group decision-making.

[CONCEPTS IN CONTEXT]

HOW SOCIAL PSYCHOLOGY EVOLVED OVER TIME

INFLUENCE	EXAMPLE
Behaviorism	Stefania's older sister is a big fan of Lady Gaga. Stefania now also really likes Lady Gaga.
Gestalt psychology	Justin is not comfortable with the homophobic slurs that he often hears one of his friends use. However, Justin believes that his other friends aren't bothered by this offensive language, so he decides not to speak up about his concerns.
Historical events	After allowing her grade 2 students to sit wherever they'd like in the classroom, Ms. O'Shea noticed a clear separation, and increased conflict, between the boys and the girls. She then created smaller groups, composed of boys and girls, to work on particular shared tasks. This effort decreased conflict, and increased cooperation, between the sexes.

IS SOCIAL PSYCHOLOGY REALLY JUST COMMON SENSE?

This focus on practical, real-world issues is one of the earliest tenets of social psychology, in part because early research in this field was prompted by horrific real-world events, such as Nazi Germany. In fact, Kurt Lewin (1951), the founder of modern social psychology, saw the inherent connection between social psychological theory and application to the real world as one of its greatest strengths: "There is nothing so practical as a good theory" (p. 169). Unfortunately, this ready application of social-psychological theories and research to daily life can also be a curse, in that people may view social psychology as simply "common sense." In truth, we rely too heavily on this notion of common sense as we tend to assume things to be more commonplace than they really are. Common to whom? is the first question. The answer is generally limited to the "us" of the group that we see ourselves as being part of, as Chapter 10 on social identity will show. The context of the situation is another limitation on how common something is. Is it common sense that completing an assignment (i.e., doing what you are told) shows a degree of moral integrity and self-discipline? If your assignment is writing an essay, it may; if your assignment is torturing a prisoner, it probably doesn't. Do too many cooks spoil the broth or do many hands make light the work? Both are statements of "common sense," but they are entirely contradictory. (Chapter 9 presents research on social facilitation and inhibition that will show just how limiting the context can be in answering such a question.) Let's now examine the biases that lead people to see the field of social psychology in this simplistic, "common sense" way, and the importance of thinking critically to combat such tendencies.

THE "I KNEW IT ALL ALONG" PROBLEM

If I told you that scientific research suggests that "opposites attract," you'd probably believe me. But you'd have had the same confidence, and agreement with the statement, if I'd said the reverse—"birds of a feather flock together." Similarly, if I told you, "absence makes the heart grow fonder," that would probably sound quite plausible. But once again, so would the opposite expression, "out of sight, out of mind."

hindsight bias – the tendency to see a given outcome as inevitable once the actual outcome is known

These examples illustrate a bias that people fall prey to frequently—the hindsight bias. Hindsight bias, or the "I knew it all along" phenomenon, refers to people's tendency to believe, once they've learned the outcome of something, that that particular outcome was obvious. Unfortunately, this bias can lead people to see social psychology as little more than common sense because once they've heard something, they see it as obvious (Richard, Bond, & Stokes-Zoota, 2001; Slovic & Fischhoff, 1977). What they don't recognize is that the exact opposite statement would also have sounded believable.

Here's an example of this problem. If I offered to pay you either $20 or $1 to perform the same behaviour, which reward would make you like that behaviour more? The behaviourist tradition believed that people would like engaging in behaviour that was reinforced with a big reward more than behaviour that was reinforced with a small reward—and you'd probably agree with this principle (surely you'd rather receive $20 than $1). But the results of a classic experiment on the phenomenon of cognitive dissonance revealed the reverse; at least in some cases, people who receive $1 for engaging in a behaviour report liking that behaviour more than those who receive $20. You'll learn more about this experiment by Festinger and Carlsmith (1959) in Chapter 6.

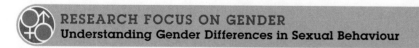

RESEARCH FOCUS ON GENDER
Understanding Gender Differences in Sexual Behaviour

To help you examine how research in social psychology contributes to our understanding of gender differences and similarities, most chapters will feature a Research Focus on Gender section that examines a particular gender-related issue in depth. For example, there is intriguing research that suggests that economic principles can explain many of the often-noted gender differences in sexual behaviour (Baumeister & Vohs, 2004). According to this view, men are interested in buying sex because sex is largely a no-cost proposition for men. For women, on the other hand, the potential cost of sex is high (pregnancy, child-rearing, or even death from childbirth), and so women are interested in using sex to gain other resources. This view of sex as a resource that is "bought" by men and "sold" by women explains a number of gender differences in sexual attitudes and behaviour, including the significant gender imbalance in prostitution (women just aren't as interested in paying for sex), the tendency for men to desire sex at earlier stages of relationships than women, and men's greater interest in one-night stands.

However, it is important to understand gender differences in sexual behaviour within the context of societal attitudes toward male and female sexuality. Empirical evidence indicates that there is a double standard that condemns premarital sexuality for women but not for men. For example, a survey of 413 Canadians between the ages of 18 to 28 found that although participants rejected the double standard personally, most participants reported that it exists at the societal level (Milhausen & Herold, 2001). In one study, researchers found that among 97 male and 192 female undergraduate students who were virgins, women reported more social pressure to remain a virgin than men (although fear of AIDS and STDs was also an influential factor in their decision). Women also reported that they were likely to stay virgins for a longer time than men (Sprecher & Regan, 1996).

EMPHASIS ON CRITICAL THINKING

The focus on the scientific method in social psychology means that you should carefully and critically examine research findings presented in this (or any) book, and especially those that are presented in the media. In other words, don't just casually believe what you read or hear, but really think about the information and whether there may be alternative explanations for a phenomenon.

Imagine that you learn there is an association between wealth and happiness (research indicates that there is, but only up to a point). Why is this? Do happy people make more money, or does having more money make people happier? Which is true? You need to carefully examine the factors that lead to this association. One possibility is that happy people engage in certain behaviours that lead to greater success in their work—such as getting along better with colleagues or persisting through difficulties—which in turn leads to more financial success. But another, equally likely, possibility is that making more money leads to greater happiness. Still another possibility is that some other factor altogether—perhaps optimism or social support—leads to both happiness and income. We can say that happiness and income correlate (or co-occur), but not that one causes the other; more data are required before we could say that.

Let's take another example. A study published in *The Archives of Pediatrics & Adolescent Medicine* reported that adolescents who frequently had dinner with their families reported lower levels of smoking, drinking, drug use, and depressive thoughts. These adolescents also had better grades (Eisenberg, Olson, Neumark-Sztainer, Story, & Bearinger, 2004). The media reported this study widely, and urged parents to have dinner with their kids as a way of preventing drug use and increasing grades. But let's think about whether this study demonstrates that having dinner as a family really has such a strong impact. Can you think of other explanations for this finding?

First, remember that this study shows that two things are *related* to each other, but it doesn't demonstrate that one thing, eating dinner together, *causes* another, less smoking and higher grades. One possibility is that parents who eat dinner with their children differ in some other way from those who don't eat dinner with their children, and that this

Corbis/SUPERSTOCK

Although research reveals that teenagers who have dinner with their family have better health habits and better grades, this finding does not prove that eating dinner together as a family *caused* those beneficial effects.

other factor leads to this relationship. For example, maybe parents who are wealthier, or more religious, or more conscientious, spend more time with their children, and these other factors (wealth, religiosity, conscientiousness) lead to better grades and less smoking.

Another possibility is that simply spending time with children is associated with better outcomes, regardless of when that time is. Research might show that parents who spend more time with their children each day, or each week, have children who have better grades and healthier behaviour. In this case, it would be the amount of time that would influence these behaviours, not whether that time was during dinner.

Still another possibility is that children who engage in unhealthy behaviour and show poor academic performance are less interested or willing to eat dinner with their families. Perhaps children who are "acting out" in some way refuse to eat dinner with their parents, even if their parents are home during the dinner hour. This example illustrates the principle of reverse causality, in which two factors are related in precisely the opposite direction than is hypothesized.

In short, all we can say is that eating a family dinner correlates with higher grades, and it shows an inverse correlation (when one increases, the other decreases) with smoking, drinking, drug use, and depressive thoughts. On the basis of this information, we are not able to say which of these factors (or variables) causes any of the others.

To help you learn how to critically examine information, Chapter 2 will describe various methods for conducting research in social psychology as well as various factors that influence research findings and the conclusions that can be drawn from them. Beginning with Chapter 3, each chapter will include a series of Questioning the Research queries that present a specific question about the results of a research study. Think carefully about your answers—this is an opportunity to sharpen your critical thinking skills.

[CONCEPTS IN CONTEXT]

WHY SOCIAL PSYCHOLOGY IS NOT JUST COMMON SENSE

THEME	EXAMPLE
The "I knew it all along" problem	Watching the news about the Vancouver riots after the Canucks' loss in June 2011, Jeremy was puzzled as to why people behaved they way they did. His sister, however, pointed out that a lot of rioters were drunk. Jeremy thought, "Ah, of course."
Emphasis on critical thinking	Naomi hears about a new book that profiles a number of highly successful people who were C-average university students. Although this book claims that C-average students are particularly successful in life, Naomi is sceptical about whether these students are actually more successful than those with a higher average. She wonders how typical these successful people are among their C-average peers and how hard the authors had to look to find them.

HOW IS SOCIAL PSYCHOLOGY CONNECTED TO OTHER FIELDS?

As described at the start of this chapter, the field of social psychology examines how people think about themselves; how people think, feel, and act in the social world; and how people's attitudes and behaviour shape the social world. But these, and related, questions are also examined in different sub-disciplines in the larger field of psychology and in other disciplines outside of psychology.

LINKS TO SUB-DISCIPLINES IN PSYCHOLOGY

Social psychology is closely connected to several sub-disciplines in the field of psychology, including personality psychology, clinical psychology, and cognitive psychology.

PERSONALITY PSYCHOLOGY. Personality psychologists focus on the role of *individual differences*, meaning the aspects of people's personality that make them different from other people, in explaining how different people feel and behave in distinct ways. We often use personality descriptions to describe other people in our social world—my friend Darren is extroverted, my co-worker Deirdra is arrogant, my boss Duane is neurotic.

Whereas personality psychologists emphasize how people's individual differences influence their attitudes, thoughts, and behaviour, social psychologists emphasize the role of the situation. For example, if you observe a person driving very aggressively, you might immediately judge that person's personality negatively ("She's a careless person" or "She only thinks about herself"). A social psychologist, on the other hand, would try to examine the role of situational factors in producing that behaviour; perhaps the person is late for a job interview, or she may be taking a sick child to the hospital. When you consider the situation (the woman was taking her sick child to the hospital), that might influence your attitude toward the aggressive driver. Do you still judge her personality as careless or self-centred? Our preference for explanations (or attributions) of events based on personality or for explanations based on situational factors varies according to our cultural background. It has been found that people from individualistic cultures give more emphasis to personality as an explanation for behaviour, and people from collectivistic backgrounds give greater weight to situational explanations (Miller, 1984; Morris & Peng, 1994).

Social psychologists examine how different people react to different situations in distinct ways. This part of social psychology focuses on the interaction of aspects of personality, such as self-esteem, need for cognition, and pro-social orientation, in influencing behaviour in a given situation. Issues of personality will be addressed throughout this book as they overlap with social psychology. For example, in Chapter 7 you'll read about how different people are persuaded by different types of advertising messages, and in Chapter 13 you'll read about how people with high levels of empathy are more likely to donate money to someone in need.

One area of research that combines social and personality psychology is the connection between stress and coping. Many studies have shown that social support (i.e., the support of friends, family, and other social networks) is important in helping people cope with stress. Researchers from the University of British Columbia have used what they call a Daily Process Method in which participants complete structured diaries about their stress and coping, twice daily, to closely monitor coping strategies over a variety of situations (DeLongis & Holtzman, 2005). Researchers have found that both personality factors and social factors influence coping, but also that the effect of personality is variable across different situations in which the stress occurs. In other words, personality is influential as well as situational variables, including social support. Personality and social psychology overlap in a great many studies, as they should if both personality and social factors are relevant to understanding social behaviour.

CLINICAL PSYCHOLOGY.   Clinical psychology is probably the best-known field within the larger field of psychology. When people think about the field of psychology, they often think about the role of clinical psychologists in diagnosing and treating mental health problems. Clinical psychology focuses on understanding and treating people with psychological disorders such as schizophrenia, depression, and phobias.

Social psychology also examines issues that are highly relevant for clinical psychology. Some social psychologists examine how the presence of very thin female models in the media can influence women's attitudes about their own bodies and thereby contribute to eating disorders (Chapter 3). In Chapter 4, you'll learn why people who blame their failures on themselves are at greater risk of experiencing depression than those who blame their failures on other people. Other social psychologists examine strategies for promoting better psychological and physical health, including ways of reducing rates of smoking (Chapter 6), strategies for increasing condom use (Chapter 7), and methods for increasing relationship satisfaction (Chapter 14).

COGNITIVE PSYCHOLOGY.   Cognitive psychology examines mental processes, including thinking, remembering, learning, and reasoning. For example, a cognitive psychologist might examine why people are more likely to buy a $200 sweater that is on sale for $50 than an identical sweater that is simply priced at $50, why some people have higher IQs than others, and why we sometimes "remember" things as having happened when they never actually did.

The *social cognitive perspective* is a combination of social psychology and cognitive psychology. This perspective refers to how we think about ourselves and the social world, with a particular focus on how we make judgements and decisions about our social environment. In some cases, our thoughts can lead us to make good, accurate decisions. In other cases, however, our thinking can lead us astray. For example, which of the following poses the greatest threat to children's safety: kidnapping by strangers or car accidents? Although many parents worry more about the former event, far more children are killed in motor vehicle accidents each year (often because they are not wearing a seatbelt or riding in a car seat) than are abducted by a kidnapper. We'll learn more about this and other errors in thinking in Chapter 5.

LINKS TO OTHER FIELDS

Social psychology is a distinct field within psychology, but it also shares a number of features with disciplines other than psychology. This section will examine the links between social psychology and philosophy, sociology, biology, anthropology, and economics.

PHILOSOPHY.   In the development of North American and European thought, the influence of ancient Greek philosophers such as Socrates, Aristotle, and Plato is still evident (Leahey, 2004). The word *psychology* derives from the Greek words for study and spirit/soul. In the Western tradition, the Greeks were the first to write about the link between thought, emotions, and behaviour in trying to explain people's actions. For example, Democritus, who lived around 400 BCE, suggested that our behaviour is essentially determined by the pursuit of pleasure and the avoidance of pain. It is easy to recognize in this the principles of reward and punishment that are central to behaviourism.

Contemporary philosophy can be described as a humanistic discipline that considers existential questions such as the meaning of life, ethics, human nature, and values. While there may be some overlap in the questions that philosophers and social psychologists address (e.g., Why do we love?), their methods for answering such questions are very different. Philosophers use analytical methods such as logic, while social psychologists rely on empirical and scientific methods. Of course, philosophical conclusions might be the basis for a hypothesis that social psychologists can then test using the scientific method.

SOCIOLOGY.   Sociology examines general rules and theories about groups, ranging from very small groups to large societies, and specifically how such groups affect people's attitudes and behaviour. Sociologists are likely to focus on broad group-level variables such as culture, social class, and ethnicity. For example, a sociologist might examine why rates of homicide in Canada are much lower than in the United States.

Similarly, social psychologists study how individual people behave in groups, as well as how one's group or culture can influence a person's behaviour. However, social psychologists are more likely to focus on the effects of immediate and specific variables, such as mood, temperature, and other people, on attitudes and behaviour, and to examine the influence of the group on the individual, not simply broader trends of the group behaviour.

BIOLOGY.   The field of biology examines the structure, function, growth, origin, and evolution of living things. Biologists examine how species evolve over time, the role of genes in influencing traits and attributes, and how individuals grow and develop over time. The link between social psychology and biology has received greater attention in recent years as research in social psychology has examined the role of biology in influencing such factors as aggression, altruism, and attraction. The sub-discipline of *evolutionary psychology* examines how biological factors can influence people's behaviour; it proposes that certain types of behaviour are "selected for" and hence have survived over time. In Chapter 12, you'll learn how evolutionary pressures influence rates of aggression, and why, from an evolutionary perspective, men tend to show higher levels of aggression than women. Chapter 13 examines the influence of evolutionary pressures on choices people make about who to help—why, in an emergency, we favour young people over the elderly, and genetically close relatives (siblings, children, and parents) over more distant relations (cousins, aunts and uncles, and grandparents). In Chapter 14, you'll read about how evolutionary psychologists explain gender differences in preferences for different characteristics in a dating partner, as well as why men and women may find their jealousy triggered by different types of infidelity.

The influence of biology on people's thoughts and feelings is also studied within the sub-discipline of **social neuroscience**, an interdisciplinary field that emerged in the early 1990s. This field examines how factors in the social world influence activity in the brain, as well as how neural processes influence attitudes and behaviour (Cacioppo et al., 2007; Harmon-Jones & Devine, 2003; Heatherton, Macrae, & Kelley, 2004). This increased focus on the role of the brain in influencing people's attitudes, thoughts, and behaviour is driven in part by the increasing availability of new techniques for studying brain activity, including positron emission tomography (PET) and functional magnetic resonance imaging (fMRI). Both of these techniques measure blood flow to particular areas of the brain, which is thought to reflect activity.

social neuroscience – a sub-discipline of social psychology examining how factors in the social world influence activity in the brain, as well as how neural processes influence attitudes and behaviour

As a result of technological advances, an increasing number of social psychologists are investigating the interaction between brain activity and experiences in the social world. For example, in Chapter 11 you'll learn that different parts of the brain are activated depending on whether people are looking at faces of their own ethnicity or a different ethnicity (Hart et al., 2000). In Chapter 14, you'll learn that particular parts of the brain are most active when people are thinking about people they love (Aron et al., 2005). Given the growing importance of the field of social neuroscience in social psychology, each chapter in this book will describe a specific research study that uses such techniques. The following Research Focus on Neuroscience describes a study showing that physical and social pain both activate the same part of the brain.

RESEARCH FOCUS ON NEUROSCIENCE
How Rejection Looks in the Brain

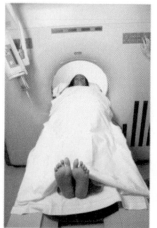

Blend Images/SUPERSTOCK
The technique used for fMRI imaging involves measuring the blood oxygen level in a given part of the brain, with the assumption that a higher level of blood oxygen is a sign of greater activity. Imagine that you are picking up a stack of heavy books, or groceries, in your arms. This muscular activity would lead to a greater flow of blood oxygen to the part of the brain responsible for moving your arms (*Cacioppo et al., 2003*).

To help you understand how the rapidly growing field of neuroscience contributes to our knowledge about social psychological theories, most chapters will feature a Research Focus on Neuroscience box that presents an in-depth look at a particular research study in neuroscience. For example, one compelling example of how techniques in neuroscience can help psychologists understand social processes comes from a clever research study conducted by Naomi Eisenberger and her colleagues (Eisenberger, Lieberman, & Williams, 2003). Participants in this study underwent brain scans in fMRI machines while they played "CyberBall," a virtual ball-tossing game in which they believed they were tossing a ball to two other participants. After a few rounds, the other two participants suddenly stopped passing the ball to one participant, which led that participant to feel ignored and excluded. Interestingly, the part of the brain that was active when participants experienced these negative emotions was precisely the same part of the brain that is activated when people experience physical pain. This research suggests that both social and physical pain share a common neurological basis.

ANTHROPOLOGY.　Anthropology examines the concept of culture, and specifically the role of culture in influencing people's attitudes and behaviour. For example, anthropologists may study the social significance of food in different cultures, the impact of culture on gender differences, and how cultures vary in their interpretations of the links between health and illness.

Social psychology originated in Western cultures, and much of the early research was therefore conducted by Western researchers using people living in Western cultures. However, in the last two decades social psychologists have shown more interest in examining the impact of culture on people's thoughts, feelings, and behaviours. Some of their work is informed by earlier anthropological research. For example, anthropologists were among the first to discuss the relative importance of the group or the individual in different cultures, or of post-Confucian values in East Asia (e.g., Benedict, 1989; Wright, 1960). These differences were then later identified and measured by Hofstede (1980, 2001) and other social psychologists, including the research group called the Chinese Culture Connection (1987) led by Canadian researcher Michael Harris Bond. The impact of culture on theory and research in social psychology will be described in detail in each chapter. For example, you'll learn about the impact of culture on rates of aggression (Chapter 12), frequency of helping behaviour (Chapter 13), and definitions of love (Chapter 14).

behavioural economics – the study of how social, cognitive, and emotional factors influence economic decisions

ECONOMICS.　Economics studies how people make trade-offs between scarce resources and how they choose between various alternatives. For example, an economist might examine how people choose between two different jobs, or the factors that lead a person to spend money now rather than save it for the future. Economists also examine why people make choices that do not maximize their well-being—such as giving money to charitable causes instead of using it themselves—and why people make cognitive errors. For example, they'll examine why a person may choose a medical treatment when it's presented as the numbers of years of life to be gained but reject it if it's presented in terms of years lost.

In particular, the field of **behavioural economics** applies research on social, cognitive, and emotional biases to understand how people make economic decisions (Ariely & Norton, 2007; Thaler, 1980). In 2002, psychologist Daniel Kahneman of Princeton University received the Nobel Prize in Economics in large part due to his focus on issues at the intersection of psychology and economics, including fairness in the marketplace (Kahneman, Knetsch, & Thaler, 1986a, 1986b, 1990). In Chapter 5, you'll learn about Kahneman's research on errors in social decision-making.

NewsCom
Professor Daniel Kahneman of Princeton University won the Nobel Prize in 2002 for his work, in collaboration with the late Amos Tversky, on decision-making.

Social psychologists also focus on how people make particular choices as well as the costs and benefits of various alternatives. In Chapter 9, you'll learn how people make decisions that will benefit themselves rather than their broader group. In Chapter 13, you'll learn about the cost-benefit analysis that people perform before they decide to help a person in need. In Chapter 14, you'll learn that physically attractive people experience many benefits that others do not, including higher starting salaries and bigger raises.

[CONCEPTS IN CONTEXT]

EXAMPLES OF THE LINK BETWEEN SOCIAL PSYCHOLOGY AND OTHER FIELDS

FIELDS WITHIN PSYCHOLOGY	SAMPLE RESEARCH QUESTION
Personality psychology	Do people who are high in neuroticism hold more negative attitudes toward others?
Clinical psychology	Do depressed people see the world in a more pessimistic way?
Cognitive psychology	Do people remember more negative behaviours performed by out-group members than by in-group members?

FIELDS OUTSIDE OF PSYCHOLOGY	SAMPLE RESEARCH QUESTION
Philosophy	How can we define or explain the experience of consciousness? What is mind?
Sociology	How do divorce rates differ as a function of ethnicity?
Anthropology	How do cultures vary in the meaning they attach to different body shapes and sizes?
Biology	How do evolutionary factors predict altruistic behaviour?
Economics	How does paying students to read influence their frequency of reading in the future?

HOW DOES SOCIAL PSYCHOLOGY APPLY ACROSS CULTURES AND SUBCULTURES?

Most of the early research in social psychology was conducted almost entirely by researchers in Western cultures, such as Canada, the United States, Australia, and western Europe. These researchers studied people and events in their own country, largely for convenience, and assumed that their general findings would apply equally well to people and events across different cultures. However, more recent research reveals that culture can have a dramatic impact on how people think about themselves and the social world (Matsumoto & Yoo, 2006). This **sociocultural perspective** describes people's behaviour and mental processes as being shaped in part by their social and/or cultural context. This section will examine the distinctions between different types of cultures and how culture can have an impact on findings and theories in social psychology.

sociocultural perspective – a perspective describing people's behaviour and mental processes as being shaped in part by their social and/or cultural context

INDIVIDUALISTIC VERSUS COLLECTIVISTIC CULTURES

Canadian and other Western cultures, such as those of the United States, Australia, and the United Kingdom, are **individualistic** cultures, meaning cultures in which independence, self-reliance, autonomy, and personal identity are valued (Hofstede, 2001; Markus & Kitayama, 1991, 1994; Noon & Lewis, 1992; Triandis, 1989). In individualistic cultures, people describe the self as a unique set of attributes and traits, and see people's behaviour as

individualistic – a view of the self as distinct, autonomous, self-contained, and endowed with unique attributes emerging largely from such traits. A person may, for example, be described as hostile, optimistic, and/or conscientious, and these traits, in turn, lead to specific patterns of behaviour. Individuals in individualistic cultures focus on expressing their own needs, goals, and preferences. In individualistic cultures, people are told to follow their dreams, struggle against blind conformity and obedience, and be all they can be. Groups are often seen as destructive forces that pressure and intimidate individuals. According to Hofstede's data (2001), the most individualistic nations in the world are, in order, the United States, Australia, the United Kingdom, Canada, the Netherlands, and Hungary (the last three countries tie at fourth, fifth, and sixth ranking).

collectivistic – a view of the self as part of a larger social network, including family, friends, and co-workers

Other cultures, in contrast, are more **collectivistic** in their orientation, and are focused on interdependence, harmony, cooperation, and social identity (Hofstede, 2001; Markus & Kitayama, 1994; Noon & Lewis, 1992; Triandis, 1989). In these cultures, the self is viewed as fundamentally integrated with one's relationships and social group, and people focus on maintaining interdependence with others. One's thoughts, feelings, and behaviours are all influenced by those of one's group. In many collectivistic cultures, a desire for independence is seen as unnatural and immature, and people may even fear being separated and different from others. Asserting one's unique needs and desires interrupts feelings of group solidarity and harmony, and hence people are willing to sacrifice their own particular wants in favour of the group. According to Hofstede (2001), the five most collectivistic nations in the world are, in order, Guatemala, Ecuador, Panama, Venezuela, and Columbia. Note that although Japan and China are highly collectivistic nations relative to North American, northern European, and similar cultures, they are considerably more individualistic than the five most collectivistic nations.

Distinctions between collectivistic and individualistic concepts are illustrated in Table 1.2.

Culture influences how people see and act in the social world, and even how people see themselves. In one study, Malaysian, Australian, and British adults were asked to complete the Twenty Statements Test (Bochner, 1994). This test simply asks people to respond 20 times to the open-ended prompt "Who are you?" and is a commonly used approach for measuring how people see, or define, themselves. Sixty-one percent of the British responses and 68 percent of the Australian responses focused on personal qualities and traits, such as "I am tall" and "I am outgoing." In contrast, only 48 percent of the Malaysian responses described personal qualities and traits, and 41 percent of the Malaysian responses referred to group memberships, including family relationships, religious group memberships, and occupational group memberships. These responses included "I am the youngest child in my family," "I am a member of a tennis club," and "I am a student." Only 18 percent of the British and 19 percent of the Australian responses described group memberships. It should be noted, however, that the differences between individualistic and collectivistic cultures are in emphasis only (Noon & Lewis, 1992): some of the British and Australian responses were expressions of social identity and some of the Malaysian responses were expressions of individual identity. Nevertheless, these different emphases do influence thoughts, feelings, and behaviour: in North America and western Europe, we shop to be distinctive, while in Japan one shops to be appropriate (Clammer, 1992).

Research that compares statements made by Americans versus statements by Indians reveals similar findings (Dhawan, Roseman, Naidu, & Rettek,

COLLECTIVISM:

Marx's "best idea"

Photo courtesy Rex Barron, www.rexbarron.com

Table 1.2	Differences Between Individualistic and Collectivistic Views of the Self	
INDEPENDENT SELF (CHARACTERISTIC OF INDIVIDUALISTIC SOCIETIES)	**INTERDEPENDENT SELF (CHARACTERISTIC OF COLLECTIVISTIC SOCIETIES)**
Be unique	Belong, fit in
Express self	Occupy one's proper place
Realize internal attributes	Engage in appropriate action
Promote own goals	Promote others' goals
Be direct: "Say what's on your mind"	Be indirect: "Read other's mind"

Source: Markus, H., & Kitayama, S. (1991). Culture and the self: Implications for cognition, emotion, and motivation. *Psychological Review, 98*, pp. 224-253.

1995). The majority of statements (65 percent) made by Americans describe their own attributes and traits. Only 34 percent of those made by Indians describe themselves. Moreover, even within the general category of self-evaluation, Americans describe feelings of self-worth and psychological attributes. In contrast, Indians are more likely to write about positive states.

WHAT'S YOUR CULTURAL ORIENTATION?

Self-Construal Scale

INSTRUCTIONS: *Rate your agreement with each of these items on a scale of 1 (strongly disagree) to 7 (strongly agree).*

1. My happiness depends very much on the happiness of others.
2. It is important for me to maintain harmony within my group.
3. The well-being of my co-workers is important to me.
4. I feel good when I cooperate with others.
5. Winning is everything.
6. It annoys me when other people perform better than I do.
7. I enjoy working in situations involving competition with others.
8. It is important for me to do my job better than others.

[RATE YOURSELF]

SCORING: Add up your scores on items 1 to 4. Then add up your scores on items 5 to 8.

INTERPRETATION: The first four items measure orientation toward collectivism. The last four items measure orientation toward individualism. People with a higher score on the first set of items than the second are more oriented toward collectivism, whereas people with a higher score on the second set of items are more oriented toward individualism (Singelis, Choo, & Hatfield, 1995).

Yim & Ebbeck (2009) compared children's preferences for group musical activities in child care centres in both a collectivistic and an individualistic society. A total of 228 young children aged 4–5 years in seven child care centres in Hong Kong and in Adelaide, Australia, participated in the study. The findings showed that there were relationships between children's cultural contexts and their musical preferences for activities including singing. Children in Hong Kong had a significantly higher level of preference for singing than did South Australian children. This reflects collectivism because the Hong Kong children's experience of singing involved activities that were more "social" than the Australian children. Particularly popular were two local social phenomena: children's participation in choirs, and the popularity of karaoke, both of which are social activities and have greater value to collectivistic cultures.

THE IMPACT OF CULTURE

Cross-cultural research, meaning research examining similar theories and findings across different cultures, sometimes reveals that people across different cultures see the world in largely the same way. For example, people in different cultures share views about what facial characteristics are attractive: prominent cheekbones, thin eyebrows, and big eyes (Cunningham et al, 1995; Langlois, Kalahonis, Rubenstein, Larson, Hallam, & Smoot, 2000).

In other cases, findings from research in Western cultures differ dramatically from those in other cultures. For example, the personality traits associated with attractiveness vary considerably across different cultures. In the United States "what is beautiful is good," whereas in Korea "what is beautiful is honest." As mentioned earlier in the chapter, research conducted in Western cultures also commonly finds that people tend to focus on the role of the person in influencing behaviour more than on the role of the situation. As you'll learn in detail in Chapter 4, the fundamental attribution error explains why if we notice a car following too closely behind us or driving too fast, we tend to make a personal or dispositional attribution for this behaviour ("That driver is a jerk!"), and not a situational attribution ("That driver must be in a hurry").

Who's Who in Contemporary Canadian Social Psychology Research

Courtesy Michael Harris Bond.

Michael Harris Bond is a Canadian-born academic who began teaching at the Chinese University of Hong Kong in 1974, and now works as Chair Professor of Psychology at the Hong Kong Polytechnic University. He was born in Toronto, completed his honours degree in psychology at the University of Toronto, and received his PhD from Stanford University. Professor Bond is a leading researcher in the field of Chinese and cross-cultural psychology and was president of the International Association for Cross-Cultural Psychology from 1998 to 2000. Among his major contributions is a multinational research project on social beliefs that assessed how people think the world works (i.e., the social axioms that people live by).

AN EXAMPLE OF CROSS-CULTURAL DIFFERENCES IN DEFINING SUCCESS

A boat docked in a tiny Mexican village. An American tourist complimented the Mexican fisherman on the quality of his fish and asked how long it took him to catch them.

"Not very long," answered the fisherman.

"But then, why didn't you stay out longer and catch more?" asked the American.

The Mexican explained that his small catch was sufficient to meet his needs and those of his family.

The American asked, "But what do you do with the rest of your time?"

"I sleep late, fish a little, play with my children, and take a siesta with my wife. In the evenings, I go into the village to see my friends, have a few drinks, play the guitar, and sing a few songs . . . I have a full life."

The American interrupted, "I have an MBA from Harvard and I can help you! You should start by fishing longer every day. You can then sell the extra fish you catch. With the extra revenue, you can buy a bigger boat."

SuperStock   SuperStock

People across cultures share relatively common views about what is attractive: prominent cheekbones, thin eyebrows, and big eyes (Cunningham et al., 1995; Langlois, Kalahonis, Rubenstein, Larson, Hallam, & Smoot, 2000).

"And after that?" asked the Mexican.

"With the extra money that the larger boat will bring, you can buy a second one and a third one and so on until you have an entire fleet of trawlers. Instead of selling your fish to a middleman, you can then negotiate directly with the processing plants and maybe even open your own plant. You can then leave this little village and move to Mexico City, Los Angeles, or even New York City! From there you can direct your huge new enterprise."

"How long would that take?" asked the Mexican.

"Twenty, perhaps twenty-five years," replied the American.

"And after that?"

"Afterward? Well, my friend, that's when it gets really interesting," answered the American, laughing. "When your business gets really big, you can start selling stocks and make millions!"

"Millions? Really? And after that?" said the Mexican.

"After that you'll be able to retire, live in a tiny village near the coast, sleep late, play with your children, catch a few fish, take a siesta with your wife, and spend your evenings drinking and enjoying yourself with your friends."

This story illustrates differences in how different cultures define success—is success gaining financial wealth or spending time with family and friends? People in individualistic cultures are more likely to define success in terms of individual accomplishments, such as acquiring great wealth, whereas those in collectivistic cultures are more likely to define success in terms of interpersonal relationships.

Although the tendency toward making a fundamental attribution error was assumed to be a general perceptual bias common to all people, cross-cultural research indicates that this bias is not commonly seen across all cultures. In fact, in many collectivistic cultures, people focus more on the role of the situation in influencing behaviour than on the role of the person (Choi, Nisbett, & Norenzayan, 1999). It turns out that the fundamental attribution error is not so fundamental after all and is actually quite culture-specific. This is just one example of how the knowledge we gain from studying one culture may not apply equally well to a different culture, and of how important it is for researchers to test theories across different cultures instead of simply assuming that people in different cultures will all respond in the same way.

SUBCULTURE AND OTHER SOCIAL OR DEMOGRAPHIC VARIABLES

Other research on culture examines differences between people who live in the same country but in different subcultures within that country. These subcultures, or different groups, could be based, for example, on region, socioeconomic status, or religion (Kashima, Kokubo, Boxall, Yamaguchi, & Macrae, 2004; Kitayama, Mesquita, & Karasawa, 2006).

Carole Peterson of Memorial University, and her colleagues compared the subcultures of Canadian children of European versus Chinese descent (Peterson, Wang, & Hou, 2009). As our understanding of who we are depends in part on our memories of ourselves, Peterson examined these children's early memories to determine differences in the two groups' perceptions of themselves. The researchers coded the memories into categories according to their content (e.g., family interactions, solitary play) and found that two of the three most frequent categories recalled by the children of Chinese descent involved a group. Conversely, two of the three most frequent categories for the children of European descent were of individual experiences. Although the children were all born in Canada, the greater emphasis on individualism in Canadian culture did not have as great an impact on the children of Chinese descent (see Figure 1.2).

FIGURE 1.2 **EARLY CHILDHOOD MEMORIES OF EUROPEAN-CANADIAN AND CHINESE-CANADIAN CHILDREN**

In this experiment, Canadian children of European and Chinese descent were asked about their early childhood memories to determine whether the individualistic nature of Canadian society had affected the children of Chinese descent (a collectivistic culture).

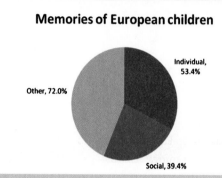

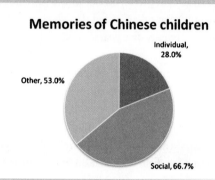

Source: Peterson, Wang, & Hou (2009).

CRITIQUES OF THE MAINSTREAM

SOCIAL CONSTRUCTIONISM. This text provides an overview of what is primarily mainstream social psychology. However, there are always dissenting voices in any discipline (if scientists always agreed, science would not advance) and this is the case in psychology too. Some psychologists even refer to themselves as critical psychologists, thereby setting themselves in opposition to the mainstream view of psychology as a science (e.g., Hepburn, 2003). One of the strongest and most influential critiques of the mainstream is **social constructionism**.

> **Social constructionism** – the view that there is no absolute reality and that our knowledge and what we understand to be reality are socially constructed

The basic idea of social constructionism is that knowledge and reality are relative to, or related to, the social circumstances and environment they come from. In other words, what we regard as reality is not absolute. Instead, it is socially constructed and exists in a particular social situation, and it is only understandable within the terms of that social situation. Still another way of saying this is that we only understand experiences of reality in relation to the concepts and categories that we have available. As Berger and Luckmann (1966) put it, "what is real to a Tibetan monk may not be 'real' to an American businessman" (p. 15). There are "hard" and "soft" versions of social constructionism (Averill, 1985). The soft version acknowledges that some psychological phenomena can be tested using a scientific approach, even though some of our reality is socially constructed.

Dittmar (1992) provides an example of scientific social psychological research that has a social constructionist perspective. She studied the symbolic significance of material possessions, but was able to measure and analyze the extent to which different types of symbolism (e.g., identity, achievement, relationships) were important for people. She did this by asking people to explain, in their own words, the significance of their important possessions. Then, using a technique known as content analysis, Dittmar quantified different aspects of the object's significance to the respondent. Such an approach is an attempt to put the focus on respondents' own representations rather than on those of the researchers. In studies like these, the categories of significance that typically emerge present the possession as a symbol for aspects of a person's identity, either in individual terms (such as personal history or personal achievement) or in terms of the person's connectedness to others (e.g., to family members, a group, or to another individual), or the categories relate to the object's use, which is often discussed in terms of control (e.g., an efficient tool), and sometimes in terms of emotional mediation (e.g., something that makes the person happy). So, material possessions symbolize identity, mediate emotions, and enhance perceived (or actual) control. Dittmar also found gender differences. Women tended to value their favoured objects in a relational and symbolic manner, while men tended toward activity-related, functional, and self-oriented concerns.

THE BIG PICTURE

INTRODUCTION

As described at the start of this chapter, social psychology examines three distinct but interrelated topics:

How the social world influences how we think about ourselves	How the social world influences our thoughts, attitudes, and behaviour	How our attitudes and behaviour shape the social world around us

WHAT YOU'VE LEARNED

This chapter has described the nature of social psychology, including the topics addressed within this field, how it has evolved over time, and how it is connected to other fields.

1. What social psychology is

This section examined the definition of social psychology, and the topics addressed within this discipline. These topics include how we think about ourselves; how we think, feel, and act in the social world; and how our attitudes and behaviour shape the social world.

2. How social psychology evolved over time

This section described how the field of social psychology has evolved over time. This discipline was heavily influenced by behaviourism, Gestalt psychology, and historical events.

3. Whether social psychology is really just common sense.

This section examined whether social psychology is just "common sense." You learned about the "I knew it all along" problem, and the importance of using the scientific method to test theories and hypotheses within

this field. This section also described how to use critical thinking to test information you are given.

4. How social psychology is connected to other fields

This section examined how social psychology is connected to fields within and outside of psychology. First, it described the connection between social psychology and other fields within psychology, including personality psychology, clinical psychology, and cognitive psychology. Next, you learned how social psychology is connected to fields outside of psychology, including sociology, biology, anthropology, and economics.

5. How social psychology applies across cultures and subcultures

This section examined the impact of culture on theory and research in social psychology. You learned about the impact of culture as well as the distinction between individualistic and collectivistic cultures.

Key Terms

behavioural economics 18
behaviourism 8
collectivistic 20
Gestalt psychology 9
hindsight bias 12
hypothesis 5
individualistic 19

positive psychology 11
scientific method 5
self-fulfilling prophecy 8
self-perception 6
self-presentation 6
social cognition 6
social constructionism 24

social influence 6
social neuroscience 17
social perception 6
social psychology 5
sociocultural perspective 19

Questions for Review

1. Describe three distinct issues examined by social psychology.

2. How have historical events influenced theory and research in social psychology?

3. Describe the "I knew it all along" phenomenon, and one strategy for critically examining information.

4. How is social psychology connected to two disciplines within psychology, and two disciplines outside of psychology?

5. Describe the major distinction between individualistic and collectivistic cultures.

Take Action!

At the end of each chapter, you'll read about five distinct ways in which you could put the information you've learned to practical use in the real world. These Take Action! ideas could include strategies for helping motivate your child to clean his or her room (Chapter 3), improving the effectiveness of sales techniques (Chapter 7), or working effectively with other students on a group project (Chapter 9).

To help you gain experience in conducting and evaluating research, each chapter will end with a series of activities that will give you exposure to research methods and techniques in social psychology. Additional activities and interactive tool are available on WileyPLUS. These activities will fall into three categories: "Participate in Research," "Test a Hypothesis," and "Design a Study."

Participate in Research

These activities will give you research experience as a participant—meaning the person who participates in a study. In these cases, you will complete a study in social psychology from the perspective of the participant, which will help give you a sense of exactly what participants themselves experience.

Test a Hypothesis

These activities will give you experience from the perspective of a researcher. In these activities, you'll be given a specific hypothesis to test that relates to a topic described in that chapter.

Design a Study

This final type of activity will give you a chance to create your own study. You'll be able to choose the type of study you want to conduct (self-report, observational/naturalistic, or experimental, and form your own hypothesis and approach to testing this hypothesis. This type of hands-on experience with research will help you better understand the challenges of conducting research in social psychology.

RESEARCH METHODS

DID YOU EVER WONDER?

Have you ever come across headlines in the media that make such ridiculous claims that they leave you wondering how they could possibly be true? Here are some examples.

Image Source/cpimages.com

- Breast implants lower cancer risk but boost suicides (*Cosmos Magazine*, September 2006)
- Attending religious services sharply cuts risk of death (Physorg.com, November 2008)
- Recession causes increase in teen dating violence (ABCNews, June 2009)
- Sugar rush. . . to prison? Study says lots of candy could lead to violence (CBC News, October 2009)

This is what happens when headline writers fail to make a distinction between correlation and causality. For instance, the first headline, which appeared in *Cosmos Magazine*, was attached to a story that detailed the work of a team of researchers from Université Laval in Quebec that collected data on more than 24,000 women in Ontario and Quebec who had breast implants for cosmetic purposes (Villeneuve et al., 2006). The researchers found that women with breast implants had a lower mortality rate (i.e., deaths from cancer and circulatory diseases) than the general population. It was also found that the suicide rate among these women was higher than in the general population. To explain these findings, the researchers argued that it is possible that women who consider breast implants are on average healthier than those in the general population. These women also tend to have higher socioeconomic status, a factor that is generally associated with better health. Furthermore, it was suggested that women who receive breast implants are likely to have lower levels of self-esteem, lower levels of self-confidence, and higher levels of depression (all factors that can contribute

MEDIA CONNECTIONS	ENVIRONMENTAL CONNECTIONS	HEALTH CONNECTIONS	LAW CONNECTIONS
	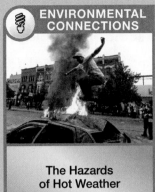		
The Growing Use of Web-Based Experiments	The Hazards of Hot Weather	Evaluating Abstinence-Only Sex Education	The Challenges of Studying Drinking and Driving

to thoughts of suicide). Additionally, some women may experience complications after implants, which could contribute to despair and further increase the chances of suicide. As you see in this example, there is not necessarily a direct link between breast implantation and suicide because there are far more risk factors associated with suicide than the *Cosmos* headline indicates. This illustrates the important difference between research that shows a correlation between two variables, and research that shows that one variable caused the other. This chapter will examine research methods such as experimental and correlational studies. You'll also find answers to these questions:

 Why are children who watch violent cartoons more likely to hit their siblings?

 Why do people underestimate their risky behaviour when answering surveys?

 Why do women eat less when they are talking with an attractive man?

 Why can university students who pretend to act as prison guards become violent very quickly?

 Why do American women tend to give more extreme answers to questions about dating than Indonesian-American female students?

These are typical questions that are examined by social psychologists using different types of research methods.

How researchers in social psychology test their ideas

The different types of correlational research methods

How experimental research is conducted

How qualitative research is conducted

The ethical issues in conducting research

How culture influences research findings

PREVIEW

Social psychology is rooted in the scientific method and therefore aims for scientific rigour. While different research methods achieve this to different degrees—a researcher will sometimes sacrifice some of the rigour of "hard science" in order to do research in a "real life" context rather than a lab—scientific research has these characteristics: it *describes* a phenomenon (for example, that people are more aggressive when it is very hot outside), *makes predictions* about it (that the rate of homicides should increase during the summer), and *explains* why it happens (many adverse environmental circumstances increase the likelihood of people acting more aggressively). In this chapter, you'll learn all about the research methods that are used in social psychology.

HOW DO RESEARCHERS IN SOCIAL PSYCHOLOGY TEST THEIR IDEAS?

This section will describe each of the steps in the research process (see Figure 2.1):

- forming a question
- searching the literature
- forming a hypothesis
- creating an operational definition
- collecting and analyzing data
- proposing or revising a theory

FORM A QUESTION

All research in social psychology, as in other scientific fields, starts with a question. Many studies in social psychology start with a question based on the observation of a real-world event. In Chapter 13, you'll learn about the murder of Kitty Genovese, which occurred while people who were watching failed to call the police. Why didn't anyone call for help? This tragic event led to numerous studies that tried to answer questions about which factors predict helping behaviours (or, in this case, not helping).

Sometimes the research questions are designed to test established theories in psychology. For example, many researchers have examined the predictors of prejudice and discrimination using, as their starting point, Realistic Conflict Theory, the belief that actual conflict between groups of people is based on competition between them for finite resources. For example, opinions such as "They're taking our jobs," an argument used against minority groups in a variety of contexts, can be seen as conflict in the form of prejudice, with jobs being the finite resource. You'll learn more about this theory in Chapter 10.

FIGURE 2.1 STEPS IN THE RESEARCH PROCESS

This figure describes each of the steps in the research process.

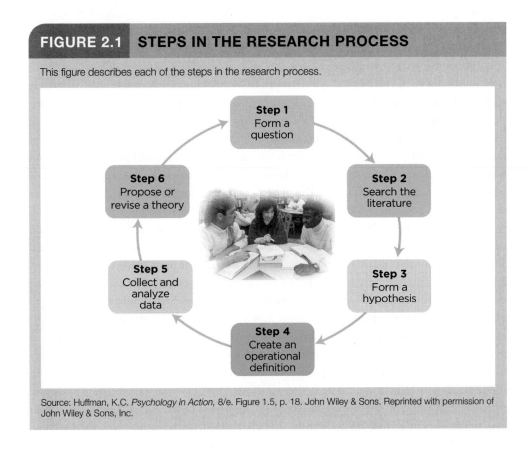

Source: Huffman, K.C. *Psychology in Action*, 8/e. Figure 1.5, p. 18. John Wiley & Sons. Reprinted with permission of John Wiley & Sons, Inc.

SEARCH THE LITERATURE

Because some ideas for research are likely to have already been studied by others, it is important to first determine what other people might have found out about the same, or similar, ideas. A literature review is not simply an introduction to an essay or report. It is an account of what other researchers have examined and found on a topic. It provides a guiding description of materials that are available on the topic. As a researcher, you therefore need to go to the library and read journal articles about research related to your question, or search on the web. Use on-line databases, such as PsychINFO and PsychLIT, that let you search for articles by a particular topic or author. Check out the library homepage at your school or ask a librarian for help.

For example, let's assume that you are interested in studying factors that are associated with information disclosure and control among those who use online social networks, such as Facebook. In order to study this topic, you have to review journal articles, chapters, and books on decision-making, specifically decisions that people make about managing their privacy. Emily Christofides, Amy Muise, and Serge Desmarais are three researchers from the University of Guelph who did exactly that. They explored empirical research that examined information disclosure and control on Facebook and identified a number of factors, such as self-esteem, trust, and need for popularity, that are associated with the disclosure and control of personal information on Facebook (Christofides, Muise, & Desmarais, 2009).

A literature review examines previous studies on a given topic, such as television violence and aggression, and attempts to reach an overall conclusion. A good literature review identifies useful articles and other sources of information that are relevant to the topic and that critically appraises them. This approach is often used when different studies have revealed different findings. The aim is to conduct a review of valid and unbiased studies. It is in the literature review that areas of controversy on the topic are identified and discussed. Without a good literature review, one risks reinventing the wheel; in other words, conducting a piece of research that you think is original, only to discover something similar has already been done.

literature review – examining previous relevant studies on a given topic and critically appraising them

FORM A HYPOTHESIS

hypothesis – a testable prediction about the conditions under which an event will occur

A **hypothesis** is a testable prediction about the conditions under which an event will occur. It is a statement about the expected cause and effect relationship between two variables, but is more specific than the original question you asked. Because a hypothesis can be directly tested, it includes a specific prediction. Usually, a hypothesis is based on previous observations and is therefore formed after reviewing existing literature on the topic. For example, in the example given above (Christofides, Muise, & Desmarais, 2009), the hypothesis was that the same personality variables that predict information disclosure would predict information control on Facebook. The two processes (disclosure and control) were predicted to be highly but negatively related to each other. The hypothesis is therefore a tentative statement about the relationship between two or more variables. In this case, the hypothesis is about the relationship between personality variables such as self-esteem, trust, and need for popularity, and behavioural tendencies toward information disclosure and information control on Facebook. It should be noted that this is a correlational study. Although the term "prediction" is used, this does not mean that one variable causes the other. Rather, the researchers were only predicting that there would be a negative correlation between the variables. Stated differently, this means that there could be another variable that influences both variables being studied. If the researchers had wanted to test for a causal relationship, they might then, for example, have decided to manipulate self-esteem (e.g., by giving subjects positive feedback on a task) to see if that leads to (causes) more disclosure. This type of study is what we call an experimental approach, and is discussed more fully below. There is also what is known as a quasi-experimental approach, which, in our example, might have involved finding groups of people with high self-esteem and groups of people with low self-esteem and predicting that the former will disclose more on Facebook. This approach is quasi-experimental because it samples pre-existing groups and then treats them as if they are different experimental groups.

CREATE AN OPERATIONAL DEFINITION

operational definition – a specific procedure or measure that one uses to test a hypothesis

An **operational definition** describes a specific procedure or measure that you'll use to test your hypothesis. For example, in their study, Christofides, Muise, and Desmarais (2009) needed a procedure for testing how people control their personal information on Facebook. They therefore developed a scale consisting of seven questions (or *items*—questions in a survey or questionnaire are always referred to as items) about how people used Facebook's privacy settings. For example, they asked, "How likely are you to say no to a Facebook friend's request in order to control who has access to your information?" Personal disclosure on Facebook is a relatively new research topic, so Christofides and colleagues had to design their own operational definition of this concept. But as there has been a great deal of research on self-esteem over the past few decades, they didn't need to develop a scale of their own for an operational definition of this concept. Instead, they used a well-established and reliable self-esteem scale, the Rosenberg Self-Esteem Scale. Researchers can define their variables in very different ways, which can influence the findings. If you have a good operational definition, your measure is valid—in other words, it measures what it's supposed to measure. If you don't, it won't. Asking people about specific examples of control and behaviour on Facebook (such as saying no to a friend request in order to control who has access to your information) is taken by these researchers to be a valid measure of people's control of personal information in this context.

COLLECT AND ANALYZE DATA

Data can be collected in different ways—by observation, through surveys, from pre-existing documents (e.g., medical records), or via experiment. To test information disclosure and information control among Facebook users, you could observe the behaviour of your friends on Facebook and record their level of disclosure online. However, it's important to note that although you would be able to collect some data by observation, it wouldn't be so easy to collect information about your friends' personality variables, such as their self-esteem, in this way. Instead of observation, Christofides, Muise, and Desmarais (2009) chose to use an online survey to collect data from more than 300 undergraduate students who were current Facebook users. This is an appropriate method of data collection as more than 90 percent of students use Facebook, so, the sample is likely to be representative of the general student population. Participants completed a survey that measured aspects of their personality including self-esteem, needs of popularity, levels of trust, and general tendency to disclose personal information.

After the data are collected, the next step is to analyze them. For many researchers, this is the best part of conducting research because they get to see if their ideas are supported by data. Students who answered the Facebook survey reported that they disclosed more information about themselves on Facebook than they did in general. The participants also reported that information control and privacy were important to them. However, the researchers didn't find support for their hypothesis that information disclosure and information control are negatively correlated. Instead, they found that the need for popularity predicted disclosure, while levels of trust and self-esteem predicted information control. In other words, disclosure and control on Facebook are affected by different aspects of personality and are not as closely related as the researchers had hypothesized.

Media Connections describes a new approach to collecting data on the Internet.

MEDIA CONNECTIONS

The Growing Use of Web-Based Experiments

Recently, social psychologists have started to conduct studies using the Internet. Web-based research has advantages over traditional methods, particularly when collecting self-report surveys. One of the greatest advantages is the ability to collect large amounts of data at low cost from many people. Web-based surveys also allow researchers to collect data from a more diverse group of participants than the typical university or college student sample because Web-based surveys tend to attract participants from a broader range of ages and backgrounds. In addition to these advantages, however, several large-scale studies of Web-based research have also found a number of problems (Gosling, Vazire, Srivastava, & John, 2004; Johnson, 2005).

First, Web-based studies are very likely to include repeat participants. In one study, approximately 4 percent of the responses were resubmitted by the same participants, meaning people completed the survey more than once. This can happen, for example, when people with more than one email account complete the same survey using different email addresses. In such instances, certain types of responses will therefore appear more common than they actually are—decreasing the accuracy of the study.

Second, participants who are completing a survey on the Web may read items carelessly—or not at all—in part because they are not being watched by an experimenter. In fact, approximately 3.5 percent of the responses to Web-based studies were submitted by individuals who had not read the response options.

This error occurs in less than 1 percent of cases in pencil-and-paper self-reports.

Third, participants who complete Web-based studies may skip items, either intentionally (they are bored) or unintentionally (they don't see the instructions at the top of the screen). In line with this view, the rate of missing data in Web-based surveys, while low (1.2 percent), is much higher than the rate for standard self-reports. In sum, although Web-based research has advantages, researchers should be aware of its potential limitations and should take steps to minimize these common errors.

© iStockphoto.com/Rich Legg

PROPOSE OR REVISE A THEORY

theory – an organized set of principles that explain observed phenomena

The final step in the research process is proposing a **theory**, meaning an organized set of principles that explain observed phenomena. Although hypotheses are specific predictions about the association between two events (such as watching violence on television and engaging in aggressive behaviour), they do not explain how or why these two events are connected. In contrast, theories give potential explanations. For example, according to social learning theory, exposure to violence on television leads to aggression through a variety of processes (e.g., modelling, which means learning through observing the actions of others, as you'll see in Chapter 12). Sometimes a study's results lead to the revision of a particular theory. At other times, they refute the theory altogether. Because theories provide one type of explanation for a given phenomenon, they also generate questions for future research—which in turn starts the research process over again. Christofides, Muise, and Desmarais (2009), the example that we have used to illustrate the six steps of the research the process, concluded in their study of Facebook users that information disclosure and information control may not be two ends of the same spectrum, as previous research had suggested, but are instead independent behaviours that are influenced by different aspects of personality. Based on the results of their study, this is their revision to pre-existing theory.

[CONCEPTS IN CONTEXT]

STEPS IN THE RESEARCH PROCESS

STEP	EXAMPLE
Form a question.	Does watching aggression on television lead children to act aggressively?
Search the literature.	What have other researchers done to examine this question?
Form a hypothesis.	Children who watch adults act aggressively on television will behave more aggressively than children who do not watch such aggression.
Create an operational definition.	Aggression will be measured as the number of times, in the 15 minutes following exposure to the aggression on television, that a child hits or pushes another child or threatens to, or says something to another that is judged to be aggressive. Violence on TV will be regarded as depictions of a person or persons who consciously commit an act which kills, injures, or causes another person suffering, against his or her will, or which inflicts damage on an inanimate object.
Collect and analyze data.	Researchers will observe children's behaviour following exposure to the aggression on television. Having decided what specific behaviours they will regard as aggression, researchers will examine whether rates of aggression are higher in children who watched the aggression on television than in children who didn't watch it.
Propose or revise a theory.	Researchers will propose a social learning theory of aggression stating that exposure to aggression leads to modelling this behaviour.

WHAT ARE THE DIFFERENT TYPES OF CORRELATIONAL RESEARCH METHODS?

Imagine that you decide to take part in a psychology study and are asked questions about your alcohol use and sexual behaviour. These questions ask for highly personal information, including whether you've had sex without a condom, whether you've consumed alcohol, and whether you've had sex after drinking. Such a study was actually performed (LaBrie & Earleywine, 2000), with students in one condition being asked to check which of each of these statements were true for them—a direct approach. In the same study, students in another condition were asked to read a group of statements and indicate how many of the statements were true for them *but not indicate* which specific statements were true—an indirect approach. Researchers then compared how many total statements were rated as true in each of these two conditions.

As predicted, researchers found that fewer students were willing to directly acknowledge risky behaviour than were willing to indirectly acknowledge such behaviour. For example, only 36 percent of students admitted to having engaged in sex without a condom after consuming alcohol when they were given a standard self-report questionnaire that directly asked about this behaviour. However, 65 percent admitted to engaging in this behaviour when they were given a questionnaire that asked this question indirectly. This study illustrates some of the challenges in designing surveys and self-report measures, which are a type of **correlational research** method for examining issues in social psychology.

Correlational research methods examine the association between two or more variables (e.g., height and weight, which are highly correlated). This section will examine the two major types of correlational research that are used in the field of social psychology: observational/naturalistic methods and self-reports/surveys. We'll see the advantages and disadvantages of each approach.

correlational research – a research technique that examines the extent to which two or more variables are associated with one another

Who's Who in Contemporary Canadian Social Psychology Research

Courtesy Serge Desmarais

Serge Desmarais is professor of Psychology at the University of Guelph, Ontario. He received his BA, MA, and PhD in social psychology from the University of Waterloo. Professor Desmarais's research interests focus on the impact of gender norms and gender socialization on women's and men's lives. His two primary areas of concentration are psychology and social justice and gender issues related to income distribution. Professor Desmarais was the recipient of a Canada Research Chair in Applied Social Psychology (2002–2007). He is the author of several scholarly papers and chapters, the co-author of two introductory psychology textbooks, the recipient of two university teaching awards and is also the former associate editor of *Canadian Psychology*.

OBSERVATIONAL/NATURALISTIC METHODS

Observational or naturalistic methods are used to describe and measure people's behaviour in everyday situations. In the observational approach, researchers observe behaviour and systematically record that behaviour (see, for example, the operational definition of aggression in the Concepts in Context: Steps in the Research Process box).

observational/naturalistic methods – a research approach that involves the observation and systematic recording of a particular behaviour

To examine adolescent sexual behaviour and other risk factors for sexually transmitted infections (STIs), Mo, Wong, and Merrick (2007) conducted naturalistic research by examining data on 44,430 adolescents aged 12 to 19 years old from the Canadian Community Health Survey (CCHS). Their analysis revealed that STIs are associated with the following: female gender; Canadian-born status; less than secondary education level; low annual family income; having multiple sexual partners; not using a condom at last sexual encounter; and a history of alcohol, tobacco, and drug use. This is an example of archival research (which is explained below), but it is still naturalistic as the data were produced in a natural context (i.e., real-life medical appointments) rather than in a laboratory.

Some researchers collect their data by observing social interactions and rating them in various ways. For example, if you were interested in examining whether boys or girls are more aggressive, you could watch children playing on a playground and count their aggressive behaviours (e.g., hitting, name calling, kicking, throwing). Researchers who use this approach try to be as unobtrusive as possible to avoid influencing the behaviour of the people who are being observed.

You can also collect naturalistic data without observing people's behaviour directly. If you were interested in examining the association between living in a fraternity and pizza consumption,

Cartoon by Paul Mason.

archival research – a research
approach that uses already recorded
behaviour

each week you could count the number of empty pizza boxes in the garbage at a fraternity and at a different type of housing situation (e.g., a student residence). If you found that fraternities had many more empty pizza boxes each week than dorms, you might conclude that there is a link between pizza consumption and fraternity life. Researchers in one clever study in the United States on the factors leading to the common cold gathered and weighed used tissues as a way of measuring mucus produced (Cohen, Doyle, Skoner, Rabin, & Gwaltney, 1997).

Another observational/naturalistic approach is **archival research**, in which researchers use already recorded behaviour, such as divorce rates, death rates, sports statistics, crime rates, weather reports, or, as we saw in our example above, statistics for sexually transmitted infections. In Chapter 4, we will look at a famous archival study in which researchers examined newspaper quotations from famous baseball players to form theories about their personalities and then measured their life expectancies (Peterson & Seligman, 1987). In Chapter 8, we will look at an archival study on the effects that publicizing suicides has on subsequent rates of suicide (Phillips, 1982). Environmental Connections describes the use of archival research to examine whether hot temperatures are associated with higher crime rates.

ENVIRONMENTAL CONNECTIONS

The Hazards of Hot Weather

Researchers who examine the impact of climate on rates of aggression often rely on archival data. In one study, Craig Anderson and colleagues examined the association between the number of hot days (days when the maximum temperature reached 32°C) in a given summer and the rate of violent crimes in 50 different American cities (Anderson, Bushman, & Groom, 1997). As predicted, hotter summers were associated with more violent crimes, including assault, property crime, and rape. Other research reveals that aggressive crimes occur more frequently in the hotter geographic regions of countries (e.g., the American south versus the northern states), and that violent crimes occur more frequently in the summer than in the winter (Anderson, 1989). In fact there is a perception of southerners being more emotionally expressive than northerners in many countries, particularly in the northern hemisphere (where the south is generally warmer). In a study conducted in 26 countries, northerners were viewed as less emotionally expressive than southerners in the United States, Switzerland, Spain, Serbia, Japan, Italy, Germany, France, and Belgium—and the effect was reversed in some southern hemisphere countries (e.g., Indonesia and Columbia). Although overall the hypothesis that people in warmer climates are more expressive was supported, there are clearly other factors at play, possibly involving specific cultural differences. For example, here in Canada samples taken from British Columbia and Quebec showed that stereotypes differentiating northerners versus southerners don't exist for Canadians. Perhaps in Canada a different grouping is more appropriate, such as Anglophones versus Francophones rather than northerner versus southerners. In England, the stereotype was opposite, with northerners being perceived as more emotionally expressive than southerners (Pennebaker, Rimé, & Blankenship, 1996).

The Canadian Press/Ryan Remiorz

A particular literature review that analyzes data from different studies that examine related hypothesis is called a **meta-analysis**. Meta-analyses use a statistical technique for combining data that have been collected by different researchers, which evens out the strengths and weaknesses of particular studies as all the data are considered simultaneously. Meta-analyses have been used to examine a variety of issues in social psychology, including attitudes toward rape (Anderson, Cooper, & Okamura, 1997), gender differences in the attributions people make for success and failure (Swim & Sanna, 1996), the link between attitudes and behaviour (Kraus, 1995), the impact of extrinsic rewards on intrinsic motivation (Deci, Koestner, & Ryan, 1999), and the extent to which conformity to social norms varies across cultures (Bond & Smith, 1996). In Chapter 4, the idea known as "belief in a just world" is discussed. This is the general view that some people hold that the world is essentially a fair place, that good things happen to good people, and so on. A meta-analysis by Wendy O'Connor from Carlton University and her colleagues found no significant difference between men and women in a meta-analysis of studies on belief in a just world (O'Connor, Morrison, McLeod, & Anderson, 1996). Note that (and this doesn't just apply to meta-analyses) research is still valid even if it doesn't produce statistically significant results. In other words, while research often reports differences between men and women, research that finds similarities is also important although under reported.

meta-analysis – a literature review that analyzes data from several studies that examine related hypothesis

ADVANTAGES.   What are the advantages of using naturalistic or observational methods? Because these methods are based on the observation of real-world phenomena, they help researchers develop hypotheses and theories. They also have internal validity and are less vulnerable to criticisms that they are artificial than some experimental studies (as you will see below). Studies using these methods are also relatively easy to conduct. They usually rely either on observing naturally occurring situations, or on analyzing already collected data, and therefore do not require extensive laboratory space, equipment, and assistance.

Naturalistic methods can also provide data about events that researchers would be unable to examine in other settings. We have already encountered the example of researchers using archival data to examine the link between temperature and rates of homicide (Anderson, Bushman, & Groom, 1997), which would be impossible to gather in any other way.

inter-rater reliability – the extent to which two or more coders agree on ratings of a particular measure

Naturalistic methods can also provide large amounts of data that researchers would never be able to collect on their own. This is particularly important, for example, when researchers are interested in examining how something has changed over time: it is unlikely that a researcher would be able to design a study and then follow the participants for 20 years (although you'll read about such a study examining the link between exposure to violence on television as a child and levels of adult aggression in Chapter 12).

off the mark.com   by Mark Parisi

NEAR AS WE CAN TELL, THE GREEN LIGHT MEANS "PROCEED" AND THE RED LIGHT MEANS "STOP AND PUT YOUR FINGER UP YOUR NOSE..."

©1992 MARK PARISI
www.offthemark.com

LIMITATIONS.   One problem with the observational approach is that the presence of the observer is likely to influence behaviour. People typically behave differently when they know that they're being watched.

The observer's own biases can also influence how they interpret the behaviour they observe. One person might interpret pushing between children on a playground as normal behaviour. Another person might see such behaviour as a sign of aggression or hostility. To help limit the problems of observer bias, researchers often have at least two people do the ratings independently, and then measure how often they agree. This is called **inter-rater reliability**.

The most important limitation Dif observational methods is that while such approaches can show whether two variables are *correlated*, or associated, with each other, they cannot tell us which

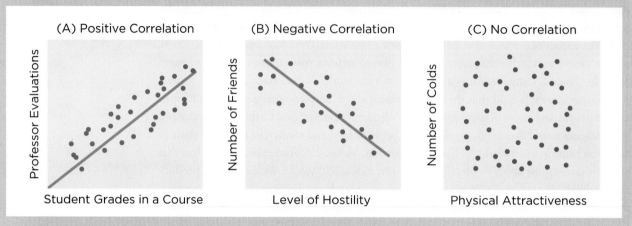

FIGURE 2.2 | TYPES OF CORRELATION

Figure A shows a positive correlation (as student grades increase, positive professor evaluations increase), Figure B shows a negative correlation (as hostility increases, number of friends decreases), and Figure C shows no correlation (as physical attractiveness increases, number of colds doesn't change).

(A) Positive Correlation — Professor Evaluations / Student Grades in a Course

(B) Negative Correlation — Number of Friends / Level of Hostility

(C) No Correlation — Number of Colds / Physical Attractiveness

Source: Kowalski & Weston, *Psychology,* fifth edition, John Wiley & Sons. Figure 2.6, page 54. Reprinted with permission of John Wiley & Sons, Inc.

variable causes the other. For example, if we find—as research shows—that students who receive better grades in a class give their professor better ratings, what can we conclude? We know there is a correlation—students who receive higher grades in a class give that professor more positive teaching evaluations (*a positive correlation*). But even though we know there is an association or correlation between these two events or variables (grades and evaluations), in other words that they tend to co-occur to some degree, we still don't know which one causes the other (or whether something else causes both of them). Does having a better professor cause you to get better grades? Or do students who are doing well in class come to like their professor more? Similarly, if you find that people who are more hostile have fewer friends (*a negative correlation*), you still can't tell if people who are mean to others have trouble making friends, or if people who don't have many friends grow to be hostile over time. Figure 2.2 shows the different types of correlations.

In some cases, we don't have to worry about the direction of the association between two variables because if one of the variables is fixed (cannot change), we can be certain that it was not caused by the other variable. For example, if we conduct a naturalistic observation study and find that men are more aggressive than women, we can be sure that the aggression did not lead to their gender (a fixed variable). Similarly, if the data regarding the two variables were collected at two different periods of time, we can be certain that the second variable could not have caused the first variable. For example, if we measure students' attendance for a social psychology class in a given semester and then measure their academic performance in the course at the end of the semester, we might find that attendance is a good predictor of academic performance in the course, but not the other way around.

However, even in cases where it is clear that one of the variables could not have caused the other, we still can't be certain that the other variable causes the correlation between the two variables. There is still a possibility that a third variable caused them both, explaining the observed association between the two variables. For example, hair loss and coronary heart disease are positively correlated: people who are bald are more likely to have coronary heart disease. However, it would be inaccurate to say that balding *causes* coronary heart disease; rather, both balding and coronary heart disease are the result of getting older (the "third variable" in this example).

SELF-REPORT OR SURVEY METHODS

Self-report or survey methods rely on asking people questions about their thoughts, feelings, and behaviour. Researchers can ask these questions directly in an interview, either in person or by telephone, or participants can complete written surveys. The Rosenberg Self-Esteem Scale that was used by Christofides, Muise, and Desmarais (2009) in the research example earlier in this chapter is a commonly used self-report measure to assess whether people generally have positive feelings about themselves (Rosenberg, 1965). You can try it in the Rate Yourself box that follows.

HOW DO YOU FEEL ABOUT YOURSELF?

Self-Esteem Scale

INSTRUCTIONS: *Rate your agreement with each of these items on a 1 to 4 scale, with 1 meaning "strongly disagree" and 4 meaning "strongly agree."*

    1. I feel that I'm a person of worth, at least on an equal plane with others.

    2. On the whole, I am satisfied with myself.

    3. I wish I could have more respect for myself.

    4. I certainly feel useless at times.

    5. At times I think I am no good at all.

    6. I feel that I have a number of good qualities.

    7. All in all, I am inclined to feel that I am a failure.

    8. I am able to do things as well as most other people.

    9. I feel that I do not have much to be proud of.

    10. I take a positive attitude toward myself.

[RATE YOURSELF]

SCORING: Indicate whether you strongly agree, agree, disagree, or strongly disagree with each of these statements. For statements 1, 2, 6, 8, and 10 give yourself 4 points for strongly agree, 3 points for agree, 2 points for disagree, and 1 point for strongly disagree. For statements 3, 4, 5, 7, and 9 give yourself 1 point for strongly agree, 2 points for agree, 3 points for disagree, and 4 points for strongly disagree. Then add up your total number of points.

INTERPRETATION: People with a higher score on this scale have higher self-esteem, meaning they see themselves overall in a more positive light than those with lower scores on this scale (Rosenberg, 1965).

One particular type of self-report or survey data is **event-recording** or **experience sampling measures** (see Table 2.1; Reis & Wheeler, 1991). For these measures, respondents report various experiences that they have at regular intervals. In some cases, respondents report on a designated set of events, such as social interactions, particular moods, etc., and they simply fill out a brief form whenever they are in these situations (noting mood, describing the event, etc.). In other cases, respondents carry a programmed watch or beeper, and write down various pieces of information (e.g., their mood, a description of the event) after they are signalled (usually several times a day).

event recording or experience sampling measures – a particular type of self-report or survey data where participants report various experiences they have at regular time intervals. Also called experience sampling.

ADVANTAGES. Survey measures have many advantages and are commonly used to collect information about the link between people's attitudes and behaviours. Surveys enable researchers to collect data from many participants at the same time, so this is a very inexpensive way to gather data. Researchers could, for example, recruit many university students to complete a

TABLE 2.1	The Rochester Interaction Record									
Intimacy	Superficial	1	2	3	4	5	6	7	Meaningful
I disclosed	Very Little	1	2	3	4	5	6	7	A Great Deal
Other disclosed	Very Little	1	2	3	4	5	6	7	A Great Deal
Quality	Unpleasant	1	2	3	4	5	6	7	Pleasant
Satisfaction	Less than expected	1	2	3	4	5	6	7	More than expected
Initiation	I Initiated	1	2	3	4	5	6	7	Other Initiated
Influence	I Influenced More	1	2	3	4	5	6	7	Other Influenced More

The Rochester Interaction Record is a commonly-used event-recording or experience-sampling measure in which participants record information about their daily interactions shortly after they occur. This measure has been used to examine frequency of conflict with a dating partner, intimate discussions, and feelings of loneliness.

Source: Reis, H.T., & Wheeler, L. (1991). Studying social interaction with the Rochester Interaction Record. In M. P. Zanna (Ed.), *Advances in Experimental Social Psychology* (Vol. 24, pp. 270–318). San Diego: Academic Press.

written survey on their attitudes towards love and their experience in romantic relationships to see if people's dating experience is associated with their views of love.

Surveys also let researchers ask questions about a range of topics—including actions, feelings, attitudes, and thoughts—that could not be assessed simply by observing people's behaviour. You can't directly measure variables such as love, empathy, or prejudice, although you could infer them indirectly by observing people's actions.

LIMITATIONS. Self-report or survey methods also have their limitations. Let's examine some factors that limit the reliability of this method.

Question wording. First, survey methods can lead to biased findings if they use leading questions. Leading questions are questions that provide some evidence of the "right answer" because of how they are phrased. For example, polls reveal that asking if the government is spending too much on welfare reveals a different answer (53 percent agreeing) than asking if the government spends too much on assistance to the poor (23 percent agreeing) (CBS News/New York Times, 1994). Table 2.2 shows some other leading questions.

Even subtle wording differences can lead to different results. Some research indicates that the order in which questions are asked can influence the responses (Schwarz, Strack, & Mai, 1991). People who are asked how happy they are with their life, and then asked how happy they are with their marriage, give very different answers than those who are asked the same two questions, but in the opposite order. The preceding question influences our interpretation of the second question, and hence influences the answer we give.

TABLE 2.2	Examples of Leading Survey Questions

QUESTION 1	QUESTION 2
Given the importance to future generations of preserving the environment, do you believe enforcement of the Canadian Environmental Protection Act should be strengthened, weakened, or left alone?	Given the fact that installing scrubbers at utility plants could increase electricity bills by 25 percent, do you believe enforcement of the Canadian Environmental Protection Act should be strengthened, weakened, or left alone?
Do you prefer your hamburgers flame-broiled or fried?	Do you prefer a hamburger that is grilled on a hot stainless steel grill or one that is cooked by passing the raw meat through an open gas flame?

Can you see how people would answer these pairs of questions in very different ways based on their wording? Most people are more in favour of enforcing the Canadian Environmental Protection Act in the first question than in the second question, and prefer flame-broiled hamburgers more in the first question than in the second.

Source: Goodwin, C. J. (1998). *Research in Psychology: Methods and Design*. New York: Wiley.

Similarly, in a study conducted in the UK, people reported a greater intention to exercise if they were first asked a question about how much they would regret not exercising, than if they were asked the regret question after they had stated their intention to exercise (Abraham & Sheeran, 2004).

Finally, providing information about who is conducting the research influences responses. More people are in favour of the statement "People should have the freedom to express their opinions publicly" when a question on this topic is asked by the Catholic Church rather than by the American Nazi Party (Ottati, Riggle, Wyer, Schwarz, & Kuklinski, 1989).

Response options.   Similarly, the response options given in a survey can influence the results. The responses provided give people an idea of what the "normal" or "typical" behaviour is, and people often don't want to appear very different from others (and they *especially* don't want to appear worse than others). They are therefore more likely to choose one of the mid-level choices as opposed to one of the more extreme (high frequency or low frequency) choices. So, if you ask people if they smoke less than 1 cigarette a day, 1 to 2 cigarettes a day, 3 to 5 cigarettes a day, or more than 5 cigarettes a day, they will give lower estimates about their cigarette smoking than if you ask if they smoke less than 10, 10 to 20, 20 to 30, or more than 30 cigarettes a day. In this first example, people will be likely to report smoking between 1 and 5 cigarettes a day (the two mid-level choices in this set of answers), whereas in the second example, people are likely to report smoking 10 to 30 cigarettes a day, again because these responses are the mid-level options. Table 2.3, using research from Germany, provides another example of how response options can influence people's reports of how much television they watch (Schwarz, Hippler, Deutsch, & Strack, 1985). Chapter 4, on social perception, describes a study from the UK showing that people strongly prefer a food that is 75 percent fat-free to one that is 25 percent fat (Sanford, Fay, Stewart, & Moxey, 2002).

Response options can have an even stronger impact on answers when participants must choose between a set of very limited response options. A story in *The New York Times Magazine* described the somewhat surprising results of a survey showing that 51 percent of Americans think, "primates are entitled to the same rights as human children" (Pollan, 2002). However, the actual survey listed only four choices: primates should be treated "like property," "similar to children," "the same as adults," or "not sure." Given these four options, some respondents may have chosen the "similar to children" answer not because this choice expressed their true feelings, but because this choice was the option that was closest to their true feelings, given the rather limited options.

TABLE 2.3	Reported Daily Television Watching as a Function of Response Options		
QUESTIONNAIRE A:		**QUESTIONNAIRE B:**	
Low-frequency options	**Reported daily use**	**High-frequency options**	**Reported daily use**
Up to ½ hour	7.4 percent	Up to 2 ½ hours	62.5 percent
½ hour to 1 hour	17.7 percent	2 ½ hours to 3 hours	23.4 percent
1 hour to 1 ½ hours	26.5 percent	3 hours to 3 ½ hours	7.8 percent
1 ½ hours to 2 hours	14.7 percent	3 ½ hours to 4 hours	4.7 percent
2 hours to 2 ½ hours	17.7 percent	4 hours to 4 ½ hours	1.6 percent
More than 2 ½ hours	16.2 percent	More than 4 ½ hours	0.0 percent

Only 16.2 percent of people reported watching more than 2 ½ hours of television daily (the highest response option given) when the response options were for a low frequency of television watching, but 37.5 percent of people reported watching this much when the options were for a high frequency of television watching.

Source: Schwarz, N., Hippler, H., Deutsch, B., & Strack, F. (1985). Response scales: Effects of category range on reported behavior and comparative judgments. *Public Opinion Quarterly, 49*, 388–395.

"What I drink and what I tell the pollsters I drink are two different things."

© Leo Cullum/ The New Yorker Collection/ www.cartoonbank.com

Inaccuracy of responses. Surveys methods are also limited by the possibility of inaccurate reporting. In some cases, people might believe they are telling the truth, but they simply may not be able to accurately recall the necessary information. For example, people may not remember how much money they donated to charity last year or how often they flossed their teeth.

Researchers who use experience sampling and event recording measures are less likely to encounter problems caused by their participants' forgetfulness. However, all types of self-report measure can experience problems if people are motivated to give inaccurate information. Why would people provide inaccurate information? People are concerned with the social desirability of their answers, particularly when the research examines highly personal or controversial topics. For example, students often report to their parents and professors that they studied and attended class more frequently than they really did. Remember the study described at the start of this section? It revealed that students' reports of how often they used a condom during sex (a highly personal topic) were less accurate if the question was asked with a more direct approach than with a less direct approach. Similarly, reports of sexual behaviour that are given retrospectively tend to be much lower than reports of sexual behaviour that are given using a daily diary approach (McAuliffe, DiFranceisco, & Reed, 2007).

covert measures – measures used by researchers that rely on participants' behaviour or reaction not directly under participants' control

To minimize the problems associated with socially desirable responding, some researchers rely on **covert measures**, meaning measures that rely on behaviours or reactions that are not directly under a person's control. Covert measures are particularly likely to be used when participants might not want to be honest in their responses. In one study, researchers examined heterosexual men's arousal in response to erotic material that featured either heterosexual couples, lesbian couples, or homosexual couples (Adams, Wright, & Lohr, 1996). Because heterosexual men would be likely to report little arousal in response to material featuring homosexual men, researchers used "penile cuffs" to measure erection strength in response to the three different types of material. Interestingly, heterosexual men who were homophobic, meaning they reported having negative feelings toward gay men, were the only participants who showed an increase in erection strength in response to the homosexual material. This study illustrates the advantages of using covert measures when studying sensitive topics such as sexual behaviour.

Because people are often reluctant to admit to racial prejudice on self-report measures, many researchers who study stereotyping use various types of covert measures (as you'll read about in detail in Chapter 11). One commonly-used covert measure is the Implicit Association Test (IAT), which is based on the assumption that it is easier—and hence faster—to make the same response to concepts that are strongly associated with each other than to concepts that are more weakly associated (Nosek, Greenwald, & Banaji, 2005). In this test, people respond to two different types of stimulus words: the first set is attitudinal words (e.g., pleasant, peaceful, ugly, happy), and the second set is the list of stereotypic target words (e.g., Caucasian names and Black names, women's names and men's names). People press one key when they see a pleasant target word and another key when they see an unpleasant target word. Research generally shows that people are faster at responding to pairs of words that they view as compatible than to incompatible pairs, and has found, in terms of prejudice, an implicit linking of Caucasian with good and Black with bad (Ranganath & Nosek, 2008). Likewise, students often respond more quickly to pairings of

Questioning the Research:

Some researchers have criticized the use of the IAT as a measure of prejudice. In particular, these researchers suggest that responses on the IAT may not reflect participants' own endorsement of a prejudicial attitude, but rather familiarity with a given stereotype, the salience of particular types of pairings, and/or cultural knowledge about a given belief (Blanton & Jaccard, 2006). What do you believe the IAT is likely to measure? How could you test your belief?

TABLE 2.4	Word Completion Test	
SAMPLE FRAGMENT	**PREJUDICED RESPONSE**	**NON-PREJUDICED RESPONSE**
_ I C E	RICE	NICE
P O L I _ E	POLITE	POLICE

This table shows a word completion task consisting of three words that could be used to test prejudiced reactions. In one study, participants who watched a tape of an Asian woman completed the word fragments in ways that were consistent with the stereotype.

Source: Gilbert, D., & Hixon, J. (1991). The trouble of thinking: Activation and application of stereotypic beliefs. *Journal of Personality and Social Psychology*, 60, 509–517.

the words "old" and "bad" than pairings of "old" and "young," suggesting that, for young people, "old" is more closely linked with "bad" than it is with "young," even though the concepts old and young are clearly related along a continuum and old is no more intrinsically connected to the concept bad than is young. Other covert measures to assess prejudice include word completion tasks (see Table 2.4), reaction times, and facial expressions (see Research Focus on Neuroscience).

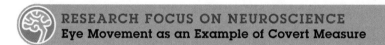

RESEARCH FOCUS ON NEUROSCIENCE
Eye Movement as an Example of Covert Measure

Research measures may be unobtrusive and still not interfere with behaviour. For example, Daniel Krupp from the University of Lethbridge has argued that eye gaze is an accurate and unobtrusive measure (Krupp, 2008). Some studies use eye gaze as a way of measuring interest, including sexual interest, which is difficult to gauge through such measures as self-report. "Dwell time," which is the length of time that an individual voluntarily examines a visual stimulus before shifting attention to a new one, has been found to correlate with genital arousal and to predict self-reported preferences for biological sex and age. Rupp and Wallen (2007) recorded heterosexual male and female participants' eye movements while participants viewed a series of sexually explicit images of heterosexual couples engaged in oral sex and intercourse. Male and female participants selectively attended to the male face, female face, and genital regions and selectively avoided the image backgrounds. In evolutionary terms, these are the most important parts of the body to pay attention to as they indicate reproductive health.

Eye gaze measurement can also indicate cultural differences. Collaborating with an international team of researchers, Takahiko Masuda from the University of Alberta found that, when judging people's emotions from their facial expressions, Japanese incorporate information from the social context more than Westerners do (Masuda et al., 2008). Participants viewed cartoons depicting a happy, sad, angry, or neutral person surrounded by other people expressing the same emotion as the central person or a different emotion. The surrounding people's emotions influenced Japanese participants' perceptions of the central person but not that of Westerners. These differences were reflected in differences in attention that were indicated by eye-tracking data: Japanese looked at the surrounding people more than Westerners did, suggesting that people from collectivist contexts really do, even at the level of eye gaze, pay more attention to context than people from individualistic contexts.

What other types of covert measures do researchers use? Researchers have measured participants' nodding in response to a persuasive communication, timed how long participants take to walk down a hallway after having been exposed to neutral versus "old" words, or observed participants' behaviour toward another person behind a one-way mirror after they've seen a violent television program. In one study conducted in the United States, participants came in to complete a two-part study that examined the association between personality and impression formation, as well as personality and taste preferences (Lieberman, Solomon, Greenberg, & McGregor, 1999). First, participants read an essay on politics that was supposedly written by another student (their partner in this study). For half the participants, this essay criticized their prevailing political orientation. The other half of the participants read an essay that supported their political views. Next, participants were told that the taste the researchers were examining that day was "spicy," and that they should pour some spicy sauce in a small cup for their partner to drink. (They were also told that their partner did not particularly like spicy foods.) As predicted, participants who read the essay that was critical of their political views gave significantly more hot sauce to their partner than those who read a supportive essay. Thus, the amount of hot sauce given was a covert way of testing participants' level of aggression.

EXAMPLES OF EACH RESEARCH APPROACH

RESEARCH METHOD	EXAMPLE
Naturalistic/Observation methods	Analyze archival data to rate the thinness of women appearing in magazines and on television over time, and the rate of diagnosed eating disorders.
Survey/Self-Report methods	Give women a questionnaire that asks them to rate how frequently they read magazines featuring thin models and how frequently they engage in various symptoms associated with eating disorders.

HOW DO YOU CONDUCT EXPERIMENTAL RESEARCH?

 Researchers conducted a study to find out if women eat less when they want to appear attractive (Mori, Chaiken, & Pliner, 1987). They brought in female university students to have a "get acquainted" conversation (designed to simulate a dating situation), and examined the effects of the "quality of the dating partner" on the amount women ate. Women in one condition were told that they were interacting with a very desirable man—he was described as being single, going to law school, and being interested in travel, athletics, and photography. Those in another condition were told they were interacting with a less desirable man—he was described as having no interests other than watching TV and no plans other than to make money. Researchers then measured how many M&Ms women ate during the conversation. As predicted, women who were talking with the undesirable man ate significantly more than those who were talking with the desirable man. In contrast, men ate about the same amount regardless of whether or not their partner was attractive. These results suggest that women present a different image to men in certain situations—when they want to appear attractive, they don't eat much.

This section will examine issues in experimental methods (such as in the study just described) as well as two factors that influence the quality of experimental research methods: internal and external validity.

EXPERIMENTAL METHODS

In **experimental methods**, researchers manipulate one or more **independent variables** and then measure the effects of the manipulations on one or more **dependent variables**. Stated differently, the dependent variable is the factor that is measured to see if it is affected by the independent variable. Students tend to confuse independent and dependent variables. One way of remembering which is which is to remember that changes in the dependent variable *depend upon* changes that you, the researcher, make to the other, independent variable; another way is to think of the independent variable as coming first in the hypothesis (changes in X produce changes in Y). The first stated variable must be independent as you have at that point ("changes in X ...") introduced no other variable for it to depend upon. In the study just described, the independent variable was the desirability of the man (highly desirable versus relatively undesirable) and the dependent variable was the number of M&Ms eaten.

This approach lets us determine systematically whether changes in the independent variable cause changes in the dependent variable, and therefore provides evidence of causality (changes in X cause changes in Y) as opposed to correlation (X and Y tend to co-occur). For example, if you want to test whether people who are injured get more help if they are alone or in groups, you could stage an emergency in front of either a lone individual or in front of a large group and then see in which situation people get help faster. In this case, the independent variable is the size of the group, and the dependent variable is the speed of help.

RANDOM ASSIGNMENT.   As the first step in conducting experiments, researchers randomly assign people to the different experimental conditions. **Random assignment** means that every person had an equal chance of being in either of the conditions: they did not get to choose which condition they wanted, and neither did the experimenter use any type of selection process to assign people to conditions (e.g., putting the first 10 people in one condition and then the next 10 people in the second condition). Instead, researchers use a truly random method of assigning people to groups, such as flipping a coin, drawing slips of paper out of a hat, or using a table of random numbers. This random assignment to conditions means you can have greater confidence that there is not a third variable causing change in both the independent and dependent variables. For example, instead of using random assignment, you may put the first 10 people in the experimental group and the next 10 people in the control condition. It is possible that in the first group, you may have more students from a first-year psychology course as a group of them walked to the experiment together after class. On the other hand, you may have more students in their second and third year in the control group as they showed up when their classes ended in the building next door. Any effect you may find between the experimental and control condition could be due to a third variable, such as maturity or some other systematic difference between first-year students and the others.

It is important to note that random sampling applies both to correlational studies and experimental studies. That is, in a well-designed study in which the results will be generalized, people should have an equal chance of participating. Recall in the Facebook study described earlier in the chapter that the researchers were interested in studying students in the researchers' university (a mid-size university in southern Ontario) who used Facebook (Christofides, Muise, & Desmarais, 2009). In carrying out the study, however, the researchers recruited participants from a pool of psychology students. Although this gave them access to a large department in their university, not all students at the university had an equal chance of participating in the study as students outside the psychology department were not contacted. Random assignment, in this instance, was not well implemented.

What would happen if you ran an experiment on the effects of watching violent television on aggression, but instead of randomly assigning children to watch a particular show you

experimental methods – a research approach that involves the manipulation of one or more independent variables and the measurement of one or more dependent variables

independent variable – the variable that is manipulated in experimental research

dependent variable – the factor that is measured to see if it is affected by the independent variable

random assignment – a technique for placing participants into the different conditions in an experiment that gives all participants equal opportunity of being placed in any of the conditions

let children choose whether they would like to watch a violent television show or a sitcom? If you then find that those who watch violent television are more aggressive than those who don't, can you be certain that watching this type of television show caused the aggression? No, because it is likely that kids who *chose* to watch violent television differ from those who did not want to watch it. Perhaps these kids are more aggressive in general, or they don't get to watch violent television much at home. Because of this uncertainty, we can't tell whether the independent variable (watching a violent television show) caused the dependent variable (intensity of aggression). This may seem like an obvious point, but some research studies do rely on such flawed designs, as illustrated in Health Connections.

HEALTH CONNECTIONS

Evaluating Abstinence-Only Sex Education

Many research studies have examined the effectiveness of abstinence-only sex education, meaning programs in which students learn only about strategies for abstaining from sexual intercourse before marriage, and not about contraceptive use. Researchers have often reported beneficial effects of these programs, such as reductions in early sexual activity (Kirby, 2002). However, these research studies often have problems that limit what we can learn. For example, one study found that an abstinence-only program led to an increase in age at first sexual encounter—but researchers eliminated girls who had sex during the program from inclusion in their analyses. Other studies have included only adolescents who had taken a pledge to refrain from sexual activity before marriage—but adolescents who make such a pledge probably differ in many ways from those who don't (Kirby, 2002). Still other studies chose to evaluate not the effectiveness of abstinence-only education on sexual behaviour, but rather the *attitudes* toward sexual behaviour. Would you be surprised to know that after having followed an abstinence-only program many adolescents report more positive attitudes about abstinence? Such studies don't measure whether such attitudes actually lead to abstinent behaviour. So, what do well-designed studies on abstinence-only education—including random assignment, inclusion of all research participants, and evaluation of sexual behaviour—reveal? Those who receive abstinence-only education are no more likely than those in a control group to abstain from sexual activity or delay the start of sexual activity (Trenholm, Devaney, Fortson, Bridgespan, & Wheeler, 2007).

Michelle D. Bridwell/PhotoEdit Inc.

CONTROL. Researchers have a lot of *control* over what happens to the participants in their experiment. Researchers choose what happens to whom and when and how. With proper use of controls, they should not have to worry about other factors having an influence on their findings, such as the participants' personalities, attitudes, and/or experiences. In the observational research described earlier, the researcher only measures—but does not control—the independent variable. For example, in the adolescent sexual behaviour study described earlier in the Observational/Naturalistic Methods section of this chapter (Mo et al., 2007), the gender of the participants, their level of education, or their family income could serve as an independent variable, but these factors are only measured. In experiments, the researchers manipulate one or more independent variables, and therefore have control over exactly what happens to the participants.

Because experiments contain multiple conditions and participants are randomly assigned to these conditions, this type of research method gives us greater confidence that the effects of the independent variable cause the effects on the dependent variable. This is an advantage of

FIGURE 2.3 A MODEL OF EXPERIMENTAL DESIGN

As shown in this figure, experiments include random assignment and the use of a control condition. These two features, which are not used in naturalistic/observation and self-report/survey methods of research, help researchers determine whether the independent variable caused the dependent variable.

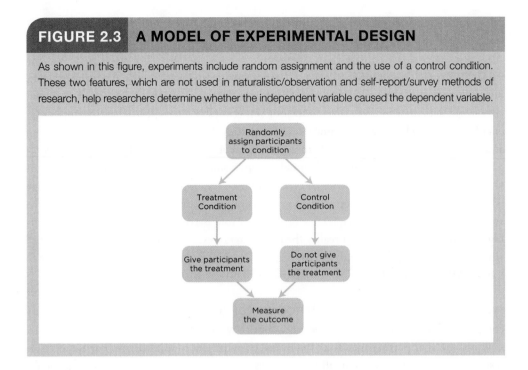

experimental research over the other research methods discussed, as the latter can show correlation, but not causation. Figure 2.3 summarizes the experimental design.

INTERNAL VALIDITY

Because experiments use random assignment and can control exactly what happens to the participants, this research approach is the only one that provides answers about causality. However, in order to be confident that the effects on the dependent variable were caused by the independent variable, we need to design experiments that are high on internal validity. **Internal validity** is the degree to which our conclusions about the effects of the independent variable on the dependent variable are valid: in other words, the extent to which the experiment demonstrates what we say it does. For example, let's say we are conducting an experiment about the effects of peer tutoring on grades, and we randomly assign some people to receive such tutoring and other people to get nothing extra. If the results show that those who received peer tutoring have better grades than those who do not, can we be sure that this effect is caused by the tutoring? Maybe those who didn't receive the tutoring were disappointed and therefore felt especially bad toward the class and simply stopped studying at all. Maybe the experimenter assumed that those who received the tutoring would do better in the class, and therefore was nicer to those people. In turn, perhaps those people who received the tutoring felt better because they were treated well by the experimenter, not due to the effects of the tutoring itself. Maybe people who received the tutoring talked about how great it was, which made those who didn't get the tutoring feel bad. In other words, there could be a variety of alternative explanations for the findings, which therefore weakens the experiment's internal validity.

Researchers often try to increase internal validity by reducing or eliminating the **demand characteristics**, meaning cues in a research setting that may inadvertently guide participants' behaviour (Aronson, Wilson, & Brewer, 1998; Orne, 1962). Participants are often focused on trying to "figure out" the goal of the study, and sometimes try to "help the researcher" by behaving in the desired way. This behaviour decreases the internal validity of the experiment because participants' behaviour is then influenced by these demand characteristics and not merely by the variables the experimenter is manipulating. There are ways of decreasing such cues, including the provision of a good cover story, providing a high-quality control condition,

internal validity – the degree to which one can validly draw conclusions about the effects of the independent variable on the dependent variable

demand characteristics – the cues in a research setting that may inadvertently guide participants' behaviour

minimizing experimenter expectancy effects, and designing studies with high experimental or psychological realism.

PROVIDE A GOOD COVER STORY. Participants in an experiment often want to figure out the purpose of the study. If participants know the purpose of the research experiment, they might act either in a way to support it or sometimes to discredit it. Therefore, researchers often try to hide the exact hypotheses of the study. For example, if you are conducting a study on how low self-esteem leads to aggression, you obviously couldn't tell your participants this since it would influence their behaviour. Some studies even use deception by providing false information to participants to minimize the impact of participant expectancy effects (we will talk more about the use of deception at the end of this chapter). In one study you'll read about in Chapter 13, researchers told participants the study was examining personality variables, but in reality the researchers were measuring how students reacted when smoke began pouring into the room as they completed their questionnaire (Darley & Latané, 1968).

PROVIDE A HIGH-QUALITY CONTROL CONDITION. In some cases, researchers can't completely disguise the nature of the study, but they can reduce demand characteristics by making sure that participants don't know exactly what the conditions are. For example, in research examining persuasion, all participants may read the same persuasive message on the value of mandatory community service programs for university students. Some participants may then be told the message was written by a high school debate student. Others will be told the message was written by a highly respected professor. If the researchers later find that those in the "professor condition" are more persuaded by the message, we can be relatively confident that knowledge of the author's identity influenced the power of the message. Why? Because the study was absolutely identical in all respects except for the one variable—the supposed author. However, to be sure, one should include a third group, or condition, known as the control condition. In this condition, participants will read the same message, but will be given no information about the author. It is important that the control condition resemble the experimental ones in all respects except the independent variable, so that you can be confident that it is the independent variable that has caused any change in the dependent variable.

MINIMIZE EXPERIMENTER EXPECTANCY EFFECTS. Another type of demand characteristic is the experimenter's own behaviour. **Experimenter expectancy effects** are produced when an experimenter's expectations about the results of the experiment influence how the experimenter behaves toward the participant, and, thereby, the results. For example, if you think that individuals from a particular ethnic group are not as intelligent or as hard working as others, you might treat them differently when you interact with them.

Experimenter expectancy effects can even influence behaviour in animals. In one clever study, an experimenter told some students that they were merely replicating a well-established finding that some rats are "maze bright" and that other rats are "maze dumb," and thus would have more trouble learning to navigate a maze (Rosenthal & Fode, 1963). The researcher then told half of the students they were working with smart rats, and the other half that they were working with dumb rats. Students then placed their rats at the start of the runway and timed them. On Day 1, the times were pretty close, but over time, the "bright" rats ran faster and faster than the dumb rats (see Figure 2.4).

Researchers typically take a number of steps to avoid introducing experimenter expectancy effects. One approach is to minimize interaction between participants and experimenters. For example, participants may receive all of their instructions in a standardized form, such as on the computer. Another strategy to protect against such problems is to keep the

experimenter expectancy effects – when an experimenter's expectations about the results of the study influence participants' behaviour and thereby affect the results of the study

Questioning the Research:

Although this study clearly demonstrated that people's expectations influenced the rats' learning, it didn't examine why. How might participants' expectations have influenced the rats' running speed?

FIGURE 2.4 CAN EXPERIMENTERS' EXPECTATIONS INFLUENCE RATS' BEHAVIOUR?

In a study to test the strength of experimenter expectancy effects, researchers asked psychology students to count the correct responses of rats as they ran through mazes. Although the rats were all the same at the beginning of the study, researchers told some students that their rats were "maze smart," and others that their rats were "maze dumb." As predicted, rats labelled as "smart" made more correct responses than those labelled as "dumb" every day of the study. In addition, the difference between numbers of correct responses increased over time, meaning the difference between the rats' scores was greater on Day 5 than on Day 1. The researchers believe that the students' expectations about the rats may have led them to treat the rats differently in subtle ways that influenced the rats' performance (Rosenthal & Fode, 1963).

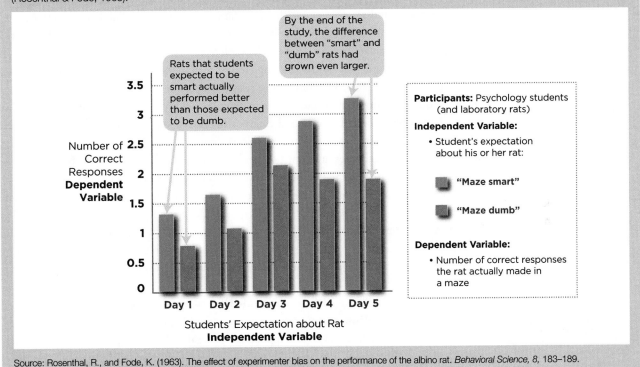

Source: Rosenthal, R., and Fode, K. (1963). The effect of experimenter bias on the performance of the albino rat. *Behavioral Science, 8*, 183–189.

experimenter blind, meaning that the experimenters who are interacting with the participants do not know which condition the participants are in.

DESIGN STUDIES THAT ARE HIGH IN EXPERIMENTAL OR PSYCHOLOGICAL REALISM.

Another way to reduce, or at least minimize, demand characteristics is to design experimental procedures with high experimental realism or psychological realism, meaning studies that are so engaging for participants that they tend to behave naturally and spontaneously. Some researchers who study marital interaction, for example, ask couples to re-enact a conflict they have had previously and videotape the re-enactment. Some couples have the tendency to get very involved in such re-enactments, in which case it is likely that they behave naturally. Of course, it is certainly possible that couples who know that their fight will later be watched by psychologists don't act as they might if they were alone.

Creating studies with high experimental or psychological realism is particularly important when experiments take place in laboratory or research settings in which experimenters have their equipment, such as video cameras, one-way mirrors, and other materials needed for the study. In these settings, participants' attitudes and behaviour may be influenced by the artificial setting (which then becomes what is known as a confounding variable), instead of by the independent variable. This can lead to problems in the study if participants who are asked to do an unusual procedure in the lab act as they think they should act, as opposed to how they otherwise would.

experimenter blind – the procedure that ensures the experimenter who is interacting with a study's participants does not know which condition the participants are in

experimental realism or psychological realism – the extent to which participants are engaged in a particular study and hence act in more spontaneous and natural ways

However, even under laboratory conditions researchers can design studies that participants find very realistic and engaging. For example, a famous study by Stanley Milgram in which people were directed to give painful electric shocks to other participants was very involving—even gripping—for participants, and it is therefore assumed that their behaviour was genuine (you'll learn more about this study in Chapter 8).

EXTERNAL VALIDITY

external validity – the degree to which there can be reasonable confidence that the same results would be obtained for other people in other situations

In order to provide useful information about real-world events and processes, research studies also need to have external validity, meaning confidence that the same results would be obtained for other people and in other situations. One famous study on the link between attachment styles in infancy and later experience in romantic relationships collected data in the United States by asking readers of a newspaper to complete a "love quiz" (Hazan & Shaver, 1987). It seems likely that those who bother to complete and mail in the quiz would have characteristics that differ (more romantic attitudes? worse relationships?) from those who wouldn't bother to take the quiz. So, the study would be low in external validity. As it turns out, however, other researchers have replicated Hazan and Shaver's findings about the link between attachment styles and relationship interaction (as you'll learn more about in Chapter 14). In other cases, researchers may find that results from a particular study that lead to a particular finding can't be obtained for other people and in other situations (meaning the study is low in external validity). External validity could also be a problem when we examine a concept in one culture and assume the findings apply to all cultures. For example, most social psychology studies were conducted in North America and western Europe and, until late 20th century, when research in cross-cultural psychology started to increase, the external validity of these findings was not questioned by many psychologists. There are, fortunately, several ways of increasing external validity.

DESIGN STUDIES THAT ARE HIGH IN MUNDANE REALISM.   Research studies need to have mundane realism, meaning they need to resemble places and events that exist in the real world so that the findings can be applied (or generalized) from an experiment to the real world. For example, there is research that has examined how susceptible university students are to getting a cold during exam period (Jemmott & Magloire, 1988). One could assume that such research might generalize widely as an example of the effects of stress on health. However, imagine an experiment in which students completed an exam and were given an electric shock each time they gave a wrong answer. Although this type of situation would probably be extremely stressful for the participant, it would have low mundane realism because it is uncommon. Therefore, it might not give us accurate information about how stress can influence health in situations that are more realistic or more common.

mundane realism – the extent to which the conditions of the study resemble places and events that exist in the real world

Conducting field experiments (experiments conducted in a natural setting) is an effective way of increasing mundane realism. For example, in Chapter 3 you'll read about a study researchers conducted on Halloween in the United States that measured how many candies children took from a bowl as a function of whether or not there was a mirror above the bowl (Gibbons, 1990). Experiments that are conducted in the field are less likely to be influenced by the particular setting in which they take place (in part because participants may not even know they are taking part in a study—an issue we'll discuss later in this chapter).

field experiments – experiments that are conducted in natural settings

USE A RANDOM OR REPRESENTATIVE SAMPLE.   Many research studies are conducted using a *convenience sample*, meaning a sample that is selected because the participants are readily accessible to the researcher (often university students who are taking an introductory psychology course!). In fact, 75 percent of all published articles in two major American psychology journals (*Personality and Social Psychology Bulletin* and *Journal of Personality and Social Psychology*) used university students as participants (Sherman, Buddie, Dragan, End, & Finney, 1999). Because students tend to be more educated, from wealthier backgrounds, and younger than the majority of the population, it is not clear whether findings based on such a sample would hold true for other people. Similarly, the majority of research in psychology is based largely on middle-class white male samples (Gannon, Luchetta, Rhodes, Pardie, & Segrist, 1992; Graham, 1992). We can be relatively confident that the findings from this type of study would apply to those in such a population in the real world, but we should be less confident that these findings would apply to populations that differ in terms of age, ethnicity, gender, income, and so on. Even apparently equivalent samples, such as university students, will have different characteristics in different cultures; in some countries students represent more of a social elite than in others. In Russia, for example, students represent only about 3.5 percent of the population (Lavric, 2008).

Another problem with the use of convenience samples is that those who take the time to participate in a study might also differ from those who don't. Therefore, their responses may not be applicable to the general population (Bradburn & Sudman, 1988). For example, a study of sexual behaviour conducted by researchers at McGill University included a number of personal topics, such as contraceptive use and attitudes to sexual behaviour (Hynie & Lydon, 1996). But who is most likely to respond to these types of questions? Probably those who are relatively comfortable discussing such sensitive issues, and with revealing personal information to strangers—people who lack this comfort may have simply refused to participate in the survey. In addition, individuals who are comfortable discussing such topics might also be more likely to engage in such behaviours, which could lead to an overestimation of the frequency of these behaviours.

Let's say that you are asked to evaluate the quality of your Social Psychology course. If you really like your professor, you are probably highly motivated to complete the survey to let others know how great this class is. Similarly, if you really hate this course (which I know is hard to imagine, but try), you are likely to want to warn others about this class, and so you would complete the survey. However, if you have mixed feelings about the class, or you don't feel strongly about it either way, you may not be very motivated to complete a survey at all.

Research studies should try to use a **random sample**, or a **representative sample**, meaning a sample that reflects the characteristics of the population in question (which may or may not be the general population). So, if you are interested in examining the frequency of drinking on university campuses, it would be a mistake to simply survey students who live in a fraternity or sorority, because research shows that these students drink more alcohol than those who live in residence halls or off-campus (Wechsler, Dowdall, Davenport, & Castillo, 1995). Instead you might want to call every tenth person in the student directory to try to recruit a sample that represents all the students at the school (e.g., an equal mix of males and females, athletes and non-athletes,).

random sample or representative sample – a sample that reflects the characteristics of the population of interest

MAKE PARTICIPATION CONVENIENT.   Another way of increasing external validity is to make participation in a research study as convenient as possible. For example, if you recruit people to participate in a smoking cessation intervention that requires them to spend every Saturday for a month travelling to a faraway place, you're probably just influencing those who are very motivated to quit and the results may therefore not be generalizable, or applicable, to the average smoker (who may lack such extreme motivation). On the other hand, if you find that attending one two-hour workshop is helping people to quit smoking, that result would probably be far more generalizable to other smokers. Many people would be willing to attend this type of program, and therefore the researchers should feel more confident that their approach could work with other people.

CONDUCT REPLICATIONS.   Finally, you should conduct the same study in different populations or locations and (if you want your results to be applicable to people in general, not just to Québécois, Canadians, or North Americans) in other cultures. For example, if you conduct the same study in a small rural high school, a medium-sized suburban high school, and a large inner-city high school, all in Canada, and you find that in all three locations students who are lonely have poorer social skills, then you can have reasonable confidence that Canadian adolescents who have poor social skills are at greater risk of feeling lonely. However, you might not be able to surmise that loneliness and poor social skills are also connected for university students or adults.

WHAT IS THE BEST APPROACH?

How do you decide which research technique to use to answer a particular question? There is no single best method, and all methods have strengths and weaknesses. Because experiments are the only technique that randomly assigns people to conditions, the experimental approach is the best method for examining whether a specific factor is likely to cause another. However, because experiments are somewhat artificial, this approach does not give us as much information about what happens in real-life situations. For their part, while naturalistic observation methods give us very accurate information about what happens in the "real world," they tell us more about how two (or more) different variables are connected than about whether one variable causes the other.

As noted, experiments are the only research method that determines whether one variable causes another. However, there are some cases in which practical and/or ethical concerns make it impossible to conduct true experiments. For example, you can't randomly assign some people to get divorced in order to determine the effects of this stressor on children's own relationship satisfaction. Researchers who are interested in the impact of divorce might instead examine differences between children whose parents are divorced and children whose parents remain married (a quasi-experimental design).

In sum, different methods are best for providing different types of information and for answering different questions. You might want to use naturalistic observation to examine whether boys tend to play in larger groups than girls, because obviously you could not answer this question using a true experimental design. On the other hand, if you are interested in examining the effectiveness of a prosocial videotape on increasing cooperation, conducting a true experiment is probably the best approach.

Finally, we can be more confident about scientific findings if researchers using different types of research methods all produce the same answer. For example, if researchers using many different approaches all examine the link between alcohol use and risky sexual behaviour and reach the same conclusion, we can be quite confident that drinking alcohol does lead to risky sexual behaviour (and it does). Concepts in Context describes how researchers could use each of the three major approaches to examine a particular topic in social psychology, in this case the link between exposure to thin ideals in the media and disordered eating.

[CONCEPTS IN CONTEXT]

EXPERIMENTAL METHODS AND STRATEGIES FOR IMPROVING INTERNAL AND EXTERNAL VALIDITY

FACTOR	EXAMPLE
Experimental methods	Randomly assign some women to read a magazine featuring thin models and others to read a magazine featuring more neutral photographs, and then rate how much they eat during a supposed "ice cream taste-test" in the second part of the study.
Internal validity	Keep experimenters blind to which types of magazines the women read, so that any differences that emerge are clearly a function of the type of magazine read.
External validity	Recruit participants without specifying the study's focus on ice cream consumption, and conduct the study with high school students, university students, and adult women.

HOW DO YOU CONDUCT QUALITATIVE RESEARCH?

In the first chapter, social constructionism was given a brief introduction. If, as social constructionists argue, there is no absolute social truth but, instead, many socially constructed realities that are equally valid, then the task of a researcher, in this view, is not to establish an absolute scientific "truth." Social constructionists are therefore associated with a different approach to research. Rather than strictly follow the scientific method, which informs the methods described above and are also known as quantitative research methods, they practise qualitative methods. However, it should not be supposed that social constructionists never conduct empirical research, or that qualitative research has no place in a scientifically rigorous research project. It is more accurate to say that there are areas of psychology that are open to experimentation and other forms of scientific, quantitative research, and other areas that are open to qualitative approaches. While qualitative research isn't in the mainstream of social psychological research, it's becoming increasingly recognized that such research has a contribution to make. For example, the *Journal of Cross-Cultural Psychology*, which had avoided publishing qualitative research since its beginning in 1970, published in 2009, for the first time, a special edition featuring qualitative approaches. We'll now briefly introduce qualitative research methods so that you are aware of their existence, which is sufficient at this stage of your psychology career.

The basic difference between qualitative and quantitative approaches is evident in their names. Quantitative approaches ask questions about quantity—"How big is the difference?" or "How strong is the correlation?"—between two variables in a survey or experiment. Quantitative data are always numbers, thereby allowing statistical analysis. Qualitative research, in contrast, asks questions about the quality of the object of research—for example, "What are the perceptions of a particular group of people about a specific topic?" Qualitative data are usually words, such as newspaper text, interviews, letters, or written responses to a researcher's question. However, qualitative data can be in other forms as well, such as photographs, magazine ads, store signs, or popular songs. Qualitative researchers consider the *meaning* of their data rather than *how much* of X and Y there is.

What, for example, could one say about the meaning, in the broadest sense, of the Tim Hortons logo? One point that can be made is that it resembles a personal signature. It therefore indicates that a man, Tim Horton, who was a national hockey hero, has given his personal validation of the product; it signifies the former hockey hero's personal seal of approval. This is a qualitative interpretation that could, for example, form part of a researcher's analysis of restaurant logos. One could then test this interpretation and convert it into a hypothesis to be tested quantitatively by verifying whether the handwritten nature of the logo gives a "personal touch" that acts positively on people's attitudes to the product. If you were interested in doing this (and this kind of knowledge is important for marketing), you could ask people about their associations with the Tim Hortons logo (and others). You might, for example, ask participants to rate, on a 7-point scale, the Starbucks and Tim Hortons logos for "personal touch," "trustworthiness," "friendliness," etc. Your hypothesis might be that the Tim Hortons logo is viewed as more personal and trustworthy than the Starbucks one. If your participants do prefer the Tim Hortons logo, it could of course be something else (e.g., the colour) that makes people warm more to it. This could be tested by asking participants (in the same questionnaire) *why* they have expressed the preferences that they have. This would produce qualitative data (i.e., their answers to this open-ended question) that would inform your interpretation of the quantitative data. This is a good example of how qualitative and quantitative approaches can be complementary rather than opposed.

There are three basic levels of qualitative analysis: the most basic is descriptive, where you describe your data by, for example, a diagram or a flow chart. The second is thematic, in which you look for themes within the data. This is the most common form of qualitative analysis within contemporary psychology, and one popular method of analysis is known as

Interpretative Phenomenological Analysis (IPA). With thematic analysis you typically consider *what* people say. At the third level of analysis, discursive, you consider *why* people say it the way they do. The best known of these methods is called Discourse Analysis. A discourse analyst might identify that in a particular report the word "flood" is paired with "immigrants," thus conveying a message of danger.

WHAT ARE THE ETHICAL ISSUES INVOLVED IN CONDUCTING RESEARCH IN SOCIAL PSYCHOLOGY?

It is mandatory for researchers to attend to ethical issues when conducting research. Here's one of the reasons why. In 1973, Phillip Zimbardo, a professor at Stanford University, conducted a study to examine the impact of the prison environment on behaviour (Haney, Banks, & Zimbardo, 1973; Haney & Zimbardo, 1998). Twenty-one university men were randomly assigned to either the "guard" or "prisoner" role, and then literally lived in a make-believe prison (set up in the basement of the psychology building). Guards were given uniforms, whistles, and billy clubs, and were instructed to enforce various prison rules. Prisoners were given uniforms and spent most of their time locked in their cells. Although all participants had completed measures of psychological well-being prior to the study, after only a few days the prison environment became highly disturbing: guards forced prisoners to perform cruel and humiliating tasks, and prisoners became extremely passive and, in some cases, depressed. Although the original experiment was planned to last for two weeks, Zimbardo called off the study after only eight days because of the extreme behaviour observed.

The consequences of participating in the Zimbardo study were substantial for both the "prisoners," who were subjected to unpleasant physical conditions and psychological pressures, and the "guards," who learned how cruel they could be to other students under particular conditions.

Dr. Philip Zimbardo

The Zimbardo prison study raised a number of concerns in the psychology community, in large part because participants clearly experienced psychological—and even physical—harm. Researchers therefore question whether this study should have been done, and whether the benefits of what was learned in this study outweighed the costs for the participants. To avoid conducting ethically questionable studies in the future, there are now careful procedures that researchers must follow when conducting scientific research. This section will examine how ethical issues are treated in conducting research in social psychology, including review by an institutional board, informed consent, deception, confidentiality, and debriefing.

REVIEW BY A RESEARCH ETHICS BOARD

Research Ethics Board – A panel of experts responsible for the ethical assessment of all research proposals conducted at an organization

First, studies now undergo an extensive review by a **Research Ethics Board (REB)** before they are implemented. This review of research plans, conducted by a panel that considers ethical concerns, is required by virtually all organizations in Canada (and in most Western countries), including hospitals, universities, universities, and government agencies. These boards review whether the potential benefits of the research are justifiable in light of possible risk of harm, including physical risks (e.g., receiving painful electric shocks, experiencing extreme heat, having to run on a treadmill) as well as psychological risks (e.g., having to give a speech, learning you are low in creativity, wearing an embarrassing T-shirt). These boards may force experimenters to make changes in the design or procedure of the research, or deny approval for a particular study altogether. As a researcher you might, for example, wonder about the effects of (falsely) telling someone his or her spouse was having an affair. However, a research review panel would never allow this type of study because of the high potential for psychological harm to the poor unsuspecting participant (and his or her spouse). Figure 2.5 shows excerpts from the *Canadian Code of Ethics for Psychologists* (2000).

FIGURE 2.5   EXCERPTS FROM THE *CANADIAN CODE OF ETHICS FOR PSYCHOLOGISTS*

In adhering to the Principle of Respect for the Dignity of Persons, psychologists would:

Informed consent

I.20   Obtain informed consent for all research activities that involve obtrusive measures, invasion of privacy, more than minimal risk of harm, or any attempt to change the behaviour of research participants.

I.21   Establish and use signed consent forms that specify the dimensions of informed consent or that acknowledge that such dimensions have been explained and are understood.

Freedom of consent

I.27   Take all reasonable steps to ensure that consent is not given under conditions of coercion, undue pressure, or undue reward.

I.28   Not proceed with any research activity, if consent is given under any condition of coercion, undue pressure, or undue reward.

In adhering to the Principle of Integrity in Relationships, psychologists would:

Avoidance of incomplete disclosure

III.23   Not engage in incomplete disclosure, or in temporarily leading research participants to believe that a research project or some aspect of it has a different purpose, if there are alternative procedures available or if the negative effects cannot be predicted or offset.

III.24   Not engage in incomplete disclosure, or in temporarily leading research participants to believe that a research project or some aspect of it has a different purpose, if it would interfere with the person's understanding of facts that clearly might influence a decision to give adequately informed consent (e.g., withholding information about the level of risk, discomfort, or inconvenience).

III.25   Use the minimum necessary incomplete disclosure or temporary leading of research participants to believe that a research project or some aspect of it has a different purpose, when such research procedures are used.

III.26   Debrief research participants as soon as possible after the participants' involvement, if there has been incomplete disclosure or temporary leading of research participants to believe that a research project or some aspect of it has a different purpose.

Source: Canadian Psychological Association, 2000. Pages 11 and 25. http://www.cpa.ca/cpasite/userfiles/Documents/Canadian%20Code%20of%20Ethics%20for%20Psycho.pdf

PROVIDE INFORMED CONSENT

Research studies now require participants to give **informed consent.** This consent refers to an individual's deliberate, voluntary decision to participate in research, based on the researcher's description of what such participation will involve. Participants don't need to hear about every single aspect of the research, but they do need to hear enough to make an educated decision about whether they would like to participate.

informed consent – an individual's deliberate, voluntary decision to participate in research, based on the researcher's description of what such participation will involve

deception – giving false information to the participants in a study

In some cases, researchers can't provide participants with accurate information about the study because giving even a few details would ruin the study. For example, in one study researchers were interested in examining honesty (Bersoff, 1999). Participants came into the lab to complete some questionnaires, and then, as they were leaving, the experimenter gave them the wrong amount of money (too much). The dependent variable was whether participants would return the money or just take it and leave. (As predicted, most participants just took the extra money and left.) Evidently, participants in this study could not give full consent to their participation, because telling them the study was examining honesty would have changed their behaviour. Such studies therefore use **deception**, which consists of giving false information to participants. Law Connections describes another type of study that involves tricky ethical considerations.

"I don't usually volunteer for experiments, but I'm kind of a puzzle freak."

© Mike Twohy/The New Yorker Collection/www.cartoonbank.com

LAW CONNECTIONS

The Challenges of Studying Drinking and Driving

When researchers study real-life behaviour that could have serious legal and/or health implications, they must take precautions to assure participants' safety. In one study, researchers from the University of Waterloo were interested in examining whether alcohol use affects people's attitudes and intentions toward drinking and driving (MacDonald, Zanna, & Fong, 1995). Male participants were randomly assigned to the sober or intoxicated condition (and all participants were of legal drinking age). Those in the intoxicated condition drank enough alcohol to reach a blood-alcohol concentration above the legal limit (the legal limit for driving while intoxicated in most Canadian provinces is 0.05, and in Quebec—it is 0.08). All participants then completed a questionnaire assessing their attitudes and intentions to drink and drive in a number of situations. The results indicated that when asked general questions about their future intentions, sober and intoxicated participants were equally negative about this behaviour. However, when a contingency was embedded in the question (e.g., "Would you drink and drive only a short distance?"), intoxicated participants were significantly less negative about drinking and driving than were sober participants. Given the researchers' concern that intoxicated participants could leave the study and drive while intoxicated—an illegal and dangerous behaviour—all participants in this condition were required to stay in the laboratory for one hour after completing the study. If a participant's blood-alcohol concentration remained above 0.05 after one hour, the experimenter then either accompanied the participant home (if he lived on campus) or provided a taxi ride home (if he lived off campus). This experiment also used only male participants because of concerns about exposing females, if pregnant, to alcohol.

Ingram Publishing/SUPERSTOCK

PROTECT CONFIDENTIALITY

Participant confidentiality needs to be protected from unauthorized disclosure, which is why surveys often use a code number instead of the person's name. Data also need to be stored in a locked room with restricted access and electronic data must be stored on a computer with sufficient security. When reports using the data are made, only group-level information is presented, as opposed to individually describing how particular people behaved. So, researchers would say that "most students who received the alcohol prevention workshop drank less," instead of "most students who received the alcohol prevention workshop drank less except for Bart Simpson, who surprisingly doubled his beer intake over the next month."

PROVIDE DEBRIEFING

debriefing – a disclosure made to participants after research procedures are completed in which the researcher explains the purpose of the study, answers questions, attempts to resolve any negative feelings, and emphasizes the study's contributions to science

After participating in a research study, participants are given a **debriefing**. This refers to a disclosure made to participants after research procedures are completed. The researcher explains the purpose of the study, answers any questions, attempts to resolve any negative feelings, and emphasizes the study's contributions to science. This is especially important in cases in which deception has been used.

STRATEGIES FOR MANAGING ETHICAL ISSUES IN CONDUCTING RESEARCH

FACTOR	EXAMPLE
Review by an institutional board	Dr. Rosenberg submits her research proposal to the Research Ethics Board. She then changes several aspects of the study design in order to meet the board's requirements.
Provide informed consent	Dr. Rosenberg describes the goals and procedures to all participants before the study begins. She also reviews the benefits and costs of participating. Finally, she lets participants know they can withdraw from the study at any time.
Protect confidentiality	Danny and Lisa, two research assistants in Dr. Rosenberg's lab, enter all data using participants' code numbers only. The forms that match participants' names and code numbers are stored in a separate lab.
Provide debriefing	After participants have completed the study, Dr. Rosenberg describes the study's goals and procedures. She emphasizes the contributions of this research to psychology theory, and the normality of the participants' actions.

HOW DOES CULTURE INFLUENCE RESEARCH FINDINGS?

Imagine that you are asked a series of questions about your attitudes. The items include "On a date, the boy should be expected to pay all expenses"; "It is alright for a girl to want to play rough sports like football"; and "Petting is acceptable on a first date." How would women from different cultures respond to these questions? Researchers examined precisely this question by asking female students in the United States from different cultural backgrounds (including Japan, Taiwan, Indonesia, and the Middle East, as well as the United States) each of these, and other, questions (Gibbons, Hamby, & Dennis, 1997). As predicted, women from the United States gave more extreme answers—meaning both high and low answers—than women from other cultures, who tended to give more moderate answers—meaning those in the middle of the possible responses. The researchers suggest that these moderate answers reflect, in part, the lack of meaning of many of these questions for those from different cultures. After all, in cultures in which arranged marriages are the norm (and dating therefore does not occur) and in those in which women are not encouraged to engage in sports, such questions simply aren't meaningful. Participants are therefore much more likely to give neutral answers because they don't know how to interpret or respond to the item.

Another contributor to this finding, however, could be the bias toward a modest or moderate style of responding to questionnaires among East Asian collectivist cultures when compared to North American norms (Fischer, 2004). It's also the case that, in responding to questionnaires, people from collectivist cultures are more likely to have a general tendency to agree with questions than are people from individualistic cultures, such as North Americans, as the greater emphasis on social harmony leads to more agreeable responding (Smith, 2004).

These findings demonstrate some of the many challenges of conducting research across different cultures, as we'll discuss throughout this textbook. Let's now examine how culture influences three particular issues in research design and methodology: the impact of question order, question wording, and the language used.

THE IMPACT OF QUESTION ORDER

In one study, researchers asked German students at the University of Heidelberg and Chinese students at Beijing University two identical questions: (1) How happy are you with your studies? and (2) How happy are you with your life as a whole? (Haberstroh, Oyserman, Schwarz, Kühnen, & Ji, 2002). However, half of the students at each school were asked the questions in that order, and half of the students were asked these questions in the opposite order. Did the question order matter? Well, for German students, the correlation between these two answers was higher when they were asked about their academic life first. For Chinese students, question order had no impact on the correlation between their responses.

How can culture impact the effect of order? For German students, academic performance plays a stronger role in self-esteem because academic achievement reflects their accomplishments. Thus, when German students first think about their academic achievements, they report having a somewhat higher overall life satisfaction. In other words, academic life satisfaction has a stronger impact on life satisfaction for German students than for Chinese students.

THE IMPACT OF QUESTION WORDING

How questions are worded in surveys can also influence responses in different ways across cultures. In one study, Canadian and Japanese participants were asked to complete a survey in which questions were worded in three distinct ways (Heine, Lehman, Peng, & Greenholtz, 2002). Participants in one condition read the question with no reference ("I have respect for the authority figures with whom I interact"); participants in another condition read the question with a reference to other Japanese ("Compared to most Japanese, I think I have respect for the authority figures with whom I interact"); and participants in yet another condition read the question with a reference to North Americans ("Compared to most North Americans, I think I have respect for the authority figures with whom I interact").

As predicted, the reference group included in the question had a significant effect on people's responses. Although there was no overall cultural difference in responses, when no reference group was included, significant effects of culture occurred when reference groups were included. When comparing themselves to people in the other culture, Canadians saw themselves as less interdependent than the Japanese. In contrast, Japanese people saw themselves as more interdependent than Canadians. These findings indicate that question wording, and in particular the type of comparison noted in the question, impacts responses in different ways for people in different cultures.

THE IMPACT OF LANGUAGE

Another subtle factor that can influence findings in cross-cultural research is the language used during testing. In one study, researchers examined differences in how Chinese and European Americans organized sets of three words (Ji, Zhang, & Nisbett, 2004). Participants were given three words and were asked to indicate which two words were most closely related and why. For example, if participants were given the words "monkey," "panda," and "banana," they could group "monkey" and "panda" because they were both animals, or they could group "monkey" and "banana" because monkeys eat bananas. Although in general Chinese people organized objects in a more relational way than European Americans (meaning they were more likely to group "monkey" and "banana" together than "monkey" and "panda" together), the responses of bilingual Chinese people were more relational when they were tested in Chinese than when they were tested in English. Other research supports this finding that the language used during testing can influence the accessibility of different types of thoughts, which in turn can impact the research findings (Trafimow, Silverman, Fan, & Law, 1997).

THE BIG PICTURE

RESEARCH METHODS

This chapter included many applications of the three "big ideas" studied in social psychology. The examples below should help you see the connection between our discussion of the self and these big ideas, and contribute to your understanding of the big picture of social psychology.

THEME	EXAMPLES
The social world influences how we think about ourselves.	• After having followed an abstinence-only program, many adolescents report more positive attitudes about abstinence although this might not lead to abstinence behaviour. • The language used during testing can influence the accessibility of different types of thoughts. For example, the responses of bilingual Chinese people were more relational when they were tested in Chinese than when they were tested in English. • When a reference group is included in a question, there is a significant effect on people's responses.
The social world influences our thoughts, attitudes, and behaviour.	• In an online survey, undergraduate students reported that they disclose more information about themselves on Facebook than they do in general. • When judging people's emotions from their facial expressions, Japanese people incorporate information from the social context more than Westerners do. • As the greater emphasis on social harmony leads to more agreeable responding, people from collectivist cultures are more likely to have a general tendency to agree with questions than are people from individualistic cultures.
Our attitudes and behaviour shape the social world around us.	• People in many countries view northerners as less emotionally expressive and southerners as more emotionally expressive. • Research generally shows that people are faster at responding to pairs of words that they view as compatible than to incompatible pairs, and in terms of prejudice, there is an implicit linking of Caucasian with good and Black with bad. • Academic life satisfaction has a stronger impact on life satisfaction for German students than for Chinese students.

This chapter has examined five key issues in conducting research in social psychology:

1. How do researchers in social psychology test their ideas?

This section examined the specific steps in the research process, including forming a question, searching the literature, forming a hypothesis, creating an operational definition, collecting and analyzing data, and proposing or revising a theory. You also learned why exposing children to images of aggression in the media is a bad idea.

2. What are the different types of correlational research methods?

This section described two distinct types of correlational research methods—observational/naturalistic methods and self-report or survey methods—as well as the strengths and limitations of each approach. You also discovered that how you ask university students about their alcohol use and sexual behaviour can influence their response.

3. How do you conduct experimental research?

This section described specific features of experimental methods, including random assignment and control. It also described the importance of designing studies with high internal and external validity. You also learned that women eat fewer M&Ms when they are talking with an attractive man than when they are talking with someone who is less attractive.

4. How do you conduct qualitative research?

This section described the distinction between qualitative and quantitative research. It also described levels of qualitative analysis, including descriptive, thematic, and discursive analyses.

5. What are the ethical issues in conducting research in social psychology?

This section described how researchers manage the ethical issues involved in conducting research in social psychology, including review by a Research Ethics Board, informed consent, deception, confidentiality, and debriefing. You also learned that university students can behave like actual prison guards (and indeed prisoners) very quickly, when they are put in this situation.

6. How does culture influence research findings?

The last section in this chapter described the role of culture in influencing research findings in social psychology. You discovered how question order, question wording, and the language used can all impact on responses in different ways for people from individualistic and collectivistic cultures.

Key Terms

archival research 36
correlational research 35
covert measures 42
debriefing 56
deception 55
demand characteristics 47
dependent variable 45
event recording or experience
    sampling measures 39
experimenter blind 49
experimental methods 45

experimental realism or psychological
    realism 49
experimenter expectancy effects 48
external validity 50
field experiments 50
hypothesis 32
independent variable 45
informed consent 55
internal validity 47
inter-rater reliability 37
literature review 31

meta-analysis 37
mundane realism 50
operational definition 32
observational/naturalistic
    methods 35
random assignment 45
random sample or representative
    sample 51
Research Ethics Board 54
theory 34

Questions for Review

1. Describe each of the steps in the scientific method.

2. Describe two advantages and two disadvantages of each of the three major methods of conducting research in social psychology: naturalistic/observation, self-report/survey, and experiments.

3. What are two ways of increasing internal validity and two ways of increasing external validity?

4. What are four ways that researchers manage ethical concerns when conducting research in social psychology?

5. Describe how people from different cultures can respond to the same questionnaire in different ways.

Take Action!

1. After observing that whenever your brother goes for a run, he seems to be in a great mood, you wonder whether exercise makes people feel good. How could you do this study using self-report methods? How could you do this study using experimental methods?

2. Dr. D'Angelo is a dentist who wants to get feedback from her patients about their satisfaction with office policy and wait times. She was planning on mailing an anonymous survey to all of her patients, but then decided that this would be too much work. She is now planning on asking patients for their thoughts about their dental care when they come in for the appointment. What is the problem with this approach?

3. Your roommate Darren wants to know if his new hypnosis tape is actually effective in helping people quit smoking. To test its effectiveness, he asks 10 of his closest friends to help him determine whether hypnosis is a good way of helping people stop smoking. He gives his five male friends the hypnosis tape, and his five female friends a music tape. One week later, he asks each person how many cigarettes they are smoking. When Darren asks you for your thoughts on his study, what problems do you see?

4. As part of a class project, you want to measure the effects on self-esteem of telling university athletes that they have failed a test on "sports intelligence." How could you design a study to ethically test this question?

5. You are interested in designing a study to test differences in attitudes toward human rights, including women's rights and gay rights, across cultures. How could you conduct such a study? What do you think you would find?

LIVE RESEARCH

Participate in Research

Activity 1 Forming a Question: The first step in research is to form a question that you'd like to inquire about. Think about your observations of your own or other people's behaviour, and factors that may influence them. Then go online to share your question with others—and see what questions other students have raised.

Activity 2 Understanding Correlation: This chapter has described the difference between correlation and causation, and the possibility of a third variable accounting for the association between two variables. Go online to read several studies that describe links between two events, and decide whether each example shows correlation or causation.

Activity 3 The Importance of Internal and External Validity: To test the impact of internal and external validity in experimental research, go online to read about several potential research studies you could conduct. Then rate whether the proposed study has problems with internal validity, external validity, or both.

Activity 4 Understanding the Ethics of Research: You've learned a lot in this chapter about the importance of following ethical guidelines when conducting research in social psychology. Go online to look at a series of proposed studies and rate whether each follows appropriate guidelines—and if not, how the study should be modified to follow these guidelines.

Activity 5 The Role of Context: To examine the impact of culture on the attributions we make, go online to briefly look at a photograph, and then list all of the items you saw in that picture.

Test a Hypothesis

One of the findings discussed in this chapter was whether students who receive better grades in a class like the professor more than those who receive worse grades. To test whether this hypothesis is true, design a survey to ask other students about their grade in a class and their liking of the professor. Do your findings support or refute the hypothesis?

Design a Study

Go online to design your own study that tests the influence of exposure to aggressive models on acts of aggression. You'll choose the type of study you want to conduct (self-report, observational/naturalistic, or experimental), choose your own independent and dependent variables, and form your own hypothesis. Then, you can share your findings with other students across the country!

3

CHAPTER

THE SELF: SELF-PERCEPTION AND SELF-PRESENTATION

DID YOU EVER WONDER?

Who are you?

What is your *self*?

How do you know?

We speak of identity, of self-awareness, of self-esteem, but our sense of self is a diffuse and complex idea. It consists of all sorts of elements, including our achievements, values, important relationships, and so on—and we can say of an item of clothing, or a car, "It's just not me." We might also sometimes find ourselves saying of our own behaviour, "It's not me to act like that—I don't know what came over me." It sounds as if we know what "me" is, but in reality this "me" is hard to pinpoint. We can also wonder how

The Canadian Press/XINHUA

changeable the self really is. And how fragile it is. If you lose someone important to you, or even a possession that means a lot to you, you might feel that you've lost "a part of yourself."

A story that exemplifies an exceptionally strong sense of self, and which "touched hearts" not just in Canada, but across the world, is that of Olympic skater Joannie Rochette. Her mother was in Vancouver to see Joannie skate in the 2010 Winter Olympics and suddenly died of a heart attack two days before Joannie was due to compete. By all accounts, not only were they very close as mother and daughter, but her mother had always been very involved in Joannie's career and training. "She has always been the most critical person about my skating, pushing me harder to improve," Joannie said of her mother before she passed away. "Even if it requires quite a big deal of humility at 22 to admit you need more of your mother, I expressed it and she drives from home to St-Leonard once a week to come to supervise with her unique eyes my training."

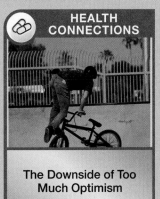
It surprised many when Joannie decided to compete, and many more when she skated almost immaculately and was in third place at the end of the first day of competition. Two days later, she had to skate again, and won the bronze medal (Almasy, S., 2010, Feb. 24).

In an email interview given to the *Christian Science Monitor* a few months before, Thérèse Rochette spoke of her daughter: "I always encouraged her to have confidence in *herself*, to believe in her dreams, to consider the progress that she has accomplished over many years. But in periods of great stress, I also have the necessary distance to remind her of a rule she knows well: above all, skate for *herself*, for her pleasure." (Bryant, 2010)

Somehow Joannie had a strong enough sense of who she was, that she was able to compete—and win a medal. We can only speculate about Joannie's competing emotions and the questions about oneself that this kind of experience can prompt, but there is something humbling and inspiring about this tragic yet heroic story.

This chapter will explain why people's feelings of self-worth are influenced not only by their own attributes, but also by their comparisons with others. You'll also find answers to these questions:

 Why are people who get fired just as happy as those who stay hired?

 Why can reading about Pamela Anderson make you feel smarter?

 Why do people see themselves as more virtuous than others?

 Why should you not worry about wearing an embarrassing t-shirt?

 Why do people in individualistic cultures tend to rate themselves as better than others, whereas people in collectivistic cultures tend to see others as better than themselves?

What do these questions have in common? They all describe findings from research in social psychology on how we see ourselves and how we present ourselves to others.

WHAT YOU'LL LEARN

How to define self-concept and self-awareness

How personal factors influence the self-concept and self-awareness

How social factors influence the self-concept

How people maintain a positive self-concept

How people present themselves to others

How culture influences self-concept, self-perception, and self-presentation

PREVIEW

Anthropologist Clifford Geertz wrote that "the Western conception of the person as a bounded, unique, more or less integrated motivational and cognitive universe, a dynamic center of awareness, emotion, judgment, and action organized into a distinctive whole and set contrastively against other such wholes and against its social and natural background, is, however incorrigible it may seem to us, a rather peculiar idea within the context of the world's cultures" (1983, p. 59).

This is a useful quote to consider, as it draws our attention to some of the assumptions that Western cultures, and therefore the psychology that developed in those cultures, hold about what a person, or self, is. For example, the self has boundaries or edges, and is distinct from its environment. Each self is also assumed to be unique. It is like a little universe of thoughts, motivations, awareness, emotion, decision-making, and behaviour. It is also a whole thing, not part of another thing. It is separate from other similar whole selves. Geertz also draws our attention to there being other ways to understand the self—namely, that outside the Western individualistic countries and the field of social science, the Western notion of self is (to use his phrase) a "rather peculiar idea."

The Western quest to understand the self can be traced back to (at least) two and a half thousand years ago (around 500 BCE), when the Greek philosopher Socrates wrote, "Know thyself," which is certainly more easily said than done. Our view of ourselves is often distorted in a variety of ways, and even knowing what "self" is can be problematic. Since the late 19th century, however, social psychologists have examined the meanings of the nature of self, and the scientific approach has now generated a large amount of information about the self, as you will also see throughout this chapter.

WHAT ARE THE SELF-CONCEPT AND SELF-AWARENESS?

This section will examine the distinction between self-concept and self-awareness. We will also review three functions of self: interpersonal tool, decision maker, and regulatory system. If someone were to ask you what you're like, what would you say? You might say "smart," "funny," "friendly," or "athletic." All of these would describe your self-concept, meaning your overall beliefs about your own attributes. According to William James, a pioneering American psychologist, self-concept is one aspect of the self, and can be referred to as the Known or the Me (James, 1890). The second aspect of the self is self-awareness, which is also called the Knower

self-concept – an individual's overall beliefs about his or her own attributes

or the I. The known is self-concept (your knowledge about who you are) and the knower is self-awareness (your act of thinking about yourself). According to James, individual sense of identity is created by combining these two aspects of the self (Aronson, Wilson, Akert, & Fehr, 2007).

Self-concept, according to the American psychologist Hazel Rose Markus (1977), is made up of distinct beliefs that we hold about ourselves and that influence what we notice about the world and how we process self-relevant information. For example, people who include being artistic as part of their schema of themselves (i.e., they see themselves as artistic) are likely to focus on the aesthetic aspects of what they encounter in the world, such as the outfits their friends are wearing, the arrangement of flowers in a vase, or the combination of colours in a spectacular sunset. On the other hand, those who are not "schematic" for art, as Markus phrases it, would be unlikely to notice such aesthetic details, or to pay attention to them if they did notice. Your self-concept has an impact on how you feel about yourself. If your overall evaluation of your attributes is positive, you'll have high **self-esteem**, just as your self-esteem will be lower if you view your attributes less favourably.

self-esteem – an individual's evaluation of his or her own worth

Research indicates that self-concept changes from childhood to adulthood. As children develop, their perceptions of themselves become increasingly differentiated and comprehensive, a process of change that is particularly evident during adolescence (Shapka & Keating, 2005). For example, if you ask a 10-year-old girl "Who are you?" you're likely to hear something concrete, such as, "I am a girl, I have long hair, I play soccer, and my best friend is Jessica." This is a concrete self-concept, which emphasizes physical or visible characteristics. In contrast, if you ask a 21-year-old university student the same question, you're likely to hear something quite different, such as, "I'm a psychology major, I believe in peace, I'm quiet, and I have a good sense of humour." This is a more abstract self-concept, which emphasizes psychological characteristics.

Self-awareness is a state of being aware of oneself as an object of one's thoughts. Duval and Wicklund (1972) suggest that when one is aware of oneself as an object it is similar to being aware of another person, animal, or object. A variety of factors can lead to self-awareness, such as standing in front of a crowd, looking in a mirror, or hearing one's voice on tape. When people are forced into being self-aware, they become motivated to change their behaviour (in order to match it to their personal standards) or to try to escape from their self-awareness (so that they don't notice the contradiction). Figure 3.1 summarizes this dynamic.

FIGURE 3.1 MODEL OF SELF-AWARENESS THEORY

According to self-awareness theory, environmental cues or personality factors can lead people to become more aware of their thoughts, feelings, and behaviour. This increase in self-awareness, in turn, leads people to think about discrepancies between their attitudes and behaviour. If self-discrepancies are found, we have one of two options: match our behaviour to our internal attitudes or reduce self-awareness.

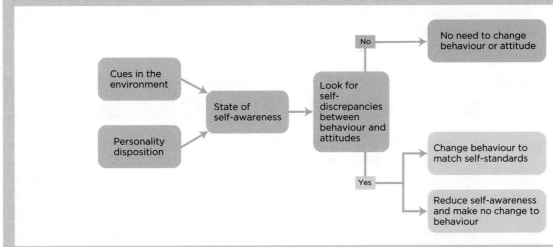

Research generally supports the idea that people who are self-aware are more likely to match their behaviour to their own personal standards. In one study conducted in the United States, Halloween trick-or-treaters were greeted at a researcher's door and left alone to help themselves from a bowl of candy (Beaman, Klentz, Diener, & Svanum, 1979). Each child was asked to only take one piece. For half the children, there was a full-length mirror right behind the bowl (which should clearly increase self-awareness), whereas for the other half there was no mirror. Thirty-four percent of those without the mirror took more than one piece of candy, compared to only 12 percent of those with the mirror.

FUNCTIONS OF SELF

SELF AS INTERPERSONAL TOOL.   In order for us to have a social life and have relationships with others around us, we need to have a relatively stable identity. Our interaction with others would otherwise consist of a series of disjointed interactions with relative strangers. For example, in the movie *50 First Dates* (2004), Lucy, the main female character played by Drew Barrymore, has lost her short-term memory and forgets people she meets and what she did the day before. In essence, Lucy doesn't have a stable sense of her self or identity. To some extent, we are who we think we are and with no knowledge of ourselves we have no sense of identity. This is an important element in people's social life and interpersonal relationships.

SELF AS DECISION MAKER.   We all make large and small decisions in order to set our priorities in life. These decisions reflect our goals and values. For example, if your goal is to attend graduate school and become a psychologist, it will be important for you to perform well in all your psychology courses. To do this, you would need to first decide to attend your psychology classes, complete the assignments, and study for exams. These small decisions are consistent with your larger goals. However, if your goal is to swim for the Canadian national team, your performance in psychology courses is not that significant in reaching your goal. You may even skip a few classes to practise your swimming. Overall, people make small and large decisions that reflect their principles, goals, and priorities.

SELF AS REGULATORY SYSTEM.   The self has to maintain itself despite the individual's diverse and sometimes contradictory goals. If you've ever been on a diet, you have undoubtedly struggled to control the urge to eat something "forbidden" (e.g., cheesecake), and have probably been unable to resist on at least one occasion. This failure to match your actual behaviour to your ideal standards occurs because it is exhausting to constantly try to exercise such restraint—sooner or later you may simply "use up" your willpower and give in to temptation (Pennebaker, 1989; Wegner, 1994). As described in Research Focus on Neuroscience, recent research suggests that different parts of the brain are activated when we make decisions about an immediate reward (e.g., eating that cheesecake right now) versus a delayed reward (e.g., promising ourselves a piece of cheesecake in a few weeks, after we've lost those stubborn 10 pounds).

RESEARCH FOCUS ON NEUROSCIENCE
Different Parts of the Brain Make Different Types of Decisions

Research in neuroscience suggests that different parts of the brain are responsible for making decisions about immediate rewards versus delayed rewards (McClure, Laibson, Loewenstein, & Cohen, 2004). In one study, researchers used functional magnetic resonance imaging (fMRI) to examine which parts of the brain were active when participants made different types of decisions. When participants made decisions about an immediate reward—such as whether to receive $10 immediately or $11 tomorrow—the part of the brain that is influenced by neural systems associated with emotions was activated. When participants made decisions about a delayed reward—such as receiving $5 in two weeks or $40 in six weeks—the part of the brain involved in abstract reasoning and calculation was activated. This study provides convincing evidence that different parts of the brain are used to make different types of decisions. As one of the authors of this study says, "Our emotional brain wants to max out the credit card, order dessert and smoke a cigarette. Our logical brain knows we should save for retirement, go for a jog and quit smoking."

Self-regulation is an important function of the self. One has to take care of one's interpersonal relationships, regulate one's emotional states, and organize information that is related to particular tasks.

Research conducted by Jennifer Campbell at the University of British Columbia suggests that some of us may have a clearer sense of self than others. Self-concept clarity is defined as the extent to which knowledge about the self is clearly or consistently defined (Campbell, 1990). Campbell and her colleagues have found that the extent to which one's knowledge of one's self is stable, and clearly and consistently defined, has important cognitive and emotional implications (Campbell, 1990).

For example, Campbell and colleagues (Campbell et al., 1996) found that people who were low in self-concept clarity were more likely to be neurotic and have low self-esteem, and were less likely to be aware of their internal states. They also tended to engage in chronic self-analysis and rumination, an involuntary, negative form of self-focus associated with threat or uncertainty (e.g., "Sometimes it's hard for me to shut off thoughts about myself"). People low in self-concept clarity were also less likely to engage in positive forms of self-focus such as reflection (e.g., "I love exploring my inner self.").

[CONCEPTS IN CONTEXT]

WHAT ARE THE SELF-CONCEPT AND SELF-AWARENESS?

FACTOR	EXAMPLE
Self as interpersonal tool	Among Jariah's group of friends, everyone knows that Jariah is a caring and helpful individual and if anyone needs help, Jariah is the first person to be approached. Jariah takes a pride in being someone who friends can turn to.
Self as decision maker	Kendis wants to become a psychology professor. He has decided that in order to achieve his goal, he has to work hard during the semester and not miss any important assignments.
Self as regulatory system	Kendis also knows that in order to achieve his goal, he has to resist the temptation to party too hard during the semester.

HOW DO PERSONAL FACTORS INFLUENCE THE SELF-CONCEPT AND SELF-AWARENESS?

This section will explain how the self-concept is influenced by a variety of factors within ourselves. What are the things that we do that make up our self-concept? We think about our thoughts, we focus on self-awareness, we regulate ourselves, we examine our own behaviour, and we interpret our motivation.

THINKING ABOUT YOUR THOUGHTS

Imagine you're trying to choose classes for next semester. You might think about English classes you've taken in the past, or about how you feel about reading literature, to help you make your decision. You're thinking about how you feel, and this gives you insight into the choice you should make. This process of thinking about your thoughts or feelings is called introspection. Introspection is often seen as influencing the self-concept.

THE HAZARDS OF INTROSPECTION.

Despite the commonsense belief that thinking about why we like something can help us understand our true attitudes, introspection is actually not a very effective way of gaining insight into our true attitudes (Dijksterhuis, 2004; Levine, Halberstadt, & Goldstone, 1996). In fact, people who analyze the reasons why they have a particular attitude (e.g., why they like their dating partner, why they prefer certain classes) show a lower correlation between their attitudes and their behaviour, meaning that their attitudes aren't very good at predicting their actual behaviour, than those who don't engage in this type of self-reflection. In one study, female participants were asked to choose a poster to take home as a thank you gift (Wilson et al., 1993). They were asked to base their selection either on their reasons for preferring a specific poster or on their "gut feeling" about a poster. When researchers contacted the students several weeks later, those who had relied on their gut feelings in making the choice reported feeling happier with their selection than those who had focused on the reasons.

Why does thinking about their preferences lead people to make decisions that aren't necessarily in their best interest? First, in many cases our feelings are a better predictor of our true preferences and even our future behaviour (Wilson, Dunn, Bybee, Hyman, & Rotondo, 1984; Wilson & LaFleur, 1995). This is why you may feel a tremendous attraction to someone who it doesn't make sense for you to be attracted to—your heart is guiding your behaviour, not your head (perhaps much to your parents' dismay). As Sigmund Freud noted, "When making a decision of minor importance, I have always found it advantageous to consider all the pros and cons. In vital matters, however . . . the decision should come from the unconscious, from somewhere within our selves (cited by Dijksterhuis, 2004; p. 586)."

OVERESTIMATION OF THE IMPACT OF EVENTS.

We often believe that various factors will influence our mood much more than they actually do (Gilbert & Wilson, 2000; Stone, Hedges, Neale, & Satin, 1985; Wilson, Laser, & Stone, 1982). In fact, in general, people are inaccurate in their **affective forecasting**, meaning that they greatly overestimate the impact that both positive and negative events will have on their mood (Wilson, Wheatley, Meyers, Gilbert, & Axsom, 2000).

affective forecasting – the process of predicting the impact of both positive and negative events on mood

For example, imagine that you're an assistant professor of psychology approaching the tenure decision—meaning the decision by your department and your university about whether you'll basically have guaranteed lifetime employment (if you're given tenure) or you'll effectively be fired (if you're denied tenure). Which of those situations would make you feel better, and how long would that feeling (good or bad) last? This is precisely the study that was done by researchers at the University of Texas at Austin to examine people's accuracy in predicting their future emotional states (Gilbert, Pinel, Wilson, Blumberg, & Wheatley, 1998). In this study, researchers asked all former assistant professors who had achieved or failed to achieve tenure in the last 10 years to rate how happy they were. Then they asked current assistant professors—who were about to come up for tenure—how they thought they'd feel a few years later if they did or did not get tenure. Although current assistant professors predicted that they'd feel worse overall later on if they didn't get tenure, reports from those who'd lived through this experience don't support this belief: in fact, several years later, those who did and did not have tenure were found to be equally happy. Similarly, university students expect to experience negative feelings for a long time following the breakup of a romantic relationship (Gilbert et al., 1998). But in reality, students whose relationships end are just as happy as those whose relationships continue. These findings suggest that people expect to feel much greater regret than they actually do, which could lead us to make faulty decisions—meaning decisions that are motivated primarily by our anticipation of great and long-lasting regret—which we never actually experience.

It's not just that people are wrong about how they'll feel after experiencing relatively minor good or bad events—like missing a train or winning a football game: We also tend to believe that major events will have a much longer lasting effect on our mood than they actually do (Wilson et al., 2000). Many Americans say they believe they'd be happier if they lived in California—given the warm climate—than in the U.S. Midwest, but overall, people who live in the Midwest are just as happy as those who live in California (Schkade & Kahneman, 1998). What does this mean at a practical level? Don't play the lottery—even if you win, you won't be happy for as long as you think.

FOCUSING ON SELF-AWARENESS

Another factor that can influence the way we see ourselves is how we compare ourselves to our own standards of behaviour.

THE PROBLEM OF SELF-DISCREPANCY. According to **self-discrepancy theory** (Higgins, 1996), our self-concept is influenced by the gap between how we see ourselves (our actual self) and how we want to see ourselves (our ideal self;). Everyone feels some discrepancy between their actual and ideal selves, but people who perceive a large discrepancy

self-discrepancy theory – the theory that our self-concept is influenced by the gap between how we actually see ourselves and how we want to see ourselves

feel less good about themselves than people who see a small discrepancy. If you see yourself as a consistent C-level student but you come from an academically successful family and you aspire to be an intellectual like your parents and siblings, you may experience a large gap between your actual and ideal selves and therefore feel very negative about yourself. On the other hand, a person who sees herself as a strong varsity tennis player and is captain of the tennis team (i.e., she *is* a strong tennis player) may perceive a relatively small gap between her actual and ideal selves.

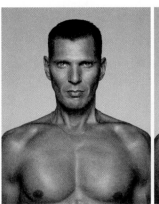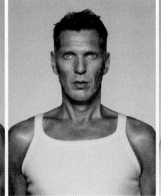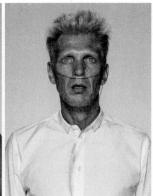

Photographer: Erwin Olaf. Courtesy: Hasted Kraeutler, New York, U.S.A.
Dutch photographer Erwin Olaf's self-portrait-50 years old "I Wish, I Am, I Will Be" captures the discrepancy between actual-self (middle) and ideal-self (left).

THE IMPACT OF SELF-AWARENESS. Self-discrepancy theory suggests that the self-concept is influenced by the gap between our actual and ideal selves. However, other researchers believe that people rarely think about such a discrepancy, and that as a result, the presence of such a discrepancy would affect the self-concept only when a person is paying attention to it (Duval & Wicklund, 1972). Specifically, according to **self-awareness theory**, people notice self-discrepancies only when they focus on their own behaviour.

self-awareness theory – when people focus on their own behaviour, they are motivated to either change their behaviour (so their attitudes and behaviour are in line) or escape from self-awareness (to avoid noticing this contradiction)

THE LIMITS OF SELF-CONTROL. Once we've spent energy on controlling our thoughts and desires, we have difficulty doing so again. In a study by Baumeister Bratslavsky, Muraven, and Tice (1998), participants who had signed up for a "taste perception" study, and were specifically told not to eat for three hours before the experiment, came into a laboratory room and saw a table with two types of food: a bowl of red and white radishes and a bowl of chocolate candies and freshly baked chocolate chip cookies. Each participant was then randomly assigned to one of the two food conditions (radishes or chocolate), and was asked to take about five minutes to taste at least two pieces of the assigned food. After this period of tasting, the experimenter returned to give the participant the second portion of the study—a problem-solving task in which participants had to trace a geometric puzzle without retracing any lines. However, the puzzle was specifically designed to be impossible to solve in order to create a frustrating situation. The experimenter then left the room, and timed how long the participant worked on the task before giving up (which was signalled by ringing a bell). As predicted, participants who were in the radish condition—and thus had to exercise great willpower in resisting eating chocolate—gave up working on the frustrating puzzle after only 8 ½ minutes, whereas participants who were in the chocolate condition—and hence may not have "used up" all their self-control when it came time to work on the puzzle—worked an average of nearly 19 minutes before giving up.

One alternative explanation for these results is that participants in the radish condition were simply hungrier than those in the chocolate condition—after all, chocolate chip cookies and chocolates are certainly more filling than radishes. However, the results of a no-food control condition, in which participants simply worked on the frustrating puzzle without seeing either of the foods, revealed that participants in this condition—who clearly would be quite hungry—spent nearly 21 minutes working on the puzzle before giving up. Thus, we can be rather confident that the results of this study are not simply due to different levels of hunger in the different conditions. Figure 3.2 describes another example of the downside of exercising high levels of self-control.

FIGURE 3.2 DOES DEPLETING MENTAL ENERGY MAKE SELF-CONTROL MORE DIFFICULT?

Experimenters asked participants to solve various word starts, for example adding letters to "BU—" to create a word. Starts could be solved with sexual words, such as BUTT, or neutral words, such as BUGS. Some students had to complete a challenging mental task before completing the word starts. As predicted, a higher percentage of students whose energy and attention were depleted completed the word starts to make sexual words.

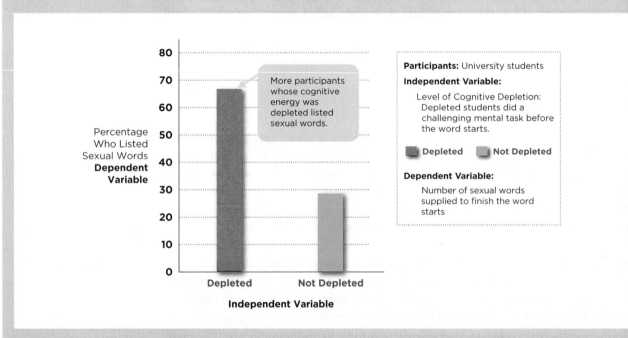

Source: Gaillot, M.T., & Baumeister, R.F. (2007). The physiology of will power: Linking blood glucose to self-control. *Personality and Social Psychology Review*, 11, 303–327

Trying to control or suppress our thoughts can also backfire and make these thoughts particularly salient (Major & Gramzow, 1999; Wegner & Gold, 1995; Wegner, Shortt, Blake, & Page, 1990). Have you ever tried to not think about something (e.g., an ex-boyfriend, a particularly gruesome scene from a movie, a failed test)? If so, then you most likely found that thoughts about this "forbidden" topic dominated your mind. Trying to suppress our thoughts can even influence our behaviour. In one study, students were shown a picture of a "skinhead" named Hein, and were asked to spend five minutes describing a typical day in his life (Gordijn, Hindriks, Koomen, Dijksterhuis, & Van Knippenberg, 2004). This study was conducted in The Netherlands, where skinheads (people with shaved heads and Nazi symbols on their clothing) are commonly seen as aggressive, racist, dumb, unhealthy, and unemployed. Some participants were specifically told not to use stereotypes (the "suppression condition"), while others were not given any instructions. Participants later completed a second part of the study. It was a word recognition task in which strings of letters were presented together and participants had to decide whether this list of letters contained an actual word. Those who had tried to suppress their skinhead stereotypes recognized words that were related to the stereotype faster than did participants who were not given the suppression instructions.

Questioning the Research:

Although Baumeister et al. (1998) found that participants' lack of self-control in the second task was due to their having had to exercise considerable self-control in the first task, can you think of another explanation for the findings?

ESCAPE FROM SELF-AWARENESS.   Although in some cases self-awareness leads people to match their behaviour to their internal standards, in other cases people choose to escape from this self-awareness and the discomfort it can bring. Efforts to escape from self-awareness can be relatively harmless. For example, dieters may choose to distract themselves from thoughts of their hunger by reading a book or talking on the phone. But in other cases people's efforts to reduce self-awareness can have dangerous consequences. In a study conducted in the U.S. by Jay Hull and Richard Young (1983), university students were given either negative or positive feedback about their IQ and then given an opportunity to taste and rate different kinds of wine. As predicted, students who were told they had low IQ scores drank more wine than those who received success feedback. These findings are in line with other findings showing that people often use alcohol to avoid thinking about themselves (Cooper, Frone, Russell, & Mudar, 1995; Steele & Josephs, 1990).

EXAMINING YOUR BEHAVIOUR

Another factor that influences how we see ourselves is our own behaviour—and research demonstrates that we look to our behaviour in particular ways to understand our self-concept.

SELF-PERCEPTION THEORY.   According to Daryl Bem's (1972) **self-perception theory**, we look at our behaviour to determine our attitudes and beliefs, in just the same way that we may examine other people's behaviour to see what they are like. If you take a number of psychology classes, you look to your behaviour and assume that you really like psychology. If you regularly choose the chocolate cake from a dessert tray, you assume that you must like chocolate. People who are led to believe that in the past they've supported a given policy tend to express positive attitudes toward that policy, whereas those who believe that they've opposed such a policy in the past tend to express negative attitudes toward it (Albarracin & Wyer, 2000; Schlenker & Trudeau, 1990).

self-perception theory – we look to our own behaviour to determine our attitudes and beliefs

Self-perception theory explains why asking people to perform a behaviour, especially with little pressure, can lead them to experience a change in self-concept. Imagine that you are with a group of friends and they decide to go bowling. Even if you haven't enjoyed bowling in the past, if you go with your friends and participate, you may find yourself feeling more positive about bowling in the future. Self-perception theory predicts that you'll experience this change in attitude because you'll look at your behaviour (e.g., "Here I am bowling") to determine your belief about bowling (e.g., "I must like bowling").

In one test of self-perception theory, researchers approached random people in the streets of two Polish cities and asked them for help with finding a non-existent address (Dolinski, 2000). Virtually everyone (94 percent) responded, typically saying "I don't know." Participants were then approached a few blocks away by a woman carrying a huge suitcase and asked if they would watch it for a few minutes while she went up to visit a friend who lived on the fifth floor. Although only 34 percent of participants in the control condition agreed to watch over the suitcase, 58 percent of the participants who had first been asked for directions agreed to keep an eye on it. These people looked at their behaviour and determined that they were indeed helpful people. They had tried to provide directions when asked, and they were now willing to help yet another stranger by watching her luggage.

RESEARCH FOCUS ON GENDER
Gender Differences in Self-Definition

Although we all have a distinct view of our own strengths and weaknesses, one difference that has emerged in various studies is that men and women tend to differ in their views of themselves (Gabriel & Gardner, 1999). For example, Bergdahl (2005) found that men overestimate their driving ability even when they're aware of their risky behaviour. Women, on the other hand, have a more realistic estimate of their driving ability, and even tend to underestimate their performance . Further, Pallier (2003) reported that when information is available about one's ability on a specific task, men and women are similar in estimating their ability. However, when this information is missing, men tend to estimate their abilities at a significantly higher level than women do.

Studies thus seem to indicate that men and women differ in their self-confidence about their ability to succeed in a task (Beyer, 1998; 2002). It has been found that, if a task was perceived as "masculine," men reported more confidence in their abilities than women do. If a task was perceived as "feminine," however, men did not show higher confidence than women. Women, on the other hand, showed lower confidence in their abilities if the task was perceived as "masculine" than "feminine." This implies that gender stereotypes and awareness of those stereotypes influence self-confidence for both men and women (Brannon, 2008).

FACIAL FEEDBACK HYPOTHESIS. Although Bem's self-perception theory focused specifically on people's tendency to judge how they feel based on their behaviour, other researchers suggest that a similar process can influence our emotions (Laird, 1974). According to the **facial feedback hypothesis**, changes in facial expression can lead to changes in emotion. For example, people who hold their faces in a smile feel happier than those who maintain a frown (Kleinke, Peterson, & Rutledge, 1998). Changes in body posture and activity can have a similar effect on mood: people who sit slumped over feel less pride than those who sit upright; people who clench their fists feel more anger than those who relax their hands; and people who lift their hands up feel more positive than those who push their hands down (Duclos et al., 1989; Stepper & Strack, 1993). Similarly, people who nod while listening to a persuasive message show more attitude change than those who shake their heads (Briñol & Petty, 2003).

How could simply changing your facial expression or body posture affect your mood? One explanation is that changes in emotion that are caused by facial (and body) feedback are simply a result of self-perception (Kleinke et al., 1998). Thus, people who are smiling may perceive themselves as happy and therefore feel happy, while those who are frowning may see themselves as angry and therefore feel angry. Another explanation is that facial expressions and body movements influence emotions by producing physiological changes in the brain (Hennenlotter et al., 2008; Izard, 1994; Zajonc, Murphy, & Inglehar, 1989). Particular facial

facial feedback hypothesis – the hypothesis that changes in facial expression can lead to changes in emotion

expressions and body movements may lead to increases or decreases in blood flow to the brain, which in turn are responsible for changes in mood.

INTERPRETING YOUR MOTIVATION

Another factor that can influence how people view themselves is the motivation they identify as being the reason for their behaviour (Amabile, Hill, Hennessey, & Tighe, 1994). If you believe that you are engaging in a given activity based on intrinsic motivation—namely, the desire to engage in the activity for its own sake, because you find it interesting or enjoy it—you see your behaviour as motivated by internal factors, such as the sheer interest you have in this task. People who work on a task for intrinsic reasons report greater task involvement, enjoyment, curiosity, and interest. They also report greater psychological well-being (Sheldon, Ryan, Deci, & Kasser, 2004). On the other hand, if you believe that you engage in a given activity based on extrinsic motivation—namely, the desire to engage in an activity for external rewards or pressures—you see your behaviour as motivated by the desire to fulfill obligations, receive a benefit, or avoid a punishment. People who work on a task for extrinsic reasons report feeling concerned with recognition, competition, and tangible rewards or benefits. The pursuit of extrinsically focused goals, such as achieving financial success, can have negative consequences on overall life satisfaction and psychological well-being (Nickerson, Schwartz, Diener, & Kahneman, 2003; Sheldon, 2005). It's important to note here that in some (e.g., East Asian) collectivistic countries, maintaining harmonious social relations is associated with psychological well-being more than it is in individualistic countries (Uchida, Norasakkunkit & Kitayama, 2004). We will discuss this further at the end of the chapter.

[RATE YOURSELF]

WHAT MOTIVATES YOU?

Work Preference Inventory

INSTRUCTIONS: *Rate each item on a scale of 1 (never or almost never true of me) to 4 (always or almost always true of me).*

1. I enjoy trying to solve complex problems.
2. I am strongly motivated by the money/grades I earn.
3. Curiosity is the driving force behind much of what I do.
4. I am strongly motivated by the recognition I can earn from other people.
5. I prefer to figure things out for myself.
6. I have to feel that I'm earning something for what I do.
7. It is important for me to be able to do what I enjoy.
8. To me, success means doing better than other people.
9. I'm more comfortable when I can set my own goals.
10. I prefer working on projects with clearly specified procedures.

SCORING: Add up your scores on the odd-numbered items to create one subscale. Then add up your scores on the even-numbered items to create a second subscale.

INTERPRETATION: This scale assesses people's focus on work for intrinsic versus extrinsic reasons (Amabile, Hill, Hennessey, & Tighe, 1994). People with higher scores on the intrinsic subscale (the odd-numbered items) than the extrinsic subscale (the even-numbered items) are more motivated by intrinsic motivations for work, whereas people with higher scores on the extrinsic subscale than the intrinsic subscale are more motivated by extrinsic motivations for work.

THE DANGERS OF OVERJUSTIFICATION. To determine why we're engaging in a particular behaviour, we tend to examine the factors that lead to that behaviour. Intrinsic motivation, as mentioned above, is usually associated with greater enjoyment of a task than extrinsic motivation. In research at Concordia University, for example, Bye, Pushkar, & Conway (2007) examined the motivations of traditional students (defined as up to 21 years of age and entering university straight from high school) and non-traditional students (defined as at least 28 years of age). They found that, overall, non-traditional students were higher on intrinsic motivation, and for both traditional and non-traditional students intrinsic motivation was associated with positive emotions.

Receiving external rewards can, however, undermine our interest in engaging in a behaviour for intrinsic reasons, a phenomenon called overjustification. This means that sometimes activities that should be intrinsically motivating, such as reading books, getting good grades, and attending classes, become less enjoyable once external motivations for such behaviours are provided. For example, some high schools have policies that require students to engage in a volunteer activity prior to graduation. While these policies were developed in part to expose students to the benefits of volunteering (for themselves and for their communities), some research shows that after being forced to volunteer students become less interested in volunteering in the future, compared to students who were given a choice about volunteering (Stukas, Snyder, & Clary, 1999). This presumably occurs because, while volunteering should be fun (e.g., intrinsically rewarding), when you are forced to volunteer you assume that the only reason you're doing it is for extrinsic reasons (e.g., fear of not graduating). See Business Connections for some important exceptions to the overjustification effect.

overjustification – the phenomenon in which receiving external rewards for a given behaviour can undermine the intrinsic motivation for engaging in this behaviour

BUSINESS CONNECTIONS

Does Giving Bonuses Enhance or Undermine Motivation?

Many businesses try to motivate their employees to work hard by providing specific incentives for good performance, such as bonuses. However, research on overjustification suggests that providing extrinsic motivation for completing a task can undermine intrinsic motivation and thereby reduce performance levels. Research with both children and adults reveals that those who receive an expected reward (e.g., are told that they will get to do a fun activity if they do three other activities first) are less creative than those who get no reward or get an unexpected reward (Amabile, Hennessey, & Grossman, 1986). Similarly, people who are motivated to make money primarily for extrinsic reasons (e.g., comparing well with others) are more depressed than those who are motivated by more intrinsic reasons (e.g., doing work one enjoys).

What can businesses do to motivate employees? Some companies have explored nonfinancial perks, such as "dress-down Fridays," more vacation days, or more flexible work schedules. However, other research suggests that people who are paid for meeting a performance standard show greater enjoyment of the task and higher performance levels (Eisenberger, Rhoades, & Cameron, 1999). Providing extrinsic motivation for vague tasks (e.g., creativity) may therefore undermine interest and performance, yet such rewards may improve performance on tasks for which clear, high standards are established. Of course, intrinsic motivation may be different for those with different self-construals. As you might expect, it has been found by researchers from McGill University that individuals with an independent self-construal orient toward personal-goal pursuit, whereas individuals with interdependent self-construal prioritize in-group goals above personal ones (Downie, Koestner, Horberg, & Haga, 2006).

Radius/SUPERSTOCK

In one of the first experimental studies to demonstrate overjustification, Mark Lepper and his colleagues at Stanford University visited a nursery school and measured children's overall interest in drawing with magic markers (Lepper, Greene, & Nisbett, 1973). Some of the children were then asked to participate in a fun study of drawing and were separated into three groups. In the first group, children were told that they would get a reward if they drew pictures with magic markers for the experimenter (and they did receive a reward). Children in the second group were simply asked to draw pictures for the experimenter (and didn't receive a reward). Finally, a third group of children was asked to draw pictures for the experimenter and then received a "surprise reward" (meaning that they didn't know they would receive a reward until after they had finished drawing). The researchers then measured the amount of time children in each group spent drawing with markers during the next class period. As predicted, children who had received the expected reward spent only 8.6 percent of their time drawing, compared to 16.7 percent for those who did not expect to receive a reward and 18.1 percent for those who received an unexpected reward. These findings suggest that providing a reward in advance of doing an activity undermines intrinsic motivation, but that providing an unexpected reward has no significant impact on such motivation.

OVERCOMING OVERJUSTIFICATION.   Although the presence of external rewards can undermine intrinsic motivation, in many cases rewards can work very well to stimulate interest (Eisenberger & Cameron, 1996). For example, providing rewards for finishing a task and/or showing high-quality work can be quite effective. Even in cases where there are external pressures, there are ways to avoid, or at least minimize, the negative consequences of such pressures. One study demonstrated that people who impose even shorter deadlines on themselves for completing a task than the external source's deadline show more task enjoyment than people who simply follow the externally imposed deadline (Burgess, Enzle, & Schmaltz, 2004). In other words, although it may seem counter intuitive, you can avoid dampening your intrinsic motivation to finish writing your psychology lab report that's due in two weeks by setting your own earlier deadline. You're also less likely to cheat. Eric Donohue from the Université du Québec à Montréal and colleagues found that elite athletes with higher intrinsic motivation are less likely to take performance-enhancing drugs (Donahue et al., 2006).

[CONCEPTS IN CONTEXT]

PERSONAL INFLUENCES ON THE SELF-CONCEPT

FACTOR	EXAMPLE
Thinking about your thoughts	While riding the bus home, Carlos was thinking why he told his friends that he thinks the social psychology course is very relevant to business and management students.
Focusing on self-awareness	Although the sign says, "Please take just one," Amy is tempted to help herself to many free samples on display at the new candy store, until she looks up and sees her own reflection in the mirror above the counter.
Regulating the self	Xavier really misses his ex-girlfriend. To help himself forget about her, he deliberately tries not to think about her—yet the more he forces himself not to think about her, the more he finds thoughts of their relationship creeping into his mind.
Examining your behaviour	Daniel spends a lot of time playing chess with friends, so he thinks he really likes chess.
Interpreting your motivation	Samantha was always eager to play basketball until her new coach decided to reward each player with a dollar for each basket the player scores.

HOW DO SOCIAL FACTORS INFLUENCE THE SELF-CONCEPT?

 Imagine that you come to the psychology department one day to participate in a study on general knowledge. First, you read a brief paragraph about a famous woman's behaviour, lifestyle, and attributes. If you are in one condition, you read about Marie Curie, a Polish scientist in the late 1800s who was the first woman to win a Nobel Prize. If you are in the other condition, you read about a very different famous woman, Canadian-born Pamela Anderson, who is most commonly known for her role in *Baywatch*, her frequent appearances in *Playboy*, and her well-publicized relationships. The paragraphs emphasize the intelligence of the former and the (alleged) lack of intelligence of the latter. Next, you complete a 16-question general knowledge test based on the game Trivial Pursuit, in which you must answer such questions as "Who painted La Guernica?" (Dali, Miro, Picasso, or Velasquez) and "What is the capital of Bangladesh?" (Dacca, Hanoi, Yangon, or Bangkok). How does reading about one of the two (very different) women influence your score on the knowledge test? As predicted, those who read about Marie Curie performed worse on the trivia test than those who read about Pamela Anderson, presumably because they saw their own knowledge very differently depending on whether they were comparing themselves to a very smart person or a less intelligent one (Stapel & Suls, 2004). This study is just one example of how factors in the social world—including actual as well as hypothetical comparison targets—can influence our feelings and behaviour. This section will describe a theory that shows the impact of social factors on the self-concept: social comparison theory.

SOCIAL COMPARISON THEORY

social comparison theory – the theory that people evaluate their own abilities and attributes by comparing themselves to other people

According to social comparison theory, people evaluate their own abilities and attributes by comparing themselves with others (Festinger, 1954). This tendency to use social comparison is especially likely in situations of uncertainty, in which it may be difficult to assess our ability in a purely objective way. If you're told that you received an 83 on an exam, you may want information on how other students did so that you can understand how your performance compares to theirs. It's almost certain that you'll feel much better if the average grade was 73 than you would if it was 93. Social comparison theory explains why so many first-year university students suddenly don't feel quite as smart as they used to: many students at universities were the academic stars of their high school, and their self-esteem drops when all of a sudden they find themselves surrounded by students who were the stars at their own high schools—what's known as the "small fish in a big pond effect" (Marsh, Kong, & Hau, 2000).

In one of the first studies of the impact of social comparison on self-concept, researchers advertised a part-time job in the campus newspaper and set up appointments for students to be interviewed (Morse & Gergen, 1970). When students showed up for the interview, they sat in the waiting room with another job applicant (who was actually a confederate of the experimenters). In one condition, the supposed job applicant seemed quite impressive. He wore a suit, appeared well groomed and confident, and carried an expensive briefcase stocked with several sharp pencils. In the other condition, the applicant seemed much less impressive. He wore a smelly sweatshirt with ripped pants and no socks. He completed the application with a small, dull pencil he managed to locate after digging through his pockets, and he seemed to have great

"Big deal, an A in math. That would be a D in any other country."

trouble even completing the application. After a few minutes the experimenter returned to the waiting room with a final form, which was a self-esteem measure. As predicted, participants' self-esteem was much higher if they had sat in the waiting room with the weak applicant than if they had sat with the impressive applicant.

Social comparison theory thus explains why we think about ourselves in very different ways depending on the nature of the comparison we're making and its significance to us. Patricia Pliner from the University of Toronto and her colleagues had female participants perform a variety of skill-related tasks. Some of the participants were given the impression that they had been outperformed on the tasks by a confederate of the researcher, while the rest of the participants performed the tasks in a non-competitive environment (Pliner, Rizvi & Remick, 2009). In a subsequent, supposedly unrelated task that was presented as a piece of consumer research being carried out for a commercial food producer, participants were invited to choose a food to eat: one of seven versions of a lasagna (the product they were supposedly testing) described as varying in nutritional and calorific content. Women who were dieters and were told they'd been outperformed chose healthier options than dieters who were not made to feel outperformed in the previous tasks. This effect was insignificant among women who weren't dieters. The authors conclude that for dieters, competition by means of food choice can provide a means of restoring self-regard when self-esteem has been threatened in some other domain.

The Media Connections box provides an example of the hazards of such comparisons.

MEDIA CONNECTIONS

What Happens When Barbies Get Smaller and GI Joes Get Bigger?

Most media images of women in Western societies show women as thin. This includes women in movies, television shows, music videos, and on magazine covers. Some would say that women are portrayed as dangerously thin. At the same time, women's magazines publish a large number of articles on weight loss, presumably in an attempt to "help" women reach this increasingly thin ideal (Andersen & DiDomenico, 1992).

In its February 2010 issue, the British magazine *Love* published shots of eight supermodels in an identical nude pose, and also released each model's measurements. *Love*'s editor Katie Brand explained the concept: "We took eight women who are generally acknowledged as the most beautiful in the world, [and] got them to show off their bodies—widely regarded as the most perfect in the world" (Press Association, 2010). Although Brand states that the idea was to show "how much they differed physically from one another" and that "'perfection' is not fixed, timeless or transcendent," the measurements of most of these women with a "perfect body" are potentially putting their health at risk. For example, British supermodel Kate Moss weighs 47.6 kilograms (105 lb) and is 172 centimetres (5'7") tall. Her body mass index (BMI) is therefore, 16.4, which is well below the "underweight" threshold according to Health Canada's risk classification. The underweight category, similar to the overweight category, is associated with an increased risk of developing health problems (Health Canada, 2003).

What are the consequences of this media focus on the thin ideal? Women who rate advertisements featuring female models in popular women's magazines feel more depressed, especially if they are already unsatisfied with their own appearance (Patrick, Neighbors, & Knee, 2004). Not surprisingly, women who are of normal weight often feel too heavy. Nearly half of women of average weight are trying to lose weight (Biener & Heaton, 1995), as are 35 percent of normal-weight girls, and 12 percent of underweight girls (Schreiber et al., 1996). It has been reported that among Canadian adults (age 20 to 64 years old), 12.3 percent of women are underweight compared to 3.9 percent of men. The problem of low body weight is particularly pronounced among Canadian women aged 20 to 24, with one in four below the healthy weight range (Nelson, 2010).

Although most research on social pressures leading to dissatisfaction with body image has focused on the prevailing thin ideal for women, men are also increasingly feeling pressure to conform to a similarly unrealistic, overly muscular ideal (Pope, Olivardia, Gruber, & Borowiecki, 1999).

(continued)

To test the evolution of the "muscular male ideal" over time, researchers examined the measurements of GI Joe action toys (the action toy with the longest continuous history) produced in 1973, 1975, and 1994. This review revealed a disturbing trend. As shown in this photo, the GI Joe action figure became much more muscular over time: although there was no change in the height of the figure, the circumference of the biceps increased from 2.1 inches (1973) to 2.5 inches (1975) to 2.7 inches (1994). These may seem like small differences, but if you translate these changes to adult male bodies, bicep circumference would increase from 12.2 inches to 16.4 inches. And the latest GI Joe (the GI Joe Extreme, introduced in 1998) has biceps that translate into 26.8 inches in adult males—larger than those of any bodybuilder in history. What do you think are the possible effects on boys of changing ideals for masculinity?

REUTERS/Mike Blake/Landov; Julie Pratt

Interestingly, such comparisons seem to occur at an automatic level (Stapel & Blanton, 2004). In one study, participants were presented a subliminal picture of either a baby girl or an elderly woman, which means that the picture passed before their eyes so quickly that they didn't realize they had seen it—i.e., it was below the threshold of their conscious awareness. Participants then rated their own age on a scale of one to seven, with one meaning "young" and seven meaning "old." As expected, participants who saw the picture of the baby rated themselves as older than did those who saw the picture of the elderly woman. This finding is particularly surprising as the participants had no conscious awareness of having seen a picture at all prior to rating their age.

We also choose particular people to serve as relevant comparison models against which to assess our own behaviour. University baseball players would be likely to compare themselves with strong players on their own team, not with a player on a Major League Baseball team. In fact, people often, perhaps for ease, rely on readily available comparisons against others to assess their own performance (Mussweiler & Rüter, 2003). For example, people often think about and compare themselves to their best friend when they are evaluating their own performance. Ironically, we make this comparison even when this friend is very different from us on a

SOCIAL INFLUENCES ON THE SELF-CONCEPT

FACTOR	EXAMPLE
Social comparison theory	Ellen was thrilled with the grade of 91 on her organic chemistry mid-term, until her roommate reported her own grade of 98.

given measure. These comparison standards are particularly important, and informative, when you're near the top of a given ability or group (Garcia, Tor, & Gonzales, 2006). For example, the second- and third-place winners in a race will be more likely to use each other as a helpful way to evaluate their personal performance than to compare themselves with those who come in 41st or 42nd place.

HOW DO PEOPLE MAINTAIN A POSITIVE SELF-CONCEPT?

Imagine that you are asked to follow water conservation practices during a drought. For example, you might be asked to shower only every other day and to flush the toilet less frequently. Then if you are asked by researchers whether you're following the recommended water conservation practices—and whether you believe most other students are following such recommendations—what will you say? One study in California revealed that students see their own behaviour as better than those of their peers (Monin & Norton, 2003). Specifically, although only 33 percent of students reported taking daily showers during the drought, students estimated that about 47 percent of other students were showering. When the ban was lifted, students still viewed their own behaviour as especially good. Although at this point 84 percent of students were showering daily, they believed that only 72 percent of their peers had returned to taking a daily shower. This study is an example of a common principle in Western social psychology. It's called the false uniqueness effect, meaning that we see our own desirable behaviour as less common than is actually the case. The false uniqueness effect is just one of several self-serving strategies that we will examine in this section. Other self-serving strategies that people use to maintain positive

www.kalastyle.com

beliefs about themselves include self-serving biases in how we process, or make sense of, our experience (e.g., misremembering), self-serving outcomes of that processing (i.e., self-serving attitudes and beliefs), self-serving comparisons with others, and self-serving behaviour.

SELF-SERVING BIASES

How well did you do on your Provincial Standardized Tests? If you're like most university students, you'll remember your scores on these tests (as well as your high school grades) as higher than they actually were (Bahrick, Hall, & Berger, 1996; Shepperd, 1993a). This tendency to misremember events in a particular direction is one of the strategies that people use to feel good about themselves. In one study, participants were first led to believe that either extroversion or introversion was a good predictor of success in university and in the workplace (Sanitioso & Wlodarski, 2004). Participants then received feedback about their own personalities and were later asked to recall this feedback for the experimenter. As expected, those who thought that extroversion was a positive trait remembered the feedback related to extraversion more accurately than the feedback related to introversion, yet those who believed that introversion predicted success showed the opposite pattern.

MISREMEMBERING.   The tendency to remember things in a self-serving way can also lead us to see change over time, even when no change has occurred. For example, people who are doing poorly in a class and get a tutor often report that their scores have improved, and they attribute this improvement to the tutor. But in reality students who do very poorly initially are likely to show some improvement over time simply because extreme values tend to become less extreme over time. In one study in the U.S., researchers collected data from 101 dating couples on their love, commitment, and satisfaction at that time, as well as how these features had changed over the last year (Sprecher, 1999). These couples were then asked these same questions every year for the next four years, so that researchers could see how relationships changed over time. Couples that stayed together throughout this time reported that their love, commitment, and satisfaction had increased over time. However, there was no evidence from the yearly reports that these features did in fact increase. Other studies with married couples show similar patterns, namely that people report increasing love for their spouse over time, whereas there is no such change when you look at actual relationship satisfaction ratings over time (Karney & Coombs, 2000).

What causes these biases in memory? This misperception occurs in part because we ignore the statistical phenomenon of regression to the average (Tversky & Kahneman, 1974), meaning that things that are initially at extreme (positive or negative) points are likely to become less extreme over time. For example, a student who gets a 100 on the mid-term exam is much more likely to receive a lower score on the next exam (particularly because a higher score is impossible), but seeing this student as doing worse over time if he or she receives a 95 on the next exam would be silly (or over-interpretation).

SEEING OUR VIEWS AS SHARED BY OTHERS.　You've already encountered the false uniqueness effect. Another way in which people see themselves in a biased way is by assuming that their views and behaviour are normative—that is, that their views and behaviours are shared by most other people. The **false consensus effect** refers to the tendency to overestimate the extent to which other people share our opinions, attitudes, and behaviours. In sum, people generally assume that anything they think or do is also what many other people think or do (Ross, Greene, & House, 1977). The false consensus effect explains why you can't believe it when your favourite television show is cancelled: surely, if you feel strongly about a given program, many other people must share your (excellent) taste. Why do we make this mistake? In part, because we usually surround ourselves with people who share our beliefs.

In one of the first demonstrations of the power of the false consensus effect, Lee Ross and his colleagues at Stanford University asked students to walk around campus for 30 minutes wearing a large cardboard sign that said "Eat at Joe's" and note the reactions they received (Ross et al., 1977). What percentage of students do you think agreed to wear the sign? Exactly 50 percent. Ross then asked all students what percentage of students they thought would agree to wear the sign. Those who had agreed to wear the sign believed that the majority of students would also agree (58 percent), whereas those who had refused to wear the sign believed that most other students would also refuse (77 percent).

People also see their own skills and abilities as relatively normative, meaning similar to that of others in their social group. For example, in one study participants were given a bogus test of "social sensitivity," which supposedly was used to assess the progress of students who were interested in careers in clinical or counselling psychology (Alicke & Largo, 1995). This test featured a number of tasks, including rating how people's traits fit together, predicting how another person would answer particular questions, and rating which word didn't fit with other words in a given set. Participants were then told either that they had passed this test, or that they had failed. When participants were then asked how they thought most other students would perform on this test, those who were told they had failed believed most of their peers would also perform poorly, but those who were told that they performed well believed that most others would also do well.

As mentioned earlier in this section, although people typically see their attitudes and undesirable behaviour as normative, they tend to see themselves as different—and particularly as better—than others on desirable abilities and behaviour (Suls & Wan, 1987).

false consensus effect – the tendency to overestimate the extent to which other people share our opinions, attitudes, and behaviours

The **false uniqueness effect**, a concept that was developed by researchers in the West, refers to the tendency for people to see themselves as more likely to perform positive acts than others, and to see ourselves as less biased, and more accurate, than others (Ehrlinger, Gilovich, & Ross, 2005). The bias occurs in part because people underestimate the number of people who engage in positive actions (e.g., donating blood) while overestimating the number of people who engage in negative actions (e.g., littering). In the water conservation study described previously, although only 33 percent of students were actually taking daily showers during the drought, participants estimated that 47 percent were showering daily (Monin & Norton, 2003).

false uniqueness effect – the tendency to underestimate the extent to which other people are likely to share our positive attitudes and behaviour

SELF-SERVING BELIEFS

People also maintain positive self-concepts by seeing themselves as more likely than other people to experience good events, and as less likely than other people to experience bad events. This phenomenon, known as **unrealistic optimism**, explains why we see ourselves as "better than average" across multiple dimensions, including having more positive personality traits (e.g., honesty, intelligence, maturity), experiencing better relationships, and being less at risk of experiencing negative events (e.g., getting divorced, experiencing an unintended pregnancy, suffering a heart attack, having a car accident; Weinstein, 1980).

unrealistic optimism – a phenomenon in which people see themselves as more likely than other people to experience good events, and less likely than other people to experience bad events

We even see ourselves as more likely to win even when the benefits that would generally help everyone's performance equally are shared by all group members (Windschitl, Kruger, & Simms, 2003). In one study, participants in the "benefit condition" were told that the instructor would spend the last two class days going over the terms on the review sheet for the final exam, whereas those in the "adversity condition" were simply told they would receive a sheet listing the terms, but that students would be responsible for learning the terms on their own. Although everyone in the class benefits from going over the terms together in class, and suffers from having to learn the terms on their own, students in the adversity condition expected to rank in the 60th percentile in their final grade whereas those in the benefit condition expected to rank in the 71st percentile. In other words, students were more likely to think they would do better than their classmates even though the benefit of the instructor's help was shared by all students in the class.

How do we maintain such optimistic illusions? In part, by describing our traits in ways that allow us to appear good (Dunning, Meyerowitz, & Holzberg, 1989; Dunning, Perie, & Story, 1991). Specifically, we see our traits in a particularly positive way, and seek out and view information that flatters us as particularly valid (Glick,

Cartoon by Mike Spicer, Copyright 2011. All rights reserved.

Gottesman, & Jolton, 1989; Kruger, 1998). For example, if you're very artistic, you're likely to pay more attention to an article that suggests creativity is a great predictor of future success than one that suggests no correlation between creativity and future success. We also assign greater importance to what we're good at than to what we're bad at. For example, students who receive a high grade in an introductory computer science course later see computer skills as more important than those who receive a low grade (Hill, Smith, & Lewicki, 1989). Although holding optimistic illusions has many benefits for psychological well-being, these beliefs can also lead to negative consequences, as described in the Health Connections box.

HEALTH CONNECTIONS

The Downside of Too Much Optimism

Although optimism is generally associated with better health (Peterson, Seligman, Yurko, Martin, & Friedman, 1998; Scheier & Carver, 1993), some intriguing research suggests that optimism can also have costs. Specifically, research by Neil Weinstein (1984, 1987) indicates that people who are unrealistically optimistic about their risk of experiencing various health problems can actually put their health at risk. For example, people generally believe that they're at less risk of experiencing many types of problems than other people, including car accidents, alcohol problems, sexually transmitted diseases, and drug addiction. Basically, people tend to believe that although risks do exist, "it won't happen to me." This tendency may be especially common in university students, who generally believe (wrongly!) that they are invulnerable to many types of problems. Unfortunately, these unrealistically positive beliefs can lead people to fail to protect themselves adequately from such problems—and thus cycle without a helmet, refuse to wear a seatbelt, or drive under the influence. In fact, a longitudinal study by Howard Friedman and colleagues (1993) found that optimists had a higher mortality rate.

This research suggests that while optimism in general is a good thing, too much optimism can have some serious drawbacks.

© iStockphoto.com/James Ferrie

HAVING HIGH PERCEIVED CONTROL

perceived control – the tendency to see uncontrollable events as at least partially under our control

In addition to, on average, seeing ourselves as more likely to experience positive events, most people also have exaggeratedly high levels of **perceived control**. This means that we see uncontrollable events as at least partially under our control (Thompson, 1999). For example, people tend to assume that they can control random events (e.g., picking lottery numbers), which is why people lose money in bets. (You almost always bet on "your" team to win, and believe that they will.) In one study, participants either chose a particular set of lottery numbers to play or were assigned specific numbers, and paid $1 for each ticket regardless of how numbers had been picked (Langer, 1975). They were then told that the tickets were all sold, but that someone who had not had a chance to purchase one wanted to do so, and would be willing to pay a premium. Would they be willing to sell their ticket to that person? Among those who had been assigned a number, the mean amount for which they sold the ticket was $1.96, but for those who had chosen the number, the mean amount was $8.17! Apparently people believed that if they chose a number, it was more likely to win, and therefore the ticket was worth more money.

We even believe that we have control in situations in which it's clearly impossible for us to have control. For example, sports fans often come to believe that their actions are influencing the outcome of a game—some people even leave the room if their team is losing, for fear that their watching of the game on television is influencing the players' performance. We may form such beliefs about our control simply because we did something one time (e.g., drink coffee, wear a certain shirt, watch the game from a particular chair) and our team won, even though the association between the two events was purely a coincidence.

MAKING OVERCONFIDENT JUDGEMENTS.   Perhaps due to our overly optimistic feelings of control over the world, we are also overconfident in our judgements (Vallone, Griffin, Lin, & Ross, 1990). In a study by David Dunning and colleagues, university students interacted briefly with a stranger and were then asked to predict how that person would behave in a particular situation and how the student's roommate would behave in the same situation (Dunning, Griffin, Milojkovic, & Ross, 1990). In both cases, students thought they would be pretty accurate in their predictions, even though it's extremely unlikely that they would be as accurate about a stranger's behaviour as about the behaviour of those they know well.

© Mike Baldwin / Cornered

Everyone knew it was a hideous style, but nothing was ever said.

© Mike Baldwin/www.CartoonStock.com

We're even overconfident in predicting our own behaviour—which explains why we use up our cell-phone minutes each month (but don't increase our monthly plan) and why we pay for yearly gym memberships (but don't regularly use the gym). In one study, students made a number of predictions about their own behaviour, such as how often they would call their parents or whether they would acquire a steady dating partner (Vallone, Griffin, Lin, & Ross, 1990). Although students estimated their accuracy at 82 percent, when researchers followed up throughout the year, the true rate of accuracy was only 68 percent. This tendency toward overconfidence means that that sometimes others' predictions about our behaviour are more accurate than our own (MacDonald & Ross, 1997). For example, people in a dating relationship typically believe that their current dating relationship will last for some time. However, the predictions of family and friends about how long this relationship will last are more accurate than those of the dating couple.

Amazingly enough, those who are least competent are most overconfident about their abilities. When students are asked to rate their own abilities in logic, grammar, and humour as compared to those of their peers, those whose actual scores placed them in the bottom 12 percent estimated that they were in the top 62 percent (Kruger & Dunning, 1999)! In sum, people who are most overconfident in their abilities are actually least competent in a given task.

Although the examples described thus far have focused on the relatively minor consequences of overconfidence, this type of self-serving belief can have substantial negative consequences. Powerful people are likely to overestimate their capabilities, particularly when they don't get valid feedback, leading to dramatic failure with consequences for many. Napoleon, the 18th century French emperor, failed in Russia, and George W. Bush, past president of the United States, failed in Iraq. On March 17, 2003, in his 15-minute speech from the White House, Bush gave Saddam Hussein 48 hours to leave the country and declared war on Iraq. One of the major justifications of this war was the supposed presence of "weapons of mass destruction" that were being hidden from United Nations inspectors. This war was launched despite strong disapproval from many Western countries, including Canada, France, Germany, and Russia. More recent evidence indicates that Iraq was in fact not hiding weapons. In this case, the overconfidence of President Bush and his advisors led to (or was used as justification for) the Iraq War.

Law Connections describes how eyewitnesses' overconfidence can also lead to negative consequences.

LAW CONNECTIONS

The Impact of Feedback on Eyewitness Confidence

People's overconfidence is particularly strong when they're given feedback that confirms their original views, a phenomenon that can have substantial consequences for the legal system. Eyewitnesses who are very confident in their judgements are, not surprisingly, particularly influential with juries (Cutler, Penrod, & Dexter, 1990; Fox & Walters, 1986). This would not be a concern were it not for the fact that after an eyewitness identifies a particular person in a police lineup or mug shot, he or she may receive feedback from a police officer regarding the selection (e.g., "Oh, good. I noticed on your identification sheet that you identified the actual murder suspect"), and people's confidence in their judgements, regardless of their accuracy, increases when they receive confirmatory feedback. In one study of this effect, participants watched a videotape from an actual in-store camera recording a robbery in which a security guard was shot and killed (Wells & Bradfield, 1999). Then, they were asked to identify the shooter from one of five pictures (none of which was the actual shooter). Those who received confirming feedback on their identification were later much more

confident about their selection of the actual shooter than those who did not receive such feedback.

TONY GENTILE/Reuters/Landov

SELF-SERVING COMPARISONS

Another strategy that people use to maintain their positive self-concepts is strategic association with successful others, a phenomenon known as **basking in reflected glory**, or BIRGing. One study found that after a university football team won a weekend game, 32 percent of the students at that school described the outcome as "we won," but only 18 percent described it as "we lost" after a weekend defeat (Cialdini et al., 1976). Students are strategically making a connection between themselves and a good outcome, but distancing themselves from a poor outcome. In another study, researchers simply counted the number of people wearing clothes with their school name or another school's name at a number of large universities on the Mondays after football games (Cialdini et al., 1976). On the Monday following a win by the home team, 64 percent of those observed were wearing school colours, compared to only 44 percent after a loss. As Cialdini eloquently notes, "We avoid the shadow of defeat and bask in the glow of victory. Even if it's reflected glory, you still get a tan."

basking in reflected glory (BIRGing) – associating with successful others to increase one's feelings of self-worth

THE BENEFITS OF DOWNWARD COMPARISON. We can also use social comparison for other reasons, including making ourselves feel better and providing means for self-improvement (Helgeson & Mickelson, 1995). In the strategy known as **downward social comparison**, people compare themselves to those who are worse off than themselves on a particular trait or attribute (who are less successful, less happy, less fortunate, etc.) as a way of making themselves feel better. For example, Bill Klein's research (1997) demonstrates that students feel much better knowing they're at a lower risk of contracting a disease than their friends, even when they learn that their odds of contracting the disease are relatively high. In this case we feel better about ourselves even after learning something potentially upsetting, simply because we see ourselves as better off than others. Similarly, women with early-stage breast cancer often choose to compare themselves to other breast cancer patients who are worse off than they themselves are—and feel better after doing so (Bogart & Helgeson, 2000; Taylor, 1989).

downward social comparison – comparing ourselves to people who are worse than we are on a given trait or ability in an attempt to feel better about ourselves

FIGURE 3.3   WHEN DO WE CHOOSE DOWNWARD SOCIAL COMPARISONS?

Participants in this experiment took a test and were given feedback intended to make them either feel good or bad about their social skills. They were then told they could take the test again, this time with a partner. As predicted, a higher percentage of people who were told they did poorly on the first test chose to retake the test with a partner who also received a mediocre score. Those who were told they did well on the first test chose to retake the test with a partner who had also received a strong score.

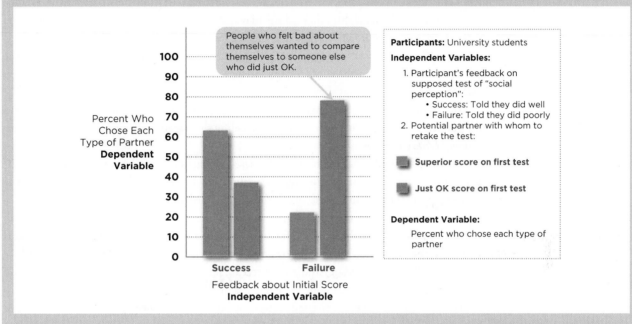

Source: Wood, J.V., Giordano-Beech, M., & Ducharme, M.J. (1999). Compensating for failure through social comparison. *Personality and Social Psychology Bulletin*, 25, 1370-1386. Used by permission of Sage Publications.

People are generally quite good at choosing comparison partners who will make them feel good about themselves. In a study conducted by Wendy Wood and her colleagues, participants were first given either success (12 or 13 out of 15) or failure feedback (3 or 4 out of 15) on a practice "social perception" test (Wood, Giordano-Beech, & Ducharme, 1999). They were then asked to take a second test, which they would take with another person in the experiment. However, they were able to choose which test they (and the other person) would take—one that the other person had already done well on ("superior" rating) or one that the other person had already done okay on ("average" rating). As shown in Figure 3.3, people who had just done well on a test were most interested in comparing themselves on a second test to someone who had done well. Those who had done poorly on the first test were most interested in comparing themselves to someone who had just done okay. In sum, people are particularly interested in engaging in downward comparison when they're feeling bad about themselves.

OVERCOMING THREATENING COMPARISONS.   There are, however, situations where you're forced to compare yourself to people who are clearly better than you, and it's therefore impossible to make self-enhancing comparisons. Although in some cases this type of comparison leads to jealousy and resentment (perhaps when a close friend experiences a better outcome than you do), we have several ways of "fighting back" when these self-esteem threats occur. First, we may emphasize various advantages that the other person may have had that led him or her to outperform us (Shepperd & Taylor, 1999).

Second, we may acknowledge that person as being extremely impressive in one domain, but derogate their abilities in other domains to compensate (Parks-Stamm, Heilman, & Hearns, 2008). In one study, women read a description of a highly successful woman who was the CEO of a company, and then rated her on various traits. Although women recognized this woman as highly competent, they rated her as unlikeable and interpersonally hostile, which presumably helps minimize the self-evaluation consequences of this type of social comparison.

Third, we may exaggerate the other person's ability and see him or her as unusually good at a given behaviour. This means that we can also be good at this behaviour—even if not quite as good. In a study conducted by Mark Alicke and his colleagues, participants and confederates both participated in an IQ test that was very difficult (students on average got 3 out of 10 items right; Alicke, LoSchiavo, Zerbst, & Zhang, 1997). The confederate was always given a score of 7. The participants knew both their scores and the confederates' scores, as did some observers (supposedly participants who were waiting to participate in the study). Observers rated the confederate's intelligence as higher than the participants', which makes sense based on what they had observed. However, participants rated the confederate as even smarter than did the observers. Once again, this strategy of "seeing the person who outperforms us as a genius" protects us from feeling the negative effects of having to make an unfavourable comparison.

Another situation in which upward social comparison can be beneficial for one's self-perception is in intimate relationships. Penelope Lockwood and her colleagues from the University of Toronto suggested that although upward comparisons to a friend may have the potential to damage the friendship (because you feel inferior, start to resent the friend's superiority, and so on), this works differently in intimate relationships where one associates with a partner rather than competes against him or her (Pinkus, Lockwood, Schimmack & Fournier, 2008). In a series of studies, the researchers used an "experience sampling" method that prompts participants to note any comparisons they have made with their partner since the last prompt. They were prompted six times a day over a two-week period. They also had to note the most significant comparison within this two-week data set and complete other measures. Although people more often make downward comparisons when comparing themselves to others (meaning that they compare a personal trait that they view the other person as being weaker in), the researchers found a different result in the case of intimate relationships, where participants were just as likely to make upward comparisons as downward comparisons to their partner. They also more often shared the results of their comparison with their partner than they did with friends, and they responded more positively to upward than to downward comparisons to their romantic partner, even for domains that are high in self-relevance, meaning the domain that they compared themselves with their partner was highly important to their idea of themselves. Participants also responded more positively to upward comparisons with their romantic partner even when the comparison had negative self-evaluative implications (i.e., reflected badly on them).

SELF-SERVING BEHAVIOUR

Because of our desire to feel good about ourselves, we often use strategies to help maintain our positive self-views. One such strategy is **self-handicapping**, which consists in creating obstacles to success so that potential failure can be blamed on these external factors as opposed to internal traits (Berglas & Jones, 1978). For example, the night before an exam, students can avoid studying and stay out really late. Then, if they do badly, they can blame their poor performance on their lack of preparation, which protects their view of their intelligence. On the other hand, if they happen to do well, what do people say? "Wow, they must be really smart to have not studied and still done so well." This is one reason that some people choose to procrastinate on a given assignment (and then pull an all-nighter). This strategy may cost them in terms of performance, but it also sets up a ready excuse for failure that protects self-esteem. After all, if you can get a C on a paper you wrote the night before, just imagine how well you could do if you'd really tried your hardest? By creating such obstacles, individuals free themselves from the pressure to perform well and as a result actually enjoy the task more

self-handicapping – a strategy in which people create obstacles to success so that potential failure can be blamed on these external factors

(Deppe & Harackiewicz, 1996). Remember, however, that self-handicapping refers to setting up obstacles to success before an event, not giving excuses after the fact.

In the first study to demonstrate use of the self-handicapping strategy, Stephen Berglas and Edward Jones (1978) randomly assigned male students to complete either solvable or unsolvable anagrams. All participants were then told that they had done well on the test, but this positive feedback was clearly confusing to those who had attempted to solve anagrams that in reality had no solution. Participants were then asked to choose whether they would prefer to take a performance-enhancing or a performance-inhibiting drug before they took another similar test. Of those who had received success feedback but had no idea why, 70 percent chose the drug that would hurt performance, compared to 13 percent of those who knew why they had done well. These findings indicate that participants who are confident in their ability on a task typically prefer to take a drug that should help them perform even better. Those who lack this confidence are much more likely to choose to take the drug that should hurt their performance—and thereby give them a ready excuse for a poor outcome.

Self-handicapping can lead to a number of negative consequences. People who self-handicap use strategies to provide explanations for less-than-successful performance, which (not surprisingly) can lead in turn to poorer performance (Hirt, Deppe, & Gordon, 1991). For example, students who tend to self-handicap report spending less time per week on academic work and engaging in less-efficient studying for exams (Zuckerman, Kieffer, & Knee, 1998). They also have lower GPAs. Similarly, they may also use alcohol before engaging in a difficult task as a way of creating a face-saving explanation for poor performance (e.g., "I would have done much better on the test, but I was drunk"; Higgins & Harris, 1988; Steele & Josephs, 1990). Finally, the use of self-handicapping can have negative effects on interpersonal relations. People who make excuses for poor performance, such as low effort or drug impairment, are rated more negatively by their peers (Rhodewalt, Sanbonmatsu, Tschanz, Feick, & Waller, 1995).

Questioning the Research:

Can you think of another explanation for the finding that people who self-handicap report having worse study habits and lower GPAs? (Hint: Is this correlation or causation?)

THE DOWNSIDE OF OVERLY POSITIVE SELF-VIEWS

This section has described a variety of strategies that people use to feel good about themselves, and in general these strategies are beneficial because people who feel good about themselves experience numerous benefits, including better physical and psychological well-being (Lipkus, Dalbert, & Siegler, 1996; Strauman, Lemieux, & Coe, 1993; Taylor & Brown, 1988). However, feeling good about yourself can have drawbacks. Under certain circumstances, people who hold overly positive views of themselves can behave more aggressively toward others and see them in a more negative light (Beauregard & Dunning, 1998; Bushman & Baumeister, 1998). They may also have poor social skills and be seen less positively by others, in part because they have difficulty responding well to any form of criticism and rejection and are seen as antagonistic (Colvin, Block, & Funder, 1995; Heatherton & Vohs, 2000; Paulhus, 1998). People who are high in self-esteem and receive failure feedback are more likely to denigrate others and exaggerate their superiority over others (Brown & Gallagher, 1992; Gibbons & McCoy, 1991). People with overly positive self-views can also engage in very destructive behaviour. Although pessimists reduce their expectations and bet smaller amounts of money after repeatedly losing when they gamble, optimists continue to have positive expectations about their likelihood of winning, even after repeatedly losing, and continue to bet large sums of money (Gibson & Sanbonmatsu, 2004).

Finally, although research in social psychology has emphasized the benefits of having perceived control for psychological and even physical well-being (e.g., Lang & Heckhausen, 2001), in some cases holding such beliefs can actually have negative consequences. For example, when women who experienced a sexual assault believe they had control over the rape—they feel they used poor judgement or should have resisted more—they experience greater distress (Frazier, 2003). Similarly, women who believe they can control whether they are assaulted again in the future also experience higher rates of distress. Women who believed they had control over the recovery process, however, did report lower levels of distress. In sum, although perceived control is usually beneficial for psychological as well as physical well-being, there is an optimal marginal error, and the illusion of control can have quite negative consequences when it is excessive.

STRATEGIES PEOPLE USE TO MAINTAIN A POSITIVE SELF-CONCEPT

FACTOR	EXAMPLE
Self-serving biases	After Ellen's softball team loses a game, most of her teammates complain about poor officiating, but after a win the team views the officials as having done a good job.
Self-serving beliefs	Because Robert is very confident that his safe driving will prevent an accident from occurring, he often neglects to wear his seatbelt.
Self-serving comparisons	Hannah plays on her high school basketball team, but isn't one of the better players. She consoles herself by remembering all the people who tried out and didn't make the team.
Self-serving behaviour	Sina just got another C on his mid-term exam, but this low grade doesn't really bother him because he knows he would have done much better if he'd had time to study before the test.

HOW DO PEOPLE PRESENT THEMSELVES TO OTHERS?

Imagine you arrive at the psychology department to participate in a study of "incidental memory." At the start of the experiment, the researcher pulls you aside from the other group members and asks you to put on a relatively embarrassing t-shirt. In one condition, the shirt features a picture of American rapper Vanilla Ice and the words "Ice, Ice, Baby." In another condition, the shirt features a picture of Barry Manilow (an American singer-songwriter who won many awards, including two Grammys). After you put on the shirt, you are then sent into a room where four or five other students are already sitting to get a questionnaire to fill out. You complete and turn in your questionnaire, and are then asked by the experimenter to estimate how many of the people in the room had noticed the t-shirt you were wearing. What would you say? Participants in exactly that study estimated that about 48 percent of the others would notice the embarrassing t-shirt, but the actual number was 23 percent (Gilovich, Medvec, & Savitsky, 2000). Why do people assume (wrongly) that more people would notice their embarrassing shirt than actually do? This error is caused largely by individuals' motivation to not only think of themselves in positive ways, but also to have others in their social world think of them in such ways (Paulhus, Bruce, & Trapnell, 1995). In turn, this motivation influences our behaviour in a variety of ways, such as the way we dress, the car we drive, where we go on vacation, the job we want to have, and much more. This section will examine self-presentation or **impression management** strategies, meaning people's efforts to create positive impressions of themselves, including self-promotion, ingratiation, and self-verification, as well as both positive and negative aspects of our tendency to focus on self-presentation.

impression management – strategies that people use to create positive impressions of themselves

SELF-PROMOTION

self-promotion – a strategy that focuses on making other people think you are competent or good in some way

The strategy of **self-promotion** focuses on making other people think you're competent or good in some way (Godfrey, Jones, & Lord, 1986). People who use self-promotion tend to agree with such statements as "I strive to look perfect to others," and "I try to keep my faults to myself" (Hewitt et al., 2003). Athletes who brag about how much they can bench press, and nerds who casually mention their exceptionally high GPA scores are trying to make you respect them.

In one study, students were asked to imagine that they were trying out for the part of Scrooge in *A Christmas Carol* (Quattrone & Jones, 1978). Some of the students were then told to imagine that they had been through the audition and had received enthusiastic applause from the director; others were not asked to imagine such an audition. Then students were asked how likely they would be to mention that they had recently received rave reviews for their performance as a lovable, generous sucker in another play (a character who is a direct opposite of the Scrooge character). Those who were confident that they had done well (i.e., those who had imagined the applause) were much more likely to comment on their prior performance, presumably to show how much more difficult their stellar performance had been. On the other hand, those who had not imagined how the audition had gone were very unlikely to divulge this information, presumably because it would hurt their efforts to convince the director that they could effectively play Scrooge.

What are the drawbacks to using self-promotion? First, competence often speaks for itself, so people who try hard to convince others that they are competent may seem less so than those who "prove it" through their actions. Bragging about your golf game, for example, may be a sign that your game could use some work. Otherwise, why would you have to try so hard to convince others of your skill?

Self-promotion can also have substantial personal consequences; although people who self-promote are seen as more competent, they're also viewed as less likeable (Godfrey et al., 1986). It has been reported that there's a gender difference in self-promotion (Rudman, 1998). That is, women who promote themselves are seen as more competent, but less likeable and less likely to be hired, whereas men don't experience such problems with self-promotion (Rudman, 1998). This suggests that self-promotion is a "double-edged sword" for women, in that it leads to higher perceived competence but lower probability of being hired.

INGRATIATION

People who use the self-promotion strategy are trying to present themselves as competent. However, those who use the ingratiation strategy are trying to be liked (Gordon, 1996; Jones, 1990). This strategy often involves complimenting or flattering someone on their clothes, their artistic ability, or whatever. One problem with ingratiation is that the more you need someone to like you, the more obvious this strategy is. If a student compliments his or her professor about how brilliant a particular lecture was and then asks for an extension on a term paper, the comment on the lecture is more likely to be perceived as insincere. However, more subtle forms of ingratiation could be effective.

ingratiation – a strategy in which people try to make themselves likeable to someone else, often through flattery and praise

Ingratiation (if it is recognized as such) can lead other people to dislike you because they see your behaviour as insincere and as being caused by an ulterior motive (e.g., desire for a promotion, a raise, or other benefits). If you ingratiate yourself to your boss while being rude to your subordinates, you might have trouble getting along with colleagues (Vonk, 1998). We quickly notice, and especially dislike, a phenomenon sometimes referred to as "the slime effect." This is one reason why likeable behaviours are seen less positively when they are enacted toward a superior than toward a subordinate, namely because people recognize the possibility that the behaviour is influenced by other motives and is merely ingratiation (Vonk, 1999).

SELF-VERIFICATION

So far we have focused on how people try to present themselves positively, but according to self-verification theory, people typically want others' perception of them to be consistent with their own perception of themselves—i.e., you want others to see you as you see

self-verification theory – the expectation that other people's perception of oneself is consistent with one's own perception of oneself yourself (Chen, English, & Peng, 2006; Sedikides, 1993; Swann, 1987; Swann & Hill, 1982). Thus, if we perceive ourselves positively, we want others to see us this way, and if we see ourselves negatively, we still want others to see us negatively, or feel more comfortable if they do. This preference for self-verification leads us to prefer to interact with those who see us as we see ourselves—even in cases in which we see ourselves negatively.

Participants in one study completed a questionnaire about themselves and indicated the extent to which they viewed themselves as likeable and competent (Swann, Pelham, & Krull, 1989). Although 80 percent of the participants saw themselves favourably, about 20 percent saw themselves less positively. A few months later, and supposedly as part of a different experiment, the participants had an opportunity to interact with one of two people who had read their original questionnaire. The participants were told that one of those people had described them as seeming socially competent and skilled whereas the other had described them as seeming less competent. Although 77 percent of the participants who saw themselves in a positive light wanted to interact with the person who saw them as highly competent, only 22 percent of those who saw themselves in a negative light preferred to interact with someone who saw them positively. In addition, the majority of those with a low self-image preferred to interact with someone who saw them in this same negative light. Although this study was conducted in a lab setting, research in more naturalistic settings reveals that roommates and married couples show similar preferences. In sum, people are more satisfied and committed to their relationships with those who see them as they see themselves, regardless of whether their view of themselves is positive or negative (Swann, Hixon, & de la Ronde, 1992).

Our desire to have other people see us as we see ourselves can lead us to act in even more extreme ways if we are "misread" by someone and want to "correct" the wrong impression (Swann, 1987). In one study, 46 women rated themselves on dominance versus submissiveness, and then played a game with a confederate of the experimenter (Swann & Hill, 1982). While they played, the confederate gave the participant either dominant or submissive feedback (e.g., "You seem like a leader, someone who likes to take charge," or "You seem like someone who likes to follow others' lead and hold back somewhat."), and the participant was then videotaped while interacting with the confederate for two minutes. Independent observers of the interactions rated participants as behaving in line with their own self-perception but found that those who received disconfirming feedback behaved even more strongly in line with how they saw themselves. That is, those who saw themselves as dominant were especially dominant in the interaction if they had received feedback suggesting that they were submissive. Those who saw themselves as submissive were especially submissive in the interaction, if they had received feedback indicating that they were dominant. In short, if the description you receive matches your own self-view, you accept it. On the other hand, if this description is not in line with how you view yourself, you are motivated to change it by going out of your way to interact differently (e.g., being even more dominant or even more submissive) the next time you interact with the person.

Although people generally are concerned with self-presentation, they differ in how much they change their behaviour in response to such concerns (Snyder, 1974; Snyder & Gangestad, 1986). Those who are high **self-monitors** readily and easily modify their behaviour in response to the demands of the situation, whereas those who are low self-monitors care little about modifying their behaviour in response to the situation and tend to maintain the same opinions and attitudes regardless of the situation. A person who is a high self-monitor is likely to behave in very different ways when with different people. For example, he or she may express support for one view when with a group of people who support that particular view, but express support for the exact opposite view when with another group of friends who oppose it. A low self-monitor, in contrast, tends to maintain the same views and behaviour regardless of the views of others, and hence shows greater consistency across situations.

self-monitoring – the extent to which one adjusts one's self-presentation in different situations

DO YOU CHANGE YOUR BEHAVIOUR IN DIFFERENT SITUATIONS?

Self-Monitoring Scale

INSTRUCTIONS: *Rate whether each item is True or False.*

☐ **1.** My behaviour is usually an expression of my true inner feelings, attitudes, and beliefs.

☐ **2.** In different situations and with different people, I often act like very different persons.

☐ **3.** I can only argue for ideas which I already believe.

☐ **4.** When I am uncertain how to act in a social situation, I look to the behaviour of others for cues.

☐ **5.** I would not change my opinions (or the way I do things) in order to please someone else or win their favour.

☐ **6.** In order to get along and be liked, I tend to be what other people expect me to be rather than anything else.

SCORING: Give yourself one point for each of the even-numbered items that you answered "True." Then give yourself one point for each of the odd-numbered items that you answered "False." Sum up your points to get your self-monitoring score.

INTERPRETATION: This scale measures people's tendency to change their behaviour across different situations and with different people (Snyder, 1974). People with higher scores are high self-monitors, who tend to change their behaviour in different situations and with different people, whereas people with low scores on this measure tend to hold the same attitudes and behaviour across different situations and with different people.

These differences in self-monitoring among people in the West have a number of consequences for how they behave in their interpersonal relationships. Compared to those who are low in self-monitoring, people who are high in self-monitoring have more dating and sexual partners, are more interested in having sex with people they're not in love with, and are more likely to have had sex with someone only once (Snyder, Simpson, & Gangestad, 1986). High self-monitors are also more willing to deceive potential romantic partners. In one American study, participants were given information about two prospective dating partners and, specifically, information about what the other person was looking for in a romantic partner (e.g., independent, gentle, self-confident, kind; Rowatt, Cunningham, & Druen, 1998). Participants then prepared their own descriptions for each of these potential partners (so the researchers could determine how much they would change their descriptions based on the preferences of potential partners). As predicted, high self-monitors were much more willing to change their presentations than low self-monitors. It's worth noting that, depending on the cultural context, maintaining a consistent self-presentation might be regarded as indicating sincerity and integrity (in individualistic societies) or a stubborn, immature refusal to adjust to different situations and relationships (in collectivist societies; Noon & Lewis, 1992)

When selecting a dating partner, high and low self-monitors also show very different preferences (Snyder, Berscheid, & Glick, 1985). In one study, male university students had to choose between two interaction partners with very different strengths and weaknesses. One potential partner was a very attractive woman (she was rated 5.75 on a 7-point scale of attractiveness). But she was described as having a reserved attitude toward strangers and being more comfortable with friends, as being more concerned with herself than with others, and as having a tendency toward moodiness. The other potential dating partner was quite unattractive (she was rated 1.88) but had a number of very positive personality traits. She was described as highly sociable, outgoing, open, good at interacting with others, emotionally stable, having a good sense of humour, and willing to listen to others and get along. As shown in Figure 3.4, high self-monitors were more likely to choose the attractive person with the negative personality, whereas low self-monitors were more likely to choose the unattractive person with the positive personality.

Questioning the Research:

The study on the influence of self-monitoring on preferences in a dating partner was conducted only with men. How do you think the findings would differ if it were conducted with women?

FIGURE 3.4 HOW DOES SELF-MONITORING IMPACT CHOICE OF DATING PARTNERS?

In this study, male university students in the U.S. who were either high or low in self-monitoring read descriptions of two potential dating partners (one physically attractive but with a negative personality, one physically unattractive but with a positive personality), and then selected one of these partners for a date. As predicted. high self-monitors preferred the physically attractive, but unsociable, partner, whereas low self-monitors chose the physically unattractive, but sociable partner.

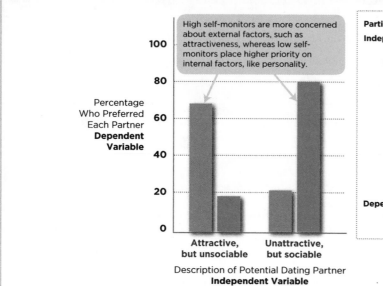

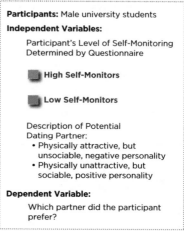

Participants: Male university students

Independent Variables:

Participant's Level of Self-Monitoring Determined by Questionnaire

■ High Self-Monitors

■ Low Self-Monitors

Description of Potential Dating Partner:
• Physically attractive, but unsociable, negative personality
• Physically unattractive, but sociable, positive personality

Dependent Variable:

Which partner did the participant prefer?

High self-monitors are more concerned about external factors, such as attractiveness, whereas low self-monitors place higher priority on internal factors, like personality.

Percentage Who Preferred Each Partner **Dependent Variable**

Attractive, but unsociable — Unattractive, but sociable

Description of Potential Dating Partner
Independent Variable

Source: Snyder, M., Berscheid, E., & Glick, P. (1985). Focusing on the exterior and the interior: Two investigations of the initiation of personal relationships. *Journal of Personality and Social Psychology*, 48, 1427–1439.

THE GOOD—AND BAD—NEWS ABOUT SELF-PRESENTATION

spotlight effect – the tendency to overestimate the extent to which one's own appearance and behaviour are obvious to others

Although people go to great lengths to present themselves in particular ways, some evidence suggests that we are overly concerned with self-presentation. Specifically, other people aren't paying as much attention to us as we often believe. So, we can relax and stop worrying about how we appear to others. In fact, people overestimate the extent to which their own appearance and behaviour are obvious to others, a phenomenon called the **spotlight effect** (remember the study on the Vanilla Ice t-shirt; Gilovich, Medvec, & Savitsky, 2000; Savitsky, Epley, & Gilovich, 2001). Similarly, although we often believe that our internal states are readily apparent to others, others typically have less access to our feelings than we think they do (Vorauer & Ross, 1999). So while you may think that the interviewer noticed your sweaty palms and could tell how nervous you were, rest assured—your secret is probably safe.

Concerns with self-presentation can also sometimes lead people to engage in crazy and potentially dangerous behaviours, such as substance abuse (Sharp & Getz, 1996). Refusing to use sunscreen because you believe you'd look more attractive with a good tan can lead to skin cancer, and failing to use condoms because you're afraid you'll appear promiscuous to a partner can lead to unintended pregnancy or even infection with an STD or AIDS (Leary, Tchividijian, & Kraxberger, 1994; Martin & Leary, 1999).

"I can't walk in these shoes, which is a problem, because I can't sit down in this skirt."

© Barbara Smaller/ The New Yorker Collection/ cartoonbank.com

STRATEGIES OF SELF-PRESENTATION

FACTOR	EXAMPLE
Self-promotion	In her bid to become class president, Newsha continues to discuss her immense leadership skills with all of her classmates.
Ingratiation	Jaime, who is one of several candidates for a promotion in his office, regularly compliments his boss on his great selection of ties.
Self-verification	Guillermo, who sees himself as very introverted and quiet, is trying to change roommates for next semester, because his current roommate, Pam, sees Guillermo as extroverted and outgoing.

HOW DOES CULTURE INFLUENCE SELF?

This section will examine how culture impacts self-perception and self-presentation, including the factors that influence the self-concept, the self-perception of motivation, the strategies used to maintain a positive self-concept, and the strategies of self-presentation.

CULTURE AND SELF-CONCEPT

There is a classic joke that "in Britain everything is permitted except that which is forbidden; in Germany everything is forbidden except that which is permitted; and in France everything is permitted even that which is forbidden" (Hofstede, 2001, p. 375). The 17th century French philosopher Pascal wrote at the beginning of a book about Michel de Montaigne, "There are truths on this side of the Pyrenees that are falsehoods on the other" (the Pyrenees being the border mountains between France and Spain; cited in Hofstede, 2001, p. 374). What Pascal wrote more than 300 years ago still rings true today. In order for us to confirm that our understanding of human behaviour applies to all humans rather than only those who live in North America or other Western nations, we should examine our theories and assumptions across the borders (i.e., in other cultures). This includes assumptions about personhood, or self.

The nature of self is a function of the culture that it develops in. Although people everywhere refer to self in connection to their body, the characteristics that are associated with the self, or our identity, vary in different cultures. This is reflected in anecdotes that are common in different societies. In Japan, for example, "The nail that stands out gets pounded down." In North America, "The squeaky wheel gets the grease." This suggests that in collectivistic societies, such as those in South American and Asian countries, conforming to duties and responsibilities is valued while non-conformist behaviours are disapproved of. On the other hand, in individualistic cultures, such as North American and western European societies, the unique characteristics of an individual are valued and considered important in understanding the person's actions.

Harry Triandis, a Greek social psychologist living in the United States, distinguishes between three aspects of self: private, public, and collective. The private self is the way a person understands him- or herself (e.g., I'm a hard-working student). The public self refers to the way that a person is perceived by others (e.g., Others think I'm smart). The collective self refers to a person's sense of belonging to a social group, such as a family, community, or ethnic group (e.g., My family knows I am the one that takes care of my aging parents). Triandis suggests that different cultures emphasize different aspects of the self. In collectivistic societies, the public and collective selves are given greater emphasis than the private self. In individualistic societies, it's the reverse, with the private self receiving greater emphasis. Romin Tafarodi from the University of Toronto and his colleagues asked Canadian, Chinese, and Japanese students to answer a set of questions about their inner self and its behavioural expression (Tafarodi, Lo, Yamaguchi, Lee, & Katsura, 2004). Their responses confirmed a weaker sense of continuity among the two East Asian samples and also that the East Asians claimed to experience self-expression in fewer activity domains than did Canadians.

Who's Who in Contemporary Canadian Social Psychology Research

Courtesy Romin W. Tafarodi

Romin W. Tafarodi is a Canadian-born academic who earned his PhD in social psychology from the University of Texas at Austin in 1994. Since then, he has taught at Cardiff University, the University of Tokyo, and the University of Toronto, where he is currently Associate Professor of Psychology. He has contributed research articles and book chapters in the areas of self, identity, and culture, and has taught undergraduate and graduate courses ranging from statistics to philosophy and media studies. He is a strong proponent of multidisciplinary and interdisciplinary scholarship in an age of increasing academic specialization.

INDEPENDENT VERSUS INTERDEPENDENT SELF-CONSTRUAL

In individualistic societies, such as Canada, the self is viewed as an independent entity. This means that the self consists of unique characteristics including abilities, values, preferences, motivations, cognitions, and other internal attributes. An **independent self-construal** conceives the self as autonomous and separate from others, and behaviour in this case is primarily organized to express one's own internal attributes. The construal of the self as independent is more common in Western societies, including North America and western Europe.

independent self-construal – a **conception of the self** as autonomous and independent from others, and behaving primarily to express its own internal attributes

On the other hand, in collectivistic societies, such as Venezuela, the self is viewed as an interdependent entity. This means that the self is more connected to its social context and acts primarily as a response to others within the social context. An **interdependent self-construal** conceives the self as connected to others, with behaviour contingent on the values, thoughts, and preferences of others. Accordingly, the self is more meaningful in a relationship and is connected to the whole. The construal of the self as interdependent is more common in South American, Asian, and African societies.

interdependent self-construal – a conception of the self as connected to others, with its behaviour contingent on the values, thoughts, and preferences of others

A conceptual presentation of self, as suggested by Markus and Kitayama (1991), is illustrated in Figure 3.5. The large circle is self and the smaller circles are others in relationships. The distances between the large and the small circles indicate the closeness of the self and others. The number of Xs in circles indicates various aspects of the self that are shared with others. As shown in Figure 3.5a, in independent self-construal there is a solid line separating the self from others (i.e., the self as autonomous), but in interdependent self-construal the large circle is separated from small circles by a dashed line (Figure 3.5b). This indicates that the interdependent self-construal is defined in relationships with specific others and that these relationships with others guide an individual's behaviour.

FIGURE 3.5   INDEPENDENT SELF AND INTERDEPENDENT SELF

This figure is a conceptual presentation of the view of self by Markus and Kitayama (1991). The Xs in circles indicate personal attributes. In the independent self, the person's individual attributes are highlighted (e.g., outgoing, analytical, adventurous). In the interdependent self, the person's relational attributes are highlighted (e.g., responsible toward siblings, generous toward co-workers, caring toward mother and father).

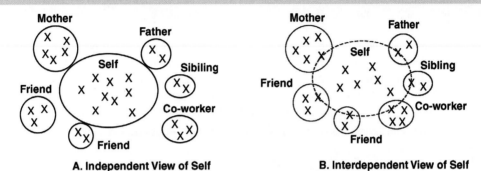

A. Independent View of Self

B. Interdependent View of Self

Source: Markus, H.R. & Kitayama, S. Culture and the self: Implications for cognition, emotion, and motivation. *Psychological Review, Vol 98 (2)*, Apr 1991, 224-253.)

FACTORS INFLUENCING THE SELF-CONCEPT

As described in Chapter 1, people in different cultures see themselves in very different ways. In individualistic cultures, such as those of Canada, the United States, and the United Kingdom, people view themselves in terms of their attitudes, skills, and traits (Bochner, 1994; Cousins, 1989; Dhawan, Roseman, Naidu, & Rettek, 1995; Rhee, Uleman, Lee, & Roman, 1995). When people are asked to respond to the question "Who am I?" (The Twenty Statements Test, Bochner, 1994, that you encountered in Chapter 2), people from individualistic cultures often describe their personal attributes and traits, such as "smart," "funny," or "shy," whereas people in collectivistic cultures tend to see themselves in terms of their group and family affiliations. The latter also describe themselves in terms of their social roles, interpersonal relationships, and group memberships, such as "a university student," "a daughter," or "a member of the Catholic church." This is because groups, rather than individuals, are regarded as the most important social unit. As you will see, this has implications for many aspects of psychological functioning.

This difference in how people define themselves, or in their self-concepts, extends to how people think about and reflect on their experiences in the world. For example, University of Waterloo researchers have found that people in individualistic cultures are more likely than those from collectivistic cultures to think about themselves in the first person, and to project their needs and feelings onto others (Cohen & Gunz, 2002). For example, when asked to describe a memory, those from individualistic cultures are much more likely to recall being at the centre of the event, whereas those from collectivistic cultures are much more likely to recall someone else being the focus (see Figure 3.6). People from individualistic cultures are also more likely to show an egocentric projection of their own emotions onto others. These cultural differences are reflected in how parents and caretakers encourage different types of behaviour. In individualistic countries, children are encouraged to speak up and use words to describe their feelings, whereas in collectivistic countries, children are encouraged to try to understand others' emotions, intentions, and motivations (Kanagawa, Cross, & Markus, 2001). In sum, individualists appear to maintain more of a focus on themselves, whereas collectivists maintain their attention on the social context in which they find themselves.

FIGURE 3.6	CULTURAL DIFFERENCES IN FIRST MEMORIES

In this study, North American and Chinese students were asked to describe their earliest childhood memory. North Americans described lengthy, specific, self-focused, and emotionally elaborate memories, with a focus on individual attributes in describing themselves (Wang, 2001). In contrast, the Chinese students' memories were brief and focused on collective activities, general routines, and emotionally neutral events. The Chinese students were also more likely to describe social roles in their self-descriptions.

American: "I have a memory of being at my great-aunt and -uncle's house. It was some kind of party; I remember I was wearing my purple-flowered party dress. There was some sort of crib on the floor, shaped kind of like this: [a sketch]. I don't know if it was meant for me or for one of my younger cousins, but I crawled into it and lay there on my back. My feet stuck out, but I fit pretty well. I was trying to get the attention of people passing by. I was having fun and feeling slightly mischievous. When I picture the memory, I am lying down in the crib, looking at my party-shoed feet sticking out of the end of the crib."

Chinese: "I used to play with friends when I was little. We went to the bush to pick up wild fruits to eat. And I watched them catch birds."

People in individualistic cultures also place a stronger emphasis than those in collectivistic cultures on having a consistent and stable self-concept, in part because, in Western cultures, the self is predominantly described in terms of one's internal traits, abilities, and attributes (Campbell et al., 1996; Suh, 2002). In line with this emphasis, people from individualistic cultures are more likely to agree with such statements as "In general, I have a clear sense of who I am and what I am," and "I seldom experience conflict between different aspects of my personality" (Campbell et al., 1996). Those from collectivistic cultures, on the other hand, are more likely to agree with such statements as "My beliefs about myself often conflict with one another," and "Sometimes I think I know other people better than I know myself." Of course, knowing more about others, which implies a degree of social sensitivity, is desirable and highly functional in a collectivistic cultural context.

Similarly, culture also influences how interested people are in engaging in social comparison. Those from collectivistic backgrounds are more interested in social comparison information than those from individualistic backgrounds (White & Lehman, 2005). This greater interest in social comparison is likely to be a result of people with a more interdependent self-concept having an overall greater focus on the thoughts, feelings, behaviours, and goals of others.

Culture also is linked with clarity in people's self-concept: Canadians have higher self-concept clarity than Japanese people, meaning that Canadians see themselves as more consistent across situations (Campbell et al., 1996). In one study, both Japanese and Canadian university students were asked to complete the Twenty Statements Test alone, with a peer, in a large group of peers, or with a higher status person such as a faculty member (Kanagawa, Cross, & Markus, 2001). Canadians reported having a clear sense of who they are and showing consistency from day to day as well as across different situations (e.g., with a faculty member, with a peer, in a group, alone). In contrast, Japanese people reported differences in self-concepts across these distinct situations, because their self-concepts are more influenced by, or adaptable to, the situation. This patterning makes sense given the individualistic emphasis on individual achievement and attributes, and the collectivistic emphasis on relationships and interdependence with others. Clarity of individual self-concept simply matters more for those in individualistic cultures; conversely, adaptability to different social contexts matters more for people from relatively collectivistic cultures.

ARE YOU CONSISTENT IN DIFFERENT SITUATIONS?

Self-Consistency Scale

INSTRUCTIONS: *Rate each item on a scale of 1 (strongly disagree) to 5 (strongly agree).*

☐ **1.** In general, I have a clear sense of who I am and what I am.

☐ **2.** My beliefs about myself often conflict with one another.

☐ **3.** I seldom experience conflict between different aspects of my personality.

☐ **4.** Sometimes I think I know other people better than I know myself.

☐ **5.** I spend a lot of time wondering about what kind of person I really am.

☐ **6.** My beliefs about myself seem to change very frequently.

☐ **7.** Sometimes I feel that I am not really the person that I appear to be.

SCORING: For items 1 and 3, give yourself the number of points equal to the rating that you assigned to the statement. Items 2, 4, 5, 6, and 7 are reverse-scored, so higher scores are converted to lower numbers (and vice versa). In other words, if you rated the statement a 5, give yourself 1 point. If you rated the statement a 2, give yourself 4 points.

INTERPRETATION: This scale assesses individuals' beliefs about their consistency across different situations (Campbell et al., 1996). Higher scores reflect greater consistency (typical of individualistic cultures), whereas lower scores reflect greater variability (typical of collectivistic cultures).

CULTURE AND SELF-PERCEPTION AND SELF-PRESENTATION

Imagine that you are assigned to work with a group of fellow students on a project for the entire semester. At the end of the project, you're asked to rate yourself and each of your classmates on sociability, intellect, and assertiveness. This method allowed researchers to examine whether individuals' self-reports were the same as, higher, or lower than the reports of other group members. How do you think your own self-ratings would compare to those given to you by your peers? Given what you've already learned in this chapter about individuals' tendency to see themselves in overly positive ways, I hope you believe that people tend to rate themselves higher than others rate them—which is precisely what researchers have demonstrated with North American samples. When Chinese college students participated in this same study, though, they rated themselves lower than group members did (Yik, Bond, & Paulhus, 1998). Although 56 percent of North American students rated themselves better than their peers rated them, only 43 percent of Chinese participants showed this type of self-enhancement. In other words, the general tendency to see one's self in extremely positive ways seems to hold true for more people in individualistic cultures than in collectivistic cultures, with the latter showing what is referred to as a modesty bias (in contrast to a self-serving bias). This section will examine how culture impacts on self-perception and self-presentation, including the factors that influence the self-concept, sources of self-motivation, the strategies used to maintain a positive self-concept, and the strategies of self-presentation.

Questioning the Research:

Although this section describes the impact of culture on how people answer the question "Who Am I?" in the Twenty Statements Test, can you think of other factors that might influence how people answer this question? (Hint: What other demographic factors might influence responses?)

HOW PEOPLE EXPERIENCE PSYCHOLOGICAL WELL-BEING

Although consistency among different aspects of the self is an important predictor of well-being in individualistic cultures, such consistency is often not associated with well-being in collectivistic cultures (Suh, 2002). East Asians are less concerned with consistency because they see the self as more of a social product, in which the person is naturally different in different situations and with different people. Moreover, in collectivistic cultures consistency may represent rigidity and a lack of flexibility. In sum, what is psychologically good and healthy is determined by one's culture—consistency is associated with well-being in Western (i.e., individualistic) cultures because, as has already been noted, it is regarded positively by others in that cultural context. However, in Eastern (or, more accurately, collectivistic) cultures, adaptability to different situations is culturally valued and is also associated with well-being. In both cases, well-being is a result of the fit between the person and the culture, and it has been suggested that psychotherapy in different cultures is aimed at restoring this person-culture fit (Noon & Lewis, 1992).

Another explanation for why consistency is a weaker predictor of well-being in collectivistic than in individualistic cultures is that these different cultures view the likelihood, direction, and cause of change in distinct ways (Choi & Nisbett, 2000; Ji, Nisbett, & Su, 2001; Peng & Nisbett, 1999). In collectivistic cultures, reality is seen as dynamic and changeable, and so change is a normal and natural part of life. In contrast, individualistic cultures expect consistency over time, and are thus surprised when change occurs. For example, Canadians are more surprised than Columbians when a "good person" (e.g., a seminary student) doesn't help someone, as well as when a "bad person" helps someone. They are also more surprised when a study's hypothesis is not supported and evidence is found instead for an alternative hypothesis. In sum, people in collectivistic cultures have a more fluid and open view of people. They are less likely to hold the view "once a criminal, always a criminal," as is often assumed to be true in individualistic cultures.

SOURCES OF SELF-MOTIVATION

Culture also impacts how people think about their motivation for engaging in behaviour (Iyengar & Lepper, 1991). Remember the "magic marker study" described earlier in this chapter, in which children's intrinsic interest in drawing with magic markers was undermined when researchers gave children rewards for such drawing)? The intrinsic motivation of North American children is undermined when they do a task for extrinsic reasons (such as getting a reward or following their parent's wishes). In collectivistic cultures, on the other hand, the focus is on the group, which can be family or any other social unit, and following the preferences of others rather than one's own doesn't necessarily undermine intrinsic interest.

In one study, researchers asked both Anglo American and Asian American elementary school children to solve a series of anagrams (puzzles in which letters are unscrambled to form

FIGURE 3.7	COMMON PROVERBS FROM DIFFERENT CULTURAL CONTEXTS

The collectivist proverb example expresses the view that it is worthwhile to bring your best to a team project. The individualist example is an adage based on a quote from Napoleon Bonaparte. It expresses the view that you should only count on yourself.

Collectivist: Motivational slogan on the wall in a Japanese Bank[1]
"You cannot win alone, but your team can."
Individualist: Saying used by some parents from a British or Anglo Canadian background
"If you want a job done well, do it yourself."

[1]Rohlen, T. (1975). The company work group. In E. Vogel (Ed.), *Modern Japanese organization and decision making*. Tokyo, Japan: Tuttle.

FIGURE 3.8   HOW DOES CULTURE IMPACT INTRINSIC MOTIVATION?

In this experiment, elementary school children were asked to solve a series of anagrams. The choice of which anagrams to work on was made either by the child, the experimenter, or the child's mother. Anglo American children worked the longest when they chose the anagrams to work on, whereas Asian American children worked the longest when anagrams were chosen by their mother.

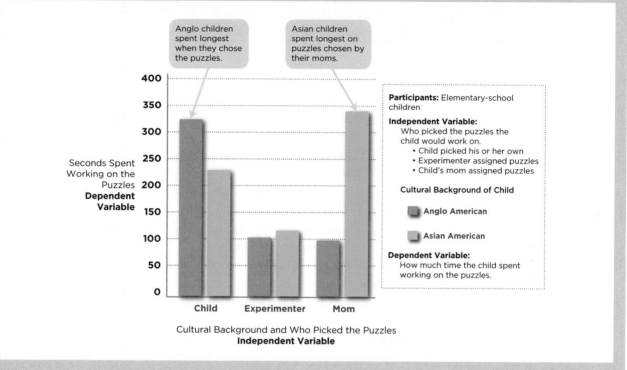

Source: Iyengar, S., Lepper, M. (1999). Rethinking the value of choice: A cultural perspective on intrinsic motivation. *Journal of Personality and Social Psychology, 76*, 349–366. Copyright © 1999 by the American Psychological Association. Reproduced. The use of APA information does not imply endorsement by APA.

words; Iyengar & Lepper, 1999). In some conditions, the children were told to choose a category of anagrams (and the colour marker to work with), in others they were told the experimenter wanted them to solve a certain set of categories, and in still another they were told their mother wanted them to solve a certain category. As shown in Figure 3.8, Anglo American children solved significantly more anagrams when they could make their own choices than when their mother or the experimenter chose for them, which is in agreement with other research showing the importance of intrinsic motivation in individualistic samples. Among Asian children, however, anagram solving was highest when the children followed their mother's choices—showing that intrinsic motivation can remain high among Asian children even when children's choices are guided by an extrinsic factor.

STRATEGIES FOR MAINTAINING A POSITIVE SELF-CONCEPT

Earlier in this chapter, you read about the strategies people use to maintain positive self-concepts, such as holding unrealistic beliefs about their ability to control events, making self-serving attributions, and seeing themselves in a particularly positive light. But many of these so-called truths about human nature may in fact best describe people in individualistic cultures, and may have less relevance for those from collectivistic cultures. For example, people from individualistic cultures are more likely than those from collectivistic cultures to believe that they have some control over how objects (such as familiar shapes on a computer screen)

self-serving attribution – the tendency to view oneself in a positive light

work together, even when the objects are interacting in a completely random way (Ji, Peng, & Nisbett, 2000). Canadians and others from individualistic cultures are also more likely to idealize or glorify their daily experiences than those in collectivistic cultures. Although daily diary studies reveal no differences between Anglo Americans and Asian Americans in how they describe their moods, in retrospective reports—meaning looking back over time through reports made at a later date—European Americans report that they're happier overall than Asians report (Oishi, 2002). What causes this difference? North Americans have a theory that "life is good," whereas Asians have a theory that "life is good and bad."

USE OF FALSE UNIQUENESS BIAS.   Similarly, the false uniqueness bias (people's tendency to see themselves as especially talented and better than others) is much more common in individualistic cultures than in collectivistic ones (Chang, Asakawa, & Sanna, 2001; Heine & Lehman, 1995; Markus & Kitayama, 1991; Stigler, Smith, & Mao, 1985). For example, in a study with Japanese, Asian Canadian, and European Canadian students, Steve Heine and Darrin Lehman from the University of British Columbia found that Canadians tended to evaluate their own university in an unrealistically positive way—meaning they rated it much better than students from other universities would rate it. In contrast, Japanese students show self-effacing biases—meaning they actually rate their own university less positively than do students who attend another school (Heine & Lehman, 1997). In fact, individuals from individualistic cultures tend to see themselves as particularly good at a task even when they receive objective information that their own performance was lower than that of other students.

These cultural differences in self-enhancement are also seen in research on individuals' expectancies for positive versus negative events. In one study, researchers asked European American university students attending the University of Michigan and Japanese students attending Shikoku Gakuin University in Japan to rate the likelihood of experiencing various events (Chang & Asakawa, 2003). Some of these events were positive, such as "meeting someone new with whom you expect to be close friends," and others were negative, such as "failing a test." They were then asked whether each event was more likely to happen to them than their sibling, more likely to happen to their sibling than to them, or equally likely to happen to both them and their sibling. Americans saw positive events as much more likely to happen to themselves than to a sibling, and negative events as much more likely to happen to a sibling than to themselves. In contrast, Japanese people saw positive events as equally likely to happen to themselves and a sibling, and negative events as much more likely to happen to themselves than their sibling. Again, this study shows a collectivistic focus on people with whom one is in a relationship (in this case, siblings) and an individualistic attention to oneself even above siblings.

CAUSES OF CULTURAL DIFFERENCES IN SELF-ENHANCEMENT.   What leads to these cultural differences in the tendency to be self-enhancing or self-effacing? Some intriguing research by Japanese psychologist Shinobu Kitayama and his colleagues suggests that North Americans perceive situations as relatively conducive to self-enhancement, whereas Japanese situations are relatively conducive to self-criticism (Kitayama, Markus, Matsumoto, & Norasakkunkit, 1997). North Americans see success situations (e.g., getting a good grade on a paper, passing other runners in a race) as more relevant to their self-esteem than failure situations (e.g., being jilted by a dating partner, receiving negative feedback from a boss). North Americans believe that their self-esteem would increase more in success situations than it would decrease in failure situations. On the other hand, Japanese respondents show the reverse pattern, by selecting a greater number of failure situations than success situations as relevant to their self-esteem and seeing failure situations as having a greater impact on self-esteem than success situations.

It has been found that North Americans are relatively likely to engage in self-enhancement, whereas Japanese people are relatively likely to engage in self-criticism (Heine et al., 2001). For example, when Canadians and Americans fail at a task, they tend to give up much more quickly on a second, similar task compared to those who succeed (presumably because they fear receiving more negative information about their ability). Yet Japanese who fail at a task actually persist longer at a second task than those who succeed (again, presumably because they are focused on self-improvement).

Why do people in individualistic cultures use strategies to maintain a positive self-concept whereas those in collectivistic cultures don't? The commonly assumed belief that people need to have a positive self-regard seems to be unique to those in individualistic cultures (Heine, Lehman, Markus, & Kitayama, 1999). There is little evidence that Japanese people need a positive self-regard, and in fact, some research suggests that a self-critical focus is more common. Steve Heine and Darrin Lehman, again with samples of Japanese, Asian Canadian, and European Canadian students, found that actual-ideal self-discrepancies were larger for Japanese than for either of the Canadian groups (Heine & Lehman, 1999). In other words, individuals' actual selves were more distant from their ideal selves for Japanese participants than for those in the individualistic cultural context of Canada, in part because feeling different from the person you'd like to be is more threatening to those in individualistic cultures than for those in collectivistic ones. Of course, if people in collectivistic cultures place more emphasis on the group, they might be expected to derive satisfaction from regard for their group (e.g., family or company) rather than from individual self-esteem.

STRATEGIES OF SELF-PRESENTATION

These cultural differences in self-perception also lead people to present themselves to others in very different ways. In one study, Japanese Americans and European Americans completed a series of tasks (anagrams, perceptual reasoning, etc.) and were told they got 65 percent correct (Akimoto & Sanbonmatsu, 1999). They were also told this was a very good score, and that they did better than 80–90 percent of other university students. When they were later asked about their performance by a confederate, Japanese students were less self-promoting and more self-effacing than European Americans (although such differences weren't found in their answers to a private, written questionnaire, meaning the Japanese students didn't actually see their performance in a less favourable light). Unfortunately, this modesty in their interaction resulted in the Japanese students being perceived as having performed less well, being less competent, and being less likely to be hired when such interactions were later rated. So, this collectivistic tendency for modesty, perhaps to promote in-group harmony and prevent jealousy, can have negative personal consequences (among individualists).

VARIATIONS WITHIN CULTURES

As we conclude the section on the impact of culture on self, it's important to make two points. First, all the cultural differences that have been described are differences in emphasis only (Markus & Kitayama, 1991). People in collectivistic cultures are also aware of their individual identity and people in individualist contexts have ties to groups such as family, a hockey team, and a nation. Second, there is more variation within a culture than between cultures. Cultures and societies are enormously heterogeneous, so there is an overlap between the ranges of scores obtained from different cultures. This is particularly the case in large nations such as Canada and the United States. In other words, although Canadians (on average) are individualistic when compared to (for example) Chinese, there are some Canadians who have values and beliefs that are more collectivistic than some relatively individualistic

Chinese. Similarly, although Columbians, on average have values that are more collectivistic than Canadians have, there are, nevertheless, some particularly individualistic Columbians who hold more individualistic values than some particularly collectivistic Canadians. To make the mistake of assuming that all Columbians are more collectivistic than all Canadians would be to commit what Hofstede (2001) refers to as the ecological fallacy, and is akin to stereotyping. The **ecological fallacy** is the error of assuming that relationships between variables at the group level are the same as relationships at the individual level. Therefore, you should remember that there is always variation within as well as between cultures.

ecological fallacy – the error of assuming that relationships between variables at the group level are the same as relationships at the individual level

THE BIG PICTURE

THE SELF: SELF-PERCEPTION AND SELF-PRESENTATION

This chapter included many applications of the three "big ideas" studied in social psychology. The examples below should help you see the connection between our discussion of the self and these big ideas and contribute to your understanding of the big picture of social psychology.

THEME	EXAMPLES
The social world influences how we think about ourselves.	• Women who see photos of highly attractive women, and men who read descriptions of socially dominant men, feel worse about their own value as a marriage partner. • People who hold their faces in a smile feel happier than those who maintain a frown.
The social world influences our thoughts, attitudes, and behaviour.	• Children who face a mirror while trick-or-treating are more likely to take only one piece of candy than those who don't face a mirror. • People who are given negative feedback about their IQ drink more wine than those who receive positive feedback. • Students whose university football team wins are more likely to wear clothes featuring their school name the following Monday than those whose football team loses.
Our attitudes and behaviours shape the social world around us.	• Students who are initially required to volunteer are less likely to volunteer later on. • People who have overly positive views of themselves are more aggressive toward others. • People who are high in self-monitoring are more likely to deceive potential romantic partners than those who are low in self-monitoring.

WHAT YOU'VE LEARNED

This chapter examined six key principles of self-perception and self-presentation.

1. How to define self-concept and self-awareness.

This section examines how we come to see and describe ourselves. Self-concept is our belief about our own attributes; the self-concept changes from childhood to adulthood. Self-concept becomes more abstract and less concrete as we get older. Self-awareness is a state of being aware of oneself. Both environmental cues and personality disposition influence self-awareness. In this section, we also discussed functions of self as interpersonal tool, decision maker, and self-regulator.

2. How personal factors influence the self-concept.

A variety of personal factors, including thinking about our thoughts, focusing on self-awareness, regulating the self, examining our behaviour, and interpreting our motivation, can influence how we see ourselves. We also demonstrated that sometimes we make errors when assessing our attitudes and feelings: assistant professors think they'll be very sad, and for a long time, if they don't get tenure, but in reality they feel just as good as those who got tenure in a few years' time.

3. How social factors influence the self-concept.

Both social comparison theory and the two-factor theory of emotion demonstrate the influence of social factors on our self-concept. You also learned that comparing your intelligence to that of Pamela Anderson is a good idea.

4. How people maintain a positive self-concept.

We use a variety of strategies to maintain a positive self-concept, including self-serving biases, self-serving beliefs, self-serving comparisons, and self-serving behaviour. For example, you learned that people see themselves as showering less frequently than others during a drought, but showering more frequently than others during normal conditions. All of these strategies help us feel good about ourselves, sometimes in the face of considerable evidence to the contrary.

5. How people present themselves to others.

People use a number of different strategies to present themselves to other people in a positive way. These strategies include self-promotion, ingratiation, and self-verification. However, we also learned that we don't need to focus quite so much on self-presentation—because other people are much less aware of our own behaviour than we believe they are. In other words, it is truly okay to wear the Vanilla Ice t-shirt.

6. How culture influences self-concept, self-perception, and self-presentation.

The last section in this chapter described the role of culture in influencing self-concept, self-perception, and self-presentation. We learned that individuals' tendency to self-enhance, meaning to rate themselves as particularly good—and certainly as better than most others—is highly influenced by culture. In sum, people from individualistic cultures tend to rate themselves in particularly positive ways, whereas those from collectivistic cultures show considerably more modesty.

Key Terms

affective forecasting 68
basking in reflected glory (BIRGing) 84
downward social comparison 84
ecological fallacy 102
facial feedback hypothesis 72
false consensus effect 80
false uniqueness effect 81
impression management 88

independent self-construal 94
interdependent self-construal 94
ingratiation 89
overjustification 74
perceived control 82
self-awareness theory 69
self-concept 64
self-discrepancy theory 69
self-esteem 65

self-handicapping 86
self-monitoring 90
self-perception theory 71
self-promotion 88
self-serving attributions 99
self-verification theory 89
social comparison theory 76
spotlight effect 92
unrealistic optimism 81

Questions for Review

1. Describe the three functions of self and the distinction between self-concept and self-awareness.

2. Describe four ways in which personal factors influence the self-concept, including the limits of each factor.

3. Describe two distinct ways in which social factors influence the self-concept, and include a research example of each.

4. We all use a variety of strategies to maintain our positive self-views. Describe four specific ways in which people

see themselves in a biased way, and at least one problem with the use of such self-presentation strategies.

5. Describe two strategies that we use to present ourselves to others. What are the advantages and disadvantages of each?

6. Describe two distinct cultural differences in strategies that people use to maintain a positive self-concept, and two explanations for these differences.

Take Action!

1. Suppose that you're trying to motivate your eight-year-old nephew to practise the guitar. What strategies might and might not work to accomplish this goal?

2. Your brother is an amazing athlete—he excels at basically every sport he tries. Unfortunately, you aren't quite as athletically gifted. What strategies can you use to avoid feeling bad about your own sports abilities in comparison to your brother's?

3. In the past year, your best friend has experienced a number of negative events, including rejection for a very desired job and the end of a long-term dating relationship. Yet she continues to feel very positive about herself. What strategies should she use to maintain a positive self-concept in the face of disappointment?

4. You have an important job interview tomorrow morning. Given your knowledge about self-presentation, what strategies will you use (and avoid) in order to make a good impression?

5. Your sister will be spending a month in Japan this summer as part of a high school exchange program. What advice might you give her when she asks how Japanese people differ from Canadians?

RESEARCH CONNECTIONS

Participate in Research

Activity 1 Rating Cartoons. Self-perception theory posits that holding different facial expressions influences mood. Go online to rate a series of cartoons while holding your face in different expressions. Then compare your ratings of the two sets of cartoons to see if the cartoons you rated while smiling had a higher overall rating than the cartoons you rated while frowning.

Activity 2 Rating Yourself. According to social comparison theory, we feel differently about ourselves depending on the types of comparisons we make. Go online to look at two sets of photos, and rate how you feel about yourself after each set. Compare your ratings to see if the photos you saw influenced how you rated yourself.

Activity 3 Testing BIRGing. To test the prevalence of BIRGing, follow the procedure used by Cialdini et al. (1976). Count the number of people you see on campus wearing school apparel the day following a loss by your university's most popular sports team versus the day after a win. Do your findings indicate students at your school BIRG (at least in relation to sports)?

Activity 4 The Power of Self-Verification. This chapter has described people's tendency to prefer feedback from others that verifies, or supports, their own self-concept. Go online to rate yourself across a series of dimensions, and then rate the type of feedback you would prefer to receive from others on these dimensions.

Activity 5 The Impact of Culture on Memory. To examine the impact of culture on memories, go online to report on your culture and describe one of your earliest memories. Then compare your response to those of students from other cultures.

Test a Hypothesis

One of the common findings in research on self-monitoring is that people with different levels of self-monitoring look for different things in a dating partner. To test whether this hypothesis is true, create several different descriptions of potential dating partners (varying such things as attractiveness, personality, income, and so on). Then ask your friends to complete the self-monitoring inventory and rate their interest in the different types of dating partners. Do your findings support or refute the hypothesis?

Design Your Own Study

Go online to design your own study that tests the strategies people use to maintain a positive self-concept. You'll be able to choose the type of study you want to conduct (self-report, observational/naturalistic, or experimental), choose your own independent and dependent variables, and form your own hypothesis. When you're done, you can share your findings with other students across the country!

SOCIAL PERCEPTION

DID YOU EVER WONDER?

On the evening of February 4, 1974, 19-year-old Patricia Hearst, daughter of wealthy American newspaper publisher Randolph Hearst, was kidnapped by a leftwing guerilla group called the Symbionese Liberation Army (SLA). Eight days later the kidnappers made their demands public, and negotiations continued until April 2 when members of the SLA published a letter in a local newspaper promising that Patricia would be released within 72 hours. A day later, however, a radio station received a tape on which Patricia made this announcement:

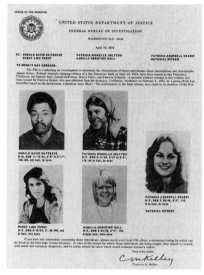

Associated Press

> I would like to begin this statement by informing the public that I wrote what I am about to say. It's what I feel. I have never been forced to say anything on any tape. . . . I have been given the choice of (1) being released in a safe area or (2) joining the forces of the Symbionese Liberation Army and fighting for my freedom and the freedom of all oppressed people. I have chosen to stay and fight . . . I have been given the name Tania after a comrade who fought alongside Che in Bolivia for the people of Bolivia. I embrace the name with the determination to continue fighting with her spirit . . . I know Tania dedicated her life to the people, fighting with total dedication and an intense desire to learn, which I will continue in the oppressed American people's revolution." (Hearst, 1982, pp. 118–121)

Twelve days after the release of the tape, members of the SLA robbed a bank in San Francisco and wounded two bystanders. Patricia was captured on a surveillance camera holding a machine gun and soon became a member of the FBI's Ten Most Wanted list. A year and half later, the FBI captured Patricia and other members of the SLA. Patricia's sensational trial started shortly after her arrest and she became, simultaneously, a celebrity, a victim, and a criminal.

HEALTH CONNECTIONS

The Role of Attributions in Prejudice against Obesity

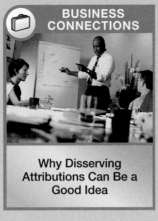

BUSINESS CONNECTIONS

Why Disserving Attributions Can Be a Good Idea

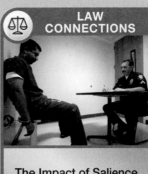

LAW CONNECTIONS

The Impact of Salience on Perceived Guilt

EDUCATION CONNECTIONS

Why Focusing on Effort over Ability Is a Good Idea

Can you imagine being a member of that jury? What would your verdict be? Her lawyer argued that Patriciahad no criminal intent during the robbery as she had been beaten, sexually assaulted, and brainwashed while in captivity and these factors resulted in identification with her captors, a phenomenon that has been observed among hostages and prisoners of war. The prosecutor, on the other hand, argued that Patricia knowingly and willingly took part in SLA actions. It was suggested that, by identifying with the SLA, Patricia was able to become more than a nondescript, conventional rich girl. She became a self-proclaimed revolutionary.

Your perceptions about Patricia's behaviour will have a strong impact on how you interpret it. If you believe that her behaviour (i.e., her participation in the bank robbery and identification with the SLA) can be attributed to internal factors, such as her personality and her values, you're more likely to find her guilty. If you believe that her behaviour can be attributed to external factors, such as being kidnapped and brainwashed, you're more likely to find her not guilty.

The jury found her guilty and she was sentenced to 35 years' imprisonment. Her sentence was later dropped to seven years and she was eventually released after 22 months. In 2001, Patricia Hearst received full pardon by U.S. President Bill Clinton. She now lives a quiet life with her bodyguard-turned-husband and two children.

In this chapter, we will discuss stories like Patricia Hearst's and other issues regarding how we interpret people's behaviour. You'll also find answers to these questions:

 Why is it a good idea to give your spouse the benefit of the doubt?

 Why do teenagers see their friends, but not themselves, as careless drivers?

 When is doing a good deed sometimes *not* a good idea?

 Why are North Americans likely to see murder as caused by crazy people, yet Chinese people are likely to blame the media?

 How frequently do we lie and to whom do we lie to?

The answers to these questions all describe findings from research on how we see other people and interpret their behaviour.

PREVIEW

social perception – how people form impressions of and make inferences about other people

Imagine that you're standing in line to buy tickets for a movie you've wanted to see, and you overhear the person in front of you describing how much they hated that movie. You now have to make a quick decision—should you see the movie you intended to see, or a different one? This decision will be driven largely by your inferences about the person whose conversation you overheard. This is an example of social perception, meaning how we form impressions of and make inferences about other people. Although the process of making attributions about someone's attitudes and behaviour may seem like a very rational and straightforward process, we aren't always very accurate in assessing the cause of another person's behaviour. North Americans and people from similarly individualistic cultures sometimes focus too much on the role of personal factors, while ignoring, or minimizing, the often considerable influence of the situation.

HOW DO WE THINK ABOUT WHY OTHER PEOPLE DO WHAT THEY DO?

Think about an occasion when someone you were dating brought up a problem in your relationship, and how you handled it. Your reaction very likely influenced your satisfaction with the relationship. Researchers Thomas Bradbury and Frank Fincham (1992) conducted a series of studies with married couples in which they asked couples to discuss a problem in their relationship and then to make attributions for the causes of these problems. For example, a negative explanation for the problem of not spending enough time together might be "You stay up all night watching TV," whereas a positive explanation might be "Our schedules aren't really in sync." The researchers found that these different types of attributions, not surprisingly, can impact approaches to resolving the conflict as well as marital satisfaction. This section will examine four major theories that describe how we think about why people engage in particular types of behaviour: the theory of naïve psychology, correspondent inference theory, the covariation theory, and Weiner's attribution theory. An intergroup perspective of attribution is also presented.

naïve psychology – Heider's theory that people practise a form of untrained psychology as they use cause and effect analyses to understand their world and other people's behaviour

HEIDER'S THEORY OF NAÏVE PSYCHOLOGY

According to Fritz Heider (1958), an Austrian psychologist who is often described as the "father of attribution theory," people practise naïve psychology as they use causal theories to understand their world and other people's behaviour. As these theories have a similar structure to scientific theories, everyone is therefore a naïve scientist. Heider's idea is based on three principles. First, people have the need to explain the cause of other people's behaviour in order to understand their motivation. For example, if your classmate helps you with your statistics assignment, you can explain her behaviour either as a reflection of her being a helpful person or of her expecting a favour in return (e.g., your vote in the next election for a student association). Second, people are motivated to try to figure out why a person acted in a given way so that they can predict how the person will act in the future. For example, if in the past you observed that Sophia helped a friend move and shared her notes with a classmate, you're likely to predict that Sophia will be helpful next time someone asks a favour of her. Third, when people make causal attributions, they make a distinction between internal and external causes of behaviour. In some cases, people make **external attributions** about the causes of others' behaviour. This means that they see the behaviour as caused by something external to the person performing the behaviour—i.e., it relates to something about

external attribution – seeing the behaviour as caused by something external to the person who performs the behaviour

the situation. For example, imagine that while driving to work one day you notice that the driver behind you seems very aggressive: she is following your car very closely, honks her horn if you delay even a few seconds when the red light turns green, and finally swerves around to pass you. You would be making a situational attribution if you were to presume that she is late for a job interview, has a sick child in the car who needs to go to the hospital, or has simply had a bad day. In other cases, people make **internal attributions** about the causes of others' behaviour, meaning that they see the person's behaviour as caused by personal factors; in other words, something specific to the person, such as traits, ability, effort, or personality. For example, you would be making a dispositional attribution about the driver's behaviour if you were to presume that she is rude, is hostile, or is very aggressive. In the story of Patricia Hearst that opened this chapter, the jury thus

© Jerry King/ www.cartoonstock.com.

internal attribution – refers to whether the person's behaviour is caused by personal factors, such as traits, ability, effort, or personality

made an internal attribution in finding her guilty as they decided that her behaviour was motivated by her desire to be rebellious and have an exciting and distinctive life.

JONES AND DAVIS'S THEORY OF CORRESPONDENT INFERENCE

Edward Jones and Keith Davis (1965) developed a theory to explain why people make the attributions they do. **Correspondent inference theory** is based on their observation that people often believe that a person's disposition corresponds to his or her behaviour. This theory predicts that people look at various factors related to a person's actions to try to infer whether an action is caused by the person's internal disposition. In a classic study, Ned Jones and his colleagues demonstrated this attribution process (Jones, Davis, & Gergen, 1961). Participants were first asked to observe a person who was describing himself in a job interview as either very extroverted or very introverted. Half of the participants were told that this applicant was interviewing for a job on a submarine (a job that requires considerable close contact with many others). The other half were told that he was applying for a job as an astronaut (a job that, at the time, required a person to spend long periods of time alone). Participants were then asked to rate the applicant's personality, and specifically his degree of extroversion. Those who saw an applicant acting in a predictable way—describing his extroversion when he was interviewing for a job on a submarine, or describing his introversion when he was interviewing for a job as an astronaut—were quite reluctant to make this rating. They were reluctant because they

correspondent inference theory – the theory that people infer whether a person's behaviour is caused by the person's internal disposition by looking at various factors related to the person's action

(rightly) attributed the person's behaviour to the situation (e.g., wanting to get the job). But when people behaved in an unexpected way (e.g., the extrovert wanting the astronaut job, the introvert wanting the job on the submarine), participants were very willing to make a dispositional attribution because they saw the person's behaviour as reflecting his true personality. This behaviour certainly isn't designed to help them win the job, they concluded. Moreover, they rated the extrovert as especially extroverted when he wanted the astronaut job and the introvert as especially introverted when he wanted the job on the submarine. In the case of Patricia Hearst, the jury inferred that Patricia had a criminal tendency based on her statement after her captivity, her participation in the bank robbery, her assumption of a new name and identity, and her romantic relationship with another member of the SLA.

Correspondent inference theory proposes that there are three factors that influence the extent to which you attribute behaviour to the person rather than the situation:

1. Does the person have the *choice* to engage in the action?
2. Is the behaviour *expected* based on the social role or circumstance?
3. What are the *intended effects or consequences* of the person's behaviour?

First, if you know that the person was forced to engage in a given behaviour, it is reasonable to assume that the action is due to the situation and not the person. For example, most students who major in psychology are required to take a course in statistics. If your friend is a psychology major and she's taking statistics, can you infer that she likes statistics? No, because her behaviour may have been caused by the situation (the requirements of the major). But what if your friend is an English major? Can you then assume that she likes statistics? Probably yes, because in this case you have much greater certainty that the behaviour was caused by the person.

Second, is the behaviour *expected* based on the social role or circumstance? Behaviour that isn't necessarily required, but is largely expected in a situation, doesn't tell us much about the person. If you see someone wearing a tuxedo at a wedding, you shouldn't infer that he's a stylish and formal dresser, because his outfit is quite likely a function of the situational requirement that he wear something formal. On the other hand, if you see someone wearing a t-shirt with a picture of a tuxedo on it at a formal wedding, you might very appropriately make a dispositional attribution for this unexpected behaviour.

Third, what are the *intended effects or consequences* of the behaviour? To make an attribution, Jones and Davis believe that people are likely to look at the effects of a person's behaviour. If there is only one intended effect, then you have a pretty good idea of why the person is motivated to engage in the behaviour. If there are multiple good effects, it's more difficult to know what to attribute the behaviour to. Imagine, for example, that a friend of yours decides to take a really boring job that pays $15,000 a year in an isolated area where she doesn't know anyone, the weather is cold, and there is a great mountain for skiing. Why did she take the job? Probably because she really likes to ski. Another friend of yours takes an interesting and challenging job that pays $80,000 in a large cosmopolitan city where he has many friends. Why did he take the job? Was it the nature of the job, the pay, the city, or the presence of his friends? In this case, it's very difficult to make an attribution because the behaviour could have been caused by a variety of factors.

In sum, according to correspondent inference theory we are best able to make a dispositional attribution, and see people's behaviour as caused by their traits, when the behaviour is freely chosen, is not a function of situational expectations, and has clear non-common effects. According to the correspondent inference theory, one question to ask about Patricia Hearst's case is whether she had the choice to engage in the bank robbery. You may say yes as some SLA members didn't take part in the robbery. The next question is whether her part in the bank robbery was based on her social role or circumstance. You might argue that Patricia's circumstance, being kidnapped and possibly beaten and brainwashed, contributed to her action.

The last question is what the consequences of her action were. Given that the bank robbery was successful and people were wounded, she committed a criminal act. The jury made a dispositional attribution by finding Patricia responsible for her action and, therefore, guilty. You may arrive at a different attribution.

KELLEY'S COVARIATION THEORY

An alternative theory of attribution was developed by Harold Kelley (1967). His **covariation theory** focuses on the factors that are present when a behaviour occurs and the factors that are absent when it does not occur. Does your sister always fall madly in love with a potential romantic partner after the first date, regardless of that person's particular traits? If so, according to covariation theory you would likely make a dispositional or personal attribution (e.g., my sister gets infatuated easily). Or does your sister typically ridicule potential romantic partners but feels very passionate about this particular partner? In this case, you would likely make a situational attribution (e.g., this person is very special). The three main components of correspondent inference theory are consensus, distinctiveness, and **consistency**. Figure 4.1 summarizes the theory with examples.

The first component of covariation theory is the **consensus** of the attitude or behaviour— whether other people generally agree or disagree with a given person. If many people agree with that person or behave in a similar manner, we're more likely to make a situational attribution than we would if few people agreed with the target individual. In the case of Patricia Hearst, if we have evidence that most other people who have been kept in captivity have reacted similarly and have identified with their captors (high consensus), then we could argue that the situation had a major impact on Patricia's behaviour. However, if there is no evidence that those who are kidnapped tend to identify with their captors (low consensus), then we could argue that Patricia had a disposition to rob a bank and identify with revolutionary urban fighters.

covariation theory – the theory that people determine the causes of a person's behaviour by focusing on the factors that are present when a behaviour occurs and absent when it doesn't occur, with specific attention on the role of consensus, distinctiveness, and consistency

consistency – information about whether a person's behaviour toward a given stimulus is the same across time

consensus – The first component of covariation theory and it refers to whether other people generally agree or disagree with a given person

FIGURE 4.1 MODEL OF COVARIATION

According to covariation theory, we use the level of consensus, distinctiveness, and consistency about a person's behaviour to explain the behaviour as mainly caused either by the person's situation or by the person's own characteristics or dispositions.

Consensus	Distinctiveness	Consistency	Attribution
High Other people all think your sister's boyfriend is great.	**High** It is unusual for her to like someone this much, so quickly.	**High** Your sister continues to like this person over time.	**Situational** This boyfriend really is special.
Low Other people think your sister's boyfriend is horrible.	**Low** Your sister quickly likes all her dating partners.	**High** Your sister continues to like this person over time.	**Dispositional** Your sister tends to fall in love quickly. This boyfriend is nothing special.
		Low Your sister quickly decides she doesn't like this guy.	**Uncertain** You can't tell if this boyfriend wasn't right or if your sister just falls in and out of love quickly.

distinctiveness – refers to whether the person generally reacts in a similar way across different situations

Second, we consider the **distinctiveness** of the person's attitude or behaviour, meaning whether the person's attitude or behaviour in this situation is highly unusual or whether the person generally reacts in a similar way across different situations. Once again, if we find out that Patricia Hearst had an interest in revolutionary movements and was a social activist before her kidnapping, then we could argue that her behaviour matched her earlier tendency (low distinctiveness). This leads us to make a dispositional attribution.

Third, we consider the consistency of the person's attitude or behaviour—i.e., whether the person's attitude and/or behaviour is similar over time. If a person's behaviour is highly consistent over time and across situations, we're likely to make a dispositional attribution. On the other hand, if a given behaviour is unusual for a particular person, we're likely to make a situational attribution. Based on Patricia's socioeconomic lifestyle, it seems reasonable to assume that if she had not been abducted she likely would not have become a member of the SLA and participated in a bank robbery. This makes her behaviour quite inconsistent with her past behaviour (i.e., low in consistency), which in turn leads us to make a situational attribution for her behaviour, and therefore conclude she isn't guilty. On the other hand, if we have reasons to believe that Patricia had tendencies to be involved in social and political activism regardless of her abduction (e.g., she was a member of a student union organization that held several demonstrations during her first year at university), then we could argue that her identification with the SLA was consistent with her past behaviour (i.e., high in consistency). This would lead us to make a dispositional attribution for her behaviour and therefore conclude that she's guilty.

In sum, according to the covariation model, we make different attributions depending on the consensus, distinctiveness, and consistency of a person's attitude and/or behaviour (Fiedler, Walther, & Nickel, 1999). If consensus and distinctiveness are low and consistency is high, we make an internal or dispositional attribution. In contrast, if consensus, distinctiveness, and consistency are all high, we make a situational attribution. Finally, in cases where a person's attitude or behaviour is low in consistency, we're unable to make any attribution, whether dispositional or situational.

WEINER'S ATTRIBUTION THEORY

Bernard Weiner developed a framework for attribution based on achievement. According to Weiner, people attribute their achievements (i.e., successes or failures) in terms of three dimensions: locus (whether the location of the cause is internal or external to the person), stability (whether the cause stays the same or can change), and controllability (whether the person can control the cause). This produces eight different types of explanation for achievement (see Table 4.1).

According to Weiner's attribution theory, people often tend to attribute their own success to internal factors (e.g., skills) and others' success to external factors (e.g., luck). Additionally, people attribute their own failure to external factors (e.g., task difficulty) and others' failure to internal factors (e.g., ability). Why do people do this? Weiner's attribution theory is based on the assumption that people want to maintain a positive self-image. People

TABLE 4.1	Causes of Success and Failure, Classified According to Locus, Stability, and Controllability			
	INTERNAL		**EXTERNAL**	
Controllability	Stable	Unstable	Stable	Unstable
Uncontrollable	Ability	Mood	Task difficulty	Luck
Controllable	Typical effort	Immediate effort	Teacher bias	Unusual help from others

Source: Weiner, 1979

therefore attribute success and failure to factors that enable them to feel good about themselves (Weiner, 1986). For example, by asserting that she chose her own course of action, and chose to stay when she had the opportunity to leave the SLA, Patty Hearst presented her membership of the group as internal (her choice) and controllable (she could have made another choice). Taking part in the subsequent bank raid enabled her to feel that her behaviour was also stable.

Weiner's theory can be applied at both individual and group levels. For example, researchers from York University tested the utility of Weiner's theory in predicting helping behaviour toward victims of natural disaster (Marjanovic, Greenglass, Struthers, & Faye, 2009). According to this theory the likelihood of helping depends on the perceived locus of causality (i.e., whether or not the victim has caused the negative event) and situational controllability (i.e., whether or not the negative event could have been predicted and prevented). Across two studies it was found that attributing responsibility to the victims of natural disaster was associated with low rates of helping (Marjanovic et al., 2009).

A variation of the three-dimensional model of attribution uses the dimensions of internal/external, stable/unstable (whether the same outcome would occur again or whether this was an isolated occurrence of this outcome), and global/specific (whether the same outcome would occur in other situations or is specific to this situation only). This model was used in a theory addressing the cognitive aspect of depression, in other words, depressive thoughts (Abramson, Seligman, & Teasdale, 1978). The suggestion is that if a person habitually explains negative outcomes (i.e., bad events), using attributions that are internal (I am to blame), stable (I always mess up!), and global (I can't do anything right), then this will be associated with depression. There is some support for the idea. For example, Martin Seligman and colleagues found a greater tendency toward repeatedly internal, stable, and global attributions for negative events among depressed students than non-depressed students. The depressed students also attributed positive events to external, unstable causes. Thus, these students not only blamed themselves for bad outcomes, but also didn't credit themselves for positive events (Seligman, Abramson, Semmel, & von Baeyer, 1979). Although it presents an attractive idea that makes intuitive sense, support for the theory is mixed as it isn't clear how generalizable the theory is. Using a community sample rather than a student sample, researchers at the University of British Columbia did *not* find that a depressive attribution style, which was measured during weeks 33 and 34 of pregnancy, predicted postpartum depression a week after birth. Although the level of clinically significant depression did increase over this period, from 2 percent to 6 percent of the sample before birth, to 10 percent to 14 percent of the sample a week after giving birth, (indicating that there was some evidence of postpartum depression within the sample), the increased incidence of depression didn't appear to be connected to a depressive attribution style (Manly, McMahon, Bradley, & Davidson, 1982).

INTERGROUP ATTRIBUTION

Attribution theories are generally framed within the context of individuals (i.e., individuals making attributions about themselves or other individuals). But attributions can also be made on an intergroup basis, which is when individuals make attributions for their behaviour based on their membership in a group (i.e., their in-group) and attributions about others' behaviour based on the others being members of a different group (i.e., an outgroup, from the perspective of the person making the judgement; Deschamps, 1983; Hewstone, 1989). Stated differently, when behaviour is explained in terms of characteristics ascribed on the basis of group membership, an **intergroup attribution** is being made. One of the characteristics of intergroup attribution is **ethnocentrism**, which refers to attributing desirable characteristics to one's own group while attributing undesirable characteristics to members of outgroups (Hewstone, 1989; Hewstone & Jaspars, 1982). Intergroup attributions are essentially attributions based on stereotypes, and

intergroup attribution – making attributions about one's own and others' behaviours based on group membership

ethnocentrism – a tendency to attribute desirable characteristics to one's own group and undesirable characteristics to outgroups.

as they are often ethnocentric they are a part of the broader subject of prejudice and discrimination, which are defined in terms of making judgements about a person based on group membership rather than individual characteristics. This topic, is discussed further in the chapter on Intergroup Relations.

RESEARCH FOCUS ON GENDER
Gender Differences in Attribution

Studies suggest that people make different attributions for men than women (Swim & Sanna, 1996). In one meta-analysis (i.e., a statistical analysis of the results of numerous different studies on the same issue), researchers found that observers tend to attribute men's successes to ability and women's successes to effort. This pattern of attributions reverses in the case of failure, with observers seeing men's poor performance as caused by bad luck or low effort and women's poor performance as caused by lack of ability. Additionally, one study of elementary school children in grade 3 and students in their first years of high school revealed consistent gender differences in beliefs about the causes of both success and failure on a math exam (Stipek & Gralinski, 1991). Compared to boys, girls rated their ability lower, and also expected to do less well. Moreover, after doing well on the math test, girls were much less likely than boys to attribute this success to their ability. Similar findings have been found among university students (Campbell & Henry, 1999). When students were asked to explain their success and failure in their courses, it was found that male students attributed their success to ability more often than female students did. Although both men and women used effort as the most common explanation for their success, women used this explanation significantly more often than men did. Such gender differences also match parents' beliefs as parents tend to attribute their sons' math performance to talent and their daughters' math achievement to effort (Raty, Vanska, Kasanen, & Karkkainen, 2002). The findings reflect the tendency for women to believe that they have to put in more effort to succeed and the tendency for men to be confident in their abilities (Brannon, 2011; Campbell & Henry, 1999).

[CONCEPTS IN CONTEXT]

FOUR ATTRIBUTION THEORIES PLUS INTERGROUP ATTRIBUTION

THEORY	EXAMPLE
Heider's theory of naïve psychology	Your sister has been especially rude to you on the phone recently. Given how unusual this type of behaviour is for her, you assume she must be going through a hard time at work.
Correspondent inference theory	Your brother has decided to quit his well-paying job as a lawyer to become a poet—much to your father's dismay. But you see this decision as the right one, because clearly your brother must be choosing a career that he truly wants to pursue.
Kelley's covariation theory	Samantha is certain she's going to enjoy reading Margaret Atwood's new book. She enjoyed all of Atwood's other books, and most of her friends rave about the new one. Even her sister who doesn't like to read at all said the new book was great.
Weiner's attribution theory	Hassan received A+ in his social psychology midterm. He says he received a high grade because he is smart and he studied hard.
Intergroup attribution theory	Mozafer encourages his friends to visit Istanbul. He says tourists have a memorable time in Turkey because Turks are hospitable, friendly, and polite.

WHAT TYPES OF ERRORS DO WE MAKE IN THINKING ABOUT OTHER PEOPLE?

Think back to when you first got your driver's licence—and how well you drove. Although most teenagers have relatively high rates of risky driving (the main reason that insurance rates are so high for young drivers), research suggests that teenagers give very different explanations for their own risky driving compared to that of their friends. In one study with 70 teenagers who had newly acquired driver's licences, researchers examined the attributions they made for their own and their friends' risky driving (Harré, Brandt, & Houkamau, 2004). As predicted, teenagers were much more likely to give situational explanations ("I was in a hurry, I was late") for their own risky driving than for their friends' driving. Similarly, dispositional attributions ("He was showing off, acting cool") were much more likely to be used to explain their friends' risky driving than their own. This section will describe two common errors that people make in attributing the causes of people's behaviour: the fundamental attribution error and the actor-observer effect.

FUNDAMENTAL ATTRIBUTION ERROR

The **fundamental attribution error** or **correspondence bias** is a very common type of attribution error in Western cultures (Allison, Mackie, Muller, & Worth, 1993; Gilbert & Malone, 1995; Jones, 1979; Van Boven, Kamada, & Gilovich, 1999). Although people may use various pieces of information about the situation (e.g., choice or distinctiveness) to interpret behaviour, Canadians and others from individualistic cultures have a strong tendency to focus on the role of personal causes in explaining behaviour while ignoring situational influences.

One study of the fundamental attribution error asked students to read a speech written by a university student that was either in favour of or opposed to Fidel Castro, the former long-time communist leader of Cuba (Jones & Harris, 1967). Some of the participants were told that the student had been allowed to choose which position to take in

fundamental attribution error (or correspondence bias) – the tendency to overestimate the role of personal causes and underestimate the role of situational causes in explaining behaviour

---

FIGURE 4.2 **DOES CHOICE IMPACT USE OF THE FUNDAMENTAL ATTRIBUTION ERROR?**

Experimenters asked students to read essays that either supported or opposed Fidel Castro and were supposedly written by students who either were given a choice about which side to write about or who had no choice. Surprisingly, participants in both conditions said that the writers were expressing true opinions, even when they were told the writer had no choice about the topic.

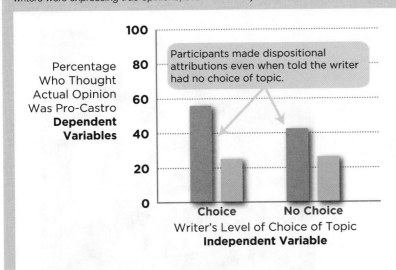

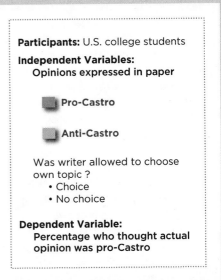

Source: Jones, E., & Harris, V. (1967). The attribution of attitudes. *Journal of Experimental Social Psychology, 3*, 1–24.

the speech. Others were told that the professor had assigned the student which position to take. As predicted, participants who were told that a student who had written a pro-Castro speech had chosen the topic were more likely to assume that the student actually liked Castro (i.e., they made a dispositional attribution) than were those who were told that the student had been assigned the topic. However, as shown in Figure 4.2, (we will examine this more later) participants still assumed that even in the assigned, no choice condition, those who took the pro-Castro side were more pro-Castro than those who took the anti-Castro side.

Why do some people make the fundamental attribution error? We believe that when people's behaviour is caused by the situation, they give obvious clues that reflect this external pressure (Lord, Scott, Pugh, & Desforges, 1997). If a person who is strongly pro-choice on the abortion issue is forced to argue the pro-life side for their high school debate team, we assume that their debate performance will be relatively weak (because they don't truly believe what they're arguing). We also believe that engaging in behaviour that is in line with attitudes is easier. So, we are particularly likely to attribute strong performance to a person's true attitude. For example, essays that are described as being in line with their writer's own attitude are seen as stronger and more persuasive than essays believed to conflict with the speaker's attitude (Gawronski, 2003a; Miller, Ashton, & Mishal, 1990). Unfortunately, and as described in the Health Connections box, the attributions we make about people's behaviour can have negative consequences.

HEALTH CONNECTIONS

The Role of Attributions in Prejudice against Obesity

Research reveals that obese people suffer a number of social and psychological consequences (or correlations). Compared to normal-weight individuals, they are rated as less likeable, have fewer dating partners, are less likely to get married, get lower grades, complete fewer years of education, earn less money, and are generally the subject of negative social attitudes (Miller et al., 1990; Ryckman, Robbins, Kaczor, & Gold, 1989). One long-term study of obese and non-obese women found that those who were obese made less money, completed fewer years of education, and were less likely to be married than their normal-weight peers (Gortmaker, Must, Perrin, Sobol, & Dietz, 1993).

Why do people who are obese experience such negative consequences? One reason is that obesity is often seen as something that is within a person's control. Obese people are seen as slow, lazy, sloppy, and lacking in willpower (Crandall, 1994). We often assume that if they wanted to lose weight, they could simply stop eating so much. In other words, we blame obese people for their weight. In one study, high school girls were shown a picture of a girl and read a short statement about her. Then they were asked to rate how much they thought they would like her (DeJong, 1980). Some of the girls saw a picture of an overweight girl, while others saw a picture of a normal-weight girl. Of those who saw the picture of the overweight girl, some were told that her weight was a result of a thyroid disorder. As predicted, participants who saw the normal-weight girl liked her more than those who saw the overweight girl. But those who saw the overweight girl and were told that she had an acceptable reason for her weight (the thyroid condition) liked her just as much as those who saw the normal-weight girl. This study suggests that it's not just the weight that makes obese people seem unattractive, but the attributions made about the causes of the weight, such as laziness.

Are obese people really different from others? No—the personality characteristics of obese and non-obese people are very similar (Poston et al., 1999).

Alamy

HOW COMPLEX ARE THE ATTRIBUTIONS YOU MAKE FOR OTHERS' BEHAVIOUR?

Attribution Complexity Scale

INSTRUCTIONS: *Rate each item on a scale of −3 (strongly disagree) to +3 (strongly agree).*

1. Once I've figured out a single cause for a person's behaviour I don't usually go any further.

2. I have found that the causes for people's behaviour are usually complex rather than simple.

3. I usually find that complicated explanations for people's behaviour are confusing rather than helpful.

4. I prefer simple rather than complex explanations for people's behaviour.

5. I don't usually bother to analyze and explain people's behaviour.

6. I don't enjoy getting into discussions where the causes for people's behaviour are being talked over.

7. I really enjoy analyzing the reasons or causes for people's behaviour.

8. I am not really curious about human behaviour.

SCORING: For items 1, 3, 4, 5, 6, and 8, give yourself the number of points equal to the rating that you assigned to the statement. Items 2 and 7 are reverse-scored, so higher scores are converted to lower numbers (and vice versa). In other words, if you rated the statement a −3, give yourself 3 points. If you rated the statement a +2, give yourself −2 points.

INTERPRETATION: This scale measures how much a person tends to think about the causes of a person's behaviour. People with higher scores tend to make internal attributions, and those with lower scores tend to make external attributions (Fletcher, Danilovics, Fernandez, Peterson, & Reeder, 1986).

"You can't blame everything on being home-schooled by bank robbers."

© P.C. Vey/ The New Yorker Collection/ www.cartoonbank.com

actor-observer effect – the tendency to see other people's behaviour as caused by dispositional factors, but see our own behaviour as caused by the situation

ACTOR-OBSERVER EFFECT

Although we have a general tendency to see people's behaviour as caused by dispositional factors, we are much less likely to see our own behaviour this way. In fact, we're very likely to focus on the role of the situation in causing our own behaviour, a phenomenon called the **actor-observer effect** (Jones & Nisbett, 1971; Krueger, Ham, & Linford, 1996; Malle & Knobe, 1997). As described at the start of this section, teenage drivers attribute their own risky driving to situational factors, such as running late. But they attribute their peers' risky driving to personal factors, such as trying to "act cool" (Harré, Brandt, & Houkamau, 2004). Similarly, in one study, both prisoners and guards were asked to rate the cause of the prisoners' offences (Saulnier & Perlman, 1981). As you might expect, prisoners tend to see their crimes as caused by the situation, whereas guards

Questioning the Research:

Do the actor-observer differences seen in the risky driving study and prisoner's study reveal true attribution differences or, alternatively, differences in self-presentation and the desire to simply appear good to the experimenter? What do you think and why? How could you test whether this effect reflects true attribution differences or simply differences in self-presentation?

tend to see these crimes as caused by dispositional factors. The following Business Connections box describes an interesting exception to this general tendency to make self-serving attributions.

BUSINESS CONNECTIONS

Why Disserving Attributions Can Be a Good Idea

Attribution theory usually describes the benefits of making internal attributions for good events (e.g., "I'm smart, which is why I did well on my French test") and external attributions for bad events (e.g., "The teacher is unfair, which is why I did poorly on my math test"). But some recent research on the types of attributions made in a business context actually shows that making disserving attributions—i.e., making internal attributions for bad events—can sometimes be a good approach (Lee, Peterson, & Tiedens, 2004). In one study, researchers examined the types of attributions contained in the corporate annual reports of 14 companies over a 21-year period. Researchers counted the number of statements that focused on the company's own role in producing a negative outcome (e.g., "The unexpected drop in earnings this year is primarily attributable to some of the strategic decisions we made last year"). Researchers also counted the number of statements that focused on external factors (e.g., "The drop in earnings this year is primarily attributable to the unexpected downturn in the domestic and international environment"). Then they examined the change in average stock price for each company one year later. Contrary to what attribution theory would generally suggest, companies that gave internal attributions for negative events reported greater increases in stock prices than those that gave external attributions. The authors suggest that because people expect organizations to be in control of their outcomes, making external attributions for failure can lead to even worse expectations.

SUPERSTOCK

ACCESS TO INTERNAL THOUGHTS AND FEELINGS.　Why does the actor-observer effect occur? One explanation is that observers can only see other people's behaviour as they don't have access to others' internal thoughts or feelings. When we consider our own behaviour as an actor, on the other hand, we obviously have access to our internal thoughts and feelings (Malle & Pearce, 2001). When you are in the midst of an important game, for example, you are likely to be highly aware of how your own nervousness is influencing your play and that you think this is an anxiety-provoking situation. Others watching you, who do not witness your thoughts about the situation being anxiety provoking, may simply think "she's nervous." Additionally, we may not know how others behave in other situations but we know how we do. In line with this view, we're less likely to make the actor-observer error with our close friends than with strangers, presumably because we have greater access to our friends' internal thoughts and feelings. We might know, for example, that they're not usually nervous in other situations, whereas we wouldn't know that of a stranger.

DESIRE TO MAINTAIN A POSITIVE SELF-IMAGE.　Motivational factors can also contribute to the actor-observer effect. As described in Chapter 3 and again in this chapter, we're highly motivated to see ourselves in positive ways. This tendency explains why women explain the success of attractive women (who presumably threaten other women's own self-concept) as due more to luck and less to ability when compared to how they explain the success of less attractive women (Försterling, Preikschas, & Agthe, 2007). We also use different explanations to describe our own and others' behaviour. For example, research with married couples demonstrates that each spouse tends to see the other as responsible for initiating a conflict (Schütz, 1999). And each spouse views his or her own behaviour as caused by the situation.

Motivational factors can also lead us to blame others for their own misfortunes, again as a way of protecting ourselves from potentially experiencing such an outcome. In fact, we tend to assume that good things happen to good people and bad things happen to bad people. This phenomenon is known as **belief in a just world** (Lerner, 1980; Lipkus, Dalbert, & Siegler, 1996). This belief is another strategy that helps maintain our idealistic self-views because it lets us see ourselves as relatively safe from harm—since surely we all see ourselves as good people (and even if we know that we've done some bad stuff, we may attribute it situationally, thereby protecting our self-image).

belief in a just world – the phenomenon in which people believe that bad things happen to bad people and that good things happen to good people

People who have a strong belief in a just world are more likely to hold negative attitudes toward poor people, and therefore see them as deserving their plight (Furnham & Gunter, 1984). One study examined the attributions given to explain poverty among people in a "developed country" (Australia) versus a "developing country" (Malawi, a small country in sub-Saharan Africa; Campbell, Carr, & MacLachlan, 2001). As predicted, Australians were much more likely than Malawians to attribute poverty to dispositional characteristics of the poor—such as laziness, lack of intelligence, and lack of ability—rather than to situational factors.

In a study conducted at Brock University with mostly female students, researchers manipulated the threat to belief in a just world by varying participants' perception of the innocence of a victim and then measuring the extent to which the victim was blamed for her situation (Hafer, Bègue, Choma, & Dempsey, 2005). All participants completed questionnaires that examined the belief that one deserves one's outcomes and the belief that outcomes are achieved by striving for long-term goals. Half of the participants were in the innocent victim condition, which was intended to create a strong threat to participants' belief in a just world. These participants heard a description about an HIV positive woman who believed she contracted the virus when a condom broke. The other half of the participants were in the non-innocent victim condition, which was intended to create a weak threat to a belief in a just world. These participants heard a description about an HIV positive woman who believed she contracted the virus when she did not use a condom. It was found that those participants who were both high on belief in deservingness of one's outcomes and high on commitment to pursuing long-term goals blamed the innocent victim more for her misfortune. This suggests that belief in a just world has more than one facet. This effect was not found when the victim was not innocent as this condition posed little threat to a belief in a just world. Under this condition the victim was considered, at least in part, responsible for her fate. The results of the study indicate that people believe in a just world because this belief allows them to commit to long-term goals that are seen as deserved. As was found in this study, the more people preserve their belief in a just world by blaming innocent victims, the more they focus on long-term and deserving goals.

Who's Who in Contemporary Canadian Social Psychology Research

Courtesy Carolyn Hafer

Carolyn Hafer is a psychology professor at Brock University. She received her PhD from the University of Western Ontario. Professor Hafer studies the social psychology of justice, particularly, the concept of the "belief in a just world." She has investigated the function of beliefs in a just world in daily life and how these beliefs influence responses to one's own misfortune. Her social justice lab is supported by several grants from the Social Sciences and Humanities Research Council of Canada. In 2004, Professor Hafer received Brock University's Chancellor's Chair Award for Research Excellence. She was President of the International Society for Justice Research from 2008–2010, and currently serves on the Executive Board as Past-President. Professor Hafer has also served on the Executive Board for the Canadian Psychological Association's Social/Personality Section, and was Associate Editor of the journal *Social Justice Research*.

COMMON ATTRIBUTION ERRORS

ERROR	EXAMPLE
Fundamental attribution error	The car behind you honks as soon as the light turns green and then speeds up and passes you. You assume this person is rude, inconsiderate, and impatient.
Actor-observer effect	You have just received a C on a chemistry test and are furious because the professor was completely unclear about what material would be covered on the exam. But when you discuss this unfair testing practice with your academic advisor, you're shocked with her advice that you should have studied the information presented in lectures as well as in the textbook.

WHY DO WE MAKE ERRORS WHEN WE THINK ABOUT OTHER PEOPLE?

Imagine that you are asked to read a brief story about a student ("Sara") who helped a professor move some heavy books and journals (Reeder, Vonk, Ronk, Ham, & Lawrence, 2004). Some participants were told that Sara helped voluntarily (e.g., she simply noticed the professor needed help). Other participants were told that Sara helped as part of her job in the psychology department. A third group of participants were told that Sara helped because she had an ulterior motive—she needed a letter of recommendation from the professor. Participants rated Sara as much more selfish, and much less helpful, in the ulterior motive condition than in the other two conditions. When an ulterior motive is provided, participants then judge her seemingly altruistic behaviour as motivated by external factors (the desire to receive a positive letter of recommendation) as opposed to internal factors. This study demonstrates one factor that influences how people make attributions for a person's behaviour: the presence of an ulterior motive. This section will describe several explanations for why people can and do err when they attribute the causes of others' behaviour, including salience, lack of cognitive capacity, belief about others' abilities, and self-knowledge.

SALIENCE

Different factors are salient (i.e., obvious) for actors and observers (Storms, 1973; Taylor & Fiske, 1975). Specifically, as the actor in an event you're very aware of the situational factors that led to your behaviour. If you're the observer of someone else's behaviour, on the other hand, what is most salient in the event is the person rather than the situation. When situational factors are salient, we're less likely to make a dispositional attribution.

In one of the earliest studies to demonstrate the power of salience on attributions, Michael Storms (1973) examined the role of salience by videotaping a conversation between two students and then having the students watch the tape from either of two perspectives. Some students watched the conversation from their own perspective (i.e., looking at the other person), and others watched it from their partner's perspective (i.e., looking at themselves; see Figure 4.3). Participants were then asked how much they attributed their own and the other person's behaviour to dispositional versus situational effects. Participants who had watched from their own perspective (i.e., they watched their partner speaking) saw their behaviour as influenced by both dispositional and situational factors. Those who watched

FIGURE 4.3 THE IMPACT OF SALIENCE ON ATTRIBUTIONS

1. Participant's conversation with another student was videotaped.

2. Participant watched one of two versions of the video, either from the perspective of the other student (making her salient) or from her own perspective.

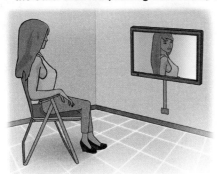

3. Participant was asked to make an attribution about the causes of his or her behaviour in the conversation.

When the participant was made salient, a dispositional attribution was more likely.

When the participant was not salient, dispositional and situational attributions were both likely.

the tape from their partner's perspective (i.e., they saw themselves speaking) saw their behaviour as caused by dispositional factors. These results show that the salience of the person influences our attributions, and that usually others are more salient to us than ourselves. Law Connections describes a real-world example of the impact of salience on attributions in the criminal justice system.

LAW CONNECTIONS

The Impact of Salience on Perceived Guilt

The tendency to attribute another person's behaviour to disposi-tional factors when that person is highly salient can have a substan-tial impact on real-life situations. Researchers in one study showed participants a videotaped police interrogation that focused in some cases on the "suspect," in other cases on the "detective," and in still other cases on both the suspect and the detective (Lassiter, Geers, Munhall, Ploutz-Snyder, & Breitenbecher, 2002; Lassiter & Irvine, 1986). As predicted, participants who watched the tape that focused only on the "suspect" were much less likely to see that person's confession as coerced than those who watched a videotape that focused on the "detective" or on both the suspect and the detective. Those who watched the videotape that focused on the suspect were also more likely to see the behaviour as caused by dispositional factors. Other research supports this view, namely that people attribute confessions to the person, not the situation (Kassin & Sukel, 1997). Moreover, simply changing the

perspective of the videotape influences jurors' verdicts, showing that an observer's perspective has substantial real-life implications (Lassiter, Geers, Handley, Weiland, & Munhall, 2002).

Spencer Grant/PhotoEdit

The role of salience in influencing the types of attributions that people make can help explain the findings from a study by Ross, Amabile, & Steinmetz (1977), who paired univer-sity students to play questioner and contestant in a simulated quiz show. Participants drew cards to choose their role, and the questioner was then given 15 minutes to come up with questions to which they knew the answers but most people did not. For example, what do the initials in W.H. Auden's name stand for? How long is the Nile River? Not surprisingly, the contestants could not answer very many of the questions. However, when questioners, contestants, and observers were asked how much general knowledge the questioners and the contestants had, only the questioners themselves seemed aware of the huge advantage of being able to come up with their own questions to ask. Questioners gave themselves and their part-ners about the same ratings of intelligence, whereas both observers and contestants rated the questioners as more intelligent than the contestants.

The researchers also found that, although participants in this study tended to see the con-testants as less bright than the questioners, contestants who missed difficult questions were seen as higher in knowledge than those who missed easy questions (Ross, et al., 1977). This effect suggests that question difficulty may be very salient for observers, and that at least in this case, they take this situational factor into account. In other words, when the challenge posed by the situation (e.g., the difficulty of the questions posed by the questioners) is highly salient, peo-ple take this external factor into account in attributing the cause of contestants' wrong answers. Question difficulty had little impact on the ratings of the questioners' general knowledge.

LACK OF COGNITIVE CAPACITY

People may initially focus on the internal factors underlying a person's behaviour, and only later adjust the weight of these factors by taking the situation into account (Gilbert & Malone, 1995; Krull, 1993). Moreover, distraction adds to people's tendency to give insufficient weight to the situation and therefore overestimate the impact of disposition. According to the **two-stage model of attribution**, we first automatically interpret another person's behaviour as caused by his or her disposition, and only later adjust our interpretation by taking into account situa-tional factors that may have contributed to the behaviour. In line with this model's predictions,

two-stage model of attribution – a model in which people first automati-cally interpret a person's behaviour as caused by dispositional factors, and then later adjust this interpretation by taking into account situational factors that may have contributed to the behaviour

FIGURE 4.4   THE TWO-STAGE MODEL OF ATTRIBUTION

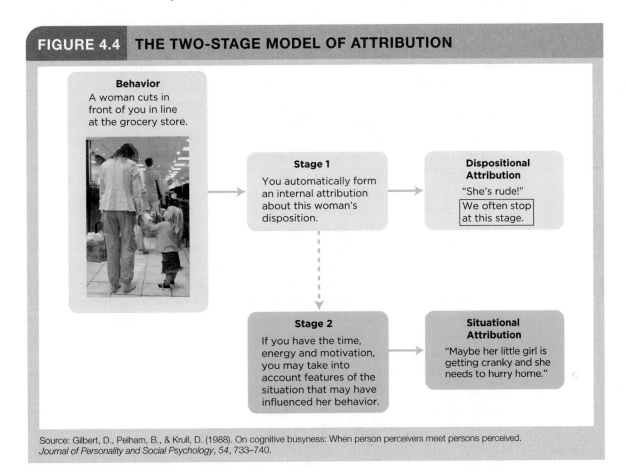

Source: Gilbert, D., Pelham, B., & Krull, D. (1988). On cognitive busyness: When person perceivers meet persons perceived. *Journal of Personality and Social Psychology, 54*, 733–740.

people who are busy or distracted when they must make an attribution are particularly likely to rely on dispositional factors and fail to take into account situational factors that may have contributed to the behaviour (Gilbert & Hixon, 1991; Gilbert & Osborne, 1989; Gilbert, Pelham, & Krull, 1988). Figure 4.4 is a schematic presentation of the two-stage model.

In one study of this model, Stephanie Tobin and Gifford Weary (2003) examined the impact of distraction on dispositional attribution that one makes. First, participants watched a video of a child who either successfully completed a series of tasks on an IQ test (in the positive comparison condition) or failed these tasks (in the negative comparison condition). Next, all participants watched a second tape of another child's performance (the main video). Some of the participants were also given an extra task to distract them while they watched the main tape. They were told to remember an eight-digit code number that appeared on the bottom of the screen just before the main video started. As predicted, participants who were not distracted showed no difference in their rating of the child's ability in the main video, regardless of which of the two comparison videos they had seen (i.e., the positive or negative comparison conditions). This is because these participants had the ability to focus on the specific performance observed in the main video. In contrast, participants who were distracted while they watched the main video rated the child's ability as greater when they saw the negative comparison video first than did participants who saw the positive comparison video first. This difference in ratings occurred because participants who were distracted (by having to remember the number throughout the experiment) used the first video as a comparison to evaluate the child's performance in the main video.

BELIEFS ABOUT OTHERS' ABILITIES AND MOTIVATIONS

The majority of research indicates that research participants tend to believe that people are unable to persuasively engage in counter-attitudinal behaviour (i.e., act in ways that go against their attitudes). There is a corresponding assumption that a person's behaviour must reflect their true attitudes, this was examined in a series of studies by Gawronski (2003b). In one study, participants were asked to imagine that a person was asked to write about a particular side of a given political topic, such as the legalization of marijuana. Participants believed that the essay would be more persuasive when the person agreed with the position instead of being against it. A second study revealed that participants were more likely to see persuasive essays as reflective of a person's true attitude (Gawronski, 2003b). This suggests that one factor that contributes to the fundamental attribution error is our erroneous belief that people simply can't effectively argue for a position they don't support.

Although our default position is to assume that people only engage in behaviour that is consistent with their true attitude, if we're given another plausible motive for a person's behaviour we're able to take situational factors into account (Fein, 1996; Fein, Hilton, & Miller, 1990; Hilton, Fein, & Miller, 1993). Providing an ulterior motive for a person's behaviour influences the attributions we make because the presence of a motive leads us to more effortful and critical thinking (Fein, 1996). In one study, participants were told that a student, Rob, had written a speech arguing in favour of or against a proposed country-wide standard stating that athletes who don't meet academic requirements will not be eligible to play on school teams (Fein et al., 1993). Some participants were told that Rob had no choice about which side to defend. Others were told that Rob was given a choice but that a professor he was working with had strongly recommended that he defend a particular side (i.e., participants were given an ulterior motive for Rob's choice). The results showed that inferring an ulterior motive actually decreased participants' bias toward making dispositional attributions for the behaviour. Specifically, students who read that Rob had no choice thought he was more in favour of the proposition when he wrote a pro speech than when he wrote a con speech. When they thought Rob had an ulterior motive, the difference disappeared, meaning they no longer believed they could tell which side he favoured. Although in this case the presence of an ulterior motive decreased participants' dispositional attributions, in other cases the presence of such a motive can actually increase such attributions—as shown in the study described at the start of this section about participants' evaluation of "Sara's" motives for helping a professor move some books.

Interestingly, we're more likely to make a dispositional attribution when we learn that a person received a positive incentive for engaging in a dishonest behaviour than when the person received a negative incentive (Greitemeyer & Weiner, 2003). In one study, participants were told that a teaching assistant agreed to add false positive teaching ratings to a faculty member's course evaluation. In some cases the faculty member offered a reward for doing so (e.g., "I will write you a strong letter of recommendation"). In other cases the faculty member threatened a punishment for refusing to do so (e.g., "I will write you a weak letter of recommendation"). Participants saw the teaching assistant as more responsible for the transgression when a positive reward was given than when a punishment was threatened. These findings suggest that people see a positive incentive as motivating only certain people (e.g., those who already have certain dispositions). A negative incentive is seen as a strong situational pressure that would influence most people's behaviour.

SELF-KNOWLEDGE

We see ourselves behaving in different ways in different situations and with different people, but we typically see other people in relatively few situations. Because we have more information about our own behaviour than we do about others' behaviour, we assume that our behaviour is more variable than do those who observe us (Kruger et al., 1996; Malle & Knobe, 1997). You may describe your own behaviour as highly influenced by situational factors (e.g., I'm shy when I'm trying to make small talk at large family parties; I'm outgoing when I'm with my friends; I'm nervous when I'm giving a class presentation), but your classmates—who see you generally only in the classroom setting—are likely to see your nervous reaction as a reflection of your disposition.

Questioning the Research:

All of the studies discussed in this section have used Western, mostly North American, university student samples. Would you expect these findings to be the same in other populations? Why or why not?

Because we have access to our own internal attitudes and beliefs, we can also give ourselves credit for having good intentions, even when we don't carry them out (Kruger & Gilovich, 2004). In one study, participants rated how much weight should be placed on a person's intentions, as opposed to behaviour, to get an accurate sense of whether a person actually possesses that trait. For example, if the trait was "thoughtfulness," participants would rate how important intentions alone were in determining whether someone was thoughtful. Participants rated each trait once for themselves, and once with another person in mind. As predicted, participants saw their own intentions to perform a given behaviour as a stronger predictor of whether they actually had this trait compared to other people's intentions. The Education Connections box describes another example of the power of the attributions we make on our behaviour.

EDUCATION CONNECTIONS

Why Focusing on Effort over Ability Is a Good Idea

Carol Dweck's (2006) research on implicit theories of intelligence reveals that the types of attributions that people make for their success and failure influence their academic motivation and performance. Some people hold a "fixed" theory of intelligence, and believe their success is based on innate ability. Others hold a "growth" or "incremental" view of intelligence, and believe their success is based on hard work and learning. People with these different mindsets show very different responses to both academic success and failure. In one study, grade 5 students completed a set of problems and were told they did very well (Mueller & Dweck, 1998). Then the children received different types of feedback attributions from the experimenter: some children were told, "You must be smart at these problems" (intelligence feedback), and others were told, "You must have worked hard at these problems" (effort feedback). On a later task, children who received praise for their intelligence showed less persistence, less enjoyment, and worse performance than children who were praised for their effort. These findings suggest that there are significant downsides to having a "fixed" theory of intelligence, including how we react to failure:

fixed-mindset individuals tend to dread failure because they see it as a negative reflection on their basic abilities, while growth mindset individuals don't mind failure as much because they realize their future performance can be improved. In turn, individuals with a growth theory may be more likely to continue working hard, even in the face of some initial setbacks.

Christina Kennedy/PhotoEdit

FINAL THOUGHTS ON ATTRIBUTION ERRORS

Although this section has focused on common errors we make in understanding people's behaviour, there is some good news . . . and some advice. First, the good news: We can overcome our tendency to make dispositional attributions when we're strongly motivated (thanks to our personality or the situation we're in) to avoid making quick and easy judgements (Webster, 1993). In fact, people do understand that the situation impacts on behaviour, and most people even believe that others make more extreme dispositional attributions—i.e., other people consider the situation even less—than they themselves do (Van Boven, White, Kamada, & Gilovich, 2003). This is similar to the self-enhancing biases described in Chapter 3—people want to see themselves as better than others.

Now, the advice: We tend to make dispositional attributions because they're quick and easy—the person's behaviour is immediately apparent although the situational factors that influenced the behaviour may be much more subtle. So it's easier to make dispositional attributions, but they're not necessarily accurate. We should therefore try to consider the role of the situation before jumping to dispositional conclusions. Is the dentist rushed and running late during your appointment? Instead of thinking she's rude and inconsiderate, perhaps you should think about situational factors that may have led to her behaviour (e.g., concern about her son who is sick at home, another patient's appointment that ran late, or an upcoming interview to hire a new dental hygienist—or all three).

[CONCEPTS IN CONTEXT]

CAUSES OF ATTRIBUTION ERRORS

ERROR	EXAMPLE
Salience	Although you feel pretty nervous during your practice job interview, you understand that this feeling is a normal reaction to the video camera taping the interview. But later on, when you watch the tape yourself, you're amazed at your very anxious appearance.
Lack of cognitive capacity	You're in the park reading the newspaper and you assume that the small child sitting alone at the playground must be shy. But after you finish your reading, you notice that some older children are building a fort in the sandbox and have excluded the small children from participating.
Beliefs about others' motivations	Jeff, a close friend of Hilary's, assumed that Hilary's newfound support of the death penalty reflected a change from her anti–death penalty views. But after he observed Hilary having a romantic late-night dinner with Bill, the head of a local pro–death penalty group, he suddenly questioned whether her attitudes had truly changed.
Self-knowledge	Luke is very nervous during the spelling bee, and he's certain that his mistake was caused by the overwhelming pressure of the large audience.

HOW DO WE FORM IMPRESSIONS OF PEOPLE BASED ON NONVERBAL BEHAVIOUR?

Imagine that you're a high school student—and that once again you've missed your curfew and must explain to your parents why you're 30 minutes late. How effectively could you lie to them about why you're late? Researchers who study social perception have examined how people detect deception. In one study, students watched a video showing a theft and then answered three questions about the video. Some were told to tell the truth about the video while others were told to lie about it (and all answers were videotaped). Researchers then coded a number of dimensions from the video, including nonverbal and verbal behaviours: smiling, gaze aversion, gestures, speech hesitations, response latency, speech rate, and speech errors. As shown in Figure 4.5, people who lied were very different in several ways from those who told the truth. The differences included rate of speech, frequency of gesturing (e.g., use of arm or hand movements to modify or supplement what they said), and use of details (e.g., sights, sounds, smells, exactly where and when the event happened, and how they felt). Clearly, both verbal and nonverbal behaviour communicate important information to others. This section will examine two distinct issues in nonverbal behaviour: the effects of communicating in nonverbal ways, and how nonverbal behaviour can aid in detecting deceptive communications.

COMMUNICATING IN NONVERBAL WAYS

We typically think of communication as involving verbal expressions. However, in many cases people communicate in nonverbal ways—including through body language, eye gaze, facial expressions, gestures, and even handshakes (Ambady & Rosenthal, 1993; Chaplin, Phillips, Brown, Clanton, & Stein, 2000; Gifford, 1991). In one study, participants watched a video of an attractive

"Say what's on your mind, Harris—the language of dance has always eluded me."

FIGURE 4.5 ARE THERE NONVERBAL CUES TO DECEPTION?

Participants watched a video and then answered questions (either lying or telling the truth) about what they had seen. Researchers then examined differences in the participants' nonverbal behaviour, including the latency period (how long it took for the participants to start talking), speech hesitations (how frequently the participants said "ah" or "uhm"), and gesturing (how frequently the participants used hand or arm gestures to illustrate what they were saying). As predicted, participants who were lying took longer to start talking, hesitated more in their speech, and used fewer gestures compared to those who were telling the truth.

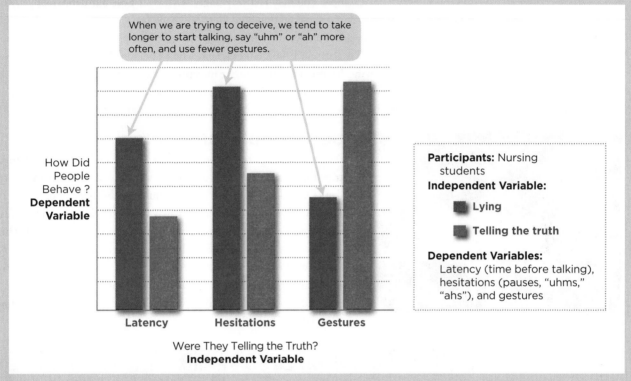

Source: Vrij, A., Edward, K., & Bull, R. (2001). Stereotypical verbal and nonverbal responses while deceiving others. *Personality and Social Psychology Bulletin, 27*, 899–909.

woman giving a speech about the value of sororities and fraternities (Marsh, Hart-O'Rourke, & Julka, 1997). In one condition, she used negative (nervous) nonverbal behaviour, including fidgeting, darting eye movements, and stroking her hair. In another condition, she used more natural nonverbal behaviour. As predicted, those who saw the negative nonverbal video rated the speaker as less likeable and less self-assured.

RESEARCH FOCUS ON NEUROSCIENCE
The Special Processing of Eye Contact

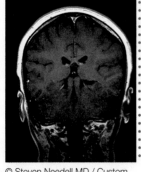

© Steven Needell MD / Custom Medical Stock Photo

The power of eye contact as a social cue is very strong. In fact, research suggests that particular parts of the brain respond to receiving eye contact. In one study participants watched a video of a person walking toward them (Pelphrey, Viola, & McCarthy, 2004). In some cases this person averts his eyes as he approaches, whereas in other conditions the person shifts his gaze toward them so that eye contact occurs. Researchers then examined the parts of the brain that were activated during each of these two conditions. Findings indicated that the mutual gaze condition led to greater activity in the superior temporal sulcus (STS) region of the brain compared to the averted gaze condition. These results suggest that different parts of the brain are involved in processing general information about faces. The STS is involved in processing the social information that is conveyed in eye gaze. The authors argued that the STS region plays a role in social perception and social cognition and is sensitive to the degree to which the action signals approach or avoidance (Pelphrey et al., 2004).

CAUSES OF ERRORS IN COMMUNICATION. Although nonverbal communication often provides important information about people's emotions, several factors can lead to lower accuracy. First, people may try to hide their emotions in order to avoid the consequences of letting others know how they're feeling (Gross, 1998; Gross & Levenson, 1993; Richards & Gross, 1999). For example, you may feel very angry with your boss but deliberately try to hide this emotion in order to avoid getting fired. Second, when facial expressions conflict with information about the situation, we interpret the emotion in line with the situation and not the expression (Carroll & Russell, 1996). For example, when a person's facial expression shows anger but he or she is in a frightening situation, we interpret the emotion as fear. Finally, people are more accurate when identifying emotions expressed by people within their own culture or by those with greater exposure to that culture (Elfenbein & Ambady, 2003).

Alamy

DETECTING DECEPTION

As shown in Figure 4.6, people often conceal or even lie about their true thoughts—and they do so on average one to two times each day (DePaulo & Kashy, 1998; DePaulo, Kashy, Kirkendol, Wyer, & Epstein, 1996). For example, they may try to hide how much they dislike someone (e.g., the boss), or they may directly misrepresent what they feel (e.g., when you tell the boss that you really don't mind staying late or working on Saturdays). And although we're often lied to, we're often unable to detect exactly when someone is lying: we're only accurate in distinguishing lies from the truth about 54 percent of the time (Bond & DePaulo, 2006).

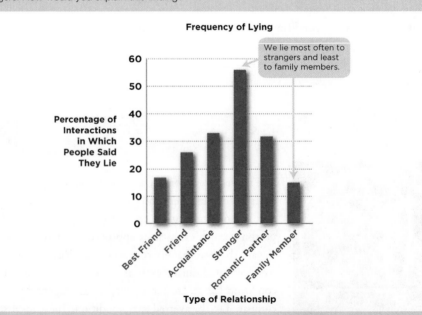

FIGURE 4.6   HOW OFTEN DO WE LIE?

We lie a lot, but more to some people than to others. In this survey, people admitted that they lie more to their romantic partners than to their best friends or family members, and they lie most often to strangers. How would you explain this finding?

Frequency of Lying

We lie most often to strangers and least to family members.

Percentage of Interactions in Which People Said They Lie

Type of Relationship

Source: DePaulo, B., & Kashy, D. (1998). Everyday lies in close and casual relationships. *Journal of Personality and Social Psychology, 74*, 63–79.

One reason why we have trouble detecting lying is that we make the fundamental attribution error, and assume that people's statements reflect their honest and trustworthy dispositions (O'Sullivan, 2003). In one study, male participants were videotaped engaging in two types of deception: one involved committing a mock crime (e.g., stealing some money) and the other involved giving a false opinion (e.g., stating a belief about the death penalty that the participant did not endorse; Frank & Ekman, 2004). When these videotapes were later shown to two groups of observers (each group saw one of the two types of deception), the proportion of people who rated the participants as truthful in one situation was correlated highly with the proportion of people who rated the same participant as truthful in the other situation. This finding suggests that some people are simply better able to appear truthful than others, perhaps because some people are better able to control their facial actions.

CUES FOR DETECTING DECEPTION.   Verbal cues can be useful for detecting deception (Ekman & Friesen, 1975). One study revealed that people who are lying make fewer references to the self (e.g., I, me, my), use more negative emotion words (e.g., hate, worthless, enemy), and use fewer "exclusive" words (e.g., but, except, without; Newman, Pennebaker, Berry, & Richards, 2003). This patterning suggests that people who are lying try to distance themselves from the lie (and hence make fewer self-references), experience greater tension and guilt (and hence use more negative emotion words), and focus their attention on creating a story (and therefore use more simplistic, and less exclusive, language).

People who are lying also describe events in shorter more general ways (e.g., "I took the bus home") than those who are telling the truth, who tend to use more intricate and elaborate descriptions (e.g., "I had planned to walk home, but then it started to rain so I decided to wait for the bus").

Nonverbal cues can also help us determine when someone is trying to deceive us (DePaulo, 1992; Frank & Ekman, 1997). People who are genuinely smiling tend to be telling the truth, but those who are putting on a false smile may be lying (Ekman & Davidson, 1997). In sum, people who are lying differ from those who are telling the truth in both the verbal and nonverbal cues they provide, but these can be relatively subtle differences and they're not consistent (i.e., some people are better at lying than others).

INDIVIDUAL DIFFERENCES IN DETECTING DECEPTION.   As well as varying in our ability to lie persuasively, we also vary in our accuracy at detecting other people's lies (Frank & Ekman, 1997). Those who are most accurate at detecting lies rely on both verbal and nonverbal cues, in contrast to most of us who rely primarily on verbal cues (see Rate Yourself).

HOW ACCURATE ARE YOU AT DETECTING DECEPTION?

Deception Detection Scale

INSTRUCTIONS: *Answer the following statements using a rating system of 1 (very uncharacteristic of me) to 9 (very characteristic of me).*

1. When people lie to me, I often catch them because their voice and eyes give them away.
2. I can usually see right through people's "acts."
3. I tend to pay attention to the appearance or behaviour of other people, from my own point of view.
4. I can figure out a lot about people just by watching them interact in social situations.
5. I like to observe and critique how others are acting in varying situations.
6. I can tell by the way a person carries him/herself whether he/she is being genuine.
7. I am alert to how other people manage their appearance.
8. I can usually tell from others' body language when they are trying to hide something from me.

[RATE YOURSELF]

SCORING: Add up your total number of points on these eight items.

INTERPRETATION: This scale measures your belief in your own ability to judge others' behaviour and determine deception. Higher scores indicate a greater belief in one's ability to detect other people's true intentions from their nonverbal communication (Sheldon, 1996).

[I WOULD YOU BELIEVE…]

UNIVERSITY STUDENTS ARE AS ACCURATE (OR INACCURATE) AS POLICE OFFICERS AT DETECTING LIES?

Who is best at detecting lies? Perhaps surprisingly, university students do as well (or rather, as poorly) as police officers, judges, and psychiatrists (Ekman & O'Sullivan, 1991; Ekman, O'Sullivan, & Frank, 1999). Interestingly, secret service agents are better at detecting lies than other people, perhaps due to their highly specialized and intensive job training, considerable experience, and interest in detecting deception. In line with this view, clinical psychologists who are particularly interested in deception (namely those who chose to attend a two-day workshop on detecting deception) showed greater accuracy than clinical psychologists without this specialized interest in deception (Ekman et al.,1999).

Questioning the Research:

Does the fact that psychologists who attended the workshop were more accurate at identifying lies mean that the workshop *led* to this accuracy? Can you think of an alternative explanation for this finding?

Finally, yet another factor that helps in detecting lying is familiarity with a person's culture, presumably because some nonverbal cues for lying are culture specific. In one study, researchers videotaped university students in the United States and Jordan telling the truth (in some cases) or lies (in other cases) about their friends (Bond, Omar, Machmoud, & Bonser, 1990). When these videotapes were shown to students in both cultures, people were better at detecting lies told by a person from their culture than lies told by someone from a different culture.

THE POWER OF FACIAL EXPRESSIONS. One of the most common and effective ways in which people communicate nonverbally is through facial expressions (Gosselin, Kirouac, & Doré, 1995; Izard, 1994; Wehrle, Kaiser, Schmidt, & Scherer, 2000). Look at the people shown in Figure 4.7 and see if you can recognize each person's emotion. People in different cultures tend to use the same facial expressions to convey a limited number of major, or basic, emotions—happiness, fear, sadness, anger, surprise, and disgust (Ekman, 1994; Russell, 1995). In one of the early studies on universally recognizable emotions, Ekman (1972) showed photographs to people from five countries (Brazil, Argentina, Chile, the United States, and Japan) and asked them to identify the emotions. The results showed a high level of agreement among participants in identifying six emotions (listed above). The researchers argued that the expressions of emotions are universal since people in these diverse cultures agreed on what emotion was being showed in the photos. Izard (1971) reported these findings with people in different cultures.

One potential limitation with the findings in the studies by Ekman (1972) and Izard (1971) was that in both cases the countries that were studied were all literate and industrialized. Perhaps the people studied in these cultures had learned how to interpret the facial expressions in the photos because of the presence of television, movies, and other forms of mass media. In response to this critique, Ekman, Sorenson, and Friesen (1969) studied two preliterate tribes of New Guinea and found results that were remarkably similar to the findings in literate societies. Tribe members were able to identify the emotions that were portrayed on the photographs, providing further evidence for the universality of emotional expression

FIGURE 4.7 FACIAL EXPRESSIONS

Tay Rees/Getty Images, Inc.

HOW NONVERBAL BEHAVIOUR INFLUENCES IMPRESSIONS

FACTOR	EXAMPLE
Communicating in Nonverbal Ways	Jerry felt pretty confident about his speech delivery during his practice at home. However, his father suggested that he try to avoid fidgeting with his hands and shuffling his feet as this makes him seem less trustworthy.
Detecting Deception	Sara really wanted to believe her boyfriend's explanation about why her birthday present was late (once again). But his vague and general description of the supposed problem and the way he expressed it somehow made her doubt his story.

and recognition. The finding that emotions are recognized across cultures suggests an evolutionary basis for this consistency, and, if this is correct, it would be logical for "important emotions" to be understood more rapidly than less important ones (e.g., anger should be recognized more quickly than happiness as it is an emotion that enables a response in a possibly dangerous situation)—which is exactly what the research shows.

HOW DOES CULTURE RELATE TO SOCIAL PERCEPTION?

Culture not only influences how people see themselves, but also how they see and make sense of the social world. Cross-cultural research shows that the tendency to attribute behaviour to dispositional factors that is commonly seen in Western cultures is much less common in other cultures. For example, in one cross-cultural study both American and Chinese students read brief accounts of two murders that received international attention (Morris & Peng, 1994). In one case, a Chinese physics student who had failed to get an academic job shot his advisor and several other people at the University of Iowa, and then killed himself. In another case, a recently fired postal worker shot his supervisor and several other people at a post office in Michigan, and then killed himself. As predicted, Americans generally blamed dispositional causes (the person was mentally imbalanced, had no grip on reality, had personality problems). The Chinese people generally blamed situational causes (e.g., America's selfish values, the media's glorification of violence, an economic recession, unhelpful supervisors). In this section, we will examine the impact of culture on the types of attributions that people make, the factors that influence these attributions, and the expression of emotion.

TYPES OF ATTRIBUTIONS

Although the fundamental attribution error is one of the most commonly described biases in the field of social psychology, and until recently was thought to describe a universal human tendency, this error is much harder to find in collectivistic cultures than in individualistic ones (Choi & Nisbett, 1998; Choi, Nisbett, & Norenzayan, 1999; Krull, Loy, Lin, Wang, Chen, & Zhao, 1999). In other words, it's not as fundamental to people as largely North American research had suggested it might be. In one study, Indian women living in Canada were asked to describe their experience of living in Canada (Moghaddam, Dittro, & Taylor, 1990). It was found that Indian women attributed both their success and failures in adjusting to life in Canada to internal causes. This finding is in contrast with research discussed above where participants from individualistic societies were more likely to attribute success to internal factors and failure to external factors.

In another study, Indian and American and participants were asked to describe the causes of positive and negative events (Miller, 1984). Americans were much more likely to rely on an actor's dispositional factors than Indians, who were much more likely to refer to situational factors influencing the actor's behaviour. For example, in explaining a situation in which a motorcycle accident occurs and the motorcycle driver (a lawyer) takes his injured passenger to the hospital but then leaves to attend to his own work, an American said, "The driver is obviously irresponsible; the driver was in a state of shock; the driver is aggressive in pursuing career success" (p. 972). An Indian, on the other hand, said, "It was the driver's duty to be in court for the client whom he's representing; secondly, the driver might have gotten nervous or confused; and thirdly, the passenger might not have looked as seriously injured as he was" (p. 972). Although both Americans and Indians described the driver's emotional state as partially at fault, the Indians were much more likely to also refer to situational factors, and Americans were more likely to refer to additional individual factors.

In sum, although people in different cultural contexts believe that dispositions do influence behaviour, people in collectivistic cultures see situations as having a more powerful impact on behaviour than do people in individualistic cultures (Choi et al., 1999). In other words, it turns out that the fundamental attribution error is not so fundamental after all. It might have been more accurately named the individualistic attribution error. However, when attribution theory and research was being developed in the 1960s and 1970s, there was no cross-cultural comparison available. The field of cross-cultural psychology only developed to the point of making substantial contributions to mainstream social psychology after the publication of Hofstede's research in the 1980s. As later chapters in this book will also show, attribution theory is not the only area of social psychology that has had to be somewhat rewritten as cross-cultural data have become available.

These cultural differences in reliance on internal attributions are found not only in laboratory studies but also in naturalistic studies that use archival data. In one study, researchers analyzed newspaper articles describing various business scandals and found that American newspapers made more references to the individual than the organization, and Japanese newspapers made more references to the organization (Menon, Morris, Chiu, & Hong, 1999). For example, in a *New York Times* article about a case of unauthorized trading, the actor was described as an "errant cowboy who attacked his work as aggressively as he hit tennis balls," whereas the Japanese newspaper wrote that "somebody should have recognized the fictitious trading since documents are checked everyday." Similarly, sports articles in Canadian newspapers and other Western societies are more likely to include dispositional attributions than such articles in Hong Kong, even when they are writing about the same sport (Lee, Hallahan, & Herzog, 1996; Markus, Uchida, Omoregie, Townsend, & Kitayama, 2006). Table 4.2 provides an example of this.

Questioning the Research:

Where do these different attribution styles come from? Do you think they reflect biological differences or what is taught in a culture, or both? How could you test these different theories?

FACTORS INFLUENCING ATTRIBUTIONS

What leads to the greater prevalence of the fundamental attribution error in individualistic cultures than in collectivistic ones? Research points to a variety of factors.

VIEW OF PERSONALITY AS CHANGEABLE.   One explanation is that in collectivistic cultures personality is seen as more changeable than in individualistic cultures. In line with this view, people from collectivistic cultures are much more likely to disagree with such statements as "Someone's personality is something about them that they can't change very much," and "A person can do things to get people to like them but they can't change their real personality," (Choi et al., 1999).

TABLE 4.2	Olympic Athletes' Attributions for Their Successful Performance
ATHLETE	**QUOTE EXPLAINING THE WIN**
Misty Hyman (American)	"I think I just stayed focused. It was time to show the world what I could do. I'm just glad I was able to do it. I knew I could beat Suzy O'Neil, deep down in my heart I believed it, and I know this whole week the doubts kept creeping in, they were with me on the blocks, but I just said, 'No, this is my night.'"
Naoko Takahsai (Japanese)	"Here is the best coach in the world, the best manager in the world, and all of the people who support me—all of these things were getting together and became a gold medal. So I think I didn't get it alone, not only by myself."

These comments are by two athletes who won Olympic gold medals in the 2000 Summer Olympics in Sidney, Australia: Misty Hyman, an American, won the women's 200-metre butterfly event, and Naoko Takahasi, from Japan, won the marathon. Although both women achieved at the highest level in their respective sport, the explanations they gave for their success differ dramatically.

Source: Markus, H., Uchida, Y., Omoregie, H., Townsend, S., & Kitayama, S. (2006). Going for the gold: Models of agency in Japanese and American contexts. *Psychological Science, 17*, 103–112.

FIGURE 4.8   HOW DOES CULTURE AFFECT FOCUS ON THE SITUATION?

What do you notice in this photo? According to research by Masuda and Nisbett (2001), Americans tend to remark on the fish, whereas Japanese people tend to remark on aspects of the background, such as the bubbles, rocks, and water.

Source: Masuda, T., & Nisbett, R. (2001). Attending holistically versus analytically: Comparing the context sensitivity of Japanese and Americans. *Journal of Personality and Social Psychology, 81*, 922–934.

STRONGER FOCUS ON THE SITUATION.   Another explanation for the greater prevalence of the fundamental attribution error in individualistic cultures is that people in collectivistic cultures pay more attention to the impact of the situation on behaviour, and therefore see more connection between events (Ji, Peng, & Nisbett, 2000; Nisbett, Peng, Choi, & Norenzayan, 2001; Norenzayan & Nisbett, 2000). A clever study by Masuda and Nisbett (2001) asked students to watch underwater scenes that included fish, plants, rocks, and sand, and then to describe what they were seeing. Japanese participants described the background and relationships between the focal fish and the background much more than Americans did. For example, they were quite likely to note that "the water was green" or "the bottom was rocky." In contrast, Americans were much more likely to describe salient objects—and were particularly likely to describe the biggest and/or fastest fish. Moreover, the Japanese students were more likely to recognize the focal object (i.e., the main fish) when it was presented with the same background than were Americans. American students were more likely to recognize the focal object than the Japanese when it was presented with no background or a novel background. This study shows the emphasis placed in these different cultures on the salient object versus the background (see Figure 4.8). In sum, collectivistic cultures engage in patterns of holistic thought—and are more attentive to relationships and context—whereas individualistic cultures engage in analytical thought and focus on themselves.

Research also shows that when people from collectivistic cultures make the fundamental attribution error, they're better able to overcome this bias than are people in individualistic cultures (Choi & Nisbett, 1998; Choi et al., 1999; Krull et al., 1999; Norenzayon & Nisbett, 2000). For example, when Choi and colleagues (1999) asked participants to read essays written by another person and rate that person's true attitude, both Americans and Koreans tended to assume that the essay reflected the person's true beliefs. However, when participants were first asked to rate an essay where the topic had been given to the essay writer by the experimenter, the Koreans were then much less likely to assume that the essay reflected the person's true beliefs, whereas the Americans' dispositional attribution didn't change. Similarly, Americans continue to make the fundamental attribution error even when the writer's lack of choice is made salient—for example, when they themselves are asked to write an essay on a topic and are given no choice, and even when the essay by the target person is almost a direct copy of the one written by the experimenter. In contrast, Korean participants make the fundamental attribution error less often when lack of choice is more salient (Norenzayan & Nisbett, 2000). In sum, Koreans are as likely as Americans to make dispositional attributions when there is no situational information, and Koreans otherwise make stronger situational attributions than Americans and are more responsive to salient situational information than Americans. Higgins and Bhatt (2001) from St. Thomas University and Camosun College, respectively, found a similar difference when they measured explanations by Indian and Canadian students for positive and negative events in the interpersonal and achievement-oriented domains. While they found that both cultural groups showed a self-serving tendency to explain negative life events with more contextual causes and to explain positive life events with more internal and controllable causes, overall, the Indian students gave more contextual causes for life events than did the Canadians.

THE IMPACT OF DISTRACTION.   Distraction also has a different impact on attribution errors in people from different cultures. As described earlier in this chapter, people tend to make more dispositional errors when they are distracted and therefore can't adjust for the situational pressure on behaviour. But is this equally true for those in collectivistic cultures? No. In one study, both American and East Asian students listened to a speech that was supposedly written by another student, who had been told by his professor to write from a particular perspective (Knowles, Morris, Chiu, & Hong, 2001). They were then asked to rate how much the speech reflected the student's true attitude. In some cases, they also had to perform a challenging computer task (hitting a particular key every time a certain letter appeared on the screen) while listening to the speech. Americans behave as expected—when they're busy, they make dispositional attributions even though the student had *no choice* about which side to write on. Students from Hong Kong, on the other hand, don't make this error, even when they're busy.

HOW DOES CULTURE INFLUENCE EXPRESSIONS OF EMOTION?

EMOTIONAL DISPLAY RULES

Although Ekman and colleagues ended the debate on the universality of emotion by demonstrating that facial expressions of emotion are universal, cultural factors do nonetheless have an influence on emotion. One difference involves **cultural display rules**, meaning the rules in a culture that govern how to express universal emotions. One of the largest studies on display rules was conducted by Matsumoto and 66 collaborators around the globe who collected data

cultural display rules – rules in a culture that govern how universal emotions should be expressed

from more than 5,000 participants in 32 countries (Matsumoto et al., 2008). While the results indicated universality in terms of expressing more emotion toward those who are closer to us (i.e., in-group members) than those who are more distant (i.e., outgroup members), cultural differences were also found. For example, it was found that participants from collectivistic cultures reported expressing more positive emotions (e.g., happiness) and fewer negative emotions (e.g., anger) toward in-group members. This is because in societies such as Japan, Malaysia, and Indonesia in-group harmony is important and while positive emotions maintain this harmony negative emotions threaten it. In contrast, participants in individualistic societies such as Canada, Denmark, and the Netherlands reported expressing more negative emotions and fewer positive emotions toward their in-group members, reflecting the lesser importance of maintaining harmony and cohesion in in-groups in these societies, which makes it more acceptable to display negative emotions.

People in individualistic cultures (e.g., Canada and Australia) are also more comfortable expressing self-reflective emotions, such as pride and guilt, than those in collectivistic cultures (e.g., Venezuela and Japan). As there is more focus on the person and individual uniqueness in individualistic societies, more value is given to the expression of self-reflective emotions. Similarly, people from collectivistic cultures show more socially engaging emotions, such as friendliness and shame, than people from individualistic cultures, who show more socially disengaging emotions, including anger and disdain (Kitayama, Mesquita, & Karasawa, 2006). This reflects the importance of harmony within groups and affiliation to a group in collectivistic cultures. Emotions that don't disturb the social connections between group members are accepted while those that are harmful are discouraged and rejected.

CHOICE OF WORDS.   Culture also influences how people talk about emotion. A study of the words that people from different cultures use when they're describing emotional events examined European Americans, Chinese Americans who were highly oriented toward American culture (e.g., born in the United States and not very proficient in Chinese), and Chinese Americans who were not oriented toward American culture (e.g., born overseas and quite proficient in Chinese; Tsai, Simeonva, & Watanabe, 2004). All participants were asked to describe their early relationships with their family, their experiences of childhood rejection, and their encounters with loss. Researchers then coded the different types of words that the participants used:

- social words (e.g., friend, mother, give, advice)
- positive emotion words (e.g., happy, good, fun)
- negative emotion words (e.g., angry, miserable, hurt)

As predicted, European Americans used fewer social words than Chinese Americans who weren't very oriented toward American culture. Chinese Americans who were oriented toward American culture used a pattern that was much more similar to that of the European Americans.

EMPHASIS ON TONE.   Finally, cross-cultural research reveals differences in people's focus on verbal content versus verbal tone. In one study, participants listened to either positive or negative words (e.g., grateful, satisfaction, pretty, sore, dislike, and anxiety) that were delivered in either a positive tone or a negative tone (Ishii, Reyes, & Kitayama, 2003). As predicted, Americans tended to focus on verbal content over verbal tone. Japanese participants showed the opposite pattern as they emphasized the tone of the delivery of the word over the word's meaning. Once again, this study provides evidence of cultural differences in the importance of different types of communication.

THE BIG PICTURE

SOCIAL PERCEPTION

This chapter included many applications of the three "big ideas" studied in social psychology. The examples below should help you see the connection between social perception and these three ideas and contribute to your understanding of the big picture of social psychology.

THEME	EXAMPLES
The social world influences how we think about ourselves.	• Prisoners see their own criminal behaviour as caused by situational factors. • People who watch a videotape of themselves engaging in a conversation see their behaviour as caused by dispositional factors. • Contestants in a quiz game give themselves lower ratings of intelligence than questioners.
The social world influences our thoughts, attitudes, and behaviour.	• We believe persuasive essays are more effective when they're written by someone who agrees with the position that the essay supports than when they're written by someone who disagrees with the position. • We see a teaching assistant as more responsible for adding false information to a teaching evaluation when he or she is given a reward for doing so rather than a punishment for refusing to do so. • People are more accurate at detecting lies that are told by a person from their own culture than lies told by a person from a different culture.
Our attitudes and behaviour shape the social world around us.	• People who are distracted when they judge a child's behaviour are more likely to make errors in attributions about the child's behaviour. • Each spouse sees the other as responsible for initiating conflict, and sees his or her own behaviour as caused by the situation. • We see people who engage in negative nonverbal behaviour as less likeable and self-assured than those who use more natural nonverbal behaviour.

WHAT YOU'VE LEARNED

This chapter has examined five key principles of social perception.

1. How we think about why other people do what they do.

We examined four theories that describe how we attribute people's attitudes and behaviour either to the person or to the situation: the theory of naïve psychology, correspondent inference theory, covariation theory, and Weiner's attribution theory. We also examined an intergroup perspective of attribution.

2. What types of errors we make in thinking about other people.

There are two distinct types of attribution errors: the fundamental attribution error and the actor-observer effect. These errors explain why prison guards focus on the dispositional causes of criminal behaviour whereas prisoners focus on situational causes—and why teenage drivers see others' risky driving as caused by their dispositions, but their own risky driving behaviour as caused by the situation.

3. Why we make errors when we think about other people.

There are several causes of attribution errors, including salience, lack of cognitive capacity, belief about others' abilities, and self-knowledge. Providing ulterior motives for good behaviour influences how people make attributions for a person's behaviour—meaning that good deeds make you seem good, unless people see this behaviour as caused by selfish motives.

4. How we form impressions of people based on nonverbal behaviour.

Nonverbal behaviour includes facial expressions, gesturing, and even handshakes. Nonverbal behaviour plays a powerful role in creating impressions and indicating deception. Some important cues for detecting lying include a faster rate of speech, more speech hesitations, and less use of detail (e.g., sights, sounds, smells, exactly where and when the event happened, and how the person felt).

5. How culture influences expressions of emotions.

The role of culture in influencing social perception includes types of attributions, factors influencing attributions, and the expression of emotion. The tendency to attribute behaviour to dispositional factors is common in individualistic cultures, but not in collectivistic ones. Finally, we saw that North Americans generally blamed dispositional causes for murder, whereas Chinese and Indian people generally blamed situational causes.

Key Terms

actor-observer effect 117
belief in a just world 119
consensus 111
consistency 111
correspondent inference theory 109
covariation theory 111

cultural display rules 135
distinctiveness 112
ethnocentrism 113
external attribution 109
fundamental attribution error/
    correspondence bias 115

internal attribution 109
intergroup attribution 113
naïve psychology 108
social perception 108
two-stage model of
    attribution 122

Questions for Review

1. Describe each of the three components of covariation theory and the three factors of correspondent inference theory, including how each of these factors impacts the attributions we make.

2. Describe the two different types of attribution errors that we make in thinking about other people, and give specific research examples of each type.

3. Describe the four distinct factors that contribute to attribution errors.

4. Describe two ways in which people communicate nonverbally, and two cues for detecting deception.

5. Describe two distinct ways in which one's culture influences the types of attributions that a person tends to make for people's behaviour, as well as two explanations for these differences.

Take Action!

1. You've just received bad news—you weren't selected for the varsity soccer team. According to attribution theory, how would you explain this disappointing event?

2. Your uncle just returned from a trip to Yellowknife and is encouraging you to take a similar trip in the very near future. You think about it but just aren't sure it's a good idea. According to covariation theory, what type of information would you need in order to make an external attribution for your uncle's enjoyment—and conclude that the trip would be right for you after all?

3. You're serving on a jury. Given your knowledge of factors that lead to attribution errors, what specific steps could you take to minimize the impact of these biases on your decision?

4. Your teenage son comes in over an hour past his curfew and claims that he ran out of gas on the way home. What are two verbal and two nonverbal cues that you could use to try to determine whether he's lying?

5. Your new colleague is from India. How might her cultural background influence both the types of attributions she makes and the way in which she expresses emotion?

RESEARCH CONNECTIONS

Participate in Research

Activity 1 Testing the Covariation Model: Kelley's covariation model describes the role of consensus, distinctiveness, and consistency in helping us understand and predict people's behaviour. Go online to test the types of attributions you make in different situations.

Activity 2 Understanding Attribution Errors: This chapter described how the attributions that we make for our behaviour are different from those we make for other people's behaviour. Go online to read several scenarios that feature either you, or another person, and rate the causes of behaviour in each situation.

Activity 3 The Impact of Distraction on Attributions: To test the impact of distractions on attribution formation, go online to watch two videos of people who are interviewing for a job and rate each person's qualifications. While watching one of the interviews, you'll have to say the alphabet backwards.

Activity 4 Judging Emotion from Facial Expressions: You've learned a lot in this chapter about the role of facial expressions and other types of nonverbal behaviour in communicating emotion. Go online to look at a series of faces and rate the emotion each person is expressing.

Activity 5 The Role of Context: To examine the impact of culture on the attributions we make, go online to briefly look at a photograph, and then list all of the items you saw in that picture.

Test a Hypothesis

One of the common findings in research on attribution theory is that people who win tend to take credit for their successes (that is, make internal attributions), whereas people who lose tend to blame their failures on external factors. To test whether this hypothesis is true, find several recent articles in a newspaper or online that summarize the previous night's sports results. Then rate the types of attributions that players make following a win versus following a loss. Do your findings support or refute the hypothesis?

Design a Study

Go online to design your own study that tests the importance of nonverbal communication. You'll be able to choose the type of study you want to conduct (self-report, observational/naturalistic, or experimental), choose your own independent and dependent variables, and form your own hypothesis. Then, you can share your findings with other students across the country!

5

CHAPTER

SOCIAL COGNITION

DID YOU EVER WONDER?

AFP/Getty Images, inc.

Few of us will ever actually compete in the Olympics, but most of us believe that if we did we'd be pretty happy just to be there, and would be even happier if we won a silver medal rather than a bronze. Some research suggests, however, that athletes who win a silver medal often react differently. In fact, in many cases the athlete who wins the bronze medal is happier than the one who wins the silver. In the 2008 Summer Olympics in Beijing, Nastia Liukin, a Russian American, narrowly beat teammate Shawn Johnson, an American artistic gymnast, for the gold medal in the All-Around. Shawn Johnson was generally viewed as the favourite, and presumably was disappointed to receive the silver. But Chinese gymnast, Yang Yilin, was clearly delighted to receive the bronze medal. Her best showing in international competition previously had been a sixth-place finish in the All-Around at the 2007 Worlds, and her teammate, Jiang Yuyuan, was widely expected to be the Chinese gymnast who was most likely to receive a medal. In this chapter, you'll find out why that is, as well as answers to the following questions:

LAW CONNECTIONS	BUSINESS CONNECTIONS	HEALTH CONNECTIONS	EDUCATION CONNECTIONS

The Power of Reconstructive Memory	The Impact of Mood on Economic Decisions	The Power of Belief	The Overwhelming Power of Teachers' Expectations

 Why do we remember an article titled "Opposites Attract" better than one titled "Researchers Examine Predictors of Attraction"?

 Why are men who "read" *Penthouse* less happy with their own dating partners?

 Why don't close relationships protect you from getting a sexually transmitted disease?

 Why can even false claims about hearing voices lead to admission to a mental hospital?

 Why do people from individualistic cultures make judgements about someone's personality much more quickly than those from collectivistic cultures?

. . . .

These questions are all answered by social psychology research findings on how we think about the social world.

WHAT YOU'LL LEARN

How cognitive shortcuts can lead to errors in thinking about the world

How presentation influences how we think about the world

How we form impressions of people

How beliefs create reality

How culture influences social cognition

PREVIEW

automatic thinking – a type of decision-making process that occurs at an unconscious or automatic level and is entirely effortless and unintentional

heuristics – mental shortcuts that are often used to form judgements and make decisions

controlled or effortful thinking – thinking that is effortful, conscious, and intentional

social cognition – how people think about the social world, and in particular how people select, interpret, and use information to make judgements about the world

Think about all the decisions you make in a typical day—what to eat, what to wear, who to see, and how to spend your time (and money). Although we naturally want to make good decisions, we're confronted almost constantly with decisions, making it truly impossible to think about and process all the relevant information in a careful and deliberative way. Instead, people often rely on **automatic thinking**, a type of decision-making process that occurs at an unconscious or automatic level and is entirely effortless and unintentional. This type of thinking relies on the use of mental shortcuts, or "rules of thumb" known as **heuristics**, which can save us time when making decisions but can also lead to inaccurate judgements. However, in some cases people can and do use a more deliberate and careful type of thinking, namely **controlled** or **effortful thinking**, which in turn can lead to more accurate judgements. We tend to use this type of thinking when we have the time and motivation necessary to make the considerable effort this type of thinking involves (Webster, Richter, & Kruglanski, 1996; Wegener & Petty, 1995). For example, when you chose which university to attend, you probably didn't make a snap judgement based on a pretty picture in a brochure. Rather, you evaluated the positive and negative features of different schools before ultimately reaching a decision. This chapter is about issues of **social cognition**, or how we think about the social world.

HOW CAN SHORTCUTS LEAD TO ERRORS IN THINKING ABOUT THE WORLD?

Imagine that as part of a psychology study you're asked to read 20 research summaries. Each of these summaries provides an article title and describes a study on the link between similarity and attraction. Sometimes, however, the findings contradict each other. Some studies describe research showing that greater similarity leads to attraction, but others find the reverse. You're then asked to carefully review all of the evidence, and form your own belief about the link between similarity and attraction. How would you determine your answer? Rationally, in making your decision, you might weigh the number of articles for and against each view and the quality of their arguments. However, participants in this actual study were heavily influenced by the titles of the articles (Bushman & Wells, 2001). Articles that had very salient titles (such as "Birds of a Feather Flock Together" and "Opposites Attract") were very influential on participants' judgements. Articles with less appealing titles ("Research Examines Similarity as a Source of Liking" and "Research Asks Who Likes Whom") were given less weight in participants' overall decision, even though the information contained in each research summary was the same (only the title changed). This study illustrates a particular type of shortcut, namely the availability heuristic, meaning the ease with which an idea comes to mind. This section will examine this and other cues that we rely on to reach decisions quickly, including intuition, availability, representativeness, the base-rate fallacy, anchoring and adjustment, and counterfactual thinking/simulation. In many instances, our use of these shortcuts can lead to errors in perceiving the world.

INTUITION

One of the most common shortcuts we use in making decisions about the world is relying on our intuition (we might call it "instinct"), instead of relying on more objective information. For example, employers often believe that they can do a better job of judging a person's future performance through interviews than they can through more objective measures, such as test scores, education, or prior experience. In fact the latter information is more reliable as it better predicts future job performance than interview ratings (Dawes, 2001). Employers (and medical schools, and universities) nonetheless have a tendency to persist in interviewing candidates because people believe so powerfully in their ability to accurately judge someone, even following only a brief interview.

intuition – a decision-making shortcut in which we rely on our instinct instead of relying on more objective information

[I WOULD YOU BELIEVE...]

DRINKING LEMONADE CAN IMPROVE DECISION-MAKING?

In one study, researchers gave participants a glass of lemonade that was sweetened either with real sugar (glucose) or Splenda® (a sugar substitute; Masicampo & Baumeister, 2008). The researchers believed that drinking actual sugar, which increases blood sugar and thereby the energy available to the brain, would lead to more careful, effortful decision-making. Participants then took part in a "consumer decision task" in which they imagined that they were searching for a new apartment, and had to choose among three options. The apartment descriptions were designed such that one apartment was clearly better than the other two choices, but making this choice required some careful thought about the relative features instead of relying on intuition. As predicted, students who drank the lemonade with real sugar were more likely to choose the "right" apartment (presumably because they were less likely to rely on quick heuristics) than those who drank the lemonade with Splenda.

Even experts don't benefit from relying on their intuition. In one study, 284 people who make their living commenting on political or economic events were contacted—the type of people who often appear on the news to predict who a political party will select as their leader, the direction of the economy, future conflicts in the Middle East, and so on (Tetlock, 2005). Philip Tetlock asked each of these people to assess the likelihood of various events occurring. Then, he rated the accuracy of each of these predictions over the next 20 years. Would you believe that these experts were quite inaccurate in their predictions—and in fact, were no more accurate at predicting future events than non-experts?

We believe that at times, however, our intuition can pay off, and particularly when it comes to multiple-choice exams, where we tend to believe that it's better to go with our first thought than to second guess ourselves. To find out whether this is a good strategy, Kruger, Wirtz, and Miller (2005) examined introductory psychology midterm exams from over 1,500 students. The researchers counted the number of times students erased an answer, and the impact of this answer change on students' final grades. Contrary to what you might believe, 51 percent of the changes were from wrong to right, whereas only 25 percent were right to wrong (and the remaining 23 percent were wrong to wrong). Given that changes from wrong to right were more frequent than right to wrong, you should probably rethink relying on your first instinct when you aren't quite sure of the answer.

AVAILABILITY

availability heuristic – a mental shortcut in which people make a judgement based on how easily they can bring something to mind

The **availability heuristic** refers to the tendency to estimate the likelihood of an event based on how easily instances of it are "available" in memory, with events that come to mind more easily being seen as more likely or prevalent (MacLeod & Campbell, 1992; Manis, Shedler, Jonides, & Nelson, 1993; Schwarz, 1998; Tversky & Kahneman, 1973, 1974). In other words, the availability heuristic means that people are more influenced by the salience of events than how often they occur. For example, do you think there are more words that start with the letter *k* than words that have *k* as the third letter? We might believe more words start with the letter *k* because it's pretty easy for us to think of these words—*king, kite, kangaroo*, etc. But this ease of recall is simply because we categorize words in our minds using the alphabet. On the other hand, it's much more difficult to count the number of words that have *k* as a third letter, even though there are many more words that have *k* as the third letter (*bike, cake, joke*) than words that start with the letter *k*.

The availability heuristic explains why people are often highly concerned about things that they really don't need to worry about, whereas they fail to worry about those things that are most likely to occur. Parents of small children often worry obsessively about very, very low probability events occurring to their children, such as abduction by strangers or rare but highly publicized illnesses such as severe acute respiratory syndrome (SARS), H5N1 (commonly called the avian flu), cholera, Lyme disease, and West Nile virus. On the other hand, they're typically less concerned about other situations or behaviours that actually pose a much greater risk to their children, such as failure to wear a helmet while bicycling, not using a seatbelt or car seat, or drowning in a bathtub or swimming pool. Statistics about the actual risks suggest we're worrying about the wrong things. Overall, the availability heuristic indicates that people are biased by information that is easy to recall, vivid, well publicized, and recent.

The availability heuristic, as with all other heuristics, involves automatic processing and uses little cognitive effort. The downside of automatic processing is that people sometimes make judgemental errors as a result of using heuristics. On the other hand, controlled cognitive processing is slower and requires some cognitive effort. The advantage of controlled cognitive processing is that it reduces errors. People engage in both types of processing depending on the importance of the decision to be made and the level of attention that is given to a decision. For example, after the explosions in Japan's nuclear power plants in March 2011, there were worldwide concerns about possible contaminated food, such as seafood, as a result of radiation. Although this fear was realistic in northeastern Japan, an area close to the power plants, it wasn't in Canada and many health agencies, including the Canadian Food Inspection Agency (CFIA), announced that Japanese products posed no risk to food in Canada (CBC News, 2011). Despite the CFIA's conclusion, it remains possible that consumers who relied on the availability heuristic at the time avoided eating Japanese food (Winnipeg Free Press, 2011). In contrast, people who engaged in controlled processing more likely made informed decisions and didn't avoid sushi at Japanese restaurants in Canada on the basis of its imagined radiation.

THE IMPACT OF PAST EXPERIENCES.   One factor that leads to use of the availability heuristic is a person's past experiences. Past experiences activate particular **schemas**, meaning mental structures that organize our knowledge about the world and influence how we interpret people and events. For example, if your cousin owns a car that is very unreliable, your schemas for that kind of car will be negative even if *Consumer Reports Canada* evaluates it as very reliable. In this case, your personal experience is more available to you, and therefore has a larger impact on your judgement than more objective information.

schemas – mental structures that organize our knowledge about the world and influence how we interpret people and events

Recent experiences are particularly likely to increase availability, which in turn influences our judgements (Bargh, Chen, & Burrows, 1996). If you've just seen a movie in which a child is kidnapped, you're more likely to then interpret ambiguous situations, such as a child fighting with an adult in a parking lot, in line with this recently activated concept. In one study, men completed a word recognition task that consisted of identifying a series of either sexist or nonsexist words about women (Rudman & Borgida, 1995). The sexist words included babe, bimbo, and playboy, whereas the nonsexist words included mother, sister, and nurturer. Next, supposedly as part of another experiment, participants then interviewed a female confederate for a job, and rated her competence. Those who had been exposed to the sexist words rated the woman as less competent than those who saw the nurturing words (4.15 versus 5.55 on a scale of 1 to 7). Therefore, even subtle factors can increase the accessibility of certain words or concepts which then influence behaviour.

Questioning the Research: Can you think of another explanation for the finding that men who are cued with sexist words then rate a woman as less competent than men who are cued with neutral words? (Hint: Is it clear that sexism is the concept that is triggered?)

As noted above, schemas influence how we interpret people and the world around us. Schemas allow us to categorize information around us in an efficient manner (Fiske & Taylor, 1991). Stereotypes are an example of schemas. For example, your stereotype of a professor might be a knowledgeable, industrious, and absent-minded person. This is your schema of a professor. There are different types of schemas. **Person schemas** are beliefs about other people, their traits, and goals (Fiske & Taylor, 1991). For example, the belief that introverts are people who are quiet, shy, and withdrawn is a person schema. You have a person schema about your best friend (e.g., generous, fun, and honest), your roommate (e.g., tidy, sensitive, and academically inclined), or about a celebrity. **Self schemas** refer to our memory, inferences, and information about ourselves (Fiske & Taylor, 1991). It has been shown that people recall behaviours that are relevant to their self schema more than behaviours that aren't (Carpenter, 1988). **Role schemas** refer to behaviours that are expected of people in particular occupations or social positions (Fiske & Taylor, 1991). For example, the role schema for musicians is that they create or play music, while for surgeons it's that they perform surgery on people. **Event schemas** refer to scripts that we have for well-known situations, and are also known simply as **scripts** (Abelson, 1981). Event schemas help us prepare for a sequence of events (Fiske & Taylor, 1991). For example, you have a script for attending a lecture, including finding a seat, taking a note pad or laptop out of your backpack, taking notes during lecture, asking questions when you need clarification, avoiding talking on your phone or texting, , and packing your belongings and leaving at the end of the lecture. These scripts enable you to expect a certain sequence of events and guide you in how to behave. Finally, **content-free schemas** are rules about processing information. So, unlike other schemas, content-free schemas are not about particular categories, but they are like logical formulation about how contents are related. For example, if A is greater than B and B is greater than C, then A must be greater than C. "Greater" is without content and could mean taller, happier, richer, or more anxious.

person schemas – beliefs about other people, their traits, and goals

self schemas – our memory, inferences, and information about ourselves

role schemas – behaviours that are expected of people in particular occupations or social positions

event schemas – scripts that people have for well-known situations which help them prepare for the expected sequence of events

content-free schemas – rules about processing information

Schemas also form the basis of a recent therapeutic development in cognitive therapy that focuses on the identification and alteration of early maladaptive schemas, defined as "self-defeating emotional and cognitive patterns that begin early in our development and repeat throughout life" (Young, Klosko, & Weishaar, 2003, p. 7). Because they begin early in life, schemas become familiar and thus comfortable. We distort our view of the events in our lives in order to maintain the validity of our schemas. Schema therapists have identified 18 common maladaptive schemas within five domains. For example, the schema labelled "self-sacrifice" is in the domain labelled "other-directedness," and is described as follows:

> Excessive focus on voluntarily meeting the needs of others in daily situations, at the expense of one's own gratification. The most common reasons are: to prevent causing pain to others; to avoid guilt from feeling selfish; or to maintain the connection with others perceived as needy. Often results from an acute sensitivity to the pain of others. Sometimes leads to a sense that one's own needs are not being adequately met and to resentment of those who are taken care of (p. 16).

THE ROLE OF UNCONSCIOUS PRIMING. This type of **priming**—meaning the process by which recent experiences increase the accessibility of a given trait or concept

priming – increase accessibility to a given concept or schema due to a prior experience (i.e., schema)—can even occur at an unconscious, or subliminal level (Bargh & Pietromonaco, 1982; Higgins, Rholes, & Jones, 1977; Zemack-Rugar, Bettman, & Fitzsimons, 2007). For example, in one study participants were exposed to words flashing subliminally that related, in one condition, to high performance (e.g., compete, win, achieve, succeed), and in the other conditions to neutral concepts (e.g., ranch, carpet, river, shampoo; Bargh, Gollwitzer, Lee-Chai, Barndollar, & Trötschel, 2001). As predicted, people who were exposed to words priming high performance later found more such words in a word-search puzzle, compared to people who had been exposed to neutral words.

Priming can influence people's physical behaviour in a variety of spheres; for example, performance of a motor task or the seeking of help in an interpersonal context. Researchers from Canada and France found that the motivation of sports science students on an unfamiliar exercise task could be influenced by subliminally priming them with words associated with autonomy and internal motivation, including *envie, volonté, liberté* (desire, willing, freedom), or with words to do with being controlled and motivated by external influences, including *contraint, obligation, devoir* (constraint, obligation, duty). Participants thought they were doing two unrelated experiments, one to do with psychology, the other with physiology. In the first, they were shown pictures and had to identify if they were the same as others shown on a computer screen (a memory task). However, before each picture appeared on the screen, a word appeared for 45 milliseconds, not long enough for participants to register having seen the word. Participants primed with autonomous motivation performed better on the subsequent exercise task, invested more effort, persisted longer during the learning period and during the free-choice period, reported more interest and enjoyment for the activity, and reported a higher level of autonomy, than did participants primed with controlled motivation (Radel, Sarrazin, & Pelletier, 2009).

A study conducted at McGill University used a similar technique to test a different type of behaviour: seeking help as a response to distress. Participants were primed with words presented subliminally on a computer screen to prompt either positive or negative interpersonal expectations. The two sets of words were *caring, helpful, supportive, accepting,* and *loving* (positive interpersonal expectations), and *critical, rejecting, nagging, hurtful,* and *distant* (negative interpersonal expectations). Participants, who were all unmarried female students, were then asked to listen to a scenario and answer a series of questions about how they would react to the situation described, one where they discover that they're accidentally pregnant. Participants primed for positive interpersonal expectations gave more reports of seeking emotional support and made less use of self-denigrating coping. Those primed for negative interpersonal expectations gave fewer reports of positive affect and of growth-oriented coping, which was measured by the endorsement of items like "I was inspired to do something creative" or "Changed or grew as a person in a good way" (Pierce & Lydon, 1998).

THE INFORMATION AVAILABLE. The amount of information we can bring to mind about a given event contributes to the availability effect (Rothman & Hardin, 1997; Schwarz et al., 1991). We often have much more information about certain outcomes than other outcomes, and we mistakenly judge the likelihood of an event occurring on the amount of information we have. For example, we often see acting as a very lucrative profession because we receive considerable information about the wealth of big movie stars, but we receive virtually no information about all of the aspiring actors who are barely making ends meet while they wait tables or park cars. Similarly, people buy lottery tickets in part due to the massive publicity the big multi-million dollar winners receive—but fail to take into account the many examples of people who repeatedly play the lottery and never win.

In one study, German researchers asked participants to recall either 12 examples of their own assertive behaviour (which was a rather challenging task) or recall just six examples of such behaviour (which was much easier; Schwarz et al., 1991). As predicted, participants who only had to recall six examples of assertive behaviour reported higher assertiveness than those who had to recall 12 examples. Why? Because participants use the ease of their recall as a guide to determine whether that trait describes them—and it is naturally much easier to recall six examples than 12. The reverse was also the case: when they were asked to think of 12 examples of themselves behaving unassertively (which is quite hard to do), participants ended up rating themselves as relatively assertive, whereas when they had to think of only six examples of behaving unassertively (which is relatively easy), they rated themselves as relatively unassertive.

In other cases, we receive incomplete information, which in turn can lead to biases in decision-making. We may receive less than complete information when we rely on friends or family members to give us information, because our loved ones tend to protect us from negative information. For example, asking your mother or your boyfriend whether your out-fit is flattering may not yield the same outcome as asking a more critical observer. Similarly, former-President George Bush was quoted by the Associated Press as saying that "the best way to get the news is from objective sources, and the most objective sources I have are people on my staff who tell me what's happening in the world" (Kinsley, 2003). His desire to receive news only from those who are most loyal, and potentially protective of him, could have led him to receive incomplete information, which in turn could have led to poor decision-making.

REPRESENTATIVENESS

The **representativeness** heuristic refers to a tendency to perceive someone or something as belonging to a particular group or category on the basis of how similar this object is to a typical object in that category. Psychologists Daniel Kahneman and Amos Tversky proposed the representativeness heuristic, arguing that people tend to make judgments about similar objects based on their salient and superficial features (Kahneman & Tversky, 1972; Tversky & Kahneman, 1974). Imagine, for example, that you're given the following description: "Steve is very shy and withdrawn, invariably helpful, but with little interest in people, or in the world of reality. A meek and tidy soul, he has a need for order and structure, and a passion for detail" (Tvesky & Kahneman, 1974, p. 1124). Is Steve an airline pilot, a librarian, or a physician? Considering that no relevant information about Steve's occupation is given, you should base your judgement on the percentage of airline pilots, librarians, and physicians that there are in society. However, this is not what participants did in Tvesky & Kahneman's study (1974). They found that people tend to ignore the probability of each of these occupations in society and instead base their judgement on how representative Steve is to the stereotype of a librarian.

representativeness – the tendency to perceive someone or something based on its similarity to a typical case

Although, in some cases, using the representativeness heuristic allows us to quickly and efficiently reach the right answer, in other cases, relying on this shortcut can lead to errors, or at least a delay in arriving at the correct answer. For example, if I ask you whether an ostrich is a bird, you might take much more time to respond than if I'd asked whether a robin is a bird. Why? Because an ostrich doesn't fit our stereotype of a bird (e.g., small, can fly, lives in a nest), but a robin does. The representativeness heuristic reflects people's cognitive error in not taking into account the probability of outcomes and being overly influenced by representativeness.

BASE-RATE FALLACY

Errors in both the availability and representativeness heuristics occur because people tend to ignore the probability of a given event, a phenomenon called the **base-rate fallacy** (Tversky & Kahneman, 1973). This fallacy explains why people are often very nervous about dying in a plane crash but they're rarely concerned about dying in a car accident. Plane crashes are highly publicized in the media and therefore much more salient and available to our minds.

base-rate fallacy – an error in which people ignore the numerical frequency, or base rate, of an event in estimating how likely it is to occur

Our reliance on the base-rate fallacy can lead us to make unwise decisions. For example, following the terrorist attack on September 11, 2001, more people in America avoided flying and chose to drive (Gigerenzer, 2004). Unfortunately, the number of people who were killed in car accidents on American roadways during the three months following September 11 was greater than the number of people killed during fatal crashes during the same three months the previous year. It's possible that a change in behaviour after the 9/11 attacks was responsible for some of those additional highway deaths, compared to the previous year.

Although most people see flying as much more dangerous than driving, more people are killed each year in car crashes than plane crashes. This illustrates the base-rate fallacy, in which people ignore the overall probabilities of an event occurring.

The Canadian Press/AP Photo/Orlando Gomez

The base-rate fallacy also explains why people make errors when they use the representativeness heuristic. For example, if you hear about a conservative man who enjoys math puzzles and prefers to spend time alone, you guess that he's an engineer, not a lawyer, because this description seems to fit the description of an engineer better than that of a lawyer. If you're then told that this description refers to a member of a large group of people, of whom 30 percent are engineers and 70 percent are lawyers, logically you should see the person as more likely to be a lawyer, simply because lawyers make up 70 percent of the sample. Even then, however, we tend to continue to see the person being described as especially likely to be an engineer simply because his description matches our image of an engineer more closely than our image of a lawyer.

ANCHORING AND ADJUSTMENT

anchoring and adjustment – a mental shortcut in which people rely on an initial starting point in making an estimate but then fail to adequately adjust from this anchor

The accessibility of information can also lead to reliance on the anchoring and adjustment heuristic, in which people rely on an initial starting point in making an estimate and then fail to adequately adjust their original decision (Mussweiler & Strack, 2000; Tversky & Kahneman, 1974). It has been found that people even fail to sufficiently adjust when the initial anchor is obviously wrong. In one study, some students were asked whether Mahatma Gandhi died before or after age 140, and other students were asked if he died before or after age 9 (Strack & Mussweiler, 1997). All students were then asked how old Gandhi was when he died. Those who had been asked the first question—with the anchor of 140—guessed on average that he was 67 years old when he died. Those who had been asked the second question—with the anchor of 9—guessed on average that he was 50 when he died. (Gandhi was 78 years old at the time of his death.)

In some cases, it makes sense to rely on the initial anchor. For example, when buying a house, the asking price (the initial anchor) is probably very relevant because it is based on a realistic appraisal of the selling prices of similar homes. However, people rely on anchors to make their judgements even when the anchor should clearly have no impact on their decision. In a classic study, researchers spun a large wheel of fortune and asked people to evaluate whether the number on which the wheel stopped was higher or lower than the percentage of African countries that belonged to the United Nations (Tversky & Kahneman, 1974). In spite of the obvious irrelevance of the anchor, people gave a higher estimate when the wheel stopped on a high number than when it stopped on a low number.

In some cases, people's tendency to use anchoring can be used in beneficial ways. In a recent study, Janiszewski & Uy (2008) demonstrated that home sellers get higher prices when they provide a precise number (such as $252,500) than a rounded number (such as $250,000). Why could the nature of the anchor in this case influence the final price of such an important purchase? The authors propose that when people are bidding on something that costs a round number (such as $20.00), they think in terms of dollars (and then whether this object is actually worth $19 or $18 or $21). But a more precise number leads people to think in smaller denominations. Thus, if something is priced at $19.85, we think whether it is worth $19.90 or $19.75. The final price for the object therefore tends to be closer to the initial price when a precise anchor has been given as opposed to a more rounded anchor.

COUNTERFACTUAL THINKING/SIMULATION

Accessibility cues not only influence our judgements and decisions about the world, but also our reactions to various events. The term **counterfactual thinking** refers to the tendency to imagine alternative outcomes to various events, which in turn can influence how people experience both positive and negative events (Davis, Lehman, Wortman, Silver, & Thompson, 1995; Davis, Lehman, Silver, Wortman, & Ellard, 1996; Medvec & Savitsky, 1997; Sanna & Turley, 1996). The amount of delight or regret you feel depends on how easily you can imagine a different outcome. When it's easy to imagine a different outcome, you experience a stronger emotional reaction to the outcome. Recall the study of Olympic athletes discussed at the beginning of this chapter that found a tendency for bronze medal winners to be happier than silver medalists. This is because the silver medalists can easily imagine a different but better outcome and regret the actual outcome, whereas bronze medalists are happier because they nearly won no medal at all. Similarly, imagine that you're taking a psychology class and are very close to receiving a 90, but you ultimately end up with an 89. You'll probably be disappointed because you can so easily imagine circumstances that would have led you to get a 90 (answering one more question correctly on the final exam, working a little harder on your term paper, and so on). On the other hand, if you're taking the class and expect to receive a mark in the 80s, you'll probably be perfectly satisfied with an 87. You would be even more satisfied than those who received an 89 and were so close to receiving a 90 (see Figure 5.1).

counterfactual thinking – the tendency to imagine alternative outcomes to various events

The use of counterfactual thinking explains why people who feel that they could have "undone" a negative event (e.g., a devastating injury, the death of a loved one) experience more distress (Davis et al., 1995; Davis et al., 1996). This is why we often feel much worse for people who die but "really shouldn't have"—such as the person who was supposed to fly on a later flight but got to the airport early and hence took the flight that crashed. As Tom Barbash (2003) writes in *On Top of the World* about employees of Cantor Fitzgerald, a firm that occupied the very top floors of the North Tower of the World Trade Center at the time of the 9/11

FIGURE 5.1 HOW DOES COUNTERFACTUAL THINKING IMPACT GRADE SATISFACTION?

In this experiment, researchers examined the role of counterfactual thinking—the ability to easily imagine another outcome—on university students' satisfaction with their grades in a psychology class. As predicted, students who received an 87 felt happier with their grades than those who earned a higher grade of 89 but narrowly missed getting a 90.

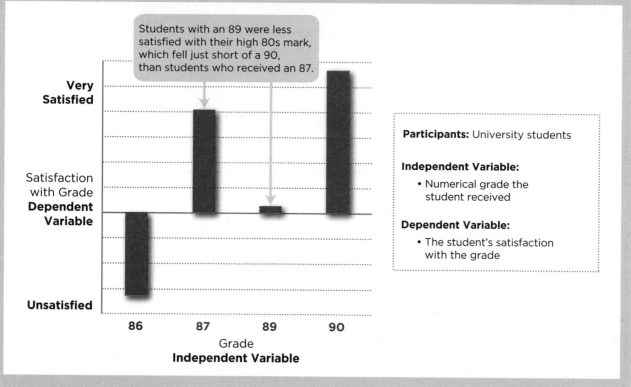

Source: Medvec, V., & Savitsky, K. (1997). When doing better means feeling worse: The effects of categorical cutoff points on counterfactual thinking and satisfaction. *Journal of Personality and Social Psychology, 72,* 1284–1296. Reprinted by permission of American Psychological Association.

terrorist attacks, those who survived the attacks often felt particularly strong guilt about their more than 600 colleagues who were killed. One executive intended to send his secretary down to the lobby to welcome a visitor, but at the last minute decided to go himself because his secretary was $7\frac{1}{2}$ months pregnant and he didn't want her to have to make the long trip down in the elevator. He made the trip to the lobby just as the plane hit the building. He lived; his secretary died. Another survivor recalls, "If it hadn't been a nice day, if I hadn't decided to walk, if I hadn't taken that particular route, or stopped to give someone directions, or if I'd taken a different elevator bank. I easily could have been in their circumstances" (p. 201). The problems associated with counterfactual thinking—and its enhancement of grief—even led to a change in the procedures used in the Israeli army. Due to the tremendous guilt soldiers felt if they traded shifts with another person who was then killed, Israeli soldiers are no longer allowed to trade shifts with each other.

FACTORS INFLUENCING THE USE OF COUNTERFACTUAL THINKING. The desire to avoid the regret caused by counterfactual thinking can also influence our behaviour, and in fact, make us less likely to act at all (Tykocinski, Pittman, & Tuttle, 1995; Tykocinski & Pittman, 1998). Imagine that a friend calls to tell you about a great new price for a concert you really want to see—a ticket typically costs $100, but if you buy it this week you'll pay only $40.

Although you intend to buy the ticket, you forget to do so for two weeks. You then learn that the special price has ended and the ticket now costs $90 (still a savings of $10, but certainly not as good a deal as the $60 savings you passed up). Students in the control condition were only asked how likely they would be to buy a concert ticket for $90 that was initially $100. They gave a rating of 6.36 (on a scale of 1 to 9, where 1 = very unlikely and 9 = very likely). Participants who were aware of having missed out on the even better deal gave a rating of 4.94. In other words, those who missed out on the great deal were much less interested in buying the ticket than those who had never heard about that deal. This is in part because they're concerned that they'll continue to be reminded of the higher cost they're paying and will therefore experience ongoing regret.

Neil Roese and James Olson from the University of Western Ontario found that self-esteem influences our use of counterfactual thinking (Roese & Olson, 1993). Participants read scenarios in which they worked with another student on a project over a three-week period. A sequence of four events was described: two events concerning the participant and two concerning the other student, with, in each case, one of the two events describing a positive contribution to the project (e.g., learning a program that was useful or finding a useful summary chapter) and the other event describing a hindrance (e.g., either family problems or exams for another course preventing a contribution). The series of events ended with either a good outcome (a high mark) or a negative outcome (a low mark). Participants then had the opportunity to imagine things that could have happened to alter the outcome (i.e., they were asked to engage in counterfactual thinking). Previous research has shown that people's counterfactual mutations (i.e., the changes that they imagine) reflect their perceptions of the cause of the actual outcome (Wells & Gavanski, 1989). When, following a successful outcome, the individual's counterfactual scenario involves a change in the individual's actions, the implication is that the individual feels responsible for the success, whereas mutating the actions of another person following success implies that this other is viewed as having been responsible for the success. Roese & Olson (1993) found that people with high self-esteem were more likely to engage in counterfactual thinking in the successful outcome scenario and could suggest more alternative actions for themselves. In other words, the people who feel good about themselves have their perception confirmed by a good outcome and find it relatively easy to exaggerate their perception of their own part in the good outcome. There was a corresponding effect for people with low self-esteem: they found it easier to generate alternative actions for themselves under conditions of failure, illustrating their perception of their own blameworthiness and confirming their low perception of themselves. As we saw earlier, this is the kind of processing that schema therapy addresses (Young et al., 2003): people can distort their perception of events to correspond with their already-held schemas, in this case either positive or negative self-related schemas.

THE BENEFITS OF COUNTERFACTUAL THINKING. This section has focused on the negative aspects of counterfactual thinking—particularly its association with regret. But counterfactual thinking can also have positive effects (Nasco & Marsh, 1999; Roese, 1994). People can use counterfactual thinking to make themselves feel better when they have narrowly missed experiencing a negative outcome. If your last-minute decision to participate in a research study for extra credit meant that you received an A− in the course instead of a B+, you might be motivated to take advantage of extra-credit points in a more timely fashion in the future. Counterfactual thinking can also serve to motivate future behaviour in a constructive and positive way when a better outcome was narrowly missed. If you narrowly missed an A− in a class, you may feel some regret, but you could also remind yourself that with just a little extra effort you could achieve an A in the future. Simply asking someone to imagine how a negative event could turn out differently in the future reduces negative feelings (Boninger, Gleicher, & Strathman, 1994).

SHORTCUTS THAT CAN LEAD TO ERRORS

FACTOR	EXAMPLE
Intuition	Nasheen is selecting a group of summer interns for the computer centre. Although he has reviewed each applicant's file, he also interviews each candidate personally because he believes his intuition is the best way to choose good employees.
Availability	Pankraz refuses to let his son go on a camping trip with his Boy Scout troop (due to fear of him contracting Lyme disease from a tick). However, he typically ignores his son's failure to wear a helmet while bicycling.
Representativeness	When the kids were picking teams, Kasimir picked the new kid, Enzo, because he was big and he looked as if he could look after himself on the ice. He ignored the fact that Enzo had just come from Italy and he couldn't skate.
Base-rate fallacy	Samantha is very scared of airplane travel, so she mostly travels by car. Although it takes much longer to drive long distances, Samantha feels it's worth it given the added safety provided by car travel.
Anchoring and adjustment	When Jane is asked whether she brushes her teeth more than 10 times a week, she estimates brushing about 13 times a week. But when she is later asked whether she brushes her teeth more than 20 times a week, she estimates brushing about 17 times a week.
Counterfactual thinking	Ricardo just received his final grade in Social Psychology: a 78, which means he made the B+ cut-off, and he is thrilled. However, his roommate Rich is extremely disappointed with his own B+ grade. Given his average of 79, he just missed getting an A−.

HOW DOES PRESENTATION INFLUENCE HOW WE THINK ABOUT THE WORLD?

Imagine that you've signed up for a psychology study on "standards of aesthetic and artistic judgement." When you arrive for the study, the researcher explains that this study examines people's views about the distinction between different types of works of art (Kenrick, Gutierres, & Goldberg, 1989). The study begins and you're shown one of the following: 16 photos of highly attractive nude women from *Playboy* or *Penthouse* magazine, or 16 photos of abstract art. All participants are then told that there is "some controversy" about whether being in a stable relationship influences people's reactions to art, so it would be helpful if they would rate both their love for their current dating partner and their level of sexual attraction to their current dating partner. As you might expect, men who've just viewed nude female centrefolds from *Playboy* and *Penthouse* report feeling less love as well as less attraction for their current partner compared to those who simply view the art slides. This example describes the **contrast effect**, which is the relative difference in intensity between two stimuli and their effect on each other. This effect applies at perceptual and cognitive levels. For example, a grey box seems darker against a white background than against a black background. Similarly, a heavy object seems lighter if you lifted an even heavier object beforehand. In contrast effect, the information or target is precisely the same in different situations, but the way we perceive that information is very different depending on how it's presented (Anderson, 1975; Simpson & Ostrom, 1976). This section will examine how different types of presentation, namely the contrast effect and framing, influence how we think about the world.

contrast effect – the relative difference in intensity between two stimuli and their effect on each other

CONTRAST EFFECT

One presentation factor that can influence decision-making is the contrast effect, in which people's beliefs about one thing are influenced by what they have just seen or heard (Anderson, 1975; Simpson & Ostrom, 1976). For example, a $70 sweater may not seem like a very good deal initially, but if you learn that the sweater was reduced from $200, all of a sudden it may seem like a real bargain. It's the contrast that "seals the deal." Research even shows that people eat more when they're eating on large plates than from small plates. The same portion simply looks larger on a small plate, and we use perceived portion size as a cue that tells us when we're full (Wansink, van Ittersum, & Painter, 2006).

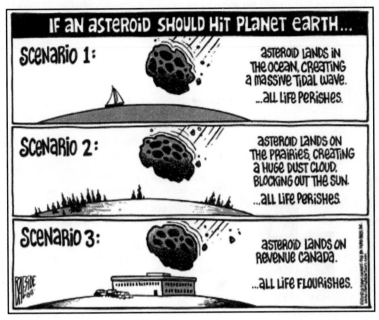

© Adrian Raeside

The contrast effect explains why media images of attractive others can influence how we judge our own and others' attractiveness. In one study, male university students who were watching TV were asked to rate a photo of a potential blind date (Kenrick & Gutierres, 1980). The students were watching either *Charlie's Angels* and its attractive female stars or another police show without attractive female stars. As predicted, those who were watching *Charlie's Angels* rated the photo as less attractive than those who were watching the other show. It has also been found that we even see ourselves as less attractive after seeing photographs of highly attractive people of the same gender as us (Brown, Novick, Lord, & Richards, 1992; Gutierres, Kenrick, & Partch, 1999).

FRAMING

The **framing** heuristic refers to the tendency to be influenced by the way an issue is *framed*—that is, how it is presented (Tversky & Kahneman, 1981). Are you more likely to use a drug with a 90 percent success rate or one with a 10 percent failure rate? These numbers both describe the same effectiveness rate, yet somehow a 90 percent success rate sounds better than a 10 percent failure rate. Similarly, students rate a medical treatment with a 50 percent success rate as more effective—and they're more likely to recommend it to members of their immediate family—than a treatment with a 50 percent failure rate (Levin, Schnittjer, Thee, 1988). Students also feel more optimistic about a person with a 90 percent chance of survival than one with a 10 percent chance of dying (Wilson, Kaplan, & Schneiderman, 1987). See Figure 5.2 for another example of how subtle differences in wording can influence people's preferences.

Framing influences how we see all sorts of daily life situations. Imagine reading a newspaper article that described a change in the unemployment rate from 9 percent to 8 percent. This story could be written in a positive way, with an emphasis on the decrease in unemployment ("We're heading in the right direction"). Alternatively, this story could be written in a negative way, with an emphasis on a continuing high rate of unemployment ("Unfortunately, unemployment rates remain high"). This type of framing influences how we interpret reality.

> **Questioning the Research:**
> Research suggests that men who see highly attractive nude centrefolds then rate their partners as less attractive. Is it likely that this brief exposure could influence long-term relationship satisfaction and attraction? Why or why not?

framing – the tendency to be influenced by the way an issue is presented

FIGURE 5.2 CAN FRAMING INFLUENCE BELIEFS ABOUT HEALTHY FOOD?

In this experiment, researchers investigated the effects of framing on participants' perceptions of the healthiness of different foods. They compared two foods, one with 5 percent of calories from fat, the other with 25 percent. Each food was described in terms of either how fat-free it was (95 percent fat-free or 75 percent fat-free) or how much fat was in the food (5 percent or 25 percent). As predicted, more participants saw the food as healthy when it was described in terms of how fat-free it was than in terms of how much fat it contained.

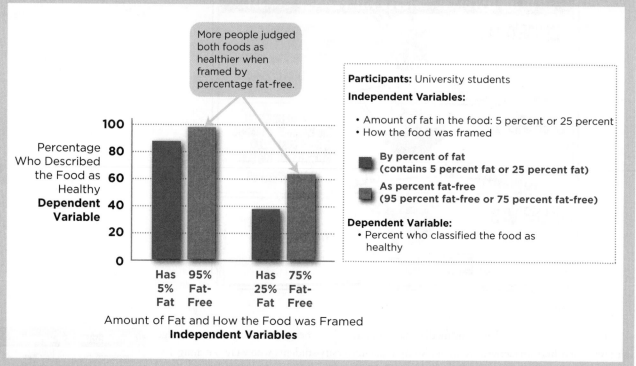

Source: Sanford, A.J., Fay, N., Stewart, A., & Moxey, L. (2002). Perspective in statements of quantity, with implications for consumer psychology. *Psychological Science*, *13*, 130–134. Used by permission.

The way health messages are framed influences how well they persuade people to engage in healthy behaviours—but in different ways for different types of behaviours (Rothman & Salovey, 1997). When the message's goal is to get people to adopt a new behaviour that will help them detect a health problem, such as cancer, framing the message negatively, meaning in terms of the costs of *not* engaging in the behaviour, is most effective. In one study, Beth Meyerowitz and Shelley Chaiken (1987) gave university women information pamphlets on breast self-examination that included either positively or negatively framed information (e.g., "Research shows that women who do breast self-examination have an increased chance of finding a tumour in the early, more treatable stage of the disease," versus "Research shows that women who do not do breast self-examination have a decreased chance of finding a tumour in the early, more treatable stage of the disease"). Women who were exposed to the negatively framed message expressed the most positive attitudes and intentions about engaging in breast self-exam and were more likely to report performing breast self-exams four months later. Similar results are found with the use of mammograms (Banks et al., 1995), amniocentesis (Marteau, 1989), skin cancer detection (Rothman, Salovey, Antone, & Keough, 1993), and HIV testing (Kalichman & Coley, 1995).

On the other hand, gain-framed messages, meaning those that emphasize the *benefits* of engaging in a behaviour, are more effective in promoting behaviour to prevent a problem from developing (Rothman & Salovey, 1997). For example, one study found that 71 percent of those who received gain-framed messages about skin cancer requested free sunscreen with an

SPF level of 15 as compared to only 46 percent of those who received the loss-framed messages (Rothman et al., 1993). Gain-framed messages are also more effective than loss-framed ones at increasing intentions to use condoms (Linville, Fischer, & Fischhoff, 1993). The Law Connections box shows another example of the power of the framing of a question.

reconstructive memory – the process by which memories of a given event are altered after the event occurred

LAW CONNECTIONS

The Power of Reconstructive Memory

The framing of a question can even influence how people remember information that they are given over time (Loftus & Palmer, 1974). The phenomenon of **reconstructive memory** describes the process in which memories of an event are altered after the event occurred. In one study, participants saw a videotape of a car accident and were then asked a series of questions about it. In one condition they were asked "How fast were the cars going when they *hit* each other?" In another condition they were asked "How fast were they going when they *contacted* each other?" In a third condition they were asked "How fast were they going when they *smashed* each other?" Although in each of the conditions participants saw the exact same video, the verb used in the question about the accident influenced their recollection of the car's speed. Those who heard "contacted" estimated a speed of only 31 miles per hour. Those who heard "hit" estimated a speed of 34 miles per hour; and those who heard "smashed" estimated a speed of 41 miles per hour. When participants were contacted a week later and asked to recall what they had seen on the video, 32 percent of those who had been asked about the accident using the word "smashed" recalled having seen broken glass, while no one in the other two groups remembered this detail. In fact, there was no broken glass in the video.

A series of studies by Elizabeth Loftus at the University of California, Irvine, demonstrates that simply asking participants to *imagine* experiencing a fictitious event can later lead them to see this experience as actually having occurred (Loftus & Pickrell, 1995). In one study, participants were asked to write a story about a time when they were lost in the mall as a child. Researchers checked with family members to confirm that this had not actually occurred, yet about 25 percent of participants later reported having actually experienced this event. Other researchers also have shown that people can be led to misremember events, including accidentally spilling a punch bowl on the parents of the bride at a wedding (Hyman, Husband, & Billings, 1995), getting their hand caught in a mousetrap as a child (Ceci, Huffman, Smith, & Loftus, 1994), and seeing Bugs Bunny at Disneyland (an impossibility since Disneyland only features Disney characters, such as Mickey Mouse; Braun, Ellis, & Loftus, 2002).

Ann Cutting/Workbook Stock/Getty Images

ERRORS CAUSED BY PRESENTATION

FACTOR	EXAMPLE
Contrast effect	Paris bought a very expensive leather jacket at her local outlet mall. Although she spent more than she intended, she reminds herself that she paid much less than the original cost listed on the price tag, so clearly she got a great deal.
Framing	Ursula prefers to order from a local restaurant as it doesn't charge for delivery and if she picks up her order, she receives a 10% discount on her bill. Ursula is less enthusiastic about another local restaurant that does not give any discount for pick up orders and charges 10% for delivery.

HOW DO WE FORM IMPRESSIONS OF PEOPLE?

Although the last section focused on factors that lead to errors in perceiving the social world, some of our most important judgements are those we make about people, which are often inaccurate. Imagine that you're asked to participate in a psychology study on "person perception," in which all you have to do is read a paragraph about a person and then rate their likelihood of having a sexually transmitted disease (STD; Conley & Collins, 2002). In some cases, the person is single and hasn't been in a serious dating relationship for a long time. In other cases, the person has been in a monogamous dating relationship for several months. However, in all cases the person described has had the exact same number of sexual partners (five) and has used condoms about half of the time. Although the relevant information (number of sexual partners and frequency of condom use) for STD risk is exactly the same in both conditions, participants overwhelmingly see the person in the relationship as less likely to have an STD than the person who is single. This example illustrates **implicit personality theory**, the theory that knowing that a person has a given trait leads us to assume that he or she also has certain other traits. This is one way in which we form impressions (sometimes wrongly) of others. This section examines factors that influence how we form impressions, including the ease of impression formation, beliefs about how traits go together, and the impact of mood.

implicit personality theory – the theory that certain traits and behaviours go together

THE EASE OF IMPRESSION FORMATION

We form impressions about other people very quickly, and based on very little information, such as their facial expression, appearance, or even a single action (Berry, 1991; Hassin & Trope, 2000). For example, try to form a mental image of a person you're going to meet for each of the following names: Jennifer, Michael, Gertrude, Sigmund. The impressions you formed likely differ greatly—because even something as subtle as a person's name can influence our expectations. Even these brief first impressions have a strong and lasting effect on our attitudes, beliefs, and behaviour. In fact, we move quickly from forming our first impressions of a person to making various inferences about what the person is like, why he or she acts in a given way, and how he or she will behave in the future. However, some people make these decisions more quickly than others (see Rate Yourself).

HOW QUICKLY DO YOU FORM IMPRESSIONS?

Need for Closure Scale

INSTRUCTIONS: *Rate each item on a scale of 1 (strongly disagree) to 6 (strongly agree).*

1. When faced with a problem, I usually see the one best solution very quickly.
2. I do not usually consult many different options before forming my own view.
3. I tend to struggle with most decisions.
4. When considering most conflict situations, I can usually see how both sides could be right.
5. When thinking about a problem, I consider as many different opinions on the issue as possible.
6. Even after I've made up my mind about something, I am always eager to consider a different opinion.
7. I always see many possible solutions to problems I face.
8. To me, success means doing better than other people.

[RATE YOURSELF]

SCORING: For items 1 and 2, give yourself the number of points equal to the rating that you assigned to the statement. Items 3, 4, 5, 6, 7, and 8 are reverse-scored, so higher scores are converted to lower numbers (and vice versa). In other words, if you rated the statement a 6, give yourself 1 point. If you rated the statement a 2, give yourself 5 points. Then sum up your total number of points on all 8 items.

INTERPRETATION: This scale measures need for closure, meaning preference for quickly reaching (and maintaining) a conclusion as well as avoiding ambiguity. People with higher scores are more decisive, whereas those with lower scores are more comfortable with ambiguity (Webster & Kruglanski, 1994).

THE POWER OF FIRST IMPRESSIONS. Because we form impressions of people so quickly, the information that we learn first has a strong influence on our overall judgement (yes, first impressions *do* matter). The **primacy** effect refers to the phenomenon of the traits that you hear about first having an influence on your interpretation of other traits (Kelley, 1950). Solomon Asch (1946) demonstrated that people see certain traits as going together. In this well-known study, participants were randomly assigned to read one of two lists of words describing a target person. The words were exactly the same in the two conditions (e.g., intelligent, skillful, industrious, determined, practical, cautious), except that in one condition the word "warm" was added to the list and in the other condition the word "cold" was added to the list. Although only a single word was different in the two lists, participants who read the list that included the word "warm" saw the person being described as happier, funnier, more good-natured, and more generous than did those who read the list that included the word "cold." Similarly, would you believe that we form different impressions when a person is described as "intelligent, industrious, impulsive, critical, stubborn, and envious" than when a person is described as "envious, stubborn, critical, impulsive, industrious, and intelligent"? This is exactly what research by Solomon Asch suggests: the first trait we hear about exerts a particularly strong impact on the impressions we form.

primacy – the tendency for information that is presented early to have a greater impact on judgements than information that is presented later

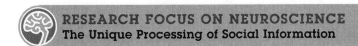

RESEARCH FOCUS ON NEUROSCIENCE
The Unique Processing of Social Information

Mitchell, Macrae, & Banaji (2004) demonstrated that different parts of the brain are used when people engage in social tasks (e.g., when forming an impression of a person) versus nonsocial tasks (e.g., remembering the order in which information about a person is given). The researchers asked 17 participants to read a series of statements about personality traits (e.g., "At the party, he was the first to start dancing on the table") and paired each of these statements with one of 18 faces. In some cases, participants were asked to form an impression of the person based on their picture and the information they read about the person. In other cases, participants were simply asked to memorize the order in which the information about a particular person was presented. Participants underwent functional magnetic resonance imaging (fMRI) scanning while performing their given task so that researchers could examine the type, and location, of brain activity that occurred in each case. The results revealed that participants used the dorsomedial prefrontal cortex (PRC) when engaging in the social task—meaning when they were asked to form an impression of a person—but used other parts of the brain (the superior frontal and parietal gyri, precentral gyrus, and the caudate) when engaging in the nonsocial task—i.e., when they were asked to simply memorize the order of the information presented. This work shows that distinct parts of the brain are used in the social cognition (i.e., neuroanatomical distinctiveness). The authors suggest that previous psychological theories may have neglected important functional differences between social and nonsocial cognitive processes in the human brain (Mitchell et al., 2004).

ACCURACY OF FIRST IMPRESSIONS. Although you might question whether first impressions could be accurate, in many cases such impressions can be remarkably right. In one of the first studies to test the accuracy of first impressions, researchers asked students to rate themselves and rate their peers around them on the first day of class, before students had had any chance to interact (Norman & Goldberg, 1966). Students' self-ratings were positively correlated with others' ratings of them, particularly on the traits of "sociable" and "responsible." More recent research supports these findings (Albright, Kenny, & Malloy; 1988; Levesque & Kenny, 1993). For example, research by Nalini Ambady reveals that even very brief (six-second) silent video clips of teachers are associated with teachers' end-of-semester evaluations from students (Ambady & Rosenthal, 1993).

In some cases, we can even make fairly accurate predictions about a person based only on seeing a picture of that person's face. In one study, participants were shown photographs of two candidates who were running for the United States Congress, and were asked to identify the face that displayed the most competence (Todorov, Mandisodza, Goren, & Hall, 2005). People's ratings of the face that was the most competent predicted the winner in the race about 70 percent of the time. Similarly, people's ratings of the power-related traits in the faces of chief executive officers (CEOs) are correlated with the company's profits (Rule & Ambady, 2008). In yet another study, participants looked at photos of men taken from online personal advertisements, and guessed whether the men were gay or straight (Rule & Ambady, 2008). Would you believe that people are 70 percent accurate in determining someone's sexual orientation just from seeing the person's photo? That's exactly what these researchers found.

THE POWER OF NEGATIVE TRAITS. The theory of primacy tells us that the first traits we encounter influence our impression more than later traits. In addition, the type of trait influences our impressions in particular ways (Coovert & Reeder, 1990; Pratto & John, 1991; Vonk, 1993). People are more strongly influenced by negative traits than they are by positive traits, a phenomenon known as **trait negativity bias**. In other words, one bad trait can destroy someone's reputation much more than one positive trait can impress people (think of baseball player Barry Bonds, for example). Trait negativity bias explains why negative information about a political candidate (e.g., inconsistent, short-tempered) has a greater effect on our impressions—and voting behaviour—than does positive information (e.g., kind, intelligent; Klein, 1991).

Why do we pay so much more attention to negative traits than positive ones? It's probably an adaptive tendency based in our evolution—we need to react to negative information, such as potential threats to our safety, faster than to positive information. If you learn that a person is likely to hurt you, this information is clearly more important to your survival than learning that a person is trying to help you. Research demonstrates that the brain reacts more strongly when evaluating negative information than when evaluating positive information (Ito, Larsen, Smith, & Cacioppo, 1998).

BELIEFS ABOUT HOW TRAITS FIT TOGETHER

When we form an overall impression of a person, we're also influenced by our general intuition or beliefs about how certain traits and behaviours go together. In doing so, we rely on implicit personality theory, which, as it was stated before, refers to our tendency to assume that if a person has a certain trait he or she also likely has certain other traits (Anderson & Sedikides, 1991; Sedikides & Anderson, 1994). For example, we often believe that highly attractive people also possess other positive traits, such as social skills, intelligence, and extraversion (Eagly, Ashmore, Makhijani, & Longo, 1991; Feingold, 1992; Langlois et al., 2000). In Chapter 14, we'll continue the discussion of implicit personality theory and how it relates to interpersonal attraction.

Implicit personality theory allows us to make judgements about the world in an efficient way, but it can also lead to some potentially dangerous errors. For example, many university students believe that people with a sexually transmitted disease must have certain other

---

trait negativity bias – the tendency for people to be more influenced by negative traits than by positive ones

Questioning the Research:

Research demonstrates that attractive people do have other positive traits, such as greater social skills and higher levels of extraversion. Do you think this association reflects correlation or causation? How could you test these two hypotheses?

personality traits and behaviours, such as blatant promiscuity, an unhealthy appearance, and many sexual partners from high-risk settings (e.g., bars in cities; Williams, Kimble, Covell, & Weiss, 1992). This is why it can be difficult to believe that someone who goes to university could have AIDS. It just doesn't fit with our beliefs about how certain traits go together. And it's one reason why many university students put themselves—and their partners—at great risk when they fail to use condoms. As described at the start of this section, people tend to see those in close relationships as less likely to have a sexually transmitted disease.

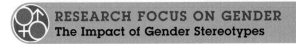

RESEARCH FOCUS ON GENDER
The Impact of Gender Stereotypes

One of the drawbacks of using shortcuts when forming impressions of people is that these shortcuts can lead us to focus on general information about a person's group or category, and to pay much less attention to specific information about the particular person. As you recall from the chapter on social perception, there is a gender difference in the attribution of success and failure. In one study, participants read information about two male and two female students at their university (Stewart, Vassar, Sanchez, & David, 2000). The information included the names of the students and several personality traits. For example, some participants read about "Kathryn, who is careless, kind, irritable, and stable." Others read an identical description of "Thomas." Then they were asked to match the names of the four students with the personality descriptions they were given. Participants with progressive attitudes toward women—meaning those who tend to agree with a statement like "Men should share in household tasks such as washing dishes and doing laundry"—made fewer errors in matching names to descriptions for female targets than for male targets. Those with more traditional attitudes toward women, on the other hand, showed the opposite tendency, and made more errors in matching names to descriptions for female targets than for male ones. These findings indicate, as predicted, that traditional men and women pay more attention to information about men and in turn are able to remember specific details about the target men described. In contrast, those with progressive values tend to focus on women's distinct features, and show greater accuracy when matching women's names and trait descriptions. The authors suggest that progressive participants were motivated to see women in more individual terms because of their belief that it's important to improve the status of women and other groups who are low in power, and because of their identification with women and feminism. Traditional participants' greater individuation of men was argued to stem from their perception of men's higher status (as confirmed by pretests) and their acceptance of the status quo (Stewart et al., 2000). Similarly, researchers from the University of Waterloo found that people who held extreme stereotypes of other groups were more likely to dismiss as atypical a person who doesn't conform to the stereotype (rather than alter their stereotype), and the more extremely the observed person deviated from the stereotype, the more likely they were to be dismissed (Kunda & Oleson, 1997)

THE IMPACT OF MOOD

Our mood exerts a strong influence on how we think about the world (Mayer & Hanson, 1995; Seta, Hayes, & Seta, 1994). People who are in a positive mood are more likely than those in a neutral mood to rely on shortcuts in thinking. Imagine that you've just learned that you've been hired for a highly desirable summer job that you had wanted for some time. You and your friend then attend a class given by a guest lecturer. Because you're already in a good mood, you're likely to see the lecturer in a particularly positive way. Our mood can even influence how we see our own behaviour (Forgas, Bower, & Krantz, 1984). In one study, researchers manipulated participants' feelings so that they were in either a good mood or a bad one. They then showed them a videotape of themselves talking to someone else (the tapes had been made the day before). As predicted, participants who were in a good mood saw themselves more positively than those who were in a bad mood. Finally, and as described in the Business Connections box, mood can even impact our decisions in substantial ways.

BUSINESS CONNECTIONS

The Impact of Mood on Economic Decisions

Mood can even have an impact on decision-making when real money is at stake. Lerner, Small, and Lowenstein (2004) first randomly assigned participants to watch one of three film clips:

- a sad clip (from *The Champ*, describing the death of a boy's mentor)
- a disgusting clip (from *Trainspotting*, showing a man diving into a filthy toilet into which he had just vomited)
- a neutral clip (from a National Geographic Special on the Great Barrier Reef)

Next, participants were randomly assigned to one of two conditions. Some were in the "sell" condition—they were given a set of highlighters and had to choose to keep the set or sell it. Other participants were in the "choice" condition—they had to choose between receiving the highlighter set or cash. Each participant was asked to rate a list of 28 choices (the amount of cash differed). The variables in the study's design—seeing either a sad movie, a disgusting movie, or a neutral movie, and being in either the "sell" condition or "choice" condition—enabled the researchers to evaluate whether mood impacts selling versus buying decisions. How did participants' mood affect their buying and selling? As predicted, mood had a dramatic impact on both types of decisions. Compared to those in the neutral condition, participants in the disgust condition had very low buying and selling prices, while those in the sadness condition had higher buying prices but lower selling prices. In sum, different emotions can have quite different—and even opposing—effects on economic decisions. What does this mean for you? Be aware that your mood can influence the economic decisions you make: the price at which you'll sell your car, how much you're willing to spend on your spring break trip, and what you'll pay for a ticket to the Stanley Cup Final.

The Canadian Press/AP Photo/Keith Srakocic

[CONCEPTS IN CONTEXT]

FACTORS THAT INFLUENCE IMPRESSION FORMATION

FACTOR	EXAMPLE
Primacy	Abraham read an article that listed several positive qualities about hybrid cars. The article talked about how hybrids are less harmful to the environment, fuel efficient, durable, cost effective, use both a gas engine and an electric battery, and some models may run gas free for their first 20 kilometres after charging. When Abraham's friend asked him what those qualities were, he could remember the first two (that hybrid cars cause less pollution and are fuel efficient) but he found it difficult to remember the qualities from the middle of the list.
Trait negativity bias	Denise's boss is considerate toward all of his employees, as well as respectful. But after Denise learned her boss was arrested for drinking and driving, she decided that he was untrustworthy and selfish.
Implicit personality theory	Given Elise's truly exceptional beauty, you're very surprised when she confides in you that she's very unhappy in her relationship with Brad. You've always assumed that people who are very attractive also have very satisfying personal relationships.

HOW DO BELIEFS CREATE REALITY?

This section will examine three distinct ways in which people's beliefs can create reality: through perceptual confirmation, belief perseverance, and self-fulfilling prophecy.

PEOPLE SEE WHAT THEY EXPECT TO SEE

One factor that leads us to create precisely the reality we expect is our tendency to see things in line with our initial expectations. Once we have a particular expectation, we interpret ambiguous events in line with our beliefs, look for information to support our view, and disregard information that contradicts it. Let's take a look at this process.

SEEING EVENTS IN LINE WITH OUR BELIEFS.   Considerable research in social psychology demonstrates that people tend to see things in line with their own beliefs and preconceptions, a phenomenon called **perceptual confirmation** (Klein & Kunda, 1992). For example, if you expect to work on a project with a person in a stigmatized group (e.g., someone suffering from schizophrenia), you're likely to see the person in a more positive way than you would if you didn't expect to work with that person. Why? Because if you believe you'll have to continue to interact with someone, you're very motivated to believe that he or she will be a good partner! This is just one example of our tendency to see what we want to see.

perceptual confirmation – the tendency for people to see things in line with their own beliefs and preconceptions

In a unique demonstration of the power of our beliefs to influence how we see the world, David Rosenhan of Stanford University and several people without mental illness (i.e., a graduate student, a painter, a housewife, and a pediatrician) went to the admissions departments of local mental hospitals (Rosenhan, 1973). They all claimed that they were hearing voices, and they were all admitted to the hospitals with a diagnosis of schizophrenia. However, once they were in the hospital as patients, they acted in a completely normal manner. How did the professional staff treat them? They continued to see them as "sick" and even interpreted their normal behaviour as symptoms of schizophrenia. For example, when one "patient" kept a journal of his experiences in the hospital, it was described as "obsessive writing behaviour" in his chart. In addition, "patients" who gathered outside the cafeteria before it opened (in a place where there was little to do) were said to be exhibiting "oral-acquisitive syndrome." In sum, once staff members believed that a given person was a patient, they interpreted the person's behaviour according to their beliefs.

The phenomenon of perceptual confirmation helps explain why people can watch the same event but see it in very different ways. If you watch a political debate or hockey game with someone who is rooting for a different person or team than you are, the bias in perception held by both of you will be evident (see Figure 5.3). People see their preferred candidate as making more intelligent points and see their favoured team as showing greater ability and morality. In fact, people feel even more supportive of their favoured political candidate after watching a debate. This suggests that such debates may do less to help candidates attract new supporters than to help their current supporters feel more positive toward them (and hence more likely to donate money and/or vote). The power of perceptual confirmation also helps explain a powerful effect in health psychology that our Health Connections box describes—the placebo effect.

HEALTH CONNECTIONS

The Power of Belief

One of the most powerful examples of the power of belief on behaviour is the placebo effect, in which physiologically inert medicines or treatments can produce very real, and even lasting, effects on physical health. The effects of placebos have been demonstrated on virtually every organ system in the body and on many diseases, including chest pain, arthritis, hay fever, headaches, ulcers, hypertension, postoperative pain, seasickness, and pain due to the common cold (Benedetti & Amanzio, 1997).

One of the most important factors predicting the effectiveness of placebos is patients' expectations about the effects of the treatment. Why? One reason is that having certain expectations about how a treatment will work leads patients to look for signs that confirm those expectations (Skelton & Pennebaker, 1982). In a recent study (Kaptchuk et al., 2010), the placebo effect was examined with patients suffering from irritable bowel syndrome (IBS). The study was a randomized, controlled three-week trial. Eighty patients were divided into two groups: one received no treatment and the other received placebo pills. Patients in the second group were instructed to take placebo pills twice a day. They were told that these pills are like sugar pills (meaning they have no active ingredients). In addition, patients in this group were told that clinical studies have shown that these pills improve IBS symptoms. This statement created an expectation among patients that they may benefit from the pills. The results indicated that the group on placebo pills showed significant improvement on their symptoms compared to the group with no treatment. The findings indicate that even when there is no deception involved in treating participants with a placebo, there are measurable physiological changes in participants' behaviour.

People's expectations about how a treatment will work can even lead to changes in their own behaviour. These changes in turn lead to some physical effect, such as the reduction of pain (Benedetti & Amanzio, 1997). If you have a bad headache and take an aspirin, which you believe will alleviate the headache, you may relax because you know the pain will soon disappear, and this relaxation will lead to a decrease in your headache.

Finally, the mere expectation of a physical change may lead to physiological changes in the body (Bandura, O'Leary, Taylor, Gauthier, & Gossard, 1987; Benedetti & Amanzio, 1997). In a study with patients who were having their wisdom teeth removed, only half were given real ultrasound therapy during their procedure (Hashish, Hai, Harvey, Feinmann, & Harris, 1988). The

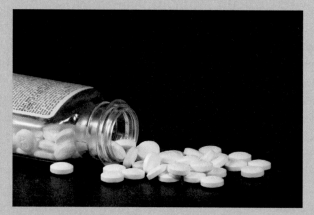
© Joe Potato Photo/iStockPhoto

others thought they were receiving this therapy but the machine was unplugged. Patients in both cases showed a decrease in pain, jaw tightness, and swelling, indicating that all these physical effects were caused simply by the expectation that they were receiving a pain-reducing therapy. This evidence suggests that the placebo effect occurs at least in part due to social-psychological principles such as perceptual confirmation and behavioural confirmation or self-fulfilling prophecy.

FIGURE 5.3   CAN OUR BELIEFS INFLUENCE WHAT WE SEE?

Researchers surveyed students who watched a roughly played football game between Princeton and Dartmouth Universities. The researchers were interested in whether perceptual confirmation would affect spectators' interpretation of the episode, meaning whether students would see the players on their team as less responsible for starting the rough play than players on the opposing team. In line with predictions, Princeton students saw Dartmouth students as much more responsible than Princeton students for starting the rough play (presumably because Princeton's star player left the game with a broken nose in the second quarter), whereas Dartmouth students saw players from both schools as starting the rough play.

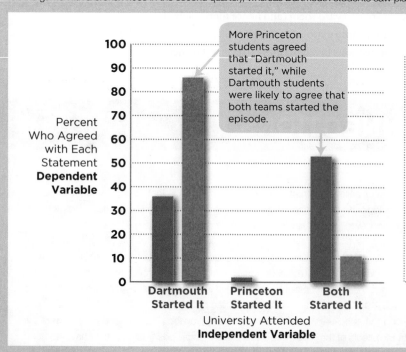

More Princeton students agreed that "Dartmouth started it," while Dartmouth students were likely to agree that both teams started the episode.

Participants: University students who watched a game between Princeton and Dartmouth at which there were many episodes of roughness

Independent Variable:
• University attended

■ Dartmouth
■ Princeton

Dependent Variable:
• Perception of which team started the rough play

Source: Hastorf, A. H., & Cantril, H. (1954). They saw a game: A case study. *Journal of Abnormal and Social Psychology, 49,* 129–134.

SEEING UNCORRELATED EVENTS AS CORRELATED. We tend to see the world in line with our expectations. This can lead us to see a correlation between two events when in reality no such association exists. This phenomenon is called **illusory correlation** (Hamilton & Gifford, 1976; McArthur, 1980). For example, people often see boy babies as more difficult than girl babies simply due to stereotypes about the correspondence between sex and personality traits.

Why do we make this error? In part, because we tend to notice events that support our belief while ignoring those that do not. For example, if you believe that bad things happen on Friday the 13th, you'll pay particular attention to such events that day and therefore "see" bad things as happening with greater frequency than normal (e.g., you stub your toe, forget to bring your homework assignment to class, have an argument with a friend). If these events happened on another day, you would be unlikely to attribute them to the calendar day.

Another factor that contributes to this error is our tendency to see two relatively rare attributes as associated, even if we have no expectation that these things should go together. This tendency has been used to explain negative stereotyping of minority groups. In one study, participants read a series of sentences that described people in either Group A or Group B (Johnson & Mullen, 1994). More of the sentences described members of Group A than Group B, and more of the sentences described positive behaviours (e.g., "Arthur, a member of Group A, carved a statue for his town's park") than negative behaviours (e.g., "Dennis, a member of Group B, hit his pet dog because he was angry"). They then were given a list of sentences without the person's name included, and had to guess whether each sentence described a person from Group A or Group B. Although the number of sentences that described positive versus negative behaviours was equivalent for those in both groups, participants were much more likely to choose negative behaviours as describing a person from Group B. This error occurs because people tend to attribute behaviour that is more rare (in this case, the negative behaviour) to members of smaller groups. In real life, for example, media often report gang violence as ethnically related, so people may think that many minority youth are gang members.

SEEING A POSITIVE OUTCOME AS MORE LIKELY. As you saw in Chapter 3 on self-perception, we have a tendency to overestimate the likelihood of positive events. We also tend to see ourselves as less likely than others to suffer bad events in the future (e.g., cancer), a phenomenon called **unrealistic optimism** (Weinstein, 1980). Unrealistic optimism is one of three positive illusions that are frequently measured within "normal" samples of people. The other two are an unrealistically positive view of the self, known as **illusory superiority** (Hoorens, 1993), and an unrealistic perception of our own control over events (Taylor & Brown, 1988, 1994). These cognitive illusions have been argued to have positive benefits in terms of mental health and health-related behaviours (Taylor & Brown, 1988; Taylor, 1991). On the other hand, the "depressive realism" construct argues that people who are depressed or dysphoric tend to be more realistic in their assessment of a situation or outcome than other people, who, because of their cognitive illusions, tend to overestimate how much control they have over matters (Taylor & Brown, 1988). Alloy and Abramson (1979) use the slogan "sadder but wiser" (p. 480) to describe this phenomenon, which other researchers have disputed (e.g., Colvin & Block, 1994). As you will see in Chapter 14 on interpersonal attraction, positive illusion has both positive and negative consequences for romantic relationships.

SEEING A GIVEN OUTCOME AS INEVITABLE. Finally, we have a tendency to see a given outcome as inevitable once we're aware of the outcome. This **hindsight bias** (also called the I-knew-it-all-along phenomenon) means that we see an event's occurrence as being completely in line with our expectations, even if we would also have seen a completely different outcome as being in line with our expectations (Hawkins & Hastie, 1990). In a study designed to demonstrate the power of the hindsight bias, students read about a dating situation that ended in one of two ways—with a marriage proposal or a rape (Carli, 1999). Although the

illusory correlation – the tendency to see a correlation between two events when in reality there is no association between them

unrealistic optimism – the tendency for people to see themselves as less likely than others to suffer bad events in the future

illusory superiority – an unrealistically positive view of the self

hindsight bias – the tendency of people to see a given outcome as having been inevitable once they know the actual outcome

story was exactly the same in the two conditions (except for the last line), people saw the ending as rather predictable in both situations, based on the details of the story (which of course were the same in both conditions). Why do people make this error? In part because they misremember details that support their argument. In other words, we fill in blanks in our memory with things that seem to make sense.

"I knew the woodpeckers were a mistake."

© Mick Stevens/ The New Yorker Collection/ www.cartoonbank.com

The hindsight bias also influences how we see many real-world events. In one study, researchers examined students' predictions about whether then-President Clinton would be convicted in his impeachment trial in 2001 (Bryant & Guilbault, 2002). As predicted, after his acquittal, students reported having believed all along that he wouldn't be convicted, even though before the announcement of his acquittal they saw conviction as rather likely. Daniel Bernstein from Kwantlen Polytechnic University and colleagues suggest that there is a connection between the errors children make as they develop a "theory of mind" and the errors made by adults in hindsight bias. They suggest that the key is faulty perspective taking (Birch & Bernstein, 2007). They found a correlation between theory of mind errors and hindsight bias in 144 preschoolers between 3 and 5 years old, independent of their age and language ability (Bernstein, Atance, Meltzoff, & Loftus, 2007).

PEOPLE MAINTAIN BELIEFS OVER TIME

Another factor that contributes to our ability to create precisely the reality we expect is our tendency to maintain our beliefs over time. We do this even when evidence suggests that these beliefs may be wrong.

belief perseverance – the tendency to maintain, and even strengthen, beliefs in the face of disconfirming evidence

EXPLAINING BELIEF PERSEVERANCE. Belief perseverance is the phenomenon in which people actively maintain and strengthen their attitudes even when they face disconfirming evidence. For example, if you believe that swimming right after you've eaten will lead to a bad cramp, you're likely to continue believing this even when evidence seems to refute it. This tendency to maintain our beliefs makes it very difficult to change a person's attitudes.

In one of the first studies to demonstrate belief perseverance, students were asked to read 25 supposed suicide notes and determine which ones were real and which ones were fake (Ross, Lepper, & Hubbard, 1975). Some of the students were led to believe that they were extremely good at distinguishing between the two types of notes (they were told that they got 24 out of 25 right, whereas most students only got 16 right). Others were led to believe that they were not very good (they were told that they got 10 right). Still others were told that they got 17 right. Then the experimenter said that all this feedback had been made up in advance because the experiment involved deception, and that actually the participants' scores had nothing to do with their answers. The experimenter went on to say that some of the notes were indeed real and that others were fake. The experimenter asked the participants how many they thought they had gotten right. Those who had been told that they got only 10 right said about 13; those who had heard that they got 17 right said 15. Those who had been told that they got 24 right said 17. This shows that even though all the participants heard that their scores were predetermined, these fake scores still influenced their assessment of their own abilities, illustrating the phenomenon of belief perseverance.

FACTORS LEADING TO BELIEF PERSEVERANCE.   Why does belief perseverance occur? First, we create causal explanations to explain the evidence. For example, students who were told that they did well may have explained their success to themselves by recalling their good intuition in other situations or the ease with which they understand people. Later, when their scores were shown to be false, they still recalled the reasons they had created to explain their success, and therefore had trouble believing that the evidence was really false.

Similarly, in another study, students read a fictitious report showing that good firefighters have either risk-seeking or cautious personalities (Anderson, Lepper, & Ross, 1980). Students then generated reasons for why this relationship might exist. For example, "You have to be willing to take risks to go into a burning building and save lives." Or "You have to be cautious so that you don't injure yourself and others by going into a burning building without really thinking of a plan." After, the students were then told that the report was fake, they persisted in believing the original (false) report and didn't realize that they could just as easily have believed the reverse if they had read the other false report. These results demonstrate that the effects of belief perseverance are particularly strong when people generate their own causal reasons as opposed to when they read explanations provided by others (Davies, 1997).

PEOPLE'S BEHAVIOUR ELICITS WHAT THEY EXPECT

We have seen that social perception involves interpreting situations or people in particular ways, sometimes based on biases. Social perception can also involve the active creation of behaviours in others based on our biases and expectations (Darley & Fazio, 1980; Hilton & Darley, 1991; Rosenthal, 1994). Specifically, **behavioural confirmation** or **self-fulfilling prophecy** refers to the process by which people's expectations about a person lead them to elicit behaviour that confirms those expectations. If you believe that the woman your brother has just started dating is rude, you may initially behave in an aloof way toward her. Then, when she acts rather distant toward you, you'll interpret her behaviour as "proof" that your initial belief was correct, and completely ignore the role that your own behaviour played in eliciting her behaviour (see Figure 5.4). The self-fulfilling prophecy is when our schema about how to act toward another person causes the person to behave in a way that is consistent with our expectations.

EXPLAINING THE PROCESS OF SELF-FULFILLING PROPHECY.   How does this process of self-fulfilling prophecy work? First, and as shown in Figure 5.4, people form expectations about what another person is like. As described at the beginning of this chapter, people form expectations about others based on even trivial and meaningless pieces of information such as a person's name, where they live, and what type of car they drive.

Second, these expectations influence how they act toward that person. We have a tendency to seek information that supports our views, which in turn can lead us to confirm these views even when the evidence doesn't support them (Snyder & Swann, 1978; Zuckerman, Knee, Hodgins, & Miyake, 1995). For example, if you're told that a new person in your dorm is introverted, you're more likely to ask questions that tend to confirm this impression (e.g., "What things do you dislike about large parties?" and "What factors make it hard for you to really

Questioning the Research:

Given the findings of this study, should we believe the standard debriefing after participating in a deceptive psychology study is effective? Is there a better approach to letting participants know they were deceived?

behavioural confirmation/self-fulfilling prophecy – the process by which people's expectations about a person lead them to elicit behaviour that confirms those expectations

FIGURE 5.4 MODEL OF A SELF-FULFILLING PROPHECY

In the cycle of behavioural confirmation or self-fulfilling prophecy, people's initial expectations about a target person actually elicit the behaviour they expect.

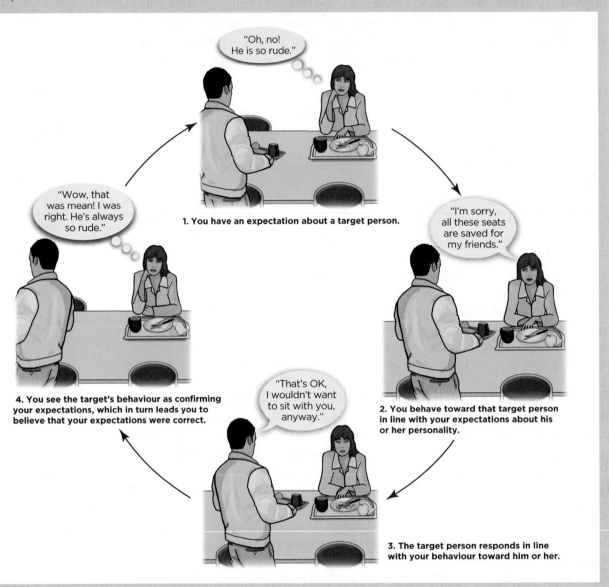

open up to people?"). On the other hand, if you're told that she's extroverted, you're more likely to ask questions that confirm this very different impression (e.g., "What would you do to liven things up at a party?" and "What types of situations do you seek out if you want to meet new people?"). Figure 5.5 illustrates this tendency to ask questions that confirm our initial belief.

Third, this behaviour may lead the person to act in ways that are consistent with the perceiver's expectations (e.g., not attending social events, talking about boring subjects). In a classic study, Mark Snyder, Elizabeth Tanke, and Ellen Berscheid (1977) asked male university students to have a phone conversation with a woman who they thought (based on a photograph they were shown) was either unattractive or attractive. Men who thought they were interacting with an attractive woman were friendlier and more outgoing. Later, researchers asked raters (who had no idea about the study's hypothesis or procedure) to evaluate the woman's responses. The raters found significant differences as a function of whether the woman was

FIGURE 5.5 HOW DO EXPECTATIONS ELICIT BEHAVIOUR?

In this experiment, researchers led participants to believe that they would be talking either to a partner with an extroverted personality or an introverted personality. Then, they noted how many questions participants asked that would elicit extroverted responses (such as "What is the most fun thing about working in groups?") or introverted responses (such as "When is the best time to work by yourself in the library?"). As predicted, participants who expected an extroverted partner asked many more extroverted questions than introverted questions, whereas those who expected an introverted partner asked somewhat more introverted questions than extroverted questions.

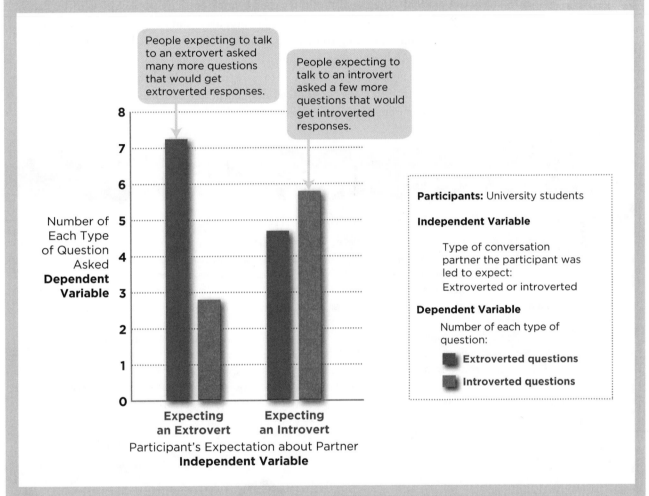

Source: Snyder, M., & Swann, W. (1978). Behavioral confirmation in social interaction: From social perception to social reality. *Journal of Experimental Social Psychology, 14*, 148–162.

thought to be attractive or not attractive. Not surprisingly, women who were treated in a friendlier manner responded in a more positive way.

Researchers from the Universities of Victoria, Manitoba, and Waterloo suggest that, at least in some social situations, the key to the self-fulfilling prophecy in terms of social acceptance ("Will they like me?") is personal warmth (Stinson, Cameron, Wood, Gaucher, & Holmes, 2009). In two studies, one correlational, the other experimental, the researchers found that anticipation of acceptance or rejection predicted personal warmth, which predicted actual acceptance. In the experimental study, they decreased the participants' expectation of being rejected by telling them that the person they were to meet was him or herself anxious about being rejected, and the result was an increase in the participants' warmth toward the other person. The researchers suggest that when people anticipate being accepted, they behave more warmly toward others, which leads to acceptance by others. Similarly, when people anticipate rejection they behave less warmly toward others, which, of course, leads to rejection.

While the self-fulfilling prophecy does exist, it's important not to overestimate its power. There is a popular belief, for example, that air accidents are associated with the full moon, and it has been suggested that the self-fulfilling prophecy plays a role in this association. Researchers from the University of Saskatchewan analyzed 93 air disasters in terms of the moon's phase and the five days centred around the four lunar phases. They found that 10 days (out of a 30 moon-day cycle) had as many, or more, accidents as the day of the full moon and that fatal aircraft accidents in Canada over an eight-year period showed no relationship to the moon's phase (Kelly, Saklofske, & Culver, 1990). This popular belief is a good example of people perceiving a false correlation.

Behavioural confirmation (self-fulfilling prophecy) can have major implications in real-world situations, including courtrooms, families, and education. For example, research by Allen Hart at Amherst College has shown that judges' beliefs influence juries' decisions even in cases in which jurors are specifically told to disregard the judge's behaviour and form their own opinions (Hart, 1995). The power of self-fulfilling prophecy can also be seen in the classroom, as described in Education Connections.

EDUCATION CONNECTIONS

The Overwhelming Power of Teachers' Expectations

In a dramatic real-life demonstration of the power of self-fulfilling prophecies, researchers told randomly selected teachers in a San Francisco elementary school that the results of an IQ test had revealed that 20 percent of their students were "late bloomers" and could be expected to do very well in the coming year (Rosenthal & Jacobsen, 1968). How effective was this manipulation? Students whose teachers had been told this improved their IQ scores by as much as 30 points. Although this study was conducted in the 1960s, more recent research reveals similar findings about the impact of teachers' expectations on student performance. For example, teachers' expectations about their students' grades have been found to be a strong predictor of students' actual grades, even controlling for previous achievement and student motivation (Smith, Jussim, & Eccles, 1999). Such expectations are a particularly strong predictor of achievement for low-achieving students (Madon, Jussim, & Eccles, 1997). Teachers' expectations are also a stronger predictor of their evaluations of their students' performance—that is, the grades they assign—than are their students' scores on standardized tests (Jussim & Eccles, 1992). This finding suggests that although teachers see (and grade) students' performance in line with what they expect, these expectations are not an accurate measure of students' true achievement. Why? Because these expectations do not predict more objective measures of performance, such as standardized test scores.

Superstock

Willliam Cousineau and Moira Luke (1990), from the University of British Columbia, examined the relationship between teachers' expectations of performance and the Academic Learning Time (ALT) of elementary students in physical education classes. ALT refers to the time that a student is on task at an appropriate level of difficulty, which has been found to correlate highly with performance. Six teachers from different schools were asked to rank their students according to how they well they expected the students to perform in physical education. Thirty-six grade six students whose teachers had rated them as high, medium, or low in terms of the teachers' performance expectations were then observed in three basketball lessons. It was found that students whose performance was expected to be high had significantly more academic learning time, which means that they were being taught more effectively. The study thus found a relationship between teachers' expectations and student performance as measured by outside observers. The differences between the students' performances is explained as being due, at least in part, to the teachers having behaved differently toward the high-expectancy students.

Is it possible to break the cycle of self-fulfilling prophecy and thereby form accurate impressions? Yes, at least in some cases. First, behavioural confirmation is less likely to occur if the perceiver's goal is to be liked by the target person (Copeland, 1994; Neuberg, Judice, Virdin, & Carrillo, 1993; Snyder & Haugen, 1994). When we want to be accurate about the target person, or want to be liked by that person, we apparently try harder to get to know the real person instead of relying on prior assumptions. In one study, participants were given a negative expectation about a person they would be interviewing, and they were then either given no particular goal for the interaction or were told to try to be liked by the interviewee (Neuberg et al., 1993). Participants in the "no goal" condition acted in a distant and challenging way during the interview. In turn, they elicited less positive answers from the interviewee, thereby confirming the negative expectation. Participants in the "be liked goal" condition, on the other hand, were much warmer and less threatening and elicited more positive responses from the interviewee, thereby disconfirming the negative expectation.

The cycle of behavioural confirmation can also be broken if targets are aware of perceivers' expectations. In these cases, the target will try actively to counter these expectations, which can help prevent self-fulfilling prophecies. In one study, pairs of students were assigned to have a conversation under different conditions (Hilton & Darley, 1985). Half the participants were told that their partner might be cold, while the other half weren't given any information about their partner. Half the partners were also told that their partner might think they were cold (i.e., they were given a forewarning). Who was most successful at refuting the (inaccurate) belief about them being cold? Those who were aware that their partner might be likely to see them as cold. Thus, making a person aware of the perceiver's assumptions can work to decrease, or even eliminate, the effects of the perceiver's expectations.

The cycle of self-fulfilling prophecy can also be broken if the perceiver's assumptions are highly inaccurate and the target therefore doesn't act in the expected way. Bill Swann and Robin Ely (1984) asked 128 women to interview individuals who were either certain or uncertain of their own extroversion. However, the perceivers were told that the target individuals were the opposite of what the individuals actually believed about themselves. (In other words, if the individual believed himself to be introverted, the perceiver was told he was extroverted.) Perceivers were also told either that the target had been rated as extroverted by all the other judges (high certainty) or by some of the other judges (low certainty). Perceivers then chose which 5 of 12 questions they would like to ask the target to judge his or her degree of extroversion. As predicted, those who expected the person to be extroverted and were very certain of this judgement asked more confirming questions than those who were less certain. Judges' ratings of the answers by the target individuals showed that behavioural confirmation does occur in interactions between high-certainty perceivers and low-certainty targets. However, when targets were quite firm in their beliefs about their own traits, they actively resisted the questions and eventually convinced the perceivers of their actual traits—thereby showing that behavioural confirmation is not inevitable.

THE GOOD NEWS ABOUT SELF-FULFILLING PROPHECY. Obviously, self-fulfilling prophecies can have many negative effects. (Chapter 11 describes some of the ways in which this cycle can lead to stereotypes and prejudice.) But here are a few encouraging words.

- We're better at judging friends and acquaintances than at judging strangers. We're also better at making judgements about how people (e.g., our roommates, co-workers) will act around us than about how they'll act in other situations. We behave in a manner prompting our friends' warmth because we know our friends are warm toward us. We're more accurate in these cases because we know the person and have lots of information about them (Madon et al., 2001).
- We can form more accurate impressions when we're motivated to be accurate and open-minded as well as when we're aware of the biases described in this chapter. Graduate students in psychology, for example, are less likely to make these errors.
- Finally, although we have described the power of self-fulfilling prophecies in leading to negative effects, such predictions can also lead to positive ones. For example, people whose dating partners treat them as special and unique may try to live up to these idealized images and, over time, become more like their partners' images of them (Snyder & Swann, 1978; Snyder et al., 1977), as in this excerpt from the book *Enchanted April*:

    "The more he treated her as though she were really very nice, the more Lotty expanded and became really very nice, and the more he, affected in his turn, became really very nice himself; so that they went round and round, not in a vicious but in a highly virtuous circle" (Von Arnim, 1922).

[CONCEPTS IN CONTEXT]

HOW BELIEFS CAN CREATE REALITY

FACTOR	EXAMPLE
Perceptual confirmation	After watching the political debate, you're delighted with the clearly superior performance of the candidate you prefer. You're later shocked, however, when the newspapers report that both candidates performed equally well.
Belief perseverance	Although you drive a large SUV, in part because you believe this type of vehicle will protect you in the event of an accident, you decide to attend a talk on campus about the dangers of SUVs. Despite the evidence presented by the speaker on their dangers (including their tendency to roll over and greater difficulty in coming to quick stops), you continue to believe that this vehicle is indeed the safest choice.
Behavioural confirmation/Self-fulfilling prophecy	Rees is babysitting for his 3-year-old niece, Jane, who he has heard is very shy and introverted. To avoid upsetting her, Rees keeps his distance and does not try to engage her in play. Surely enough, Jane spends most of the time playing entirely on her own. At the end of the afternoon, Rees remarks to his brother that Jane sure is shy.

HOW DOES CULTURE INFLUENCE SOCIAL COGNITION?

Another factor that influences social cognition is culture. People from different cultures think about the social world in different ways. In Chapter 4 on social perception, we talked about cultural differences in attributional style. As you will recall, in general, people from collectivistic cultures place greater emphasis on situational factors in explaining their social world, while people from individualistic cultures emphasize dispositional factors. Whereas people from collectivist cultures can, and do, see each other in terms of personality traits, a large body of evidence suggests that they rely on traits to a lesser degree than do individualists in their understanding of themselves and others (Heine & Buchtel, 2009).

In one study, researchers asked both Anglo-Americans and Mexican Americans to read a series of sentences describing a person's behaviour, and then judge whether this person had a given trait (Zàrate, Uleman, & Voils, 2001). For example, one sentence read, "He took his first calculus test when he was 12" and the trait that participants reacted to was "smart." Another sentence read, "She left a 25 percent tip for the waitress" and the trait was "generous." As predicted, Anglo-Americans made the trait judgements much more quickly than did Mexican Americans. This reflects Anglo-Americans' strong tendency to emphasize the role of traits in leading to behaviour—as well as the tendency of those from collectivistic cultures to take situational factors into account. This section will examine the impact of culture on cognitive errors and our beliefs about traits.

COGNITIVE ERRORS

Not surprisingly, culture influences the availability of different events/concepts. This is, in part, because one's country of origin influences what is known and therefore what is easily brought to mind. As a simple example, people in different cultures will think of different things if you ask them to name a food they like or a movie they've seen. This is simply because our culture influences what we're exposed to and therefore what types of experiences come easily to mind. Try the exercise in Figure 5.6 for a compelling example of how culture impacts availability.

Differences in what cultures value also leads to differences in cognitive errors. For example, in a study conducted by Steven Heine and Darrin Lehman from UBC, it was found that unrealistic optimism, one of the three self-enhancing cognitive illusions, is found less frequently among Japanese students than among Canadian students (Heine & Lehman, 1995). The authors suggest that self-enhancing biases like unrealistic optimism are found less among people from collectivistic societies because the attention to the individual that self-enhancement engenders is not valued in interdependent cultures.

FIGURE 5.6   AVAILABILITY EXERCISE

Follow the directions listed below very carefully. You'll be truly amazed at what you find.

1. Pick a number from 1 to 9.

2. Subtract 5 from that number.

3. Multiply that number by 3.

4. Square that number (meaning multiply that number by itself).

5. Add the digits in your number until you get only one digit (e.g., if you have the number 65, add 6 + 5 = 11, then add 1 + 1 = 2).

6. If the number is less than 5, add 5. If the number is greater than or equal to 5, subtract 4.

7. Multiply this number by 2.

8. Subtract 6 from this number.

9. Now, map the digit of the number to a letter in the alphabet (1 = A, 2 = B, 3 = C, etc.)

10. Pick a country that starts with that letter.

11. Take the second letter in the country name and think of a mammal that begins with this letter.

12. Think of the colour of that mammal.

Now, turn to the end of this chapter and see if I've correctly guessed your country and mammal!

Who's Who in Contemporary Canadian Social Psychology Research

Courtesy Steven J. Heine

Steven J. Heine is a professor at the University of British Columbia. He received his BA from the University of Alberta and his master's and PhD from the University of British Columbia. In his research, Professor Heine examines psychological processes that are universal and those that are limited to certain cultural groups. He has specifically investigated similarities and differences between Japanese and North Americans on self-enhancing and self-improving motivations. Professor Heine has received many awards, including the Distinguished Scientist Early Career Award from the American Psychological Association in 2003 and the Early Career Award from the International Society of Self and Identity in 2002.

Culture also influences the frequency of counterfactual thinking (Morris & Peng, 1994). In one study, for example, students in the graduate physics program at the University of Michigan read a true story about a graduate student who had killed his advisor on a university campus. They were then asked to consider a series of scenarios that were similar to the scenario that actually occurred. These scenarios changed either a piece of information about the person or a piece of information about the situation. For example, in one condition participants were asked, "What if Lu's advisor had worked harder to prepare him for the dissertation defence and job market?" (a change regarding the situation). In another they were asked, "What if Lu had not been mentally imbalanced?" (a change regarding the person). Participants then rated how likely it was that the murder would have occurred in the slightly changed scenario. As predicted, Chinese participants judged the murder much less likely to occur under changes in the situation than did Americans. Because Americans, much like Canadians, focus on the person's disposition, they believed that this "murderous disposition" would have led to the killing regardless of the situational factors. In other words, people from individualistic cultures focus on the person's internal disposition, which they see as largely fixed. In turn, people from collectivistic cultures are much more likely to engage in counterfactual thinking because they focus more on the situation—and therefore are more likely to see how features of the situation could change the outcome.

IN THE NEWS

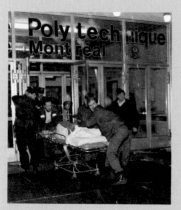

THE CANADIAN PRESS/Shaney Komulainen

The Challenge of Attribution: On December 6, 1989, 25-year-old Marc Lépine shot 28 people, killing 14 women at the École Polytechnique in Montreal before killing himself. Lépine claimed that he was fighting feminism and that he specifically targeted women. Canadians have debated various interpretations of the events. Many have characterized the massacre as anti-feminist and as a representation of societal violence against women (situational interpretation), while others have pointed to the abuse he experienced in childhood and his mental state (personal interpretation).

BELIEFS ABOUT TRAITS

As described in Chapter 4, people from collectivistic cultures are more likely to explain a person's behaviour as being caused by the situation. People from collectivistic cultures place relatively less emphasis, compared to those from individualistic cultures, on dispositional factors. This difference reflects, in part, cross-cultural differences in how individuals view traits. In other words, cultures differ in their beliefs about whether traits predict behaviour and whether traits stay consistent over time. For example, a Canadian university student would tend to see a person's behaviour, such as study habits, types of friends, and style of dress, as largely determined by person's internal traits, and would see these traits as predicting behaviour over time and across different situations. On the other hand, a university student from Venezuela might see such behaviour as heavily influenced by the person's immediate situation, and would therefore not believe that such behaviour would necessarily continue over time and in different situations.

In one study, researchers examined beliefs about personality in both Mexican and American university students (Church et al., 2003). While participants in both cultures reported holding strong beliefs about the stability of traits, the Americans' beliefs were more strongly held. Specifically, Americans reported greater agreement with statements such as "People who are friendlier now than others will probably remain friendlier than others in the future as well" and "For most persons, success at their job will depend a lot on their personality characteristics." As described at the start of this section, this strong belief about the power of traits leads people from individualistic cultures to make judgements about people's personality much more quickly than those in collectivistic cultures (Zàrate et al., 2001).

SELF-CONSTRUAL AND FIELD DEPENDENCE. Markus and Kitayama (1991) proposed that people think differently depending on whether their self-construal is interdependent or relatively independent. People whose sense of self is interdependent construe (i.e., define) themselves in terms of contexts and relationships with others. Internal attributes, such as personality traits, are less salient for individuals who construe their identity in ways that focus on interdependence. On the other hand, those who construe their identity in independent terms perceive their self as autonomous and separate from others. Internal attributes, including individual attitudes and preferences, are more salient for people who are high in independent self-construal (Matsumoto & Juang, 2010). This difference applies not only to understanding oneself and others, but to all aspects of one's environment.

John Berry (1976), a Canadian cross-cultural psychologist from Queen's University, proposed that survival in different environments requires different perceptual and cognitive skills. This implies that being socialized in cultures that foster an interdependent self-construal is related to context dependency and holistic thinking, while being socialized in cultures that foster an independent self-construal is related to analytical thinking. This has been shown in the contrast between what is referred to as "field dependence" and "field independence." People who are **field dependent** have greater difficulty in identifying a figure that is embedded in a larger background but are better able to perceive the whole image as one holistic figure. In contrast, people who are **field independent** have a greater ability to identify a target figure and separate it from its larger background.

field dependent – having more difficulty in identifying an embedded figure in a larger background but greater ability to perceive an image as one holistic figure

field independent – having the ability to identify an embedded figure and separate it from a larger background

Witkin and Berry (1975) used the Embedded Figures Test (see Figure 5.7) to examine these concepts cross-culturally. They found that respondents from the Temne of West

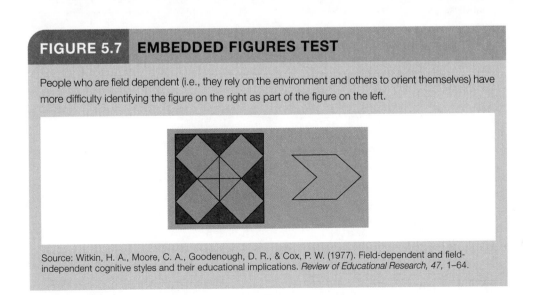

FIGURE 5.7 EMBEDDED FIGURES TEST

People who are field dependent (i.e., they rely on the environment and others to orient themselves) have more difficulty identifying the figure on the right as part of the figure on the left.

Source: Witkin, H. A., Moore, C. A., Goodenough, D. R., & Cox, P. W. (1977). Field-dependent and field-independent cognitive styles and their educational implications. *Review of Educational Research, 47*, 1–64.

Africa, whose survival depends on collective action, had more difficulty in identifying a series of shapes hidden in a larger background than do people from more individualistic societies. The Temne thus showed field dependence. Ji, Peng, and Nisbett (2000) found that East Asian students in the U.S. were more field dependent than American students. In other words, East Asians tend to think holistically while North Americans tend to think analytically (Nisbett, Peng, Choi, & Norenzayan, 2000). Kühnen, Hannover, Roeder and colleagues (2001) also reported that Malay and Russian students were more field dependent than German and American students. Nsamenang (1992) reported a similar difference between Africans and North Americans. Overall, people from collectivistic cultural backgrounds attend more to the context in their social and physical environment than do people from individualistic cultural backgrounds.

THE BIG PICTURE

SOCIAL COGNITION

This chapter included many applications of the three "big ideas" studied in social psychology. The examples below should help you see the connection between social cognition and these big ideas and contribute to your understanding of the big picture of social psychology.

THEME	EXAMPLES
The social world influences how we think about ourselves.	• A B+ grade feels much worse when we narrowly miss receiving an A- than when we narrowly miss receiving a B. • We see a recorded performance of ourselves more positively if we're in a good mood rather than a bad mood. • We see ourselves as less attractive after seeing photographs of highly attractive people of the same gender as us.
The social world influences our thoughts, attitudes, and behaviour.	• People who are subliminally cued with words related to the elderly walk more slowly than those who are cued with neutral words. • People are much more likely to choose a medical treatment with a 50 percent success rate than a 50 percent failure rate. • People are much more influenced by negative information about a political candidate than positive information.
Our attitudes and behaviour shape the social world around us.	• Men who believe they're talking with an attractive woman elicit more positive behaviour from her than those who believe they're talking with a less attractive woman. • People's expectations about the person they're talking to influence the types of questions they ask that person, which in turn confirms their initial expectation. • People whose dating partners treat them as special and unique over time grow to be more like their partners' images of them.

WHAT YOU'VE LEARNED

This chapter examined five key principles of social cognition.

1. How can shortcuts lead to errors in thinking about the world?

The first section described various errors, or shortcuts, that we make when we think about the world. These shortcuts include intuition, availability, representativeness, base-rate fallacy, anchoring and adjustment, and counterfactual thinking. And you learned that people are more influenced by articles with catchy titles ("Opposites Attract") than by those with more neutral ones ("Researchers Examine Predictors of Attraction"). You also learned about schemas and different types of schemas.

2. How does presentation influence how we think about the world?

The next section examined various errors caused by presentation, and specifically how the same information can be seen very differently when it is described in different ways. We learned specific ways in which presentation can impact judgements, including the contrast effect and framing. This section revealed that spending a lot of time "reading" pornographic magazines makes your own (non-airbrushed) partner seem less sexually appealing, and that people prefer 90 percent fat-free food over food that is 10 percent fat.

3. How do we form impressions of people?

This chapter also examined factors that influence the impressions we form of other people. These factors include the power of first impressions, the strength of negative information, and implicit personality theories. This section explained why people see people who are in close relationships as less likely to have an STD than those who are single, even when rates of lifetime sexual behaviour are identical.

4. How do beliefs create reality?

Next, we examined ways in which people's beliefs can create the reality they expect. These factors include perceptual confirmation, belief perseverance, and behavioural confirmation/self-fulfilling prophecy.

5. How does culture influence social cognition?

Finally, we examined the role of culture in predicting how we think about the world. This section described how culture influences what is easily accessible in our thinking as well as our beliefs about traits. Beliefs about traits lead people from individualistic cultures to make judgements about an individual's personality much more quickly than those from collectivistic cultures.

Key Terms

anchoring and adjustment 148
automatic thinking 142
availability heuristic 144
base-rate fallacy 147
behavioural confirmation/
   self-fulfilling prophecy 165
belief perseverance 164
content-free schemas 145
contrast effect 152
controlled or effortful thinking 142
counterfactual thinking 149

event schemas 145
field dependent 173
field independent 173
framing 153
heuristics 142
hindsight bias 163
illusory correlation 163
illusory superiority 163
implicit personality theory 156
intuition 143
perceptual confirmation 161

person schemas 145
primacy 157
priming 145
reconstructive memory 155
representativeness 147
role schemas 145
schemas 144
self schemas 145
social cognition 142
trait negativity bias 158
unrealistic optimism 163

Questions for Review

1. Describe four ways in which shortcuts can lead to errors in thinking about the world.

2. Describe two ways in which presentation influences how we think about the world.

3. Describe how we form impressions of other people, including the role of first impressions and the power of negative impressions.

4. Describe two distinct ways in which people's beliefs can create reality, and two ways in which people can, at times, overcome the power of such beliefs.

5. Describe how one's culture influences counterfactual thinking and beliefs about traits.

Take Action!

1. Your boyfriend has to travel across the country this summer for a family reunion. Unfortunately, he's deeply afraid of flying because of the many news reports about airplane crashes. What could you tell him about his errors in thinking so that he worries less about flying?

2. You have a summer internship with an advertising agency. Your first assignment is to design a campaign to increase the sales of a new chocolate bar. How could you use framing to market this product?

3. This semester you're taking a course with Professor Adams, who your roommate warned you is a bad lecturer and unfair grader. So far you've tended to agree with your roommate's judgement of most things, and of Professor Adams, but after reading this chapter you're wondering whether some social cognitive biases may have influenced your reaction to this professor. Which biases do you think might be responsible for your negative impression?

4. Think of a time when your initial expectations of a person may have led to their confirmation. What could you have done differently in this situation to avoid initiating the process of self-fulfilling prophecy?

5. Your sister is spending the summer on an exchange program with a Japanese family. What could you tell her to expect in terms of cultural differences in thinking about the social world?

RESEARCH CONNECTIONS

Participate in Research

Activity 1 The Impact of Counterfactual Thinking: This chapter described how counterfactual thinking influences our experience of positive and negative events. Go online to read various scenarios about an event, and rate how you think you'd feel in each situation.

Activity 2 The Influence of Framing: One subtle influence on the choices we make is how these choices are presented, or framed. Go online to test the influence of framing on the choices you make regarding your health-related behaviours.

Activity 3 The Power of First Impressions: This chapter described how people's judgements of how competent political candidates are for office is highly correlated with the outcome of these races. Go online to test whether your view of how competent candidates are accurately predicts the winner of the most recent federal election.

Activity 4 The Hazards of Perceptual Confirmation: You learned in this chapter about how we see things in line with our expectations. Go online to read a description of a person, and then rate this person's attributes to see if your expectations guide your answers.

Activity 5 The Impact of Culture on Social Cognition: The final section of this chapter described how people from different cultures vary in how strongly they believe in the power of people's personal traits. Go online to rate your agreement with various statements about people's traits—then see how other students rate their own agreement.

Test a Hypothesis

One of the common findings in research on social cognition is that low probability events are much more likely to appear in the media (such as plane crashes and kidnapping) than high probability events (such as car crashes and drowning). To test whether this hypothesis is true, search your newspaper for the frequency of various health risks to see whether some types of events are more commonly reported than others. Then go online to report your findings to other students.

Design a Study

Go online to design a study that tests how shortcuts in thinking can lead to errors. You'll be able to choose the type of study you want to conduct (self-report, observational/naturalistic, or experimental), choose your own independent and dependent variables, and form your own hypothesis. Then you can share your findings with other students across the country!

Answer to Figure 5.6: Availability Exercise

Is it a grey elephant from Denmark? How did we know? The complicated mathematical calculations ultimately lead everyone to the number 4, which then maps onto the letter D. Most North Americans immediately think of Denmark, while people from other parts of the world often more readily think of the Dominican Republic or Djibouti.

ATTITUDE FORMATION AND CHANGE

DID YOU EVER WONDER?

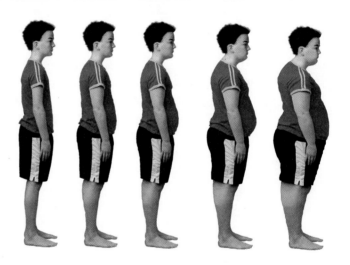

Obesity is a major health problem in industrialized countries, including Canada, the United States, the UK and other western European nations, and Australia. In Canada, the prevalence of people who are overweight and obese has increased in the past 20 years for both sexes and among all age groups. Alarmingly, overweight and obesity rates are increasing most rapidly among Canadian children. Children from low-income families and those from multi-ethnic and urban neighbourhoods are particularly at risk for obesity (Canadian Institute for Health Information, 2004). Two major contributors to this high rate of obesity are the consumption of unhealthy food and physical inactivity. With the rising cost of health care and the impact of obesity on both physical and psychological well-being, we may therefore wonder how we can develop more positive attitudes about healthy foods and physical activities, and in so doing, reduce child obesity. In this chapter, we'll find an answer to this question as we examine how attitudes are formed and changed. You'll also find answers to the following questions:

MEDIA CONNECTIONS	HEALTH CONNECTIONS	ENVIRONMENTAL CONNECTIONS	BUSINESS CONNECTIONS
		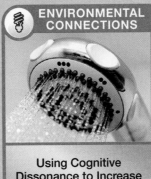	
The Dangerous Impact of Media Images of Tobacco and Alcohol Use	Using Cognitive Dissonance to Create a Change in Health Behaviour	Using Cognitive Dissonance to Increase Water Conservation	Consumer Purchasing Attitudes and Behaviours Related to Food

 Why does describing an elderly woman lead you to oppose sex and nudity on television?

 Why do people with prejudiced attitudes often not show prejudiced behaviour?

 Why might you be really interested in participating in a group discussion on the sex lives of animals?

 Why does describing a love of the arts make some people oppose research on chronic disease prevention?

 Why do European Canadians justify the choices they make for themselves, whereas Asian Canadians justify the choices they make for their friends?

WHAT YOU'LL LEARN

How attitudes are formed

When attitudes predict behaviour

When engaging in a behaviour leads to attitude change

The alternatives to cognitive dissonance theory

How culture impacts attitude formation and change

PREVIEW

attitudes – positive and negative evaluations of people, objects, events, and ideas

We quickly and constantly form **attitudes**, which are defined as the positive and negative evaluations we hold about each of the following:

- people (e.g., "I can't stand Derek Jeter.")
- objects (e.g., "Indian food is my favourite cuisine.")
- events (e.g., "Halloween is my favourite holiday.")
- ideas (e.g., "I am in favour of the global reduction of nuclear weapons.")

As these examples illustrate, attitudes include three distinct components: affect, cognition, and a behavioural tendency (an inclination to behave in a particular way; Rosselli, Skelly, & Mackie, 1995). It is not the behaviour itself, but the tendency toward it, that is part of the attitude. You may, for example, love Indian food and therefore have an inclination toward eating it, but never get the chance to. Psychologists have long been interested in the link between attitudes and behaviour, primarily because we tend to assume that attitudes lead to behaviour (e.g., if you have a positive attitude toward the Green Party, you will vote for them). But perhaps surprisingly, our attitudes are not always a very good predictor of our behaviour (although a supporter of the Green Party, you might vote strategically for a party that you think has a better chance of winning) Moreover, in some cases, changing our behaviour can actually precede and then lead to a change in our attitude.

HOW DO WE FORM ATTITUDES?

Attitude is one of the most studied topics in social psychology. Several decades ago, Gordon Allport described attitude as "probably the most distinctive and indispensable concept in contemporary American social psychology" (Allport, 1954, p. 43). Not surprisingly, over the last few decades attitude has been defined and evaluated in different ways. In 1935, Allport in fact offered one of the early definitions of attitude, describing it as "a mental and neural state of readiness, organized through experience, exerting a directive and dynamic influence upon the individual's response to all objects and situations with which it is related" (Allport, 1935, p. 810). Later, Daryl Bem defined attitudes as "likes and dislikes" (Bem, 1970, p. 14). Then, in the 1990s, attitude was defined as "a psychological tendency that is expressed by evaluating a particular entity with some degree of favor or disfavor" (Eagly & Chaiken, 1993, p. 1). Today, researchers regard attitude as an abstract construct that cannot be viewed but can be inferred from people's behaviour and their self-report (Schwarz & Bohner, 2003). In this view, attitudes are presumed to guide our actions and choices.

Although you probably don't realize it, attitudes are formed very quickly—and often without conscious awareness. They are also, to some extent, malleable (i.e., they can be shifted and changed). Simply making certain things salient can have a noticeable influence on attitudes. Researchers in one study asked participants to write a description of a particular person, including the person's hobbies, personality traits, and general character (Kawakami, Dovidio, & Dijksterhuis, 2003). To write these descriptions, they had to imagine this person in some detail, including what it must be like to be that person. Some participants were told to describe an elderly woman and others were asked to describe a young woman. After finishing these descriptions, participants rated their own attitudes toward a variety of topics, such as feelings about spending more money on health care and beliefs about whether sex and nudity should be shown on television. As predicted, participants who had described an elderly woman reported attitudes that were more consistent with those of elderly people than those who had described a young woman. This example shows how information that is made prominent (i.e., salient) influences our attitudes. It also helps explain the success of charity advertising campaigns that provide specific information about what your money will contribute toward (e.g., your money will buy a goat for this family in this village and it will change their lives in this way).

"Oh great. Not only do we have a virus, but now the computer has developed an attitude."

© Teresa McCracken/ www.cartoonstock.com

This section will examine the different ways in which people acquire their attitudes: through information, classical conditioning, operant conditioning, and observational learning or modelling.

One of the most common ways in which people form attitudes is through the information they receive from their social environment. Children, for example, often develop their initial attitudes based on the attitudes that their parents and other role models express. On the positive side, this means that parents who love books, or enjoy gardening, are likely to pass these attitudes on to their children. On the negative side, this process can also lead to adopting negative attitudes as children who hear their parents express prejudiced views are very likely to adopt these same attitudes. As described in our Research Focus on Neuroscience, negative information has a particularly strong impact on our attitudes.

IN THE NEWS

Peter Dazeley/Photographer's Choice RF/Getty Images

In 2007, the province of Quebec announced that in the fight against the "obesity epidemic" it will reduce junk food in schools. Philippe Couillard, Health Minister of the time, said that as part of the government plan, access to junk food will be limited and healthy food habits will be encouraged (CBC, September 12, 2007).

RESEARCH FOCUS ON NEUROSCIENCE
The Power of Negative Information

Although both positive and negative information influences people's evaluations of an object, a situation, or person, negative information seems to have a stronger influence— a phenomenon described as the negativity bias (Ito, Larsen, Smith, & Cacioppo, 1998). One of the explanations for the negativity bias is that negative information should be more important to our survival than positive information—we should respond more quickly to

off the mark.com by Mark Parisi

WHY SO NEGATIVE?

painful stimuli, for example, than pleasant ones. In order to test whether the negativity bias occurs even at a neurological level, researchers in one study showed participants positive images (photographs of a bowl of chocolate ice cream and a pizza), and negative images (a dead cat and a decomposing cow). Participants were asked to determine whether the pictures were positive, negative, or neutral. Researchers then evaluated brain waves to measure electrocortical activity in response to each type of image. As predicted, participants showed larger brain waves, indicating greater brain activity, in response to the negative photographs. This research demonstrates that the negativity bias is seen even at a neurological level—as the waves for negativity were steeper than the ones for positivity. This provides one explanation for why people form stronger attitudes in response to negative information about an object or person than to positive information. You might wonder if the positive and negative images were balanced in intensity; in other words, is a picture of a decomposing cow as intensely displeasing as chocolate ice cream is pleasing? In fact the researchers did check for this in advance by selecting images with clearly positive and negative evaluations (obtained in a preliminary study) and which produced similar levels of self-reported arousal (from the same preliminary study).

CLASSICAL CONDITIONING

classical conditioning – a type of learning in which a neutral stimulus is repeatedly paired with a stimulus that elicits a specific response, and eventually the neutral stimulus elicits that response on its own

Attitudes can also be formed based on a simple association between an object or person and a pleasant or unpleasant event (Cacioppo, Marshall-Goodell, Tassinary, & Petty, 1992; Walther, 2002). This type of learning is called **classical conditioning**, which is defined as learning in which a neutral stimulus leads to a specific reaction after the stimulus is repeatedly paired with another stimulus that naturally leads to that reaction (see Figure 6.1). As you may remember from your introduction to psychology course, classical conditioning was first demonstrated by the Russian physiologist Ivan Petrovich Pavlov (1849–1936) in his famous classical conditioning study showing that dogs will start to salivate simply in response to hearing a bell ring, if that ring is first rung repeatedly just before the presentation of food. This observation has generated many empirical studies on attitude formation and other psychological concepts (see Chapter 14, Interpersonal Attraction and Social Relationships). For example, you may form a positive attitude toward the new neighbour who owns a sheltie-poodle mixed breed dog simply because you grew up with a sheltie-poodle dog and you're now associating the pleasant memory of your dog, and consequently the positive mood, with the new neighbour.

mere exposure – the phenomenon by which the greater the exposure that we have to a given stimulus, the more we like it

One way in which attitudes can be conditioned is through **mere exposure**, meaning the more we are exposed to something, the more we like it, regardless of whether or not we interact with it (Abrams & Greenwald, 2000; Bornstein, 1989; Harmon-Jones & Allen, 2001; Moreland & Zajonc, 1982). In other words, just the fact that it is around (merely being exposed to it) commends it to us. The repeated exposure is regarded as a form of classical conditioning because the stimulus that one is being repeatedly exposed to is considered to be the conditioned stimulus (CS). The unconditioned stimulus (US) is the absence of negative stimuli or aversive consequences (Zajonc, 2001). When CS and US are paired on several occurrences, in other words, when the person does not suffer from negative experiences, then a conditioned response (CR) or *liking* is attached to CS. Have you ever heard a song on the radio and really disliked it initially, but then, over time, as you hear it again, and again, and again, you actually grow to like it? This is an example of the power of simply being exposed to something repeatedly. This phenomenon helps explain why we prefer mirror-image pictures of ourselves—because that is how we normally see ourselves—whereas our friends prefer reverse-mirror-image pictures of us—because that is how they normally see us (Mita, Dermer, & Knight, 1977).

FIGURE 6.1 CLASSICAL CONDITIONING

Classical conditioning helps explain why a previously neutral stimulus, such as the smell of a given perfume, initially creates no reaction but over time, through pairing with something that does create a reaction, can lead to that reaction entirely on its own.

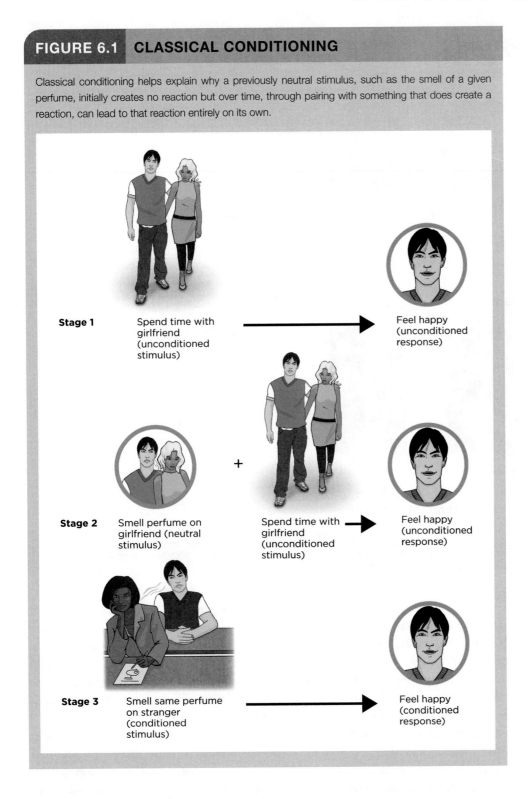

Stage 1 Spend time with girlfriend (unconditioned stimulus) → Feel happy (unconditioned response)

Stage 2 Smell perfume on girlfriend (neutral stimulus) + Spend time with girlfriend (unconditioned stimulus) → Feel happy (unconditioned response)

Stage 3 Smell same perfume on stranger (conditioned stimulus) → Feel happy (conditioned response)

The examples above all involve stimuli that a person is conscious of being exposed to. In **subliminal persuasion**, the stimulus that influences the person's attitude is presented so rapidly that it is below the person's level of conscious awareness (Bornstein & D'Agostino, 1992; Murphy & Zajonc, 1993; Zajonc, 1968). In one study, for example, participants saw a series of photographs of a woman engaging in various activities (e.g., getting into a car, sweeping a floor, sitting in a restaurant, studying; Krosnick, Betz, Jussim, & Lynn, 1992). Right before they saw two of the pictures of the woman, another picture was flashed subliminally (i.e., without the participants being aware that they had seen it). In some cases, the subliminal picture was of

subliminal persuasion – a type of persuasion that occurs when stimuli are presented at a very rapid and unconscious level

FIGURE 6.2 CAN SUBLIMINAL PRIMING INFLUENCE ATTITUDES?

In this experiment researchers showed participants photos of a woman so quickly they could only perceive them subliminally. They later showed the participants another photo of the woman and asked them about their attitudes toward her and how they would rate her personality. People who saw positive photos subliminally rated the woman's attitudes and personality more positively than people who saw negative photos.

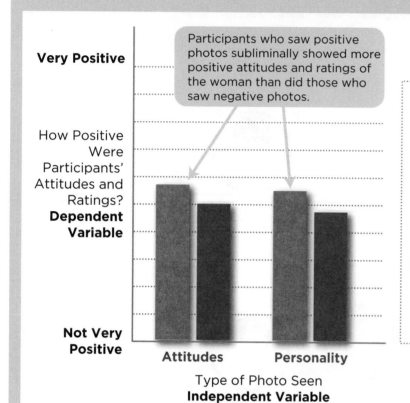

Source: Krosnick, J., Betz, A., Jussim, L., & Lynn, A. (1992). Subliminal conditioning of attitudes. *Personality and Social Psychology Bulletin, 18*, 152–162.

something positive (a child with a Mickey Mouse doll, a couple in a romantic setting, a pair of kittens), and in other cases, the picture was of something negative (a bucket of snakes, a dead body on a bed, a bloody shark). All participants were then asked to rate their attitude toward the woman and their beliefs about her personality. As predicted, those who saw positive subliminal images presented right before the pictures of the woman had a more positive attitude toward her than those who saw the negative subliminal pictures, even though the participants had no conscious awareness of having seen the pictures (see Figure 6.2).

Subliminal processing can also strengthen the attitudes we already hold. Erin Strahan, Steven Spencer, and Mark Zanna of the University of Waterloo found that people who were already thirsty were more motivated to drink after being exposed to subliminal thirst-related messages. Similarly, people who felt sad were more motivated to seek company after subliminal messages or primes related to positive social interactions (Strahan, Spencer, & Zanna, 2002). Sports psychologists from the University of Ottawa and the University of Grenoble have also found that subliminal processing of words that suggest autonomous motivation resulted in better performance on a subsequent exercise task than words that suggest controlled (i.e., forced) motivation. In other words, better performance was associated with subliminal exposure to the idea of doing things out of a sense of autonomy rather than because one is somehow compelled to. The words evoking autonomy were *envie, volonté, liberté, choisir* (desire, will, freedom, choosing); the words evoking being controlled were *contraint, obligation, devoir, obéir* (constraint, obligation, duty, obey). The words were chosen based on previous studies using words to characterize these two motivational orientations (Radel, Sarrazin, & Pelletier, 2009). Participants were asked to look at two pictures on a computer screen and indicate whether or not they were identical, but before the pictures were shown, the words priming either type of motivation were quickly flashed on the screen. The authors discuss the findings in terms of athletes' unconscious motivation.

A different application of the use of subliminal messaging is, for example, in advertising. It is important to note, however, that although subliminal processing has some impact on people's behaviour, deliberate attempts to manipulate it, as through advertising, don't always work. It should not be viewed as a reliably effective tool in influencing behaviour.

OPERANT CONDITIONING

Have you ever decided to wear your jeans in a particular way (maybe low-rise, or with a big rip in the knee) because you knew your friends would approve? Most of us have experience with conforming to the attitudes of our peers. This type of conditioning, **operant conditioning**, describes a type of learning in which people are rewarded or punished for engaging in a specific behaviour (Skinner, 1938). Operant conditioning can also influence attitude formation—and attitude expression. For example, if a little boy who wants a doll for Christmas is ridiculed by his parents, he is likely to form a negative attitude toward dolls, whereas a little girl who wants the same present and is praised by her parents will form a positive attitude toward dolls. Parents initially have the power to form their children's attitudes through operant condition-ing, which is one reason why most children express attitudes that are similar to those of their parents. By adolescence, however, peers often reward and punish particular attitudes—which is one of the factors that lead to high levels of conformity (e.g., of clothing, musical preferences, and behaviours) in this age group. Research Focus on Gender describes gender differences in political attitudes as well as some potential causes of such differences.

Operant conditioning influences people's attitudes—and behaviour. It might even help you in your dating relationship. Researchers in one study examined the level of rewards received by each partner in a dating relationship, such as doing favours for one another, help-ing with projects, and so on (Berg & McQuinn, 1986). As predicted, couples who exchanged a high number of rewards were more likely to still be dating four months later than couples who exchanged few rewards.

> **operant conditioning** – a type of learning in which behaviour that is rewarded increases, whereas behaviour that is punished decreases

> **Questioning the Research:**
>
> This section describes the benefits of operant condition-ing in influencing attitudes and behaviour. Can you think of a drawback to this approach of influencing attitudes? (Hint: What did you learn in Chapter 3 about the dangers of overjustification?)

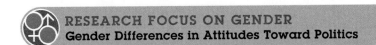

RESEARCH FOCUS ON GENDER
Gender Differences in Attitudes Toward Politics

One area in which men and women may differ is in their attitudes toward social and political issues. To investigate gender differences in attitudes toward these issues, researchers examined data from a large interview survey of approximately 1,700 respondents in the United States between 1973 to 1998 (Eagly, Diekman, Johannesen-Schmidt, & Koenig, 2004). Participants were asked their attitudes toward several topics, including gun control, the death penalty, abor-tion, reducing income differentials between the rich and the poor, gay rights, and the legaliza-tion of marijuana. The results indicated stable gender gaps with regards to social and political issues. Compared to men, women tended to have more socially compassionate attitudes, such as opposing the death penalty, reducing the income differentials between the rich and poor, and favouring gun control. Women also tended to have more traditionally moral attitudes, such as disapproval of divorce, abortion, and opposing the legalization of marijuana. These gender differences do not simply line up in terms of liberalism versus conservatism: women are more liberal than men on issues of social compassion and rights, but more conservative than men on issues of traditional morality.

The authors explained these differences based on women's greater responsibilities in domestic domains and generally their lower power in society relative to men. According to social role theory (Eagly, Wood, & Diekman, 2000), the social roles that men and women occupy influence their attitudes, their ideology, and their social identity. For example, women tend to assume greater family obligations, which is consistent with gender role expectation. This, in turn, is reflected in their conservative attitudes on issues of traditional morality, support of policies in favour of children, and education. Additionally, women generally have lower power in society, which is reflected in their greater empathy with those in disadvantaged circumstances and a greater commitment for social equality.

OBSERVATIONAL LEARNING/MODELLING

observational learning/modelling – a type of learning in which people's attitudes and behaviour are influenced by watching other people's attitudes and behaviour

Operant conditioning typically involves a direct or conscious process (e.g., dating couples do not provide rewards for each other entirely by accident), but attitudes can be formed in a more subtle way through **observational learning** or **modelling** (Bandura, 1986). This type of learning occurs when people form attitudes by watching how others act toward an object or person, and in turn adopt those views themselves. By observing how others feel, for example, children may learn that they should have a negative attitude toward broccoli or a positive attitude toward candy. This is one of the many reasons that frequent television advertisements for fast foods and sweets contribute to childhood obesity. In line with this view, children who are raised by an overweight mother have more positive attitudes toward overweight people, whereas those who are raised by a thin mother have more positive attitudes toward thin people (Rudman, Phelan, & Heppen, 2007). Similarly, researchers at the University of Guelph have demonstrated that children's intentions regarding their future safety behaviour (such as wearing a bicycle helmet, using a seatbelt, and wearing sunscreen) are heavily influenced by their observations of their parents' behaviour (Morrongiello, Corbett, & Bellissimo, 2008). This indicates that attitudes are learned and that observing others facilitates such learning.

Charles Beyl

Modelling is most effective at shaping our attitudes when we're observing someone who is similar to us. Why? Because those who we identify with serve as more effective models for our own behaviour. Albert Bandura of Stanford University put this notion into practice when he used modelling to try to help dog-phobic children become more comfortable with dogs (Bandura, Grusec, & Menlove, 1967). Nursery-school age children who were scared of dogs watched a little boy play with a dog for 20 minutes a day. After only four days, 67 percent were willing to climb into the playpen with a dog and remain alone with it after everyone else left the room. This comfort remained one month later. Moreover, the change in attitude was even greater, when, in a similar study, the children watched television clips that showed children interacting with the dogs.

While observational learning or modelling is most effective when we directly observe our parents, siblings, or friends engaging in a behaviour, it can also work to shape attitudes when we don't know the person who is expressing the attitude or engaging in the behaviour (Bandura, 1986).

Because attitudes are often influenced by what people observe in the media, including television, movies, and videos, some television campaigns feature celebrities promoting a particular cause, such as the importance of staying in school or doing volunteer work. In other cases, storylines on long-running television programs are used to influence people's attitudes. For example, in Mexico nearly one million people participated in a literacy program after watching characters in a popular drama participate in such a program. In one particularly creative use of modelling, in South Africa *Sesame Street* now features an HIV-positive orphan named Kami, who is a Muppet. This character is a normal five-year-old child, who says things like, "I love to tell stories and fly kites. And even though I have HIV, my friends know it's OK to play with me!" Children who watch this show may develop more positive attitudes toward people who are infected with HIV. In Tanzania, storylines have emphasized the costs of having too many children and have encouraged women to adopt methods of birth control. In Kenya, a radio soap opera includes fictional storylines on the negative consequences of female circumcision and domestic violence. The hope is that these stories and programs will help people to form positive attitudes toward the use of birth control and negative attitudes toward female circumcision and domestic violence.

On the other hand, the media can also shape harmful attitudes. Children who watch more television request more toys than those who watch less television, presumably because more exposure to toy advertisements leads to more positive attitudes toward these products (Chamberlain, Wang, & Robinson, 2006). Non-smoking teenagers who watch movies in which characters smoke show a more positive view of smokers' social status as well as greater intentions to smoke than those who see the same films with the smoking edited out (Pechmann & Shih, 1999). The Media Connections box describes some potentially dangerous impacts on young children of media images of smoking and alcohol consumption.

MEDIA CONNECTIONS

The Dangerous Impact of Media Images of Tobacco and Alcohol Use

The media play a substantial role in influencing people's attitudes. In addition to entertaining people, they educate, provide role models, and offer guidelines about how to behave (Nelson, 2010). For example, people's attitudes toward smoking and alcohol use are partly shaped by the media and this influence is particularly strong on young children. One study in the *Journal of the American Medical Association* examined the presence of tobacco products (cigarettes, cigars, and pipes) in 50 G-rated animated children's films, including *Bambi*, *Lady and the Tramp*, and *The Lion King* (Goldstein, Sobel, & Newman, 1999). Tobacco use was portrayed in 56 percent of the films, including all seven films released in 1996 and 1997 (the latest years included in the study). "Good characters" were as likely to use tobacco as "bad" ones. Smoking is often portrayed as glamorous and cool and adolescents who view smoking in movies are more likely to start smoking themselves (Dalton et al., 2003). Similarly, television provides numerous examples of the link between fun and drinking (Grube & Wallach, 1994). Alcohol advertisements typically show young, attractive people drinking in appealing settings (e.g., at parties, on the beach) and having a very good time—they don't show senior citizens drinking while they play shuffle board. One study with grade 5 and grade 6 students found that kids who had more awareness of television beer advertisements (e.g., they could identify the type of beer advertised even when its name was blocked) viewed drinking more favourably and had greater intentions to drink as adults (Grube & Wallach, 1994). This research shows the strong influence of the media on children's attitudes toward smoking as well as alcohol use.

In general, empirical studies have found a link between the appearance of smoking and drinking in films and television and the engagement of individuals in this behaviour. However, researchers have noted a decline in such behaviours in the media without a corresponding decline among young adults (Ling, Neilands, & Glantz, 2009). Adding to the complexity of the data, our attitudes toward smoking change over time. Look at the two ads in this box. The top one, although effective in the 1970s, would be less effective and possibly offensive today. The one on the bottom is part of an anti-smoking ad that was published in fashion magazines in 2006 aimed at women. Smoking might have been associated with being cool and sexy in the past but it is seen as unhealthy and unfashionable now.

What are your attitudes toward smoking and drinking? Can you think of images you have seen in the media and how they might have impacted your attitudes? If your attitude to smoking is negative, what other messages have you received about smoking (e.g., through parent modelling) and what type of attitude learning are these messages examples of (review the different types of learning above)?

Image Courtesy of The Advertising Archives

Printed with the permission of the Cancer Society of Finland, courtesy of Bob Helsinki

HOW MUCH DO ATTITUDES MATTER?

This section has described ways in which attitudes are formed, including relatively direct methods, such as information and operant conditioning. We also covered indirect methods for forming attitudes: classical conditioning, and observational learning or modelling. The Would You Believe feature describes another factor that can influence our attitudes—our genes.

OUR ATTITUDES ARE ROOTED IN OUR GENES?

A growing amount of research in personality psychology demonstrates that our genes can influence intelligence as well as various aspects of our behaviour, including alcoholism. There is also research in social psychology that suggests our genes can influence our attitudes (Bouchard, 2004; Tesser, 1993). A study of twins (comparing monozygotic twins with dizygotic, or identical, twins) by James Olson and his colleagues from the University of Western Ontario and the University of British Columbia found a significant genetic component for attitudes relating to preservation of life, equality, athleticism, leadership, and sensory experiences (Olson, Vernon, Harris, & Jang, 2001). Although the exact genetic mechanism that influences attitudes is unknown, researchers believe broad genetic characteristics, such as sensation seeking and cognitive reasoning, may be responsible for these effects. In other words, our general genetic tendencies toward particular types of behaviours—such as a preference for highly arousing activities (e.g., rock climbing, car racing)—may in turn influence more specific attitudes by exposing us to particular environmental factors which also influence development. The old nature versus nurture debate is, on the whole, redundant now. We are products of an interaction between our genetic make-up and our environment that starts even before we are born.

But social psychologists are most interested in attitude formation as a way of predicting what people will do in the future—and as you might guess, our attitudes are not always a very good predictor of our behaviour. Early efforts at HIV prevention, for example, focused on providing people with straightforward information about the factors leading to the spread of HIV (e.g., unprotected sex, sharing needles) with the assumption that this information would lead to changes in attitudes, which in turn would lead to changes in behaviour. In some cases, providing information did lead to changes in attitudes, but people's attitudes were often a poor predictor of their behaviour. The next section examines when attitudes do, and do not, predict behaviour.

HOW ATTITUDES ARE FORMED

METHOD OF ATTITUDE FORMATION	EXAMPLE
Classical conditioning	You feel happy whenever you smell cinnamon because you associate this scent with your mother's kitchen.
Operant conditioning	A child develops a negative attitude toward the pink bicycle he wanted after his grandmother ridicules that preference.
Observational learning/modelling	A university student forms a positive view of cigarettes because his two best friends smoke.

WHEN DO ATTITUDES PREDICT BEHAVIOUR?

In a classic study of the gap between attitudes and behaviour, Richard LaPiere, a sociologist at Stanford University in the 1930s, travelled around the United States with a young Chinese couple (LaPiere, 1934). During the time of LaPiere's study, widespread prejudice against Chinese people was quite common, and many restaurant and hotel managers expressed negative attitudes toward Chinese people. To test how well these attitudes would predict behaviour, LaPiere took this couple on a 10,000 mile trip throughout the United States, which included visits to 251 restaurants, campgrounds, and hotels. What happened? In all 184 restaurants, the Chinese couple was accepted—and they were received with considerable hospitality in 72 of the restaurants. In visits to 66 hotels, they were refused only once. Two months after the trip, LaPiere wrote to all of the places they had visited and asked whether they would accept Chinese patrons. Although about 49 percent of establishments did not respond to the questionnaire, of those who responded, 91 percent said they would not accept such guests, even though such a couple had clearly been served within the last few months. This study shows that the attitude-behaviour link is not always as strong as we think. This section will examine each of the factors that influence the attitude-behaviour link: strength, accessibility, specificity, and social norms.

STRENGTH

Attitudes vary in their strength, and strong attitudes are more likely to predict behaviour than weak ones (Kraus, 1995; Krosnick, Boninger, Chuang, Berent, & Carnot, 1993). Stronger attitudes are highly important to the person, and are often formed on the basis of direct experience. Let's take a look at these two elements.

Questioning the Research:
If people are more likely to donate money to causes they see as important, does this reveal correlation or causation? Can you think of another explanation for this association?

IMPORTANCE. First, and not surprisingly, attitudes on topics that are highly *important* to us are more predictive of our behaviour (Crano, 1997). Many people believe that children learn better in high-quality schools, and that having high-quality schools is important for our society. However, people with young children in school, or who soon will be, are probably more likely to act on these attitudes (e.g., vote to pay higher taxes, donate money to local school boards) than those who will not be affected directly by the quality of schools in their area. Similarly, 23.7 percent of people who see global warming as an important issue report contributing money on behalf of this cause, compared to only 8 percent of those who don't see it as an important issue (Visser, Krosnick, & Simmons, 2003).

DIRECT EXPERIENCE. Second, attitudes that are formed on the basis of *direct experience* are likely to be stronger and are therefore better predictors of behaviour (Fazio & Zanna, 1981; Millar & Millar, 1996; Regan & Fazio, 1977). For example, if you're asked about your attitude toward reporting a student whom you saw cheating on a midterm, your attitude will be more predictive of your behaviour if you have actually been in that situation and had to decide whether to report the person to your professor. If you've never been in this situation, you might believe that you'd act in a certain way, but it's more difficult to predict what you would actually do.

In one study on the impact of direct experience on the attitude-behaviour link, Russell Fazio and Mark Zanna (1978) from the University of Waterloo asked students about their attitudes toward psychology experiments. It was found that if students had actually participated in psychology experiments, their attitudes were more likely to predict their future participation than if students had not participated. In other words, the link between attitudes and behaviour was much stronger for those who had participated in psychology experiments than those who had only read about them. In the case of LaPiere's study of attitudes and behaviour toward Chinese people, some of the people who responded to the questionnaire may not have served the Chinese couple in the first instance and may never have met a Chinese person, so their attitude wasn't a good predictor of their behaviour. Furthermore, of those who had met a Chinese person before, their image of Chinese people may have been very different from the Chinese people who were in front of them.

ACCESSIBILITY

The *ease* or *accessibility* with which one's attitude comes to mind can also influence the attitude-behaviour link (Krosnick, 1989). People who are well informed about a topic are likely to have greater attitude-behaviour consistency than those who are poorly informed, because having a lot of information about a topic increases the accessibility of attitudes about this topic. For example, if you're asked to think about various political issues (e.g., abortion, capital punishment, global warning), the attitudes that come more quickly to your mind are likely to be better predictors of your behaviour in response to these attitudes than if it takes some time for you to recall what you think about the issues. When people with a less accessible attitude encounter the attitude object (such as the Chinese couple), they may act before they've had time to access their attitude, increasing the chance that their behaviour won't be in line with the attitude.

Situational factors can also influence accessibility, and in turn the attitude-behaviour link. As described in Chapter 3, situational factors that increase self-awareness can lead people to engage in behaviour that is in line with their attitudes, perhaps in part because factors that increase self-awareness may also increase the accessibility of one's attitude. For example, Canadian researchers have found that participants who are given a chance to think about their past behaviours prior to expressing their attitudes later show a higher correlation between these attitudes and their subsequent behaviour (Zanna, Olson, & Fazio, 1981). It has also been found that people who watch themselves in a mirror engage in more moral behaviour— presumably because the mirror reminds them of their own positive attitude toward honesty (Batson, Thompson, Seuferling, Whitney, & Strongman, 1999). Finally, simply asking someone to express his or her attitude repeatedly also increases accessibility of that attitude, which in turn should increase the likelihood that this attitude will predict behaviour (Holland, Verplanken, & van Knippenberg, 2003).

On the other hand, situational factors that decrease self-awareness, and/or impair cognition, can weaken the attitude-behaviour link (MacDonald, MacDonald, Zanna, & Fong, 2000; MacDonald, Zanna, & Fong, 1995). Tara MacDonald and her colleagues conducted a study on the effects of alcohol use on intentions to use condoms (MacDonald, Zanna, & Fong, 1996). Fifty-four male Canadian undergraduates were randomly assigned to either the sober or the intoxicated condition. Both groups watched a video and then answered questions, but those in the intoxicated condition were first given three alcoholic drinks. The 10-minute video featured two undergraduates, Mike and Rebecca, who meet at a campus bar, dance and drink with friends, and then walk home to Rebecca's apartment. Mike and Rebecca then begin to get physical, at which point they discuss the fact that neither of them has condoms, and the only nearby store is closed. Rebecca discloses that she is on the pill, so pregnancy prevention is not the issue. At this point the video stops, and students are then asked to answer a series of questions as if they were experiencing the situations in the video.

The findings of this study provide strong (and scary) evidence that alcohol impairs decision-making. First, both sober and intoxicated students saw having unprotected sex in this situation as foolish. On a scale of 1 to 9, sober students rated this behaviour as extremely foolish (8.08) as did intoxicated students (7.67). Similarly, sober students rated this behaviour as extremely irresponsible (8.04) as did intoxicated students (7.83). However, while sober participants were fairly unlikely to report they would engage in sex in this situation (3.83), intoxicated students were very likely to report that they would indeed have sex in this situation (6.78). In fact, only 21 percent of the sober participants reported that they were even fairly likely to have sex in this situation, compared to 77 percent of the intoxicated participants. Although this study doesn't test what students would actually do in this situation, it suggests that alcohol use may lead people to engage in behaviour that they recognize as foolish and irresponsible (and/or to be more honest about it). Thus, in cases in which people are not so focused on or aware of their actual attitudes, people are less likely to show a strong correlation between their attitudes and behaviour. Therefore, the more accessible an attitude is, the stronger the relation between attitude and behaviour.

SPECIFICITY

Consider what might have happened if LaPiere had included a photograph of the young, well-dressed Chinese couple when he asked whether the restaurants and hotels would serve this particular couple. Would the link between attitudes and behaviours have been stronger? It is quite possible, because attitudes toward a specific behaviour show a stronger link to that behaviour than attitudes that are more general (Ajzen & Fishbein, 1977). The correlation between the attitude "How do you feel about using condoms?" and actual condom use is a lot lower than the correlation between the attitude "How do you feel about using condoms every time you have sex in the next month when you are with a new partner?" and actual condom use (Sheeran, Abraham, & Orbell, 1999).

SOCIAL NORMS

Social norms – the implicit and explicit rules that a specific group has for its members on values, beliefs, attitudes, and behaviours.

Social norms, meaning the implicit and explicit rules that a specific group has for its members on values, beliefs, attitudes, and behaviours. These rules influence whether our attitudes predict our behaviour, in part because our behaviour is often heavily influenced by others in our group (Trafimow & Finlay, 1996). For example, you may have a negative attitude toward smoking but you may choose to smoke when you're with certain friends who smoke. You may do this because you're worried that if you refuse to smoke, it will offend them, or you might be ridiculed. Social norms about a particular attitude are also more likely to lead to behaviour because attitudes that are held by those in our social network are stronger, and thus more resistant, to change (Visser & Mirabile, 2004). In terms of LaPiere's study, people's willingness to serve the Chinese couple might have been more strongly predicted by their attitudes if the social norms against Chinese people were particularly powerful.

In one study, researchers examined the impact of exposure to sexual content on television on adolescents' perceived social norms regarding sexual activity (Martino, Collins, Kanouse, Elliott, & Berry, 2005). As predicted, adolescents who reported watching television shows that included high levels of sexual content believed that more of their friends were sexually active. Most importantly, adolescents who believed that more of their friends were sexually active were more likely to report engaging in sexual activity themselves one year later.

Two theories that emphasize the role of social norms in predicting behaviour are the theory of planned behaviour and the prototype/willingness model.

theory of planned behaviour – a theory that describes people's behaviour caused by their attitudes, subjective norms, and perceived behavioural control

THEORY OF PLANNED BEHAVIOUR. As shown in Figure 6.3, the **theory of planned behaviour** developed by Icek Ajzen and Martin Fishbein (1977) describes behaviour as influenced by *intentions*, meaning whether a person plans to engage in a given behaviour. Intentions, in turn, are influenced by a combination of *attitudes* (positive or negative feelings about engaging in a particular behaviour), *subjective norms* (your beliefs about whether other people would support you in engaging in a new behaviour), and *perceived behavioural control* (the extent to which you believe yourself capable of successfully enacting a behaviour). (See the Rate Yourself box for examples of each of these dimensions.) For example, whether you wear sunscreen each time you go to the beach is influenced by whether you intend to wear sunscreen. These intentions, in turn, are influenced by your attitudes (how positively or negatively you feel about wearing sunscreen), your subjective norms (how you think your friends and parents will feel about you wearing sunscreen), and your perceived behavioural control (your confidence in your own ability to actually put on sunscreen).

The theory of planned behaviour is a particularly strong predictor of behaviour when that behaviour is relatively easy for a person to control (e.g., taking vitamins, voting, having a

FIGURE 6.3   PLANNED BEHAVIOUR

According to the theory of planned behaviour, our attitudes, subjective norms, and perceived behavioural control influence our intentions to engage in a behaviour, which in turn influence whether we actually do engage in that behaviour (Ajzen & Fishbein, 1977). In addition, perceived behavioural control also has a direct impact on whether we engage in that behaviour.

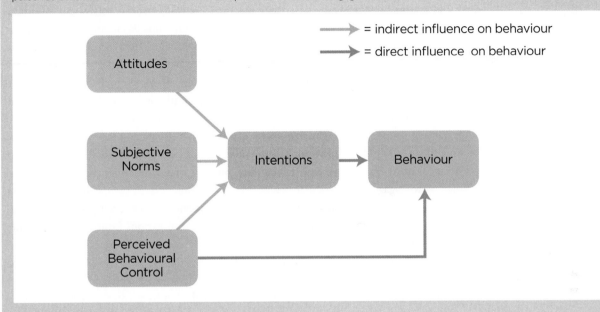

CONDOM USE

Self-Efficacy Scale

INSTRUCTIONS: *These questions ask about your own feelings about using condoms in specific situations. Rate each item on the following scale: strongly disagree = 0, disagree = 1, undecided = 2, agree = 3, strongly agree = 4.*

  1. I feel confident in my ability to put a condom on myself or my partner.

  2. I feel confident in my ability to suggest using condoms with a new partner.

  3. I feel confident that I could remember to use a condom even after I have been drinking.

  4. I feel confident that I could stop to put a condom on myself or my partner even in the heat of passion.

  5. I feel confident in my ability to persuade a partner to accept using a condom when we have intercourse.

  6. I feel confident in my ability to use a condom correctly.

  7. I feel confident I could purchase condoms without feeling embarrassed.

  8. I feel confident that I could use a condom with a partner without "breaking the mood."

  9. I feel confident I could remember to carry a condom with me should I need one.

  10. I feel confident I could use a condom during intercourse without reducing any sexual sensations.

[RATE YOURSELF]

SCORING: Sum up your total number of points on all 10 items.

INTERPRETATION: This scale measures condom use self-efficacy, meaning confidence that one could effectively use condoms. People with higher scores are more confident in their ability to carry out this behaviour, whereas those with lower scores are less confident (Brafford & Beck, 1991).

mammogram; Madden, Ellen, & Ajzen, 1992). This theory is less effective, however, at predicting more spontaneous behaviour (e.g., smoking a cigarette at a party, putting on a seatbelt, using a condom).

prototype/willingness model – a model that describes the role of prototypes in influencing a person's willingness to engage in the behaviour in a given situation

PROTOTYPE/WILLINGNESS MODEL. The **prototype/willingness model** extends the theory of planned behaviour by describing not only the role of social norms and intentions in predicting behaviour, but also the role of prototypes (Gibbons & Gerard, 1995; Gibbons, Gerrard, Blanton, & Russell, 1998; Gibbons, Gerrard, & McCoy, 1995). Prototypes are social images of what people who engage in the behaviour are like. This model also describes the willingness to engage in the behaviour in a given situation. If, for example, you see students who drink and drive as rather stupid and careless, you should be less likely to engage in this behaviour yourself because your prototype of people who do this behaviour is negative. On the other hand, if you see people who drink and drive as rather daring and independent, you may be more likely to engage in this behaviour because, in this case, your prototype is positive. An important feature of the prototype/willingness model is that it describes the role of people's willingness to engage in a particular behaviour. This willingness, in turn, is influenced by an individual's attitudes, subjective norms, prior experience with this behaviour, and prototypes.

The prototype/willingness model is a good predictor of various health-risk behaviours, including smoking, engaging in unprotected sexual intercourse, and exercising (Blanton et al., 2001; Gibbons, Gerrard, Cleveland, Wills, & Brody, 2004; Ouellette, Hessling, Gibbons, Reis-Bergan, & Gerrard, 2005). In one study, researchers asked teenagers to "think for a minute about the type of person your age who drinks alcohol frequently," and then rate your image of that person (e.g., smart, popular, boring, self-confident, independent, confused, etc.; Gerrard et al., 2002). Next, the participants rated their own willingness to drink alcohol in various situations. As predicted, those who didn't drink alcohol rated the drinker prototype more negatively than those who did drink. This suggests that helping teenagers form negative images about those who choose to drink may be one avenue for decreasing underage drinking.

THE TRANS-THEORETICAL MODEL OF BEHAVIOUR CHANGE (TTM)

The trans-theoretical model (TTM) – a model that views a change in behaviour as a progression through a series of stages, including pre contemplation, contemplation, preparation, action, and maintenance.

The **trans-theoretical model** of behaviour change extends the theory of planned behaviour to an individual's readiness to engage in healthy behaviours, such as stopping smoking. Developed by James Prochaska of the University of Rhode Island and colleagues in 1977, the model views a change in behaviour as a progression through a series of stages:

- Stage 1 is precontemplation. At this stage, people are not intending to change their behaviour in the near future (i.e., within the next six months) and are therefore not ready to make a change.
- Stage 2 is contemplation. At this stage, people are intending or getting ready to change their behaviour in the near future (within the next six months).
- Stage 3 is preparation. At this stage, people are ready to take action in the immediate future, usually within the next month.
- Stage 4 is action. At this stage, people have changed their behaviour within the last six months and are working hard to move forward.
- Stage 5 is maintenance. At this stage, people work hard to avoid a relapse and are aware of situations that may tempt them to slip back.

In a study of 756 smokers, Prochaska, Diclemente, Velicer, and Rossi (1993) compared different self-help programs in smoking cessation. They found that "providing smokers interactive feedback about their stages of change, decisional balance, processes of change, self-efficacy, and temptation levels in critical smoking situations" was more effective than providing general self-help feedback (p. 404). In other words, participants who received individualized manuals that matched their stage were more successful in quitting smoking than people who received a general self-help program. This indicates that changing behaviour is most effective if interventions are matched with the individual stages of behaviour change. Although this approach is now used to treat many problem behaviours, some researchers have questioned the effectiveness of interventions that use a stage-based approach in changing smoking behaviour (Riemsma et al., 2003).

Questioning the Research:

Most of the research on the prototype/willingness model has collected data on teenagers and young adults. Do you think this model would apply equally well to predicting behaviour in older populations? Why or why not?

WHY (AND WHEN) ATTITUDES DO MATTER

This section has described factors that influence the link between people's attitudes and their behaviour. By understanding these factors, we can make a better guess about when a person's attitude will predict his or her behaviour, and when it will not. Researchers can design strategies for increasing these factors as a way of changing someone's behaviour. For example, the knowledge that accessibility of an attitude is an important predictor of behaviour could lead health educators to design promotional materials (e.g., brochures, posters, signs, etc.) that are designed to increase the accessibility of various attitudes (e.g., driving sober, using condoms, not smoking).

[CONCEPTS IN CONTEXT]

FACTORS INFLUENCING THE ATTITUDE-BEHAVIOUR LINK

FACTOR	EXAMPLE
Strength	Reggie, who feels very passionately that abortion is an individual choice, is quite likely to volunteer her time to support an organization devoted to this cause.
Accessibility	Although E.J. believes that it is a good idea to vote, he wasn't sure if he was going to find the time to vote in the federal election. However, on election day, he was repeatedly asked by others whether he had voted, which finally led him to make a trip to his local polling station.
Specificity	Sonya's attitude toward studying on a Saturday night while her friends are partying is a much stronger predictor of her studying behaviour on Saturday night than of her general attitude toward studying.
Social norms	Neda's negative attitude toward drinking and driving typically leads her to refuse to drive after drinking. However, when she is with her high school friends, who do not share this attitude, she sometimes drives after drinking.
Trans-theoretical Model of Behaviour Change (TTM)	At the third attempt, Leonor has quit smoking for almost a year. She avoids staying late at pubs as she has learned that once she has a few drinks, she would be tempted to have a smoke.

WHEN DOES ENGAGING IN A BEHAVIOUR LEAD TO ATTITUDE CHANGE?

Although we often describe attitudes as leading to behaviour, at least under some circumstances the link between attitudes and behaviour can go in both ways. In other words, in some cases our behaviour can form our attitudes. In one of the first studies to demonstrate how effort justification (i.e., justifying the effort we put into a task) can lead to attitude change, Elliott Aronson and Judson Mills (1959) conducted a study with female university students on the impact of severity of initiation on liking for a group. Women were invited to participate in a discussion group on sex (which was seen as an exciting thing to do), but in order to be in the group, you had to go through a form of initiation (this initiation was supposedly just to make sure that everyone in the group would be comfortable talking). In the mild initiation condition, women read out loud a list of 12 sexually oriented words (e.g., petting, kissing, necking)—a somewhat embarrassing task, but one that was not particularly unpleasant. In the severe initiation condition, on the other hand, participants read a list of highly sexually oriented words as well as two vivid sexual passages from novels. Participants in the control condition were included in the group without having gone through either initiation. Then, all participants were given headphones to listen to a portion of the group discussion (supposedly to prepare them for their own participation the following week). What did they hear? A very boring discussion of "secondary sex behaviour in lower animals." But what did the women in the different conditions think? As predicted, those who had endured a lot to get into the group (the severe condition) liked the group discussion more than those in either of the other groups. In this section, we will examine ways that behaviour changes attitudes.

COGNITIVE DISSONANCE THEORY

cognitive dissonance theory – a theory that describes attitude change as occurring in order to reduce the unpleasant arousal people experience when they engage in a behaviour that conflicts with their attitude or when they hold two conflicting attitudes

One of the best-known and important theories in social psychology is cognitive dissonance theory, which was developed by Leon Festinger (1957). According to this theory, when a person holds two conflicting cognitions or engages in a behaviour that conflicts with a cognition, he or she experiences an unpleasant psychological state of arousal (or dissonance). Imagine that you are a member of a student organization that encourages recycling, but one day you toss an empty soda can into the nearest trash bin instead of carrying the can until you find a recycling bin. This act should create a state of cognitive dissonance because you've engaged in a behaviour (throwing a can into a trash bin) that is not in line with your attitude (that recycling is important).

According to Leon Festinger (1957), people are highly motivated to reduce the dissonance caused by holding inconsistent attitudes, or engaging in counter-attitudinal behaviour. But how can we reduce such dissonance, or negative arousal? One way is by changing our behaviour so that it is in line with our attitudes (e.g., you could go back and put the can in the recycling bin). However, it is often hard to "undo" behaviours after the act, making this method of reducing dissonance relatively uncommon.

Another way to reduce the unpleasant arousal caused by inconsistency is to decide that this inconsistency isn't really a problem, because these attitudes and/or behaviours aren't very important (Simon, Greenberg, & Brehm, 1995). For example, if you engage in some types of counter-attitudinal behaviour under conditions of high choice, you could later see your attitude and behaviour as less important (e.g., "Well, I smoke, but that's not nearly as dangerous as driving without my seatbelt"). However, this strategy of *trivialization* isn't used very often, because it isn't as effective with highly important decisions (e.g., "Well, it really doesn't matter whom I marry").

Finally, and most commonly, we can reduce feelings of inconsistency by changing our attitudes to match our behaviour, or by changing one attitude to match another. For example, once you have stated an attitude, or engaged in a behaviour, that goes against an attitude you hold, you are likely to change your initial attitude so that you feel consistent. If a smoker is trying to quit but she relapses, later she may see smoking as less risky (Gibbons, Eggleston, & Benthin, 1997).

In general, people have difficulty admitting that their attitudes were wrong, so once they've stated an attitude they often find ways to continue to justify that attitude as the correct one. For example, at the start of the Iraq war, some Canadians (and Americans and Britons) supported the policy of war because they believed that Iraq had weapons of mass destruction. However, once later information revealed that Iraq did not in fact have such weapons, many of these people continued to justify their original attitude, either by saying that Iraq could eventually have developed them or that liberating the Iraqi people from Sadam Hussein was also a good reason for going to war.

This section will examine four distinct reasons why we might change our attitudes as a result of cognitive dissonance: insufficient justification, insufficient deterrence, effort justification, and post-decision dissonance.

INSUFFICIENT JUSTIFICATION. The first study to demonstrate the impact of cognitive dissonance on attitude change was conducted by Leon Festinger and his colleague Merrill Carlsmith (1959). Each participant came into the lab to take part in a study on performance and was given an extremely boring task to complete—to move each of 48 spools of thread a quarter turn in one direction, then another quarter turn, then another quarter turn, and then back again to their starting position, for an entire hour. Then, after the participant was finally told that the experiment was finished, the experimenter asked for a favour. He explained that this experiment was not really on "measures of performance," as the participant had been told, but was actually on the influence of expectations about a task on how people see the task. The participant was further told that, being in the control condition, he or she was not given any prior expectation about what to expect, but the next participant, who was due to arrive any minute, was in the "positive expectation" condition. Moreover, the experimenter explained, the research assistant who was supposed to give the next student the positive expectations was running late, and it would be appreciated if the participant would be willing to stay and just tell the next participant that the experiment was really fun and exciting. Some of the participants were offered $20 (a considerable sum in the 1950s) to lie to the next participants, whereas others were offered only $1 to tell this lie. All participants agreed to lie, and after doing so, they were asked by the experimenter what they thought of the experiment (on a 1 to 25 scale, with 1 indicating very unenjoyable).

What do you think happened? Contrary to reward theory, those who were given $20 admitted that they found the task boring, as did those who were given no money. But what about those who were given $1 to lie? As shown in Figure 6.4, they actually claimed they sort of liked the task!

This experiment demonstrates that receiving insufficient justification for engaging in an attitude-discrepant behaviour can lead to attitude change. In other words, if you engage in a behaviour that is counter-attitudinal, you must make some kind of a justification. If the external justification is high ("Well, I did get $20") you will attribute your behaviour to external

---

FIGURE 6.4 **CAN RECEIVING A SMALL REWARD LEAD TO GREATER ENJOYMENT?**

In a classic experiment, Festinger & Carlsmith (1959) had participants do a boring task. Then they paid each one to tell the next participant that the experiment was enjoyable. According to a behaviourist model, those who were paid $20 should find the task more enjoyable than those who were paid only $1. However, these findings showed the reverse: Participants who were paid $1 enjoyed participating in the study more than those who were paid $20, providing support for cognitive dissonance theory.

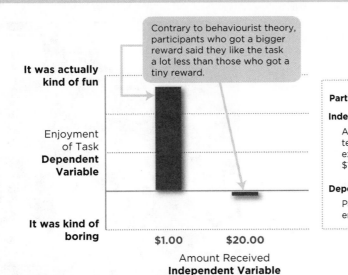

Contrary to behaviourist theory, participants who got a bigger reward said they like the task a lot less than those who got a tiny reward.

It was actually kind of fun

Enjoyment of Task
Dependent Variable

It was kind of boring

$1.00 $20.00

Amount Received
Independent Variable

Participants: University students

Independent Variable:
Amount participants were paid to tell the next participant that the experment was enjoyable: either $1 or $20

Dependent Variable
Participants' ratings of their actual enjoyment of the study

Source: Festinger, L., & Carlsmith, J. (1959). Cognitive consequence of forced compliance. *The Journal of Abnormal and Social Psychology, 58*, 203–210.

factors and not change your attitude ("Boy, that task really was boring, but worth it for $20"), but if the external justification is low ($1), you must explain your behaviour using internal factors ("Well, I must have at least liked the task a little").

Although the Festinger and Carlsmith (1959) study demonstrated the negative effects of insufficient justification—that is, that people convince themselves they like something they didn't really enjoy—this principle can also be used to promote positive behaviours. For example, Michael Leippe and Donna Eisenstadt (1994) found that asking "white" students to write an essay in favour of a policy doubling funds for academic scholarships for minority students (at the cost of such scholarships for white students) led the students to become more supportive of this policy. Similarly, and as described in the following Health Connections box, cognitive dissonance can be used to promote changes in unhealthy behaviours.

HEALTH CONNECTIONS

Using Cognitive Dissonance to Create a Change in Health Behaviour

Some researchers have used cognitive dissonance as a way of promoting healthier behaviours. Alexandra Peterson and her colleagues from the University of Western Ontario conducted a study inducing dissonance in smokers by asking them to deliver a speech in front of a camera on the dangers of smoking that, participants were told, would later be shown to high school students as part of an anti-smoking campaign (Peterson, Haynes, & Olson, 2008). In this case, dissonance was operationalized (created) by inducing the participants' awareness of their own hypocrisy as smokers giving such a speech. To help them write the speech, participants were given an information sheet on the dangers of smoking, and all participants ended up including all the points on the sheet in their speeches. As a control measure, an additional group of participants (also smokers) were given the information sheet, but cognitive dissonance was not induced in their case as they were not asked to behave hypocritically by giving the anti-smoking speech.

The results showed that some of the participants in the cognitive dissonance condition subsequently reported a greater intention to quit smoking, but only those with high self-esteem. Those with low self-esteem did not report a greater intention to quit smoking even after making the hypocritical speech. The authors interpret the results as demonstrating that, at least among individuals with relatively high self-esteem, dissonance resulting from hypocrisy can be used to encourage young smokers to strengthen their behavioural intention to quit smoking (Peterson et al., 2008).

This effect doesn't apply only to smokers. In a second study, the results were similar for students (not specifically smokers) who were asked to write a speech on healthy behaviours that they were told would be used in a public health promotion campaign that would identify them as the author. Cognitive dissonance was induced by making participants' own health behaviour salient to them, on the assumption that most people in a student sample would feel that they should behave in a healthier manner. As with the smokers in the previous study, those with high self-esteem subsequently reported a greater intention to improve their healthy

behaviours (Peterson et al., 2008). The authors suggest that individuals with high self-esteem typically feel more dissonance than those with low self-esteem, because the former have higher expectations for themselves (e.g., they expect their actions to be rational and consistent with their attitudes).

Findings such as these add to the complexity of our understanding of cognitive dissonance: at least under some circumstances, dissonance is more likely to lead to improved (or changed) behaviour for those with high self-esteem, but not those with low self-esteem. These findings also resonate with Ajzen & Fishbein's (1977) theory of planned behaviour, in which perceived behavioural control is an important predictor of attitudes predicting behaviour. In other words, people will behave in a manner consistent with their attitudes, or will change their behaviour to reduce dissonance, if they think that they are capable of making the change (i.e., they have high self-esteem), but not if they don't feel capable.

Digital Vision/ Getty Images, inc.

INSUFFICIENT DETERRENCE/PUNISHMENT. Although offering an insufficient reward for a behaviour is one way of creating attitude change, such change can also occur if you offer an insufficient deterrence for not doing something desirable (Aronson & Carlsmith, 1963; Freedman, 1965). In one study, children were brought into the lab and shown a bunch of toys. Most of the toys were pretty common (e.g., blocks, dolls, Etch A Sketch®), but there was one really cool toy: Robby the Robot. Robby the Robot walked by himself, moved his arms, and made a noise, and this toy was novel for all the children. After showing the children all the toys, the experimenter said he needed to go get something from another room and he'd be back in five minutes. In one condition, he told the children that they could play with any of the toys except Robby the Robot, and that if they played with Robby they would be in big trouble (severe deterrent). In the other condition, they were just told to play with any of the toys they wanted, except Robby. What happened? Well, all children did avoid playing with Robby the Robot, but when they were asked to rate the toys at the end of the study, evidence for self-persuasion occurred. As expected, those who received the severe threat still liked Robby a lot, but those who received only a mild threat didn't report liking Robby that much at all. This study shows the effect of *insufficient deterrence* on leading to attitude change.

The effects of insufficient deterrence on attitude change last over time. Six weeks after children participated in the "Robby the Robot" study, a different experimenter brought the same children into the lab to participate in a new study on creativity in drawing (Freedman, 1965). While she was scoring their drawing test, she said they could play with any toy in the room, including the robot. Of those who previously had received the strong threat, 77 percent played with the robot now, yet only 33 percent of those who previously had received the mild threat played with the robot. These findings suggest that the attitude change produced by the mild threat condition was indeed long-lasting and internally based.

EFFORT JUSTIFICATION. Have you ever spent a lot of time and energy on something and then ultimately achieved it, but found it wasn't worth the effort? Well, you probably haven't had this experience. Why? Because this kind of inconsistency arouses cognitive dissonance. So if you have this feeling, you work quickly to justify the effort you spent. This was demonstrated by the research at the start of this section on the impact of mild versus severe initiations on interest in participating in a (surprisingly boring) sex discussion group. Similarly, in a more recent study, students who were asked to perform an embarrassing task—in this case walking across a campus quad wearing a grass skirt, coconut bra, and hat featuring plastic fruit—had estimated that the distance they have to travel was less under conditions of high choice than under conditions of low choice (Balcetis & Dunning, 2007). Our desire to justify our effort—and thus avoid the uncomfortable experience of cognitive dissonance—explains a variety of real-world phenomena, including why we stay in bad relationships far too long, why people are so attached to their fraternity/sorority, and why contestants on television report that this highly embarrassing experience was so worthwhile.

In line with the predictions of research on effort justification, simply forcing someone to undergo a challenging task can facilitate attitude and behaviour change. One study with overweight participants examined the impact on weight loss of engaging in high versus low effort cognitive tasks (Axsom & Cooper, 1985). Participants in this study completed several tasks that were completely unrelated to weight loss, but were high in effort in one condition and low in effort in the other condition. In both conditions participants engaged in auditory, visual and reading tasks. Effort was manipulated by varying the difficulty and duration of these tasks (e.g., 10 minutes in the low effort condition versus 50 minutes in the high effort condition). Participants completed these tasks during five experimental sessions. Participants' weight was measured at the last session and at the six-month follow-up session. It was found that those who completed the high effort task lost an average of 8.55 pounds, whereas those who completed the low effort task showed no weight change. The authors argued that participants who were in the high effort condition perceived the goal of their task, which was losing weight, as more attractive and they pursued the goal regardless of how successful they were during the five experimental sessions. In Chapter 9 you will encounter a similar finding in relation to group membership: people feel greater commitment to groups that are harder to join. The Environmental Connections box describes yet another way in which cognitive dissonance theory can lead to behaviour change.

ENVIRONMENTAL CONNECTIONS

Using Cognitive Dissonance to Increase Water Conservation

Elliot Aronson and his colleagues conducted a clever study in which they used cognitive dissonance to increase water conservation (Dickerson, Thibodeau, Aronson, & Miller, 1992). Female swimmers were asked to help with a water conservation project as they exited the pool and headed to the locker room. In one condition, participants were asked several questions about water conservation, including whether they took as short a shower as they could. They were also asked to sign a flyer stating that they took short showers. In two other conditions, participants were either asked the questions about water conservation or were asked to sign the flyer. Finally, in the control condition participants did not answer questions or sign the flyer. Female researchers then followed the women into the locker room and surreptitiously timed the length of their showers. As predicted, participants who both signed the flyer and answered the questions took significantly shorter showers than those who did neither of these acts (220.5 seconds versus 301.8 seconds). Participants who did only one act (signed the flyer or answered questions) took showers that were midway between those in the control condition and those who completed both acts (148 seconds in both of these conditions). These findings demonstrate that reminding people of their past behaviour that conflicts with their attitude (meaning that they have taken long showers but are in favour of water conservation) encourages behaviour change (meaning shorter showers).

© iStockPhoto

JUSTIFYING DECISIONS/POST-DECISION DISSONANCE. People often have to make difficult decisions, and after they do so, they may experience some dissonance because choosing one appealing option also means giving up another appealing option (Harmon-Jones & Harmon-Jones, 2002; Schultz, Léveillé, & Lepper, 1999; Simon, Krawczyk, & Holyoak, 2004). People often resolve this dissonance by changing their attitudes toward both of the alternatives as a way of reducing this discomfort (Brownstein, Read, & Simon, 2004). For example, if you are torn between buying one of two cars, each of which has some pluses and some minuses, after you've bought one of the cars you may experience some discomfort because in making this decision you're very aware of what you've given up in the process. In this instance, people would tend to increase their positive feelings toward the alternative they've chosen (e.g., "I am so happy driving this SUV because I feel so safe"), and at the same time, increase their negative feelings toward the alternative they've rejected (e.g., "I can't believe anyone still buys a minivan—they just look so dorky"). Amazingly enough, this decrease in liking for highly rated alternatives that we've rejected is seen in children as young as four years old and even in monkeys (Egan, Santos, & Bloom, 2007). This finding that attitude change occurs following rejection of an alternative even in these populations suggests that the drive to reduce dissonance may be a fundamental aspect of human psychology that occurs even without extensive experience in decision-making and the ability to engage in highly sophisticated cognitive reasoning.

To test the impact of post-decision dissonance on evaluations of various alternatives, Jack Brehm recruited women to rate different consumer products (e.g., a coffee pot, toaster, radio; Brehm, 1956). After the women rated the items, they were told they could take one of the items home. Participants in the high-dissonance condition were given a difficult choice between two items that they rated very close together. Participants in the low-dissonance condition were given an easy choice, between items they rated pretty far apart. They then received their gift, read a few research papers about the products, and then re-rated the products. What do you think happened? In the low-dissonance condition, ratings didn't change very much. But in the high-dissonance condition, participants' ratings of the two objects that they had previously rated very similarly and had just chosen between were now much further apart. Similarly, people who are asked to choose between two jobs (each of which has some good features and some bad features) initially rate these jobs as rather equal in appeal (Simon et al., 2004). However, once they have been forced to select one job and reject the other, the difference in how much they like the two jobs becomes significantly greater as they justify their decision.

REVISIONS TO DISSONANCE THEORY

Because cognitive dissonance theory is one of the most famous theories in the field of social psychology, researchers have continued to investigate the precise conditions under which attitude change through cognitive dissonance does and does not occur. Two of the most commonly discussed revisions to the original theory are the "new look" at dissonance theory and the self-standards model.

THE "NEW LOOK." According to the "new look" at dissonance theory created by Joel Cooper and Russell Fazio (1984), four steps are necessary for people to experience attitude change following dissonance:

1. negative or aversive consequences
2. personal responsibility
3. physiological arousal and discomfort
4. attribution of that arousal to their own behaviour

First, attitude change only occurs if a person experiences *negative or aversive consequence* for their behaviour (e.g., lying to someone, doing something embarrassing; Johnson, Kelly, & LeBlanc, 1995; Scher & Cooper, 1989). For example, if you try to mislead someone into thinking the upcoming task is fun when it's actually boring (like the classic Festinger & Carlsmith study on turning spools of thread), but the other participant is unconvinced, you don't experience negative consequences, and therefore don't experience dissonance and don't change your attitude (Cooper & Worchel, 1970).

Second, attitude change occurs only when a person takes *personal responsibility* for the negative consequences of their action. Previous research had shown that if people are aware of the unwanted negative consequences of their actions when they decide to act, they feel a greater sense of personal responsibility (and dissonance). Using this finding, participants in a study were required to deliver a counter-attitudinal speech, with some participants made aware that their speech was going to be used to change others' opinions (i.e., a negative consequence/personal responsibility) and other participants not told this (i.e., no personal responsibility; Goethals, Cooper, & Naficy, 1979). In the study's results, only those who were aware of the potential negative consequences of their action before they made the speech, and who therefore felt a sense of responsibility for their action, showed attitude change.

FIGURE 6.5　A NEW LOOK AT DISSONANCE

According to the "new look" at dissonance theory, engaging in a behaviour that contradicts your attitude (such as throwing a can into a trash bin instead of a recycling bin if you are strongly pro-recycling) can lead you to change your attitude to match your behaviour, but only if certain conditions are met. These conditions are experiencing negative consequences for engaging in the behaviour, taking personal responsibility for engaging in the behaviour, feeling uncomfortable arousal for engaging in that behaviour, and, finally, attributing the arousal to engaging in that behaviour. If, and only if, all of these conditions are met, you then experience dissonance and change your attitude to match your behaviour (such as feeling that recycling isn't really that important; Cooper & Fazio, 1984).

Engage in a behaviour that contradicts your attitude

Step 1. Experience negative or aversive consequences

Step 2. Take personal responsibility

Step 3. Experience physiological arousal and discomfort

Step 4. Attribute that arousal to his/her own behaviour

Change attitude to match the behaviour

Third, attitude change should occur only in cases where a person experiences *physiological arousal and discomfort* (Elkin & Leippe, 1986; Elliot & Devine, 1994). To test this part of the new look at dissonance theory, researchers randomly assigned participants to one of three conditions (Steele, Southwick, & Critchlow, 1981):

1. One group of participants gave their attitudes toward a tuition raise (the control condition).
2. Another group of participants wrote an essay in favour of raising tuition (which would lead to dissonance), and then tasted and rated different types of water.
3. The final group of participants wrote the same essay, but then tasted and rated different types of vodka.

As predicted, participants who tasted different types of water showed a significant increase in positive attitudes toward the tuition raise—the typical dissonance effect. However, participants in the dissonance alcohol condition showed almost no attitude change. These students reduced their arousal by drinking, so didn't experience the arousal that would be necessary for them to change their attitude.

Fourth, attitude change should occur only when a person *attributes that arousal to his or her own behaviour*. If you attribute your arousal to some external factor (e.g., wearing weird glasses, seeing a funny cartoon, anticipating painful shocks, believing you have been given a stimulating drug), there is no dissonance, and in turn, no attitude change (Cooper, Fazio, & Rhodewalt, 1978; Croyle & Cooper, 1983; Fried & Aronson, 1995; Losch & Cacioppo, 1990; Pittman, 1975). Testing for the impact of arousal on attitude change, Zanna and Cooper (1974) gave student participants a pill (a placebo or sugar pill), which some students were told would probably lead them to experience some arousal. As expected, those who attributed their arousal to the pill didn't show any attitude change following the dissonance-inducing task (writing a counter-attitudinal essay). Those who weren't told about the pill's supposed tendency to cause arousal showed the predicted attitude change.

Although the new look at dissonance theory generated much interest among social psychologists, some recent research points to a few weaknesses in this theory. Specifically, the evidence now suggests that people can show attitude change after engaging in an attitude-inconsistent behaviour even in the absence of any aversive consequences (Harmon-Jones, 2000). In one study, participants drank an unpleasant beverage (Kool-Aid with vinegar) and then wrote a sentence saying they liked it, either under conditions of high choice (e.g., the participants could choose which side to write on, although the experimenter pointed out that he was in need of more people to write that they liked the beverage) or low choice (the participants were told they had been randomly assigned to write that they liked the beverage; Harmon-Jones, Brehm, Greenberg, Simon, & Nelson, 1996). Although participants in both choice conditions then simply threw the paper away (and therefore didn't experience any negative consequences), those who wrote the sentence under a condition of high choice reported liking the beverage more than those who wrote under a condition of low choice (see Figure 6.6). In contrast, those who tasted a pleasant beverage showed no difference in rating in the two conditions.

FIGURE 6.6   CAN GREATER CHOICE LEAD TO GREATER ATTITUDE CHANGE?

In this experiment, participants were asked to taste either a delicious or a really nasty-tasting drink, and write a sentence saying they liked it. Some participants were given less freedom than others about writing the sentence. As predicted participants who had no choice about the position they took on the drink reported liking the unpleasant drink much less than those who "chose" to write they liked it.

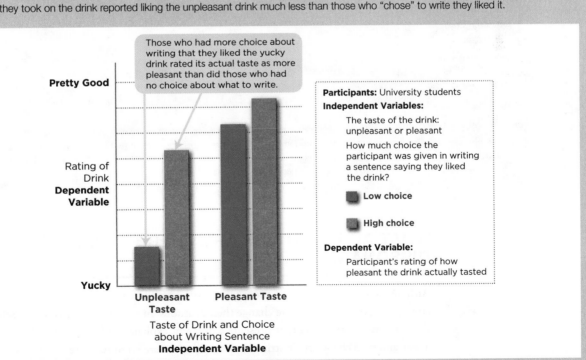

Source: Harmon-Jones, E., Brehm, J., Greenberg, J., Simon, L., & Nelson, D. (1996). Evidence that the production of aversive consequences is not necessary to create cognitive dissonance. *Journal of Personality and Social Psychology, 70*, 5–16.

SELF-STANDARDS MODEL. Jeff Stone and Joel Cooper (Stone, 2003; Stone & Cooper, 2001, 2003) created the self-standards model of cognitive dissonance. This model proposes that people experience discomfort whenever they see their behaviour as deviating from some type of important personal or normative standard, but that the strategy they use to reduce this dissonance will depend on the thoughts about the self that are currently accessible. Attitude change will occur, as a way of reducing this dissonance, when no self-relevant thoughts are available or, especially, when self-relevant thoughts are available that are directly relevant to the behaviour. For example, if you write an essay in favour of decreasing funding for handicapped services at your university, you then become even more in favour of this decrease if you are given positive feedback about your personal attributes that are relevant to the context (e.g., in this case, your lack of compassion for handicapped services) as a way of justifying your behaviour. On the other hand, attitude change won't occur when you receive positive feedback about your personal attributes that are irrelevant to the given behaviour (e.g., your creativity), because in this case your focus is shifted away from your own personal standards of behaviour.

Can watching others engage in inconsistent behaviour lead us to change our own attitudes? A recent study shows exactly that. Students who see another student make a counter-attitudinal speech advocating for tuition increases become more supportive of that issue themselves (Norton, Monin, Cooper, & Hogg, 2003). This effect is particularly strong when participants know that the speaker disagrees with the position. Why does experiencing such "vicarious dissonance" lead to attitude change? Apparently we can feel uncomfortable when we watch someone else, particularly someone whom we respect, engage in counter-attitudinal behaviour, and this discomfort leads us to change our own attitudes to reduce this dissonance.

self-standards model – a model that proposes people experience discomfort whenever they see their behaviour as deviating from some type of important personal or normative standard, but that the strategy they use to reduce this dissonance will depend on what thoughts about the self are currently accessible

Questioning the Research:

Should experiencing "vicarious dissonance" lead to as much attitude change as experiencing dissonance from our own actions? Why or why not?

[CONCEPTS IN CONTEXT]

COGNITIVE DISSONANCE THEORY AND REVISIONS TO DISSONANCE THEORY

THEORY	EXAMPLE
Cognitive dissonance theory	Joe goes through a humiliating and painful fraternity initiation. He then develops a tremendous love for his fraternity.
The "new look" at dissonance theory	As part of a class project, Shadi writes an essay proposing a decrease in scholarship aid for university students (even though she disagrees with this proposal). Shadi is relieved to learn that the essays will be thrown out immediately. She continues to oppose the reduction in scholarship aid.
Self-standards model	Étienne writes a paper proposing a decreased emphasis on recycling on campus as part of a business internship. Although he disagrees with this policy change, Étienne is very pleased when he receives an "A" on his paper—along with very positive comments on his writing. Étienne continues to oppose this change in emphasis.

WHAT ALTERNATIVES ARE THERE TO COGNITIVE DISSONANCE THEORY?

Although cognitive dissonance theory has existed for some time, there are other theories that attempt to explain why people change their attitudes. In a study designed to test self-affirmation theory, an alternative that presents a different explanation for how people resolve dissonance and thus change their attitudes, participants were recruited based on measures of their appreciation of the arts, with researchers only choosing participants who had either very high scores or very low scores (Steele & Liu, 1983). To create dissonance, participants were first asked to write an essay that opposed giving high priority to funding for research on chronic diseases and handicaps and their treatment. Next, all participants rated their appreciation of beauty in the arts, literature, architecture, and so on. Finally, participants rated the strength of their essay. As predicted, participants who strongly valued the arts rated their essays as very strong, giving themselves an average of 24.4 on a scale of 1 to 31 points. Researchers expected this result as participants' rating of their appreciation of the arts after writing the essay had given them an opportunity to affirm an important part of themselves, their love and appreciation of the arts, and by doing so resolve their dissonance without resorting to rating their essays as poor in quality. On the other hand, participants who were low on valuing the arts, and therefore didn't experience a self-affirmation boost by rating their love and appreciation for the arts after writing the essay, rated their essays an average of 8.5. In other words, they resorted to rating their essays as poor in order to resolve the dissonance they experienced from writing a counter-attitudinal essay. Self-affirmation theory thus offers an alternative explanation for how dissonance can be resolved. In this section, we will examine this theory further, as well as two other theories that propose alternatives to cognitive dissonance theory—self-perception theory and impression management theory.

SELF-PERCEPTION THEORY

According to Bem's (1967) **self-perception theory**, people don't actually change their attitudes but simply look to their own behaviour to determine what their attitudes are. In other words, we don't change our attitudes as a way of resolving tension or justifying our behaviour, as posited by cognitive dissonance theory. Instead, we see our behaviour as providing important information about our true attitudes. To test this theory, Daryl Bem told participants about the Festinger and Carlsmith study in which participants turned spools of thread and were then asked to lie to new participants about having enjoyed the task. Bem asked his participants to guess the attitudes of the participants in the Festinger and Carlsmith study. As he predicted, his participants guessed that those who had received $20 for telling others that they had liked the task had lied for the money. The participants also guessed that those who had received only $1 must have actually liked the task (Who would lie for just a dollar?). In other words, they reached conclusions by predicting attitude from behaviours.

self-perception theory – the theory that people infer their attitudes by simply observing their behaviour

Stuart Valins conducted a very clever study to test the effect of self-perception of attitudes on behaviour (Valins, 1966). Male university students were shown "centrefold pictures" of beautiful naked women while they were "hooked up" to electrodes that supposedly measured their heartbeats, and this information was provided to the participants as they looked at the pictures. The fictitious heartbeat information was actually controlled by the experimenter, and during one randomly selected photo, the heartbeats would speed up. The men assumed that their heartbeat was fastest in response to that particular photo. When the experiment was over, the researcher let the men pick one of the pictures to take home: men overwhelmingly chose the photo that they thought they liked the most, based on their perceived heartbeat rate. This study demonstrates the power of self-perception in determining our attitudes—participants clearly looked to their "behaviour" (e.g., their supposed heart rate) to determine their attitude.

IMPRESSION MANAGEMENT THEORY

Impression management theory is based on the idea that individuals try to maintain impressions that are consistent with the perceptions they want to convey to others. According to impression management theory, people aren't motivated to be consistent in their behaviours and attitudes, but rather to appear consistent (Baumeister, 1982). In other words, we don't want to be seen as hypocritical and therefore try to show others that our attitudes and behaviours are in line, even if they are not. In one study, participants who wrote a counter-attitudinal essay under "public conditions" (e.g., they had to put their name, phone number, address, and major on the essay), even under no-choice conditions, showed just as much attitude change as those who were exposed to the typical dissonance condition (e.g., they were given high choice

impression management theory – a theory that individuals try to maintain impressions that are consistent with the perceptions they want to convey to others

and their essay remained anonymous; Baumeister & Tice, 1984). These findings suggest that concerns about self-presentation can also influence attitude change as participants in the no-choice condition should not have experienced enough dissonance for their attitudes to change as greatly as did the attitudes of those who had no choice about writing the essay.

Although there are cases in which stating attitudes anonymously decreases the effects of cognitive dissonance, supporting the notion that people are concerned about managing others' impressions of them, impression management theory can't explain other research findings. For example, people are also more likely to change their attitudes following an interaction with an unattractive (e.g., rude and unpleasant) experimenter than an attractive one (Rosenfeld, Giacalone, & Tedeschi, 1984). This finding suggests, in line with cognitive dissonance theory, that people show more attitude change when they have to justify their reasons for engaging in a given behaviour—and interacting with a rather unappealing experimenter should require more justification than interacting with a more pleasant one. In contrast, impression management theory would predict that greater attitude change occurs in front of the attractive experimenter, a situation where you would be more motivated to appear consistent as one presumably cares more about the impression on those one likes. Similarly, impression management theory cannot easily explain the results of experiments with children, such as in the Robby the Robot study. These children were too young to be motivated to appear consistent to the experimenter. Moreover, why did they still not play with Robby the Robot later with a different experimenter—i.e., in a situation that frees them from a need to appear consistent to an experimenter?

SELF-AFFIRMATION THEORY

Claude Steele posits that engaging in attitude-discrepant behaviour makes people feel bad about themselves, and they are therefore motivated to revalidate the integrity of their self-concept (Steele & Liu, 1983). **Self-affirmation theory** thus describes how people can reduce the arousal caused by cognitive dissonance by affirming a different part of their identities, even if that identity is completely unrelated to the cause of the arousal. Contrary to the original cognitive dissonance theory, this validation can be achieved in a number of ways, including but not limited to resolving dissonance. As described in the study at the start of this section, participants who valued the arts and were able to affirm this part of themselves rated their essays opposing research for chronic disease treatment as stronger than those who didn't value the arts (and thus did not experience self-affirmation from rating their attitudes about the arts; Steele & Liu, 1983). Self-affirmation theory thus suggests that the participants in Festinger and Carlsmith's study could have resolved their dissonance in a variety of ways (e.g., donating money to a charity, helping someone in distress). In these cases, participants would feel better about themselves, and then not feel the need to change their attitudes to be in line with their behaviour.

In another study testing self-affirmation theory, Steele and colleagues gave participants positive or negative feedback about a personality test and then had participants rate 10 popular music albums (Steele, Spencer, & Lynch, 1993). Participants were allowed to keep either their fifth- or six-rated album, whichever they preferred. After they selected the album to keep, they then re-rated all the albums. What would dissonance theory predict? That after making a decision, they'd like the chosen album even more than the unchosen album (remember they were awfully close). This was true for most participants. However, and in line with self-affirmation theory, participants who had received positive feedback on the personality test didn't change their ratings. This study was replicated using participants with high and low self-esteem, and half of the participants were given a test that made their self-esteem salient. Most people again increased their rating of their chosen album, but those with high self-esteem who had this self-esteem made salient didn't show this inflation in their rating of the album they chose.

Other studies have also found links between self-affirmation and self-esteem. Jeff Schimel from the University of Alberta and colleagues investigated in three different studies whether affirming the self intrinsically would reduce threats to self-esteem (Schimel, Arndt, Banko, & Cook, 2004).

self-affirmation theory – a theory that describes how people can reduce the arousal caused by cognitive dissonance by affirming a different part of their identities, even if that part is completely unrelated to the cause of the arousal

In the first two studies, they found that on a math task (made potentially threatening to female participants by making salient the stereotype that women are less good at math than men) the opportunity to receive some self-affirmation prior to the task improved performance, as self-handi-capping (i.e., creating obstacles for oneself in anticipation of failing a task) was reduced. In line with self-affirmation theory, being able to feel good about an aspect of the self is thus viewed as having acted as a buffer against the threat to a different aspect of the self. Finally, in the third study, Schimel and colleagues found that people felt less anxious about potentially threatening social interactions when they were first given the opportunity to receive self-affirmation.

Overall, self-affirmation appears to function as a coping mechanism to bolster threatened self-esteem. Other Canadian researchers have also found evidence for this. In a study of people with low self-esteem, it was found that self-affirmation reduced their tendency to lower their estimates of their performance in situations where they expected immediate feedback on their performance and lowering their estimation protected them from the interpersonal threat that is inherent in such feedback (Spencer, Fein, & Lomore, 2001). The researchers conclude that the findings suggest that people can cope with threats to interpersonal aspects of the self by affirming other important aspects of the self.

Although self-affirmation may be a way to reduce dissonance without changing one's atti-tude, some evidence suggests that people prefer to resolve inconsistency directly by chang-ing their behaviour to make it less inconsistent, rather than get rid of dissonance indirectly (e.g., by self-affirming; Stone, Wiegand, Cooper, & Aronson, 1997). For example, if people are reminded of their failure to volunteer, and then given an opportunity to resolve this discrep-ancy directly (e.g., donate money to the homeless) or indirectly (e.g., buy condoms to show they are careful), 67 percent of people donate, but only 11 percent purchase condoms.

WHICH THEORY IS RIGHT?

This is an ongoing question. Currently, cognitive dissonance theory and self-affirmation theory are seen as more likely explanations of behaviour leading to attitude change than impression manage-ment theory and self-perception theory. However, and as described in this section, researchers con-tinue to examine the specific conditions under which behaviour change leads to attitude change.

[CONCEPTS IN CONTEXT]

ALTERNATIVES TO COGNITIVE DISSONANCE THEORY

THEORY	EXAMPLE
Self-perception theory	A student realizes that she must be attracted to the teaching assistant in her English literature course because she tries to sit beside him every day in class.
Impression management theory	Aneta is a vegetarian who agrees to eat veal during a psychology experiment on taste preferences. She falsely reports liking veal to the experimenter so that she appears consistent.
Self-affirmation theory	Steve feels bad about himself for littering after he left his coffee cup by the tree where he was sitting in the park. However, after he signs up to donate blood, he no longer sees littering as that big a deal.

HOW DOES CULTURE IMPACT ATTITUDE FORMATION AND CHANGE?

Another factor that influences attitude formation and change is culture. In one study, European and Asian Canadians were asked to rate in terms of preference 10 types of dinner entrees avail-able at nearby restaurants (Hoshino-Browne et al., 2005). Half of the participants were asked to think about their own preferences in making these ratings. The other half were asked to think about a close friends' preferences. They were then forced to make a difficult decision—to decide between receiving a gift certificate for their fifth or sixth favourite restaurant. Next, they were asked to re-rate the entree options. In line with previous research, European Canadians showed a greater distinction in their two ratings of the entrees that were originally their fifth and sixth choices when they made the ratings based on their own preferences compared to their friend's preferences. Asian Canadians, on the other hand, showed a significantly greater distinction between the two ratings when they considered their friend's preferences compared to their own. In other words, European Canadians felt the need to justify the choices they made on their own behalf, and Asian Canadians felt the need to justify the choices they made on their friend's behalf. This section will examine the impact of culture on attitudes and cognitive dissonance.

BUSINESS CONNECTIONS

Consumer Purchasing Attitudes and Behaviours Related to Food

Changing consumer purchasing behaviours about food in today's global market is important for ethical and environmental reasons. Essentially, consumers' choices in purchases have an effect on the world around them; a purchase can represent support for or against genetically modified food, chemicals in food, organic food, sustainable agriculture, local food systems, ethical treatment of animals, fair trade, farmers' markets, and so forth (Codron, Siriex, & Reardon, 2006). In this way, researchers are interested in understanding how consumers develop attitudes toward food purchases with the intention of encouraging people to think critically, purchase selectively and, hopefully, have an impact on important environmental and social issues (Johnston, 2008). Research with consumers in Denmark found consumption practices are frequently influenced by habits or routine, as well as by intentional reflection and choice (Halkier, 2001).

To understand ethical consumerism in Canada, Beagan (from Dalhousie University), Ristovski-Slijepcevic, and Chapman (from the University of British Columbia, 2010) explored four groups of consumers in Eastern and Western Canada with the intention of assessing how routine versus reflective choices influence food purchases. To do this, Punjabi Canadians in British Columbia, African Canadians in Nova Scotia, and European Canadians in both provinces (i.e., N.S. & B.C.) were asked to discuss how they make food purchases, a qualitative study. The results indicated that the European Canadians in B.C. were more likely to actively engage in discussions about ethical food consumption in comparison to the other three groups, including European Canadians in N.S. who showed little interest in the issue of ethical consumption. For the African and Punjabi Canadians, a higher priority was placed on maintaining ethno-cultural heritage through food practices than on ethical consumption. For these two groups the emphasis in food consumption was on tradition and historical considerations. The study indicates that there are regional differences in attitudes and practices toward ethical food consumption within Canada.

Additionally, there are differences that reflect cultural attitudes and behaviour toward food.

Maintaining ethno-cultural heritage through food practices could be observed not only among different ethnic groups in Canada, but also cross-culturally. For example, in many Western societies people have negative attitudes toward particular foods (some with high protein) such as brains, heart, kidneys, and liver, while in other societies they are part of a typical diet (Mulatu & Berry, 2001). Additionally, in Canada and other Western nations the concept of health is associated with eating right, exercising regularly, and avoiding addictive substances (Mulatu & Berry, 2001). This perspective is based on individual lifestyle choices and overlaps with the biomedical model of health. However, in non-Western societies, including Aboriginal and Asian cultures, health is associated with living spiritual harmony between one's self and the natural surroundings (Chen & Swartzman, 2001; Mulatu & Berry, 2001). This perspective is more holistic, is linked to both internal and external factors, and is based on traditional health systems and religious beliefs.

Scorpion, seahorse, starfish, millipede, and other delicacies for sale at a Beijing market.

© Russell Sneddon/Alamy

ATTITUDES

Culture influences the factors that predict attitudes as well as attitude-behaviour consistency. Let's look at each of these factors.

FACTORS PREDICTING ATTITUDES.   People in collectivistic cultures are more influenced than individualists by social norms, such as their beliefs about what their peers are doing (Cialdini, Wosinska, Barrett, Butner, & Gornik-Durose, 1999). In other words, they are concerned about what others in their group think. On the other hand, people in individualistic cultures are more influenced than collectivists by information about what they've done in the past. In other words, they are concerned about and assume personal consistency in behaviour. This is because dispositional traits (i.e., our "core inner self") are perceived as relatively stable. The self in individualistic cultures is seen as independent and stable, whereas in collectivistic cultures the self is more interdependent and is seen as less stable because it is considered preferable to adjust to different situations and relationships (Markus & Kitayama 1991; Noon & Lewis, 1992).

In one study, university students in the United States and Poland (a relatively collectivistic society compared to the U.S.) were asked about their willingness to complete a marketing survey without pay (Cialdini, Wosinska, Barrett, Butner, & Gornik-Durose, 1999). Half of the students in each group were first asked to consider their own prior history of compliance with requests. The other half were first asked to consider information regarding other students' compliance. Although both one's own prior history and others' prior history influenced compliance in students from both countries, one's own history had a greater impact on compliance for Americans, whereas others' compliance had a greater impact on Polish students.

Other people's behaviour is a stronger influence on individuals' behaviour in collectivistic cultures than in individualistic ones.

© Dennis Cox/Alamy

ATTITUDE-BEHAVIOUR CONSISTENCY.   People in different cultures also differ in the extent to which they show attitude-behaviour consistency (Kashima, Siegal, Tanaka, & Kashima, 1992). As described previously, consistency between one's attitudes and behaviour is seen as more important in individualistic cultures. Individualistic cultures emphasize the role of stable internal traits in predicting attitudes as well as behaviour, but collectivistic cultures emphasize the power of the situation in influencing attitudes and behaviour. Japanese people, in other words, don't believe in attitude-behaviour consistency as strongly as Australians do.

COGNITIVE DISSONANCE

Although the phenomenon of cognitive dissonance is one of the most famous theories in social psychology, the majority of research on this effect has been conducted in Western societies. Because cognitive dissonance results from holding two inconsistent attitudes, or an attitude that conflicts with one's behaviour, cultures in which such self-consistency is not valued may not experience cognitive dissonance so readily, or potentially not at all (Choi & Choi, 2002; Markus & Kitayama, 1991). Specifically, if one's self is based on one's social roles and relationships, having inconsistencies between two attitudes, or between one's attitudes and behaviour, simply may not lead to negative feelings about the self. Collectivistic cultures may have a greater tolerance of behavioural or attitudinal contradiction, and are likely to attribute inconsistencies in one's attitudes and behaviours to the situation as opposed to the person.

To examine the effects of creating two inconsistent attitudes in people in different cultures, Steve Heine and Darrin Lehman (1997) from the University of British Columbia recruited Japanese living in Canada and European Canadians to participate in a "marketing study." Participants completed a personality test and were asked to evaluate various music CDs. They then received feedback on their personality test, which was either positive (e.g., they scored better than 85 percent of others) or negative (e.g., they scored better than 25 percent of others). Those in the control condition received no feedback. Finally, as a thank-you gift that they could take home they were invited to choose between two CDs that they had rated closely, and were then asked to again rate all the CDs in order to measure any change in their ratings. As explained for similar studies earlier in the chapter, asking people to choose between two highly desirable items is a common way of creating dissonance. As shown in Figure 6.7, European Canadians who received negative feedback showed a large change in their ratings of the CDs, as did those who received no feedback, although to a lesser extent. In contrast, the ratings by Japanese participants were not affected by the feedback, nor did their ratings change from simply having had to make a difficult choice between two closely rated CDs. Thus, dissonance reduction, by changing the ratings of the CDs, is simply not used by Japanese participants to counter self-esteem threats, and making a difficult choice just doesn't impact Japanese participants in the same way that it affects people from Western societies, such as Canada.

FIGURE 6.7 CAN NEGATIVE FEEDBACK LEAD TO ATTITUDE CHANGE?

In this experiment, Japanese and Canadian participants were asked to listen to and rate music CDs and then take what they were told was a personality test. After researchers gave the feedback about their supposed results of the test, they asked students to rate the CD again. As predicted, Canadians who received no feedback or, especially, negative feedback showed a larger change in ratings of the CDs than those who received positive feedback, whereas the ratings given by Japanese participants were not affected by the type of feedback received.

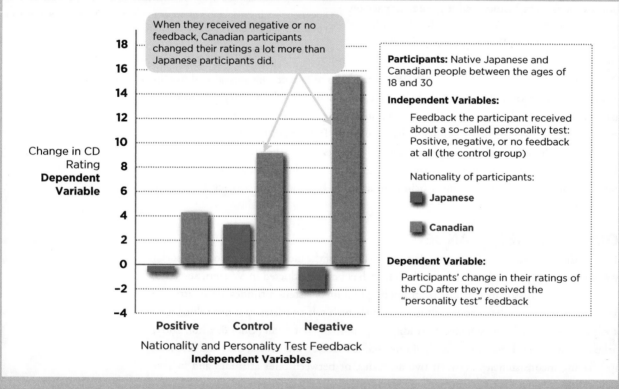

Source: Heine, S., & Lehman, D. (1997). Culture, dissonance, and self-affirmation. *Personality and Social Psychology Bulletin, 23*, 389–400. Used by permission of Sage Publications.

Research also indicates that the factors that create cognitive dissonance are different in individualistic cultures and collectivistic ones. As described at the start of this section, European Canadians experience dissonance when they are forced to make a difficult decision for themselves (Hoshino-Browne et al., 2005). In contrast, Asian Canadians experience dissonance when they make a difficult decision about their friend's preferences.

Finally, the factors that lead to feelings of dissonance seem to differ as a function of culture. One series of studies used the standard free choice paradigm in which participants had to choose between two closely rated CDs, and then had to re-rate both the chosen and unchosen CD (Kitayama, Snibble, Markus, & Suzuki, 2004). European American participants consistently showed the standard (European North American) pattern, in which they rated the chosen CD much higher than the CD not chosen. However, Japanese Americans showed little difference in their rating of the two CDs unless they had also been forced to think about other people (in one study, to also rate how other students would rate the CDs; in another study, to also rate how someone they liked would rate the CDs). Thus, unlike the European Americans, Japanese Americans did not justify their choices by showing a spread of ratings unless they were primed to think about other people. This finding suggests that dissonance in European Americans is caused by a concern about their competence, but dissonance in Japanese people is caused by a concern about possible rejection by others.

THE BIG PICTURE

ATTITUDE FORMATION AND CHANGE

This chapter included many applications of the three "big ideas" studied in social psychology. The examples below should help you see the connection between these three ideas and attitude formation and change, and contribute to your understanding of the big picture of social psychology.

THEME	EXAMPLES
The social world influences how we think about ourselves.	• We like a boring task more if we get paid $1 to do it than if we get paid $20. • Men prefer the centrefold picture in which they *believe* they showed a stronger physiological arousal.
The social world influences our thoughts, attitudes, and behaviour.	• We like songs on the radio that we hear frequently. • Dating relationships with high levels of reward are more likely to continue over time. • Adolescents who watch television shows with high sexual content see their friends as more sexually active.
Our attitudes and behaviour shape the social world around us.	• People who give high levels of rewards to their dating partners are more likely to maintain those relationships over time. • People who are concerned about global warning are more likely to donate to that cause. • Participants are more likely to vote when their attitudes toward a given political party are highly accessible.

This chapter has examined five key principles of attitude formation and change.

1. How do we form attitudes?

We initially form attitudes through information, classical conditioning (including mere exposure and subliminal persuasion), operant conditioning, and observational learning (or modelling). You also learned that even just having a person describe an elderly person can lead the person to form attitudes that are in line with those of a senior citizen.

2. When do attitudes predict behaviour?

There are several factors that influence the link between attitudes and behaviour, and in particular when attitudes do—and do not—lead to behaviour. We learned specific factors that strengthen the attitude-behaviour connection, such as strength, accessibility, specificity, and social norms. We also saw that people who hold prejudiced attitudes won't necessarily behave in line with those beliefs—as demonstrated by the study that involved a Chinese couple visiting various hotels and restaurants.

3. When does engaging in a behaviour lead to attitude change?

This section described cognitive dissonance theory and factors leading to this theory. You learned about factors that lead to attitude change following dissonance, including insufficient justification, insufficient deterrence, effort justification, and justifying dissonance. You also

learned about two revisions to this theory—the "new look" at dissonance theory and the self-standards model. You further learned that people who suffer through an embarrassing initiation to participate in a group discussion on sex (that in reality turns out to be very boring) report liking this group much more than those who only experience a mild initiation.

4. What alternatives are there to cognitive dissonance theory?

This section examined several theories that provide an alternative explanation for the findings seen in research testing cognitive dissonance theory. These alternatives include self-perception theory, impression management theory, and self-affirmation theory.

5. How does culture impact attitude formation and change?

This section described how culture influences the attitudes we form, as well as the factors that lead to cognitive dissonance. You learned that for people in collectivistic cultures attitudes are more strongly influenced by social norms than they are for people in individualistic cultures. You also learned that European Canadians justify the choices they make for themselves, whereas Asian Canadians justify the choices they make for their friends.

Key Terms

attitudes 180	observational learning/	self-standards model 204
classical conditioning 182	modelling 186	social norms 192
cognitive dissonance theory 196	operant conditioning 185	subliminal persuasion 183
impression management	prototype/willingness model 194	theory of planned behaviour 192
theory 205	self-affirmation theory 206	trans-theoretical model (TTM) 194
mere exposure 182	self-perception theory 205	

Questions for Review

1. Describe two ways in which people acquire attitudes.
2. Describe two factors that increase the attitude-behaviour link.
3. What are three different factors that can lead to cognitive dissonance?
4. Which explanation for self-persuasion do you find most convincing, and why? Which explanation is least convincing, and why?
5. Describe how culture impacts attitudes and cognitive dissonance.

Take Action!

1. You want your daughter to develop gender-neutral attitudes and behaviour. What are three specific steps you could take to help accomplish this goal?
2. You're working with a local political organization to increase voting on university campuses. What strategies might you use to increase the likelihood that students'

positive attitudes toward voting will lead them to actually vote?

3. You're trying to get your niece to clean her room. How could you use principles of cognitive dissonance to accomplish this goal?

4. After writing a required term paper that argues for increasing university tuition, you experience dissonance. According to self-affirmation theory, how could you eliminate this arousal?

5. You have a summer internship with an international marketing company and are asked to collect survey data from people in Canada and Venezuela (highly individualistic and collectivistic societies, respectively). What strategies should be most effective at increasing compliance with the request to complete a survey in each of these countries?

RESEARCH CONNECTIONS

Participate in Research

Activity 1 The Power of Subliminal Processing: This chapter has described how attitudes can be formed even at an unconscious, or subliminal, level. Go online to complete a brief task that includes subliminal processing to see how even information that is processed unconsciously can influence your attitudes.

Activity 2 The Link Between Strength and Accessibility: You learned in this chapter about the link between attitude strength and attitude accessibility. Go online to complete an assessment of your own attitudes to judge how strength and accessibility are correlated.

Activity 3 Using Cognitive Dissonance to Create Behaviour Change: This chapter described how creating cognitive dissonance can lead to healthier behaviour, including increased condom use, and more water conservation. You can go online to complete several exercises designed to create feelings of cognitive dissonance in you—and then see how your behavioural intentions change.

Activity 4 The Power of Self-Affirmation: You learned in this chapter about how engaging in self-affirmation about one aspect of your life can help you resolve feelings of conflict about other aspects—and thereby reduce attitude change. Go online to participate in an exercise that creates conflict, and then provides an opportunity for self-affirmation, to see the impact of self-affirmation on your attitudes.

Activity 5 The Impact of Culture on Attitudes: The final section of this chapter described how culture influences attitude formation and change, and in particular the different impact of social norms on attitudes in different cultures. Go online to complete a survey on your attitudes, and the impact of social norms on these attitudes—and then see how other students rate their own attitudes and influences on these attitudes.

Test a Hypothesis

One of the common findings in research on attitude formation is that attitudes are often formed by images we see in the media. To test whether this hypothesis is true, watch two different children's programs—one designed to appeal to girls and one designed to appeal to boys—and count the number of gender stereotypic references in the advertisements shown during each program. Go online to report your findings.

Design a Study

Go online to design your own study testing how and when attitudes can predict behaviour. You'll be able to choose the type of study you want to conduct (self-report, observational/ naturalistic, or experimental), choose your own independent and dependent variables, and form your own hypothesis. Then you can share your findings with other students across the country!

PERSUASION

DID YOU EVER WONDER?

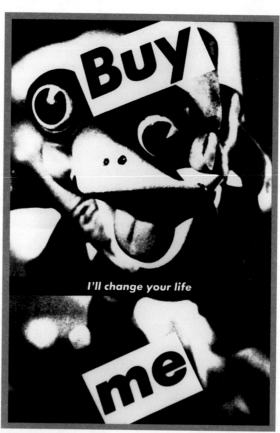

© Barbara Kruger. Courtesy: Mary Boone Gallery, New York.

Why do some advertising campaigns work and not others? In the developed countries, electronic media, print, radio, and television are a central part of most people's lives. In these countries, the television commercial is generally considered the most effective mass-market advertising format. Because a single commercial can be broadcast repeatedly for weeks, months, and even years, companies often spend tremendous amounts of money to produce a single advertisement. Advertisements are used to sell virtually all goods and services, from breakfast cereals to cars to laundry detergents to political candidates. Many television advertisements feature catchy jingles (songs

<table>
<tr>
<td>

**ENVIRONMENTAL
CONNECTIONS**

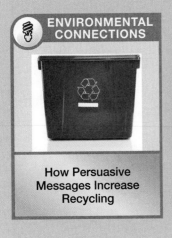

**How Persuasive
Messages Increase
Recycling**

</td>
<td>

**LAW
CONNECTIONS**

**The Benefits of "Stealing
the Thunder"**

</td>
<td>

**HEALTH
CONNECTIONS**

**Why Having Bad Breath
Is Worse Than Dying**

</td>
<td>

**BUSINESS
CONNECTIONS**

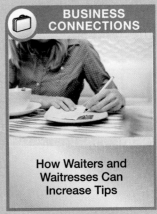

**How Waiters and
Waitresses Can
Increase Tips**

</td>
</tr>
</table>

or melodies) or catchphrases (e.g., "keeps going and going and going . . ." or "I am Canadian") that generate sustained appeal and remain in the minds of television viewers long after the span of the advertising campaign. This chapter examines factors that influence the persuasiveness of television commercials and other advertisements. You'll also find answers to the following questions:

 Why are people more convinced by familiar metaphoric phrases than literal phrases that mean the same thing?

 Why are people who drink coffee highly critical of studies that suggest caffeine is unhealthy?

 Why do people tip better when their bill is placed on a tray with a credit card emblem?

 Why do warning labels about violence on a television program increase interest in watching the program?

 Why are different persuasive messages used in different cultures?

PREVIEW

persuasion – communication that is designed to influence a person's attitudes and behaviour

Why do advertisements for beer feature young and highly attractive people? Why do we care that Tyler Seguin agreed to wear Bauer hockey equipment beginning with the 2010–11 NHL season? Does having a 21-year age minimum for alcohol use, as is the case in the United States, versus an 18-year minimum age (Quebec, Alberta, and Manitoba) or 19-year minimum age (the rest of Canada) increase teenagers' interest in drinking? This chapter examines each of these topics in the area of **persuasion**, meaning communications that are designed to influence people's attitudes and behaviour. These communications can be deliberate attempts to influence attitudes in general, such as through the advertisements we see on television, in magazines, and on billboards, and they can be less formal, such as the arguments you hear from a friend who wants you to vote for a particular provincial candidate. In this chapter, you'll learn about the factors that influence the effectiveness of persuasion techniques, the strategies for resisting persuasion attempts, and the influence of culture on persuasion.

HOW DO WE PROCESS PERSUASIVE MESSAGES?

Imagine that you're asked to listen to a persuasive message, such as a speech by a politician or an advertisement for a car. Would you believe that the rate of delivery of the speech could be more influential than the messages that are presented?

In one study, researchers asked participants to listen to a speech supposedly made by another student (Smith & Shaffer, 1995). In one condition, the speech included strong arguments. In another condition, the speech consisted of weak arguments. In addition, half of the participants in each condition heard the speech at a moderate rate of speech. The other half of participants heard the speech at a very high rate of speech. Who was most persuaded? Participants who heard weak arguments at a normal rate of speech were, not surprisingly, least persuaded. However, participants who heard weak arguments at a

IN THE NEWS

THERE'S PROBABLY NO GOD.
NOW STOP WORRYING AND ENJOY YOUR LIFE.

Brought to you by the Okanagan branch of the Centre for Inquiry Canada
Our nation's voice for atheists and skeptics
Sponsored by the Kamloops Centre for Rational Thought
www.cficanada.ca

Atheist ads: These ads were from a controversial campaign on public transport vehicles that started in the UK and spread to other countries, including Canada. The cities of Toronto, Ottawa, Calgary, and Montreal accepted and ran the atheist ads. Halifax's Metro Transit initially rejected the "Probably No God" ads on the basis that they were offensive, but said it would reconsider Humanist Canada's "You Can Be Good without God" if the organization "toned down the message." Vancouver and Victoria, B.C., and London, Ontario, do not accept religious advertising on their buses, and so rejected this atheist advertising. Kelowna, BC, which had originally rejected the ads has recently reinstated them.

fast rate were just as persuaded as those who heard strong arguments at either a normal or fast rate. The faster delivery is more amenable to peripheral than central processing as it gives you (the audience) less time to think about the content of the message.

In another study, researchers from HEC Montreal examined how voice and gender influence credibility in a banking telemarketing context. They found that voice characteristics significantly affected attitudes toward an advertisement. When listening to a recorded mock telemarketing message for an ATM card offered by a Canadian bank, student participants found a voice more credible (either a man's or a woman's) if it spoke with moderate intensity, no marked voice intonation, and at a fast speech rate (Chebat, El Hedhli, Gélinas-Chebat, & Boivin, 2007). These studies provide support for the idea that how an argument is presented has an influence on people, rather than just the argument itself. This section examines two distinct routes to persuasion, the factors that influence the type of processing used, and the route that is most effective in leading to persuasion.

ROUTES TO PERSUASION

The **elaboration likelihood model (ELM)** of persuasion (shown in Figure 7.1) argues that people focus on different aspects of a persuasive message based on their involvement in the message content (Petty & Cacioppo, 1986). When people think carefully about a communication message and are influenced by the strength of the arguments, they're using the **central** or **systematic route**. An example of this would be when, because you're thinking about buying a car, you decide to read the latest issue of *Consumer Reports* and then test drive several cars, evaluate their different features, and so on.

In contrast, the **peripheral** or **heuristic route** to persuasion is when people don't think carefully about a communication message and are influenced by superficial characteristics. For example, if you see a television ad in which an attractive man or woman drives a sleek-looking car very fast down winding roads in scenic areas, you might make your decision based on these superficial characteristics.

elaboration likelihood model (ELM) – a model describing two distinct routes (central and peripheral) that are used to process persuasive messages

central or **systematic route processing** – a type of processing of persuasive messages that occurs when people have the ability and motivation to carefully evaluate the arguments in a persuasive message

peripheral or **heuristic route processing** – a type of processing of persuasive messages that occurs when people lack the ability and motivation to carefully evaluate a persuasive message, and therefore are influenced only by superficial cues

FACTORS THAT INFLUENCE TYPE OF PROCESSING USED

What factors influence which route of persuasion you use? There are two distinct factors— your ability to focus and your motivation to focus.

FIGURE 7.1   ELABORATION LIKELIHOOD MODEL OF PERSUASION

According to the elaboration likelihood model of persuasion, attitudes can be formed through either of two routes (Petty & Cacioppo, 1986). The central, or systematic, route involves careful consideration of the quality of the argument put forward in the message. The peripheral, or heuristic, route involves reliance on the message's superficial features. The route that is used depends on the person's ability and motivation to process the message.

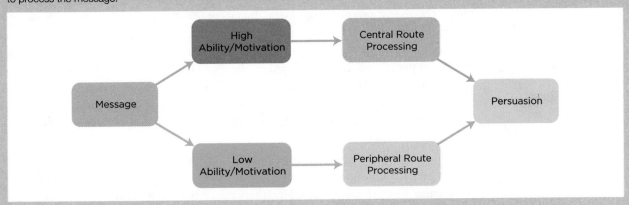

ABILITY TO FOCUS. If you are distracted, and therefore have limited *ability to focus*, it is difficult to concentrate on central messages that require greater processing, and you may therefore rely on peripheral cues (Petty, Wells, & Brock, 1976). People tend to automatically accept information they receive, and only later process that information and decide whether to reject it (Gilbert, Krull, & Malone, 1990; Gilbert, Tafarodi, & Malone, 1993). For example, if people are interrupted immediately after hearing some information, or are under intense time pressure, they're more likely to (incorrectly) accept this information as true simply because they lack the motivation and opportunity to engage in more careful processing.

In one study, students read either a strong or weak argument in favour of a 20 percent increase in school tuition (Petty et al., 1976). The strong messages emphasized the benefits for education (e.g., improving teaching, lowering class sizes, hiring better teachers). The weak messages emphasized the benefits for the campus yards (e.g., hiring more gardeners, getting more flowers, and so on). Some students listened to these messages without distraction. Others listened to the messages while also performing a difficult computer task. Those who had no distraction were persuaded by the strong messages but not by the weak messages, as one would predict. Those who were distracted were somewhat persuaded by both types of messages, presumably because they didn't have a chance to generate counter-arguments to the weak messages.

Even subtle factors that increase people's ability to concentrate can lead to higher rates of central or systematic processing. In one study, half of the participants consumed an orange juice drink that contained caffeine and the other half consumed the same drink but without the caffeine (Martin, Laing, Martin, & Mitchell, 2005). All participants then read a strong message opposing voluntary euthanasia and rated their agreement with this position. As the researchers had selected participants for this study based on their positive attitude toward voluntary euthanasia, this message opposed their current belief. Which participants were most convinced? Those who had consumed caffeine—and were presumably therefore more aroused and alert—were more persuaded by this counter-attitudinal message.

peripheral cues – cues that are associated with the context of a message rather than the content. These cues include length of the message, the source of the message, and the speed at which the message is delivered.

MOTIVATION TO FOCUS. But even if you have the ability to focus, you may not have the *motivation to focus* on processing central messages if you are uninvolved or uninterested in the message (Chaiken, 1980; Fabrigar, Priester, Petty, & Wegener, 1998; Maheswaran & Chaiken, 1991). With no motivation, you are likely to rely on **peripheral cues**, such as the length of the message, the source of the message, and the speed at which the message is delivered (Smith & Shaffer, 1991, 1995).

In one study, it was found that even the familiarity of the phrases used in a message can influence persuasion (Howard, 1997). To test their hypothesis, researchers asked students to read two phrases and to rate their agreement with each phrase, and researchers also manipulated the students' involvement with the task. Each pair of phrases included one familiar metaphoric phrase, and a second, more literal, statement that meant the same thing. For example, one pair of phrases was "Finding yourself between a rock and a hard place" (familiar phrase) and "Having to choose between undesirable alternatives" (literal phrase). Another pair of phrases was "Don't put all your eggs in one basket" (familiar phrase) and "Don't risk everything on a single venture" (literal phrase). Participants' involvement with the rating task was manipulated by informing some of them that the task was a test of their language skills and that the results of their test would be compared with the results of a national sample. This had the effect of increasing those students' involvement.

It was expected that those in the condition of high involvement would report no difference between messages containing familiar versus literal phrases. This is because when participants are motivated to consider different phrases, they notice that both messages have identical meanings. However, when participants are not motivated to examine the messages in detail, they are less likely to devote cognitive resources to the task and are more likely to accept familiar phrases. This is exactly what was found. People whose involvement with a message was low were more persuaded by familiar phrases than by the literal phrases. These participants relied on the peripheral cues, and therefore were more persuaded by the familiar phrases. On the other hand, high involvement participants were equally persuaded by both phrases. These participants weighed the meaning of the phrases—which were of course identical—in making their decision. Howard (1997) also found that when participants were distracted by having to also note the body language of others who were present and listening to the message, the familiar phrase was more persuasive. These findings show that when people are not motivated to examine a message in an objective manner, or when they are distracted and have fewer cognitive resources to devote to considering the message, they are more likely to be persuaded by peripheral cues.

Peripheral cues can also include the presumed expertise of the person delivering the message—i.e., the message source. In a study by Richard Petty and his colleagues (Figure 7.2), students listened to a speaker promoting the benefits of mandatory exams for all students

FIGURE 7.2   DOES PERSONAL INVOLVEMENT INFLUENCE THE TYPE OF PROCESSING USED?

In this experiment, university students listened to arguments in favour of requiring students to pass an examination in order to graduate from university. The hypothesis was that when the message people listen to involves them highly at a personal level, they will use central processing, and hence are more persuaded by strong arguments than weak ones, regardless of who delivers the argument. In contrast, people who are less personally involved with the message will use peripheral route processing, and hence are more influenced by the expertise of the speaker than by the strength of the message. Both hypotheses were supported.

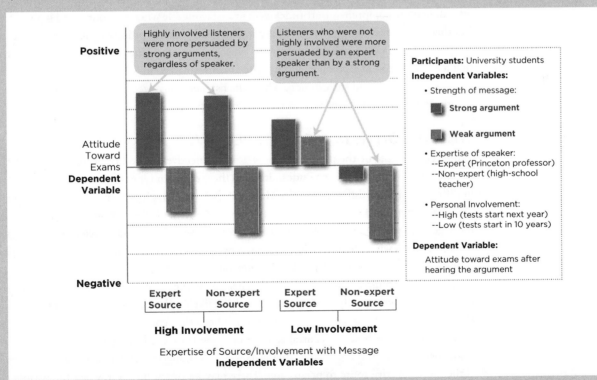

Source: Petty, R. E., Cacioppo, J. T., & Goldman, R. (1981). Personal involvement as a determinant of argument-based persuasion. *Journal of Personality and Social Psychology, 41*, 847–855.

before graduation (Petty, Cacioppo, & Goldman, 1981). This study included three distinct independent variables:

- expertise of the speaker—some students were told the person was an education professor at Princeton, whereas others were told he was a high school teacher
- message strength—some students heard a strong argument based on research, and others heard a weak argument based on personal anecdotes
- personal involvement—some students were very involved in the message because they were told the exams would start next year; others were told they would not be implemented for 10 years

For those who were not very involved and who, therefore, were less likely to employ central processing and more likely to rely on peripheral processes, the primary factor that predicted attitude was the expertise of the speaker. They were more positive about the exams when the message was delivered by a professor than by a high school student, regardless of the strength of the argument. For those who were highly involved (and who therefore made the cognitive effort to employ central processing), the strength of the argument was the major predictor of attitudes.

If an argument is difficult to understand, this may also lead people to rely on peripheral processing. Carolyn Hafer and her colleagues from Brock University examined the influence of complex language in a message to people who disagreed with the view being expressed (Hafer, Reynolds, & Obertynski, 1996). They varied argument strength, wording complexity/comprehensibility, and source status (i.e., the status of the person making the argument). They found that when arguments were easy to comprehend, attitudes were more favourable when the arguments were strong. In other words, when the arguments were comprehensible, central processing was possible and stronger arguments were therefore appreciated. When arguments were difficult to comprehend, attitudes were more favourable when the source had high status. In other words, the complexity of the arguments made central processing less productive, so peripheral factors were given more weight. This and the other studies described above show that a combination of factors, including who is delivering the message, how strong and complex the message is, and the extent to which the listener is involved and motivated to examine the message, influence the persuasiveness of a message.

WHICH ROUTE IS MORE EFFECTIVE?

Is the central route or the peripheral route a more effective method of persuasion? Both are effective at changing people's attitudes, although these different types of processing are effective in different ways for different people. Messages that are of high personal relevance motivate us to pay attention, and as long as we have the ability (i.e., no distractions), we process such messages centrally. On the other hand, messages that are of low personal relevance or that we need to process while distracted are processed peripherally. Interestingly, the same cue can be processed in different ways (depending on motivation and ability): white teeth in a toothpaste ad, for example, could be processed centrally (because white teeth could be a sign of an effective toothpaste) or peripherally (because white teeth are likely to be a cue of attractiveness). Finally, although persuasion can and does occur through both the central and peripheral routes, attitude change that is based in central route processing is longer lasting and more resistant to future persuasion efforts (Chaiken, 1980; Mackie, 1987), suggesting that, in the long term, this is the more effective route to persuasion. There may be times, however, when the peripheral route will do. If you're trying to incite a crowd to protest, for example, you'll probably be more successful whipping them up with some peripheral processing than by presenting cogent arguments that require central route processing. The Environmental Connections box describes the benefits of persuasive messages that lead to central route processing.

ENVIRONMENTAL CONNECTIONS

How Persuasive Messages Increase Recycling

Several studies have examined the use of persuasive messages to increase recycling of newspapers and aluminum cans (Werner, Byerly, White, & Kieffer, 2004; Werner, Stoll, Birch, & White, 2002). In one study, researchers placed a recycling notice on the wastebaskets in some classrooms and hallways and a different sign on the wastebaskets in other classrooms and hallways of several large university buildings (Werner et al., 2004). Both signs requested that people refrain from putting their newspapers in the trash, and provided information about the location of the nearest recycling bin. Signs in the validation condition, so called because it validated participants' possible complaint about inconvenience, also included the following statement: "We are sorry for the inconvenience, but please recycle your newspaper." Signs in the persuasion condition read, "It is important, so please recycle your newspaper." The signs remained in place for three weeks and were then removed. The researchers counted the percentage of newspapers that were recycled in each building by counting the number of newspapers placed in recycling bins and the number of newspapers that were placed in trash cans. This percentage was counted prior to the placement of the signs, during the period in which the signs were in place, and in the two-week follow-up period after the signs had been removed. The validation condition revealed a 9 percent increase in recycling, indicating that validating another's complaint can be persuasive.

However, the persuasion condition produced a 17 percent increase. While both of these increases were significantly higher than the increase observed in the control condition (3 percent), in which there were no signs, in this particular context, alerting people to the seriousness of pro-environmental actions (e.g., "It is important") is more effective than validating their experience.

© iStockphoto.com/gabyjalbert

DIFFERENT ROUTES TO PERSUASION

ROUTE	EXAMPLE
Central route processing	Lilly is deciding which university to attend. She visits the three schools she is considering, compares their programs, and calls current students to ask for their opinions.
Peripheral route processing	Reza is in a bar and is deciding which beer to order. He remembers a funny radio commercial he heard for a particular beer and decides to order that one.

WHAT FACTORS INFLUENCE PERSUASION?

Imagine that you read an article describing the link between coffee use and a disease you've never heard of before. How would you react to this information? Liberman and Chaiken (1992) tested precisely this when they asked participants to read an article about coffee use and "fibrocystic disease" (a fictional disease described in the article as being associated with breast cancer). Some participants read a version of the article in which medical research suggests a very strong link between caffeine use and the disease (a "strong report"). Other participants read a version of the article in which medical research doesn't support the link (a "weak report"). Participants—which included both those who drink coffee regularly and those who never do—were then asked to evaluate the article, including their beliefs about the link between caffeine use and the disease, the strength of the report, and their intention to reduce their own caffeine consumption. As predicted, those who drank coffee found both the strong and weak reports much less convincing than those who didn't drink coffee. The researchers speculate that those who drank coffee—and therefore found the information personally relevant—were threatened by the information, and therefore processed the message in a highly defensive way. This section examines the factors that influence the effectiveness of persuasive messages: the source who delivers the message, the content of the message, and the audience who receives the message.

SOURCE: WHO DELIVERS THE MESSAGE

The *source* of persuasion refers to the person or persons who deliver the message, such as the spokesperson for a given product, the actor who appears in an advertisement, or a person who gives a speech. The source's attractiveness, similarity, and credibility can each influence how persuasive the message appears to people.

ATTRACTIVENESS. First, and not surprisingly, *attractive* and *likeable* sources are more persuasive than unattractive and less likeable ones. Why? Because we assume that if attractive people buy a particular car, or drink a particular pop, or use a particular shampoo, we might become more attractive by engaging in this same behaviour! In one study, researchers recruited attractive and unattractive people to ask students to sign a petition (Eagly & Chaiken, 1975). Attractive people were successful in getting signatures 41 percent of the time, compared to only 32 percent of the time for the unattractive people. This is partly because people assume that attractive people have positive qualities such as honesty, generosity, intelligence, and agreeableness (see Chapter 14 to learn more about why attractiveness is so appealing.) Likeable people are especially persuasive in videotaped and audiotaped messages, compared to written ones (Chaiken & Eagly, 1983). Unlikeable people, on the other hand, are more persuasive in writing, suggesting that the likeability of the person delivering the message is an especially important predictor of how people respond to television advertising.

SIMILARITY. Would you be more persuaded to buy a particular running shoe if your good friend swears by it or if Jamaican sprinter, three-time World and Olympic gold medalist, world record and Olympic record holder Usain Bolt swears by it? Research says your good friend is more similar to you and therefore more persuasive (Wilder, 1990). Because you have more in common with our friend, you believe the shoe is more likely to work for you. This is why advertisements on TV try to feature people who are similar to the target audience (e.g., a tired housewife, busy executive, and so on). In one study, students at the University of California at Santa Barbara (UCSB) read a strong speech either about gun control or euthanasia (Mackie, Gastardo-Conaco, & Skelly, 1992). Some students were told the writer was a fellow UCSB student. Others were told the writer attended the University of Manitoba. Students' attitudes changed in the direction of the message they read when the speech was delivered by a student who supposedly attended their school. They were not influenced at all when the message was delivered by someone who attended a different school. Why are similar sources more persuasive? One reason is that we remember messages presented by in-group members better than those presented by outgroup members (Wilder, 1990). We tend to know the in-group members more than the outgroup members and are therefore more likely to trust them and be persuaded by them.

Another reason involves identification. We're more persuaded by people who we identify with (and this is why, under some circumstances, for example, if we want running shoes for actual running, we may be persuaded by Usain Bolt, but if we want them to look cool among our friends, an in-group member would be a better person to identify with). We can even be influenced by identification with fictional characters. Researchers from the University of Waterloo examined whether identifying with a film character who smokes increases associations of the self with smoking (Dal Cin, Gibson, Zanna, Shumate, & Fong, 2007). Undergraduate men were randomly assigned to view film clips in which the male protagonist either smoked or didn't smoke. They found that greater identification with the smoking protagonist predicted stronger associations between the self and smoking (for both smokers and non-smokers) and increased smokers' intention to smoke. These results suggest that exposure to smoking in movies is causally related to changes in smoking-related thoughts, and that identification with protagonists is an important feature of persuasion.

Messages delivered by similar sources can be persuasive even if the message feels somewhat coercive. In one study, students read an essay that was supposedly written by another student at their school (Silvia, 2005). This essay described the very negative attitude of their university toward its students, and included several strongly worded statements requesting agreement with these points (e.g., "I know I will persuade you about this"). Some of the participants were told the other student shared their first name and birth date. Other participants were given the other student's first name and birth date (that were intentionally different from their own). Researchers then asked participants for their agreement with the essay. Students who believed they shared a first name and birth date with the author of the essay rated their agreement with the essay an average of 6.18 (where 1 = not at all, and 7 = very much). Students who didn't believe they had this similarity rated the essay an average of 4.19. This shows that when people perceive that they have something in common with another person (e.g., first name, birth date), they assume they share other commonalities and, therefore, agree more with that person.

The power of similar sources in leading to persuasion is one explanation for the nearly $182 million in annual revenue earned by a company you've probably never heard of—Vector Marketing, which sells Cutco kitchen knives. The strategy this company uses is to recruit people (mostly university students) to attend an orientation session in which they learn how to make face-to-face sales calls to sell knives. Sellers are encouraged to sell the knives first to family members and friends (supposedly as a way of gaining experience in pitching the product). Then, at the end of these sales presentations, the sellers are told to ask for referrals to other people who might want to buy these knives—and what could be more persuasive than receiving a call about a product that your friend suggested you would want to hear about?

The Tupperware Brands Corporation and their home party was a pioneer in using this technique. Tupperware kitchen and home products are sold at homes, schools, and other community locations where the host invites family, friends, colleagues, and neighbours. The Tupperware representative is also present at these parties and everyone is aware that the host receives a percentage of the sale. The success of this method stems mainly from the act of buying from a friend rather than an unknown salesperson. The Tupperware Brands Corporation has been so successful with this strategy that it abandoned its retail outlets.

CREDIBILITY.   Sources who appear *credible*, meaning competent and trustworthy, are more persuasive than those who lack credibility (Chaiken & Maheswaran, 1994; Maddux & Rogers, 1980; Priester & Petty, 1995; Verplanken, 1991). This is why doctors are often quoted in advertisements for health-related products. For children between the ages of 7 and 10, best friends are particularly influential. Barbara Morrongiello and Tess Dawber from the University of Guelph had children choose between risky or non-risky alternatives in a variety of play situations. Having made their choice, their best friend was able to persuade them to make the other choice approximately half the time (Morrongiello & Dawber, 2004). Peers in general (not just best friends) are also influential with this age group (Christensen & Morrongiello, 1997).

We're also more convinced by sources that we believe are trustworthy, meaning those who don't have an ulterior motive for convincing us. Thus, if someone tries to convince you to join a health club and you're aware that the person will receive a month's free membership if you join, you're more likely to question his or her credibility as a proponent of the club. Our concern about people's ulterior motives helps explain why we see expert witnesses who are paid for their testimony as less believable than those who volunteer (Cooper & Neuhaus, 2000).

People who argue unexpected positions—meaning those that seem to go against their own self-interests—are often especially persuasive because they're seen as highly credible (Wood & Eagly, 1981). Messages that favour a view that goes against participants' expectations are seen as more factually-based than those that subscribe to the expected side, and therefore lead to greater attitude change. Alice Eagly and colleagues asked participants to listen to a political speech accusing a large company of polluting a local river (Eagly, Wood, & Chaiken, 1978). Some participants were told the speechmaker was a pro-environmental candidate who was addressing an environmental protection group. Others were told that he was a pro-business candidate addressing company supporters. When was the speech most persuasive? When it was delivered by the pro-business candidate, because, in this case, he seemed most sincere and credible. The environmentalist was seen as biased.

The credibility of a speaker is particularly influential when people have recently been exposed to another persuasive message (Tormala & Clarkson, 2007). Specifically, when people have just received a persuasive message from a source with low credibility, they're more persuaded by a message from a moderately credible source than if they had first received a message from a source with high credibility (see Figure 7.3). This study indicates that how we evaluate the credibility of a source is influenced not just by the source's credentials, but also by the credentials of other sources we have recently seen.

Repeated exposure to a persuasive message can also lead individuals to attribute the message to a more credible source. In one study, researchers exposed some participants to a statement regarding a food legend five times, and other participants only two times (Fragale & Heath, 2004). All of the statements were false. For example, one statement was "Star-Kist Tuna was recalled in Minnesota and Wisconsin after consumers found that the cans contained cat food and not tuna." Another statement was "Coca-Cola is just as effective as paint thinner at dissolving paint." Participants were then asked whether the statement was originally reported by *Consumer Reports* or by the *National Enquirer*. Those who heard the statement five times were more likely to believe it came from *Consumer Reports* than those who only heard the statement twice. In sum, simple repetition can lead information to be wrongly attributed to a more credible source.

Even non-credible sources can become more persuasive over time, a phenomenon known as the **sleeper effect** (Pratkanis, Greenwald, Leippe, & Baumgardner, 1988). This occurs because over time, people may remember the message, but not remember the speaker. For example, you might read something in *Glamour* and initially discount it because of its source,

sleeper effect – the phenomenon by which a message that initially is not particularly persuasive becomes more persuasive over time because people forget its source

---

FIGURE 7.3 EXAMPLES OF HIGH-AND LOW-CREDIBILITY SOURCES

The following examples show what a writing sample from a person with high credibility and a person with low credibility would look like. These are the types of messages shown to participants in the Tormala and Clarkson study.

HIGH-CREDIBILITY SOURCE	LOW-CREDIBILITY SOURCE
The passage you are about to read was taken from a message written by Professor Kenneth Sturreck, PhD. Dr. Sturreck is a Distinguished Professor of Education Sciences at Queen's University and is world renowned for his work in this area. The passage you will read is an editorial excerpt submitted by Dr. Sturreck to the *Chronicle of Higher Education*.	The passage you are about to read was taken from a message written by Kenneth Sturreck. Kenneth (age 14) is in his first year at Maude Johnson High School in Winnipeg, Manitoba. The passage you will read is an editorial submitted by Kenneth to his high school newspaper.

but a few months later you might recall the information, but forget that you read it in *Glamour* and therefore believe it. In one study on the power of the sleeper effect, participants heard a message by a credible or a non-credible source, and then reported their attitude change (Hovland & Weiss, 1951). Immediately after the message, those who heard the credible speaker had much greater attitude change than those who heard the non-credible speaker. However, when participants reported their attitudes again four weeks later, there was no difference in attitude change between the high-and low-credibility speaker. Similarly, some advertisements in magazines appear as if they are articles. Although people may initially realize that the article is an advertisement, they may still read it and over time forget that it was just an ad.

CONTENT OF THE MESSAGE

The message content, meaning the arguments that are presented and whether they're strong or weak, obviously influences persuasion. Some messages are based on providing information (e.g., "This bleach will get your clothes their whitest"). Other messages are based on positive emotion (e.g., "Don't these people drinking Molson look happy?"), and still others are based on fear (e.g., public health ads against unsafe sex or smoking). So, which factors influence the effectiveness of a message?

LENGTH.   We often think that long messages are more persuasive than short ones, but the link between message length and persuasiveness is complex (Harkins & Petty, 1981). Long messages are more effective if they are strong and processed centrally, but less effective if they're weak and processed peripherally (Petty & Cacioppo, 1984; Wood, Kallgren, & Preisler, 1985). However, long messages that include weak or irrelevant messages can have less impact than short, strong, and focused messages, particularly if people are using central route processing (Friedrich, Fetherstonhaugh, Casey, & Gallagher, 1996). The Law Connections box describes another way in which message content can influence persuasion.

> **Questioning the Research:**
>
> This section described factors that influence persuasion, but these factors can't all be present at the same time. For example, similarity is often very different from expertise. How do you think these factors combine in influencing persuasiveness?

LAW CONNECTIONS

The Benefits of "Stealing the Thunder"

One common strategy in the legal system is for lawyers to volunteer the weaknesses in their own case, particularly if they believe their opponent will raise these issues as part of their own case. This approach, often referred to as "stealing the thunder," is seen as a highly effective way of reducing the impact of negative information. To test whether presenting both sides of the argument is indeed an effective strategy, researchers presented participants with one of three trial transcripts: "no thunder" (e.g., no hidden information), "thunder" (e.g., information presented by one side but not the other), and "stolen thunder" (e.g., information presented by both sides; Williams, Bourgeois, & Croyle, 1993). As predicted, those who read the "stolen thunder" version saw the lawyer who presented this damaging information about his own client as more credible, and were less likely to think the client was guilty than those who heard that information presented only by the other lawyer (although participants who read the "no thunder" version were the least likely to see the client as guilty). These findings suggest that presenting two-sided messages can be a very

effective approach in the legal system, as long as one is reasonably confident that the opposing side will present the information anyway. It should be noted that presenting a two-sided argument is best whenever the audience is intelligent and paying attention (i.e., using the central route to persuasion).

Corbis/SUPERSTOCK

DISCREPANCY. The discrepancy between the message and the audience's original attitude can also impact its persuasiveness (Wegener, Petty, Detweiler-Bedell, & Jarvis, 2001). Messages that differ excessively from people's attitudes are likely to be ignored. For example, some messages about safer sex for high school students are ineffective because they say "no sex, ever" (see "Would You Believe . . ." for a vivid example of the drawbacks to highly discrepant messages). The message "Always use a condom if you have sex" may be more realistic. Similarly, and as described at the start of this section, heavy coffee drinkers are more critical of a study supposedly showing a link between caffeine consumption and disease than those who don't drink coffee. Presumably this is because coffee drinkers don't want to believe they're engaging in a health-damaging behaviour (Liberman & Chaiken, 1992; Sherman, Nelson, & Steele, 2000). This is a good example of implementing a strategy to reduce cognitive dissonance (which you will remember from Chapter 6).

[WOULD YOU BELIEVE...]

VIRGINITY PLEDGES HAVE NO EFFECT ON RATES OF SEXUALLY TRANSMITTED DISEASES?

One popular set of interventions to prevent the spread of sexually transmitted diseases (STDs) and unwanted pregnancies is to encourage adolescents to make a pledge to abstain from sex until marriage.

To examine the effect of making such a pledge on rates of STDs, researchers examined data collected from a sample of over 15,000 adolescents in the United States (Brückner & Bearman, 2005). Participants were asked about their sexual behaviour, including whether they had taken a pledge to remain a virgin until marriage, and, for those who had become sexually active, when they had first had sex and their number of sexual partners. In addition, researchers collected urine samples from the participants to test directly for STDs.

This data revealed several interesting findings. First, those who made a virginity pledge did become sexually active at a later age than those who didn't make a pledge. On average, those who didn't make a virginity pledge began having sex at age 17, compared to age 19 for those who made a virginity pledge. Although those who made the pledge tended to have sex later than those who didn't, the majority of both pledgers and non-pledgers did have sex prior to marriage: 88 percent of the pledgers and 99 percent of the non-pledgers. Most importantly, there were no differences in STD rates between those who made a pledge and those who didn't. What explains this lack of difference in STD rates? Although those who made a virginity pledge started having sex at a later age and had fewer sexual partners than those who didn't make a pledge, they were also less likely to use a condom when they first had sex and were less likely to see a doctor because they were worried about having an STD. This study indicates a potential downside to a reliance on virginity pledges—although they do delay the onset of sexual activity, they're not likely to lead to abstinence before marriage and don't decrease the likelihood of contracting an STD.

This tendency to refute messages that differ too greatly from our original attitude helps explain why attitudes tend to become more extreme over time; people gather support for their own beliefs and ignore disconfirming evidence (Miller, McHoskey, Bane, & Dowd, 1993; Pomerantz, Chaiken, & Tordesillas, 1995). In a classic study of this phenomenon, researchers asked students who were either for or against the death penalty to read two fictitious studies: one that showed that the death penalty deterred homicides and one that showed no deterrent effect (Lord, Ross, & Lepper, 1979). After reading these studies, participants were asked what changes had occurred in their attitudes toward capital punishment. Even though everyone had read the same two studies, participants became more extreme in their attitudes: those who were somewhat in favour of capital punishment now strongly supported it, while those who were somewhat against it now more strongly opposed it. How does reading information about both sides of an issue lead to greater attitude extremity? One factor that contributes to this extremity is that people tend to see evidence that supports their view as quite strong, and evidence that opposes their view as quite weak (see Figure 7.4). For example, people who are high in prejudice against homosexuals rated a fake (unbeknownst to them) scientific study that supported negative views about gay people as more convincing than a study that refuted these views (Munro & Ditto, 1997). People who are low in prejudice against homosexuals

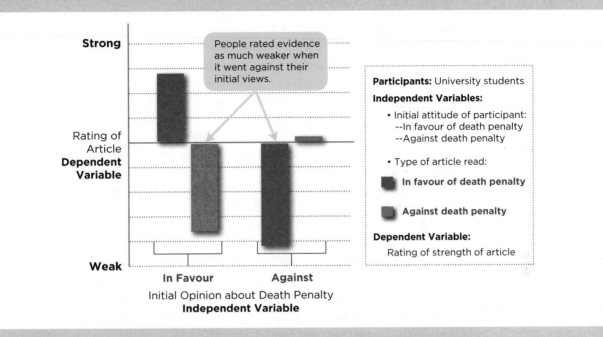

FIGURE 7.4   HOW PERSUASIVE ARE ARGUMENTS THAT CONTRADICT OUR INITIAL VIEWS?

In this experiment, participants were asked to read fictional studies that either supported or refuted their initial views about the death penalty. As predicted, participants rated an article that supported their initial view as stronger than an article that contradicted their initial view.

Source: Lord, C. G., Ross, L., & Lepper, M. R. (1979). Biased assimilation and attitude polarization: The effects of prior theories on subsequently considered evidence. *Journal of Personality and Social Psychology, 37*, 2098–2109.

gave opposite ratings. In sum, people rate information that supports their own views as more convincing than information that goes against those views (Biek, Wood, & Chaiken, 1996; Edwards & Smith, 1996; Giner-Sorolla & Chaiken, 1994, 1997).

AUDIENCE

Individual difference factors, such as age, gender, and personality traits, can influence the persuasiveness of messages.

DEMOGRAPHIC FACTORS.   People in their late adolescent and early adult years are most influenced by persuasive messages, which may in part explain why this demographic group is coveted by television executives (Krosnick & Alwin, 1989; Sears, 1986). Compared to adults, university students have less stable attitudes and a stronger tendency to comply with authority, which means their attitudes and behaviour are more easily influenced. However, Penny Visser and Jon Krosnick (1998) found that people in early and late adulthood (they had a sample ranging from 18 to 89 years) are more responsive to persuasive messages than those in middle adulthood. In follow-up studies, they found that attitude importance, certainty, and perceived quantity of attitude-relevant knowledge are greater in middle adulthood; in other words, middle-aged adults are more confident of their knowledge, of their own correctness, and of the importance of the attitude than younger or older adults. Other research suggests that older adults are more persuaded by messages that focus on meaningful goals (e.g., "Take time for the ones you love" and "Capture those special moments"), whereas younger adults show no such preference (Fung & Carstensen, 2003). Research Focus on Gender describes gender differences in susceptibility to persuasion.

Research on the impact of gender on persuasion suggests overall that men and women use different strategies to influence others (Lips, 2008). Several organizational studies have found that men tend to use direct and assertive strategies to influence their subordinates, whereas women are more likely to use indirect and less assertive strategies (Ansari, 1989; Goodyear, 1990). However, although it has been shown that women are more likely to *report* using submissive strategies than men (Carli, 1999), Canadian researchers Karen Korabik, Galen Baril, and Carol Watson (1993) found that, at least in a laboratory setting, this gender difference in self-report didn't match actual behaviours when participants role-played a series of scenarios in the role of manager. While female participants without management experience described their own conflict management style as more integrating, obliging, and compromising than did men, their behaviour in the role-plays didn't show such differences when rated by those in the subordinate roles. It has also been found that, overall, although men and women report using different strategies to influence others, they don't seem to differ in their preference in using particular strategies. For example, both men and women prefer to use "reason and logic," followed by "simply state my desires," "offer to compromise," and "convince, persuade, and coax" (White & Roufail, 1989).

One reason for a gender difference in the usage of influence strategies is that social expectations for men and women differ (Lips, 2008). Linda Carli (1999) argues that women are less likely to be perceived as competent and that this therefore makes them less likely to rely on competency as an influence strategy. That is, women are less likely to use their capabilities, performance, and abilities as effective methods to influence others. Additionally, even when women are perceived as competent, they're less likely to be perceived as having legitimate authority, such that when they try to use a direct strategy to exert influence, they're more likely to be resisted. Thus, the use of direct and assertive strategies by women exposes them to a greater risk of social disapproval than does men's usage of the same strategies. Perhaps this is one reason that women are more likely to report or possibly use submissive strategies. Korabik and colleagues (1993) also found that use of more assertive strategies by female managers was viewed less positively by subordinates than were the same strategies used by male managers.

It is important to note that gender differences in using influence strategies also tend to be concealed by power differences (Sagrestano, 1992). That is, those who hold power use more direct influence strategies, regardless of their gender.

PERSONALITY.   Personality factors can also influence how people respond to certain types of persuasive messages (DeBono, 1987; Jarvis & Petty, 1996; Snyder & DeBono, 1985). One study examined the impact of *self-monitoring*—which tends to result in people changing their attitudes and behaviour to fit the situation—on how people respond to image-based and information-based magazine ads (Snyder & DeBono, 1985). In ads for Irish Mocha Mint coffee, the image ad said, "Make a chilly night a cozy evening," whereas the information ad said, "A delicious blend of three great flavours—coffee, chocolate, and mint." As predicted, high self-monitors (people who tend to change their behaviour to fit different situations as they are more image conscious) were willing to pay an average of $14 for the product in the image ads but only $12 for the product in the information ads. On the other hand, low self-monitors (people who tend to stay the same regardless of their specific situation) were willing to pay an average of $13 for the product in the information ads and only $11 for the product in the image ads. This shows that people who are more image conscious are more likely to be influenced by ads that appeal to image than by those that simply offer information.

There are other individual difference variables that influence susceptibility to messages. For example, people tend to regulate their behaviour either by focusing on their ideals, wishes, or aspirations, and on bringing about positive outcomes, or by focusing on duties, responsibilities, and obligations, and avoiding negative outcomes. Sunghwan Yi from the University of Guelph and Hans Baumgartner from Pennsylvania State University found that the perceived persuasiveness of a message was increased when there was a match between a person's regulatory focus and the content of the message. Messages emphasizing positive outcomes ("If you eat plenty of fruits and vegetables, you will avoid malfunctions of the immune system and you will reduce the risks of bad health") were more persuasive for those who focused on positive outcomes. Conversely, people who focused on avoiding negative outcomes were more influenced by messages presenting a negative outcome ("If you don't eat enough fruits and vegetables, it may cause malfunctions of the immune system and you will risk bad health"; Yi & Baumgartner, 2009).

Another personality factor that can influence responsiveness to persuasive communications is people's need to think about things (Cacioppo & Petty, 1982; Jarvis & Petty, 1996). Those who are high in need for evaluating are less likely to answer "no opinion" on surveys, and are more likely to express evaluative thoughts when looking at new things (e.g., "I would not hang this in my home," and "I really like the colours"). In the Rate Yourself box, the Need for Cognition scale measures people's enjoyment of engaging in careful and effortful processing of information and, as you might predict, those who are high in need for cognition (i.e., those who enjoy thinking carefully about information) tend to think about the information presented in a message more thoroughly, or in other words, to engage in central route processing. These high need for cognition people are more persuaded by strong messages (Cacioppo, Petty, & Morris, 1983), presumably because they appreciate the strength of the argument as they have used central route processing and considered it properly. Additionally, researchers from Algoma University College, Sault Ste. Marie, found that people who are low in need for cognition are more persuaded by attractive sources of persuasive messages. They attribute more desirable characteristics to them, again associating peripheral processing with cues that work like rules of thumb and therefore require little thought (e.g., "Attractive people are good, so I believe this person"; Perlini & Hansen, 2001).

[RATE YOURSELF]

DO YOU ENJOY THINKING AND PROBLEM SOLVING?

Need for Cognition Scale

INSTRUCTIONS: *Rate each item on a scale of −4 (strongly disagree) to +4 (strongly agree).*

1. I really enjoy a task that involves coming up with new solutions to problems.
2. I appreciate opportunities to discover the strengths and weaknesses of my own reasoning.
3. I would prefer my life to be filled with puzzles that I must solve.
4. I enjoy thinking about an issue even when the results of my thought will have no effect on the outcome of the issue.
5. I tend to set goals that can be accomplished only by expending considerable mental effort.
6. I am usually tempted to put more thought into a task than the job minimally requires.
7. I appreciate opportunities to discover the strengths and weaknesses of my own reasoning.
8. I usually end up deliberating about issues even when they do not affect me personally.

SCORING: Sum up your total number of points on all 8 items.

INTERPRETATION: This scale assesses the extent to which people engage in and enjoy thinking about and carefully processing information (Cacioppo & Petty, 1982). People with higher scores are more interested in engaging in thinking, whereas those with lower scores are less interested.

Those who are low in need for cognition, meaning those who like to conserve mental resources, are more persuaded by peripheral cues, such as the expertise of the speaker, the reaction of other people, and the length of the message (Cacioppo & Petty, 1982). In one study, students listened to audiotapes that contained either high-or low- quality arguments, and then rated their agreement with the message (Axsom, Yates, & Chaiken, 1987). Students who scored low on the Need for Cognition scale were more likely to be influenced by the reaction of others in the audience (e.g., whether others seemed to support the argument) than were those who scored high on the Need for Cognition scale.

People who are low in need for cognition are also more influenced by other peripheral cues, such as the attractiveness or popularity of the speaker. In one study, researchers showed students a 20-minute clip of the film *Die Hard* (Gibson & Maurer, 2000). Half of the students saw a clip in which the lead character, played by Bruce Willis, smokes. The other half saw a clip in which he didn't smoke. Among non-smokers, those who were low in need for cognition and saw the lead character smoke reported more willingness to become friends with a smoker than those who were high in need for cognition.

Expanding on the above three major factors related to persuasion (i.e., source, message, audience), Robert Cialdini describes six principles that influence the effectiveness of persuasive messages. These principles are discussed below.

SIX PRINCIPLES OF PERSUASION

Psychologist Robert Cialdini identified six principles for successfully influencing people (2001):

1. *Reciprocation.* We comply with the requests of those who have done us a favour. This principle is universal and applies to most social behaviours, including pro-social behaviour (e.g., we help those who have helped us), self-disclosure (e.g., we disclose to those who reveal to us), cooperation/competition (e.g., we cooperate with those who cooperate with us and compete with those who compete with us), and compliance (we tend to be persuaded by those who have complied with our request in the past).

2. *Social Validation.* We comply with a request if other people and those who are similar to us are also complying. In other words, we tend to follow many others and similar others. This principle is particularly effective when the social situation is unclear. When we are uncertain about what to believe or how to act we follow the lead of similar others.

3. *Consistency.* Once we take a position, we tend to comply with requests that are consistent with that position. For example, if you describe yourself as a generous person, you're more likely to donate a couple of dollars next time someone collects money for a charity.

4. *Friendship/Liking.* We're more likely to comply with the requests of friends and others whom we like. There are factors that increase such liking, including the other's attractiveness, their similarity to us, compliments we receive from them, and their cooperation.

5. *Authority.* We tend to comply with the requests of those who are authority figures. For example, we're more likely to buy a particular drink if our favourite actor or comic book character is promoting it rather than someone who we are disinterested in. The advertisement in Figure 7.5 features a Canadian actor, Ryan Reynolds, playing a well-known fictional superhero, Green Lantern, promoting drinking milk. This ad could be persuasive if you like either Ryan Reynolds or Green Lantern. Of course, if you do not particularly identify with these characters, the ad may not be effective for you.

6. *Scarcity.* We value opportunities and products that are less available. The power of scarcity is used in sales techniques such as limited offers and creating deadlines so customers are pushed to make immediate purchases.

FIGURE 7.5   PERSUASION THROUGH AUTHORITY

This "Got Milk?" advertisement invokes a comic book superhero, Green Lantern, who is played by Canadian actor, Ryan Reynolds. This provides two reasons to buy milk: 1) to be like a super hero, and 2) to be like a film star.

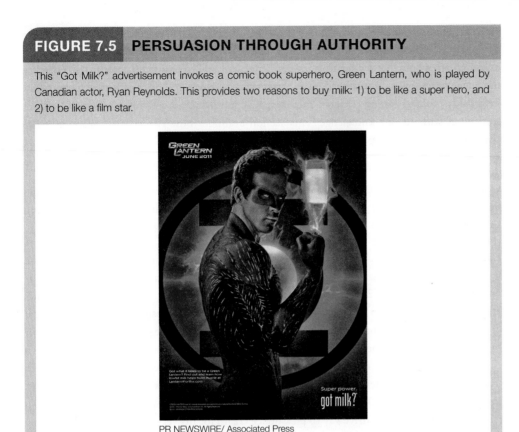

PR NEWSWIRE/ Associated Press

[CONCEPTS IN CONTEXT]

FACTORS INFLUENCING PERSUASION

FACTOR	EXAMPLE
Source	Michelle was selecting a new toothpaste to buy. In making her decision, she remembered a recent advertisement about the kind of toothpaste used by most dentists.
Message	In deciding who to vote for, Sally remembered that she had heard one candidate being interviewed and found his arguments to be long-winded and complex, so she voted for the other candidate.
Audience	Bruce, who is low in need for cognition, was persuaded by the car advertisement that featured an attractive model driving the car really fast.

HOW CAN SUBTLE FACTORS INFLUENCE PERSUASION?

Although this chapter has focused up to now on the presence of relatively obvious features of messages that influence persuasion (either persuasiveness or susceptibility to persuasion), subtle cues can also lead to persuasion. In one study, diners at a restaurant were presented with their bill on one of two types of trays (McCall & Belmont, 1996). On the basis of prior research, which suggested that people estimate higher product values in the presence of credit-related cues, the researchers hypothesized that customers would tip more in the presence of what they called a "credit cue." In one condition, the tray featured a credit card emblem, such as Visa or

American Express. In the other condition, the tray was blank. Researchers then examined the size of tip left in each of these conditions, with the hypothesis that the presence of the credit card emblem would cue higher tips. As predicted, customers tipped on overage 4.29 percent more when their bill was presented on a tip tray with a credit card emblem than on a blank tray. This study provides strong evidence that even very subtle factors can influence our behaviour, sometimes without our knowledge. This section examines how two subtle factors influence persuasion: emotional appeals and subliminal processing.

THE IMPACT OF EMOTIONAL APPEALS

One strategy that is often used to influence people's attitudes and behaviour is to create messages that try to arouse particular emotions. Two types of messages that illustrate the use of emotion are fear-based appeals and positive emotion appeals.

FEAR-BASED APPEALS. The use of negative emotion, and particularly fear, is common in some types of persuasive messages. One study of AIDS public service announcements on television found that 26 percent of the announcements used fear (Freimuth, Hammond, Edgar, & Monohan, 1990). Persuasive messages that use fear are designed to create the threat of impending danger or harm caused by engaging in a behaviour (e.g., drug use, smoking) or by failing to engage in a behaviour (e.g., not using a condom, not wearing a seatbelt). This is a common way to try to persuade people to change health-related behaviours (Higbee, 1969). These messages sometimes use scary verbal statements and may show graphic, even disgusting, images (see Figure 7.6). One television ad promoting the use of seatbelts shows a young man backing his car out of the driveway to pick up ice cream for his very pregnant wife, but failing to wear a seatbelt and then being hit by a speeding car. In some countries, including Canada and Australia, television ads may include even more graphic images, such as dead bodies and crash survivors learning how to walk again. Research Focus on Neuroscience describes how negative emotions can influence voting choices.

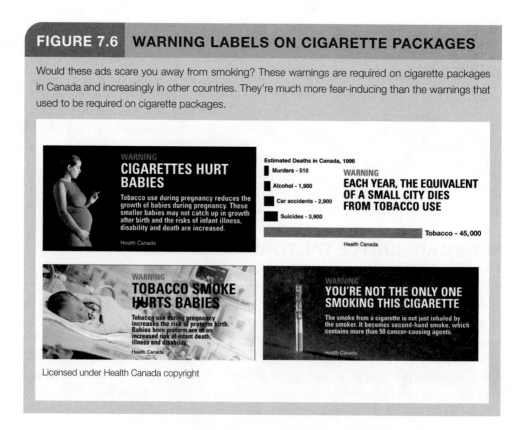

FIGURE 7.6 WARNING LABELS ON CIGARETTE PACKAGES

Would these ads scare you away from smoking? These warnings are required on cigarette packages in Canada and increasingly in other countries. They're much more fear-inducing than the warnings that used to be required on cigarette packages.

Licensed under Health Canada copyright

RESEARCH FOCUS ON NEUROSCIENCE
The Influence of Emotion in the Ballot Box

In one study, the brain activity of participants was examined as they listened to statements made by political candidates (Westen, Blagov, Harenski, Kilts, & Hamann, 2006). The brain areas responsible for reasoning did not show increased activity while participants listened to the politician's speeches, but the brain areas that controlled emotions did show increased activity. This finding suggests that unconscious feelings and emotions may have a stronger influence on our voting behaviour than more conscious and rational thoughts. Researcher Drew Westen noted that "the skillful use of fear is unmatched in leading to enthusiasm for one candidate and causing voters to turn away from another" (*Newsweek*, 2010, April 6).

Fear-based messages are designed to increase people's feelings of vulnerability to various health problems, and thereby motivate them to change their behaviour. But most evidence suggests that this approach is not particularly effective. One study of Project DARE (Drug Abuse Resistance Education), a commonly used fear-based drug prevention program for children that was developed in the United States and is used in Canada, found that this program has little effect on preventing or reducing drug use. In fact it's often less effective than programs that focus simply on social skills (Ennett, Tobler, Ringwalt, & Flewelling, 1994). Similarly, a fear-arousing mass media campaign in Australia to promote condom use led to an increase in anxiety, but had little effect on knowledge or behaviour (Rigby, Brown, Anagnostou, Ross, & Rosser, 1989; Sherr, 1990). Ironically, people who receive high fear messages often report that they're very influenced, but in reality show lower levels of attitude and behaviour change than those who receive positive approaches (Janis & Feshbach, 1953).

But sometimes fear appeals can lead to behaviour change, in part because such messages can increase feelings of vulnerability and thereby lead to more careful processing of the information presented (Baron, Logan, Lilly, Inman, and Brennan, 1994). David Hammond from the University of Waterloo and an international research team compared health warnings and their effects in Canada, the U.S., Australia, and the UK. The larger, more graphic warnings, such as those on Canadian cigarette packages (which were also introduced in the UK during the study) produced more motivation to give up smoking than did the smaller text warnings in the U.S. (Hammond et al., 2007). Another study found that 86 percent of those who saw a scary video on lung cancer reported trying to stop or cut down their smoking, as compared to only 33 percent of those who saw a control video (Sutton & Eiser, 1984). The Health Connections box describes other factors that can increase the effectiveness of fear-based appeals.

Questioning the Research:

This study found that people who saw a scary movie on lung cancer reported trying to quit smoking more than those who didn't see the movie. Are you confident that people were reporting their behaviour accurately? Why or why not?

HEALTH CONNECTIONS

Why Having Bad Breath Is Worse Than Dying

Because many people, especially teenagers, aren't very concerned about long-term consequences, fear-based messages that emphasize the long-term consequences of a behaviour are usually ineffective. Many university students say that having an unplanned pregnancy would be worse than getting HIV, partly because pregnancy leads to an instant problem, whereas developing HIV is a much more distant problem. Additionally, young people feel that HIV and AIDS can be taken care of with medication.

Overall, the lack of concern about long-term consequences compared to short-term ones explains why people who learn that tanning can cause skin cancer still tan for the short-term benefit of looking healthier and more attractive (Broadstock, Borland, & Gason, 1992; Leary & Jones, 1993). Similarly, one study with 19 young drug sniffers (who often go on to use intravenous drugs) found that none were concerned about AIDS as a reason for not using IV drugs—they simply didn't want to lose control over their lives due to addiction (des Jarlais, Friedman, Casriel, & Kott, 1987).

In contrast, fear appeals that focus on the short-term consequences of a behaviour can be quite effective (Klohn & Rogers, 1991). For example, smoking prevention messages for teenagers that emphasize the immediate physiological and social consequences of smoking, such as the financial cost of smoking, rejection by potential dating partners who don't like the smell of smoke, and having stained teeth and bad breath, yield better results. In fact, emphasizing minor but short-term consequences is more effective in changing attitudes toward smoking than emphasizing the serious long-term health consequences (Pechmann, 1997). Similarly, Jones and Leary (1994) found that university students were more persuaded to use sunscreen after reading an essay describing the short-term negative effects of tanning on appearance (e.g., increasing wrinkles, scarring, aging, and so on) than an essay describing the long-term negative effects (e.g., the health risks of tanning, prevalence of different types of skin cancer).

© iStockphoto.com/.shock

Fear-based messages are most likely to change behaviour when they force people to actually imagine having a particular disease or problem, and thereby lead to heightened vulnerability. One public service announcement designed to enhance people's perceived vulnerability to HIV featured an attractive Hispanic man saying the following: "Do I look like someone who has AIDS? Of course not. I am Alejandro Paredes. I finished school. I have a good job. I help support my family. My kind of guy doesn't get AIDS, right? Well, I have AIDS, and I don't mind telling you it's devastating. If I had a second chance, I'd be informed. Believe me" (Freimuth et al., 1990, p. 788). This appeal is clearly designed to increase people's vulnerability to HIV, and to eliminate the use of various cognitive defences against this information (e.g., only poor people get HIV, only people who look unhealthy have HIV, and so on).

The importance of feeling personally vulnerable to a disease helps explain why personal testimonials can be more effective than objective statistics at increasing risk perception and thereby motivating behaviour change. In one study, researchers compared the effectiveness of two distinct types of messages that described the risk of acquiring the hepatitis virus and were designed to promote the acceptance among homosexual men (a group at high risk of acquiring this virus) that they are at risk (De Wit, Das, & Vet, 2008). One of the messages emphasized statistical evidence about the prevalence of the virus and the particularly large rates of hepatitis among gay men. The other message featured a person describing how he had been infected with this virus, even though he had believed he wasn't vulnerable. Researchers then examined perceived risk and intention to receive a vaccination for hepatitis. The narrative message was more effective at increasing intentions to receive a vaccination than the statistical one. In general, research evidence suggests that fear messages may be helpful if the audience is provided with specific means of preventing the feared outcome.

Interestingly, providing the opportunity to self-affirm can also lead to greater acceptance of fear messages. In one study, women read a leaflet describing the link between excessive alcohol use and breast cancer (Harris & Napper, 2005). Half of these women were frequent drinkers (14 alcoholic drinks per week). The other half were infrequent drinkers. The women were randomly assigned to one of two conditions. In the self-affirmation condition, women wrote about their most important value and how this value influenced their behaviour in daily life. In the control condition, women wrote about how their least important value might be important to another student. All participants then read the leaflet, which summarized recent research on the link between alcohol consumption and breast cancer and emphasized that excessive drinking can be hazardous. Next, participants reported their personal risk of developing breast cancer, ease of imagining themselves developing breast cancer, and intention to reduce alcohol consumption. As predicted, women who were excessive drinkers and had the opportunity to self-affirm their most important value prior to reading the leaflet showed greater acceptance of the alcohol consumption–breast cancer link than those who were in the control condition. Similarly, smokers who write about important values, a commonly used way of triggering self-affirmation, are more accepting of information that smoking harms health (Crocker, Niiya, & Mischkowski, 2008).

Self-affirmation also seems to enable an individual to objectively evaluate information that would otherwise evoke a defensive reaction. Researchers from the University of Colorado and the University of Waterloo found that "affirmed" and "non-affirmed" participants rated the persuasiveness of arguments varying in strength, that either agreed or disagreed with their own attitudes. Among participants who rated their attitudes as personally important, self-affirmation decreased bias and increased sensitivity to argument strength (Correll, Spencer, & Zanna, 2004).

THE POWER OF POSITIVE EMOTION

Although fear is one way to persuade people, so is using *positive emotion messages* (Janis, Kaye, & Kirschner, 1965; Mackie & Worth, 1989; Petty, Schumann, Richman, & Strathman, 1993). In fact, people who are in a good mood (e.g., those eating snack foods, watching an upbeat program, listening to pleasant music) are more easily persuaded than those who aren't. The Business Connections box describes how putting people in a good mood can lead customers to tip more.

"I forget the name of the product, but the jingle on TV goes something like 'Ya-dee-dum-dee-rah-te-dum-dee-rah-dee-dum.'"

© Warren Miller/ The New Yorker Collection/ www.cartoonstock.com

BUSINESS CONNECTIONS

How Waiters and Waitresses Can Increase Tips

Creating positive emotions can persuade people to be more generous in one common daily life situation—tipping at a restaurant. Several studies demonstrate that small behaviours that activate positive moods in customers lead to significantly higher tipping. In one study, bartenders gave customers their bill along with a small advertisement card, a joke card, or no card (the control condition; Gueguen, 2002). As predicted, customers who received the joke card were more likely to tip than those who received no card or the advertisement card. In another study, waitresses left one of three messages on the cheques, or no message at all, after customers finished their meals (Seiter & Gass, 2005). All three messages were designed to produce a good mood, but they varied in the specific content of the message: "Have a Nice Day," "United We Stand," "God bless America." People who received the "United We Stand" message left significantly higher tips (20 percent) than those who received the "God bless America" message (18 percent), no message (16 percent), or the "Have a Nice Day" message (16 percent). "God bless America" and "United We Stand" were both presented with little American flag stickers and they were both supposed to appeal to patrons' patriotism.

The authors are unable to explain why one patriotic message worked better than the other. Simply learning the server's name also increases tipping. In one study, couples that arrived at a restaurant were randomly assigned to one of two conditions (Garrity & Degelman, 1990). In condition one, the server introduced herself by name. In the other condition, she didn't. The tipping rate was substantially higher when the customers learned the server's name (23 percent) than when they didn't (15 percent). Again, the authors aren't able to explain their findings, but explanations in terms of likeability (they seem more likeable if they introduce themselves) or identification (we identify more with a person whose name we know than someone anonymous in the role of server) that we have already discussed seem to present possible explanations.

© Corbis Super RF / Alamy

Why do positive messages lead to persuasion? People who are in a good mood want to maintain this positive feeling, and thus are less likely to process information carefully. In turn, they tend to rely on shortcut peripheral cues, such as availability of a given argument, when evaluating a message (Ruder & Bless, 2003). If you're feeling very happy, you may simply agree with whatever message you hear, regardless of message quality. In fact, even nodding one's head, a type of cue of happiness or agreement, while listening to a persuasive message leads to more persuasion than shaking one's head (Briñol & Petty, 2003). This tendency to rely on peripheral route processing is particularly likely when people are concerned that focusing on the message's content will disrupt their good mood (e.g., when the message is depressing). This tendency isn't found when the message is uplifting (Wegener, Petty, & Smith, 1995). As shown in Figure 7.7, students who are in a happy mood when they receive a positive message are more convinced by strong arguments than weak ones, yet argument strength has no impact on persuasion when those who are in a happy mood receive a negative message (e.g., a message involving a tuition raise).

In contrast, people who are in a sad mood tend to rely on the overall number of arguments they can generate for a given position. So, they rely on the content of the arguments generated in forming an attitude, not simply on how easily these arguments came to mind. Thus, people who are in a sad or neutral mood are more likely to use the central route, and carefully evaluate the content of a persuasive message (Bless, Bohner, Schwarz, & Strack, 1990).

Under some circumstances, humour can be a way of enhancing persuasiveness. Michael Conway from Concordia University and Laurette Dubé from McGill University examined the use of humour in persuasive messages on threatening topics that were designed to promote preventive health behaviours. The messages focused on the use of sunscreen to prevent skin cancer in one study and the use of condoms to prevent AIDS in another. Both men and women who scored high on traits of masculinity expressed greater intention to adopt the particular behaviour when the message was presented with humour than when it was not. The authors suggest that this is because "high-masculinity" individuals are particularly averse to experiencing distress (Conway & Dubé, 2002). In a study using a management training exercise, Jim Lyttle of York University in Toronto found that different forms of humour were found to be variably persuasive. Messages including ironic wisecracks and self-effacing humour were more persuasive than without the inclusion of these forms of humour (Lyttle, 2001).

FIGURE 7.7 DOES MOOD IMPACT PROCESSING?

To study whether mood influenced the type of processing used to consider arguments, the researchers in this experiment had university students watch some funny television clips (such as from the David Letterman show) and then read messages involving either good news—a tuition decrease—or bad news—a tuition increase. As predicted, happy people were more convinced by strong arguments than weak arguments regarding a message that conveyed good news (suggesting central processing). However, the strength of the argument had no effect on people's attitudes when the message conveyed bad news (suggesting a reliance on peripheral processing). Researchers suggested that using peripheral-route processing helps happy people avoid focusing too closely on depressing messages and allows them to maintain a good mood.

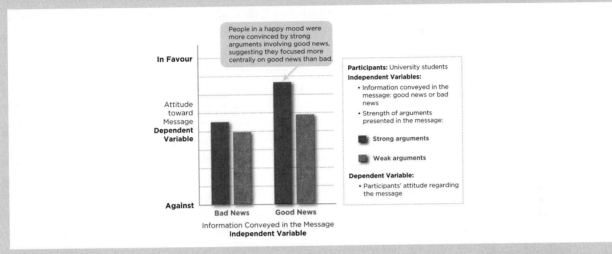

Source: Wegener, D. T., Petty, R. E., & Smith, S. M. (1995). Positive mood can increase or decrease message scrutiny: The hedonic contingency view of mood and message processing. *Journal of Personality and Social Psychology, 69,* 5–15.

THE IMPACT OF SUBLIMINAL MESSAGES

You may have heard about a famous example of real-world persuasion in which Coke and popcorn sales at a movie theatre increased dramatically after the words "Eat Popcorn" and "Drink Coke" were flashed very briefly on the screen. Although this story was later determined to be a hoax, there is some evidence that at least in some cases **subliminal persuasion**, meaning persuasion that occurs when stimuli are presented so rapidly that the observer is not conscious of having viewed them, can influence people's attitudes and behaviour.

subliminal persuasion – a type of persuasion that occurs when stimuli are presented very rapidly at an unconscious level

The belief that subliminal priming can influence what people buy is demonstrated in a study conducted in the Netherlands (Karremans, Stroebe, & Claus, 2006). Dutch participants were asked to assist in a marketing study in which they would evaluate different types of products. During the first part of the study, participants completed a computer task in which they were primed with either the word "Lipton Ice" or a control word that contained the same letters (e.g., "Npeic Tiol"). Next, participants were asked to indicate which of two brand names they would prefer if they were offered a drink now. One of those brand names was Lipton Ice and the other was Spa Rood (a type of mineral water common in the Netherlands). Participants were also asked to rate how thirsty they were at that moment. The researchers found no difference in intention to drink Lipton Ice as a function of the prime condition for those who were not thirsty. However, among participants who were thirsty, those who received the Lipton Ice prime showed a strong preference for this brand over the other brand. This research reveals that subliminal persuasion can influence consumer preferences, at least in the short-term and when the consumer is open, or susceptible, to the message. Overall, research on subliminal priming suggests it works mainly when a person is already "primed" or in a receptive state, such as being thirsty.

Similarly, researchers from the University of Waterloo found that subliminally priming a goal-relevant cognition (thirst or sadness in different studies) influenced behaviour and enhanced the persuasiveness of an ad for a relevant product when people were motivated to pursue the goal (when they were thirsty, or when they expected to interact with another person). The researchers concluded that subliminal priming can be used to enhance persuasion, but only when certain conditions are met (when participants are already primed). Both the priming of goal-relevant cognitions and the motive to pursue the goal were necessary for ads targeting the goal to be more persuasive (Strahan, Spencer, & Zanna, 2002).

Clearly, there are limits to the effects of subliminal processing. Although you can buy many commercially produced self-help CDs—which claim they can help you stop smoking or improve your memory—research provides no support for claims that subliminal processing can have such powerful effects. In one study, researchers gave students one of two types of tapes to listen to for the next three weeks (Greenwald, Spangenberg, Pratkanis, & Eskenazi, 1991). Some participants received tapes they were told would improve their memory, whereas others received tapes they were told would improve their self-esteem. However, researchers gave half of the participants the type of tape they were not expecting—meaning some of those who thought the tape would help their memory were given a tape that was actually supposed to help their self-esteem. Researchers then measured memory and self-esteem changes three weeks later. Although participants believed that the tape they received had a positive impact, with those who believed they received a memory tape reporting better memory and those who believed they received a self-esteem tape reporting better self-esteem, there were no actual differences in self-esteem or memory after exposure to a particular tape. This research suggests that there are clear limits to the power of subliminal persuasion.

Although the effectiveness of subliminal messages is debated and their use is banned in several countries, including Canada and the UK, some companies still use them. For example, there was an investigation in Ontario about subliminal messages that were appearing in some video slot machines in casinos. It was found that winning jackpot symbols were flashed at players for a fifth of a second, which was considered long enough for the brain to register the message but not to process it consciously. Although it isn't known if the flashing jackpot signs were influencing gamblers' behaviour, the investigation led to the casino operator pulling 87 video slot machines from casinos in Ontario (CBC News, February 26, 2007). Finally, there are, of course, alternatives to subliminal advertising. Advertisers continue to spend billions of dollars a year trying to increase people's exposure to certain products in the belief that increased exposure should increase sales (we first encountered the idea that mere exposure can lead to more positive attitudes in Chapter 6).

[CONCEPTS IN CONTEXT]

HOW SUBTLE FACTORS CAN IMPACT PERSUASION

FACTOR	EXAMPLE
Emotional appeals	Dupal knew that smoking was bad for his health, but he just couldn't seem to break the habit. After seeing a photograph of a cancer-ridden lung, however, he stopped smoking. Dupal hasn't had a cigarette in over six months.
Subliminal processing	Monique was feeling thirsty as she watched *Canadian Idol*. After repeatedly seeing the judges drink a Diet Coke on the show, Monique decided to buy a Diet Coke herself.

HOW CAN YOU RESIST PERSUASION?

Although we have focused on factors that influence how people process persuasive messages, in some cases the attempt at persuasion can backfire. In one study, students read descriptions of several fictitious made-for-television films (Bushman & Stack, 1996). Half of these films described a violent film, and the other half described a non-violent film. In addition, some of the movies included the warning label "This film contains some violent content. Viewer discretion is advised," while others included only the information label "This film contains some violence." Students then rated how interested they were in seeing each film. As predicted on the basis of what the authors call "forbidden fruit theory" (i.e., you want what you can't have or, in this case, if they warn you off it, it must be worth a look), participants were more interested in watching the violent films with the warning labels than those with the information labels. This study describes one example of the way in which attempts at persuasion can backfire. Attempts to persuade people can also fail under other conditions. This section will describe four factors that influence our ability to resist persuasion: forewarning, reactance, inoculation, and attitude importance.

FOREWARNING

First, it's often easier for people to resist attempts at persuasion when they receive forewarning that others are trying to persuade them (Chen, Reardon, Rea, & Moore, 1992). **Forewarning** refers to making people aware that they will soon receive a persuasive message. For example, telling teenagers that they're going to hear a speech on "why teenagers should not drive" leads to less change than telling them they're going to hear a speech on driving in general (Freedman & Sears, 1965). Researchers have found that forewarning about an upcoming persuasion attempt allows people to construct counter-arguments and is particularly effective for resisting persuasion (Zuwerink & Cameron, 2003).

forewarning – making people aware that they will soon receive a persuasive message

Forewarning about an upcoming persuasion attempt is especially useful if it includes specific training on evaluating the features of persuasive messages. In one study, half of the participants received information on how to critically evaluate the legitimacy of the source that delivers a message (Sagarin, Cialdini, Rice, & Serna, 2002). For example, participants read the following:

Many ads use authority figures to help sell the product. But how can we tell when an authority figure is being used ethically or unethically? For an authority to be used ethically it must pass two tests. First, the authority must be a real authority, and not just someone dressed up to look like an authority. Second, the authority must be an expert on the product he or she is trying to sell. (p. 530).

Participants then rated six advertisements (three featuring legitimate authorities and three featuring illegitimate authorities). As predicted, participants who received the training rated the ads containing the illegitimate authorities as more manipulative and less persuasive than those who had received no training (the control condition).

With or without training, consumers can be active, sceptical readers of persuasion attempts. When people recognize an emotional "tactic" in an ad, this can have a significant impact on an ad's intended effect. June Cotte from the University of Western Ontario and her colleagues examined a commonly employed emotional tactic, the guilt appeal. They found that credible guilt advertisements that aren't overtly manipulative induce guilt feelings and positive attitudes. However, when consumers infer manipulative intent by the marketer, they don't feel guilty and instead develop negative attitudes toward the sponsor of the advertisement and the advertisement itself (Cotte, Coulter, & Moore, 2005).

REACTANCE

reactance – the idea that people react to threats to their freedom to engage in a behaviour by becoming even more likely to engage in that behaviour

Knowing about an upcoming persuasion attempt also motivates us to resist whatever the message is because of what is called reactance, or the boomerang effect (Brehm, 1966; Brehm & Brehm, 1981; Edwards & Bryan, 1997). **Reactance** refers to the feeling that people have when their freedom is threatened and they want to restore their freedom. If your parents really hate someone you're dating and try to break it off, how might you react? You might become even more attached to this person as a reaction against your parents' attempts to restrict your freedom. In these cases, persuasion backfires, as described in the study at the start of this section on the use of warning labels on violent films. Reactance explains why banning television violence or using warning labels on particular television shows or movies can increase people's interest in watching these programs (Bushman & Cantor, 2003; Bushman & Stack, 1996; Pennebaker & Sanders, 1976). Reactance also explains why students drink more alcohol after receiving a high threat message about the dangers of alcohol consumption than after receiving a low threat message (Bensley & Wu, 1991).

One factor that can lead people to react against a persuasive message is having the opportunity to engage in the behaviour that is forbidden by the message (Albarracin, Cohen, & Kumkale, 2003). In one study, university students read one of two messages about an alcohol-type beverage. One of the messages urged students to completely abstain from consuming the beverage; the other message urged students to consume the beverage in moderate amounts. Some participants then had the opportunity to try the beverage. When participants later reported their future intentions regarding that beverage, those who hadn't tried the beverage reported similar levels of intending to consume the beverage in the future regardless of which message they had read. However, among those who had tried the beverage, those who had read the message urging complete abstinence reported stronger intentions to try the beverage again in the future than those who read the message urging moderate consumption. This research suggests that messages that emphasize moderation may be more effective than those that emphasize abstinence—because if people do engage in the behaviour, abstinence messages are much less effective than moderation messages.

INOCULATION

inoculation – the idea that exposure to a weak version of a persuasive message strengthens people's ability to later resist stronger versions of the message

People are better able to resist persuasion after they have been exposed to a weak version of a persuasive message. Such exposure helps people defend against a message as it gives them practice in defending their views, a process called **inoculation** (much, for example, like having a measles inoculation; McGuire, 1964). This practice allows people to better defend against a stronger version of the message later on, and even increases attitude certainty (Tormala & Petty, 2004). For example, people who are first asked to write, and then refute, reasons opposing "equal opportunity for all" are then more resistant to future anti-equality messages (Bernard, Maio, & Olson, 2003). Thus, if you're a university student who has always been in favour of the Green Party, you'll be more able to resist persuasive messages from the Conservative Party if you've been exposed to weak versions of these messages beforehand and if, in the past, you've responded to challenges to your political preference. Those who have never had to defend their views will be less able to offer such resistance.

Persuasive messages may be particularly effective when they provide direct counter-arguments that refute the common reasons that people give for not engaging in the target behaviour. In one study, researchers created four different types of messages to promote organ donation (Siegel et al., 2008). Counter-argument messages refuted common myths about organ donation; emotional messages described the significant impact organ donors can have on the lives of others; motivating action messages emphasized the importance of acting on one's desire to sign up as a donor; and dissonance messages emphasized the inconsistency that results when people believe that organ donation is good to do, but then fail to sign up. Posters with these messages were then placed at multiple locations, including a library, hospital, university and community college, directly above a computer terminal on which people could register as organ

FIGURE 7.8 CAN PROVIDING COUNTER-ARGUMENTS INCREASE PERSUASION?

In this experiment, researchers chose public locations in which to display posters with four different types of messages promoting organ donation. As predicted, the counter-argument message led to the greatest number of registrations, suggesting that refuting counter-arguments can be a particularly effective persuasive approach.

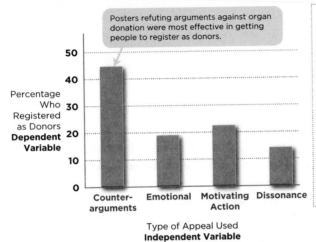

Posters refuting arguments against organ donation were most effective in getting people to register as donors.

Participants: General public

Independent Variable:

Type of appeal used

- **Counter-arguments** - refuted organ-donation myths
- **Emotional** - described impact on the lives of others
- **Motivating Action** - emphasized acting on desire to sign up
- **Dissonance** - emphasized inconsistency of believing organ donation is good, but failing to sign up

Dependent Variable:

Percentage of people registered as organ donors

Source: Siegel, J. T., Alvaro, E. M., Crano, W. D., Lac, A., Ting, S., & Jones, S. P. (2008). A quasiexperimental investigation of message appeal variations on organ donor registration rates. *Health Psychology, 27*, 170–178.

donors. Researchers then counted the number of individuals who signed up in each location. In each location, the counter-argument message led to the greatest number of registrations, indicating that this approach was particularly effective (see Figure 7.8). Thus, persuasive messages may be most effective, at least at increasing this type of altruistic health-related behaviour, when they specifically refute arguments against engaging in the targeted behaviour.

ATTITUDE IMPORTANCE

Finally, even in cases that expose us to messages that are designed to change our attitudes, all attitudes are not created equal: attitudes that are important to us are more resistant to persuasion. In one study, people who were in favour of allowing gay people to serve in the military listened to a message that opposed this position (Zuwerink & Devine, 1996). People who considered this attitude highly important were more resistant to this attempt at persuasion than those who deemed the attitude low in importance. Similarly, people who are highly aware of their attitudes are more resistant to persuasion than those who are less aware of their attitudes (Wood, 1982). Leandre Fabrigar and his colleagues from Queen's University conducted two experiments to examine the impact of attitude accessibility (i.e., how aware a person is of his or her attitude toward something) on participants' consideration of attempts to persuade them. In the first experiment, they measured the accessibility of attitudes toward nuclear power before presenting student participants with a persuasive message that contained either strong or weak arguments against the use of nuclear power. In the second, the accessibility of attitudes toward vegetarianism was experimentally manipulated by varying the number of times participants expressed their attitudes toward vegetarianism. In both cases, the researchers found that the quality of an argument had a greater impact on persuasion when the participants could access their attitudes more easily, suggesting that increased attitude accessibility leads to greater acceptance of relevant persuasive messages (Fabrigar et al., 1998).

Who's Who in Contemporary Canadian Social Psychology Research

Leandre Fabrigar is Associate Professor of Psychology at Queen's University. He received his undergraduate degree from Miami University and his MA and PhD from Ohio State University in the U.S. In his lab (Fab Lab), Professor Fabrigar conducts research on attitudes and persuasion, including the role of affect and cognition in persuasion, the impact of attitude structure on susceptibility to persuasion, and attitude-behaviour consistency. Professor Fabrigar has received awards for excellence in graduate and undergraduate teaching, has published numerous journal articles and book chapters, and has been consulting editor of several journals, including the *Personality and Social Psychology Bulletin* and the *Journal of Experimental Social Psychology*.

Similarly, people who consider a message in terms of how it relates to their important values show greater resistance to attempts to change these attitudes (Blankenship & Wegener, 2008). For example, people who read a persuasive message and reflect on how that message relates to their important values, such as loyalty, freedom, and self-respect, are more resistant to weak arguments than those who reflect on their less important values.

However, even if attitudes are important to us, it still takes effort to resist persuasion attempts. The amount of self-control that we have therefore plays a key role in determining whether we are influenced by persuasion attempts (Burkley, 2008). In one study, university students read an essay about a new university policy to shorten summer vacation to only one month—a policy that students generally rated as undesirable. Half of the students simply read the essay and then rated their agreement with the new policy. The other students completed a challenging task that required considerable self-control prior to reading the essay. These students were asked to squeeze a handgrip shut for as long as possible, a task which becomes very difficult for the forearm to maintain, and thus requires considerable self-control to avoid releasing the grip. Students who first exercised self-control on the handgrip task rated the policy more positively than did those who simply read the essay, presumably because the former had already used up their ability to engage in self-control and thus were more persuaded by the essay.

Questioning the Research:

This study suggests that important attitudes are more resistant to persuasion than less important ones. What other factors might explain the greater resistance of highly important attitudes? (Hint: How might important attitudes differ from less important attitudes?)

[CONCEPTS IN CONTEXT]

WAYS TO RESIST PERSUASION

FACTOR	EXAMPLE
Forewarning	Lily was looking forward to the school assembly until she learned that the topic was promoting abstinence. Lily is now certain that this assembly will present silly arguments and has already started developing counter-arguments to refute this abstinence message.
Reactance	Mohammad, who is 14-years-old, was somewhat interested in seeing a new R-rated movie. After his father refused to allow him to see it, Mohammad became extremely interested in seeing it.
Inoculation	Susan is president of the student association at her university. In preparation for a speech she is giving to the student body, she asks her friends to criticize the points she'll be making and practises defending them.
Attitude importance	Mario is a strong proponent of affirmative action policies and has been involved in several local and national initiatives to implement such policies. Although Mario is sometimes confronted with information that refutes the benefits of affirmative action, he remains convinced in his views.

HOW DOES CULTURE INFLUENCE PERSUASION?

Have you ever looked at the advertisements in magazines from other countries? If not, you might be surprised at how culture affects persuasive messages. Magazine advertisements in most Western nations appeal to individual benefits and preferences, and personal success and independence to a greater extent than advertisements in most Eastern nations. To test the impact of culture on the types of persuasive messages presented, Heejung Kim and Hazel Markus (1999) examined advertisements from popular American and Korean magazines. As shown in Figure 7.9, they rated whether the advertisements appealed to conformity values (e.g., emphasizing tradition, group norms, social roles, and trends) or uniqueness (e.g., rejecting tradition and group norms, emphasizing choices, freedom, and uniqueness). As predicted, although some ads from both countries emphasized both types of messages, advertisements in Korea were much more likely to focus on conformity, in-group benefits, harmony, and family integrity, whereas advertisements from the U.S. were much more likely to focus on uniqueness. This section will examine how culture impacts the types of persuasive messages used and the effectiveness of different persuasive messages.

TYPES OF PERSUASIVE MESSAGES USED

Commercial advertisements tend to reflect the distinct values and beliefs of a given culture and emphasize its prevailing themes (Aaker, Benet-Martinez, & Garolera, 2001; Han & Shavitt, 1994). In one study, Jennifer Aaker and her colleagues at the Stanford University School of Business asked Japanese, Spanish, and American men and women to describe the personality attributes associated with various commercial brands (e.g., "If Coca-Cola was a person, how would you describe him/her?" or "If Porsche was a person, how would you describe him or her?"). Although some of these attributes were similar in all three societies, such as excitement, competence, and sophistication, other attributes varied by culture:

- The attribute ruggedness appeared in ratings by Americans, but not by Japanese or Spanish participants.
- The attribute passion appeared in Spanish ratings but not American ratings.
- Both Japanese and Spanish participants were more likely to rate commercial brands on harmony-oriented values (e.g., peacefulness).
- The Americans rated commercial brands on more individualistic values (e.g., competence).

These results indicate that commercial brands have meanings that are culturally common and others that are culturally specific. Research has shown that people from East Asian and Latin cultures tend to value cooperation and harmony more than people from North American

---

FIGURE 7.9   **EXAMPLES OF AD SLOGANS IN KOREA VERSUS THE UNITED STATES**

ADS REFLECTING CONFORMITY (KOREA)	ADS REFLECTING UNIQUENESS (UNITED STATES)
"Our ginseng drink is produced according to the methods of a 500-year-old tradition."	"Choose your own view."
"Our company is working toward building a harmonious society."	"Ditch the Joneses."
"Seven out of ten people are using this product."	"The Internet isn't for everybody. But then again, you are not everybody."

Source: Kim, H., & Markus, H. R. (1999). Deviance or uniqueness, harmony or conformity? A cultural analysis. *Journal of Personality and Social Psychology, 77(4)*, 785–800.

cultures (Schwartz, 1994). It's therefore not surprising that peacefulness emerged as an attribute in ratings by Japanese and Spanish people. Additionally, considerable research has shown that people from North American cultures give more value to independence and self-assertion (Marin & Marin, 1991; Triandis, Marin, Lisansky, & Betancourt, 1984). Consequently, it might be expected that competence and ruggedness would emerge as attributes in the United States but not in Japan and Spain.

THE EFFECTIVENESS OF DIFFERENT PERSUASIVE MESSAGES

Different types of persuasive messages are effective in different cultures. In individualistic societies, certain characteristics of the source, such as being an expert, increase the source's credibility and the message's persuasiveness. In collectivistic societies, other factors, including being an older male and part of a famous family, increase credibility and therefore persuasiveness.

The effectiveness of different persuasive principles also varies across culture. Morris, Podolny, and Ariel (2001) examined Cialdini's six principles of persuasion in China, Germany, Spain, and America using participants who were employees of Citibank, a multinational cooperation. The study had a natural experimental setting as it took place in the workplace, the structure of the company was the same in all four nations, and the employees were local. The researchers found that when the participants were asked if they were willing to help a co-worker on a task, the main reason for feeling obliged to help the co-worker differed across the four countries. In China, authority was the primary reason for complying with the co-worker's request, with more willingness to offer help when the co-worker had high status and was a member of the participant's unit. This reflects China's high score on Hofstede's (2002) "power distance" cultural dimension, compared to the other four countries. Power distance refers to how much people endorse an unequal power balance in society and respect those with power. In Germany, consistency was the main reason for offering assistance, with the German employees being more likely to offer help if the co-worker's request was consistent with the organization's rules. Hofstede (2002) argues that Germans give high weight to official regulations and organizational rules and are therefore more inclined to agree to requests that are consistent with official policy. In Spain, liking and friendship was the primary reason for complying with a co-worker's request. If the Spanish worker was a friend of the person who was asking for a favour, or liked him or her, the participant was more likely to offer assistance. This reflects the notion of the Spanish word *simpatia*, which has no equivalent in English and characterizes Spanish cultures (Rodrigues & Assmar, 1988). People in "simpatia" cultures express high concern with the social well-being of others, giving high value to friendship and being actively friendly. In America, reciprocity was the primary reason for helping a co-worker. That is, the American workers felt obligated to comply with a request from someone who had done some favour for them in the past. As you recall from previous chapters, the United States is the most individualistic society, where fulfilling individual needs and desires takes precedence over group goals and requirements. Americans, therefore, are more inclined to meet someone else's wishes if the person has already fulfilled their wish and request.

It has also been found that advertising techniques differ across cultures. Specifically, advertising appeals that stress interdependence and togetherness lead to more favourable brand attitudes among Chinese people than do appeals that stress independence and autonomy (Wang, Bristol, Mowen, & Chakraborty, 2000). For example, Chinese participants reacted more positively to an advertisement for a watch that ended, "The ALPS watch. A reminder of relationships" than to one that ended, "The ALPS watch. The art of being unique." Americans, on the other hand, show the reverse pattern, and find appeals stressing independence more appealing than those stressing interdependence.

Finally, people in subgroups within a broader culture can also be influenced in different ways by different types of persuasion attempts (Marin, Marin, Perez-Stable, Otero-Sabogal, 1990). In one study, researchers examined the impact of different factors on intentions to quit smoking among both Hispanic smokers and non-Hispanic smokers in the United States. Family-related attitudes were a greater influence on Hispanics' attitudes toward quitting, whereas the effects of withdrawal from cigarettes was a greater influence on non-Hispanics' attitudes toward quitting. This research points to the importance of designing persuasive messages that fit with individuals' cultural norms and values.

THE BIG PICTURE

PERSUASION

This chapter included many applications of the three "big ideas" studied in social psychology. The examples below should help you see the connection between persuasion and these big ideas and contribute to your understanding of the big picture of social psychology.

THEME	EXAMPLES
The social world influences how we think about ourselves.	• Adolescents who make a "virginity pledge" see themselves (wrongly) as less at risk of having an STD. • Women who have the opportunity to self-affirm see their risk of developing breast cancer as higher than women who do not first self-affirm.
The social world influences our thoughts, attitudes, and behaviour.	• People who hear a weak persuasive message at a fast rate are more persuaded than those who hear the message at a normal or slow rate. • People who hear persuasive messages delivered by highly attractive speakers are more persuaded than those who hear messages delivered by less attractive speakers. • People are more interested in seeing a movie that includes a warning label than movies that include a label with information, but no warning about the content.
Our attitudes and behaviour shape the social world around us.	• Our feelings about the death penalty influence how we perceive studies that describe research on this issue. • Coffee drinkers are more critical of a study supposedly showing a link between caffeine consumption and disease than those who don't drink coffee. • Waiters and waitresses who leave a patriotic message with their bills receive better tips.

WHAT YOU'VE LEARNED

This chapter has examined five key principles of persuasion.

1. How do we process persuasive messages?

This section described two distinct routes to persuasion: central route processing and peripheral route processing. It also described the factors that influence which route we use when processing a persuasive message, including our ability to focus and our motivation to focus, and which message is more effective in different cases. You also learned that messages delivered at a fast pace can be effective even if they consist of weak arguments.

2. What factors influence persuasion?

This section described the factors that influence persuasion—the source, the message, and the audience. Source factors that influence persuasion include attractiveness, similarity, and credibility. Message factors include the length of the message, the discrepancy of the message, and the emotions aroused by the message. Audience factors that influence the persuasiveness of the message include demographic factors and personality. You also learned that people who drink coffee are much more critical of research describing the health risks of caffeine than those who don't drink coffee. Because they're more critical, they feel much less threatened by the information.

3. How can subtle factors influence persuasion?

This section described how subtle factors can influence persuasion. You learned about how both negative appeals, such as those based on fear, and positive appeals, such as those based on happiness and positive emotion, can be persuasive. This section also described how subliminal processing can sometimes lead to persuasion. You also learned that providing a bill on a tray with a credit card emblem leads to higher rates of tipping.

4. How can you resist persuasion?

This section described the strategies for resisting persuasion. You learned about forewarning (letting someone know a persuasion attempt is coming), reactance (the tendency to resist persuasion attempts), inoculation (the benefits of exposure to weak versions of a persuasive message in allowing us to overcome persuasion attempts), and attitude importance (how attitudes that we consider important are more resistant to persuasion attempts). You also learned that including warning labels on violent films leads to increased interest in seeing those films.

5. How does culture influence persuasion?

This section described how culture influences persuasion. You learned that the types of persuasive messages used are different in different cultures, with messages in individualistic cultures emphasizing uniqueness and messages in collectivistic cultures emphasizing conformity. The effectiveness of different persuasive messages also differs across cultures. In turn, messages that emphasize uniqueness are seen as more persuasive in collectivistic cultures, and those emphasizing conformity are seen as more persuasive in individualistic cultures.

Key Terms

central or systematic route processing 217
elaboration likelihood model (ELM) 217
forewarning 239
inoculation 240
peripheral cues 218

peripheral or heuristic route processing 217
persuasion 216
reactance 240
sleeper effect 224
subliminal persuasion 237

Questions for Review

1. List the two routes to persuasion, and give an example of each.

2. Describe how message, source, and audience factors can influence persuasion.

3. Describe how both positive and negative emotions can influence persuasion.

4. Describe four ways in which we can resist persuasion.

5. Describe how culture impacts persuasion.

Take Action!

1. As part of a group project in your marketing class, you need to create advertisements for different types of products: a car, laundry detergent, beer, and a hockey skate. Which route to persuasion, central or peripheral, would you recommend using for each product, and why?

2. Imagine that you're asked to help with a university-wide campaign to increase seatbelt use. How would you create a persuasive message for the university student audience? What source characteristics should be most effective? What types of messages would you recommend?

3. To help master his Spanish, your younger brother has decided to purchase a set of subliminal tapes to play while he sleeps. What would you tell him about the effectiveness of subliminal messages?

4. You're a principal at a local high school, and you want to help your students resist being persuaded by all the advertising messages for alcohol they see. What strategies might you use to help your students resist these persuasion attempts?

5. You're trying to get a summer internship with an advertising company, and are asked to submit a sample of an advertisement for a new car. What type of advertisement would you design for an individualistic culture? How would you change the advertisement if it were to be shown in a collectivistic culture?

RESEARCH CONNECTIONS

Participate in Research

Activity 1 The Impact of Message Relevance on Persuasion: This chapter has described how we process some messages in a central or systematic way, and others in a peripheral or heuristic way. Go online to read various advertisements, and rate how you think you would process each type of advertisement.

Activity 2 The Influence of the Source on Persuasion: One influence on the effectiveness of a persuasive message is the source who delivers that message. Go online to test the source's influence on how persuaded you are by different messages.

Activity 3 The Power of Negative Information: This chapter described how people's views about candidates for political office are more influenced by emotional factors than rational factors. Go online to view campaign ads that rely on negative information and rate their effectiveness.

Activity 4 Strategies for Resisting Persuasion: You learned in this chapter about how we sometimes react against messages that try to change our behaviour. Go online to read a series of persuasive messages and test which ones you might react against.

Activity 5 The Impact of Culture on Persuasion: The final section of this chapter described how people from different cultures are influenced by different types of persuasive messages. Go online to rate how persuasive you find different advertising messages—then see how students from different countries rate these same messages.

Test a Hypothesis

One of the common findings in research on persuasion is that different types of messages are effective for different types of people. To test whether this hypothesis is true, find two different types of advertisements for the same product. Then, ask different people to rate how effective they find each of the ads to be. Go online to report your results to other students.

Design a Study

Go online and design your own study to test how various factors can influence persuasion. You'll be able to choose the type of study you want to conduct (self-report, observational/naturalistic, or experimental), choose your own independent and dependent variables, and form your own hypothesis. Then you can share your findings with other students across the country!

SOCIAL INFLUENCE: NORMS, CONFORMITY, COMPLIANCE, AND OBEDIENCE

DID YOU EVER WONDER?

In October 2010, the University of Alberta newspaper *The Gateway* broke a story about hazing activities at the school's chapter of the Delta Kappa Epsilon (DKE) fraternity (Eldridge, 2010). Allegedly, during a pledge weekend in January of 2010 at the DKE house near the Edmonton campus, students were submitted to a weekend of traumatic initiation activities.

These activities, *The Gateway* article reported, included locking pledges into a plywood box, referred to as "the Hilton," which is sometimes covered in food or urine. During an off-campus dinner, students were forced to eat intentionally disgusting food that in some cases caused them to vomit, and then they were pressured to eat their own vomit in order to clear their plates. Pledges were also deprived of water and sleep during the weekend initiation and forced to listen to loud, repetitive music, a combination that led to hallucination for some participants (Eldridge, 2010, Petz, 2010). *The Gateway* also obtained a video of the initiation rituals, which included a scene of a group of young men circling around a male student and berating him.

Dan McKechnie/urbanobscure.com

HEALTH CONNECTIONS	MEDIA CONNECTIONS	ENVIRONMENTAL CONNECTIONS	LAW CONNECTIONS

Why Misperceiving the Thinness Norm Can Lead to Eating Disorders

Why Publicizing Suicides May Be a Bad Idea

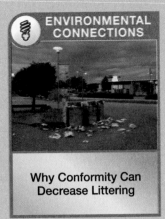

Why Conformity Can Decrease Littering

The Impact of Compliance on False Identifications and False Confessions

The incident led to a five-year suspension of student privileges for DKE and made them ineligible to register as a student group at the University of Alberta. Additionally, charges were made against the DKE chapter concerning abuse of students' safety and dignity (Bocari, 2011). The story shocked members of the University of Alberta community and other Canadians. Unfortunately this type of initiation is not an uncommon occurrence and not at all unfamiliar to Delta Kappa Epsilon.

DKE is one of the oldest fraternities, founded in 1844 at Yale University, and has an estimated 85,000 members in North America. Although on the DKE website the objectives of DKE include "advancement and encouragement of intellectual excellence" and "development of a spirit of tolerance and respect for the rights and views of others," the fraternity group has been the centre of some controversy in the past few years. In the same year as the incident at the University of Alberta, Yale's DKE chapter was accused of having their pledges march through campus yelling sexist chants, such as "no means yes," and other obscenities against women. Consequently, the Yale's DKE chapter was suspended for five years. Similarly, the DKE chapter of the University of Mississippi was suspended in 2007 after a student from the university accused fraternity members of making racial slurs. Why do some fraternities make their members go through bizarre and gruelling initiation practices such as these? How could hazing be tolerated in fraternity life? In this chapter, you'll learn how social psychological factors contribute to our understanding of this kind of harmful behaviour. You'll also find answers to these questions:

 Why is it a good idea to ask a question in class?

 Why do people sometimes ignore offensive remarks (when they shouldn't)?

 Why are we more helpful to someone who shares our birthday?

 Why are you likely to obey anyone who wears a uniform?

 Why do Americans prefer a pen with an unusual colour, while Asians prefer a pen with a common colour?

PREVIEW

social norms – unspoken but shared rules of conduct in a formal or informal group

conformity – the tendency to change our perceptions, opinions, or behaviours in ways that are consistent with perceived group norms

compliance – changes in behaviour that are caused by a direct request

obedience – behaviour that is produced by the commands of authority figures

Think about the clothes you're wearing, the music you listen to, the way you wear your hair, and the laptop you're using. All of these choices are influenced by social norms, meaning unspoken but shared rules of conduct within a particular formal or informal group. Although these examples describe relatively minor ways in which the social world influences our attitudes and behaviour, in some cases the social world exerts a powerful and direct impact on our behaviour. For example, teenagers may feel pressure from others in their social groups to drink alcohol or smoke. This type of conformity, meaning changing our opinions or behaviours to meet perceived group norms, can occur because people fear the consequences of deviating from the norm. In some cases the social world can even lead us to obey orders that may harm or kill people—or ourselves. This type of social influence describes compliance, meaning behaviour that is elicited by direct requests, and obedience, meaning behaviour that is produced by the commands of authority figures. This chapter will examine how these different types of social influence impact our attitudes and behaviour.

HOW DO SOCIAL NORMS INFLUENCE BEHAVIOUR?

Think about a time when you were in class and didn't understand what the professor was explaining. When your professor asked if there were any questions, how did you respond? If you're like many students, you did nothing. Why? Dale Miller and Cathy McFarland (1987) conducted a study to examine precisely this issue. They first asked participants to read an article in preparation for taking part in a discussion with other students. The article was deliberately written in a confusing manner, and was virtually incomprehensible to anyone without extensive knowledge of the topic. Students were told to come see the experimenter if they had any serious problems in understanding the paper. After finishing the article, participants then completed a survey that asked them questions about the clarity of the article and, most importantly, what percentage of other people in the study they believed would ask the experimenter questions about the article. Although no participants in the study asked the experimenter a question, students assumed that 37 percent of other students would ask questions. In a follow-up to this study, researchers examined participants' beliefs about the factors that inhibited them and others from asking a question. As predicted, participants believed their own behaviour was motivated by fear of embarrassment, but saw other people's behaviour as motivated by having a greater understanding of the article. This research provides one example of an error we can make in interpreting the social world—that is, we often see our own behaviour as different from other people's behaviour and as caused by different factors. This section will examine errors we make in perceiving social norms, as well as the power of norms and the pressure we feel to conform to them.

THE POWER OF SOCIAL NORMS

Social norms influence your values, beliefs, and behaviours. For example, when you came to university you may have found that people dressed differently, or listened to different types of music, or had different views about political or social issues than you did. It's also likely that at least in some ways you changed your own attitudes or behaviour to conform to the ones that were the norm at your university. In many cases, these norms serve as helpful guides to appropriate behaviour: stopping at a red light, waiting in line for your turn at a coffee shop, and raising your hand before asking a question in your psychology lecture. These are all examples of norms that regulate our behaviour in socially acceptable ways.

© Global Integration

Social psychologists distinguish between two kinds of social norms (Cialdini, Reno, & Kallgren, 1990; Reno, Cialdini, & Kallgren, 1993). **Descriptive norms** describe how people behave in a given situation. On many university campuses students follow a variety of descriptive norms of behaviour. These norms might include how they spend Saturday nights, what types of clothes they wear, and how much they study. On the other hand, **injunctive norms** (or prescriptive norms, as they are also known) describe what people *ought* to do in a given situation, meaning the type of behaviour that is approved of in a given situation. Reporting cheating to a professor might be an injunctive norm, even if this norm doesn't actually describe people's typical behaviour. Not showing up naked in a classroom is another example of an injunctive norm.

Norms often influence our attitudes and behaviour in very subtle ways. In one study, researchers at Columbia University examined how social norms influence teenagers' taste in music (Salganik, Dodds, & Watts, 2006). Over 14,000 teenagers were recruited from Internet sites and asked to participate in a study of music preferences. Half of the teenagers were simply asked to listen to some obscure rock songs and download the ones they liked—they received no information about the songs (which were taken from a website

descriptive norms – norms that describe how people behave in a given situation

injunctive norms – norms that describe what people ought to do in a given situation, meaning the type of behaviour that is approved of in the situation

where unknown bands post their music). The other teenagers were also asked to listen to these same obscure songs, but in this case they saw, in addition to the title of the songs, the number of times the songs had been downloaded by others (a measure of how popular each song was). Researchers found that simply knowing how many other people had downloaded a song influenced how likely others were to download the song, clearly showing that social norms influenced music ratings. The Would You Believe box describes another real-world example of the power of social norms.

JUST HEARING ABOUT AN ILLNESS CAN MAKE YOU SICK?

Many professors who teach abnormal psychology report that as they describe the various clinical disorders (depression, schizophrenia, etc.) many students suddenly recognize these relatively rare disorders in people they know—their parents, siblings, friends, roommates, and sometimes even themselves. This reaction is sometimes called medical students' disease because medical students, who learn about rare and unusual symptoms, often start diagnosing themselves with multiple disorders.

This reaction can sometimes lead to the phenomenon of mass psychogenic illness, in which large numbers of people, typically in a relatively small and isolated group, all report similar symptoms. For example, students in a school may hear about a virus that is "going around" or a suspected case of food poisoning, and many will suddenly report experiencing related symptoms. This is not—at least not usually—just a case of students trying to get a vacation! Instead, researchers believe that drawing people's attention to a particular type of symptom leads them to engage in careful (even too careful) monitoring of their bodies and to interpret various minor symptoms, such as a headache or nausea, as caused by the suspected problem. In one case, a teacher at a Tennessee high school first noticed an odour and complained of various symptoms (headache, nausea, dizziness, shortness of breath; Jones et al., 2000). Soon many students and staff members experienced similar symptoms, and the school was evacuated. However, a specific medical or environmental explanation for the symptoms was never found, suggesting that the teacher's reaction had led people to believe that they too were experiencing such effects. How does this happen? It's caused in part by people's tendency to look to others to see how they should react in a given situation—if others look anxious, "emotional contagion" may then occur (Gump & Kulik, 1997).

People quickly acquire the norms of a new environment even if they don't know them when they first enter the environment. In fact, people are most likely to acquire norms when they're in new situations. They look to older and/or more established group members to form their own attitudes and behaviours. This applies to political, environmental, family, and other social attitudes. Similarly, university students' attitudes become more similar to those living closest to them in a dormitory over the course of a semester, particularly in the case of attitudes that are seen as highly important (Cullum & Harton, 2007).

GREGORY

"Sure, I follow the herd—not out of brainless obedience, mind you, but out of a deep and abiding respect for the concept of community."

Alex Gregory/The New Yorker Collection/www.cartoonbank.com

Interestingly, however, people seem largely unaware of the impact of social influence (Nolan, Schultz, Cialdini, Goldstein, & Griskevicius, 2008). In one study, researchers asked 810 participants about the frequency of their energy conservation measures, their motivation for such behaviour, and their beliefs about other people's energy conservation behaviour. Although beliefs about others' energy conservation behaviour were highly correlated with individuals' own behaviour, participants saw such norms as much less important in determining their behaviour than other factors, such as protecting the environment. This research suggests that even in cases where our behaviour is influenced by our perception of social norms, we aren't necessarily aware of this influence.

ERRORS IN PERCEIVING SOCIAL NORMS

Although people are generally motivated to adhere to the norms of their group, at times they make errors in perceiving these norms. The term **pluralistic ignorance**, which was coined by Daniel Katz and Floyd Allport (1931), refers to a misperception that occurs when each individual in the group privately rejects a group's norms but believes that the other members of the group accept these norms (Miller & McFarland, 1987). They may go along with the norm because they falsely assume that others' behaviour has a different cause (acceptance of the norm) than one's own behaviour (fear of embarrassment). The study at the start of this section described how pluralistic ignorance is demonstrated in many university classes. Often a professor will ask, "Are there any questions?" and no one raises their hand. Each person assumes that everyone else in the class really understands the material, which is why they aren't asking any questions. But many individuals actually do have questions and believe that they're the only one who isn't raising their hand due to embarrassment and fear of looking stupid.

In a study of the factors that can impede the initiation of dating relationships, Jacquie Vorauer from the University of Manitoba and Rebecca Ratner (1996) examined why students often fail to "make the first move" in initiating a romantic relationship. They gave university students a series of questionnaires that assessed how frequently a fear of rejection had been an obstacle in their pursuit of a relationship, as well as how often they believed such fear inhibited others from pursuing a relationship with them. For example, in one questionnaire participants were asked to imagine that they were at a party and were introduced to a single person who could be a potential romantic partner, and that they talked alone with this person toward the end of the evening. Then the students were asked to imagine that neither person specifically expressed interest in a romantic relationship, and to explain this lack of expressed interest. Although 74 percent of the students reported that fear of rejection would explain their failure to express direct interest in the other person, 71 percent believed that lack of interest on the part of the other person would best be explained by the person's lack of interest in them. The study thus shows how pluralistic ignorance can interfere with the formation of a romantic relationship—because each person simply assumes that the other isn't interested in a relationship, although his or her own (identical) behaviour is driven by fear of rejection. Other misunderstandings between romantic partners are explained in a similar study by Vorauer, Cameron, Holmes, and Pearce (2003). They found that fear of rejection prompts individuals to exhibit what they call a "signal amplification bias," referring to people's perception that their overtures communicate more romantic interest to potential partners than is actually the case.

Unfortunately, misperceiving the social norms of one's environment can have substantial consequences. A number of studies have demonstrated that university students often believe that there is too much alcohol use on campus (Prentice & Miller, 1993). They also believe (wrongly) that other students approve of that amount of alcohol. This is problematic as people's estimate of the frequency of alcohol use among their peers influences their own use, even if these estimates are inaccurate (Baer & Carney, 1993; Baer, Stacy, & Larimer, 1991; Marks, Graham, & Hansen, 1992). Similarly, men who believe that other men believe in rape

pluralistic ignorance – a particular type of norm misperception that occurs when each individual in the group privately rejects the group's norms, but believes that others accept these norms

myths, such as "Women often provoke rape through their appearance or behaviour," are more likely to report behaving in a sexually aggressive way (Bohner, Siebler, & Schmelcher, 2006). In Chapter 10, you'll learn about another consequence of pluralistic ignorance—less interaction between members of different ethnic groups. While members of each group would like to have more contact with members of the other groups, they believe that this interest is not shared by the members of those other ethnic groups (Shelton & Richeson, 2005). The Health Connections box describes another way in which misperceiving social norms can have negative consequences.

HEALTH CONNECTIONS

Why Misperceiving the Thinness Norm Can Lead to Eating Disorders

Research conducted by Sanderson, Darley, and Messinger (2002) demonstrates that misperceiving the thinness norm can have substantial consequences. The thinness norm refers to the perception that it's common to be thin and the accompanying belief that other people are thinner than oneself. In one study, the researchers surveyed 120 students on their eating habits, body image, exercise motivations, and their attitudes regarding the campus thinness norm. They also asked women about their perceptions of other women at their university based on these measures. As predicted, women thought that other women weighed less, exercised more frequently and for more extrinsic reasons, and desired a smaller body than they themselves do. For example, women have an average body-mass index (BMI) of 22 but believe that other women have a BMI of about 20.5. Similarly, women report exercising about four hours a week but believe that other women exercise about five and a half hours a week. Finally, and most importantly, women who feel that they don't meet the campus thinness norm are more likely to experience symptoms of eating disorders, such as an extreme focus on thinness, binge eating, and purging. These findings indicate that feeling deviant from the norm is associated with a variety of negative consequences.

® ThinkStock/Superstock

THE PRESSURE TO CONFORM TO SOCIAL NORMS

Questioning the Research:

Research demonstrates that there is an association between people feeling that they're deviating from valued social norms and people feeling alienated from the environment that values those norms. Can you think of an explanation for these findings? (Hint: Is this correlation or causation?)

The pressure to conform to social norms is often very powerful, in part because people who deviate from the norm often experience negative consequences such as embarrassment, awkwardness, and even hostile behaviour from others (Kruglanski & Webster, 1991). Students who believe that they deviate from the campus norm of alcohol use, for example, feel alienated from campus life and report less interest in attending university reunions later on (Prentice & Miller, 1993). Because of the unpleasant consequences of deviating from the norm, we're motivated to learn and adhere to the norms of our group. An example of this is teenagers who may feel pressure to shoplift when they're with a group of friends who are shoplifting. Even if they're worried about the legal consequences of getting caught, they may be more worried about the social consequences of refusing to go along with their group.

In a classic study of the consequences of rejecting group norms, Stanley Schachter asked groups of students to engage in a group decision-making task (1951). Students met to discuss the case of Johnny Rocco, a juvenile delinquent who was awaiting sentencing for a minor crime, and were supposed to determine the appropriate punishment for him. Each group consisted of several actual participants, plus three students who were acting as confederates of the experimenter and were playing particular roles during the group discussion. One confederate was the "mode": he went along with the group position throughout the discussion. Another confederate was the "slider": he initially chose a position of extreme deviation from the group, but then gradually moved toward the group's modal position. The third confederate was the "deviate": he chose a position of extreme deviation and maintained that position throughout the discussion. After the 45-minute discussion, students rated how much they liked each person in the group, with 1 being the person they liked most, and 9 being the person they liked least. Not surprisingly, people liked the deviate least (6.11, compared to 4.47 for the mode and 4.76 for the slider). This research shows that deviation from the norm can have real consequences for people.

Even watching someone else experience rejection can lead to greater conformity. Perhaps you witnessed bullying or a student being excluded from a social group when you were in high school. Although you may not have taken an active part in the incident, and possibly were not in favour of such behaviour, you may have stayed silent. This is a common phenomenon in bullying, as others watch someone experience rejection but avoid intervention out of fear that they could suffer the same consequence. In a study conducted by researchers at the University of Western Ontario, participants watched one of two humorous videotapes (Janes & Olson, 2000). Some participants watched a videotape in which one person made fun of another person's appearance—such as saying, "His acne was so bad as a teenager we used to call him 'pizza face.'" Other participants watched a videotape in which a person made fun of himself such as saying, "My acne was so bad as a teenager they used to call me 'pizza face.'" Still other participants watched a videotape in which a comedian made jokes that weren't directed at anyone (the control condition). All participants then saw a cartoon and rated how funny they thought it was. However, before providing their rating, participants learned that other students had rated the cartoon as very funny (when in reality it was not funny at all). What did participants' own ratings of the cartoon show? Those who had watched the self-ridicule tape rated the cartoon as not funny, as did those who had watched the comedian make jokes that weren't directed at anyone (see Figure 8.1). On the other hand, those who had watched the tape that ridiculed the other person conformed to what they thought were the ratings of other students and rated the cartoon as very funny. Janes and Olson's study thus shows that when we watch someone being ridiculed or rejected by a group of people, we're more likely to adopt the group norm and not express our opinion.

The examples thus far have mostly described the negative emotions that can be felt by people when they deviate from the social norms of their group. While avoiding such negative consequences can motivate someone to follow group norms, in some cases people's desire to conform to social norms can also result in more positive behaviours. In one study, Robert Cialdini and colleagues compared different types of messages given to hotel guests to encourage them to reuse their towels—something that is very beneficial in conserving energy costs (Goldstein, Cialdini, & Griskevicius, 2008). In one condition, hotel guests received the standard pro-environmental message: "Help Save the Environment: You can show your respect for nature and help save the environment by reusing your towels during your stay." Other guests received a similar message, but with a focus on social norms: "Join Your Fellow Guests in Helping to Save the Environment: Almost 75 percent of guests who are asked to participate in our new resource savings program do help by using their towels more than once. You can join your fellow guests to help save the environment by reusing your towels during your stay." About 35 percent of those who received the first message reused their towels. However, about

FIGURE 8.1 DO WE CONFORM MORE AFTER SEEING OTHERS REJECTED?

In this experiment, university students were shown two videos. The first showed a comedian either telling jokes ridiculing another person, the comedian ridiculing himself, or the comedian making jokes that didn't ridicule anyone. The second video was a cartoon that was not at all funny. Before watching the cartoon, however, the students were told that other viewers had rated the cartoon as very funny. As predicted, those who had watched the video where the comedian ridiculed someone else conformed more to the other participants' rating of the cartoon than did those who had watched the self-ridiculing comedian or those who had watched the comedian make jokes that weren't directed at anyone, suggesting that watching someone else be rejected makes us more likely to conform to group norms.

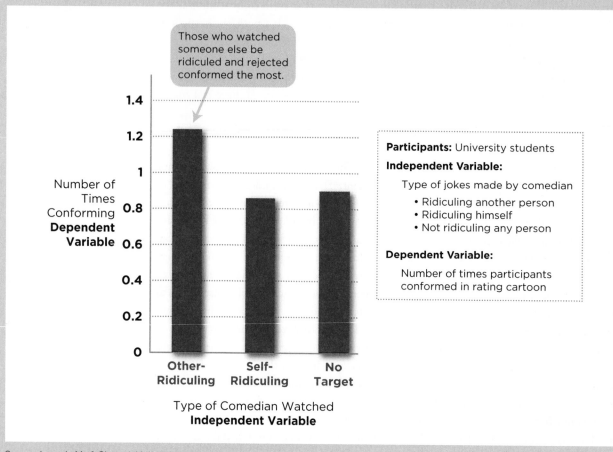

Source: Janes, L. M., & Olson, J. M. (2000). Jeer pressures: The behavioral effects of observing ridicule of others. *Personality and Social Psychology Bulletin, 26,* 474–485.

45 percent of those who received the second message reused their towels, indicating that learning about other people's behaviour was effective at changing behaviour.

Similar norm-based education campaigns have been carried out on many university campuses. For example, campaigns to reduce rates of binge drinking on university campuses have emphasized the message that most students have fewer than five drinks when they party, which can be an effective way of reducing drinking (Perkins, 2002; Perkins & Craig, 2006; Schroeder & Prentice, 1998). Similarly, research reveals that telling university women that other women on campus actually eat more and weigh more than the former might believe they do leads to a reduction in symptoms of eating disorders (Mutterperl & Sanderson, 2002). In sum, giving people accurate information about various norms can reduce misperceptions and thereby improve health.

EXAMPLES OF THE INFLUENCE OF SOCIAL NORMS

FACTOR	EXAMPLE
The power of social norms	When Hassan's family moves and he must attend a new high school, he suddenly changes his style of dress and music preferences to fit those of his new peers.
Errors in perceiving social norms	Sonja's belief that most other students rarely study until the night before an exam leads her to procrastinate on her own work, sometimes with disastrous consequences.

WHAT FACTORS LEAD TO CONFORMITY?

Think about a time when you heard someone say something inappropriate, perhaps expressing a racist, sexist, or homophobic slur. How did you respond? Although you may not know it, your response was probably influenced by the presence of other people. To test the impact of other people on individuals' reactions in precisely this situation, researchers in one study asked men (really confederates) to make a sexist remark in front of female participants (Swim & Hyers, 1999). For example, in one condition a man said, "Yeah, we definitely need to keep the women in shape," and in another, he said, ". . . one of the women can cook." Women then had a chance to react to this remark. Only 16 percent of the women responded with a direct verbal comment, although 91 percent had negative thoughts about the person who had made the remark, showing that concern about the social pressures and costs of responding directly influenced their behaviour. This study demonstrates the power of other people in influencing our behaviour, and in particular how we often conform to others' behaviour. This section will examine the types of influence that lead to conformity, the factors that increase or reduce conformity, and the role of minority influence in eliciting conformity.

WHY WE CONFORM

Conformity can be produced by two distinct types of influence: informational influence and normative influence. Let's look at each of these.

INFORMATIONAL INFLUENCE.

Informational influence refers to influence that leads a person to conform to the behaviour of others because the person believes that the others are correct in their judgements and the person also wants to be correct (Deutsch & Gerard, 1955; Kelly, Jackson, Hutson-Comeaux, 1997; Reno et al., 1993). This type of influence might occur when you're new to a situation and therefore look to others for accurate information. For example, if you're trying to decide what course to take next semester, you might ask students in their third or fourth year for their thoughts about a given course.

informational influence – the influence that produces conformity when a person believes others are correct in their judgements, and the person wants to be right

One of the first studies to demonstrate the impact of informational influence on social norms was conducted by Muzafer Sherif (1936). This study used the autokinetic effect: when a stationary dot of light is shown on a wall in a dark room, the dot appears to move even though in reality it doesn't. When individuals are alone in the room and are asked to guess how far the dot is moving, their guesses differ greatly. But when individuals are in a group, so that they know the responses of others, their estimates of how far the dot is moving converge over time. This shows how people can influence one another and thus create a group norm. People use other people's beliefs as a way of getting information about the situation, and believe that these people are correct in their judgements. When Sherif tested participants alone again after they had been in the group, their estimates of the dot's movement remained close to the group norms rather than reverting back to the original estimates they had made when they were alone. This study demonstrated **private conformity**, where people change their private view (i.e., what they believe) and thereby conform to the group norm because they believe that others are right.

Private conformity has also been demonstrated under a different experimental condition. MacNeil and Sherif (1976) had a four-person group in the laboratory experiencing the autokinetic effect. Three of the individuals were confederates and only one person was a real participant. The confederates were told to establish an arbitrary norm: for example, to report that the light moves an average of 12 inches over a series of trials. After completing the task, the group had a break and one of the confederates left the group and was replaced by a real participant. Then, the new group continued completing the same judgement over a series of trials and the same norm continued with only two confederates. The group had another break and again one of the confederates was replaced by a real participant. By the fourth series of trials, all the group members were real participants. This process continued for 11 changes or "generations," with the oldest member of the group replaced each time by a naïve participant. It was found that it took 11 generations before the group norm started to shift. This clever demonstration indicates that norms develop within a group and, in the absence of other influences, they are resistant or slow to change. Additionally, group norms continue to influence group members long after those who instigated the norm are gone.

NORMATIVE INFLUENCE. Normative influence, on the other hand, describes influence that produces conformity when a person fears the negative social consequences of appearing deviant (Reno et al., 1993). Let's say you're with a group of friends and someone pulls out a pack of cigarettes, lights a cigarette, and offers cigarettes to everyone in the group. Also let's assume that you are not a smoker but everyone else accepts a cigarette and begins to smoke. If you accept a cigarette and smoke, it is not because you have all of a sudden gained some information that smoking is harmless (informational influence). Rather, it is because you decided to go along with the group norms (normative influence). This is why people often don't react to sexist remarks, as demonstrated in the study at the start of this section (Swim & Hyers, 1999).

In a famous study by Solomon Asch (1951), participants arrived for an experiment on visual discrimination that was being conducted in a group of six or seven people. The design of the experiment is a simple one: Participants look at a target line and then at three other comparison lines, and say which line is the same length as the target line (see Figure 8.2). They go through two sets of lines; the judgements are really easy; and all the participants identify the same line as being the same length as the target line. On the third set, however, the first person identifies what is clearly a wrong answer. As a participant, you would be tempted to laugh because it is so obvious that it's wrong, but then the next person gives the same (wrong) answer, and so does the next person. At this point, what do you think? More importantly, what do you do? Thirty-seven percent of the time, participants actually gave the wrong answer in order to conform to the rest of the group, with 50 percent of participants giving the wrong answer at least half the time. This study revealed **public conformity**, meaning when people conform because they want to publicly agree with others, even though in reality, they realize that their answer is incorrect. Why do people give the wrong answer when they clearly know it's wrong? This study represents attributional and behaviour dilemma for participants: first, they must determine why their peers, who are actually confederates of the experimenter, are giving different judgements from their own, and second, they must determine what their own dissent would imply about themselves and their peers.

---

private conformity – when people rethink their original views, and potentially change their minds to match what the group thinks

normative influence – the influence that produces conformity when a person fears the negative social consequences of appearing deviant

public conformity – when people's overt behaviours are in line with group norms

FIGURE 8.2   DOES GROUP PRESSURE INCREASE CONFORMITY?

Participants in Asch's famous experiment joined a group that was shown cards with lines on them, as shown in this figure. Other group members were confederates of the experimenter and who sometimes gave the wrong answer when askedwhich comparison line matched the standard. Even though participants knew the group answer was wrong, they often went along with the group and gave the wrong answer, rather than disagree by providing the correct answer.

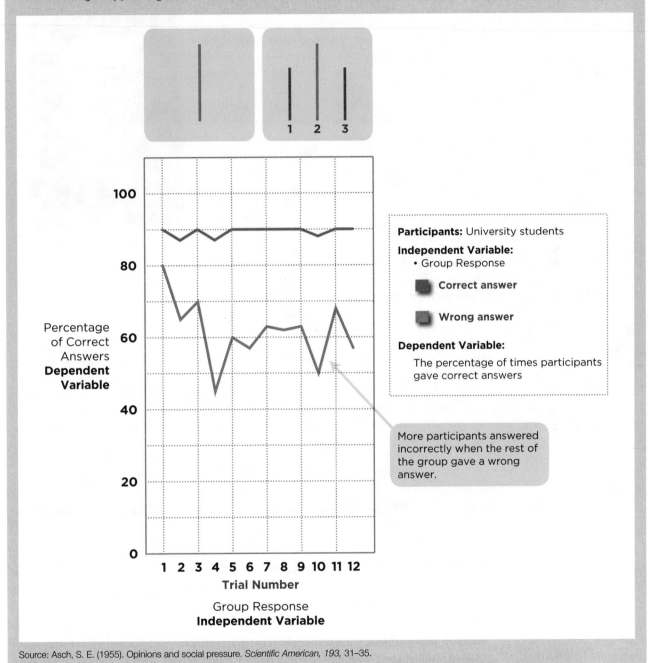

Source: Asch, S. E. (1955). Opinions and social pressure. *Scientific American, 193*, 31–35.

This study received a great deal of publicity because it seemed like such a remarkable show of conformity: after all, it occurred in a situation in which the people didn't know each other, wouldn't receive rewards for making certain answers, and had no real stake in the study. It also raised the fear that the pressure to conform would be even stronger in cases where individuals really cared about the consequences of their behaviour. The Media Connections box describes a very dangerous consequence of conformity.

MEDIA CONNECTIONS

Why Publicizing Suicides May Be a Bad Idea

Studies have found a relationship between reports of suicide and the number of similar deaths that follow (Phillips, 1982). Psychologists refer to this phenomenon as the "Werther effect," a reference to German writer Johann Wolfgang von Goethe's 1774 novel *The Sorrows of Young Werther*, in which the hero shoots himself in the head. After the novel was released, young men across Europe started copying the main character, prompting some countries to ban the book. It has been reported that in the months that follow nationally televised feature news stories about suicide more people die than in the months that aren't preceded by such stories (Phillips & Carstensen, 1986). Moreover, the number of suicides increases only in those places where the suicide was highly publicized—and the more widespread the publicity, the greater the increase.

Psychologists and sociologists believe that some people who hear about another's self-inflicted death decide to imitate the suicide, copying the particular way in which the person died. This tendency is particularly strong among adolescents, who tend to be more impressionable and easier to influence toward conformity. Loren Coleman discusses this phenomenon in her book *Copycat effect: How the media and popular culture trigger the mayhem in tomorrow's headlines* (2004). For example, after Kurt Cobain, the lead singer of the American grunge band Nirvana, committed suicide in April 1994, copycat suicides followed in the same year both in North America and overseas. Twenty-year-old Gaston Lyle Senac, an American, killed himself after pointing a shotgun at himself, telling his friends, "Look, I'm just like Kurt Cobain," and then pulling the trigger. Twenty-two-year-old Australian Brian Lever left behind a poem about Cobain. An unnamed teen in southern Turkey killed himself in imitation of Cobain. A 16-year-old Lebanese youth shot himself in his bedroom, where the walls were covered with posters of Cobain. In Ireland, a 16-year-old left behind a note

CP Photo/David Lazarowych/Pool

in which she wrote that she had "done it for Kurt." And in Canada three teenagers from Quebec took a cross-continental trip that ended in British Columbia, where they committed suicide in their car and left a journal with Cobain's lyrics. Moreover, it didn't stop there. After the story about the three teenagers from Quebec was released, another teenager from Quebec (17 years old) jumped from the Jacques Cartier Bridge off the island of Montreal while listening to Nirvana on a Walkman. Soon after, two more youths (one 17 and the other 19) committed suicide, this time at Niagara Falls, and they too were labelled as Cobain-related suicides. The series of suicides continued in Canada and other parts of the world in subsequent years (Coleman, 2004).

There is a similar "copycat" effect in relation to mass murders of the type witnessed at Columbine in 1999. "One week after Columbine, on April 28, 1999, one student, Jason Lang (pictured), 17, was killed, and one other student was wounded at W. R. Myers High School in Taber, Alberta, Canada. This was the first fatal high school shooting in Canada in 20 years. The shooter was a 14-year-old boy. Exactly a month after Columbine, on May 20, 1999, at Conyers, Georgia, six students were injured at Heritage High School when classmate Thomas Solomon, 15, opened fire." (Coleman, 2004, p. 176)

FACTORS THAT INCREASE CONFORMITY

Researchers have investigated factors that influence conformity, including group size, standing alone, demographic variables, and motivation for accuracy.

GROUP SIZE. First, there is the role of *group size* (Asch, 1951; Campbell & Fairey, 1989; Gerard, Wilhelmy, & Conolley, 1968; Knowles, 1983; Mullen, 1983). It might make intuitive sense to expect that larger groups exert a more powerful influence. In Asch's experiments, when participants responded in the presence of only one confederate, almost no one gave the wrong answer about which line was the same size as the target line. However, when the opposition increased to two people, the proportion of participants giving the wrong answer on at least one trial jumped to 14 percent. When the opposition increased to three, 32 percent of participants bowed to the pressure to conform on at least one trial. Additional increases beyond four did not, however, increase conformity: so a group of four is better at producing conformity than a group of two, but a group of 17 is not better than a group of 10. In fact this depends to some extent on the type of influence the group is exerting in a particular situation. University of British Columbia researchers found that group size was much more important when the influence was normative rather than informational (Campbell & Fairey, 1989). Group size has also been found to influence our willingness to express a minority opinion. In a series of studies, John Bassili (2003) from the University of Toronto found that people who held a minority opinion expressed their views less quickly than those expressing a majority viewpoint. In addition, the larger the number of people holding the majority viewpoint, the longer the delay before an individual would express a minority viewpoint.

The presence of particular group members may also influence conformity. As described by **social impact theory**, people we are close to have more impact on us than those who are more distant (Latané, 1981; Latané, Liu, Nowak, Bonvento, & Zhang, 1995). This is why as a university student you increasingly conform to the norms of your university and decreasingly conform to the norms of your high school. We also conform more in the presence of powerful and vocal group members (Miller & McFarland, 1991; Miller & Prentice, 1994; Perrin & Spencer, 1981). For example, Klofas and Toch (1982) found that prison guards and prisoners who held the most hardline positions, and were not representative of the majority, were likely to define themselves as spokespersons for the group, thereby creating the illusion that all prison guards and prisoners held more hardline positions than they actually did.

social impact theory – the theory that people we are close to have more impact on us than people who are more distant

We also conform more in groups that are attractive to us (i.e., when we want to feel as if we belong) as demonstrated by Romin Tafarodi, from the University of Toronto, and colleagues (Tafarodi, Kang, & Milne, 2002). They argued that second generation immigrants tend to want to feel part of the wider (in this case, Canadian) society. If they are members of a visible minority, however, awareness of their physical distinctiveness (relative to the Euro-Canadian majority) may appear to them as an "ethnifying" obstacle to assimilation or integration. The researchers' hypothesis was that because of this obstacle, there would be even greater conformity (as if trying harder to "fit in"). Their participants were Chinese Canadian university students who were either born in Canada or who had arrived in childhood. The study was described to them as examining identity and aesthetic judgement and gave them the task of rating a series of abstract paintings in terms of how much they liked them. Some participants performed the task in front of a mirror, in order to make their physical appearance salient to them, while others had no mirror. Some were also provided with normative ratings (i.e., the average rating) for one of three ethnic groups: European Canadians, Chinese Canadians, and Nigerians in Canada. As hypothesized, those who performed in front of a mirror, and who had therefore been reminded of their Chinese ethnicity, appeared to align themselves with the Euro-Canadian majority by shifting their ratings toward those of this majority.

STANDING ALONE.   Although both the size of the group and the nature of its members influence rates of conformity, the single biggest predictor of conformity is whether a participant must take the lone deviant position, meaning to stand alone. In Asch's experiment, when another person in the group gave the truthful answer, the pressure to conform was drastically reduced (Allen & Levine, 1969, 1971; Nemeth & Chiles, 1988). Even after the "supporter" left the room on some pretext, participants were better able to resist the pressure to conform. In fact, even when another person in the group gives another—or more extreme—wrong answer, the pressure to conform is drastically reduced. If the person who deviates seems to be incompetent (wears thick glasses, complains of being unable to see the lines well, and so on), having anyone else stand up to the majority decreases conformity. When a group appears unanimous, it's at its strongest. When someone breaks the unanimity, others feel better able to do so as well.

demographic variables – varying characteristics of an individual, sample group, or population.

DEMOGRAPHIC VARIABLES. Demographic variables, such as age and gender, also influence conformity (Eagly & Carli, 1981; Eagly, Wood, & Fishbaugh, 1981). Conformity is highest in adolescence, when there is real pressure to fit in, and lower in children and older adults (Berndt, 1979; Brown, Clasen, & Eicher, 1986; Gavin & Furman, 1989). Peer pressure, for example, is identified by adolescents as a major predictor of misconduct (e.g., drug/alcohol use, unprotected sex, and minor delinquent behaviour; Brown et al., 1986). Gender also seems to be relevant in rates of conformity as the Research Focus on Gender shows.

"Gee, Tommy, I'd be lost without your constant peer pressure."

Jack Ziegler/The New Yorker Collection/www.cartoonbank.com

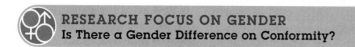

RESEARCH FOCUS ON GENDER
Is There a Gender Difference on Conformity?

Research indicates that there is a gender difference in rates of conformity. Specifically, women are more likely than men to agree with others in group decision-making tasks, and are less likely than men to dissent from the group. However, the size of these gender differences in conformity varies across types of situations. First, both men and women are particularly likely to conform in unfamiliar situations (Eagly & Carli, 1981; Eagly, Wood, & Fishbaugh, 1981). For example, women may conform more in conversations about hockey, whereas men may conform more in conversations about child-rearing. However, gender role, which refers to behavioural and social norms that are expected from men and women, has been found to be related to conformity. People with more masculine gender roles, regardless of their gender, conform less than people with more feminine gender roles (Maslach, Santee, & Wade, 1987). That is, those who identify with characteristics that are traditionally associated with men, such as competence, achievement, power, and autonomy, are less likely to conform regardless of whether they are men or women. This difference is due in part to gender differences in social roles: men are often focused on demonstrating their independence from others, whereas women are often focused on fostering cooperation in their interactions.

Another factor that may lead to gender differences in conformity is the type of persuasion strategy used (Guadagno & Cialdini, 2002). Specifically, women tend to be more influenced by face-to-face persuasion attempts than by email persuasion attempts, perhaps because it's more difficult for women to resist agreeing with others during direct face-to-face communication than during a more distant persuasion attempt. On the other hand, men show no differences in how they respond to these two distinct types of communication.

Therefore, the answer to the question, "Is there a gender difference on conformity?" is "It depends." In different situations, men and women conform differently. Also, depending on the individual's gender identity, conformity varies.

MOTIVATION.   Another factor that can influence conformity is *task importance*: on easy tasks people don't need to look to group members for the answer, whereas on harder tasks they may feel less sure about their answer. In one study, students participated in groups of three (one participant, two confederates) and were asked to serve as eyewitnesses to a crime, after which they had to identify the perpetrator in a lineup (Baron, Vandello, & Brunsman, 1996). In some cases the task was very difficult (they saw each picture once for only a second). In other cases it was quite easy (they saw each picture twice for a total of 10 seconds). The experimenters also varied the students' motivation to perform well. In some cases they were told that this was only a pilot test, whereas in other cases they were given money for being right. As shown in Figure 8.3, in cases of low motivation (the pilot test), students conformed about one-third of the time, regardless of the difficulty of the task (note that this is very similar to the rate of conformity in the Asch study). On the other hand, in cases of high motivation (they could receive extra cash), they conformed rarely on easy tasks (when they probably felt confident that they knew the right answer) but conformed frequently on difficult tasks (when they probably felt less confident and really wanted to be right).

Interestingly, social motives seem to influence conformity in different ways for men and women (Griskevicius, Goldstein, Mortensen, Cialdini, & Kenrick, 2006). In one study, researchers measured participants' conformity to the opinions of other members of a group on a task involving rating artistic images. In one condition, participants were asked to imagine an anxiety-provoking situation prior to rating the images, such as being in a dark house alone late at night and hearing a noise from an intruder. In another condition, participants were asked to imagine a highly romantic situation, such as spending a day at the beach with a desirable partner and kissing that person passionately, prior to rating the images. Compared to those in a control condition (which involved no imagining prior to completing the rating), both men and women who imagined the anxiety-provoking scene showed greater conformity. On the other hand, men and women reacted in very different ways to imagining the romantic situation. For women, imagining a romantic situation increased conformity, but for men, imagining this scene led to lower levels of conformity. The authors propose that men who fail to conform to the norm may be more attractive to potential dating partners, perhaps because they appear independent, suggesting that being nonconformist is a way for men to attract mates. In contrast, conforming to social norms, which indicates agreeableness, may be a way for women to attract mates.

THE POWER OF MINORITY INFLUENCE

Can individuals who are in the minority on a particular view or norm sometimes convince others to go along with them? Although **minority influence** is much less common (or much less obvious) than majority influence, it does occur. If it didn't, ideas in society wouldn't change; there would be no new political developments, no shifts in fashion, no advances in philosophy or science. Research on minority influence was initiated by French researcher

minority influence – a process in which a small number of people in a group lead an overall change in the group's attitude or behaviour

FIGURE 8.3   DOES CONFORMITY INCREASE WHEN THE TASK IS DIFFICULT AND IMPORTANT?

In this study, participants were placed in groups of three, with two of the three being confederates of the experimenter. The group witnessed pictures of the person on the left committing a crime and had to pick the suspect from a lineup of pictures, like the one shown below on the right. The confederates chose the wrong person from the lineup. As predicted, conformity was highest when the task was difficult and it was important to choose correctly.

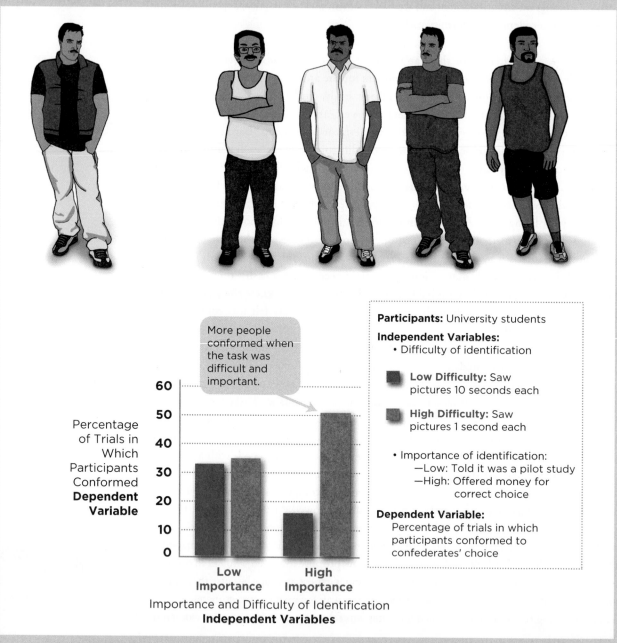

Participants: University students

Independent Variables:
• Difficulty of identification

Low Difficulty: Saw pictures 10 seconds each

High Difficulty: Saw pictures 1 second each

• Importance of identification:
—Low: Told it was a pilot study
—High: Offered money for correct choice

Dependent Variable:
Percentage of trials in which participants conformed to confederates' choice

More people conformed when the task was difficult and important.

Percentage of Trials in Which Participants Conformed **Dependent Variable**

Importance and Difficulty of Identification
Independent Variables

Source: Baron, R. S., Vandello, J. A., & Brunsman, B. (1996). The forgotten variable in conformity research: Impact of task importance on social influence. *Journal of Personality and Social Psychology, 71*, 915–927.

Serge Moscovici in a series of studies which reversed the Asch paradigm by having a minority of two confederates influence a majority of four naïve participants (e.g., Moscovici, Lage, & Naffrechoux, 1969; Moscovici & Personnaz, 1980). Instead of the length of lines, the stimuli were 36 coloured slides. All were blue, but they varied in brightness. Participants were randomly allocated to either a consistent, inconsistent, or control condition. In the consistent condition, the two confederates described all 36 slides as green. In the inconsistent condition, the two confederates described 24 of the 36 slides as green and the remaining 12 slides as blue. In the control condition, there were no confederates. Minority influence was measured by the percentage of naïve participants who yielded to the confederates by calling the blue slides green. In the consistent condition, 8.42 percent of the participants answered "green" and 32 percent conformed at least once. In the inconsistent condition, 1.25 percent of the participants answered "green." In the control condition, only 0.25 percent of the participants answered "green." Thus, the consistent condition showed the greatest yielding to minority influence, although less in quantitative terms than typically produced by the majority in the Asch studies. In a follow-up study, however, it was found that both experimental groups were more likely to report ambiguous blue/green slides as green than the control group. This suggests that the minority influence is more lasting than the behavioural conformity produced in the studies on majority influence.

Moscovici (1976) suggests that this experiment demonstrates the difference between "conversion" (i.e., genuine change in belief) and mere conformity, a qualitatively different type of influence. There is an argument that corresponds with the distinction between normative and informational influence, with majorities said to exert more of the former and minorities more of the latter. This view is supported by a study in which participants not only gave a judgement on the colour of the slide (blue or green), but after each slide were shown a white screen and were asked to report the colour of the after-image that they saw on it (Moscovici & Personnaz, 1980). For blue slides, the after-image should be yellow/orange, while for green slides it should be red/purple. Those exposed to the minority influence reported after-images closer to the purple end of the spectrum, suggesting that the influence was at a perceptual, unconscious level (as most people don't know what the after-images are for different colours).

One factor that increases the power of minority influence is the consistency of the minority's position: people who are unwavering in their view attract attention from others and make their argument especially salient (Maass & Clark, 1984, 1986; Nemeth, Mayseless, Sherman, & Brown, 1990; Tanford & Penrod, 1984). Such expression also gives majority group members the idea that the person is not going to yield, which may then put pressure on others to compromise on their own views. When a person is very firm in his or her beliefs (particularly if the individual is in the minority), it can make others think that that individual might actually be right. In fact, majorities usually influence people by eliciting public conformity (because people don't want to appear deviant from the norm), but minorities may lead to private conformity, which occurs when people rethink their original views, and change their minds (Wood, Lundgren, Ouellette, Busceme, & Blackstone, 1994; Wood, Pool, Leck, & Purvis, 1996).

Minority influence can be particularly effective when delivered by a person who is already well established within a group, in part because a certain amount of acceptance has already been granted to them (Bray, Johnson, & Chilstrom, 1982; Clark & Maass, 1988; Hollander, 1958, 1960). In one study, students with moderate views on abortion were exposed to messages by in-group members (those who attended their university) or outgroup members (those who attended a different university; Clark & Maass, 1988). Those who heard minority views expressed by members of their in-group were more likely to be persuaded, in part because in-group members are seen as more credible. Minority opinions expressed by in-group members are also seen more positively and are subjected to less counter-argument (Alvaro & Crano, 1997). However, minority influence is weaker in large groups than in small ones, in line with social impact theory (Clark & Maass, 1990).

Questioning the Research:

This study examined the power of minority influence by comparing persuasion by students who attended one's own university versus those who attended a different university. Is this distinction a good strategy for measuring minority influence? Why or why not? What might be a better approach to examining influence by a minority member of an in-group versus an outgroup?

"Straight, but not narrow" bumpersticker. Gay, lesbian, and bisexual groups often include "allies," heterosexuals who are supportive of gay rights, in part because mainstream members can increase the likelihood of minority influence.

Mark Owens/John Wiley & Sons

When minority influence does occur, it can have a beneficial effect on the quality of the decision. Specifically, because minority influence leads to the expression of a wider range of arguments, and more original arguments, from multiple perspectives, hearing about a minority viewpoint leads to newer and more original thoughts (Martin, 1996; Mucchi-Faina, Maass, & Volpato, 1991; Peterson & Nemeth, 1996). Minority messages are also processed more extensively, particularly when they oppose the recipient's attitude (Erb, Bohner, Rank, & Einwiller, 2002). In this way, minority influence can improve thinking, as portrayed in the classic film *12 Angry Men*, in which one man on a jury persuades the other jury members to accept his point of view despite being, initially, in a minority of one against 11.

THE BENEFITS OF CONFORMITY

You probably wouldn't feel comfortable wearing jeans at a wedding, or a tuxedo or ball gown at a soccer game. Although, in individualist societies, we think of conformity as a bad thing, meaning that people who conform are seen as weak and dependent, conformity is very much a part of our lives. While many of the salient examples of conformity focus on its dangers (e.g., suicides, fraternity hazing, sexual assault), conformity has real utility and can also be used for worthwhile purposes. Examples might include a fraternity that mandates community service, or a university campus in which expressions of racist or sexist attitudes are clearly rejected, or a neighbourhood in which recycling is the norm. See the Environmental Connections box for another example of the benefits of conformity.

ENVIRONMENTAL CONNECTIONS

Why Conformity Can Decrease Littering

Seeing someone else picking up litter (e.g., a fast-food bag) in a parking lot reduces the percentage of people who throw flyers from their windshields on the ground, from 43 percent to 9 percent (Kallgren, Reno, & Cialdini, 2000). In one study, researchers watched participants' behaviour in a parking lot that was cluttered with trash, cigarette butts, and paper cups (Reno et al., 1993). In half of the cases, a confederate walked by and threw a piece of paper on the ground. In the other half, the confederate walked by and picked up a piece of trash and put it in a trashcan. When the (unknowing) participants reached their cars, they found a "please drive safely" flyer on the windshield. In the control condition, where there was no confederate, over one-third of the participants littered (38 percent). Similarly, when the confederate modelled the act of littering, 30 percent of participants also littered. On the other hand, when the confederate instead modelled the act of picking up litter,

Tove, Jan/Johner Images/Getty Images, Inc.

only 4 percent of participants littered. This research reveals the power of making certain types of norms salient as a strategy for improving the environment.

[CONCEPTS IN CONTEXT]

EXAMPLES OF FACTORS LEADING TO CONFORMITY

FACTOR	EXAMPLE
TYPES OF INFLUENCE	
Informational influence	Abbas, who has not been in Canada long, is trying to decide which candidate to vote for in the upcoming election. To help him choose, Abbas asks his friends who have lived in Canada longer and have similar political views to his own what they think of the different candidates.
Normative influence	Jill smokes when she is with her high school friends because everyone else is doing it.
INFLUENCES ON CONFORMITY	
Group size	Aviva always voices her opinion about which type of food she prefers to eat when she goes out to dinner with one or two friends, but when she goes out with a large group of people she typically defers to whatever the others seem to want.
Standing alone	After Brittany saw someone cheating during the final exam in her physics class, she wasn't sure what to do because no one else seemed to be reporting the act. But after hearing that another student had come forward to report the cheating, she decided to go talk to the professor about what she had seen.
Demographic variables	Peter, a 16-year-old in high school, conforms to the behaviour of his friends. However, his younger brother, Brian (aged 10), conforms neither to Peter's friends' behaviour nor to his own friends' behaviour.
Motivation	Juan often agrees with his friends when they're talking about their favourite sports teams, even when he disagrees with their opinions. However, when they're discussing politics, he adamantly expresses his opinion even when it goes against those of his friends.
Minority influence	Jasmine's strong views about the importance of distribution requirements in course selection at her school were originally opposed by other students, but after she forcefully and consistently described the benefits of her plan, many people came to share her views.

WHAT FACTORS LEAD TO COMPLIANCE?

Imagine that a stranger asks you for a favour—how likely would you be to agree? Would you believe that something as small as sharing the same date of birth as that stranger would increase your willingness to do the favour? In one study, participants signed up for what they believed was a study on astrology (Burger, Messian, Patel, del Prado, & Anderson, 2004). When they arrived for the study, they met someone who they believed to be another participant (but who was actually a confederate). As the experimenter began to pass out the questionnaires, she asked for each participant's birthday as a way of determining their astrological sign. After each participant responded, the confederate provided her own birthday. In half of the cases, the confederate gave the same birthday as the participant (who typically commented on this coincidence). In the other cases, the confederate gave a birthday that was different from the participant's. After the completion of the questionnaires, the experimenter thanked each person for participating and left the room. The confederate then asked each participant for a favour—to read an eight-page essay for an English class and provide a critique. As predicted, more than 62 percent of those who believed they shared a birthday with the confederate agreed to provide this critique, compared to only 34 percent of those who believed they didn't share a birthday. As well as sharing a birthday, sharing a first name and having fingerprint similarities produced the same increased tendency to compliance. This study is one example of how very subtle factors, in this case a superficial, coincidental, and relatively inconsequential perceived similarity, can influence behaviour.

This section will examine how strategies can be used to induce **compliance**. These factors include reciprocity, consistency and commitment, and scarcity.

RECIPROCITY

reciprocity – a mutual exchange between two people

One of the most straightforward strategies that leads to compliance is **reciprocity**, meaning the pressure to reciprocate someone else's behaviour. So, if someone does something nice for us, we tend to do something nice for that person (Regan, 1971; Uehara, 1995). Reciprocity is universal, meaning that a reciprocation norm applies cross-culturally. Reciprocity also applies to most social behaviours, including pro-social behaviour (e.g., we help those who have helped us), self-disclosure (e.g., we disclose to those who reveal to us), cooperation/competition (e.g., we cooperate with those who cooperate with us and compete with those who compete against us), and compliance (we tend to be persuaded by those who have complied with our request in the past). Reciprocity explains why if you agree with someone on an initial topic, that person is more likely to agree with you later on a different topic. On the other hand, if you refuse to change your initial position, that person is likely to resist your influence later (Cialdini, Green, & Rusch, 1992). Reciprocity explains the effectiveness of both the door-in-the-face and that's-not-all techniques.

door-in-the-face technique – a compliance technique where one first asks for a big request, and then asks for a smaller request which then seems more reasonable

THE DOOR-IN-THE-FACE TECHNIQUE.   In using the **door-in-the-face technique**, you first make a big request (a really outrageous one), and then make a smaller request (Cialdini et al., 1975). The beauty of this strategy is that the second request seems pretty reasonable in comparison to the first request, and people are therefore much more likely to comply.

In one study on the power of the door-in-the-face technique, Cialdini and colleagues asked a group of university students to serve as chaperones for a group of juvenile delinquents during a day trip to the zoo (Cialdini et al., 1975). Only 17 percent agreed. When another group of students was first asked to serve as counsellors to juvenile delinquents for two hours a week for two years, an even larger commitment, they all refused. However, these students were then asked to help with the day trip to the zoo. This time, 50 percent agreed.

© Dana Fradon/The New Yorker Collection/www. cartoonbank.com

THE THAT'S-NOT-ALL TECHNIQUE.   Another technique that relies on reciprocity is the **that's-not-all technique**. In this strategy, the influencer begins with an inflated request and then decreases its apparent size by offering discounts or bonuses (Pollock, Smith, Knowles, & Bruce, 1998). In one study, Burger (1986) set up a booth at a university fair to sell cupcakes. Some people who approached the table were told that the cupcakes cost 75 cents. Others were told that they cost $1, but then the price was quickly reduced to 75 cents. Seventy-five percent of the people who were offered the "reduced price" bought the cupcakes, compared to 44 percent of those who were only offered the same but regular price of 75 cents. This is in part due to the norm of reciprocity (e.g., someone does something nice for you by lowering the price, so you do something nice for that person by buying the item).

that's-not-all technique – a compliance technique in which the influencer begins with an inflated request, and then decreases its apparent size by offering discounts or bonuses

The that's-not-all technique is more effective with low-cost items than with higher-cost ones, presumably because we're more likely to be persuaded by subtle cues to spend small amounts of money but think through larger purchases more rationally (Pollock et al., 1998). One study found that the that's-not-all technique led 76 percent of people to buy a small box of chocolates, compared to only 45 percent in the control condition. However, this technique had no impact on willingness to buy a large (and more expensive) box of chocolates (18 percent versus 24 percent).

CONSISTENCY AND COMMITMENT

Another factor that leads to compliance is people's desire to appear consistent. Once we've committed to engaging in a behaviour, we follow through on that, or related, behaviours to appear consistent. This factor explains the effectiveness of the foot-in-the-door and lowballing techniques.

FOOT-IN-THE-DOOR.   This approach is almost the exact opposite of the door-in-the-face technique. The **foot-in-the-door technique** refers to a two-step technique for inducing compliance: first a small request is made, and then a second, larger request is made (Beaman, 1983; DeJong & Musilli, 1982; Schwarzwald, Bizman, & Raz, 1983). Sometimes these requests are made by the same experimenter, and sometimes they're made by different experimenters. The percentage of participants who agree to the second, larger request is typically much larger than the percentage of people who would agree to the larger request if it were not preceded by a smaller request. In one U.S. study, participants were asked to write a one- or two-sentence message about homelessness on a petition that was supposedly going to their senator (Burger & Caldwell, 2003). Two days later, another experimenter called to ask them to donate two hours of time that weekend to help with a food drive. Thirty-two percent of those who were only asked this larger request agreed to help with the food drive, compared to 51 percent of those who were first asked to sign the petition.

> **foot-in-the-door technique** – a two-step compliance technique in which an influencer first asks someone to perform a small request, and then asks for a larger request

In a classic study of this technique, researchers in southern California went door to door asking people to agree to a small request (Freedman & Fraser, 1966). For example, in one case people were asked to put a small, three-inch-square sign near their front door that said, "Be a Safe Driver"; in another case, they were asked to put up a sign saying, "Keep California Beautiful"; and in two other cases they were asked to sign a petition that was being sent to senators about either safe driving or keeping California beautiful. Most of the people approached by the researchers agreed to these requests. Two weeks later, another experimenter went to the same houses and asked residents to put a public service billboard on their front lawn that said, "Drive Carefully." The sign was very large and poorly lettered, and almost totally blocked the front lawn and their house—as was clearly shown in a photograph shown to the residents. Who agreed to allow this ugly sign on their front lawn? Only about half of those who had either signed a petition (on a same or different topic) or put a "Keep California Beautiful" sign by their door agreed to the new request. However, 76 percent of those who had put the "Be a Safe Driver" sign by their door agreed to the new request.

This effect was replicated by Patricia Pliner and colleagues from the University of Toronto (Pliner, Hart, Kohl & Saari, 1974). In this case, researchers called at houses in a Toronto suburb and requested donations for a charitable organization. Some residents had been approached the evening before and were either asked to wear a lapel pin the next day to help publicize the funding drive (a small prior request) or to both wear the pin and persuade a member of their household to do the same (a moderate prior request). Forty-six percent of those who hadn't been approached the day before donated to the charity, whereas 75 percent and 81 percent of those who had been asked a small or moderate request, respectively, gave donations. In other words, a larger prior request was more effective in this instance—you get your foot further in the door that way.

According to Freedman and Fraser (1966), those who agreed with the first request in their study came to see themselves as the type of person who supports safe driving and is willing to put a sign up to help out others. In turn, this new self-image later convinces them to allow the huge sign to be placed on their lawn. A similar argument applies to the study by Pliner, Hart, Kohl, & Saari, (1974). Those who see themselves as supporters of the charity by agreeing to wear a pin are more likely to continue their perceived support when asked for a larger favour (a donation). The self-image of being helpful or charitable occurs and then influences future behaviour—even, as the following study shows, when the first attempt isn't successful. In one study, people on the street were approached at random and asked for help with finding a non-existent address (Dolinski, 2000). Virtually everyone (94 percent) at least responded, typically saying, "I don't know," but no one could actually help in this situation as the street didn't exist. Participants were then approached a few blocks later by a woman carrying a huge suitcase and they were asked if they would just watch the luggage for a few minutes while she went up to visit a friend who lived on the fifth floor. How many people simply walking down the street would agree to such a request? Not that many— about 34 percent. But what about when they were first asked to help with directions? People who had been asked by the first confederate agreed to watch the woman's luggage 58 percent of the time, suggesting that the foot-in-the-door effect may work in part because it allows people to form an image of themselves as helpful even if their helpful intentions are not carried out.

It should be noted, however, that the explanation that self-perception is the determining factor is not entirely proven. Donald Gorassini and James Olson from the University of Western Ontario manipulated self-perceptions of helpfulness in experimental settings. They found that the self-rating helpfulness did not predict foot-in-the-door effect (i.e., increased helping). In other words, no link was found between self-perception helpfulness and compliance to a large request (Gorassini & Olson, 1995).

Who's Who in Contemporary Canadian Social Psychology Research

James Olson is a professor at the University of Western Ontario. He received his BA and his MA from Carleton University and his PhD from the University of Waterloo. Professor Olson's current research interests include justice (e.g., the influence of self-presentation motives on the expression of discontent), social cognition (e.g., social comparison), humour (e.g., the role of self-perception in judgements of funniness), and attitudes (e.g., dissonance theory). Professor Olson is the recipient of several awards and is a co-organizer of the Ontario Symposium on Personality and Social Psychology, an ongoing series of conferences on personality and social psychology topics.

lowballing – a two-step technique in which the influencer secures agreement with a request, but then increases the size of that request by revealing hidden costs

LOWBALLING. The term **lowballing** describes a two-step technique in which the influencer secures compliance with a request but then increases the size of that request by revealing hidden costs (Burger & Petty, 1981; Cialdini, Cacioppo, Bassett, & Miller, 1978). Lowballing is commonly used by car dealers. Imagine that you and the car dealer reach an agreement to purchase a particular car at a particular price. But after you've reached the agreement, you learn that the purchase price doesn't include many of the features you might expect (e.g., floor mats, a radio, air conditioning), so the true price is higher. Although the deal has now changed, most people feel compelled to pay the additional fees because they've already committed to buying the car.

The lowballing technique works because once someone has agreed to a request they feel committed to follow through, even when the nature of that request changes. In one study, researchers asked students to participate in a psychology study that would begin at 7 a.m. (Cialdini et al., 1978). Only 31 percent agreed. A different approach was taken with other students. First they were simply asked to participate in a psychology study (nearly all agreed). Then the researchers informed them that the study would begin at 7 a.m. In this condition 56 percent of the students agreed to participate. Why? Because once they've agreed to the request, it's hard for them to tell the experimenter that they've changed their mind.

As the following study shows, lowballing only works when the same person makes the request both times (Burger & Petty, 1981). People apparently feel some obligation to the person with whom they have initially negotiated, and thus tend to honour that agreement. When research participants are told that they can receive extra credit for completing a series of math problems, most agree (65% to 70%). However, when they're next told that the professor refused to allow such credit and asked whether they would still be willing to complete the problems, 85 percent of those who are asked by the same experimenter agree. In contrast, only 21 percent of those who are asked by a different experimenter agree to complete the problems.

Questioning the Research:

Can you think of an alternative explanation for these findings? (Hint: In the second condition, the time of the day is clearly the reason for saying no and maybe participants feel uncomfortable admitting this.)

SCARCITY

Yet another factor that leads to compliance is **scarcity**, meaning limiting people's opportunity to act, either in terms of time ("This sale ends on Saturday") or number ("Only two left"). This factor explains the effectiveness of the deadline and hard-to-get techniques.

scarcity – a compliance technique in which the opportunity to act is limited in terms of the time to act or number of opportunities

DEADLINE.   Many compliance techniques in the real world rely on creating the illusion (often false) of a strict deadline by which time you need to have acted. For example, often when you tour a health club, you're told that if you join right away you'll get the lowest price, and that if you don't sign up immediately you'll end up paying more later. Similarly, advertisements for some stores continually note that the store is going out of business, and hence buying now is essential. Oddly enough, the stores continue to be in business . . . but continue to use the threat of going out of business to motivate sales.

In a clever demonstration of the power of scarcity in increasing the perceived attractiveness of a given item, Jamie Pennebaker and his colleagues asked people in a bar to rate the average attractiveness of all people of their same gender or the opposite gender (Pennebaker et al., 1979). Some people were asked early in the evening (9 p.m.), some were asked in the middle of the evening (10:30 p.m.), and some were asked at the end of the evening (midnight, with the bar closing at 12:30 a.m.). Although the attractiveness of the same-gender people showed a slight decrease over the course of the evening, the attractiveness of opposite-gender people rose remarkably as the time remaining for meeting someone decreased.

Questioning the Research:

Can you think of another explanation for the finding that people of the opposite sex increase in their attractiveness later in the evening?

HARD TO GET.   In other cases, the perceived scarcity of an object leads people to act more quickly or to pay more because of their concern that the desired object will soon be unavailable (Worchel, Lee, & Adewole, 1975). It's not unusual, for example, for some popular items at Christmas time to suddenly become hard to find, whether toys, electronic gadgets and games, sports items, or other accessories, with the result that people wait long hours for new shipments to arrive and are willing to pay higher prices.

The hard-to-get effect works in part because it leads such objects to appear more desirable. One research study demonstrated the power of scarcity in increasing the appeal of an object: people rated a chocolate chip cookie as tasting better when they saw it being taken from a jar containing only two cookies than when they saw it being taken from a jar containing 10 cookies (Worchel et al., 1975). Similarly, companies that advertise only a few job vacancies are perceived as paying a higher salary than those advertising many job vacancies (Highhouse, Beadle, Gallo, & Miller, 1998).

THE SERIOUS CONSEQUENCES OF COMPLIANCE

Although most of this section has focused on the power of compliance to elicit relatively inconsequential behaviours, this type of social influence can also elicit much more serious behaviours. As described in the Law Connections box, compliance pressures can even lead people to confess to crimes they didn't commit. One of the most famous examples of compliance leading to false confessions occurred in 1990, when five African American and Hispanic teenagers living in Harlem were found guilty of the rape and assault of a 28-year-old investment banker who was jogging in Central Park. Four of the five defendants had made lengthy videotaped confessions to the crime. Thirteen years later, a serial rapist who was in prison for another crime confessed to the crime. After a DNA match was made connecting this person to the crime, the defendants' convictions were vacated and they were released from prison.

LAW CONNECTIONS

The Impact of Compliance on False Identifications and False Confessions

In the legal system, compliance pressures can lead to false identifications. Specifically, when eyewitnesses are asked to identify a suspect in a lineup, the instructions they receive influence their response (Malpass & Devine, 1981). Those who are asked to choose a person from a lineup are much more likely to wrongly identify a person (when the actual suspect is not in the lineup) than those who are asked to choose someone but are specifically told that the suspect may not be in the lineup. Moreover, eyewitnesses who receive confirming feedback—namely, those who hear "Good, you identified the suspect" following their identification—overestimate how good a look they had at the suspect as well as how clearly they were able to make out facial details (Wells, Olson, & Charman, 2003). This increase in confidence about their identification can make them even more compelling witnesses when they later appear in a trial.

Compliance pressures can even lead people to wrongly identify themselves as guilty of an offence they didn't commit (Kassin, 2005; Kassin & Kiechel, 1996). In one study of the power of pressure on eliciting false confessions, researchers asked participants to perform a relatively simple computer task that was supposedly designed to test spatial awareness. Before the beginning of the task, they were warned not to press a particular button on the keyboard because doing so would cause the computer to crash and the data to be lost. About one minute after the participant began the task, the computer screen suddenly went blank and the experimenter rushed in and accused the participant of pressing the forbidden key. Although in reality not a single person had touched this key, over 69 percent of the participants ultimately were willing to sign a confession saying that they had done so. When participants were working on the task in a high-speed condition and their mistake was supposedly seen by an eyewitness, then 100 percent of the participants agreed to sign the confession. This study provides strong evidence that compliance pressure can have dangerous real-world consequences. Researchers are currently examining strategies for reducing this type of compliance pressure to avoid convicting people—based on a false confession—for crimes they didn't commit.

mbbirdy/ Vetta/ Getty Images, Inc.

WHAT FACTORS LEAD TO OBEDIENCE?

Bickman (1974) studied obedience by asking people on the street to comply with some type of request, such as picking up a paper bag, standing on the opposite side of a sign, or giving someone a dime. In half of the cases, the requester wore ordinary clothes. In the other cases he wore a security guard's uniform. Regardless of the request, many more people obeyed the request when the person was wearing a uniform (92 percent) than when he was wearing street clothes (42 percent), presumably because the uniform signifies legitimate authority. This section will examine factors that increase obedience, as well as the ethical issues involved in conducting scientific research on obedience.

EXAMPLES OF STRATEGIES FOR INDUCING COMPLIANCE

STRATEGY	EXAMPLE
RECIPROCITY	
Door-in-the-face	Vivian asks her parents if they will buy her a car when she graduates from university. When they say no, she asks if they will give her $1,000 as a down payment on a car.
That's-not-all	As Alton is standing in a store trying to decide whether to buy a new television, the salesperson comes over to him and whispers that there is an overstock of this particular model and he can give a 10-percent discount. Alton agrees to the purchase and hands the clerk his credit card.
CONSISTENCY AND COMMITMENT	
Foot-in-the-door	Glenda asks her neighbour to buy a box of Girl Guide cookies. After she agrees, Glenda asks if she'd like to contribute $20 to the annual Girl Guide fundraiser.
Lowballing	Aden agreed to buy his first car for $15,000. After the initial contract was prepared, the car dealer told him that the safety package is not included in the price. Aden agreed to pay an extra $2,000 for the safety package as this feature would ensure his and his car's safety.
SCARCITY	
Deadline	Monisha is looking for an apartment. After showing her an apartment, the landlord tells her that he gives a $100 discount to tenants who put down a deposit the same day they see the apartment. Although Monisha originally intended to spend the next week looking at different apartments, she decides to sign a lease for this apartment today.
Hard to get	Hitesh is trying to decide if he should go to a concert with his friends and he suddenly learns that the concert only has two tickets remaining. Although he really isn't sure whether he wants to spend the money, he buys a ticket because he's worried that the event will soon sell out.

FACTORS THAT INCREASE OBEDIENCE

In the early 1960s, Stanley Milgram at Yale University began a series of experiments to examine the factors that predict obedience to authority (1963, 1974). This study, which marked Milgram's first line of research as a new professor, was based on his interest in discovering the processes that led to the Nazi actions carried out by people who were simply obeying orders. He was interested in what led people to be willing to give and follow such orders, and whether similar levels of obedience could be found in the United States.

In a series of experiments, Milgram brought ordinary men into his lab to participate in what was supposedly a study of memory. After a participant arrived at the lab, he was greeted by Milgram and introduced to another person, who was supposedly another participant but in reality was a confederate of Milgram's. The experimenter then explained the

Archived of the History of American Psychology – University of Akron
The shock generator used in Milgram's research was designed to look very realistic and thereby convince participants that they were truly giving electric shocks to another participant.

study, which both were told was designed to test the impact of punishment on speed of learning. The participants were told that one person would serve as the "teacher" and administer shocks to the other person (the "learner") when the learner gave a wrong answer.

The learner was always a confederate who would receive the "shocks." The "teacher" was told to start by giving the learner the lowest level of shock (15 volts) and to increase the shock level each time the learner made a mistake.

As the study progressed, the learner continued to give wrong answers and the teacher continued to increase the intensity of the shocks. At the 75-volt level, the learner began to cry out after each shock, and by 150 volts the learner asked to be let out of the experiment (see Table 8.1). Moreover, he began claiming that his heart was bothering him, suggesting a major negative consequence of continuing the experiment. But each time the participant hesitated or turned to the experimenter for advice, he received a prompt that prodded him to continue. These prompts continued until the teacher simply refused to continue or reached the highest level of volts (450, which was marked "XXX dangerous").

Much to Milgram's surprise, the vast majority of the participants in his study were willing to give another innocent participant the maximum level of electric shocks—in fact, 65 percent of the participants fully obeyed the experimenter's orders to the highest level. This extremely high rate of obedience was shocking to many, including psychiatrists whom Milgram had consulted before the experiment and who had predicted that approximately 1 percent of the participants would obey.

To examine the factors that led to this high rate of obedience, Milgram conducted a series of follow-up studies that varied different factors in his original study. He found that some factors affected the rate of obedience more than others.

PERSON FACTORS. First, although initially Milgram and many others assumed that only people who were cruel and sadistic would give high levels of shocks, this study provided little evidence that *person* factors mattered. Most people in the Milgram study did show full obedience, but the vast majority of those who did so really struggled with obeying the researcher: They pleaded with the experimenter, they perspired, they trembled, and so forth. They weren't enjoying it or finding it easy. As Milgram describes,

> I observed a mature and initially poised businessman enter the laboratory smiling and confident. Within 20 minutes he was reduced to a twitching, stuttering wreck, who was rapidly approaching a point of nervous collapse. He constantly pulled on his earlobe and twisted his hands. At one point he pushed his fist into his forehead and muttered, "Oh God, let's stop it." And yet he continued to respond to every word of the experimenter, and obeyed to the end (Milgram, 1963, p. 377).

An identical study with women participants showed that 65 percent also reached the 450-volt level. Although some personality characteristics may increase obedience, this behaviour is not primarily a function of the person (Elms & Milgram, 1966).

Although most descriptions of the Milgram study emphasize the high rates of obedience, it is also true that a sizable minority of participants didn't give the highest levels of shocks, indicating that the nature of the person does matter. So who is most likely to obey authority? One personality factor that predicts obedience is *authoritarianism*, a trait that describes people who are submissive and uncritical in their acceptance of the morality of authority (Blass, 1991). As you might imagine, people who were high in authoritarianism did show higher rates of obedience in the Milgram studies. Research on authoritarianism has declined as the Second World War has receded further into history. However, in the late 1980s Bob Altemeyer at the University of Manitoba did rewrite the scale produced in the 1950s by Adorno and colleagues as the Right Wing Authoritarianism scale (Altemeyer, 1988). More recently, Altemeyer and Hunsberger (2005) found links between right wing authoritarianism and religious fundamentalism.

TABLE 8.1	The "Learner's" Protests	
VOLT LEVEL	**LEARNER'S PROTEST**	**PERCENTAGE OF TEACHERS WHO STOPPED**
75 volts	Ugh!	0
95 volts	Ugh!	0
105 volts	Ugh (louder)	0
120 volts	Ugh! Hey, *this* really hurts.	0
135 volts	Ugh!	0
150 volts	Ugh!! Experimenter! That's all. Get me out of here. I told you I had heart trouble. My heart's starting to bother me. Get me out of here, please. My heart's starting to bother me. I refuse to go on. Let me out.	0
165 volts	Ugh! Let me out! (*shouting*)	0
180 volts	Ugh! I can't stand the pain. Let me out of here! (*shouting*)	0
195 volts	Ugh! Let me out of here. Let me out of here. My heart's bothering me. Let me out of here! You have no right to keep me here! Let me out! Let me out of here! Let me out! Let me out of here! My heart's bothering me. Let me out! Let me out!	0
210 volts	Ugh!! Experimenter! *Get* me out of here. I've had enough. I *won't* be in the experiment any more.	0
225 volts	Ugh!	0
240 volts	Ugh!	0
255 volts	Ugh! Get me *out* of here.	0
270 volts	(*Agonized scream.*) Let me out of here. Let me out of here. Let me out. Do you hear? Let me out of here.	0
285 volts	(*Agonized scream.*)	0
300 volts	(*Agonized scream.*) I absolutely refuse to answer any more. Get me out of here. You can't hold me here. Get me out. Get me out of here.	12.5
315 volts	(*Intensely agonized scream.*) *I told you I refuse to answer*. I'm no longer part of this experiment.	10
330 volts	(*Intense and prolonged agonized scream.*) Let me out of here. Let me out of here. My heart's bothering me. Let me out, I tell you. (*Hysterically.*) Let me out of here. Let me out of here. You have no right to hold me here. Let me out! Let me out! Let me out! Let me out of here! Let me out! Let me out!	5
345 volts	(No response)	2.5
360 volts	(No response)	2.5
375 volts	(No response)	2.5
390 volts	(No response)	0
405 volts	(No response)	0
420 volts	(No response)	0
435 volts	(No response)	0
450 volts	(No response)	65

Participants in the Milgram study were faced with a very unwilling learner and were forced to choose whether to obey the authority figure (the experimenter) who was telling them to continue, or the learner, who was insisting that they stop.

Source: Milgram, S. (1974), Obedience to Authority; An Experimental View. New York: Harper Collins.

HOW MUCH DO YOU BELIEVE IN OBEYING AUTHORITIES?

INSTRUCTIONS: *Rate your agreement with each of the following statements on a scale of 1 (strongly disagree) to 7 (strongly agree).*

1. Obedience and respect for authority are the most important virtues children should learn.

2. What this country needs most, more than laws and political programs, is a few courageous, tireless, devoted leaders in whom the people can put their faith.

3. Most of our social problems would be solved if we could somehow get rid of the immoral, crooked, and feeble-minded people.

4. People can be divided into two distinct classes: the weak and the strong.

5. What the youth needs most is strict discipline, rugged determination, and the will to work and fight for family and country.

SCORING: Add up your scores on each of these items.

INTERPRETATION: This scale measures the degree of authoritarianism, meaning people's belief in and support of the policies and decisions made by powerful authorities. People with higher scores (25–35) have a greater belief in the power of authorities than those with lower scores (5–15) (Adorno, Frenkel-Brunswick, Levinson, & Sanford, 1950).

AUTHORITY FACTORS. A factor that did influence rates of obedience was the nature of the *authority*. Although a scientist is not typically seen as a significant authority figure (e.g., compared to a military leader or work supervisor), apparently in this context the experimenter was seen as the definitive authority. When Milgram ran this study in Bridgeport, Connecticut, in a rundown lab that was not associated with Yale, the rate of obedience dropped to 48 percent. When the experimenter was an ordinary person (supposedly just another participant), the rate of obedience dropped to 20 percent. In other cases, obedience occurs based on even more subtle cues, such as the person's dress—as described in the study at the start of this section (Bushman, 1988).

IN THE NEWS

The Canadian Press/AP Photo/Brian Bohannon

McDonald's. In April of 2004, workers at a McDonald's restaurant in Mount Washington, Kentucky, obeyed a series of orders delivered over the phone by a person they believed was a police officer. This officer was supposedly investigating whether a McDonald's worker had stolen a customer's purse. Following the officer's instructions, the store manager ordered an 18-year-old female employee to remove all her clothing in an effort to find the stolen items. The victim later sued McDonald's for failing to protect her during her ordeal; in October 2007, she was awarded over $5 million in punitive damages and expenses.

PROCEDURE FACTORS. Another factor that contributed to the high rate of obedience in Milgram's studies was the *procedure* that was used, including the location of the victim and the experimenter. Milgram carried out 18 variations of his research and manipulated the proximity between the teacher, the learner, and the experimenter in some cases. When the learner was in the adjoining room, as was the case in the original study, 65 percent of participants reached the 450-volt level (Miller, Collins, & Brief, 1995). When the learner was in the same room as the teacher, only 40 percent of the participants reached the 450-volt level. When the teacher was required to force the learner's hand onto a metal shock plate, the rate of obedience dropped to 30 percent. And when the experimenter was not in the same room but instead gave his instructions by telephone, the rate of obedience was only 21 percent (some participants even lied and stayed at the 15-volt level).

People are also much more willing to convey orders to harm someone else than to actually carry out such orders (Kilham & Mann, 1974). In this case, the person's responsibility is reduced even more. It was also found that when a supposed participant disobeyed, so did most others (90 percent). Moreover, when participants are given the option of whether to give a shock or not, most do not. People also refuse to continue when two experimenters disagree. And they refuse to obey another participant who tells them to continue.

Although these findings show that some aspects of the procedure and the nature of the authority decrease obedience, a lot of people are still willing to obey. Why? In part because Milgram's procedure was designed to produce obedience. First, the participants didn't have personal responsibility for the victim (Tilker, 1970; Blass, 1996). As described previously, the researcher gave the orders and thus took full responsibility for what was occurring, allowing the participants to absolve themselves of blame.

Second, there was a gradual escalation of shock levels, meaning that people could initially feel fine about obeying the request, and obey repeatedly before the frightening implications of the procedure were clear (Gilbert, 1981). Most people would not initially give a 450-volt shock, but once you've given 15 volts, and then 30 and then 45, how do you decide when to stop? This is like the foot-in-the-door technique in that participants had no easy way to justify a decision to stop giving shocks at a certain point. In line with this view, people who defy authority tend to do so early on; that is, those who ultimately disobey tend to resist authority more quickly (Modigliani & Rochat, 1995). Interestingly, in a meta-analysis of data from several of Milgram's studies, Canadian researcher Dominic Packer found that participants were most likely to stop obeying orders at the 150-volt level (Packer, 2008). What is unique about this voltage level? It was at this level that the victim first asked to be released, thus providing participants with an alternative request to comply with. Packer suggests that participants who disobeyed at 150 volts saw the learner's right to terminate the experiment as overriding the experimenter's wish to continue.

Third, although the participant could *hear* the victim, he couldn't *see* him—people who have more feedback (audio and visual) are more likely to behave in a responsible way (Tilker, 1970). In general, however, it has been found that people tend to ignore such situational factors and attribute evil to the victim—right in line with people's tendency to make the fundamental attribution error (Safer, 1980).

ETHICAL ISSUES

The Milgram studies generated a tremendous amount of interest among social psychologists for several reasons. First, these results were completely unexpected—even experts predicted that very few people would go along with the authority figure to such a dangerous extent. Second, the variations of the experiment that Milgram conducted provided considerable information about the influence of various factors in producing obedience, and therefore enabled researchers to distinguish among the effects of the participant, the procedure, and the authority. Perhaps most important, these studies also generated considerable debate about the ethics of such experiments. Many researchers were horrified that this study was even conducted—it obviously exposed people to psychological harm during the experiment, and it is certainly possible that such effects lingered, perhaps permanently (Baumrind, 1985).

In response, Milgram claimed that the debriefing following his study was very thorough and was designed to leave the participants feeling good about themselves and their behaviour. In a follow-up questionnaire returned by 92 percent of the participants, 44 percent claimed that they were "very glad to have participated in the experiment" and 40 percent said that they were "glad to have participated." Only 1 percent were "sorry" or "very sorry" to have participated. Milgram sent each participant a five-page report describing the value of this study. Moreover, an independent psychiatrist examined the 40 participants who were thought to be at greatest risk of experiencing harm, and none of them showed any signs of long-term damage. Nevertheless, the full extent of the harm, or even potential harm, of having participated in this study remains unknown.

REPLICATIONS OF MILGRAM'S STUDY

Meeus and Raaijmakers (1986) conducted a modification of Milgram's study 20 years later at the University of Utrecht in the Netherlands. The study was different from Milgram's in several ways, including a change from physical violence (i.e., administering shocks) to psychological violence (i.e., administering verbal insults). The authors argued that in modern Western societies of the 1980s, psychological rather than physical violence is more likely to be used to exert power. To create psychological violence, the participants were told to make the learner nervous and disturbed by making negative remarks during the test. These remarks were about the learner's performance and had to become increasingly provocative to produce tension in the learners.

Participants were Dutch males and females between 18 and 55 years of age. The researchers asked participants to read various test questions over a microphone to a supposed job applicant who was actually a confederate of the researcher. They were told that if the learner did well, he would get the job, and otherwise wouldn't. The researchers told the participants that they were interested in examining how the job applicant would react under pressure, so they wanted them to harass the applicant by saying things like "If you continue like this, you will fail" and "This job is much too difficult for you." As the "interview" continued, the applicant protested. He pleaded with them to stop, then refused to tolerate the abuse, and was clearly showing signs of tension. He eventually just stopped answering the questions. How many of the participants continued to read the 15 stress-inducing statements? None of them did in a control group (which lacked an authority urging them to continue), but 92 percent did so when the experimenter prodded them along (and took responsibility for the results). The obedience rate in Meeus and Raaijmakers' study was considerably higher than in Milgram's studies, indicating that it's easier to obey orders that urge psychological rather than physical violence.

Additionally, a partial replication of Milgram's experiment was conducted by Jerry Burger (2009) from Santa Clara University in the United States. To ensure ethical consideration and the well-being of participants, several changes were made to the original study. One important change was modifying the range of shock in the generator's shock machine. In the new study the highest shock that participants could deliver was 150 volts instead of 450. The 150-volt point in the original study was where the learner protested in pain and demanded to be released. Milgram's finding was that the majority of those who delivered shocks after this point continued until the end. It was therefore assumed in the new experiment that most participants who delivered the 150-volt shock would have continued until the maximum level if the opportunity had been presented. By stopping at 150 volts, participants were protected against excessive psychological pressure and stress, which was present in the original study. Another modification in the new study was informing the participants (three times) that they could withdraw from the study at any time and would still receive $50 for their participation.

The participants in Burger's study comprised 29 men and 41 women, with their ages ranging from 20 to 81 years, for an average age of 42.9 years. The majority of the participants were White Caucasian (54.3 percent) while 18.6 percent were Latin/Hispanic and 12.9% were Asian/Indian. Seventy percent of the participants ended up delivering the maximum shock of 150 volts, which is similar to Milgram's study as more than two-thirds of the participants delivered the maximum shock. Additionally, Burger (2009) found neither gender nor ethnicity differences in the rates of obedience. Overall, the results showed that people obey authority at the same rate now as they did half a century ago.

REAL-WORLD EXAMPLES OF OBEDIENCE

One of the most frightening acts of obedience during recent years occurred in the 1970s in Jonestown, Guyana. The People's Temple was a cult-like organization that was based in San Francisco and drew its members mostly from poor people in that city. In 1977 the Reverend

THIS HAS BEEN A TEST OF THE EXTREMELY ANNOYING NOISES SYSTEM.

Dave Coverly/The Cartoonist Group

Questioning the Research:

This study was designed to examine rates of obedience while avoiding the ethical constraints of the Milgram study. Do you think this study provides important information about people's willingness to obey authority that is comparable to what was found in the Milgram study and other real-life examples of obedience to authority? Why or why not?

Associated Press
Social-psychological principles explain why more than 900 people obeyed the order to kill themselves at Jonestown.

Jim Jones, their leader, moved the group to a remote jungle settlement in South America, and most of his followers joined him. They lived in relative obscurity until 1978, when Congressman Ryan of California went to Guyana to investigate the cult's activities at the urging of relatives of some of its members. Three members of Ryan's party, including a member of the cult who was trying to defect, were shot and killed as they tried to leave Jonestown. Since this act would clearly lead to the arrest and imprisonment of Jones, and hence the abolition of the cult, he decided to require his followers to commit mass suicide. He prepared large vats of strawberry Flavor-Aid laced with cyanide, and ordered his followers to drink the Flavor-Aid. Although a few people escaped or resisted, virtually all of the 910 followers complied with his order and killed themselves. In one particularly dramatic case, a young woman helped her baby drink some of the poison and then drank some herself.

When the mass suicide at Jonestown occurred, most people questioned why so many people would willingly kill themselves. But social-psychological principles clearly tell us why (Osherow, 2004). First, Jim Jones was very charismatic, a powerful leader who had obviously convinced all those people to leave their homes and live in the jungle. Second, most of the people were poor and uneducated, and may have appreciated the safety of having someone else control many aspects of their lives in exchange for the security and salvation Jones promised. Third, and probably most important, they were in a place that was totally alien, both physically and socially. They were isolated from others. And as we know from research on the power of norms, people are most likely to look to others for guidance in their own behaviour when they are in unfamiliar situations. Those who may have had doubts probably considered the situation, and when they saw other people drinking the poison, seemingly without question, they probably assumed that it was the right thing to do.

Obedience has led to dangerous consequences in many other real-life cases, such as the My Lai Massacre during the Vietnam War (see Figure 8.4) and the activities of terrorist groups, such as al Qaeda. Obedience also plays a role in fraternity initiation, as described at the start of this chapter.

Although these real-world examples of obedience may seem very different from one another, they actually share many common features that likely contributed to the obedience shown in each case. First, the people in many of these situations are in very uncertain, and isolated, surroundings, which increases their dependence on the group. In turn, any doubts

FIGURE 8.4   THE MY LAI MASSACRE

Some of the most horrible acts of obedience have occurred during times of war. During the Vietnam War, a group of American soldiers approached a Vietnamese village and proceeded to round up men, women, and children. The following interview by Mike Wallace of the TV program *60 Minutes* describes one soldier's view of this event, known as the My Lai Massacre.

Mike Wallace:	How many people did you round up?
Soldier:	Well, there was about forty, fifty people that we gathered in the center of the village. And we placed them in there, and it was like a little island, right there in the center of the village, I'd say.
Mike Wallace:	What kind of people—men, women, children?
Soldier:	Men, women, children.
Mike Wallace:	Babies?
Soldier:	Babies. And we huddled them up. We made them squat down and Lieutenant Calley came over and said, "You know what to do with them, don't you?" And I said yes. So I took for granted that he just wanted us to watch them. And he left, and came back about ten or fifteen minutes later and said, "How come you ain't killed them yet?" And I told him that I didn't think you wanted us to kill them, that you just wanted us to guard them. He said, "No. I want them dead." So . . .
Mike Wallace:	He told this to all of you, or to you particularly?
Soldier:	Well, I was facing him. So, but the other three, four guys heard it and so he stepped back about ten, fifteen feet, and he started shooting them. And he told me to start shooting. So I started shooting. I poured about four clips in the group.
Mike Wallace:	You fired four clips from your . . .
Soldier:	M-16.
Mike Wallace:	And that's how many clips—I mean, how many . . .
Soldier:	I carried seventeen rounds to each clip.
Mike Wallace:	So you fired something like sixty-seven shots?
Soldier:	Right.
Mike Wallace:	And you killed how many? At that time?
Soldier:	Well, I fired them automatic, so you can't . . . You just spray the area on them and so you can't know how many you killed cause they were going fast. So I might have killed ten or fifteen of them.
Mike Wallace:	Men, women, and children?
Soldier:	Men, women, and children.
Mike Wallace:	And babies?
Soldier:	And babies.

As this interview describes, people can commit horrible acts when they're ordered to do so by an authority figure. Obedience to an authority is especially likely during times of war, in which soldiers must rely on their commanders for guidance, are isolated from family and friends, and experience constant stress.

about the actions of the group are quelled, and a mindset of "us versus them" (group members versus those outside the group) is created. These strategies for creating obedience are used regularly by leaders of cults (as we saw in the case of Jim Jones) and in military settings (as seen in the case of prisoner abuse in the Abu Ghraib prison in Iraq in Chapter 10). These situational factors can then lead seemingly normal people to behave in really atrocious ways, as you learned about from Zimbardo's prison study that was described in Chapter 2 (Haney, Banks, & Zimbardo, 1973; Haney & Zimbardo, 1998). As Nasra Hassan, a Muslim from Palestine who spent four years studying terrorists describes, "What is frightening is not the abnormality of those who carry out the suicide attacks, but their sheer normality" (2001). Her research reveals that suicide bombers are typically young men who often have had a friend or relative killed by the other side. These findings mean that eliminating suicide bombers is not as simple as identifying mentally dysfunctional people, but rather changing the situational factors that create terrorists.

STRATEGIES FOR RESISTING OBEDIENCE

What can we do to help people defy unjustified demands by authority figures? Are people who defy authority different in some way from those who obey? Although several researchers have examined factors in the participants who defied the experimenter in Milgram's studies, there are no associations between defiance and personality factors or religious beliefs (Modigliani & Rochat, 1995). Participants who defied the authority in the Milgram studies are simply ordinary people who chose to deliberate about what they were being asked to do—and that deliberation allowed them to defy the situational pressures and disobey.

This description of the participants who disobeyed in the Milgram study is very similar to the one of people who defied authorities' orders in Nazi Germany and helped the targeted people (Rochat & Modigliani, 1995). Many of these helpers were ordinary people who recognized a need to help people who were being persecuted. They often began helping by performing a very small action, and these early modest steps escalated to larger and more risky acts of assistance.

One factor that can help people stand up to the pressure exerted by authorities is knowing about the power of influence (Richard, Bond, & Stokes-Zoota, 2001). You should therefore be better able to defy unjustified authority after taking a social psychology class. People who are aware of the situational pressures that lead people to obey authorities are more likely to stand up to such authorities themselves—they are willing to act as whistleblowers even in the face of a strong authority. People who are better educated are also more likely to disobey military orders (Hamilton, Sanders, & McKearney, 1995).

Another factor that helps people defy authority is having another person who disobeys with them. As we saw in the case of the Asch study, because people do not like to "stand alone," having other people on their side (as a group, or even just one other person) helps those who wish to defy authority (Rochat & Modigliani, 1995). It may not have been enough for the soldier at My Lai to defy the lieutenant, but one can speculate about what might have happened if the soldier had spoken up. Would other soldiers have joined him, making it much less likely that the massacre would have occurred? It's possible. There is power in numbers, and this means that if you disagree with something or someone, you should speak out.

People are especially likely to disobey authority if they see such acts modelled by other authority figures. In a variation of the original study, Milgram examined how people would respond when two experimenters disagreed about whether the "teacher" should continue shocking the "learner." As predicted, virtually no one chooses to continue shocking the learner when one authority disagrees with the other.

In a famous real-world example of conflicting authorities, the pastors of a village in France gave a sermon in response to Hitler's request that all refugees be turned over to the police and sent to Germany (Rochat & Modigliani, 1995). In this sermon, they noted, "We appeal to all our brothers in Christ to refuse to cooperate with this violence, and in particular, during the days that will follow, with the violence that will be directed at the British people ... We shall resist whenever our adversaries demand of us obedience contrary to the orders of the Gospel" (p. 199). The initial act of public resistance on the part of two pastors initiated a confrontation between members of Hitler's Third Reich and the people of Le-Chambon-sur-Lignon village that lasted four years—until the day of the German Army's surrender in Paris on August 25, 1944.

Finally, although this section has focused on the hazards of obeying an *unjustified* authority, we should remember that obeying an authority can, in many cases, be good. Nurses may have to obey orders to give a patient an injection or administer some other medical procedure. Prison guards may need to obey orders to place a prisoner in solitary confinement. In these cases, obedience enables a legitimate institution to fulfill its role in society for the greater good.

EXAMPLES OF FACTORS LEADING TO OBEDIENCE

FACTOR	FINDING
Participant	Most of the evidence suggests that the characteristics of the participant (i.e., the person who is being asked to obey) do not have a strong influence on obedience. One exception is the characteristic of authoritarianism: people who are more authoritarian are also somewhat more obedient than others.
Authority	The nature of the authority figure (i.e., the person demanding obedience) clearly affected obedience in the Milgram studies. Although rates of obedience were quite high when the authority figure was seen as an expert, they dropped substantially when another participant served as the authority.
Procedure	Another factor that contributed to the high rate of obedience in the Milgram studies was the *procedure* used, in other words what, specifically, people were being asked to do and how they were asked to do it. When the participant and the learner were in the same room (i.e., when the results of their actions were more clearly evident to participants), levels of obedience dropped, and when participants had to physically administer the shock by moving the "learner's" arm, the level of obedience dropped further. Similarly, when the experimenter simply gave instructions by phone (i.e., was more distant and, therefore, easier to disobey), obedience dropped substantially.

HOW DOES CULTURE AFFECT SOCIAL INFLUENCE?

Cross-cultural studies show that not only are there cultural differences in the level of conformity, compliance, and obedience, there are also cultural differences in the way these concepts are viewed. It has been shown that people from individualistic cultures value conformity less than people from collectivistic cultures (Punetha, Giles, & Young, 1987). What may be perceived as unimaginative surrender to the group in one context is perceived as having enough moral discipline to put the group ahead of one's self in the other context.

Heejung Kim and Hazel Markus of Stanford University conducted an unusual naturalistic study (Kim & Markus, 1999). Researchers went to San Francisco airport and asked both European Americans and Chinese Americans who were waiting for a flight if they would complete a brief survey. They told them they would receive a pen in exchange for helping. After they completed the survey, the researcher reached into a large bag and pulled out five pens for the participants to select from. In some conditions, three of the pens were one colour and two were the other colour, and in other conditions four of the pens were one colour and the fifth was a different colour. The researcher simply noted which colour the participants chose. The researchers hypothesized that European Americans would tend to choose a more uncommon colour pen (e.g., the pen which there were only one or two of, depending on the condition) than would Chinese Americans. As predicted, European Americans picked the more uncommon colour 74 percent of the time, whereas Chinese Americans only chose the unique colour 24 percent of the time.

CONFORMITY

One of the major differences between individualistic and collectivistic cultures is the emphasis and value they place on conformity (Markus & Kitayama, 1994). In individualistic cultures, conformity is seen as a sign of weakness (e.g., giving in to others, ignoring one's own opinions and beliefs). In individualistic cultures, conformity is also often seen as a bad thing for another reason—people want to stand out and be different, and we admire people who differentiate themselves from the crowd. "The squeaky wheel gets the grease" is a common expression meaning that people should complain in order to get their needs met.

In contrast, people in collectivistic cultures often place a particular value on fitting in with others and conforming to social norms, and therefore conformity is seen as a sign of self-control, maturity, tolerance, and respect for others (Markus & Kitayama, 1994). The Korean word for conformity means maturity and inner strength (Kim & Markus, 1999). In line with this value, a common expression in Japan is "The nail that stands out gets pounded down," clearly indicating the importance of conforming. Kim and Markus point out that people in the United States regularly order precisely what they want in restaurants and even in coffee shops (e.g., "I'll have a decaffeinated latte with skim milk"). However, ordering in such a specific manner in Korea is unheard of—and doing so would convey that this person does not get along well with others and is not sensitive to the waiter's needs.

The different levels of conformity, compliance, and obedience in different cultures is related to the eco-cultural characteristics of a society. Berry (1979) has shown that in agricultural societies conformity is high. In these societies, conformity is functional as survival of a group depends on fulfilling one's responsibilities and conforming to the group norms. On the other hand, in hunting and gathering societies conformity is low. In these societies, being independent and self-reliant is functional because exploring the environment is essential for one's survival. Therefore, conformity in these societies is viewed as weakness and is a sign of deficiency.

People's rights and responsibilities and therefore their levels of conformity and obedience vary across cultures. This difference is also reflected in the rights and responsibilities of students that are outlined by universities and colleges. Table 8.2 compares documents produced

TABLE 8.2　Students' Rules of Conduct: Examples from Canada and Cameroon

UNIVERSITY OF GUELPH IN CANADA	UNIVERSITY OF BUEA IN CAMEROON
You have the responsibility not to engage in activities likely to endanger the health or safety of yourself or another person.	No student shall engage his/her fellow student or any member of the University or public in physical scuffles.
You have the responsibility to treat all members of the University community with respect and without harassment, bullying or hazing.	Respect and obey constituted authorities of the University.
You have the responsibility not to destroy, tamper with, deface or vandalize, monopolize, unlawfully access, remove or possess property not your own, including, but not limited to, library material, computing facilities, telecommunication systems and emergency telephones.	No item of furniture should be moved out of the Common Room, Restaurant, Classrooms or Library without permission. The full cost of lost or damaged property will be borne by the student responsible for such loss or damage. All students should contribute to the cleanliness of the faculties put at their disposal. They should avoid littering and should make maximum use of the dustbins provided.
The purchase, possession and/or consumption of liquor by those under the age of 19 is prohibited. Consumption or open possession of liquor is prohibited on campus other than in those areas where it has been specifically permitted, or in licensed premises.	No liquor may be sold or consumed on the University Campus before noon. Any student found drunk or misbehaving under the influence of alcohol either on or off campus shall be severely disciplined.
You have the responsibility not to interfere with the normal functioning of the University, nor to intimidate, interfere with, threaten or otherwise obstruct any activity organized by the University, including classes, or to hinder other members of the University community from being able to carry on their legitimate activities, including their ability to speak or associate with others.	The University expects students to conduct themselves decently and responsibly at all times, whether on or off campus.
You have the responsibility to abide by the Federal and Provincial statutes pertaining to illegal drugs and controlled substances. The possession, use or trafficking of illegal drugs or controlled substances is prohibited, and each activity may form the basis of a separate charge.	The possession and/or consumption of any dangerous drug is prohibited. Any student found contravening this regulation shall be summarily dismissed from the University.
No parallel expectation.	While it is not required that students appear in suits and ties or expensive clothes, they should be neat and presentable at all times. This applies especially to their appearance in class and in the restaurant.
No parallel expectation.	No student may be absent from class without prior authorization except for reasons of health which should be justified. Students are to be punctual to class, show due respect to their teachers and maintain order and quiet in the class.

This table shows selected rights and responsibilities of Canadian and Cameroonian students as outlined by their respective universities.

by a Canadian university (University of Guelph) and a Cameroonian university (University of Buea). What are the differences and similarities between these two universities?

Not surprisingly, studies reveal that the rates of conformity on an Asch-type paradigm are even higher in collectivistic countries than in individualistic countries (Bond & Smith, 1996). A meta-analysis of 133 studies from 17 different countries revealed that collectivistic countries tend to show higher rates of conformity than individualistic countries. Among the Bantu tribe of Zimbabwe, 51 percent of participants conformed in this paradigm, significantly higher than the conformity rate in individualistic countries. One examination of conformity rates across cultures revealed a range of 18 percent to 60 percent. Similarly, Chinese and Japanese participants are more likely to use the mid point of rating scales than are Canadians and Americans (Chen, Lee, & Stevenson, 1995). This reflects a tendency for Canadians and Americans to express individual preferences rather than try to fit in with the group.

Because people in collectivistic cultures pay more attention to their own and others' behaviour to ensure conformity to valued norms, they're less influenced by question wording than are those in individualistic cultures (Ji, Schwarz, & Nisbett, 2000). For example, in one study Chinese and American students were asked how frequently they experienced various activities or events, such as going to the library, catching a cold, and having a nightmare. In some conditions, participants gave open-ended answers. In other conditions, they responded based on a low-frequency or high-frequency scale. As predicted, Americans were much more influenced in their responses by the frequency scale that was used than were the Chinese. The explanation for this result is that collectivistic cultures value monitoring one's own and others' behaviour, and hence Chinese students pay more attention to their behaviour and have a more accurate recall of their behaviour. Autobiographical memory is therefore more accurate in collectivistic cultures.

COMPLIANCE

The degree to which different factors influence compliance and persuasion varies across culture as shown in Morris, Podolny, and Ariel's (2001) study examining six factors of compliance (i.e., reciprocity, scarcity, consistency, friendship/liking, consensus, and authority) in China (Hong Kong), Germany, Spain, and America. In another study demonstrating variations in compliance across cultures, Bontempo, Lobel, and Triandis (1990) asked Brazilian and American students how they would respond to various hypothetical situations involving helping others, such as helping a sick friend, loaning someone money, or encouraging someone to change an unhealthy behaviour. Although in both cultures people report a similar willingness to help others, the Brazilians reported a sincere enjoyment of providing such assistance whereas Americans reported little satisfaction. Moreover, Brazilians were equally likely to engage in the helping behaviour whether it would be done anonymously or in public (see Figure 8.5). The Americans were much more likely to say they would do the behaviour in a public situation than in an anonymous one. Once again, Americans apparently help out of obligation, particularly if they might receive public scrutiny for not helping, whereas the Brazilians help out of an intrinsic desire to help their group members.

People's attitudes and norms are more in line with those of others in collectivistic cultures than in individualistic ones. In one study, university students in Poland (a relatively collectivistic culture) and the United States were asked about their willingness to complete a marketing survey without pay (Cialdini, Wosinska, Barrett, Butner, & Gornik-Durose, 1999). Half of the students in each group were first asked to consider their own prior history of compliance with requests, whereas the other half were first asked to consider information regarding other students' compliance. Although both their own prior history and others' history influenced compliance in students in both countries, their own history had a greater impact on compliance for Americans whereas others' compliance had a greater impact on Polish students.

Subtle differences in wording have a greater impact on compliance in collectivistic cultures than in individualistic ones. In one study, participants from Korea and the United States imagined what they would say in various situations where they would have to make

FIGURE 8.5 HOW DOES CULTURE AFFECT COMPLIANCE?

Researchers in this experiment asked students in Brazil and the United States how they would respond to various requests for help. As predicted, Brazilians are equally likely to engage in the helping behaviour whether it would be done anonymously or in public, whereas Americans are much more likely to perform helping behaviour in a public situation than in an anonymous one.

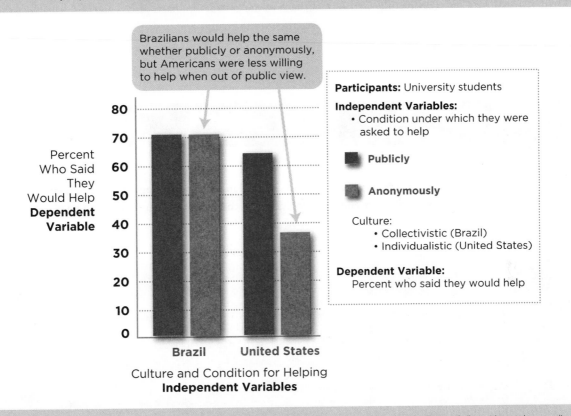

Source: Bontempo, R., Lobel, S., & Triandis, H. (1990). Compliance and value internalization in Brazil and the U.S.: Effects of allocentrism and anonymity. *Journal of Cross-Cultural Psychology, 21,* 200–213.

a request (e.g., borrowing money, asking for the time, Holtgraves & Yang, 1992). Although, overall, Americans were more polite than Koreans, the Koreans' use of language was more responsive to the specific features of the situation (e.g., power of the target of the request, degree of acquaintance between themselves and the target,). This may be due to there being strong distinctions in collectivistic cultures between people in different groups, resulting in more variability overall in social interactions. People in collectivistic cultures are therefore more sensitive and attuned to the situation.

Finally, Koreans' usage of politeness strategies was more sensitive to relational cues, whereas Americans' usage of politeness strategies was more sensitive to the message's content (Ambady, Koo, Lee, & Rosenthal, 1996). These findings emerge because the content of communications is very important in cultures that focus on directness and accuracy, and where relationships are based on equality. On the other hand, in cultures that pay particular attention to hierarchies and relationships, the roles of the target and speaker also convey meaning, and hence people are less focused on the content of the message.

OBEDIENCE

Finally, rates of obedience also differ as a function of culture. In one study, participants from the United States, Russia, and Japan read surveys that described different acts of obedient behaviour in the workplace (Hamilton & Sanders, 1995). These acts included things like obeying orders to dump fertilizer that will lead to a toxic waste spill, and obeying orders to not carry out adequate tests of a new drug due to time pressure. Participants then rated how responsible the person was for engaging in the behaviour. As predicted, participants from collectivistic cultures (Japan, Russia) were more likely to excuse the person for engaging in the behaviour than North Americans. These findings are in line with those you've learned about earlier in this book, such as the greater emphasis placed on the role of the situation in collectivistic cultures compared to the greater emphasis placed on the role of the person in individualistic cultures.

THE BIG PICTURE

SOCIAL INFLUENCE

This chapter included many applications of the three "big ideas" studied in social psychology. The examples below should help you see the connection between social influence and these big ideas and contribute to your understanding of the big picture of social psychology.

THEME	EXAMPLES
The social world influences how we think about ourselves.	• We think that students in general drink too much and we assume, therefore, that we're less comfortable with the amount of drinking on campus than other students. We don't realize that a lot of other students are also uncomfortable with the amount of drinking on campus. • We believe that our fear of looking stupid inhibits us from asking questions in class, and we believe that other students don't ask questions because they don't have any. • We admit to making an error we didn't make if we're under time pressure and another person claims to have seen us commit the error.
The social world influences our thoughts, attitudes, and behaviour.	• We adopt the political attitudes of our friends. • We pay more for a car than we should—due to the necessary "add-ons" the dealer describes. • We laugh at offensive jokes, even though we don't find them funny.
Our attitudes and behaviour shape the social world around us.	• When we feel strongly about a position, we convince others to support our view. • We eat less than we want to in public settings (to conform to the perceived thinness norm), which then strengthens the prevalence of that (false) norm for others. • We ask our parents for an outrageous curfew, and thereby are granted a later curfew than we typically have.

WHAT YOU'VE LEARNED

This chapter has examined four key principles of social influence, including social norms, conformity, compliance, and obedience, as well as the impact of culture on each of these types of social influence.

1. How do social norms influence behaviour?

This section examined how social norms influence behaviour in multiple ways. You learned about the power of social norms, the pressure people feel to conform to norms, and the errors people make in perceiving norms. You also learned why it's probably a good idea to ask a professor a question when you don't understand the course material.

2. What factors lead to conformity?

This section described factors that influence conformity. You learned about the two types of influence: informational influence and normative influence. Next, you learned about different influences on conformity, including group size, standing alone, demographic variables, and motivation. Finally, you learned about minority influence and the benefits of conformity. You also discovered that people can find jokes offensive, but fail to confront the joke teller for fear of the consequences.

3. What factors lead to compliance?

This section described five strategies that people use to gain compliance. You learned about the foot-in-the-door technique, the door-in-the-face technique, lowballing, scarcity, and reciprocity. You also learned that we are more likely to comply with requests from those who are similar to ourselves—for example, if they share our birthday.

4. What factors lead to obedience?

This section described factors that lead to obedience. You learned about the factors that led to obedience in the Milgram study, and that personality factors have little to do with whether we obey, but that procedure and authority factors have a significant impact. You learned about ethical issues in conducting research on obedience, real-world examples of obedience, and strategies for resisting obedience. You also learned that most people will obey an order from a person in a uniform—even when that person gives an order that has nothing to do with his or her position of authority.

5. How does culture affect social influence?

The last section in this chapter described the impact of culture on social influence. You learned that people in collectivistic cultures place a greater value on fitting in with and conforming to social norms than people in individualistic cultures. You learned that the factors that motivate compliance, and the rates of obedience, differ from one culture to another.

Key Terms

compliance 250
conformity 250
demographic variable 262
descriptive norms 251
door-in-the-face technique 268
foot-in-the-door technique 269
informational influence 257

injunctive norms 251
lowballing 270
minority influence 263
normative influence 258
obedience 250
pluralistic ignorance 253
private conformity 258

public conformity 258
reciprocity 268
scarcity 271
social impact theory 261
social norms 250
that's-not-all technique 268

Questions for Review

1. Describe the impact of social norms on behaviour, including the power of social norms and the errors we make in perceiving norms.

2. Name four influences on conformity.

3. Explain the factors that lead to compliance.

4. Describe two factors that increased obedience in the Milgram studies and one factor that didn't.

5. How does culture influence conformity, compliance, and obedience?

Take Action!

1. Your roommate is depressed because she feels stupid in her classes (when no one else has questions about the material that she really is not understanding) and because the man of her dreams hasn't asked her out (even though they've talked intimately together on several occasions). How would you cheer her up by describing the potential role of pluralistic ignorance in these two problems?

2. You're on the school board committee, and the committee has been asked to reach a decision about how to balance the school budget. Your own ideas for how to accomplish a balanced budget differ from those of the other people on the committee. How best could you convince others to adopt your proposed strategies?

3. You're trying to recruit volunteers for a community service fair at your university. Describe three approaches that you could use to induce compliance. Which approach would be most effective and why?

4. Your younger sister calls you because she's worried about her upcoming sorority initiation. She has heard that upper-class students often command pledges to obey orders to engage in embarrassing tasks. How could you advise her to handle this situation?

5. Your cousin has just been hired to work in China following his graduation. What might you tell him about the importance of conforming to social norms in this culture to help him fit in?

RESEARCH CONNECTIONS

Participate in Research

Activity 1 The Power of Social Norms: This chapter has described how people often feel compelled to act in ways that are in line with the norms of their group. Go online to read about various norms, and rate how much pressure you would feel to conform to different norms.

Activity 2 The Impact of Normative Influence: One factor that influences conformity is normative influence, meaning our beliefs about what other people think or feel. Go online to test how your responses to a situation might be influenced by your perception of others' attitudes.

Activity 3 Strategies of Compliance: This chapter described a number of different strategies of compliance that are often used in daily life. Go online to test how you would respond to different compliance techniques.

Activity 4 The Impact of the Situation on Obedience: You learned in this chapter about factors that influence obedience, and how we often underestimate the power of situational factors in leading to such obedience. Go online to read a description of a person obeying an authority, and then rate what you see as the cause of the person's behaviour.

Activity 5 The Impact of Culture on Social Influence: The final section of this chapter described how people from different cultures vary in how they are impacted by social influence. Go online to rate your agreement with various statements about conformity—then see how other students, including those from other cultures, rate their own agreement.

Test a Hypothesis

One of the common findings in research on social influence is that women tend to conform more than men (at least on some topics). To test whether this hypothesis is true, create a survey that describes different types of norms and the extent to which people feel compelled to conform to particular norms. Give this survey to both men and women, and then go online to report your findings to other students.

Design a Study

Go online to design your own study that tests the impact of different factors on conformity. You'll be able to choose the type of study you want to conduct (self-report, observational/naturalistic, or experimental), choose your own independent and dependent variables, and form your own hypothesis. Then you can share your findings with other students across the country!

9

CHAPTER

GROUP PROCESSES

DID YOU EVER WONDER?

AGF s.r.l. / Rex Features

In the early months of 2011, the world witnessed uprisings in several Arab nations in the Middle East and Africa, including Tunisia, Egypt, Morocco, and Libya. A wave of demonstrations swept through these countries, as people in the thousands demanded change and expressed rejection of their authoritarian rulers, who in turn were slow to realize the depth of the discontent. For example, in an interview with Christiane Amonpour for ABC news, Muammar Qaddafi, the ruler of Libya for over 40 years, said, "No demonstrations at all in the streets! No, no one against us. Against me for what? . . . They love me, all my people with me, they love me all. They will die to protect me, my people" (Amanpour, 2011). How do leaders sometimes fail to understand the situation so badly? How do they lose touch with the reality of their country? Although in explaining these complex political situations many factors should be considered, part of the explanation lies in understanding group processes and in particular a phenomenon called groupthink. These rulers had all surrounded themselves with like-minded advisors and aids who constantly reinforced the world-views and decisions of the rulers (Davidson, 2011). Among such governing groups, alternative views are rarely presented and discussed, leading to a different perception

LAW CONNECTIONS

The Dynamics of Jury Deliberation

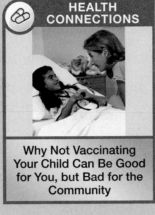

HEALTH CONNECTIONS

Why Not Vaccinating Your Child Can Be Good for You, but Bad for the Community

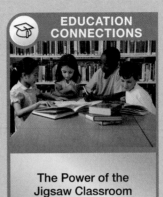

EDUCATION CONNECTIONS

The Power of the Jigsaw Classroom

ENVIRONMENTAL CONNECTIONS

Caring about the Environmental Impact of Cars

of reality. This chapter will examine the different intragroup (i.e., within the group) processes, including groupthink. You'll also find answers to these questions:

 Why do restaurants impose mandatory tipping charges for large groups?

 Why do people tend to make riskier decisions when they're part of a group?

 What are some of the characteristics of a good leader?

 Why are people less cooperative when they play "the Wall Street game" than when they play "the community game"?

 Why do Chinese students perform better when they work in pairs than when they work alone?

PREVIEW

We all interact in groups on a regular, even daily, basis. Sometimes these interactions are informal—we watch a movie with other people in the theatre, we attend a concert with a group of friends, we spend a day at a crowded beach. At other times these interactions are more formal and structured: we collaborate on projects with co-workers, we play sports in teams in front of groups of supporters, we serve on a jury and reach a verdict. These group settings influence our attitudes, decisions, and behaviour, even in the absence of the group, and can lead to both positive and negative outcomes. We have already looked at some intra-group processes: majority and minority influence. In this chapter, we'll consider more intra-group processes to describe ways in which both informal and formal groups influence people's behaviour, both for better and for worse.

HOW DO GROUPS INFLUENCE BEHAVIOUR?

Most human activities are performed in a group. People play in groups (e.g., music bands, running groups, sports teams), work in groups (e.g., army squads, managerial teams, juries), and socialize in groups (e.g., dinner parties, study groups, volunteer teams). Our well-being depends on our relationships with the people we socialize with. Understanding groups—both what they are and how they influence us—is therefore important, both for people in general and for the researchers who strive to deepen our understanding of groups and their dynamics. Many of the social processes that we have looked at so far could be described as interpersonal, in other words as happening between two or more people. However, many social processes also involve groups of people, as opposed to numbers of individuals. Some of these processes happen within a group and are called **intragroup** processes. Others, those that occur between groups of people, are known as **intergroup** processes. In this chapter, we'll focus largely on the intragroup processes.

intragroup processes – processes that happen within a group

intergroup processes – processes that occur between groups of people

Turner (1982) states that a group exists when "two or more individuals . . . perceive themselves to be members of the same social category" (p. 15). The term "group" has also been defined as two or more people who have a common fate or some degree of interdependence, who co-exist within a social structure, or who have face-to-face or some other form of interaction (Bales, 1950; Sherif & Sherif, 1969). British psychologist Rupert Brown later extended Turner's definition, proposing that "a group exists when two or more people define themselves as members of it and when its existence is recognized by at least one other" (Brown, 2000, p. 3). The notion of interconnectedness, or shared outcomes, is an important aspect of a group. Shoppers at a mall, then, would not be considered a group. If there were a disaster, however, and the shoppers found themselves trapped together with a common predicament, they might then become a group. Similarly, spectators at a sporting event may not be a group, but those that support the same team may be as they then have a common group identity.

Although all these definitions describe aspects of group characteristics, Brown's definition is considered the most parsimonious, and it also has the advantage of referring to a group in relation to other groups, rather than just as a system on its own. For both these reasons, Brown's definition is the one that we favour in this chapter.

Think about a time when you had dinner in a restaurant with a group of people. How did you tip? According to research in social psychology, probably not very well. In one study, researchers examined the impact of group size on the size of the tip left at a restaurant (Lynn & Latané, 1984). Groups of diners were surveyed as they left an International House of Pancakes restaurant. Researchers asked them how many people were in their group, the amount of their bill, and the size of the tip they had left. As predicted, single people were the most generous (tipping an average of 19 percent) and parties of four or more were the least generous (tipping an average of 11 percent). This phenomenon is precisely why many restaurants impose a "mandatory tip" on large parties: as the group size increases, each individual person slightly reduces the size of his or her tip, expecting that others will pick up the slack. If you've ever worked as a waiter, this finding won't surprise you.

This section will examine this and other ways in which groups and the presence of other people influence behaviour, including social facilitation, social loafing, and cohesion. It should be noted, however, that groups can also cause shifts in attitudes, norms (discussed later in this chapter), and motivations. For example, it has been suggested that the support that is available to learners in a second-language group influences the learner's competence in using the language, as well as the person's feelings of connectedness to the members of the language group (Genesee, Rogers, & Holobow, 1983; Leets & Giles, 1992). Among English speakers learning Spanish, those who had feelings of low self-determined motivation also tended to perceive themselves as being criticized by the Spanish speakers (Clement, Noels, & Macintyre, 2007; Noels & Rollin, 1998).

Who's Who in Contemporary Canadian Social Psychology Research

New Light Photography

Kim Noels is a professor at the University of Alberta. She received her BA and PhD from the University of Ottawa. In her research, Professor Noels examines the social psychology of language as it relates to intercultural relations and communication. Professor Noels has investigated motivation to learn languages and how the learner's motivation is influenced by others (e.g., members of the language community) She also examines the relation between language learning and ethnic identity as they relate to cross-cultural adaptation. Professor Noels is an active member of the Canadian Psychological Association (CPA) and past chair of the International and Cross-Cultural Psychology Section of the CPA.

SOCIAL FACILITATION

In some cases, the presence of others can have a positive influence on an individual's behaviour. This phenomenon was first noticed by Norman Triplett (1898), a psychologist who observed that cyclists were faster when they raced with other cyclists than when they raced alone. In one of the first experimental studies to test this idea, Triplett asked children to wind string on a fishing reel as fast as they could. Children who performed this task in the presence of other children wound the string significantly faster than those who performed the task alone. This effect is known as **social facilitation**.

In other cases, however, researchers have noted that the presence of other people can also lead to poorer performance (Bond & Titus, 1983). For example, people who perform a

social facilitation – when people do better on a task in the presence of others than when they're alone

difficult task (such as typing their name backwards with various letters interspersed between the letters of their name) do so more slowly in front of other people than when they're alone (Schmitt, Gilovich, Goore, & Joseph, 1986). This is referred to as **social inhibition**.

social inhibition – when people do worse on a task in the presence of others than when they're alone.

How can the presence of others lead to a better performance in some cases and worse performance in others? According to Robert Zajonc's theory of social facilitation, the mere presence of other people increases our physiological arousal (meaning energy or excitement), and this arousal enhances whatever a person's dominant tendency is on a particular task (Blascovich, Mendes, Hunter, & Salomon, 1999; Bond & Titus, 1983; Zajonc, 1965; Zajonc & Sales, 1966). On well-learned or easy tasks, the dominant response is the correct one—to make that shot, to solve the simple addition problems, or to solve easy anagrams. High arousal therefore leads to better performance on tasks that are simple or well learned (see Figure 9.1). On the other hand, high arousal leads to poorer performance on tasks that are difficult or less familiar. This theory thus explains why people perform better on some tasks in the presence of a group, compared to when they're alone, but worse on others.

Why does the presence of others lead to arousal? Research points to three explanations: the mere presence of others, evaluation apprehension, and distraction.

Japanese violinist Taro Hakase is among the top violinists in the world and has performed with many popular artists internationally. He should perform better in front of a larger crowd than when alone, whereas less-skilled violinists should show the reverse effect.

ANDY RAIN/EPA /Landov

MERE PRESENCE. One explanation for social facilitation is that the mere presence of other people is energizing (Zajonc, 1965). For example, you might prefer to take an aerobics class with other people than do aerobics to a video in your living room. In this case, you simply feel more energetic, alert, and aroused in their presence than you would by exercising alone.

A classic study on social facilitation was conducted using cockroaches as participants (Zajonc, Heingartner, & Herman, 1969). Researchers constructed two mazes: one was very simple (a straight path from one end of the box to the other), and the other was more complex (it included multiple paths that led in different directions). In one condition, the cockroaches were alone as they scurried from one end of the maze (with a bright light which

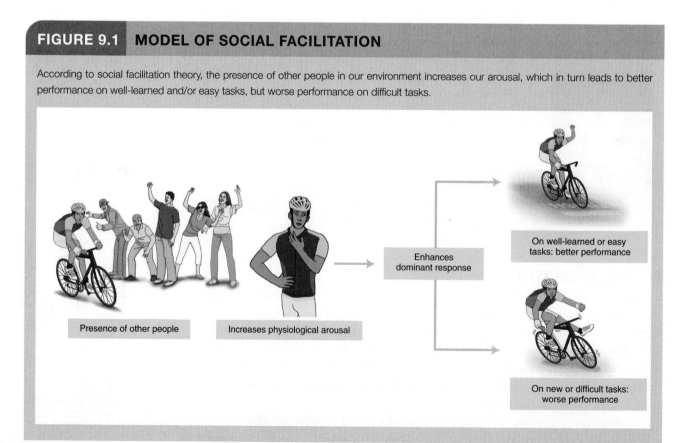

FIGURE 9.1   MODEL OF SOCIAL FACILITATION

According to social facilitation theory, the presence of other people in our environment increases our arousal, which in turn leads to better performance on well-learned and/or easy tasks, but worse performance on difficult tasks.

Presence of other people

Increases physiological arousal

Enhances dominant response

On well-learned or easy tasks: better performance

On new or difficult tasks: worse performance

they disliked) to the other (which was darkened). In the other condition, the cockroaches were observed by (or, at least, were in the presence of) other cockroaches as they completed the maze (the other cockroaches were placed in "audience boxes" that lined the maze). As predicted by social facilitation, cockroaches performed the simple maze faster in the presence of other cockroaches than they did alone. However, the presence of other cockroaches disrupted performance on the more complex maze: they were slower in the presence of other cockroaches than when they were alone. Social facilitation effects for easy tasks in the presence of others are not limited to humans and cockroaches: they've also been reported in animals. For example, chickens and fish eat more, and rats eat and copulate more, when they're in the presence, respectively, of other chickens, fish, and rats (Hogg & Vaughan, 2002). In sum, the presence of others serves as a source of arousal, which in turn causes social facilitation for easy tasks.

EVALUATION APPREHENSION. Other researchers believe that social facilitation is caused not simply by the mere presence of other people in an environment, but rather by people's concern about being evaluated by this audience (e.g., evaluation apprehension; Henchy & Glass, 1968). In one of the first studies to test this explanation for social facilitation, Cottrell and colleagues asked people to pronounce various nonsense words (a relatively easy task) under one of three conditions (Cottrell, Wack, Sekerak, & Rittle, 1968). Participants in one condition were alone; participants in another condition were in front of an audience of two confederates (who could see the words that the participant was trying to pronounce); and participants in the third condition were in front of an audience of two confederates who were blindfolded (and thus could not see the words), creating a mere presence condition. As predicted, participants were more accurate in the audience condition than in either the alone or mere presence condition. This finding indicates that the presence of an evaluating audience is a stronger influence on performance than the mere presence of others in an experimental setting. However, it's important to note that this study, as with other studies conducted in laboratory settings, might have limited generalizability to real-life situations.

Unfortunately, the presence of a supportive audience can lead to worse performance on difficult or unfamiliar tasks. In one study, students took a math test while either a friend or a stranger watched (Butler & Baumeister, 1998). Although students felt less stress when taking the test in front of a friend than in front of a stranger, they made more errors and took longer to complete it when the friend was present. This research suggests that we may "choke under pressure" of our audience's high expectations. The Would You Believe box describes a real-world case in which people's concern about how others will evaluate them impacts on their performance.

THE "HOME FIELD ADVANTAGE" CAN BE A DISADVANTAGE?

You've probably heard of the "home field advantage." But did you know that playing at home can in some cases be a *disadvantage*? Research demonstrates that teams usually perform better at home, but they play badly when they must play decisive games at home (Baumeister & Steinhilber, 1984; Schlenker, Phillips, & Boniecki, 1995a, 1995b). Under these conditions, such as having to win a game to win a championship series, the intense pressure from supportive fans may disrupt performance. Choking is especially likely if the team has the opportunity to win the championship at home. What is usually a well-rehearsed behaviour (playing the sport), and therefore is subject to facilitation effects, may become an unfamiliar situation (playing for the championship), even to a professional, and therefore be subject to social inhibition.

DISTRACTION. Another explanation for the effect of arousal on performance is that the presence of other people is distracting—even when they're not evaluating our performance—decreasing our ability to focus on a particular task (Baron, Moore, & Sanders, 1978; Groff, Baron, & Moore, 1983; Huguet, Galvaing, Monteil, & Dumas, 1999). If we're performing an easy task, this distraction isn't a problem. However, if we're performing a complex task, this distraction impairs our performance. For example, people who are leaving a parking space take longer to leave when someone is waiting for the spot than when no one is waiting (Ruback & Juieng, 1997). More importantly, teenage drivers, who are likely to find driving more difficult than more experienced older drivers, show significantly more crashes when they're driving with passengers than when driving alone (Chen, Baker, Braver, & Li, 2000).

In one study, researchers asked participants to perform either a difficult or an easy task that was supposedly in preparation for a task they would later be completing with other participants (Markus, 1978). The easy task was taking off and putting on their own shoes. The difficult task was putting on and taking off ill-fitting socks, shoes, and a lab coat provided by the experimenter. In the alone condition, people performed the task alone; in the incidental audience condition, people performed the task in front of an inattentive person (a confederate), who was facing away from the participant and working on a different task; and in the audience condition, they performed the task in front of the experimenter, who was watching. In all conditions, participants were not aware that they were being timed, and believed that they were performing the task only in preparation for engaging in the real task of the experiment. As predicted, the mere presence of another person influenced participants' behaviour. It took less time for participants to complete the easy task when an audience was present than when they were alone. However, it took more time for participants to complete the difficult task when an audience was present than when they were alone (see Figure 9.2). Markus (1978) argues that evaluation apprehension did not lead to the social facilitation effect, because in the

FIGURE 9.2 HOW DOES THE PRESENCE OF OTHERS AFFECT TASK SPEED?

In this experiment, students were unaware that they were being timed while doing either an easy task or a hard task. As predicted, the mere presence of an audience, whether or not they were watching, made participants take less time to perform an easy task and more time to perform a difficult task, providing support for mere presence as an explanation for the social facilitation effects found in this study.

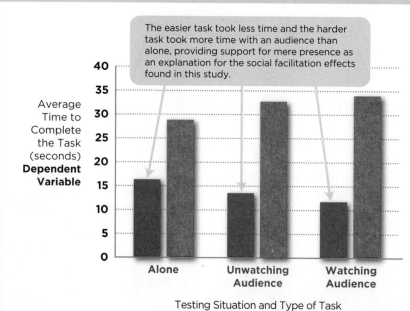

The easier task took less time and the harder task took more time with an audience than alone, providing support for mere presence as an explanation for the social facilitation effects found in this study.

Participants: University students

Independent Variables:
Testing situation
 • Alone
 • Unwatching audience
 • Watching audience

Type of task
 ■ Easy
 ■ Difficult

Dependent Variable:
How long it took to perform the task

Average Time to Complete the Task (seconds) **Dependent Variable**

Testing Situation and Type of Task
Independent Variables

incidental audience condition the confederate was in no position to evaluate the participant and yet the same effect was found as in the audience condition. Bernard Guerin (1986), from the University of Queensland in Australia, reviewed all relevant studies and found only 13 that tested for "mere presence" (without any other variables) and concluded that the mere presence of others produces the social facilitation/inhibition effects only when the presence of others produces some sense of uncertainty in the participant, either because the others' behaviour is unpredictable or because it cannot be monitored.

SOCIAL LOAFING

In social facilitation, an individual is completing a task in the presence of others. But what happens when people work together in a group toward producing a common group goal and the individual's own performance is not measured or evaluated? Think about a time when you worked with other people on a group project. Did all members pull their own weight or did some people slack off? In group situations, when people are not individually accountable for their performance, people, or at least people from individualistic cultures, are often tempted to reduce their effort.

The term **social loafing** describes this group-produced reduction in individual output on tasks where contributions are pooled (Hoeksema-van Orden, Gaillard, & Buunk, 1998; Karau & Williams, 1993; Kerr, 1983). In one study, students alone or in groups of two, four, or six were put in soundproofed rooms and asked to clap and cheer as loudly as possible (Latané, Williams, & Harkins, 1979). Each student made the most noise when alone, and the least noise when in a group of six. Similarly, and as described at the start of this section, restaurants often impose a mandatory tip when people are dining in large groups, precisely because of the (realistic) concern that social loafing will lead to lower tips (Boyes, Mounts, & Sowell, 2004; Lynn & Latané, 1984).

> **social loafing** – a group-produced reduction in individual output on easy tasks where contributions are pooled

What factors influence social loafing? According to the **collective effort model**, people are motivated to exert effort in group tasks only when they believe their distinct efforts are identifiable, that these efforts will make a difference in the group's success, and when they'll experience positive outcomes (Jackson & Williams, 1985; Karau & Williams, 1993; Kerr, 1983; Williams & Karau, 1991). Let's examine each of these factors.

> **collective effect model** – a model which describes people's motivation to exert effort in group tasks as depending on whether they believe their distinct efforts will be identifiable, their efforts will make a difference in the group's success, and they'll experience positive outcomes

IDENTIFIABLE CONTRIBUTIONS. First, one factor that influences social loafing is whether people believe that their own contribution will be recognized (Shepperd, 1993b; Weldon & Gargano, 1988; Williams, Harkins, & Latané, 1981). When people socially loaf, they do it in part because they can "hide in the crowd." Making their outputs identifiable decreases people's tendency to withdraw effort in a group setting. People don't socially loaf when their own outputs will be evaluated, especially if these outputs will be compared to others' outputs, or if they'll receive individual feedback about their efforts (Harkins & Jackson, 1985; Hoeksema-van Orden et al., 1998). For example, if you're working on a group project but each person takes responsibility for writing a separate part of the report—and the professor will know which part each group member did—you'll be more motivated to expand your effort than if your contribution is pooled together with everybody else's efforts. This finding helps explain why swimmers on a relay team post faster times, compared to when swimming individual events, when their own time is identified, but slower when only the time of the team as a whole is identified (Williams, Nida, Baca, & Latané, 1989).

CONTRIBUTIONS' IMPACT. Another factor that influences social loafing is whether you believe your efforts will have an impact on the group's performance—in other words, if you work harder, better performance will result (Kerr & Bruun, 1983). People who must perform a difficult and unique task for the group don't reduce their effort, even when their individual output won't be evaluated. In this case, they feel they can make a unique and important contribution to the group effort (Harkins & Petty, 1982; Karau & Williams, 1993;

Shepperd, 1993b; Shepperd & Taylor, 1999). On the other hand, people who believe their efforts aren't necessary for the success of the group tend to display less effort. People who believe their partner is capable of good performance but lazy (and therefore is just choosing not to expend effort) are particularly likely to reduce their own effort (Kerr, 1983). After all, nobody wants to be the "sucker" who does all the work while others rest. This is one reason why many students fear group projects—they're concerned that they'll end up being the one who does all the work for the group.

TASK IMPORTANCE.   People are also motivated to work hard on a group task if the task is highly important to them (Karau & Williams, 1993; Shepperd, 1993b; Shepperd & Taylor, 1999). If you're working on a group lab report for your social psychology class, and you hope your professor will write a letter of recommendation for you for graduate school, you're likely to work hard on the project even if others in your group aren't contributing much. In one study, students who were told to evaluate a proposal for implementing mandatory senior comprehensive exams were much more likely to loaf if the proposal would not be implemented for six years, or would be implemented at a different school, than if the proposal could be implemented at their own school the following year—and therefore affect them personally (Brickner, Harkins, & Ostrom, 1986).

In cases where the task is very important, people can be highly motivated to work hard even when their own contributions won't be identifiable—especially when they believe that other group members aren't going to work to produce a high-quality product. In this case, **social compensation** occurs, meaning people work harder on a project to compensate for poor performance or social loafing by others (Williams & Karau, 1991). In one study, university students were told that they would work with a partner on either a math test or a verbal test (Plaks & Higgins, 2000). In some cases, the students were told that the partner was a female student, in other cases that the partner was a male student, and in still other cases participants were not told the gender of their partner. As shown in Figure 9.3, participants worked harder on a group task when they had low expectations about their partner's competence (e.g., a woman working on a math test, a man working on a verbal test) than if they had high expectations about their partner's competence (e.g., a man working on a math test, a woman working on a verbal test). These findings suggest that people try to compensate when they expect their partner to perform poorly.

While the preceding discussion explains what social loafing is and why it occurs, our discussion of social loafing does not end here. As we'll see later in this chapter in the section on the influence of culture on intragroup processes, social loafing is one of the areas that best demonstrates the ethnocentrism of North American social psychology prior to the development of cross-cultural psychology in the wake of Hoftstede's (1980) research.

GROUP COHESION

Although this section has focused to some extent on how group processes can lead to negative behaviours, groups can also foster positive effects. Group cohesion refers to the morale, team spirit, and solidarity of the members of the group. Cohesiveness is an essential characteristic that transforms a collection of individual people into members of a group (Hogg & Vaughan, 2002). Highly cohesive groups perform better than less cohesive ones (Cota, Evans, Dion, Kilik, & Longman, 1995; Mullen & Copper, 1994). In the 2002 and 2010 Winter Olympics, the Canadian men's and women's hockey teams won gold medals, demonstrating the importance of team cohesion. One study examined the level of cohesion and attitudes about the army among members of 60 military platoon leadership teams (Mael & Alderks, 1993). Squad members who perceived their platoon as more cohesive showed greater job involvement, higher motivation to perform well, a stronger intent to continue their career with the army, and greater confidence in the effectiveness of the platoon. Most importantly, cohesion was also associated

social compensation – the notion that if a project is important to you, you may work even harder to compensate for the poor performance or social loafing of others

Questioning the Research:

This research suggests that creating a highly cohesive team will lead to better performance. Can you think of an alternative explanation for the cohesion-performance link? (Hint: Does this research distinguish between correlation and causation?)

FIGURE 9.3 HOW DOES SOCIAL COMPENSATION IMPACT TASK PERFORMANCE?

Researchers in this experiment told university students that they would work with a partner on a test. Some students were told they would work with a male partner, some with a female partner, and others were not told the gender of the partner.

As predicted, participants worked harder on a group task when they had low expectations about their partner's competence (e.g., a woman working on a math test, a man working on a verbal test) than if they had high expectations about their partner's competence (e.g., a man working on a math test, a woman working on a verbal test).

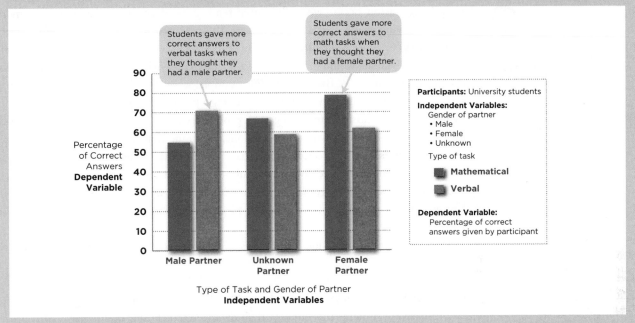

Source: Plaks, J. E., & Higgins, E. T. (2000). Pragmatic use of stereotyping in teamwork: Social loafing and compensation as a function of inferred partner-situation fit. *Journal of Personality and Social Psychology, 79*, 962–974.

with higher ratings of performance, including planning, preparing, and executing eight practice combat missions. As noted above, higher cohesion is also associated with better performance for sports teams (Patterson, Carron, & Loughead, 2005). Robert Klassen and Lindsey Krawchuk (2009) from the University of Alberta have suggested that we become susceptible to the effects of group cohesiveness in early adolescence. They found that cohesion affected group performance among groups of 13-year-olds, but not groups of 11-year-olds, which suggests that working effectively in a group is a developmental process and something that is learned.

[CONCEPTS IN CONTEXT]

EXAMPLES OF THE INFLUENCE OF GROUPS ON BEHAVIOUR

FACTOR	EXAMPLE
Social facilitation	When Yan goes bowling (a game at which he excels), he performs even better when in front of his friends than when alone, but when he plays pool (a game at which he's pretty weak), he performs much better alone than in front of anyone.
Social loafing	As part of a community service project, Janine's sorority is spending a day cleaning up a local park. Because there are so many women in her group, Janine figures that no one will really notice if she shows up late and leaves early.
Cohesion	Team cohesion in the wake of a national disaster was cited by many pundits as one of the reasons that the Japanese women's soccer team defeated both Germany and the United States to win the 2011 FIFA Women's World Cup.

HOW DO INTRAGROUP PROCESSES INFLUENCE DECISION-MAKING?

This section examines how group processes influence decision-making. We'll look at two phenomena that can lead groups to err in their decisions: group polarization and groupthink.

GROUP POLARIZATION

group polarization – when the initial tendencies of group members become more extreme following group discussion

risky shift – a process by which groups tend to make riskier decisions than individuals would make alone

Group polarization occurs when the initial tendencies of group members become more extreme following group discussion (Isenberg, 1986; Moscovici & Zavalloni, 1969; Myers & Kaplan, 1976; Teger & Pruitt, 1967). This process can lead groups to make riskier decisions than individuals would make alone—a phenomenon originally described as the **risky shift** (Wallach, Kogan, & Bem, 1962). For example, when people must choose between a relatively safe choice or a risky choice (e.g., making a particular chess move, trying a difficult play in the last seconds of a football game), groups are much more willing to make a risky choice than are individuals who must act alone, assuming that the direction of the group's initial tendency is in the direction of the risky decision. If the group's initial tendency is toward caution, the group becomes more cautious. Polarization, in other words, is toward a more extreme version of the group's initial individual views, not toward risk *per se*. However, when groups are inclined toward risk, the process of polarization does make them take greater risks.

Why does group discussion lead groups to polarize in their views? Research points to two explanations.

HEAR MORE PERSUASIVE ARGUMENTS. First, during discussions group members hear persuasive arguments that support their own views, including points they hadn't previously considered, which can intensify their views (Isenberg, 1986). For example, you may enter a discussion with the opinion that you're opposed to changing the degree requirements at your university. After hearing additional persuasive arguments that support your original view, you're likely to be even more strongly opposed. Simply repeating arguments during a group discussion can also lead to greater attitude polarization (Brauer, Judd, & Gliner, 1995).

Group members are also particularly likely to hear a greater number of persuasive arguments because they deliberately look for views that support their position. In one study, researchers asked managers from banks and industrial companies to read a case study about a company that was deciding whether to invest a considerable sum in starting production in a developing company (Schulz-Hardt, Frey, Lüthgens, & Moscovici, 2000). Participants were put in small groups and asked to discuss the company's situation and reach a group decision. The groups were told that additional information about the decision was available, including articles both in favour of and against the investment. Groups were given a list of these articles, which were written by experts on the economy, and could request any articles that they wanted. What type of information did groups want? As predicted, groups that consisted of individuals with the same view were more interested in receiving articles that supported their decision than articles that opposed it. In contrast, groups that consisted of individuals with more discrepant views showed less interest in receiving articles that supported their eventual decision and more interest in receiving articles that opposed it.

LEARN GROUP NORMS. Group polarization can also occur following discussion because such discussion leads us to more accurately assess the norms of our group (Isenberg, 1986). Prior to group discussion, we may have an inaccurate understanding of the group members' views on a given topic, both in the position held and its strength, and such discussion can therefore increase how accurately we perceive their views. Moreover, because most people want to fit in with, but also be "better than," other members of their group, we may come to express even more extreme attitudes as a way of demonstrating that our views are strong and in the right direction. Knowing the group norms can thus lead us to becoming more confident in our own views.

To examine the effects of group discussion on individuals' own attitudes, researchers asked 24 female university students to privately (in writing) rate the attractiveness of men in magazine photos (Baron, Hoppe, Kao, & Brunsman, 1996). Then the women read their ratings aloud in groups of three, with two of the women actually being confederates but all three supposedly having completed the same task. In the positive corroboration condition, the confederates agreed with the participant's view; in the contradiction condition, they disagreed with the participant's view; and in the control condition, the confederates didn't provide their responses aloud. Next, participants were told they could look at the photographs again for a longer period of time, and that they could change their ratings if they found their views had changed. In the positive corroboration condition, participants significantly increased their rating; in the contradiction condition, they significantly decreased their rating; and in the control condition, participants' ratings also increased, but less strongly than when they received positive corroboration. The Law Connections box describes a real-world example of the hazards of relying on group norms.

LAW CONNECTIONS

The Dynamics of Jury Deliberation

Many of the errors in group decision-making that have been described so far can have a major impact on jury deliberations. For example, group discussion may exaggerate the initial biases of the jury members (Kaplan & Miller, 1978; Myers & Kaplan, 1976). Information that is consistent with the members' initial preferences is more likely to be discussed, whereas non-confirming information is more likely to be ignored (Stasser & Titus, 1985). In one study, juries spent more time discussing information that supported their preferred outcome, and less time discussing information that disputed this outcome (Sommers, Horowitz, & Bourgeois, 2001). Jurors may also weigh information that favours their preferred outcome more heavily than non-confirming information as a way of supporting their desired verdict. They may even ignore information that contradicts their preferred verdict.

What can help jury decision-making? Interestingly, juries that include group members of varied ethnicity are more likely to have in-depth discussions than all-White juries (Sommers, 2006). In one study, researchers compared the quality of deliberation in all-White versus diverse ethnicity mock juries. Diverse groups discussed a wider variety of information than all-White groups. In addition,

compared to those in all-White groups, Whites in diverse groups cited more case facts, made fewer errors, and were more likely to discuss the impact of racism on the trial. These findings suggest that diverse juries engage in better decision-making processes than the members of all-White juries.

© Image Source/SUPERSTOCK

GROUPTHINK

Another common problem with group decision-making is the development of **groupthink**, a group decision-making style introduced at the start of this chapter that is characterized by an excessive tendency among group members to seek concurrence, consensus, and unanimity, as opposed to making the best decision (Janis, 1972, 1982; Tetlock, Peterson, McGuire, Chang, & Field, 1992). Groups who show this decision-making style overestimate the

groupthink – a group decision-making style that is characterized by an excessive tendency among group members to seek concurrence, consensus, and unanimity, as opposed to making the best decision

morality and invulnerability of their group, and ignore or even stifle discrepant views. This decision-making style can in turn lead group members with discrepant views to avoid stating them for fear of rejection from the group. As described at the beginning of this chapter, groupthink might have contributed to the worldview of some Arab rulers that appeared to blind them from what was really happening in their countries. Groupthink is also thought by some to have contributed to the U.S. decision to invade Iraq.

© Harley Schwadron/www.CartoonStock.com

OVERESTIMATE INVULNERABILITY AND MORALITY. As already stated, the groupthink decision-making style is more likely to occur when groups overestimate their invulnerability and morality (Janis, 1982). Groups may see their chosen course of action as highly likely to succeed, and as being based in the group's fundamental goodness and morality. For example, one of the factors that led to the escalation of the Vietnam War was the belief that democracy was inherently better than communism, and hence Americans were bound to win the war.

CLOSED-MINDEDNESS. Another factor that contributes to groupthink is closed-mindedness, meaning when group members won't hear dissenting views from outgroup members (i.e., people who are not part of the group; Tetlock et al., 1992). This type of group isolation means that no efforts are made to seek information from outgroup members, and any information that is received is dismissed as unimportant. Groups with a strong and rigid leader are at greater risk of closed-mindedness, in part because such leaders may be unwilling to seek outside information.

PRESSURE TOWARD UNIFORMITY. The third factor that contributes to groupthink is pressure toward uniformity (Janis, 1982; Kameda & Sugimori, 1993). This pressure is especially common among groups that are highly cohesive, meaning those that are composed of people from similar backgrounds (Hogg, Hains, & Mason, 1998). When referring to a series of controversial decisions made during George W. Bush's presidency, including war on terrorism and invading Iraq, Ken Auletta of *The New Yorker* said, "This is a cohesive White House staff, dominated by people whose first loyalty is to Team Bush" (2004).

Unfortunately, cohesiveness can hurt performance in some cases, such as when creative, innovative ideas are needed. In one study, groups of university students were asked to recommend a solution for a case study in automobile production where there had been a drop in productivity by some assembly-line workers who produced instrument panels. (Turner, Pratkanis, Probasco, & Leve, 1992). Some of the groups were made highly cohesive (e.g., they wore name tags that displayed their name and their group's name), while others were low in cohesiveness. Some of these groups were also put under high threat conditions (e.g., they were told that experts would use the videotape of their group's discussion to evaluate dysfunctional group processes), whereas others were

"All those in favor say 'Aye.'"
"Aye."
"Aye."
"Aye."
"Aye."
"Aye."

© *The New Yorker* Collection 1979 Henry Martin from cartoonbank.com. All Rights Reserved

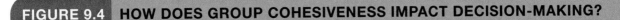

FIGURE 9.4 HOW DOES GROUP COHESIVENESS IMPACT DECISION-MAKING?

In this experiment, groups were asked to recommend solutions for increasing the productivity of automobile production workers. It was hypothesized that pressure toward uniformity in highly cohesive groups would lead to poorer quality solutions.

The results partly supported this hypothesis: when threat levels were high, cohesive groups did make poorer suggestions, but under a low threat level, cohesive groups made higher quality suggestions.

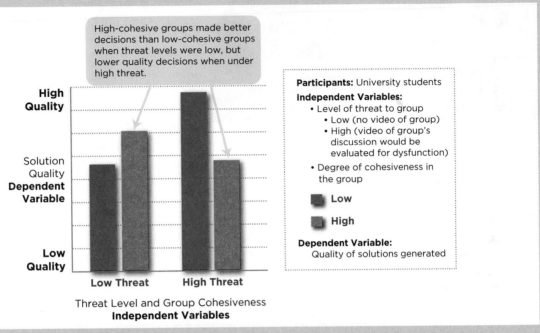

Source: Turner, M. E., Pratkanis, A. R., Probasco, P., & Leve, C. (1992). Threat, cohesion, and group effectiveness: Testing a social identity maintenance perspective on groupthink. *Journal of Personality and Social Psychology, 63*, 781–796.

not given this threat. As shown in Figure 9.4, highly cohesive groups made somewhat higher quality decisions than non-cohesive groups under conditions of no threat, but much lower quality decisions under conditions of high threat.

What are the critical elements of groupthink? According to Glen Whyte of the Rotman School of Management in Toronto, the lack of caution and the preference for risk that characterize groups that are prone to groupthink are associated with a perception of exaggerated capability (i.e., the group thinks it's more able than it really is). This exaggerated sense of group efficacy, facilitated by group polarization, leads to critical decisions crystallizing around a decision option that is likely to fail (Whyte, 1998).

SOLUTIONS TO GROUPTHINK

Although this section has focused on the various factors that lead groups to make faulty decisions, people in groups can work together to make good decisions. First, group members, and in particular group leaders, need to encourage open contributions from all group members as well as to emphasize the importance of open criticism. Groups with a norm of engaging in constructive criticism make better decisions (Postmes, Spears, & Cihangir, 2001), and criticism from in-group members is often easier for people to accept than criticism from out-group members (Hornsey & Imani, 2004). Encouraging open contributions and criticism is particularly important in cases in which not all group members have the same information. Group members also need to regularly seek input from non–group members.

Second, groups should deliberately recruit diverse members. Although groups that consist of people from diverse backgrounds (in terms of ethnicity, gender, religion, age, and so on) can have problems with miscommunication and misunderstanding, such groups have

Questioning the Research:

In the Turner et al. (1992) study, the groups consisted of university students who didn't know each other previously and were brought together for a psychology study. How do you think the results would be different if this study was done with a real group, i.e., one in which people expected to interact in the future and could experience consequences for the quality of their decision?

© Diane Diederich/iStockPhoto

Diversity isn't just politically correct and fair to people who have traditionally faced discrimination: it leads to better decision-making.

a broader range of opinions, attitudes, and thoughts. As long as the group has good communication, this diversity can lead to greater flexibility and creativity as well as better decisions. Antonio and colleagues (2004) examined the content of group discussions between groups consisting of all-White European university students in the U.S. versus those consisting of a majority of White European university students and one African American university student. As predicted, the presence of an African American student in the group led to a greater integration of different perspectives and viewpoints.

Finally, training a person in the group about the dangers of biased group decision-making and having this person inform other group members about these issues can also be effective (Larson, Foster-Fishman, & Keys, 1994). Even forewarning participants about the information that different people have can increase effective decision-making (Stasser, Stewart, & Wittenbaum, 1995; Stewart & Stasser, 1995). All of these factors can help reduce the likelihood of groupthink, which the *New York Times* has described as showing "the ways that smart people working collectively can be dumber than the sum of their brains" (Schwartz, 2003).

[CONCEPTS IN CONTEXT]

EXAMPLES OF HOW GROUP PROCESSES INFLUENCE DECISION-MAKING

FACTOR	EXAMPLE
Group polarization	At the start of the discussion, Justin thought that requiring high school students to do mandatory community service was probably not a great idea. But after discussing it with other students, Justin became strongly opposed to the requirement.
Groupthink	The board of trustees developed a plan to renovate the university museum at a cost of $2 million—a plan they believed would be welcomed by the university community. When the plan was announced, both faculty and students were very upset that these much-needed funds were not being used to hire more professors and provide more scholarships to students. Faculty and students engaged in public protest against the planned renovation.

HOW DO LEADERS GUIDE AND MOTIVATE THE GROUP?

Think about a group that you once belonged to (or currently belong to)—a student government organization, a community service program, an athletic team—and the leader of that group. Was this person an effective leader? If so, what was he or she like? One study examined the characteristics of effective group leaders by asking students to participate in a series of group interaction tasks (Sorrentino & Field, 1986). Students first attended five weekly sessions consisting of group problem-solving activities, such as planning a project and ranking the importance of materials that would be needed if the group had to survive in a desert. These sessions were recorded so that researchers could rate each participant's interaction.

Participants also rated their impressions of their own and other group members' contributions to the problem-solving tasks. Group members who were oriented toward both achievement and interpersonal dynamics were given the highest scores on all measures. These individuals characteristically took pride in accomplishment, had high self-confidence, and established friendly relations with other group members while seeking their approval. Participants with these characteristics were also rated higher on objective behavioural measures, such as the quantity of verbal participation, and they were most likely to be chosen as the leader of the group by other participants.

In some cases, group leaders are chosen in a formal process, such as an election by group members, or an appointment by those in higher positions. In other cases, leaders emerge informally and gradually, as the group interacts over time. Regardless, group leaders have an important influence on the group decision-making process and outcome of discussions (Albright & Forziati, 1995; Chemers, Watson, & May, 2000; Kaiser, Hogan, & Craig, 2008). They play a particularly important role in guiding and motivating the group.

So what makes a good leader? Theory and research points to three popular models: the trait (or "great person") model, transactional versus transformational leadership, and the contingency model.

TRAIT OR "GREAT PERSON" MODEL

The trait or "great person" model of leadership, describes good leaders as emerging based on specific personality traits, such as intelligence, dominance, and extroversion (Zaccaro, 2007). For example, Pierre Trudeau, who was Canada's fifteenth prime minister and was known for his charisma and confidence, is an excellent example of a leader with a strong personality and who was a dominant figure in Canadian political history. People with particular leadership characteristics (e.g., initiative) have been rated by judges as more effective at leading groups on diverse tasks, including an artistic task, a logical/spatial task, a social task, and a creative task (Albright & Forziati, 1995). One study on leadership effectiveness in military cadets demonstrated that individuals who were high in leadership efficacy (e.g., skilled in terms of initiative, decisiveness, judgement, communication, and so on) were rated higher in leadership potential by both their supervisors and peers (Chemers et al., 2000). Similarly, in a study by researchers from the Royal Military College of Canada and University of Western Ontario, measures of traits indicating dominance in recruits at the Canadian Forces Recruiting Centres predicted evaluations by the recruits' instructors both nine months into the recruits' training and nine months later (Bradley, Nicol, Charbonneau, & Meyer, 2002). Dominance also predicted leadership performance four years later. Another characteristic that predicted performance in training (after nine months) and leadership performance (after four years) was an "internal" locus of control orientation (i.e., the perception that events in one's life are under one's control).

TRANSACTIONAL VERSUS TRANSFORMATIONAL LEADERS

Other accounts of leadership focus on the difference between transactional and transformational leaders. Transactional leaders reward desirable behaviours by group members and act once mistakes or problems occur (Burns, 1978). In contrast, transformational leaders foster trust among group members, build identification with and excitement about higher-level group goals, and examine new approaches for problem-solving. Although both transactional and transformational leaders can be successful, groups with transformational leaders tend to have better performance (Bass, Avolio, Jung, & Berson, 2003). Transformational leadership may be more effective because it creates intrinsic motivation (Charbonneau, Barling, & Kelloway, 2001). Sports teams with transformational coaches, for example, create higher levels of intrinsic motivation in their players, which in turn leads to better performance.

CONTINGENCY MODEL

The contingency model of leadership emphasizes the importance of having a match between the leader's specific traits and the demands of a particular situation (Kaplan & Kaiser, 2003; Peters, Hartke, & Pohlmann, 1985; Vroom & Yago, 2007). According to this model, some people are *task-oriented*, meaning they focus on organizing projects, setting standards, and achieving goals. Task-oriented leaders are good at keeping others focused on the work at hand and maintaining group effort. Other leaders are described as *people-oriented* or *relationship-oriented*, meaning that they focus on building a supportive, caring, and democratic work environment. People-oriented leaders seek out feedback and contributions from group members, validate people's contributions, and facilitate teamwork. Lester B. Pearson, Canada's fourteenth prime minister, is an example of a task-oriented leader. In helping resolve the 1956 Suez Crisis, he was praised for the skill with which he established an international police force, ending hostilities between Israel, the United Kingdom, and France on one side and Egypt on the other. In 1957, Pearson received the Nobel Peace Prize for his peacekeeping role in the conflict.

RESEARCH FOCUS ON GENDER
Women as Leaders

Across the world, more and more women are being seen in leadership positions, including as heads of state. Although women have the potential to be strong leaders, they don't receive the opportunity to develop this potential as often as men do (Brannon, 2011).

Most research on the effectiveness of women's leadership style has been conducted in the workplace or in laboratory settings using university students. Meta-analyses of the research on gender and leadership in the workplace show that, in general, men and women in managerial positions—i.e., in a position of power with a leadership role—show similar leadership styles (Eagly, Johannesen-Schmidt, & van Engen, 2003; Eagly & Johnson, 1990). Van Engen and Willemsen (2004) reported that in male-dominated workplaces both men and women show a masculine leadership style in, for example, focusing on a specific task. However, researchers have found differences. For example, women are more likely to reward subordinates, invest time in team building, and engage in consulting (Catalyst, 2005; van Engen & Willemsen, 2004). In general, men tend to act in a more autocratic or directive style and women tend to act in a more democratic or participatory style (Eagly & Johnson, 1990).

Marie-Hélène Budworth from the University of Toronto and Sara Mann from the University of Guelph have documented that behaviours that are successful for men in the workplace are not equally successful for women (Budworth & Mann, 2010). Specifically, tendencies toward modesty and lack of self-promotion are hypothesized to perpetuate the lack of female involvement in top management positions. To get to the top you need to be good at self-promotion, but self-promotion is viewed as a less positive attribute in women.

Roya Ayman from the Illinois Institute of Technology and Karen Korabik from the University of Guelph (2010) suggest that without including the roles of gender and culture our understanding of leadership is limited. These researchers argue that as most theories of leadership have been developed in North America they suffer from **ethnocentrism**, the belief that one's cultural values are shared by others, and have only been validated among male leaders. Research indicates that leadership is neither a gender- nor a culture-neutral concept. In fact, women who adopt a masculine leadership style in a male-dominated environment tend to receive a negative evaluation, especially from men (Ayman & Korabik, 2010).

ethnocentrism – the belief that one's cultural values are shared by others

Female leaders from around the world (from left to right): Johanna Siguroardottir, prime minister of Iceland since 2009; Laura Chinchilla Miranda, president of Costa Rica since 2010; Julia Gillard, prime minister of Australia since 2010; Ellen Johnson-Sirleaf, president of Liberia since 2006.

Bloomberg via Getty Images, Inc.; Yuri Cortez/AFP/Getty Images, Inc.; Jun Sato/WireImage/Getty Images, Inc.; Issouf Sanago/AFP/Getty Images, Inc.

[CONCEPTS IN CONTEXT]

EXAMPLES OF THE POWER OF LEADERSHIP

FACTOR	EXAMPLE
Trait or "great person" model	Abila has strong communication skills, is friendly, and is extroverted. She was nominated for organizing a campaign to raise awareness about AIDS in Africa.
Transactional leader	Darren has been working at a large company for one year. He has only talked to his manager once after making an error in preparing a financial statement and his manager called him into her office.
Transformational leader	Steve's boss holds monthly meetings encouraging employees to express their opinions about the company's strategic planning.
Contingency model	Akiko is a focused and task-oriented person. She was elected to represent students at her university senate in order to increase funding for the students' association.

HOW DO GROUPS HANDLE SOCIAL DILEMMAS?

In a study by Liberman, Samuels, and Ross (2002), university students were asked to play a game in which they could win some money. Each person played with a partner, and on each trial the player could choose to either cooperate with the other player or to compete against him or her. If both players cooperated, each person would win $0.40. If both competed, they would receive nothing. However, if one person chose to cooperate and the other to compete, the person who cooperated would lose $0.20 and the person who competed would win $0.80. Although all participants played the same game, it was described to them in different ways. Half were told that it was "the Wall Street game," which was designed to increase the tendency to compete. The other half were told that it was "the community game," which was designed to increase the tendency to cooperate. As predicted, participants were much more likely to cooperate when they were playing the "community game" than when they were playing "the Wall Street game." Why does a simple label change people's behaviour? Labels create expectations about how our partner will behave in a situation, and our behaviour is influenced by these expectations. In this case, the "community game" label actually helped resolve what is known as a social dilemma.

A social dilemma is a situation in which what is best for the individual, or one group, is in conflict with what is best for another individual or group. Development of the Alberta oil sands provides an example of a more complex social dilemma. In 2008, the Canadian arm of

social dilemma – situations where if all individuals make self-interested choices the result will be the worst possible outcome for everyone.

Deloitte Consulting produced a paper on the development of Alberta's oil sands called "The Producers' Dilemma," which argued that "oil companies increasingly face a difficult choice. If they each, acting in their own self-interest, continue to invest in production at current rates, a host of problems—labour shortages, rising costs, infrastructure deficits, increased public concern about environmental issues—will increase production costs and encourage construction delays, which in turn means that investors could see lower (or at least sub-optimal) returns on their investment" (Alberta Venture Magazine, 2008). In other words, the company found its short-term interests to be in conflict with many other interests, including its own long-term interests. This section will describe factors that influence social dilemmas, as well as some solutions to such dilemmas.

TYPES OF SOCIAL DILEMMAS

In all social dilemmas, what is best for the individual is not what is best for the group (and vice versa). However, the specific nature of the dilemma can differ, including whether the dilemma is between groups or between individuals and whether the dilemma involves reducing a common resource or sustaining a common good or service. The following is a description of three types of social dilemmas: common resource dilemmas, the public good dilemma, and the prisoner's dilemma.

COMMON RESOURCE DILEMMAS. Common resource dilemmas are a type of social dilemma in which a resource, such as water, land, natural fish stocks, or oil, can be reduced—and even eliminated—by overuse (Edney, 1980; Komorita & Parks, 1995). In this case, each person can take moderate amounts of a common resource, but if everyone takes as much as they want, the resource will eventually be depleted. For example, during times of drought, people in affected communities are urged to take short showers, wear clothes for longer periods of time without washing them, and flush the toilet less frequently. However, individual people may be reluctant to comply with these recommendations in part because they believe that their own use of water is relatively minimal. But if everyone chooses to ignore the water restriction recommendations, eventually the water could run out, leading to serious problems for everyone. This situation is referred to as the *tragedy of the commons*.

In a famous demonstration of a resource dilemma in action, several participants sat around a table on which there was a bowl of 60 nuts (Edney, 1979). The experimenter explained that every 10 seconds he would double the number of nuts in the bowl, and that each participant's goal was to get as many nuts as possible. Any participant could reach into the bowl and grab nuts at any time. Participants could have effectively managed their resource by removing only 30 nuts, and then waiting for the experimenter to double the nuts (returning to the original amount), so that every 10 seconds they could take another 30 nuts (in theory forever). However, 65 percent of the groups never got past the first 10 seconds as someone instantly grabbed at the nuts, leading the other participants to follow suit, and at 10 seconds no nuts remained in the bowl to be doubled (two times zero equals zero).

common resource dilemma – a social dilemma in which each person can take as much as he or she wants of a common resource, but if everyone takes as much as they want, the resource will eventually be completely depleted

"Leave some shells for less fortunate children."

public goods dilemma – a type of social dilemma where each person must decide what to contribute to a common pool of resources that will not exist unless people contribute to it

PUBLIC GOODS DILEMMA. Another type of social dilemma is the **public goods dilemma**, in which a public good or service needs to be sustained over time (Komorita & Parks, 1995).

This type of dilemma refers to a situation in which each person can take freely of the resource, and must decide whether and what to contribute to the common pool of resources. If a sufficient number of people contribute to the common pool, others can benefit because the resource will be available to them even if they don't contribute. However, if not enough people contribute to the common pool, the resource can disappear completely. In fact, the best choice for each individual is to not contribute, but hope that others do.

There are many real-world examples of public goods dilemmas:

- Many people take for granted that blood will be available for them if they ever need a transfusion, but have never donated their own blood for others' use.
- Many people don't contribute to the Canadian Cancer Society but could benefit from research on cancer treatment funded by those who do donate.

PRISONER'S DILEMMA.   The **prisoner's dilemma** refers to the situation in which two people may choose to either cooperate with each other or compete (Pruitt & Kimmel, 1977). We saw an example of this in the game played by two students in the study by Lieberman, Samuels, & Ross (2002). In the classic situation, each person is better off competing with his or her partner, but only if the partner cooperates. Let's say two men are caught robbing a liquor store. They are separated, and each is told that if he confesses and the other one does not, he will go free whereas his partner will get a 10-year sentence. On the other hand, if his partner confesses and he doesn't, he gets a 10-year sentence. What's the worst option? If both people confess, each person could get a 10-year sentence. In contrast, the best option for the group (meaning both people together) is for both people to cooperate (i.e., pleading not guilty). If they both cooperate, each person may receive a relatively short prison sentence (not as good as having no prison sentence, but certainly better than receiving a 10-year sentence). The prisoner's dilemma paradigm therefore describes a situation in which the best outcome for each individual person leads to the worst outcome for his or her partner (Figure 9.5). The prisoner's dilemma represents a dilemma (not surprisingly) for participants because each person's best option depends on the option chosen by the other person.

Gerard Seijts from the University of Manitoba and Gary Latham from the University of Toronto recently collaborated to examine individual performance in a social dilemma where participants had to decide how best to invest an amount of money (Seijts & Latham, 2010). The dilemma for participants was whether to invest their individual sum of money in their personal account, where the contribution would stay the same, or to invest it in the group/joint account, where the contribution would be doubled and all participants regardless of their contribution would receive an equal share. The results of the study suggest that three factors will facilitate group performance (i.e., earn more money for the group): (1) individual and group goals should be compatible rather than conflicting; (2) there should be commitment to group goals; and (3) the belief that cooperation leads to positive outcomes should be fostered. The researches noted that facilitating group performance in larger groups (seven- versus three-person groups) is more challenging: participants in larger groups in the study reported higher self-serving personal goals, lower levels of collective goal commitment, and lower levels of group outcome expectations than did participants in smaller groups.

SOLUTIONS TO SOCIAL DILEMMAS

Social dilemmas involve a conflict between what is best for a person and what is best for his or her group. Social dilemmas present challenging issues to solve, but the following strategies can help resolve them successfully:

- Regulate the use of resources.
- Engage in open communication.

prisoner's dilemma – the situation in which two people may choose to either cooperate with each other or compete

FIGURE 9.5 SAMPLE PRISONER'S DILEMMA PAYOFF MATRIX

In prisoner's dilemma paradigms, the best outcome for each person is to compete (plead guilty) while the partner cooperates (pleads not guilty), whereas the worst outcome is to cooperate while the partner competes. However, both people jointly are best off if they both cooperate and plead not guilty.

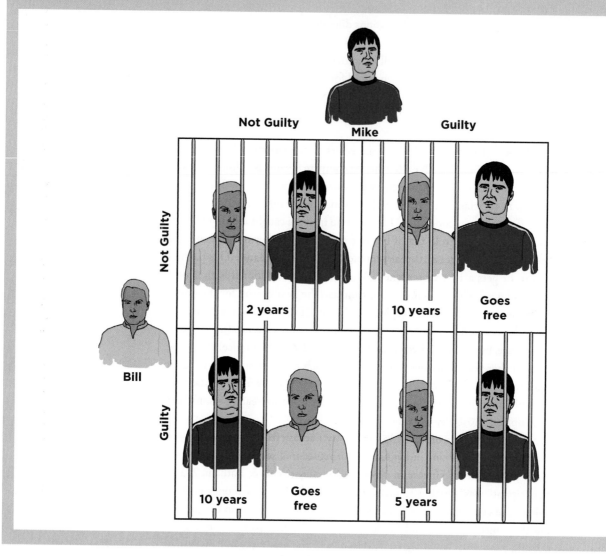

- Activate altruistic motives.
- Create small, connected groups.
- Create consequences for competition.

Let's examine each of these approaches.

REGULATE THE USE OF RESOURCES. One strategy is to set up a formal way to *regulate* the use of limited resources (Sato, 1987; van Dijk, Wilke, & Wit, 2003). Solutions of this type often involve creating a structural system, such as an organization or a leader, to allocate resources fairly. For example, the Canadian Environmental Protection Agency is in charge of setting rules about pollution because we don't trust companies to regulate their own pollution levels. Similarly, the Health Connections box describes why many countries have compulsory vaccinations—in part because parents are less likely to have children vaccinated without such regulations.

HEALTH CONNECTIONS

Why Not Vaccinating Your Child Can Be Good for You, but Bad for the Community

Many countries have compulsory immunization requirements. Others, like Canada, try hard to influence parents to have their children vaccinated, without actually making it illegal not to. For example, babies in Canada are not allowed to attend school without certain vaccinations. Although these vaccines are very effective at preventing disease, they do pose a very small risk to each individual baby—a few babies each year suffer seizures and even death as a result of receiving a vaccination. According to Health Canada, "Serious side effects such as severe allergic reactions can occur, but are extremely rare, and occur in Canada less often than once per million doses of vaccine" (Health Canada, 2009).

As a parent, the ideal choice is clearly to have all other babies vaccinated but not to have your own baby vaccinated. After all, if all other babies are vaccinated, there's no way your child can acquire one of these diseases, and you could then avoid exposing your child to even the very small risk of such a vaccination. But think about what would happen if each parent chose to refuse the vaccination for his or her own child—many babies would then develop these diseases, leading to the death of many more children.

Keith Brofsky/Getty Images, Inc.

Setting up ways to regulate the use of resources is particularly important because people often over-consume resources due to biased perceptions about their fair share. Herlocker, Allison, Foubert, and Beggan (1997) assigned participants to either a three-person or twelve-person group. Participants were then told that the group needed to share resources (such as blocks or sand), and that each group member could take as many units of a given resource as they desired. After participants selected the amount of resources they wanted, they were asked to estimate how much of the total pool of resources they had selected. Although participants admitted to intentionally taking more of the resource than their fair share, they also underestimated the proportion of the resource as a whole that they had taken.

ENGAGE IN OPEN COMMUNICATION.   Another strategy that groups can use to solve social dilemmas is communication, especially face-to-face (Bornstein, Rapoport, Kerpel, & Katz, 1989; Dawes, 1980; Drolet & Morris, 2000; Kerr & Kaufman-Gilliland, 1994). Face-to-face group discussion helps increase cooperative behaviour in social dilemmas, in part because such discussion leads group members to see others as wanting to cooperate and enables people to make commitments to cooperate (Bouas & Komorita, 1996; Kimmel, 1980; Orbell, van de Kragt, & Dawes, 1988). Communication can also clear up misunderstandings that could impede cooperation (Tazelaar, van Lange, & Ouwerkerk, 2004).

One study found that repeating one's intention to cooperate in a prisoner's dilemma interaction led to more cooperation, greater liking, and more trust (Lindskold, Han, & Betz, 1986). Moreover, people who expect cooperation from a partner are more creative and flexible problem-solvers—58 percent of those who expect cooperation in a negotiation reach a solution, compared to only 25 percent of those who expect conflict (Carnevale & Probst, 1998).

One reason why communication increases cooperation is that group discussion can lead group members to develop an internalized personal norm for behaving cooperatively. For example, if group members discuss the advantages of limiting how many fish a person can catch, some people will follow this agreement based on their own internalized norms, even without a clear monitor for such behaviour (Kerr, Garst, Lewandowski, & Harris, 1997). Even subtle cues can lead to cooperation, such as knowing that someone similar to you cooperated (Parks, Sanna, & Berel, 2001), or as described at the start of this section, describing a prisoner's dilemma game as "the community game" instead of "the Wall Street game" (Liberman, Samuels, & Ross, 2002). The Education Connections box describes a unique approach to creating cooperative interaction in the classroom.

EDUCATION CONNECTIONS

The Power of the Jigsaw Classroom

The "jigsaw" classroom is a technique designed by Elliot Aronson and his colleagues to bring children from different backgrounds together to work toward a common goal (Aronson & Bridgeman, 1979; Slavin & Cooper, 1999; Weigel, Wiser, & Cook, 1975). This technique involves dividing students within a classroom into small learning groups, and then giving each child in that small group one piece of information to learn.

For example, as part of a history lesson each child in the group might be given information about a different stage of a historical figure's life. Because each member of the group only has one piece of information, group members need to work together to learn the information possessed by each student. This process gives each child a chance to explain his or her material to the other students, and helps students focus on asking questions and listening to one another. In this way, the jigsaw technique changes the classroom environment into one in which children cooperate together toward the common goal of mastering the material, instead of competing against one another to share the right answer.

Research on cooperative learning programs reveals that this approach can be very effective (Blaney, Stephan, Rosenfield, Aronson, & Sikes, 1977; Lucker, Rosenfield, Sikes, & Aronson, 1977). Children in jigsaw classrooms show greater liking for their classmates and greater increases in self-esteem than those in other classrooms. Jigsaw classrooms have led to greater academic performance on the part of minority students and no differences in the academic performance of majority (White European) students. In fact, after two weeks of the jigsaw technique the gap between performance by majority and minority students dropped from 17 percentage points to about 10 percentage points.

What leads to the beneficial effects of the jigsaw technique? First, children who participate in jigsaw groups tend to increase their participation and interest in school activities (Blaney et al., 1977). Second, children gain in empathy and perspective-taking. Finally, children may change the attributions they make for others' behaviour (Stephan, Presser, Kennedy, & Aronson, 1978). They may begin to give others credit for their successes (e.g., he really is smart) and to remove blame for failures (e.g., that was a ridiculously hard question). In other words, they start to use the same attributions to explain others' successes and failures that they use to explain their own.

Digital Vision/Media Bakery

ACTIVATE ALTRUISTIC MOTIVES.   Another approach to solving social dilemmas is to get people to activate altruistic or moral motives, meaning the motive to help others and behave in a moral way (Dawes, 1980; Lynn & Oldenquist, 1986). In a study conducted in the United Kingdom, Mark van Vugt found that when people consume water in a variable rate system (in which case they are charged for the water they consume), there was no difference in the consumption of water between people who identified highly with their community and people who felt little attachment to their community (van Vugt, 2001). In contrast, when people were on a fixed rate for their water consumption (in which case they pay the same amount regardless of how much water they consume), those with low identification with their community used more water than people with high community attachment (see Figure 9.6). The study supports the moderating effects of community identification on the use of a communal resource (i.e., water), particularly when there is no financial incentive associated with use (fixed rate). Simply feeling respected by other people in one's group increases cooperation, especially for people who are more concerned about fitting in with others in the group

(De Cremer, 2002). The Environmental Connections box describes how individuals who are aware of the problems caused by car use—pollution, noise, energy consumption—are more likely to use public transport.

ENVIRONMENTAL CONNECTIONS

Caring about the Environmental Impact of Cars

Some environmental psychologists are interested in why commuters continue to rely on their cars even though they know that cars pose a threat to the environment, including global warming, acid rain, resource depletion, noise pollution, and congestion (Lowe, 1990). In this type of environmental research, the focus is on how commuters deal with the conflict between their short-term individual interests (e.g., autonomy) that are at odds with long-term collective interests (e.g., saving the environment). Research on this type of commuter dilemma has found that commuters who possess prosocial attitudes are more likely to use public transportation than commuters who are self-focused (van Lange, van Vugt, Meertens, & Ruiter, 1998).

Joireman, van Lange, and van Vugt (2004) examined motives and attitudes that might lead more people to decide to use public transit systems. This research found that the strongest effect for increased use of public transportation was a high level of consciousness about future consequences and, more specifically, high awareness of the harmful impact that commuting by car has on the environment.

Canadian Press/Mario Beauregard

FIGURE 9.6 HOW DOES COMMUNITY IDENTIFICATION IMPACT COOPERATION?

This study measured how much water people used in a community that encouraged water conservation. The hypothesis was that people who identify strongly with community goals would conserve water, regardless of whether they paid a fixed or variable rate. As predicted, people with a variable rate used about the same amount of water regardless of their community identification, whereas, under a fixed consumption rate, people who identified highly with their community used much less water than those who didn't identify as strongly.

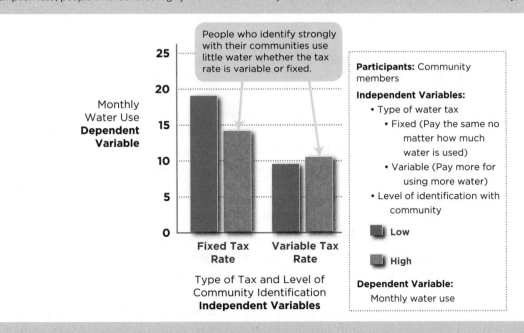

Source: van Vugt, M. (2001). Community identification moderating the impact of financial incentives in a natural social dilemma: Water conservation. *Personality and Social Psychology Bulletin, 27,* 1440–1449. Used by permission of Sage Publications.

CREATE SMALL, CONNECTED GROUPS.   Creating small, connected groups is yet another strategy that reduces competition and increases cooperation in social dilemmas (Dawes, 1980; Edney, 1980). People in small groups are less selfish than those in large groups, perhaps because they can more directly see the consequences of their good (and bad) behaviour in small groups (Brewer & Kramer, 1986). For example, you might find yourself more willing to toss litter on a public highway than on a street in your neighbourhood.

How can social dilemmas be solved when groups are very large, such as all the people who live in a given town or attend a specific university? In these cases, it may be difficult for people to directly see the benefits of cooperation, but other strategies can work to increase cooperation. One approach is making a superordinate group identity salient. This involves creating a focus on what all people in the group have in common (e.g., we're all members of this university community; Kramer & Brewer, 1984). Another effective approach is to divide the larger community into subgroups. For example, universities could increase recycling efforts by reporting the percentage of trash recycled by each dorm instead of simply reporting the overall percentage of recycling at the school.

tit-for-tat – a strategy in a prisoner's dilemma situation whereby one starts with cooperation, and then does whatever one's partner does on each subsequent interaction (e.g., cooperate after cooperation and compete after competition from one's partner)

CREATE CONSEQUENCES FOR COMPETITION.   One way to create consequences for competing is to use the **tit-for-tat** strategy, which involves starting with cooperation, and then doing whatever your partner does on each interaction (e.g., cooperate after your partner cooperates and compete after he or she competes). Although cooperators can be taken advantage of, and competition has the potential for greater rewards, the tit-for-tat strategy leads to better overall outcomes for both members in a social dilemma, in part because it helps people protect themselves. After all, people who always cooperate are likely to be exploited by their partners (Komorita, Chan, & Parks, 1993).

Creating consequences for competition as well as rewards for cooperation can increase cooperation in social dilemmas, particularly among those who are initially competitive (Komorita & Barth, 1985; Komorita, Parks, & Hulbert, 1992; Sheldon, 1999). For example, people who receive a bonus for cooperating show more cooperation than those who receive a negative incentive. Research Focus on Neuroscience describes how cooperation even seems to be rewarding on a neurological level.

RESEARCH FOCUS ON NEUROSCIENCE
How Cooperation Looks in the Brain

Although you might imagine that cooperation is simply something we learn through experience, some research suggests that there are neurological benefits to engaging in cooperative behaviour. In one study, researchers examined the areas of the brain that are activated when people are cooperating (Rilling et al., 2002). Thirty-six women played multiple rounds of a prisoner's dilemma game with another woman. On each trial, participants could cooperate with their partner or compete with their partner. As is typical in prisoner's dilemma games, participants received the best outcomes for themselves when they competed and their partner cooperated. To view the neurological consequences of the participants' choices, researchers used fMRI to scan the players' brains throughout the trials. The scans revealed that when both participants cooperated the brain areas that are associated with reward processing were activated. Moreover, this type of activation wasn't present during any of the other pairings of cooperative/competitive behaviour. This finding suggests that cooperating with someone, even at some cost to oneself, is positively reinforcing at a neurological level: in other words, cooperating feels good in the brain.

There is a clear downside, however, to creating negative consequences as a strategy for encouraging cooperation, as the use of such consequences can undermine people's trust that others are internally motivated to cooperate (Mulder, van Dijk, De Cremer, & Wilke, 2006). In turn, people may trust other group members less when they believe their cooperative behaviour is motivated by the external fear of the consequences of failing to cooperate. This is particularly likely when trust within a group is initially high.

[CONCEPTS IN CONTEXT]

EXAMPLES OF TYPES OF SOCIAL DILEMMAS AND THEIR SOLUTIONS

FACTOR	EXAMPLE
TYPES OF SOCIAL DILEMMAS	
Common resource dilemma	If each person waters his or her lawn during a drought, soon there won't be enough water for anyone to shower.
Public goods dilemma	Neil always takes a few cents from the "take a penny, leave a penny" jar to help pay his order at the local coffee shop. However, Neil has never left any change in the jar for others.
Prisoner's dilemma	Simon is accused of cheating on an exam, and is told that he'll receive a lesser punishment if he identifies another person who also cheated. However, he'll receive the maximum punishment if he chooses not to identify another student who cheated and that person identifies Simon as having cheated.
SOLUTIONS TO SOCIAL DILEMMAS	
Regulate use of resources	Toll booths are used to require people to pay for use of the road.
Engage in open communication	Bringing two groups together who both want access to a local park on a given day may help them reach a compromise that will work well for both sides.
Activate altruistic motives	Reminding people at holiday times of those who are less fortunate may lead people to contribute more money to charitable organizations.
Create small, connected groups	Creating a competition between different classrooms in an elementary school for picking up litter can lead each classroom to work together for the common good.
Create consequences for competition	When Abdi and Nahid argue over their shared toys, their mother takes the toys away for one week.

HOW DOES CULTURE RELATE TO INTRAGROUP PROCESSES?

To examine the impact of priming different types of cultural symbols on cooperation in a prisoner's dilemma task, researchers recruited Chinese American participants and had them play the game under different conditions (Wong & Hong, 2005). Participants in one condition were primed with Chinese cultural symbols (such as a dragon and a person performing kung fu). Participants in the other condition were primed with American icons (such as the American flag and a scene at a football game). Then the participants played a prisoner's dilemma game with either a friend or a stranger. As predicted, participants were more likely to cooperate with friends when Chinese cultural knowledge was activated than when American cultural knowledge was activated: 77 percent versus 53 percent. In contrast, participants showed a similarly low level of cooperation with strangers after both Chinese and American culture priming (63 percent versus 59 percent). These findings indicate that priming different cultures influences people's behaviour, and in particular their willingness to cooperate with a friend in a social dilemma. This section will examine the ways in which culture impacts social influence in group settings, including in social loafing and social dilemmas.

SOCIAL LOAFING

For decades, the findings on social loafing appeared very robust. On a variety of tasks, the social loafing effect was found over and over again, to the extent that social psychology text-books used to describe it as a universal phenomenon and would confidently say, "When in groups, people loaf." However, as the sub-discipline of cross-cultural psychology developed after the first publication of Hofstede's (2001) research, it became evident that not all people loaf in all groups. It would be more accurate to say something like "When in unimportant groups, working on trivial tasks, individualists loaf." There are two points to be made here: The first is that the experimental settings often used trivial tasks with no consequences outside the experiment and the "experimental groups" themselves didn't have a strong group identity—i.e., people were randomly assigned to a "group" and told that they're now a group. We have already seen that if either the task or the group has significance for people (which is more often the case in real life than in experimental settings), loafing effects are reduced. The second point involves culture. In collectivistic cultures, individuals may be particularly motivated to have their group seem competent, regardless of whether their own individual input is identified (Karau & Williams, 1993). For people in collectivistic cultures, group harmony and success may be more important than individual performance (and they could also be evaluated poorly by group members for loafing).

In order to examine the impact of culture on social loafing, researchers assigned 80 Chinese and 72 American children in grades six and nine to complete a task either alone or in pairs (Gabrenya, Wang, & Latané, 1985). This task involved listening to a series of tones that were played through stereo headphones, and noting whether the tones were played to the left ear, right ear, or both. Although culture had no effect on the rate of social loafing by grade six students, culture did impact performance for the grade nine students. Specifically, American students in grade nine had fewer errors when working on the task alone than when working in pairs, demonstrating their tendency to socially loaf when working in pairs. In contrast, Chinese students in grade nine had fewer errors when working on the task in pairs, showing "social striving," meaning they performed better when working with a partner than when working alone. Similarly, using an Israeli sample but measuring independent and inter-dependent self-construal (i.e., individual sense of self in relation to others), Erez & Somech (1996) found less loafing among those with a more interdependent self-construal. It should not be assumed, however, that collectivism always leads people to make more effort in any group. Because groups are more important to collectivists, so is the distinction between in-groups ("us") and outgroups ("them"). Working with management trainees from the U.S., Hong Kong, and Israel, Earley (1993) found that individualists worked harder on their own (the usual social loafing effect) but collectivists worked harder when they were working with someone from an in-group, but not with people from outside their group. The conclusion, then, is that collectivists don't loaf as long as they're in a group they regard as "us." If they're stuck with a group of "them," they'll loaf.

Using a largely Dutch sample, Klehe and Anderson (2007) examined the relation between social loafing and the cultural dimensions of individualism-collectivism and power distance. As you recall from Chapter 1, individualism refers to valuing independence, self-reliance, autonomy, and personal identity in a given culture, and collectivism refers to valuing interdependence, harmony, cooperation, and social identity. Power distance, another cultural dimension proposed by Hofstede (2001), refers to the degree of comfort with and acceptance of hierarchical relationships. In their study, Klehe and Anderson (2007) found the predicted effect for collectivism (reduced motivation to loaf), but they also found that power distance predicted more loafing in situations where there was a temptation to loaf (i.e., where the task was not pleasant). It appears to be the case that people who are high on power distance (i.e., they respect hierarchical relationships) and who have an inclination to loaf will loaf, unless there is someone higher in the hierarchy instructing them not to.

SOCIAL DILEMMAS

Given the greater emphasis on fulfilling individuals' needs in individualistic cultures compared to collectivistic ones, research on how people solve social dilemmas reveals considerable differences across cultures. In one study, researchers examined rates of cooperation among groups in Japan and in the United States (Wade-Benzoni et al., 2002). Participants in both countries completed a social dilemma exercise in which they needed to manage a real-life crisis in the shark fishing industry. This crisis involved overfishing, meaning that fishing industries were catching sharks faster than the sharks could reproduce, thus causing the resource to rapidly deplete. The groups were asked to allocate resources between different interests, including commercial fishing and recreational fishing. As predicted, groups of Japanese decision-makers agreed to harvest less and more equally allocate resources than groups of American decision-makers. What led to these differences? One factor was expectation: Americans expected others to act more competitively than the Japanese did, and this expectation contributed to Americans' less cooperative behaviour.

THE BIG PICTURE

GROUP PROCESSES

This chapter included many applications of the three "big ideas" studied in social psychology. The examples below should help you see the connection between group influence and these big ideas and contribute to your understanding of the big picture of social psychology.

THEME	EXAMPLES
The social world influences how we think about ourselves.	• People are less self-aware when in a group than when alone. • In conflict situations, we see our own goals as just and fair. • People underestimate the proportion of resources that they take from a common pool.
The social world influences our thoughts, attitudes, and behaviour.	• We "choke" in front of a supportive audience, and we make more errors on a math test when we take the test in front of a friend than in front of a stranger. • If our contributions will be pooled together, we exert more effort on a task when working with a low-ability partner. • We get more extreme in our views following discussion with others.
Our attitudes and behaviour shape the social world around us.	• We see people in other groups in a simplistic and stereotypical way. • We feel more positively toward others once we have worked together on a common goal. • We take goods from a common pool even when we don't contribute to that pool.

This chapter examined factors in group processes, and in particular the power of groups on influencing behaviour, decision-making, and social dilemmas.

1. How do groups influence behaviour?

This section examined ways in which groups influence behaviour. You learned about social facilitation, and three explanations for this effect (distraction, evaluation apprehension, and mere presence). This section also described social loafing and the impact on social loafing of identifiable contributions, contributions having impact, and task importance. Finally, this section examined the link between cohesion and group performance. You also learned why most restaurants impose a mandatory tip on groups of five or more.

2. How do intragroup processes influence decision-making?

This section examined how the group process influences decision-making. You learned about group polarization and the factors that contribute to it, including hearing a larger number of persuasive arguments and learning group norms. This section also described the factors leading to groupthink, including overestimating the group's invulnerability and morality, closed-mindedness, and pressure toward uniformity.

3. How do leaders guide and motivate the group?

This section examined three models of leadership: the trait or "great person" model, transformational versus transactional leadership, and the contingency model. You also learned that people who are oriented toward both achievement and interpersonal dynamics are the most effective leaders.

4. How do groups handle social dilemmas?

This section examined how groups handle social dilemmas, in which the needs of the individual conflict with the needs of the group. You learned about types of resource dilemmas, including the common resource dilemma, the public goods dilemma, and the prisoner's dilemma. This section also described solutions to social dilemmas, including regulating resources, communicating, creating small and connected groups, activating altruism, and having consequences. You also learned that describing a prisoner's dilemmas game as "the Wall Street game" leads to higher levels of competition than describing it as "the community game."

5. How does culture relate to intragroup processes?

This section examined the relation between culture and group processes, including social loafing and social dilemmas.

Key Terms

collective effect model 297
common resource dilemma 308
ethnocentrism 306
group polarization 300
groupthink 301
intergroup processes 292

intragroup processes 292
prisoner's dilemma 309
public goods dilemma 308
risky shift 300
social compensation 298
social dilemma 307

social facilitation 293
social inhibition 294
social loafing 297
tit-for-tat 314

Questions for Review

1. What are four ways in which groups influence behaviour?

2. Describe how group processes influence decision-making.

3. Describe three models of leadership.

4. What are three types of social dilemmas, and what are some solutions to such dilemmas?

5. Describe how culture influences social loafing and social dilemmas.

Take Action!

1. You're a professor assigning a group project. What do you do to make sure all students give the project their all?

2. You're the president of a student group that must make recommendations to the university administration about strategies for improving the quality of education

and student life. What strategies could you use to avoid problems associated with group decision-making, such as group polarization and groupthink?

3. You're working with people from different cultures on a project. How might you work to increase everyone's contributions to the project?

RESEARCH CONNECTIONS

Participate in Research

Activity 1 The Impact of the Task on Social Facilitation: This chapter described how physiological arousal can lead us to perform better on some tasks, but worse on others. Go online to test how arousal could influence your performance on different types of tasks.

Activity 2 The Importance of Leadership: One factor that influences how well groups function is the style and characteristics of the group leader. Go online to rate how well you think different leadership strategies would work for your groups.

Activity 3 The Complexity of Social Dilemmas: You learned in this chapter about different types of social dilemmas and how groups handle social dilemmas. Go online and identify an example of a social dilemma involving common resources (e.g., water, land, air). Then identify how individual action could protect the common resource.

Activity 4 The Relation of Culture to Intragroup Processes: The final section of this chapter described how culture influences social interaction in group settings. Go online to examine different strategies that are used cross-culturally in resolving social dilemmas. Then see how people from different cultures rate these distinct strategies.

Test a Hypothesis

One of the common findings in research on group processes is that individuals in groups exert less overall effort than individuals working alone. To test whether this hypothesis is true, recruit some friends to work on a brainstorming task. Tell half of your friends to come up with various ideas as a group, and tell the others to come up with ideas individually. This approach will let you see whether people in groups do socially loaf, and thereby come up with fewer ideas than those who work individually. Then, go online to report your findings to other students.

Design a Study

Go online to design your own study testing the factors that can lead to groupthink. You'll be able to choose the type of study you want to conduct (self-report, observational/naturalistic, or experimental), choose your own independent and dependent variables, and form your own hypothesis. Then you can share your findings with other students across the country!

10

INTERGROUP RELATIONS

DID YOU EVER WONDER?

Terry Jones is a preacher at a church called the Dove World Outreach Center in Gainesville, Florida. Though the church has a membership of only 50 people, Jones has managed to make himself known worldwide. In 2010, he announced that he wanted to launch "International Burn a Koran Day" on the ninth anniversary of the September 11, 2001 attacks against the United States. He said that his plan to burn Korans and organize an anti-Muslim rally was to memorialize the September 11 attacks. The announcement received extensive media and political attention both nationally and globally. Jones was even called the "anti-pastor" on the BBC, a label that was then picked up by other media. Many governments around the world, including both the Canadian and American governments, condemned the pastor's statement. American religious leaders from such organizations as the National Association of Evangelicals and the Theological Education Institute in Connecticut broadly rejected the plan.

In an open letter to the *Huffington Post*, a group of American veterans of the wars in Afghanistan and in Iraq stated that, "When citizens here participate in hateful rhetoric and intolerance toward Muslims, it leaves soldiers over there exposed" (Muskus, 2010). Demonstrations were organized in several Muslim countries, including Pakistan, Indonesia, Palestine, Somalia, and India (a non-Muslim majority country) protesting Jones's intentions. Political Muslim fundamentalists also seized the opportunity to mobilize the masses against America more generally, and a wave of violence was reported in Muslim countries.

Though Jones cancelled his plans for "International Burn a Koran Day," in March 2011, he held a mock "Trial of the Koran" in his church where he burned a copy of the

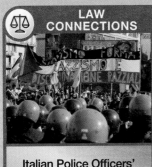
LAW CONNECTIONS

Italian Police Officers' Perception of Crowd Conflict

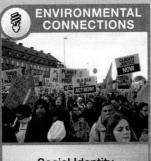
ENVIRONMENTAL CONNECTIONS

Social Identity and Environmental Activism

BUSINESS CONNECTIONS

Using Mediation and Arbitration to Resolve Conflict

HEALTH CONNECTIONS

Being Alive Well

religious text. This led to a violent reaction in Afghanistan the following month. Protestors there attacked a United Nations compound in northern Afghanistan, killing four Nepalese guards and three UN staff (one Norwegian, one Swede, and one Romanian). How do views leading to such inflammatory and extreme acts develop? Why are there such grave misunderstandings between some Muslims and non-Muslim groups? This chapter will examine some of the theories that address these questions, as well as explanations of collective action or crowd behaviour—i.e., what happens when people congregate *en masse*. You'll also find answers to these questions:

 Why did people in the riot in Vancouver following the Canucks' Stanley Cup loss feel less compelled to follow normal rules of behaviour?

 Why does receiving a D on an exam when you thought you deserved a B make you feel more angry than when you receive the same mark but didn't think you deserved better?

 Why would mediation have been a better negotiation strategy than arbitration in reaching a deal between the Canada Post Corporation and the postal workers' union?

 Why is the modern Canadian health-care system sometimes not appropriate for those with different conceptions of health (e.g., First Nation Canadians)?

PREVIEW

Imagine that you're representing a students' association in your university at a meeting with the chairperson of the psychology department. As you speak to the chair, you're engaging in an example of intergroup behaviour if you behave and respond toward this other person in a manner that results from your, and the other person's, group memberships. In this case, you may make certain assumptions, and make adjustments in your manner that reflect your role as a student representative. Another example of intergroup behaviour would be attacks by skinheads in eastern Europe on Roma gypsies simply because they're Roma gypsies, and even if the act is carried out by one skinhead against one gypsy (DiManno, 2009). While this act does represent behaviour at the individual level, because one individual is acting against another individual, it's also intergroup behaviour because the individual is acting as a member of a right-wing fascist group against a member of the Roma people, another group. Both examples, then, are instances of intergroup relations, which have been defined as "the way in which people in groups perceive, think about, feel about, and act toward people in other groups" (Hogg, 2006, p. 479).

intergroup relations – the way in which people in groups perceive, think about, feel about, and act toward people in other groups

Many of the topics that are discussed in this book, including stereotypes, prejudice, and aggression, relate to intergroup relations as they are examples of attitudes and behaviours that can happen simultaneously at both the interpersonal and intergroup levels. This chapter will examine the role that social psychological factors play in both positive intergroup relations and intergroup conflict.

HOW DO DIFFERENT THEORIES EXPLAIN INTERGROUP RELATIONS?

One important aspect of intergroup relations is the collective behaviour of people in a crowd. There are abundant examples of both national and international mobilization of crowds in countries around the world. A recent and more local example happened in late June 2010 when hundreds of people protested in downtown Toronto against the G20 summit. Although the demonstrations were for the most part peaceful, there were incidents of tension and confrontation between police and demonstrators, with some police cars set on fire and some stores and businesses vandalized. According to CTV News (2010), heavily armed riot police used tear gas and rubber bullets to disperse the crowds. The police also arrested more than 600 protestors and, according to a *Globe and Mail* report, riot police boxed in hundreds of people soaking in the rain (Galloway & Mehler Paperny, 2010). The arrest of hundreds of demonstrators is considered to be one of the largest mass arrests in Canadian history. How are we to understand this event and other similar events? Why do people in a crowd behave the way they do? Studying people's behaviour in crowds or studying the collective action of people when they're part of a large mass can be difficult. This is particularly the case as there are many factors that influence people's behaviour in crowds, including each individual's motivation and goals in being part of the crowd, the presence of others who share those motivations and goals, the presence of others who oppose them, the cues that are present in the environment, and the individual's perception of an injustice being carried out against him- or herself and the group. In this chapter, we will examine some of these factors. We begin with crowd behaviour as an inherent example of intergroup relations.

THE CANADIAN PRESS/Darren Calabrese

Police standing off against protestors in downtown Toronto during the G20 summit on Saturday, June 26, 2010.

EARLY RESEARCH AND THEORIES OF CROWD BEHAVIOUR

One of the earliest theories of crowd behaviour was suggested by Gustav Le Bon (1896), French social psychologist. Le Bon observed riots in France and argued that when people become part of a crowd they "descend several rungs on the ladder of civilization" (p. 32). People act instinctively and become irrational. According to Le Bon (1896), three characteristics are associated with the processes that seem to be specific to crowds:

1. Anonymity: People in a crowd become anonymous and are therefore less responsible for their actions.
2. Suggestibility: When people's social constraints are loosened, they become more suggestible. When one or a few individuals start to act on their aggressive impulses (as anonymity allows them to do), others copy due to their heightened suggestibility, giving in to their own urges to act unreasonably and aggressively.
3. Contagion: The irrationality and acts of violence are contagious and sweep through the crowd (due to the heightened suggestibility of crowd members).

In other words, Le Bon (1896) argued that people "go mad" (i.e., become irrational) in crowds—that crowd behaviour is destructive, pathological, and should be controlled. Similarly, McDougall (1920) characterized crowds as violent, impulsive, suggestible, and emotional. Both Le Bon and McDougall described crowds as possessing a group mind. Under the influence of the collective mind ("mental unity"), people are less responsible for their actions, act based on instinct, become less intelligent, and become more violent. Le Bon and McDougall, therefore, had a negative perception of crowds and believed that a crowd has to be controlled and managed.

An alternative view was suggested by Floyd Allport (1924), who argued that "there is no psychology of groups which is not essentially and entirely a psychology of individuals" (p. 6). Allport rejected the idea of a group mind and suggested that "the individual in the crowd behaves just as he would behave alone only more so" (p. 295). If Le Bon thought crowds made people mad, Allport thought crowds allowed people to be bad. Regardless, both agreed that crowds are destructive and harmful. The Law Connections box reports on a study of how Italian police officers perceive unruly crowds.

LAW CONNECTIONS

Italian Police Officers' Perception of Crowd Conflict

Research has found that crowd conflict can be understood by using the elaborate social identity model (Stott & Reicher, 1998), which is based on social identity theory (Tajfel & Turner, 1979) and self-categorization theory (Turner, 1987). This model suggests that crowds recognize that everyone in the crowd shares a common social identity based on their intergroup relations with the out-group (i.e., those who oppose what the crowd represents). Crowd conflict can occur (1) when physical force is used and the police perceive it as legitimate but the crowd doesn't, or (2) when the crowd feels that it has the power to use its collective force to resist police action.

Prati and Pietrantoni (2009) surveyed 352 Italian police officers about crowd conflict and the attributions of responsibility they made for the behaviour of people in the crowd. All participants were male and had been in police service on aver-age 6.95 years. It was found that while police officers perceived the crowd as being heterogeneous (comprising distinct individu-als), they at the same time made a distinction between individu-als based on whether they belonged to a minority or majority group within the crowd. The police officers believed that crowd conflict arose because the minority group had violent tenden-cies and were able to manipulate the majority group, who were less self-conscious in the crowd due to anonymity, diffused responsibility or accountability, and increased perceptions of group cohesion. In other words, police officers believed that people in a crowd tend to be irrational but not necessary violent. As crowd violence increased, however, police officers then per-ceived the crowd as a homogeneous threat and every person as potentially dangerous. As expected, it was found that when the police officers perceived the crowd as a homogeneous threat, they were more likely to treat crowd members as a single body, in other words not as distinct individuals but as homogeneous beings, rather like herd animals (Prati & Pietrantoni, 2009). Additionally, it was found that the police officers didn't perceive themselves as responsible for the initiation or development of violence involving crowds.

In sum, the attributions that police officers hold and the prac-tices that stem from them are important in understanding how police forces respond to crowds and their approach to maintaining public order. Reicher, Stotto, Cronin, and Adang (2004) developed guidelines for crowd policing. These include (1) education about the social identities of different groups in the crowd, (2) facilitation of crowd aims, (3) differentiation of crowd members, and (4) proper communication with crowd members. Implementing such meth-ods and holding group sessions for police officers with a psycholo-gist after crowd conflict to discuss the officers' experiences could increase understanding of the complexity of crowd dynamics (Prati & Pietrantoni, 2009).

These findings indicate that police officers, in general, adhere to the classical view of crowd behaviour (i.e., with crowds providing anonymity and diffused responsibility), which in turn relates to bad policing and negative attributions toward crowds. The results also support the elaborate social identity model (i.e., development of a new identity) and how the model could be used to train police officers.

AP Photo/Alberto Pellaschiar

DEINDIVIDUATION

In reaction to Allport's position, other psychologists, including Muzafer Sherif (1936), Solomon Asch (1952), and Philip Zimbardo (1969), argued that social groups and crowds in particular have characteristics that cannot be understood by studying individuals. These psy-chologists argued that studying group process should not be abandoned. Zimbardo (1969) offered the theory of deindividuation. According to Zimbardo, when people are in large groups, they're less likely to follow normal rules of behaviour. This is partly because people in large groups become anonymous and there is a sense of diffusion of individual responsi-bilities. It's easy to see the roots of Zimbardo's "deindividuation" in Le Bon's "anonymity." In Zimbardo's view, anonymity is a social circumstance that leads to the psychological state of deindividuation.

deindividuation – the tendency to not follow normal rules of behav-iour as a result of losing one's self awareness

You're no doubt aware that there are times when you're more self-conscious than at other times. Deindividuation occurs when one loses this awareness of oneself as a distinct indi-vidual, and one therefore feels less compelled to follow normal rules of behaviour (Diener, 1979; Festinger, Pepitone, & Newcomb, 1952; Mullen, 1986; Postmes & Spears, 1998). Deindividuation is more likely to occur in group settings, and contributes to the tendency of groups of people to engage in highly destructive actions. For example, lynchings, riots, and acts of vandalism all occur in group settings (Mullen, 1986; Watson, 1973). Perhaps you recall the riot in Vancouver after the Vancouver Canucks lost game seven of the Stanley Cup hockey series to the Boston Bruins in June 2011. Canadians were shocked at the images released after the riot depicting seemingly normal people vandalizing, damaging, and looting properties. City officials estimated the cost to be in the millions. Why did some people set fire to cars, overturn parked cars, throw beer bottles at giant television screens, and steal goods from stores? What factors lead to deindividuation? Research points to several contributing factors, including anonymity, accountability, and a decrease in self-awareness. We'll now examine each of these factors separately.

REUTERS/MIKE CARLSON
Riots in downtown Vancouver on June 15, 2011

ANONYMITY. One factor that contributes to deindividuation is *anonymity* (Rehm, Steinleitner, & Lilli, 1987). Group settings provide anonymity because each individual is less distinguishable. Anonymity is also enhanced in situations where people wear uniforms or they paint or cover their face, which makes the person less identifiable. Anonymity is understood to be a social circumstance that is a precursor of deindividuation.

In 1973, Philip Zimbardo conducted a study that is known as the Stanford Prison Experiment (Haney, Banks, & Zimbardo, 1973; Haney & Zimbardo, 1998). We referred to the study in Chapter 2, when we discussed the ethical issues surrounding conducting this experiment. In this study, 24 male university students from Canada and the U.S. were selected from more than 70 applicants who responded to a local newspaper ad on a study of the psychological effects of prison life (Social Psychology Network, 2011). These participants were selected based on diagnostic interviews and personality tests and were considered to be healthy and intelligent with no history of crime or drug abuse. The participants were divided into two groups using random assignment to be either a "guard" or a "prisoner." Random assignment is an important feature of the study because, at the beginning of the study, there were no systematic differences between the guards and the prisoners.

The study was set up in the basement of the psychology building at Stanford University and simulated a prison. The study began with nine guards and nine prisoners, with the other participants on call in case they were needed. The prisoners were blindfolded, picked up from their residence by the city police, and brought to the basement of the psychology building. Guards were given uniforms, reflective sunglasses, whistles, and billy clubs. Prisoners were given uniforms and were referred to by their prisoner number. All these instructions were intended to increase deindividuation for the participants.

Soon, students who were acting as guards became abusive and forced prisoners to perform cruel and humiliating tasks. The prisoners, although rebellious at first, became extremely passive within days and, in some cases, highly depressed. Overall, the results indicated that participants soon identified with the roles they were given; guards acted aggressively and prisoners became submissive. The original experiment, which was planned to last for two weeks, was terminated after only six days because of the extreme behaviour.

In another study, Zimbardo found that female university students who wore identical white coats and hoods, similar to the Ku Klux Klan (KKK) uniform, gave longer electric shocks to another participant than those who wore their own clothes and were identified with a large name tag (Zimbardo, 1969). Again, the anonymity of wearing the white coat and hood appeared to facilitate aggression.

Do these findings demonstrate that becoming anonymous by wearing a uniform or costume increases aggressive behaviour?

Questioning the Research:

How do you think you would have behaved if you were a prisoner or guard in Zimbardo's experiment?

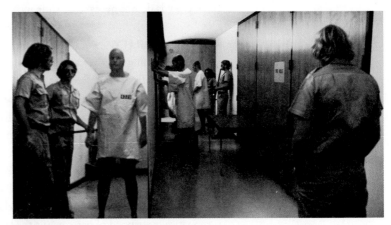

Dr. Philip Zimbardo
Images of the Stanford Prison Experiment

IN THE NEWS

(© AP/Wide World Photos)

Prisoner Abuse: Between October and December 2003, American soldiers in charge of the Abu Ghraib prison in Iraq engaged in systematic abuse of prisoners in their charge. This abuse included pouring cold water on naked detainees, beating detainees, threatening detainees with rape, and using military dogs to intimidate detainees. Although you might be tempted to blame the soldiers for these actions, research in social psychology indicates that situational factors played a major role in their behaviour.

Fortunately, no, at least not always. Although there are anthropological accounts of some warriors who paint or cover their faces mutilating their enemies more than some who don't cover their faces (Watson, 1973), and there are examples of police brutality while on duty (and the significance of anonymity is emphasized by reports of police removing their identifying numbers before entering a situation such as the G20 protests; Galloway and Mehler Paperny, 2010), research indicates that the cues in the social environment are important in increasing or decreasing aggressive behaviour.

One such study was conducted by Robert Johnson and Leslie Downing (1979). Participants were American female undergraduate students who were told that they had to evaluate the learning of another participant (actually a confederate) and administer a shock whenever the learner made an error. Participants were randomly assigned to one of the four conditions: individuation (identifiable), deindividuation (non-identifiable), prosocial cue, and antisocial cue. In the individuation condition, participants wore a large name tag, whereas in the deindividuation condition no name tag or identifying information was worn. All participants also donned a white coat that was referred to either as an old nurse uniform (the prosocial cue condition) or as something that looked rather like a KKK uniform (the antisocial cue condition). The results indicated a significant effect for costume cues. As shown in Figure 10.1, participants who wore what was referred to as the nurse uniform administered significantly fewer shocks than those who wore what was referred to as the KKK costume. Additionally, there was an interaction between costume cues and deindividuation. It was found that deindividuation increased prosocial response when prosocial cues were present. That is, participants in the nurse uniform delivered significantly less shock when they were deindividuated. However, deindividuation did not increase the antisocial response when participants wore the KKK uniform. The study indicates that deindividuation does not always increase antisocial behaviour. In particular, if there are positive cues in the environment, such as a nurse uniform, deindividuation can actually increase prosocial behaviour. Overall, when anonymous, although one may be less self-conscious, one becomes more responsive to the cues in the situation, rather than simply behaving more aggressively, and especially if the social cues promote prosocial behaviour. Significantly, neither Le Bon nor Zimbardo included crowds of pilgrims or large religious congregations in their explanations of crowd behaviours. Such crowds do not necessarily slide into either "badness" or "madness."

ACCOUNTABILITY. Another factor that contributes to deindividuation is *accountability* (or lack of it), meaning whether a person expects to be held responsible for his or her actions (Nadler, Goldberg, & Jaffe, 1982). Because people in group settings are less likely to be identified, they feel less accountable and therefore more uninhibited in their behaviour than individuals who are acting alone. You may typically feel uncomfortable littering or being wasteful but if everyone else in your group is doing so, this discomfort may fade away. In line with this view, as the size of the group increases, so does its level of violence (Leader, Mullen, & Abrams, 2007). In one study, Zimbardo (1969) abandoned two cars: one in the Bronx in New York City, where he judged that "anonymity ruled," the other in Palo Alto, California, where he judged that a sense of community dominated. The car in the Bronx was quickly vandalized (within 10 minutes of leaving it) and systematically stripped of parts, while the latter remained untouched. Zimbardo argued that the anonymity of the Bronx facilitated this behaviour by making people feel less accountable.

FIGURE 10.1 HOW DOES DEINDIVIDUATION AFFECT ANTISOCIAL BEHAVIOUR?

In this study, American female undergraduate students were randomly assigned to one of four conditions: individuation (identifiable), deindividuation (non-identifiable), prosocial cue, and antisocial cue. All participants then had the opportunity to deliver an electric shock to a learner (a confederate) following each error the learner made. The participants could increase (+3, +2, +1) or decrease (−3, −2, −1) the intensity of the shock from the base level. One main finding was that participants in a KKK uniform administered more shocks than participants in a nurse uniform. It was also found that deindividuation facilitated prosocial behaviour for those wearing a nurse uniform but had insignificant effects on the antisocial behaviour of those wearing a KKK uniform.

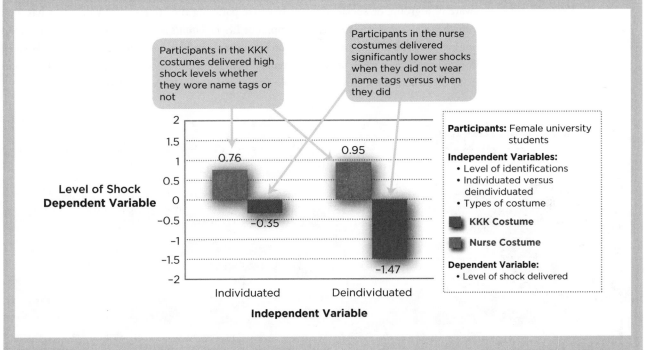

Source: Johnson R. & Downing, L. (1979). Deindividuation and valence of cues: effects on prosocial and and antisocial behavior. *Journal of Personality and Social Psychology, 37*, 1532–1538.

DECREASE IN SELF-AWARENESS.   Group settings also lead to a decrease in *self-awareness*, which in turn leads to deindividuation (Diener, 1979; Prentice-Dunn & Rogers, 1980, 1982). People in a group have less of a sense of themselves as distinct individuals. As described in Chapter 3, this decrease in self-awareness leads people to be less focused on matching their behaviour to their normal standards (Duval & Wicklund, 1972; Wicklund & Frey, 1980).

In one study, researchers told participants that they needed help with two tasks, and that the participant would do one task while another student would do the other task (Batson, Thompson, Seuferling, Whitney, & Strongman, 1999). One of the tasks was very appealing—and allowed participants to earn raffle tickets toward a desirable prize. The other task was very boring and had no positive rewards. The participant was then given the option of flipping a coin to decide who would do which task. About two-thirds of the students chose to flip the coin; most of the other one-third simply assigned the more appealing task to themselves. However, 24 of the 28 students who performed the supposedly fair coin toss declared themselves as having won the appealing task—a very unlikely event. When participants who chose to flip the coin were asked to do so in front of a mirror, the results of the coin toss then became fair. In this condition, exactly half the participants declared themselves having won the appealing task and the other half the boring task. This research points to the impact of self-awareness on people's behaviour—and our willingness to engage in less moral behaviour when self-awareness is low.

You likely noticed that anonymity, deindividuation, and decreased self-awareness are overlapping constructs. As was stated above, a situation in which a person is anonymous is likely to be one in which the person is less individually self-conscious, or self-aware, which is how deindividuation is defined. The question that is raised, then, is what happens when people become less aware of themselves as individuals (anonymous, deindividuated)? Le Bon believed that people regress to a more primitive (mad) state. Allport believed they become the selfish grasping (bad) individual that they really are underneath the veneer of social constraints. An alternative view is that as you become less aware of your individual identity you become more aware of a group, or social, identity. If you're parading the streets after your team has won (whether it's Team Canada at the Olympics or *Les Habitants* in the NHL), you're neither mad nor bad, but you are aware of being Canadian (or Canadien). Additionally, it's worth keeping in mind that every week at sports events, religious meetings, concerts, raves, weddings, and many other occasions, crowds of people gather without violence inevitably erupting.

[CONCEPTS IN CONTEXT]

CROWD BEHAVIOUR

FACTOR	EXAMPLE
Anonymity	Joel took part in a large demonstration protesting against building a new Walmart in his town. He got caught up in the excitement of the situation and found himself turning over a garbage can in the street when someone smashed a store window.
Accountability	When Neda walks her dog, Ziggy, late at night, she tends not to pick up after him as she knows that no one can see her and she won't get a ticket.
Decrease in self-awareness	Gwynneth finds himself less self-aware when he is drinking in a bar where music is loud and there are many people around.

SOCIAL IDENTITY THEORY

During our discussion above, you may have noticed that effects like deindividuation are intragroup processes. However, an important aspect of crowd behaviour—one that was overlooked by Le Bon, Allport, Zimbardo, and others—is its intergroup dimension (Reicher, 1984; Reicher & Potter, 1985). Stephen Reicher, a British psychologist, argued that in many crowd situations there are at least two groups. This simple point was virtually ignored in all previous theories of crowd behaviour. For example, in the example of the G20 summit demonstration in Toronto, there were demonstrators, but there were also a large number of police, and these two groups were interacting. In other words, each group was acting in response to the behaviour (or even the expected behaviour) of the other group. This occurs even when people are protesting in the absence of another group, such as the police, a rival group of sports fans, or a rival group of political supporters. They're usually protesting against another group, perhaps a ruling elite. Reicher's insight has finally moved research into crowd behaviour beyond the "mad or bad" discussions that are over a century old now; he asserted that crowd behaviour is often intergroup behaviour, in which terms the behaviour can make more sense—it is not simply mad or bad.

The other important insight about crowds, which follows from the idea of crowd behaviour as intergroup behaviour, is that people in a crowd do not lose their identity in some way but instead assume a new social identity as a member of a particular group. According to Reicher (1984), people in a crowd, although they may lose some personal identity, adopt (if only temporarily) a stronger sense of social identity. Therefore, in crowds there is a change of identity rather than loss of identity. Reicher's argument is based on the social identity theory of Tajfel (1982), which is we will explain next.

This alternative view of crowd behaviour helps explain the behaviour of demonstrators and police in Toronto during the 2010 G20 summit. The police adopted the identity and role of protecting the local and foreign government delegates. This shared identity created norms of conduct in that specific situation. The police acted by dispersing, intimidating, and arresting many demonstrators (who they perceived as a threat to the group they were entrusted with protecting, i.e., the state and non-demonstrating majority). On the other hand, demonstrators shared a different social identity. They came together for a specific purpose (i.e., protesting against the G20 summit) and reacted to what they perceived as police aggression by targeting police property and vandalizing local shops and businesses (perceiving that the police, as representatives and guardians of the capitalist status quo, had violated their right to peaceful protest). Therefore, although both groups (police and demonstrators) were exposed to the same environment, their group membership (and their expectations of, and the behaviour of, the other group) determined the behaviour they engaged in.

In sum, when people are in a group, and that group membership is salient, it's their group goal and group identity that regulate their behaviour. Additionally, when examining collective behaviour, it's important to realize that "the crowd" doesn't exist in isolation; rather it can represent one group and there is often another group involved as well—even if that group isn't physically present (e.g., Tamil Sri Lankans demonstrating against the Sinhalese government by blockading the Gardiner Expressway in Toronto; Bonoguore & Lewington, 2009). Therefore, as Brown (2000) notes, to understand what goes on inside a crowd, it's important to examine crowds from an intergroup perspective. This is not to say that other perspectives are wrong or irrelevant, but to ignore the intergroup aspect of crowd behaviour is to ignore one of its important elements. Social identity theory, as we will now see, helps explain this aspect of crowd behaviour and other social behaviour (see Environmental Connections).

According to **social identity theory**, each person strives to enhance his or her self-esteem, which is composed of both personal identity and social identity (Tajfel, 1982). Because our group memberships influence our thoughts, feelings, and behaviour, we're motivated to affiliate with successful groups as a way of increasing our own feelings of self-worth (Smith & Henry, 1996; Smith & Tyler, 1997; Snyder, Lassegard, & Ford, 1986). In turn, people can feel good about themselves by calling attention to their connection to successful people or groups (e.g., Indian Canadians who see the success of comedian Russell Peters, or those affected by cancer who watched Jack Layton became the leader of the official opposition while fighting the disease). In sum, people favour their in-groups over their outgroups in order to enhance their self-esteem. Figure 10.2 presents the theory.

social identity theory–a theory that posits that each person strives to enhance his or her self-esteem, which is composed of two parts: a personal identity and a social identity

Social identity theory also posits that threats to one's self-esteem increase the need for in-group favouritism (Tajfel, 1982). Therefore, people whose group is threatened and those who feel bad about themselves develop more in-group identification and are more likely to derogate outgroup members (Branscombe & Wann, 1994; Esses & Zanna, 1995; Forgas & Fiedler, 1996; Marques, Abrams, Paez, & Martinez-Taboada, 1998). In-group favouritism and outgroup derogation are particularly likely to occur under specific conditions—that is, if status of the group is being threatened, if the status of the individual within a group is being threatened, and if the group is small.

STATUS OF THE IN-GROUP.   Groups that are threatened with inferiority take particular pleasure at another group's failure—even if that failure will not directly benefit them in any way. In one study, researchers examined how Dutch soccer fans felt after their German rivals lost to the Croatian team in the 1998 FIFA World Cup (Leach, Spears, Branscombe, & Doosje, 2003). Dutch soccer fans who had first thought about how poorly their team typically did in the World Cup experienced greater pleasure with the German loss than did fans who hadn't first thought about their national team's chronic inferiority. Of course, the Dutch team got to the final although they lost to Spain.

FIGURE 10.2 MODEL OF SOCIAL IDENTITY THEORY

According to social identity theory, self-esteem is influenced by individuals' personal identity, which comes from their personal achievements, group achievements, in-group favouritism, and outgroup derogation.

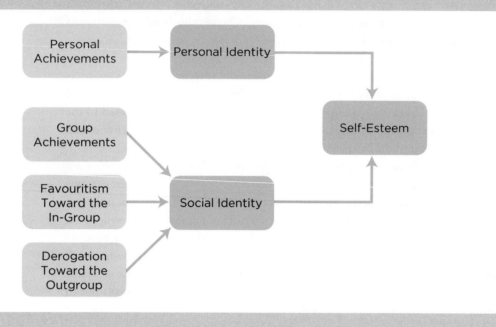

ENVIRONMENTAL CONNECTIONS

Social Identity and Environmental Activism

Social identity theory has been used to examine pro-environmental behaviour. A study in Australia looked at how environmental activism and environmental behaviour are related to social identity. Dono, Webb, and Richardson (2010) hypothesized that social identity would be related to environmental activism and that this relation would be mediated by (i.e., expressed through) environmental behaviour. Specifically, individuals who consider the environment to be socially important (they believe in activism) and identify with this social position (it forms part of their social identity) are more likely to perform pro-environmental behaviours. Pro-environmental behaviours consist of three dimensions: "consumer behaviour" (e.g., making a special effort to buy products made from recycled materials), "willingness to sacrifice" (e.g., being willing to pay higher taxes to protect the environment), and "environmental citizenship" (e.g., reading publications written by environmental groups).

Participants in the study were predominantly female students attending an Australian university. As expected, positive correlations between social identity and the three components of environmental behaviour (consumer behaviour, willingness to sacrifice, and environmental citizenship) were found. The findings indicated that the relation between environmental behaviour and social identity is indirect.

Courtesy of Matthew Whitby

The findings also indicated that the social identity of being an environmental activist is most strongly related to willingness to protest or read publications written by environmental groups and less strongly related to consumer behaviour and a willingness to pay more for environmental products (Dono et al., 2010). The findings suggest the potential usefulness of social identity theory in understanding pro-environmental behaviour.

STATUS WITHIN THE GROUP.   People who have a marginal status in their in-group are more likely to derogate outgroup members, particularly in the presence of in-group members (Noel, Wann, & Branscombe, 1995). People who feel their identity is threatened in some way often act in a hostile way toward members of other groups, presumably in an attempt to increase their own feelings of self-worth. In a study conducted in Italy, men interacted with a virtual partner, who was either traditional or feminist, on a social interaction task, without the men knowing that she was virtual (Maass, Cadinu, Guarnieri, & Grasselli, 2003). The traditional partner wanted to be a teacher, and decided not to be a lawyer because it was a career path more appropriate for men, and wanted to have time to have a family. The feminist partner wanted to be a bank manager, was "not afraid to compete with men," and worked with a group that defended women's rights. As part of the study, participants were asked to send each other photographic images (including pornographic or neutral images) and to respond to these images. The pornographic images were rated "high" or "low" on offensiveness (on the basis of ratings by 10 male students). It was found that men sent more, and more offensive, pornographic images to the feminist woman than to the traditional woman. The authors suggest that this occurred because the feminist woman represented a threat to male dominance and social status and therefore threatened men's group-based (i.e., gender-based) self-esteem.

GROUP SIZE.   The smaller the group, the greater the tendency for people to be loyal to it, which is why minority groups tend to have greater group loyalty than majority groups (Brewer & Pickett, 1999). For example, groups of minority students are much more commonly formed (such as the Iranian Students' Association, Women's Centre, Gay and Lesbian Alliance) than those of majority groups (you probably haven't heard about a White Student Union, or Heterosexual Alliance). Research Focus on Gender examines the impact on women in business when in the minority in a male-dominated group.

RESEARCH FOCUS ON GENDER
The Dynamics of Group Behaviour Based on the Ratio of Males and Females in a Group

One of the characteristics of the changing pattern of the workforce is a higher percentage of women who are now entering organizations that were once dominated by men (Hewstone et al., 2009). One of the first researchers to explore the dynamics of group behaviour based on the ratio of males to females was Rosabeth Moss Kanter in 1977. Her work with gender ratio group dynamics identified four types of proportions for group composition: uniform groups (e.g., all one gender), skewed groups (e.g., predominantly one gender with a few token members of the opposite gender), tilted groups (e.g., a majority of one gender versus a minority of the other), and balanced groups (e.g., equitable numbers of both genders; Kanter, 1997). Kanter studied the impact of proportionate membership of groups in a Fortune 500 company's sales force where 20 women worked with 300 men. This was a token group study because the women in this study often worked alone with a group of 10 to 12 men. Kanter found three perceptual phenomena that influenced group dynamics: visibility, polarization, and assimilation. Visibility was high for these women as they were often the only one in their category (i.e., female) and therefore had to contend with a greater degree of attention in comparison to the men, where, the greater the number of men, the less surprising, unique, or noteworthy each man was. Polarization, or exaggeration of differences, is the tendency for the dominant group (in this case the men), to notice their own commonalities with the others of their group (the other men) and, conversely, their differences from the minority members or member (the token woman). The limited number of token women prevents the men from exaggerating the differences between them, which in turn reinforces the men's perception of in-group commonalities. Assimilation is the term Kanter uses for the process of perceiving or misperceiving the token woman's characteristics to be more like a category characterization (e.g., a stereotype) than they actually are. Compared to women in balanced groups, women in token groups have been found to be more likely to experience discrimination (Nieva & Gutek, 1981).

More recent research on group proportionality has recognized that both gender and group size can moderate the perceived variability of the other group members (Rubin, Hewstone, Crisp, Voci, & Richards, 2004). In testing Kanter's previous findings, Hewstone and colleagues (2009) hypothesized that women would suffer greater visibility, polarization, and assimilation in male-skewed than male-tilted settings. Using the survey method, these researchers collected 188 responses from full-time academic staff in 20 departments of a British university that fit the different categories (i.e., skewed and tilted), with 12 females and 77 males in the male-skewed condition and 32 females and 67 males in the male-tilted condition. The results showed greater polarization and assimilation of women than men, although not greater visibility. Furthermore, it was found that more women than men in academia reported polarization and assimilation in both work environments.

These studies indicate that in diverse work settings, perceptions of group variability are affected by the relative sizes of the majority and minority. Additionally, there are biases as a result of group proportion. One might therefore conclude that it is important for minority and majority groups to be informed about these biases to ensure that all individuals have the same opportunity to achieve equal status and power within an organization (Hewstone et al., 2009). Such conditions facilitate harmonious intergroup relations and help make organizations and other groups more effective.

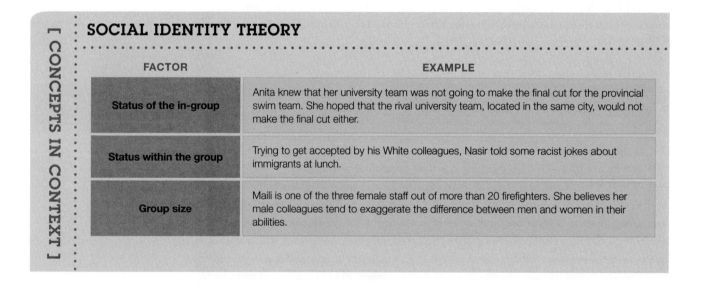

[CONCEPTS IN CONTEXT]

SOCIAL IDENTITY THEORY

FACTOR	EXAMPLE
Status of the in-group	Anita knew that her university team was not going to make the final cut for the provincial swim team. She hoped that the rival university team, located in the same city, would not make the final cut either.
Status within the group	Trying to get accepted by his White colleagues, Nasir told some racist jokes about immigrants at lunch.
Group size	Maili is one of the three female staff out of more than 20 firefighters. She believes her male colleagues tend to exaggerate the difference between men and women in their abilities.

HOW DOES INTERGROUP CONFLICT DEVELOP?

An important aspect of intergroup relations is the conflict that occurs between groups, or intergroup conflict. In Chapter 12 on aggression, there are several theories that explain aggressive behaviour among individuals. Relative deprivation theory is another theory that applies both to individuals and conflict between groups. In this section, we examine realistic conflict theory and relative deprivation theory that attempt to explain intergroup conflict.

REALISTIC CONFLICT THEORY

realistic conflict theory – a theory that describes conflict between different groups as resulting from individuals' self-interest motives in competition for jobs, land, power, and other resources

One of the causes of group conflict is direct competition for limited resources (Esses, Jackson, & Armstrong, 1998; Jackson, 1993). **Realistic conflict theory** posits that the animosity between different groups, such as that between Blacks and Whites, men and women, immigrant and local workers, and French and English Canadians, is a result of individuals' self-interest motives in terms of competition for jobs, land, and power (Correll & Park, 2005; Coser, 1956; Sherif, 1966). For example, White American students have been found to have a more positive attitude toward Asian Americans when they believe they'll be working with an Asian American student on a chemistry project (in which case this partner is assumed to offer an advantage) than when they believe they'll be working with an African American partner (African Americans, it would seem, are assumed not to be good chemists—or at least not as good as Asian Americans) and competing against an Asian American student (Maddux, Galinsky, Cuddy, & Polifroni, 2008). In the second case, Whites are concerned about being out performed by an Asian student, who indeed represents a realistic threat to their own achievement, and they therefore show more prejudiced beliefs. One implication of this study is the notion that shifting people's group memberships— in other words, making "one of them" into "one of us"—can help overcome negative intergroup relations. Imagine a Black player on one soccer team and a White player on the opposing team coming to blows during a match. If a White player on the Black player's team then joins the fray, whose side will he be on? Almost certainly that of his teammate rather than that of the person with similar skin colour.

A classic study by Muzafer Sherif (1966) used a group of 11-year-old boys at a summer camp to examine the role of competition in creating and reducing conflict between groups. The boys arrived at camp and after a few days were divided into two groups so that friend-ships that had formed were split, with friends put in different groups. At this point, the two groups should have been friendly toward one another as there were many already-existing friendships across the two groups. After the split, however, the members of each group then interacted completely apart from the other group, doing their own activities, creating their own names (Rattlers and Eagles), and so on. This first phase of the experiment constituted the stage of group formation. Then, the two groups participated in competitive activities, such as football, tug-of-war, and a treasure hunt. An intense rivalry quickly developed. Group flags were burned, cabins were ransacked, and food fights in the dining hall became common-place. This second stage of the experiment involved competitive contact between the groups, leading, quickly and easily, to intergroup conflict. In the last part of the experiment, a series of superordinate goals were created, the attainment of which required that all the boys from both groups combine their resources. For example, in one situation they all helped pull a truck that was stuck outside of the camp and was bringing food. Pooling resources to achieve these superordinate goals that were important for both groups and that neither group could achieve by itself led to intergroup cooperation (the third stage of the experiment). This study reveals just how quickly competition can lead to conflict, even among groups of very similar people with no prior history of conflict. Additionally, the study indicates that when the reason for competition has ceased and new tasks that require a new and larger group are introduced, cooperation can develop. Figure 10.3 is a schematic representation of realistic conflict theory (Taylor & Moghaddam, 1994). As you see in the figure, Sherif was able to show the stages of realistic conflict theory in his experiment by (1) formation of group that was based on interpersonal friendship and led to development of group culture, (2) inter-group conflict that was created due to intergroup competition and led to aggression and, (3) intergroup cooperation that was developed due to presence of superordinate goals and transformed intergroup hostility to cooperation.

An example of biased perceptions contributing to the escalation of competition into con-flict is the perception about conflict in Israel. Both Israelis and Palestinians see their goals (e.g., establishing a Jewish state in their ancient homeland, establishing a Palestinian state in the West Bank and Gaza, respectively) as crucially important and inherently just. At the same time, both Israelis and Arabs see the other side as the aggressor in each of the four major wars between them (1948, 1956, 1967, 1973). However, both Israel and Palestine technically fired first in two of the wars. Shamir and Shikaki (2002), in a collaboration between Hebrew

FIGURE 10.3 **REALISTIC CONFLICT THEORY**

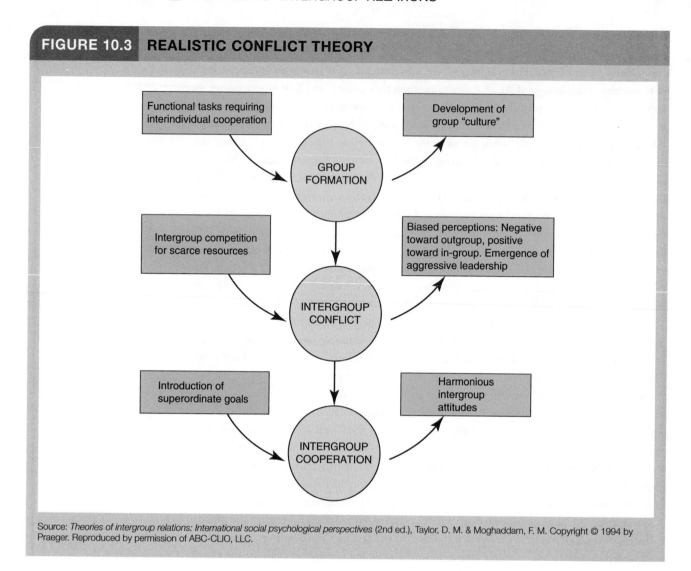

Source: *Theories of intergroup relations: International social psychological perspectives* (2nd ed.), Taylor, D. M. & Moghaddam, F. M. Copyright © 1994 by Praeger. Reproduced by permission of ABC-CLIO, LLC.

University of Jerusalem and the Palestinian Center for Policy and Survey Research, provide evidence from two surveys of Israeli Jews and Palestinians, in which the two groups both consider the violent behaviour of the other side to be terrorism, while simultaneously seeing the violent behaviour of their own side as justified.

This simultaneous view of our own side's actions as just and fair and those of the other side as evil and selfish, even when the outward behaviour may be identical, describes the phenomenon of mirror-image perception (Bronfenbrener, 1961; Pettigrew, 2003; Tobin & Eagles, 1992). In **mirror-image perception** each group sees its own behaviour as caused by the same factor—that is, the actions of the other side. Table 10.1 presents examples of this in terms of the conflict in Israel.

mirror-image perception – reciprocal view when each group sees its own behaviour as caused by the actions of the other side.

RELATIVE DEPRIVATION THEORY

relative deprivation – the feelings of discontent caused by the belief that one fares poorly compared to people in other groups

Relative deprivation, meaning the discontent that is caused by the belief that one fares poorly compared to people in other groups, offers another explanation for group conflict (Ellemers & Bos, 1998; Olson, Herman, & Zanna, 1986). Derived from realistic conflict theory and frustration-aggression theory, relative deprivation theory instead emphasizes a group's perception of its circumstances. Whereas realistic conflict theory discusses actual resources that one group has and the other does not (e.g., a prize at Sherif's camp or disputed territory in Israel), relative deprivation is the perception that one has less than one is entitled to. Stated differently,

Table 10.1	EXAMPLES OF MIRROR IMAGE PERCEPTIONS ABOUT CONFLICT IN ISRAEL	

Both Palestinians and Israelis show mirror-image perception in how they view the acts which the other side initiated and those which they initiated.

INCIDENT	PERCENTAGE OF RESPONDENTS WHO BELIEVED ACT WAS TERRORISM	
	Israeli Jews	Palestinians
Acts Perpetrated by Israelis		
Assassination of Palestinian leader Abu Ali Mustafaav	19	92
Israeli police shooting of 13 Israeli Arab demonstrators	19	90
Acts Perpetrated by Palestinians		
Assassination of Israeli Minister Rechavam Zeevi	96	11
Shooting on Giloh neighbourhood by Palestinians	90	13

Source: Shamir and Shikaki (2002). Determinants of reconciliation and compromise among Israelis and Palestinians. *Journal of Peace Research, 39(2)*, 185–202.

it is the difference between the person or group's perception of reality and their expectation of what should be, with this expectation often caused by comparison with other people or groups.

This tendency can occur even in the absence of **absolute** or **realistic deprivation**, meaning when one's basic welfare needs, such as food, housing, education, and health care, are unmet. British psychologist Rupert Brown (2000) highlights the distinction between relative and realistic deprivation when he writes that "people are discontented not necessarily because they are hungry or poor, but because they are hung*rier* or poo*rer* than they believe they should be" (p. 226). As this belief is often formed by comparison with others—with one group perceiving themselves to be unfairly disadvantaged relative to another group—relative deprivation can be the basis for intergroup conflict and group protest (e.g., "They're taking our jobs"; Berkowitz, 1972).

> absolute or realistic deprivation – the belief that one's own resources are directly threatened by people in other groups

The history of relative deprivation goes back to the mid–twentieth century when Stouffer, Suchman, DeVinney, Star, and Williams (1949) conducted a large-scale study examining the attitudes and morale of the American soldier. One of the findings was that air force personnel expressed more complaints about promotion than did the military police. This was a surprising finding as the air force had more officers, including corporals and sergeants, while the military police had more privates, so the opportunity for promotion was better in the air force than the military police. Additionally, while most personnel in the air force received promotion, few in the military police did. Stouffer and colleagues argued that because most personnel in the air force received promotion, those who didn't receive promotion felt relatively deprived by comparison with others. On the other hand, because most personnel in the military police did not receive promotion, few felt deprived.

However, the theory of relative deprivation was only formally developed and proposed by James A. Davis in 1959. He argued that there are three preconditions for relative deprivation to happen: not possessing *x*, wanting *x*, and feeling entitled to *x*. In 1976, Faye Crosby expanded on Davis's work and suggested a model that included more specific preconditions under which relative deprivation is experienced. As is outlined in Figure 10.4, she proposed that for a feeling of discontent to be experienced, a person must be aware that someone else has *x*. This is an important precondition, as not being aware of *x*, it is hard to feel deprived of it. The next condition is that a person must want *x*. This condition highlights that *x* has to be valued; otherwise lack of it doesn't create deprivation. The third condition is feeling entitled to have *x*. This implies that only when a person feels that he or she deserves or has a right to *x* will the feeling of deprivation happen. For example, as Crosby notes, if you receive a D on an exam and feel that it should have been a B, you'll experience relative deprivation. On the other hand, if you feel that the D is merited, although you may feel disappointed, you're unlikely to

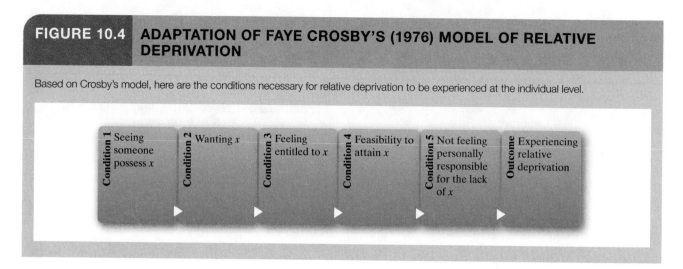

FIGURE 10.4 ADAPTATION OF FAYE CROSBY'S (1976) MODEL OF RELATIVE DEPRIVATION

Based on Crosby's model, here are the conditions necessary for relative deprivation to be experienced at the individual level.

experience relative deprivation. The fourth condition is feeling that x is attainable. If it's impossible to attain x, relative deprivation is less likely to occur. On the other hand, if it's perceived that x is obtainable, difficulty in obtaining x will lead to relative deprivation. For example, if you think it's possible to have a rock star lifestyle (vacationing in expensive locations, partying with famous people, getting exorbitant amounts of money, etc.), then in comparison to your student lifestyle you may feel deprived of a more glamorous life. However, if you don't think in those terms, thinking about a rock star lifestyle is more like wishful thinking, which won't evoke deprivation. The final condition is that of not feeling personally responsible for the lack of x. This condition highlights that the person does not assume any responsibility for not having x. If you don't blame yourself for the lack of x, you can believe yourself entitled to have x, and the lack of x as therefore unjust. You would then experience deprivation. On the other hand, if you blame yourself for not having x, you'll also believe that you don't deserve to have x, and will therefore not experience relative deprivation. It's important to note that some researchers have argued that not all preconditions are critical for relative deprivation to happen (see Taylor & Moghaddam, 1994, for a review).

The first researcher who examined the relation between relative deprivation and integroup relations (i.e., in the group context rather than that of the individual) was Walter Runciman (1966). He made a distinction between two forms of relative deprivation:

1. Fraternalistic relative deprivation refers to feeling deprived as a result of comparing the status of one's group with that of another group.
2. Egoistic relative deprivation refers to feeling deprived as a result of comparing one's status with that of similar others.

Empirical findings support the distinction between these two forms of relative deprivation and indicate that fraternalistic, not egoistic, relative deprivation is associated with intergroup attitudes and conflict (Guimond & Dubé-Simard, 1983; Vanneman & Pettigrew, 1972). Fraternalistic deprivation has been found to be the best predictor of negative attitudes of Anglo-Americans toward African Americans (Vanneman & Pettigrew, 1972), negative attitudes of Muslims toward Hindus (Tripathi & Srivastava, 1981), and separatist attitudes of French Canadians (Guimond & Dubé-Simard, 1983).

Similarly, people who experience relative deprivation have more negative attitudes toward outgroup members, as do participants who believe they're more advantaged than others (Guimond & Dambrun, 2002). Students who are told they'll have a much more difficult time finding jobs in the future are more likely to hold prejudicial attitudes toward immigrants and express stronger support for restrictive immigration policies than those who are told that finding jobs is going to be much easier in the future. These findings suggest that negative attitudes toward another group can be caused by intergroup competition for resources (in line with relative deprivation theory), but can also be used to justify the preferential treatment of one's own group.

[CONCEPTS IN CONTEXT]

INTERGROUP CONFLICT

FACTOR	EXAMPLE
Realistic conflict theory	Yaone and Mario are neighbours and have been friends for years, but their fathers have started arguing over a strip of land that links their homes. It's developing into a family feud and Yaone and Mario no longer have a good word for each other.
Relative deprivation theory	Sara, who was born in Newfoundland, feels that Canada should endorse stricter policies toward immigration. She thinks that communities in provinces of what she calls "real Canadians" are under-resourced, while resources are "thrown at" immigrant groups in the cities of the wealthier provinces.

HOW CAN INTERGROUP CONFLICT BE RESOLVED?

Although, as we have seen, there are many factors that contribute to intergroup conflict, there are fortunately many approaches that help reduce such conflict. In this section, we'll look at various strategies that can lead to conflict reduction: increasing contact between groups, GRIT (graduated and reciprocated initiatives in tension-reduction), bargaining, and integrative solutions. You should keep in mind that these strategies apply to intragroup as well as intergroup conflicts.

INCREASED INTERGROUP CONTACT

Informal contact with people from different backgrounds can be an effective strategy for reducing prejudice as it is associated with more positive feelings toward members of a variety of outgroups (Pettigrew, 1997). A variety of studies support this finding:

- Heterosexuals who have friendships with gay men have more positive attitudes toward gay men (Vonofakou, Hewstone, & Voci, 2007).
- University students who have good relationships with their grandparents have more positive attitudes toward older adults (Harwood, Hewstone, Paolini, & Voci, 2005).
- White students who are randomly assigned to a Black roommate show more positive attitudes and reduced anxiety toward Blacks than those who have a White roommate (Shook & Fazio, 2008).
- Christians who have more contact with Muslims have stronger intentions to have future contact with Muslims (including living near Muslims, marrying a Muslim, and working for a Muslim; Henry & Hardin, 2006).

Even people who *know* an in-group member who has an outgroup friend have less negative attitudes toward that group, as do those who observe an in-group–outgroup friendship (Wright, Aron, McLaughlin-Volpe, & Ropp, 1997).

Questioning the Research:

One study is described as showing that university students who have good relationships with their grandparents have more positive attitudes toward older adults. Can you think of an alternative explanation for this finding? (Hint: Does it show correlation or causation?)

Increasing contact between people from different groups doesn't necessarily reduce conflict, however. In Sherif's study of children away at camp, bringing the two groups together for activities such as a shared meal was an opportunity for further hostility between the groups. Increased contact is most likely to be beneficial when other conditions are met, including providing equal status contact, pursuing a superordinate goal that requires a contribution from both groups, and forming a common group identity. Let's look at these factors.

EQUAL STATUS CONTACT.   According to Allport's *contact hypothesis*, one of the simplest and most effective ways to resolve group conflict is to increase interaction between people in different groups (Dixon, Durrheim, & Tredoux, 2005; Gaertner et al., 1999; Slavin & Madden, 1979). However, bringing people from different groups together to interact in unequal ways, such as members of one group tutoring or working for members of another group, can maintain or increase conflict between groups. Reducing conflict between groups instead needs to involve *equal status contact*, meaning that each group member contributes to the interaction on a level playing field. By itself, however, equal status contact is sometimes not enough as it can just as easily provide an opportunity for rivalry.

SUPERORDINATE GOALS.   A more effective strategy for resolving conflict is to bring different groups together to work on a cooperative task so that the group outcome depends on the input of all members of both groups, making them interdependent. A task that requires input from the members of the different groups introduces what Sherif referred to as a **superordinate goal**. In Sherif's (1966) study, animosity between the two groups of boys was finally reduced by creating a series of problems that required cooperation among all members of both groups, making them interdependent. For example, in one case the camp truck "broke down" and the strength of everyone was needed to pull it up the hill; in another case they all had to pool their money to rent a movie they all wanted to see (there was no Netflix when Sherif did this study, making renting a movie a far more expensive proposition). Developing this type of common goal, which requires the cooperation of members of both groups, is an effective way of breaking down intergroup hostility (Gaertner et al., 1999; Slavin & Madden, 1979). It also leads to the development of a single shared group identity (i.e., the process turns two groups into one group), although these are probably what are called "nested identities," meaning when one can see oneself, in different circumstances, as a member of different groups—e.g., as a Torontonian (the Leafs against the Habs) or as a Canadian (Team Canada against the Russian national team), depending on what game is playing.

superordinate goal – a goal that can only be achieved if the members of both groups cooperate

In sum, then, contact between people in different groups is most effective in reducing prejudice when the interaction occurs between members of equal status groups who work cooperatively because they're interdependent in terms of some outcome (Desforges et al., 1997; Dixon, Durrheim, & Tredoux, 2005; Dovidio, Gaertner, & Validzic, 1998). Desforges and colleagues (1991) provides another example of this, as people who engaged in a cooperative interaction with a person who they believed was formerly a patient hospitalized for psychiatric illness subsequently adopted more positive, less prejudiced attitudes toward people who were once psychiatric patients.

Contact with people from different groups is especially beneficial in terms of positive intergroup relations when people see this contact as personally relevant, valuable, and important (van Dick et al., 2004). People who see intergroup contact as important in helping them broaden their horizons and gain insight into other cultures experience a greater reduction in prejudice from having this contact than people who don't see value in such contact. In other words, reducing prejudice occurs not just through having acquaintances from outgroups, but through seeing the presence of these outgroup colleagues (or even friends) as important to oneself.

FORM A COMMON GROUP IDENTITY.   In Sherif's studies, after several failed attempts at reducing hostility, it was the introduction of superordinate goals that finally brought the groups together. In real conflict, one cannot make the camp truck break down, but finding common ground between two groups can lead to a reduction in conflict (Cohen & Insko, 2008; Gaertner et al., 1999; Slavin & Madden, 1979; Swaab, Postmes, Beest, & Spears, 2007). For example, countries that are at odds with each other may realize they can work together on common goals, such as the safety of their citizens, the management of terrorism, and the reduction of the threat of nuclear war (Rubin, 1989). Canadian researchers Michael Wohl from Carleton University and Nyla Branscombe, now at the University of Kansas, examined how increasing the inclusiveness of group categorizations (from ethnic group identity to human identity as one's group) leads to greater forgiveness (Wohl & Branscombe, 2005). The researchers asked Jewish university students to reflect on one of two statements. In one condition, students thought about the Holocaust as an event in which the Germans behaved aggressively toward Jews. In the other condition, students thought about the Holocaust as an event in which some people behaved aggressively toward other people. Participants then rated their willingness to forgive Germans for the Holocaust. As predicted, Jewish students who reflected on the Holocaust as an event that involved aggression by some people toward other people were much more willing to forgive Germans for this tragedy than Jewish students who reflected on the Holocaust as an event that involved aggression by German people toward Jewish people. In other words, seeing the aggressors and victims as having a shared identity lessened Jewish students' hostility toward the aggressors' other identity, that of being German.

Common ground, like a superordinate goal, is a step toward a common group identity. As described by Gaertner and Dovidio's **common in-group identity model**, when group members believe they have a shared identity (a sense of belonging that encompasses both groups), a reduction in prejudice is more likely (Gaertner et al., 1999; Gaertner, Mann, Dovidio, Murrell, & Pomare, 1990; Gaertner, Mann, Murrell, & Dovidio, 1989). A sports team in Montreal with a unique roster provides a real-life example. Featured on the front page of one of Canada's national newspapers, the team came together to share their "common love" for "Canada's game" (Peritz, 2010). What makes this roster of hockey players so special? The founder of the team, Khalid Mrini, a businessman from Morocco who lives in Montreal, had the idea of launching a hockey team recruiting the best Moroccan ex-pat players from all over the world, whether they were Muslim or Jewish. The coach and about one-third of the 15 players are Jewish and the others, including the captain, are Muslim. In an interview, Mrini said, "We don't have weapons, we have sweat. And whether your name is Eli or Mohammed doesn't matter, you're going to embrace after you score a goal." The common bond (i.e., the love of hockey and their team—which is what gives them a shared identity and a superordinate common goal) between these two religious groups led the teammates to their harmonious relationship.

Simply emphasizing a superordinate category can reduce biases (Hornsey & Hogg, 2000). Creating a superordinate category is a recategorization of original categories in an attempt to reduce subgroup divisions. For example, the division between some religious groups could be de-emphasized by creating a superordinate identity that unites the religious groups based on a common group identity such as world peace, environmental protection, or family protection.

One example of such recategorization was a worldwide demonstration that happened in early 2009 against the Israeli government in response to the military conflict in the Gaza Strip. During the three-week war that began in late December 2008 between Israel and Palestine, more than 1300 Palestinians and 13 Israelis were killed. Some 4,000 homes were also destroyed or badly

common in-group identity model – a reduction in prejudice is more likely when group members believe they have a shared identity

WireImage/Getty Images, Ltd
Chromeo is an electro funk music duo from Montreal. The two childhood friends jokingly refer to themselves as "the only successful Arab/Jewish partnership since the dawn of human culture."

FIGURE 10.5 FORMING A NEW GROUP WITH CROSS-CATEGORICAL MEMBERSHIP

damaged, leaving tens of thousands of people homeless (BBC, 2010; United Nations, 2009). Reaction to the conflict, in this instance, was not simply a continuation of the tension between Muslims and Jews, or Arabs and Israelis. When some Jewish groups participated in these demonstrations, carrying signs such as, "Jews against the war on Gaza," a different identity, although provisional, was given to the same dispute that typically divided Muslim and Jewish groups. The new common identity that united these groups in protest was based on upholding human rights and opposing war.

S. Safdar

By creating a superordinate goal that crosses categories, groups are more likely to be united.

Similarly, in fostering conflict some religious leaders emphasize the division between groups and stress categorization. A videotaped statement of Osama Bin Laden (1998) encouraging Jihad against Americans provides an extreme example: "The ruling to kill Americans and their allies—civilians and military—is an individual duty for every Muslim who can do it in any country in which it is possible to do it . . . We—with God's help—call on every Muslim who believes in God and wishes to be rewarded to comply with God's order to kill Americans and plunder their money whenever and wherever they find it. God willing, America's end is near." These words of hatred reflect, among other things, categorical thinking that attempts to create problematic subgroup divisions. For people like Bin Laden, contrary to reality, Americans and Muslims are two independent categories with no common characteristics. In fact there are as many Muslims in the U.S. as there are in the country of Oman, some 2.5 million as of 2009 (Pew Research Center, 2009). As Figure 10.5 shows, recategorization creates distinctive identities that can encourage cooperation rather than division.

GRIT (graduated and reciprocated initiatives in tension-reduction) – a strategy for resolving conflict that involves unilateral and persistent efforts to establishing trust and cooperation between opposing parties

GRIT STRATEGY

The strategy known as **GRIT** (which stands for graduated and reciprocated initiatives in tension-reduction) refers to a particular approach to resolving conflict that involves unilateral and persistent efforts in order to establish trust and cooperation between opposing parties (Linskold & Han, 1988; Osgood, 1962). In this case, one party announces its intention to reduce conflict, and invites the other party to reciprocate. Then the first party carries out its tension-reducing activities as planned, even if there is no immediate response. This increases the party's credibility and may put pressure on the other party to respond accordingly. Once the other party acts, the first party quickly reciprocates. If the other party retaliates, the first party then quickly retaliates *at the same level*.

Participants who use the GRIT strategy are more likely to reach optimal agreements and feel differently about their interaction partner than those who use competitive strategies. In one study, 90 percent of those who used this strategy reached an agreement, compared to 65 percent of those in a typical competitive interaction (Lindskold & Han, 1988). Participants who use GRIT also reach agreements faster and form more positive expectations regarding future interactions.

One of the most dramatic and effective examples of GRIT was in the late 1980s when, after decades of cold war and fruitless arms reduction talks, Soviet President Mikhail Gorbachev began a process of unilateral arms reduction in the USSR and its satellite countries and waited for the West to respond. Another real-world example of the use of GRIT comes from the peace process in Northern Ireland starting in the 1990s where, in the particularly troubled city of Derry (in terms of bombings and killings), a local community group fostered small unilateral steps by the British security forces and the IRA (a paramilitary group who regarded themselves as being at war with the British government over the status of Northern Ireland as part of the United Kingdom). This involved, at an early point, drawing up a list of moves that either side could make as they began to trust the other's intentions: for example, the army could stop indiscriminate house searches through a whole area, while the IRA could stop taking over people's homes as hiding places to ambush soldiers. Over a period of years, trust developed between the sides that they were serious about wanting to reduce conflict and violence in Derry decreased to a fraction of its former level (Lampen & Lampen, 2009).

© Crispin Rodwell
www.crispinrodwell.com

BARGAINING

Bargaining means seeking an agreement through direct negotiation between both sides in a conflict, and is commonly used to resolve conflict. When you're buying a car or a house, you often negotiate the price, with each side having opposing goals (i.e., you want to pay less, while the seller wants to receive more). Bargaining is difficult because you need to strike the right balance between being tough (and getting the other side to compromise) and being reasonable (not suggesting a price that is so low that the other party walks away).

People who appear tough during negotiations are more likely to secure a good deal. In one study, participants acted as sellers negotiating the price and warranty of cell phones with a buyer (van Kleef, De Dreu, & Manstead, 2004). In some cases, participants were told that the buyer was very angry, having supposedly said, "This is a ridiculous offer—it really pisses me off." In other cases, participants were told that the buyer seemed happy with the offer, having supposedly said, "This is going pretty well; I can't complain." Researchers then measured how information about the buyers' moods influenced participants' negotiating demands. As predicted, participants who believed the buyer was angry offered better prices than those who believed the buyer was happy.

One problem with using bargaining to resolve conflict is that people who misrepresent their needs can gain a real advantage in bargaining situations (O'Connor & Carnevale, 1997; Schweitzer, DeChurch, & Gibson, 2005; Steinel & De Dreu, 2004). People who misrepresent their own motives can trick others into making bad decisions—decisions that hurt themselves and advantage the other person. For example, a parent whose sole motivation is to pay low alimony may pretend to want full custody as a way of then compromising on custody to get lower

bargaining – a very commonly used approach to resolving conflict at an individual level, whereby an agreement is sought through direct negotiation between both sides in the conflict

mediation – a particular type of bargaining in which a neutral third party tries to resolve a conflict by facilitating communication between the opposing parties and offering suggestions

arbitration – resolution of a conflict by a neutral third party who studies both sides and imposes a settlement

alimony. This may lead the other parent to fight for custody and potentially negotiate toward lower alimony. About 28 percent of people in negotiations misrepresent what they want, and these people tend to get better outcomes. However, the overall joint outcome is better when both people are honest.

The Business Connections box describes two other approaches to resolving conflict: **mediation**, in which a neutral third party tries to resolve a conflict by facilitating communication and offering suggestions, and **arbitration**, in which a neutral third party studies both sides and then imposes a settlement.

BUSINESS CONNECTIONS

Using Mediation and Arbitration to Resolve Conflict

Mediation is a commonly used strategy for resolving conflict between labour and management in business disputes (Brett, Goldberg, & Ury, 1990; Emery & Wyer, 1987; Shapiro & Brett, 1993). Mediators first help parties rethink the conflict so that they understand the costs of continuing it (e.g., people will lose their jobs; businesses will lose money) and the benefits of ending the conflict. Mediators also try to decrease misperceptions, and help people on the opposing sides find common ground, or find superordinate goals that everyone wants to achieve. Because a key factor in successful mediation is trust between the parties, a mediator can be useful in getting each side to identify and rank its goals, and then ideally reach a compromise. Because the use of a mediator can lead to greater flexibility and perspective-taking, as well as collaboration (e.g., seeing the conflict as a joint problem that must be solved), this approach can often lead to beneficial outcomes for both parties.

© Mike Flanagan/www.CartoonStock.com

As in mediation, arbitration uses a neutral third party to help two sides reach an agreement. However, unlike mediation, in arbitration the third party studies both sides and then imposes a settlement (Lind, Kanfer, & Early, 1990). People are generally less satisfied with arbitration than mediation because each party has little control over the outcome. A recent example was the Canadian postal strike in June 2011, in which the government passed a bill that ordered postal workers back to work pending the outcome of arbitration. The Canadian Union of Postal Workers, however, said the legislation was unfair because it imposed a wage increase that was lower than Canada Post's last offered. The legislation also imposed a selection process where each side provides their final offer and the arbitrator selects one in its entirety rather than finding a middle ground (Campion-Smith, 2011). Ultimately, Canada Post workers were dissatisfied with this form of arbitration as their key issues were not addressed.

Mediation tends to produce better results than arbitration. One study found that 77 percent of those who participated in mediation to resolve a dispute were satisfied with the procedure, compared to 45 percent of those who used arbitration (Brett & Goldberg, 1983). This greater satisfaction is due in part to people's ability to help control and develop the outcome of mediation decisions. However, combining these two strategies can be an effective way of resolving disputes. In some cases people first use mediation, and then follow with arbitration if an agreement is not reached (McGillicuddy, Welton, & Pruitt, 1987). This approach leads to more problem-solving and less competition and hostility than straight mediation, where negotiation just ends if an agreement is not reached.

INTEGRATIVE SOLUTIONS

An **integrative solution** is a negotiated resolution to a conflict. All parties obtain outcomes that are superior to what they would have obtained from an equal division of the contested resources (De Dreu, Koole, & Steinel, 2000). Although it seems as if this approach would be relatively easy to reach, because both parties benefit, misperceptions often hinder such agreements. One review of research found that in over 20 percent of negotiations that could have resulted in integrative agreements, the participants agreed to terms that were worse for each.

Imagine that you're negotiating the terms for a new job and you're more interested in vacation time than a big salary. When you're dissatisfied with the offer that the company proposes, you suggest a compromise of what you prefer. Instead of suggesting two additional vacation weeks and no salary increase, you suggest a small increase in salary and one additional vacation week. Why didn't you suggest your preference? Because you believe the company wouldn't agree to such terms, even though you don't know what the company really wants and it might in fact prefer this option but mistakenly assume that you would prefer a higher salary. When the company agrees to your suggested compromise, both you and the company end up less satisfied than if you had agreed on the three extra vacation days and no salary increase (the integrative solution).

How can integrative agreements be reached? One of the best ways is by letting both sides honestly discuss their goals and needs (Swaab et al., 2007; Thompson & Hrebec, 1996; Thompson, Peterson, & Brodt, 1996). Through open communication and trying to understand the other party's point of view, people may come to see that there are opportunities for joint benefits. Although we often think that what we want is very clear, sometimes these goals are not so obvious to the other side (Vorauer & Claude, 1998). In fact, people often fail to realize that they have compatible interests and settle for a choice that is worse for both (e.g., a lose-lose agreement) simply because they don't share information. This failure to recognize the possibility of integrative solutions is particularly likely when people negotiate under time pressure, and thus focus more on the immediate consequences of a negotiation than the longer-term outcomes (Henderson, Trope, & Carnevale, 2006).

Another factor that can lead to integrative agreements is perspective-taking, meaning understanding the viewpoint of the other side (Galinsky, Maddux, Gilin, & White, 2008). People who are better at perspective-taking, such as those who agree with the statement "I believe that there are two sides to every question and try to look at them both," are more likely to reach creative agreements that benefit both sides.

Finally, another strategy for resolving conflict (one that is perhaps too often overlooked) is to apologize. By apologizing, people publicly acknowledge that their behaviour was wrong (according to a value system that is reaffirmed by the apology) and caused harm. They also indicate an intention to repair a relationship that has been threatened by their actions and, especially if their victims accept the apologies, they reduce their blame (Schleien, Ross, H. & Ross, M., 2010). There is a stereotype that women apologize more than men, but is this really the case? Karina Schumann and Michael Ross (2010) found, using daily diaries, that women did indeed report making more apologies than men. However, they also reported more transgressions that required an apology. Compared to men, therefore, women in fact did not apologize for a greater proportion of reported transgressions. Rather than suggesting that men commit fewer transgressions than women, however, Schumann and Ross hypothesized that men have a higher threshold for what they judge to be offensive enough to require an apology. In a separate study, they therefore asked participants to rate both imaginary and recalled examples of offensive behaviour in terms of their offensiveness (Schumann & Ross, 2010). As Schumann and Ross had hypothesized they would, men rated the offences as less severe than women did.

Research from the University of Waterloo looked at apologies in sibling disagreements among young children (Schleien, Ross, & Ross, 2010). The researchers coded apologies in

integrative solution – a negotiated resolution to a conflict in which all parties obtain outcomes that are superior to what they would have obtained from an equal division of the contested resources

40 families when children were 2 1/2 and 4 1/2 years old, and again two years later. They found that, at these young ages, sibling apologies were rare, generally simple in form, and more frequent after physical harm than after rights violations or verbal harms. Spontaneous apologies were more frequent than apologies mandated by parents, and spontaneous apologies increased with age, as did reconciliation following apologies. By age 6, children reacted more favourably to spontaneous apologies than to parent-mandated apologies, demonstrating their sensitivity to this one indicator of the apologizer's sincerity. Even as young as 6 years, a sincere apology can lead to reconciliation.

[CONCEPTS IN CONTEXT]

STRATEGIES FOR RESOLVING INTERGROUP CONFLICT

FACTOR	EXAMPLE
Increased intergroup contact	The president of the University of Istanbul brought opposing student groups, which included the Kurds and the Turks, together to lobby for a new student centre.
GRIT	In an effort to reach out to his grumpy neighbour, Daryl makes the first effort to be friendly. When his neighbour responds with a similarly friendly gesture, Daryl quickly reciprocates by engaging in yet another friendly outreach.
Bargaining	Igor is trying to negotiate a price for a new car from a car dealer. In order to secure the best deal, he suggests a price that is lower than what he thinks the dealer will accept, but not so low that she doesn't take him seriously.
Integrative solutions	Two sisters are fighting over an orange. Their father (with the wisdom of Solomon) cuts it in half and gives half the orange to each of his daughters. This is a compromise solution, but if he had asked why they wanted it he could have come to a more integrative solution that better served both their wishes: one wanted to eat the flesh, but the other only wanted the peel for baking cookies.

HOW DOES CULTURE RELATE TO INTERGROUP RELATIONS?

As we have seen in previous chapters, people from collectivistic and individualistic societies differ on many dimensions. Culture influences the way people define themselves (i.e., as having an interdependent vs. independent self) and the significance attributed to in-groups versus outgroups. Culture also influences norms and values (e.g., cooperation vs. competition, or conformity vs. independence). Consequently, culture and its important dimension of collectivism/individualism relate to positive and negative intergroup relations.

People from collectivistic societies make a strong distinction between their group and other groups, us versus them, in-group versus outgroup (Triandis & Trafimow, 2001). Collectivists define themselves as part of the in-group and are more likely to cooperate with the in-group (Altocchi & Altocchi, 1995). Because the focus in collectivistic societies is on the in-group, it is "natural" in such societies to dislike and avoid outsiders (Triandis & Trafimow, 2001, p. 378; Triandis & Triandis, 1962; Triandis, 1972).

This pattern of thinking isn't acceptable in individualistic societies, where it is viewed as prejudice, and assumed that prejudice is a bad thing. The view instead from an individualistic perspective is that attention should be paid to personal characteristics rather than group memberships. As people from individualistic societies define themselves more as individuals than as members of a group, the difference between in-groups and outgroups is less sharply defined (Triandis & Trafimow, 2001).

Compared to people from individualistic societies, people from collectivistic societies pay less attention to individual attributes and they see members of in- and outgroups as homogeneous (Triandis, McCusker, & Hui, 1990; Triandis & Trafimow, 2001). Therefore, people are more likely to engage in intergroup rather than interpersonal relations in many situations. On the other hand, people from individualistic societies focus on individual attributes and emphasize the uniqueness of individuals. They're more likely to see members of their group as relatively heterogeneous, although they do still see their outgroup as relatively homogeneous (Triandis, McCusker, & Hui, 1990; Triandis & Trafimow, 2001). This means that individualists engage in both interpersonal and intergroup relations depending on the situation (Triandis & Trafimow, 2001). To put it another way, everyone engages in both interpersonal and intergroup behaviour, but collectivists have a greater tendency toward intergroup interactions across more situations.

It has also been suggested that collectivists are more likely to engage in ethnocentrism than individualists (Lee & Ward, 1998; Triandis & Trafimow, 2001). Ethnocentrism refers to the tendency to believe that one's ethnic or cultural group is preferable and that all other groups should be evaluated in relation to one's ethnicity. In a study with Thai, Indian, and Chinese participants, researchers from Chulalongkorn University in Thailand found that regardless of nationality those who were more collectivistic also showed a tendency to be more ethnocentric (Kongsompong, Powtong, & Sen, 2010). This tendency is also found in people who are more collectivistic but living in predominantly individualistic societies, as they also show more ethnocentrism. Yoo & Donthu (2005) found this tendency toward ethnocentrism expressed in consumer choices in relation to Japanese products, where there was a correlation with collectivism among U.S. consumers.

RESEARCH FOCUS ON NEUROSCIENCE
The Link between Culture and the Brain

Culture provides members of a society with guidelines about the appropriate way to understand and behave within their society (Hofstede, 2001). The brain's plasticity, however, makes it extremely likely that culture and the brain's neural processes are interwoven, rather than culture being something purely outside the individual. Cultural practices are constrained by our neural abilities, while at the same time our brain adapts to cultural practices (Ambady & Bharucha, 2009).

Advances in theoretical and methodological approaches in three fields have allowed neuroscientists to begin exploring the bidirectional interactions between culture and biology: cultural psychology, human neuroscience, and molecular science (Chiao et al., 2010). Cultural psychology has developed theories and methods for identifying cultural traits that characterize the diversity seen in social groups around the world (Norenzayan & Heine, 2005). Human neuroscience has developed techniques for mapping neural processes related to psychological processes (Handy, 2005). Finally, molecular genetics has developed techniques for understanding the association between variability in single genes and genome-wide maps as they relate to neural, mental, and cultural processes (Chiao et al., 2010).

Having mapped the human genome, scientific evidence indicates that only 0.2 to 0.4 percent of the genome varies across individuals (Tishkoff & Kidd, 2004). Nevertheless, cultural variation is evident in the observed frequencies of common variants and polymorphisms (multi-gene traits). As individuals adapt to their environment, they develop and use cultural traits, which over time are refined by cognitive and neural responses to the environment, thus creating culturally determined neurobiology (Boyd & Richerson, 1985).

A recent study by Chiao and Blizinsky (2010) examined data compiled from 124 peer-reviewed publications on 50,135 individuals living in 29 countries. Using Hofstede's individualism–collectivism cultural dimension, these researchers examined the frequencies of alleles (or gene variants) of 5-HTTLPR (a polymorphic region that relates to the transportation of serotonin in the gene that codes for how serotonin is transported in the brain). Polymorphism (or variation) for 5-HTTLPR has been linked to many neuropsychiatric disorders. The researchers found that collectivistic cultures were significantly more likely to be comprised of individuals carrying the short allele of 5-HTTLPR, which has been related to decreased frequencies of anxiety and mood disorders. These researchers suggest that collectivistic values increase social harmony (at least with one's in-group members) and encourage giving social support to others (again, within the in-group) in order to lower the prevalence of chronic life stress that may trigger negative emotions and psychopathology (Chiao & Blizinsky, 2010).

GROUP CONFLICT

Culture also influences how individuals view the causes of conflict and which strategies they use to resolve conflict. In one study, researchers asked both American and Chinese students to read several hypothetical scenarios involving conflict (e.g., a mother-daughter disagreement, a decision to go to school or have fun; Peng & Nisbett, 1999). Then, the participants rated how they would resolve the situation. Seventy-four percent of Americans gave an answer that assigned blame exclusively to one side. In contrast, only 28 percent of the Chinese people responded in a way that assigned fault to one side.

Two studies suggest that Canadians might be good compromisers. In a comparison of Turks and Canadians conducted by researchers from York University, Turks reported refraining from conflict, postponing conflict, and employing persuasion to a greater extent than did Canadians, whereas Canadians were more likely to compromise, appeal to third-party assistance, and give priority to the other party in the conflict (Cingöz-Ulu & Lalonde, 2007). Similarly, Zhenzhong Ma from the University of Windsor found that Chinese people used avoidance more often as an approach to resolve conflicts in the workplace than Canadians, who used a more compromising approach (Ma, 2007).

Does the ability to see both sides in a conflict lead people in collectivistic cultures to achieve better resolutions to conflict? In a word, yes. Participants from the United States and Hong Kong participated in two-party negotiations (Arunachalam, Wall, & Chan, 1998). Hong Kong negotiators achieved higher joint outcomes as well as higher individual outcomes than American negotiators. Similarly, research examining differences in decision-making strategies used by managers in the United States, Japan, and Hong Kong indicates that Japanese leaders are more willing to listen to different perspectives on a problem than Americans (Cosier, Schwenk, & Dalton, 1992). In addition, compared to American leaders, Japanese leaders tend to exert less control over the decision-making process, which in turn, leads to better decision-making.

Cultural differences may also influence the effectiveness of negotiations between people from different cultures. Because people from individualistic and collectivistic cultures may vary in the assumptions they make about others' perspectives, these misunderstandings could make it difficult to reach a compromise (Kimmel, 1994). People from individualistic cultures typically assume that others see negotiation as a business activity, as primarily a form of verbal communication, and that time and deadlines are important. On the other hand, those from collectivistic cultures, such as people in Asia and the Middle East, may see negotiation as a social activity that is built on a trusting relationship, that communication is often nonverbal, and that because building a relationship takes time, deadlines are not particularly important. In line with this view, Asians pay less attention to verbal expressions and more attention to nonverbal expressions than do Americans (Ambady, Koo, Lee, & Rosenthal, 1996; Ishii, Reyes, & Kitayama, 2003; Markus & Kitayama, 1991).

People in different cultures also vary in the extent to which they focus on verbal content versus verbal tone (Ishii, Reyes, & Kitayama, 2003). In one study with Americans and Japanese, Americans had more trouble ignoring vocal content than vocal tone, showing that

Americans focus more on content (e.g., see it as more important, relevant, etc.). In contrast, Japanese people showed greater difficulty ignoring vocal tone than verbal content. This different preference can lead to misunderstandings when information in cultures is conveyed in different ways. Think about the numerous ways you could say the word "yes"—with great excitement (Yes!), resignation (yes...), confusion (yes?). If an English speaker from an individualistic society relies on content more than tone, all these variants of yes would be largely understood in the same way. In contrast, if a non-English speaker from a collectivistic society relies more on tone, he or she would ignore the verbal content, and interpret the tone of the answer in very different ways.

ACCULTURATION

The contemporary world is characterized by people moving from one cultural context to another. People move from rural to urban settings, from one city to another, or from one nation to another. People move for a variety of reasons, including war, poverty, education, work, and personal reasons such as love, illness, or duty. Immigrants generally experience difficulties in their journey. The psychological study of immigrants and immigration has been an important area of investigation, particularly in recent years, and is formally called the study of acculturation (Smith, Bond, & Kagitcibasi, 2006).

One of the well-accepted definitions of acculturation was offered by three anthropologists in the 1950s. According to this definition, **acculturation** is what happens "when groups of individuals having different cultures come into continuous first hand contact, with subsequent changes in the original cultural pattern of either or both groups" (Redfield, Linton, & Herskovits, 1936, p. 149). Given that acculturation involves at least two groups that are in contact, the topic of acculturation is considered to be within the realm of intergroup relations (Liebkind, 2001).

acculturation – behavioural and psychological changes that happen when groups of individuals having different cultures come into continuous first hand contact.

Who's Who in Contemporary Canadian Social Psychology Research

Courtesy John W. Berry

John W. Berry is a professor Emeritus at Queen's University in Kingston, Ontario. He received his PhD from the University of Edinburgh. Professor Berry's current research interests are focused on the psychology of intercultural relations, including acculturation, immigration, and multiculturalism. Professor Berry is the recipient of many honorary awards, including Doctorat Honoris Causa from the University of Geneva and Doctor Honoris Causa from the University of Athens. He is also an honorary professor at Inner Mongolian Normal University, Hohot, and at Northwest Normal University, Lanzhou, both in China.

The two main models of acculturation examine the topic either as a linear process or in terms of cultural pluralism. The linear process is based on the assumption that as individuals learn the values and behaviours of a new culture, they lose their original cultural values and behaviours (Berry, 1997; Nguyen, Messe, & Stollak, 1999; Sayegh & Lasry, 1993). This is a unidirectional model, which is also equated with assimilation (Nguyen et al., 1999). The cultural pluralism model is based on the assumption that members of an ethnic group can maintain their heritage culture while also adapting to the mainstream society (Berry, 1997; Laroche, Kim, Hui, & Tomiuk, 1998). This is a bi-dimensional model as it recognizes that members of ethnic groups may maintain their heritage culture in varying degrees and also adopt the new culture in varying degrees.

FIGURE 10.6 **VARIETIES OF INTERCULTURAL STRATEGIES IN IMMIGRANT GROUPS AND IN THE RECEIVING SOCIETY**

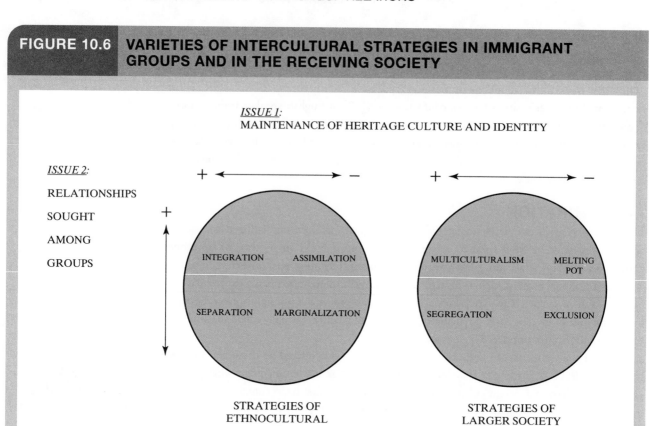

Source: Berry, J.W. (2001). A psychology of immigration. *Journal of Social Issues, 57,* 615–631.

John Berry, a Canadian psychologist from Queen's University, is a key contributor to research on the bi-dimensional acculturation model. In an impressive line of work, Berry (2001; 2003) has proposed and validated four acculturation strategies based on the two dimensions. According to Berry, there are two focal questions to which immigrants and newcomers to any society have to respond. The first is how much one values maintaining one's original cultural identity and characteristics. The second is how much one values contact and participation with another group (i.e., the larger society). If the answer to both of these questions is highly, the individual wants **integration**, defined as the tendency to maintain one's own culture and also participate in the larger society. If the answer to the first question is highly and the answer to the second question is very little, the individual desires **separation**, defined as the tendency to maintain one's own culture but to reject, or not participate in, the larger society. If the answer to the first question is very little and the answer to the second question is highly, the individual desires **assimilation**, defined as the tendency to abandon one's original culture and participate in the larger society. Lastly, if the answers to both questions are very little, the individual is opting for **marginalization**, defined as the tendency to neither maintain one's own culture nor participate in the larger society. Figure 10.6 shows these acculturation strategies: the left side shows the perspective of immigrant groups, and the right side shows the perspective of the receiving society.

It is important to note that immigrants and non-dominant cultural groups do not always have a choice in how they acculturate. The acculturation strategies of ethnic groups are constrained by what the dominant group endorses (Berry & Safdar, 2007). For example, it has been found that when Greeks emigrate, although they lose part of their family values, this loss is less extensive in Canada, where multiculturalism is the official policy, than in Europe, where assimilationist policies are predominant (Georgas, Berry, Shaw, Christakopoulou, & Mylonas,

integration – the tendency to maintain one's own culture and also participate in the larger society

separation – the tendency to maintain one's own culture but to reject, or not participate in, the larger society

assimilation – the tendency to abandon one's original culture and participate in the larger society

marginalization – the tendency to neither maintain one's own culture nor participate in the larger society

1996). Therefore, in examining the above acculturation strategies, it's important to understand the policies and restrictions that the national society imposes on immigrants. Integration, for example, can only be successful when the larger society is accepting of its immigrants' cultures (Berry 2001; Phinney, Berry, Vedder, & Liebkind, 2006).

When integration is sought by the larger society, multiculturalism is the result that represents a strategy of "mutual accommodation" (Berry, 2001, p. 620). When assimilation is sought by the larger society, the melting pot is a representation of the larger society enforcing its values. When separation is demanded by the larger society, segregation is the result as it involves limited contact with minorities and immigrants. Finally, when marginalization is imposed by the larger society, exclusion is the outcome and involves systematic exclusion of a group from having rights and opportunities (Berry 2001; Phinney et al, 2006).

Overall, the results of many studies indicate that integration is the most adaptive strategy and marginalization the least adaptive strategy, while assimilation and separation are intermediate acculturation strategies (Berry, 1997; Berry & Sabatier, 2010; Scottham & Dias, 2010). For example, Phinney, Chavira, and Williamson (1992) found that among high school and university students integration was positively associated with self-esteem and assimilation was negatively related to self-esteem. The authors argued that their results are consistent with the social identity theory in that rejecting one's heritage culture has a negative influence on one's self-esteem. Similarly, in a large cross-cultural study of immigrant youth, it was found that integration was positively related to psychological adaptation (i.e., higher self-esteem, higher life satisfaction, and lower psychological problems) and sociocultural adaptation (i.e., school adjustment and lower behavioural problems; Vedder, van de Vijver, & Liebkind, 2006). However, other researchers, including Floyd Rudmin (2003), a Canadian researcher currently at the University of Tromso in Norway, have criticized Berry's model, arguing that there is no clear evidence that integration is the most adaptive acculturation strategy.

In sum, research on the acculturation of immigrants indicates that in order to increase immigrants' success in their new society and reduce intergroup conflict, it is important to accept cultural diversity and have an "even playing-field" for all groups in the larger society (Berry, 1997).

BURKA   NIQAB   HIJAB   ASSIMILATION

Anthony Jenkins - The Globe and Mail/ The Canadian Press

HEALTH CONNECTIONS

Being Alive Well

When you think about health or being healthy, do you think about not being ill? Is absence of disease an indication of health? If your answer is yes, this is a biomedical view of health and is often how North Americans perceive themselves as healthy. For many Western cultural groups, the perception of being healthy is related to medicine and biological fitness (Crawford, 1985, 1994; Lupton, 1995). The Western perspective of health is very much about the body, about the image of the body, and the exercise regimen we put our body through. Do you think this perception of health is shared in other cultures? Adelson (1998) asked this exact question of the Cree (Iyiyuu) of Whapmagoostui (Great Whale River), located approximately 1,400 kilometres north of Montreal, Quebec, in the subarctic Canadian boreal forest.

For the Cree of Whapmagoostui, there is no word that means health, at least not in the way that North Americans use the word. Instead, the Cree people use the word *miyupimaatisiiun*, which translates to "being alive well" and is a much more inclusive concept. "Being alive well" is different from "health" as it goes beyond the biomedical sense of health and is instead a statement of how one lives, performs his or her activities, interacts with others, and accomplishes his or her goals. "Being alive well" is also strongly related to Cree food, *iyiyuumiichim*.

When asking about someone's health, a Cree adult would most likely reflect on his or her relationship to the land and animals. One might hear that this person "is eating well." This response is more complex than one might assume as it implies that one has been eating bush food. Bush food is food gathered from the land, not the grocery store. As such, it means that this person has had a good hunting season, which in turn implies that he or she has the physical strength, skills, and ability required to hunt and prepare the meat and hides. In this manner, being healthy or "being alive well" speaks to ideals that can only be enacted through all that which is immediately understood as "being Cree" (Adelson, 1998, p. 17). In sum, among the Cree people, health, in addition to being about lack of illness, is about the quality of one's connections with members of the in-group and the environment, expressing a different, more collectivistic set of values than the dominant North American society's values.

Leigh Turner (2005) from McGill University argues that different conceptions of health can lead to important misunderstandings when patients from one cultural context encounter a doctor from another. The importance of culturally sensitive health care is increasingly recognized and programs attempting to provide culturally sensitive health care represent examples of cultural adaptation from the dominant society (in this case Canadian health-care providers); but they are also aimed at promoting cultural adaptation on the part of the patient from another culture (native or migrant). Making health-care services more sensitive to cultural differences is a positive step as it increases people's use of those services.

© Megapress / Alamy
Cree elders cooking traditional wild game.

THE BIG PICTURE

INTERGROUP RELATIONS

This chapter included many applications of the three "big ideas" studied in social psychology. The examples below should help you see the connection between intergroup relations and these big ideas, and contribute to your understanding of the big picture of social psychology.

THEME	EXAMPLES
The social world influences how we think about ourselves.	• People in a crowd, although they may lose some personal identity, adopt (if only temporarily) a stronger sense of social identity. • People can feel good about themselves by calling attention to their connection to successful people or groups. • People who feel their identity is threatened in some way often act in a hostile way toward members of other groups, presumably in an attempt to increase their own feelings of self-worth.
The social world influences our thoughts, attitudes, and behaviour.	• When people are in large groups, they're less likely to follow normal rules of behaviour. • Individuals who have the social identity of being an environmental activists are more likely to perform pro-environmental behaviours, such as willingness to pay more for environmental products. • Heterosexuals who have friendships with gay men have more positive attitudes toward gay men.
Our attitudes and behaviour shape the social world around us.	• As a result of individuals' self-interest motives in terms of competition for jobs, land, and power, animosity between different groups could develop. • When a group of people perceive themselves to be unfairly disadvantaged relative to another group, intergroup conflict and group protest may happen. • Contact between people in different groups reduces prejudice when the interaction occurs between members of equal status groups who work cooperatively to achieve a shared outcome

WHAT YOU'VE LEARNED

This chapter examined intergroup relations in terms of social identity theory and cultural factors. Factors that lead to group conflicts and approaches to reduce conflict were also discussed.

1. What factors influence the behaviour of people in a crowd?

One of the earliest theories of crowd behaviour described three characteristics that are associated with crowds: anonymity, suggestibility, and contagion. According to the theory of deindividuation, when people are in large groups, they're less likely to follow normal rules of behaviour. This is due to decreased self-awareness, anonymity, and lack of accountability.

2. How does social identity theory contribute to understanding group relations?

According to social identity theory, people have individual and social identities. Social identity is based on group membership. When people become a member of a group, the group membership becomes salient, and it is their group goal and group identity that regulates their behaviour. You also learned why derogating the outgroup can make you feel better both about your group and yourself.

3. What factors lead to intergroup conflicts?

Conflict between groups happens when people are competing for resources (i.e., realistic conflict theory) or when they perceive that their circumstances are deteriorating (i.e., relative deprivation theory). You also learned that when students are told that they'll have a much harder time finding jobs in the future they're more likely to hold negative attitudes toward immigrants than students who are told that finding jobs is going to be much easier in the future.

4. How can we reduce intergroup conflict?

There are several approaches that lead to reductions of intergroup conflict. These include increasing intergroup contact on an equal status basis, forming common goals, and recategorization. Other approaches include the GRIT strategy, bargaining, and integrative solutions. You also learned that when group members believe they have a shared identity (a sense of belonging that encompasses both groups), they're less likely to view members of the other group negatively.

5. How does culture relate to intergroup relations?

Culture influences people's perceptions of themselves, groups, and people's norms and values. Culture also influences the importance that people give to distinctions between their in-group and outgroups. It has been suggested that people from collectivistic societies are more likely to engage in ethnocentrism than people from individualistic societies. Additionally, conflict is viewed and resolved differently by people with different cultural backgrounds. You also learned about the bi-dimensional acculturation model and four acculturation strategies.

Key Terms

absolute/realistic deprivation 335
acculturation 347
arbitration 342
assimilation 348
bargaining 341
common in-group identity model 339
deindividuation 324

GRIT 340
integration 348
integrative solution 343
intergroup relations 322
marginalization 348
mediation 342
mirror-image perception 334

realistic conflict theory 332
relative deprivation 334
separation 348
social identity theory 329
superordinate goal 338

Questions for Review

1. What factors influence deindividuation?
2. How does social identity theory differ from previous theories in explaining crowd behaviour?
3. Describe two theories that explain intergroup conflict.
4. Discuss two strategies that are used in reducing intergroup conflict.
5. How are collectivistic and individualistic societies different in terms of ethnocentrism?

Take Action!

1. You're organizing a student demonstration. What do you do to make sure it remains peaceful?

2. You're interested in comparing students who identify themselves as feminist versus those who don't. How do you measure "feminist" as a social identity?

3. You're a member of a committee that has been assigned the task of understanding a conflict between Muslim and Hindu student organizations. How do you show that the two groups have simplistic and possibly stereotypic perceptions of each other?

4. You've been hired as a mediator between labour and management in a business dispute. What two things could you do to reduce conflict between the opposing parties?

5. Your neighbour is a new immigrant from Syria. What advice could you give him about a successful acculturation strategy that he could adopt?

LIVE RESEARCH

Participate in Research

Activity 1 The Power of Crowds: This chapter described the characteristics of people in crowds. Go online to identify the characteristics of a rioting crowd in London, England, in August 2011. Which theory or theories are more useful in explaining the behaviour of those who were involved?

Activity 2 Social Identity: You learned in this chapter about individual and social identities. Go online to identify the social identities of French Canadians versus English Canadians.

Activity 3 Group Conflict: This chapter described two causes of group conflict: realistic conflict theory and relative deprivation theory. Go online to test how each theory explains the conflict between two groups in a dispute.

Activity 4 Strategies for Reducing Group Conflict: You learned in this chapter about factors that reduce conflicts between groups. Go online to read about a number of different strategies that could be used to reduce group conflicts, and rate the effectiveness of each approach.

Activity 5 The Impact of Culture on Stereotypes: The final section of this chapter described how people from different cultures vary in their perception of groups and how to resolve group conflict. Go online to rate your views about people in different groups—then see how other students rated their views.

Test a Hypothesis

The contemporary understanding of crowd behaviour is that people in crowds assume a new social identity. To examine this hypothesis, read accounts of recent demonstrations in your region. Then, go online to report your findings to other students.

Design a Study

Go online to design your own study testing the importance of social identities in a crowd. You'll be able to choose the type of study you want to conduct (self-report, observational/naturalistic, or experimental), choose your own independent and dependent variables, and form your own hypothesis. Then you can share your findings with other students across the country!

11 CHAPTER

STEREOTYPE, PREJUDICE, AND DISCRIMINATION

DID YOU EVER WONDER?

Carl Beam, The North American Iceberg, 1985. National Gallery of Canada, Ottawa. © CARCC 2011. Photo © NGC.

Internationally, Canada is known for its multicultural policy, its acceptance of cultural diversity, its democracy, and its peaceful global policy. However, Canadian history includes dark chapters of discrimination and racism. One notably shameful phase in Canadian history is the treatment of Aboriginal peoples. During the period of colonization, there was a move to educate Aboriginal people by European settlers. The goal of civilizing the Aboriginal population led to the development of residential schools in the mid 1800s. These schools, which were modelled after similar boarding schools in the United States, had as their motto "Kill the Indian in him and save the man" (Bear, 2008; Hutchings, 2011). The motto was put into practice by separating the Aboriginal children from their families and communities. Religious groups such as the Anglican, Catholic, Presbyterian, and United churches received funding from the government to run these schools. As the funding was typically insufficient, students were generally malnourished and were exposed to diseases such as tuberculosis. There are reports that the death rate in residential schools ranged from 24 percent (Hutchings, 2011) to 50 percent (Bryce, 1922). Yet, the worst aspect of these schools was the sexual, emotional, and physical abuse that happened in them (Hutchings, 2011).

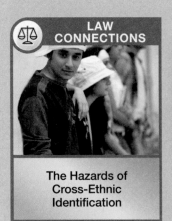

LAW CONNECTIONS

The Hazards of Cross-Ethnic Identification

EDUCATION CONNECTIONS

Reducing the Effects of Stereotype Threat in the Classroom

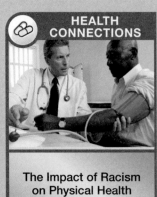

HEALTH CONNECTIONS

The Impact of Racism on Physical Health

BUSINESS CONNECTIONS

Examining the Effects of Affirmative Action Policies

Although most residential schools closed in the 1970s, it wasn't until late 1996 that the last residential school closed (CBC, 2008). In 1998, the Canadian government issued an official apology referred to as the Statement of Reconciliation and committed $350 million to address the healing needs of Aboriginal families. Over the last few decades, the Canadian federal government has taken a series of steps to address the injustices and inequalities of the past. However, the living standard of Aboriginal people in Canada is far lower than that of other Canadians. Aboriginal people have a lower average life expectancy, education level, and average income, and have higher levels of unemployment, infant mortality, and suicide than other Canadians. Arguably their suffering is related to the racist policies that they were subjected to (Henry, Tator, Mattis, & Rees, 1995). In 2008, Canadian Prime Minister Stephen Harper, in his speech offering apology to those who suffered abuse in the residential school system, estimated that there are approximately 80,000 survivors or former students in Canada (Harper, 2008).

In this chapter we will examine factors that contribute to prejudice and discrimination and their consequences for minority groups, including the Aboriginal peoples of Canada. You'll also find answers to these questions:

 How can discriminating against someone make you feel good?

 How can watching commercials make women more likely to avoid math and science careers?

 Why does a shooter fire faster when seeing a Black man than a White man?

 Why does adopting more tolerant views about women and gay people reduce discrimination against gay people?

 Why do negative stereotypes about memory loss in older adults make them more likely to forget?

PREVIEW

stereotype – a belief that associates a whole group of people with a certain trait

A belief that associates a whole group of people with a certain trait is called a **stereotype**. We all hold such beliefs. We typically rely on stereotypes on a regular basis to describe people who differ from us in some way. You probably have a stereotype for what type of person drives a BMW convertible, a Jeep, or a Honda Accord. You may believe that blondes have more fun, that left-handed people are creative, or that Miss Universe contestants aren't so bright.

prejudice – hostile or negative feelings about people based on their membership in a certain group

discrimination – behaviour directed against people solely because of their membership in a particular group

Although stereotypes may sometimes be relatively harmless, or even positive, they may lead to **prejudice**, meaning hostile or negative feelings about people based on their membership in a certain group, and **discrimination**, meaning behaviour directed against individuals solely because of their membership in a particular group. This chapter will examine social psychological factors that contribute to stereotyping, prejudice, and discrimination, the consequences of being stereotyped, and strategies for overcoming these harmful effects.

WHAT FACTORS CONTRIBUTE TO STEREOTYPING AND PREJUDICE?

Think about a time when you behaved badly toward someone of a different nationality, gender, sexual orientation, age, or ability. What factors might have motivated your behaviour? Research in psychology suggests that we may engage in negative behaviour toward others when we feel bad about ourselves. To examine whether people whose self-esteem is threatened are more likely to express prejudice, Steve Fein and Steve Spencer of the University of Waterloo conducted a study at a school where there was a strong negative stereotype about Jewish American women, but not about Italian American women. Participants came into the lab and were first given either positive or negative feedback about their intelligence. They were next asked to evaluate a job candidate based on her resumé, a photograph, and a videotape of her interview. In half of the cases, the woman was named Maria D'Agnostino and portrayed as Italian. The other times, she was named Julie Goldberg and portrayed as Jewish. As predicted, participants who had received negative feedback about their own intelligence rated Julie Goldberg's personality more negatively (even though all of the materials were the same) than those who rated Maria D'Agnostino. There were no differences in ratings of the candidates for those who had received positive feedback. Researchers also found that those who had rated the Jewish woman more negatively had a greater boost in their self-esteem following the experiment (Fein & Spencer, 1997).

Another study from the University of Waterloo took a more complex approach to the concept of self-esteem in relation to the expression of prejudice by distinguishing explicit and implicit self-esteem (Jordan, Spencer, & Zanna, 2005). Explicit self-esteem, which is measured in self-reports, is defined as self-esteem that one has expressed about oneself. Implicit self-esteem is defined as one's evaluation of oneself that may exist largely outside of one's awareness. The measurement of implicit self-esteem needs subtler methods, such as computer-based reaction time tasks that require responses that are difficult to control (Jordan, Spencer, & Zanna, 2003). Using these methods, previous studies had established that individuals who consciously feel positive about themselves (i.e., they have high explicit self-esteem) but who harbour self-doubts and insecurities at less conscious levels (i.e., they have low implicit self-esteem) behave more defensively by, for example, rationalizing their decisions more (Jordan, Spencer, Zanna, Hoshino-Browne, & Correll, 2003). Jordan and colleagues (2005) found that when participants' self-esteem was threatened by negative feedback on a bogus intelligence test, those with high explicit self-esteem but relatively low implicit self-esteem recommended a more severe punishment for an Aboriginal student who started a fist fight than for a White student who started a fist fight. It appears that the threat to such participants' fragile self-esteem resulted in prejudiced behaviour in the form of harsher judgements of an outgroup member.

The above results indicate that receiving a blow to one's self-esteem can lead to the expression of prejudice, and, in the case of Fein and Spencer (1997), that the expression of this prejudice can then boost one's self-esteem. This section will discuss this and other ways in which social psychological factors contribute to stereotypes and prejudice, including social learning, social categorization, and cognitive biases.

SOCIAL LEARNING

As we learned in Chapter 6, people form attitudes through broad learning principles, such as classical conditioning, operant conditioning, and modelling (Bandura, 1986). Children may receive rewards and punishments for expressing particular attitudes or engaging in particular behaviours toward others. For example, a child who uses a derogatory term for *gay* or *lesbian* and is then punished learns that using the expression is unacceptable and should be less likely to use such a stereotypical term again. Similarly, children often form their attitudes about people in different groups by watching (and listening) to their parents. If a child hears a parent express negative attitudes about people who hold different religious beliefs from their own, or sees a parent avoid interactions with people with such beliefs, the child is likely to form negative beliefs about people in this group and potentially to act in a more biased way toward them in the future (Towles-Schwen & Fazio, 2001).

Parents aren't the only people who can serve as models—we often look to others for guidance in forming our attitudes and behaviour. Hearing someone express prejudiced attitudes, watching someone engage in discrimination, or observing someone respond favourably to a joke that involves a stereotype all contribute to the formation and maintenance of stereotypes (Crandall, Eshleman, & O'Brien, 2002). For example, Whites who hear someone express racist views express weaker antiracist positions than those without such exposure (Blanchard, Crandall, Brigham, & Vaughn, 1994).

Parents who have friends from different backgrounds and express tolerant and accepting attitudes toward other groups model non-prejudicial attitudes for their children.

© Radius/SUPERSTOCK

Social learning is one explanation for why people are often willing to express certain types of prejudice, but not others (Crandall et al., 2002). For example, many people feel relatively comfortable expressing prejudice against racists, drug addicts, KKK members, child molesters, terrorists, and ex-convicts. However, they're unlikely to feel comfortable expressing prejudice against people in other stigmatized groups, such as people who are blind or elderly, or immigrants. People therefore learn to avoid discriminating against those in the "not acceptable" category, but may show a high level of prejudice toward people in groups that are socially acceptable to discriminate against. Similarly, many people who consider themselves unprejudiced because they consciously avoid discriminating against people based on their ethnicity or gender may feel comfortable telling a joke about a pedophile or a "red-neck."

Believing that other people agree with our stereotypes also increases the strength and accessibility of these stereotypes, and thereby makes them more resistant to change (Stangor, Sechrist, & Jost, 2001; Wittenbrink & Henly, 1996). In one study, White students first rated their attitudes toward Blacks (Sechrist & Stangor, 2001). Some students were then told that these beliefs were common—that 81 percent of the students at their school shared their beliefs. Other students were told that these beliefs were uncommon—that only 19 percent of the students at their school shared their beliefs. Receiving information about the normality of their views influenced participants' beliefs about the percentage of Blacks who possessed positive traits (such as athletic, hardworking, musical, and emotionally expressive) as well as negative traits (such as poor, violent, irresponsible, and uneducated). Specifically, students who were high in prejudice and who received information that their views were shared by others believed that a greater percentage of Blacks possessed more negative traits and fewer positive traits than did those who learned that their views weren't shared by others. Receiving information about the normality of their views also influenced the White students' behaviour, such as how close they sat to a Black student.

In a study conducted by researchers at the University of Manitoba (Vorauer & Sasaki, 2010), participants, who were all European/White Canadians, were told that the study was about examining how exchanged information between two people affect their perceptions of each other. Participants were informed that they would be exchanging written information with their partner who was in a room around the corner. All participants filled out brief personal information questionnaires which was exchanged with their partner. The participants then received their partner's information, which indicated that he or she was an Aboriginal Canadian. Participants were divided into two groups. Those in the multicultural condition read a half-page passage about ethnic issues in Canada that emphasized the value of multiculturalism and diversity. Those in the control condition didn't read the passage. All participants were asked to answer a series of questions, including an extended personal information sheet, which was going to be exchanged with their partner. Warmth was assessed in terms of disclosing detailed and intimate information to their partner, expression of liking of their partners, and overall total number of words in their answers. As shown in Figure 11.1, it was found that the low prejudice students (which was assessed prior to the study through mass testing) in the multicultural condition were more likely to express more warmth toward the Aboriginal student than the low prejudice

FIGURE 11.1 DOES AWARENESS OF MULTICULTURALISM AFFECT PREJUDICIAL BEHAVIOUR?

In this study, the level of warmth that European/White Canadian students expressed toward an Aboriginal Canadian partner was measured as a function of student's level of prejudice and ideology condition. It was found that ideologies that promote other groups (i.e., multiculturalism) are beneficial for those who have a positive tendency toward outgroup members. That is, those with low prejudice express more warmth toward their Aboriginal partner after reading a multicultural message. On the other hand, those who have negative tendency toward the outgroup (i.e., high prejudice), are more likely to feel threatened after reading a multicultural message and express less warmth toward their Aboriginal partner.

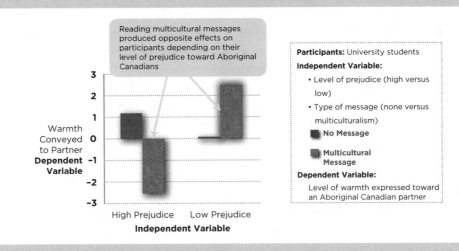

Source: Vorauer, J. D., & Sasaki, S. J. (2010). In need of liberation or constraint? How intergroup attitudes moderate the behavioral implications of intergroup ideologies. *Journal of Experimental Social Psychology, 46*, 133–138.

students in the control condition (no message). Additionally, the high prejudice students in the multicultural condition expressed less warmth than high prejudice students in the control condition. This is consistent with the research hypotheses as it is believed that although reading a passage on multiculturalism led all participants to perceive themselves to be different from their partners, it increased the feeling of threat among those with high prejudice. It is possible that participants with low prejudice were inspired by the multiculturalism ideology and paid more attention to attributes of their partners and tried to exhibit more warmth. The study indicates that ideological ideas such as those in the multicultural message should be tailored to particular individuals to increase the effectiveness of such messages.

Who's Who in Contemporary Canadian Social Psychology Research

Courtesy Jacquie Vorauer

Jacquie Vorauer received her undergraduate degree from the University of British Columbia and her master's and PhD from the University of Waterloo. She is now a faculty member at the University of Manitoba. Professor Vorauer has published extensively in the area of intergroup relations and the factors that influence people's interactions with outgroup members. Her research interests centre on people's beliefs about how they are viewed by others. She also examines how evaluative concerns affect people's interactions with outgroup members. Professor Vorauer served as an associate editor at the *Journal of Personality and Social Psychology* in 2006 and an associate editor at the *Journal of Experimental of Social Psychology* in 2005 and 2010.

SOCIAL CATEGORIZATION

social categorization – the practice of classifying people into in-groups or outgroups based on attributes that the person has in common with the in-group or outgroup

Another factor that contributes to stereotyping and prejudice is our tendency to quickly classify people into groups on the basis of common attributes, which is called **social categorization**. All groups are necessarily either groups that we are in, in which case they are in-groups (i.e., people like us), or groups that we are not in, in other words outgroups (e.g., people not like us; Billig & Tajfel, 1973). This type of social categorization can even be done on meaningless grounds, such as eye colour, shoe size, or the province in which a person was born. This classification of people into two groups (us and them) has two consequences that contribute to stereotyping—the outgroup homogeneity effect and in-group favouritism.

outgroup homogeneity effect – people's tendency to underestimate the variability of outgroup members compared to the variability of in-group members

OUTGROUP HOMOGENEITY EFFECT. The **outgroup homogeneity effect** refers to people's general tendency to see outgroup members as very similar to one another, while seeing members of their in-group as more diverse (Judd & Park, 1988; Judd, Ryan, & Park, 1991; Mullen & Hu, 1989; Ostrom & Sedikides, 1992). For example, we may see students who attend a different school as a single group of very similar people (e.g., students at *that other school*), but divide people at our school into athletes, musicians, artists, and so on.

Why do people hold such different beliefs about in-group versus outgroup members? One reason is that we typically have less exposure to and familiarity with people in the outgroup than those in our in-group (Harasty, 1997; Park, Ryan, & Judd, 1992). Greater familiarity with a group leads to seeing greater differentiation and variability within the group (Linville, Fischer, & Salovey, 1989). For example, later in the semester, women who joined sororities saw less variability in the women in other sororities than they had perceived earlier in the semester, presumably as they spent more time with women in their own sorority (Ryan & Bogart, 1997). In fact, babies as young as nine months are better at discriminating between faces within their own ethnic group than those from other ethnic groups, suggesting that the outgroup homogeneity effect occurs quite early in life (Kelly et al., 2007). We are not born with this characteristic, however—it is learned. Korean children who are adopted by White French families between the ages of three and nine years are better at recognizing White faces than Asian ones (Sangrigoli, Pallier, Argenti, Ventureyra, & de Schonen, 2005). In contrast, Korean children who grow up in Korea recognize Korean faces better than White ones. The Law Connections box describes another real-world example of the hazards of the outgroup homogeneity effect.

LAW CONNECTIONS

The Hazards of Cross-Ethnic Identification

On the morning of June 22, 2006, a 17-year-old woman was waiting for a bus in a small town close to Toronto (Brown, 2008). A young male riding a bicycle approached her and started talking to her but then grabbed her and sexually assaulted her. The young woman screamed and, according to her testimony, "freaked out." The male then rode off on his bike. The entire incident took about 10 minutes. Although she told her mother about the incident, she didn't report it to the police. Three months later, on September 20, 2006, the young woman saw the same man on the same bike she had seen when she was assaulted. She called the police and later gave a videotaped statement about the crime. The male was said to be between 17 and 24 years old and was of East Indian or Pakistani descent with a slight Pakistani accent. In the course of the police investigation, the victim was provided with a photo

lineup, which included a photo of a young man (Mr. GS) who was a student at the same high school that the victim was attending. The young woman identified Mr. GS as the perpetrator, which led to Mr. GS's arrest. A year later, after reviewing all the evidence in court, Mr. GS was found not guilty. It became evident that the perpetrator was not Mr. GS.

This is just one example of a case in which witnesses have identified a person of a different ethnicity as the perpetrator of a crime, and were later found to have identified the wrong person. You will have heard the phrase "They all look the same." Who you will have heard it applied to will depend on your ethnicity, but rest assured, whatever your ethnicity, there are others to whom you and the members of your ethnicity all look the same. Errors in cross-ethnic identification have been documented by researchers, including a study conducted in Canada that found that Caucasian and Asian students were more accurate at recognizing faces of their own ethnicity than recognizing faces of other ethnicities (Ng & Lindsay, 1994) and another that found Caucasian and First Nations students more accurate in indentifying faces of their own ethnicity than faces of other ethnicities (Corenblum & Meissner, 2006; Jackiw, Arbuthnott, Pfeifer, Marcon, & Meissner, 2008).

People tend to see outgroup members as looking very similar to one another, and they show greater accuracy for recognizing in-group members than outgroup members. This phenomenon is called the **cross-ethnic identification bias**, or cross-racial bias (Meissner & Brigham, 2001; Slone, Brigham, & Meissner, 2000; Sporer, 2001). Why does this misidentification occur? One explanation is that people engage in deeper processing when seeing a person from the same ethnicity than someone from a different ethnicity (Chance & Goldstein, 1981). Another factor could be familiarity (as you spend time among *them*, you start to be able to tell them apart). Regardless of the process that leads to cross-ethnic identification bias, this perceptual error can lead to significant problems in eyewitness identification, which is a serious issue. Psychologists now testify in court about the dangers of relying on eyewitness testimony, especially in the absence of other corroborating evidence. Given the potential for errors, and their consequences, this bias is an important phenomenon that should be considered in Canada's highly multicultural and multi-ethnic society.

> **cross-ethnic identification bias** – the tendency to see outgroup members as looking very similar to one another, and showing greater accuracy for recognizing in-group members than outgroup members

IN-GROUP FAVOURITISM.　Social categorization also leads to people's tendency to discriminate in favour of those in their in-group versus their outgroup (Brewer, 1979; Chatman & von Hippel, 2001; Reynolds, Turner, & Haslam, 2000). In general, people evaluate their in-group more positively than their out group, a phenomenon called **in-group favouritism**. For example, jurors give shorter sentences to those in the same ethnic group as themselves who are accused of crimes (Sommers & Ellsworth, 2000). People not only judge their in-group more favourably, they're also more confident in their judgement. In a study conducted at the Université de Québec à Montréal, people of African or Chinese descent living in Canada, as well as French Canadians, were shown a series of photographs of faces on a computer screen (Beaupré & Hess, 2006). They were then asked to rate the intensity of the emotional expression on the images and their level of confidence in their rating. It was found that participants were more confident in judging the emotional expression of faces that were members of their cultural in-group than those of outgroups. Amazingly enough, this in-group favouritism has also been found to occur when groups are based on meaningless criteria, such as the number of dots people see in a picture or the letters they choose at random from a bag (Crisp, Hewstone, & Rubin, 2001).

> **in-group favouritism** – the tendency to evaluateone's in-group more positively than outgroups

What factors contribute to in-group favouritism? One factor is self-interest: we're motivated to favour those in our in-group because those people are more likely to favour us in return (Vivian & Berkowitz, 1992, 1993). This preference for those in our in-group is acquired early in life and remains fairly stable: although self-reported prejudice decreases over time, White 6-year-olds show the same pro-White, anti-Black bias on subtle tests as older children and adults (Baron & Banaji, 2006). We even rate words referring to our in-group (e.g., we, us) more positively than those referring to outgroups (e.g., they, them), suggesting that this preference for those in our in-group occurs at an automatic level (Otten & Wentura, 1999; Perdue, Dovidio, Gurtman, & Tyler, 1990).

In-group favouritism is also more likely when people heavily identify with the group, and when group norms are salient (Gagnon & Bourhis, 1996; Levin & Sidanius, 1999; Marques, Abrams, Paez, & Martinez-Taboada, 1998). Whites who identify strongly with their White ethnic identity and think about how an affirmative action policy will affect Whites are less supportive of affirmative action than those who identify less strongly with their ethnic identity or who think about how this policy will affect Blacks (Lowery, Unzueta, Knowles, & Goff, 2006).

social dominance orientation – a personality trait that indicates preference to maintain hierarchy within and between groups

Another factor that contributes to in-group favouritism is a person's level of **social dominance orientation**, a personality variable that shows preference for maintaining hierarchy both within groups and between groups (see the Rate Yourself box; Guimond, Dambrun, Michinov, & Duarte, 2003; Pratto, Sidanius, Stallworth, & Malle, 1994; Whitley, 1999). Not surprisingly, people who are high in social dominance orientation are more likely to engage in-group favouritism, in part because those who want to maintain the superior position of their own in-group are particularly motivated to derogate outgroup members and reward in-group members as a way of maintaining that superiority.

[RATE YOURSELF]

DO YOU SEE SOME GROUPS AS HIGHER IN STATUS THAN OTHERS?

Social Dominance Orientation Scale

INSTRUCTIONS: *Rate each item on a scale of 1 (strongly disagree) to 7 (strongly agree).*

☐ **1.** Some groups of people are simply inferior to other groups.

☐ **2.** It's okay if some groups have more of a chance in life than others.

☐ **3.** Sometimes other groups must be kept in their place.

☐ **4.** In getting what you want, it is sometimes necessary to use force against other groups.

☐ **5.** Inferior groups should stay in their place.

☐ **6.** To get ahead in life, it is sometimes necessary to top other groups.

☐ **7.** If certain groups stayed in their place, we would have fewer problems.

☐ **8.** It's probably a good thing that certain groups are at the top and other groups are at the bottom.

SCORING: Sum up your total number of points on all of these items.

INTERPRETATION: This scale measures individuals' preferences for hierarchy within a given social system. People with higher scores believe that groups vary in their social status, and that some groups will necessarily dominate over others (Sidanius & Pratto, 2001). People with lower scores believe that groups are equal in status and hierarchy, and that one group should not dominate another. Scores under 13 are considered low, whereas scores over 20 are considered high in social dominance orientation (Son Hing, Bobocel, Zanna, & McBride, 2007).

In turn, those who believe that their own group should be dominant over other groups are more prejudiced against people in lower-status groups, including against women, homosexuals, and minority group members. This prejudice may come, at least in part, from a strong motivation to internalize beliefs that legitimize the group differences (e.g., some men are motivated to believe that women are less intelligent than they are; Guimond, 2000). In one study, White participants rated the percentage of Blacks who they believed held various traits (e.g., poor, violent, intelligent; Strube & Rahimi, 2006). Those who were high on social dominance orientation held the least positive views of Blacks, and also believed that other students held the same views.

COGNITIVE BIASES

As described in Chapter 5, people often use shortcuts in their thinking, and these faulty problem-solving strategies can lead to stereotyping and prejudice. Such cognitive biases include illusory correlation, the ultimate attribution error, the contrast effect, perceptual confirmation, and the confirmation bias.

ILLUSORY CORRELATION.   One cognitive bias that contributes to stereotyping is **illusory correlation**, which describes the tendency to overestimate the association between variables that are only slightly or not at all correlated (Hamilton & Gifford, 1976; Hamilton & Rose, 1980; Johnson & Mullen, 1994; McConnell, Sherman, & Hamilton, 1994). Because people pay particular attention to things that are novel or unique, people who are distinctive are more salient—they basically stick out more. In turn, behaviours committed by members of small groups or groups that are distinctive receive more attention and are more memorable than the same behaviours committed by members of common groups (Risen, Gilovich, & Dunning, 2007). People then overestimate how frequently the distinctive behaviour is performed by that group. As Anne Frank wrote in her diary, "What one Christian does is his own responsibility, what one Jew does is thrown back at all Jews" (Frank, 1993, p. 239).

illusory correlation – the tendency to overestimate the association between variables that are only slightly or not at all correlated

Here is a real-world example of the impact of illusory correlation. Fewer people in the world are homosexual than heterosexual, and child molestation is (fortunately) a relatively rare behaviour. However, because both homosexuality and child molestation are therefore more distinctive behaviours, people often see them as going together more frequently than they actually do (and are therefore more likely to hold the belief that homosexuals are particularly likely to engage in inappropriate sexual behaviour with children). In reality, of course, heterosexual men are statistically the most likely to abuse children.

ULTIMATE ATTRIBUTION ERROR.   Another cognitive bias that can lead to stereotypes and prejudice is the **ultimate attribution error**, which describes people's tendency to make different attributions for success and failure depending on whether the individual is part of their in-group or an outgroup (Hewstone, 1990; Hewstone & Ward, 1985; Pettigrew, 1979). Specifically, people tend to make dispositional, or internal, attributions for negative behaviour by those in an outgroup, whereas they tend to make situational, or external, attributions for the same behaviour if it's committed by someone in their in-group.

ultimate attribution error – an error in which people make dispositional attributions for negative behaviour and situational attributions for positive behaviour by outgroup members, yet show the reverse attributions for successes and failures for their in-group members

In one study, Black and White university students read a scenario in which a Black or a White person was fired (Chatman & von Hippel, 2001). Both Blacks and Whites showed in-group favouritisms, judging the firing as caused by internal factors, such as personality and intelligence, for outgroup members but by external factors, such as situational pressures and circumstances beyond the person's control, for in-group members.

Why do we make these different attributions for negative things that occur to people in our in-group versus those in our outgroup? In part because these attributions help us feel safe in an often unpredictable world. For example, if we believe that women who are raped have "asked for it" in some way, perhaps due to drinking alcohol, wearing skimpy clothing, or walking alone late at night, we can feel that this type of bad thing won't happen to us. This phenomenon, known as belief in a just world, refers to the assumption that bad things happen to bad people and good things happen to good people (Lerner, 1980).

Unfortunately, this tendency to make different attributions for in-group versus outgroup members can lead to scapegoating and "blaming the victim" (Lerner & Miller, 1978). In one study, participants read about the behaviour of a young woman who was friendly to a man at a party (Janoff-Bulman, Timko, & Carli, 1985). Half of the participants then read that she had been raped by that man later in the evening. All participants then rated how appropriate her behaviour at the party had been. Those who didn't read about the rape saw her behaviour as appropriate, whereas those who learned she had been raped saw her same behaviour as inappropriate. This research shows how extensively people can interpret the same information differently, in this case in a way that makes them feel that the victim's behaviour caused the attack.

CONTRAST EFFECT. As you learned in Chapter 5, people perceive stimuli that are different from expectations as more different than they actually are (Fiske, Bersoff, Borgida, Deaux, & Heilman, 1991; Jussim, Coleman, & Lerch, 1987). For example, if you expect that women will be passive and gentle, when you encounter a woman who is assertive and strong she may seem especially tough and aggressive. Describing the same tendency, Stephen Carter, a Black man and law professor at Yale University, notes in his book *Reflections of an Affirmative Action Baby* that "like a flower blooming in winter, intellect is more readily noticed where it is not expected to be found" (Carter, 1993, p. 54). Thus, if you believe that football players are dumb, when you encounter one who gets an A on an exam, you may see him as even smarter than another student with the same grade.

What accounts for these overly positive (or negative) perceptions of average behaviour? According to the **shifting standards model**, people within a group are more often compared to others within that group than to people in other groups (Biernat, 2003; Biernat & Manis, 1994; Biernat, Manis, & Nelson, 1991). For example, a woman may be described as a great athlete because her skills are better than those of most other women even if these skills are only average compared to men's abilities. One study revealed that softball managers respond with greater enthusiasm for good performance by a woman—such as hitting a single—than the same performance by a man (Biernat & Vescio, 2002). However, they also favour men over women with comparable skills for favoured infield positions and batting order.

While it is therefore easier for minority group members to make minimum standards (due to shifting standards), these positive evaluations based on lowered standards can, not surprisingly, be insulting. As described by one Black employee working in a largely White environment:" They were astonished that I could write a basic memo. Even the completion of an easy task brought surprised compliments" (Biernat, 2003, p. 55). Minority group members also must work harder to prove that their performance is based on ability (Biernat, Crandall, Young, Kobrynowicz, & Halpin, 1998; Biernat & Kobrynowicz, 1997). As Carter (1993) eloquently describes, Blacks "really do have to work twice as hard to be considered half as good" (p. 58).

PERCEPTUAL CONFIRMATION. Perceptual confirmation, meaning the tendency to see things in line with one's expectations, is another process that can lead to harmful stereotyping, and helps explain why members of minority groups have to "jump through more hoops." A study conducted at the University of British Columbia demonstrates this effect. Tasha Riley and Charles Ungerleider tested whether pre-service teachers (i.e., student teachers) made discriminatory judgements about Aboriginal students. Fifty pre-service teachers were asked to assess the records of 24 students and recommend their placement in remedial, conventional, or advanced programs. It was found that the pre-service teachers systematically devalued the performance of students who they were led to believe were of Aboriginal ancestry in comparison with their non-Aboriginal counterparts, even though the student records were otherwise identical (Riley & Ungerleider, 2008). Having been told these children were of Aboriginal origin, the teachers saw poorer performance in identical records. The authors suggest that although Canada has pursued a policy of multiculturalism and Canadians regard themselves as tolerant, they are discriminatory in relation to Aboriginal Canadians.

Perceptual confirmation occurs in part because we interpret ambiguous information as supporting our stereotypes, and thereby see the same behaviour in a very different way depending on our expectations (Hilton & von Hippel, 1990; Kunda & Sherman-Williams, 1993; Kunda, Sinclair, & Griffin, 1997). Perceptual confirmation leads people to see pseudo

shifting standards model – a model that posits that people within a group are more often compared to others within that group rather than to people in other groups

perceptual confirmation – the tendency to see things in line with one's expectations

patients' behaviour at a mental hospital as abnormal (Rosenhan, 1973), view other athletic teams as more unfairly aggressive than their own (Hastorf & Cantril, 1954), and underestimate 11-month-old girl infants' crawling ability and overestimate such behaviour in boys (Mondschein, Adolph, & Tamis-LeMonda, 2000).

Because stereotypes lead people to recall information about a person that is consistent with their expectations, they interpret and encode that information in distinct (i.e., stereotypical) ways. In one study, all participants saw a video about a child (Hannah) who was either from a poor background or a rich background (Darley & Gross, 1983). Half of the participants were also given additional information by watching her answer a series of academic problems in an inconsistent way (she got some right and some wrong). Then all participants rated Hannah's academic ability. Those who hadn't seen Hannah's academic performance seemed reluctant to judge her ability based simply on her socioeconomic status. However, those who saw the video of her academic performance readily judged her ability, even though the video provided ambiguous information, and her socioeconomic status did appear to influence their judgements. Specifically, those with negative expectations (e.g., those who thought Hannah was poor) rated her lower on work habits, motivation, and cognitive skills than did those who hadn't seen the video. Those with positive expectations (e.g., those who thought Hannah was rich) rated her somewhat higher if they had seen the video. In this case stereotypes didn't have a direct effect on performance expectations, but clearly made participants more willing to use irrelevant information to interpret behaviour in line with their stereotype.

Researchers have also found that we require fewer examples to confirm our beliefs about a trait that is highly stereotypical of a person in a given outgroup than for a person in our in-group (Biernat & Ma, 2005). For example, if a young person misplaces his or her keys, we assume that person is just being forgetful. But if an older person misplaces his or her keys, we assume that person may be experiencing serious memory loss.

CONFIRMATION BIAS.   Confirmation bias describes the tendency to search for information that supports one's initial view. When people have expectations about a particular person, they address few questions to that person, and hence acquire relatively little information that could disprove their assumptions (Trope & Thompson, 1997). People may also ask questions that are designed to confirm their expectations, which protects them from gaining and using disconfirming information. For example, if you're meeting people from Sweden for the first time, you might ask them about their love of ice hockey, cold weather, and saunas, whereas if you're meeting people from Brazil for the first time, you might ask them about their love of spicy foods, festive music, and carnivals. Do you see the confirmation bias at work here?

confirmation bias – the tendency to search for information that supports one's initial view

We also ignore information that disputes our expectations. We're more likely to remember (and repeat) stereotype-consistent information and to forget or ignore stereotype-inconsistent information, which is one way stereotypes are maintained even in the face of disconfirming evidence (Lyons & Kashima, 2003; O'Sullivan & Durso, 1984). If you learn that your new Swedish friends hate hockey and love sailing, and that your new Brazilian friends dislike spicy foods and love rap music, you're less likely to remember this new stereotype-inconsistent information.

What's the good news? People who are unprejudiced pay more attention to stereotype-disconfirming information than stereotype-confirming information (Wyer, 2004). In one study, participants read four brief descriptions of a target person, and then selected one person to learn more about in a subsequent task. Some of these descriptions included stereotypical information (e.g., a Black person who is uneducated and has a menial job). Others included information that disconfirmed stereotypes (e.g., a Black person who is educated and has a white-collar job). Of those who were unprejudiced (as assessed by scores on a racism scale), 68 percent chose to receive more information about a stereotype-disconfirming person. Of participants who were prejudiced, 77 percent chose to receive more information about a person who was stereotype-confirming. People who are unprejudiced also make different attributions for behaviour—seeing stereotype-confirming behaviour as situational rather than internal, and stereotype-disconfirming behaviour as dispositional.

RESEARCH FOCUS ON GENDER
The Development of Gender Stereotypes

Gender stereotypes are the stereotypical evaluation of an individual based on the person's gender. Children show signs of gender stereotyping as young as 3 years old (Martin & Little, 1990). Such stereotyping includes making judgements about another child's toy or the colour of her dress. For example, Ruble, Lurye, and Zosuls (2007) reported that by age 4, children show strong gender stereotypes. They reported that some girls go through a phase of liking "pink frilly dresses" but boys do not. This gender colour distinction partly reflects current cultural norms as many little girls receive compliments when they wear "pink frilly dresses." Such preferences also indicate that children actively interpret their social world, including gender categorization. Children learn that gender is an important social categorization which applies to them and that certain behaviours, preferences, and characteristics are associated with one gender but not the other.

Parents have a tendency to dress girls in pink and boys in blue.

© Eric Gevaert / Alamy

Gender stereotypes and gender socialization limit the achievement expectations of both boys and girls. Mendez and Crawford (2002) reported that, even among gifted students, boys show higher aspirations in their career choice than girls. Additionally, as researchers from the University of Calgary found, young women anticipate more potential work-family conflict than young men do (Singer, Cassin, & Dobson, 2005). These researchers found that among graduate students enrolled in clinical or counselling psychology programs in Canada, more women reported that their career would be disrupted by child-rearing responsibilities than men did. Women also reported lower expectations in terms of salary than men, which may be reflected in the fact that women, in general, negotiate lower salaries than men.

There are some indications, however, that occupational aspirations among high school girls have become more ambitious (Francis, 2002). Moreover, more young women are now aspiring to pursue a career in male-dominated fields, although the reverse is not true (Lips, 2008). In general, when gender stereotypes and socialization become weaker and less restrictive, both genders benefit as boys and girls learn to base their occupational ambition more on their talents and less on their gender roles (Lips, 2008).

ASSESSING PREJUDICE

In order to examine the prevalence of prejudice about different groups, as well as the factors that contribute to prejudice, researchers need to be able to assess such beliefs. This section will examine three ways in which researchers in psychology measure prejudice: self-report measures and two covert measures.

SELF-REPORT MEASURES.   As you learned in Chapter 2, self-report measures are commonly used to examine people's attitudes, beliefs, and behaviours. This approach is direct and can be cost-effective since it's possible to gather data from many people relatively quickly. Many self-report measures of prejudice exist, including the Modern Racism Scale (McConahay, 1986), the Homosexuality Attitudes Scale (Kite & Deaux, 1986), and the Modern Sexism Scale (Swim, Aikin, Hall, & Hunter, 1995). The Rate Yourself box provides an example of a scale that can be used to assess people's willingness to rely on stereotypes.

[RATE YOURSELF]

HOW MUCH DO YOU ACCEPT STEREOTYPES?

Acceptance of Stereotypes Scale

INSTRUCTIONS: *Rate each item on a scale of 0 (strongly disagree) to 6 (strongly agree).*

  1. Stereotypes are useful in daily life even though they are not always correct.

  2. Stereotypes can be harmful but they are essential for interacting with members of real groups.

  3. To hold a stereotype does not necessarily mean that you are looking down on someone.

  4. In daily life, there's so much to pay attention to, it helps if you can make a few assumptions about a person.

  5. People differ so much from one another, it is impossible to generalize about them.

  6. If we did not stereotype each other, there would be a lot less conflict in the world.

  7. If you hold a stereotype about people you'll never be able to see them for who they really are.

  8. Stereotypes have too much influence on our behaviour toward others.

SCORING: First, add up your points on items 1, 2, 3, and 4. Then add up your points on items 5, 6, 7, and 8. Subtract your summed score on the second set of items from your summed score on the first set of items to get your final score.

INTERPRETATION: This scale assesses people's general acceptance of stereotypes. People with higher scores have a greater willingness to rely on stereotypes when interacting with other people, whereas those with lower scores are less willing to rely on such beliefs (Carter, Hall, Carney, & Rosip, 2006).

Although self-report measures of stereotypes can provide useful information, these measures are also problematic for testing something as sensitive as prejudice and discrimination. As you can probably imagine, people are often reluctant to express prejudice about people in other groups, and thus may deliberately misreport their answers as a way of appearing more accepting and tolerant than they actually are.

COVERT MEASURES.   Because people are often unwilling to express prejudiced beliefs openly, researchers who study prejudice and discrimination have developed covert, or indirect, methods of assessing such beliefs and behaviours. One such method is the bogus pipeline, which is just a fake lie-detector test. Participants are hooked up to a mechanical device and told that it assesses their true beliefs by detecting any false information they give. Having been told this, participants are more likely to give honest responses to avoid the discomfort of getting caught in a lie.

The Implicit Association Test (IAT) is another commonly used covert method of testing people's prejudice about individuals in different groups. This test is based on the assumption that it's easier—and therefore faster—to make the same response to concepts that are strongly associated with each other than to concepts that are weakly associated (Nosek, Greenwald, & Banaji, 2005). Because people are faster at responding to the compatible pairs (i.e., strongly associated concepts) than the incompatible ones, it's often assumed that a quick response indicates that the two concepts are implicitly linked for that individual. For example, students often respond more quickly to a pairing of the words "fat" and "bad" (which are often closely linked in people's minds) than the words "thin" and "bad" (which are typically less closely linked). (For a better understanding of how the test works, you can visit the following website and take the test yourself: https://implicit.harvard.edu/implicit.) Although the IAT is the most widely used covert method for assessing people's attitudes toward members of different groups, some researchers have criticized its validity, particularly when it is used to provide specific information about a given person's degree of prejudice (Blanton & Jaccard, 2006).

[CONCEPTS IN CONTEXT]

FACTORS LEADING TO STEREOTYPING AND PREJUDICE

FACTOR	EXAMPLE
Social learning	Jimmy is in grade two and has a good friend named Isabella. After Jimmy is ridiculed by children on his bus for liking a girl, he refuses to play with Isabella anymore.
Social categorization	Yvette just joined a sorority and is having fun getting to know the other members. She feels very glad to have joined, and although it includes a wide range of women with different interests, she's starting to see them as a group, and herself as one of them.
Cognitive biases	Sierra volunteers at a local senior citizens centre one afternoon a week. In this role, she insists on carrying groceries for Mr. Maglione, even after he insisted he was perfectly capable of carrying the groceries himself. Sierra sees Mr. Maglione's white hair and wrinkled skin, and assumes that he must need assistance.
Assessing prejudice	Samantha is interested in knowing whether her new roommate, Amir, holds prejudiced beliefs about homosexuals. Instead of asking her roommate about this, Samantha observes Amir's behaviour when she introduces him to her gay friend.

WHAT ARE THE CONSEQUENCES OF STEREOTYPING, PREJUDICE, AND DISCRIMINATION?

Unfortunately, stereotypes can have real consequences. In one study, researchers randomly assigned female university students to watch one of two sets of television commercials (Davies, Spencer, Quinn, & Gerhardstein, 2002). Some women watched gender stereotypic television commercials, in which a woman jumped on her bed with joy after discovering a new acne product or drooled in anticipation of trying a new brownie mix. Other women watched counter-stereotypic commercials, in which a woman impressed someone with her knowledge of automotive engineering or spoke intelligently about her concerns related to health care. All women then completed a math test. As predicted, women who had watched the gender stereotypic commercials performed worse on the math test than those who had watched the counter-stereotypic commercials (19 percent correct compared to 31 percent correct). This research demonstrates just one example of the negative, and at times lasting, consequences of being stereotyped. This section will examine how the use of stereotypes leads to this, and other, negative consequences, including behavioural confirmation/self-fulfilling prophecy, stereotype threat, reduced psychological well-being, and reverse discrimination.

SELF-FULFILLING PROPHECY

People's expectations not only lead them to see things in line with their beliefs (i.e., perceptual confirmation), but also to interact with a person in ways that elicit expected behaviours (Darley & Fazio, 1980). As described in Chapter 5, self-fulfilling prophecy, or behavioural confirmation, refers to the tendency to seek, interpret, and create information that verifies our own beliefs. If you believe that a person isn't very bright, you're likely to ask questions that confirm this expectation. On the other hand, if you think you're talking to a smart person, you might ask different questions.

In a classic study, researchers asked White students at Princeton University to interview both Black and White Princeton undergraduates for a job (Word, Zanna, & Cooper, 1974). As predicted, interviewers who interacted with Black applicants interacted in very different ways from those who interacted with White applicants, including sitting further away, making more speech errors, and having less eye contact with the Black applicants. Next, the researchers trained students to interview job applicants using the distinct styles shown by those who had interviewed Whites versus Blacks. In other words, some students were trained to interview in the style used when people had interviewed the White students (sitting closer to the applicant, using correct grammar, and having good eye contact). Others were trained to interview in the style used when people had interviewed the Black students (sitting further away, making frequent speech errors, having little eye contact). These students then interviewed a new group of only White job applicants. Can you predict the findings?

The White applicants who were interviewed by someone using the style used with Black applicants in the first part of the study performed worse than those who were interviewed in the style used with White applicants in the first part. Specifically, those who were interviewed "as if Black" sat further from the interviewer, made more speech errors, and were seen as less calm and composed than those who were interviewed "as if White." Most importantly, applicants who were interviewed "as if Black" were seen by independent judges as less adequate for the job. This study demonstrates that people's expectations about other people can lead them to engage in behaviours that elicit behaviour that supports these expectations—a vicious, and dangerous, cycle.

How do people's expectations about others elicit the behaviour they expect? If you're interested in someone, your expectation that that person will or will not return your interest can affect the outcome. People who expect acceptance have a tendency to be warmer toward the person of interest, which can lead to acceptance; while people who expect rejection have a tendency to be cold or withdrawn, which in turn leads to less acceptance. These tendencies were examined in a study by researchers from the University of Waterloo and the University of Manitoba. To test whether one's level of interpersonal warmth is an important component of the self-fulfilling prophecy, the researchers had single male students engage in a videotaped face-to-face conversation with an attractive female confederate. In the experimental condition, the male students received information prior to the conversation indicating that the female confederate was not critical of other people. The control group received no such information. It was expected that this type of disclosure would increase the male students' anticipated acceptance and reduce their expectation of being rejected. Later on, female students reviewed the videos of these interactions and found that male students in the experimental condition showed a greater degree of "warmth" in their

Questioning the Research:

This classic study was conducted in 1974. Do you think researchers today would find the same differences in terms of how White interviewers interact with Black versus White job applicants?

interactions than the control group. These findings indicate the power of expectations in eliciting certain behaviours.

STEREOTYPE THREAT

stereotype threat – the fear that one's behaviour may confirm an existing cultural stereotype, which then disrupts one's performance

Another negative consequence of stereotyping is **stereotype threat**, which refers to when minority group members (it could also apply to majority groups, but is more likely for minority groups) fear that they may behave in a manner that confirms existing cultural stereotypes (Steele, 1997). This apprehension, in turn, interferes with their ability to perform well, and thus leads them to confirm the negative stereotype about their group. For example, if a woman is told that she's about to take a test on spatial reasoning that women typically do poorly on, that awareness may make her nervous and thus lead her to do less well on the test.

In the first study to demonstrate the stereotype threat effect, Claude Steele and Joshua Aronson (1995) randomly assigned Black and White university students at Stanford University to one of three groups before taking a verbal SAT test. Some received diagnostic information ("this test examines the factors associated with high versus low ability"), and some received non-diagnostic information ("this test examines methods of problem-solving"). Findings indicated, as predicted, that Blacks did just as well as Whites when the test was non-diagnostic, but did much worse than Whites when the test was presented as diagnostic. All of these students were smart—they were Stanford students—but the Black students may have felt more nervous about taking a diagnostic test given the stereotypes of Blacks as underachievers. In other words, because the Black students were aware of the racial stereotype (i.e., that Blacks tend to underperform academically) their performance on the test that measured academic ability was impaired by the stereotype. This indicates that when minorities (in this case, Black students) are in a threatening environment, their performance tends to worsen.

The impact of stereotype threat on academic tasks has been demonstrated by people in a variety of different types of stereotyped groups, including the following:

- high school girls and university women taking math tests described as diagnostic of math ability (Keller & Dauenheimer, 2003; Spencer, Steele, & Quinn, 1999)
- White males who take a math test after comparing their math ability to that of Asian males (Aronson et al., 1999)
- Latino men and women who take a math test described as diagnostic of their ability (Gonzales, Blanton, & Williams, 2002)
- children from low socioeconomic backgrounds who take intellectual tests described as diagnostic of their overall intellectual ability (Croizet & Claire, 1998)

Stereotype threat can also influence the same person in different ways, depending on which aspect of the person's identity is made salient. As Figure 11.2 shows, a study by Margaret Shih at Harvard University and her colleagues found that Asian women do better on math tests when their ethnic identity is primed, but worse when their sex is primed (Shih, Pittinsky, & Ambady, 1999).

Although in many cases researchers create stereotype threat by describing a test as diagnostic of the person's true aptitude, it can also be activated in more subtle ways. As described at the start of this section, women who saw gender stereotypic commercials performed worse on a math test than those who had watched the counter-stereotypic commercials (Davies et al., 2002). Women who watched the gender stereotypic commercials also showed less interest in careers requiring quantitative skills (such as engineer, mathematician, computer scientist, accountant) than those who watched the counter-stereotypic ads. It has also been found that simply being the only person of your gender or ethnicity in a

FIGURE 11.2 CAN IDENTITY SALIENCE IMPACT PERFORMANCE?

In this study, female Asian American students wrote about an aspect of their identity (either their Asian or their female identity), and then took a math test. When students' attention was focused on their female identity, they performed worse on the test than when their attention was focused on their Asian identity.

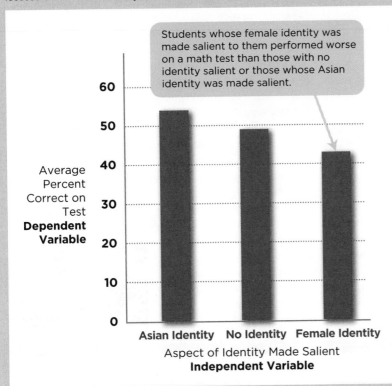

Students whose female identity was made salient to them performed worse on a math test than those with no identity salient or those whose Asian identity was made salient.

Average Percent Correct on Test
Dependent Variable

Aspect of Identity Made Salient
Independent Variable

Participants: Asian American female university students

Independent Variable:

Which aspect of their identity was made salient to them

- Asian identity
- None
- Female identity

Dependent Variable:

How well they did on a math test

Source: Shih, M., Pittinsky, T. L., & Ambady, N. (1999). Stereotype susceptibility: Identity salience and shifts in quantitative performance. *Psychological Science, 10,* 80–83.

group can activate stereotype threat, and thus disrupt performance, particularly for members of disadvantaged or stereotyped groups (Sekaquaptewa & Thompson, 2002). This was demonstrated by Michael Inzlicht, now at the University of Toronto, and his colleague Talia Ben Zeev (2000, 2003). These researchers found that female participants tended to perform worse on a math test when they were in a minority condition (i.e., one female and two males in a group) compared to when they were in a non-minority condition (i.e., three females in a group). This happens because when people are in a minority, they are (and feel) more conspicuous. Additionally, members of a minority may feel a responsibility to represent their group. If you can remember the effects of social inhibition, you won't be surprised that the self-consciousness and evaluation apprehension that are present in these situations inhibit performance (Inzlicht & Ben-Zeev, 2000, 2003). However, and as indicated in the Education Connections box, subtle manipulations can also minimize the negative effects of stereotype threat.

"Ah, Harding—perhaps you can give us some input from the straight community."

EDUCATION CONNECTIONS

Reducing the Effects of Stereotype Threat in the Classroom

Historically, in Canada, women were stereotyped as being less capable of achieving at the university level than men. In the 1970s, only 32 percent of university students were women, compared to 58 percent in 2001 (Frenette & Zeman, 2007). While women proved the old stereotype wrong, the one area of academics where women have not excelled is in mathematics and related domains (Evangelauf, 1993). In situations where math is a central component, women are perceived to be unequal to men in their ability to use math skills on such tasks as taxes, accounting, or even calculating a waiter's tip. Women's weak ability to do math is a widely known stereotype in some societies (Eccles, Jacobs, & Harold, 1990; Swim, 1994), one that most women are subjected to throughout their schooling.

According to stereotype threat research, gender-based math differences are more likely due to differences in gender-role socialization. Steven Spencer from the University of Waterloo and colleagues examined gender difference in math performance and found that women did as well as men on easy tests, but did substantially worse than men on difficult tests (Spencer, Steele, & Quinn, 1999). But is it possible that the threat of the "math" stereotype affected women's ability on the difficult test as they knew it was cognitively demanding and expected to do worse because of the stereotype?

In two follow-up studies, these same researchers manipulated the gender-based stereotype by explaining to the experimental group in both studies that the test had never shown gender differences in the past (Spencer et al., 1999). For the control group, in one study the participants were told that the test they were about to work on had shown gender differences in the past (thus increasing awareness of the stereotype about women's math ability) while in the other study they were told nothing. As expected, when women were told that no gender difference existed on the test they performed as well as men. In contrast, they underperformed when they were presented with evidence that either stated or didn't mention a gender bias. These findings indicate that awareness of a stereotype threat creates apprehension or anxiety that disrupt women's math performance. In sum, when the gender stereotype was nullified, the performance difference was eliminated.

Researchers are now investigating how stereotype threat leads to decreased performance. One explanation is that stereotype threat leads to lower working memory capacity. In line with this view, Latino students who are told that a memory test is highly predictive of intelligence recall fewer words on the test than those who aren't given this information (Schmader & Johns, 2003). Another explanation is that such threat increases anxiety, which in turn disrupts performance (Inzlicht & Ben Zeev, 2003). Support for this explanation is found in research demonstrating that being the only representative of one's group in a situation leads to lower levels of performance. More recent research has examined how stereotype threat is associated with the activation of particular parts of the brain (Krendl, Richeson, Kelley, & Heatherton, 2008). This work indicates that although women who are solving math problems usually show activation in a part of the brain that controls mental math tasks (not surprisingly), those who are under conditions of threat instead show activation in a part of the brain that regulates emotions. This finding suggests that women under conditions of stereotype threat may focus more on the social and emotional consequences of confirming negative stereotypes about their group, and less on successfully computing the math problems, thus bringing about exactly what they fear.

REDUCED PSYCHOLOGICAL WELL-BEING

rejection-identification model – a model which proposes that people in disadvantaged groups experience a negative impact on their well-being when they perceive prejudice and discrimination against themselves

Members of low status groups are, not surprisingly, more likely than those in high status groups to report experiencing personal discrimination (Major et al., 2002; Schmitt, Branscombe, Kobrynowicz, & Owen, 2002). According to the **rejection-identification model**, perceiving prejudice and discrimination negatively impacts psychological well-being. People who interpret others' negative behaviour toward them as prejudice (e.g., when receiving a speeding ticket, failing to get a desired job, or being told an apartment they want to rent is unavailable) experience depression, sadness, and helplessness (Branscombe, Schmitt, & Harvey, 1999; Schmitt & Branscombe, 2002). Observing blatant discrimination toward a member of our own group can also lead to impaired cognitive abilities (Salvatore & Shelton, 2007). As described in the Health Connections box, experiencing discrimination can lead to negative effects on physical health as well.

HEALTH CONNECTIONS

The Impact of Racism on Physical Health

One of the most dangerous consequences of prejudice and discrimination is its impact on physical health. Black Americans have higher rates of coronary heart disease (CHD) and hypertension than do White Americans, and these differences may be caused in part by the constant exposure to discrimination and racism (Clark, Anderson, Clark, & Williams, 1999; Mendes, Major, McCoy, & Blascovich, 2008). Perceived discrimination is also associated with other negative health effects. Researchers from the University of Guelph surveyed immigrants living in rural and urban Ontario and found that perceived discrimination was linked to higher levels of adverse psychological and physical symptoms (Safdar, Fuller, & Lewis, 2007; Safdar, Rasmi, Dupuis & Lewis, 2008). That is, those who reported high perceived discrimination against themselves and their in-group also reported higher levels of health and stress symptoms, including insomnia, back pain, and feelings of loneliness. Those who reported high perceived discrimination also reported more social and cultural difficulties in adapting to Canadian society. These difficulties include having troubles in making friends, finding accommodation, going shopping, and even dealing with people in authority (Safdar et al., 2007). Additionally, it was found that

perceived discrimination was the most important factor in predicting health and stress symptoms, surpassing such factors as levels of education, age, gender, occupation, and years living in Canada (Safdar et al., 2007). In sum, experiencing discrimination is associated with negative physical as well as psychological symptoms and the relation is well documented in stress and coping literature (Clark, Anderson, Clark, & Williams, 1999; Dion, Dion, & Pak, 1992).

© Science Photo Library / Alamy

Although, overall, members of minority groups report experiencing more personal and group discrimination than do members of majority groups, those who strongly identify with their minority group report feeling more discrimination, as well as more psychological distress, than those who don't identify as strongly with their group (Operario & Fiske, 2001; Sellers & Shelton, 2003). For example, women who experience minority status in relation to men and thereby believe that gender discrimination is likely are more likely to experience lower psychological well-being, especially if they strongly identify with their in-group (Schmitt et al., 2002). In contrast, men who in general do not perceive they have minority status show no effect on their well-being of perceiving gender discrimination, regardless of their level of in-group identification.

SOCIAL COSTS OF ATTRIBUTIONS TO PREJUDICE. People who attribute poor behaviour to prejudice can also experience social costs. For example, Blacks who attribute failing grades to discrimination are seen less favourably than those who are seen as taking responsibility for their poor performance, suggesting that the social costs of making attributions to discrimination are substantial (Kaiser & Miller, 2001). Members of minority groups are often aware of the personal costs of reporting discrimination to members of majority groups. In a study by Stangor, Swim, Van Allen, and Sechrist (2002), university students completed a creativity test and were told that their performance was indicative of the success they would have in their future career. Participants then were provided with a written evaluation of their performance, which included the supposed gender and ethnicity of the evaluator. Everyone received a failing grade. The study was designed so that women received their evaluation from a supposedly male evaluator and men received their evaluation from a supposedly female evaluator. Similarly, White Anglo participants received their evaluation from someone who was said to be Black, and Black participants received their evaluation from someone said to have a White Anglo background. Participants were then asked to provide either private or public feedback about the extent to which they felt their evaluator was biased or had discriminated against them. As expected, members of stigmatized groups (women and Blacks) reported that a failing grade was caused by discrimination when they made the judgement privately and in front of another stigmatized group member. However, when they had to give feedback out loud or in front of members of nonstigmatized groups, they were more likely to report that their failure was due to lack of ability. This pattern of results was not found for members of nonstigmatized groups (men and White Anglos).

STRATEGIES FOR MINIMIZING THE EFFECTS OF PREJUDICE. Although people in stigmatized groups can develop low self-esteem, members of minority groups often avoid internalizing negative stereotypes about their own group and thereby protect their self-esteem (Crocker & Major, 1989; Guimond, 2000). How can they avoid the negative effects of prejudice? Research points to several effective strategies.

First, people can disengage from and ignore negative feedback (Crocker, Voelkl, Testa, & Major, 1991; Major, Spencer, Schmader, Wolfe, & Crocker, 1998). The correlation between self-esteem and academic outcomes increases over time among White adolescents, but decreases among Black adolescents, suggesting a separation between feelings about the self and academic feedback (Osbourne, 1995).

Second, members of low status groups can compare their outcomes to those of others in their in-group as opposed to those in their outgroup. Women executives, for example, may be aware that they are not receiving the same salary or promotions as their male counterparts, but may feel encouraged about their career prospects when they compare themselves to other women.

Third, people can devalue the dimensions on which their group doesn't do so well and value those dimensions in which their group excels. Athletes are likely to emphasize the positive effects of physical abilities and downplay the importance of musical aptitude, whereas members of singing groups are likely to show the reverse pattern.

Fourth, people in low status groups can increase their identification with the in-group, perhaps as a way of increasing self-esteem and thereby well-being (Branscombe et al., 1999; Major et al., 2002; Schmitt et al., 2002). For example, people with body piercings who feel discriminated against by the mainstream report greater group identification, which in turn leads to higher self-esteem (Jetten, Branscombe, Schmitt, & Spears, 2001). This identification also influences how people react to discrimination. People who identify with their group react to discrimination by feeling angry at the outgroup, whereas people who don't really identify with their in-group often feel angry at themselves after being discriminated against (Hansen & Sassenberg, 2006).

REVERSE DISCRIMINATION

reverse discrimination – preferential treatment of people in stereotyped groups

Reverse discrimination occurs when people show preferential treatment to those in stereotyped groups (Fajardo, 1985; Harber, 1998). Reverse discrimination can lead people to prefer candidates from under-represented groups over those from other groups, and to justify such preferences on seemingly objective criteria. Although in some cases members of disadvantaged groups may be seen as especially good, they can also be seen as especially bad—in sum, they're often evaluated more extremely, or as especially good if good, but especially bad if bad (Branscombe, Wann, Noel, & Coleman, 1993; Linville & Jones, 1980). In one study, participants were instructed to give a certain number of shocks to another participant (a confederate who was either Black or White), but they could choose the intensity of the shocks (Rogers & Prentice-Dunn, 1981). The confederate behaved as either friendly or hostile, and the researchers found that friendly Black confederates received lower severity shocks than friendly White confederates, showing that participants "bent over backwards" to show how "not racist" they were. However, when the confederate was hostile, the reverse was found, with hostile Blacks receiving shocks of much greater intensity than hostile Whites. Thus, reverse discrimination may benefit members of stereotyped groups, but it only occurs under certain conditions.

THE HAZARDS OF POSITIVE STEREOTYPES

Recent research suggests that stereotypes consist of two basic dimensions—competence and warmth (see Table 11.1; Fiske, Cuddy, Glick, & Xu, 2002; Fiske, Xu, Cuddy, & Glick, 1999). These two dimensions are associated with groups differently, depending on their social status:

- People who belong to high status groups (e.g., rich people, Asians, Jews) are seen as highly competent (e.g., intelligent, aggressive, competitive), but not as particularly warm (e.g., honest, warm, sensitive; Fiske et al., 2002; Lin, Kwan, Cheung, & Fiske, 2005).
- People who belong to low status groups (e.g., elderly people, housewives) are seen as incompetent but warm (Fiske et al., 1999; Fiske et al., 2002).
- People who belong to very low status groups (e.g., poor people, homeless people) are seen as low in competence and low in warmth (Fiske et al., 2002).

We also react differently to people in the different groups (Cuddy, Fiske, & Glick, 2007). We pity those who are in low competence but high warmth groups, and envy those who are in low warmth and high competence groups. Harris and Fiske (2006) also found that when people think about people who belong to groups that are seen as low in warmth and competence, such as drug addicts and the homeless, portions of the brain that are responsible for encoding disgust are activated. These perceptions of disgust suggest that we dehumanize members of certain groups, which can help explain such atrocities as hate crimes, genocide, and prisoner abuse.

Although positive stereotypes may seem harmless, they can also have detrimental effects. Researchers Peter Glick and Susan Fiske developed a theory of sexism that distinguishes between different types of attitudes that people could have about women (see Table 11.2; Glick & Fiske, 1996, 2001). **Hostile sexism**, which describes feelings of hostility toward women based on their threat to men's power, is what we more typically think of as prejudice

hostile sexism – feelings of hostility toward women based on their threat to men's power

Table 11.1	Dimensions of Stereotypes	
	COMPETENCE	
Warmth	Low	High
High	elderly people, housewives, disabled people, people with mental disability	in-group members, students, Whites, middle-class people
Low	poor people, welfare recipients, homeless people	Asians, Jews, rich people, feminists

Table 11.2	Views Reflecting Hostile or Benevolent Sexism

HOSTILE SEXISM

Most women interpret innocent remarks or acts as being sexist.

Most women fail to appreciate all that men do for them.

Women seek to gain power by getting control over men.

Women exaggerate problems they have at work.

Once a woman gets a man to commit to her, she usually tries to put him on a tight leash.

BENEVOLENT SEXISM

Many women have a quality of purity that few men possess.

Women should be cherished and protected by men.

Women, as compared to men, tend to have a more refined sense of culture and good taste.

Men should be willing to sacrifice their own well-being in order to provide financially for the women in their lives.

Every man ought to have a woman whom he adores.

Source: Glick, P., & Fiske, S. T. (1996). The ambivalent sexism inventory: Differentiating hostile and benevolent sexism. *Journal of Personality and Social Psychology, 70,* 491–512.

against women. People who are high in hostile sexism have negative attitudes toward women, such as believing that women are inherently less intelligent than men. On the other hand, **benevolent sexism** describes holding positive, but patronizing, views of women. People who are high on benevolent sexism have seemingly positive attitudes toward women, such as believing that women are more considerate and are better listeners. Although men tend to be higher on hostile sexism than women, both men and women commonly endorse benevolent sexism (Glick et al., 2000).

benevolent sexism – having positive, but patronizing, views of women

Aversive prejudice is another form of contemporary prejudice that is expressed in the form of unprejudiced beliefs about a group while at the same time having unconscious negative attitudes toward the group (Dovidio & Gaertner, 2004). One of the conditions under which aversive prejudice is more likely to be expressed is the condition of ambiguity. This is demonstrated in a study by Paula Brochu and Victoria Esses (2009), researchers from the University of Western Ontario, who examined students' attitudes toward overweight individuals and their beliefs about weight being something that a person can control as predictors of participants' level of support for a medical policy in the UK that denied surgery to overweight patients. The medical policy was set by three health-care agencies in the UK that in 2005 ruled to deny surgery to people with a body mass index (BMI) over 30. The information about the policy was presented in a way that could either justify or question the policy. Therefore, participants could interpret the policy according to their prejudiced feelings. Although most participants didn't support the policy, it was found that those who scored high on a weight prejudice scale (such as feeling disgust and repulsion when seeing an overweight person) were less likely to perceive the new policy in the UK as discriminatory and were more likely to agree that a similar policy should be adopted in Canada. Additionally, it was found that when weight control beliefs were taken into account, the weight prejudice attitudes were more powerful predictors of agreement with the policy. This is in line with the theory of aversive prejudice. In this study, the information about the policy having been provided to the participants so that they could either support or question it allowed prejudiced participants to support the policy without appearing biased (Brochu & Esses, 2009).

aversive prejudice – conscious endorsement of unprejudiced beliefs about a group while at the same time holding unconscious negative attitudes toward the group

[CONCEPTS IN CONTEXT]

THE CONSEQUENCES OF STEREOTYPING, PREJUDICE, AND DISCRIMINATION

FACTOR	CONSEQUENCE
Self-fulfilling prophecy	Professor Garnaut believes that athletes are less intelligent than other students. He therefore avoids calling on athletes in class, and uses more simplistic examples when discussing course material with athletes during office hours. As the athletes become aware of his attitude, they expect they'll do poorly in his class and therefore make less effort—they "know" it's not worth it. Professor Garnaut's views about athletes' intelligence are confirmed when these students do poorly on the final exam.
Stereotype threat	Deepa is the only female student taking her engineering exam in a room with 10 male students. She feels quite nervous because she feels out of place being the only woman in the room and is disappointed when she receives a very low score on the exam—she had performed at a much higher level on her practice tests.
Reduced psychological well-being	Dr. Denstedt gets quite down when she thinks about her salary being somewhat lower than the salary of her male counterparts.
Reverse discrimination	Jane works in human resources and knows about the pervasiveness of prejudice through a psychology course she took in university. If there's a candidate from a visible minority for a job opening, she's likely to overlook minor errors in the application form and offer the person the job. She justifies this by thinking that the candidate must have had to overcome more obstacles as a member of a visible minority.
The hazards of positive stereotypes	When Pieta learns that her new roommate is Asian Canadian, she's disappointed. She was hoping for a sociable, outgoing roommate. She consoles herself a bit when she realizes that her new roommate will at least serve as a good role model for studying more.

IS STEREOTYPING INEVITABLE?

Can stereotypes influence behaviour, even among people who believe themselves to be unprejudiced? Researchers in psychology have examined this phenomenon for many years. In one study, researchers asked both White and Black participants to play a video game (Correll, Park, Judd, & Wittenbrink, 2002). Participants were told to shoot armed targets and to not shoot unarmed targets. Results revealed that both Black and White participants made the decision to shoot an armed target more quickly if the target was Black than if it was White, and made the decision to not shoot an unarmed target more quickly if the target was White rather than Black. It's worth noting, however, that studies like this one, which was conducted in the United States, may not replicate in Canada. Kimberley Clow from the University of Ontario Institute of Technology and Victoria Esses from the University of Western Ontario gave Canadian student participants an open-ended questionnaire that asked them to list the characteristics that they thought described 15 different social groups: Chinese, Blacks, Pakistanis, Italians, Natives, Jews, homosexuals, men, women, teachers, leaders, terrorists, criminals, beggars, and doctors. It was found that not a single participant in this Canadian sample described Blacks with terms related to violence or crime. And this wasn't simply a case of the participants not wanting to appear prejudiced, as several participants did describe Natives as angry, alcoholics, and parasites. Much of the negative content of the Black stereotype that is found in the United States just didn't apply to the Black stereotype in this Canadian sample (Clow & Esses, 2007).

Correll et al. (2002) does nonetheless point to the influence of stereotypes on real-life situations,and may partially explain why Blacks are at greater risk of being accidentally shot by a police officer who is making a split-second decision. This section will examine evidence that stereotyping is inevitable, including the automatic activation of stereotypes, the difficulty of suppressing stereotypes, the active maintenance of stereotypes, and the persistence of subtle forms of discrimination.

STEREOTYPES ARE ACTIVATED AUTOMATICALLY

Stereotypes are activated automatically and without conscious awareness, even among people who describe themselves as unprejudiced (Bargh & Chartrand, 1999; Greenwald & Banaji, 1995). Patricia Devine (1989) conducted one of the first studies demonstrating this automatic activation of stereotypes. Participants were exposed at an unconscious level to words (or "primes") related to stereotypes of Blacks (e.g., poor, slavery, Harlem, jazz), and then read a paragraph about a man, Donald, who engaged in several ambiguously hostile behaviours, such as demanding his money back from a store clerk and refusing to pay the rent until his apartment was painted. Participants who had been primed with the stereotypically Black words judged Donald's behaviour as more aggressive than those who were primed with neutral words, suggesting that unconscious priming of Black stereotypes activated the general Black stereotype, which in turn led to the ambiguous behaviour being seen in a negative way.

This type of automatic activation of stereotypes occurs not just for ethnicity, but for other characteristics, including age (Kawakami, Young, & Dovidio, 2002; Perdue & Gurtman, 1990) and gender (Banaji & Greenwald, 1995; Ito & Urland, 2003; Rudman, Ashmore, & Gary, 2001). Thomas Mussweiler (2006) from Germany demonstrated in three studies that stereotypic movements trigger a stereotype that is associated with such movements. In the first study, participants in the experimental condition were induced to act in a way that cues obesity (by asking them to wear a heavy life vest and ankle weights while they performed a series of movements). Participants in the control condition performed the same movements but without wearing life vests and weights. All participants were then given a one-page description of a target person named Beate whose characteristics were described in ambiguous terms. Some of Beate's characteristics related to the overweight stereotype and some were unrelated. Participants were then asked to rate her on 15 characteristics. It was found that the experimental group (those who had worn the life vests and ankle weights) described Beate as having more stereotypic characteristics associated with obesity, such as unhealthy, sluggish, and lazy, than did control participants (see Figure 11.3). Mussweiler (2006) reported similar findings in subsequent studies, where participants in the experimental condition were asked to pedal a bicycle slowly and then had to rate the characteristics of an ambiguously described elderly target person. As expected, these participants described the target as having more stereotypic characteristics associated with the elderly, such as slow, forgetful, and scatter-minded, compared to the control group, who were asked to pedal at a normal speed. Research Focus on Neuroscience describes how techniques in neuroscience can be particularly useful in examining how the brain responds to pictures of people from different backgrounds.

Questioning the Research:

Can you think of another explanation for why people who are unconsciously exposed to stereotypes of Black people then judge another person's behaviour as more hostile? Does this study *prove* that exposure to these words activates the general Black stereotype?

RESEARCH FOCUS ON NEUROSCIENCE
How the Brain Responds to Gender and Ethnicity Categorization

Some of the most recent research examining issues in stereotypes, prejudice, and discrimination has been conducted using the tools of neuroscience (Eberhardt, 2005). These techniques are particularly well suited for examining these issues as people have a tendency to express less prejudicial attitudes than they actually feel. Neuroscience techniques can therefore be

FIGURE 11.3 CAN BEHAVIOUR LEAD TO STEREOTYPING?

In this study, people either wore a heavy life vest and ankle weights while they performed a series of movements or performed such movements without wearing the life vest and ankle weights. They were then asked to rate a target person. As predicted, participants who wore the vest and weights described the target person as having more traits associated with obesity than did those whose actions had not been designed to cue obesity.

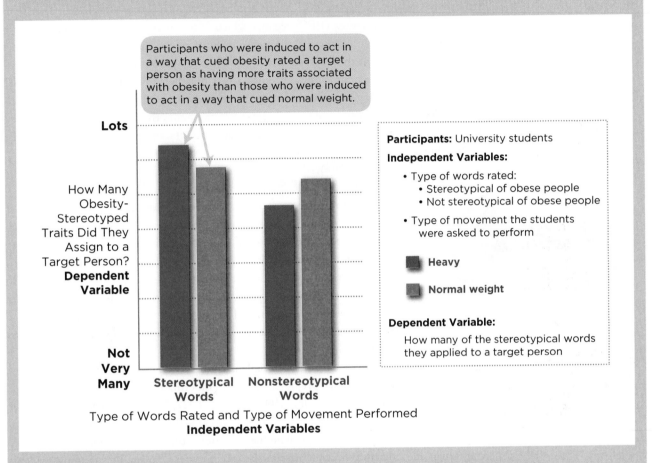

Source: Mussweiler, T. (2006). Doing is for thinking! Stereotype activation by stereotypic movements. *Psychological Science, 17*, 17–21.

extremely useful in answering questions about whether prejudiced responses occur automatically and how such responses can be reduced.

Mitchell, Ames, Jenkins, and Banaji (2008) used functional magnetic resonance imaging (fMRI) to examine the pattern of neural activity when stereotypes were triggered. In this study, 17 participants responded to a series of questions during fMRI scanning. Researchers used two sets of items: stereotypical items (e.g., "likes shopping for clothes," or "likes action movies") and nonstereotypical items (e.g., "likes Coke better than Pepsi"). During scanning, participants were shown pictures of a man or a woman and were asked to estimate how likely the person would be to endorse the statement. It was found that when a gender stereotype was used in regard to the target image's preference (e.g., the female target likes shopping for clothes), there was more activation in the right frontal cortex compared to when a gender stereotype was not used. This indicates the important role that the frontal cortex plays in the retrieval of categorical knowledge. The researchers suggest that gender stereotyping, as a form of social categorization, may involve the same neural processes as other forms of categorical knowledge (Mitchell et al., 2008, p. 600).

In another study, researchers asked 20 participants to perform the implicit association test (IAT) for gender and ethnicity while their brain was being scanned using fMRI
(Knutson, Mah, Manly, & Grafman, 2007). For the gender IAT, participants classified names
as either male or female (e.g., Mary, John) and then classified words as either weak or strong
(e.g., feather). For the ethnicity IAT, participants classified names as typically White or Black
and then classified words as either pleasant or unpleasant. It was found that when participants made stereotypic associations about gender and ethnicity, there was higher activity in
the medial prefrontal cortex (PFC) regions, which function as an emotional-motor system
that responds to potential danger in the environment (Gallese, Keysers, & Rizzolatti, 2004).
The researchers suggest that representation of well-learned associations about social groups
within this part of the brain allows for quick access to beliefs toward social groups that are
perceived as threatening or negative. In sum, these studies show that stereotyping and automatic thinking can be traced to several regions of the brain, that stereotyping involves the
same type of categorization that we use for inanimate objects, and that stereotypes can invoke
an emotional response.

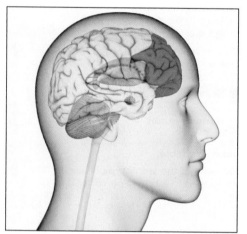

Dorling Kindersley/Getty Images, Inc.

STEREOTYPES ARE HARD TO SUPPRESS

You might think that one effective strategy for reducing the negative effects
of stereotypes and prejudice would be to try to actively suppress them.
Unfortunately this approach is quite ineffective. For example, elderly
people, who report a stronger desire than younger people to control prejudiced reactions, rely more on stereotypes, even when instructed not to
(von Hippel, Silver, & Lynch, 2000). Suppressing stereotypes also uses
up considerable energy and effort, so someone who initially resists using
stereotypes later performs worse on cognitive tasks (Gailliot, Plant, Butz,
& Baumeister, 2007).

Trying to inhibit initially prejudicial responses can also lead someone
to show more prejudice later on (Liberman & Forster, 2000; Monteith,
Sherman, & Devine, 1998; Wegner, 1997; Wyer, Sherman, & Stroessner,
2000). Benoit Monin and Dale Miller (2001) conducted a study to examine whether people who have the opportunity to show how unprejudiced
they are in one situation show increased use of stereotypes later on. In this study, students
first rated five applicants for a starting position at a large consulting firm. Each candidate
was briefly described (e.g., GPA, major, university, photo), and in all cases the "best candidate" was clear (one person had attended the best school and had the highest GPA). In
some cases, the best candidate was a White woman. In other cases, he was a Black man,
and in other cases he was a White man (the control condition). In this first part of the
study, students overwhelmingly chose this "best candidate" in all conditions (regardless of
the applicant's gender or ethnicity). In the second part of the study, participants were told
that they had one more hiring task to solve. The situation was that a police chief in a small
town in a rural area had to hire a new police officer for a department that was racist (or
sexist). A prior officer (who was Black or female, depending on the condition) had complained of a hostile work environment and had quit, and the police chief was well aware
that a White male would fit best with the other officers. Participants were asked if, given
the circumstances, ethnicity (or gender) should be considered as a factor in hiring a new
officer for the position. The researchers found that students who had been able to show
how unprejudiced they were in the first task by recommending the Black or female applicant were more likely to agree that ethnicity (or gender) should be a factor in this second
condition than those who had chosen the White man in the first case. This suggests that
participants who had already established that they were unprejudiced felt that they could
afford to exhibit otherwise unexpressed prejudice in the second scenario. It is possible to

rationalize decisions such as this by arguing, for example, that the goal is to protect female and Black candidates by keeping them out of the sexist or racist environment.

DISCONFIRMING EVIDENCE IS IGNORED

Even when people meet others who disconfirm their stereotypes, they can maintain the prior stereotypes by creating a separate category for them, a process called **subcategorization**, which impedes stereotype change (Hewstone, Macrae, Griffiths, & Milne, 1994; Kunda & Oleson, 1995). For example, one study with high school students found that after the creation of a police-schools liaison program designed to change adolescents' negative stereotypes about police officers, students became more positive about those officers who participated in the program (Hewstone, Hopkins, & Routh, 1992). Unfortunately, these beliefs didn't generalize to other police officers. The students simply categorized their school police officers differently from police in general.

subcategorization – the maintenance of prior beliefs by creating separate categories for people who disconfirm these stereotypes

However, encountering stereotype-inconsistent information can decrease the strength of a stereotype if the information is dispersed across different group members rather than being concentrated in a small number of people (Hewstone et al., 1994; Kunda & Oleson, 1997; Queller & Smith, 2002). In one study, participants received three pieces of information (one stereotype-consistent, one stereotype-inconsistent, and one neutral) about a number of corporate lawyers, and then rated how stereotypical this group of lawyers was (Weber & Crocker, 1983). Some participants read descriptions in which the inconsistent information was distributed across all the lawyers, whereas others read descriptions in which this information was clustered in a small number of lawyers. Those who read about the scenario in which all the lawyers had some stereotype-inconsistent information revised their general stereotype of the lawyer group. In contrast, those who read about the scenario in which some lawyers had stereotype-inconsistent information just dismissed those lawyers as atypical, and hence did not change their overall impression of lawyers. In sum, people who see high dispersion of a stereotype-inconsistent trait among the

© Tom Cheney / The New Yorker Collection / www.cartoonbank.com.

members of a group become less confident in holding stereotypes about particular individuals in the group (Ryan, Judd, & Park, 1996). Stereotype-inconsistent behaviour has been found to be especially effective in reducing stereotypes when it's attributed to stable internal causes (Wilder, Simon, & Faith, 1996). In other words, if the behaviour is perceived to be something that stays the same (e.g., a person's character) rather than involving something temporary about the situation (e.g., a particular social pressure), stereotype inconsistent behaviour is highly effective in reducing stereotypes.

SUBTLE DISCRIMINATION PERSISTS

Although stereotypes of women, homosexuals, and Blacks are less prevalent today than they have been in the past (Diekman & Eagly, 2000), more subtle types of discrimination remain (Devine & Elliot, 1995; Dovidio & Gaertner, 2000; Swim et al., 1995). For example, subtle discrimination based on ethnicity and religion may have led to delays in foreign government responses following flooding in Pakistan (see In the News). Similarly, and as described in the Business Connections box, while blatant sexism against women has largely disappeared, people continue to engage in more subtle forms of sexism, such as denying that women continue to experience discrimination, feeling antagonistic toward women's demands, and opposing policies that are designed to help women in education and work settings.

IN THE NEWS

FAROOQ NAEEM/AFP/Getty Images, Inc.

Unequal Disasters: In August 2010, Pakistan experienced the worst monsoon rains it had seen in 80 years (BBC News, 2010b). The flooding crisis affected about 20 million people, left about 6 million homeless, and killed more than 1,600 people. Some villages were completely submerged and many districts were evacuated (Gronewold, 2010). The flood's widespread destruction and its claim on human lives, crops, businesses, and industry required immediate international mobilization, yet the level of response, in terms of both public and private funding, was low and slow to come. Siri Agrell (2010), Urban Affairs reporter for the *Globe and Mail,* wrote that the total fundraising for the Pakistan floods was $229 million for an affected population of 14 million (i.e., $16.36 of funding per person), whereas in response to the earthquake in Haiti in January 2010, $3.3 billion was donated for an affected population of 3 million (i.e., $1,087.33 of funding per person). Similarly, the total fundraising for the Indian Ocean earthquake/tsunami in 2004 was $6.2 billion for an affected population of 5 million ($1,249.80 of funding per person)! Why were international donors snubbing Pakistan? Is it possible that religion and ethnicity contributed to delays in the response from the public and governments? Pakistan is a Muslim country with a different culture and language from Western donor countries. Pakistan is also a neighbouring country of Afghanistan, where many Western countries, including Canada, are fighting against the Taliban.

BENEVOLENT DISCRIMINATION.

Benevolent discrimination underlies views that, for example, women are pure, fragile, and good at nurturing. Although seemingly positive (albeit patronizing) because they flatter women on their feminine nurturing qualities, these beliefs serve to undermine women's abilities, rights, and freedoms and ultimately threaten their social status. Researchers at the University of Winnipeg conducted a study of benevolent discrimination in regard to First Nations students. The participants were students at the university who thought they were taking part in a study organized by the campus newspaper on the qualities that are needed for success in various organizational roles at the newspaper. After being "randomly" assigned the role of editor, participants had to look at one of two sets of pictures and rate them for possible publication. One of the sets of pictures evoked the stereotype of First Nations Canadians as being lazy and incompetent. Participants then had to assess an essay for potential publication. The essay was purportedly by either a First Nations student or a non–First Nations student, although the essays were identical and had errors. Participants were also given either of two samples of "good writing" to read, supposedly to help them assess the essay, but the sample article either provided evidence that intelligence is largely innate (genetic) or learned (environmental). All together, then, the study manipulated three variables: a prime for awareness of the stereotype of First Nations people (the set of photographs), a prime for the view that intelligence is innate versus learned (the sample of "good writing"), and an essay submission from a First Nations or non–First Nations student. When asked afterwards how much of their time, as editor, they would give to help the essay writer, those who had been primed with the First Nations stereotype and support for the theory of innate intelligence were prepared to give more time to assist the First Nations author. While it is possible that this response could reflect benevolence rather than benevolent prejudice, when these same participants were asked how likely they would be to recommend the author to work on their team, they were less inclined to recommend the First Nations author than they were to recommend the non–First Nations author (see Figure 11.4). As the essays had been identical, this appears to be a discriminatory judgement: although these participants had appeared to be more benevolent to the First Nations author by being prepared to spend more time helping the author, this willingness actually betrays the participants' assumption that the First Nations author simply needed more help as, when it came down to it, these participants were less likely to give that person a recommendation (Werhun & Penner, 2010).

FIGURE 11.4   DOES ETHNICITY AFFECT OUR WILLINGNESS TO HELP?

In order to examine benevolent discrimination in regard to First Nations students, researchers from the University of Winnipeg assigned participants the role of editor and had them examine photographs that depicted the stereotype of First Nations people as lazy, and read articles discussing the view that intelligence is innate versus learned. Participants then read an essay submission from a First Nations or non–First Nations student. When asked afterwards how much of their time, as editor, they would give to help the essay writer, those who had been primed with the First Nations stereotype and read the article supporting the view that intelligence is innate were prepared to give more time to assist the First Nations author. The same participants, however, were less likely to recommend the writing of the First Nations candidate for potential publication. Participant responses were based on the Likert scale of 1–7 (1 being not very willing and 7 being very willing).

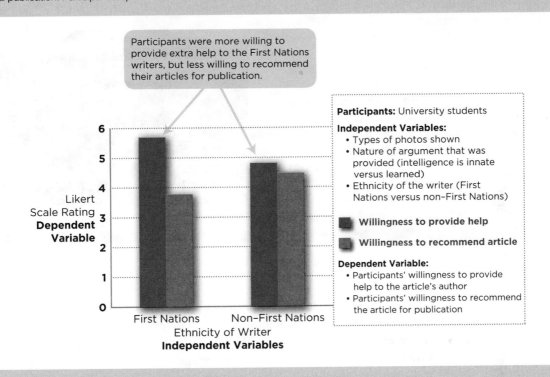

Source: Werhun, C. G., & Penner, A. J. (2010). The effects of stereotyping and implicit theory on benevolent prejudice toward Aboriginal Canadians. *Journal of Applied Social Psychology, 40,* 899–916.

BUSINESS CONNECTIONS

Examining the Effects of Affirmative Action Policies

Affirmative action policies, meaning policies that are designed to combat discrimination and promote equal opportunity for members of all groups, have received considerable attention in both the legal system and psychology (Crosby & Franco, 2003). The goal of affirmative action is to increase the representation of "qualified" marginalized groups who have faced discrimination due to systematic institutionalized barriers. Affirmative action legislation is a government's attempt to eliminate structural barriers that traditionally exist in the workplace or in educational organizations. One of the myths about affirmative action is that it's a preferential selection of members of minority groups with

no regard for their qualifications. In fact, although affirmative action is targeted to groups who have suffered from systematic discrimination, it is designed to benefit only those members of the marginalized group who are qualified for a particular position.

Unfortunately, affirmative action policies can also lead to costs for the people that they're designed to help. For example, women who believe that they were hired as managers because of their gender have less organizational commitment, less satisfaction with their work, and less satisfaction with their supervisor and co-workers (Chacko, 1982). The affirmative action label also affects the perceived competence of female and minority group hirees, meaning that other people see those who potentially benefited from such policies as less capable than those who are assumed to have been hired based entirely on their own merits (Crosby, Iyer, Clayton, & Downing, 2003; Heilman, Block, & Lucas, 1992).

Does this mean that affirmative action policies should be eliminated? No: most research suggests that overall affirmative action programs benefit both majority and minority group members, and that the potential negative costs of such policies can be eliminated or at least reduced (Crosby et al., 2003). First, affirmative action policies need to take into account an individual's distinct qualifications as well as the person's ethnicity and/or gender, which reduces the potential negative effects that beneficiaries of such policies may experience (Heilman, Block, & Lucas, 1992). Second, emphasizing the substantial institutional and societal barriers that many members of minority groups face, and thereby portraying such policies as simply "levelling the playing field," can serve to reduce negative feelings about such programs that may be felt by members of majority groups. In fact, even people who strongly endorse principles of merit, and thereby typically reject affirmative action programs, are supportive of such programs in cases where there is such a high level of workplace discrimination that qualified members of minority groups are deprived of job opportunities. Leanne Son Hing from the University of Guelph and Ramona Bobocel and Mark Zanna from the University of Waterloo demonstrated this in two studies, one measuring participants' pre-existing perceptions of actual workplace discrimination, and the other experimentally inducing perceptions of discrimination (Son Hing, Bobocel, & Zanna, 2002).

The Canadian Press/Peter Bregg

Stereotypes can influence how people are treated, albeit often in subtle ways. In one study, confederates applied for jobs at local stores, and wore either a hat saying "Gay and Proud" or "Texan and Proud" (Hebl, Foster, Mannix, & Dovidio, 2002). Although those wearing the "Gay and Proud" hats were not discriminated against in formal ways (e.g., they were not less likely to be told there were no jobs available or to be hired), they were responded to more negatively in informal ways—the average interaction time was nearly six and a half minutes with the nonstigmatized applicants, but only a little over four minutes for the gay and lesbian applicants.

People may also justify acts of discrimination in creative ways to avoid appearing prejudiced. In one study, male and female participants read a description of an applicant—either "Michael" or "Michelle"—who had applied for a position as a police chief (Uhlmann & Cohen, 2005). Half of the participants in each of these conditions read that the applicant was streetwise, meaning tough, had worked in rough neighbourhoods, and got along well with other officers. The other half of the participants read that the applicant was educated, meaning well schooled and experienced in administration. Participants then rated the strength of the applicant's credentials as well as the importance of the characteristics "streetwise" and "educated" in their hiring decision. The results revealed that the importance of the criteria used to evaluate the candidate differed depending on the candidate's gender. If the male applicant was described as educated, the criterion "educated" was seen as more important than when the female applicant was described as educated. In contrast, if the female candidate was described as streetwise, the "educated" characteristic was seen as much more important in the hiring decision than when the male candidate was described as streetwise. This study reveals that stereotypes do influence hiring decisions—and that male applicants are typically preferred—but that people justify these decisions using other factors. In sum, we've clearly come a long way, but there is still progress to be made.

[CONCEPTS IN CONTEXT]

PERSPECTIVES ON WHETHER STEREOTYPING IS INEVITABLE

FACTOR	EXAMPLE
Stereotypes are activated automatically	Yu Peng is reading a newspaper article about a woman who's on welfare. She immediately assumes the woman is Black, and is surprised to later read that she's White.
Stereotypes are hard to suppress	Jimmy is working late and is very tired. When evaluating a set of job applications, he rates the male applicants as more qualified than the female applicants, although their overall qualifications are virtually identical.
Disconfirming evidence is ignored	Jean-François's new co-worker, Mary Jean, is from Calgary. Jean-François had assumed that people from Alberta are all socially conservative and politically right wing, and thus is surprised to learn that Mary Jean is liberal and a supporter of the Green Party. Jean-François now sees Mary Jean as an odd exception, and continues to believe that, in general, people from Alberta are socially conservative.
Subtle discrimination persists	Mohammed and Yasmeen are trying to get a sales clerk's attention at a department store. They notice that the clerk helps other people who haven't been waiting as long as they have before she finally helps them.

HOW CAN SOCIAL AND COGNITIVE INTERVENTIONS HELP OVERCOME PREJUDICE?

Although the last section described stereotypes as inevitable, the use of stereotypes can be reduced. In one study, researchers examined the effects of believing that men and women are equal on reducing anti-gay prejudice (Dasgupta & Rivera, 2006). Participants read some information about a university student who they were told would be interviewing them about their attitudes toward politics. Some participants read that the interviewer was a member of the university's gay students alliance. Other participants read that the interviewer was a member of a fraternity. Participants were then interviewed by the student (who was really a confederate of the experimenter). Participants who held traditional beliefs about the roles of women and homosexuals in society showed discriminatory behaviour in the interview with the student who was gay—less eye contact, less smiling, and less comfort overall. Those who held more egalitarian views about the role of women and homosexuals showed more positive behaviour. This is consistent with the prediction that anti-gay attitudes lead to anti-gay behaviour for those who are not motivated to hold egalitarian views and therefore are not able to control their subtle behaviour. This section will examine this as well as ways in which social and cognitive interventions can help people overcome their reliance on stereotypes, including providing training and education, and being motivated to avoid stereotyping. (Other ways to reduce stereotyping and intergroup conflict were described in Chapter 10 on intergroup relations.)

PROVIDE TRAINING AND EDUCATION

Stereotypes can also be controlled through education and training, including through taking another person's perspective, learning considerable information about a person, and receiving training in statistical reasoning.

TAKE ANOTHER PERSON'S PERSPECTIVE.   Taking the perspective of a person in a stereotyped group can help decrease the prevalence of stereotyping (Esses & Dovidio, 2002). In one study, participants were asked to write about a day in the life of an elderly man (Galinsky

& Moskowitz, 2000). Some were asked to suppress their stereotypes of the elderly, whereas others were asked to take the perspective of the man while they wrote. Later, in a second task, those who had taken the perspective of the elderly man were less likely to recall stereotypes than those who had tried to suppress their stereotypes. Similarly, White participants who watched a videotape showing examples of racial discrimination and then imagined the victim's feelings showed greater decreases in prejudice than those who didn't engage in this perspective-taking (Dovidio et al., 2004).

Encouraging people to take the perspective of an outgroup member is more effective if the perspective-taking is targeted at an emotional rather than a cognitive level. Victoria Esses from the University of Western Ontario and John Dovidio from Colgate University asked participants either to focus on their emotions or their thoughts while they watched a video clip involving discrimination against African Americans. Compared to those who were asked to focus on their thoughts, the researchers found a greater subsequent willingness to engage in intergroup contact with African Americans among those who had been asked to focus on their emotions as they watched the video clip (Esses & Dovidio, 2002).

In a clever demonstration to help children experience what discrimination feels like, Jane Elliott, an elementary school teacher in Iowa, told her students that "blue-eyed people were better than brown-eyed people" and on a later day reversed this by saying that brown-eyed people were better than blue-eyed people (Elliott, 1977). She described numerous positive features of the high status group (e.g., "George Washington had blue eyes"), gave students in this group preferential treatment (e.g., let them sit in the front of the classroom), and forbade students in the different groups from playing with each other at recess. This exercise helped students understand how it feels to be the target of prejudice and discrimination, and, as you might expect, Elliott very quickly created a divided classroom. Children in the majority group ridiculed the kids in the other group, refused to play with them, and behaved aggressively toward them on the playground. Children in the minority group became depressed, withdrawn, and self-conscious. Perhaps most importantly, children performed worse on tests when they were members of the minority group than when they were members of the majority group.

Is this type of demonstration an effective technique for reducing prejudice? It is, but only for individuals who actually participate in the exercise—simply hearing a lecture or watching a video doesn't appear to reduce prejudicial attitudes (Byrnes & Kiger, 1990).

LEARN CONSIDERABLE INFORMATION ABOUT A PERSON. People who have considerable personal information about another person also tend to rely less on stereotypes than those who are unable to make clear distinctions among different group members based on their individuality (Locksley, Borgida, Brekke, & Hepburn, 1980; Postmes & Spears, 2002). For example, when you hear only that a person is a male or female, you rely much more on the use of stereotypes than when you have more information about the person and their actions.

Learning information about one member of a group can also help people think about a group in a more diverse way, and thereby decrease reliance on stereotypes (Wolsko, Park, Judd, & Wittenbrink, 2000). For example, exposing people to admired Black people and disliked Whites, as well as positive Black stereotypes (e.g., a family barbecue, music) reduces prejudice (Dasgupta & Greenwald, 2001; Wittenbrink, Judd, & Park, 2001). Similarly, exposing people to information about famous female leaders as well as seeing women in leadership positions decreases automatic stereotypes about women (Dasgupta & Asgari, 2004).

PROVIDE TRAINING IN STATISTICAL REASONING. Training in statistical reasoning, including gaining knowledge about how we can erroneously think certain things go together, reduces the formation of stereotypes (Schaller, Asp, Rosell, & Heim, 1996). As described previously, police officers are initially more likely to mistakenly shoot (in a video game) unarmed

Blacks than unarmed White suspects (Plant, Peruche, & Butz 2005). However, after repeated training with the computer program that reveals that the ethnicity of the suspect is unrelated to whether a weapon is present, officers are able to eliminate their biases. This study demonstrates that training reduces police officers' biases toward shooting unarmed Blacks—a finding with very important real-world implications.

Even a simple shift, such as in how people think about inequality, can impact stereotypes. Whites who think about ethnic inequality, such as White privilege, show lower racism than those who think about it as Black disadvantages (Powell, Branscombe, & Schmitt, 2005). Similarly, it is expected that framing inequality as a disadvantage faced by Aboriginal peoples enables European Canadians to interpret it as an outgroup issue with little self-relevance, where as focusing on the privileges of European Canadians may help them focus on the advantages of their in-group membership, leading to more guilt and lower racism.

BE MOTIVATED TO AVOID STEREOTYPING AND PREJUDICE

Stereotypes are, at least to some extent, within our control, meaning that people who are motivated can reduce their reliance on stereotypes (you can test your own motivation to avoid prejudice in the Rate Yourself exercise on this page; Legault, Green-Demers, Grant, & Chung, 2007). For example, women tend to express less prejudice toward gay men and lesbians than do men (Ratcliff, Lassiter, Markman, & Snyder, 2006). This gender difference is partly a function of women's greater internal motivation to respond without prejudice. Similarly, Patricia Devine's research reveals that individuals can stop stereotyping or acting based on stereotypes (Plant & Devine, 1998). People who are high on internal motivation to respond without prejudice (e.g., "I attempt to act in non-prejudiced ways toward Black people because it is personally important to me") and low on external motivation (e.g., "I attempt to appear non-prejudiced toward Black people in order to avoid disapproval from others") show lower levels of ethnic bias on implicit tests and on self-reports (Amodio, Harmon-Jones, & Devine, 2003; Devine, Plant, Amodio, Harmon-Jones, & Vance, 2002).

HOW MOTIVATED ARE YOU TO AVOID PREJUDICE?

Motivation to be Non-Prejudiced Scale

INSTRUCTIONS: *Rate each item regarding the extent to which each reason corresponds to your ultimate reason for avoiding prejudice on a scale of 1 (does not correspond at all) to 7 (corresponds exactly).*

1. I am motivated to avoid prejudice because I would feel guilty if I were prejudiced.
2. I am motivated to avoid prejudice because biased people are not well liked.
3. I am motivated to avoid prejudice because I am tolerant and accepting of differences.
4. I am motivated to avoid prejudice because striving to understand others is part of who I am.
5. I am motivated to avoid prejudice because I would feel bad about myself if I were prejudiced.
6. I am motivated to avoid prejudice because I get more respect/acceptance when I act unbiased.
7. I am motivated to avoid prejudice because I value non-prejudice.
8. I am motivated to avoid prejudice because tolerance is important to me.

SCORING: Sum up your total number of points on all of these items.

INTERPRETATION: This scale measures individuals' motivation to avoid prejudice. People with higher scores are more motivated to avoid prejudice against others, whereas those with lower scores are less motivated (Legault et al., 2007).

[RATE YOURSELF]

So, what factors can help people avoid stereotyping? Let's review a few strategies, including increasing self-awareness, adopting egalitarian goals, being motivated to be accurate, and avoiding trying too hard.

INCREASE SELF-AWARENESS. People who don't want to hold prejudiced attitudes feel guilty when they believe they're behaving in a discriminatory way (Devine, Monteith, Zuwerink, & Elliot, 1991; Song Hing, Li, & Zanna, 2002; Macrae, Bodenhausen, & Milne, 1998). In turn, pointing out their stereotypical attitudes leads them to self-reflection, which can motivate them to change such beliefs. For example, telling White people that they had negative reactions to pictures of Blacks leads them to feel guilty and to inhibit such reactions later on (Monteith, Ashburn-Nardo, Voils, & Czopp, 2002). Similarly, making straight people aware of the discrepancies between their attitudes and behaviours regarding gay people leads low prejudiced people to exert greater control over their prejudiced responses. Specifically, once these discrepancies are activated, people who are low in prejudice feel bad and inhibit their response to a gay joke (Monteith, 1993). In sum, heightened self-focus reduces the expression of stereotypes, at least in participants who have a personal desire to avoid using stereotypes.

ADOPT EGALITARIAN GOALS. People with egalitarian goals, meaning a focus on avoiding the use of stereotypes, are able to control automatic stereotype activation (Moskowitz, Gollwitzer, Wasel, & Schaal, 1999). As described at the start of this section, people who held traditional beliefs about the roles of women and homosexuals in our society showed discriminatory behaviour when they believed they were interacting with a gay student (Dasgupta & Rivera, 2006). In contrast, those with more tolerant views about the role of women and homosexuals avoided engaging in such behaviour. In sum, stereotypes may be the dominant response, but they can be controlled in some situations and by some people.

BE MOTIVATED TO BE ACCURATE. Because stereotypes are shortcuts that let us focus our energy on other things, we're especially likely to use stereotypes when we're under time pressure—this is one reason why powerful people, who tend to have more responsibility and thus are more likely to use cognitive shortcuts, often rely more on stereotypes (Fiske, 1993). People make immediate stereotypes about a person when they interact with the person only briefly, but interactions as long as 15 minutes with the person that also provide more information lead to the inhibition of stereotypes (Kunda, Davies, Adams, & Spencer, 2002). This shows that stereotypes are automatically and quickly activated, but that they're also short lived.

Fortunately, when people need to form an accurate impression of someone, they tend not to simply rely on quick and easy judgement rules like stereotypes (Neuberg, 1989; Pendry & Macrae, 1994; Weary, Jacobson, Edwards, & Tobin, 2001). Those who are motivated to be accurate gather more information and do so in a less biased way, which in turn improves their performance. For example, if you're told that you'll work with the person on a joint task and that you can win money for performing well on the task, you'll pay more attention to the person's actual characteristics and rely less on stereotypes (Neuberg & Fiske, 1987).

AVOID TRYING TOO HARD. In some cases, people's efforts to appear nonbiased can backfire and actually lead people to behave less warmly toward members of other groups (Norton, Somers, Apfelbaum, Pura, & Ariely, 2006; Vorauer, 2005). In one study, White participants believed they would discuss either ethnic backgrounds or love and relationships with either a White or Black partner (Goff, Steele, & Davies, 2008). White participants sat closer to Black partners than to White partners when they expected to discuss love and relationships, but sat further away when they expected to discuss ethnicity. Just the threat of appearing racist may lead Whites to stand further away from Blacks.

[CONCEPTS IN CONTEXT]

WAYS IN WHICH SOCIAL AND COGNITIVE INTERVENTIONS CAN HELP OVERCOME PREJUDICE

FACTOR	EXAMPLE
Provide training and education	Angela, a Methodist, thought of Jewish people as being very different from herself. But after reading Anne Frank's diary in school, she learned that Jewish girls shared many of her same hopes and fears.
Be motivated to avoid using stereotypes	Rosalina was surprised to learn that she responded differently to photographs of other Latinos than she did to photos of Blacks. She now makes a conscious effort to respond in a similar way to people of all ethnicities.

HOW DOES CULTURE RELATE TO PREJUDICE AND STEREOTYPES?

DEGREE OF PREJUDICE

Prejudice can vary across cultures in terms of degree (more or less prejudiced) and content (what characteristics are ascribed to the person). In terms of degree, Melanie Morrison from the University of Saskatchewan and colleagues found negative attitudes toward homosexuals to be less evident in a Canadian than an American sample (Morrison, Morrison, & Franklin, 2009). Why do you think this and other differences between countries and cultures exist in terms of their degree of prejudice?

The "racial democracy theory" holds that the degree of racial tension that has been evident in the United States has been largely absent in Latin American societies and that, by extension, people from these societies are less prejudiced (Peña, Sidanius, & Sawyer, 2004). Peña and colleagues (2004) tested this by using implicit and explicit measures of prejudice in the United States, Cuba, Puerto Rico, and the Dominican Republic against Blacks and Whites. In general, the results showed significant racial prejudice against Blacks and in favour of Whites in all four nations. However, participants from the United States actually displayed lower implicit and explicit racial prejudice than participants in each of the three Latino nations. Overall, the results contradicted the thesis of racial democracy and suggested that Latin America may not be nearly as egalitarian as the theory suggests. Combining data from several major international studies (including Hofstede's, 2001), Garcia and colleagues found more ethnocentrism and more sexism among individuals who were more collectivistic (Garcia, Posthuma, & Roehling, 2009). Recall from Chapter 10 on intergroup relations that researchers have found that, regardless of nationality, among participants who were from Thailand, China, and India, those who were more collectivist also showed a tendency to be more ethnocentric (Kongsompong, Powtong, & Sen, 2010).

CONTENT OF STEREOTYPES

We have already seen that the stereotypes associated with the social category "Black" are not identical in Canada and the United States (Clow & Esses, 2007). This would suggest that, at least to some extent, the content of stereotypes varies across cultures. Stereotypes that a person holds about their own group are called **auto-stereotypes**; stereotypes about other groups are called **hetero-stereotypes**. Some common hetero-stereotypes (if you're neither Italian nor

auto-stereotype – a stereotype that one holds about one's own group

hetero-stereotype – stereotypes about other groups

Japanese) include "Italians are emotional" and "Japanese are quiet." You're also likely familiar with the stereotypes about your own group, which are called auto-stereotypes. For example, Canadians are aware of the stereotype that "Canadians are polite." Studies indicate that a group's auto-stereotypes overlap with the hetero-stereotypes that other groups hold toward the particular group. In one study, students in Italy, France, Germany, Russia, the United Kingdom, and the United States were asked to rate how typical certain traits were of individuals in each of these six nations (Peabody, 1985). It was found that there was a substantial overlap between the hetero- and auto-stereotypes. That is, participants generally rated Germans as hard working, English as self-controlled, and Americans as self-confident.

In another multinational study that included researchers from McMaster University, students were asked to provide hetero-stereotypes of Canadians, Australians, Americans, British, and Nigerians (McAndrew et al., 2000). Again, significant agreement on national hetero-stereotypes was found. The American participants perceived Canadians to be friendlier than they perceived Nigerians, the British, and themselves to be, although they perceived Australians as friendlier than any of the others. They also perceived Canadians as more generous than themselves. Canadians also agreed with most of these opinions. They saw themselves as friendlier than Nigerians, the British, and Americans. Overall, Canadian participants had a positive auto-stereotype. They saw themselves as the least aggressive, most open-minded, and second-most friendly (behind Australians) of the different countries in the study. The Canadian stereotype of Americans, however, was less positive. They saw Americans as the most aggressive, most closed-minded, most selfish, most patriotic, least religious, least friendly, and least polite of the target nations. Overall, there was significant agreement on the national stereotypes across nations (McAndrew et al., 2000).

People are aware of the stereotype that older people experience memory loss. But would you believe that the mere presence of this stereotype can *cause* such memory loss? Researchers examined whether the negative American stereotypes about aging would impact memory scores in older Americans, but not among older people in groups in which this stereotype was not present (Levy & Langer, 1994). Participants were from three groups: Americans who could hear, Americans who were deaf (who presumably would be less aware of cultural stereotypes), and Chinese who could hear (and who live in a culture in which older people are honoured). In each of these three groups, participants were divided equally between younger adults (ages 15 to 30) and older adults (ages 59 to 91). All participants completed several memory tests. As predicted, memory scores didn't differ across the three groups for the younger participants, indicating that memory was equally good across Americans who could hear, Americans who were deaf, and Chinese people who could hear. However, in the older age group, memory scores among the deaf American participants and the Chinese participants were significantly higher than among the hearing American participants. These findings suggest that the negative American stereotypes about memory in older adults may actually create a self-fulfilling prophecy in which memory loss is greater than in cultures in which a negative stereotype doesn't exist.

meta-stereotype – a person's beliefs about the stereotypes that outgroup members hold about the person's own group

Meta-stereotypes are another type of cross-cultural stereotype content. Introduced by Jacquie Vorauer and colleagues, a **meta-stereotype** is a person's beliefs about the stereotypes that outgroup members hold about the person's own group, rather than what the person personally believes about his or her group (Vorauer, Main, & O'Connell, 1998). For example, a White Canadian heterosexual man may expect to be seen as submissive and polite by Americans; as arrogant, selfish, and materialistic by First Nations people; and as uptight and conservative by homosexual Canadians. In Vorauer and her colleagues' research, White Canadians gave ratings on the extent to which they thought that First Nations people would believe that White Canadians and First Nations people possessed a series of traits. The researchers confirmed that White Canadians hold a negative meta-stereotype about how they're viewed by Aboriginal Canadians. Note that the researchers used the evaluation of First

Nations people's characteristics as a baseline against which they compared what participants imagined First Nations people hold about White Canadians.

RELIANCE ON COGNITIVE BIASES

People in collectivistic cultures show more evidence of in-group favouritism. In one study, researchers asked Korean children in grade six to resolve a conflict between two people with different goals (Han & Park, 1995). The children with a collectivistic orientation were much more likely to show greater discrimination between members of their in-group and members of outgroups than children with an individualistic orientation.

TYPES OF STEREOTYPES

As described at the start of this section, cultures vary in the stereotypes they hold about different people. We will now compare the stereotypes against certain groups that are held in different countries.

STEREOTYPES ABOUT PEOPLE WHO ARE OVERWEIGHT. As described in Chapter 5, collectivistic cultures emphasize the role of situations, not just dispositions, in influencing behaviour. In turn, people in collectivistic cultures should put less blame on obese people for their weight, and thereby show lower levels of prejudice and discrimination than people in individualistic cultures, who would be expected to place greater emphasis on the role of personal responsibility in determining weight. In one study, Chris Crandall and his colleagues examined nearly 1,000 people from six different countries for anti-fat prejudice and belief about weight being within a person's control (Crandall, D'Anello, Sakalli, Lazarus, Nejtardt, & Feather, 2001). They examined both individualistic cultures (the United States, Australia, Poland) and collectivistic cultures (Venezuela, Turkey, India).[1] The participants were asked to complete questionnaires on anti-fat prejudice, the cultural value of fatness, and belief about controllability of weight. The results indicated that the belief that weight is controllable was related to negative evaluations of fat people. Moreover, a negative evaluation of fat people was more related to a rejection of fat people in individualistic countries than in collectivistic countries. It was also found that cultural values against fat people and prejudice against fat people were more closely related to each other in the individualistic countries than in the collectivistic countries. In other words, in individualistic countries, the tendency to see fatness as controllable led to greater prejudice. This is in part because people place more emphasis on the individual's autonomy and choice in individualistic countries and, therefore, are more likely to hold individual people responsible for their weight and to see weight as controllable (see Figure 11.5).

In a longitudinal study of obese men in Sweden, it was found that obese men are 40 percent less likely to start university and 50 percent less likely to graduate from university than normal weight men (Karnehed, 2008). This educational lag was evident even after the researchers adjusted for intelligence, parental education, and parental socioeconomic position. Additionally, obese Swedish men were 35 percent more likely to receive a disability pension compared to their normal weight counterparts. The researcher attributed her findings to a number of factors, including discrimination in Swedish society against obese people. She speculated that obese individuals might internalize the negative attitudes toward obesity in their society, which may lead to low self-esteem that then affects educational performance and performance in the workplace.

There are, however, cultures where carrying more weight is clearly valued. For example, Harter (2004) reported for BBC News that in rural Mauritania young girls are force fed

[1]Although Poland scores much lower than the United States and Australia on the individualistic dimension, the authors categorized Poland as an individualistic country for the purposes of this study as it scores higher than India, Venezuela, and Turkey.

FIGURE 11.5 HOW DOES CULTURE INFLUENCE ANTI-FAT ATTITUDES?

Researchers asked students from a collectivistic culture, Mexico, and an individualistic one, the United States, about their attitudes toward fat people and being fat. As predicted, Americans reported much greater prejudice against fat people than did Mexicans, in part because Americans are more likely to hold individual people responsible for their weight because they see weight as controllable.

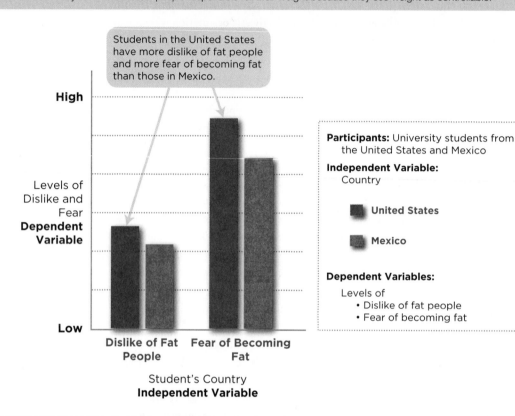

Students in the United States have more dislike of fat people and more fear of becoming fat than those in Mexico.

Participants: University students from the United States and Mexico

Independent Variable: Country

■ **United States**

■ **Mexico**

Dependent Variables:
Levels of
• Dislike of fat people
• Fear of becoming fat

Levels of Dislike and Fear
Dependent Variable

High

Low

Dislike of Fat People   Fear of Becoming Fat

Student's Country
Independent Variable

Source: Crandall, C. S., & Martinez, R. (1996). Culture, ideology, and antifat attitudes. *Personality and Social Psychology Bulletin, 22*, 1165–1176.

You may initially categorize someone in a wheelchair based largely on what you see as his or her disability. However, if you're motivated to form an accurate impression of the person, you'll focus more on the person's actual characteristics and rely less on stereotypes.

© Photodisc/SUPERSTOCK

because fat women are traditionally viewed as more desirable. Although in modern Mauritania only about 11 percent of girls are treated this way, more than a third of women were force fed as children a generation ago. This reflects the belief that fat women are a symbol of wealth and beauty and can find a good husband. Mauritania is one of the few African countries where girls receive more food than boys (Harter, 2004).

STEREOTYPES ABOUT WOMEN. Cross-cultural psychologists have examined development and socialization of gender stereotypes in many nations. One study of preschoolers in 25 countries found that aggression is one of the best-known characteristics of the male stereotype and it is learned at a very early age. Similarly, nurturance, including being affectionate and soft-hearted, is one of the important stereotypic female characteristics (Williams & Best, 1990). Gender stereotype learning begins by age 5, accelerates in early school years, and peaks during adolescence (Best, 2010; Williams & Best, 1990). Socialization within a culture plays a critical role in gender stereotype development. In a given culture, parents' expectations influence children's sex-role behaviours and children's gender stereotypes reflect those of their parents (Best, 2004; 2010). Nonetheless, there are cultural differences in gender stereotypes and knowledge of stereotypical masculine or feminine behaviours. Hofstede (2001) found that in countries where the dominant culture is feminine, gender roles are less clearly delineated than in predominantly masculine countries. It's more acceptable, therefore, for a father to stay at home and be a "house husband" in Sweden or the Netherlands than in Japan or Italy.

Researchers Peter Glick and Susan Fiske developed a theory of sexism that distinguishes between hostile sexism and benevolent sexism, which we saw earlier, and tested their theory in 19 different countries (Glick & Fiske, 1996, 2001; Glick et al., 2000; Glick et al., 2004). In some ways, sexist beliefs are very similar across different cultures:

- Hostile and benevolent sexism are correlated in all cultures, with hostile sexism predicting negative traits (e.g., uncooperative, rude, indecisive) and benevolent sexism predicting positive traits (e.g., cooperative, courteous, decisive).
- Although women show more rejection of hostile sexism than do men across cultures, both men and women commonly endorse benevolent sexism.
- Both men and women see men in more negative ways across cultures, but also see men as having more power.

These hostile and benevolent attitudes toward women reflect and support gender inequality by describing men as inherently dominant.

In other ways, cross-cultural comparisons reveal different beliefs about women. Specifically, mean scores on both types of sexism in a given culture are inversely related to gender equality (i.e., there is less equality where there is more sexism) in such measures as women's empowerment (e.g., representation in high-powered roles in a society) and development (e.g., longevity, education, standards of living; Glick et al., 2004). In highly sexist cultures, women are also more likely to endorse benevolent sexism, and even more than men do in such cultures. This finding suggests that women may accept benevolent sexism as the lesser of two evils when they're in a culture with generally negative attitudes toward women, and may be motivated to endorse this type of sexism as a way of gaining protection from men. Unfortunately, benevolent sexism can legitimize hostile sexism by allowing men to hold condescending attitudes toward women, and can thereby undermine women's efforts to achieve true equality.

This perception of women as needing protection, and as part of the property of their families, can have dangerous, and even deadly, consequences. The term "honour killing" refers to an act of violence, usually murder, committed by male family members against female family members who are seen as having brought dishonour upon the family. This dishonour can be caused by refusing to enter into an arranged marriage, dating or marrying a person outside of their family's ethnic and/or religious community, seeking a divorce, or committing adultery. These killings are supported not only by men in the family, but also by other women, due to the perception in these cultures that the family is the property and asset of men. Cultures in which "honour" is highly valued are also more inclined to tolerate violence against women within a relationship. In a comparison of "high honour" ("Latinos" and "Southern Anglos" in the U.S., and Chileans) and "low honour" ("Northern Anglos" in the U.S. and "Anglo-Canadians"), a combined Canadian and American research team including Ruth

People in individualistic cultures (such as the United States) versus collectivistic cultures (such as Mexico) differ in how they attribute the causes of obesity to internal versus external factors.

Vojtech Vlk/Age Fotostock America, Inc.

IN THE NEWS

The Canadian Press/ HO-Globe and Mail

Honour Killing: In 2007, 16-year-old Aqsa Parvez (pictured) was the victim of an honour killing in Mississauga, Ontario. Aqsa was beginning to rebel against her traditional upbringing, no longer wanting to wear her hijab and wanting to dress in Western clothes and have the same freedoms as the other girls in her high school. She tried to get away from her family to escape the family conflict but was murdered by her father and brother to save family pride. Similar Islamic honour killings have happened around the world in countries such as Pakistan, Jordan, and Egypt. In 2006, Banaz Mahmod, a 20-year-old Muslim woman living in England, was strangled with a boot lace, stuffed into a suitcase, and buried in a garden after her father learned that she had fallen in love with the "wrong man."

Grandon from the University of Waterloo found that participants in their study from honour cultures were relatively more favourable toward a woman who stayed in an abusive relationship, and rated the husband and his abusive actions more positively when the conflict was jealousy related (perceived flirting), than did participants from subcultures without strong honour traditions (Vandello, Cohen, Grandon, & Franiuk, 2009).

Honour killings can occur even in cases in which the woman has no responsibility for the "dishonouring" behaviour. For example, in some cultures a single woman who is raped will be unable to garner a bride price if she marries. Moreover, women who are raped can be seen as worthless burdens that bring dishonour to their family—and may even be killed for this act of "allowing" themselves to be raped.

THE BIG PICTURE

STEREOTYPE, PREJUDICE, AND DISCRIMINATION

This chapter included many applications of the three "big ideas" studied in social psychology. The examples below should help you see the connection between these big ideas and stereotype, prejudice, and discrimination, and contribute to your understanding of the big picture of social psychology.

THEME	EXAMPLES
The social world influences how we think about ourselves.	• A woman who is told that she's about to take a test on spatial reasoning that women typically do poorly on, gets nervous, which may interfere with her ability to perform well. • People's expectations about other people can lead them to engage in behaviours that elicit behaviour that supports these expectations. • Children from low socioeconomic backgrounds who take intellectual tests described as diagnostic of their overall intellectual ability perceive stereotype threat.
The social world influences our thoughts, attitudes, and behaviour.	• Children whose parents express prejudiced attitudes and behaviours are likely to form those attitudes themselves. • Men who have prejudiced attitudes toward women ask female job applicants fewer questions about their strengths than they ask male job applicants. • People who are primed with Black faces are more likely to misidentify tools as guns than those who are primed with White faces.
Our attitudes and behaviour shape the social world around us.	• We see people in our in-groups as different and unique, but see people in outgroups as very similar to one another. • White students who interview job applicants "as if they are Black" elicit worse performance than those who interview applicants "as if they are White." • People who are told that they'll work with another person on a joint task and can win money for performing well pay more attention to the person's actual characteristics and rely less on stereotypes of the person's in-group.

This chapter examined social psychological factors that contribute to stereotyping, prejudice, and discrimination.

1. What factors contribute to stereotyping and prejudice?

This section examined a number of social psychological factors that contribute to stereotyping and prejudice. These factors include social learning from parents and peers, social categorization, and cognitive biases, such as illusory correlation, the ultimate attribution error, the contrast effect, perceptual confirmation, and confirmation bias. You also learned why discriminating against another person after you've received negative feedback about your intelligence can make you feel better.

2. What are the consequences of stereotyping, prejudice, and discrimination?

This section examined various negative consequences of being stereotyped. These consequences include behavioural confirmation or self-fulfilling prophecy, stereotype threat, reduced psychological well-being, reverse discrimination, and the hazards of positive stereotypes. You also learned that women who watch gender-stereotypic commercials underperform on a math test.

3. Is stereotyping inevitable?

This section reviewed evidence that stereotyping is inevitable. Stereotypes can be seen as inevitable in part because such stereotypes are activated automatically and are hard to suppress. In addition, disconfirming evidence is ignored, and although blatant prejudice is rare, subtle discrimination persists. You also learned that both Black and White participants correctly shot an armed target more quickly if the target was Black than White, and refrained from shooting an unarmed target more quickly if the target was White than Black.

4. How can social and cognitive interventions help overcome prejudice?

This section examined several ways in which stereotypes can be overcome. These strategies include providing training and education, and being motivated to avoid using stereotypes. You also learned that people who have egalitarian motives act more positively toward a homosexual person than those without such motives.

5. How does culture relate to prejudice and stereotypes?

This section examined the relation of culture to prejudice and stereotypes. First, we examined the reliance on cognitive biases, such as the ultimate attribution error and in-group favouritism, across different cultures. Next, we examined the prevalence of different stereotypes in different cultures, and specifically the prevalence of fat bias and sexism. You also learned why older hearing Americans perform worse on memory tests that older Chinese people or deaf Americans.

Key Terms

auto-stereotype 389
aversive prejudice 376
benevolent sexism 376
confirmation bias 365
cross-ethnic identification
    bias 361
discrimination 356
hetero-stereotype 389

hostile sexism 375
illusory correlation 363
in-group favouritism 361
meta-stereotype 390
outgroup homogeneity effect 360
perceptual confirmation 364
prejudice 356
rejection-identification model 372

reverse discrimination 374
shifting standards model 364
social categorization 360
social dominance orientation 362
stereotype 356
stereotype threat 370
subcategorization 381
ultimate attribution error 363

Questions for Review

1. Describe four social psychological factors that lead to stereotypes.
2. Name three negative consequences of stereotypes and prejudice.
3. Describe two pieces of evidence suggesting that stereotypes occur automatically.
4. What are the strategies for helping reduce stereotypes, prejudice, and/or discrimination?
5. Describe cultural differences in the prevalence of different stereotypes.

Take Action!

1. Your sister recently had twins and wants very much to raise them to have tolerant and accepting attitudes toward people from different backgrounds. What advice would you give her?

2. After you overhear a friend tell a sexist joke, you have an argument about whether stereotypes are truly harmful to members of low status and disadvantaged groups. What information could you give him about the dangers of stereotyping?

3. Your father is attending a male friend's commitment ceremony to another man this weekend. He is not very comfortable with the idea of two men getting married. What advice would you give him about overcoming his negative attitudes and behaviour?

4. Think about your high school and identify some examples of discrimination. Based on your knowledge of social and cognitive interventions to reduce stereotypes, what strategies could you implement to help reduce prejudice and discrimination?

5. Your grandparents are planning a trip to Egypt. What might you tell them to expect about stereotypes and prejudice toward women?

RESEARCH CONNECTIONS

Participate in Research

Activity 1 The Power of Social Categorization: This chapter described how quickly and easily we divide people into those who are like us (our in-group) and those who are different from us (our outgroup). Go online to rate which types of people you would place into each category.

Activity 2 The Hazards of Positive Stereotypes: You learned in this chapter about the hazards of even positive stereotypes about individuals in particular groups. Go online to rate the characteristics of different groups to see what types of stereotypes you hold.

Activity 3 The Automatic Activation of Stereotypes: This chapter described how stereotypes are activated at an automatic and unconscious level. Go online to test how readily your stereotypes of others can be activated using a version of the IAT.

Activity 4 Strategies for Reducing Prejudice: You learned in this chapter about factors that reduce people's reliance on stereotypes. Go online to read about a number of different strategies that could be used to reduce prejudice, and rate the effectiveness of each approach.

Activity 5 The Relation of Culture to Stereotypes: The final section of this chapter described how people from different cultures vary in the types of stereotypes they hold. Go online to rate your views about people in different groups—then see how other students rate their own views.

Test a Hypothesis

One of the common findings in research on stereotypes and prejudice is that we learn stereotypes from what we see in the media. To test whether this hypothesis is true, watch several children's television programs and count the number of sex-stereotyped behaviours that boys and girls engage in. Then go online to report your findings to other students.

Design a Study

Go online to design your own study testing the factors that contribute to stereotyping and prejudice. You'll be able to choose the type of study you want to conduct (self-report, observational/naturalistic, or experimental), choose your own independent and dependent variables, and form your own hypothesis. Then you can share your findings with other students across the country!

12

CHAPTER

AGGRESSION

DID YOU EVER WONDER?

In late August 2010, the story of a massacre by a Mexican drug gang made the news globally. It was the biggest massacre in Mexico's drug war to date, with 72 people (58 men and 14 women) murdered at a ranch in northern Mexico near the border of the United States. The bodies of some of the victims, migrants from South and Central America, were piled on top of each other. It was reported that Zetas, the drug gang responsible for the massacre, kidnapped the migrants and shot them after they refused to pay the gang for crossing its territories. It's not uncommon for Mexico's drug traffickers to kidnap illegal migrants and threaten to kill them unless they pay fees.

AFP / Getty Images

Drug gangs also demand ransoms from relatives of immigrants in the United States. A similar event happened about two months earlier, in June 2010, when police discovered the bodies of 55 people in an abandoned mine in a different part of Mexico. As Mexico's ambassador in London, Eduardo Medina-Mora, said in an interview, the violence and massacres that have happened in Mexico aren't just a national problem, but are also "a global issue" (BBC News, 2010; Castillo & Stevenson, 2010).

HEALTH CONNECTIONS

The Link between Alcohol Use and Aggression

MEDIA CONNECTIONS

The Hazards of Violent Pornography

LAW CONNECTIONS

The Power of Penalties and Treatment Programs

EDUCATION CONNECTIONS

The Problem of Bullying

A different type of violence stunned the world in July 2011. A Norwegian extremist bombed a government building in downtown Oslo and went on a shooting spree at a youth camp of the liberal Labour Party on the Island of Utoya, outside of Oslo. By the time he was arrested, he had killed 77 people. His motivation wasn't drug trafficking, nor was he a member of an illegal gang. The 32-year-old Norwegian killer was an extreme-right activist who had anti-Muslim, anti-immigrant, and anti-feminist views. He believed that pro-immigrant policies are helping Muslims take over Europe and considered the current politicians to be traitors. The prime minister of Norway, Jens Stoltenberg, whose office was bombed, responded to the massacre with a strong message, "We must never stop standing up for our values . . . our answer to violence is even more democracy, more humanity, but not more naiveté" (CBC News, 2011). Do you think that this sort of thing could ever happen in your hometown?

Violence and aggression happen at national, group, and individual levels, through, for example, wars, gang conflicts, and personal assaults. Unfortunately, this kind of behaviour isn't just characteristic of modern societies, but of all (or almost all) societies. This chapter will describe factors that explain aggressive behaviour in the North American context and cross-culturally. You'll also find answers to these questions:

Why are prisoners who are high in testosterone more likely to violate prison rules?

How can the mere presence of a gun lead to more aggression?

Why might watching violent television lead you to see other people as evil?

Why is saying you're sorry often a good idea?

Why are North American hockey players more aggressive than their European counterparts?

PREVIEW

emotional or **hostile aggression** – aggression in which one inflicts harm for its own sake on another

instrumental aggression – aggression in which one inflicts harm in order to obtain something of value

Although people use the word aggression regularly in daily life, it can be surprisingly hard to define exactly what this word means. Is accidentally hurting someone aggressive? Is crashing into someone during a hockey game aggressive? Is yelling at someone aggressive? In social psychology, researchers have defined aggression differently depending on the theoretical framework that they use. Researchers also distinguish between different types of aggression. **Emotional** or **hostile aggression** refers to aggression that is inflicted simply to cause harm. Examples of hostile aggression include a jealous lover striking out in a rage or soccer fans having a brawl in the stands after a game. In contrast, **instrumental aggression** describes inflicting harm in order to obtain some goals or something of value. People who kill others in self-defence, or to gain money or attention, are motivated by instrumental aggression.

DEFINITION OF AGGRESSION

aggression – physical or verbal behaviour that is intended to harm another individual who is motivated to avoid such treatment

One of the most widely used definitions of **aggression** defines it as a form of behaviour that is intended to harm another individual who is motivated to avoid such treatment (Baron, 1977; Baron & Byrne, 1999). Based on this definition, (1) aggression is a behaviour that harms others, (2) harming others is intentional rather than accidental, and (3) the victim of the aggressive behaviour is motivated to avoid the harm, meaning the harm is unwanted rather than sought out. Although this definition doesn't specify the means by which harm is done, it does highlight the actual aggressive act, the perpetrator's intention to harm, and the victim's desire to avoid the harm. Based on this definition, aggressive acts don't include accidents (e.g., unintentionally hitting someone with an errant golf ball), or assertive acts (e.g., asking for a refund for your new but defective television), but they would include acts where there was an intention to harm, even when there was no actual harm.

From a behavioural perspective, aggressive behaviour results in physical and personal injuries (Bandura, 1973) and from a cognitive perspective, aggression is behaviour that is intended to harm another individual (Scherer, Abeles, & Fischer 1975). The conceptual difference between these two perspectives is that Bandura focuses on the outcomes of behaviour, while Scherer and colleagues take a more cognitive-motivational approach, focusing on the intention of the perpetrator. In the following section, we examine aggression from biological and social perspectives.

HOW DO BIOLOGICAL FACTORS INFLUENCE AGGRESSION?

One of the most basic and fundamental factors that influences aggression is biological make-up. Jim Dabbs and his colleagues at Georgia State University examined rates of testosterone and misbehaviour in male prison inmates (Dabbs, Carr, Frady, & Riad, 1995). Researchers collected saliva samples from 692 male inmates to measure levels of testosterone. They also examined data on the type of crime for which each inmate was serving time (robbery, assault, drug offences, and so on), and whether the inmate had received a disciplinary report for violating prison rules during his incarceration.

These data revealed that men who had committed violent crimes, such as rape and assault, had higher testosterone levels than men who had committed property crimes, such as burglary and theft. In addition, men with higher testosterone levels had violated more rules while in prison. This study suggests that testosterone levels are associated with men's aggressive behaviour, including the type of criminal activity that led to their incarceration as well as their patterns of misbehaviour while incarcerated.

This section will examine the role of biological factors in predicting aggression, including explanations that focus on instincts and evolution, as well as genetics and hormones.

INSTINCT AND EVOLUTIONARY THEORIES

Theories that view aggression as innate share a common perspective as they describe something within the person as being responsible for aggressive tendencies; aggression is therefore viewed as "built in" or a "hardwired" part of who we are, and therefore is not a learned behaviour. Let's examine two of the most famous theories.

FREUD'S DEATH WISH.   Sigmund Freud (1930) believed that people possess a powerful death wish or drive. In order to cope with this unconscious desire, people need to channel this energy in some direction. One possibility is for them to turn this energy inward—and thereby engage in self-destructive behaviour. Another option is to turn this energy outward—and thereby engage in aggression against other people.

Freud (1933) also saw aggression as a type of energy that builds up over time until it's released, a process called catharsis. Catharisis, which is a Greek word meaning cleansing, is the release of suppressed energy or emotion. In the context of aggression, it refers to a type of energy that builds up over time until it is released. This view of aggression was accepted for a long time, and led to considerable practical advice. For example, the idea that people should "blow off some steam" to relieve built-up tension is based in the idea of catharsis. This view is often promoted by the mass media and accepted by the general public. In the movie *Analyze This*, a psychiatrist played by Billy Crystal tells his mafia client, "You know what I do when I'm angry? I hit a pillow. Try that." People who are angry may hear a friend tell them, "Blow off some steam," "Get it off your chest," or "Don't bottle up anger inside." In sum, the popular view is that releasing one's anger is beneficial.

catharsis – release of suppressed energy or emotion

Scientific evidence suggests, however, that catharsis may not actually be an effective way of dealing with aggressive feelings. Researchers have found that engaging in aggressive behaviour doesn't reduce aggressive feelings, and in some cases may even increase them (Bushman, Baumeister, & Phillips, 2001; Bushman, Baumeister, & Stack, 1999). For example, participants who were asked to kill one bug initially as part of a "practice task" later killed fewer bugs during a timed "extermination task" than those who were asked to kill five bugs during the practice task, suggesting that higher levels of initial aggressive behaviour can lead to increasing levels of aggression later on (see Figure 12.1; Martens, Kosloff, Greenberg, Landau, & Schmader, 2007). Why is catharsis so ineffective? In part

FIGURE 12.1 DOES CATHARSIS INCREASE AGGRESSION?

Researchers in this experiment asked participants to kill bugs in a "practice task," and then gave participants another opportunity to kill bugs in a later "extermination task." The results did not support the catharsis theory: people who expressed a large amount of aggression engaged in more, not less, aggression later on.

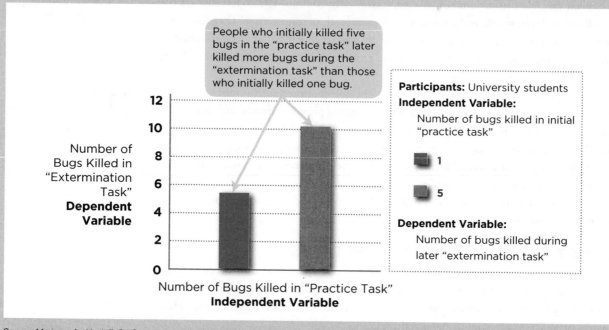

People who initially killed five bugs in the "practice task" later killed more bugs during the "extermination task" than those who initially killed one bug.

Number of Bugs Killed in "Extermination Task"
Dependent Variable

Number of Bugs Killed in "Practice Task"
Independent Variable

Participants: University students
Independent Variable:
Number of bugs killed in initial "practice task"

1

5

Dependent Variable:
Number of bugs killed during later "extermination task"

Source: Martens, A., Kosloff, S., Greenberg, J., Landau, M. J., & Schmader, T. (2007). Killing begets killing: Evidence from a bug-killing paradigm that initial killing fuels subsequent killing. *Personality and Social Psychology Bulletin, 33*, 1251–1264. Used by permission of Sage Publications.

because imagining or observing aggression may actually feel good, which can then become rewarding.

LORENZ'S INSTINCT THEORY OF AGGRESSION. Konrad Lorenz, an ethologist who studied animals in their natural habitat, saw aggression as a natural and instinctively motivated behaviour (Lorenz, 1966, 1974). According to Lorenz's **instinct theory of aggression**, people's innate desire to be aggressive toward others. This instinct toward aggression develops because only aggressive animals can ensure that they and their offspring will survive (e.g., by securing food, shelter, territorial advantages, protection from predators, and so on).

instinct theory of aggression – a theory that describes aggression as innate biological drive

Although there is a distinction between Lorenz's theory and theories of sociobiology and evolutionary psychology, these theories overlap in their understanding of aggressive behaviour in terms of natural selection. For example, Lorenz's theory and other theories of sociobiology and evolutionary psychology propose that the drive for aggression is evolutionarily adaptive because those who are aggressive have a greater likelihood of living (both themselves and their offspring). These theorists suggest that this is why in virtually all societies men are more aggressive than women (because aggression is how men obtain status and hence the best females). Put forward by Martin Daly and Margo Wilson (1996), two researchers at McMaster University, this theory also explains why parents are much more likely

"My first choice, of course, is to solve things amicably."

AGGRESSION IS OFTEN CAUSED BY A LOVED ONE?

Child abuse and neglect is a serious issue that can lead to long-lasting problems, including aggression, dating violence, criminal behaviour, substance abuse, emotional problems, and even suicide. In 2008, of an estimated 235,842 child-maltreatment-related investigations conducted in Canada, 74 percent focused on possible incidents of abuse or neglect that may have already occurred and 26 percent dealt with concerns about the risk of future maltreatment (Public Health Agency of Canada, 2008). Given that in some cases, abuse can be fatal, these statistics are alarming.

Perhaps most surprisingly, abuse and neglect are often perpetrated by a child's parents. In fact, 79 percent of deaths from abuse or neglect are caused by a parent. These deaths can be caused by a single act of abuse, such as suffocation or drowning, or repeated abuse over time, such as extended malnourishment, repeated beating, or shaking. What could possibly lead parents to abuse their child? Parents who abuse and neglect their children are often normal psychologically, but are under severe stress, perhaps due to financial pressures, crowded living conditions, and inadequate social support (Belsky, 1993; Malinosky-Rummell & Hansen, 1993; Peterson & Brown, 1994). They may also have been abused themselves.

to abuse and murder stepchildren, who they don't share genes with, than biological children. It also explains why sexual jealousy, caused by men's concern that they will expend resources on another man's child, often leads to aggression (Buss, 1995; Buss & Shackleford, 1997; Wilson & Daly, 1996).

Women are also at substantial risk of experiencing aggression at the hands of a loved one. There were 198 female victims of homicide in Canada in 2004. On average, 182 females were killed every year in Canada between 1994 and 2003. Sixty-two of these homicides in 2004 were female victims of spousal homicide. Of these, 27 women were killed by their legally married husband, 20 by a common-law partner, and 15 by a separated or divorced husband. Among solved homicides involving victims age 15 and older in 2004, half of all women were killed by someone who they had had an intimate relationship with at some point, either through marriage or dating. The comparative figure for men is 8 percent. It is estimated that 7 percent of women who experienced spousal violence between 1999 to 2004 were in a relationship with their current or previous spouse (Statistics Canada, 2006). Rates of spousal abuse were highest among certain segments of the population: those age 15 to 24; those in relationships of three years or less; those who had separated; and those in common-law unions (Statistics Canada, 2006). Women who experience abuse often suffer long-term emotional and physical health consequences. These include effects of physical injury, such as traumatic brain injury, and emotional problems, such as depression (Jackson, Philip, Nuttal, & Diller, 2002; Rennison & Welchans, 2000).

A particular type of aggression that women are more likely than men to experience is sexual assault. About one in 10 sexual assaults is reported to police, meaning that only a small proportion of sexual offences are formally documented through law enforcement (Brennan & Taylor-Butts, 2008). The prevalence of sexual assault in Canada has, therefore, been difficult to quantify. The small fraction of sexual assaults that is reported to police indicates a rate of 73 per 100,000 (Brennan & Taylor-Butts, 2008). As Figure 12.2 shows, provincial rates of police-reported sexual offences vary, with Saskatchewan having the highest rate and Prince Edward Island the lowest. Overall, sexual offences were highest in Nunavut (756), Northwest Territories (518), and Yukon (203; Brennan & Taylor-Butts, 2008). Different explanations have been suggested for variations in sexual assault across Canada, including police training, the availability of victim services, attitudes toward sexual assaults, and age demographic of the victims (Kong, Johnson, Beattie, & Cardillo, 2003).

The majority of sexual offences in Canada are of a less severe nature, although they could still be traumatizing for their target. Victimization data indicate that most sexual

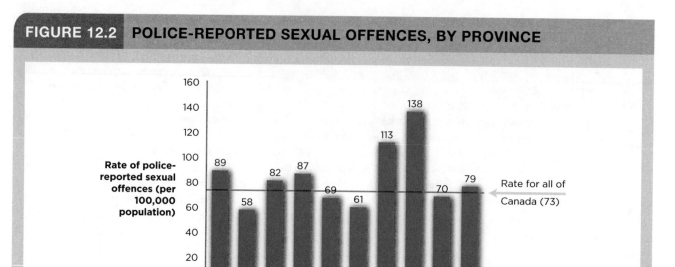

FIGURE 12.2 **POLICE-REPORTED SEXUAL OFFENCES, BY PROVINCE**

Source: Brennan, S. & Taylor-Butts, A. (2008). *Sexual Assault in Canada 2004 and 2007*. Canadian Centre for Justice Statistics. http://www.statcan.gc.ca/pub/85f0033m/85f0033m2008019-eng.pdf. Retrieved on September 6, 2011.

assaults involve unwanted sexual touching (81 percent) rather than more severe sexual attacks (19 percent). Among the incidents that came to the attention of police in 2007, the large majority (86 percent) were what police classify as level 1, the least serious form of sexual assault, but which can still include rape if no weapon was involved. (Level 2 is sexual assault with a weapon, and level 3 is aggravated sexual assault.) It has been reported that sexual victimization rates were dramatically higher among those age 15 to 24, compared to those 55 and over (Brennan & Taylor-Butts, 2008). Additionally, over half of the sexual assaults that were reported to police in 2007 involved victims under the age of 18. When victims of sexual assaults that were not reported to police were asked why they didn't report it, a majority of victims (58 percent) said that they didn't think the incident was important enough. Few of the sexual assault victims who completed the General Social Survey (GSS) filed formal reports with police, but most (72 percent) did confide in friends and many (41 percent) turned to family and other informal sources of support (Brennan & Taylor-Butts, 2008). Similar to victims of other forms of violent crime, sexual assault victims commonly experienced anger, confusion, and frustration as a result of their victimization (Brennan & Taylor-Butts, 2008).

GENETICS

Considerable research points to the role of genetic factors in influencing aggression (DiLalla & Gottesman, 1991). One meta-analysis suggests that up to 50 percent of the variance in aggression may be caused by genetic factors (Miles & Carey, 1997). In support of the view that genetics influences aggression, marked individual differences in rates of aggression are seen even by age 3 (Deluty, 1985; Olweus, 1979).

Other evidence that suggests the role of genetics in predicting aggressive behaviour comes from longitudinal research indicating that children who are highly aggressive early in life are more likely to be aggressive later. For example, both boys and girls who are rated as aggressive by their teachers at age 13 are more likely to have engaged in delinquent law-breaking behaviour by age 26 (Stattin & Magnusson, 1989). In one study, Rowell Huesmann and his colleagues examined over 600 8-year-olds, and then followed these children 22 years later (Huesmann, Eron, Lefkowitz, & Walder, 1984). People who were the most aggressive at the beginning of the study were also the most aggressive at the end of the study, showing that aggression is remarkably stable. Those who were aggressive as children were more likely to be involved in more serious aggressive acts later on, including criminal behaviour, spousal abuse, and traffic violations.

Although research on the stability of rates of aggression over time can be interpreted as providing support for a genetic view of the causes of aggression, environmental factors are also very likely to stay stable over time. Thus, merely finding stability in rates of aggression isn't enough to prove that genetics alone explains aggressive behaviour.

HOW AGGRESSIVE ARE YOU?

The Aggression Questionnaire

INSTRUCTIONS: *Rate each item on a scale of 1 (extremely uncharacteristic of me) to 5 (extremely characteristic of me).*

1. Once in a while I can't control the urge to strike another person.
2. I have become so mad that I have broken things.
3. Given enough provocation, I may hit another person.
4. If I have to resort to violence to protect my rights, I will.
5. I tell my friends openly when I disagree with them.
6. I often find myself disagreeing with people.
7. My friends say that I'm somewhat argumentative.
8. When people annoy me, I may tell them what I think of them.

[RATE YOURSELF]

SCORING: Sum up your total number of points on the first four items. Then sum up your total number of points on the second four items.

INTERPRETATION: The first four items measure physical aggression, whereas the next four items measure verbal aggression. People with higher scores on the first four items have higher levels of physical aggression than those with lower scores. People with higher scores on the last four items have higher levels of verbal aggression than those with lower scores (Buss & Perry, 1992). A study conducted by Paul Tremblay from the University of Western Ontario and his colleagues with 2,647 Canadian students (Tremblay, Graham, & Wells, 2008) indicated that average physical aggression scores for male students would be around 9.04, and around 6.92 for women. Average verbal aggression scores for male students would be around 11.2, and 10.48 for female students. Note that the gender difference is greater for physical aggression than verbal aggression.

CAUTIONARY NOTE: The scale in this form is not a diagnostic tool. Rather, it serves as an example of the type of questions that are asked to determine aggression.

There are four subscales (physical aggression, verbal aggression, anger, and hostility) on Buss & Perry's (1992) scale. The eight questions in the Rate Yourself box are made up of four of the nine items on the physical aggression subscale and four of the five items for the verbal aggression subscale.

HORMONES

In virtually all societies, males are more aggressive than females. One theory about the causes of these gender differences in aggression is the presence of the male sex hormone testosterone (Mazur & Booth, 1998; Olweus, Mattsson, Schalling, & Löw, 1988; Susman, Inoff-Germain, Nottelmann, & Loriaux, 1987). In line with this view, people who are highly aggressive have higher levels of testosterone than those who are less aggressive. Boys age 5 to 11 who are aggressive show higher levels of testosterone (Chance, Brown, Dabbs, & Casey, 2000) and delinquent and violent people have higher testosterone levels than do university students (Banks & Dabbs, 1996). Among inmates convicted of homicide, those with higher testosterone levels more often knew their victims and planned their crimes ahead of time (Dabbs, Riad, & Chance, 2001). As described at the start of this section, men with higher levels of testosterone are also more likely to commit personal crimes than property crimes, and are more likely to violate rules while they are in prison (Dabbs et al., 1995).

Testosterone levels are also correlated with levels of violence in women. Dabbs and Hargrove (1997) examined the correlation between testosterone levels and rates of aggression in female prison inmates. As predicted, women who were rated as highly aggressive by guards (including such behaviours as being physically aggressive toward others and repeatedly breaking rules) had higher levels of testosterone than those who were neutral or passive in their behaviour. Research Focus on Gender describes other gender differences in aggression.

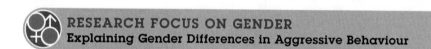

RESEARCH FOCUS ON GENDER
Explaining Gender Differences in Aggressive Behaviour

Who is more aggressive, men and boys or women and girls? Most of us see this as an easy question—surely boys and men are much more aggressive than girls and women. And research evidence generally supports this view—men commit the vast majority of homicides (Knight, Fabes, & Higgins, 1996), and even among small children, boys show more physical aggression, meaning acts intended to inflict physical harm, than girls (Hyde, 1984; Loeber & Hay, 1997). This gender difference may be due in part to genetic and evolutionary factors, including men's higher levels of testosterone and their historical role in protecting women (especially during periods of pregnancy and nursing).

But biology and evolution are not the only explanations for gender differences in aggression. According to **social learning theory**, behaviours are learned through modelling, rewards and punishments. It has been argued that males and females are taught different things about the costs and benefits of aggression (Eagly & Steffen, 1986). Specifically, boys who use their fists to fight may receive social rewards (admiration from parents and peers), whereas girls who engage in this behaviour may be punished (Rodkin, Farmer, Pearl, & Van Acker, 2000). In fact, highly aggressive boys are often seen as cool and athletic, and may be among the most popular children in elementary school classrooms.

Although men are usually more aggressive than women, these gender differences are not large, and the differences in more recent studies are smaller than in older ones (Hyde, 1984). Gender differences in aggression differ substantially for distinct types of aggression. Men and boys have much higher rates of physical aggression than women and girls, but only slightly higher rates of verbal aggression (meaning verbal expressions intended to hurt someone else) and have lower rates of relational aggression (meaning behaviours that are intended to disrupt relationships; Archer, 2004; Archer & Coyne, 2005; Buss & Perry, 1992; Crick, Casas, & Mosher, 1997; Crick & Grotpeter, 1995). Similarly, men are more likely than women to initiate aggression causing physical injury or pain, but women are more likely than men to initiate aggression producing psychological or social harm,

social learning theory – a theory that describes behaviour as learned by observing or modelling others' behaviour as well as by the presence of punishments and rewards, or reinforcements

suggesting that gender differences in aggression are caused largely by social roles and learning (Archer, 2000; Eagly & Steffen, 1986; Jenkins & Aubé, 2002) and by what is measured as aggressive behaviour.

Gender differences in aggression are also larger in more naturalistic studies than in experimental ones, and when behaviour is measured through observation rather than self-report (Hyde, 1984). A meta-analysis by Bettencourt and Miller (1996) revealed that unprovoked men are more aggressive than women, but differences among provoked men and women are small, indicating that provocation reduces the impact of gender role norms on aggression. Similarly, Lightdale and Prentice (1994) found that gender differences in aggression appear when people are identifiable in a given situation, but not when they're anonymous—suggesting that girls appear less aggressive than boys only when they believe their behaviour will be noticed. They're also less aggressive in a mixed-gender context. Comparing an all-girls school and a mixed-gender school in Colombia, researchers from Concordia University found higher levels of physical and relational aggression for the girls in the all-girls school and the conventional gender differences in the mixed school, where boys showed more physical aggression and girls showed more relational aggression (Velasquez, Santo, Saldarriaga, Lopez, & Bukowski, 2010).

How do high testosterone levels contribute to aggression? High testosterone leads to an increased readiness to respond assertively to provocation and threats, and makes people more impatient and irritable, which can lead to aggression (Olweus et al., 1988). Dabbs, Strong, & Milun (1997) found that people high in testosterone experience more arousal and tension, and higher levels of frustration, in daily life. In their study, participants were asked to keep daily records of their thoughts and activities for a four-day period. People who were high in testosterone reported experiencing more arousal and tension than those who were low in testosterone, and felt frustrated when they were unable to accomplish their goals.

Some evidence suggests that it may not be testosterone alone that leads to higher rates of aggression, but rather the presence of testosterone along with some other variable (Dabbs & Morris, 1990). In line with this view, men with high income levels have relatively low rates of adult delinquency regardless of their level of testosterone, whereas men with low income show low delinquency if they have low levels of testosterone, but high rates of adult delinquency if they have high levels of testosterone. Why? Perhaps because men with high income can dominate people in other ways (e.g., driving a nicer car, wearing nicer clothes, living in a nicer house). Similarly, men who are high in testosterone and high in fearlessness are the best at fighting fires, suggesting that personality and hormone levels together interact to produce the aggressiveness that is necessary to perform effectively under this unique type of pressure (Fannin & Dabbs, 2003).

Other evidence suggests that the link between aggression and testosterone is bidirectional. In other words, testosterone can increase levels of aggression, but aggression, or even aggressive cues, can also lead to increases in testosterone levels. In line with this view, some intriguing research indicates that men who handle a gun for 15 minutes show higher increases in testosterone, and behave more aggressively toward another participant, than those who handle a child's game (Klinesmith, Kasser, & McAndrew, 2006).

Finally, testosterone is not the only hormone that may be associated with aggression. Other evidence points to the role of the neurotransmitter *serotonin* in aggression (Bernhardt, 1997; Davidson, Putnam, & Larson, 2000). Animals that are aggressive have been shown to have low serotonin levels, and low serotonin levels have been shown to make animals overreact to aversive stimuli, increasing their risk of experiencing frustration and aggression (Bernhardt, 1997). It has also been hypothesized that a portion of the brain that is responsible for emotion regulation, principally through serotonin production, is damaged in individuals who show

Questioning the Research:

Although these studies describe high levels of testosterone as leading to aggressive behaviour, can you think of an alternative explanation for this association? (Hint: Do the studies indicate causation, correlation, or both?)

impulsive violence, suggesting that they engage in aggression because they are unable to appropriately regulate their feelings (Davidson et al., 2000). The Health Connections box describes the impact of alcohol use on aggressive behaviour.

HEALTH CONNECTIONS

The Link between Alcohol Use and Aggression

The link between alcohol use and aggression is consistent in both field and laboratory research (Bushman & Cooper, 1990; Hull & Bond, 1986). For example, in one study, 50 percent of murderers were found to have been drinking prior to committing their crime (Bushman, 1993), and men who abuse alcohol are at increased likelihood of abusing their spouse (Coker, Smith, McKeown, & King, 2000; Murphy & O'Farrell, 1996). Similarly, people who are intoxicated give higher levels of shocks to an opponent, even when not provoked, than do sober people (Bailey & Taylor, 1991). Research with student samples from six Canadian universities (from Atlantic, Eastern, Central, and Western Canada) found that alcohol consumption was significantly related to the severity of aggressive incidents that the students reported experiencing at bars and parties (Tremblay et al., 2008). Additionally, a high score on the physical aggression subscale of the aggression scale discussed earlier interacted with the quantity of alcohol consumed as a predictor of the severity of the individual's aggressive behaviour in bars. In other words, people who are more aggressive temperamentally are more likely to behave aggressively as they consume more alcohol in bars.

Why does alcohol use lead to such high levels of aggression? One reason is that alcohol use leads to disinhibition, meaning a weakening or removal of inhibitions that normally restrain people from acting on their impulses (Ito, Miller, & Pollock, 1996; Steele & Southwick, 1985). For example, people may normally be inhibited from acting aggressively due to fear of the consequences and/or the belief that they have a responsibility to act in a controlled manner. Intoxication, however, reduces such concerns. Alcohol use also interferes with information processing by impairing people's ability to think straight, draw accurate conclusions, and integrate pieces of information (Bailey & Taylor, 1991; Laplace, Chermack, & Taylor, 1994; Steele & Josephs, 1988). In line with this view, researchers from the University of Waterloo have found that men who have been drinking have trouble seeing their dating partner's side of a conflict, and thus feel more anger toward their partner (MacDonald, Zanna, & Holmes, 2000).

Alcohol exposure may also lead to more aggression at a subconscious level. In one study, participants were primed with alcohol-related images (e.g., a beer bottle or martini glass), images of weapons, or images of plants (Bartholow & Heinz, 2006). Next, they had to recognize a series of aggression-related and neutral words. Participants who were primed with alcohol-related images or images of weapons recognized aggressive words faster than neutral words, whereas those who were primed with images of plants showed no difference in how quickly they recognized these distinct types of words. Similarly, it was found exposure to alcohol advertisements, compared to neutral advertisements, led people to interpret the behaviour of a target person as more hostile. These findings suggest that exposure to alcohol-related images, even in the absence of alcohol consumption, can increase aggressive thoughts, and in turn, can potentially lead to aggressive behaviour. A study led by researchers from the University of Western Ontario revealed the importance of contextual factors in the connection between alcohol consumption and aggression (Kathryn, Bernards, Osgood, & Wells, 2006). The researchers observed drinking and aggression at bars in Toronto and found that a permissive environment and people hanging around after closing time were predictors of both the frequency and severity of aggression. It was also found that unwanted sexual contact (e.g., grabbing, holding), physical contact (e.g., pushing, punching, slapping) and non-physical contact (e.g., swearing at, demeaning, challenging someone), and people having two or more drinks were predictors of the frequency but not the severity of aggression. Furthermore, it was found that lack of staff monitoring was a predictor of patron aggression; and that having more and better coordinated staff was a predictor of more severe staff aggression. Clearly, while these findings do indicate that alcohol plays a part in aggression, they also indicate that a variety of contextual factors are relevant. The same research team argue elsewhere that more attention needs to be paid to group dynamics in understanding the connection between aggression and alcohol (Kathryn, Osgood, Wells, & Stockwell, 2006).

ACE STOCK LIMITED/Alamy

[CONCEPTS IN CONTEXT]

FACTORS LEADING TO AGGRESSION

FACTOR	EXAMPLE
Instinct and evolutionary theories	Hong Li sees life as "kill or be killed," and wants to make sure that he comes out ahead. He reacts angrily when he sees his girlfriend talking to other men, and tries to quickly interrupt such conversations.
Genetics	Like the father he never met, Matt was aggressive as a child—unlike his adoptive siblings, he was always fighting with other children on the playground. Now 16, he has just been arrested for assault.
Hormones	Carlos is high in testosterone. He experiences high levels of tension in daily life, is easily frustrated, and responds very assertively to even mild provocation.

HOW DO SOCIAL PSYCHOLOGICAL FACTORS INFLUENCE AGGRESSION?

Given the limitations of the theories that relate aggression to genetic and biological factors, researchers have also examined how social psychological factors influence aggression. In one study, participants were told that researchers were examining how a liking for sports was related to attitudes and personality (Dienstbier et al., 1998). Participants were then randomly assigned to two conditions.

In the weapon condition, participants watched a brief video of a fishing program and then practised casting with a fishing rod. Next, participants watched a brief video of target-shooting, and then practised holding and aiming a rifle and a pistol.

In the sport condition (the control condition), participants watched a brief video of gymnastics, and then held a football and imagined throwing it. Next, participants watched a video of an exciting basketball slam-dunk contest, and then held and imagined dunking a basketball.

All participants then read several scenarios about first-offence crimes, such as vandalism, robbery, and drug offences, and recommended a sentence for the offence. As predicted, participants who completed the survey in a room with weapons (the weapon condition) recommended longer sentences than those who were in a room with sports equipment (the sport condition): an average of 4.4 years compared to 3.4 years. Apparently the presence of such an object serves to "prime" aggression or, in essence, increase the likelihood of an aggressive act.

This section will examine several theories that explain how psychological factors influence aggression, including frustration-aggression theory, cognitive-neoassociation theory, excitation transfer theory, social learning theory, and the general aggression model.

FRUSTRATION-AGGRESSION THEORY

The **frustration-aggression theory** is one of the earliest social-psychological theories regarding aggression, and it incorporates the Freudian idea of aggression as a basic impulse (Berkowitz, 1989; Dollard, Doob, Miller, Mowrer, & Sears, 1939; Geen, 1968). This theory states that frustration, which is caused when people are prevented from having something they want, always leads to the desire to be aggressive, and that all aggression is caused by some form of frustration.

In line with the predictions of this theory, frustrating events can lead to aggression. In one study, researchers hired students to call strangers on the phone to request donations to a

frustration-aggression theory – a theory that frustration always leads to the desire to behave aggressively, and that aggression is caused by frustration

NEW LISTINGS FROM
FRUSTRATION HOUSE

#397 –
This picture-perfect hat can be yours! Guaranteed to make you look like a million bucks for only... $2.99
SORRY, NONE LEFT

#421 –
The most interesting, witty, inspiring, entertaining, and enlightening book ever written on this planet! Just $3.11
SOLD OUT

#599 –
World-famous L'Escargot© cookware. Impossible to make a mistake, even if you are the world's worst cook. $5.29
DISCONTINUED ITEM

#758 –
Elegant one-family town house on N.Y.C.'s historic upper East Side. Lots of light, space, garden in back. $79.99
LAST ONE

©Roz Charst/ The New Yorker Collection/
www.cartoonbank.com

displacement – people's tendency to aggress against others when the source of frustration is unavailable

charity (Kulik & Brown, 1979). Half of the students were led to believe that most people would contribute. The other half were led to believe that most people would refuse to contribute. Students who expected most people to contribute showed much higher levels of aggression (e.g., slamming the phone down, using a harsher tone) in response to a negative response than those who expected few people to contribute. Students who had high expectations for donations were more frustrated because they were unable to fulfill the goal they expected to achieve—and thus showed higher levels of aggression than those who initially had low expectations and therefore didn't experience the same frustration caused by failing to meet their goals.

DISPLACEMENT. Frustration-aggression theory states that when people are frustrated, they have a need or drive to be aggressive toward the object of their frustration. However, it also states that when the target or cause of the frustration is not available, people use **displacement**, which means they transfer their anger onto whatever target is available (Marcus-Newhall, Pedersen, Carlson, & Miller, 2000). So, for example, if you were to fail a mid-term that you felt well prepared for, you would likely feel frustrated and might therefore be motivated to express aggression in some way. As you cannot take out your anger on your professor, who you blame for deliberately asking obscure questions, you instead go home and scold your cat, dog, or partner, or some other more appropriate target.

Unfortunately, displaced aggression is particularly likely to target particular people—"designated victims"—in society, such as immigrants, the unemployed, welfare recipients, and so on. Ervin Staub (1996) suggests that mass killings are often rooted in frustration caused by economic and social difficulties. These frustrations lead to scapegoating and a "blame the victim" mentality in which people blame those in a particular group and thereby both discriminate against them and show them aggression.

To examine the factors that lead people to displace anger from one person to another, researchers created a situation in which participants were deliberately provoked (Pedersen, Gonzales, & Miller, 2000). Participants listened to either mild or irritating music, completed either easy or difficult anagrams, and were given either neutral or negative feedback by the experimenter (as a manipulation of the provocation). Next, they interacted with a confederate who also gave them either negative or neutral feedback about their performance. Finally, they were asked to rate the performance of a research assistant they had seen on videotape, another confederate, who had performed poorly (mispronouncing names, stumbling over words, etc.) or performed well on the task.

As predicted, participants who completed the difficult task while listening to the irritating music, were given negative feedback by the experimenter, and received negative feedback from the confederate gave the highest level of negative ratings of the research assistant. Although participants didn't show aggression when they only received negative feedback from the experimenter after having done a difficult task, when such feedback was also followed by negative feedback from the confederate, participants displaced their anger caused by the feedback onto the research assistant (see Figure 12.3). Displacement of aggression is particularly common when the person is provoked and then given the opportunity to think about this provocation—which maintains, and could even intensify, the person's negative mood (Bushman, Bonacci, Pedersen, Vasquez, & Miller, 2005). Thinking about, or ruminating upon, one's anger has been shown by researchers from British Columbia to have a distinct effect over and above the anger itself in the expression of aggression (Peled & Moretti, 2010).

FIGURE 12.3 DOES PROVOCATION LEAD TO ANGER DISPLACEMENT?

In this experiment, researchers provoked some participants by making them do a difficult task and then giving them negative feedback on it. Participants then met a confederate who offered some of them a trigger for aggression by also giving negative feedback. As predicted, people who were provoked displaced their frustration onto a new person who triggered their aggression, supporting the theory that we displace our anger.

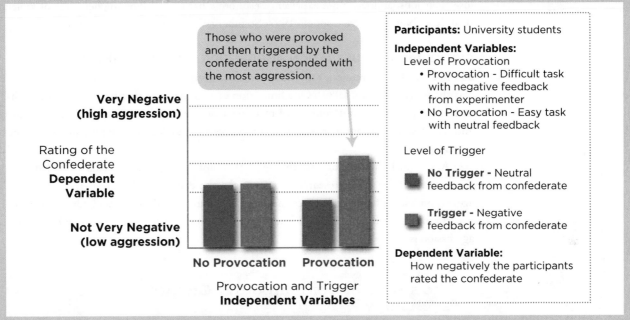

Source: Pedersen, W. C., Gonzales, C., & Miller, N. (2000). The moderating effect of trivial triggering provocation on displaced aggression. *Journal of Personality and Social Psychology, 78,* 913–927. Copyright © 2000 by the American Psychological Association. Reproduced with permission. The use of APA information does not imply endorsement by the APA.

THE IMPACT OF RELATIVE DEPRIVATION. The theory of relative deprivation was first discussed in Chapter 10 on intergroup relations. The theory explains stereotype, prejudice, and aggression. Relative deprivation refers to discontent caused by the belief that one fares poorly compared to people in other groups (Ellemers & Bos, 1998; Olson, Herman, & Zanna, 1986). The perceived injustice that arises from a situation of relative deprivation could lead individuals to experience frustration. This is why professional athletes who make millions of dollars a year may feel angry about their salary—they're not comparing what they make to what most people make, but rather to what many of their highly publicized team-mates may be making. In fact, decreasing the income discrepancy in a country—meaning the difference in income between the very wealthy and the very poor—increases the overall hap-piness in a country, in part by reducing the negative effects of social comparison (Hagerty, 2000). Similarly, some researchers believe that the increase in television watching has led to increases in violent crime, in part due to the impact of relative deprivation (e.g., seeing what other people had; Hennigan et al., 1982). This is especially true because television often shows middle-and upper-class people.

In line with this view, aggressive behaviour increases when people are in difficult finan-cial situations. In an early test of this relationship, Carl Hovland and Robert Sears (1940) examined the link between the price of cotton in 14 states in the American south from 1882 to 1930 and the number of lynchings of African Americans. As predicted, there was a strong negative correlation between the price of cotton (a major aspect of the economy during this time) and the number of lynchings, meaning that the more financial pressure people were under, the more lynchings there were.

This research suggests that people displace their frustration caused by poor economic conditions onto minority group members. Researchers in a study using complex statistical procedures revealed that the rate of lynching was particularly high when a period of poor economic growth followed a period of strong growth (Hepworth & West, 1988). Although some researchers have questioned the conclusions of the studies showing a link between economic conditions and lynchings (Green, Glaser, & Rich, 1998), other work finds that people who lose their jobs, and therefore experience economic hardships, show higher rates of violence (Catalano, Novaco, & McConnell, 1997; Steinberg, Catalano, & Dooley, 1981).

CRITIQUES OF FRUSTRATION-AGGRESSION THEORY. Although frustration can and does lead to aggression, more recent research has called into question some aspects of this theory (Berkowitz, 1989). One limitation of this theory is that frustration doesn't have to lead to aggression, but could lead to other emotions, such as disappointment, sadness, and depression. In other words, aggression represents only one of the possible responses to frustration.

A second limitation of this theory is that not all aggression stems from frustration (Berkowitz, 1989). Most researchers now make the distinction between emotional/hostile aggression and instrumental aggression (see Bushman & Anderson, 2002, for an exception). Frustration is much more likely to lead to emotional or hostile aggression, than instrumental aggression is.

Who's Who in Contemporary Canadian Social Psychology

Courtesy D. Taylor

Don Taylor received his PhD from the University of Western Ontario. He is currently a professor of psychology at McGill University. Professor Taylor conducts both laboratory and field research on the plight of disadvantaged groups in society. His theoretical interests include cultural identity, prejudice and stereotypes, and perceptions of discrimination at both the personal and group levels. Professor Taylor's work includes research on ethnic groups in urban centres in Canada and the United States, South Africa, the Philippines, and Indonesia. By far his most committed and long-term research has focused on Aboriginal groups, both First Nations and Inuit, in Canada. He has served on the editorial boards of several journals, including *Group Processes and Intergroup Relations* and the *International Journal of Intercultural Relations*. His most recent book is entitled *The Quest for Identity*, which is published by Praeger.

COGNITIVE-NEOASSOCIATION THEORY

cognitive-neoassociation theory – a theory that describes aggression as caused by experiencing negative affect of any kind, which in turn evokes aggression-related thoughts, memories, feelings, and ideas

Another theory explaining aggression suggests that experiencing a negative mood or affect activates anger-related thoughts and feelings as well as aggressive behaviour (Berkowitz, 1984, 1990). This **cognitive-neoassociation theory** proposes that any event that leads to negative affect, such as heat, pain, unpleasant noises and odours, crowding, and so on, can lead to aggression. For example, if you're in a bad mood because you recently failed an exam, you might be more likely to respond angrily to a salesman who knocks on your door. Such triggers to aggressive behaviour could include observing the following types of aggression:

- aggression in daily life (e.g., watching two children fight on a playground)
- aggression in the media (e.g., watching a television show in which cartoon characters behave aggressively)
- reading a story containing aggressive acts (e.g., an action comic book)

There are a variety of studies on how different factors can lead to negative mood or affect and thereby increase aggression.

HOT TEMPERATURES.   Numerous studies demonstrate that as the temperature increases, so does the incidence of aggressive acts, including murder, rape, domestic violence, and assault (Anderson, 1989, 2001; Anderson & DeNeve, 1992; Cohn, 1993). In one study, Anderson and colleagues examined the association between the number of hot summer days (days the maximum temperature reached at least 32 degrees Celsius) and the rate of violent crimes in 50 different American cities (Anderson, Bushman, & Groom, 1997). As predicted, hotter summers were associated with more violent crimes, including assault, property crime, and rape. Research in laboratory settings reveals similar findings: participants are more hostile to confederates when they're in hot rooms (32 degrees Celsius) versus rooms at a more comfortable temperature (Griffit, 1970; Griffit & Veitch, 1971). Why do high temperatures increase aggression? Research suggests that high temperatures lead to physiological arousal and increased hostile feelings and thoughts, which may increase the likelihood of aggression (Anderson, Deuser, & DeNeve, 1995). However, if we're aware that some of the physiological changes we experience are produced by increases in temperature, we're less likely to become aggressive. Ehor Boyanowsy from Simon Fraser University replicated previous findings linking temperature to aggression. The study also found that when participants could see a thermometer on the wall in front of them, drawing their attention to the temperature, they did not become more aggressive with increased temperature (Boyanowsky, 1999).

Some research suggests that the link between heat and aggression is curvilinear, meaning that at extremely high temperatures aggression decreases. Although warmer cities have higher violent crime rates than cooler ones, violence decreases somewhat at very high temperatures (Anderson & Anderson, 1996; Bell, 1992). Cohn and Rotton (1997, 2000) tried to explain this evidence by analyzing the relationship between heat and aggression during the day (when temperatures are at their highest) versus in the evening. Using data from Minneapolis and Dallas, two American cities, the researchers found that most assaults happen in the late evening or early morning, when temperatures are somewhat lower. This suggests a curvilinear function, with assaults reaching a peak at moderately high temperatures, but then decreasing.

Other researchers have criticized Cohn and Rotton's conclusions, noting that these data ignore the time of day, which itself is likely to have a strong impact on the frequency of aggression (Bushman, Wang, & Anderson, 2005a, 2005b). In line with this view, a reanalysis of the data used by Cohn and Rotton reveals that during the night (between 9 p.m. and 3 a.m.), increasing temperature was associated with increasing frequency of assault. In contrast, there was no association between temperature and frequency of assault during the day (3 a.m. to 9 p.m.).

OTHER UNPLEASANT CONDITIONS.   Aggression is also produced when people experience other bad conditions (e.g., pollution, threatened self-esteem, crowding, pain, noise, poverty; Baumeister, Bushman, & Campbell, 2000; Fleming, Baum, & Weiss, 1987). For example, people who are experiencing pain (by holding one of their hands in a bucket of painfully cold water) report having higher feelings of irritation and annoyance toward another student (Berkowitz, Cochran, & Embree, 1981). Various environmental factors, including ozone levels, cigarette smoke, wind speed, and humidity, are associated with rates of aggression, as evidenced by calls to police for assistance during assaults (Rotton & Frey, 1985; Zillman, Baron, & Tamborini, 1981). Feeling personally rejected or ostracized can also lead to more aggressive behaviour (Twenge, Baumeister, Tice, & Stucke, 2001).

CUES TO AGGRESSION.   According to the cognitive-neoassociation theory, another factor that can trigger aggressive behaviour is the mere presence of an object associated with aggression (Berkowitz, 1984). In a classic demonstration of the power of a weapon to elicit

"Or maybe you're at the office and you discover that somebody has been using the copy machine for personal purposes."

Questioning the Research:

The correlation between owning a gun and the likelihood of killing someone—or one's self—with the gun is clear. But is there an alternative explanation for this association? (Hint: Are people randomly assigned to have guns?)

aggression, Berkowitz and LePage (1967) conducted a study in which male participants were first provoked and then invited to deliver shocks to a confederate. In one condition, sports items (a racquet and balls) were in the room. In the other condition, a revolver and rifle were in the room. In which context did the participant behave more aggressively? When the gun was present. This is called the "weapons effect." Similarly, and as described at the start of this section, participants who handled a rifle and pistol gave higher sentencing recommendations than those who held a basketball and football.

Obviously this finding has important implications. Although it's true that "guns don't kill people, people do," the mere presence of a gun seems to be able to elicit aggressive responses from others, particularly if they're ready to be aggressive and don't have strong inhibitions against such behaviour. A study in the *New England Journal of Medicine* reported that having a gun at home triples the person's risk of being killed (Kellermann, Rivara, Rushforth, & Banton, 1993). Similarly, John Sloan and colleagues (1988) examined the rate of murder in Seattle, Washington, and Vancouver, British Columbia. Although these two cities are very similar in many regards, including population, climate, economy, and overall crime rate, Seattle has twice the murder rate of Vancouver. One possible explanation? Vancouver severely limits handgun ownership. Similarly, in Washington, D.C., the number of homicides and suicides committed with firearms declined after the 1976 Firearms Control Regulations Act, which restricts the licensing of handguns, came into effect (Loftin, McDowall, Wiersema, & Cottey, 1991). Other research indicates that following the purchase of a handgun, the gun owner's risk of suicide is significantly higher—as much as 57 times higher than the rate in the general population (Wintemute, Parham, Beaumont, Wright, & Drake, 1999).

EXCITATION TRANSFER THEORY

arousal-affect/excitation transfer model – a model describing aggression as influenced by both the intensity of the arousal and the type of emotion produced by the stimulus

According to the **arousal-affect/excitation transfer model**, aggression is influenced by both the intensity of the arousal and the type of emotion produced by the stimulus (Zillman, 1983). In other words, any type of arousal can be interpreted as aggression if a person is in a situation that cues aggression. This is based on Schachter and Singer's two-factor theory of emotion, which you will read about in Chapter 14. In one study, researchers randomly assigned some men to engage in mild exercise (a slow ride on a stationary bike) and others to engage in strenuous exercise (a more strenuous bike ride; Zillman, Katcher, & Milavsky, 1972). Those who engaged in strenuous exercise and were provoked by a confederate delivered higher intensity shocks to the confederate than those who engaged in mild exercise and were therefore less aroused. In sum, if we're physiologically aroused (for whatever reason), and if our environment tells us we're angry, we'll act aggressively.

Guns don't kill people, but their mere presence may make people more likely to kill people. Scott Olson/Getty Images.

Why does arousal lead to aggression? People misattribute to the situation their feelings of arousal caused by other sources. In other words, if there are cues to aggression in the situation, they interpret their arousal as aggression.

SOCIAL LEARNING THEORY

As you learned in Chapter 6, Bandura's social learning theory posits that behaviour is learned by observing or *modelling* others' behaviour as well as by the presence of punishments and rewards, or *reinforcements* (Bandura 1973, 1983). Both of these factors can lead to aggressive behaviour.

MODELLING.   Children can learn to engage in aggressive behaviour through watching such behaviour, either in real life or through television and movies (Bandura, Ross, & Ross, 1963).

In Al Bandura's classic study of the power of modelling on aggression in children, children were first shown a video of an adult throwing around, punching, and kicking an inflatable Bobo doll (Bandura et al., 1963). The video was very unusual and specific in terms of the behaviour and words modelled (e.g., the adult sat on the doll, punched it in the nose, hit him with a wooden mallet, and said "Sock him in the nose" and "Hit him down"). The researcher then observed the children's behaviour following a frustrating event (the children were shown some very attractive toys but then told that these toys were being saved for another child, and were instead given some less interesting toys to play with). As expected, children who had watched the adult behave aggressively toward the Bobo doll replicated much of that behaviour, even using the exact same words and actions. Figure 12.4 shows an advertisement developed by the Adults and Children Together (ACT) against Violence national media campaign in the U.S. to educate parents about the ease with which children model aggressive behaviour to educate parents about the ease with which children model aggressive behaviour.

REINFORCEMENT.   In addition to learning how to model specific behaviours through observation, children may also receive positive reinforcement for being aggressive (Bandura, 1973, 1983). For example, a young child who grabs a toy from another is positively rewarded because she has won the toy. The same is true when the elementary school bully takes other children's lunch money. The bully has been rewarded (he has the lunch money) for being aggressive. A child who learns that aggression leads to a good outcome (e.g., the aggressive child succeeds in getting the desired toy from a classmate) is more likely to engage in such behaviour in the future than a child who sees aggression as having negative consequences (e.g., if the aggressive

FIGURE 12.4   DOMESTIC VIOLENCE AFFECTS CHILDREN

This type of public service advertisement is designed to remind parents that their behaviour models behaviour for their children—and by increasing parents' awareness hopefully decreases how often their children will see such aggression.

child received a time out; Boldizar, Perry, & Perry, 1989). Moreover, aggressive children are more confident that aggression will lead to tangible rewards, such as reducing mistreatment by others, and are less concerned about aggression leading to negative outcomes, such as experiencing peer rejection (Boldizar, Perry, & Perry, 1989; Perry, Perry, & Rasmussen, 1986).

In one study, participants played one of three versions of a car racing video game (Carnagey & Anderson, 2005).

- In one version, violence was rewarded—participants received points for killing pedestrians and race opponents.
- In another version, violence was punished—participants lost points for killing pedestrians and race opponents.
- In the third version, there was no violence—killing others was not an option.

Participants who were rewarded for violence showed increased hostile emotions, aggressive thinking, and aggressive behaviour. Punishment (losing points) had no effect on aggressive thinking or behaviour, but did increase hostile emotions.

GENERAL AGGRESSION MODEL

general aggression model – a model proposing that both individual differences and situational factors lead to aggression-related thoughts, feelings, and/or physiological arousal

Craig Anderson and colleagues have combined the various theories on factors that increase the likelihood of aggression into an overall model called the **general aggression model** (Anderson, Anderson, & Deuser, 1996; Lindsay & Anderson, 2000). As shown in Figure 12.5, this model proposes that both individual difference variables (e.g., genetic factors, personality traits, hostility)

FIGURE 12.5 THE GENERAL AGGRESSION MODEL

The general aggression model describes the role of both individual differences (such as traits, beliefs, and skills) and situational factors (such as pain, frustration, and the presence of guns) in leading to aggression-related thoughts, mood, and arousal. In turn, the presence of such thoughts, mood, and arousal can lead people to appraise situations in ways that lead to aggressive behaviour.

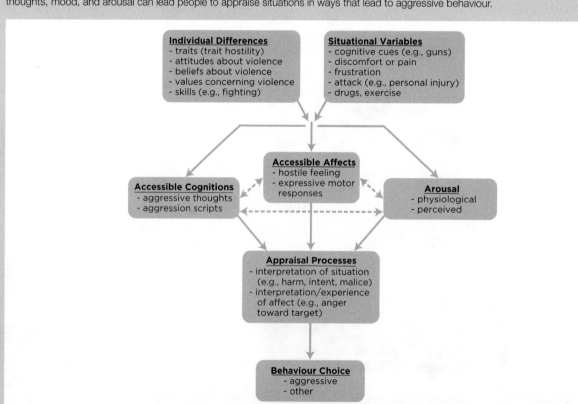

Source: Anderson, C. A. (1997). Effects of violent movies and trait hostility on hostile feelings and aggressive thoughts. *Aggressive Behavior, 23*, 161–178.

and situational variables (e.g., the presence of guns, frustration, negative affect, exposure to violence in the media) can lead to aggression-related thoughts, aggression-related feelings, and/or physiological arousal. In turn, these thoughts, feelings, and arousal can lead to aggressive behaviour, depending on how people appraise or interpret the situation.

What is the evidence for this model? First, people do vary in their general tendency toward aggression. In one study (an earlier version of which is described in detail in the next section), pairs of participants competed in a reaction time task that led to giving and receiving punishment—a loud blast of unpleasant noise—to and from each other (Anderson, Buckley, & Carnagey, 2008). Participants who were higher on trait aggressiveness gave louder noise blasts than did those who were lower in aggressiveness. Those who are high in aggressiveness are also more likely to interpret neutral words (e.g., alley, police, animal) as having an aggressive component (Bushman, 1996).

Second, exposure to cues to aggression, such as an aggressive word, a photo of a weapon, a violent movie or video game, or even songs with violent lyrics, can trigger aggressive thoughts and feelings (Anderson, 1997; Anderson et al., 2003; Anderson, Carnagey, & Eubanks, 2003). People who watch a violent movie, or play a violent video game, interpret neutral stories in a more aggressive way and recognize aggressive words more quickly compared to people who watch a nonviolent movie (Bushman, 1998; Giumetti & Markey, 2007). Male undergraduates who frequently play violent video games interpret their partner's behaviour in a competitive game as more aggressive than those without such exposure, and this perception, in turn, leads them to behave more aggressively (Bartholow, Sestir, & Davis, 2005). Similarly, people who see pictures of weapons recognize aggressive words more quickly compared to those who see pictures of plants (Anderson, Benjamin, & Bartholow, 1998).

Finally, this activation of aggressive thoughts and feelings can lead to aggressive behaviour (Anderson & Bushman, 2001; Bushman & Anderson, 2002). In one study, participants were randomly assigned to play either a violent or nonviolent version of the video game *Doom* (Sheese & Graziano, 2005). After completing the video game task, they were asked to play a prisoner's dilemma-type game in which they could choose to either cooperate with their partner for moderate mutual gain or compete with their partner for the possibility of greater personal gain. As predicted by the general aggression model, participants who

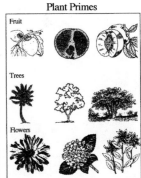

Participants who see a weapon prime are much faster at recognizing aggressive words than those who see a plant prime.

Source: Anderson, C. A., Benjamin, A. J. J., & Bartholow, B. D. (1998). Does the Gun Pull the Trigger? Automatic priming effects of weapon pictures and weapon names. *Psychological Science, 9,* 308–314.

[CONCEPTS IN CONTEXT]

FACTORS THAT LEAD TO AGGRESSION

FACTOR	EXAMPLES
Frustration-aggression theory	Luis's computer crashes just as he is about to finish writing a 10-page paper that he hadn't saved along the way. In his frustration at losing all that work, he throws his stapler across the room, breaking a window.
Cognitive-neoassociation theory	Maria is driving to work behind a car that has a bumper sticker of a handgun. Later, when a car in front of her at a red light doesn't move when the light turns green, Maria honks her horn loudly.
Excitation transfer theory	After running for 30 minutes on the treadmill, Pierre's heart is beating quickly. As he heads to the locker room to shower, a woman accidentally bumps into him in the hall. Pierre rudely snaps, "Watch where you're going, lady!"
Social learning theory	Katya's older sister, Lena, threatened to hit anyone who sat in "her seat" at the back of the school bus. Katya now makes the same threat to ensure that she can sit in her favourite seat.
General aggression model	Jason enjoys playing violent video games. After playing such games, he tends to interpret other people's behaviour as hostile, which in turn leads him to act aggressively toward them.

had first played the violent video game were much more likely to choose to compete than those who had played the nonviolent video game.

HOW DO THE MEDIA INFLUENCE AGGRESSION?

People are exposed to acts of aggression on TV, in movies, on the Internet, in magazines, and through other media outlets. Not surprisingly, exposure to aggressive acts in the media is associated with aggression in daily life. Both lab studies and longitudinal field research suggest that exposure to violence on television contributes to aggression (Anderson, 1997; Christakis & Zimmerman, 2007; Friedrich-Cofer & Huston, 1986; Wood, Wong, & Chachere, 1991). In fact, the relationship between watching aggression on television and aggressive behaviour is as strong as the link between smoking and cancer (Bushman & Anderson, 2001).

In one study to examine the effects of media violence on aggression, men and women were randomly assigned to play either a violent video game (*Mortal Kombat*) or a nonviolent game (*PGA Tournament Golf*; Bartholow & Anderson, 2002).

Mortal Kombat is a violent and popular game where the player's goal is to fight and kill other characters one at a time in various rounds of the game. *PGA Tournament Golf* is a game where the player competes on a simulated golf course using as few strokes as possible. After playing one of these two games for 10 minutes, participants competed with a confederate in a reaction time task that allowed for punishment and retaliation (a burst of loud noise through headphones). Participants who played the violent game chose higher intensities of noise levels than those who played the nonviolent game, and this effect was particularly strong for men.

This study describes one way in which exposure to violence in the media can lead to aggression in daily life. This section will examine several factors that contribute to the link between media violence and aggression, including modelling aggression, priming aggressive thoughts and emotions, creating physiological arousal, and reducing reactions to aggression.

PROVIDES AGGRESSIVE MODELS

One clear way in which exposure to violence on television can lead to aggression is via modelling (Huesmann, 1986; Josephson, 1987). As described in the previous section, people who are exposed to media violence learn aggressive ways to act and that such behaviour can get them rewards. One study with over 2,000 high school students revealed that students who watch wrestling on television are more likely to engage in fighting with peers (DuRant, Champion, & Wolfson, 2006). In several tragic cases, attempts to mimic aggressive events seen on television and in the movies have led to death. For example, in July 2007, a 12-year-old from Alberta was convicted of murdering her parents and younger brother. She was the youngest person to be convicted of multiple murders in Canada. In February 2008, a 14-year-old from California shot a 15-year-old classmate inside school. In July 2010, two teenage boys from Florida shot a 17-year-old classmate. Each of these events received widespread media coverage and were followed by more incidents. Time and place proximity of these rare cases suggest the likelihood that the later events followed in the wake of publicity of the earlier events.

George Spears and Kasia Seydegart (2004) of ERIN research in Ontario conducted a national study of Canadian children's and adolescents' experience with media. Their primary conclusion was that parental supervision of media use and family discussion of media issues have significant effects on kids' opinion regarding media violence. When families and significant others provide a framework for thinking about violence in media, kids are better equipped to assess any negative impact.

Why does exposure to violence in the media lead to aggression in real life? One explanation is that television shows and movies portray the world as full of people who are evil and violent (Berkowitz, 1984; Bushman, 1998). This view, in turn, creates a suspicious and cynical worldview, which can increase the likelihood of aggressive behaviour. People who have a sinister worldview may feel more fearful and mistrustful of others (e.g., assuming that others will hurt them) and take steps to protect themselves (e.g., buy a gun). They may also interpret ambiguous situations in a more aggressive way (e.g., in how they respond to a masked person walking down the street on a Saturday night). Additionally, Don Taylor (2011) from McGill University suggests that violence in media not only prompts copycat behaviour, but it also has influence on everyone as it gradually changes the norm. That is, due to exposure to violent television, what was considered inappropriate and unacceptable becomes socially acceptable.

In one study, grade three and grade five children were randomly assigned to watch either an aggressive or non-aggressive television show (Thomas & Drabman, 1978). Then they heard descriptions of conflict situations and were asked how they believed the average child would act in these situations. Children who had first seen an aggressive television show were more likely to believe that other children would act aggressively than those who had seen a non-aggressive show.

PRIMES AGGRESSIVE THOUGHTS AND FEELINGS

As described earlier in the description of the general aggression model, exposure to violence in the media primes aggressive thoughts and feelings, which in turn can lead to aggressive behaviour (Anderson & Bushman, 2001; Anderson & Dill, 2000; Zillman & Weaver, 1999). As discussed above, participants who played *Mortal Kombat* behaved more aggressively than those who played the nonviolent game by giving their partner louder blasts of sound (Bartholow & Anderson, 2002).

In one study, male participants were told they would assist with two different market surveys—one about music preferences and one about taste preferences (Fischer & Greitemeyer, 2006). First, participants listened to either a song that contained anti-women lyrics (such as "Superman" by Eminem) or more neutral lyrics (such as "It's My Life" by Bon Jovi). Next, as part of the taste preferences study, participants were asked to prepare a sample of hot sauce for another participant to try. However, they first heard the other participant (actually a confederate of the experimenter) express a dislike of hot spices. Participants were also told that this other person would have to consume the entire sample, and that they should administer however much hot sauce they wanted.

As Figure 12.6 explains, participants who heard the anti-women lyrics gave more hot sauce to female confederates than to male confederates. The type of lyrics had no impact on the amount of hot sauce given to male confederates suggesting, perhaps, that the lyrics specifically modelled aggressive behaviour toward women, as opposed to aggression in general.

Even the media publication of real-world events can have a substantial influence on aggression (Phillips, 1977, 1979). Sociologist David Phillips has conducted several studies examining the link between boxing matches and murder rates (Phillips, 1983, 1986). Using archival data, Phillips analyzed the change in homicide rates following heavyweight championship prizefights. These data revealed that immediately after prizefights, the number of homicides increased by 12.5 percent, and these increases were largest after heavily publicized fights. Not only do murders increase following fights, but murders of people of the same race as the person who lost the fight show a particularly sharp increase—if a White person loses the fight, more White people are killed, whereas if a Black person loses the fight, more Black people are killed. Why would heavily publicized fights lead to increases in aggression? Phillips theorizes that people match their behaviours to those that they see publicized in the media. This doesn't mean that seeing these behaviours in the media leads people to do something they wouldn't ordinarily have done (e.g., commit homicide), but rather that this exposure prompted or triggered pre-existing aggressive impulses (in line with several of the theories of aggression described earlier in this chapter).

CREATES PHYSIOLOGICAL AROUSAL

Watching highly violent television leads to physiological arousal for most people (Bushman & Geen, 1990). Exposure to violence in the media leads to increases in heart rate, blood pressure,

Questioning the Research:

Although Fischer and Greitemeyer (2006) found that anti-women lyrics had influence on aggressive behaviour of men toward women, can you think of another explanation for the findings?

FIGURE 12.6 DO ANTI-WOMEN LYRICS PRIME AGGRESSION TOWARD WOMEN?

Experimenters primed male university students with song lyrics, then gave them the opportunity for aggression against a confederate: making that person eat hot chili sauce. As predicted, men who listened to anti-women lyrics poured more hot sauce for women confederates than those who listened to neutral lyrics, suggesting that song lyrics can prime us for aggression toward targeted group members.

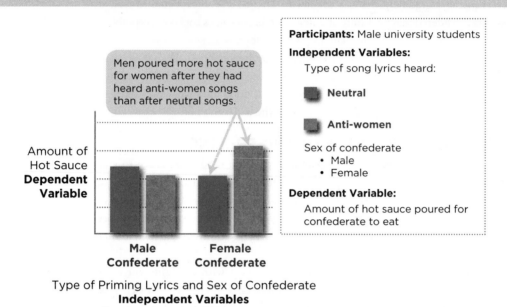

Source: Fischer, P., & Greitemeyer, T. (2006). Music and aggression: The impact of sexual aggressive song lyrics on aggression-related thoughts, emotions, and behavior toward the same and the opposite sex. *Personality and Social Psychology Bulletin, 32*, 1165–1176.

and the skin's conductance of electricity, which in turn can increase aggression. In one meta-analysis, researchers examined the impact of video game violence on physiological arousal (Anderson & Bushman, 2001). These studies revealed that exposure to violence in a video game does increase physiological arousal, including blood pressure and heart rate.

How does physiological arousal lead to aggression? First, arousal can energize, or heighten, whatever a person is already feeling, and thus increase the likelihood that a person will act on his or her feelings. Second, arousal can lead someone to misattribute the cause of this arousal, and thus react more strongly if provoked by another person. These factors explain why someone who is watching an aggressive sporting event (and thus feeling some arousal) may act aggressively toward other fans at the slightest provocation—for example, when another person accidentally spills beer on him. The excitation transfer model that we discussed earlier in the chapter overlaps with the explanation that physiological arousal leads to aggression.

To examine the effect of watching aggression on physiological arousal, participants in one study watched one of three videotapes (Bushman & Geen, 1990). Two of the videotapes featured violent clips, including fist fights and gun battles. The third videotape featured no violence. Researchers measured participants' blood pressure and pulse rate before starting the videotape, three times (at two-minute intervals) during the videotape, and again at the end of the videotape. As predicted, the violent videotape increased participants' blood pressure.

REDUCES REACTIONS TO AGGRESSION

Although exposure to violence in the media can initially lead to physiological arousal (and in turn, increased levels of aggression), repeated exposure to violence over time can reduce people's psychological and physiological reactions to aggressive images (Geen, 1981). This process is called **desensitization** or **disinhibition**. Researchers believe that repeated exposure to

Questioning the Research:

Although considerable research shows that children who watch more violent television engage in greater aggression, does this show that media viewing causes aggression? Why or why not?

desensitization or **disinhibition** – the reduction of physiological reactions to a stimuli (e.g., violence) due to repeated exposure to the stimuli (e.g., violence)

violence in the media leads people to become accustomed to such images, which decreases their impact. Research Focus on Neuroscience describes how such exposure to aggression can decrease brain activity in response to violent stimuli.

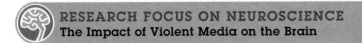

RESEARCH FOCUS ON NEUROSCIENCE
The Impact of Violent Media on the Brain

Davidson, Putnam, and Larson (2000) introduced functional imaging to the study of aggression and found that a circuit consisting of the orbital frontal cortex, amygdala, and anterior cingulate cortex varies in activity level in such a way as to suggest a neural correlate of aggression. Support for their hypothesis comes from studies in forensic psychology demonstrating that individuals with tendencies toward criminal and aggressive behaviour show reduced activity in the neural circuitry of emotion regulation (Birbaumer et al., 2005). Recent research in neuroscience reveals how exposure to violence in the media can have an impact in brain activity (Carnagey, Anderson, & Bartholow, 2007). In one study, researchers examined event-related potentials in the brain (measured brain response to thoughts or perceptions) while participants were looking at either violent or nonviolent photographs (Bartholow, Bushman, & Sestir, 2006). Participants with a high history of exposure to violent video games had lower brain reactivity in response to violent photographs, presumably because they were desensitized to such images. Unfortunately, reduced brain activity in response to violent stimuli predicted increased aggression in a later task. Other research suggests that playing violent video games leads to decreased activity in the portion of the brain that inhibits behaviour and suppresses emotional reactions (Weber, Ritterfeld, & Mathiak, 2006). These findings suggest that exposure to violence in the media could lead to increased rates of aggression over time, at least in part because such exposure may decrease neurological responses to such images.

In line with this view, people who are repeatedly exposed to violence in the media show lower levels of arousal in response to images of aggression (Berkowitz, 1984). In fact, people who watch two violent films in a row become less aroused during the second one than do adults who watch a violent film after first watching a nonviolent film (Drabman & Thomas, 1974, 1975). Exposure to violence can even lead people to show little physiological arousal while engaging in aggressive behaviour. Participants who are angered by a confederate and watch 15 minutes of a television program with many aggressive acts show the highest levels of aggression but the lowest pulse rates (Thomas, 1982).

Desensitization can also reduce people's inhibitions about engaging in aggressive behaviour. Research with children (ranging from kindergarten to grade five) reveals that those who watch a violent film are more tolerant of real-life aggression than those who watch a nonviolent film (Drabman & Thomas, 1974, 1975). In one study, children in grade three watched either a detective film or a nonviolent baseball movie. They then were asked to watch a supposedly real classroom and to seek adult assistance if any problems emerged. When problems occurred—meaning the younger children became disruptive and aggressive—children who had watched the violent detective film took longer to seek adult help than those who had watched the nonviolent film. Similarly, and as described in the Media Connections box, exposure to sexually explicit images of women desensitizes men to such images, which in turn can lead to aggression against women. Dano Demaré from the University of Manitoba and colleagues tested the interrelationship of pornography use, anti-women attitudes, and propensity for sexual violence using a statistical technique called structural equation modelling on data gathered from Canadian male undergraduates (Demaré, Lips, & Brière, 1993). The model that best fit the data was one where use of sexually violent pornography and having anti-women attitudes predicted self-reported likelihood of rape and likelihood of using sexual force, as well as self-reported history of having achieved sexual intercourse by use of coercion and force. Use of nonviolent pornography was not associated with potential or actual sexual aggression. The findings suggest the potential roles of both attitudes and sexually violent pornography in the occurrence of sexual aggression.

MEDIA CONNECTIONS

The Hazards of Violent Pornography

Although exposure to pornography is often described as relatively harmless, watching violent pornography, meaning materials that portray women as "enjoying" being victimized, can lead to aggression toward women (Linz, Donnerstein, & Penrod, 1988; Malamuth & Check, 1983). Why? In part because men who watch sexually violent movies become desensitized to the images of violence against women. In one study, men watched three violent R-rated slasher films—showing violence against women as well as sexual images—over the course of a week (Mullin & Linz, 1995). Participants then watched a videotape featuring a victim of domestic violence describing her assault and injury, and rated their beliefs about the victim of domestic violence, including the degree of her injuries and the extent to which her own behaviour had caused the assault. Compared to those who had not seen the violent movies, men who had watched these films expressed less sympathy for this victim of domestic violence. Other studies have also found that men who see a sexually violent movie show more acceptance of violence against women, less sympathy for women who are the victim of such violence, and more acceptance of rape myths (see Table 12.1; Donnerstein & Berkowitz, 1981; Linz, Donnerstein, & Penrod, 1984, 1988; Malamuth & Check, 1985). They also give more shocks to female confederates compared to those who watch neutral or erotic pornography (Donnerstein, 1980).

What's the good news? Men differ in how they respond to sexually explicit and violent films: some men show greater sexual arousal when watching aggressive portrayals of sexual situations, but most do not (Malamuth, Check, & Brière, 1986). Men who show greater sexual arousal in response to violent pornography often show a desire to experience dominance during sex, an overall hostility toward women and conflict with women, as well as positive attitudes toward violence against women (Malamuth, 1983, 1986; Malamuth, Linz, Heavey, Barnes, & Acker, 1995). Narcissistic men also enjoy films showing consensual affection followed by rape more than other men do (Bushman, Bonacci, van Dijk, & Baumeister, 2003). On the other hand, some men who imagine engaging in sexual aggression are able to resist acting on these urges (Dean & Malamuth, 1997). Men who are sensitive to others' feelings are able to inhibit their desire to behave aggressively, whereas those who are more self-centred don't.

AFP/Getty Images

TABLE 12.1	Rape Myths

1. Any healthy woman can successfully resist a rapist if she really wants to.

2. Many women have an unconscious wish to be raped, and may then unconsciously set up a situation in which they are likely to be attacked.

3. If a girl engages in necking or petting and she lets things get out of hand, it's her own fault if her partner forces sex on her.

4. One reason that women falsely report a rape is that they frequently have a need to call attention to themselves.

5. When women go around braless or wearing short skirts and tight tops, they're just asking for trouble.

Men who watch sexually aggressive films are more likely to agree with these statements than those who watch more neutral films (Burt, 1980).

FACTORS THAT LEAD TO THE MEDIA-AGGRESSION LINK

FACTOR	EXAMPLE
Provides aggressive models	Betty watches wrestling on television every Friday night. She later performs some of these wrestling moves on her brother when they're fighting.
Primes aggressive thoughts and feelings	Pedro enjoys listening to rap music, including music that contains anti-women lyrics. After listening to such music, Pedro acts more aggressively toward his female friends.
Creates physiological arousal	Devon just went to see *The Texas Chainsaw Massacre*, and feels his heart racing. When another driver cuts him off leaving the parking lot of the movie theatre, Devon lays on his horn and makes a rude gesture.
Reduces reactions to aggression	Lucinda used to find violent movies very scary and upsetting. But now that she's gone to a few violent movies with her friends, she realizes they aren't really so scary.

HOW CAN WE REDUCE AGGRESSION?

Aggression is prevalent in the real world and in the media, and is triggered by a number of distinct biological and psychological factors. In spite of this, aggressive behaviour can be controlled. In one study, university students performed poorly on some tasks that became difficult because of errors in the instructions provided by the research assistant (Ohbuchi, Kameda, & Agarie, 1989). After completion of the tasks, participants experienced one of three scenarios:

- The assistant apologized for the errors in the instructions.
- The director of the project told the students that he knew their poor performance was caused by administrative errors (thus removing their responsibility for the poor performance).
- There was no apology at all.

Not surprisingly, students were considerably less angry when the assistant apologized, regardless of whether the student was going to be held responsible for their poor performance. What does this study show? Basically that just saying you're sorry does help. This section will examine this and other ways of reducing aggression, including punishing aggressive behaviour, modelling non-aggressive responses, training in communication and problem-solving skills, and increasing empathy.

PUNISHING AGGRESSIVE BEHAVIOUR

Punishment, meaning providing unpleasant consequences, is one of the most common ways of trying to reduce aggression. Punishment can refer to giving a child a time out for having a temper tantrum, giving a driver a speeding ticket, or suspending a high school student for violating a school dress code. The Law Connections box describes programs in which punishment is a useful way of decreasing aggressive behaviour.

punishment – the provision of unpleasant consequences to try to reduce a negative behaviour

LAW CONNECTIONS

The Power of Penalties and Treatment Programs

Within the legal system, punishment is used regularly as a response to aggressive behaviour. In Canada, the rate of spousal homicide has declined for both men and women since the 1970s (Statistics Canada, 2007). This decline has been attributed to several factors, including safe houses or shelters for victims, counselling, and financial aid (Fedorowycz, 1999). Lisa Jewell and Stephen Wormith from the University of Saskatchewan conducted a meta-analysis on the effectiveness of treatment programs for male perpetrators of domestic violence (Jewell & Wormith, 2007). They found that the strongest predictors of whether someone would complete a treatment program were the person's employment status, age, and referral source. Individuals who were employed, older, and court mandated were more likely to remain in treatment than those who were unemployed, younger, or not court mandated. Other correlates of attrition that indicated modest differences between those who completed treatment and those who didn't were previous domestic violence offences, income, drug use, and criminal history. Individuals who were attending domestic violence treatment after their first partner assault offence or who had higher incomes were significantly more likely to complete treatment. In contrast, individuals who had a criminal history prior to attending domestic violence treatment or had drug problems were more likely to drop out of treatment. Men who had more education, were married, were White, or didn't have problems with alcohol also completed treatment at a somewhat higher rate than persons who were less educated, were unmarried, were members of a minority group, or had problems with alcohol. More men completed a cognitive-behavioural program than a feminist educational program, although the better educated they were, the more likely they were to complete a feminist educational program.

© Dana White/Photo Edit

Although punishment may sometimes reduce aggression, it also models the use of aggression, which can be problematic. Parents who use more harsh discipline techniques during their children's early years have more aggressive children, in part because children are more likely themselves to use aggressive responses in future interactions (Weiss, Dodge, Bates, & Pettit, 1992). One meta-analysis on the consequences of corporal punishment, such as spanking, revealed several negative outcomes, including increased delinquency and antisocial behaviour for children and increased likelihood of abusing one's own child or spouse as an adult (Gershoff, 2002). Spanking also led to less internalization of moral standards of behaviour, presumably because children attribute their positive behaviour to fear of punishment as opposed to intrinsic motives.

As was described in Chapter 6 in terms of attitude formation and change, cognitive dissonance theory predicts that implementing severe punishment for an offence can lead people to believe the only reason that they're not behaving aggressively is because they fear punishment (as opposed to a true concern with avoiding such behaviour).

MODELLING NON-AGGRESSIVE RESPONSES

Although children can learn aggressive responses from watching various models, they can also learn and model non-aggressive responses. This approach is what has led parenting books to emphasize the use of "time outs" and other non-aggressive approaches to discipline. Exposing children to compelling pro-social television programs can also help reduce aggression.

Parents can further help their children by discussing the problems of television modelling (Huesmann, Eron, Klein, Brice, & Fischer, 1983). In one study, 169 grade one and grade three children who watched a lot of violent television were randomly assigned to receive a control

Questioning the Research:

Research suggests that children who are spanked show higher levels of aggressive behaviour than those who are not. Does this mean that spanking children *leads* to aggressive behaviour? Can you think of an alternative explanation for this association?

condition or education about the unrealistic and unacceptable nature of television violence. Two years later, children who received this education were rated as less aggressive by their peers than those in the control condition. Although children in both groups showed an increase in aggression over time, those in the education group showed a significantly smaller increase.

TRAINING IN COMMUNICATION AND PROBLEM-SOLVING SKILLS

Training in communication and problem-solving skills can reduce aggression. Because much of what we see in the media shows destructive and violent ways of handling aggression, one way to reduce aggression is to show people how to respond constructively to frustrating situations (DuRant, Treiber, Getts, & McCloud, 1996). In the United States, the Peaceful Conflict Resolution and Violence Prevention Program was designed to reduce violence in school settings by training children in identifying situations that could result in violence, developing their skills in problem-solving, communication, and conflict resolution, and providing them with strategies for effective management of anger without fighting (DuRant, Barkin, & Krowchuk, 2001). Schools that implemented this program showed decreases in the use of violence by students, whereas those without such programs showed increases. Similar programs have been used in Canadian schools and were also found to be effective (Cunningham et al., 1998; Stevahn, Munger & Kealey, 2005). The Education Connections box describes another school-based approach to preventing aggression.

EDUCATION CONNECTIONS

The Problem of Bullying

Bullying is a serious problem in many schools in Canada and other countries (Nansel et al., 2001). Research conducted in Canada, the United States, and Europe indicates that about 10 to 15 percent of children age 11 to 15 report bullying others on a weekly basis (Duncan, 1999; Public Safety Canada, 2010; Sourander, Helstela, Helenius, & Piha, 2000). Reports on bullying show that males were more likely than females to both bully and be bullied, although females were more likely than males to be psychologically or verbally bullied. According to Statistics Canada (2007), 16 percent of Toronto youths in grades seven to nine had been bullied on more than 12 occasions during the years prior to the survey. In general, bullying has been found to be more common in younger children (grades six to eight) than in older children (grades nine and 10). Bullies and victims of bullying have trouble adjusting to their environment, both socially and psychologically, and show distinct patterns of poor adjustment. Bullies tend to be poorer students and to engage in substance abuse, whereas the victims of bullies tend to have difficulty making friends and feel lonely. So-called "cyberbullying" is also increasing at dramatic rates, as teenagers spend more time interacting in chat rooms, instant messaging, and socializing on Facebook and other social networking sites (Ybarra, Mitchell, Wolak, & Finkelhor, 2006).

Although the problem of bullying was largely ignored, researchers are now beginning to examine some strategies for coping with this serious problem, in part due to people's grave concern over school violence in general (Olweus, 1995). Dan

Olweus developed a school-based intervention program that includes creating greater awareness of bullying as a problem, developing class rules against bullying, increasing supervision of children during lunch and recess, and holding serious talks with bullies and victims. When this program was used in middle and junior high schools in the Netherlands, bully-related problems decreased by 50 percent, as did other antisocial behaviour (e.g., vandalism, fighting, stealing). This program also led to more positive attitudes toward school, improved social relationships, and greater order and discipline in the classroom.

Laurence Mouton/Getty Images

One of the most effective communication strategies for reducing aggressive behaviour is an apology (Ohbuchi, Kameda, & Agarie, 1989; Weiner, Amirkhan, Folkes, & Verette, 1987). Receiving a direct apology from a person who criticizes you dramatically minimizes aggressive tendencies, especially if you're able to attribute such criticism to external factors (e.g., the person was in a bad mood) and uncontrollable factors (e.g., her car broke down; Baron, 1990; Weiner et al., 1987). As described at the start of this section, people are considerably less angry when someone apologizes for making an error.

Although expressing anger in an aggressive, violent, and destructive manner leads to increased aggression, letting someone know that you're angry can also be an effective way of reducing anger. The benefit of opening up to someone is due at least in part to the insights and self-awareness that often come from such self-disclosure. Thus, processing intense feelings helps to reduce one's need to behave aggressively. Moreover, while ruminating about a problem increases the feeling of anger, distracting oneself from it reduces anger (Rusting & Nolen-Hoeksema, 1998). In one study, participants were angered, and then hit a punching bag while they either thought about the person who upset them (rumination group) or thought about becoming physically fit (distraction group; Bushman, 2002). Compared to people in the no punching bag control condition as well as those in the distraction condition, those in the rumination condition felt angry, and engaged in more aggressive behaviour in a later task.

INCREASING EMPATHY

Another factor that can help reduce aggression is to increase empathy for others (Bandura, Barbaranelli, Caprara, & Pastorelli, 1996; Miller & Eisenberg, 1988). People find it difficult to inflict pain purposely on another human being, which is why we dehumanize people in times of war. Thus, if we feel empathy toward others, we feel guilty if we hurt them, and therefore find it much harder to behave aggressively toward them (Baumeister & Campbell, 1999). For example, people give less severe shocks to a person who has just self-disclosed to them, indicating that feeling empathy reduces the need to be aggressive (Ohbuchi, Ohno, & Mukai, 1993). Similarly, as children with greater empathy for others are less likely to behave aggressively toward them, training children in perspective taking can be a useful way of reducing their aggressive behaviour.

In one study to test the power of empathy on reducing aggression, participants were told they would be interacting with a partner in a series of tasks (Konrath, Bushman, & Campbell, 2006). Participants in one condition were told that they shared a birthday with their partner; participants in the other condition were not given any information indicating similarity to their partner. All participants then wrote an essay about abortion (endorsing whichever side they preferred). In both conditions, this essay received harsh criticism from their partner, including statements such as "This is one of the worst essays I have ever read." Participants then engaged with their partner in a reaction time task in which the slower person received an unpleasant blast of noise (a reliable and subtle way of measuring aggression that we saw used in other studies in this chapter), with participants choosing the level of noise their partner would receive. Those who believed they shared a birthday with their partner chose significantly softer levels of noise than those who weren't given information about similarity to their partner.

Our desire for aggression is also reduced when we learn information that shows us that a person should not be held fully responsible for his or her actions, in part because such information helps us understand and empathize with the person (Kremer & Stephens, 1983). For example, people who learn information that helps explains a person's aggressive behaviour *before* being insulted by this person show less physiological arousal and less annoyance than those who only learn about such circumstances after receiving the insult (Johnson & Rule, 1986). Similarly, learning that a person's aggressive behaviour was unintentional or was provoked leads to lower levels of aggression and anger.

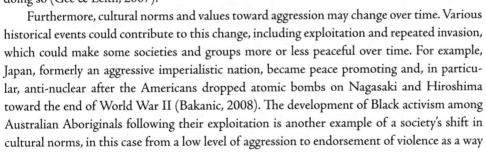

[CONCEPTS IN CONTEXT]

FACTORS THAT REDUCE AGGRESSION

FACTOR	EXAMPLE
Punishing aggressive behaviour	Dr. Vernon is a high school principal. At the start of the year, she instituted a policy in which any student who fights on school grounds receives a mandatory one-week suspension. Fighting has been dramatically reduced.
Modelling non-aggressive responses	Linda and her sister Diana frequently fight—about who is faster, who sits in which seat in the car, and who is better at hopscotch. Their father suggests they watch *Sesame Street* to learn some effective ways of cooperating. After just a few weeks, Linda and Diana are getting along much better.
Training in communication and problem-solving skills	Robert was very angry after his boss, Lianne, was critical of his performance during a meeting. His anger disappeared after Lianne apologized for her negative remarks, explaining that she received disappointing news that day.
Increasing empathy	Alison was upset when her friend, Ling, failed to respond to two invitations to a party, and vowed not to call her again. When Alison learned that Ling had been very busy taking care of her sick mother, she immediately called Ling and offered to run errands for her.

HOW DOES CULTURE RELATE TO AGGRESSION?

Attitudes toward aggression vary among cultures, within cultures, and over time. As you will read in this section, not all cultures value nonviolent behaviour to the same degree, and the prevalence of aggression differs across cultures. Using archival data, Chris Gee and Larry Leith from the University of Toronto discovered that North American–born NHL hockey players played more aggressively than European-born NHL players, but that being more aggressive had no impact on a player's success. In other words, players didn't have to be more aggressive to succeed. The authors conclude that the difference has to do with different social learning experiences in the different cultural contexts. In North America, violence in hockey is more acceptable, and players therefore learn from early on to play violently—and are rewarded for doing so (Gee & Leith, 2007).

Furthermore, cultural norms and values toward aggression may change over time. Various historical events could contribute to this change, including exploitation and repeated invasion, which could make some societies and groups more or less peaceful over time. For example, Japan, formerly an aggressive imperialistic nation, became peace promoting and, in particular, anti-nuclear after the Americans dropped atomic bombs on Nagasaki and Hiroshima toward the end of World War II (Bakanic, 2008). The development of Black activism among Australian Aboriginals following their exploitation is another example of a society's shift in cultural norms, in this case from a low level of aggression to endorsement of violence as a way to revive Aboriginals' dignity (Rowley, 1971; as cited in Hogg & Vaughan, 2002).

One example of how attitudes to aggression vary cross-culturally is in relation to aggression, or physical violence, toward children; in other words, the extent to which it's considered acceptable for an adult to hit a child. Some people think all violence against children is an abuse of their human rights. Others think it can be acceptable, if it's of the right intensity and for the right reasons. Section 43 of the Criminal Code of Canada states that any use of force that harms a child is a criminal act, unless it "is part of a genuine effort to educate the child, poses no reasonable risk of harm that is more than transitory and trifling, and is reasonable under the circumstances." According to Canada's Department of Justice website, Section 43 also "provides that a parent, teacher or person acting in the place of a parent is justified in using force to correct a child that is under his or her care provided that the force used is reasonable in all of the circumstances" (Department of Justice Canada, 2004). In 2004, the Canadian Foundation for Children, Youth and the Law challenged Section 43, arguing that it "violates children's Charter rights to security of the person, equality and . . . constituted cruel and unusual punishment." Ultimately, the Supreme Court of Canada decided that Section 43 of the Criminal Code is constitutional; it found that Section 43 does not violate a child's rights to security of the person and equality, and is not cruel and unusual punishment (Department of Justice Canada, 2004).

Douglas (2006) looked at the acceptability of corporal punishment across cultures. The literature indicates that people are more likely to approve of corporal punishment if they are male, less educated, and older. Otherwise, what most influences a person's view of corporal punishment for a child is how acceptable it is in the person's culture and the person's experience of violence as a child. Essentially, then, people's attitudes are guided by their socialization, which consists of an individual's social learning in a particular cultural context. Douglas had access to data from several Canadian university sites as well as American, European, Asian, and South American sites. Table 12.2 presents some of the findings.

Table 12.2	Corporal Punishment Approval Rates By Country							
	APPROVAL OF SPANKING A CHILD				APPROVAL OF SLAPPING A TEEN			
REGIONAL SITE	TOTAL	MEN	WOMEN	REGIONAL SITE		TOTAL	MEN	WOMEN
Total sample	40.0	50.7	35.5	Total sample		33.0	41.4	29.1
South Korea, Pusan	85.0	85.0	85.1	India, Pune		71.8	71.9	71.8
USA, Washington, DC	78.2	91.7	76.0	Portugal, Braga		70.8	72.8	67.7
USA, Louisiana, Grambling	77.3	79.2	76.3	USA, Washington, DC		63.2	75.0	61.3
Singapore	69.5	77.0	66.3	South Korea, Pusan		55.5	62.0	51.7
India, Pune	66.0	50.0	73.2	Switzerland, Fribourg, German speaking		55.3	64.7	52.3
USA, Texas, Nacogdoches	63.2	77.4	57.8	USA, Louisiana, Grambling		53.9	50.0	56.3
USA, Texas, non-Mexican American	62.0	71.3	54.3	USA, Texas, Mexican American		48.6	51.6	46.6
Portugal, Braga	60.8	68.9	48.5	Singapore		42.7	52.7	38.4
USA, Texas, Mexican American	58.9	60.0	58.1	Mexico, Northern		40.8	50.0	39.0
USA, Mississippi, Jackson	57.9	43.5	59.6	USA, Texas, non-Mexican American		40.5	47.2	34.9
USA, Ohio, Cincinnati	54.7	58.1	51.5	USA, Mississippi, Jackson		38.4	26.1	39.9
Mexico, Northern	54.4	57.9	53.7	Canada, Toronto		37.6	48.8	31.9
USA, Indiana, Terre Haute	49.6	59.7	45.6	Brazil, Sao Paulo		37.0	44.0	33.5
Switzerland, Fribourg, German speaking	44.7	55.9	41.1	USA, Ohio, Cincinnati		36.5	35.5	37.4
Canada, Toronto	43.7	53.7	38.7	Scotland, Glasgow		34.7	52.8	31.2
Brazil, Sao Paulo	41.6	48.3	38.3	USA, Indiana, Terre Haute		32.6	41.8	29.0
China, Hong Kong	35.8	50.0	26.5	USA, Texas, Nacogdoches		32.5	32.3	32.5
New Zealand, Christchurch	35.5	28.6	37.6	Israel, Emek Yezreel		27.7	24.2	28.5
Canada, London	35.0	42.9	28.1	Canada, London		27.5	37.5	18.8
USA, Utah, Logan	31.1	43.3	23.9	Freiburg, Germany		25.9	40.3	15.8
Germany, Freiburg	28.4	44.8	16.8	China, Hong Kong		25.9	34.2	20.5
Canada, Hamilton	27.8	40.5	25.7	Canada, Hamilton		25.5	35.1	23.9
Australia, Adelaide	27.4	45.7	22.8	USA, Pennsylvania, Small College		22.8	32.7	19.7
Scotland, Glasgow	26.0	50.0	21.3	Australia, Adelaide		22.6	41.3	17.9
Canada, Winnipeg	25.0	46.7	22.4	USA, New Hampshire, Durham		22.5	29.1	19.6
USA, Pennsylvania, Small College	24.5	30.9	22.5	The Netherlands, Amsterdam		20.7	30.0	17.4
Israel, Emek Yezreel	24.4	25.8	24.1	Belgium, Flemish speaking		19.9	35.1	15.2

Switzerland, Fribourg, French speaking	23.9	34.7	19.2	New Zealand, Christchurch	19.8	21.4	19.4
USA, New Hampshire, Durham	23.6	33.0	19.3	Switzerland, Fribourg, French speaking	19.3	26.4	16.2
The Netherlands, Amsterdam	21.3	37.5	15.7	Canada, Montreal	17.3	23.3	15.7
Belgium, Flemish speaking	16.2	30.7	11.7	USA, Utah, Logan	16.7	23.9	12.4
Canada, Montreal	12.5	13.3	12.2	Canada, Winnipeg	12.9	26.7	11.2

The data in this chart show the percentage of people surveyed from each geographic area who agreed or strongly agreed with hitting children as a form of discipline *(N = 7,371)*.

Source: Douglas, E. M. (2006). Familial violence socialization in childhood and later life approval of corporal punishment: A cross-cultural perspective. *American Journal of Orthopsychiatry 76*, 23–30.

PREVALENCE OF AGGRESSION

Rates of aggression differ substantially across different cultures. A recent report by the United Nations Office on Drugs and Crimes indicated that Canada is among the countries with a relatively low level of homicide (UNODC, 2010). Our "southern neighbour," the United States, however, is one of the most violent countries compared to other Western nations. The rate of violence in the United States is much higher than in other similar Western countries, including Canada, Australia, and virtually every European country (Lore & Schultz, 1993). However, compared to the rest of the world, the U.S. is among the countries with a medium level of homicide, while Russia and Mexico are among the countries with a high level of homicide (see Figure 12.7). Unfortunately, there are countries with a homicide level that is more extreme, including South Africa and Colombia. The wide national differences in homicide rate are not based on geography or the difference between Western and Eastern nations as there are countries with low and high levels of homicide in Africa, Europe, and America. What factors explain this wide variation in homicide rates?

FIGURE 12.7 HOMICIDE RATES FROM AROUND THE WORLD

As you can see from the homicide statistics for 2003-2008 reported by the United Nations Office on Drugs and Crimes, there is a wide variation in the level of homicide around the world with Columbia having one of the highest and Norway one of the lowest levels of homicide.

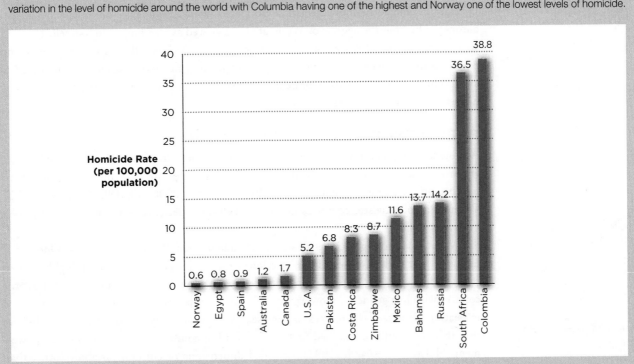

Does orientation toward individualism versus collectivism influence rates of aggression? It's difficult to determine. Some data suggest that collectivistic cultures show higher rates of aggression, including the total number of violent crimes and homicides (Bond, 2004). Higher rates of aggression may be due to the greater distinctions drawn between in-group and out-group members in collectivistic cultures.

However, other data suggest that peer-directed aggression is lower in collectivistic cultures than in individualistic ones (Bergeron & Schneider, 2005). In one study, researchers examined rates of aggression across a range of studies collected in 28 countries with over 42,000 participants. This data revealed that countries that were high on individualism have higher rates of aggression. Apparently people in societies that place a high value on the needs of the group as opposed to the needs of the individual show lower levels of aggression—at least toward their (in-group) peers.

The influence of culture on the development of aggressive behaviour appears early in life. In one study, 4-year-old children from Indonesia, Germany, Sweden, and the United States were asked to tell two stories using two separate sets of toys (Farver, Welles-Nystoem, Frosch, Wimbarti, & Hoppe-Graff, 1997). The first set of toys had neutral themes and included family figures such as a mother, father, and three children and cars. The second set of toys had aggressive themes and included police figures, motorcycles, cars, and handcuffs. Children's narratives were analyzed in terms of the number of aggressive words, complexity, story characteristics, and length. Results indicated that narratives of American children had more aggressive content and unfriendly characters compared to narratives of Swedish, German, and Indonesian children. Additionally, it was found that boys in all cultures told stories with more aggressive characteristics and aggressive content than girls.

The contrast found in children's narratives cross-culturally were reflections of their knowledge and experience of aggression in their culture. American children live in a society that has a rate of violence 10 to 20 times higher than that of other industrialized countries, including Sweden and Germany, and it has higher rates of violence than some developing countries, such as Indonesia. Children who live in a violent society experience and interpret life differently than those who live in a more peaceful society. Additionally, child-rearing norms in America tend to be individualistically oriented, with an emphasis on independence and autonomy. In America, aggression is tolerated and viewed as standing up for oneself. This is in sharp contrast with child-rearing norms in Indonesia, which is collectivistically oriented and places greater value on cooperation and group harmony. In Indonesia, children are urged to avoid conflict and are rewarded for being able to calm themselves and to settle a dispute using negotiation (Williams, 1991).

PREVALENCE OF DOMESTIC VIOLENCE

Although the data on rates of aggression in collectivistic cultures versus individualistic ones are mixed, data on rates of domestic violence strongly indicate that this type of behaviour is substantially higher in collectivistic cultures (Archer, 2006; Vandello & Cohen, 2003). Women in collectivistic countries are more likely to experience physical violence by their husbands.

What leads to higher rates of domestic violence in collectivistic cultures? One explanation is that collectivistic cultures are lower on gender equality, which is highly related to attitudes regarding aggression toward women (Acher, 2006). For example, in Egypt, a country with low gender empowerment, 70 percent of people believe that a man is justified in beating his wife if she refuses to have sex. In contrast, only 1 percent of people believe that this act would be justified in New Zealand, a country with high gender empowerment. Hofstede's research (1991) identified dimensions of cultural variability other than individualism-collectivism. Two others may be relevant in the present context. One, which

Hofstede labels "power distance," is the extent to which status and hierarchical relationships are more valued. Where men have more status, and this status is more accepted, they're in a position to abuse that status. Hofstede also labelled another dimension specifically to signal its relevance to gender relations: "masculinity-feminity." In Hofstede's terms, the more feminine nations (Scandinavia, the Netherlands) maintain differences in gender stereotypes with less emphasis than the masculine nations (e.g., Japan). Rates of domestic violence might be better explained by analysis in relation to either of these constructs rather than individualism-collectivism.

Another explanation is that collectivistic cultures tend to hold more traditional values, including an emphasis on loyalty and self-sacrifice as well as unquestioned acceptance of religion (Archer, 2006). In turn, a "good wife" is one who is obedient to her husband—a woman who remains in an abusive relationship would therefore be seen as strong and loyal. In an individualistic culture, a woman who stays in an abusive relationship would be seen as passive and foolish.

These differences in rates of domestic violence are also seen within subcultures of the United States. In one study to examine the impact of subculture on perceptions of domestic violence, researchers recruited participants from both northern and southern states, as well as participants from Hispanic backgrounds (within the United States, Southerners and Hispanics are more collectivistic than Northerners; Vandello & Cohen, 2003). As part of the study, participants overheard a physical confrontation between a student (supposedly another participant in the same study) and her boyfriend. The confrontation ended with the boyfriend aggressively slamming his partner against a wall, which the participants overheard. The victim (a confederate) then walked into the room to complete the study, and remarked on the abuse, saying, "He really cares about me. I guess that's just how he shows it, you know?" The confederate then noted the participants' response, and specifically whether the participants expressed tolerance for the abuse. As predicted, 29 percent of participants from the southern states and 24 percent of Hispanic participants expressed some tolerance for the abuse, in contrast to only 10 percent of participants from the northern states. These findings suggest that people in different cultures differ in how they view abuse against a dating partner.

SUBCULTURAL DIFFERENCES IN AGGRESSION

Bonta (1997) reported that peaceful societies are found throughout the world, such as the Paliyan people in India, the !Kung children of Namibia and Botswana, and Amish, Hutterite, and Mennonite people in Canada and the United States. These societies share certain common principles, including an intense focus on intergroup cooperation, avoidance of competition, and the inhibition of emotions. Similarly, in certain cultures in Tahiti and among the Inuit of Canada, there are no words for aggression or aggressive acts, and children are taught that violent acts are unacceptable. Disputes are handled via alternative means, such as singing abusive songs about the other, or engaging in contests in which the first one who breaks a stick with a rock is considered the braver.

Another peaceful society is Semai, in Malaysia. The Semai are nonviolent people who have an extremely low level of interpersonal aggression (Price & Crapo, 2002). Several characteristics separate Semai society from other groups in Malaysia. The Semai treat their children differently. They believe that children learn by themselves rather than believing that adults have to teach children actively. They believe that if a child isn't willing to learn, punishment won't be effective. Therefore, children have no aggressive models. Semai do not hit their children and they believe that

In Tahiti, dance is a common form of competition.

© Douglas Peebles/DanitaDelimont.com

physical aggression is dangerous. They socialize their children in a nonviolent manner and encourage their children to fear anger. As was documented by Dentan, the Semai have such a nonviolent self-image that they don't simply say that anger is bad, but instead believe they don't get angry (1968, cited by Price & Crapo, 2002).

In the early 1950s, the British started recruiting troops from the Semai in response to the Communist uprising. Initially, the Semai didn't understand the role they were expected to play and many British expected that the Semai wouldn't make good soldiers. However, historical accounts indicate that when the Semai were removed from their normal cultural environment and perceived themselves as not accountable for their behaviour, they were capable of violence (Price & Crapo, 2002). When the Semai returned home, however, they resumed their traditional nonviolent and gentle way of life despite their military experience. The Semai experience indicates that although everyone is capable of violent outbursts, when cultural norms frame aggression as unacceptable and violence is viewed as taboo, people generally behave non-aggressively (Price & Crapo, 2002).

Members of the Semai tribe from Malaysia.

AFP/Getty Images

As the section on domestic violence showed, rates of aggression can vary within a country. More generally, for example, in the United States rates of some types of aggression are higher in the South than in the Northeast and Midwest (Cohen, 1996; Nisbett, 1993). People in the South are more likely than those in other parts of the country to have a gun in their home, and to see having a gun as an important aspect of their protection. Southerners see having a gun as making their home safer rather than more dangerous, whereas Northerners see *not* having a gun as making their home safer. In fact, 67 percent of Southerners have guns/revolvers in their homes compared to 50 percent of non-Southerners, and 40 percent of Southerners keep guns for protection compared to only 23 percent of non-Southerners. The southern states are also more likely to carry out the death penalty than the northern states: 94 percent of southern states allow capital punishment, versus only 43 percent of northern states, and between 1977 and 1991, 69 percent of southern states carried out an execution compared to only 13 percent of northern states.

One explanation for such differences is that the culture of honour in the American South promotes certain types of aggressive acts, meaning those that serve to protect one's self and defend one's honour (Cohen & Nisbett, 1994). This culture may have developed due to the prevalence of herding animals as a means of economic support. Because animals are difficult to patrol over large plots of land, people need to be able to use force to protect their animals from theft, and developing a reputation as someone who would use force to protect his or her livelihood would be an important strategy for protecting such an investment.

In line with this view, Southerners do not endorse violence more generally than Northerners, but they do see defending one's honour (with aggression) as necessary following insults and for protection. Compared to people from the North, those from the South are more likely to agree that a person has the right to kill in order to "defend his home" and to hit a drunk who bumps into a man and his wife.

In a clever study to test regional differences in views about the appropriateness of different types of aggression, researchers sent letters from a fictitious job applicant to employers all over the United States (Cohen & Nisbett, 1997). In the letter, the job applicant admitted having been convicted of a felony, and asked for an application for employment from the organization. In some cases, the applicant reported having *accidentally* killed a man who had been having an affair with his fiancée and then bragged about it in a bar (an "honour killing"), and in other cases the applicant admitted having stolen a car to sell in order to pay off debts. Researchers then measured whether the organization responded, and if so, how encouraging

FIGURE 12.8   DOES SUBCULTURE IMPACT AGGRESSION FOLLOWING PROVOCATION?

Experimenters insulted some men from northern and southern U.S. backgrounds, and then measured how close they came to bumping into another person before turning away. As predicted, Southerners came closer than Northerners to bumping someone after they had been called an "asshole," supporting the idea that a culture of honour in the South permits aggression in response to insults.

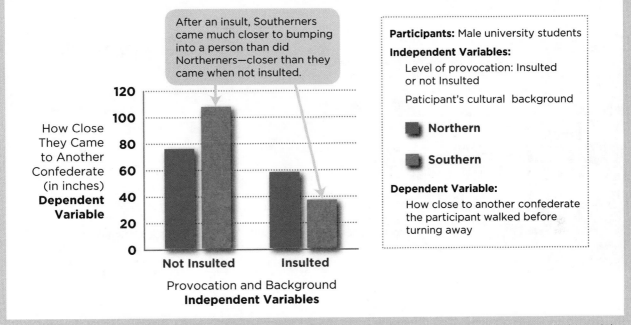

Source: Cohen, D., Nisbett, R. E., Bowdle, B. F., & Schwarz, N. (1996). Insult, aggression, and the southern culture of honor: An 'experimental ethnography'. *Journal of Personality and Social Psychology, 70*, 945–960.

and understanding the response was. As predicted, the theft letters were responded to with about the same tone in the North, South, and West, but honour killing letters were responded to with much more warmth in the South and West than in the North.

Although much of the evidence for the link between culture in the American south and aggression relies on correlational research, experimental research also suggests subcultural differences in how people understand types of aggression. In one study, researchers examined how culture influenced how men responded to an insult (Cohen, Nisbett, Bowdle, & Schwarz, 1996). They recruited male students who had grown up in the North or South to participate in a study supposedly on "human judgement." The participant completed a brief questionnaire and was then supposed to bring the questionnaire to a table in the hall. To get to the table the participant had to pass a person standing in the hall filing papers into a file cabinet, and that person, a confederate, had to shut the cabinet in order to allow the participant to pass. After the participant passed the second time (after dropping off the questionnaire to the experimenter), the person acted as if he was annoyed, said "asshole," and deliberately bumped the participant with his shoulder.

At the conclusion of the study the participant then walked down the same narrow hall toward a different confederate. The dependent variable was how close the participant came to bumping into the confederate before yielding (e.g., a game of chicken). As shown in Figure 12.8, Southerners moved out of the way sooner in the control condition than when they'd been insulted. In contrast, Northerners' behaviour was relatively similar regardless of whether they'd been insulted. Finally, while Southerners reacted more aggressively when provoked, they were also more polite than Northerners (i.e., they yielded sooner) in the control condition.

THE BIG PICTURE

AGGRESSION

This chapter included many applications of the three "big ideas" studied in social psychology. The examples below should help you see the connection between aggression and these big ideas, and contribute to your understanding of the big picture of social psychology.

THEME	EXAMPLES
The social world influences how we think about ourselves.	• Boys learn that engaging in physical aggression makes them seem cool, athletic, and popular. • Some professional athletes who make millions of dollars a year feel underpaid when they compare themselves to other professional athletes. • Children who are spanked are less likely to internalize moral standards of behaviour than those who receive other forms of punishment.
The social world influences our thoughts, attitudes, and behaviour.	• When we're frustrated, we're more likely to act aggressively. • When we're hot, we're more likely to act aggressively. • Children who see aggression on television are more likely to act aggressively.
Our attitudes and behaviour shape the social world around us.	• Children who are highly aggressive are more likely to engage in spousal abuse, criminal behaviour, and traffic violations as adults. • When we feel empathy for someone, we're less likely to behave aggressively toward them. • Children who are exposed to violent films are less likely to seek adult assistance when other children behave aggressively.

This chapter described factors that influence aggression as well as factors that can be used to reduce aggression.

1. How do biological factors influence aggression?

This section examined the role of biological factors in influencing aggression. You learned about two instinct and evolutionary theories that predict aggression: Freud's death wish and Lorenz's instinct theory of aggression. This section also examined the impact of genetics and hormones on rates of aggression. You also learned that male inmates with higher levels of testosterone are more likely than those with lower levels of testosterone to have committed crimes against a person than property crimes, and are more likely to have violated rules in prison.

2. How do psychological factors influence aggression?

This section described the role of psychological factors in influencing aggression. You learned about the frustration-aggression theory, including the role of displacement and relative deprivation, as well as critiques of this theory. This section also described the impact on aggression of negative affect, including heat, arousal, and other negative conditions, and aggressive cues. Finally, this section described how social learning theory explains aggression, and in particular the influence of modelling and reinforcement. You also learned that people who completed a survey in a room with a weapon recommended longer prison sentences than those who were in a room with a piece of sports equipment.

3. How do the media influence aggression?

This section examined four factors that explain the link between media exposure and aggression. You learned about modelling, priming of aggressive thoughts and feelings, physiological arousal, and desensitization. You also learned that playing violent games leads to more aggression than playing nonviolent games, especially for men.

4. How can we reduce aggression?

This section examined strategies for reducing aggression. These strategies include punishing aggressive behaviour, modelling non-aggressive responses, training in communication and problem-solving skills, and increasing empathy. You also learned that simply saying you're sorry to someone you've harmed (even unintentionally) reduces aggression.

5. How does culture relate to aggression?

This section examined cultural differences in aggression. First, you learned that the prevalence of aggression differs dramatically across different cultures. Next, you learned that rates of aggression against women differ across cultures. Finally, you learned that subcultures differ in their perception of different types of aggression, and specifically whether aggression is more acceptable if it protects one's honour.

Key Terms

aggression 400
arousal-affect/excitation transfer model 414
catharsis 401
cognitive-neoassociation theory 412

desensitization (disinhibition) 420
displacement 410
emotional (or hostile) aggression 400
frustration-aggression theory 409
general aggression model 416

instinct theory of aggression 402
instrumental aggression 400
punishment 423
social learning theory 406

Questions for Review

1. Describe how biological factors, including instinct and evolutionary factors, genetics, and hormones, can influence aggression.

2. What are three psychological factors that influence aggression?

3. Describe four ways in which the media influence aggression.

4. What are four effective ways of reducing aggression?

5. Describe cultural differences in the prevalence and causes of aggression.

Take Action!

1. Your next door neighbour's 8-year-old son is impatient, irritable, and aggressive. What would you predict about his level of aggression as a teenager?

2. Your roommate has just jogged on the treadmill for 45 minutes while watching a boxing match on television and is now driving home. How might he react when a driver cuts him off?

3. Given what we know about the effects of media violence on aggression, should we adopt limits of violence for television, music, movies, and video games? Why or why not?

4. You want to discipline your child for hitting a friend. What approaches might work, and what approaches might not?

RESEARCH CONNECTIONS

Participate in Research

Activity 1 The Risk of Aggression by a Loved One: This chapter described how children are most at risk of experiencing violence from parents. Search your local newspaper for instances of aggression against a child, and count the percentage of acts carried out by a parent versus a stranger. Then go online to report your findings.

Activity 2 The Impact of Frustration on Aggression: Frustration is thought to influence rates of aggression. Go online to read a series of scenarios and rate how likely you would be to behave aggressively in each situation.

Activity 3 The Impact of Media Violence: This chapter described the impact of violence in the media on rates of aggression. To examine the prevalence of acts of aggression in the media, watch several television programs and count the number of acts of aggression. Then go online to report your findings.

Activity 4 Reducing Aggression: You learned in this chapter about factors that reduce aggression. Go online to read about various strategies for reducing aggression, and then rate how effective you believe each approach would be.

Activity 5 The Relation of Culture to Aggression: The final section of this chapter described how culture influences the definition and prevalence of aggression. Go online to rate how aggressive you see different behaviours as being. Then see how other students, including those from different cultures, rate such behaviours.

Test a Hypothesis

One of the common findings in research on aggression is that children's programs frequently portray acts of aggression, which in turn can lead to aggressive behaviour. To test whether this hypothesis is true, watch several children's television programs geared to different groups (such as age, or gender) and count the number of acts of aggression. Then, go online to report your findings to other students.

Design a Study

Go online to design your own study that tests how aversive stimuli can lead to aggression. You'll be able to choose the type of study you want to conduct (self-report, observational/naturalistic, or experimental), choose your own independent and dependent variables, and form your own hypothesis. Then, you can share your findings with other students across the country!

13

ALTRUISM AND PROSOCIAL BEHAVIOUR

DID YOU EVER WONDER?

During the Second World War, more than 1,800 Jewish refugees found shelter and safety in Albania, a predominantly Muslim country. In fact, Albania's Jewish community was one of few Jewish communities in Europe that actually grew in number during the Holocaust years. Ali Sheq Pashkaj (pictured along with photos of his father) and his family housed a Jewish prisoner in their home for two years. Ali's father helped the prisoner escape from a German transport truck driven by Nazi soldiers when it was parked outside the family's general store. His father got the Nazi soldiers drunk and slipped the Jewish prisoner a note inside a melon that told him to hide in the forest. Ali's father faced torture and death threats from the soldiers once the prisoner's escape was discovered, but he continued to insist on his innocence until the soldiers eventually left.

Courtesy of Norman H. Gershman

Even before the war began, when Jews were already fleeing Nazi Germany and Austria, King Zog of Albania issued 400 Albanian passports to help the refugees. A much larger number of Jews passed through Albania on their way to other countries during the war. Those who were unable to obtain foreign visas were allowed to stay in

HEALTH CONNECTIONS

The Amazing Generosity of Living Organ Donors

EDUCATION CONNECTIONS

What Are the Consequences of Requiring Volunteerism?

MEDIA CONNECTIONS

Does Watching *Sesame Street* Lead to Prosocial Behaviour?

LAW CONNECTIONS

The Impact of Ethnicity on Guilt

Albania. What led Albania's Muslim population to open their homes, sometimes at great risk to themselves, to a community of people with whom they shared such a long historical conflict? The Albanian concept of *besa*, which means "to keep the promise," offers an explanation. Central to how most Albanians live their personal and family lives is the promise, expressed as an Albanian folk principle, to take responsibility for others in their time of need. An Albanian engineer, who was interviewed by the CBC when it reported this story, explains: "As a deep-rooted belief in Albanian culture, *besa* is a moral pledge to live honestly and truthfully and to sacrifice oneself for what is right" (CBC, Nov. 17, 2010; Canadian Jewish News, Nov. 21, 2010).

Prosocial behaviour, like that of Albania's Muslims, can be seen during any period in history and in any culture. According to Statistics Canada, Canadians donated some $10 billion in 2007, which is $1.1 billion more than they did in 2004. It was reported that about 84 percent of Canadians age 15 and over donated money and about 46 percent of the population did volunteer work. In total, people volunteered roughly 2.1 billion hours to help others! Clearly, Canadians are committed to giving back to their communities. They give generously, and the number of donors is growing. But why would someone donate money, or time, to help people they don't even know? This chapter will describe factors that explain altruism and prosocial behaviour. You'll also find answers to these questions:

. . . .

 Why does seeing the word "God" increase prosocial behaviour?

 Why is it that the bigger the crowd, the less likely you are to get help?

 Why do different motives drive people to volunteer at an HIV clinic?

 Why is it better for women to ask for directions than for men to ask for directions?

 Why are people in India as willing to donate bone marrow to a stranger as to a family member, whereas Americans by far prefer donating bone marrow to family members?

. . . .

WHAT YOU'LL LEARN

How personal factors influence helping

How situational factors influence helping

Whether pure altruism exists

Who gets help when they are in need

How culture influences helping

PREVIEW

prosocial behaviour – any behaviour that has the goal of helping another person

What do all of the "Did You Ever Wonder" questions at the beginning of this chapter have in common? They all refer to findings from research in social psychology on factors that influence **prosocial behaviour**, meaning any type of action that is intended to benefit someone other than oneself, such as cooperating, sharing, and comforting (Batson, 1998). In some cases, such behaviour is motivated by a desire to improve one's own circumstances. For example, if a child shares a favourite toy with a sibling because her father has promised her a cookie, the child's motivation for helping is not to improve her brother's well-being, but rather to improve her own well-being—to get the cookie. At other times, helping behaviour can be motivated by a desire to improve another person's well-being with no thought of benefit to the self. For example, a man who jumps onto a subway track to save a stranger who has fallen and is about to be hit by a train is concerned with the other person's welfare (a true story that you'll learn about later in this chapter). This type of helping is called **altruism**. This chapter will examine how both personal and situational factors influence helping, whether true altruism actually exists, the people who are most likely to get help, and the impact of culture on helping.

altruism – helping without expectation of personal gain

HOW DO PERSONAL FACTORS INFLUENCE HELPING?

Many people do things on a regular basis to help others: they give money to benefit schools, religious organizations, and social and political causes; they volunteer their time with animal shelters, foster children, and soup kitchens; they jump into cold water, burning buildings, and crushed cars to save people. But what motivates people to provide such help? You might be surprised that even very small things can motivate prosocial behaviour. In one study by researchers at the University of British Columbia, participants were asked to unscramble 10 five-word sentences (Shariff & Norenzayan, 2007). In one condition, these sentences contained words that were conceptually related to religion, such as God, prophet, and sacred. In the other condition, these sentences contained neutral words that were unrelated to religion. Participants then completed a game with another participant (actually a confederate of the experimenter) in which they could reward their partner with anywhere from zero to 10 one-dollar coins (and keep any remaining coins for themselves). As predicted, people who unscrambled the sentences containing cues to religion were more generous than those who solved the sentences with the neutral words: they left, on average, $4.22, compared to $1.84, and 64 percent left $5 or more, compared to only 12 percent leaving $5 or more in the neutral condition. This study demonstrates that just cueing religious words can increase helping, which suggests that people who are more religious might be more likely to engage in prosocial behaviour. This section will examine the role of personal factors, including evolutionary factors, personality, and religion, in predicting helping.

HOW ALTRUISTIC ARE YOU?

Altruism Scale

INSTRUCTIONS: *Rate on a scale from 1 (never) to 5 (very often) the frequency with which you have carried out each of these acts.*

☐ **1.** I have given directions to a stranger.

☐ **2.** I have given money to charity.

☐ **3.** I have offered to help a handicapped or elderly stranger across a street.

☐ **4.** I have donated blood.

☐ **5.** I have done volunteer work for a charity.

☐ **6.** I have helped carry a stranger's belongings (books, parcels, etc.).

☐ **7.** I have allowed someone to go ahead of me in a lineup (at a Xerox machine, in the supermarket).

☐ **8.** I have helped push a stranger's car out of the snow.

SCORING: Add up your scores on all eight of these items to get an overall total sum.

INTERPRETATION: This scale measures the consistency of people's altruistic behaviour across situations (Rushton, Chrisjohn, & Fekken, 1981). Higher scores indicate more frequent altruistic behaviour, whereas lower scores indicate less frequent altruistic behaviour.

EVOLUTIONARY FACTORS

People sometimes act in altruistic ways to help someone, even at great personal cost. When is this likely to happen? According to the evolutionary perspective, people act this way when such behaviour will help ensure the survival of their genes, which can then be passed on (Burnstein, Crandall, & Kitayama, 1994). In other words, your act of altruism might lead to your own death, but if this act results in the survival of your child, your genes will live on. Remember, evolutionary theory views behaviour as shaped by the motivation to ensure the survival of one's genes. Therefore, it explains why people might engage in behaviour that is costly to themselves—in terms of time and effort and even personal safety—but helps ensure the welfare of someone else who shares their genes. An "altruistic gene" would continue to be passed on, because parents who lacked this gene would be less likely to have children who survived to pass on their own "selfish genes." In sum, this theory of kinship selection is used to explain why parents may self-sacrifice (that is, put themselves in positions of great danger) for the benefit of their children.

kinship selection – the idea that we're more likely to help those we are genetically related to

EVIDENCE FOR KINSHIP SELECTION.

If altruistic behaviour is driven at least in part by the motivation to have one's own genes survive, we should find that people will behave more altruistically toward those who could potentially reproduce and pass on their own genes (Segal, 1993; Kruger, 2003). Is there evidence that people are more likely to help those who are closely related to them (and share more genes) than people who are distantly related (and share fewer genes)? If a grizzly bear is attacking your family group, are you more likely to help your children and your siblings than your cousins and uncles? Are identical twins (who share all the same genes) more helpful to one another than fraternal twins (who share only 50 percent of their genes)? This principle of kin selection was succinctly expressed by the early evolutionary theorist J.B.S. Haldane, who is quoted as having said, "I would lay down my life for two brothers or eight cousins"(Connolly & Martlew, 1999, p. 10).

In one study, university students responded to a series of hypothetical dilemmas in which someone needed help (Korchmaros & Kenny, 2006). Some dilemmas involved life-or-death situations. For example, two of the participants' family members are asleep in a burning building, and there is time to save only one of them. Other cases involved everyday favours. For example, two of the participants' family members need help running errands, and there is time to help only one of them. Researchers also manipulated the type of relationship between the participants and the person who needed help: their degree of genetic relatedness, emotional closeness, perceived similarity, and frequency of interaction. Findings indicated that relationship factors, including emotional closeness and similarity, influence helping, in part because genetic factors lead to these relationship factors. In other words, we help those who we feel are similar to us and emotionally close. Put differently, we tend to feel similar and close to our relatives and therefore are more inclined to help them.

Moreover, people should also be more likely to help those who are likely to reproduce and pass on their genes as opposed to those who are in poor health (and therefore unlikely to survive) and those who are very old (and therefore unlikely to reproduce; Burnstein et al., 1994). A series of studies by Eugene Burnstein and his colleagues provides support for this hypothesis. In life-or-death situations, people more often choose to give help to those who are closely related than to those who are distantly related, to the young over the old, to the healthy over the sick, and to pre-menopausal women over post-menopausal women.

EVIDENCE FOR RECIPROCAL PROSOCIAL BEHAVIOUR.   But people do show prosocial behaviour even to non-relatives. You probably help your friends and neighbours even though you share no genetic material. What explains this type of helping? According to the reciprocal prosocial behaviour perspective, people help others to increase the odds that they, in turn, will be helped by those others (Trivers, 1971, 1985; Kruger, 2003). In other words, you're probably willing to loan your class notes or give a ride to your friend because you'd like to depend on that person for help at some future time. This tendency to help those who help us is shown even among animals that live in social groups, such as monkeys, cats, and fish. In sum, because helping others leads them to reciprocate, this type of cooperation among group members, regardless of their genetic connection, increases survival.

RESEARCH FOCUS ON GENDER
Are Men or Women More Helpful?

Men and women vary in their likelihood of helping in different types of situations (Becker & Eagly, 2004; Eagly & Crowley, 1986; Eagly, 1987; Johnson, Danko, Darvill, & Bochner, 1989). Men are more likely than women to help in situations that call for brave, heroic behaviour (e.g., rescuing someone from a burning building). For example, men receive 91 percent of the Carnegie Hero Medals, which specifically are given to Canadian and American civilians who risk their lives to save a stranger. Similarly, the vast majority of people who are publicly recognized in the media for some type of heroic behaviour, such as stopping a robbery or rescuing a drowning child, are men (Huston, Ruggiero, Conner, & Geis, 1981). Moreover, these gender differences in helping are found across a range of cultures, including in Australia, Egypt, and Korea (Johnson et al., 1989).

Why are men more likely to help in these dramatic life-and-death cases? One explanation is that men experience fewer costs for helping than women do—men who help are larger and have more training than men who don't help, suggesting that they expect helping to cost them less. Men may also benefit from some behaviour—women prefer risk-prone brave males over risk-averse non-brave males, and men are well aware of this preference (Kelly & Dunbar, 2001). Another explanation for this supposed gender difference is that women help in different ways, such as taking someone to a weekly doctor's appointment.

Lips (2008) argues that gender differences in helping behaviour are largely related to gender role factors and the situation where helping is required. Men and women are more helpful in situations where helping is viewed as gender-role appropriate. For example, men are

Questioning the Research:

This study suggests that people are more likely to help those who are similar and emotionally close to them, and therefore provides support for the kinship selection model of helping. But can you think of another explanation for these findings? (Hint: How reliable is self-report in this case?)

more likely to help in dangerous situations and when an audience is present (Hamilton, 2001; Lips, 2008). This is because men are perceived to be physically stronger than women and the presence of an audience is a reminder of gender role appropriate behaviour and the norm that men are supposed to be courageous (Lips, 2008).

PERSONALITY

We often assume that people who engage in highly altruistic behaviour, such as spending tremendous amounts of time volunteering, making substantial donations to charitable organizations, and especially risking one's life to help others, have distinct personality characteristics. For example, Oskar Schindler, a German man who rescued over 1,300 Jews during the Holocaust, literally risked his life by hiding Jewish people from the Nazis. Michael Ashton from Brock University and colleagues at the University of Western Ontario researched helping behaviour in the context of the five major personality dimensions (openness, conscientiousness, extroversion, agreeableness, and emotional stability) and found that agreeableness was the characteristic that predicted altruism. However, a distinction was drawn between what the researchers called "kin altruism" (behaving in a way that benefits a genetic relative's chances of survival or reproduction at some cost to one's own chances) and "reciprocal altruism" (acting in a way that benefits an unrelated individual at some expense to oneself, with the expectation that the recipient will return such assistance in the future). The finding that agreeableness correlated with altruism applied to both forms. However, kin altruism correlated negatively with emotional stability, whereas reciprocal altruism and emotional stability correlated positively (Ashton, Paunonen, Helmes, & Jackson, 1998).

In general, people show an increase in empathy and prosocial behaviour as they mature, but individuals also vary considerably in their frequency and types of helping (Davis, Luce, & Kraus, 1994; Matthews, Batson, Horn, & Rosenman, 1981; Rushton, Fulker, Neale, Nias, & Eysenck, 1986; Zahn-Waxler, Radke-Yarrow, Wagner, & Chapman, 1992). The Health Connections box describes another example of a very helpful, even life-saving, behaviour some people engage in—organ donation.

HEALTH CONNECTIONS

The Amazing Generosity of Living Organ Donors

One of the major medical advances of the 20th century was doctors' ability to transplant organs, including kidneys, livers, lungs, and hearts, from one person to another. Although organ transplantation has allowed many people who have malfunctioning organs to live, the number of people who need organs is considerably higher than the number of organs available for donation—11 to 12 people on waiting lists die each day before an organ becomes available. Although in most cases organ donations come from people who have died, living people can also donate some organs, such as a kidney (because we have two), or a portion of an organ, such as a piece of their liver. Organ donation is an example of altruism that is not well explained by the evolutionary theories of kinship selection or reciprocal altruism. What could motivate someone to perform this type of selfless act? In fact there are several factors that increase people's intent to donate their own organs (Morgan, Miller, & Arasaratnam, 2003). These include positive attitudes toward organ donation, a general desire to help others, and knowing someone who has donated or received an organ.

empathy – the ability to understand other people's perspectives and respond emotionally to other people's experiences

EMPATHY. People who are generally altruistic share some common traits. First, they are high in **empathy**, meaning they tend to understand other people's perspectives, and respond emotionally to other people's experiences (Batson & Oleson, 1991; Dovidio, Piliavin, Gaertner, Schroeder, & Clark, 1991; Eisenberg et al., 2002; Eisenberg & Miller, 1987). As shown in the Rate Yourself box, people vary in how much empathy they have for other people, and those who are empathic are more likely to take the perspective of others, and, when someone is suffering, to try to help ease that suffering.

HOW EMPATHIC ARE YOU?

Emotional Empathy

INSTRUCTIONS: *Rate each item on a scale of −4 (very strong disagreement) to +4 (very strong agreement).*

1. It makes me sad to see a lonely stranger in a group.
2. I tend to get emotionally involved with a friend's problems.
3. Seeing people cry upsets me.
4. I become very involved when I watch a movie.
5. I am very upset when I see an animal in pain.
6. I really get involved with the feelings of the characters in a novel.
7. The people around me have a great influence on my moods.
8. I cannot continue to feel okay if the people around me are depressed.

SCORING: Sum up your total number of points on these eight items.

INTERPRETATION: This scale measures emotional empathy, meaning the extent to which people understand other people's perspectives and respond emotionally to others' experiences. Higher scores indicate higher levels of emotional empathy, whereas lower scores indicate lower levels of emotional empathy (Mehrabian & Epstein, 1972).

In turn, people with higher levels of empathy engage in more prosocial behaviour, including donating money to charitable causes (Davis, 1983) and spending time helping people in need (Otten, Penner, & Altabe, 1991). For example, Carlo and colleagues (1991) found that people who were high in empathy were much more likely to agree to switch places with another subject who was doing an upsetting task than those who were low on empathy (Carlo, Eisenberg, Troyer, Switzer, & Speer, 1991). Individual differences in empathy and altruism appear even in children: children who feel sad when they see others feeling sad or being picked on are more helpful to children in a hospital burn unit than those who show less empathy for others (Knight, Johnson, Carlo, & Eisenberg, 1994).

What makes some people more empathic than others? Some evidence points to a genetic link (Davis et al., 1994; Rushton et al., 1986). The link between empathy and behaviour is more similar in identical twins—who share all their genes—than in fraternal twins—who share only half of their

IN THE NEWS

Barry W. Wallace

Modest in life, generous in donation: When Roberta Langtry died at the age of 89, she left $4.3 million to the Nature Conservancy of Canada. Her donation was the largest gift to an environmental organization in Canadian history. What is remarkable about Roberta Langtry was that she lived a modest life despite her multimillion dollar wealth. Her closest friends and neighbours had no idea that Miss Langtry had such a large fortune. She was an elementary school teacher who lived in a one-storey home in east Toronto and drove a 15-year-old Volvo. The Conservancy plans to use the money to safeguard a rural area north of Toronto.

genes. In fact, research comparing empathy in response to others' distress using identical and fraternal twin samples suggests that as much as 70 percent of people's response to distressing situations may be rooted in genetics.

MORAL REASONING.   Another personality factor that influences helping is an individual's level of **moral reasoning** (Eisenberg & Miller, 1987). When deciding whether to engage in a particular action, some people focus on their own needs and the concrete consequences of their actions (e.g., whether they will avoid punishment or receive a reward). Others are more concerned about adhering to moral standards regardless of external social controls (e.g., whether their actions will help someone else, even if they conflict with a person's own motives).

Consider the following dilemma: "A girl named Mary was going to a friend's birthday party. On her way, she saw a little girl who had fallen down and hurt her leg. The girl asked Mary to go to her house and get her parents so the parents could take her to the doctor. But if Mary did run and get the child's parents, she would be late for the birthday party and miss the ice cream, cake, and all the games. What should Mary do? Why?" (Eisenberg, 1982, p. 231). Research using this and other moral dilemmas shows that the use of higher-level reasoning is associated with greater empathy and altruism. For example, children who use higher-level moral reasoning are more likely to choose to anonymously donate part of their earnings from participating in a study to children seen in a UNICEF poster (Eisenberg et al., 1987).

In another study, four- and five-year-old children saw a film about two children who fall from a jungle gym and get hurt (Miller, Eisenberg, Fabes, & Shell, 1996). They then had the option of playing on their own with some very attractive toys or putting loose crayons into boxes to be packed up and sent to the hospital for the injured children. Children who are high on both empathy and moral reasoning are the most likely to help the injured children and forgo their own playing time.

Parents' direct teaching of prosocial behaviour can influence children's moral reasoning (Eisenberg, Fabes, Schaller, Carlo, & Miller, 1991; Fabes, Eisenberg, & Miller, 1990). Parents who teach their children about helping through perspective taking and empathy are more likely to foster higher levels of moral reasoning than those who focus on helping as a way of gaining rewards or avoiding punishment (Hoffman, 1994). For example, a parent can foster moral reasoning by saying, "If you don't share your toys with that child, she'll feel sad." It's less effective for a parent to say, "If you don't share your toys with that child, I'll give you candy" or "I'll be disappointed." Similarly, parents who use positive behaviour, including positive feelings toward their child as well as positive discipline strategies (e.g., firmness, reasoning, calm), create more prosocial behaviour in their children over time (Knafo & Plomin, 2006). Although we learn morality, we are, to some extent, "hardwired" in our ability to learn it. Dennis Krebs (2008) from Simon Fraser University suggested that our capacity for moral reasoning may have evolved as it produces more effective social groups.

RELIGION

How does religion influence prosocial behaviour? Some religious teachings emphasize the importance of engaging in cooperative and prosocial behaviour (Batson, 1983). Other religions emphasize the importance of "brotherly love," and encourage people to treat others as they would like others to treat them (i.e., "Do unto others as you would have them do unto you"). Religious beliefs are also associated, in some studies, with more altruistic behaviour. For example, university students who describe themselves as more religiously committed spend more time volunteering with various campus organizations (Benson, Dehority, Garman, Hanson, Hochschwender, Lebold, et al., 1980; Hansen, Vandenberg, & Patterson, 1995). As described at the start of this section, even cueing people with religious words can increase prosocial behaviour.

moral reasoning – a personality factor that describes the extent to which a person's willingness to help depends on larger moral standards rather than the person's needs and the expected consequences for him or her of helping

But religion does not always lead to more helping. In fact, people who hold strong and conservative religious beliefs are very likely to help those who they believe deserve help, but not to help those whom they consider undeserving (Skitka & Tetlock, 1993). Researchers Lynne Jackson from Wilfrid Laurier University and Victoria Esses from the University of Western Ontario found that religious fundamentalists are more likely to help some people (e.g., those who are seen as deserving of help), but less likely to help those whose behaviour contradicts behaviours that are acceptable to their religion (e.g., that of homosexuals, or single mothers; Jackson & Esses, 1997). Other researchers have also found that people who are highly religious are less likely to help someone who is gay (Batson, Floyd, Meyer, & Winner, 1999).

Who's Who in Contemporary Canadian Social Psychology Research

Courtesy Dennis Krebs

Dennis Krebs is a professor of psychology, a Woodrow Wilson Fellow, and Fellow of Stanford University's Center for Advanced Study in the Behavioral Sciences. He received his undergraduate degree from the University of British Columbia and his MA and PhD from Harvard University, where he also taught for several years before returning to his native British Columbia to teach at Simon Fraser University. He has published several books and more than 90 articles, most of which address issues of altruism and morality. Additionally, Professor Krebs was a recipient in 2007 of the prestigious 3M Teaching Fellowship. Each year 10 such fellowships are given to Canadian teachers in higher education who demonstrate leadership and commitment to university teaching.

[CONCEPTS IN CONTEXT]

HOW PERSONAL FACTORS INFLUENCE HELPING

FACTOR	EXAMPLE
Evolution	Domingo and his 10-year-old son, Jerome, were trapped in their house during a fierce hurricane. Rescuers finally came, but they only had room for one more person in the boat. Domingo immediately put his son in the boat.
Personality	Lisa has volunteered once a week at a nursing home for the past two years. She recognizes the loneliness of the patients she visits, and believes that her visits really help them.
Religion	Theresa regularly attends a church whose minister encourages church members to provide help to those in need of assistance. Theresa therefore decides to volunteer at a soup kitchen one Saturday morning each month.

HOW DO SITUATIONAL FACTORS INFLUENCE HELPING?

On March 13, 1964, a 28-year-old woman named Kitty Genovese was returning home after work to her apartment in New York City at 3 a.m. (Rosenthal, 1964). When she was within 32 metres of her apartment building, an attacker stabbed and raped her on the street. Two times the attacker ran away, in fear that someone was coming, and both times he came back and continued to stab her. It was a loud, long, tortured death. Although it was 3 in the morning, 38 neighbours in her building were awakened by her screams, and watched what was happening (lights went on, windows were open). After 30 minutes, one person called the police. But by then, it was too late—Kitty Genovese was dead. Her death became a media sensation as people searched for a cause for this apparent indifference on the part of her neighbours. Was it because it occurred in a big city? Was it because the people in her building were cruel or thoughtless? This incident led to a series of studies in social psychology that examined how situational factors can influence helping behaviour at an unconscious level.

Before examining these factors, it's important to note that more than 40 years after Kitty Genovese's murder, three British psychologists, Rachel Manning, Mark Levine, and Alan Collins (2007), examined court transcripts of Winston Moseley, the murderer, and other legal documents related to the case and described a different scenario surrounding Kitty Genovese's murder. First, it's suggested that not all of the 38 neighbours were eyewitnesses and some only heard the attack. The evidence suggests that only about half a dozen saw the incident and none of the eyewitnesses watched Kitty for the full 30 minutes. Second, the three witnesses who testified in court said that they didn't perceive the situation as an emergency as Kitty Genovese and Winston Moseley were standing close together and none of the witnesses saw any stabbing. Third, in 1964 there was no 911 system and contacting police was therefore more difficult then than now, and the evidence also suggests that such phone calls were not always welcomed by the police. In sum, Manning and colleagues challenge the power of Kitty Genovese's story and argue that the story was over publicized in social psychology textbooks. Nevertheless, although the presence of 38 witnesses is being questioned, there is evidence that Kitty Genovese was murdered while there were witnesses, and this story is the historical context that led to extensive study of why people fail to help when they should.

This section will examine two models that describe how situational factors influence whether help is given—the decision-making process model and the arousal/cost-reward model—as well as the influence of three additional situational factors that may influence helping behaviour—mood, modelling, and the environment.

DECISION-MAKING PROCESS MODEL

According to the **decision-making process model** developed by Latané and Darley (1970), a number of features of emergencies make it difficult to get help. First, because emergencies are rare and unusual events, people don't have a lot of experience in handling emergencies, and therefore may not have direct personal experience in how to cope. As you may recall from Chapter 6, the link between attitudes and behaviour is stronger when you have direct personal experience with something, and therefore people's good intentions (e.g., "I would step in and save the person") may go awry.

decision-making process model – a model that describes helping behaviour as a function of five distinct steps

Second, because emergencies themselves differ widely, even when people have direct experience in handling one type of emergency, they're not likely to have experience in handling other types of emergencies, which all require different types of help. For example, saving someone who is drowning requires jumping into water, swimming to the person, and dragging him or her out. Helping someone with a flat tire requires assisting with changing the tire (or perhaps just making a phone call to CAA or a tow truck).

Third, emergencies are unforeseen. Because they occur suddenly, people aren't able to think through various options and develop plans of action.

According to the model of the decision-making process proposed by Latané and Darley (see Figure 13.1), helping behaviour occurs only when a person takes five distinct steps—and if the person at any point fails to take a particular step, he or she will not provide aid. These five steps are to notice that something is happening, interpret it as an emergency, take responsibility for providing help, decide how to help, and provide help.

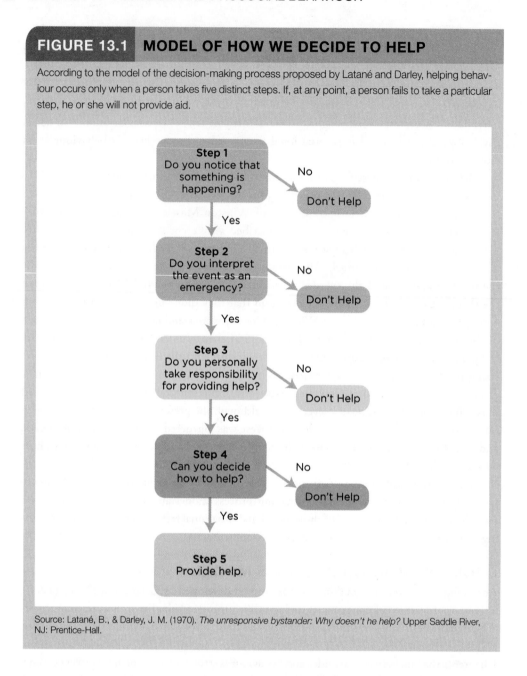

FIGURE 13.1 MODEL OF HOW WE DECIDE TO HELP

According to the model of the decision-making process proposed by Latané and Darley, helping behaviour occurs only when a person takes five distinct steps. If, at any point, a person fails to take a particular step, he or she will not provide aid.

Step 1
Do you notice that something is happening?

No → Don't Help

Yes

Step 2
Do you interpret the event as an emergency?

No → Don't Help

Yes

Step 3
Do you personally take responsibility for providing help?

No → Don't Help

Yes

Step 4
Can you decide how to help?

No → Don't Help

Yes

Step 5
Provide help.

Source: Latané, B., & Darley, J. M. (1970). *The unresponsive bystander: Why doesn't he help?* Upper Saddle River, NJ: Prentice-Hall.

NOTICE SOMETHING IS HAPPENING. First, you need to notice that something is happening. This can actually be surprisingly hard to do, because people are often self-focused. Noticing an event may be particularly difficult for people who live in a big city, and therefore are used to blocking out all kinds of stimuli (e.g., noise, strangers). As mentioned later in this chapter, this is the basis of the "urban overload" hypothesis of Milgram (1970). In some cases, people simply aren't paying attention and aren't aware of emergencies that may be occurring.

In one clever study showing the extent of people's ability to not notice, John Darley and Daniel Batson (1973) asked seminary students, who by nature should be motivated to help others, to give a speech at a nearby building. This speech was on a parable from the Bible on the Good Samaritan, and specifically describes a person who altruistically gives time and care to a wounded man (who is, importantly, an outgroup member) lying on the side of the road. As the seminary students walked to the building where they would give the speech, they passed a stranger (who was actually a confederate of the experimenters) who was slumped in a doorway, coughing and groaning. Who provided help? The only significant factor predict-ing help was time pressure: men who were in a hurry were very unlikely to help, while those who were not in a hurry were quite likely to provide help. People are also more likely to give help when they witness a clear and vivid emergency than when they see something less clear (Piliavin, Piliavin, & Broll, 1976). In one study, 89 percent of people helped when they directly saw a person fall down a flight of stairs or slump to the floor in a faint, but only 13 percent of people helped when they saw only the aftermath of such an event (e.g., a person holding and rubbing their ankle).

INTERPRET IT AS AN EMERGENCY.   Second, even if you notice an event, you need to interpret it as an emergency in order to provide help. As people often interpret events as "non-emergencies," however, they fail to act. In 1993 two 10-year-old boys in England took a 2-year-old from a shopping mall, and carried him two miles away. The little boy was fighting the older kids the entire time, and many people witnessed the children walking away, but interpreted the scene as siblings fighting and didn't try to intervene. Sadly, the older boys beat the toddler to death. In a study where attacks were staged, researchers found that more than three times as many people tried to stop a man from assaulting a woman when they thought the two were strangers (the woman yelled, "Get away from me; I don't know you") than when they thought they were romantically involved (the woman yelled, "Get away from me; I don't know why I ever married you;" Shotland & Straw, 1976). In sum, situations with greater ambiguity lead to less help (Shotland & Heinold, 1985).

People often look to the crowd to see how others are responding, and therefore fail to inter-pret an event as an emergency themselves (Darley & Latané, 1968; Latané & Rodin, 1969). As described in Chapter 8 on social influence, when people are in a new or unfamiliar situation, they often look to see how other people are responding. So, if you're unsure whether a person is truly in need of help, you may look to see what other people are doing before deciding how you should act. However, if each person is looking to others to judge how to interpret the situ-ation, and no one wants to be seen as the person who overreacts (and thus feels embarrassed), the person in need may receive no help at all. This phenomenon is called pluralistic ignorance, (see Chapter 8). It is a misperception that people have of others. In the context of helping, it is the assumption that each person has that because others are not reacting, there is no emergency.

Bibb Latané and John Darley (1968) conducted one of the first studies on the impact of situational factors on people's interpretation of emergencies. They brought students into the lab to participate in a simple questionnaire study. Some of the students were placed in a room alone to complete the questionnaire. Others were placed in a room with two other subjects. A few minutes after students starting answering the questionnaire, an unusual event occurred: smoke started pouring into the room. The researchers wanted to examine what students would do in the face of this seemingly obvious "emergency." Of the participants who were alone in the room, virtually all of them stood up to investigate the source of the smoke, and then left the room to report it to the experimenter. But what happened when three sub-jects were together in the room? In most cases, no one reported the smoke during the next six minutes (when the researchers officially ended the study)! In fact, of the 24 people in the eight groups, only one person reported the smoke within the first four minutes. And remem-ber, this smoke was not a subtle effect: by the end of the six-minute trial, the smoke was so thick that the subjects were constantly waving the smoke away from their faces just to read the questionnaire!

What types of things help people label events as an emergency? One clear sign is a direct cry for help, such as a scream. Clear cues to distress increase the likelihood that the person will get help (Clark & Word, 1972; Gaertner & Dovidio, 1977; Yakimovich & Saltz, 1971). In one study, researchers created either an ambiguous emergency, in which participants heard a loud crash but no verbal cues indicating pain, or an unambiguous emergency, in which participants heard a loud crash and groans of pain (Clark & Word, 1972). Students who heard the unambiguous emergency helped regardless of whether they were alone or in a group. Those who heard the ambiguous emergency were much more likely to help if they were alone than if they were in a group.

TAKE RESPONSIBILITY FOR PROVIDING HELP.   Third, you need to take responsibility for providing help. Even when people recognize that a situation is indeed an emergency, they may assume that other people in the situation will help, and that they themselves therefore don't need to act. This is referred to as **diffusion of responsibility**, the belief that other people present in a situation will assume responsibility (Latané & Nida, 1981). Diffusion of responsibility contributes to the **bystander effect**, which refers to people's tendency to be less likely to help in an emergency situation when there are other people present than when the person witnessing the emergency is alone. As the number of potential helpers increases, the likelihood of help decreases.

diffusion of responsibility – the belief that other people present in a situation will assume responsibility, which contributes to the bystander effect

bystander effect – the situation whereby people are less likely to help in emergency situations when there are other people present than if the person who could help is alone, resulting in a decreased likelihood of help being given

John Darley and Bibb Latané (1968) created a clever study to directly test diffusion of responsibility. After being taken to one of a series of small rooms that were connected by intercoms, participants were told that they would be talking about personal problems that university students face and that, to protect confidentiality, the experimenter would not be listening to the conversation. Some participants talked with just one other person, others were in groups of three, and still others were in groups of six. Early in the conversation, one participant (actually a confederate) would mention that he had trouble with a seizure disorder that was sometimes triggered by stress. Later in the conversation, this person's speech would become slurred and he would ask for help, saying that he was going to die. So who helped him? Eighty-five percent of the participants who were alone with that person got help immediately, as did all who were with just one other person (perhaps not wanting that person to think they were mean?). However, only 62 percent of those with two others and 68 percent of those with five others in the group helped. Clearly they assumed that someone else would help.

What's the good news? People who believe that they're the only one who could provide help to a person are more likely to help, even if they think others are aware of the need for assistance (Bickman, 1971). For example, if you believe that other people are aware of a person's need for help, but that those other potential helpers are too far away to help, you're much more likely to help than if you think the other people are as available as you are. Even arbitrarily giving a person responsibility in a situation can increase the person's likelihood of helping. In one study, a researcher asked people on a beach to watch over his radio while he went on a walk (Moriarty, 1975). Only 20 percent of the bystanders who were not given responsibility later tried to prevent a staged theft of the radio, yet 94 percent of those who had been explicitly asked intervened in some way! Similarly, one study with a group of 177 Halloween trick-or-treaters (age 4 to 13 years old) manipulated responsibility by asking either one child, each child, or no child to take responsibility for donating some of their candy to hospitalized children (Maruyama, Fraser, & Miller, 1982). Giving

IN THE NEWS

Adam Krawesky (inconduit.com)

Bystander intervention: When someone does offer help, others are likely to follow. On January 24, 2006, in the heart of Toronto's Kensington market, a conflict between a driver stuck in traffic and a passing cyclist erupted and was eventually broken up by first one passerby and then others, as recorded by a series of photographs in the magazine *Toronto Life*, which reported the story. The fight occurred when the driver tossed the remains of an unfinished Jamaican meat patty from his lunch onto the street and cyclist Leah Hollinsworth responded by tossing the food back into the man's car. The magazine describes what followed: "The driver, who was never identified, stepped out of his car and tossed two cups of hot Tim Hortons coffee at Hollinsworth, hitting her square in the back. The two tussled briefly and the motorist drove away but returned a few minutes later, attacking both her and her bike before bystanders finally separated them" (Preville, 2008).

a child personal responsibility increased the likelihood of the child donating candy and increased the number of candies donated.

DECIDE HOW TO HELP.   Fourth, you need to decide how to help, such as by calling 911, providing CPR, or jumping into a pool. People with relevant skills help more than people without such skills or training. In a study by Cramer and colleagues (1988), participants were either education students or nursing students, and were either alone or with another participant (Cramer, McMaster, Bartell, & Dragna, 1988). As they were filling out a questionnaire, they heard a man fall from a ladder outside the room, and scream out in pain. What percentage helped in the education condition? Those who were alone were much more likely to help than those who were with a nonresponding other. The percentage of nursing students who helped was basically the same whether they were alone or with others. This doesn't mean that nursing students are simply nicer people—rather it means that because they knew what to do they were more willing to get involved even if the other person with them didn't help.

Unable to resuscitate the stranger with his breath, Leon quickly grabbed his leaf blower.

© John McPherson/ www.CartoonStock.com

PROVIDE HELP.   Fifth, you need to actually provide help. This step can be difficult due to audience inhibition. In other words, people can be reluctant to help because they might fear making a bad impression in front of others, either by appearing stupid or overly cautious. What factors can get rid of audience inhibition? Well, being familiar with both the context and the other people in that context are important factors. In one study, students came into the lab in either pairs or groups of four (Rutkowski, Gruder, & Romer, 1983). In half the cases, the students had 20 minutes to "get to know each other," and were then supposed to work on some problems individually. In the other cases, the students didn't have such a conversation. As they were working, a workman supposedly fell from a ladder outside, and clearly needed help. Who helped? In line with other findings, those who were in pairs were more likely to help than those in larger groups. But among those in groups, those who had had a chance to first talk were much more likely to help than those who were with complete strangers.

STRATEGIES FOR GETTING HELP.   So, what can you do to make sure you get help if you experience or witness an emergency while you're in a large group?

- First, identify one person in the crowd, and call out to that person directly (e.g., "Hey, the woman in the red dress—I need help"). This strategy eliminates the problems caused by diffusion of responsibility, because that specific person is then identified as the person who needs to provide help.
- Second, clearly label the situation as an emergency (e.g., "I'm having trouble breathing"). This approach eliminates the problem caused by misinterpretation of the situation.
- Finally, give instructions on how exactly the person should help (e.g., "Hey, you in the red shirt, call 911").

AROUSAL/COST-REWARD MODEL

The **arousal/cost-reward model** uses rational, cost-benefit analysis to predict prosocial behaviour. According to this model, people are motivated to behave altruistically to help decrease the arousal that they experience when they see other people experiencing pain and suffering (Dovidio et al., 1991; Piliavin, Rodin, & Piliavin, 1969; Piliavin, Dovidio, Gaertner, & Clark, 1981). If you hear a baby crying, you might be motivated to pick up the baby so that it will stop crying, not due to any particular concern for the child, but rather to avoid having to hear the unpleasant sobbing.

arousal/cost-reward model – a model that describes helping behaviour as caused in part by the physiological arousal that people experience when they see someone in need of help and in part by their calculation of the costs and rewards of providing such help

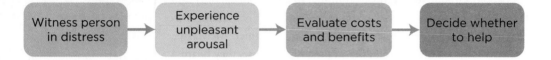

FIGURE 13.2 THE AROUSAL/COST-REWARD MODEL OF HELPING

According to this model, people who see an emergency will experience unpleasant arousal (due to seeing others in distress), and then weigh the anticipated costs and benefits of helping to determine whether to act.

Witness person in distress → Experience unpleasant arousal → Evaluate costs and benefits → Decide whether to help

One study found that people who reported feeling shock, terror, or horror when hearing about a major fire in Australia donated significantly more money to the victims than did people who didn't experience such intense emotions (Amato, 1986). Similarly, the people who give the most help are those whose physiological responses show them to be particularly distressed when seeing someone in trouble (Krebs, 1975). In sum, individuals who experience shock and distress at watching something unpleasant may be motivated to help simply to reduce their own distress.

According to this model, even when people experience unpleasant arousal in response to seeing others in pain, they still compute the relative costs and benefits of helping before deciding to take action. (This model is similar to the *social exchange model* of relationship satisfaction described in Chapter 4). For example, you may calculate the potential rewards to yourself and the victim (e.g., receiving a reward from the victim, becoming a hero, feeling good about yourself), as well as the potential costs (e.g., you yourself might die, you will lose time, you could be embarrassed).

IMPACT OF COSTS. Do the costs of helping influence altruistic behaviour? Yes (Piliavin & Piliavin, 1972; Piliavin, Piliavin, & Rodin, 1975; Wagner & Wheeler, 1969). In a study on a subway car in Philadelphia, three confederates watched as another confederate walked to the end of a car using a cane, and then fell to the ground. In some cases he just lay still, but in others he lay still and started bleeding from the mouth (using some red dye he bit into). The other confederates timed how long it took someone to help him. As predicted, people were significantly less likely to help and took longer to help when he was bleeding than when he was not bleeding. (Given the HIV epidemic that has arisen since the time of this study, the impact on helping of seeing blood would probably be even greater today.) Although bleeding may imply personal harm, even non–life-threatening costs can decrease helping. As described earlier, Darley and Batson (1973) found that seminary students who were going to give a speech (ironically on the Good Samaritan) were much more likely to help if they were early for their presentation than if they were late.

Unfortunately, teaching someone about the personal costs of prosocial behaviour can lead to a decrease in helping. Frank and colleagues (1993) asked students at both the beginning and the end of the semester how they would respond to several different helping situations (e.g., what they would do if they found an addressed envelope with $100 in it; Frank, Gilovich, & Regan, 1993). Of students in an astronomy class, 10 percent became less helpful over the course of the semester (not

IN THE NEWS

Getty Images

The Costs of Helping: On January 2, 2007, Wesley Autrey, a 50-year-old construction worker, dived onto the subway tracks to save a man who had suffered a seizure and fallen onto the tracks. Although Mr. Autrey didn't know the man who had fallen onto the tracks, he risked his own life by jumping just in front of a subway train to hold the man down as five subway cars rolled just inches above them. "I don't feel like I did something spectacular; I just saw someone who needed help," Mr. Autrey said. "I did what I felt was right." This is a very unusual perspective (Buckley, 2007).

a very large decrease in helpfulness). Of those in an economics class, who presumably learned about the financial and personal costs of helping as part of course material, 28 percent became less helpful (a much more substantial drop in their rate of helping).

IMPACT OF BENEFITS.   Although the costs of prosocial behaviour decrease the likelihood of helping, the benefits or rewards of prosocial behaviour increase helping. That's why your parents give you an allowance—to reward you for helping around the house. Even hearing "thank you" can be a reward. One study found that subjects who were told "thank you" for exchanging roles with another subject (who was really a confederate) continued to be more helpful throughout the experiment than did those who didn't receive this expression of appreciation (McGovern, Ditzian, & Taylor, 1975). Similarly, more than 93 percent of those who received a kind thank you for giving a person directions later helped another person who had dropped a small bag (Moss & Page, 1972). In contrast, only 40 percent of those who were treated rudely when they were giving directions (the confederate interrupted them and expressed a preference to just ask someone else) later helped. Children seem to be especially motivated by rewards. In one study, children who received praise for generosity were still more generous two weeks later (Rushton & Teachman, 1978).

But receiving certain types of rewards for prosocial behaviour can actually lead to a decrease in helping. In one study children were given either a few pennies or praise for helping (Smith, Gelfand, Hartmann, & Partlow, 1979). When the children were later asked why they helped, those who received pennies reported it was to get the money. In contrast, those who simply received praise reported they had helped due to concern about another person's welfare.

Similarly, Richard Fabes and his colleagues (1989) examined altruistic behaviour in children whose mothers said they often used rewards to get their child to engage in prosocial behaviour. The researchers gave half of the children a reward for helping children in a hospital (by making games for them). The others did not receive such a reward. When the children were then given a second chance to help these sick children, all of those who did not receive a reward helped compared to 44 percent of those who received a reward.

What causes this difference in helping behaviour? Research suggests that when a reward is given, it undermines children's spontaneous helping (again, this is the phenomenon of *overjustification*, as you learned about in Chapter 3). In other words, giving a reward leads children to attribute their altruistic behaviour to external, as opposed to internal, factors. The Education Connections box describes another way in which creating rewards can deter prosocial behaviour.

EDUCATION CONNECTIONS

What Are the Consequences of Requiring Volunteerism?

Did your high school require you to volunteer in order to graduate? An increasing number of schools are doing just that. Proponents of these programs describe the advantages for students and the community: Students gain exposure to people who are often less fortunate than themselves and learn skills for interacting with people from different backgrounds and with different experiences. Community organizations, including hospitals, nursing homes, and homeless shelters, gain valuable and much-needed support. But mandatory volunteer programs can also have significant drawbacks. The main problem with these programs is that requiring students to engage in altruistic behaviour can lead people to make extrinsic, as opposed to intrinsic, attributions for this behaviour. For example, a person who had always enjoyed volunteering on his or her own could now come to see volunteering as something one only does when required to.

© Frances Roberts / Alamy

MOOD

Another situational factor that influences prosocial behaviour is mood. Interestingly, both good and bad moods can lead to helping, as you'll see in this section.

good mood effect – when people are in a good mood, they are more likely to help

GOOD MOOD EFFECT. The **good mood effect** refers to the finding that helping behaviour increases when people are in a good mood (Carlson, Charlin, & Miller, 1988). For example, people are more helpful after they're offered a cookie (Isen & Levin, 1972), are told they're especially intelligent (Weyant, 1978), find a dime (Isen & Levin, 1972), listen to a tape that makes them feel good about themselves (Rosenhan, Salovey, & Hargis, 1981), or listen to uplifting music (North, Tarrant, & Hargreaves, 2004)! In fact, tipping is better on sunny days, presumably because we're happier when the sun is shining (Cunningham, 1979).

In one study, researchers approached people in a shopping mall and asked them for change for a dollar (Baron, 1997). In some cases the people were asked right in front of a "good-smelling" store (e.g., Cinnabon). In other cases they were asked in front of a "neutral-smelling" store (e.g., Gap). Fifty-six percent helped when they were in front of a good-smelling store, as compared to only 19 percent of those in front of a neutral-smelling store.

What is it about a good mood that leads to helping? First, people who are in good moods want to maintain them, and seeing someone else who is in need could destroy the mood (Isen & Levin, 1972; Wegener & Petty, 1994). In other words, we may help people in need in part to maintain our own good mood. Another reason why a good mood leads to helping may be that people who are in a good mood focus more on the positive aspects of situations, such as the benefits of helping, rather than the negative aspects, such as the costs (Isen & Simmonds, 1978). So, being in a good mood may make the benefits of helping much more salient than the costs. A third possibility for why a good mood leads to helping is that people who are in a good mood experience increased self-awareness, which in turn leads us to try to match our behaviour to our internal values (as you learned about in Chapter 3; Carlson et al., 1988; Duval, Duval, & Neely, 1979; Hoover, Wood, & Knowles, 1983). For example, people who are looking at themselves in a mirror are more helpful than those who are not looking at themselves (Batson et al., 1999).

BAD MOODS. Although good moods can increase the likelihood of prosocial behaviour, so can bad moods (Regan, Williams, & Sparling, 1972). In one study, an experimenter stopped a woman on the street and asked her to take his picture with a very expensive-looking camera (Cunningham, Steinberg, & Grev, 1980). He mentioned that the camera was sensitive, but that all she needed to do was aim and push one button. However, when she pushed the button, the camera didn't work. In some cases, he dismissed the problem by saying, "The camera acts up a lot." In other cases, he tried to make the woman feel guilty by saying she had jammed the camera by pushing too hard. Then, as the woman walked down the street, she noticed another person whose groceries were falling from a shopping bag. Who took advantage of this new opportunity to help? Only 15 percent of those who didn't feel guilty compared to 55 percent of those who believed they had broken the camera.

One reason why bad moods increase helping is our desire to make up for whatever we did that caused this negative feeling. In the case of the Cunningham et al. (1980) study in which participants thought they'd broken an expensive camera, helping someone else allows them to restore their positive self-image. Similarly, people who have been told they did badly on an IQ test help more, presumably to raise their self-esteem (Yagi & Shimizu, 1996).

Bad moods can also increase helping even when we aren't trying to make up for our own wrongdoing. For example, people who are asked to imagine the grief and worry that one of their close friends would experience if the friend was dying of cancer later help more (Thompson, Cowan, & Rosenhan, 1980). We may simply want to make ourselves feel better by doing something good to counteract any overall bad feeling, regardless of its cause. As you will see later in the chapter, this is the core of the negative-state relief hypothesis (Cialdini et al., 1987; 1990).

There is an important exception, however, to this tendency for bad moods to increase helping: when we have been socially excluded, we're less likely to help (Twenge, Baumeister, DeWall, Ciarocco, & Bartels, 2007). Jean Twenge and her colleagues examined how people who believe that other participants in a psychology study have rejected them as potential interaction partners react when they're later asked to help. Socially rejected people donate less money to a student fund, cooperate less in a game with another student, are less likely to volunteer for future psychology studies, and are less helpful when a researcher drops a bunch of pencils. These findings point to the negative impact of social rejection on the likelihood of helping in many different contexts.

MODELLING

People can increase their altruistic behaviour when such behaviour is modelled for them by their parents, peers, or even media figures (Grusec & Skubiski, 1970; Hornstein, Fisch, & Holmes, 1968; Rushton, 1975; Sprafkin, Liebert, & Poulos, 1975). As described in Chapter 6, children learn a great deal about social behaviours by watching—and imitating—others' behaviour (Bandura, 1986). Many civil rights activists in the 1960s reported having parents who had very high moral standards, suggesting that the activists' prosocial behaviour was caused, at least in part, by modelling (Schroeder, Penner, Dovidio, & Piliavin, 1995).

Seeing other people engage in helping behaviour gives us role models to follow, shows us the rewards of helping, and reminds us of the value of helping to society. In one study, a woman stood beside a car with a flat tire in a neighbourhood in California (Bryan & Test, 1967). In the experimental condition, motorists observed a model of helping behaviour: a man changing a flat tire for a woman one quarter of a mile earlier along the road. Although most people didn't stop in either the experimental or control (no model) conditions, 10 times as many people stopped after seeing the model. Similarly, watching another person donate to a Salvation Army kettle increased donations by 7 percent (Bryan & Test, 1967). As described in the Media Connections box, exposure to positive models on television can lead to prosocial behaviour.

MEDIA CONNECTIONS

Does Watching *Sesame Street* Lead to Prosocial Behaviour?

Much evidence points to the hazards of exposing young children to violent and aggressive television. But can watching positive models on television lead children to engage in prosocial behaviour? To answer this question, Mares and Woodard (2005) conducted a meta-analysis by first gathering data from many studies in which children were exposed to positive behaviour on television and then measuring the effects of this exposure on four behaviours:

- positive interactions (friendly play or peaceful conflict resolution)
- altruism (sharing, donating, offering help, and comforting)
- stereotype reduction (exposure to counter-stereotypic portrayals of gender and ethnicity)
- aggression (verbal and/or physical aggression)

As predicted, children who watched prosocial content behaved more positively as measured by all four behaviours. Males and females were equally affected by exposure to prosocial content. However, the older children in these studies (around age 7) benefited more than the younger children (as young as age 3). For example, 6-year-olds who see a television show modelling helping behaviour, such as a boy helping a dog, are much more likely to help in a later task than those who see a different episode of the same show (Sprafkin et al., 1975). Younger children may lack the cognitive ability to understand the nature of prosocial acts. This research suggests that television has the potential to lead to positive social interactions and outcomes.

Exposure to highly altruistic models can also decrease helping in some cases. People who see moderately helpful models and are then asked to help may agree to the request, but judge their motivation for such behaviour to be externally based (e.g., due to social pressure; Thomas, Batson, & Coke, 1981). In turn, people who see highly altruistic models actually see themselves as less altruistic than those who are exposed to more moderately helpful models. Similarly, you may see yourself as very helpful if you volunteer at a homeless shelter one Sunday afternoon while your roommate plays video games, but you'll probably see yourself as much less helpful if your other roommate volunteers all day every Saturday.

ENVIRONMENTAL FACTORS

Environmental factors, such as the location of an emergency, influence prosocial behaviour. Folk wisdom tells us that people are friendlier in rural towns than in large cities. We often think of people who live in country settings as more helpful and cooperative, and think of those who live in urban environments as more aloof and egocentric. But do these stereotypes give an accurate portrayal of these opposing environments? In large part, yes. People in small towns are more likely than those in urban areas to help others in a variety of small ways, including giving the time of day, participating in a survey, providing directions, returning a lost letter, and giving change (Amato, 1981, 1983; Levine, Martinez, Brase, & Sorenson, 1994; Steblay, 1987). People in small towns are also more likely to provide help in more serious situations, including helping an injured person and a lost child. In one study, a man limped down the street and then fell down with a cry of pain. He lifted the leg of his pants to reveal a heavily bandaged leg that was bleeding profusely. When this incident was staged in a small town, about half the pedestrian witnesses helped. But when this incident was staged in a large city, only 15 percent of those who witnessed the incident helped.

Why do people in cities help less? According to the **urban overload hypothesis** (Milgram, 1970), because people in cities are exposed to greater stimulation, they have a desire to keep to themselves more and this causes them to be less helpful—in short, they learn to block things out. For example, people who see someone with an arm in a large cast drop several boxes of books are much less likely to help the person when there's lots of noise from a power lawn

urban overload hypothesis – the hypothesis that people who live in urban areas are constantly exposed to stimulation, which in turn leads them to decrease their awareness of their environment

"Here I was, all this time, worrying that maybe I'm a selfish person, and now it turns out I've been suffering from compassion fatigue."

© David Sipress/ The New Yorker Collection/
www.cartoon.bank.com

mower than when there's no such competing stimulus. Only 15 percent help in the former situation, as compared to 80 percent in the latter (Mathews & Canon, 1975). There are also other factors at play. People who live in cities are likely to be less similar to each other (given the greater diversity of cities), to be more anonymous (so less accountable for their actions/ inactions), and to be greater in number (creating diffusion of responsibility). It does not appear that people in cities are generally meaner or have been raised differently (e.g., people who are raised in cities versus small towns are equally likely to help or not help, depending on where they live when the help is required)!

[CONCEPTS IN CONTEXT]

HOW SITUATIONAL FACTORS INFLUENCE HELPING

MODEL	EXAMPLE
Decision-making model	Steve and Joilene are walking across campus late at night. They hear screams coming from an open window. At first they discuss whether they should call the police. Then they notice several other people walking nearby who also have clearly heard the screams, but have not reacted at all to the noise. So, they decide the screams must just be someone having some fun, and continue on home.
Arousal/cost-reward model	Paiva walks out of a store and notices a small puppy playing near a busy road. She goes over to the dog. The dog isn't wearing a collar, and clearly seems to be lost. Paiva knows she should take the dog to a shelter, but she's running late for a job interview. She gets into her car and drives away.
Mood	Ji Ling has just received a compliment from her boss about a proposal she submitted, and is feeling very happy. When a man on the subway asks her for change to buy food, she hands him a dollar.
Modelling	Russell hates to donate blood. But after his roommate announces his own intention to donate (following a televised plea for more blood from a local hospital), Russell agrees to donate.
Environment	Camille has recently moved to Montreal from Huntingdon, a small town in Quebec. When she drops a stack of papers on the street, she's surprised that no one stops to help her pick them up—which she is certain would have happened in Huntingdon where she grew up.

DOES PURE ALTRUISM EXIST?

Think about a time when you helped someone. Were your actions motivated by a genuine desire to help, or a desire to make yourself feel better? Researchers in social psychology disagree about the factors that motivate prosocial behaviour. In one study, researchers examined the motivations of volunteers who worked at an AIDS service organization (Stürmer, Snyder, & Omoto, 2005). The volunteers completed questionnaires prior to starting their volunteer training, after completing their training but before starting their volunteer work, and again after three months and six months of service. The questionnaires examined volunteers' motivations for helping, level of empathy, and amount of help actually provided. Findings indicated that empathy was the best predictor of helping for volunteers who were homosexual. On the other hand, it was found that the best predictor of helping for volunteers who were heterosexual was interpersonal attraction or their feelings about the person they were helping—meaning whether they liked and respected the person and enjoyed spending time with him or her. Because all of the clients who were receiving help were homosexual, if the volunteer was also homosexual then the client was an in-group member and the primary motivation for helping was empathy. In contrast, if the volunteer was heterosexual, then the client was an outgroup member and the primary motivation for helping was interpersonal attraction. So, do people help out of true empathy for others or for other reasons? This section will compare two distinct hypotheses: the empathy-altruism hypothesis and the negative-state relief hypothesis. We will also discuss the positive psychology of helping.

EMPATHY-ALTRUISM HYPOTHESIS

empathy-altruism hypothesis – the idea that when we feel empathy for a person, we will help that person even if we incur a cost in doing so

According to the **empathy-altruism hypothesis**, some helpful actions are genuinely motivated by a desire to do good for others (Batson, 1991). Infants cry more when they hear another infant crying, suggesting that empathy may be a natural part of human nature (Hoffman, 1981). For example, even one-day-old infants cry in response to hearing other infants' cry, and this noise produces even more distress than hearing tapes of their own cries (Martin & Clark, 1982). In turn, empathic concern for a person in need produces an altruistic motive for helping.

When a person doesn't adopt another person's perspective but notices that person's distress, the observer may still be motivated to relieve the person's distress in order to relieve the observer's own concern. Rather than being altruistic, this type of motive for helping is egoistic, because the goal of the behaviour is not to ease the other person's burden, but to relieve one's own distress. Daniel Batson (1991) believes that most helping is motivated by self-focused concerns, but that true altruism does exist.

As shown in Figure 13.3, when individuals take the perspective of the person in need, they will feel concern and therefore be motivated to help relieve the person's distress. As described at the start of this section, gay men help people who are HIV positive due to feelings of empathy, presumably because they identify with them. Heterosexual men, on the other hand, help largely due to their own feelings of satisfaction. Research Focus on Neuroscience describes how different portions of the brain are activated when imagining your own experience of an emotion versus taking someone else's perspective.

FIGURE 13.3   THE ROLE OF DIFFERENT MOTIVATIONS IN HELPING

According to Batson's model, people can help for either egoistic or altruistic motives, depending on whether they adopt the other person's perspective and therefore feel empathy.

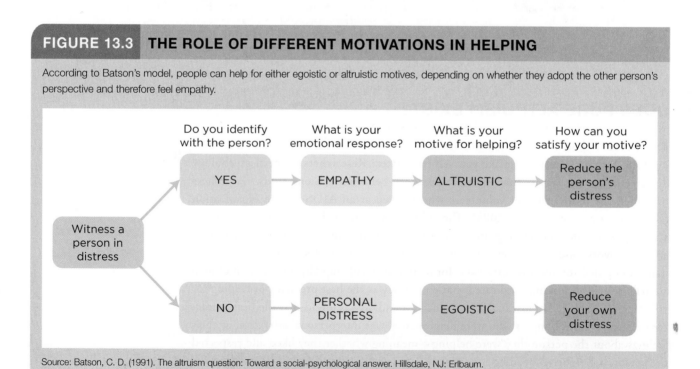

Source: Batson, C. D. (1991). The altruism question: Toward a social-psychological answer. Hillsdale, NJ: Erlbaum.

RESEARCH FOCUS ON NEUROSCIENCE
How Perspective-Taking Looks in the Brain

According to the empathy-altruism hypothesis, one key factor that influences whether a person engages in prosocial behaviour is whether that person can adopt someone else's perspective. Recent research in neuroscience has examined whether different parts of the brain process emotions when we're imagining ourselves experiencing them compared to when we're imagining other people experiencing them. In one study, participants were given short written statements that described social emotions (Ruby & Decety, 2004). These social emotions included the following:

- shame (someone opens the toilet door that you have forgotten to lock)
- irritation (someone knocks over a coffee cup on your clothes)
- pride (a job promotion is promised to you)

Then the participants were asked to imagine how they would feel if they were in those situations, and how their mothers would feel in those situations. Researchers used PET (positron emission tomography) scans of the participants' brains to show which portions of the brain were activated when participants imagined each type of social emotion from both their own and their mother's perspective. When participants adopted their mother's perspective, portions of the brain that are associated with perspective-taking processes were activated. This research provides evidence that different portions of the brain process different types of emotion-relevant stimuli, depending on whether we're thinking about these emotions from our own perspective or another person's.

A development in neuroscience that some authors regard as a very important step is the discovery of mirror neurons (Fogassi, 2011). These are neurons that fire when the organism (they've been observed in a variety of species from primates to birds) does something, but also when it observes another organism doing something. There is something happening in the brain that responds in a mirror-like way to the actions of others as well as when we perform the act ourselves. In humans, brain activity that is consistent with the behaviour of mirror neurons has been found in the premotor cortex, the supplementary motor area, the primary somatosensory cortex, and the inferior parietal cortex. This indicates that we have a sophisticated system of mirror neurons which seems likely to be the basis of imitation and, hence, of the learning that takes place in language acquisition, the learning of one's culture, and the theory of mind and of empathy. Research on mirror neurons and their functions is still at a relatively early stage, but scientist V.S. Ramachandran (2009) predicts that "mirror neurons will do for psychology what DNA did for biology: they will provide a unifying framework and help explain a host of mental abilities that have hitherto remained mysterious and inaccessible to experiments."

Batson and his colleagues have conducted several studies to distinguish between people's motivations to help make themselves feel better (i.e., egoism) versus motivations to help make others feel better (i.e., altruism). What determines which motivation a person will have in a given situation? People may feel empathy with a person based on their own personality (i.e., whether they're generally high in empathy). People may also feel empathy due to something about the other person (i.e., feeling a special connection to the person in need of help, such as sharing similar interests). Let's examine research on each of these processes.

IMPACT OF EMPATHIC MOTIVES. In one of the earliest studies to test the empathy theory of helping, Miho Toi and Daniel Batson (1982) had students listen to a recording that described another student, Carol Marcy, who had broken both her legs in a car accident. Carol needed a tutor for her psychology class so that she could graduate on time. In some cases, students were told that regardless of their decision about whether or not to help her, they would continue to see Carol over the course of the semester, making the cost of not helping (that is, feeling guilty and ashamed) relatively high. In other cases, students were told that it was unlikely they would ever see Carol again, making the cost of not helping quite low.

So, who chose to help Carol? Students with generally empathic motives helped at about equal levels regardless of whether the cost of helping was high or low—81 percent and 71 percent, respectively. Students with generally egoistic motives who thought the cost of not helping would be high were also very likely to help—76 percent. However, students who were motivated by egoistic concerns and who believed the cost of not helping would be low were very unlikely to help: only 33 percent of the students in this condition agreed to serve as a tutor.

Empathic motives can also be created simply by imagining one's self in another person's place, which in turn creates helping behaviour (Batson et al., 2003). In one study, participants were asked to assign both themselves and another student to research tasks. In each case, one task was more desirable than the other, and participants were given the option of simply choosing the task they preferred or flipping a coin to choose who would do which task. Before making the decision about which task each person would do, participants in one condition were asked to complete a perspective-taking exercise in which they were told to "imagine how the other participant will likely feel when told which task he or she is to do." Participants in the control condition were not asked to complete this imagination task. In line with predictions, 75 percent of students in the control condition assigned the more desirable task to themselves. In contrast, only 42 percent of those in the perspective-taking condition assigned the more desirable task to themselves. This study provides compelling evidence that imagining yourself in someone else's shoes can increase prosocial behaviour.

IMPACT OF FEELING SIMILAR. Feeling similar to someone else also increases empathy, and in turn, helping. In one of the first studies to test the empathy-altruism hypothesis, Daniel Batson and his colleagues at the University of Kansas conducted a study to examine the impact of empathy on altruism (Batson, Duncan, Ackerman, Buckley, & Birch, 1981). The participants in this study (one a student, the other a confederate, and both female) were told that the study involved the effects of unpleasant conditions on task performance, and that one person would be randomly chosen to be the learner and the other the observer. The "subjects" then drew lots and, because of the setup, the student always ended up as the observer. While in the observation room, the student then saw the confederate being hooked up to some scary equipment. Next, the confederate "received some shocks" and appeared uncomfortable. Then she told the experimenter about a frightening experience she had had as a child in which she was thrown from a horse onto an electric fence. Elaine, the confederate, next expressed a willingness to continue, but the experimenter wasn't sure if that made sense. So the experimenter asked the observing student (the real participant) if she would be willing to trade places with Elaine. At the beginning of the study, half of the subjects were told that they and Elaine were very similar in values and interests. The other half were told they were very different. In addition, half of the subjects were told that they could leave after witnessing two of the 10 trials during which Elaine would receive random shocks, and the others were told they would need to watch all 10 trials.

So who switched places? As shown in Figure 13.4, among those who felt little or no empathy for Elaine, the difficulty of the escape made all the difference. Specifically, those who were in the difficult escape condition (they would have to witness all 10 trials) were moderately likely to switch, and those in the easy escape condition were very unlikely to help. In contrast, most of the high-empathy (similar) subjects helped, regardless of whether they had an easy or difficult escape.

FIGURE 13.4 HOW DOES EMPATHY IMPACT HELPING?

In this experiment, participants were asked to trade places with a person who was receiving electrical shocks. As predicted, a higher percentage of participants who were similar to the victim helped regardless of whether they were able to leave the experiment quickly or had to remain through all the trials, suggesting that their behaviour was truly motivated by empathic concern for the victim.

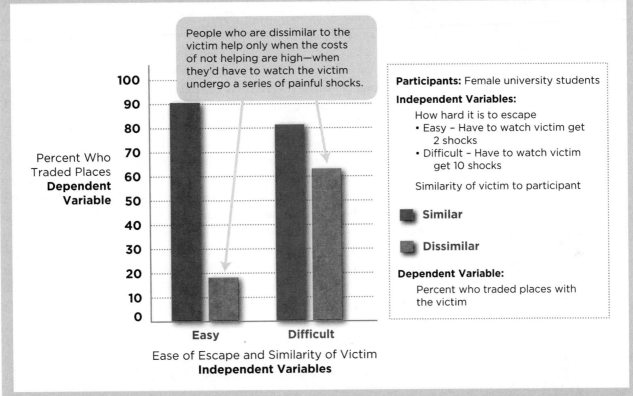

Source: Batson, C.D., Duncan, B.D., Ackerman, P., Buckley, T., & Birch, K. (1981). Is empathic emotion a source of altruistic motivation? *Journal of Personality and Social Psychology*, *40*, 290–302.

Research also reveals that empathy is a particularly strong predictor of helping behaviour when the helper and the target belong to the same cultural group (Stürmer, Snyder, Kropp, & Siem, 2006). In this case, feeling similar to the person who is in need of help increases feelings of empathy, which in turn increases helping behaviour (hence the significance of the Good Samaritan being Samaritan rather than Jewish, like the sick person at the roadside). For example, students who themselves have been through a difficult romantic breakup feel more empathy for another person who has experienced such a breakup (Baston, Sympson, Hindman, & Decruz, 1996). Similarly, students who feel similar in terms of personality and beliefs to a young woman who they're told is a cancer patient are more supportive and warmer toward her than those who feel less similar (Westmaas & Silver, 2006).

NEGATIVE-STATE RELIEF HYPOTHESIS

In contrast to the empathy-altruism model, the **negative-state relief hypothesis** describes people's altruistic behaviour as being motivated by expected benefits in terms of their mood (Cialdini, Kenrick, & Baumann, 1982; Cialdini et al., 1987). According to this model, people feel bad when they see someone suffering and they offer help to relieve their own distress. The negative-state relief hypothesis views helping as egoistic because prosocial behaviour is seen as being motivated by selfish motives, such as making oneself feel better, gaining respect from others, or even obtaining tangible rewards (Batson, 1998). For example, you may be motivated to help build a Habitat for Humanity house because it will give you something to write about

negative-state relief hypothesis – a hypothesis that people are motivated to help others in order to relieve their own negative feelings

"Hey, there's Sara, padding her college-entrance résumé!"

© Edward Koren/ The New Yorker Collection/
www.cartoonbank.com

on a university application, or you may be motivated to donate to a local hospital because your name will be mentioned publicly. In other words, people help because it makes them feel better about themselves (not to make other people feel better), and helping is therefore based on egoistic factors.

This motive for prosocial behaviour is illustrated by a famous story about Abraham Lincoln (Sharp, 1928). As Lincoln was in a carriage crossing over a bridge, he noticed a number of baby pigs who were in great danger of drowning. He quickly jumped out of the carriage, ran to the pigs, and carried them to safety. When he returned to the carriage and was praised for his generosity, he remarked that "that was the very essence of selfishness. I should have had no peace of mind all day had I gone on and left that suffering old sow worrying over those pigs. I did it to get some peace of mind" (Sharp, 1928, p. 75).

Although helping for selfish reasons doesn't really fit our definition of true altruism, this type of motivation may ironically lead to providing more help (Omoto & Snyder, 1995). Allen Omoto and Mark Snyder (1995) examined the motivations of people who volunteered to help persons with AIDS, and then measured how long the volunteers continued to work. People who were motivated to work for more altruistic motives (e.g., wanting to help others, wanting to contribute to their community) were less likely to continue volunteering than those who were motivated by more selfish concerns (e.g., wanting to make friends, wanting to learn more about HIV prevention). The Would You Believe box describes a perhaps surprising way in which helping other people increases our own happiness.

[WOULD YOU BELIEVE . . .]

SPENDING MONEY ON OTHER PEOPLE AND BEING COMPASSIONATE TOWARD THEM MAKES US HAPPY?

The egoistic-model of helping suggests that helping others makes us happy, and that helping is therefore motivated by our desire to make ourselves feel better. In line with this view, recent research reveals that helping others may make us happier than helping ourselves. In one study, researchers asked a national sample of American adults to rate their general happiness, and to report how much they spent in a typical month on four distinct types of items: bills and expenses, gifts for themselves, gifts for others, and donations to charity (Dunn, Aknin, & Norton, 2008). Although the amount that people spent on themselves was not related to overall happiness, people who spent more money on other people (either through gifts to those they knew or contributions to charities) reported higher levels of happiness. Next, these researchers examined how employees spent an unexpected profit-sharing bonus from their company, and whether their spending decisions predicted happiness six to eight weeks later. As predicted, employees who spent the money on other people (buying something for someone else or donating it to charity) experienced greater happiness than those who spent the money on themselves (paying bills or the mortgage or buying something for themselves). Finally, researchers conducted a very clever experimental study. In this study, participants were given an envelope containing $20 and were told they needed to spend the money by 5 p.m. that day. Some participants were told they needed to spend the money on a bill, expense, or gift for themselves; others were told they needed to spend the money on a gift for someone else or as a donation to a charity. Researchers then asked participants to return to the psychology department that day at 5 p.m. to report their happiness. As predicted, participants who spent the money on someone else were happier than those who spent the money on themselves. All of this research points to what may be a surprising conclusion: spending money on other people makes us happier than spending money on ourselves.

People also feel good about themselves if they behave in a loving, compassionate manner toward another. Beverley Fehr from the University of Winnipeg and Susan Sprecher asked people to recall a specific experience of compassionate love and to indicate how they were affected on several dimensions (mood, self-esteem, closeness to others; Sprecher & Fehr, 2006). Overall, the results indicated that people reap many positive benefits from experiencing compassionate love for others. While it can't be assumed in this context that compassionate love is the same as altruism, the focus on the other person does suggest some overlap between the two ideas.

According to the negative-state relief, or egoistic, model of helping, helping occurs under two conditions: if one is in a bad mood, and if helping can lead to an improvement in mood. Let's examine each of these two conditions.

HELPING OCCURS TO RELIEVE ONE'S OWN BAD MOOD.   Although this hypothesis predicts that people who are in a bad mood will be motivated to help others in order to make themselves feel better, if they can feel better in some other way, they won't help. To test this aspect of the negative-state relief hypothesis, Bob Cialdini and his colleagues made participants believe they had accidentally ruined a graduate student's data (Cialdini, Darby, & Vincent, 1973). Some of the participants later participated in a positive event (received praise for doing well), and others didn't. As predicted, more than 70 percent then helped in another situation when they felt guilty and had no other way of making themselves feel better. In contrast, fewer than 30 percent of those who had received praise for their performance helped on the subsequent task. Those who received praise for their performance didn't need to help, because they already felt better. Even the expectation that you will soon feel better can decrease helping. For example, people who feel sad due to their empathy for another person but who believe their sadness will soon be alleviated by listening to a comedian's performance are less likely to help than those who don't expect their mood to soon change (Schaller & Cialdini, 1988).

Developmental psychology offers additional evidence for the negative-state relief model of helping. As described earlier in the chapter, young children don't yet understand that helping can improve their mood, and therefore can't have the expectation of egoistic benefits (Eisenberg & Miller, 1987). It follows that children should therefore be less motivated to help due to the expectation of improving their own mood than teenagers should be, as teenagers understand the personal benefit of helping. To test this hypothesis, Cialdini and Kenrick (1976) asked children (ages 6 to 8) and teenagers (ages 15 to 18) to think of something very sad (such as the death of a favourite pet) or something neutral. They were then given a chance to help other students by sharing some of the prizes they had won in a game. As predicted, young children, who didn't yet see the connection between helping others and feeling good themselves, donated about half as many prizes in the sad condition as in the neutral condition. In contrast, teenagers, who understand that behaving altruistically can feel good, donated over four times as many prizes in the sad condition as in the neutral condition.

Questioning the Research:

This study suggests that teenagers understand that helping can lead to improvements in their own mood, which in turn leads older children to engage in higher levels of helping behaviour than younger children. Can you think of another explanation for the findings? (Hint: Could teenagers just be more motivated to appear good than younger children?)

HELPING WON'T OCCUR IF MOOD IMPROVEMENT IS IMPOSSIBLE.   Another egoistic explanation for helping behaviour is that empathic people feel sad when they see others in need, and the empathic person is motivated to help purely to relieve this unpleasant state (Cialdini et al., 1987). As a result, people will be motivated to help others only when they believe that helping will relieve their bad feelings—in other words, why go through the trouble of helping if you're not going to feel better?

To test this proposition, researchers asked some students to remember their most personally distressing memories (to put them in a sad mood), asked others to remember the route they had taken to school (to put them in a neutral mood), and asked still others to remember a positive memory (to put them in a happy mood; Manucia, Baumann, & Cialdini, 1984). The participants then drank a cup of "memory drug" called Mnemoxine (it was actually flat tonic water). The researchers told half of the students in each condition that the drug would have no mood-related side effects, and told the others that a standard side effect of the drug was to chemically preserve for 25 minutes whatever mood the person was in when taking the drug. The experimenter then left the room to get some forms, at which point a confederate appeared and asked the students to make some calls to invite people to donate

FIGURE 13.5 HOW DOES MOOD IMPACT HELPING?

Experimenters put students in sad, neutral, or happy moods, and then led them to believe their mood could either change or remain the same way for the next 25 minutes, before giving them an opportunity to help. A higher percentage of sad participants helped than happy or neutral mood participants when they believed helping could lead to mood improvements, suggesting that we help in order to reduce our own negative feelings.

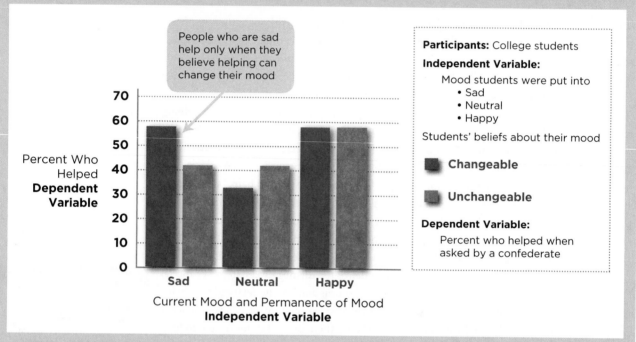

Source: Manucia, G.K., Baumann, D. J., & Cialdini, R.B. (1984). Mood influences on helping: Direct effects or side effects? *Journal of Personality and Social Psychology, 46*, 357–364.

blood. The dependent variable was the percentage of students who agreed to help make the calls. As shown in Figure 13.5, students who were in a sad mood and believed that helping would improve their mood were much more likely to help than those who believed that helping would not improve their mood because they had been told that their mood was set by the drug to remain unchanged.

COMPARING THE MODELS

There is considerable debate among social psychologists about the presence of true altruism. Researchers continue to examine the conditions that lead to altruistic behaviour, and whether such behaviour is motivated by egoistic or altruistic factors. One study by Bob Cialdini and his colleagues found that the conditions that lead to empathy also lead to a greater sense of overlap with other people. In turn, empathy for others may really be aimed at helping one's self (Cialdini, Brown, Lewis, Luce, & Neuberg, 1997). Not surprisingly, Batson and his colleagues dispute this (Batson et al., 1997). Is the debate on egoistic versus altruistic motivations for helping settled? Not at all.

Although these models may seem to contradict one another, they do agree that at times people engage in helping for egoistic reasons. The main difference between these models is that the empathy-altruism hypothesis describes the self-benefits of helping as unintended consequences, whereas the negative-state relief hypothesis describes these benefits as the primary motivation for helping. What are these benefits to the self? They can be grouped into three categories: reduction of aversive arousal, fear of punishment for not helping, and desire for reward. Let's examine each of these categories.

REDUCTION OF AVERSIVE AROUSAL. The most common egoistic explanation for helping is that people want to reduce the unpleasant arousal they experience when hearing or seeing someone who is in distress. This is why Abraham Lincoln helped the drowning pigs, and why even strangers want to comfort crying babies on airplanes. However, Batson and his colleagues (1981) argue that people who feel empathy for the person in distress help even when they could avoid hearing the person in distress by leaving. Although people who don't feel a connection to the victim help only when they're forced to continue listening to the suffering, people who feel genuine empathy help regardless of whether they have an easy or difficult escape from the situation.

FEAR OF PUNISHMENT FOR NOT HELPING. Another egoistic explanation for helping is that people know that helping is "the right thing to do," and hence are worried about feeling guilty or ashamed if they don't help. Once again, in this case helping would really be motivated by a desire to not feel lousy about one's behaviour, rather than by a true desire to improve another person's welfare (Schaller & Cialdini, 1988). Although this is a tough question to directly test, Batson and his colleagues created a clever study to do just that (Batson et al., 1988). They specifically told participants that most people in their situation did *not* help. Did this knowledge decrease helping behaviour? Not at all for people who felt empathy for the victim.

DESIRE FOR REWARD. Finally, as discussed earlier in the chapter, people learn fairly early in life that they can receive rewards for helping. In turn, people may behave altruistically only when they believe that others will notice—and think less of them if they don't help—and helping is therefore again motivated by a self-focused concern (Fultz, Batson, Fortenbach, McCarthy, & Varney, 1986). To test this explanation for helping behaviour, some students were made to feel empathy for a person in distress and others were not. Then, some students were given an opportunity to help this person. Regardless of whether anyone—including the person who was in trouble—would know that the student declined to help, people who were high in empathy were much more likely to offer help. This finding showing that people demonstrate the same kind of altruistic behaviour regardless of whether they believe someone else is watching provides strong evidence that the helping is not simply motivated by an expectation of personal benefits.

PREDICTING LONG-TERM HELPING

Although helping may be motivated by either empathic or egoistic factors, helping that is motivated by empathy is most likely to lead to long-term helping. In December 2001, researchers at the University of Tennessee conducted a study to examine the frequency of helping and motivation for helping following 9/11 (Piferi, Jobe, & Jones, 2006). In this sample of university students, 62 percent reported giving some type of aid to those involved in the attacks. The most common types of support provided were sending money (66 percent), praying (35 percent), and donating blood (24 percent). What motivated this aid? (Remember, this study took place in Tennessee, and only 7 percent of the sample even knew someone who lived in New York or Washington.)

- Thirty-four percent of those who gave support reported they were motivated to relieve their own personal pain due to the event.
- Twenty-two percent reported they were motivated to give because they would expect others to help them if the roles were reversed.
- Approximately 20 percent reported providing help because they recognized that other people were suffering.
- Another 19 percent felt it was the patriotic thing to do.
- Fifteen percent felt it was their duty to give.
- Approximately 12 percent helped because they knew someone who was involved.

When researchers followed up with these participants one year later and asked whether they were still giving, 80 percent of those who helped for other-focused reasons (that is, they recognized that others were suffering) were still giving. However, fewer than half of those who were helping for any other reason were still giving one year later.

POSITIVE PSYCHOLOGY OF HELPING

It's well established that helping, or social support, is beneficial to the recipient, but it may also be beneficial to the helper. Research indicates that there are benefits of volunteerism to the person who is volunteering. The mental health benefits of volunteerism include reduction in depressive symptoms (Musick & Wilson, 2003), happiness, and enhanced well-being (Krueger, Hicks, & McGue, 2001). Oman, Thoresen, and McMahon (1999) have data suggesting that volunteers live longer than non-volunteers. Post (2005) reviews a growing body of research and concludes that a strong correlation exists between the well-being, happiness, health, and longevity of people who are emotionally and behaviourally compassionate. There is one important caveat, however: helping has positive effects on the helper as long as he or she is not overwhelmed by the helping tasks.

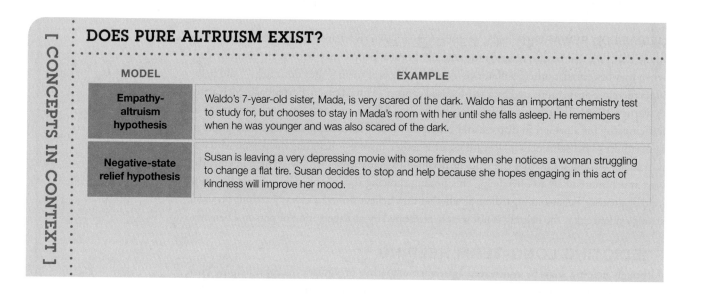

[CONCEPTS IN CONTEXT]

DOES PURE ALTRUISM EXIST?

MODEL	EXAMPLE
Empathy-altruism hypothesis	Waldo's 7-year-old sister, Mada, is very scared of the dark. Waldo has an important chemistry test to study for, but chooses to stay in Mada's room with her until she falls asleep. He remembers when he was younger and was also scared of the dark.
Negative-state relief hypothesis	Susan is leaving a very depressing movie with some friends when she notices a woman struggling to change a flat tire. Susan decides to stop and help because she hopes engaging in this act of kindness will improve her mood.

WHO GETS HELP WHEN THEY ARE IN NEED?

Think about a time when a stranger asked you for help. Maybe he or she needed directions, change for a dollar, or the time of day. Did you help? If not, why not? Research in social psychology suggests that aspects of the person as well as your relationship to the person influence whether you'll help. In one study, both male and female researchers asked people for help in 120 bus stations across the United States (Pearce, 1980). The requests for help were relatively minor: "Do you have the time?" and "Where can I stay in this city?" Some of the people who requested help were "familiar strangers," meaning they had ridden on the bus with the people they asked for help and therefore looked familiar. Others who requested help were "unfamiliar strangers"—they asked for help from people who had never seen them before.

Who was most likely to receive help? Familiar strangers were helped more than total strangers. Females were helped significantly more often than males. This section will describe why both familiarity and gender influence getting help. We'll examine how person factors, social norms, and relationship factors influence getting help.

PERSON FACTORS

Some people are much more likely to receive help than others. This section will examine the impact of person factors—including gender, age, attractiveness, and personality—on receiving help.

GENDER. Gender has a strong influence on who gets help, with women being more likely than men to receive help (Bruder-Mattson & Hovanitz, 1990; Good, Dell, & Mintz, 1989). As described at the start of this section, strangers are more likely to respond to simple questions (e.g., "What time is it?", "Where's the nearest post office?") when they're asked by females (Pearce, 1980).

This gender difference doesn't mean that people aren't willing to help men, but rather that men may be less interested in or even willing to receive help than women (Barbee, Cunningham, Winstead, & Derlega, 1993; Eagly & Crowley, 1986). The often-cited example of men's failure to ask for directions illustrates this point. Seeking help is more threatening to men, and in this way has more costs. In line with this view, men are more likely than women to worry about how people will react if they request help (Bruder-Mattson & Hovanitz, 1990). The potential costs of helping for men—admitting weakness, depending on others—may simply be too high. In an application of Latané and Darley's (1970) decision-making process model, Magdalena Cismaru and colleagues from the University of Regina examined 12 advertising campaigns that encouraged bystander intervention (Cismaru, Jensen, & Lavack, 2010). The campaigns all addressed domestic violence, and the authors analyzed the content of the campaigns in terms of the decision-making process that a bystander needs to go through before intervening. They produced a series of recommendations for such campaigns and concluded that although the campaigns did draw on important aspects of the theory of bystander intervention, such as challenging social norms, emphasizing bystander responsibility, implying bystander capability, and stressing the need for intervention, they were contradictory in many respects.

"We've been wandering in the desert for forty years. But he's a man—would he ever ask directions?"

© Peter Steiner/ The New Yorker Collection/ www.cartoonbank.com

AGE. Another demographic factor that influences how much help we want as well as how much help we get is age (Shell & Eisenberg, 1992). As you might expect, children are very willing to seek help. The authors suggest that this is because younger children are used to receiving help—because they legitimately need a lot of help—and so don't see asking for help as a sign of weakness. However, as children get older, they become aware that requesting help can show weakness and dependence on others, and they therefore become more reluctant to seek help.

ATTRACTIVENESS. Perhaps not surprisingly, attractive people get more help (Benson, Karabenick, & Lerner, 1976). Attractive people are more likely to receive directions, assistance mailing a letter, and change for a dollar (Wilson, 1978; Wilson & Dovidio, 1985). People also spend more time giving directions to attractive people than to unattractive people (Harrell, 1978).

The situations just mentioned all describe helping in a situation where there is direct interaction and the potential rewards for helping an attractive person are clear. An attractive person might appreciate the help, and the helper might benefit by getting future interactions with that person. But attractive people also get more help in situations where there is no possibility of future interaction. In one study, a stamped, completed application to psychology graduate school was left in a phone booth (Benson et al., 1976). There was a photo of the applicant, who in some cases was very attractive and in some cases was very unattractive. The attractive applicant got help 47 percent of the time versus 35 percent of the time for the unattractive applicant.

PERSONALITY. Personality factors, such as shyness, anxiety, and self-esteem, also influence the likelihood of receiving help (DePaulo, Dull, Greenberg, & Swaim, 1989). For example, people who are socially anxious receive lower levels of social support from their friends (Caldwell & Reinhart, 1988). Bella DePaulo and colleagues found that shy people were less effective than non-shy people at getting people to return a questionnaire. When they make phone calls, they sound less warm and confident, and speak less fluently. This behaviour elicits fewer responses. Although shy and non-shy people didn't differ in their frequency of asking for help, shy people were especially reluctant to ask for help from a member of the opposite sex.

Self-esteem has a mixed effect on the likelihood of receiving help. On the one hand, people who are high in self-esteem are generally less willing to ask for help, in part because they don't want to feel weak or dependent (Nadler, Mayseless, Peri, & Chemerinski, 1985). Also, people who are high in self-esteem and get unsolicited help feel particularly bad (Nadler, Altman, & Fisher, 1979)!

On the other hand, people with high self-esteem are more likely to receive—and benefit from—social support: a study with university students found that those with high self-esteem were more likely to receive social support from their families than those with low self-esteem (Caldwell & Reinhart, 1988).

SOCIAL NORMS

Social norms also influence helping. Let's examine two norms that are associated with prosocial behaviour: the norm of reciprocity and the norm of social responsibility.

NORM OF RECIPROCITY. As you learned in Chapter 8, according to the **norm of reciprocity**, people usually give back to people who have given to them (Wilke & Lanzetta, 1970, 1982). Social marketers, who use commercial marketing techniques to promote the adoption of positive health or social behaviours (such as helping out the less fortunate), often rely on the norm of reciprocity to motivate people to make donations they might otherwise not have made. For example, charitable organizations often send out small "gifts," such as greeting cards, address labels, and wrapping paper. The organization hopes that, in return for this gift, people will feel obligated to give a donation to thank them for their generosity. Similarly, waiters often use the norm of reciprocity to encourage better tipping: customers who receive a small piece of candy with their bill tip more than customers who don't receive candy (Strohmetz, Rind, Fisher, & Lynn, 2002).

One clever study by Dennis Regan (1971) examined the norm of reciprocity in an experimental setting. Two students (one subject and one confederate) worked on a task, and were then given a short break. In one condition, the confederate returned from the break with two sodas—one for himself and one for his partner. At the end of the study, the confederate asked the subject whether he would like to buy some raffle tickets, which could earn the confederate a nice prize. Subjects who received the soda bought twice as many tickets as those who didn't receive the soda—and in fact ended up spending nearly five times as much as the confederate did on the soda!

NORM OF SOCIAL RESPONSIBILITY. The **norm of social responsibility** describes people's obligation to help those who are in need of assistance, even if the helper has no expectation of later receiving help from the person being helped (Berkowitz & Daniels, 1963). For example, are you motivated to give money to a person who is homeless, or to hold a door open for a person in a wheelchair? If so, you have a sense of social responsibility. According to Bierhoff, Klein, and Kramp (1991), people with a greater sense of social responsibility are more likely to help victims of a traffic accident than those who are lower on this measure.

Questioning the Research:
This study suggests that people who are socially anxious receive little social support from their friends. Can you think of an alternative explanation for this association? (Hint: Is this link correlation or causation?)

norm of reciprocity – the idea that we should help those who are in need of assistance, because they will then help us in the future

norm of social responsibility – the idea that we have an obligation to help those who are in need of assistance

In the summer of 2010, a group of billionaires led by Warren Buffett, Bill Gates, and Melinda Gates started a campaign. The group announced that they would donate half or more of their wealth to a charitable organization. The Giving Pledge list was created and the wealthiest individuals were invited to commit giving part of their wealth to a charitable organization either during their lifetime or after their death. Although the pledge has no legal weight, it is a moral commitment and involved a public announcement. Although the donors are all billionaires, the Giving Pledge list is aimed at inspiring all individuals to give back to society. What motivates these individuals is a sense of social responsibility.

People are especially likely to help another person if they see the need for help as caused by something beyond the person's control. For example, in 2010, Canadians donated more than $113 million to Haiti after the massive earthquake that the country experienced. Canada was praised for its generous donation, which all together totalled about $311 million, including emergency aid provided by Ottawa. Former U.S. president Bill Clinton, who was coordinating the international aid in Haiti, commended Canada, saying, "I'll bet you on a per-capita basis they're the number one in the world helping Haiti" (AFP, 2010, Feb. 8).

But we don't always help people who need help: when we believe the person is responsible for the predicament, we may be much less likely to help (Meyer & Mulherin, 1990; Schmidt & Weiner, 1988). For example, in the early years of the AIDS epidemic, people were much more motivated to donate money to groups for persons with HIV who were not seen as responsible for acquiring the disease (e.g., people who became infected through a blood transfusion, infants who were infected through their mothers) than to groups supporting other people with HIV (e.g., IV drug users, gay men; see Weiner, Perry, & Magnusson, 1988).

Why do people see some people as "deserving" of help, and others as not? As you read in Chapter 4, the attributions people make about why a person has a need for help influence whether they give help (Weiner, 1980, 1986). The phenomenon known as belief in a just world describes our tendency to assume that good things happen to good people and bad things happen to bad people (Lerner, 1980; Lipkus, Dalbert, & Siegler, 1996). In turn, we're more likely to help someone if we don't see that person as responsible for their current situation (Skikta, 1999). For example, conservatives generally see poverty as caused by a lack of intelligence and moral standards, whereas liberals tend to see poverty as caused by unjust social practices and structures. These differing views on the causes of poverty help explain why liberals tend to favour, whereas conservatives tend to oppose, increased spending on social programs.

The attributions that we make even for people's minor requests can influence whether, and how much, we help. Schmidt and Weiner (1988) presented students with a scenario about a classmate asking to borrow lecture notes. Students were much more likely to help the person who was wearing an eye patch and dark glasses—presumably because this person was unable to take his own notes due to circumstances beyond his control—than the person who admitted he missed class to go to the beach!

RELATIONSHIP FACTORS

Although the chapter has focused until now on personal factors that influence helping, in many cases such behaviour is not simply a function of aspects of the other person, but also of the connection between that person and ourselves. This section will examine the impact of relationship factors on who we help, including similarity and friendship.

SIMILARITY. We're most likely to help those who are similar to us—in dress, gender, nationality, and attitudes (Dovidio & Morris, 1975; Holloway, Tucker, & Hornstein, 1977; Krebs, 1975). In a series of studies in Boston, Paris, and Athens, researchers examined helping behaviour for natives of the country, foreigners who spoke the language, and foreigners who didn't speak the language (Feldman, 1968). The types of helping behaviour included giving directions, mailing a letter, and being correctly charged for a cab ride. Results consistently showed that people help those who are most similar. For example, 24 percent of the time, natives were not given directions, and natives were never given wrong directions. In contrast, foreigners were not helped in 35 percent of the instances when they asked for help, and were actually given wrong directions 10 percent of the times they asked. So, only about half the time do foreigners get useful help. As described in the Law Connections box, jurors tend to favour defendants of their own ethnicity (Sommers & Ellsworth, 2000).

However, there are studies that find no effect for ethnicity in helping behaviour. For example, in a series of studies by Richard Bourhis and colleagues (2007) from the University of Montreal, cross-cultural helping was measured by asking pedestrians for directions in the streets of Montreal. Four field experiments were conducted, in 1977, 1979, 1991, and 1997. The results indicated that neither the ethnicity of the experimenter (Black or White) nor the language that the experimenter was using (English or French) had any effect on the experimenter being given accurate directions.

⚖ LAW CONNECTIONS

The Impact of Similarity of Ethnicity on Guilt

Jury decision-making is a complex process that requires people to process diverse pieces of information—often with some pointing to the defendant's guilt and others to his or her innocence—and ultimately reach a decision with substantial consequences. We would all like to believe that this process is fair and just—that jurors make decisions based purely on the stated facts of the case. However, individuals often show a bias in their decision-making, and in particular tend to favour defendants of their own ethnicity (Sommers & Ellsworth, 2000). In a series of studies, Sam Sommers and Phoebe Ellsworth at the University of Michigan gave White and Black university students in the U.S. identical trial summaries, and asked the students to rate the defendant's guilt. White students were more likely to see the Black defendant as guilty than the White defendant. Black students showed the opposite pattern.

Jeffrey Pfeifer from the University of Regina and James Ogloff from Monash University in Australia investigated whether the prejudices of mock jurors in Canada would result in the same differences in criminal sanctions given by the jurors as the ones given by jurors in research in the United States. English Canadian participants (ages 18 to 45 years) read a transcript of a sexual assault trial that varied the ethnic background of both the victim and the defendant (i.e., English, French, or First Nations). When they were asked to rate the guilt of the defendant on a 7-point scale, they found him guiltier if he was French or First Nations than if he was English Canadian. However, and perhaps encouragingly, when they were asked (as in a court) to simply rate him guilty or not guilty, there was no indication of prejudice in the mock jurors' decisions (Pfeifer & Ogloff, 2003).

© moodboard / Alamy

Even similarity based on relatively superficial characteristics—such as the sports team one roots for—can lead to greater helping. In a study conducted in England, participants who were soccer fans were recruited to take part in a study (Levine, Prosser, Evans, & Reicher, 2005). Unbeknownst to the participants, only those who had specifically identified themselves as fans of the Manchester United soccer team were invited to participate in the study. Participants came into the psychology department to complete a series of questionnaires and were then told to walk to another part of the building to complete the next part of the study. As the participants rounded a hallway, they saw another person (really a confederate of the experimenter) slip and fall, and then cry out while holding his ankle. In some conditions, this person was wearing a soccer jersey for Manchester United. In other conditions, he was wearing a soccer jersey for Liverpool (a rival team). In the third (control) condition, he was not wearing a shirt from any team. Researchers then examined whether participants stopped and helped the injured person. As predicted, participants were much more likely to help someone who was wearing a Manchester United shirt than either of the other shirts. Ninety-two percent of those wearing a Manchester United shirt got help, compared to only 33 percent of those wearing a rival team's shirt and 30 percent of those wearing a neutral shirt. This study provides compelling evidence that we're more likely to help those who are similar to ourselves.

FRIENDS.   Not surprisingly, people are more likely to help those they know and care about than strangers, and are more likely to help those with whom they have a communal relationship, meaning a relationship in which people expect mutual responsiveness to each others' needs. In contrast, we're much less likely to help those with whom we have an **exchange relationship**, meaning a relationship in which people desire and expect strict reciprocity. In one study, participants were paired with either a friend or a stranger for a study on task performance, but the participants were to complete the task without help from each other and while in different rooms (Clark, Mills, & Powell, 1989). Participants in one condition (the "needs" condition) were told that the lights in their room would change whenever the other person needed help (although these lights were totally irrelevant for the participants in completing the task and could be ignored). Participants in the "inputs" condition were told that the lights would change whenever the other person had made a substantial contribution to the task (and again the participants could ignore the lights without consequence). The dependent variable was how often the participants looked at the lights. In support of the hypotheses, participants looked more at the lights in the "needs" condition when the person was a friend, and looked more at the lights in the "inputs" condition when the person was a stranger.

exchange relationships – a relationship in which people desire and **expect** strict reciprocity

We also help friends create the distinct impressions they want to present to others. In one study, people were asked to describe a friend to another person (Schlenker & Britt, 1999). When talking about the friend to an attractive, opposite-sex individual, the friend was described in a manner consistent with the qualities that the opposite-sex person preferred. On the other hand, when talking about the friend to an unattractive opposite-sex individual, the friend was described as lacking the qualities this person preferred.

BUT NOT ALWAYS.   Although we tend to behave more altruistically toward people we're close to, in some cases closeness can backfire. According to the **self-evaluation maintenance model**, one's own self-concept can be threatened if someone performs better than us on a task that is relevant to our sense of esteem (Tesser, 1980).

self-evaluation maintenance model – the theory that our self-concept can be threatened if someone performs better than us on a task that is relevant to our sense of esteem

In one study, people either came in with a friend to participate or participated with a stranger (Tesser & Smith, 1980). Some participants were asked to perform a task high in relevance to them, relating to their verbal skills and leadership. Other participants were asked to perform a task low in relevance to them (i.e., not relating to them). After completing the task, participants were given a negative feedback, that is they did "a little below average." The participant was then asked to help the friend or stranger do well on the task by giving some helpful clues, with the participant being free to choose how helpful the clues should be. What did the researchers find? When participants were in the high relevance task, they were more likely to give less helpful clues to their friend than to a stranger. However, when they were in the low relevance task, they were more likely to give more helpful clues to their friend than to a stranger! According to the self-esteem maintenance model, we're not always more helpful to our friends and family members. When the relevance of a particular domain is high and it's important for us to perform well, we're reluctant to help a friend who may outperform us. This occurs because we compare our performance to our friend's performance and if the friend outperforms us we look bad to ourselves and our self-esteem drops. In contrast, if the relevance of the domain is low, we're more likely to help a friend than a stranger. This occurs as we tend to bask in the reflected glory of the friend and, therefore, the closer the friend is to us, the more likely we will be to help. For example, based on this model it would be predicted that Serena and Venus Williams are competitive and possibly less helpful to each other in tennis as both are tennis world champions. However, the two sisters are more likely to bask in each other's glory when it comes to other domains such as modelling, design, and musical ability.

Although there may be times when we don't help our friends enough (in an effort to protect our own feelings of self-worth), at other times we help our friends too much, meaning that we provide more help than is really needed (Gilbert & Silvera, 1996). This type of *overhelping* can make you appear altruistic but also make the other person seem needy, weak, and dependent. For example, giving a job candidate a series of very easy questions (e.g., "softballs"), such as "Are you an honest person?" and "Do you generally get along with co-workers?" can undermine the person's true job potential, because the person isn't given the opportunity to "show what they can do." This type of hindering of a person's performance leads observers to attribute success to external, as opposed to internal, factors. For example, after you give your roommate extensive feedback on her essay for medical school, others may interpret her admission as being due to your substantial assistance with her application rather than to her strong grades.

THE DOWNSIDE OF RECEIVING HELP

In most cases, receiving help is good. When people are in need of help, they want to receive it. Supportive help—help given by someone who isn't similar to us and given in a way that doesn't make us feel inferior or dependent—leads to positive reactions (Fisher, Nadler, & Whitcher-Alagna, 1982). For example, when you ask your parents to loan you money to buy a car or proofread your resumé before a big job interview, you're probably happy if they help. This type of help can lead to increases in self-esteem and positive mood, and make us feel good about ourselves as well as the person who helped us (Deci, La Guardia, Moller, Scheiner, & Ryan, 2006). We're especially appreciative of help when we believe that the decision to help was made based on the helper's positive feelings about us (Ames, Flynn, & Weber, 2004).

However, we react negatively to receiving help when it makes us feel inferior to and dependent on the helper (Ackerman & Kendrick, 2008; Nadler & Fisher, 1986; Reinhardt, Boerner, & Horowitz, 2006; Searcy & Eisenberg, 1992; Seidman, Shrout, & Bolger, 2006). For example, African American students experience a substantial drop in self-esteem if they're offered unsolicited (and unneeded) help, yet Anglo-American students don't (Schneider, Major, Luhtanen, & Crocker, 1996). African American students probably experience this drop because they're concerned that their helper assumed they would need help because of their ethnicity. Similarly, for older adults, receiving social support, such as physical assistance, is associated with depressive symptoms and vision problems (Reinhardt et al., 2006). These adults may recognize the need for support, but aren't happy to need it. Social support therefore seems to be most helpful when it is invisible, meaning when it's accomplished outside of the person's awareness, or when it can be reciprocated, thereby making the person feel less dependent on the support giver (Bolger & Amarel, 2007; Gleason, Iida, Bolger, & Shrout, 2003). Similarly, Ellen Ryan and Ann Anas from McMaster University and a colleague found that customers (either seated or in a wheelchair) who were "overhelped" by a retail salesperson rated the encounter as less satisfying and viewed the salesperson as less effective (Ryan, Anas, & Gruneir, 2006).

We also react negatively to receiving help if the help comes from people who are similar to ourselves, especially if they're helping us with a task that we really care about (Nadler, 1987;

Nadler, Fisher, & Itzhak, 1983). So, if you're a varsity tennis player and your teammate offers to help you with your serve, you may feel uncomfortable about receiving this unwanted help. However, you might be very willing to have this same teammate help you with your chemistry lab report (assuming you're not both chemistry majors, of course). This is one of the main drawbacks to peer tutoring programs—because students are on a similar level, it can be difficult for one person to help another.

Finally, people react negatively to receiving help when they don't believe they'll have a way of repaying the help (Nadler & Fisher, 1986). Consistent with the norm of reciprocity, people like to be involved in relationships in which both people give and receive at roughly equal levels. If you receive considerable help, but have no way of repaying the helper, you may feel guilty, which can then have a negative impact on the relationship.

[CONCEPTS IN CONTEXT]

WHO GETS HELP WHEN THEY'RE IN NEED

FACTOR	EXAMPLE
Person	Hailey just agreed to buy four boxes of Thin Mint Girl Scout cookies. Although Hailey is on a diet and doesn't really want cookies in the house, the little girl who sold her the cookies was very cute. Hailey just didn't see how she could say no.
Social norms	Lindsay really had no need for a new calendar. But after she received a free one as a gift from a local charity, she felt compelled to make a small donation.
Relationship	Jerome is walking in a large city. He is asked several times for money by older and dishevelled homeless people. Each time he refuses. Then, before asking Jerome for a few dollars, a young man comments that he roots for the team on Jerome's baseball hat. Jerome gives him two dollars.

HOW DOES CULTURE INFLUENCE HELPING?

Cultural norms and experiences have an influence on both the frequency and types of prosocial behaviour that people engage in. In this section, we'll discuss some of the influences of culture on prosocial behaviour.

Studies show that in all cultures, helping behaviour is more likely to be given to an in-group member than an outgroup member (Triandis, 1994). In collectivistic cultures, however, members of in-groups are even more likely to be helped than outgroup members, compared to the rates of helping in individualistic cultures. In some cultures, moreover, all outsiders are seen as belonging to outgroups and they're therefore less likely to be helped. In still other cultures, outsiders are given tentative inclusion in the in-group until their membership in the group is determined more definitely. Harry Triandis (1994), a Greek American social psychologist, reports that outsiders are welcomed in traditional Greek villages with the people generally being very helpful toward them. In fact, a tentative helpful gesture is made in an attempt to check if the person can be trusted and included in the in-group. A foreigner is therefore more likely to get help in the village than is a Greek stranger because the foreigner has the potential to become an in-group member while the Greek stranger is perceived as clearly not being a member of the in-group. However, in general, in collectivistic countries outsiders are less likely to receive help even when the cost of helping is minimal.

In one study, both American university students and students from India read a hypothetical scenario in which a person is said to need a bone marrow transplant and the participant is described as being a potential donor (Baron & Miller, 2000). Both Americans (67 percent) and

Indians (72 percent) felt obligated to help by providing bone marrow if the person was said to be a member of the student's family. However, 76 percent of Indians saw donating as "morally required" even if the person in need was a stranger. Only 29 percent of Americans saw donating to a stranger as "morally required." This study demonstrates that norms for helping behaviour are different across cultures. This following sections will examine cultural differences in these social norms for helping behaviour, including differences regarding the frequency of helping, norms for helping, and motivations for helping.

FREQUENCY OF HELPING

To examine differences across cultures in the likelihood of helping, Robert Levine and his colleagues examined three types of helping behaviour in large cities in 23 countries (Levine, Norenzayan, & Philbrick, 2001). The three behaviours included assisting a blind person across the street, retrieving an "accidentally" dropped pen, and picking up a pile of magazines for a person with a hurt leg. As shown in Table 13.1, the rates of helping differed dramatically from one country to another (Canada, unfortunately, wasn't included in this multinational study).

TABLE 13.2	Percentage Rates of Helping across Cultures		
COUNTRY	**BLIND PERSON**	**DROPPED PEN**	**HURT LEG**
Brazil	100	100	80
Costa Rica	100	79	95
Malawi	100	93	65
India	92	63	93
Austria	75	88	80
Spain	100	76	63
Denmark	67	89	77
China	63	75	92
Mexico	92	55	80
El Salvador	92	89	43
Czech Republic	100	55	70
Sweden	58	92	66
Hungary	67	76	70
Romania	92	66	48
Italy	75	35	80
Thailand	42	75	66
Bulgaria	80	69	22
Netherlands	58	54	49
Singapore	50	45	49
U.S.	75	31	28
Malaysia	53	26	41

The rates of helping in each type of situation differed considerably across countries, from a high rate of overall helping in Brazil to a low overall rate in Malaysia (Levine et al., 2001).

What factors generally predicted helping across countries? The most consistent predictor of helping was the country's economic productivity: people in countries where earnings are *higher* actually helped *less*. People from countries with high rates of economic stability may have more negative attitudes about helping others than people from countries in which more people experience stressful financial situations and people therefore empathize more with those who need assistance. The most helpful countries (Brazil, Costa Rica, Malawi, and India) would all have been regarded as developing countries when the data were collected.

On average, people in cities from Latin America and Spain were more helpful than other international cities. Spanish and Latin American cultures are defined by their concern for the well-being of others, which includes a focus on being friendly, polite, and helpful to strangers (Levine et al., 2001).

Jennifer Bell and colleagues from the University of Alberta conducted a study on helping behaviour in Canada (Bell, Grekul, Lamba, Minas, & Harrell, 1995) and examined the willingness of Canadian students to tutor another student or to allow the student to borrow their lecture notes. The researchers found that the students were more willing to help by lending their notes or tutoring before an exam if the request came from a friend or from someone who they had frequent contact with, and if the person wasn't in competition with the helper. These findings were muddied somewhat, however, by the helpful Canadian student participants, many of whom refused to lend their notes and instead suggested going to photocopy them. The authors viewed this alternative means of helping as a "low cost" option—by accompanying the other student to the photocopier the lender didn't risk losing the notes.

Although there are national differences in prosocial behaviour, there are findings that appear to be universal rather than culturally proscribed. In particular, it has been found that people in large cities are generally unhelpful. Hedge and Yousif (1992) found no cultural differences between the United Kingdom and Sudan in the helping behaviour of people living in cities. In both countries, when helping was costly and the situation wasn't an emergency, people were less helpful in cities than in rural areas.

Studies have found that in some cases people from collectivistic cultures are less likely to seek help—and therefore less likely to receive help—than people from individualistic cultures. Specifically, people from collectivistic cultures may be less willing to seek social support when dealing with stressful events, because they're worried about the negative implications of support seeking on their interpersonal relationships (Kim, Sherman, Ko, & Taylor, 2006; Taylor et al., 2004). For example, support seeking could lead to burdening others with one's own problems, feeling embarrassed and losing face, or receiving criticism and poor evaluations from others. In line with this view, research reveals that Asian Americans and Koreans seek social support less frequently, and find such support less helpful, than do European Americans. This research indicates that cultural norms regarding relationships influence the use of social support as a method for handling stress.

In another multinational collaboration, Robert Levine and researchers from Israel focused on the value "embeddedness," a concept similar to collectivism as embedded cultures focus on the welfare of the in-group, and limit concern for outsiders' well-being (Knafo, Schwartz, & Levine, 2009). In this 21-nation study, researchers found a strong negative correlation between the embeddedness of a culture and people's willingness to offer help to a stranger (i.e., someone who wasn't an in-group member).

NORMS FOR HELPING

These differences in the rates of helping in different countries are due in part to the different norms for helping in different cultures. As you read at the beginning of the chapter, among Albanians *besa* is a norm for helping guests that will increase the likelihood of help being offered in Albania.

In one study, Americans and people from India were asked whether people in different situations have an obligation to help others (Miller, Bersoff, & Harwood, 1990). In some conditions, the help needed was minimal, such as giving directions or providing a ride to the train station. In other conditions, the help needed was extreme, such as donating blood or driving someone to the hospital. When the need to help was extreme or moderate, both Americans and people from India felt that help must be offered, but when the need to help was only mild,

FIGURE 13.6 HOW DOES CULTURE IMPACT NORMS FOR HELPING?

Researchers asked students from a collectivistic culture, India, and an individualistic one, the United States, how obligated they felt to help people with various needs. As predicted, in collectivistic cultures people viewed helping as required in more situations than did people from individualistic cultures.

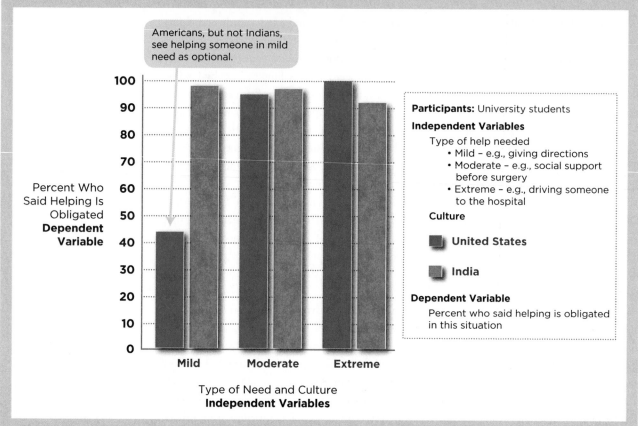

Source: Miller, J.G., Bersoff, D.M., & Harwood, R.L. (1990). Perceptions of social responsibilities in India and in the United States: Moral imperatives or personal decisions? *Journal of Personality and Social Psychology, 58*, 33–47.

people from India were much more likely than Americans to say that help must be offered (see Figure 13.6). Similarly, and as described at the start of this section, people from India are much more likely than Americans to see donating bone marrow as "morally required," even to a stranger.

Cultures also differ in how they view the norm of reciprocity, with a specific difference in the extent to which prosocial behaviour is influenced by concerns about reciprocity in helping (Miller & Bersoff, 1994). Americans see reciprocity (e.g., helping someone who has helped them) as a matter of personal choice. In contrast, people in collectivistic cultures see reciprocity as a moral imperative: when people receive help from another person, they then feel obligated to offer help to that person later on. On the other hand, people from India give less weight than Americans to rewards, payments, and self-interest in explaining altruistic behaviour.

MOTIVATIONS FOR HELPING

People in different cultures also vary in their motivations for helping. Researchers in one study compared Icelandic and Chinese children's motivations for helping (Keller, Edelstein, Schmid, Fang, & Fang, 1998). Children read a story in which a child had to choose between spending time with a long-time friend and going to a movie with a new friend. Then they answered a series of questions about the choice the child in the story should make, and why this choice was the right one. Compared to the Chinese children, the Icelandic children focused more on self-interest concerns (e.g., a desire to see the movie), and obligation (e.g., she's made a promise). The Chinese children focused more on altruistic and relationship concerns, such as taking the other person's needs into account (e.g., the new child doesn't know anyone else) and the quality of the friendship (e.g., they have been friends a long time).

THE BIG PICTURE

LINKING ALTRUISM AND PROSOCIAL BEHAVIOUR TO THE "BIG IDEAS"

This chapter included many applications of the three "big ideas" studied in social psychology. The examples below should help you see the connection between altruism and prosocial behaviour, and these big ideas, and contribute to your understanding of the big picture of social psychology.

THEME	EXAMPLES
The social world influences how we think about ourselves.	• Children who receive money for helping then describe their helping as motivated by this reward. • We give our friends less help if their success will make us look (and feel) bad. • Older adults who receive physical assistance experience higher rates of depression, because they're concerned about the perception that they need such support.
The social world influences our thoughts, attitudes, and behaviour.	• We tip more when we receive candy with our dinner bill. • We're more likely to help change a flat tire when we've just seen another person model this behaviour. • People in small towns get help faster than those in big cities.
Our attitudes and behaviour shape the social world around us.	• People with higher levels of empathy engage in more prosocial behaviour, including donating money to charitable causes and spending time helping people in need. • We help other people so that they'll follow the norm of reciprocity and help us when we're in need. • When smoke pours into a room, people in the room act as if they don't recognize the emergency—leading each other to ignore the emergency because nobody is reacting.

This chapter has examined five key principles of altruism and prosocial behaviour.

1. How do personal factors influence helping?

The first section examined how personal factors influence helping behaviour. We examined three factors that explain why people help those in need, including evolutionary factors, personality, and religion. You also learned that cueing people with religious words can increase prosocial behaviour.

2. How do situational factors influence helping?

We described several different situational factors that influence helping. You learned about the arousal/cost-reward model, which describes helping as influenced by the arousal caused by seeing someone in need as well as the costs and benefits of providing that help. In addition, this section described the impact of mood, modelling, and environmental factors on prosocial behaviour. You also learned that the large number of people who watched Kitty Genovese's attack partially explains why she didn't receive help.

3. Does pure altruism exist?

This section examined two competing views on whether true altruism exists. You learned about the empathy-altruism model that describes helping as motivated, at least at times, by true feelings of empathy for a person in need. This section also described the egoistic model, which describes helping as emerging from individuals' own selfish motives. You also learned that interpersonal attraction motives drive volunteerism with HIV patients for heterosexual people, and empathy-based motives drive such volunteerism for homosexual people.

4. Who gets help when they are in need?

This section described factors that impact whether people get help when they're in need. These factors include person factors (such as gender, age, attractiveness, and personality), social norms (such as reciprocity and social responsibility), and relationship factors (such as similarity and friendship). You also learned that women are more likely to get help than men are.

5. How does culture influence helping?

The final section examined the impact of culture on helping. You learned how culture impacts prosocial behaviour, including the frequency of helping, motivations for helping, and factors that increase helping. You also learned why people in India are as willing to donate bone marrow to a stranger as to a family member, but people in the United States are much more willing to donate to a family member than to a stranger.

Key Terms

altruism 440
arousal/cost-reward model 451
bystander effect 450
decision-making process
    model 447
diffusion of responsibility 450
empathy 444

empathy-altruism hypothesis 458
exchange relationships 471
good mood effect 454
kinship selection 441
moral reasoning 445
negative-state relief hypothesis 461
norm of reciprocity 468

norm of social responsibility 468
prosocial behaviour 440
self-evaluation maintenance
    model 471
urban overload hypothesis 456

Questions for Review

1. What are two personal factors that lead people to help those in need?

2. Describe each of the steps in the decision-making process model and the arousal/cost-reward model that predict when people will get help.

3. What are the empathy-altruism and egoistic models of helping? Which theory of altruism do you find more convincing, the egoistic or empathic perspective, and why?

4. Describe two types of people who are more likely to get help, and two types of people who are less likely to get help.

5. What is the impact of culture on the frequency, norms, and motivations of helping?

Take Action!

1. You are the parent of a 3-year-old girl. What two things could you do to help her become more altruistic?

2. Based on your knowledge of the decision-making process model for helping, what three things would you tell people to do if they need help in an emergency?

3. You're in charge of a blood drive for your sorority. How could you call upon people's empathy motives and egoistic motives to encourage them to show up and donate blood? Which approach should be more effective, and why?

4. Your roommate, Bill, is writing a lab report for his social psychology class. He would like a friend to read it over before he hands it in, and wonders whether it would be better to ask Susie (a friend who is a psychology major and is also in this same class) or Cindy (a friend who is a biology major). Who would you recommend, and why?

5. Your brother is travelling abroad to Japan for the first time. What would you tell him about his likelihood of receiving help if he needs it, and the factors that would motivate such help?

RESEARCH CONNECTIONS

Participate in Research

Activity 1 The Impact of Relatedness on Helping: This chapter has described how we're more likely to help people who share genes with us, and close relatives are therefore more likely to be helped than distant relatives or non-relatives. Go online to read about various people who need help, and rate how likely you would be to help in each situation.

Activity 2 Testing the Arousal/Cost-Benefit Model of Helping: One model that predicts helping behaviour is the arousal/cost-benefit model, which describes how the decision to help is influenced in part by the potential costs and benefits of helping in that particular situation. Go online to rate the costs and benefits of helping in different situations to see how these factors may influence your own prosocial behaviour.

Activity 3 The Impact of Empathy on Helping: This chapter described the importance of feeling empathy for another person in our decision of whether or not to help. Go online to read about various people who are in need of help, and then rate how much you empathize with each person—and how likely you would be to help.

Activity 4 Examining the Factors that Impact Who Gets Help: You learned in this chapter about the types of people who are more, and less, likely to receive help. Go online to read descriptions of people, and then rate how likely you would be to help each person.

Activity 5 The Impact of Culture on Helping: The final section of this chapter described how people from different cultures vary in how likely they are to help in different situations. Go online to rate how likely you would be to offer different types of help to a stranger—then see how other students rate their own likelihood of helping in these different situations.

Test a Hypothesis

One of the common findings in research on altruism is that people who are in a good mood are more likely to help than those who are in a neutral mood. To test whether this hypothesis is true, design a study in which you first create a good mood in some people (for example, through giving people a piece of candy, or smiling at them) but not in others. Then, measure whether those who are in a good mood are more likely to help someone. You can then go online to report your findings to other students.

Design a Study

Go online to design your own study testing the factors that influence helping behaviour. You'll be able to choose the type of study you want to conduct (self-report, observational/naturalistic, or experimental), choose your own independent and dependent variables, and form your own hypothesis. Then you can share your findings with other students across the country!

14

INTERPERSONAL ATTRACTION AND CLOSE RELATIONSHIPS

DID YOU EVER WONDER?

During the G20 summit meeting in Toronto, hundreds of social activists marched on the streets of downtown Toronto protesting against the summit. The media covered numerous stories of the demonstrators and the police reaction to them. However, there was another story, one with a different flavour, that was also covered by reporters. An article in the *Globe and Mail* drew a link between being passionate for a cause and falling in love, using headings throughout the article such as, "Protest Dating," "Hook Ups are Bound to Happen," and "Demonstrating for Love" (Dea, June 25, 2010). Several people who had met during this or other demonstrations and subsequently "hooked up" were interviewed for the article, and as one of the protesters said

Photo by Sarah Dea

in her interview, "It [the demonstration] is not a dating service but a lot of people are young and single." One story was about two graduate students from York University who met on the picket lines during the strike at their university. They started dating and fell in love. The couple later took part in other demonstrations, including the G20 summit. Although such stories highlight the importance that having similar attitudes has in attraction, they also serve as examples of the effect on attraction that physiological

 LAW CONNECTIONS	 MEDIA CONNECTIONS	 HEALTH CONNECTIONS	 BUSINESS CONNECTIONS
Benefits of Physical Attractiveness in Occupation and Crimes	Does the Internet Facilitate Intimacy or Inhibit It?	Why We Get by with a Little Help from Our Friends (and Pets)	The Impact of Culture on Attitudes about Work

arousal from one source can have when it's (mis)attributed to another source. This chapter will describe factors that impact on interpersonal attraction and close relationships. You'll also find answers to these questions:

 Why are secret affairs often very exciting?

 Why do we feel different about those we love compared to those we are *in* love with?

 Why do couples who engage in novel tasks report more satisfaction in their relationships than those who engage in mundane tasks?

 Why are men more concerned about their partner having sex with someone, and women more concerned about their partner falling in love with someone?

 Why do Israeli children have very good best friends, and Arab children very good friendship networks?

WHAT YOU'LL LEARN
· ·

What predicts interpersonal attraction

What love is

What predicts relationship satisfaction

Common problems in close relationships

How culture influences interpersonal attraction and close relationships

PREVIEW
· ·

The need to form close interpersonal bonds with others is a fundamental part of human nature (Baumeister & Leary, 1995; Reis & Collins, 2004; Reis, Collins, & Berscheid, 2000). As noted by William James in 1920, "Human beings are born into this life span of which the best thing is its friendships and intimacies." We care about what other people think of us, we want to form close and intimate relationships, and we feel sad when these relationships end. Close relationships can also have a number of psychological as well as physical benefits; people in a close relationship are happier and even live longer than those who aren't. Although we all have many types of close relationships (e.g., friends, family members, romantic partners), most North American university students report feeling closest to a romantic partner (Berscheid, Snyder, & Omoto, 1989). In this chapter, we will focus primarily on romantic relationships.

> For love is as strong as death.
> Its passions are as cruel as the grave
> And its flashes of fire are the very flame of God.
> ("The Song of Songs," c. 900–300 BCE)

· ·

WHAT FACTORS LEAD TO ATTRACTION?

Have you, or someone you know, ever tried to hide a romantic relationship from others? If so, you probably know that just trying to keep it secret makes the relationship more exciting and romantic. Dan Wegner and his colleagues at the University of Virginia conducted a series of studies to examine the special allure of "secret relationships" (Wegner, Lane, & Dimitri, 1994). They hypothesized that keeping a secret may increase relationship excitement because people have to exert time and energy suppressing their desire to talk about the relationship to others. To test this hypothesis, unacquainted students were told that they would play a communication game with a partner. Some students were told that they should communicate with their partner using their feet (e.g., by tapping their feet under a table to convey information) so that they could beat the other couple seated with them at the table. In one condition, all four participants were told that one couple would be communicating in this way. In the other condition, the other participants weren't told about this secret form of communication. Researchers then measured attraction for the partner. As predicted, participants who played "footsie" with their partner and kept this communication secret showed higher levels of attraction for each other than couples that sat near each other without touching. Couples who played "footsie" in secret also reported higher levels of attraction for each other than those who played "footsie" when the others at the table were aware of this behaviour. These findings suggest that keeping a secret with one's partner leads to increased attraction. This section will examine this and other factors that influence interpersonal attraction, including physical attractiveness, similarity (a relationship factor), and proximity (a situational factor).

PHYSICAL ATTRACTIVENESS

We are drawn to physically attractive people. Aesthetic appeal is desirable and leads to positive affect (Kenrick, Groth, Trost, & Sadalla, 1993). We like to look at things that we find visually appealing, and hence people show a general preference for objects that they find attractive. This preference influences not only the people we choose to date, but also the cars we buy, the paintings we like to look at, and the clothes we wear. Infants as young as two to three months of age show a preference for looking at pictures of attractive people rather than less attractive people (Langlois, Ritter, Roggman, & Vaughn, 1991). Moreover, people from diverse backgrounds and cultures generally agree on what is physically attractive—and that physical attractiveness is associated with many benefits.

THE BENEFITS OF PHYSICAL ATTRACTIVENESS.

Not surprisingly, the attractiveness of the other person plays a large part in determining attraction in interpersonal relationships. Physically attractive people experience many benefits, including a greater likelihood of being hired for a job, higher starting salaries, and bigger raises (Biddle & Hamermesh, 1998; Frieze, Olson, & Russell, 1991; Hamermesh & Biddle, 1994; Marlowe, Schneider, & Nelson, 1996). For example, using a 5-point scale of attractiveness, it was found that each point on the scale corresponded to an additional $2,100 per year in earnings for a woman, and an additional $2,600 a year for a man (Frieze et al., 1991). Attractiveness can also contribute to job security. Researchers in one study examined teaching evaluations for 463 courses taught by 94 faculty members at the University of Texas at Austin (Hamermesh & Parker, 2005). Professors who were the most attractive received, on average, evaluations of about 4.5 (on a 5-point scale). Those who were the least attractive received evaluations of about 3.5. Because tenure in universities is determined in part by teaching evaluations, these findings mean that attractive professors have a distinct advantage in keeping their jobs. In Law Connections, we have further explained the benefits of physical attractiveness both in the workplace and in the legal system.

LAW CONNECTIONS

Benefits of Physical Attractiveness in Occupation and Crime

ABC-TV / THE KOBAL COLLECTION / FELD, DANNY

Many people admire, even envy, those people who are physically beautiful. A great deal of research has found that people's attitudes and inferences are influenced by an individual's physical attractiveness (Hosoda, Stone-Romero, & Coats, 2003). Past research has demonstrated that attractive people are assumed by others to have more positive personality traits and, therefore, will experience a more positive life than unattractive people

(Dion, Berscheid & Walster, 1972). Physically attractive people are more likely to be hired for a job, have higher starting salaries, and receive bigger raises (Biddle & Hamermesh, 1998; Frieze, Olson, & Russell, 1991; Hamermesh & Biddle, 1994; Marlowe, Schneider, & Nelson, 1996). For example, an interview study of over one thousand employed Canadians found that attractive respondents earned higher salaries than less attractive respondents (Roszell, Kennedy & Grabb, 1989). For each point one rises on a 1 to 5 scale of attractiveness, respondents' income was $1,988 higher than less attractive respondents. This finding was truer for men, older respondents, and those in occupations held traditionally by men and less likely for women, younger respondents, and those in occupations traditionally held by women.

(continued)

Furthermore, the physical attractiveness has benefit for those who commit crimes. It has been found that the attractiveness of the defendant impacts decisions made in the legal system, including likelihood of receiving a guilty verdict and the severity of the sentence given (DeSantis & Kayson, 1997; Downs & Lyons, 1991; Lieberman, 2002; Mazzella & Feingold, 1994). In one study, researchers studied the court cases of 74 defendants in criminal court. People who were attractive received significantly lower penalties than those who were less attractive (Stewart, 1980; 1985).

When interpreting these results, one should use caution and understand that there are cultural differences in the salience of the physical attractiveness stereotype. We will discuss the role of sociocultural factors in relation to physical attractiveness later in the chapter. Other possibilities that may explain these findings, at least in the North American context, include the tendency for unattractive people to commit more crimes, the perception that crimes are committed by attractive people must be less serious, and the belief that what is beautiful is good and, therefore, attractive people would not commit serious crimes.

Some studies have found that the effects of physical attractiveness in a courtroom could be reduced by increasing jury deliberation (MacCoun, 1990). Marc Patry (2008) from Saint Mary's University found that mock jurors are more likely to find a physically attractive defendant guilty after deliberation than after no deliberation. Patry argued that jury deliberation increases the evidence-based decision-making and decreases pre-existing bias. Therefore, when there is no deliberation, bias in favour of physically attractive defendants leads to finding the person not guilty. However, this bias is not present when there is a jury deliberation. In fact, Patry (2008) found after a jury deliberation, attractive defendants were more likely to be found guilty than unattractive defendants, perhaps because attractive people are held to a higher standard and are more harshly punished when they do not live up to those standards. It should be noted that one limitation of mock jury studies like including Patry's experiment, is that participants are not real jurors who deal with actual cases. Therefore, the findings may not be generalizable to real world settings.

WHY DOES PHYSICAL ATTRACTIVENESS LEAD TO ATTRACTION?

BIOLOGICAL EXPLANATIONS. Humans have evolved preferences for physical features that indicate health or reproductive success. People who are beautiful have a symmetrical face and a well-proportioned body, signifying by virtue of these characteristics that they're more likely to be healthy, have genetic superiority in terms of vulnerability to disease, and, therefore, be reproductively fit (Fisher, 2004).

Researchers have also found that when heterosexual men look at an attractive female the area of the brain that is activated is the same area that is associated with other types of rewards, including monetary gain and drugs, suggesting that when men see a beautiful woman they may be experiencing reward in a similar way to winning a cash prize or getting high (Aharon et al., 2001).

Although you may believe that different people find different characteristics attractive, what people find beautiful is quite consistent. If you find yourself in a remote area of Africa and judge who you consider to be a physically attractive man or woman among those around you, a local would probably agree with you. For example, prominent cheekbones, thin eyebrows, and big eyes are commonly viewed as attractive. These preferences are found among people in different ethnic groups within a given culture (for example, in Canada, among Caucasians, Asians, First Nations peoples, and descendants of people from the Caribbean). They're also found across different cultures (Langlois et al., 2000). In one study, researchers examined ratings of beauty made by American college students and foreign college students who had newly arrived in the United States from various countries (Japan, China, Guatemala, Panama, etc.; Cunningham, Roberts, Barbee, Druen, & Wu, 1995). Ratings of beauty were very similar across students from these different backgrounds.

One reason for this consistency in what is seen as attractive is that people prefer faces that are "average" as opposed to "distinct" (Langlois & Roggman, 1990; Rhodes, Halberstadt, Jeffery, & Palermo, 2005). This may seem like an odd finding, but people find composite photos (those that are made up of multiple different photos) more attractive than the individual faces that make up the composite (although the most attractive single faces are still seen as

FIGURE 14.1   THE ATTRACTIVENESS OF AVERAGE FACES

Judith Langlois and colleagues (Langlois & Roggman, 1990; Langlois, Roggman, & Musselman, 1994) used image morphing technology called Morph Age to create images that were composites of multiple faces. To do this, they used images of university male and female students. They took facial photos and defined the curves of different features such as eyebrows, hairline, irises, nose, mouth, and lip line. Then, they used Morph Age to create averages of these facial features. They repeated the process five times, first combining two 2-face morphs creating 4-face morphs. Second, they combined two 4-face morphs creating 8-face morphs. Next, they combined two 8-face morphs creating 16-face morphs. Finally, they combined two 16-face morphs creating 32-face morphs. Langlois and colleagues found that participants rated composite faces of male and female as significantly more attractive than the individual faces that were used to create the composite.

AVERAGED CAUCASIAN FEMALE FACES

  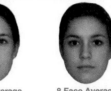

| 2 Face Average | 4 Face Average | 8 Face Average | 16 Face Average | 32 Face Average |

Source: "Averaged Caucasian Female Faces" from Langlois social development lab, online: http://homepage.psy.utexas.edu/homepage/group/langloislab/averagenessbeauty.html (accessed September 16, 2011).

more attractive than the composite). Do you find this difficult to believe? See how you would rate the photos in Figure 14.1. Moreover, our preference for "average" faces is not unique; people even find average dogs and birds more attractive than unique ones (Halberstadt, 2006; Halberstadt & Rhodes, 2000).

Composite photos are also rated as more familiar, leading to a possible explanation put forward by Philip Cooper and Daphne Maurer from McMaster University for people's preference for composite photos. As composite pictures may resemble internal face prototypes that we form from experience—a kind of composite mental picture—they may therefore seem more familiar to us than faces that are more distinct and unique, and, as described later in the chapter (recall the mere exposure effect from Chapter 6), we tend to like what we are familiar with (Cooper & Maurer, 2008). Another possible explanation for people's preference for composite pictures is that these pictures tend to be more symmetrical because they average the slight differences between people. People do find symmetry attractive (Halberstadt & Rhodes, 2000; Rhodes, Sumich, & Byatt, 1999). For example, Shackelford and Larsen (1997) found that people with symmetrical faces were rated as more physically attractive and as healthier and more dominant/extroverted. Even within pairs of identical twins, the more symmetrical twin was rated as more attractive (Mealey, Bridgstock, & Townsend, 1999). There is even evidence from researchers at Lakehead University that women's ability to detect facial symmetry increases when they're menstruating, suggesting that they may be more susceptible to attractive (symmetrical) men at this time (Oinonen & Mazmanian, 2007).

SOCIO-PSYCHOLOGICAL EXPLANATIONS. People may want to associate with attractive people because such relationships could lead to social profit (e.g., you look good if your date is good looking; Geiselman, Haight, & Kimata, 1984). In fact, people who are standing with others who are attractive do seem more attractive than those who are standing with unattractive people. This is one reason why attractive people have more dating and sexual experience (Langlois et al., 2000).

In an experimental study by Sigall and Landy (1973), it was found that both male and female participants rated a man who was with an attractive girlfriend more favourably than when he was with an unattractive woman. Participants formed an enhanced impression of a man with a beautiful woman in terms of confidence, friendliness, and likeability. Furthermore,

Sigall and Landy (1973) found that when participants were associated with a beautiful woman the participants believed that others had an enhanced impression of them in terms of confidence, talent, and sociability than when they were associated with an unattractive woman.

People hold a "what is beautiful is good" stereotype. In other words, we see attractive people as also having a variety of other positive traits (Eagly, Ashmore, Makhijani, & Longo, 1991; Feingold, 1992; Langlois et al., 2000). Attractive people are rated as higher in intelligence and social competence, and are seen as better adjusted and more extroverted/dominant. Charlene Ryan, Joel Wapnick, and their colleagues from McGill University have even found that pianists (both concert pianists and grade six students) who were rated as physically attractive were also rated higher on aspects of their technical performance than pianists judged to be less attractive (Ryan, Wapnick, Lacaille & Darrow, 2006; Wapnick, Mazza & Darrow, 2000). Attractive people are also expected to have better lives (e.g., happier marriages, more prestige, more social success). As discussed in Chapter 7, attractive people are more persuasive. So, for better or for worse (perhaps depending on your own level of attractiveness), people do judge books by their covers.

Attractive people also tend to possess greater social skills, so they may be more fun to be around. One explanation for this link between attractiveness and social skills is that people who are attractive are consistently treated better, including having more positive interactions, fewer negative interactions, and more help, attention, and rewards (Zebrowitz, Collins, & Dutta, 1998). Additionally, when interacting with an attractive person, people elicit nurturing and sociable behaviour. In other words, the social stereotypes of the perceiver that attractive people are friendly and likeable leads to behaviour by the target individual confirming the stereotype (i.e., self-fulfilling prophecy). For example, in a study it was found that women who are called by men who believe these women are attractive (based on a photograph that the men are given) are much more socially engaging and friendly on the phone compared with women who are called by men who believe they are unattractive (Snyder, Tanke, & Berscheid, 1977).

In turn, these frequent and positive interactions could lead attractive individuals to develop greater social skills. In one study, pairs of unacquainted male and female college students were asked to have a conversation (Stiles, Walz, Schroeder, & Williams, 1996). Those who were attractive and who were interacting with an attractive partner engaged in more self-disclosure.

But do attractive people really have more desirable characteristics? In a word, yes (on average). Attractive people are less lonely, less anxious, more popular, more sexually experienced, and even smarter (Diener, Wolsic, & Fujita, 1995; Feingold, 1992; Langlois et al., 2000). Not surprisingly, they also feel better about themselves. It's worth noting, though, that we not only think that beauty is good, but also think that what is good is beautiful. Sampo Paunonen at the University of Western Ontario found that women were rated as more attractive in appearance when raters were led to believe that the target was honest than when they were told she was dishonest (Paunonen, 2006).

"Would you mind taking a picture of me with your girlfriend?"

Questioning the Research:

How can it be that people seem *more* attractive when they're with very attractive people when the contrast effect would lead us to the hypothesis that being with a highly attractive person would make the other person seem *less* attractive by comparison?

According to evolutionary psychologists, men and women have evolved different mate preferences because these preferences maximize their reproductive success (Buss, 1989; Buss & Schmitt, 1993). Specifically, there is a differential parental investment: women spend more time caring for an offspring and therefore have to be more selective than men, who can reproduce with little subsequent investment. As women who are pregnant or nursing may have difficulty in securing their own resources, they need to have partners with resources to provide for them and their child. Women are therefore motivated to look for and maintain relationships with men who have high levels of education and well-paying jobs (Buss & Shackelford, 1997). This is why men may go out of their way to emphasize the resources they could provide to a potential partner, such as saying they intend to go to law school, driving an expensive car, or paying for dinner. Some intriguing research even suggests that women's preferences for resources may vary depending on their likelihood of becoming pregnant, as described in the Would You Believe box.

[WOULD YOU BELIEVE…]

WOMEN ESPECIALLY PREFER ATTRACTIVE MEN DURING THEIR TIMES OF PEAK FERTILITY?

Women's preference for men with resources may be particularly strong during times of peak fertility, when conception is most likely to occur. One study examined women's preferences for different men as a function of whether they were currently in a fertile versus non-fertile period of their menstrual cycle (Gangestad, Simpson, Cousins, Garver-Apgar, & Christensen, 2004). In this study, women saw brief segments of videotaped interviews with various men, who varied on a number of characteristics, including social presence (e.g., athletic presentation, eye-contact, composure, lack of self-deprecation, and lack of nice-guy self-presentation) and direct competitiveness (e.g., derogation of other men, lack of mentioning a nice personality, lack of laughing). Then the women rated each man in terms of his attractiveness for a short-term mate (meaning he would be appealing for a short-term sexual affair) as well as a long-term mate (meaning he would be appealing in terms of a long-term relationship). In line with predictions from evolutionary theory, women who are in a fertile period of their cycle prefer men with both social presence and direct competitiveness when they're imagining a short-term mate. However, fertility is not associated with such preferences when women are considering a longer-term mate. Women at times of peak fertility are also more concerned with the attractiveness of potential mating partners, suggesting that those who are most likely to conceive are more focused on how physically attractive their partners are (Beaulieu, 2007). These findings suggest that during times of fertility, women show a particular preference for sexual partners with traits that indicate masculinity, dominance, and attractiveness.

Research also indicates that women may behave in particularly appealing ways during times of fertility, perhaps in an attempt to attract a desirable mate. In one unusual study, researchers calculated the tips earned by strippers through lap dancing during different times of their monthly cycle (Miller, Tybur, & Jordan, 2007). As predicted, strippers earn more tips during the time in their monthly cycle when they're ovulating (about $15 an hour more than at other points in their cycle), presumably because this is when women are most interested in having sex. Moreover, strippers who were taking birth control pills—which work by inhibiting ovulation—didn't have an earning peak halfway through their cycle.

According to evolutionary theory, men's short-term sexual strategy is based on obtaining many partners (to spread their genes as widely as possible), whereas women seek partners who will stick around and provide (helping them ensure the survival of their genes post-natally). Meeting a person who might be good for a short-term affair (easy sexual access) could intensify men's short-term romantic desires, but not women's. In a series of studies to test this hypothesis, men's and women's attraction to various partners was tested as a function of the type of partner (e.g., easy sexual access versus relationship exclusivity; Schmitt, Couden, & Baker, 2001). During some interviews, participants were exposed to an experimental confederate exhibiting cues to easy sexual access (e.g., "I'm kind of a flirt really. Lately, though, my dates have been calling me too much, you know what I mean, especially the night after"). In other cases, they were exposed to a person cueing more difficult sexual access (e.g., "I don't like to waste time on dates, though, unless it's with someone interested in the same thing I am—a long-term, exclusive relationship"). In the context of short-term mating, men rated targets who exhibited cues to easy sexual access as more desirable than did women.

CRITIQUES OF THE EVOLUTIONARY PERSPECTIVE.   Although these evolutionary-based explanations for gender differences in attraction may seem to "make sense," some researchers point out flaws in this theory. First, these gender differences are much more pronounced when you ask people for their preferences in short-term and casual dating situations than in long-term and more committed ones (Kenrick, Sadalla, Groth, & Trost, 1990; Kenrick et al., 1993). No real difference between what men and women want in the context of long-term relationships has been identified—both prefer exclusive partners. Similarly, there are no gender differences in the desirability of a potential marriage partner based on his or her sexual experience. In terms of dating potential, women valued men more highly who had moderate sexual experience. On the other hand, men placed the highest value on women with high sexual experience (Sprecher, McKinney, & Orbuch, 1991).

Additionally, both men and women prefer physical attractiveness in a short-term mate (Li, Bailey, Kenrick, & Linsenmeier, 2002; Li & Kenrick, 2006), and both men and women are more selective when selecting a long-term partner than a short-term partner (Stewart, Stinnett, & Rosenfeld, 2000). Moreover, some research suggests that people report sex differences in the importance of attractiveness and earning potential, but their actual interest in real-life partners (i.e., their behaviour rather than self-report, what they do rather than what they say they do) shows no gender differences on these traits (Eastwick & Finkel, 2008). Research Focus on Gender describes gender differences in terms of sexual behaviour.

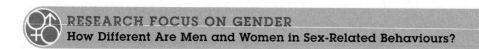

RESEARCH FOCUS ON GENDER
How Different Are Men and Women in Sex-Related Behaviours?

Although people in general show a preference for physically attractive dating partners, men and women differ in the extent to which they prefer attractive partners (Buss & Schmitt, 1993; Feingold, 1990, 1991; Fletcher, Tither, O'Loughlin, Friesen, & Overall, 2004). As you might expect, men place more importance on physical attractiveness in a dating partner than women do. One out of every three men advertising in personals requests an attractive partner, whereas only one in seven women make such a request (Koestner & Wheeler, 1988; Rajecki, Bledsoe, & Rasmussen, 1991). Similarly, women's ads tend to offer physical attractiveness (e.g., describe what they looked like), suggesting that they're aware of what men are hoping to find in a dating partner. Men also prefer partners who are younger than themselves (Buss, 1989; Rajecki et al., 1991). These preferences for a physically attractive partner are generally found in homosexual as well as heterosexual men (Bailey, Gaulin, Agyei, & Gladue, 1994; Kenrick, Keefe, Bryan, Barr, & Brown, 1995).

In contrast, women give more weight than men to traits that signify resources, such as wealth, ambition, character, and status (Buss & Schmitt, 1993; Feingold, 1992). Compared to men, women are more willing to date and marry someone who is not good looking, is older by five or more years, earns more, and has more education (Buss, 1989; Rajecki et al., 1991; Sprecher, Sullivan, & Hatfield, 1994). In line with this preference, women's personal ads are much more likely than men's to request professional status in a partner (Koestner & Wheeler, 1988; Rajecki et al., 1991). Women are also attracted to men who are confident (another potential cue to resources), but men don't really care about women's dominance (Sadalla, Kenrick, & Vershure, 1987).

Data on gender differences in preferences for sexual partners also reveal mixed results. For example, if you ask men and women for their desired number of lifetime sexual partners, there are large differences—men want an average of 7.69, compared to women, who want an average of 2.78 (Pederson, Miller, Putcha-Bhagavatula, & Yang, 2002). These general findings about gender differences in desire for sexual variety are found across diverse cultures, again providing support for an evolutionary theory (Schmitt et al., 2003). However, the majority of both men and women report the ideal number of partners over the next 30 years is one, and 99 percent of both men and women say they want to ultimately settle down (in the next five years) with a single partner. In sum, although men are more interested than women in having multiple sexual partners, if you ask people to think about the number of sexual partners they'd like to have over the next 30 years, these gender differences largely disappear.

Another critique of the evolutionary argument is that women generally don't prefer men who have stereotypically masculine traits and high levels of resources. Specifically, both men and women see androgynous dating partners as more desirable, and feminine characteristics as better than masculine ones (Green & Kenrick, 1994; Ickes, 1993). For example, prosocial men (those who are willing to help others) are rated higher in physical and sexual attractiveness, social desirability, and dating desirability than non-prosocial men (Jensen-Campbell, Graziano, & West, 1995). On the other hand, dominant men are not rated higher than prosocial men on any measures of attraction.

Pat Barclay (2010) from the University of Guelph found that when female university students perceived men as altruistic this increased the men's perceived desirability as potential dating partners (i.e., for a short-term relationship or a single date). There was no such effect for men, with a female student's perceived altruism not adding to her attractiveness as a potential dating partner. However, both men and women desired altruistic characteristics in their partner for more committed (i.e., long-term) relationships. It is important to note that Barclay's study is derived from evolutionary theory (as are several of the others cited in this section) and although the study shows the desirability of altruism, it does not address the relative importance of altruism versus other traits like attractiveness, dominance, or status.

Comstock Images/Getty Images, Inc.
Women aren't just interested in men with resources—they also want men who are caring.

A related finding is that women don't just want men with resources—they want men with particular character traits, such as talent and ambition, which in turn may lead to the acquisition of resources (Hanko, Master, & Sabini, 2004). In one study, participants read about a man who had a net worth of $14 million. Some people read that he had earned this fortune by winning the lottery. Others read that he had earned this money through selling a dot-com company. Women, but not men, rated the lottery winner as less attractive than the dot-com creator. These findings suggest that even when women show a preference for men with resources, this preference is heavily influenced by their assumptions about the man's ability to acquire these resources (or, more simply, "resources + luck" is worth less than "resources + perceived ability").

There are researchers who point to a sociocultural explanation for these gender differences in mate preferences (Eagly & Wood, 1999). Alice Eagly and Wendy Wood argue that these preferences simply reflect long-standing gender differences in societal roles. With men having greater opportunity to pursue economic resources (such as education and jobs), women have traditionally needed to look for men with such resources because they don't have access to these benefits themselves. In line with this view, men and women were more similar in their mate preferences in the 1990s than they were earlier in the 20th century (Buss, Shackelford, Kirkpatrick, & Larsen, 2001). In the 1990s, both sexes, but especially men, placed greater importance on finding a partner with good financial resources. Both men and women also increased in the importance they placed on finding a physically attractive partner. So, while women may have originally needed to find men with high resources, they now have the luxury of looking for partners with other traits (and vice versa, with men now also having the luxury to seek a partner who is both good looking and capable of providing resources).

Further evidence for the role of sociocultural differences in influencing mate preferences is found in research showing that gender differences in mate preferences differ across different societies (Eagly & Wood, 1999). In societies where women have little access to resources, such as Kenya, Pakistan, and Haiti, the women continue to show a strong preference for wealthy, well-educated, and high-status men. But in societies where women have considerable access to resources, such as Norway, Australia, and the United States, such preferences are minimal. For example, when researchers examine societies in which women participate equally with men in economic, political, and decision-making roles, women are less concerned about how much their partners make. These data indicate that as women gain power and resources, they're less focused on choosing mates who also have power and resources.

Because men can produce children with many different women, it has also been argued, they prefer partners who are more likely to produce healthy children (Buss & Shackelford, 1997). They also devote more time and energy to finding—and keeping—partners who are

FIGURE 14.2 CHANGING MODELS OF PHYSICAL ATTRACTIVENESS OVER TIME

As shown in this figure, what is seen as attractive has varied considerably over time, from the rather heavy woman portrayed in the painting, to Marilyn Monroe, who was seen as a paragon of attractiveness in the 1950s, to the very thin model who may be seen as representing attractiveness today.

Sources: (a) *Helena Fourment in a Fur Wrap*, 1636–38 by Peter Paul Rubens (1577–1640) Kunsthistorisches Museum, Vienna, Austria/ The Bridgeman Art Library; (b) ©Sunset Boulevard/Corbis; Antonio de Moraes Barros Filho/WireImage/Getty Images, Inc.

young and healthy, because these traits are seen as cues of health and more fertility (see Figure 14.2). In support of this evolutionary argument, men do show a preference for women with particular types of bodies (those whose waists are narrower than their hips), perhaps because this hourglass figure is associated with fertility (Singh, 1993, 1995). For example, men judge women with a low waist-to-hip ratio (meaning a narrow waist relative to hip size) as more attractive than those with higher ratios (meaning a large waist relative to hip size). They also rate these figures as higher in attractiveness, health, and reproductive fitness.

CONTRAST EFFECT. We're attracted to physically attractive individuals, but how attractive we find them also depends on the attractiveness of those whom we compare them to (Kenrick & Gutierres, 1980; Kenrick, Gutierres, & Goldberg, 1989; Kenrick, Neuberg, Zierk, & Krones, 1994). In other words, a particular dating partner might look very attractive when you're comparing him or her to other university students, but could somehow seem less attractive when compared to movie stars and models. As you read in Chapter 5, our evaluations of a particular object are often influenced by the other objects used in the comparison—a $200 sweater may not seem like a bargain until you find a very similar sweater that sells for $300.

The contrast effect can have a strong impact on ratings of attractiveness (Kenrick et al., 1994). In one study, men were asked to rate the attractiveness of a woman they could supposedly go on a blind date with (Kenrick & Gutierres, 1980). Half of the men rated the prospective blind date candidate as they were watching *Charlie's Angels* (a television show featuring three attractive crime-fighting women who often wore bikinis). The other half rated this woman while they were watching a television show that featured less attractive actors. As predicted, the same blind date candidate was rated much more highly when the men were watching the neutral show than when they were watching *Charlie's Angels*. Similarly, men who looked at centrefolds from *Playboy* and *Penthouse* then rated their own partners as lower in attractiveness

(Kenrick et al., 1989). The contrast effect can also have consequences for relationship longevity: the commitment of men who are in dating relationships decreases when they see a group of attractive women (Kenrick et al., 1994).

The contrast effect can also influence women's ratings of their partners. Women's commitment to their current relationship decreases once they see a group of dominant men (Kenrick et al., 1994). As noted earlier in this chapter, women are particularly interested in partners with resources, and dominant men are seen as more likely to have resources. In sum, how attractive a person finds his or her own and other potential partners is a function not only of the target's desirability, but also of the desirability of other people in the environment who are used for comparison.

SIMILARITY. We like people who are similar to ourselves, including those who share our attitudes, values, and interests, as well as those who share demographic characteristics (e.g., age, ethnicity, religion, economic background; Botwin, Buss, & Shackelford, 1997; Caspi & Herbener, 1990). In one study, students were given fictional data about another student's attitudes, and were then asked to rate how much they liked this other student (Byrne, 1997). Those who thought the other person shared none of their attitudes rated the person an average of 4.41 (on a 14-point scale, where a higher number indicates greater liking). Those who thought they shared half of their attitudes gave an average rating of 7.20. Finally, those who thought they shared all of their attitudes rated the person an average of 13.00. We also tend to seek and find partners who are at roughly our own level of physical attractiveness: this is referred to as the **matching hypothesis** (Feingold, 1988; Kalick & Hamilton, 1986).

matching hypothesis – people's tendency to seek and find partners who are roughly at their own level of physical attractiveness

Why does similarity lead to attraction? In part because people who share our important traits and values make us feel good about ourselves. After all, we're motivated to like ourselves and our views, so it's rewarding when someone else feels the same way. We also see similar people as more likeable and attractive (Moreland & Zajonc, 1982), in part because we believe similar others will like us (Condon & Crano, 1988). Having a partner who shares our valued attitudes also reduces the potential for conflict. Just imagine the consequences of dating a person who disagreed with your major political and religious beliefs.

Similarity in a romantic partner also leads to happiness (Botwin et al., 1997; Byrne, 1997; Luo & Klohnen, 2005). In one study, 93 cohabiting and married couples described their attitudes and relationship satisfaction (Aube & Koestner, 1995). When researchers asked these couples to report their relationship satisfaction 15 months later, those who were similar in attitudes had greater satisfaction.

"We laugh at the same things."

© Bernard Schoenbaum/ The New Yorker Collection/ www. cartoonbank.com

COMPLEMENTARITY. Although similarity is a strong predictor of attraction, can *complementarity* also lead to attraction? Despite the proverb "opposites attract," little research shows that people are attracted to those who are fundamentally different from themselves. In fact, qualities in a partner that are different from one's own are initially arousing and exciting, but can later be strongly disliked (the "fatal attraction" effect; Felmlee, 1995, 1998). Students who rated traits in their partner as "different" and "exciting" are more likely to experience dissatisfaction later on than those who rated their partners as similar in personality and/or interests. In sum, qualities that we initially see as unusual and exciting can eventually cause irritation.

Based on the self-evaluation maintenance (SEM) model, our self-concept can be threatened if our friends or our partner outperform us (Tesser, 1980). This is particularly damaging if we make comparisons in a domain that is central to our self-concept. For instance, if you and your romantic partner both strive to be good musicians and being an accomplished musician is a central part of who you are, it's inevitable that you'll engage in a comparison of

Questioning the Research:

This research shows a correlation between similarity and attraction, but it does not, of course, prove whether people develop greater attraction to each other *because* they're similar to one another or if a third variable explains this association. Can you think of some alternative explanations for this association between similarity and attraction?

your accomplishments as musicians and find that one of you is likely to be better, or more successful, than the other. According to the SEM model, this comparison process has a negative effect on one of the partners, and the relationship is likely to suffer as a result. The theory predicts that liking and attraction increase when friends and partners are successful in different domains and, thus, are less likely to compete in the same domain (Tesser, 1980; Tesser & Smith, 1980). In sum, similarity in attitudes and complementarity in performance domains increase liking and attraction.

reciprocity – in-kind response to the behaviour of others

RECIPROCITY. Another strong predictor of attraction is **reciprocity.** In general, reciprocity means in-kind response to the behaviour of others: that is, a positive behaviour in response to a positive behaviour and a negative behaviour in response to a negative behaviour. In this context, reciprocity means that people are attracted to people who they think are attracted to them (i.e., who reciprocate their attraction; Aron, Dutton, Aron, & Iverson, 1989). People often report starting a friendship or dating relationship because the other person liked them—we all like to be liked, and therefore are attracted to those who like us. Interestingly, having someone grow to like you more over time can lead to especially strong feelings of attraction. In a study by Aronson and Linder (1965), two "subjects" (one was a genuine participant and the other a confederate of the researcher) talked over seven sessions, and the participant received the confederate's rating of the participant's personality after each session. Those who were told that they were never liked by the confederate (28 negative things were said) and those who were told that they had been liked by the confederate but no longer were (8 positives, 14 negatives) didn't like the confederate very much. However, those who were told that they were always liked by the confederate (28 positives) liked the confederate quite a bit, and those who were told that they weren't liked by the confederate at first but now were liked (8 negatives, followed by 14 positives) liked the confederate the most. This is true even though in the latter condition fewer positive things were said and more negative things were said than in the "always liked" condition.

Believing that someone likes you can also lead to greater self-disclosure over time (Collins & Miller, 1994). This is the quid pro quo of mutual exchange. We feel happy when people share things with us because it implies trust and respect in the relationship (Miller, 1990; Taylor, Gould, & Brounstein, 1981). In turn, we disclose more to people who disclose to us. We also like people who disclose to us, and like them even more after we disclose to them. In one study, 202 college students engaged in brief get-acquainted conversations with a stranger (Vittengl & Holt, 2000). Students who engaged in greater self-disclosure during the conversation showed a more positive mood after the conversation, including greater happiness and excitement, as well as greater liking for their conversation partner.

You may be questioning these findings about the power of reciprocity—after all, doesn't conventional wisdom tell us that it's better to play "hard to get"? Well, playing hard to get means walking a very fine line: we are indeed *more* interested in dating people who seem selective or choosy in their partner selections than those who seem indiscriminate (Eastwick, Finkel, Mochon, & Ariely, 2007), but we are *less* interested in pursuing potential dating partners who seem "impossible to get" (Walster, Walster, Piliavin, & Schmidt, 1973). So, be careful in the use of this strategy—it can backfire. Perhaps being selective in who you appear "hard to get" to is the best strategy. In one study, male college students read information about five women who were potential dating partners. One woman appeared to everyone as a very difficult person to date (she had given all of the prospective dating partners she evaluated low ratings). One appeared very easy for all men to date (she had given all of the men high ratings). And one appeared easy for the participant to date, but hard for others to date (i.e., she had only rated the participant highly). The majority of participants saw the "selectively hard" woman as friendlier and warmer as well as less problematic to date, and 59 percent chose this woman from the five options they were given. Of course, all this means is that if a woman finds a particular man attractive and wants to attract him, she should flirt with him and not with other men ("Duh!").

PROXIMITY. Some of the earliest research on the predictors of interpersonal attraction revealed that we're attracted to those who are familiar to us (Festinger, Schachter, & Back, 1950). One reason that proximity tends to lead to attraction is simply that you're more likely to meet and get to know, and therefore become attracted to, people who live or work near you. Proximity to another person is strongly associated with the number of "memorable interactions" (Latané, Niu, Nowack, Bonevento, & Zheng, 1995).

The attraction caused by proximity is not simply due to the opportunity to meet and interact with people, but also due to the familiarity that comes with seeing these people repeatedly over time (Bornstein, 1989; Harmon-Jones & Allen, 2001; Moreland & Zajonc, 1982). In fact, the more we're exposed to something, the more we like it, a phenomenon called mere exposure (as you recall from Chapter 6). Richard Moreland and Scott Beach (1992) conducted a very clever study to test the power of mere exposure on interpersonal attraction. Four women who were similar in age and appearance were randomly assigned to attend a certain number of class sessions of a social psychology course. One of the women attended the class five times, another attended 10 times, a third attended 15 times, and the fourth never attended the class. Each time the woman attended the class, she entered the back of the classroom and walked to the front to take a seat so that a majority of students could see her. During the last week of class, all of the students in the class rated the attractiveness of each of the four women. As predicted, women who attended the class more times were rated as more attractive.

Yet another explanation for the impact of proximity on attraction is ease of maintaining the relationship. It simply takes less effort to manage a friendship with someone who lives next door or across the hall than with someone who lives in a different city or province. Relationships can indeed persist over great distances, but usually only important ones (e.g., with relatives or very close friends). The Internet does, however, make it easier to "meet" and develop relationships with people who may be physically distant but in virtual proximity, as the Media Connections box shows.

MEDIA CONNECTIONS

Does the Internet Facilitate Intimacy or Inhibit It?

With our increased reliance on the Internet for communication over the last 20 years, researchers have started examining how Internet use influences interpersonal relationships. One concern that has been expressed is that the Internet can discourage real (as opposed to virtual) relationships—people may be spending time online (e.g., "talking" in chat rooms, updating their status, sending emails, shopping) instead of spending time interacting with real people and thereby forming real relationships.

Does time on the Internet lead to gaining relationships? Not really. One survey found that only 22 percent of respondents (all of whom had been using the Internet for two or more years) had made a new friend online—and, as you might imagine, more than 22 percent of people make a new friend in real life during this amount of time. The Internet may also have different effects on different people. For example, some evidence suggests that greater Internet use is associated with positive outcomes, such as increased community involvement and decreased loneliness, for extroverts, but the reverse for introverts

(Kraut et al., 2002). Similarly, adolescents who are lonely and socially anxious are more likely to use the Internet to interact with strangers as opposed to close friends (Gross, Juvonen, & Gable, 2002). This means the Internet may be serving as a means to connect with those who are not part of one's daily life, which in turn could impair the formation of normal social relationships.

© M4OS Photos / Alamy

On the other hand, other research points to the value of the Internet in helping people meet and form relationships (Bargh, McKenna, & Fitzsimons, 2002; McKenna & Bargh, 1998, 2000; McKenna & Green, 2002). For example, McKenna and colleagues

(continued)

found that 63 percent of respondents had spoken on the telephone with someone they'd met on the Internet, and 54 percent had met in person. Of those who began a romantic relationship via the Internet, 71 percent were still in these relationships two years later. And, surprisingly, people who first meet online express greater liking for one another than those who first meet in person

(McKenna et al., 2002). Less positively in terms of relationships, the social networking site Facebook is reported to have been cited in approximately one fifth of divorce cases in the UK (the *Daily Telegraph*, 2009). Couples are said to use the website to find evidence of cheating or flirting, which has then led to marital breakdown.

PREDICTORS OF ATTRACTION IN FRIENDSHIP

Although this section has focused on the predictors of interpersonal attraction in romantic relationships, many of these factors also predict attraction in friendships. For example, similarity is a strong predictor of attraction and satisfaction in friendships (Cash & Derlega, 1978; McKillip & Reidel, 1983; Morry, 2005). In one study, researchers examined satisfaction in randomly assigned roommate relationships (Carli, Ganley, & Pierce-Otay, 1991). People with roommates who were similar to themselves in personality and physical attractiveness were more likely to choose to room again with the person the following year. Similarly, Kuperschmidt and colleagues found that as similarity across age, gender, academic, and social attributes increased in third- and fourth-grade students, so did friendship (Kuperschmidt, DeRosier, & Patterson, 1995).

Proximity is another strong predictor of attraction in friendships. In one of the first studies to examine the role of proximity, Leon Festinger and his colleagues (1950) investigated friendship patterns in a large apartment complex in which residents were simply given apartments as they became available—they didn't choose where exactly they would live within the building. Many more people reported developing friendships with those who lived near them, such as next door to them or in their hall, than with those who lived farther away. For example, 41 percent of the residents said a next-door neighbour was their best friend, 22 percent had a best friend two doors away, and 10 percent found a best friend at the end of their hall. More recently, and as shown in Figure 14.3, students who were randomly assigned to sit next to

FIGURE 14.3   DOES PROXIMITY INFLUENCE ATTRACTION?

Students were randomly assigned to sit next to someone, or in the same row as someone, in a psychology class for a semester. Researchers then measured the liking for that student a year later. As predicted, students who were assigned to sit in neighbouring seats for a semester felt friendlier toward each other than those who sat farther apart.

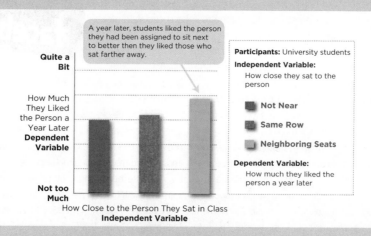

Source: Back, M.D., Schmukle, S. C., & Egloff, B. (2008). Becoming friends by chance. *Psychological Science, 19*, 439–440.

someone in a psychology class for a semester liked that person more a year later than they did those who weren't sitting in such close proximity (Back, Schmukle, & Egloff, 2008). Once again, proximity breeds attraction—even in friendships.

FACTORS THAT INFLUENCE ATTRACTION

FACTOR	EXAMPLE
Physical attractiveness	Sarah's roommate, Jen, is very attractive. She receives much attention from others, including frequent invitations to parties, numerous phone calls, and even two job offers.
Similarity	Your brother just got engaged to his long-time girlfriend, Cheryl. You're certain they'll have a great marriage because they have so much in common: they both love bowling, dogs, the beach, and movies.
Reciprocity	Roberto was flattered when Antonio, a good-looking international student from Brazil, invited him to his birthday celebration. Soon after, they started dating each other.
Proximity	Norman and Melba live in adjoining apartments. They met one day on the elevator on the way to the laundry room and have been dating ever since.

WHAT IS LOVE?

Think about different relationships in your own life—with parents, siblings, friends, and dating partners. How would you describe the type of love you feel for each person? To examine this question, researchers in one study asked participants to list all of the people in their social world who fit into one of two categories: *love* and *in love* (Meyers & Berscheid, 1997). As predicted, participants saw these different types of relationships in very different ways. First, they listed more people in the "love" category (nine to 10 people) than in the "in love" category (generally one person). Second, although both men and women reported being "in love" with the same number of people, women reported "loving" more people than did men. Beverley Fehr from the University of Winnipeg and James Russell from the University of British Columbia asked Canadian students to rate different types of love in terms of how prototypical of the concept of love each type was (Fehr & Russell, 1991). Of 20 possible types of love, the students chose, in the following order, these five as being the strongest prototypes of love: maternal love, parental love, friendship, sisterly love, and romantic love. So, what exactly is love, and how is it defined differently by different people? To answer this question, we will examine four theories about love: triangular theory, the love styles theory, arousal-attribution theory, and reward theory.

TRIANGULAR THEORY

According to Robert Sternberg (1986; 1997), there are three distinct components of love: *passion*, *intimacy*, and *commitment*. Sternberg's passion consists of deep physical attraction to the person as well as constant thoughts about—and even obsession with—the person (see Figure 14.4). This type of love is also related to sexual desire (Regan, 2000). On the other hand, the component of intimacy consists of great liking and emotional closeness to another person (again, this component is similar to companionate love). Finally, the third component, commitment, refers to your degree of connection and responsibility to the other person.

As shown in Figure 14.4, the three components of love lead to seven possible types of love: people can experience love as only one of the three components, as any two of the

FIGURE 14.4   TRIANGULAR MODEL OF LOVE

According to the triangular model of love, passion, intimacy, and commitment are each distinct components of love, and relationships may have one, two, or all three of these components (Sternberg, 1986; 1997).

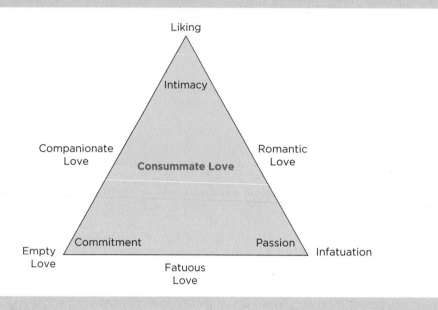

companionate love – a stable, calm, and dependable kind of love that may include quiet intimacy, stability, shared attitudes/values/life experiences, and high levels of self-disclosure

components, or as all three of the components. Romantic love, such as that shown in many movies, includes the components of passion and intimacy. **Companionate love** includes the components of intimacy and commitment.

HOW STRONGLY DO YOU FEEL PASSIONATE LOVE?

The Passionate Love Scale

INSTRUCTIONS: *Rate each item on a scale of 1 (strongly disagree) to 6 (strongly agree).*

1. I sense my body responding when ____ touches me.

2. I would feel deep despair if _____ left me.

3. I possess a powerful attraction for _____ .

4. _____ always seems to be on my mind.

5. I eagerly look for signs indicating _____'s desire for me.

6. I would rather be with _____ than anyone else.

7. I melt when looking deeply into _____'s eyes.

8. No one else could love _____ like I do.

9. For me, _____ is the perfect romantic partner.

10. Sometimes I feel I can't control my thoughts; they are obsessively on _____ .

[RATE YOURSELF]

SCORING: Sum up your total score on these 10 items.

INTERPRETATION: This scale measures passionate love, meaning the cognitive, emotional, and behavioural reactions we have toward a person we love (Hatfield & Sprecher, 1986). Higher scores indicate more intense feelings, whereas lower scores indicate less intense feelings.

TABLE 14.1	Love Styles
The love styles model describes the three primary styles of love (*eros*, *storge*, and *ludus*) and the three secondary styles (*pragma*, *mania*, and *agape*; Hendrick & Hendrick, 1986).	
Eros (passionate love)	My lover and I were attracted to each other immediately after we first met.
Ludus (uncommitted love)	I try to keep my lover a little uncertain about my commitment to him/her.
Storge (friendship love)	It's hard for me to say exactly when our friendship turned into love.
Mania (obsessive love)	I considered what my lover was going to become in life before I committed myself to him/her.
Pragma (practical love)	When things aren't going right with my lover and me, my stomach gets upset.
Agape (selfless love)	I try to always help my lover through difficult times.

Although the triangular theory of love describes all three components of love as defining complete love (*consummate love*), people can experience other types of love that have only one or two of the three components (Sternberg, 1986). A relationship with only passion and intimacy is a type of fleeting romantic love (such as a brief but intense summer fling), and a relationship with intimacy and commitment is described as companionate love (and may represent some marriages that have lasted for considerable time). However, relationships that include all three components are the happiest and most long-lasting (Whitley, 1993).

CHANGES IN LOVE ACROSS RELATIONSHIP STAGES. Scores on each of the love components tend to change over time in a relationship. In one study, researchers examined scores on each of the three components over time in 446 individuals in a romantic relationship (Lemieux & Hale, 2002). As predicted by the triangular model, intimacy and passion scores were lowest for those who were casually dating. These scores were higher for participants who were engaged, but lower again for those who were married. Not surprisingly, commitment scores increased at each of these three levels of relationship seriousness.

LOVE STYLES THEORY

The love styles theory classifies types of love in a different way (Hendrick & Hendrick, 1986, 1993, 1995; Lee, 1988). The love styles theory (as shown in Table 14.1) includes six distinct love styles: *eros* (passionate love), *ludus* (uncommitted love), *storge* (friendship love), *mania* (obsessive love), *pragma* (practical love), and *agape* (selfless love). People with an *eros* love style are drawn to romantic partners with specific physical qualities (the "type" they prefer), have an intense focus on their dating partners, and tend to be high in self-esteem (Campbell, Foster, & Finkel, 2002). The *ludus* style views romantic relationships as a playful sort of game in which everyone has fun and no one gets too serious. The *storge* love style is similar to companionate love—it describes love as a secure and trusting friendship. *Pragma* is a very practical, or pragmatic, type of love. People who have this love style aren't looking for great excitement and passion, but rather security and the appropriate "fit." *Mania* is similar in some ways to our concept of romantic love, including passion. But this type of love also includes negative elements, such as jealousy and obsession, and is seen most commonly in those with low self-esteem. Finally, *agape*, the rarest of the love styles, describes love as giving and selfless. People who have *agape* love are more concerned about their partner's well-being than their own well-being.

IMPACT ON RELATIONSHIPS. These love styles are also associated with relationship preferences in interaction, satisfaction, and longevity. First, people tend to prefer dating partners who have similar love styles to their own (Davis & Latty-Mann, 1987; Hahn & Blass, 1997). Participants in one study read brief descriptions of potential dating partners. Each of

Questioning the Research:

This research indicates that the experience of love is different for people depending on the type of relationship. But does this finding indicate correlation or causation? Can you think of some alternative explanations for this association?

these partners described themselves as having characteristics of one of the six love styles. Then participants were asked which person they preferred to date. As predicted, people generally preferred dating partners who were similar to themselves on love styles.

Love styles also influence interaction within ongoing dating relationships. In one study, members of 57 university student dating couples completed measures of their love styles as well as relationship satisfaction (Hendrick, Hendrick, & Adler, 1988). For men, high scores on *eros* and low scores on *ludus* were associated with high satisfaction. For women, high scores on *eros* and low scores on *mania* were associated with high satisfaction. Findings from the two-month follow-up revealed that couples that stayed together were higher on *eros* and lower on *ludus*. In sum, lasting relationships involved both passionate and committed love.

AROUSAL ATTRIBUTION THEORY

Arousal attribution or the misattribution of physiological arousal is evident in many real-life situations. One of the most poignant examples of this effect was seen in the years following the 9/11 terrorist attacks. Many firefighters who survived these attacks came to the aid of women who lost their firefighter husbands. This support was intended to provide these widows with the type of assistance their husbands would have provided, such as managing home repairs, mowing the lawn, and helping with the children. But in several cases, the firefighters ultimately left their own wives and families and began romantic relationships with the widows of their former colleagues (CBS News, 2003). These relationships can be explained at least partially by the misattribution of arousal caused by grief and sadness, which then gets misinterpreted as deep romantic love.

excitation transfer – when the arousal caused by one stimulus is added to the arousal from a second stimulus and the combined arousal is erroneously attributed to the second stimulus

Attraction is physiological arousal, which can lead to excitation transfer (Allen, Kenrick, Lindner, & McCall, 1989; Foster, Witcher, Campbell, & Green, 1998; Zillman, Katcher, & Milavsky, 1972). **Excitation transfer** occurs when the arousal caused by one stimulus is added to the arousal from a second stimulus and the combined arousal is attributed (erroneously) to the second stimulus. This misattribution of arousal from one source to a second source (the two factors) is based on Schachter's two-factor theory of emotion (Schachter & Singer, 1962).

passionate love – an intense, exciting, and all-consuming type of love, which includes constant thoughts about the person, powerful physical attraction, and intense communication

Passionate love is an emotional state in which arousal is interpreted as attraction to a romantic stimulus. Hatfield and Sprecher (1986) describe passionate love in terms of the interaction between mind and body. **Passionate love** is an intense, exciting, and all-consuming type of love, which includes cognitions (e.g., constant thoughts about the person), emotions (e.g., a powerful physical attraction), and behaviour (e.g., intense communication). Passionate love describes your first crush and initial stages of love in new relationships—when you can't get the person out of your mind (see the Rate Yourself box).

According to arousal attribution theory, passionate feelings should increase when we're aroused. This point was demonstrated in a Canadian field study by Donald Dutton and Arthur Aron (1974; 1989) from the University of British Columbia. The experiment was conducted on two bridges in Vancouver. One bridge (the experimental bridge) was long, narrow, wobbly, and was suspended 230 feet over Capilano Canyon. The other bridge (the control bridge) was solid, wide, and was 10 feet above a small river. Male participants who crossed the bridge were approached by either a female or a male interviewer. Participants were told that the interviewer was working on a project for his or her psychology course and were asked if they were willing to complete a questionnaire about creative expression. Participants were also asked to write a brief story, which later was analyzed for sexual imagery. When the participants completed the questionnaire, the researcher thanked them and gave a phone number at which to reach the researcher and invited the participants to call if they would like to know more about the study. The results indicated a gender effect as more participants accepted the phone number from the female than from the male interviewer. The female interviewer was also contacted more often than the male interviewer. More

FIGURE 14.5   DOES PHYSIOLOGICAL AROUSAL IMPACT ATTRACTION?

Men walked across either a sturdy or a shaky bridge to an experimenter who asked them to fill out a questionnaire. After they finished completing the questionnaire, the experimenter, who was either male or an attractive female, thanked them for their participation, and then gave participants a phone number to reach the experimenter if they had any questions about the study. Although men who crossed either bridge were quite unlikely to later call a male experimenter with questions, men who crossed a shaky bridge to the female experimenter were quite likely to later call her—perhaps because they misattributed their physiological arousal that was caused by the shaky bridge to feelings of attraction to the woman.

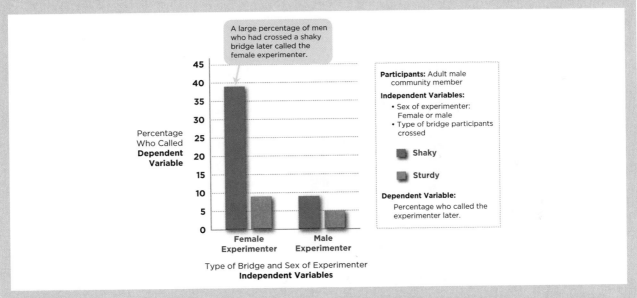

Source: Dutton, D.G., & Aron, A.P. (1974). Some evidence for heightened sexual attraction under conditions of high anxiety. *Journal of Personality and Social Psychology, 30,* 510–517.

importantly, the results indicated that compared to those who crossed the control bridge, significantly more people who crossed the experimental bridge called the female interviewer. As shown in Figure 14.5, men who crossed the shaky bridge to the female experimenter were much more likely to call than those in any of the other conditions. These men misattributed the physiological arousal caused by the situation (i.e., the shaky bridge and their fear of falling) to the female experimenter, and hence were probably calling to act on their feelings of attraction. Do you see a parallel between the findings of this study and the opening story of this chapter? Participating in a demonstration, rallying on the street, and marching with hundreds of other people create physiological arousal causing excitation, which could transfer to another person, leading to attraction.

Another study, White, Fishbein, and Rutstein (1981), also examined attraction as a function of arousal and physical attractiveness. Male participants listened to one of three audiotapes that varied in the arousal they would elicit. The negative arousal tape was a horrific description about a missionary who was being mutilated while his family was watching. The positive arousal tape was a selection from comedian Steve Martin's album *A Wild and Crazy Guy.* The neutral tape was an excerpt about the circulatory system of frogs from a biology textbook.

Next, participants were told that they were going to meet with a female participant on a brief date and talk about their reactions to the audiotape they had just heard. After being told this, they then watched a videotape of a potential date, who was either an attractive woman (wearing tight clothes, makeup, saying how she wanted to meet someone) or an unattractive woman (wearing baggy clothes, awful makeup, with a scarf over her head, saying that she had a bad cold). The men then rated how attracted they were to each woman (measured with four items on a 9-point scale).

FIGURE 14.6 DOES ATTRACTIVENESS INFLUENCE AROUSAL AND PHYSICAL ATTRACTION?

Male participants listened to a tape eliciting either negative arousal, positive arousal, or no arousal. Participants then rated their level of romantic attraction to a female participant who was either attractive or unattractive. Results indicated that participants reported higher romantic attraction to the attractive female confederate than to the non-attractive confederate, particularly when they were in the two arousal conditions.

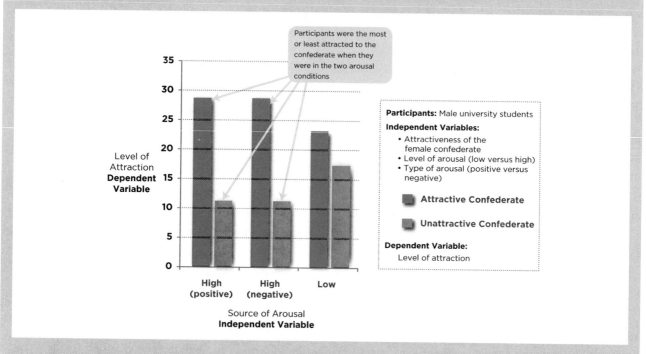

Source: White, G. L., Fishbein, S., & Rutsein, J. (1981). Passionate love and the misattribution of arousal. *Journal of Personality and Social Psychology, 41,* 56–62.

As shown in Figure 14.6, participants reported higher romantic attraction to the attractive female confederate than to the non-attractive confederate. Additionally, when the female confederate was attractive, the level of romantic attraction was the highest in the two arousal conditions, produced either by positive or negative tapes. When the female confederate was unattractive, the level of romantic attraction was the lowest in the two arousal conditions. This indicates that participants associated their arousal, which was produced by listening either to a funny or a disturbing tape, to their liking of the woman. If the woman was attractive, the highly aroused men reported they were highly attracted to her compared to men who were not aroused (whether or not the stimulus to the arousal was positive/humorous or negative/horrific). If the woman was unattractive, the highly aroused men reported they disliked her more than did men who were not aroused. This implies that the theory of passionate love and arousal attribution can be extended to a theory of aversion: arousal makes attractive people seem more attractive and makes us more aversive toward people we find unattractive.

REWARD THEORY

The basic principle of reward theory is that we like the people who are present when we experience reward (Lott & Lott, 1974). This type of association is called classical conditioning. As explained in Chapter 6 on attitudes, classical conditioning refers to the association of a neutral stimulus with another stimulus in order to get a given reaction. For example, you may feel good (an unconditioned response) every time you dance (an unconditioned stimulus). The link between dancing and feeling good is an association that you haven't learned. As it

FIGURE 14.7　CLASSICAL CONDITIONING

Classical conditioning helps explain why a previously neutral stimulus, such as the smell of a given perfume, initially creates no reaction, but over time, through pairing with something that does create a reaction, can lead to that reaction entirely on its own.

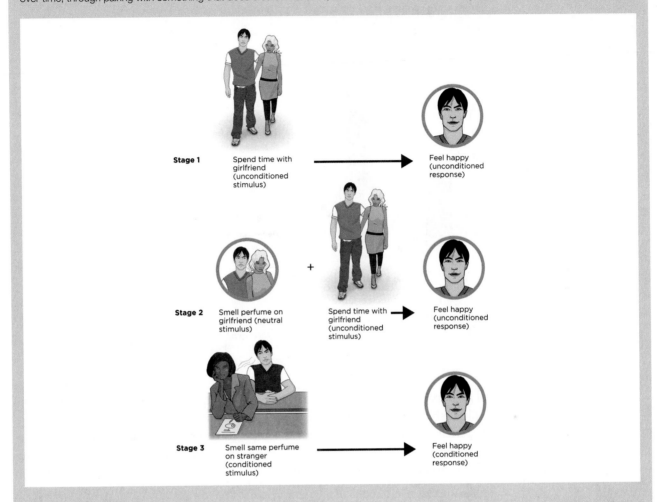

Stage 1　Spend time with girlfriend (unconditioned stimulus)　→　Feel happy (unconditioned response)

Stage 2　Smell perfume on girlfriend (neutral stimulus)　+　Spend time with girlfriend (unconditioned stimulus)　→　Feel happy (unconditioned response)

Stage 3　Smell same perfume on stranger (conditioned stimulus)　→　Feel happy (conditioned response)

involves an unconditioned stimuli and an unconditioned response, it comes naturally to you. If, however, the stimulus is repeatedly paired with a specific person over time, that person (a conditioned stimulus) will come to elicit the same positive feeling (now a conditioned response). This positive response could be called attraction as you now feel an attraction toward that person because you associate the person with the positive feeling. Note that the person doesn't need to cause the positive response. In other words, the person doesn't need to play music, to be a dance instructor, or even to dance with you to be liked. Rather if he or she is around every time you dance, you'll associate this person with the positive feeling. In general, if you consistently feel good when you're around a particular person, you end up liking that person. See Figure 14.7 for another example of classical conditioning.

A study conducted at Kansas State University provides support for a relationship between attraction and positive conditions, such as air temperature (Griffitt, 1970). In this study, 40 male and female undergraduate students read information about a stranger whose attitudes were similar to their own on either 25 percent or 75 percent of issues. The participants had to rate their attraction to the stranger based on this information. Half of the participants sat in a room with a normal temperature where the environment was considered pleasant, and the other half sat in a room that was hot, humid, and unpleasant.

FIGURE 14.8 DOES ROOM TEMPERATURE AFFECT LEVEL OF ATTRACTION?

Participants read information about a stranger whose attitudes were either similar to their own or different. Participants next had to sit in a room that either had a pleasant temperature or was hot and unpleasant and rate how much they liked the stranger. It was found that participants who sat in the room with a pleasant temperature liked the stranger more than those who sat in the hot room.

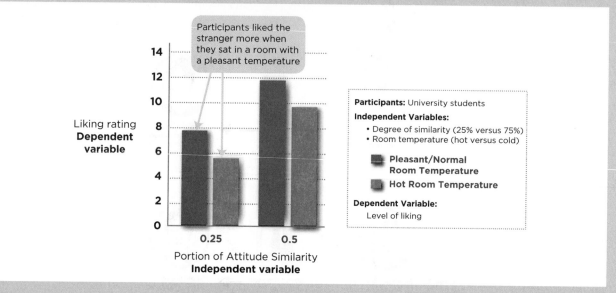

Source: Griffitt (1970). Environmental effects on interpersonal affective behavior. Ambient effective temperature and attraction. *Journal of Personality and Social Psychology, 15,* 240–244.

All participants sat in the room for 45 minutes and completed the study. Not surprisingly, the results of the study indicated that participants liked the stranger who was more similar to them (75 percent similar attitudes) than less similar (25 percent similar attitudes). The more important finding of the study, however, was that participants who were sitting in the normal temperature room liked the stranger even more than those who were sitting in the hot and humid room (see Figure 14.8). According to Griffitt, the feelings that the participants experienced due to temperature manipulation while in the room came to be associated with the stranger. Under the hot conditions, participants had the most negative feelings toward the stranger, and under the normal and pleasant conditions participants had the most positive feelings toward the stranger.

WHY DOES LOVE MATTER?

Experiencing love, however we define it, is very important for our psychological and physical well-being (Reis & Aron, 2008). Being in love makes us feel better about ourselves, which translates into higher levels of self-esteem and self-efficacy (Aron, Paris, & Aron, 1995). Just thinking about a close relationship helps people cope with threatening information about themselves (Kumashiro & Sedikides, 2005).

Developing loving close relationships is good for our physical well-being. One study of over 1,000 patients with confirmed heart disease found that those with a spouse or close confidant had lower rates of mortality (Williams, Kimble, Covell, & Weiss, 1992). Eighty-two percent of those who were married or had a close confidant lived for at least five years, compared to only 50 percent of those without such support. Similarly, women in highly satisfying marriages experienced better health than those in marriages with low satisfaction or who were single, widowed, or divorced (Gallo, Troxel, Matthews, & Kuller, 2003). The Health Connections box describes the benefits of a particular type of relationship—with our pets—on our physical well-being.

HEALTH CONNECTIONS

Why We Get by with a Little Help from Our Friends (and Pets)

You probably already know that close relationships make you feel happy. Did you also know that these relationships can make you healthier? People who have close interpersonal relationships experience positive health outcomes, including greater psychological well-being, greater physical well-being, faster recovery from illness, and, most importantly, lower rates of mortality (Allen, 2003; Stroebe & Stroebe, 1996). For example, among men who received heart surgery, those who were married requested less pain medication and recovered more quickly (Kulik & Mahler, 1989). Married patients who received high support were also released an average of 1.26 days sooner than those who received low support.

But we don't just benefit from having social support from people. Even pets can provide us with helpful support (Allen, Blascovich, Tomaka, & Kelsey, 1991). In one study, 938 people aged 65 or older were interviewed by telephone about their health status, social support, pet ownership, and frequency of doctor visits (Siegel, 1990). People with pets had fewer doctor visits. Pet ownership was particularly beneficial for those who experienced many stressful events. Those who had experienced many stressful events and didn't have a pet had an average of 10.37 doctor visits during the year compared to 8.38 for those who had a pet. Under circumstances of experimentally produced stress (a cold pressor and an arithmetic task), it has been found that pet owners had significantly lower heart rate and blood pressure levels during a resting baseline, significantly smaller increases (i.e., reactivity) from baseline levels during the mental arithmetic and cold pressor circumstances, and faster recovery than people without pets. Reactivity was lowest and recovery fastest when the pet was present in the room (Allen, Blascovich, & Mendes, 2002).

© Louise Heusinkveld / Alamy

These studies all point to the benefit of social support, even from our pets, for psychological and physical well-being.

Finally, love even seems to be processed at a neurological level. Participants who are asked to think about their romantic partner while in a functional magnetic resonance imaging (fMRI) machine show distinct patterns of brain activation (Aron, Fisher, Mashek, Strong, Li, & Brown, 2005; Bartels & Zeki, 2000; Fisher, Aron, Mashek, Li, & Brown, 2002). Feelings of romantic love may neurologically resemble the impact of a drug, which could help explain the intensity of romantic feelings (see Research Focus on Neuroscience). It could also help explain the intensity that occurs when love goes awry—jealousy, stalking, and spousal homicide.

 RESEARCH FOCUS ON NEUROSCIENCE
The Brain in Love

"Have you just fallen madly in love?" This question was posted on the psychology bulletin board on the SUNY Stony Brook campus in New York. Students who had fallen in love within the previous few months and had strong and vivid passionate feelings toward their beloved were invited to take part in the study. Dr. Helen Fisher (2004) was the researcher behind the study. She was interested in looking at the brains of those who were in love. After a screening process, 20 participants were selected to take part in the study. On the day of the experiment, participants were asked to bring a picture of their beloved and a picture of a neutral person. Each participant was then put in an fMRI machine that records blood flow in the brain and shows the brain cells that are active. The brain was scanned multiple times while the participant was looking at the picture of the beloved, than the picture of a neutral person, and counting backwards, as a distraction task between viewing the two photos. It was found that when participants were looking at the picture of their beloved, than the

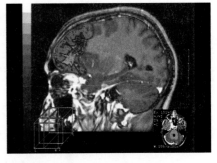

Photo Researchers
Brain scan showing emotional activity.

caudate nucleus, a large c-shaped part of the brain, was very active. The caudate nucleus is part of the brain's reward system and is associated with pleasure, motivation, focused attention, and arousal. Additionally, when the participants were gazing at the photo of their beloved, there was a high level of activity in the ventral tegmental area (VTA), which produces and distributes dopamine to many parts of the brain.

It was also found that romantic love is produced by specific chemicals in the body (Fisher, 2004). People who are in love have elevated levels of dopamine and norepinephrine, and a low level of serotonin. High dopamine is associated with excessive energy and sleeplessness (e.g., talking about the beloved all night), focused attention (e.g., remembering the smallest details about the beloved), dependency (e.g., craving the union with the beloved), and sexual desire and exclusivity. High norepinephrine is associated with loss of appetite and increased memory (e.g., cherishing moments spent with the beloved). Low serotonin is associated with obsession. Romantic lovers cannot stop thinking about each other and as their love affair intensifies, their obsessive thinking also increases.

[CONCEPTS IN CONTEXT]

THEORIES OF LOVE

THEORY	EXAMPLE
Triangular theory	Kent and Rory have been married for six years. They share great intimacy and are highly committed to the relationship. But after the birth of their second child, they feel lower levels of passion.
Love styles theory	Alexandra and Adrian were close friends in university. They continued to talk and see each other frequently after graduation, and over time their friendship evolved into a romantic relationship.
Arousal attribution theory	Aldéric just returned from his morning run when in the elevator he met his attractive new neighbour, Alexis. The next day he asked her out.
Reward theory	Donatien's favourite hobby is cooking. He attends a cooking class three times a week and met Émilie there. After six months, Donatien and Émilie started dating.

WHAT PREDICTS A HAPPY AND HEALTHY RELATIONSHIP?

How happy are you in your current (or were in your most recent) romantic relationship? Do you know what makes you happy? Some research in social psychology suggests that one important predictor may be the amount of time and energy we have put into the relationship (Drigotas, Safstrom, & Gentilia, 1999). Because our relationships have a significant impact on our psychological—and even physical—well-being, we want to be in happy and healthy relationships. This section will examine two models of relationship satisfaction and maintenance: **attachment styles**, **positive illusions**, social norms, and social exchange theory.

attachment styles – the expectations that a person has about a relationship partner, based largely on the person's early experiences with his or her caregivers

positive illusions – the notion that people tend to see their romantic partners as well as their relationships in highly idealized ways

ATTACHMENT STYLES

Research in developmental psychology demonstrates that children form close attachments to their parents and those who care for them (Bowlby, 1982, 1988). These attachment bonds give children a sense of security, and thereby provide reassurance in unfamiliar and upsetting

Table 14.2	Models of Attachment Styles
The attachment style model links research in developmental psychology to research in social psychology and is one of the most studied theories in the field of close relationships. Which of the following descriptions best describes you?	
Secure	I find it relatively easy to get close to others and am comfortable depending on them and having them depend on me. I don't often worry about being abandoned or about someone getting close to me.
Avoidant	I am somewhat uncomfortable being close to others. I find it difficult to trust them completely, difficult to allow myself to depend on them. I am nervous when anyone gets too close, and, often, love partners want me to be more intimate than I feel comfortable being.
Anxious	I find that others are reluctant to get as close as I would like. I often worry that my partner doesn't really love me or won't want to stay with me. I want to merge completely with another person, and this desire sometimes scares people away.

Source: Hazan, C., & Shaver, P. (1987). Romantic love conceptualized as an attachment process. *Journal of Personality and Social Psychology, 52*, 511–524.

situations. However, the precise nature of the parent-child attachment varies, with some children forming a secure attachment and others forming an insecure attachment bond (Ainsworth, Blehar, Waters, & Wall, 1978; Bowlby, 1982, 1988). Children with a secure attachment bond have parents who are available and responsive to their children's needs, and hence the children feel comfortable depending and relying on their parents and comfortable with exploring new situations.

In contrast, children who form an insecure attachment bond can have an anxious/ambivalent attachment or an avoidant attachment. A third style of anxious attachment has also been identified by Main & Solomon (1986), known as disorganized insecure attachment. This is relatively infrequent, however, with estimates of its occurrence at around 5 percent (Main & Solomon, 1986). Children with an anxious/ambivalent attachment have parents who are inconsistent in how they respond to their child's needs; they are available, and even intrusive, at times, but are unavailable at other times. These children have difficulty trusting and relying on others, although they want very much to have intimate and close relationships. On the other hand, children with an avoidant attachment have parents who are consistently unavailable, and may even be rejecting or dismissive of the child. These children, not surprisingly, seem not to need or desire close relationships, and may reject such closeness even when it's offered.

It would appear that the attachment style that we develop in childhood, as a result of the parenting style we are exposed to, becomes a kind of blueprint for how we expect relationships to be throughout life, and we tend to have some consistency between our attachment style as a child and our attachment style in adult relationships. Research by Cindy Hazan and Phil Shaver (1987) revealed that individuals also report having attachment styles toward romantic partners in adulthood that resemble childhood attachment styles (Brennan & Shaver, 1995; Feeney, 1996; Feeney & Collins, 2001). Approximately 59 percent of adults classify themselves as secure, about 25 percent classify themselves as avoidant, and only 11 percent classify themselves as ambivalent (with the remaining 5 percent showing roughly equal scores on two attachment styles; Mickelson, Kessler, & Shaver, 1997; see Table 14.2). Adults with a secure attachment style feel comfortable getting close to others, and don't worry about becoming overly dependent or about being abandoned by their partners. Those with an anxious attachment style want desperately to have close relationships, but they are less trusting of others and fear that their partner will leave them, and hence can become jealous and possessive. Individuals with an avoidant attachment style are less interested in close relationships and less invested in them. They rarely seek support from their dating partners and pull away from them in stressful situations. Attachment styles are fairly stable across different relationships, meaning that people who are secure in one relationship are likely to be secure in all of their relationships (Brumbaugh & Fraley, 2006). Anna Doyle and colleagues from Concordia University found that Canadian teenagers who had an insecure attachment totheir mother also tended to have an insecure attachment to their romantic partners (Doyle, Lawford, & Markiewicz, 2009).

THE IMPACT OF ATTACHMENT STYLES ON DATING INTERACTION.

Individuals' attachment styles are associated with their interactions and experiences in dating relationships (Carnelley, Pietromonaco, & Jaffe, 1996; Davila, Bradbury, & Fincham, 1998). For example, individuals with a secure attachment style give more support to their partners during anxiety-provoking situations. In contrast, individuals with anxious attachment styles give little support to their partners, perhaps because they're so focused on their own needs (Collins & Feeney, 2000). Although most of the work on attachment styles has examined heterosexual couples, recent research suggests that secure attachment is also associated with greater relationship satisfaction in gay and lesbian couples (Elizur & Mintzer, 2003). Since the federal Civil Marriage Act was passed into law on July 20, 2005, same-sex marriage has been legal nationwide in Canada. Heather MacIntosh and colleagues from the University of Ottawa examined the impact of legalized marriage on same-sex couples. With a combination of qualitative and quantitative methods, they assessed relationship satisfaction and attachment in 26 married lesbian or gay male couples and interviewed 15 of these couples to determine the impact of legalized marriage on their relationships and to explore their views about the support they received from society and their communities (MacIntosh, Reissing, & Andruff; 2010). The quantitative analysis showed that the 26 couples had significantly higher levels of relationship satisfaction and significantly less attachment-related anxiety and avoidance compared to normative data for married heterosexual couples. Despite some challenges and struggles, the participants indicated that marriage had an overwhelmingly positive effect on their lives.

Not surprisingly, individuals' attachment styles are associated with the experience of and strategies for managing conflict. People who are securely attached are more open and supportive when discussing a conflict with their dating partner (Creasey & Ladd, 2005; Simpson, Rholes, & Phillips, 1996; Simpson, Rholes, & Nelligan, 1992). Specifically, people who are securely attached show these characteristics when discussing conflicts with their partner:

- They're less anger-prone.
- They endorse more constructive anger goals.
- They report more adaptive responses and more positive affect in anger episodes.
- They attribute less hostile intent to others.
- They expect more positive outcomes than insecure people.

For example, one study with both dating and married couples found that those with secure attachment models were more likely to forgive their partner for misbehaviour, which in turn predicted relationship satisfaction (Kachadourian, Fincham, & Davila, 2004). People who are securely attached seem to have a functional response to anger, which is rooted in a rational analysis of the situation (rather than a paranoid or uncontrollably hostile reaction), and have more constructive responses to anger.

On the other hand, people with insecure attachment styles have much more difficulty managing interpersonal conflict. In a study of 123 dating couples, researchers examined how individuals with different attachment styles respond to major problems in their relationships (Simpson et al., 1996). As predicted, those with an anxious orientation perceived their partner and their relationship less positively after discussing a major conflict. Observer ratings also revealed that anxious women had greater stress and anxiety, whereas avoidant men were rated as less warm and supportive. Insecure attachment is also associated with more negative attributions for one's partner's behaviour, which in turn leads to poorer communication (Pearce & Halford, 2008). People with insecure attachment styles also experience greater physiological stress reactions to interpersonal conflict than securely attached people (Powers, Pietromonaco, Gunlicks, & Sayer, 2006).

People with an anxious attachment style also perceive more conflict with their dating partner than do others, which can escalate the severity of conflict (Campbell, Simpson, Boldry, & Kashy, 2005). Researchers from the University of Western Ontario and the University of Minnesota have found that anxiously attached people tend to perceive more frequent and severe daily conflict in their romantic relationships than do less anxious people, report feeling more hurt by these conflicts, and believe that conflicts forecast a more negative future for their relationships (Simpson, Campbell, & Weisberg, 2006). In another study, participants read about a negative behaviour by a hypothetical dating partner (Collins, Ford, Guichard, & Allard, 2006). These behaviours included "didn't respond when you tried to cuddle" and "left you standing alone at a party where you didn't know anyone." Those with an anxious attachment style see these negative behaviours more negatively than do those with secure or avoidant attachment styles. They also responded to these negative behaviours by acting more negatively themselves, which in turn is likely to lead to conflict and decreased satisfaction over time. This is one reason why people with an anxious attachment style are more likely to be unsatisfied in their dating relationships.

Recent research in neuroscience suggests that attachment styles influence our ability to suppress negative thoughts about interpersonal interactions (Gillath, Bunge, Shaver, Wendelken, & Mikulincer, 2005). In this study, 20 women completed measures of attachment styles, and then participated in an fMRI procedure. They were asked to think about—and stop thinking about—various negative relationship scenarios. These scenarios included breaking up with one's dating partner, having a fight with one's dating partner, and experiencing the death of one's dating partner. In line with the predictions, people who had anxious models of attachment showed greater activation in areas of the brain that are associated with sadness when they were thinking about the negative events compared to people who had more secure attachments. Anxious participants also showed lower levels of activation in the area of the brain responsible for regulating emotions. These findings suggest that people who have an anxious attachment style react more strongly to thoughts of loss and are less able to regulate these negative emotions.

THE IMPACT OF ATTACHMENT STYLES ON SEXUAL EXPERIENCE.   Attachment styles are associated in distinct ways both with the types of sexual experiences people have and with their motives for having sex (Davis, Shaver, & Vernon, 2004; Gentzler & Kerns, 2004; Schachner & Shaver, 2004; Schmitt, 2005). Those with anxious models of attachment tend to have sex as a way of reducing insecurity and fostering intense intimacy (Schachner & Shaver, 2004). For example, they're likely to report engaging in sex to make their partner love them more and to feel valued.

On the other hand, those with avoidant models of attachment tend to have sex to increase their status and prestige among peers (Schachner & Shaver, 2004). They tend to report engaging in sex in response to peer pressure, including fitting in with others and bragging about it. Individuals with avoidant attachment styles have more sexual experiences—they're more accepting of casual sex and are less likely to engage in sex within the context of a committed relationship (Gentzler & Kerns, 2004). How do you get over a relationship if it breaks down? One way is to find someone else. Stephanie Spielmann from the University of Toronto and colleagues found that focusing on someone new may help anxiously attached individuals overcome their attachment to an ex-romantic partner, suggesting one possible motive behind so-called rebound relationships (Spielmann, MacDonald, & Wilson, 2009).

Who's Who in Contemporary Canadian Social Psychology Research

Courtesy Jessica Cameron

Jessica J. Cameron is an associate professor at the University of Manitoba. Professor Cameron received her undergraduate degree from the University of Manitoba and her PhD from the University of Waterloo. The primary focus of Professor Cameron's research is the interpersonal dynamics of (in)security, exploring a wide range of topics including relationship initiation, perceptions of communication, and social perceptions. In 2010, Professor Cameron became chair of the Social and Personality Psychology section of the Canadian Psychological Association as well as associate editor of the *Journal of Social and Personal Relationships*.

POSITIVE ILLUSIONS

As described in Chapter 3, people tend to see themselves in an overly positive light (e.g., as more athletic, intelligent, and attractive than others than they actually are). According to research on close relationships, people extend these idealized self-views to both their relationships and their relationship partners (Klohen & Mendelsohn, 1998; Martz et al., 1998; Murray, Holmes, & Griffin, 1996; Neff & Karney, 2005). Specifically, people see their romantic partners as particularly attractive and intelligent, and rate them even more highly on these traits than their partners rate themselves. Even when people recognize a negative trait in a partner, they miraculously see this trait in a positive way (e.g., stubbornness is seen as "conviction"; Murray & Holmes, 1996).

People also describe their own romantic relationships as better than other people's relationships. They're more optimistic in their expectations about their dating relationships than are their roommates and parents about these same relationships. In addition, people list fewer current or future "relationship challenges" than the parents see in their children's relationships (Buunk & van der Eijnden, 1997; MacDonald & Ross, 1999; Rusbult, Van Lange, Wildschut, Yovetich, & Verette, 2000). People who engage in this type of love illusion are happier and are more likely to have their relationship last. Holding such idealized views of one's relationship partner is actually associated with increased satisfaction and relationship longevity.

WHY POSITIVE ILLUSIONS CAN BE GOOD. How can holding such positive illusions lead to happy relationships? First, people may deliberately ignore "the bad," and thereby minimize conflict (e.g., not recognize when their partner is attracted to someone else). In one study, dating couples were asked to rate and discuss pictures of six opposite-sex people who they might interact with in a dating context (Simpson, Ickes, & Blackstone, 1995). These discussions were videotaped, and then each partner viewed the tape and reported what they were thinking and what they thought their partner was thinking at each point in the discussion. As hypothesized, dating partners who were close and secure about their relationship were the least accurate in assessing their partners' thoughts during this potentially relationship-threatening task, suggesting that inaccuracy can be a defence (i.e., that the head may be protecting the heart).

People who are in relationships also tend to ignore or devalue other potential partners, which in turn helps protect them from threats to their relationship (Lydon, Fitzsimons, & Naidoo, 2003; Miller, 1997). For example, college students who are in dating relationships rate attractive people (who could presumably threaten their current relationship) as less physically and sexually attractive than do college students who are single (Simpson, Gangestad, & Lerman, 1990; see Figure 14.9).

FIGURE 14.9 DOES RELATIONSHIP THREAT DECREASE RATINGS OF ATTRACTION?

People in both serious and casual dating relationships were asked to rate the attractiveness of an available dating partner after being told either that the person was interested in them or that the person wasn't attracted to them. As predicted, people in casual dating relationships were more interested in a potential partner when they learned that this person was interested in them (a high threat condition), whereas those who were in exclusive relationships were actually less interested in this person who posed a threat to their relationship.

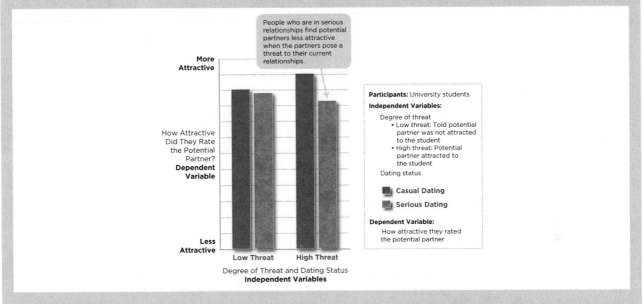

Source: Bazzini, D. G., & Shaffer, D. R. (1999). Resisting temptation revisited: Devaluation versus enhancement of an attractive suitor by exclusive and nonexclusive daters. *Personality and Social Psychology Bulletin, 25,* 162–176.

THE DOWNSIDE OF POSITIVE ILLUSIONS.   Illusions aren't always beneficial, however. In fact, Bill Swann and his colleagues at the University of Texas at Austin found that dating couples experience greater satisfaction when their partner sees them in an idealized way, but married couples are happiest when their spouse sees them as they see themselves (Swann, de la Ronde, & Hixon, 1994). Couples in both types of relationships completed measures describing their own attributes (e.g., intelligence, attractiveness, athletic skills) and their partners' attributes, as well as measures of intimacy. Individuals in dating relationships who saw their partners in a favourable light (regardless of how the partners viewed themselves) had greater satisfaction. But individuals in marital relationships who saw their partners as they saw themselves had greater satisfaction. Seeing one's partner in a positive light seems to be an important predictor of satisfaction early in a relationship, but accuracy seems to be more important over time. Why? Probably because it's good and relaxing to be with someone who likes us for who we are, and understands us (De La Ronde & Swann, 1998). It's also probably good for marital functioning to recognize your spouse's weaknesses (e.g., a spouse who isn't good with numbers). In line with this view, more recent research reveals that individuals who see their spouse's strengths and weaknesses more accurately are less likely to get divorced (Neff & Karney, 2005).

Positive illusions can also lead to greater disappointment when these high expectations don't pan out. Researchers James McNulty and Benjamin Karney (2004) examined expectations, satisfaction, and problem-solving skills in newly married couples over four years. Their findings reveal that couples whose expectations matched their problem-solving skills were more satisfied over time. Those who had high expectations and strong skills did experience high levels of satisfaction, as did those with lower expectations and weaker skills. However, those with high expectations and low skills experienced the lowest levels of satisfaction. In sum, although positive illusion is important in maintaining relationships the marginal error of this illusion should be at a reasonable degree. For example, it's threatening if your partner thinks you're an extrovert when in reality you're really shy. That said, your partner could have accurate knowledge of your strengths and weaknesses while still viewing you in a favourable way.

SOCIAL NORMS APPROACH

According to the social norms perspective, we like those who follow the same social norms and rules that we value and practise. Imagine that you're helping your dating partner with a statistics assignment. How would you react if, after you finish, he or she gave you $20 for the time you spent helping out? Would you feel offended or would you like your partner more? The social norms approach examines rules and norms that govern social relationships. Margaret Clark and Judson Mills (1979; 1993) studied interpersonal attraction using social norms. These researchers distinguished between exchange and communal relationships. Exchange relationships are between colleagues, acquaintances, and distant relatives. Communal relationships are between lovers, family members, and close friends. The rules that govern these relationships are different. In exchange relationships, a benefit is given with the expectations of a comparable benefit in return. That is, giving and receiving benefits are part of the exchange. For example, if you lend your lecture notes to a classmate, you expect that the person will lend you his or her notes if you miss a future class. On the other hand, in communal relationships, a benefit is given to fulfill the needs of the person we care for. Helping your boyfriend or girlfriend on an assignment is an example of a communal relationship, where you help to express your concern, not because you expect a payment.

Clark and Mills (1993) have argued that there are qualitative and quantitative differences between exchange and communal relationships. In communal relationships, there are various levels of strength. This refers to how motivated the person is to respond to the other person's needs. For instance, you would be more motivated to respond to the needs of your child than to the needs of your best friend. Similarly, you're more motivated to meet the needs of your best friend than the needs of other friends. The more motivated we are to respond to the needs of another person, the more connected we are to that person and the stronger the relationship (Clark & Mills, 1993). In exchange relationships, there is a cost line. That is, there is a maximum point for giving a benefit. This maximum point or limitation is considerably lower in an exchange relationship than a communal relationship. For example, you may lend your notes to a classmate, you may watch her bag, share your lunch, and even lend her money for a taxi, but you are not going to pay for her spring break holiday.

Clark and Mills (1979; 1993) have shown that we like those who follow the rules that are specific to each relationship. Following communal norms with our romantic partner, family, and close friends increases liking and sustains those relationships. Following exchange rules with acquaintances increases our liking of those individuals. This basic principle was demonstrated in an empirical study by Clark and Mills (1979). Participants were single male undergraduate students who worked on a vocabulary task using letter tiles. While participants were working on the task, they could see an attractive woman (a confederate) working on a similar task in a different room through a monitor. All participants were told that after they finished the task they were going to meet the woman and talk about their common interests. Half of the participants were told that the woman was married and that her husband would pick her up after the study. This condition was the exchange relationship condition as it was assumed that single men desire an exchange relationship with a married woman. The other half of the participants were told that the woman was single, new to the university, and didn't know many people. This condition was the communal relationship condition as it was assumed that single men desire a communal relationship with an attractive woman who is also single and available. When the participants finished their task, the experimenter asked them if they wished to give their extra tiles to the woman who was seemingly working on a more difficult task. All participants agreed. The female confederate responded by either transferring some of her points to

FIGURE 14.10   DOES FOLLOWING NORMS INFLUENCE LEVEL OF ATTRACTION?

Male participants worked on a vocabulary task using letter tiles and were told that after they finished the task they were going to meet an attractive woman who was working on the same task in a different room. Participants were either told that the woman was married (exchange relationship condition) or that she was single (communal condition). After the task was finished, participants had the opportunity to give their extra tiles to the woman. In response, the female confederate either transferred some of her points to the participants or just thanked the participants. It was found that participants liked the woman more in the exchange condition where credit was transferred. However, in the communal condition it was found that participants liked the woman more where credit wasn't transferred.

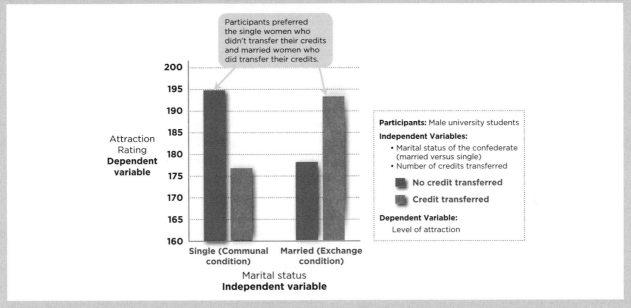

Source: Clark, M. S., & Mills, J. (1979). Interpersonal attraction in exchange and communal relationships. *Journal of Personality and Social Psychology, 37*, 12-24.

the participants (benefit condition) or by thanking the participants without any payment (no benefit condition). Later, participants' liking of the female confederate was measured.

As expected, it was found that in the exchange-benefit condition participants liked the woman more than in the exchange-no-benefit condition. Additionally, in the communal-no-benefit condition, participants liked the woman more than in the communal-benefit condition (see Figure 14.10). In sum, our liking of another person is a function of the appropriateness of the benefit for the type of relationship.

social exchange theory – the theory that people's satisfaction in a relationship is determined by the costs and rewards of the relationship

SOCIAL EXCHANGE THEORY

Social exchange theory is a very rational and practical approach to attraction and relationship satisfaction that is rooted in principles of economics (Bui, Peplau, & Hill, 1996; Clark & Grote, 1998; Le & Agnew, 2003; Rusbult, Martz, & Agnew, 1998). According to this theory, people are happiest in their relationships when the benefits of these relationships are greater than their costs. What are the rewards of close relationships? These benefits include companionship, sex, happiness, economic support, and intimacy. In contrast, the costs of close relationships include time, energy, lack of freedom to date other people, feelings of dependence, and stress and worry regarding the relationship.

"I've done the numbers, and I will marry you."

© William Hamilton/ The New Yorker Collection/ www.cartoonbank.com

THE IMPACT OF COMPARISON LEVEL.   Social exchange theory also proposes that relationship success or failure is influenced not only by the overall costs and benefits in the relationship, but also by the expectations

TABLE 14.3	Calculating the Costs and Benefits of a Relationship

This table describes how Jenny might decide whether to stay in a relationship with Juan. According to social exchange theory, Jenny would calculate the costs and benefits of her relationship, and stay with Juan if the benefits outweigh the costs, but exit the relationship if the costs outweigh the benefits.

BENEFITS	COSTS
Her boyfriend Juan is considerate when she's feeling sad.	He gets jealous when she spends time with friends.
He cooks her dinner regularly.	He's always borrowing money from her.
He shares her interest in NASCAR racing.	He's pretty messy.

comparison level – the expected outcome of a relationship, meaning the extent to which a person expects his or her relationship to be rewarding

people have regarding the costs and benefits of intimate relationships (Thibaut & Kelley, 1959). The degree that we like someone is determined by estimating the cost of receiving rewards from the other person. If the cost is low, we like the other person. If, however, the cost is too high, we're less likely to be attracted to the other person. The term **comparison level** refers to the expected outcome of a relationship, meaning the extent to which a given person expects his or her relationships to be rewarding (see Table 14.3). A person who has had many unpleasant relationships could have a very low comparison level—and in turn, might be happy even in relatively poor relationships. In contrast, a person who has a high comparison level has high expectations for the quality of his or her close relationships, and would exit relationships that do not meet these expectations.

comparison level for alternatives (CLalt) – a calculation regarding the expected benefits and costs that a person could receive from having a relationship with various other partners

Social exchange theory also proposes that people make a similar type of calculation regarding the expected benefits and costs they could receive from having a relationship with various alternative partners, called the **comparison level for alternatives**, or **CLalt** (Thibaut & Kelley, 1959). Individuals will be committed to their relationships when the overall benefits and costs of their current relationship are greater than that provided by alternative relationships, but will choose to leave the relationship if their alternative options are more appealing (Drigotas & Rusbult, 1992). In line with this theory, a study by Caryl Rusbult and John Martz (1995) found that battered women who had few alternatives in life (due to low levels of education, little money, and/or no job) were more likely to feel committed to their relationship and to return to their abusive partner.

Although most of the research testing the social exchange model of relationships was conducted on heterosexual couples, research with same-sex couples points to very similar findings (Kurdek, 1992, 2000). In one study, researchers examined relationship quality in four types of couples: married heterosexual couples, non-married heterosexual couples, male homosexual couples, and female homosexual couples (Kurdek & Schmitt, 1986). All couples lived together and had no children in the home. Findings revealed that married heterosexual couples, gay male couples, and lesbian couples all reported greater love for their partner and more relationship satisfaction than cohabitating heterosexual couples. For each type of couple, greater relationship satisfaction was associated with seeing few alternatives to the relationship, reporting many attractions of the relationship, feeling high attachment to one partner, and engaging in high levels of shared decision-making. These findings provide further evidence that the factors that predict satisfaction in homosexual relationships are the same ones that predict satisfaction in heterosexual relationships (Gottman et al., 2003).

Janet Kimber/Getty Images, Inc.
The predictors of relationship satisfaction are very similar for heterosexual and same-sex couples: relationships with many benefits and fewer costs are more satisfying for everyone.

THE IMPACT OF INVESTMENT. Finally, social exchange theory also includes the component of **investment**, meaning the resources devoted to a relationship that cannot be retrieved (e.g., time, energy, self-disclosure; Le & Agnew, 2003; Rusbult, 1980, 1983). These investment factors influence individuals' commitment to their present relationship, and thereby their willingness to tolerate costs. For example, if you've been in a relationship for only a few weeks, and hence have little investment in this relationship, you would be quite likely to end the relationship in the face of a substantial problem (e.g., finding evidence of your partner's infidelity). On the other hand, if you've been in a relationship for many years, and have great investment in

investment – the resources devoted to a relationship that cannot be retrieved

FIGURE 14.11   EQUITY THEORY

Equity theory proposes that relationship satisfaction is a function of the relative costs and benefits of the relationship for each partner, and that couples in which both partners experience a similar ratio of costs to benefits experience greater satisfaction.

$\dfrac{\text{Person A's costs}}{\text{Person A's benefits}} = \dfrac{\text{Person B's costs}}{\text{Person B's benefits}}$	$\dfrac{\text{Person A's costs}}{\text{Person A's benefits}} \begin{array}{c} > \\ < \end{array} \dfrac{\text{Person B's costs}}{\text{Person B's benefits}}$
Equitable Relationship	**Inequitable Relationship** (Person A is underbenefiting and Person B is overbenefiting)

this relationship (e.g., own a house with a person, have children with this person), you would be more likely to try to maintain the relationship even if the costs of the relationship are greater than the benefits at a particular point in time.

BUT IS IT REALLY EQUITY THAT MATTERS?   According to social exchange theory, attraction and satisfaction are largely functions of each person's costs and benefits in the relationship. But according to equity theory, the ratio of costs and benefits for each part- ner is a better predictor of satisfaction than simply the overall costs and benefits (Hatfield, Greenberger, Traupmann, & Lambert, 1982; Walster, Walster, & Traupmann, 1978). People are most attracted to a relationship when the ratio between benefits and contributions is simi- lar for both partners. In other words, people could be equally happy in a relationship in which they give little to their partner and receive little from their partner and one in which they give a lot and receive a lot—in both cases, the equity between the two partners is equivalent.

equity theory – the theory that relationship satisfaction depends on the ratio of costs and benefits for each partner in a relationship

In contrast, relationships that lack equity are less attractive and are associated with dis- tinct types of dissatisfaction (Van Yperen & Buunk, 1990; Walster et al., 1978). People who feel they give more than their partners (that they're underbenefited) often feel (understand- ably) angry and resentful. Just think about a relationship you might have had in which you found yourself having to always be the one who initiated plans, offered assistance, and paid for dinner—you probably felt somewhat resentful. On the other hand, people who are in a relationship in which they receive more than they give (they're overbenefited) may feel guilty and uncomfortable (see Figure 14.11).

Interestingly, some research on the impact of social support in intimate relationships reveals that men and women react in distinct ways to relationships that lack equity (Väänänen, Buunk, Kivimäki, Pentti, & Vahtera, 2005). Researchers examined the amount of support given and received in a relationship as well as the frequency of missing work due to illness. For women, giving more support than they received (an underbenefited relationship) was associ- ated with fewer sick days. In contrast, for men, receiving more support than they gave (an overbenefited relationship) was associated with fewer sick days. This research suggests that the impact of equity on satisfaction may be different for men and women.

STRATEGIES FOR INCREASING RELATIONSHIP SATISFACTION

So, what can you do to experience greater satisfaction in your interpersonal relationships? First, increase the number of rewarding and positive behaviours in the relationship (Gottman & Levenson, 1992). This seems like a very simple strategy, but it works: even if the relationship has some problems, increasing the number of positives or rewards about the relationship will enhance satisfaction, in part by changing the costs-benefits ratio (in line with social exchange and equity theories). Couples with many rewarding interactions are less likely to break up, and couples who increase the rewards in their relationships experience greater satisfaction (Berg & McQuinn, 1986; Gottman & Levenson, 1992; Rusbult, 1983).

What else might you do to make your relationship more satisfying? Engage in new and arousing activities with your partner to maintain relationship excitement over time. Many surveys reveal that marital satisfaction decreases over time—with sizeable drops occurring after the first year of marriage and after the seventh or eighth years—perhaps because people simply get bored (Kurdek, 1999). Research by Art Aron and his colleagues (2000) suggests that people need to combat the boredom that may arise in a relationship after the newness and exhilaration have decreased. In one study, married couples were randomly assigned to one of three conditions: one group did no activity (control condition), one group rolled a ball back and forth (mundane task), and one group did unusual activities such as tying their partner's arms and legs together and having them crawl across the floor carrying a pillow between their legs (the novel task). Oddly enough, couples that struggled and laughed their way through the novel task reported more satisfaction in their relationship than did those in the other two groups. Why did engaging in these tasks lead to greater satisfaction? Perhaps cognitive dissonance ("I look really stupid, so this must be worth it") or arousal-excitation theory ("My heart is beating fast so I must love my partner") was responsible.

Last, but not least, remember that relationships can be very rewarding, but they take considerable attention and energy to maintain (Harvey & Omarzu, 1997). We need to "mind our relationships," and not simply take them—and our partners—for granted. As Leo Tolstoy described in *Anna Karenin*,

"He was happy; but, having embarked on married life, he saw at every step that it was not at all what he had anticipated. At every turn he felt like a man who, after admiring the smooth, happy motion of a boat on a lake, suddenly finds himself in it. It was not enough to sit still without rocking the boat—he had to be on the look-out and never forget the course he was taking, or that there was water beneath and all around. He must row, although his unaccustomed hands were made sore. It was one thing to look on and another to do the work, and doing it, though very delightful, was very difficult" (p. 56).

[CONCEPTS IN CONTEXT]

THEORIES OF RELATIONSHIP SATISFACTION

FACTOR	EXAMPLE
Attachment styles	Tabitha has been dating Russ for one year, but she's not very happy with their relationship. She becomes very worried if Russ is even a few minutes late to pick her up for a date. Tabitha then becomes convinced that he doesn't really love her, and this concern often leads to an intense fight.
Positive illusions	Beth has recently started dating Eric. She feels so lucky to be dating someone who is just perfect in many ways. Eric sometimes is a little cheap (he insists on eating only in fast-food restaurants), which Beth sees as a wonderful sign of how concerned he is about saving for their future.
Social norms approach	Emma helped her professor to organize her research lab throughout the semester. She was disappointed when she received a thank-you card instead of money for her many hours of work in the lab.
Social exchange theory	Fabiola and Gustave have been happily married for 10 years. Their relationship is not perfect—they at times have vigorous fights—but they both see the benefit of love and stability that their relationship provides as far outweighing its costs.

WHAT ARE SOME COMMON PROBLEMS IN CLOSE RELATIONSHIPS?

Although the previous section described how relationships bring us much joy and happiness (as well as better health), people also experience various problems and challenges in their relationships. Let's take a look at an example of one problem: jealousy. In one study on jealousy, participants imagined their dating partner flirting with someone else at a party (Dijkstra & Buunk, 1998). Some participants were asked to imagine their partner flirting with someone who is very physically attractive. Others were asked to imagine their partner flirting with someone who is high in dominance, meaning a person who is self-confident, influential, and powerful. Participants then reported how jealous they would feel. As predicted, men are more jealous when they imagine their partner flirting with someone who is high in dominance than someone who is highly physically attractive. Women show the reverse pattern: they experience greater jealousy when they believe their partner is flirting with someone who is highly attractive. Some researchers explain this difference using an evolutionary perspective (as we will see below). This section will examine common problems in close relationships: conflict, jealousy, loneliness, and relationship dissolution.

CONFLICT

One of the most important things couples have to manage in close relationships is conflict, because it is natural for all close relationships to experience some conflict (Holmes & Murray, 1996; Jensen-Campbell & Graziano, 2000). Married couples have an average of two to three disagreements per month (McGonagle, Kessler, & Schilling, 1992), and adolescents report having one to two conflicts per day—usually with a friend, sibling, or parent (Jensen-Campbell & Graziano, 2000). Although conflict is a part of all close relationships, people handle relationship conflicts in very different ways—and how they handle conflict is a major predictor of relationship satisfaction and longevity. Let's examine some common strategies that couples use in managing conflict.

TYPOLOGY OF RESPONSES. Carol Rusbult and her colleagues at the University of North Carolina at Chapel Hill describe four major types of response that people use in handling conflict (Drigotas, Whitney, & Rusbult, 1995; Rusbult & Zembrodt, 1983; Rusbult, Zembrodt, & Gunn, 1982). One constructive strategy is **voice**, meaning talking things over with your relationship partner to try to solve the conflict (see Table 14.4). For example, if your partner continually comes home late from the office, you could discuss with your partner how this tardiness makes you upset, and try to reach a solution to this problem (e.g., perhaps your partner could bring work home from the office).

Table 14.4	Responses to Relationship Dissatisfaction
Not surprisingly, people who have high relationship investment and satisfaction are more likely to use a constructive strategy for resolving conflicts (Drigotas et al., 1995).	
Voice	Discussing problems, seeking help from a friend or therapist, suggesting solutions, changing oneself or attempting to change a partner. For example, "We talked things over and worked things out" or "I tried my hardest to make things better."
Loyalty	Praying for improvement, supporting a partner in the face of criticism, continuing to wear symbols of a relationship (a ring, a locket). For example, "I loved her so much that I ignored her faults," "I just waited to see if things would get better and went out with him when he asked me," or "I prayed a lot and left things in God's hands."
Neglect	Letting things fall apart, ignoring a partner or spending less time together, criticizing a partner for things unrelated to the problem. For example, "Mostly my response was silence to anything he might say, ignoring him if we were around other people" or "We seemed to drift apart—we might have exchanged five to 10 words in a week."
Exit	Separating, actively abusing a partner, threatening to leave, screaming shrewishly at a partner. For example, "I told him that I couldn't take it anymore and that it was over" or "I slapped her around a bit, I'm ashamed to say."

Other strategies that are used to handle relationship problems are destructive. **Neglect**, meaning giving up on the relationship and withdrawing from it emotionally, is one type of destructive strategy, and **exit**—leaving the relationship—is another. **Loyalty**, where the partner remains committed to the relationship and simply waits patiently for things to get better. Loyalty sounds as if it could be a good strategy, but this approach isn't associated with favourable consequences, possibly because it's a less visible and more indirect strategy (Rusbult, Zembrodt, & Gunn, 1982).

THE FOUR HORSEMEN OF THE APOCALYPSE. John Gottman, a professor at the University of Washington, has conducted extensive research on relationship conflict (Gottman & Levenson, 2002). His research uses a variety of measures (physiological, nonverbal, verbal, and questionnaire) and large samples of couples that are followed over time. This research has revealed four styles of conflict that are particularly destructive in a marriage:

- *criticism*: complaining about some features of the spouse or the relationship
- *contempt*: acting as if sickened or repulsed by one's partner
- *defensiveness*: protecting the self
- *stonewalling*: emotionally withdrawing and refusing to participate in conversation

All of these strategies can lead to increased isolation and withdrawal. In fact, Gottman calls them "The Four Horsemen of the Apocalypse," meaning that the end of the relationship, or apocalypse, will follow with these four negative styles of conflict—the four horsemen riding in. In support of this model, Huston and Vangelisti (1991) found that relationships in which there are high levels of negative behaviour by either spouse, including criticizing, complaining, and becoming angry and impatient, lead to lower satisfaction over time in wives (though not husbands).

The *stonewalling* approach is part of another commonly observed conflict behaviour called the **demand/withdraw interaction pattern**. This pattern refers to the relatively common situation in which one partner attempts to start a discussion by criticizing, complaining, or suggesting change and the other partner then attempts to end this discussion—or avoid the issue—by maintaining silence or withdrawing from the situation (Christensen & Heavey, 1990; Verhofstadt, Buysee, De Clercq, & Goodwin, 2005). In a heterosexual relationship, the man is more likely to withdraw from conflict and the woman is more likely to take a leading role in initiating conflict, and discussion of conflict. This gender difference is explained in part by socialization pressures that lead women to have higher expectations for closeness in a relationship than do men. Other researchers explain this gender difference by noting the typical power imbalance in marriage, in which men tend to receive more benefits than women—and therefore have less interest in making changes. And sadly, avoiding communication and withdrawing from conflict leads to relationship dissatisfaction (Bodenmann, Kaiser, Hahlweg, & Fehm-Wolfsdorf, 1998; Weger, 2005).

demand/withdraw interaction pattern – a relatively common situation in which one partner is nagging, critical, and insistent about discussing the relationship problems while the other partner is withdrawn, silent, and defensive

NEGATIVE ATTRIBUTIONAL TRAPS. The attributions people make for events in their relationships can also be classified as constructive, or relationship-enhancing, or destructive to the relationship (Bradbury & Fincham, 1992; Bradbury, Beach, Fincham, & Nelson,1996; Karney & Bradbury, 2000). As described in Chapter 4, people readily make attributions, or create explanations, for events they observe in the world, and people usually make beneficial attributions for the events that happen to themselves and their loved ones. In turn, people in happy relationships make beneficial attributions for their partners' behaviour, such as creating external excuses for misbehaviour and internal explanations for positive behaviour. So, when your partner comes home late (again), you might attribute this behaviour to an external factor (e.g., her boss is so demanding), and when your partner surprises you with a special gift, you might attribute this behaviour to an internal factor (e.g., he is so thoughtful).

In contrast, **negative attributional traps** occur when people explain their partner's positive behaviour in negative ways (Graham & Conoley, 2006; McNulty & Karney, 2001). In one study, married couples rated their trust in their partner, discussed a common relationship problem, and then rated the beliefs about their partner's behaviour during the discussion (Miller & Rempel, 2004). Researchers then contacted the couples again two years later and showed them the same videotape. Once again, they rated their beliefs about their partners' motives. As predicted, people who initially had made negative attributions about their partner's behaviour reported less trust in their partner two years later. Similarly, people who initially reported lower trust made more negative attributions later on. People who make negative attributions for their partner's behaviour experience lower marital satisfaction, in part because this type of explanation for behaviour tends to increase relationship conflict (Fincham & Bradbury, 1992; Kubany, Bauer, Muraoka, & Richard, 1995). Negative attributional traps can therefore have a significant and lasting impact on relationship satisfaction. Using an observational method, Amielle Julien and colleagues from the Université de Québec à Montréal examined conflict, social support, and relationship quality among heterosexual, gay male, and lesbian couples (Julien, Chartrand, Simard, Bouthillier, & Bégin, 2003). They found that heterosexual, gay male, and lesbian couples did not differ in their levels of communication behaviours. In both the conflict and the support domains, they exhibited similar levels of negative and positive behaviours. The three types of couples also showed similar levels of perceived support following support discussions. The similarities in observed communication are consistent with much of the empirical findings in studies that have used self-report methods for comparing heterosexual, gay male, and lesbian couples.

negative attributional traps – explaining a partner's behaviour in negative ways

STRATEGIES FOR EFFECTIVE CONFLICT RESOLUTION. Because conflict and disagreements are part of all close relationships, couples need to learn strategies for managing conflict in a healthy and constructive way (Honeycutt, Woods, & Fontenot, 1993). Some couples just avoid and deny the presence of any conflict in a relationship. However, denying the existence of conflict results in couples failing to solve their problems at early stages, which can then lead to even greater problems later on. Not surprisingly, expressing anger and disagreement initially leads to lower marital satisfaction (Gottman & Krokoff, 1989). However, these patterns predict increases in marital satisfaction over time. This research suggests that working through conflicts is an important predictor of marital satisfaction.

So, what can you do to manage conflict in your own relationships? First, try to understand the other person's point of view and put yourself in his or her place (Arriaga & Rusbult, 1998; Honeycutt et al., 1993). People who are sensitive to what their partner thinks and feels experience greater relationship satisfaction. For example, Arriaga and Rusbult (1998) found that among people in dating relationships as well as marriages, those who can adopt their partner's perspective show more positive emotions, more relationship-enhancing attributions, and more constructive responses to conflict.

Second, because conflict and disagreements are an inevitable part of close relationships, people need to be able to apologize to their partner and forgive their partner for wrongdoings (Fincham, 2000; McCullough et al., 1998; McCullough, Worthington, & Rachal, 1997). Apologies minimize conflict, lead to forgiveness, and serve to restore relationship closeness. In line with this view, spouses who are more forgiving show higher marital quality over time (Paleari, Regalia, & Fincham, 2005). Interestingly, apologizing can even have positive health benefits (Witvliet, Ludwig, & Vander Laan, 2001). For example, when people reflect on hurtful memories and grudges, they show negative physiological effects, including increased heart rate and blood pressure, compared to when they reflect on sympathetic perspective-taking and forgiving.

"O.K., we'll try it your way—let's ignore any problems that come up in the next twenty years and see what happens."

© David Sipress/ The New Yorker Collection/ www. cartoonbank.com

JEALOUSY

Jealousy is a common problem in relationships because people naturally fear threats—real or perceived—to their relationships (Parrot & Smith, 1992). We react with more jealousy to high levels of threat (e.g., your partner finds someone attractive) than low levels of threat (e.g., your partner has a work colleague he spends time with), and with more jealousy to threats to our self-esteem (e.g., your partner sees someone wearing clothes like yours and comments on how good they look; DeSteno, Valdesolo, & Bartlett, 2006; Sharpsteen, 1995).

GENDER DIFFERENCES IN THE CAUSES OF JEALOUSY. Although both men and women experience jealousy, they differ in exactly when they'll experience it and what will cause it (Buss, Larsen, Westen, & Semelroth, 1992). According to the evolutionary psychology perspective, jealousy is an adaptation to the different reproductive issues faced by men versus women. Men, on the one hand, should be more concerned about a partner's sexual infidelity, because they could end up raising another man's child. In line with this view, most research suggests that men's jealousy is a primary cause of aggression toward women. In the words of O. J. Simpson, accused of the murder of his ex-wife, "Let's say I committed this crime. Even if I did do this, it would have to have been because I loved her very much, right?" (Farber, 1998). Women, on the other hand, should be more concerned about a partner's emotional infidelity, because men who are emotionally involved with a different partner could start devoting resources to this new relationship. In other words, if a man becomes involved in a new relationship, he would likely provide support for the children in this new relationship and therefore have less (if any) available to help children from an earlier relationship.

In turn, men and women react in different ways to sexual versus emotional infidelity (Buss et al., 1999; Buunk, Angleitner, Oubaid, & Buss, 1996). In a series of studies by David Buss and colleagues (1992) to test this hypothesis, men and women were asked whether they would be more upset if their romantic partner formed a deep emotional attachment or had sexual intercourse with someone else. Sixty percent of the men reported that they would be more upset by a partner's sexual infidelity, whereas 83 percent of the women felt that emotional infidelity would be worse (see Figure 14.12). As described at the beginning of this section, men and women also report feeling jealous in response to different people who threaten the relationship: men are more concerned when their partner is talking to someone highly dominant, and women are more concerned when their partner is talking to someone highly attractive.

Research using measures of physiological arousal, such as heart rate and sweat, reveals gender differences that are similar to those found by Buss et al. (1992) when imagining sexual infidelity versus emotional infidelity. Moreover, cross-cultural research reveals similar patterns (Buss et al., 1999; Buunk et al., 1996), again suggesting that evolutionary factors are responsible for this discrepancy.

CRITIQUES OF THE EVOLUTIONARY PERSPECTIVE. However, some recent research contradicts some of the gender differences in reactions to infidelity (sexual and emotional) found by Buss and his colleagues. First, some researchers suggest that these gender differences in jealousy are a result of the different expectations that men and women have about the pairings of emotional and sexual infidelity (Harris & Christenfeld, 1996; DeSteno & Salovey, 1996). According to this *"double-shot" hypothesis*, men believe that if their partner is engaging in sexual infidelity, she's also very likely to have some type of emotional commitment to that relationship, whereas they don't assume that a partner who is emotionally involved with someone is necessarily involved in a sexual relationship. In contrast, women who learn that their mate is emotionally involved with someone are very likely to assume that he's also sexually involved, whereas they don't assume that a man who is sexually involved with someone is also emotionally involved.

Other recent challenges to the evolutionary explanation for the gender differences call into question the method used. Buss finds strong gender differences when people answer

FIGURE 14.12 — DO MEN AND WOMEN DIFFER IN THEIR RESPONSES TO DIFFERENT TYPES OF INFIDELITY?

Men and women were asked whether they would be more upset if their romantic partner formed a deep emotional attachment or had sexual intercourse with someone else. As predicted, a higher percentage of men said they would be more upset by a partner's sexual infidelity than emotional infidelity, whereas a higher percentage of women felt that emotional infidelity would be more upsetting.

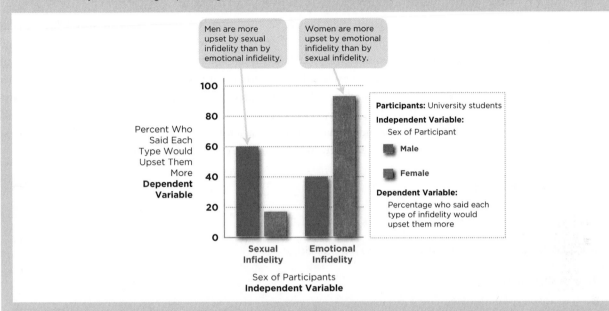

Source: Buss, D.M., Larsen, R.J., Westen, D., & Semmelroth, J. (1992). Sex differences in jealousy: Evolution, physiology, and psychology. *Psychological Science, 3,* 251–255.

hypothetical scenarios (e.g., "Which would bother you more?"), but when participants recall actual incidents of infidelity by a partner both men and women are more focused on a partner's emotional, as compared to sexual, infidelity (Harris, 2002). Moreover, gender differences in jealousy aren't found in people who have actually experienced infidelity (Berman & Frazier, 2005). This research suggests that hypothetical accounts are very different than what people actually experience. Still other research reveals that the gender differences in jealousy emerge only when participants are given the forced choice phrasing (that is, "Which of the two types of infidelity would be worse?"). In contrast, when participants are asked to rate each type of jealousy on a 1-to-7 scale, both men and women report greater jealousy in response to sexual infidelity (DeSteno, Bartlett, Braverman, & Salovey, 2002; Sabini & Green, 2004). All of these findings suggest that the method used to assess reactions to infidelity may influence whether gender differences in response to types of infidelity are found—suggesting that such differences may reflect the method used, and not fundamental differences in reactions.

Researchers have even raised concerns about how to interpret the findings from studies that use physiological measures, which are used in part to eliminate the problems associated with biased self-report. As noted previously, compared to women, men tend to show greater physiological reactivity, such as heart rate and blood pressure, when they imagine sexual infidelity (Harris, 2000, 2002). However, this greater physiological reactivity also occurs when men imagine sexual scenes that do *not* include infidelity. In other words, and perhaps not surprisingly, the increases in physiological arousal seen in men who think about sexual infidelity may simply measure increases in arousal caused by thinking about sex in general, not infidelity in particular.

Still other research points to the impact of the sample studied on the conclusions researchers reach. Gender differences in reactions to jealousy are more common in the university student population than in non-student samples (Sabini & Green, 2004). These findings therefore call into question the idea that gender differences in jealousy are rooted in evolutionary factors.

LONELINESS

The absence of interpersonal relationships, which can lead to a state of loneliness, is a common problem. People who are lonely feel left out of social events, isolated from others, and lacking in close interpersonal relationships (see the Rate Yourself box; Archibald, Bartholomew, & Marx, 1995; Berg & McQuinn, 1989; Berg & Peplau, 1982). Researchers often distinguish between different types of loneliness. *Social loneliness* describes people who lack the presence of close others and a social network. People who are socially lonely don't get invited to parties, rarely have plans for dinner with friends, and can't easily call on a friend for assistance with moving or other practical tasks. In contrast, *emotional loneliness* refers to the lack of a romantic partner (Green, Richardson, Lago, & Schatten-Jones, 2001). People who are emotionally lonely may have a strong friendship network, but lack a very close and intimate romantic relationship. Although social and emotional loneliness are moderately correlated, a person can experience one type of loneliness without the other.

HOW LONELY ARE YOU?

The UCLA Loneliness Scale

INSTRUCTIONS: *Rate each item on a scale of 1 (never) to 4 (often).*

- **1.** I lack companionship.
- **2.** There is no one I can turn to.
- **3.** My interests and ideas are not shared by those around me.
- **4.** I feel left out.
- **5.** I am no longer close to anyone.
- **6.** I feel isolated from others.
- **7.** No one really knows me well.
- **8.** My social relationships are superficial.
- **9.** I am unhappy being so withdrawn.
- **10.** People are around me but not with me.

[RATE YOURSELF]

SCORING: Sum up your total number of points on all 10 items.

INTERPRETATION: This scale assesses the extent to which a person is experiencing loneliness. People with higher scores feel more lonely, whereas those with lower scores feel less lonely (Russell, Peplau, & Cutrona, 1980).

Loneliness is associated with major consequences, including lower immune competence, higher blood pressure, and higher levels of stress hormones (Hawkley, Burleson, Berntson, & Cacioppo, 2003; Uchino, Cacioppo, & Kiecolt-Glaser, 1996). One recent study with college students revealed that students who have high levels of loneliness have a weaker immune response to the flu vaccine, meaning they're at greater risk of developing the flu even following a vaccination (Pressman et al., 2005).

What leads to loneliness? Research points to three main factors: poor social skills, negative self-views, and negative expectations. Let's examine each of these explanations.

THE IMPACT OF POOR SOCIAL SKILLS. People who are lonely often have poor social skills, which impairs the formation of positive interpersonal relationships (Berg & Peplau, 1982; Jones, Carpenter, & Quintana, 1985). It's also important to note that people who have poor social

FIGURE 14.13   MODEL OF SELF-FULFILLING PROPHECY

People who are lonely may expect rejection in social interactions, and may therefore act in ways that elicit this behaviour.

skills are also more lonely. Therefore, the relation could go either way. Additionally, people who are lonely also engage in less self-disclosure and react negatively to other people's self-disclosure, which in turn inhibits self-disclosure from their partner (Rotenberg, 1997; Solano, Batten, & Parish, 1982). In turn, people who don't reciprocate self-disclosure appropriately experience more discomfort and less liking from their interaction partners. Interestingly, heterosexual people who are lonely engage in very little self-disclosure with opposite-sex others (impairing the natural quid pro quo of self-disclosure in close friendships), but inappropriately high self-disclosure with same-sex others.

THE IMPACT OF NEGATIVE SELF-VIEWS.   Lonely people generally have negative self-views (Christensen & Kashy, 1998). They often experience other negative emotions, including anxiety, depression, and shyness (Jones et al., 1985). They have trouble trusting others and a fear of intimacy (Rotenberg, 1994; Sherman & Thelen, 1996), suggesting that they may have insecure attachment models (Duggan & Brennan, 1994). For example, lonely people show greater accuracy for remembering negative feedback about themselves (Frankel & Prentice-Dunn, 1990). In contrast, non-lonely people show greater accuracy for remembering positive feedback.

THE IMPACT OF NEGATIVE EXPECTATIONS.   Lonely people also have extremely negative expectations about their interactions with others as shown in Figure 14.13 (Bruch, Hamer, & Heimberg, 1995; Meleshko & Alden, 1993). They often feel nervous and inhibited during social interactions, in part because they expect that others are forming a negative impression of them, and hence interact in a highly self-protective way. In one study, both lonely and non-lonely people watched videotapes of their own interactions with friends (Duck, Pond,

Leatham, 1994). Compared to non-lonely people, lonely people tended to evaluate the communication quality lower and draw more negative conclusions about their own friendships. In sum, lonely people may be extremely critical of their own communication patterns, which in turn leads to dissatisfaction with their behaviour in relationships.

RELATIONSHIP DISSOLUTION

Romantic breakups are understandably difficult—the end of such a relationship is stressful and disruptive. These breakups can lead to negative psychological outcomes, including sadness, depression, and anger (Sbarra & Emery, 2005). People who are left or "dumped" typically experience increased distress, compared to those who initiate the breakup.

NEGATIVE IMPACT OF DIVORCE. Relationship dissolution is particularly hard when it involves children. Children who experience their parents' divorce experience negative outcomes, including higher conflict in their own marriages, more negative attitudes toward marriage, and a decreased likelihood of being in a close relationship (Segrin, Taylor, & Altman, 2005).

Why do children of divorce experience such negative, and lasting, consequences? One explanation is that divorce is disruptive to children's lives in a number of ways, including changes in the family's economic status and adjusting to living in a single-parent home. Thus, some people have argued that couples need to "stay together for the sake of the children," and that people should try to stay together if at all possible in order to avoid the disruption for the children. (Keep reading to find out whether this is actually a good idea or not.)

Another explanation is that divorce may lead children to develop negative beliefs about relationships. After all, findings indicate that the children of divorced parents are themselves more likely to experience a divorce, so it may be that children whose parents divorce develop more negative attitudes about marriage in general and about their potential spouse in particular.

Children whose parents get divorced (or have high levels of conflict) may also model their own relationships on such patterns, and thereby experience negative marriages themselves. After all, children who grow up and observe their parents' frequent fights may experience negative consequences and beliefs about relationships regardless of whether the parents eventually choose to divorce. In one study, researchers examined 297 parents and their adult married children (Amato & Booth, 2001). Findings indicated that children whose parents' marriage had a lot of conflict also had a lot of conflict (and less happiness and more problems and instability) in their own marriages. What accounts for this relationship? Children's perceptions of their parents' marriage were a significant predictor of their own marital problems (probably due to observational learning). This is true regardless of whether parents ultimately got divorced. Similarly, research with adolescents indicates that parental marital status is not strongly related to children's psychological adjustment, but that the level of conflict that children perceived in their parents' marriage was a strong predictor of the children's well-being (Enos & Handal, 1986).

BENEFITS OF RELATIONSHIP BREAKUP. When a relationship breaks up, people with secure attachment models experience less distress than those with anxious or avoidant attachment models (Davis, Shaver, & Vernon, 2003; Sbarra, 2006). People may also experience benefits, as Table 14.5 shows.

Even divorce can have some positive outcomes. For example, individuals whose parents divorced report more positive relationships with their mothers, greater social support, and more independence than those with intact families (Riggio, 2004). Divorce may therefore bring some benefits to children as they struggle with their mother to adapt to changes brought on by the divorce and take on greater responsibility at an earlier age. Interestingly, individuals who experience the divorce of their parents also report less anxiety about their own personal relationships than those whose parents' marriage is still intact. In this way, they may come to understand that relationships don't last forever, and that people may still be happy even if a valued relationship ends.

Table 14.5	Positive Changes Caused by Relationship Breakups

Although relationship breakups typically cause tremendous sadness, they can also teach us valuable things about ourselves that will help us in our future relationships (Tashiro & Frazier, 2003).

Category	Example
Person positive	Through breaking up, I found I can handle more on my own. I am more self-confident.
Other positives	I've learned what I do and don't want in a relationship partner. I'm a lot more cautious in choosing a romantic partner.
Relational positives	I know not to jump into a relationship too quickly. I learned many relationship skills that I can apply in the future (e.g., the importance of saying you're sorry).
Environment positives	I rely on my friends more. I forgot how important friends are when I was with him. I also concentrate more on school now. I'm putting so much more time and effort toward it.

[CONCEPTS IN CONTEXT]

COMMON RELATIONSHIP PROBLEMS

FACTOR	EXAMPLE
Conflict	Kayla is very eager to discuss the problems in her marriage. But every time she tries to start a discussion with her husband, Jack, he simply walks away.
Jealousy	Al's girlfriend Gisèle is on a trip with some friends. He knows that these friends enjoy going out dancing and drinking at bars, and he's worried that Gisèle may become interested in dating someone she meets on the trip.
Loneliness	Naomi is just starting university, and she very much wants to make new friendships. But Naomi feels pretty bad about herself. She doubts that most other people would even want to be her friend.
Dissolution	After 12 years of marriage, Jesse and Marc have just decided to divorce. They're worried about the effects of this decision on their son, Matthias. After talking with a counsellor, however, they realize that their constant fighting may already be causing him problems. They agree that an environment with less conflict would be better for him, and they start working on an amicable divorce.

HOW DOES CULTURE INFLUENCE ATTRACTION AND CLOSE RELATIONSHIPS?

Think about your own friendships. Would you say you're more satisfied with your best friendship, or with your friendships in general? Research in social psychology suggests that your culture may influence your answer to this question. In one study, researchers examined friendships among both Arab (more collectivistic) and Jewish (more individualistic) grade four and five students in Israel (Scharf & Hertz-Lazarowitz, 2003). Arab students tended to have better quality peer relationships in general. In contrast, Jewish students tended to have better quality best-friend relationships. These findings make sense given the relative importance placed on connectedness and reciprocity in collectivistic cultures (and hence, strong social networks), as well as the relative importance placed on independence, autonomy, and personal relationships in individualistic ones. This study demonstrates that the predictors of friendship satisfaction are different for people in different cultures. This section will examine this and other ways in which culture impacts on people's views about attraction and close relationships, including their definition of beauty, the nature of love, and definitions of friendship.

DEFINING BEAUTY

Researchers have documented cultural differences in the meaning of attractiveness. In a study by Daibo, Murasawa, and Chou (1994), for example, Japanese and Korean participants were compared in regard to what they considered to be physically attractive. In Japan, large eyes, small mouths, and a small chin were judged attractive. In Korea, large eyes, a small, thin face, and a small, high nose were considered attractive. The findings indicate that the two cultures apply different standards for attractiveness.

However, on the whole, people across different cultures agree on what is attractive. In a meta-analysis reviewing 1,800 articles, Langlois et al. (2000) found that participants across and within cultures agree about what is attractive. These findings, along with others (Cunningham et al., 1995), suggest that there is a universal standard for what is considered attractive. People from diverse cultures show a consistent preference for faces that are "average" as opposed to "distinct," and for those with "baby faces" (McArthur & Berry, 1987). People across cultures also show particular gender differences in what they want in a mate, with men preferring young and attractive partners and women preferring older and wealthier partners (Buss, 1989; Buss & Schmitt, 1993; Feingold, 1992). These findings suggest there are some universal features that we look for in mates.

Newscom
Wedding of cricket star Shoaib Malik and Sania Mirza

But cultures do vary in the stereotypes they hold about attractiveness. Although the "what is beautiful is good" stereotype holds true across different cultures, the precise meaning of "what is good" varies from culture to culture (Wheeler & Kim, 1997). In Korea, people who are beautiful are seen as higher in integrity and concern for others. In the United States, on the other hand, people who are beautiful are seen as higher in dominance and assertiveness.

Dion, Pak, and Dion (1990) from the University of Toronto, argued that physical attractiveness is less salient in collectivistic than individualistic societies. This is because collectivistic values emphasize the group rather than the individual. As a result, group related attributes such as family and social networks are considered to be more important than individual attributes such as physical attractiveness. In an experiment, Dion and colleagues (1990) asked participants of Chinese ethnicity in Toronto to report their impressions of a person based on the person's photograph, which varied in physical attractiveness. It was found that Chinese students who had high involvement with their ethnic community were less likely to give the photo a positive attractiveness rating than those who had low involvement with their ethnic community. The researchers argued that being involved with the Chinese community reinforced collectivistic values, which reduced the likelihood of their group members stereotyping based on physical attractiveness (Dion et al., 1990).

THE NATURE OF LOVE

Cultures have very distinct views about the importance of different types of love (Dion & Dion, 1993, 1996; Simmons, vom Kolke, & Shimizu, 1986). Cultures may even differ in how they define love. For example, people in individualistic cultures, such as the United States and Italy, overwhelmingly see "passionate love" as exciting and positive. On the other hand, those in China see "passionate love" as both positive and negative—as a type of "sad love." In one study, researchers examined lyrics of popular love songs in the United States and China (Rothbaum & Tsang, 1998). They rated the songs on several dimensions, including the degree of intense desire, negative outcomes, suffering, and dependence. Western love songs were more likely to focus on the two lovers as isolated from others (e.g., "There is nobody here, it's just you and me, the way I want it to be"). In contrast, Chinese love songs were more likely to include negative views of love, such as love connected to suffering (e.g., "Not knowing that tragedy has been predestined . . . Can't forget the commitment we had made . . . I call to you with the endless pain in my heart").

IMPORTANCE OF LOVE FOR MARRIAGE. Cultures also differ considerably in the relative importance placed on love as a precursor to marriage, with people in individualistic cultures seeing love as a more important component of marriage than people in collectivistic cultures (see Table 12.7; Dion & Dion, 1996; Levine, Sato, Hashimoto, & Verma, 1995; Sprecher, Sullivan, & Hatfield, 1994). Levine and colleagues (1995) asked university students in 11 countries—Australia, Brazil, England, Hong Kong, India, Japan, Mexico, Pakistan, the Philippines, Thailand, and the United States—to rate the importance of love for marriage. It was found that participants from Western nations (Australia, Brazil, England, Mexico, and the U.S.) valued the importance of love for establishing a marriage more than the participants from Eastern nations (India, Pakistan, the Philippines, and Thailand). Japan and Hong Kong, two Eastern countries with highly developed economies, fell between these two groups. Overall, it was found that participants considered love to be more important in marriage if they came from nations that are economically prosperous, have an individualistic culture, have higher rates of divorce, and have lower fertility rates.

Kenneth Dion and Karen Dion (1993) from the University of Toronto studied love styles among students. They found that Chinese and other Asian students scored significantly higher on *storge* (companionate love) than did Anglo-European students. Goodwin and Findlay (1997) also examined love styles among students, this time in the UK, and found that Chinese students from Hong Kong endorsed pragmatic and logical love more than the British students did. Chinese students also endorsed less erotic love than the British students.

People in individualistic cultures also expect more from marital relationships (Hatfield & Sprecher, 1995). Individualistic cultures emphasize personal fulfillment in marriage, and thus focus on the impact of individual factors, such as personality and attractiveness, on relationship satisfaction (Goodwin & Findlay, 1997). They're choosy in their preferences for dating and marriage partners, and see individuals as having an inherent right to choose a spouse on their own, even if this choice conflicts with the wishes of family and friends (Sprecher et al., 1994).

Dion & Dion (1993) suggest that, paradoxically, some of the psychological elements of individualism make the likelihood of realizing desired outcomes like romantic love or personal fulfillment in marriage more difficult. Dion & Dion (1991) also found that among Canadian students an individualistic value orientation was associated with a "ludic" style of love (a playful, noncommittal approach), but also with lesser likelihood of describing actual romantic love experiences as having been tender, deep, and rewarding.

In contrast, collectivistic cultures emphasize the importance of intimacy across a network of family relationships, not just within marriage (Dion & Dion, 1993; Simmons et al., 1986). For example, while only about 5 to 10 percent of people from Western nations would marry a person they didn't love, 50 percent of respondents from India and Pakistan said they would do so (see Figure 14.15).

Chinese people also value social or parental conformity more than Americans do. Family approval of a relationship influences individuals' commitment to that relationship in Indonesia, but not in Australia (MacDonald & Jessica, 2006). Moreover, the families of both partners in the couple have more influence over the future of a romantic relationship in

FIGURE 14.15 WHO MARRIES FOR GOOD QUALITIES, BUT NOT FOR LOVE?

Students were asked, "If a man (woman) had all the other qualities you desired, would you marry this person if you were not in love with him (her)?" (Levine et al., 1995). About half of those in the collectivistic cultures of India and Pakistan would agree to marry this person. In contrast, very few of those in the individualistic cultures of the United States, England, and Australia would agree to do so.

	India	Pakistan	U.S.	England	Australia
Yes	49.0%	50.4%	3.5%	7.3%	4.8%
No	24.0%	39.1%	85.9%	83.6%	80.0%
Undecided	26.9%	10.4%	10.6%	9.1%	15.2%

collectivistic cultures than in individualistic ones. Researchers from Canada, the Netherlands, and the UK have found that research participants from countries with collectivist cultures accept more parental influence in their choice of partner than do those from individualistic cultures (Buunk, Park, & Duncan, 2010).

These differences in views about the importance of love in marriage lead to different views about the cause of relationship dissolution. In individualistic countries, people are more willing to dissolve a marriage that isn't working, because the primary goal of marriage is seen as being the happiness and fulfillment of both spouses (Hatfield & Sprecher, 1995; Sprecher et al., 1994). On the other hand, in collectivistic countries, marriage may be seen as a way to join two families in order to benefit them both, and hence the happiness of the spouses may be less important. Arranged marriages cultivate the existing social structure, expand socio-economic and political links between families, and preserve the control of more elderly generations over younger generations (Gupta, 1976). A famous historical example of this type of union is the marriage of Marie Antoinette, who was Austrian and married off by her family to French royalty with the hope that this marriage would improve relations between the two countries.

SATISFACTION IN ARRANGED MARRIAGES. Arranged marriage is the most common type of marriage around the world. In many cultures, marriages are initiated by family members. Not surprisingly, couples in arranged, or family-initiated, marriages report some differences in their patterns of interaction compared to people in couple-initiated marriages. A study of couples in Turkey revealed that those in family-initiated marriages reported fewer interactions alone with their partner and lower levels of disclosure in their relationship compared to people in couple-oriented relationships (Hortacsu & Oral, 2001).

How does the type of marriage impact relationship satisfaction? Some research indicates that marital satisfaction is lower in arranged marriages than in couple-initiated ones. For example, one study with over 500 Chinese women compared marital satisfaction in arranged marriages and "love matches" (Xiaohe & Whyte, 1990). Women in love matches reported greater satisfaction than those in arranged marriages. It's important to note, however, that marital satisfaction may not be related to overall life satisfaction in collectivistic cultures. Additionally, other research indicates no differences in relationship satisfaction between those living in arranged marriages and marriages of choice (Myers, Madathil, & Tingle, 2005).

MANAGING CONFLICT. People in different cultures rely on different types of strategies for managing conflict. For example, Banu Cingöz-Ulu and Richard Lalonde from

York University examined the conflict resolution styles of Canadians and Turks in a variety of relationships. They found differences in two strategies: "giving in" and using help from a third party. Canadian participants tended to vary their strategy more according to the relationship than did Turks. Canadians reported giving in significantly more often to their romantic partners than to their same-sex friends, whereas Turkish participants didn't differ in how much they gave in to their romantic partners and same-sex friends. Canadian participants also used third-party help significantly more often for conflicts in their romantic relationships than they did for conflicts in their same same-sex and opposite-sex friendships (Cingöz-Ulu & Lalonde, 2007). These results seem at odds with previous research that has found that people from individualistic cultures use more direct and confrontational strategies (e.g., persuading, dominating) and that people from collectivistic cultures use more indirect strategies (e.g., avoiding, compromising, and third-party help). In fact, the authors suggest that there are more similarities than differences across the two cultures, and that the differences that do exist are determined more by the nature of the relationship than by culture.

Yum (2004) examined the types of responses to conflict in both individualistic (American) and collectivistic (South Korean) samples. Members of collectivistic cultures tend to use more relationship-maintaining strategies (e.g., loyalty, voice) and use fewer relationship-destructive strategies (e.g., exit, neglect) than those in individualistic cultures. These findings make sense given the great focus on maintaining relationships and showing loyalty and respect in collectivistic cultures. Individualistic cultures, on the other hand, emphasize the importance of engaging in behaviours to satisfy one's own personal needs and goals. As is shown in Table 14.6, people from collectivistic and individualistic societies differ in how they would handle a conflict between their romantic partner and their parents.

> **Questioning the Research:**
>
> Although this study suggests that love is more important for marriage in individualistic than collectivistic cultures, can you think of an alternative explanation for this association? (Hint: What else might differ across these different cultures?)

Table 14.6 How Would You Handle a Parent-Fiancé Conflict?

People in different cultures vary considerably on how they would handle conflicts between their parents and their fiancé, with a higher percentage of Australians and Americans reporting that they would most likely do nothing, and a higher percentage of Greek and Hong Kong participants reporting that they would most likely tell the fiancé to fit in.

	Australia	U.S.	Greece	Hong Kong
Nothing	52%	28%	14%	3%
Tell fiancé that he or she should make a greater effort to "fit in with the family"	26%	28%	76%	79%

Source: Triandis, H. C., Chen, X. P., & Chan, D. K. (1998). Scenarios for the measurement of collectivism and individualism. *Journal of Cross-Cultural Psychology, 29*, 275-289.

THE NATURE OF FRIENDSHIPS Friendships in individualistic cultures often include concepts describing personal stimulation, such as creative, active, and energetic, and they direct activities (Maeda & Ritchie, 2003). People in individualistic cultures tend to want friends who are independent (e.g., "not a whiner"). In fact, too much dependence in a friendship is seen as a sign of personal weakness.

People in individualistic cultures tend to distinguish between types of friendships (Adams & Plaut, 2003). As described at the start of this section, people in individualistic cultures report having high-quality "best friendships," and are likely to depend heavily on a small number of friends. An international team including researchers from the University of Saskatchewan found that emotional reliance on friends, meaning willingness to confide in and rely on our friends, is higher in the United States and Russia and lower in South Korea and Turkey (Ryan, La Guardia, Solky-Butzel, Chirkov, & Kim, 2005).

In contrast, friendships in collectivistic cultures often emphasize comfort and ease (Maeda & Ritchie, 2003). For example, research on friendships in Ghana revealed that such relationships focus on practical support, advice, and interdependence (Adams & Plaut, 2003).

Similarly, studies of friendships in Japan suggest an emphasis on providing self-esteem support (e.g., "encourages me"). As described in the Business Connections box, people in collectivistic cultures also tend to focus on interpersonal concerns in larger social networks, including workplace relationships.

BUSINESS CONNECTIONS

The Impact of Culture on Attitudes about Work

Canada is a culturally diverse country with 19.2 percent of Canadians born in another country (Statistics Canada, 2006). When discussing economics, many debates touch on the different attitudes of people with different ethnicities have toward work. The idea is that newcomers arrive in Canada with work attitudes and approaches to work that are different than non-immigrants' attitudes. To explore this, Bauder (2006) interviewed 509 individuals from predominantly Chinese-speaking, Punjabi-speaking, and English-speaking neighbourhoods in Vancouver. He found that immigrants are focused more on economic survival and less on their careers than non-immigrants. Female immigrants were on average more oriented toward economic survival and less toward career-development than non-immigrant women. In a slightly different manner, male immigrants had stronger comprehensive work attitudes but were less career-oriented than non-immigrant men. Furthermore, rural immigrants were even less career-oriented than urban

The Canadian Press/Aaron Harris

immigrants. It appears that newcomers often adjust based on strategic responses to the context of particular social and economic interests of the individual, a social group, the state, and a range of labour market factors (Bauder, 2003).

THE BIG PICTURE

LINKING ATTRACTION AND CLOSE RELATIONSHIPS

This chapter included many applications of the three "big ideas" studied in social psychology. The examples below should help you see the connection between interpersonal attraction and close relationships and these big ideas, and contribute to your understanding of the big picture of social psychology.

THEME	EXAMPLES
The social world influences how we think about ourselves.	• Thinking about a close relationship helps us cope with threatening information about ourselves. • Married couples feel happiest in their relationships when their partner sees them as they see themselves.
The social world influences our thoughts, attitudes, and behaviour.	• Attractive professors get higher teaching evaluations. • People in an inequitable marriage are more likely to leave for an alternative relationship.
Our attitudes and behaviour shape the social world around us.	• People with an anxious attachment style see negative behaviour as worse than do those with secure or avoidant attachment styles. In turn, they respond to negative behaviour by acting more negatively themselves, which leads to conflict. • People who are lonely engage in less self-disclosure, which in turn inhibits self-disclosure from their partner.

This chapter has examined five key principles of interpersonal attraction and close relationships.

1. What factors lead to attraction?

This section examined different predictors of interpersonal attraction. Physical attractiveness influences attraction, as do relationship factors (similarity, complementarity, and reciprocity), and situational factors (physiological arousal, proximity, and the contrast effect). You also learned why "secret relationships" can lead to particularly high levels of attraction.

2. What is love?

This section described theories of love. These include the triangular theory (passion, intimacy, commitment), the love styles model (*ludus, eros, mania, agape, storge, pragma*), arousal-attribution theory, reward theory, the social norms approach, and social exchange theory. And you learned that we see relationships with people we "love" as different from those with people we are "in love" with.

3. What predicts a healthy and happy relationship?

This section described two models that predict satisfaction in relationships: the attachment styles model (secure, anxious/ambivalent, anxious/avoidant) and the positive illusions approach.

4. What are some common problems in close relationships?

This section described several common problems that emerge in close relationships. These topics include constructive and destructive approaches to managing conflict, gender differences in reactions to infidelity, the causes and correlates of loneliness, and the hazards and benefits of relationship dissolution.

5. How does culture influence attraction and close relationships?

The last section in this chapter described the role of culture in influencing interpersonal attraction and close relationships. We examined cultural differences in defining beauty, the nature of love, and the nature of friendship. Finally, you learned that people in individualistic cultures report having higher-quality "best friend" relationships, and those in collectivistic cultures report having higher-quality peer relationships in general.

Key Terms

attachment styles 504	equity theory 513	positive illusions 504
companionate love 496	excitation transfer 498	reciprocity 492
comparison level 512	investment 512	social exchange theory 511
comparison level for alternatives (CLalt) 512	matching hypothesis 491	
demand/withdraw interaction pattern 516	negative attributional traps 517	
	passionate love 498	

Questions for Review

1. Why do most people prefer to date attractive partners? Provide four specific reasons.

2. Explain how each of the models of love conceptualizes the distinct types of love.

3. Describe each of the three models that predict relationship satisfaction.

4. What are four common problems in close relationships?

5. Describe how culture influences how people see love and marriage.

Take Action!

1. Let's say your roommate is interested in dating a woman in his history class. What three things would you suggest to help him establish a relationship with her?

2. Your aunt and uncle have been married for 30 years. Based on your knowledge of triangular theory, what love components are likely to be highest in their relationship right now?

3. Your older sister recently started a new dating relationship. According to social exchange theory, what types of things should she do to increase her relationship satisfaction?

4. Imagine that you're getting married. What two approaches might you use when managing conflict in this relationship, and what two approaches would it be good for you to avoid?

5. Your co-worker has a friend from India who is planning on having an arranged marriage. Your co-worker makes a number of rude remarks about her friend's approach to marriage. What could you tell her about the cultural differences in marriage as well as the predictors of marital satisfaction?

RESEARCH CONNECTIONS

Participate in Research

Activity 1 Are Average Faces Most Attractive?: This chapter described how people see composite faces, meaning those that are made up of many different faces, as more attractive than single faces. Go online to look at different faces and rate how attractive you find each one—then find out whether you too see composite photographs as more attractive.

Activity 2 Testing the Triangular Theory of Love: This chapter examined the three distinct components of love, according to triangular theory. Go online to rate your feelings of intimacy, passion, and commitment to see what type of love you have in your current (or had in your most recent) relationship.

Activity 3 The Impact of Attachment Styles on Dating Patterns: This chapter described the impact of attachment styles on patterns of dating as well as interactions in romantic relationships. Go online to test your own attachment style and see how this style may influence your dating patterns and interactions.

Activity 4 Gender Differences in Jealousy: You learned in this chapter about the impact of gender on reactions to different types of infidelity. Go online to read about different types of infidelity, and then rate how upset you would be in each situation.

Activity 5 The Impact of Culture on Love: The final section of this chapter described how people from different cultures vary in how strongly they believe that love is an essential part of marriage. Go online to rate your agreement with the importance of love in marriage, and the absence of love in leading to divorce. Then see how other students rated their own agreement.

Test a Hypothesis

As you learned in this chapter, men and women tend to look for different characteristics in dating partners. To test whether this hypothesis is true, find personal ads for dating either online or in a local newspaper, and calculate the percentage of men and women who are looking for particular traits (such as attractiveness, wealth, or intelligence). Then, go online to report your findings to other students.

Design a Study

Go online to design your own study that will test factors that predict interpersonal attraction. You'll be able to choose the type of study you want to conduct (self-report, observational/naturalistic, or experimental), choose your own independent and dependent variables, and form your own hypothesis. Then you can share your findings with other students across the country!

GLOSSARY

absolute or realistic deprivation the belief that one's own resources are directly threatened by people in other groups

acculturation behavioural and psychological changes that happen when groups of individuals having different cultures come into continuous first hand contact

actor-observer effect the tendency to see other people's behaviour as caused by dispositional factors, but see our own behaviour as caused by the situation

affective forecasting the process of predicting the impact of both positive and negative events on mood

aggression physical or verbal behaviour that is intended to harm another individual who is motivated to avoid such treatment

altruism helping without expectation of personal gain

anchoring and adjustment a mental shortcut in which people rely on an initial starting point in making an estimate but then fail to adequately adjust from this anchor

arbitration resolution of a conflict by a neutral third party who studies both sides and imposes a settlement

archival research a research approach that uses already recorded behaviour

arousal/cost-reward model a model that describes helping behaviour as caused in part by the physiological arousal that people experience when they see someone in need of help and in part by their calculation of the costs and rewards of providing such help

arousal-affect/excitation transfer model a model describing aggression as influenced by both the intensity of the arousal and the type of emotion produced by the stimulus

assimilation the tendency to abandon one's original culture and participate in the larger society

attachment styles the expectations that a person has about a relationship partner, based largely on the person's early experiences with his or her caregivers

attitudes positive and negative evaluations of people, objects, events, and ideas

automatic thinking a type of decision-making process that occurs at an unconscious or automatic level and is entirely effortless and unintentional

auto-stereotype a stereotype that one holds about one's own group

availability heuristic a mental shortcut in which people make a judgement based on how easily they can bring something to mind

aversive prejudice conscious endorsement of unprejudiced beliefs about a group while at the same time holding unconscious negative attitudes toward the group

bargaining a very commonly used approach to resolving conflict at an individual level, whereby an agreement is sought through direct negotiation between both sides in the conflict

base-rate fallacy an error in which people ignore the numerical frequency, or base rate, of an event in estimating how likely it is to occur

basking in reflected glory (BIRGing) associating with successful others to increase one's feelings of self-worth

behavioural confirmation/self-fulfilling prophecy the process by which people's expectations about a person lead them to elicit behaviour that confirms those expectations

behavioural economics the study of how social, cognitive, and emotional factors influence economic decisions

behaviourism a theory of learning that describes people's behaviour as acquired through conditioning

belief in a just world the phenomenon in which people believe that bad things happen to bad people and that good things happen to good people

belief perseverance the tendency to maintain, and even strengthen, beliefs in the face of disconfirming evidence

benevolent sexism having positive, but patronizing, views of women

bystander effect the situation whereby people are less likely to help in emergency situations when there are other people present than if the person who could help is alone, resulting in a decreased likelihood of help being given

catharsis release of suppressed energy or emotion

central or systematic route processing a type of processing of persuasive messages that occurs when people have the ability and motivation to carefully evaluate the arguments in a persuasive message

classical conditioning a type of learning in which a neutral stimulus is repeatedly paired with a stimulus that elicits a specific response, and eventually the neutral stimulus elicits that response on its own

cognitive dissonance theory a theory that describes attitude change as occurring in order to reduce the unpleasant arousal people experience when they engage in a behaviour that conflicts with their attitude or when they hold two conflicting attitudes

cognitive-neoassociation theory a theory that describes aggression as caused by experiencing negative affect of any kind, which in turn evokes aggression-related thoughts, memories, feelings, and ideas

collective effect model a model which describes people's motivation to exert effort in group tasks as depending on whether they believe their distinct efforts will be identifiable, their efforts will make a difference in the group's success, and they'll experience positive outcomes

collectivistic a view of the self as part of a larger social network, including family, friends, and co-workers

common in-group identity model a reduction in prejudice is more likely when group members believe they have a shared identity

common resource dilemma a social dilemma in which each person can take as much as he or she wants of a common resource, but if everyone takes as much as they want, the resource will eventually be completely depleted

companionate love a stable, calm, and dependable kind of love that may include quiet intimacy, stability, shared attitudes/values/ life experiences, and high levels of self-disclosure

comparison level for alternatives (CLalt) a calculation regarding the expected benefits and costs that a person could receive from having a relationship with various other partners

comparison level the expected outcome of a relationship, meaning the extent to which a person expects his or her relationship to be rewarding

compliance changes in behaviour that are caused by a direct request

confirmation bias the tendency to search for information that supports one's initial view

conformity the tendency to change our perceptions, opinions, or behaviours in ways that are consistent with perceived group norms

consensus The first component of covariation theory and it refers to whether other people generally agree or disagree with a given person

consistency information about whether a person's behaviour toward a given stimulus is the same across time

content-free schemas rules about processing information

contrast effect the relative difference in intensity between two stimuli and their effect on each other

controlled or effortful thinking thinking that is effortful, conscious, and intentional

correlational research a research technique that examines the extent to which two or more variables are associated with one another

correspondent inference theory the theory that people infer whether a person's behaviour is caused by the person's internal disposition by looking at various factors related to the person's action

counterfactual thinking the tendency to imagine alternative outcomes to various events

covariation theory the theory that people determine the causes of a person's behaviour by focusing on the factors that are present when a behaviour occurs and absent when it doesn't occur, with specific attention on the role of consensus, distinctiveness, and consistency

covert measures measures used by researchers that rely on participants' behaviour or reaction not directly under participants' control

cross-ethnic identification bias the tendency to see outgroup members as looking very similar to one another, and showing greater accuracy for recognizing in-group members than outgroup members

cultural display rules rules in a culture that govern how universal emotions should be expressed

debriefing a disclosure made to participants after research procedures are completed in which the researcher explains the purpose of the study, answers questions, attempts to resolve any negative feelings, and emphasizes the study's contributions to science

deception giving false information to the participants in a study

decision-making process model a model that describes helping behaviour as a function of five distinct steps

deindividuation the tendency to not follow normal rules of behaviour as a result of losing one's self awareness

demand characteristics the cues in a research setting that may inadvertently guide participants' behaviour

demand/withdraw interaction pattern a relatively common situation in which one partner is nagging, critical, and insistent about discussing the relationship problems while the other partner is withdrawn, silent, and defensive

demographic variables varying characteristics of an individual, sample group, or population

dependent variable the factor that is measured to see if it is affected by the independent variable

descriptive norms norms that describe how people behave in a given situation

desensitization or disinhibition the reduction of physiological reactions to a stimuli (e.g., violence) due to repeated exposure to the stimuli (e.g., violence)

diffusion of responsibility the belief that other people present in a situation will assume responsibility, which contributes to the bystander effect

discrimination behaviour directed against people solely because of their membership in a particular group

displacement people's tendency to aggress against others when the source of frustration is unavailable

distinctiveness refers to whether the person generally reacts in a similar way across different situations

door-in-the-face technique a compliance technique where one first asks for a big request, and then asks for a smaller request which then seems more reasonable

downward social comparison comparing ourselves to people who are worse than we are on a given trait or ability in an attempt to feel better about ourselves

ecological fallacy the error of assuming that relationships between variables at the group level are the same as relationships at the individual level

elaboration likelihood model (ELM) a model describing two distinct routes (central and peripheral) that are used to process persuasive messages

emotional or hostile aggression aggression in which one inflicts harm for its own sake on another

empathy the ability to understand other people's perspectives and respond emotionally to other people's experiences

empathy-altruism hypothesis the idea that when we feel empathy for a person, we will help that person even if we incur a cost in doing so

equity theory the theory that relationship satisfaction depends on the ratio of costs and benefits for each partner in a relationship

ethnocentrism a tendency to attribute desirable characteristics to one's own group and undesirable characteristics to outgroups; the belief that one's cultural values are shared by others.

event recording or experience sampling measures a particular type of self-report or survey data where participants report various experiences they have at regular time intervals. Also called experience sampling.

event schemas scripts that people have for well-known situations which help them prepare for the expected sequence of events

exchange relationships a relationship in which people desire and expect strict reciprocity

excitation transfer when the arousal caused by one stimulus is added to the arousal from a second stimulus and the combined arousal is erroneously attributed to the second stimulus

experimental methods a research approach that involves the manipulation of one or more independent variables and the measurement of one or more dependent variables

experimental realism or psychological realism the extent to which participants are engaged in a particular study and hence act in more spontaneous and natural ways

experimenter blind the procedure that ensures the experimenter who is interacting with a study's participants does not know which condition the participants are in

experimenter expectancy effects when an experimenter's expectations about the results of the study influence participants' behaviour and thereby affect the results of the study

external attribution seeing the behaviour as caused by something external to the person who performs the behaviour

external validity the degree to which there can be reasonable confidence that the same results would be obtained for other people in other situations

facial feedback hypothesis the hypothesis that changes in facial expression can lead to changes in emotion

false consensus effect the tendency to overestimate the extent to which other people share our opinions, attitudes, and behaviours

false uniqueness effect the tendency to underestimate the extent to which other people are likely to share our positive attitudes and behaviour

field dependent having more difficulty in identifying an embedded figure in a larger background but greater ability to perceive an image as one holistic figure

field experiments experiments that are conducted in natural settings

field independent having the ability to identify an embedded figure and separate it from a larger background

foot-in-the-door technique a two-step compliance technique in which an influencer first asks someone to perform a small request, and then asks for a larger request

forewarning making people aware that they will soon receive a persuasive message

framing the tendency to be ¬influenced by the way an issue is presented

frustration-aggression theory a theory that frustration always leads to the desire to behave aggressively, and that aggression is caused by frustration

fundamental attribution error (or correspondence bias) the tendency to overestimate the role of personal causes and underestimate the role of situational causes in explaining behaviour

general aggression model a model proposing that both individual differences and situational factors lead to aggression-related thoughts, feelings, and/or physiological arousal

Gestalt psychology a theory that proposes objects are viewed holistically

good mood effect when people are in a good mood, they are more likely to help

GRIT (graduated and reciprocated initiatives in tension-reduction) a strategy for resolving conflict that involves unilateral and persistent efforts to establishing trust and cooperation between opposing parties

group polarization when the initial tendencies of group members become more extreme following group discussion

groupthink a group decision-making style that is characterized by an excessive tendency among group members to seek concurrence, consensus, and unanimity, as opposed to making the best decision

hetero-stereotype stereotypes about other groups

heuristics mental shortcuts that are often used to form judgements and make decisions

hindsight bias the tendency of people to see a given outcome as having been inevitable once they know the actual outcome

hostile sexism feelings of hostility toward women based on their threat to men's power

hypothesis a testable prediction about the conditions under which an event will occur

illusory correlation the tendency to overestimate the association between variables that are only slightly or not at all correlated

illusory superiority an unrealistically positive view of the self

implicit personality theory the theory that certain traits and behaviours go together

impression management theory a theory that individuals try to maintain impressions that are consistent with the perceptions they want to convey to others

impression management strategies that people use to create positive impressions of themselves

independent self-construal a conception of the self as autonomous and independent from others, and behaving primarily to express its own internal attributes

independent variable the variable that is manipulated in experimental research

individualistic a view of the self as distinct, autonomous, self-contained, and endowed with unique attributes

informational influence the influence that produces conformity when a person believes others are correct in their judgements, and the person wants to be right

informed consent an individual's deliberate, voluntary decision to participate in research, based on the researcher's description of what such participation will involve

ingratiation a strategy in which people try to make themselves likeable to someone else, often through flattery and praise

in-group favouritism the tendency to evaluate one's in-group more positively than outgroups

injunctive norms norms that describe what people ought to do in a given situation, meaning the type of behaviour that is approved of in the situation

inoculation the idea that exposure to a weak version of a persuasive message strengthens people's ability to later resist stronger versions of the message

instinct theory of aggression a theory that describes aggression as innate biological drive

instrumental aggression aggression in which one inflicts harm in order to obtain something of value

integration the tendency to maintain one's own culture and also participate in the larger society

integrative solution a negotiated resolution to a conflict in which all parties obtain outcomes that are superior to what they would have obtained from an equal division of the contested resources

interdependent self-construal a conception of the self as connected to others, with its behaviour contingent on the values, thoughts, and preferences of others

intergroup attribution making attributions about one's own and others' behaviours based on group membership

intergroup processes processes that occur between groups of people

intergroup relations the way in which people in groups perceive, think about, feel about, and act toward people in other groups

internal attribution refers to whether the person's behaviour is caused by personal factors, such as traits, ability, effort, or personality

internal validity the degree to which one can validly draw conclusions about the effects of the independent variable on the dependent variable

inter-rater reliability the extent to which two or more coders agree on ratings of a particular measure

intragroup processes processes that happen within a group

intuition a decision-making shortcut in which we rely on our instinct instead of relying on more objective information

investment the resources devoted to a relationship that cannot be retrieved

kinship selection the idea that we're more likely to help those we are genetically related to

literature review examining previous relevant studies on a given topic and critically appraising them

lowballing a two-step technique in which the influencer secures agreement with a request, but then increases the size of that request by revealing hidden costs

marginalization the tendency to neither maintain one's own culture nor participate in the larger society

matching hypothesis people's tendency to seek and find partners who are roughly at their own level of physical attractiveness

mediation a particular type of bargaining in which a neutral third party tries to resolve a conflict by facilitating communication between the opposing parties and offering suggestions

mere exposure the phenomenon by which the greater the exposure that we have to a given stimulus, the more we like it

meta-analysis a literature review that analyzes data from several studies that examine related hypothesis

meta-stereotype a person's beliefs about the stereotypes that outgroup members hold about the person's own group

minority influence a process in which a small number of people in a group lead an overall change in the group's attitude or behaviour

mirror-image perception reciprocal view when each group sees its own behaviour as caused by the actions of the other side

moral reasoning a personality factor that describes the extent to which a person's willingness to help depends on larger moral standards rather than the person's needs and the expected consequences for him or her of helping

mundane realism the extent to which the conditions of the study resemble places and events that exist in the real world

naïve psychology Heider's theory that people practise a form of untrained psychology as they use cause and effect analyses to understand their world and other people's behaviour

negative attributional traps explaining a partner's behaviour in negative ways

negative-state relief hypothesis a hypothesis that people are motivated to help others in order to relieve their own negative feelings

norm of reciprocity the idea that we should help those who are in need of assistance, because they will then help us in the future

norm of social responsibility the idea that we have an obligation to help those who are in need of assistance

normative influence the influence that produces conformity when a person fears the negative social consequences of appearing deviant

obedience behaviour that is produced by the commands of authority figures

observational learning/modelling a type of learning in which people's attitudes and behaviour are influenced by watching other people's attitudes and behaviour

observational/naturalistic methods a research approach that involves the observation and systematic recording of a particular behaviour

operant conditioning a type of learning in which behaviour that is rewarded increases, whereas behaviour that is punished decreases

operational definition a specific procedure or measure that one uses to test a hypothesis

outgroup homogeneity effect people's tendency to underestimate the variability of outgroup members compared to the variability of in-group members

overjustification the phenomenon in which receiving external rewards for a given behaviour can undermine the intrinsic motivation for engaging in this behaviour

passionate love an intense, exciting, and all-consuming type of love, which includes constant thoughts about the person, powerful physical attraction, and intense communication

perceived control the tendency to see uncontrollable events as at least partially under our control

perceptual confirmation the tendency to see things in line with one's expectations, beliefs, or preconceptions

peripheral cues cues that are associated with the context of a message rather than the content. These cues include length of the message, the source of the message, and the speed at which the message is delivered.

peripheral or heuristic route processing a type of processing of persuasive messages that occurs when people lack the ability and motivation to carefully evaluate a persuasive message, and therefore are influenced only by superficial cues

person schemas beliefs about other people, their traits, and goals

persuasion communication that is designed to influence a person's attitudes and behaviour

pluralistic ignorance a particular type of norm misperception that occurs when each individual in the group privately rejects the group's norms, but believes that others accept these norms

positive illusions the notion that people tend to see their romantic partners as well as their relationships in highly idealized ways

positive psychology a recent branch of psychology that studies individuals' strengths and virtues

prejudice hostile or negative feelings about people based on their membership in a certain group

primacy the tendency for information that is presented early to have a greater impact on judgements than information that is presented later

priming increase accessibility to a given concept or schema due to a prior experience

prisoner's dilemma the situation in which two people may choose to either cooperate with each other or compete

private conformity when people rethink their original views, and potentially change their minds to match what the group thinks

prosocial behaviour any behaviour that has the goal of helping another person

prototype/willingness model a model that describes the role of prototypes in influencing a person's willingness to engage in the behaviour in a given situation

public conformity when people's overt behaviours are in line with group norms

public goods dilemma a type of social dilemma where each person must decide what to contribute to a common pool of resources that will not exist unless people contribute to it

punishment the provision of unpleasant consequences to try to reduce a negative behaviour

random assignment a technique for placing participants into the different conditions in an experiment that gives all participants equal opportunity of being placed in any of the conditions

random sample or representative sample a sample that reflects the characteristics of the population of interest

reactance the idea that people react to threats to their freedom to engage in a behaviour by becoming even more likely to engage in that behaviour

realistic conflict theory a theory that describes conflict between different groups as resulting from individuals' self-interest motives in competition for jobs, land, power, and other resources

reciprocity a mutual exchange between two people; an in-kind response to the behaviour of others

reconstructive memory the process by which memories of a given event are altered after the event occurred

rejection-identification model a model which proposes that people in disadvantaged groups experience a negative impact on their well-being when they perceive prejudice and discrimination against themselves

relative deprivation the feelings of discontent caused by the belief that one fares poorly compared to people in other groups

representativeness the tendency to perceive someone or something based on its similarity to a typical case

Research Ethics Board A panel of experts responsible for the ethical assessment of all research proposals conducted at an organization

reverse discrimination preferential treatment of people in stereotyped groups

risky shift a process by which groups tend to make riskier decisions than individuals would make alone

role schemas behaviours that are expected of people in particular occupations or social positions

scarcity a compliance technique in which the opportunity to act is limited in terms of the time to act or number of opportunities

schemas mental structures that organize our knowledge about the world and influence how we interpret people and events

scientific method a technique for investigating phenomena, acquiring new knowledge, and/or correcting previous knowledge

self schemas our memory, inferences, and information about ourselves

self-affirmation theory a theory that describes how people can reduce the arousal caused by cognitive dissonance by affirming a different part of their identities, even if that part is completely unrelated to the cause of the arousal

self-awareness theory when people focus on their own behaviour, they are motivated to either change their behaviour (so their attitudes and behaviour are in line) or escape from self-awareness (to avoid noticing this contradiction)

self-concept an individual's overall beliefs about his or her own attributes

self-discrepancy theory the theory that our self-concept is influenced by the gap between how we actually see ourselves and how we want to see ourselves

self-esteem an individual's evaluation of his or her own worth

self-evaluation maintenance model the theory that our self-concept can be threatened if someone performs better than us on a task that is relevant to our sense of esteem

self-fulfilling prophecy the process by which people's expectations about a person lead them to elicit behaviour that confirms these expectations

self-handicapping a strategy in which people create obstacles to success so that potential failure can be blamed on these external factors

self-monitoring the extent to which one adjusts one's self-presentation in different situations

self-perception theory the theory that people infer their attitudes by simply observing their behaviour

self-perception how we think about ourselves

self-presentation how people work to convey certain images of themselves to others

self-promotion a strategy that focuses on making other people think you are competent or good in some way

self-serving attribution the tendency to view oneself in a positive light

self-standards model a model that proposes people experience discomfort whenever they see their behaviour as deviating from some type of important personal or normative standard, but that the strategy they use to reduce this dissonance will depend on what thoughts about the self are currently accessible

self-verification theory the expectation that other people's perception of oneself is consistent with one's own perception of oneself

separation the tendency to maintain one's own culture but to reject, or not participate in, the larger society

shifting standards model a model that posits that people within a group are more often compared to others within that group rather than to people in other groups

sleeper effect the phenomenon by which a message that initially is not particularly persuasive becomes more persuasive over time because people forget its source

social categorization the practice of classifying people into ingroups or outgroups based on attributes that the person has in common with the in-group or outgroup

social cognition how people think about the social world, and in particular how people select, interpret, and use information to make judgements about the world

social cognition how we think about the social world, and in particular how we select, interpret, and use information to make judgements about the world

social comparison theory the theory that people evaluate their own abilities and attributes by comparing themselves to other people

social compensation the notion that if a project is important to you, you may work even harder to compensate for the poor performance or social loafing of others

social constructionism the view that there is no absolute reality and that our knowledge and what we understand to be reality are socially constructed

social dilemma situations where if all individuals make self-interested choices the result will be the worst possible outcome for everyone

social dominance orientation a personality trait that indicates preference to maintain hierarchy within and between groups

social exchange theory the theory that people's satisfaction in a relationship is determined by the costs and rewards of the relationship

social facilitation when people do better on a task in the presence of others than when they're alone

social identity theory a theory that posits that each person strives to enhance his or her self-esteem, which is composed of two parts: a personal identity and a social identity

social impact theory the theory that people we are close to have more impact on us than people who are more distant

social influence the impact of other people's attitudes and behaviours on our thoughts, feelings, and behaviour

social inhibition when people do worse on a task in the presence of others than when they're alone

social learning theory a theory that describes behaviour as learned by observing or modelling others' behaviour as well as by the presence of punishments and rewards, or reinforcements

social loafing a group-produced reduction in individual output on easy tasks where contributions are pooled

social neuroscience a sub-discipline of social psychology examining how factors in the social world influence activity in the brain, as well as how neural processes influence attitudes and behaviour

social norms the implicit and explicit rules that a specific group has for its members on values, beliefs, attitudes, and behaviours

social norms unspoken but shared rules of conduct in a formal or informal group

social perception how people form impressions of and make inferences about other people and events in the social world

social psychology A scientific study of the way in which a person's thoughts, feelings, and behaviours are influenced by the real, imagined, or implied presence of others

sociocultural perspective a perspective describing people's behaviour and mental processes as being shaped in part by their social and/or cultural context

spotlight effect the tendency to overestimate the extent to which one's own appearance and behaviour are obvious to others

stereotype threat the fear that one's behaviour may confirm an existing cultural stereotype, which then disrupts one's performance

stereotype a belief that associates a whole group of people with a certain trait

subcategorization the maintenance of prior beliefs by creating separate categories for people who disconfirm these stereotypes

subliminal persuasion a type of persuasion that occurs when stimuli are presented at a very rapid and unconscious level

superordinate goal a goal that can only be achieved if the members of both groups cooperate

that's-not-all technique a compliance technique in which the influencer begins with an inflated request, and then decreases its apparent size by offering discounts or bonuses

trans-theoretical model (TTM) a model that views a change in behaviour as a progression through a series of stages, including pre contemplation, contemplation, preparation, action, and maintenance

theory of planned behaviour a theory that describes people's behaviour caused by their attitudes, subjective norms, and perceived behavioural control

theory an organized set of principles that explain observed phenomena

tit-for-tat a strategy in a prisoner's dilemma situation whereby one starts with cooperation, and then does whatever one's partner does on each subsequent interaction (e.g., cooperate after cooperation and compete after competition from one's partner)

trait negativity bias the tendency for people to be more influenced by negative traits than by positive ones

two-stage model of attribution a model in which people first automatically interpret a person's behaviour as caused by dispositional factors, and then later adjust this interpretation by taking into account situational factors that may have contributed to the behaviour

ultimate attribution error an error in which people make dispositional attributions for negative behaviour and situational attributions for positive behaviour by outgroup members, yet show the reverse attributions for successes and failures for their in-group members

unrealistic optimism the tendency for people to see themselves as less likely than others to suffer bad events in the future

urban overload hypothesis the hypothesis that people who live in urban areas are constantly exposed to stimulation, which in turn leads them to decrease their awareness of their environment

REFERENCES

Aaker, J. L., Benet-Martínez, V., & Garolera, J. (2001). Consumption symbols as carriers of culture: A study of Japanese and Spanish brand personality constucts. *Journal of Personality and Social Psychology, 81*, 492–508.

Aaker, J. L., & Williams, P. (1998). Empathy versus pride: The influence of emotional appeals across cultures. *Journal of Consumer Research, 25*, 241–261.

ABC News (2007). *Primetime Basic Instincts 5: The Milgram Experiment re-Visited*. [Television series episode].

Abelson, R. P. (1981). The psychological status of the script concept. *American Psychologist, 36*, 715–729.

Abraham, C., & Sheeran, P. (2004). Deciding to exercise: The role of anticipated regret. *British Journal Health Psychology, 9*, 269–278.

Abrahamson, A., Baker, L., & Caspi, A. (2002). Rebellious teens? Genetic and environmental influences on the social attitudes of adolescents. *Journal of Personality and Social Psychology, 83*, 1392–1408.

Abrams, R., & Greenwald, A. (2000). Parts outweigh the whole (word) in unconscious analysis of meaning. *Psychological Science, 11*, 118–124.

Abramson, L.Y., Seligman, M.E.P. & Teasdale, J.D. (1978). Learned Helplessness in Humans: Critique and Reformulation. *Journal of Abnormal Psychology, 87(1)*, pp. 49–74.

Ackerman, J. M., & Kenrick, D. T. (2008). The costs of benefits: Help-refusals highlight key trade-offs of social life. *Personality and Social Psychology Review, 12*, 118–140.

Adams, G., & Plaut, V. C. (2003). The cultural grounding of personal relationship: Friendship in North American and West African worlds. *Personal Relationships, 10*, 333–347.

Adams, H., Wright, L., & Lohr, B. (1996). Is homophobia associated with homosexual arousal? *Journal of Abnormal Psychology, 105*, 440–445.

Adelson, N. (1998). Health beliefs and the politics of Cree well-being. *Health, 2*, 5–22.

Adorno, T. W., Frenkel-Brunswik, E., Levinson, D. J., & Sanford, R. N. (1950). *The Authoritarian Personality*. New York: Harper & Row.

Agrell, S. (Aug. 16, 2010). Why Western donors are snubbing Pakistan after giving to Haiti. *Globe and Mail*. Retrieved from http://www.theglobeandmail.com/news/world/why-western-donors-are-snubbing-pakistan-after-giving-to-haiti/article1675172/

Aharon, I., Etcoff, N., Ariely, D., Chabris, C. F., O'Connor, E., & Breiter, H. C. (2001). Beautiful faces have variable reward value: fMRI and behavioral evidence. *Neuron, 32*, 537–551.

Ainsworth, M. S., Blehar, M. C., Waters, E., & Wall, S. (1978). *Patterns of Attachment: A Psychological Study of the Strange Situation*. Oxford, UK: Erlbaum.

Ajzen, I., & Fishbein, M. (1977). Attitude-behavior relations: A theoretical analysis and review of empirical research. *Psychological Bulletin, 84*, 888–918.

Akimoto, S., & Sanbonmatsu, D. (1999). Differences in self-effacing behavior between European and Japanese Americans: Effect on competence evaluations. *Journal of Cross-Cultural Psychology, 30*, 159–177.

Albarracín, D., & Wyer, R. (2000). The cognitive impact of past behavior: Influences on beliefs, attitudes, and future behavioral decisions. *Journal of Personality and Social Psychology, 79*, 5–22.

Albarracín, D., Cohen, J. B., & Kumkale, G. T. (2003). When communications collide with recipients' actions: Effects of the post-message behavior on intentions to follow the message recommendation. *Personality and Social Psychology Bulletin, 29*, 834–845.

Albright, L., & Forziati, C. (1995). Cross-situational consistency and perceptual accuracy in leadership. *Personality and Social Psychology Bulletin, 21*, 1269–1276.

Albright, L., Kenny, D., & Malloy, T. (1988). Consensus in personality judgments at zero acquaintance. *Journal of Personality and Social Psychology, 55*, 387–395.

Alicke, M., & Largo, E. (1995). The role of the self in the false consensus effect. *Journal of Experimental Social Psychology, 31*, 28–47.

Alicke, M., LoSchiavo, F., Zerbst, J., & Zhang, S. (1997). The person who out performs me is a genius: Maintaining perceived competence in upward social comparison. *Journal of Personality and Social Psychology, 73*, 781–789.

Allen, J. B., Kenrick, D. T., Linder, D. E., & McCall, M. A. (1989). Arousal and attraction: A response-facilitation alternative to misattribution and negative-reinforcement models. *Journal of Personality and Social Psychology, 57*, 261–270.

Allen, K. (2003). Are pets a healthy pleasure? The influence of pets on blood pressure. *Current Directions in Psychological Science, 12*, 236–239.

Allen, K. M., Blascovich, J., & Mendes, W. B. (2002). Cardiovascular reactivity and the presence of pets, friends, and spouses: The truth about cats and dogs. *Psychosomatic Medicine 64*, 727–739.

Allen, K. M., Blascovich, J., Tomaka, J., & Kelsey, R. M. (1991). Presence of human friends and pet dogs as moderators of autonomic responses to stress in women. *Journal of Personality and Social Psychology, 61*, 582–589.

Allen, V. L., & Levine, J. M. (1969). Consensus and conformity. *Journal of Experimental Social Psychology, 5*, 389–399.

Allen, V. L., & Levine, J. M. (1971). Social support and conformity: The role of independent assessment of reality. *Journal of Experimental Social Psychology, 7*, 48–58.

Allison, S.T., Mackie, D.M., Muller, M.M., & Worth, L.T., (1993), Sequential Correspondence Biases and Perceptions of Change: The Castro Studies Revisited. *Personality and Social Psychology Bulletin, 19 (2)*, 151–157.

Alloy, L. B., and Abramson, L. Y. (1979). Judgment of contingency in depressed and nondepressed students: Sadder but wiser? *Journal of Experimental Psychology: General, 108*, 441–485.

Allport, F. H. (1924). *Social psychology*. New York: Houghton Mifflin.

Allport, G. W. (1954). *Handbook of social psychology*. Reading, MA.: Addison-Wesley.

Almasy, S. (2010, Feb. 24). Days after mother's death, Olympic figure skater pushes on. *CNN*. Retrieved from http://www.cnn.com/2010/SPORT/02/24/olympics.rochette/index.html

Altemeyer, B. (1988). *Enemies of freedom: Understanding right-wing authoritarianism*. The Jossey-Bass social and behavioral science series and The Jossey-Bass public administration series. San Francisco, CA, US: Jossey-Bass.

Altemeyer, B. & Hunsberger, B. (2005). Fundamentalism and Authoritarianism. Chapter in Paloutzian, R.F. & Park, C.L. (Eds.). *Handbook of the psychology of religion and spirituality.* (pp. 378–393). New York, NY, US: Guilford Press.

Altocchi, J., & Altocchi, L. (1995). Polyfaceted psychological acculturation in Cook Islanders. *Journal of Cross-Cultural Psychology, 26*, 426–440.

Alvaro, E. M., & Crano, W. D. (1997). Indirect minority influence: Evidence for leniency in source evaluation and counterargumentation. *Journal of Personality and Social Psychology, 72,* 949–964.

Amabile, T., Hill, K., Hennessey, B., & Tighe, E. (1994). The Work Preference Inventory: Assessing intrinsic and extrinsic motivational orientations. *Journal of Personality and Social Psychology, 66,* 950–967.

Amanpour, C. (2011). 'My people love me': Moammar Gadhafi denies demonstrations against him anywhere in Libya (February 28, 2011). *ABC News.* Retrieved from http://abcnews.go.com/International/christiane-amanpour-interviews-libyas-moammar-gadhafi/story?id=13019942

Amato, P. R. (1981). The effects of environmental complexity and pleasantness on prosocial behaviour: A field study. *Australian Journal of Psychology, 33,* 285–295.

Amato, P. R. (1983). Helping behavior in urban and rural environments: Field studies based on a taxonomic organization of helping episodes. *Journal of Personality and Social Psychology, 45,* 571–586.

Amato, P. R. (1986). Emotional arousal and helping behavior in a real-life emergency. *Journal of Applied Social Psychology, 16,* 633–641.

Amato, P. R., & Booth, A. (2001). The legacy of parents' marital discord: Consequences for children's marital quality. *Journal of Personality and Social Psychology, 81,* 627–638.

Ambady, N., & Bharucha, J. (2009). Culture and the Brain. *Current Directions in Psychological Science, 18,* 342–345.

Ambady, N., Koo, J., Lee, F., & Rosenthal, R. (1996). More than words: Linguistic and nonlinguistic politeness in two cultures. *Journal of Personality and Social Psychology, 70,* 996–1011.

Ambady, N., & Rosenthal, R. (1993). Half a minute: Predicting teacher evaluations from thin slices of nonverbal behavior and physical attractiveness. *Journal of Personality and Social Psychology, 64,* 431–441.

Ames, D. R., Flynn, F. J., & Weber, E. U. (2004). It's the thought that counts: On perceiving how helpers decide to lend a hand. *Personality and Social Psychology Bulletin, 30,* 461–474.

Amodio, D. M., Harmon-Jones, E., & Devine, P. G. (2003). Individual differences in the activation and control of affective race bias as assessed by startle eyeblink response and self-report. *Journal of Personality and Social Psychology, 84,* 738–753.

Andersen, A., & DiDomenico, L. (1992). Diet vs. shape content of popular male and female magazines: A dose-response relationship to the incidence of eating disorders? *International Journal of Eating Disorders, 11,* 283–287.

Anderson, C., Bushman, B., & Groom, R. (1997). Hot years and serious and deadly assault: Empirical tests of the heat hypothesis. *Journal of Personality and Social Psychology, 73,* 1213–1223.

Anderson, C., Lepper, M., & Ross, L. (1980). Perseverance of social theories: The role of explanation in the persistence of discredited information. *Journal of Personality and Social Psychology, 39,* 1037–1049.

Anderson, C., & Sedikides, C. (1991). Thinking about people: Contributions of a typological alternative to associationistic and dimensional models of person perception. *Journal of Personality and Social Psychology, 60,* 203–217.

Anderson, C.A. (1989). Temperature and aggression: Ubiquitous effects of heat on occurrence of human violence. *Psychological Bulletin, 106,* 74–96.

Anderson, C. A. (1997). Effects of violent movies and trait hostility on hostile feelings and aggressive thoughts. *Aggressive Behavior, 23,* 161–178.

Anderson, C. A. (2001). Heat and violence. *Current Directions in Psychological Science, 10,* 33–38.

Anderson, C. A., & Anderson, K. B. (1996). Violent crime rate studies in philosophical context: A destructive testing approach to heat and southern culture of violence effects. *Journal of Personality and Social Psychology, 70,* 740–756.

Anderson, C. A., Anderson, K. B., & Deuser, W. E. (1996). Examining an affective aggression framework: Weapon and temperature effects on aggressive thoughts, affect, and attitudes. *Personality and Social Psychology Bulletin, 22,* 366–376.

Anderson, C. A., Benjamin, A. J. J., & Bartholow, B. D. (1998). Does the gun pull the trigger? Automatic priming effects of weapon pictures and weapon names. *Psychological Science, 9,* 308–314.

Anderson, C. A., Berkowitz, L., Donnerstein, E., Huesmann, L. R., Johnson, J. D., Linz, D., et al. (2003). The influence of media violence on youth. *Psychological Science in the Public Interest, 4,* 81–110.

Anderson, C. A., Buckley, K. E., & Carnagey, N. L. (2008). Creating your own hostile environment: A laboratory examination of trait aggressiveness and the violence escalation cycle. *Personality and Social Psychology Bulletin, 34,* 462–473.

Anderson, C. A., & Bushman, B. J. (2001). Effects of violent video games on aggressive behavior, aggressive cognition, aggressive affect, physiological arousal, and prosocial behavior: A meta-analytic review of the scientific literature. *Psychological Science, 12,* 353–359.

Anderson, C. A., Carnagey, N. L., & Eubanks, J. (2003). Exposure to violent media: The effects of songs with violent lyrics on aggressive thoughts and feelings. *Journal of Personality and Social Psychology, 84(5),* May 2003, 960–971.

Anderson, C. A., & DeNeve, K. M. (1992). Temperature, aggression, and the negative affect escape model. *Psychological Bulletin, 111,* 347–351.

Anderson, C. A., Deuser, W. E., & DeNeve, K. M. (1995). Hot temperatures, hostile affect, hostile cognition, and arousal: Tests of a general model of affective aggression. *Personality and Social Psychology Bulletin, 21,* 434–448.

Anderson, C. A., & Dill, K. E. (2000). Video games and aggressive thoughts, feelings, and behavior in the laboratory and in life. *Journal of Personality and Social Psychology, 78,* 772–790.

Anderson, K., Cooper, H., & Okamura, L. (1997). Individual differences and attitudes toward rape: A meta-analytic review. *Personality and Social Psychology Bulletin, 23,* 295–315.

Anderson, N. (1975). On the role of context effects in psychophysical judgment. *Psychological Review, 82,* 462–482.

Anthony, T., Copper, C., & Mullen, B. (1992). Cross-racial facial identification: A social cognitive integration. *Personality and Social Psychology Bulletin, 18,* 296–301.

Antonio, A. L., Chang, M. J., Hakuta, K., Kenny, D. A., Levin, S., & Milem, J. F. (2004). Effects of racial diversity on complex thinking in college students. *Psychological Science, 15,* 507–510.

Archer, J. (2000). Sex differences in aggression between heterosexual partners: A meta-analytic review. *Psychological Bulletin, 126,* 651–680.

Archer, J. (2004). Sex differences in aggression in real-world settings: A meta-analytic review. *Review of General Psychology, 8,* 291–322.

Archer, J. (2006). Cross-cultural differences in physical aggression between partners: A social-role analysis. *Personality and Social Psychology Review, 10,* 133–153.

Archer, J., & Coyne, S. M. (2005). An integrated review of indirect, relational, and social aggression. *Personality and Social Psychology Review, 9,* 212–230.

Archibald, F. S., Bartholomew, K., & Marx, R. (1995). Loneliness in early adolescence: A test of the cognitive discrepancy model of loneliness. *Personality and Social Psychology Bulletin, 21,* 296–301.

Ariely, D., & Norton, M. (2007). Psychology and experimental economics: A gap in abstraction. *Current Directions in Psychological Science, 16,* 336–339.

Aron, A., Dutton, D. G., Aron, E. N., & Iverson, A. (1989). Experiences of falling in love. *Journal of Social and Personal Relationships*, 6, 243–257.

Aron, A., Fisher, H., Mashek, D. J., Strong, G., Li, H., & Brown, L. L. (2005). Reward, motivation, and emotion systems associated with early-stage intense romantic love. *Journal of Neurophysiology*, 94, 327–337.

Aron, A., Norman, C. C., Aron, E. N., McKenna, C., & Heyman, R. E. (2000). Couples' shared participation in novel and arousing activities and experienced relationship quality. *Journal of Personality and Social Psychology*, 78, 273–284.

Aron, A., Paris, M., & Aron, E. N. (1995). Falling in love: Prospective studies of self-concept change. *Journal of Personality and Social Psychology*, 69, 1102–1112.

Aronson, E., & Bridgeman, D. (1979). Jigsaw groups and the desegregated classroom: In pursuit of common goals. *Personality and Social Psychology Bulletin*, 5, 438–446.

Aronson, E., & Carlsmith, J. (1963). Effect of the severity of threat on the devaluation of forbidden behavior. *The Journal of Abnormal and Social Psychology*, 66, 584–588.

Aronson, E., & Linder, D. (1965). Gain and loss of esteem as determinants of interpersonal attractiveness. *Journal of Experimental Social Psychology*, 1, 156–171.

Aronson, E., & Mills, J. (1959). The effect of severity of initiation on liking for a group. *The Journal of Abnormal and Social Psychology*, 59, 177–181.

Aronson, E., Wilson, T., & Brewer, M. (1998). *Experimentation in social psychology. The Handbook of Social Psychology 4th ed., Vols. 1 and 2* (pp. 99–142). New York: McGraw-Hill.

Aronson, J., Lustina, M. J., Good, C., Keough, K., Steele, C. M., & Brown, J. (1999). When White men can't do math: Necessary and sufficient factors in stereotype threat. *Journal of Experimental Social Psychology*, 35, 29–46.

Arriaga, X. B., & Rusbult, C. E. (1998). Standing in my partner's shoes: Partner perspective taking and reactions to accommodative dilemmas. *Personality and Social Psychology Bulletin*, 24, 927–948.

Arunachalam, V., Wall, J., & Chan, C. (1998). Hong Kong versus U.S. negotiations: Effects of culture, alternatives, outcome scales, and mediation. *Journal of Applied Social Psychology*, 28, 1219–1244.

Asch, S.E. (1946). Forming impressions of personality. *The Journal of Abnormal and Social Psychology*, 41, 258–290.

Asch, S. E. (1951). Effects of group pressure upon the modification and distortion of judgment. In H. Guetzkow (Ed.) *Groups, Leadership and Men: Research in Human Relations* (pp. 177–190). Pittsburgh, PA: Carnegie Press.

Asch, S. E. (1952). *Social Psychology*. Englewood Cliffs, NJ: Prentice Hall.

Asch, S. E. (1955). Opinions and social pressure. *Scientific American*, 193, 31–35.

Aube, J., & Koestner, R. (1995). Gender characteristics and relationship adjustment: Another look at similarity-complementarity hypotheses. *Journal of Personality*, 63, 879–904.

Auletta, K. (2004, January 19). Bush's Press Problem. *The New Yorker*. Retrieved from http://www.newyorker.com/archive/2004/01/19/040119on_onlineonly02

Averill, J.R., (1985). The social construction of emotion: With special reference to love. In K. Gergen & K. Davis (Eds.), *The social construction of the person* (pp. 89–109). New York: Springer-Verlag.

Axsom, D. (1989). Cognitive dissonance and behavior change in psychotherapy. *Journal of Experimental Social Psychology*, 25, 234–252.

Axsom, D., & Cooper, J. (1985). Cognitive dissonance and psychotherapy: The role of effort justification in inducing weight loss. *Journal of Experimental Social Psychology*, 21, 149–160.

Axsom, D., Yates, S., & Chaiken, S. (1987). Audience response as a heuristic cue in persuasion. *Journal of Personality and Social Psychology*, 53, 30–40.

Ayman, R., & Korabik, K. (2010). Leadership: Why gender and culture matter. *American Psychologist*, 65, 157–170.

Back, M. D., Schmukle, S. C., & Egloff, B. (2008). Becoming friends by chance. *Psychological Science*, 19, 439–440.

Baer, J. S., & Carney, M. M. (1993). Biases in the perceptions of the consequences of alcohol use among college students. *Journal of Studies on Alcohol*, 54, 54–60.

Baer, J. S., Stacy, A., & Larimer, M. (1991). Biases in the perception of drinking norms among college students. *Journal of Studies on Alcohol*, 52, 580–586.

Bahrick, H., Hall, L., & Berger, S. (1996). Accuracy and distortion in memory for high school grades. *Psychological Science*, 7, 265–271.

Bailey, D. S., & Taylor, S. P. (1991). Effects of alcohol and aggressive disposition on human physical aggression. *Journal of Research in Personality*, 25, 334–342.

Bailey, J. M., Gaulin, S., Agyei, Y., & Gladue, B. A. (1994). Effects of gender and sexual orientation on evolutionarily relevant aspects of human mating psychology. *Journal of Personality and Social Psychology*, 66, 1081–1093.

Bakanic, E. D. (2008). The end of Japan's nuclear taboo. *Bulletin of the Atomic Scientists – Web Edition*, 9 June 2008. Retrieved from http://www.thebulletin.org/web-edition/features/the-end-of-japans-nuclear-taboo

Balcetis, E., & Dunning, D. (2007). Cognitive dissonance and the perception of natural environments. *Psychological Science*, 18, 917–921.

Bales, R. F. (1950). *Interaction process analysis: A method for the study of small groups*. Chicago: Univ. of Chicago Press.

Banaji, M. R., & Greenwald, A. G. (1995). Implicit gender stereotyping in judgments of fame. *Journal of Personality and Social Psychology*, 68, 181–198.

Bandura, A. (1973). *Aggression: A Social Learning Analysis*. Englewood Cliffs, NJ: Prentice-Hall.

Bandura, A. (1983). Self-efficacy determinants of anticipated fears and calamities. *Journal of Personality and Social Psychology*, 45, 464–469.

Bandura, A. (1986). *Social foundations of thought and action: A social cognitive theory*. Englewood Cliffs, NJ: Prentice-Hall.

Bandura, A., Barbaranelli, C., Caprara, G. V., & Pastorelli, C. (1996). Mechanisms of moral disengagement in the exercise of moral agency. *Journal of Personality and Social Psychology*, 71, 364–374.

Bandura, A., Grusec, J. E., & Menlove, F. L. (1967). Vicarious extinction of avoidance behavior. *Journal of Personality and Social Psychology*, 5, 16–23.

Bandura, A., O'Leary, A., Taylor, C., Gauthier, J., & Gossard, D. (1987). Perceived self-efficacy and pain control: Opioid and non-opioid mechanisms. *Journal of Personality and Social Psychology*, 53, 563–571.

Bandura, A., Ross, D., & Ross, S. (1963). Imitation of film-mediated aggressive models. *The Journal of Abnormal and Social Psychology*, 66, 3–11.

Banks, S., Salovey, P., Greener, S., Rothman, A., Moyer, A., Beauvais, J., Epel, E. (1995). The effects of message framing on mammography utilization. *Health Psychology*, 14, 178–184.

Banks, T., & Dabbs, J. M. J. (1996). Salivary testosterone and cortisol in delinquent and violent urban subculture. *Journal of Social Psychology*, 136, 49–56.

Barbash, T. (2003). *On top of the world: Cantor Fitzgerald, Howard Lutnick, and 9/11: A story of loss and renewal*. New York: Harper Collins.

Barbee, A. P., Cunningham, M. R., Winstead, B. A., & Derlega, V. J. (1993). Effects of gender role expectations on the social support process. *Journal of Social Issues, 49*, 175–190.

Barclay, P. (2010). Altruism as courtship display: some effects of third-party generosity on audience perceptions. British Journal of Psychology, *101*, 123–135.

Bargh, J. A., & Chartrand, T. L. (1999). The unbearable automaticity of being. *American Psychologist, 54*, 462–479.

Bargh, J. A., Chen, M., & Burrows, L. (1996). Automaticity of social behavior: Direct effects of trait construct and stereotype activation on action. *Journal of Personality and Social Psychology, 71*, 230–244.

Bargh, J. A., McKenna, K. Y. A., & Fitzsimons, G. M. (2002). Can you see the real me? Activation and expression of the 'true self' on the Internet. *Journal of Social Issues, 58*, 33–48.

Bargh, J., & Pietromonaco, P. (1982). Automatic information processing and social perception: The influence of trait information presented outside of conscious awareness on impression formation. *Journal of Personality and Social Psychology, 43*, 437–449.

Bargh, J., Gollwitzer, P., Lee-Chai, A., Barndollar, K., & Trötschel, R. (2001). The automated will: Nonconscious activation and pursuit of behavioral goals. *Journal of Personality and Social Psychology, 81*, 1014–1027.

Baron, A. S., & Banaji, M. R. (2006). The development of implicit attitudes: Evidence of race evaluations from ages 6 and 10 and adulthood. *Psychological Science, 17*, 53–58.

Baron, J., & Miller, J. G. (2000). Limiting the scope of moral obligations to help: A cross cultural investigation. *Journal of Cross-Cultural Psychology, 31*, 703–725.

Baron, R. A. (1977). *Human aggression.* New York: Plenum.

Baron, R. A. (1990). Countering the effects of destructive criticism: The relative efficacy of four interventions. *Journal of Applied Psychology, 75*, 235–245.

Baron, R. A. & Byrne, D. (1999). *Social Psychology: Understanding human interaction* (9th ed). Boston: Allyn & Bacon.

Baron, R. A. (1997). The sweet smell of . . . helping: Effects of pleasant ambient fragrance on prosocial behavior in shopping malls. *Personality and Social Psychology Bulletin, 23*, 498–503.

Baron, R. A. & Byrne, D. (1999). *Social Psychology: Understanding human interaction* (9th ed). Boston: Allyn & Bacon.

Baron, R. S., Hoppe, S. I., Kao, C. F., & Brunsman, B. (1996). Social corroboration and opinion extremity. *Journal of Experimental Social Psychology, 32*, 537–560.

Baron, R. S., Logan, H., Lilly, J., Inman, M., & Brennan, M. (1994). Negative emotion and message processing. *Journal of Experimental Social Psychology, 30*, 181–201.

Baron, R. S., Moore, D., & Sanders, G. S. (1978). Distraction as a source of drive in social facilitation research. *Journal of Personality and Social Psychology, 36*, 816–824.

Baron, R. S., Vandello, J. A., & Brunsman, B. (1996). The forgotten variable in conformity research: Impact of task importance on social influence. *Journal of Personality and Social Psychology, 71*, 915–927.

Bartels, A., & Zeki, S. (2000). The neural basis of romantic love. *Neuroreport: For Rapid Communication of Neuroscience Research, 11*, 3829–3834.

Bartholow, B. D., & Anderson, C. A. (2002). Effects of violent video games on aggressive behavior: Potential sex differences. *Journal of Experimental Social Psychology, 38*, 283–290.

Bartholow, B. D., Bushman, B. J., & Sestir, M. A. (2006). Chronic violent video game exposure and desensitization to violence: Behavioral and event-related brain potential data. *Journal of Experimental Social Psychology, 42*, 532–539.

Bartholow, B. D., & Heinz, A. (2006). Alcohol and aggression without consumption: Alcohol cues, aggressive thoughts, and hostile perception bias. *Psychological Science, 17*, 30–37.

Bartholow, B. D., Sestir, M. A., & Davis, E. B. (2005). Correlates and consequences of exposure to video game violence: Hostile personality, empathy, and aggressive behavior. *Personality and Social Psychology Bulletin, 31*, 1573–1586.

Bass, B. M., Avolio, B. J., Jung, D. I., & Berson, Y. (2003). Predicting unit performance by assessing transformational and transactional leadership. *Journal of Applied Psychology, 88*, 207–218.

Bassili, J. N. (2003). The minority slowness effect: Subtle inhibitions in the expression of views not shared by others. *Journal of Personality and Social Psychology, 84*, 261–276.

Batson, C. D. (1983). Sociobiology and the role of religion in promoting prosocial behavior: An alternative view. *Journal of Personality and Social Psychology, 45*, 1380–1385.

Batson, C. D. (1991). *The altruism question: Toward a social-psychological answer.* Hillsdale, NJ: Erlbaum.

Batson, C. D. (1998). Altruism and prosocial behavior. In D. Gilbert, S. Fiske, & G. Lindzey (Eds.), *Handbook of social psychology* (pp. 282–316). New York: McGraw-Hill.

Batson, C. D., Duncan, B. D., Ackerman, P., Buckley, T., & Birch, K. (1981). Is empathic emotion a source of altruistic motivation? *Journal of Personality and Social Psychology, 40*, 290–302.

Batson, C. D., Dyck, J. L., Brandt, J. R., Batson, J. G., Powell, A. L., McMaster, M. R., et al. (1988). Five studies testing two new egoistic alternatives to the empathy-altruism hypothesis. *Journal of Personality and Social Psychology, 55*, 52–77.

Batson, C. D., Floyd, R. B., Meyer, J. M., & Winner, A. L. (1999). "And who is my neighbor?": Intrinsic religion as a source of universal compassion. *Journal for the Scientific Study of Religion, 38*, 445–457.

Batson, C. D., Lishner, D. A., Carpenter, A., Dulin, L., Harjusola-Webb, S., Stocks, E. L., et al. (2003). ". . . As you would have them do unto you": Does imagining yourself in the other's place stimulate moral action? *Personality and Social Psychology Bulletin, 29*, 1190–1201.

Batson, C. D., & Oleson, K. C. (1991). Current status of the empathy-altruism hypothesis. In M. S. Clark (Ed.), *Review of Personality and Social Psychology* (Vol. 12, pp. 62–85). Newbury Park, CA: Sage.

Batson, C. D., Sager, K., Garst, E., Kang, M., Rubchinsky, K., & Dawson, K. (1997). Is empathy-induced helping due to self-other merging? *Journal of Personality and Social Psychology, 73*, 495–509.

Batson, C. D., Sympson, S. C., Hindman, J. L., & Decruz, P. (1996). "I've been there, too": Effect on empathy of prior experience with a need. *Personality and Social Psychology Bulletin, 22*, 474–482.

Batson, C. D., Thompson, E. R., Seuferling, G., Whitney, H., & Strongman, J. A. (1999). Moral hypocrisy: Appearing moral to oneself without being so. *Journal of Personality and Social Psychology, 77*, 525–537.

Bauder, H. (2003). Cultural representations of immigrant workers by service providers and employers. *Journal of International Migration and Integration, 4*, 415–38.

Bauder, H. (2006). Origin, employment status and attitudes towards work: Immigrants in Vancouver, Canada. *Work, Employment and Society, 20*, 709–729.

Baumeister, R. (1982). A self-presentational view of social phenomena. *Psychological Bulletin, 91*, 3–26.

Baumeister, R., Bratslavsky, E., Muraven, M., & Tice, D. (1998). Ego depletion: Is the active self a limited resource? *Journal of Personality and Social Psychology, 74*, 1252–1265.

Baumeister, R., & Tice, D. (1984). Role of self-presentation and choice in cognitive dissonance under forced compliance: Necessary or sufficient causes? *Journal of Personality and Social Psychology, 46*, 5–13.

Baumeister, R., & Vohs, K. (2004). Sexual economics: Sex as female resource for social exchange in heterosexual interactions. *Personality and Social Psychology Review, 8*, 339–363.

Baumeister, R. F., Bushman, B. J., & Campbell, W. K. (2000). Self-esteem, narcissism, and aggression: Does violence result from low self-esteem or from threatened egotism? *Current Directions in Psychological Science, 9,* 26–29.

Baumeister, R. F., & Campbell, W. K. (1999). The intrinsic appeal of evil: Sadism, sensational thrills, and threatened egotism. *Personality and Social Psychology Review, 3,* 210–221.

Baumeister, R. F., & Leary, M. R. (1995). The need to belong: Desire for interpersonal attachments as a fundamental human motivation. *Psychological Bulletin, 117,* 497–529.

Baumeister, R. F., & Steinhilber, A. (1984). Paradoxical effects of supportive audiences on performance under pressure: The home field disadvantage in sports championships. *Journal of Personality and Social Psychology, 47,* 85–93.

Baumrind, D. (1985). Research using intentional deception: Ethical issues revisited. *American Psychologist, 40,* 165–174.

Bazzini, D. G., & Shaffer, D. R. (1999). Resisting temptation revisited: Devaluation versus enhancement of an attractive suitor by exclusive and nonexclusive daters. *Personality and Social Psychology Bulletin, 25,* 162–176.

BBC News (2010, Aug. 6). Pakistan's flooding sweeps south. *BBC News.* Retrieved from http://www.bbc.co.uk/news/world-south-asia-10889925

BBC News (2010, August 25). Murdered bodies found in Mexico 'were migrants.' Retrieved from http://www.bbc.co.uk/news/world-latin-america-11090563

BBC News (2010, Sept. 21). UN faults Israel, Hamas probes into Gaza conflict. *BBC News.* Retrieved from http://www.bbc.co.uk/news/world-middle-east-11384476

Beagan, B. L., Ristovski-Slijepcevic, S., & Chapman, G. E. (2010). People Are Just becoming More Conscious of How Everything's Connected: 'Ethical' Food Consumption in Two Regions of Canada. *Sociology, 44,* 751–769.

Beaman, A., Klentz, B., Diener, E., & Svanum, S. (1979). Self-awareness and transgression in children: Two field studies. *Journal of Personality and Social Psychology, 37,* 1835–1846.

Beaman, A. L. (1983). Fifteen years of foot-in-the-door research: A meta-analysis. *Personality and Social Psychology Bulletin, 9,* 181–196.

Bear, C. (2008, May 12). American Indian boarding schools haunt many. *NPR news.* Retrieved from http://www.npr.org/templates/story/story.php?storyId=16516865.

Beaulieu, D. A. (2007). Avoiding costly mating mistakes: Ovulatory shifts in personal mate value assessment. *Journal of Social and Personal Relationships, 24,* 441–455.

Beaupré, M. G., & Hess, U. (2006). An in-group advantage for confidence in emotion recognition judgments: The moderating effect of familiarity with the expressions of out-group members. *Personality and Social Psychology Bulletin, 32,* 16–26.

Beauregard, K., & Dunning, D. (1998). Turning up the contrast: Self-enhancement motives prompt egocentric contrast effects in social judgments. *Journal of Personality and Social Psychology, 74,* 606–621.

Becker, S. W., & Eagly, A. H. (2004). The heroism of women and men. *American Psychologist, 59,* 163–178.

Begley, S. (April 6, 2010). *Fear and Loathing in the Voting Booth.* Newsweek. Retrieved from http://www.newsweek.com/2010/04/05/fear-and-loathing-in-the-voting-booth.html

Bell, J. Grekul, J., Lamba, N., Minas, C. & Harrell, W. W. (1995) The impact of cost on student helping behavior. *Journal of Social Psychology, 135,* 49–57.

Bell, P. A. (1992). In defense of the negative affect escape model of heat and aggression. *Psychological Bulletin, 111,* 342–346.

Belsky, J. (1993). Etiology of child maltreatment: A developmental-ecological analysis. *Psychological Bulletin, 114,* 413–434.

Bem, D. (1967). Self-perception: An alternative interpretation of cognitive dissonance phenomena. *Psychological Review, 74,* 183–200.

Bem, D. J. (1972). Constructing cross-situational consistencies in behavior: Some thoughts on Alker's critique of Mischel. *Journal of Personality, 40,* 17–26.

Benedetti, F., & Amanzio, M. (1997). The neurobiology of placebo analgesia: From endogenous opioids to cholecystokinin. *Progress in Neurobiology, 52,* 109–125.

Benedict, R. (1989). *The chrysanthemum and the sword.* Boston: Houghton Mifflin. First published 1946.

Bensley, L. S., & Wu, R. (1991). The role of psychological reactance in drinking following alcohol prevention messages. *Journal of Applied Social Psychology, 21,* 1111–1124.

Benson, P. L., Dehority J., Garman, L., Hanson, E., Hochschwender, M., Lebold, L., et al. (1980). Intrapersonal correlates of nonspontaneous helping behavior. *Journal of Social Psychology, 110,* 87–95.

Benson, P. L., Karabenick, S. A., & Lerner, R. M. (1976). Pretty pleases: The effects of physical attractiveness, race, and sex on receiving help. *Journal of Experimental Social Psychology, 12,* 409–415.

Berg, J. H., & McQuinn, R. D. (1986). Attraction and exchange in continuing and noncontinuing dating relationships. *Journal of Personality and Social Psychology, 50,* 942–952.

Berg, J. H., & McQuinn, R. D. (1989). Loneliness and aspects of social support networks. *Journal of Social and Personal Relationships, 6,* 359–372.

Berg, J. H., & Peplau, L. A. (1982). Loneliness: The relationship of self-disclosure and androgyny. *Personality and Social Psychology Bulletin, 8,* 624–630.

Bergdahl, J. (2005). Sex differences in attitudes toward driving. A survey. Social Science Journal, 42, 595–601.

Berger, P. & Luckmann, T. (1966). *The social construction of reality.* Garden City: Doubleday.

Bergeron, N., & Schneider, B. H. (2005). Explaining cross-national differences in peer- directed aggression: A quantitative synthesis. *Aggressive Behavior, 31,* 116–137.

Berglas, S., & Jones, E. E. (1978). Drug choice as a self-handicapping strategy in response to noncontingent success. *Journal of Personality and Social Psychology, 36,* 405–417.

Berkowitz, L. (1972). Frustrations, comparisons, and other sources of emotion arousal as contributors to social unrest. *Journal of Social Issues, 28,* 77–91.

Berkowitz, L. (1984). Some effects of thoughts on anti- and prosocial influences of media events: A cognitive-neoassociation analysis. *Psychological Bulletin, 95,* 410–427.

Berkowitz, L. (1989). Frustration-aggression hypothesis: Examination and reformulation. *Psychological Bulletin, 106,* 59–73.

Berkowitz, L. (1990). On the formation and regulation of anger and aggression: A cognitive-neoassociationistic analysis. *American Psychologist, 45,* 494–503.

Berkowitz, L., Cochran, S. T., & Embree, M. C. (1981). Physical pain and the goal of aversively stimulated aggression. *Journal of Personality and Social Psychology, 40,* 687–700.

Berkowitz, L., & Daniels, L. R. (1963). Responsibility and dependency. *The Journal of Abnormal and Social Psychology, 66,* 429–436.

Berkowitz, L., & LePage, A. (1967). Weapons as aggression-eliciting stimuli. *Journal of Personality and Social Psychology, 7,* 202–207.

Berman, M. I., & Frazier, P. A. (2005). Relationship power and betrayal experience as predictors of reactions to infidelity. *Personality and Social Psychology Bulletin, 31,* 1617–1627.

Bernard, M. M., Maio, G. R., & Olson, J. M. (2003). The vulnerability of values to attack: Inoculation of values and value-relevant attitudes. *Personality and Social Psychology Bulletin, 29,* 63–75.

Berndt, T. J. (1979). Developmental changes in conformity to peers and parents. *Developmental Psychology, 15,* 608–616.

Bernhardt, P. C. (1997). Influences of serotonin and testosterone in aggression and dominance: Convergence with social psychology. *Current Directions in Psychological Science, 6,* 44–48.

Bernstein, D. M., Atance, C., Meltzoff, A. N., & Loftus, G. R. (2007). Hindsight bias and developing theories of mind. *Child Development. 78,* 1374–1394.

Berry, D. (1991). Accuracy in social perception: Contributions of facial and vocal information. *Journal of Personality and Social Psychology, 61,* 298–307.

Berry, J. & Safdar, S. (2007). Psychology of diversity: Managing of diversity in plural societies. In A. Chybicka & M. Kazmierczak (Eds.), *Appreciating diversity: Cultural and gender issues* (pp. 19–36). Cracow, Poland: Impuls.

Berry, J. W. (1976). *Human ecology and cognitive style: Comparative studies in cultural and psychological adaptation.* New York: Sage.

Berry, J.W. (1979). A cultural ecology of social behaviour. In L. Berkowitz (ed.), Advances in experimental social psychology, (Vol. 12, pp. 177–206). New York: Academic Press.

Berry, J. W. (1997). Immigration, acculturation, and adaptation. *Applied Psychology: An International Review, 46,* 5–68.

Berry, J. W. (2001). A Psychology of Immigration. *Journal of Social Issues, 57,* 615–631.

Berry, J. W. (2003). Conceptual approaches to acculturation. In K. Chun, P. Balls-Organista, and G. Marin (Eds.). *Acculturation: Advances in Theory, Measurement and Application* (pp. 17–37). Washington: APA Books.

Berry, J. W., & Sabatier, C. (2010). Acculturation, discrimination, and adaptation among second generation immigrant youth in Montreal and Paris. *International Journal of Intercultural Relations, 34,* 191–207.

Berscheid, E., Snyder, M., & Omoto, A. M. (1989). The Relationship Closeness Inventory: Assessing the closeness of interpersonal relationships. *Journal of Personality and Social Psychology, 57,* 792–807.

Bersoff , D. (1999). Why good people sometimes do bad things: Motivated reasoning and unethical behavior. *Personality and Social Psychology Bulletin, 25,* 28–39.

Best, D. L. (2004). Gender roles in childhood and adolescence. In U. P. Gielen & J. L. Roopnarine (Eds.), *Childhood and adolescence in cross-cultural perspective* (pp. 199–228). Westport, CT: Greenwood.

Best, D. L. (2010). The contributions of the Whitings to the study of the socialization of gender. *Journal of Cross-Cultural Psychology, 41,* 534–545.

Bettencourt, B. A., & Miller, N. (1996). Gender differences in aggression as a function of provocation: A meta-analysis. *Psychological Bulletin, 119,* 422–447.

Bickman, L. (1971). The effect of another bystander's ability to help on bystander intervention in an emergency. *Journal of Experimental Social Psychology, 7,* 367–379.

Bickman, L. (1974). The social power of a uniform. *Journal of Applied Social Psychology, 4,* 47–61.

Biddle, J. E., & Hamermesh, D. S., (1998). Beauty, productivity, and discrimination: Lawyers' looks and lucre. *Journal of Labor Economics, 16,* 172–201.

Biek, M., Wood, W., & Chaiken, S. (1996). Working knowledge, cognitive processing, and attitudes: On the determinants of bias. *Personality and Social Psychology Bulletin, 22,* 547–556.

Biener, L., & Heaton, A. (1995). Women dieters of normal weight: Their motives, goals, and risks. *American Journal of Public Health, 85,* 714–717.

Bierhoff, H. W., Klein, R., & Kramp, P. (1991). Evidence for the altruistic personality from data on accident research. *Journal of Personality, 59,* 263–280.

Biernat, M. (2003). Toward a broader view of social stereotyping. *American Psychologist, 58,* 1019–1027.

Biernat, M., Crandall, C. S., Young, L. V., Kobrynowicz, D., & Halpin, S. M. (1998). All that you can be: Stereotyping of self and others in a military context. *Journal of Personality and Social Psychology, 75,* 301–317.

Biernat, M., & Ma, J. E. (2005). Stereotypes and the confirmability of trait concepts. *Personality and Social Psychology Bulletin, 31,* 483–495.

Biernat, M., & Manis, M. (1994). Shifting standards and stereotype-based judgments. *Journal of Personality and Social Psychology, 66,* 5–20.

Biernat, M., Manis, M., & Nelson, T. E. (1991). Stereotypes and standards of judgment. *Journal of Personality and Social Psychology, 60,* 485–499.

Billig, M., & Tajfel, H. (1973). Social categorization and similarity in intergroup behaviour. *European Journal of Social Psychology, 3,* 27–52.

Biernat, M., & Vescio, T. K. (2002). She swings, she hits, she's great, she's benched: Implications of gender-based shifting standards for judgment and behavior. *Personality and Social Psychology Bulletin, 28,* 66–77.

Bin Laden, Osama. (1998). Declaration of war against the Americans occupying the land of the two holy places. MidEastWeb. Retrieved from http://www.mideastweb.org/osamabinladen1.htm

Birbaumer, N., Veit, R., Lotze, M., Erb, M., Hermann, C., Grodd,W., & Flor, H. (2005). Deficient fear conditioning in psychopathy: A functional magnetic resonance imaging study. *Archives of General Psychiatry, 62,* 799–805.

Birch, S. A. J. & Bernstein, D. M. (2007). What can children tell us about hindsight bias: A fundamental constraint on perspective-taking? *Social Cognition. 25,* 98–113.

Blanchard, F. A., Crandall, C. S., Brigham, J. C., & Vaughn, L. A. (1994). Condemning and condoning racism: A social context approach to interracial settings. *Journal of Applied Psychology, 79,* 993–997.

Blaney, N., Stephan, C., Rosenfield, D., Aronson, E., & Sikes, J. (1977). Interdependence in the classroom: A field study. *Journal of Educational Psychology, 69,* 121–128.

Blankenship, K. L., & Wegener, D. T. (2008). Opening the mind to close it: Considering a message in light of important values increases message processing and later resistance to change. *Journal of Personality and Social Psychology, 94,* 196–213.

Blanton, H., & Jaccard, J. (2006). Arbitrary metrics in psychology. *American Psychologist, 61,* 27–41.

Blanton, H., VandenEijnden, R., Buunk, B., Gibbons, F., Gerrard, M., & Bakker, A. (2001). Accentuate the negative: Social images in the prediction and promotion of condom use. *Journal of Applied Social Psychology, 31,* 274–295.

Blascovich, J., Mendes, W. B., Hunter, S. B., & Salomon, K. (1999). Social "facilitation" as challenge and threat. *Journal of Personality and Social Psychology, 77,* 68–77.

Blass, T. (1991). Understanding behavior in the Milgram obedience experiment: The role of personality, situations, and their interactions. *Journal of Personality and Social Psychology, 60,* 398–413.

Blass, T. (1996). Attribution of responsibility and trust in Milgram's obedience experiment. *Journal of Applied Social Psychology, 26,* 1529–1535.

Bless, H., Bohner, G., Schwarz, N., & Strack, F. (1990). Mood and persuasion: A cognitive response analysis. *Personality and Social Psychology Bulletin, 16,* 331–345.

Bocari, M. (2011, January 27). DEK gets five-year suspension. *Edmonton Sun.* Retrieved from http://www.edmontonsun.com/news/edmonton/2011/01/27/17058106.html

Bochner, S. (1994). Cross-cultural differences in the self concept: A test of Hofstede's individualism/collectivism distinction. *Journal of Cross-Cultural Psychology, 25,* 273–283.

Bodenmann, G., Kaiser, A., Hahlweg, K., & Fehm-Wolfsdorf, G. (1998). Communication patterns during marital conflict: A cross-cultural representation. *Personal Relationships, 5,* 343–356.

Bogart, L., & Helgeson, V. (2000). Social comparisons among women with breast cancer: A longitudinal investigation. *Journal of Applied Social Psychology, 30,* 547–575.

Bohner, G., Siebler, F., & Schmelcher, J. (2006). Social norms and the likelihood of raping: Perceived rape myth acceptance of others affects men's rape proclivity. *Personality and Social Psychology Bulletin, 32,* 286–297.

Boldizar, J. P., Perry, D. G., & Perry, L. C. (1989). Outcome values and aggression. *Child Development, 60,* 571–579.

Bolger, N., & Amarel, D. (2007). Effects of social support visibility on adjustment to stress: Experimental evidence. *Journal of Personality and Social Psychology, 92,* 458–475.

Bond, C., & DePaulo, B. (2006). Accuracy of deception judgments. *Personality and Social Psychology Review, 10,* 214–234.

Bond, C., Omar, A., Mahmoud, A., & Bonser, R. (1990). Lie detection across cultures. *Journal of Nonverbal Behavior, 14,* 189–204.

Bond, C. F., & Titus, L. J. (1983). Social facilitation: A meta-analysis of 241 studies. *Psychological Bulletin, 94,* 265–292.

Bond, M. H. (2004). Culture and aggression: From context to coercion. *Personality and Social Psychology Review, 8,* 62–78.

Bond, R., & Smith, P. B. (1996). Culture and conformity: A meta-analysis of studies using Asch's (1952b, 1956) line judgment task. *Psychological Bulletin, 119,* 111–137.

Boninger, D., Gleicher, F., & Strathman, A. (1994). Counterfactual thinking: From what might have been to what may be. *Journal of Personality and Social Psychology, 67,* 297–307.

Bonoguore, T., & Lewington, J. (2009, May 11). Premier tells protestors not to block roads. *Globe and Mail.* Retrieved from http://v1.theglobeandmail.com/servlet/story/RTGAM.20090511.wprotest0511/BNStory/National/undefined

Bonta, B. D. (1997). Cooperation and competition in peaceful societies. *Psychological Bulletin, 121,* 299–320.

Bontempo, R., Lobel, S., & Triandis, H. (1990). Compliance and value internalization in Brazil and the U.S.: Effects of allocentrism and anonymity. *Journal of Cross-Cultural Psychology, 21,* 200–213.

Bornstein, G., Rapoport, A., Kerpel, L., & Katz, T. (1989). Within- and between-group communication in intergroup competition for public goods. *Journal of Experimental Social Psychology, 25,* 422–436.

Bornstein, R., & D'Agostino, P. (1992). Stimulus recognition and the mere exposure effect. *Journal of Personality and Social Psychology, 63,* 545–552.

Bornstein, R. F. (1989). Exposure and affect: Overview and meta-analysis of research, 1968–1987. *Psychological Bulletin, 106,* 265–289.

Bothwell, R. K., Brigham, J. C., & Malpass, R. S. (1989). Crossracial identification. *Personality and Social Psychology Bulletin, 15,* 19–25.

Botwin, M. D., Buss, D. M., & Shackelford, T. K. (1997). Personality and mate preferences: Five factors in mate selection and marital satisfaction. *Journal of Personality, 65,* 107–136.

Bouas, K. S., & Komorita, S. S. (1996). Group discussion and cooperation in social dilemmas. *Personality and Social Psychology Bulletin, 22,* 1144–1150.

Bouchard, T. (2004). Genetic influence on human psychological traits: A survey. *Current Directions in Psychological Science, 13,* 148–151.

Bowlby, J. (1982). Attachment and loss: Retrospect and prospect. *American Journal of Orthopsychiatry, 52,* 664–678.

Bowlby, J. (1988). *A Secure Base: Parent-child Attachment and Healthy Human Development.* New York: Basic Books.

Boyanowsky, E. (1999). Violence and aggression in the heat of passion and in cold blood: The Ecs-TC syndrome. *International Journal of Law and Psychiatry. Special Issue: Current issues in law and psychiatry, 22(3-4),* 257–271.

Boyd, R., & Richerson, P. J. (1985). *Culture and the Evolutionary Process.* Chicago: Univ. of Chicago Press.

Boyes, W. J., Mounts, W. S. J., & Sowell, C. (2004). Restaurant tipping: Free-riding, social acceptance, and gender differences. *Journal of Applied Social Psychology, 34,* 2616–2628.

Bradburn, N., & Sudman, S. (1988). *Polls & Surveys: Understanding What They Tell Us.* San Francisco, CA: Jossey-Bass.

Bradbury, T. N., & Fincham, F. D. (1992). Attributions and behavior in marital interaction. *Journal of Personality and Social Psychology, 63,* 613–628.

Bradbury, T. N., Beach, S. R. H., Fincham, F. D., & Nelson, G. M. (1996). Attributions and behavior in functional and dys-functional marriages. *Journal of Consulting and Clinical Psychology, 64,* 569–576.

Bradley, J. P., Nicol, A. A. M., Charbonneau, D., & Meyer, J. P. (2002). Personality correlates of leadership development in Canadian Forces officer candidates. *Canadian Journal of Behavioural Science, 34,* 92–103.

Brafford, L., & Beck, K. (1991). Development and validation of a condom self-efficacy scale for college students. *Journal of American College Health, 39,* 219–225.

Brannon, L. (2011). *Gender: Psychological perspectives* (6th ed.). Boston: Allyn & Bacon, Pearson.

Branscombe, N. R., Schmitt, M. T., & Harvey, R. D. (1999). Perceiving pervasive discrimination among African Americans: Implications for group identification and wellbeing. *Journal of Personality and Social Psychology, 77,* 135–149.

Branscombe, N. R., & Wann, D. L. (1994). Collective self-esteem consequences of outgroup derogation when a valued social identity is on trial. *European Journal of Social Psychology, 24,* 641–657.

Branscombe, N. R., Wann, D. L., Noel, J. G., & Coleman, J. (1993). In-group or out-group extremity: Importance of the threatened social identity. *Personality and Social Psychology Bulletin, 19,* 381–388.

Brauer, M., Judd, C. M., & Gliner, M. D. (1995). The effects of repeated expressions on attitude polarization during group discussions. *Journal of Personality and Social Psychology, 68,* 1014–1029.

Braun, K., Ellis, R., & Loftus, E. (2002). Make my memory: How advertising can change our memories of the past. *Psychology & Marketing, 19,* 1–23.

Bray, R. M., Johnson, D., & Chilstrom, J. T. (1982). Social influence by group members with minority opinions: A comparison of Hollander and Moscovici. *Journal of Personality and Social Psychology, 43,* 78–88.

Brehm, J. (1956). Postdecision changes in the desirability of alternatives. *The Journal of Abnormal and Social Psychology, 52,* 384–389.

Brehm, J. W. (1966). *A Theory of Psychological Reactance.* New York: Academic Press.

Brehm, J. W., & Brehm, S. S. (1981). *Psychological Reactance.* New York: Wiley.

Brennan, K. A., & Shaver, P. R. (1995). Dimensions of adult attachment, affect regulation, and romantic relationship functioning. *Personality and Social Psychology Bulletin, 21,* 267–283.

Brennan, S. & Taylor-Butts, A. (2008). *Sexual Assault in Canada 2004 and 2007.* Canadian Centre for Justice Statistics. Retrieved from http://www.statcan.gc.ca/pub/85f0033m/85f0033m2008019-eng.pdf

Brett, J. M., & Goldberg, S. B. (1983). Grievance mediation in the coal industry: A field experiment. *Industrial and Labor Relations Review, 37,* 49–69.

Brett, J. M., Goldberg, S. B.,& Ury,W. L. (1990). Designing systems for resolving disputes in organizations. *American Psychologist, 45,* 162–170.

Brewer, M. B. (1979). In-group bias in the minimal intergroup situation: A cognitive motivational analysis. *Psychological Bulletin, 86,* 307–324.

Brewer, M. B., & Kramer, R. M. (1986). Choice behavior in social dilemmas: Effects of social identity, group size, and decision framing. *Journal of Personality and Social Psychology, 50,* 543–549.

Brewer, M. B., & Pickett, C. L. (1999). Distinctiveness motives as a source of the social self. In T. Tyler, R. Kramer, & O. John (Eds.), *The psychology of the social self* (pp. 71-87). Mahwah, NJ: Erlbaum.

Brickner, M. A., Harkins, S. G., & Ostrom, T. M. (1986). Effects of personal involvement: Thought-provoking implications for social loafing. *Journal of Personality and Social Psychology, 51,* 763–770.

Briñol, P., & Petty, R. E. (2003). Overt head movements and persuasion: A self-validation analysis. *Journal of Personality and Social Psychology, 84,* 1123–1139.

Broadstock, M., Borland, R., & Gason, R. (1992). Effects of suntan on judgements of healthiness and attractiveness by adolescents. *Journal of Applied Social Psychology, 22,* 157–172.

Brochu, P. M. & Esses, V. M. (2009). Weight prejudice and medial policy: Support for an ambiguously discriminatory policy is influenced by prejudice-colored glasses. *Analyses of Social Issues and Public Policy, 9,* 117–133.

Bronfenbrenner, U. (1961). The mirror-image in Soviet-American relations. *Journal of Social Issues, 17,* 45–56.

Brown, B. B., Clasen, D. R., & Eicher, S. A. (1986). Perceptions of peer pressure, peer conformity dispositions, and self-reported behavior among adolescents. *Developmental Psychology, 22,* 521–530.

Brown, D. (2008). Ontario Court of Justice between: Her Majesty the Queen and Gurakbal Singh Bains. Retrieved from http://www.yourbestdefence.com/sexual_assault_acquittal.htm

Brown, J., & Gallagher, F. (1992). Coming to terms with failure: Private self-enhancement and public self-effacement. *Journal of Experimental Social Psychology, 28,* 3–22.

Brown, J., Novick, N. Lord, K., Richards, J. (1992). When Gulliver travels: Social context, psychological closeness, and self-appraisals. *Journal of Personality and Social Psychology, 62,* 717–727.

Brown, R. (2000). *Group processes* (2nd ed.). Oxford: Blackwell.

Brownstein, A., Read, S., & Simon, D. (2004). Bias at the racetrack: Effects of individual expertise and task importance on predecision reevaluation of alternatives. *Personality and Social Psychology Bulletin, 30,* 891–904.

Bruch, M. A., Hamer, R. J., & Heimberg, R. G. (1995). Shyness and public consciousness: Additive or interactive relation with social interaction? *Journal of Personality, 63,* 47–63.

Brückner, H., & Bearman, P. (2005). After the promise: The STD consequences of adolescent virginity pledges. *Journal of Adolescent Health, 36,* 271–278.

Bruder-Mattson, S. F., & Hovanitz, C. A. (1990). Coping and attributional styles as predictors of depression. *Journal of Clinical Psychology, 46,* 557–565.

Brumbaugh, C. C., & Fraley, R. C. (2006). Transference and attachment: How do attachment patterns get carried forward from one relationship to the next? *Personality and Social Psychology Bulletin, 32,* 552–560.

Bryan, J. H., & Test, M. A. (1967). Models and helping: Naturalistic studies in aiding behavior. *Journal of Personality and Social Psychology, 6,* 400–407.

Bryant, F., & Guilbault, R. (2002).'I knew it all along' eventually: The development of hindsight bias in reaction to the Clinton impeachment verdict. *Basic and Applied Social Psychology, 24,* 27–41.

Bryant,C.C.(2010,Feb.23).Olympic Figure Skater Joannie Rochette, in her mother's words. *Christian Science Monitor.* Retrieved from http://www.csmonitor.com/World/Olympics/2010/0223/Olympic-figure-skater-Joannie-Rochette-in-her-mother-s-words

Bryce, P. (1922). *The story of a national crime.* Report for the Department of Indian Affairs (DIA). Retrieved from http://canadiangenocide.nativeweb.org/mort_rate_index.html

Buckley, C. (2007, January 3). Man Is Rescued by Stranger on Subway Tracks. *The New York Times.* Retrieved from http://www.nytimes.com/2007/01/03/nyregion/03life.html

Budworth, M-H., & Mann, S. (2010). Becoming a leader: The challenge of modesty for women. *Journal of Management Development, 29,* 177–186.

Bui, K. T., Peplau, L. A., & Hill, C. T. (1996). Testing the Rusbult model of relationship commitment and stability in a 15-year study of heterosexual couples. *Personality and Social Psychology Bulletin, 22,* 1244–1257.

Burger, J. M. (1986). Increasing compliance by improving the deal: The that's-not-all technique. *Journal of Personality and Social Psychology, 51,* 277–283.

Burger, J. M. (2009). Replicating Milgram would people still obey today? American Psychologists, 64, 1–11.

Burger, J. M., & Caldwell, D. F. (2003). The effects of monetary incentives and labeling on the foot-in-the-door effect: Evidence for a self-perception process. *Basic and Applied Social Psychology, 25,* 235–241.

Burger, J. M., Messian, N., Patel, S., del Prado, A., & Anderson, C. (2004). What a coincidence! The effects of incidental similarity on compliance. *Personality and Social Psychology Bulletin, 30,* 35–43.

Burger, J. M., & Petty, R. E. (1981). The low-ball compliance technique: Task or person commitment? *Journal of Personality and Social Psychology, 40,* 492–500.

Burgess, M., Enzle, M., & Schmaltz, R. (2004). Defeating the potentially deleterious effects of externally imposed deadlines: Practitioners' rules-of-thumb. *Personality and Social Psychology Bulletin, 30,* 868–877.

Burkley, E. (2008). The role of self-control in resistance to persuasion. *Personality and Social Psychology Bulletin, 34,* 419–431.

Burns, R. B. (1978). The relative effectiveness of various incentives and deterrents as judged by pupils and teachers. *Educational Studies, 4,* 229–243.

Burnstein, E., Crandall, C., & Kitayama, S. (1994). Some neo-Darwinian decision rules for altruism: Weighing cues for inclusive fitness as a function of the biological importance of the decision. *Journal of Personality and Social Psychology, 67,* 773–789.

Burt, M. R. (1980). Cultural myths and support for rape. *Journal of Personality and Social Psychology, 38,* 217–230.

Bushman, B. J. (1988). The effects of apparel on compliance: A field experiment with a female authority figure. *Personality and Social Psychology Bulletin, 14,* 459–467.

Bushman, B. J. (1993). Human aggression while under the influence of alcohol and other drugs: An integrative research review. *Current Directions in Psychological Science, 2,* 148–152.

Bushman, B.J. (1996). Individual differences in the extent and development of aggressive cognitive-associative networks. *Personality and Social Psychology Bulletin, 22,* 811–819.

Bushman, B. J. (1998). Priming effects of media violence on the accessibility of aggressive constructs in memory. *Personality and Social Psychology Bulletin, 24,* 537–545.

Bushman, B. J. (2002). Does venting anger feed or extinguish the flame? Catharsis, rumination, distraction, anger and aggressive responding. *Personality and Social Psychology Bulletin, 28,* 724–731.

Bushman, B. J., & Anderson, C. A. (2001). Media violence and the American public: Scientific facts versus media misinformation. *American Psychologist, 56,* 477–489.

Bushman, B. J., & Anderson, C. A. (2002). Violent video games and hostile expectations: A test of the general aggression model. *Personality and Social Psychology Bulletin, 28,* 1679–1686.

Bushman, B., & Baumeister, R. (1998). Threatened egotism, narcissism, self-esteem, and direct and displaced aggression: Does self-love or self-hate lead to violence? *Journal of Personality and Social Psychology, 75,* 219–229.

Bushman, B. J., Baumeister, R. F., & Phillips, C. M. (2001). Do people aggress to improve their mood? Catharsis beliefs, affect regulation opportunity, and aggressive responding. *Journal of Personality and Social Psychology, 81,* 17–32.

Bushman, B. J., Baumeister, R. F., & Stack, A. D. (1999). Catharsis, aggression, and persuasive influence: Self-fulfilling or self-defeating prophecies? *Journal of Personality and Social Psychology, 76,* 367–376.

Bushman, B. J., Bonacci, A. M., Pedersen, W. C., Vasquez, E. A., & Miller, N. (2005). Chewing on it can chew you up: Effects of rumination on triggered displaced aggression. *Journal of Personality and Social Psychology, 88,* 969–983.

Bushman, B. J., Bonacci, A. M., van Dijk, M., & Baumeister, R. F. (2003). Narcissism, sexual refusal, and aggression: Testing a narcissistic reactance model of sexual coercion. *Journal of Personality and Social Psychology, 84,* 1027–1040.

Bushman, B. J., & Cantor, J. (2003). Media ratings for violence and sex: Implications for policymakers and parents. *American Psychologist, 58,* 130–141.

Bushman, B. J., & Cooper, H. M. (1990). Effects of alcohol on human aggression: An integrative research review. *Psychological Bulletin, 107,* 341–354.

Bushman, B. J., & Geen, R. G. (1990). Role of cognitive emotional mediators and individual differences in the effects of media violence on aggression. *Journal of Personality and Social Psychology, 58,* 156–163.

Bushman, B. J., & Stack, A. D. (1996). Forbidden fruit versus tainted fruit: Effects of warning labels on attraction to television violence. *Journal of Experimental Psychology: Applied, 2,* 207–226.

Bushman, B. J., Wang, M. C., & Anderson, C. A. (2005a). Is the curve relating temperature to aggression linear or curvilinear? Assaults and temperature in Minneapolis reexamined. *Journal of Personality and Social Psychology, 89,* 62–66.

Bushman, B. J., Wang, M. C., & Anderson, C. A. (2005b). Is the curve relating temperature to aggression linear or curvilinear? A response to Bell (2005) and to Cohn and Rotton (2005). *Journal of Personality and Social Psychology, 89,* 74–77.

Bushman, B., & Wells, G. (2001). Narrative impressions of literature: The availability bias and the corrective properties of meta-analytic approaches. *Personality and Social Psychology Bulletin, 27,* 1123–1130.

Buss, A. H., & Perry, M. (1992). The aggression questionnaire. *Journal of Personality and Social Psychology, 63,* 452–459.

Buss, D. M. (1989). Sex differences in human mate preferences: Evolutionary hypotheses tested in 37 cultures. *Behavioral and Brain Sciences, 12,* 1–49.

Buss, D. M. (1995). Evolutionary psychology: A new paradigm for psychological science. *Psychological Inquiry, 61,* 1–30.

Buss, D. M., Larsen, R. J., Westen, D., & Semmelroth, J. (1992). Sex differences in jealousy: Evolution, physiology, and psychology. *Psychological Science, 3,* 251–255.

Buss, D. M., & Schmitt, D. P. (1993). Sexual Strategies Theory: An evolutionary perspective on human mating. *Psychological Review, 100,* 204–232.

Buss, D. M., & Shackelford, T. K. (1997). From vigilance to violence: Mate retention tactics in married couples. *Journal of Personality and Social Psychology, 72,* 346–36.

Buss, D. M., Shackelford, T. K., Kirkpatrick, L. A., Choe, J. C., Lim, H. K., Hasegawa, M., et al. (1999). Jealousy and the nature of beliefs about infidelity: Tests of competing hypotheses about sex differences in the United States, Korea, and Japan. *Personal Relationships, 6,* 125–150.

Buss, D. M., Shackelford, T. K., Kirkpatrick, L. A., & Larsen, R. J. (2001). A half century of mate preferences: The cultural evolution of values. *Journal of Marriage & the Family, 63,* 491–503.

Butler, J. L., & Baumeister, R. F. (1998). The trouble with friendly faces: Skilled performance with a supportive audience. *Journal of Personality and Social Psychology, 75,* 1213–1230.

Buunk, A. P., Park, J. H. & Duncan, L.A. (2010). Cultural variation in parental influence on mate choice. *Behavior Science Research, 44(1),* pp. 23–40.

Buunk, B. P., Angleitner, A., Oubaid, V., & Buss, D. M. (1996). Sex differences in jealousy in evolutionary and cultural perspective: Tests from the Netherlands, Germany, and the United States. *Psychological Science, 7,* 359–363.

Buunk, B. P., & van der Eijnden, R. J. J. M. (1997). Perceived prevalence, perceived superiority, and relationship satisfaction: Most relationships are good, but ours is the best. *Personality and Social Psychology Bulletin, 23,* 219–228.

Byrne, D. (1997). An overview (and underview) of research and theory within the attraction paradigm. *Journal of Social and Personal Relationships, 14,* 417–431.

Byrnes, D. A., & Kiger, G. (1990). The effect of a prejudice reduction simulation on attitude change. *Journal of Applied Social Psychology, 20,* 341–356.

Cacioppo, J., Amaral, D., Blanchard, J., Cameron, J., Carter, C., Crews, D. (2007). Social neuroscience: Progress and implications for mental health. *Perspectives on Psychological Science, 2,* 99–123.

Cacioppo, J., Marshall-Goodell, B., Tassinary, L., & Petty, R. (1992). Rudimentary determinants of attitudes: Classical conditioning is more effective when prior knowledge about the attitude stimulus is low than high *Journal of Experimental Social Psychology, 28,* 207–233.

Cacioppo, J. T., Berntson, G. G., Lorig, T. S., Norris, C. J., Rickett, E., & Nusbaum, H. (2003). Just because you're imaging the brain doesn't mean you can stop using your head: A primer and set of first principles. *Journal of Personality and Social Psychology, 85,* 650–661.

Cacioppo, J. T., & Petty, R. E. (1982). The need for cognition. *Journal of Personality and Social Psychology, 42,* 116–131.

Cacioppo, J. T., Petty, R. E., & Morris, K. J. (1983). Effects of need for cognition on message evaluation, recall, and persuasion. *Journal of Personality and Social Psychology, 45,* 805–818.

Caldwell, R. A., & Reinhart, M. A. (1988). The relationship of personality to individual differences in the use of type and source of social support. *Journal of Social & Clinical Psychology, 6,* 140–146.

Campbell, C. R. & Henry, J. W. (1999). Gender differences in self-attributions: Relationships of gender to attributional consistency, style, and expectations for performance in a college course. *Sex Roles, 41,* 95–104.

Campbell, D., Carr, S., & MacLachlan, M. (2001). Attributing 'third world poverty' in Australia and Malawi: A case of donor bias? *Journal of Applied Social Psychology, 31,* 409–430.

Campbell, J., Trapnell, P., Heine, S., Katz, I., Lavallee, L., & Lehman, D. (1996). Self-concept clarity: Measurement, personality correlates, and cultural boundaries. *Journal of Personality and Social Psychology, 70,* 141–156.

Campbell, J.D. (1990). Self-esteem and clarity of the self-concept. *Journal of Personality and Social Psychology. 59(3),* 538–549.

Campbell, J. D., & Fairey, P. J. (1989). Informational and normative routes to conformity: The effect of faction size as a function of norm extremity and attention to the stimulus. *Journal of Personality and Social Psychology, 57,* 457–468.

Campbell, L., Simpson, J. A., Boldry, J., & Kashy, D. A. (2005). Perceptions of conflict and support in romantic relationships: The role of attachment anxiety. *Journal of Personality and Social Psychology, 88,* 510–531.

Campbell, W. K., Foster, C. A., & Finkel, E. J. (2002). Does self-love lead to love for others?: A story of narcissistic game-playing. *Journal of Personality and Social Psychology, 83,* 340–354.

Campion-Smith, B. (2011, June 30). Backroom talks came close to ending postal standoff. *Toronto Star.* Retrieved from http://www .thestar.com/news/canada/politics/article/1017004--backroom-talks-came-close-to-ending-postal-standoff

Canadian Atheist Bus Campaign. Retrieved from http://atheistbus.ca/

Carli, L. (1999a). Cognitive reconstruction, hindsight, and reactions to victims and perpetrators. *Personality and Social Psychology Bulletin, 25,* 966–979.

Carli, L. L. (1999b). Gender, interpersonal power, and social influence. *Journal of Social Issues, 55,* 81–99

Carli, L. L., Ganley, R., & Pierce-Otay, A. (1991). Similarity and satisfaction in roommate relationships. *Personality and Social Psychology Bulletin, 17,* 419–426.

Carlo, G., Eisenberg, N., Troyer, D., Switzer, G., & Speer, A. L. (1991). The altruistic personality: In what contexts is it apparent? *Journal of Personality and Social Psychology, 61,* 450–458.

Carlson, M., Charlin, V., & Miller, N. (1988). Positive mood and helping behavior: A test of six hypotheses. *Journal of Personality and Social Psychology, 55,* 211–229.

Carnagey, N. L., & Anderson, C. A. (2005). The effects of reward and punishment in violent video games on aggressive affect, cognition, and behavior. *Psychological Science, 16,* 882–889.

Carnagey, N. L., Anderson, C. A., & Bartholow, B. D. (2007). Media violence and social neuroscience: New questions and new opportunities. *Current Directions in Psychological Science, 16,* 178–182.

Carnelley, K. B., Pietromonaco, P. R., & Jaffe, K. (1996). Attachment, caregiving, and relationship functioning in couples: Effects of self and partner. *Personal Relationships, 3,* 257–277.

Carnevale, P. J., & Probst, T. M. (1998). Social values and social conflict in creative problem solving and categorization. *Journal of Personality and Social Psychology, 74,* 1300–1309.

Carpenter, S. L. (1988). Self-relevance and goal-directed processing in the recall and weighting of information about others. *Journal of Experimental Social Psychology, 24,* 310–332.

Carroll, J., & Russell, J. (1996). Do facial expressions signal specific emotions? Judging emotion from the face in context. *Journal of Personality and Social Psychology, 70,* 205–218.

Carter, J. D., Hall, J. A., Carney, D. R., & Rosip, J. C. (2006). Individual differences in the acceptance of stereotyping. *Journal of Research in Personality, 40,* 1103–1118.

Carter, S. L. (1993). *Reflections of an affirmative action baby.* New York: Basic Books.

Cash, T. F., & Derlega, V. J. (1978). The matching hypothesis: Physical attractiveness among same-sexed friends. *Personality and Social Psychology Bulletin, 4,* 240–243.

Caspi, A., & Herbener, E. S. (1990). Continuity and change: Assortative marriage and the consistency of personality in adulthood. *Journal of Personality and Social Psychology, 58,* 250–258.

Castillo, E. & Stevenson, M. (August 26, 2010). Mexican drug cartel massacres migrants. *Globe & Mail.* Page A12.

Catalano, R., Novaco, R., & McConnell, W. (1997). A model of the net effect of job loss on violence. *Journal of Personality and Social Psychology, 72,* 1440–1447.

CBC News (2007, February 26). Ontario removes video slot machines flashing winning images. *CBC News.* Retrieved from http://www.cbc.ca/canada/story/2007/02/25/video-lottery

CBC News (2008, May 16). Residential schools: A history of residential schools in Canada. *CBC News.* Retrieved from http://www.cbc.ca/news/canada/story/2008/05/16/f-faqs-residential-schools.html

CBC News (2011, March 23). Japan radiation fears limit food exports. *CBC News.* Retrieved from http://www.cbc.ca/news/world/story/2011/03/23/japan-food-water-safety.html

CBC News (2011, July 22). Norway island camp massacre claims 80. *CBC News.* Retrieved from http://www.cbc.ca/news/world/story/2011/07/22/oslo-blast.html

CBS News. (2003, Dec. 2). Firemen divorce for 9/11 widows. *CBS News.* Retrieved from http://www.cbsnews.com/stories/2003/12/02/earlyshow/living/main586338.shtml

Ceci, S., Huffman, M., Smith, E., & Loftus, E. (1994). Repeatedly thinking about a non event: Source misattributions among preschoolers. *Consciousness and Cognition: An International Journal, 3,* 388–407.

Chacko, T. I. (1982). Women and equal employment opportunity: Some unintended effects. *Journal of Applied Psychology, 67,* 119–123.

Chaiken, S. (1980). Heuristic versus systematic information processing and the use of source versus message cues in persuasion. *Journal of Personality and Social Psychology, 39,* 752–766.

Chaiken, S., & Eagly, A. H. (1983). Communication modality as a determinant of persuasion: The role of communicator salience. *Journal of Personality and Social Psychology, 45,* 241–256.

Chaiken, S., & Maheswaran, D. (1994). Heuristic processing can bias systematic processing: Effects of source credibility, argument ambiguity, and task importance on attitude judgment. *Journal of Personality and Social Psychology, 66,* 460–473.

Chamberlain, L. J., Wang, Y., & Robinson, T. M., (2006). Does children's screen time predict requests for advertised products? Cross-sectional and prospective analyses. *Archives of Pediatrics & Adolescent Medicine, 160,* 363–368.

Chance, J. E., & Goldstein, A. G. (1981). Depth of processing in response to own- and other-race faces. *Personality and Social Psychology Bulletin, 7,* 475–480.

Chance, S. E., Brown, R. T., Dabbs, J. M. J., & Casey, R. (2000). Testosterone, intelligence and behavior disorders in young boys. *Personality and Individual Differences, 28,* 437–445.

Chang, E., & Asakawa, K. (2003). Cultural variations on optimistic and pessimistic bias for self versus a sibling: Is there evidence for self-enhancement in the West and for self-criticism in the East when the referent group is specified? *Journal of Personality and Social Psychology, 84,* 569–581.

Chang, E., Asakawa, K., & Sanna, L. (2001). Cultural variations in optimistic and pessimistic bias: Do Easterners really expect the worst and Westerners really expect the best when predicting future life events?. *Journal of Personality and Social Psychology, 81,* 476–491.

Chaplin, W., Phillips, J., Brown, J., Clanton, N., & Stein, J. (2000). Handshaking, gender, personality, and first impressions. *Journal of Personality and Social Psychology, 79,* 110–117.

Charbonneau, D., Barling, J., & Kelloway, E. K. (2001). Transformational leadership and sports performance: The mediating role of intrinsic motivation. *Journal of Applied Social Psychology, 31,* 1521–1534.

Chatman, C. M., & von Hippel, W. (2001). Attributional mediation of in-group bias. *Journal of Experimental Social Psychology, 37,* 267–272.

Chebat, J-C., El Hedhli, K., Gélinas-Chebat, C., & Boivin, R. (2007). Voice and persuasion in a banking telemarketing context. *Perceptual and Motor Skills, 104*(2), 419–437.

Chemers, M. M., Watson, C. B., & May, S. T. (2000). Dispositional affect and leadership effectiveness: A comparison of self-esteem, optimism, and efficacy. *Personality and Social Psychology Bulletin, 26*, 267–277.

Chen, C., Lee, S., & Stevenson, H. W. (1995). Response style and cross-cultural comparisons of rating scales among East Asian and North American students. *Psychological Science, 6*, 170–175.

Chen, H. C., Reardon, R., Rea, C., & Moore, D. J. (1992). Forewarning of content and involvement: Consequences for persuasion and resistance to persuasion. *Journal of Experimental Social Psychology, 28*, 523–541.

Chen, L. H., Baker, S. P., Braver, E. R., & Li, G. (2000). Carrying passengers as a risk factor for crashes fatal to 16-and 17-year-old drivers. *Journal of the American Medical Association, 283*, 1578–1582.

Chen, S., English, T., & Peng, K. (2006). Self-verification and contextualized self-views. *Personality and Social Psychology Bulletin, 32*, 930–942.

Chiao, J. Y., & Blizinsky, K. D. (2010). Culture-gene coevolution of individualism-collectivism and the serotonin transporter gene (5-HTTLPR). *Proceedings of the Royal Society B: Biological Sciences, 277*, 529–537.

Chiao, J. Y., Hariri, A. R., Harada, T., Mano, Y., Sadato, N., Parrish, T. B., et al. (2010). Tools of the Trade: Theory and methods in cultural neuroscience. *Social Cognitive and Affective Neuroscience, 5*, 356–361.

Chinese Culture Connection (1987). Chinese values and the search for culture-free dimensions of culture. *Journal of Cross-Cultural Psychology, 18*(2), 143–164.

Choi, I., & Choi, Y. (2002). Culture and self-concept flexibility. *Personality and Social Psychology Bulletin, 28*, 1508–1517.

Choi, I., & Nisbett, R. (1998). Situational salience and cultural differences in the correspondence bias and actor-observer bias. *Personality and Social Psychology Bulletin, 24*, 949–960.

Choi, I., & Nisbett, R. (2000). Cultural psychology of surprise: Holistic theories and recognition of contradiction. *Journal of Personality and Social Psychology, 79*, 890–905.

Choi, I., Nisbett, R., & Norenzayan, A. (1999). Causal attribution across cultures: Variation and universality. *Psychological Bulletin, 125*, 47–63.

Christakis, D. A., & Zimmerman, F. J. (2007). Violent television viewing during preschool is associated with antisocial behavior during school age. *Pediatrics, 120*, 993–999.

Christensen, A., & Heavey, C. L. (1990). Gender and social structure in the demand/withdraw pattern of marital conflict. *Journal of Personality and Social Psychology, 59*, 73–81.

Christensen, P. N., & Kashy, D. A. (1998). Perceptions of and by lonely people in initial social interaction. *Personality and Social Psychology Bulletin, 24*, 322–329.

Christensen, S. & Morrongiello, B. A. (1997). J The influence of peers on children's judgments about engaging in behaviors that threaten their safety. *Journal of Applied Developmental Psychology, 18*(4), 547–562.

Christofides, E., Muise, A., & Desmarais, S. (2009). Information disclosure and control on Facebook. Are they two sides of the same coin or two different processes? *CyberPsychology & Behaviour, 12* (3). 341–345.

Church, A., Ortiz, F., Katigbak, M., Avdeyeva, T., Emerson, A., Vargas Flores, J., et al. (2003). Measuring individual and cultural differences in implicit trait theories. *Journal of Personality and Social Psychology, 85*, 332–347.

Cialdini, R. B. (2001). *Influence: Science and practice* (4th ed.). Boston: Allyn and Bacon.

Cialdini, R. B., Brown, S. L., Lewis, B. P., Luce, C., & Neuberg, S. L. (1997). Reinterpreting the empathy-altruism relationship: When one into one equals oneness. *Journal of Personality and Social Psychology, 73*, 481–494.

Cialdini, R. B., Borden, R. J., Thorne, A., Walker, M., Freeman, S., & Sloan, L. (1976). Basking in reflected glory: Three (football) field studies. *Journal of Personality and Social Psychology, 34*, 366–375.

Cialdini, R. B., Caccioppo, J. T., Bassett, R., & Miller, J. A. (1978). Low-ball procedure for producing compliance: Commitment then cost. *Journal of Personality and Social Psychology, 36*, 463–476.

Cialdini, R. B., Darby, B. L., & Vincent, J. E. (1973). Transgression and altruism: A case for hedonism. *Journal of Experimental Social Psychology, 9*, 502–516.

Cialdini, R. B., Green, B. L., & Rusch, A. J. (1992). When tactical pronouncements of change become real change: The case of reciprocal persuasion. *Journal of Personality and Social Psychology, 63*, 30–40.

Cialdini, R. B., & Kenrick, D. T. (1976). Altruism as hedonism: A social development perspective on the relationship of negative mood state and helping. *Journal of Personality and Social Psychology, 34*, 907–914.

Cialdini, R. B., Kenrick, D. T., & Baumann, D. J. (1982). *Effects of mood on prosocial behavior in children and adults.* In N. Eisenberg-Berg (Ed.), *Development of Prosocial Behavior* (pp. 339–359). New York: Academic Press.

Cialdini, R. B., Reno, R. R., & Kallgren, C. A. (1990). A focus theory of normative conduct: Recycling the concept of norms to reduce littering in public places. *Journal of Personality and Social Psychology, 58*, 1015–1026.

Cialdini, R. B., Schaller, M., Houlihan, D., Arps, K., Fultz, J., & Beaman, A. L. (1987). Empathy-based helping: Is it selflessly or selfishly motivated? *Journal of Personality and Social Psychology, 52*, 749–758.

Cialdini, R. B., Vincent, J. E., Lewis, S. K., Catalan, J., Wheeler, D., & Darby, B. L. (1975). Reciprocal concessions procedure for inducing compliance: The door-in-the-face technique. *Journal of Personality and Social Psychology, 31*, 206–215.

Cialdini, R. B., Wosinska, W., Barrett, D. W., Butner, J., & Gornik-Durose, M. (1999). Compliance with a request in two cultures: The differential influence of social proof and commitment/consistency on collectivists and individualists. *Personality and Social Psychology Bulletin, 25*, 1242–1253.

Cingöz-Ulu, B., & Lalonde, R. N. (2007). The role of culture and relational context in interpersonal conflict: Do Turks and Canadians use different conflict management strategies? *International Journal of Intercultural Relations, 31*, 443–458.

Cismaru, M., Jensen, G. & Lavack, A.M. (2010). If the noise coming from next door were loud music, you'd do something about it: Using mass media campaigns encouraging bystander intervention to stop partner violence. *Journal of Advertising, 39*, 69–82.

Clammer, J., 1992. Aesthetics of the self: Shopping and social being in contemporary urban Japan. In R. Shields (Ed.), *Lifestyle shopping*. London: Routledge.

Clark, M. S., & Grote, N. K. (1998). Why aren't indices of relationship costs always negatively related to indices of relationship quality? *Personality and Social Psychology Review, 2*, 2–17.

Clark, M., S., & Mills, J. (1979). Interpersonal attraction in exchange and communal relationships. Journal of Personality and Social Psychology, 37, 12–24.

Clark, M., S., & Mills, J., (1993). The difference between communal and exchange relationships: What it is and is not. Personality and Social Psychology Bulletin, 19, 684–691.

Clark, M. S., Mills, J., & Powell, M.C. (1986). Keeping track of needs in communal and exchange relationships. *Journal of Personality and Social Psychology, 51*, 333–338.

Clark, R. D., & Maass, A. (1988). The role of social categorization and perceived source credibility in minority influence. *European Journal of Social Psychology, 18*, 381–394.

Clark, R. D., & Maass, A. (1990). The effects of majority size on minority influence. *European Journal of Social Psychology, 20*, 99–117.

Clark, R. D., & Word, L. E. (1972). Why don't bystanders help? Because of ambiguity? *Journal of Personality and Social Psychology, 24*, 392–400.

Clark, R., Anderson, N. B., Clark, V. R., & Williams, D. R. (1999). Racism as a stressor for African Americans: A biopsychosocial model. *American Psychologist, 54*, 805–816.

Clement, R., Noels, K. A., & Macintyre, P. D. (2007). Three variations on the social psychology of bilinguality: Context effects in motivation, usage and identity. In A. Weatherall, B. Watson, & C. Gallois (Eds.). *Language, discourse, and social psychology* (pp. 51–77). Melbourne, Australia: Palgrave MacMillan.

Clow, K. A., & Esses, V. M. (2007). Expectancy effects in social stereotyping: Automatic and controlled processing in the Neely paradigm. *Canadian Journal of Behavioural Science, 39*, 161–173.

Codron, J. M., Siriex, L. & Reardon, T. (2006). Social and Environmental Attributes of Food Products in an Emerging Mass Market: Challenges of Signalling and Consumer Perception, with European Illustrations. *Agriculture and Human Values, 23*, 283–97.

Cohen, D. (1996). Law, social policy, and violence: The impact of regional cultures. *Journal of Personality and Social Psychology, 70*, 961–978.

Cohen, D., & Gunz, A. (2002). As seen by the other... Perspectives on the self in the memories and emotional perceptions of Easterners and Westerners. *Psychological Science, 13*, 55–59.

Cohen, D., & Nisbett, R. E. (1994). Self-protection and the culture of honor: Explaining Southern violence. *Personality and Social Psychology Bulletin, 20*, 551–567.

Cohen, D., & Nisbett, R. E. (1997). Field experiments examining the culture of honor: The role of institutions in perpetuating norms about violence. *Personality and Social Psychology Bulletin, 23*, 1188–1199.

Cohen, D., Nisbett, R. E., Bowdle, B. F., & Schwarz, N. (1996). Insult, aggression, and the southern culture of honor: An 'experimental ethnography'. *Journal of Personality and Social Psychology, 70*, 945–960.

Cohen, G. L., Garcia, J., Apfel, N., & Master, A. (2006). Reducing the racial achievement gap: A social-psychological intervention. *Science, 313*, 1307–1310.

Cohen, G. L., Garcia, J., Purdie-Vaughns, V., Apfel, N., & Brzustoski, P. (2009). Recursive processes in self-affirmation: Intervening to close the minority achievement gap. *Science, 324*, 400–403.

Cohen, S., Doyle, W. J., Skoner, D. P., Rabin, B. S., & Gwaltney, J. M. Jr., (1997). Social ties and susceptibility to the common cold. *Journal of the American Medical Association, 277*, 1940–1944.

Cohen, T. R., & Insko, C. A. (2008). War and peace: Possible approaches to reducing intergroup conflict. *Perspectives on Psychological Science, 3*, 87–93.

Cohn, E. G. (1993). The prediction of police calls for service: The influence of weather and temporal variables on rape and domestic violence. *Journal of Environmental Psychology, 13*, 71–83.

Cohn, E. G., & Rotton, J. (1997). Assault as a function of time and temperature: A moderator-variable time-series analysis. *Journal of Personality and Social Psychology, 72*, 1322–1334.

Cohn, E. G., & Rotton, J. (2000). Weather, seasonal trends and property crimes in Minneapolis, 1987–1988. A moderator-variable time-series analysis of routine activities. *Journal of Environmental Psychology, 20*, 257–272.

Coker, A. L., Smith, P. H., McKeown, R. E., & King, M. J. (2000). Frequency and correlates of intimate partner violence by type: Physical, sexual, and psychological battering. *American Journal of Public Health, 90*, 553–559.

Coleman, L. (2004). *The Copycat Effect: How the Media and Popular Culture Trigger the Mayhem in Tomorrow's Headlines.* Simon and Schuster. (p. 176.)

Collin, C. A., Di Sano, F. & Malik, R. (1994). Effects of confederate and subject gender on conformity in a color classification task. *Social Behavior and Personality. 22(4)*, 355–364.

Collins, N. L., & Feeney, B. C. (2000). A safe haven: An attachment theory perspective on support seeking and caregiving in intimate relationships. *Journal of Personality and Social Psychology, 78*, 1053–1073.

Collins, N. L., Ford, M. B., Guichard, A. C., & Allard, L. M. (2006). Working models of attachment and attribution processes in intimate relationships. *Personality and Social Psychology Bulletin, 32*, 201–219.

Collins, N. L., & Miller, L. C. (1994). Self-disclosure and liking: A meta-analytic review. *Psychological Bulletin, 116*, 457–475.

Colvin, C., Block, J., & Funder, D. (1995). Overly positive self-evaluations and personality: Negative implications for mental health. *Journal of Personality and Social Psychology, 68*, 1152–1162.

Colvin, C. R. and Block, J. (1994). Do positive illusions foster mental health? An examination of the Taylor and Brown formulation. *Psychological Bulletin, 116*, 3–20.

Condon, J. W., & Crano, W. D. (1988). Inferred evaluation and the relation between attitude similarity and interpersonal attraction. *Journal of Personality and Social Psychology, 54*, 789–797.

Conley, T., & Collins, B. (2002). Gender, relationship status and stereotyping about sexual risk. *Personality and Social Psychology Bulletin, 28*, 1483–1494.

Connolly, K. & Martlew, M. (Eds.). (1999). Altruism. In *Psychologically speaking: A book of quotations.* Leicester: BPS Books.

Conway, M. & Dubé, L. (2002). Humor in persuasion on threatening topics: Effectiveness is a function of audience sex role orientation. *Personality and Social Psychology Bulletin. 28(7)*, 863–873.

Cooper, J. (1980). Reducing fears and increasing assertiveness: The role of dissonance reduction. *Journal of Experimental Social Psychology, 16*, 199–213.

Cooper, J., & Fazio, R. H. (1984). *A new look at dissonance theory.* In L. Berkowitz (Ed.), *Advances in Experimental Social Psychology* (Vol. 17, pp. 229–266). New York: Academic Press.

Cooper, J., Fazio, R., & Rhodewalt, F. (1978). Dissonance and humor: Evidence for the undifferentiated nature of dissonance arousal. *Journal of Personality and Social Psychology, 36*, 280–285.

Cooper, J., & Neuhaus, I. M. (2000). The 'hired gun' effect: Assessing the effect of pay, frequency of testifying, and credentials on the perception of expert testimony. *Law and Human Behavior, 24*, 149–171.

Cooper, J., & Worchel, S. (1970). Role of undesired consequences in arousing cognitive dissonance. *Journal of Personality and Social Psychology, 16*, 199–206.

Cooper, M., Frone, M., Russell, M., & Mudar, P. (1995). Drinking to regulate positive and negative emotions: A motivational model of alcohol use. *Journal of Personality and Social Psychology, 69*, 990–1005.

Cooper, P. A. & Maurer, D. (2008). The influence of recent experience on perceptions of attractiveness. *Perception. 37(8)*, 1216–1226.

Coovert, M., & Reeder, G. (1990). Negativity effects in impression formation: The role of unit formation and schematic expectations. *Journal of Experimental Social Psychology, 26*, 49–62.

Copeland, J. (1994). Prophecies of power: Motivational implications of social power for behavioral confirmation. *Journal of Personality and Social Psychology, 67*, 264–277.

Corenblum, B., & Meissner, C. A. (2006). Recognition of faces of ingroup and outgroup children and adults. *Journal of Experimental Child Psychology, 93,* 187–206.

Correll, J., & Park, B. (2005). A model of the ingroup as a social resource. *Personality and Social Psychology Review, 9,* 341–359.

Correll, J., Park, B., Judd, C. M., & Wittenbrink, B. (2002). The police officer's dilemma: Using ethnicity to disambiguate potentially threatening individuals. *Journal of Personality and Social Psychology, 83,* 1314–1329.

Correll, J., Spencer, S. & Zanna, M.P. (2004). An affirmed self and an open mind: Self-affirmation and sensitivity to argument strength. *Journal of Experimental Social Psychology. 40(3),* 350–356.

Coser, L. A. (1956). *The functions of social conflict.* Glencoe, IL: Free Press.

Cosier, R. A., Schwenk, C. R., & Dalton, D. R. (1992). Managerial decision making in Japan, the U.S., and Hong Kong. *International Journal of Conflict Management, 3,* 151–160.

Cota, A. A., Evans, C. R., Dion, K. L., Kilik, L., & Longman, R. (1995). The structure of group cohesion. *Personality and Social Psychology Bulletin, 21,* 572–580.

Cotte, J., Coulter, R. & Moore, M. (2005). Enhancing or disrupting guilt: The role of ad credibility and perceived manipulative intent. *Journal of Business Research. 58(3),* 361–368.

Cottrell, N. B., Wack, D. L., Sekerak, G. J., & Rittle, R. H. (1968). Social facilitation of dominant responses by the presence of an audience and the mere presence of others. *Journal of Personality and Social Psychology, 9,* 245–250.

Cousins, S. (1989). Culture and self-perception in Japan and the United States. *Journal of Personality and Social Psychology, 56,* 124–131.

Cramer, R. E., McMaster, M. R., Bartell, P. A., & Dragna, M. (1988). Subject competence and minimization of the bystander effect. *Journal of Applied Social Psychology, 18,* 1133–1148.

Crandall, C. (1994). Prejudice against fat people: Ideology and self-interest. *Journal of Personality and Social Psychology, 66,* 882–894.

Crandall, C. S., D'Anello, S., Sakalli, N., Lazarus, E., Nejtardt, G. W., & Feather, N. T. (2001). An attribution-value model of prejudice: Anti-fat attitudes in six nations. *Personality and Social Psychology Bulletin, 27,* 30–37.

Crandall, C. S., Eshleman, A., & O'Brien, L. (2002). Social norms and the expression and suppression of prejudice: The struggle for internalization. *Journal of Personality and Social Psychology, 82,* 359–378.

Crandall, C. S., & Martinez, R. (1996). Culture, ideology, and antifat attitudes. *Personality and Social Psychology Bulletin, 22,* 1165–1176.

Crano, W. (1997). Vested interest, symbolic politics, and attitude-behavior consistency. *Journal of Personality and Social Psychology, 72,* 485–491.

Crawford, R. (1985). A cultural account of "health": Control, release, and the social body. In J. McKinlay (Ed.), *Issues in the political economy of health care* (pp. 60–101). London: Tavistock.

Crawford, R. (1994). The boundaries of the self and the unhealthy other: Reflections on health, culture and AIDS. *Social Science and Medicine, 38,* 1347–1365.

Creasey, G., & Ladd, A. (2005). Generalized and specific attachment representations: Unique and interactive roles in predicting conflict behaviors in close relationships. *Personality and Social Psychology Bulletin, 31,* 1026–1038.

Crick, N. R., Casas, J. F., & Mosher, M. (1997). Relational and overt aggression in preschool. *Developmental Psychology, 33,* 579–588.

Crick, N. R., & Grotpeter, J. K. (1995). Relational aggression, gender, and social-psychological adjustment. *Child Development, 66,* 710–722.

Crisp, R. J., Hewstone, M., & Rubin, M. (2001). Does multiple categorization reduce intergroup bias? *Personality and Social Psychology Bulletin, 27,* 76–89.

Crocker, J., & Major, B. (1989). Social stigma and self-esteem: The self-protective properties of stigma. *Psychological Review, 96,* 608–630.

Crocker, J., Niiya, Y., & Mischkowski, D. (2008). Why does writing about important values reduce defensiveness? Self-affirmation and the role of positive other-directed feelings. *Psychological Science, 19,* 740–747.

Crocker, J., Voelkl, K., Testa, M., & Major, B. (1991). Social stigma: The affective consequences of attributional ambiguity. *Journal of Personality and Social Psychology, 60,* 218–228.

Croizet, J., & Claire, T. (1998). Extending the concept of stereotype and threat to social class: The intellectual underperformance of students from low socioeconomic backgrounds. *Personality and Social Psychology Bulletin, 24,* 588–594.

Crosby, F. (1976). A model of egoistical relative deprivation. *Psychological Review, 83,* 85–113.

Crosby, F. J., & Franco, J. L. (2003). Connections between the ivory tower and the multicolored world: Linking abstract theories of social justice to the rough and tumble of affirmative action. *Personality and Social Psychology Review, 7,* 362–373.

Crosby, F. J., Iyer, A., Clayton, S., & Downing, R. A. (2003). Affirmative action: Psychological data and the policy debates. *American Psychologist, 58,* 93–115.

Croyle, R., & Cooper, J. (1983). Dissonance arousal: Physiological evidence. *Journal of Personality and Social Psychology, 45,* 782–791.

CTV News (2010). Corralled for 4 hours, crowd dispersed by G20 police. *CBC News.* Retrieved from http://www.ctv.ca/CTVNews/TopStories/20100627/g20-protests-100627/

Cuddy, A. J. C., Fiske, S. T., & Glick, P. (2007). The BIAS map: Behaviors from intergroup affect and stereotypes. *Journal of Personality and Social Psychology, 92,* 631–648.

Cullum, J., & Harton, H. C. (2007). Cultural evolution: Interpersonal influence, issue importance, and the development of shared attitudes in college residence halls. *Personality and Social Psychology Bulletin, 33,* 1327–1339.

Cunningham, C.E., Cunningham, L.J., Martorelli, V.,Tran, A., Young, J. & Zacharias, R. (1998) The effects of primary division, student-mediated conflict resolution programs on playground aggression. *Journal of Child Psychology and Psychiatry. 39(5),* 653–662.

Cunningham, M. R. (1979). Weather, mood, and helping behavior: Quasi experiments with the sunshine samaritan. *Journal of Personality and Social Psychology, 37,* 1947–1956.

Cunningham, M. R., Roberts, A. R., Barbee, A. P., Druen, P. B., & Wu, C. (1995). "Their ideas of beauty are, on the whole, the same as ours": Consistency and variability in the cross-cultural perception of female physical attractiveness. *Journal of Personality and Social Psychology, 68,* 261–279.

Cunningham, M. R., Steinberg, J., & Grev, R. (1980). Wanting to and having to help: Separate motivations for positive mood and guilt-induced helping. *Journal of Personality and Social Psychology, 38,* 181–192.

Cutler, B., Penrod, S., & Dexter, H. (1990). Juror sensitivity to eyewitness identification evidence. *Law and Human Behavior, 14,* 185–191.

Dabbs, J. M. J., & Hargrove, M. F. (1997). Age, testosterone, and behavior among female prison inmates. *Psychosomatic Medicine, 59,* 477–480.

Dabbs, J. M. J., Riad, J. K., & Chance, S. E. (2001). Testosterone and ruthless homicide. *Personality and Individual Differences, 31,* 599–603.

Dabbs, J. M. J., Strong, R., & Milun, R. (1997). Exploring the mind of testosterone: A beeper study. *Journal of Research in Personality*, 31, 577–587.

Dabbs, J. M., Carr, T. S., Frady, R. L., & Riad, J. K. (1995). Testosterone, crime, and misbehavior among 692 male prison inmates. *Personality and Individual Differences*, 18, 627–633.

Dabbs, J. M., & Morris, R. (1990). Testosterone, social class, and antisocial behavior in a sample of 4,462 men. *Psychological Science*, 1, 209–211.

Daibo, I., Murasawa, H., & Chou, Y. (1994). Attractive faces and affection of beauty: A comparison in preference of feminine facial beauty in Japan and Korea. *Japanese Journal of Research on Emotion*, 1(2), 101–123.

Dal Cin, S., Gibson, B., Zanna, M. P., Shumate, R., & Fong, G. T. (2007). Smoking in movies, implicit associations of smoking with the self, and intentions to smoke. *Psychological Science*, 18, 559–563.

Dal Cin, S., MacDonald, T., Fong, G.T., Zanna, M.P., & Elton-Marshall T.E. (2006). Remembering the message: The use of a reminder cue to increase condom use following a safer sex intervention. *Health Psychology*. 25(3), 438–443.

Dalton, M., Sargent, J., Beach, M., Titus-Ernstoff, L., Gibson, J., Aherns, M., et al. (2003). Effect of viewing smoking in movies on adolescent smoking initiation: A cohort study. *Lancet*, 362, 281–285.

Daly, M., & Wilson, M. I. (1996). Violence against stepchildren. *Current Directions in Psychological Science*, 5, 77–81.

Darley, J. M., & Batson, C. D. (1973). "From Jerusalem to Jericho": A study of situational and dispositional variables in helping behavior. *Journal of Personality and Social Psychology*, 27, 100–108.

Darley, J. M., & Fazio, R. H. (1980). Expectancy confirmation processes arising in the social interaction sequence. *American Psychologist*, 35, 867–881.

Darley, J. M., & Gross, P. H. (1983). A hypothesis-confirming bias in labeling effects. *Journal of Personality and Social Psychology*, 44, 20–33.

Darley, J. M., & Latané, B. (1968). Bystander intervention in emergencies: Diffusion of responsibility. *Journal of Personality and Social Psychology*, 8, 377–383.

Das, E. H. H. J., De Wit, J. B. F., & Stroebe, W. (2003). Fear appeals motivate acceptance of action recommendations: Evidence for a positive bias in the processing of persuasive messages. *Personality and Social Psychology Bulletin*, 29, 650–664.

Dasgupta, N., & Asgari, S. (2004). Seeing is believing: Exposure to counterstereotypic women leaders and its effect on the malleability of automatic gender stereotyping. *Journal of Experimental Social Psychology*, 40, 642–658.

Dasgupta, N., & Greenwald, A. G. (2001). On the malleability of automatic attitudes: Combating automatic prejudice with images of admired and disliked individuals. *Journal of Personality and Social Psychology*, 81, 800–814.

Dasgupta, N., & Rivera, L. M. (2006). From automatic antigay prejudice to behavior: The moderating role of conscious beliefs about gender and behavioral control. *Journal of Personality and Social Psychology*, 91, 268–280.

Davidson, L. (2011). *Egypt: The groupthink problem—an analysis.* The Naked Truth In A Confused World. Retrieved from http://thenakedtruthinaconfusedworld.blogspot.com/2011/02/egypt-groupthink-problem-analysis-by-dr.html

Davidson, R. J., Putnam, K. M., & Larson, C. L. (2000). Dysfunction in the neural circuitry of emotion regulation—a possible prelude to violence. *Science*, 289, 591–594.

Davies, M. F. (1997). Belief persistence after evidential discrediting: The impact of generated versus provided explanations on the likelihood of discredited outcomes. *Journal of Experimental Social Psychology*, 33, 561–578.

Davies, P. G., Spencer, S. J., Quinn, D. M., & Gerhardstein, R. (2002). Consuming images: How television commercials that elicit stereotype threat can restrain women academically and professionally. *Personality and Social Psychology Bulletin*, 28, 1615–1628.

Davila, J., Bradbury, T. N., & Fincham, F. (1998). Negative affectivity as a mediator of the association between adult attachment and marital satisfaction. *Personal Relationships*, 5, 467–484.

Davis, C. G., Lehman, D. R., Silver, R. C., Wortman, C. B., & Ellard, J. H. (1996). Self-blame following a traumatic event: The role of perceived avoidability. *Personality and Social Psychology Bulletin*, 22, 557–567.

Davis, C. G., Lehman, D. R., Wortman, C. B., Silver, R. C., & Thompson, S. C. (1995). The undoing of traumatic life events. *Personality and Social Psychology Bulletin*, 21, 109–124.

Davis, D., Shaver, P. R., & Vernon, M. L. (2003). Physical, emotional, and behavioral reactions to breaking up: The roles of gender, age, emotional involvement, and attachment style. *Personality and Social Psychology Bulletin*, 29, 871–884.

Davis, D., Shaver, P. R., & Vernon, M. L. (2004). Attachment style and subjective motivations for sex. *Personality and Social Psychology Bulletin*, 30, 1076–1090.

Davis, J. (1959). A formal interpretation of the theory of relative deprivation. *Sociometry*, 22, 280–296.

Davis, K. E., & Latty-Mann, H. (1987). Love styles and relationship quality: A contribution to validation. *Journal of Social and Personal Relationships*, 4, 409–428.

Davis, M. H. (1983). Empathic concern and the muscular dystrophy telethon: Empathy as a multidimensional construct. *Personality and Social Psychology Bulletin*, 9, 223–229.

Davis, M. H., Luce, C., & Kraus, S. J. (1994). The heritability of characteristics associated with dispositional empathy. *Journal of Personality*, 62, 369–391.

Dawes, R. M. (1980). Social dilemmas. *Annual Review of Psychology*, 31, 169–193.

Dawes, R. M. (2001). *Everyday irrationality: How pseudoscientists, lunatics, and the rest of us fail to think rationally.* Boulder, CO: Westview Press.

De Cremer, D. (2002). Respect and cooperation in social dilemmas: The importance of feeling included. *Personality and Social Psychology Bulletin*, 28, 1335–1341.

De Dreu, C. K. W., Koole, S. L., & Steinel, W. (2000). Unfixing the fixed pie: A motivated information-processing approach to integrative negotiation. *Journal of Personality and Social Psychology*, 79, 975–987.

De Hoog, N., Stroebe, W., & De Wit, J. B. F. (2005). The impact of fear appeals on processing and acceptance of action recommendations. *Personality and Social Psychology Bulletin*, 31, 24–33.

De La Ronde, C., & Swann, W. B. J. (1998). Partner verification: Restoring shattered images of our intimates. *Journal of Personality and Social Psychology*, 75, 374–382.

De Wit, J. B. F., Das, E., & Vet, R. (2008). What works best: Objective statistics or a personal testimonial? An assessment of the persuasive effects of different types of message evidence on risk perception. *Health Psychology*, 27, 110–115.

Dea, S. (2010). Demonstrating love. *The Globe and Mail*, June 25, 2010, pp. L1, L3.

Dean, K. E., & Malamuth, N. M. (1997). Characteristics of men who aggress sexually and of men who imagine aggressing: Risk and moderating variables. *Journal of Personality and Social Psychology*, 72, 449–455.

DeBono, K. G. (1987). Investigating the social-adjustive and value-expressive functions of attitudes: Implications for persuasion processes. *Journal of Personality and Social Psychology*, 52, 279–287.

Deci, E. L., La Guardia, J. G., Moller, A. C., Scheiner, M. J., & Ryan, R. M. (2006). On the benefits of giving as well as receiving autonomy support: Mutuality in close friendships. *Personality and Social Psychology Bulletin, 32*, 313–327.

Deci, E., Koestner, R., & Ryan, R. (1999). A meta-analytic review of experiments examining the effects of extrinsic rewards on intrinsic motivation. *Psychological Bulletin, 125*, 627–668.

DeJong, W. (1980). The stigma of obesity: The consequences of naive assumptions concerning the causes of physical deviance. *Journal of Health and Social Behavior, 21*, 75–87.

DeJong, W., & Musilli, L. (1982). External pressure to comply: Handicapped versus nonhandicapped requesters and the foot-in-the-door phenomenon. *Personality and Social Psychology Bulletin, 8*, 522–527.

DeLongis, A. & Holtzman, S. (2005). Coping in context: The role of stress, social support, and personality in coping. *Journal of Personality. Special Issue: Advances in Personality and Daily Experience. 73(6)*, 1633–1656.

Delta Kappa Epsilon (2011). *Objects*. Retrieved from http://www.dke.org/site/about_dke/objects.php

Deluty, R. H. (1985). Consistency of assertive, aggressive, and submissive behavior for children. *Journal of Personality and Social Psychology, 49*, 1054–1065.

Demaré, D., Lips, H.M. & Briere, J. (1993). Sexually violent pornography, anti-women attitudes, and sexual aggression: A structural equation model. *Journal of Research in Personality. 27(3)*, 285–300.

Department of Justice Canada (2004). Fact sheet: Section 43 of the *Criminal Code* (corporal punishment)—The Canadian Foundation for Children, Youth and the Law v. The Attorney General of Canada. *Department of Justice Canada*. Retrieved from http://www.justice.gc.ca/eng/news-nouv/fs-fi/2004/doc_31114.html

DePaulo, B. M., Dull, W. R., Greenberg, J. M., & Swaim, G. W. (1989). Are shy people reluctant to ask for help? *Journal of Personality and Social Psychology, 56*, 834–844.

DePaulo, B., & Kashy, D. (1998). Everyday lies in close and casual relationships. *Journal of Personality and Social Psychology, 74*, 63–79.

DePaulo, B., Kashy, D., Kirkendol, S., Wyer, M., & Epstein, J. (1996). Lying in everyday life. *Journal of Personality and Social Psychology, 70*, 979–995.

Deppe, R., & Harackiewicz, J. (1996). Self-handicapping and intrinsic motivation: Buffering intrinsic motivation from the threat of failure. *Journal of Personality and Social Psychology, 70*, 868–876.

DeSantis, A., & Kayson, W. A. (1997). Defendants' characteristics of attractiveness, race, and sex and sentencing decisions. *Psychological Reports, 81*, 679–683.

Deschamps, J. C. (1983). Social attribution. In J. Jaspars, F. D. Fincham an M. Hewstone (eds.), Attribution theory and research: conceptual, developmental and social dimensions (pp. 223–40). London: Academic Press.

Desforges, D. M., Lord, C. G., Pugh, M. A., Sia, T. L., Scarberry, N. C., & Ratcliff, C. D. (1997). Role of group representativeness in the generalization part of the contact hypothesis. *Basic and Applied Social Psychology, 19*, 183–204.

Desforges, D. M., Lord, C. G., Ramsey, S. L., Mason, J. A., Van Leeuwen, M. D., West, S. C., et al. (1991). Effects of structured cooperative contact on changing negative attitudes toward stigmatized social groups. *Journal of Personality and Social Psychology, 60*, 531–544.

desJarlais, D. C., Friedman, S. R., Casriel, C., & Kott, A. (1987). AIDS and preventing initiation into intravenous (IV) drug use. *Psychology & Health, 1*, 179–194.

DeSteno, D. A., & Salovey, P. (1996). Evolutionary origins of sex differences in jealousy? Questioning the 'fitness' of the model. *Psychological Science, 7*, 367–372.

DeSteno, D., Bartlett, M. Y., Braverman, J., & Salovey, P. (2002). Sex differences in jealousy: Evolutionary mechanism or artifact of measurement? *Journal of Personality and Social Psychology, 83*, 1103–1116.

DeSteno, D., Valdesolo, P., & Bartlett, M. Y. (2006). Jealousy and the threatened self: Getting to the heart of the green-eyed monster. *Journal of Personality and Social Psychology, 91*, 626–641.

Deutsch, F., & Lamberti, D. (1986). Does social approval increase helping?. *Personality and Social Psychology Bulletin, 12*, 149–157.

Deutsch, M., & Gerard, H. B. (1955). A study of normative and informational social influences upon individual judgment. *The Journal of Abnormal and Social Psychology, 51*, 629–636.

Devine, P. G. (1989). Stereotypes and prejudice: Their automatic and controlled components. *Journal of Personality and Social Psychology, 56*, 5–18.

Devine, P. G., & Elliot, A. J. (1995). Are racial stereotypes really fading? The Princeton trilogy revisited. *Personality and Social Psychology Bulletin, 21*, 1139–1150.

Devine, P. G., Monteith, M. J., Zuwerink, J. R., & Elliot, A. J. (1991). Prejudice with and without compunction. *Journal of Personality and Social Psychology, 60*, 817–830.

Devine, P. G., Plant, E. A., Amodio, D. M., Harmon-Jones, E.,& Vance, S. L. (2002). The regulation of explicit and implicit race bias: The role of motivations to respond without prejudice. *Journal of Personality and Social Psychology, 82*, 835–848.

Dhawan, N., Roseman, I., Naidu, R., & Rettek, S. (1995). Self-concepts across two cultures: India and the United States. *Journal of Cross-Cultural Psychology, 26*, 606–621.

Dickerson, C., Thibodeau, R., Aronson, E., & Miller, D. (1992). Using cognitive dissonance to encourage water conservation. *Journal of Applied Social Psychology, 22*, 841–854.

Diekman, A. B., & Eagly, A. H. (2000). Stereotypes as dynamic constructs: Women and men of the past, present, and future. *Personality and Social Psychology Bulletin, 26*, 1171–1188.

Diener, E. (1979). Deindividuation, self-awareness, and disinhibition. *Journal of Personality and Social Psychology, 37*, 1160–1171.

Diener, E., Wolsic, B., & Fujita, F. (1995). Physical attractiveness and subjective well-being. *Journal of Personality and Social Psychology, 69*, 120–129.

Dienstbier, R. A., Roesch, S. C., Mizumoto, A., Hemenover, S. H., Lott, R. C., & Carlo, G. (1998). Effects of weapons on guilt judgments and sentencing recommendations for criminals. *Basic and Applied Social Psychology, 20*, 93–102.

Dijksterhuis, A. (2004). Think different: The merits of unconscious thought in preference development and decision making. *Journal of Personality and Social Psychology, 87*, 586–598.

Dijkstra, P., & Buunk, B. P. (1998). Jealousy as a function of rival characteristics: An evolutionary perspective. *Personality and Social Psychology Bulletin, 24*, 1158–1166.

DiLalla, L. F., & Gottesman, I. I. (1991). Biological and genetic contributors to violence: Widom's untold tale. *Psychological Bulletin, 109*, 125–129.

DiManno, R. (2009, September 12). No hope for Roma in Czech ghettos. *Toronto Star*. Retrieved from http://www.thestar.com/news/article/694756

Dion, K. K., Berscheid, E., & Walster, E. (1972). What is beautiful is good. *The Journal of Personal and Social Psychology, 24*, 285 – 290.

Dion, K. K., & Dion, K. L. (1996). Cultural perspectives on romantic love. *Personal Relationships, 3*, 5–17.

Dion, K. K., Pak, A. W., & Dion, L. D. (1990). Stereotyping physical attractiveness: A sociocultural perspective. *Journal of Cross-cultural Psychology, 21*, 158 – 179.

Dion, K. L., & Dion, K. K. (1993). Gender and ethnocultural comparisons in styles of love. *Psychology of Women Quarterly*, Gender and culture, *17*, 463–473.

Dion, K. L., Dion, K. K., & Pak, A. (1992). Personality-based hardiness as a buffer for discrimination-related stress in members of Toronto's Chinese community. *Canadian Journal of Behavioral Science, 24*, 517–536.

Dion, K. K. & Dion, K.L. (1991). Psychological individualism and romantic love. *Journal of Social Behavior & Personality. 6(1),* 17–33.

Dion, K. K. & Dion, K.L. (1993). Individualistic and collectivistic perspectives on gender and the cultural context of love and intimacy. *Journal of Social Issues. 49(3),* 53–69.

Dittmar, H. (1992). *The social psychology of material possessions: To have is to be.* London: Prentice-Hall.

Dixon, J., Durrheim, K., & Tredoux, C. (2005). Beyond the optimal contact strategy: A reality check for the contact hypothesis. *American Psychologist, 60,* 697–711.

Dolinski, D. (2000). On inferring one's beliefs from one's attempt and consequences for subsequent compliance. *Journal of Personality and Social Psychology, 78,* 260–272.

Dollard, J., Doob, L. W., Miller, N. E., Mowrer, O. H., & Sears, R. R. (1939). *Frustration and Aggression.* New Haven, CT: Yale University Press.

Donahue, E. G., Miquelon, P., Valois, P., Goulet, C., Buist, A., & Vallerand, R.J. A Motivational Model of Performance-Enhancing Substance Use in Elite Athletes, *Journal of Sport & Exercise Psychology, 2006,* 511–520.

Donnerstein, E. (1980). Aggressive erotica and violence against women. *Journal of Personality and Social Psychology, 39,* 269–277.

Donnerstein, E., & Berkowitz, L. (1981). Victim reactions in aggressive erotic films as a factor in violence against women. *Journal of Personality and Social Psychology, 41,* 710–724.

Dono, J., Webb, J., & Richardson, B. (2010). The relationship between environmental activism, pro-environmental behaviour and social identity. *Journal of Environmental Psychology, 30,* 178–186.

Douglas, E. M. (2006). Familial violence socialization in childhood and later life approval of corporal punishment: A cross-cultural perspective. *American Journal of Orthopsychiatry 76,* 23–30.

Dovidio, J. F., & Gaertner, S. L. (2004). Aversive racism. In M. P. Zanna (Ed.), *Advances in experimental social psychology* (Vol. 36, pp. 1–52). New York: Elsevier.

Dovidio, J. F., Gaertner, S.L., & Validzic, A. (1998). Intergroup bias: Status, differentiation, and a common in-group identity. *Journal of Personality and Social Psychology, 75,* 109–120.

Dovidio, J. F., & Morris, W. N. (1975). Effects of stress and commonality of fate on helping behavior. *Journal of Personality and Social Psychology, 31,* 145–149.

Dovidio, J. F., ten Vergert, M., Stewart, T. L., Gaertner, S. L., Johnson, J. D., Esses,V. M., et al. (2004). Perspective and prejudice: Antecedents and mediating mechanisms. *Personality and Social Psychology Bulletin, 30,* 1537–1549.

Downie, M., Koestner, R., Horberg, E. & Haga, S. (2006). Exploring the Relation of Independent and Interdependent Self-Construals to Why and How People Pursue Personal Goals. *The Journal of Social Psychology. 146(5),* 517–531.

Downs, A. C., & Lyons, P. M. (1991). Natural observations of the links between attractiveness and initial legal judgments. *Personality and Social Psychology Bulletin, 17,* 541–547.

Doyle, A.B., Lawford, H., & Markiewicz, D. (2009). Attachment style with mother, father, best friend, and romantic partner during adolescence. *Journal of Research on Adolescence. 19(4),* 690–714.

Drabman, R. S., & Thomas, M. H. (1974). Exposure to filmed violence and children's tolerance of real life aggression. *Personality and Social Psychology Bulletin, 1,* 198–199.

Drabman, R. S., & Thomas, M. H. (1975). Does TV violence breed indifference? *Journal of Communication, 25,* 86–89.

Drigotas, S. M., & Rusbult, C. E. (1992). Should I stay or should I go? A dependence model of breakups. *Journal of Personality and Social Psychology, 62,* 62–87.

Drigotas, S. M., Safstrom, C. A., & Gentilia, T. (1999). An investment model prediction of dating infidelity. *Journal of Personality and Social Psychology, 77,* 509–524.

Drigotas, S. M., Whitney, G. A., & Rusbult, C. E. (1995). On the peculiarities of loyalty: A diary study of responses to dissatisfaction in everyday life. *Personality and Social Psychology Bulletin, 21,* 596–609.

Drolet, A. L., & Morris, M. W. (2000). Rapport in conflict resolution: Accounting for how face-to-face contact fosters mutual cooperation in mixed-motive conflicts. *Journal of Experimental Social Psychology, 36,* 26–50.

Duck, S., Pond, K., & Leatham, G. (1994). Loneliness and the evaluation of relational events. *Journal of Social and Personal Relationships, 11,* 253–276.

Duclos, S., Laird, J., Schneider, E., Sexter, M., Stern, L., & Van Lighten, O. (1989). Emotion-specific effects of facial expressions and postures on emotional experience. *Journal of Personality and Social Psychology, 57,* 100–108.

Duggan, E. S., & Brennan, K. A. (1994). Social avoidance and its relation to Bartholomew's adult attachment typology. *Journal of Social and Personal Relationships, 11,* 147–153.

Duncan, R. (1999). Peer and sibling aggression: An investigation of intra- and extra-familial bullying. Journal of *Interpersonal Violence, 14(8),* 871–886.

Dunn, E. W., Aknin, L. B., & Norton, M. I. (2008). Spending money on others promotes happiness. *Science, 319,* 1687–1688.

Dunning, D., Meyerowitz, J., & Holzberg, A. (1989). Ambiguity and self-evaluation: The role of idiosyncratic *trait* definitions in self-serving assessments of ability. *Journal of Personality and Social Psychology, 57,* 1082–1090.

Dunning, D., Perie, M., & Story, A. (1991). Self-serving prototypes of social categories. *Journal of Personality and Social Psychology, 61,* 957–968.

DuRant, R. H., Barkin, S., & Krowchuk, D. P. (2001). Evaluation of a peaceful conflict resolution and violence prevention curriculum for sixth-grade students. *Journal of Adolescent Health, 28,* 386–393.

DuRant, R. H., Champion, H., & Wolfson, M, (2006). The relationship between watching professional wrestling on television and engaging in date fighting among high school students *Pediatrics, 118,* 265–272.

DuRant, R. H., Treiber, F., Getts, A., & McCloud, K. (1996). Comparison of two violence prevention curricula for middle school adolescents. *Journal of Adolescent Health, 19,* 111–117.

Dutton, D. G., & Aron, A. P. (1974). Some evidence for heightened sexual attraction under conditions of high anxiety. *Journal of Personality and Social Psychology, 30,* 510–517.

Dutton, D. G., & Aron, A. P., (1989). Romantic attraction and generalized liking for others who are sources of conflict-based arousal. *Canadian Journal of Behavioural Science, 21,* 246–257.

Duval, S., & Wicklund, R. (1972). *A Theory of Objective Self Awareness.* New York: Academic Press.

Duval, S., Duval, V. H., & Neely, R. (1979). Self-focus, felt responsibility, and helping behavior. *Journal of Personality and Social Psychology, 37,* 1769–1778.

Eagly, A. H. (1987). *Sex Differences in Social Behavior: A Social-role Interpretation.* Hillsdale, NJ: Lawrence Erlbaum.

Eagly, A. H., Ashmore, R. D., Makhijani, M. G., & Longo, L. C. (1991). What is beautiful is good, but . . . : A meta-analytic review of research on the physical attractiveness stereotype. *Psychological Bulletin, 110,* 109–128.

Eagly, A. H., & Carli, L. L. (1981). Sex of researchers and sex-typed communications as determinants of sex differences in influenceability: A meta-analysis of social influence studies. *Psychological Bulletin, 90,* 1–20.

Eagly, A. H., & Chaiken, S. (1975). An attribution analysis of the effect of communicator characteristics on opinion change: The case of communicator attractiveness. *Journal of Personality and Social Psychology, 32,* 136–144.

Eagly, A. H., & Crowley, M. (1986). Gender and helping behavior: A meta-analytic review of the social psychological literature. *Psychological Bulletin, 100,* 283–308.

Eagly, A. H., Johannesen-Schmidt, M. C., & van Engen, M. L. (2003). Transformational, transactional, and laissez-faire leadership styles: A meta-analysis comparing women and men. *Psychological Bulletin, 129,* 569–591.

Eagly, A. H., & Johnson, B. T. (1990). Gender and leadership style: A meta-analysis. *Psychological Bulletin, 108,* 233–256.

Eagly, A. H., & Steffen, V. J. (1986). Gender and aggressive behavior: A meta-analytic review of the social psychological literature. *Psychological Bulletin, 100,* 309–330.

Eagly, A. H., & Wood, W. (1999). The origins of sex differences in human behavior: Evolved dispositions versus social roles. *American Psychologist, 54,* 408–423.

Eagly, A. H., Wood, W., & Chaiken, S. (1978). Causal inferences about communicators and their effect on opinion change. *Journal of Personality and Social Psychology, 36,* 424–435.

Eagly, A. H., Wood, W., & Diekman, A. B. (2000). Social role theory of sex differences and similarities: A current appraisal. In T. Eckes & H.M. Taunter (Eds.), *The developmental social psychology of gender* (pp.123–174). Mahwah, NJ: Erlbaum.

Eagly, A. H., Wood, W., & Fishbaugh, L. (1981). Sex differences in conformity: Surveillance by the group as a determinant of male nonconformity. *Journal of Personality and Social Psychology, 40,* 384–394.

Eagly, A., Diekman, A., Johannesen-Schmidt, M., & Koenig, A. (2004). Gender gaps in sociopolitical attitudes: A social psychological analysis. *Journal of Personality and Social Psychology, 87,* 796–816.

Earley, P. C. (1993). East meets West meets Mideast: Further explorations of collectivistic and individualistic work groups. *Academy of Management Journal, 36,* 319–348.

Eastwick, P. W., & Finkel, E. J. (2008). Sex differences in mate preferences revisited: Do people know what they initially desire in a romantic partner? *Journal of Personality and Social Psychology, 94,* 245–264.

Eastwick, P. W., Finkel, E. J., Mochon, D., & Ariely, D. (2007). Selective versus unselective romantic desire: Not all reciprocity is created equal. *Psychological Science, 18,* 317–319.

Eberhardt, J. L. (2005). Imaging race. *American Psychologist, 60,* 181–190.

Eccles, J. S., Jacobs, J. E., & Harold, R. E. (1990). Gender role stereotypes, expectancy effects, and parents' socialization of gender differences. *Journal of Social Issues, 46,* 183–201.

Edney, J. J. (1979). The nuts game: A concise commons dilemma analog. *Environmental Psychology & Nonverbal Behavior, 3,* 252–254.

Edney, J. J. (1980). The commons problem: Alternative perspectives. *American Psychologist, 35,* 131–150.

Edwards, K., & Bryan, T. S. (1997). Judgmental biases produced by instructions to disregard: The (paradoxical) case of emotional information. *Personality and Social Psychology Bulletin, 23,* 849–864.

Edwards, K., & Smith, E. E. (1996). A disconfirmation bias in the evaluation of arguments. *Journal of Personality and Social Psychology, 71,* 5–24.

Egan, L., Santos, L., & Bloom, P. (2007). The origins of cognitive dissonance: Evidence from children and monkeys. *Psychological Science, 18,* 978–983.

Ehrlinger, J., Gilovich, T., & Ross, L. (2005). Peering into the bias blind spot: People's assessments of bias in themselves and others. *Personality and Social Psychology Bulletin, 31,* 680–692.

Eisenberg, M.E., Olson, R.E., Neumark-Sztainer, D., Story, M., & Bearinger, L.H. (2004). Correlations between family meals and psychosocial well-being among adolescents. *Archives of Pediatrics & Adolescent Medicine, 158,* 792–796.

Eisenberg, N. (1982). *The Development of prosocial behavior.* New York: Academic Press.

Eisenberg, N., Fabes, R. A., Schaller, M., Carlo, G., & Miller, P. A. (1991). The relations of parental characteristics and practices to children's vicarious emotional responding. *Child Development, 62,* 1393–1408.

Eisenberg, N., Guthrie, I. K., Cumberland, A., Murphy, B. C., Shepard, S. A., Zhou, Q., et al. (2002). Prosocial development in early adulthood: A longitudinal study. *Journal of Personality and Social Psychology, 82,* 993–1006.

Eisenberger, N., Lieberman, M., & Williams, K. (2003). Does rejection hurt? An fMRI study of social exclusion. *Science, 302,* 290–292.

Eisenberg, N., & Miller, P. A. (1987). The relation of empathy to prosocial and related behaviors. *Psychological Bulletin, 101,* 91–119.

Eisenberg, N., Shell, R., Pasternack, J., Lennon, R., Beller, R., & Mathy, R.M. (1987). Prosocial development in middle childhood: A longitudinal study. *Developmental Psychology, 23,* 712–718.

Eisenberger, R., & Cameron, J. (1996). Detrimental effects of reward: Reality or myth? *American Psychologist, 51,* 1153–1166.

Ekman, P. (1994). Strong evidence for universals in facial expressions: A reply to Russell's mistaken critique. *Psychological Bulletin, 115,* 268–287.

Ekman, P., & O'Sullivan, M. (1991). Who can catch a liar? *American Psychologist, 46,* 913–920.

Ekman, P., O'Sullivan, M., & Frank, M. (1999). A few can catch a liar. *Psychological Science, 10,* 263–266.

Ekman, P., Sorenson, E.R., & Friesen, W.V. (1969). Pancultural elements in facial displays of emotion. *Science, 164,* 86–88.

Eldridge, A. (2010, October 25). New information brought forward about hazing at the U of A DKE fraternity. *The Gateway.* Retrieved from http://thegatewayonline.ca/articles/news/2010/10/22/new-information-brought-forward-about-dke-hazing

Elfenbein, H., & Ambady, N. (2003). When familiarity breeds accuracy: Cultural exposure and facial emotion recognition. *Journal of Personality and Social Psychology, 85,* 276–290.

Elizur, Y., & Mintzer, A. (2003). Gay males' intimate relationship quality: The roles of attachment security, gay identity, social support, and income. *Personal Relationships, 10,* 411–435.

Elkin, R. A., & Leippe, M. R. (1986). Physiological arousal, dissonance, and attitude change: Evidence for a dissonance arousal link and a 'Don't remind me' effect. *Journal of Personality and Social Psychology, 51,* 55–65.

Ellemers, N., & Bos, A. E. R. (1998). Social identity, relative deprivation, and coping with the threat of position loss: A field study among native shopkeepers in Amsterdam. *Journal of Applied Social Psychology, 28,* 1987–2006.

Elliot, A. J., & Devine, P. G. (1994). On the motivational nature of cognitive dissonance: Dissonance as psychological discomfort. *Journal of Personality and Social Psychology, 67,* 382–394.

Elms, A. C. & Milgram, (1966) Personality characteristics associated obedience and defiance toward authoritative command. *Journal of Experimental Research in Personality 1,* 282–289.

Emery, R. E., & Wyer, M. M. (1987). Child custody mediation and litigation: An experimental evaluation of the experience of parents. *Journal of Consulting and Clinical Psychology, 55,* 179–186.

Ennett, S. T., Tobler, N. S., Ringwalt, C. L., & Flewelling, R. L. (1994). How effective is drug abuse resistance education? A meta-analysis of Project DARE outcome evaluations. *American Journal of Public Health, 84,* 1394–1401.

Enos, D. M., & Handal, P. J. (1986). The relation of parental marital status and perceived family conflict to adjustment in White adolescents. *Journal of Consulting and Clinical Psychology*, 54, 820–824.

Erb, H., Bohner, G., Rank, S., & Einwiller, S. (2002). Processing minority and majority communications: The role of conflict with prior attitudes. *Personality and Social Psychology Bulletin*, 28, 1172–1182.

Erez, M., & Somech, A. (1996). Is group productivity loss the rule or the exception? Effects of culture and group-based motivation. *Academy nf Management Journal*, 39, 1513–1537.

Esses, V. M., & Dovidio, J. F. (2002). The role of emotions in determining willingness to engage in intergroup contact. *Personality and Social Psychology Bulletin*, 28, 1202–1214.

Esses, V. M., Jackson, L. M., & Armstrong, T. L. (1998). Intergroup competition and attitudes toward immigrants and immigration: An instrumental model of group conflict. *Journal of Social Issues*, 54, 699–724.

Esses, V. M., & Zanna, M. P. (1995). Mood and the expression of ethnic stereotypes. *Journal of Personality and Social Psychology*, 69, 1052–1068.

Evangelauf, J. (1993). Number of Minority Students in Colleges Rose by 9% from 1990 to 1991, U.S. Reports; Fact File: State-by-State Enrollment by Racial and Ethnic Group, Fall 1991. *Chronicle of Higher Education*, 39, 30–31.

Fabes, R. A., Eisenberg, N., & Miller, P. A. (1990). Maternal correlates of children's vicarious emotional responsiveness. *Developmental Psychology*, 26, 639–648.

Fabes, R. A., Fultz, J., Eisenberg, N., May-Plumlee, T., & Christopher, F. S. (1989). Effects of rewards on children's prosocial motivation: A socialization study. *Developmental Psychology*, 25, 509–515.

Fabrigar, L. R., Priester, J. R., Petty, R. E., & Wegener, D. T. (1998). The impact of attitude accessibility on elaboration of persuasive messages. *Personality and Social Psychology Bulletin*, 24, 339–352.

Fajardo, D. M. (1985). Author race, essay quality, and reverse discrimination. *Journal of Applied Social Psychology*, 15, 255– 268.

Fannin, N., & Dabbs, J. M. J. (2003). Testosterone and the work of firefighters: Fighting fires and delivering medical care. *Journal of Research in Personality*, 37, 107–115.

Farber, C. (1998). Whistling in the dark. *Esquire*, 129, 54–64, 119–120.

Farver, J. M., Welles-Nystroem, B., Frosch, D. L., Wimbarti, S., & Hoppe-Graff, S. (1997). Toy stories: Aggression in children's narratives in the United States, Sweden, Germany, and Indonesia. *Journal of Cross-Cultural Psychology*, 28(4), 393–420.

Fazio, R. H., & Zanna, M. (1981). *Direct experience and attitude-behavior consistency*. In L. Berkowitz (Ed.), *Advances in Experimental Social Psychology* (Vol. 14, pp. 161–202). San Diego, CA: Academic Press.

Fazio, R. H. & Zanna, M.P. (1978). Attitudinal qualities relating to the strength of the attitude-behaviour relation. *Journal of Experimental Social Psychology*, 14, 398–408.

Fedorowycz, O. (1999). Homicide in Canada, 1998. *Juristat*, 19(1), Cat. 85-002-XIE.

Feeney, B. C., & Collins, N. L. (2001). Predictors of caregiving in adult intimate relationships: An attachment theoretical perspective. *Journal of Personality and Social Psychology*, 80, 972–994.

Feeney, J. A. (1996). Attachment, caregiving, and marital satisfaction. *Personal Relationships*, 3, 401–416.

Fehr, B., & Russel, J. A. (1991). The concept of love viewed from a prototype perspective. *Journal of Personality and Social Psychology*, 60, 425–438.

Fein, S. (1996). Effects of suspicion on attributional thinking and the correspondence bias. *Journal of Personality and Social Psychology*, 70, 1164–1184.

Fein, S., Hilton, J., & Miller, D. (1990). Suspicion of ulterior motivation and the correspondence bias. *Journal of Personality and Social Psychology*, 58, 753–764.

Fein, S., & Spencer, S. J. (1997). Prejudice as self-image maintenance: Affirming the self through derogating others. *Journal of Personality and Social Psychology*, 73, 31–44.

Feingold, A. (1988). Matching for attractiveness in romantic partners and same-sex friends: A meta-analysis and theoretical critique. *Psychological Bulletin*, 104, 226–235.

Feingold, A. (1990). Gender differences in effects of physical attractiveness on romantic attraction: A comparison across five research paradigms. *Journal of Personality and Social Psychology*, 59, 981–993.

Feingold, A. (1991). Sex differences in the effects of similarity and physical attractiveness on opposite-sex attraction. *Basic and Applied Social Psychology*, 12, 357–367.

Feingold, A. (1992). Good-looking people are not what we think. *Psychological Bulletin*, 111, 304–341.

Feldman, R. E. (1968). Response to compatriot and foreigner who seek assistance. *Journal of Personality and Social Psychology*, 10, 202–214.

Felmlee, D. H. (1995). Fatal attractions: Affection and disaffection in intimate relationships. *Journal of Social and Personal Relationships*, 12, 295–311.

Felmlee, D. H. (1998). 'Be careful what you wish for . . .': A quantitative and qualitative investigation of 'fatal attractions.' *Personal Relationships*, 5, 235–253.

Festinger, L. (1954). A theory of social comparison processes. *Human Relations*, 7, 117–140.

Festinger, L. (1957). *A Theory of Cognitive Dissonance*. Oxford, England: Row, Peterson.

Festinger, L. & Carlsmith, J. (1959). Cognitive consequences of forced compliance, *The Journal of Abnormal and Social Psychology*, 58, 203–210.

Festinger, L., Pepitone, A., & Newcomb, T. (1952). Some consequences of de-individuation in a group. *The Journal of Abnormal and Social Psychology*, 47, 382–389.

Festinger, L., Schachter, S., & Back, K. (1950). *Social Pressures in Informal Groups: A Study of Human Factors in Housing*. New York: Harper.

Fiedler, K., Walther, E., & Nickel, S. (1999). Covariation-based attribution: On the ability to assess multiple covariates of an effect. *Personality and Social Psychology Bulletin*, 25, 607–622.

Fincham, F. D. (2000). The kiss of the porcupines: From attributing responsibility to forgiving. *Personal Relationships*, 7, 1–23.

Fincham, F. D., & Bradbury, T. N. (1992). Assessing attributions in marriage: The Relationship Attribution Measure. *Journal of Personality and Social Psychology*, 62, 457–468.

Fischer, P., & Greitemeyer, T. (2006). Music and aggression: The impact of sexual-aggressive song lyrics on aggression-related thoughts, emotions, and behavior toward the same and the opposite sex. *Personality and Social Psychology Bulletin*, 32, 1165–1176.

Fischer, R. (2004). Standardization to account for cross-cultural response bias: A classification of score adjustment procedures and review of research in JCCP. *Journal of Cross-cultural Psychology*, 35(3), 263–282.

Fisher, H. (2004). *Why we love: The nature and chemistry of romantic love*. New York: Henry Holt.

Fisher, H. E., Aron, A., Mashek, D., Li, H., & Brown, L. L. (2002). Defining the brain systems of lust, romantic attraction, and attachment. *Archives of Sexual Behavior*, 31, 413–419.

Fisher, J. D., Nadler, A., & Whitcher-Alagna, S. (1982). Recipient reactions to aid. *Psychological Bulletin*, 91, 27–54.

Fiske, S. T., Bersoff, D. N., Borgida, E., Deaux, K., & Heilman, M. E. (1991). Social science research on trial: Use of sex stereotyping research in Price Waterhouse v. Hopkins. *American Psychologist, 46,* 1049–1060.

Fiske, S. T., Cuddy, A. J. C., Glick, P.,& Xu, J. (2002). A model of (often mixed) stereotype content: Competence and warmth respectively follow from perceived status and competition. *Journal of Personality and Social Psychology, 82,* 878–902.

Fiske, S. T., & Taylor, S. E. (1991). *Social cognition* (2nd ed.), New York: McGraw-Hill.

Fiske, S. T., Xu, J., Cuddy, A. C., & Glick, P. (1999). (Dis)respecting versus (dis)liking: Status and interdependence predict ambivalent stereotypes of competence and warmth. *Journal of Social Issues, 55,* 473–489.

Fiske, S.T. (1993). Controlling other people: The impact of power on stereotyping. *American Psychologist, 48,* 621–628.

Flegal, K. M., Carroll, M. D., Kuczmarski, R. J., & Johnson, C. L., (1998). Overweight and obesity in the United States: Prevalence and trends, 1960–1994. *International Journal of Obesity and Related Metabolic Disorders, 22,* 39–47.

Fleming, I., Baum, A., & Weiss, L. (1987). Social density and perceived control as mediators of crowding stress in high-density residential neighborhoods. *Journal of Personality and Social Psychology, 52,* 899–906.

Fletcher, G., Danilovics, P., Fernandez, G., Peterson, D., & Reeder, G. (1986). Attributional complexity: An individual differences measure. *Journal of Personality and Social Psychology, 51,* 875–884.

Fletcher, G. J. O., Tither, J. M., O'Loughlin, C., Friesen, M., & Overall, N. (2004). Warm and homely or cold and beautiful? Sex differences in trading off traits in mate selection. *Personality and Social Psychology Bulletin, 30,* 659–672.

Fogassi, L. (2011). The mirror neuron system: How cognitive functions emerge from motor organization. *Journal of Economic Behavior & Organization, 77,* 66–75.

Forgas, J. P., Bower, G. H., & Krantz, S. E. (1984). The influence of mood on perceptions of social interactions. *Journal of Experimental Social Psychology, 20,* 497–513.

Forgas, J. P., & Fiedler, K. (1996). Us and them: Mood effects on intergroup discrimination. *Journal of Personality and Social Psychology, 70,* 28–40.

Foster, C. A., Witcher, B. S., Campbell, W. K., & Green, J. D. (1998). Arousal and attraction: Evidence for automatic and controlled processes. *Journal of Personality and Social Psychology, 74,* 86–101.

Försterling, F., Preikschas, S., & Agthe, M. (2007). Ability, luck, and looks: An evolutionary look at achievement ascriptions and the sexual attribution bias. *Journal of Personality and Social Psychology, 92,* 775–788.

Fox, S., & Walters, H. (1986). The impact of general versus specific expert testimony and eyewitness confidence upon mock juror judgment. *Law and Human Behavior, 10,* 215–228.

Fragale, A. R., & Heath, C. (2004). Evolving informational credentials: The (mis)attribution of believable facts to credible sources. *Personality and Social Psychology Bulletin, 30,* 225–236.

Francis, B. (2002). Is the future really female? The impact and implications of gender for 14–16 year olds' career choices. *Journal of Education and Work, 15,* 75–88.

Frank, A. (1993). *Anne Frank: Diary of a young girl.* New York: Bantam.

Frank, M., & Ekman, P. (2004). Appearing truthful generalizes across different deception situations. *Journal of Personality and Social Psychology, 86,* 486–495.

Frank, R., Gilovich, T., & Regan, D. T. (1993). Does studying economics inhibit cooperation?. *Journal of Economic Perspectives, 7,* 159–171.

Frankel, A., & Prentice-Dunn, S. (1990). Loneliness and the processing of self-relevant information. *Journal of Social & Clinical Psychology, 9,* 303–315.

Frazier, P. (2003). Perceived control and distress following sexual assault: A longitudinal test of a new model. *Journal of Personality and Social Psychology, 84,* 1257–1269.

Freedman, J. (1965). Long-term behavioral effects of cognitive dissonance. *Journal of Experimental Social Psychology, 1,* 145–155.

Freedman, J. L., & Fraser, S. C. (1966). Compliance without pressure: The foot-in-the-door technique. *Journal of Personality and Social Psychology, 4,* 195–202.

Freedman, J. L., & Sears, D. O. (1965). Warning, distraction, and resistance to influence. *Journal of Personality and Social Psychology, 1,* 262–266.

Freimuth, V. S., Hammond, S. L., Edgar, T., & Monahan, J. L. (1990). Reaching those at risk: A content-analytic study of AIDS PSAs. *Communication Research, 17,* 775–791.

Frenette, M., & Zeman, K. (2007). Why are most university students women? Evidence based on academic performance, study habits and parental influences. *Statistics Canada.* Retrieved from http://www.statcan.gc.ca/pub/11f0019m/11f0019m2007303-eng.pdf.

Freud, S. (1930). *Civilization and Its Discontents.* New York: W.W. Norton.

Freud, S. (1933). *New Introductory Lectures on Psychoanalysis.* New York: W.W. Norton.

Friedman, H., Tucker, J., Tomlinson-Keasey, C., Schwartz, J., Wingard, D., & Criqui, M. (1993). Does childhood personality predict longevity? *Journal of Personality and Social Psychology, 65,* 176–185.

Friedrich-Cofer, L., & Huston, A. C. (1986). Television violence and aggression: The debate continues. *Psychological Bulletin, 100,* 364–371.

Friedrich, J., Fetherstonhaugh, D., Casey, S., & Gallagher, D. (1996). Argument integration and attitude change: Suppression effects in the integration of one-sided arguments that vary in persuasiveness. *Personality and Social Psychology Bulletin, 22,* 179–191.

Frieze, I. H., Olson, J. E., & Russell, J. (1991). Attractiveness and income for men and women in management. *Journal of Applied Social Psychology, 21,* 1039–1057.

Fultz, J., Batson, C. D., Fortenbach, V. A., McCarthy, P. M., & Varney, L. L. (1986). Social evaluation and the empathy-altruism hypothesis. *Journal of Personality and Social Psychology, 50,* 761–769.

Fung, H. H., & Carstensen, L. L. (2003). Sending memorable messages to the old: Age differences in preferences and memory for advertisements. *Journal of Personality and Social Psychology, 85,* 163–178.

Furnham, A., & Gunter, B. (1984). Just world beliefs and attitudes towards the poor. *British Journal of Social Psychology, 23,* 265–269.

Gabrenya, W. K., Wang, Y., & Latané, B. (1985). Social loafing on an optimizing task: Cross-cultural differences among Chinese and Americans. *Journal of Cross-Cultural Psychology, 16,* 223–242.

Gabriel, S., & Gardner, W. (1999). Are there 'his' and 'hers' types of interdependence? The implications of gender differences in collective versus relational interdependence for affect, behavior, and cognition. *Journal of Personality and Social Psychology, 77,* 642–655.

Gaertner, S. L., & Dovidio, J. F. (1977). The subtlety of White racism, arousal, and helping behavior. *Journal of Personality and Social Psychology, 35,* 691–707.

Gaertner, S. L., Dovidio, J. F., Rust, M. C., Nier, J. A., Banker, B. S., Ward, C. M., et al. (1999). Reducing intergroup bias: Elements of intergroup cooperation. *Journal of Personality and Social Psychology, 76,* 388–402.

Gaertner, S. L., Mann, J. A., Dovidio, J. F., Murrell, A. J., & Pomare, M. (1990). How does cooperation reduce intergroup bias? *Journal of Personality and Social Psychology, 59,* 692–704.

Gagnon, A., & Bourhis, R. Y. (1996). Discrimination in the minimal group paradigm: Social identity or self-interest? *Personality and Social Psychology Bulletin, 22,* 1289–1301.

Gailliot, M. T., Plant, E. A., Butz, D. A., & Baumeister, R. F. (2007). Increasing self-regulatory strength can reduce the depleting effect of suppressing stereotypes. *Personality and Social Psychology Bulletin, 33,* 281–294.

Gailus, J. (2008). The Oilsands Producer's Dilemma. Alberta Venture Magazine. Retrieved from http://albertaventure.com/2008/04/the-oilsand-producers-dilemma/

Galinsky, A. D., Maddux, W. W., Gilin, D.,& White, J. B. (2008). Why it pays to get inside the head of your opponent: The differential effects of perspective taking and empathy in negotiations. *Psychological Science, 19,* 378–384.

Galinsky, A. D., & Moskowitz, G. B. (2000). Perspective-taking: Decreasing stereotype expression, stereotype accessibility, and in-group favoritism. *Journal of Personality and Social Psychology, 78,* 708–724.

Gallese V., Keysers C., Rizzolatti G. (2004). A unifying view of the basis of social cognition. *Trends in Cognitive Science, 8,* 396–403.

Gallo, L. C., Troxel, W. M., Matthews, K. A., & Kuller, L. H. (2003). Marital status and quality in middle-aged women: Associations with levels and trajectories of cardiovascular risk factors. *Health Psychology, 22,* 453–463.

Galloway, G., & Mehler Paperny, A. (2010, November 3). Nearly 100 Toronto police officers to be disciplined over G20 summit conduct. *The Globe and Mail.* Retrieved from http://www.theglobeandmail.com/news/national/toronto/nearly-100-toronto-officers-to-be-disciplined-over-summit-conduct/article1784884/%20/.

Gangestad, S. W., Simpson, J. A., Cousins, A. J., Garver-Apgar, C. E., & Christensen, P. N. (2004). Women's preferences for male behavioral displays change across the menstrual cycle. *Psychological Science, 15,* 203–206.

Gannon, L., Luchetta, T., Rhodes, K., Pardie, L., & Segrist, D. (1992). Sex bias in psychological research: Progress or complacency? *American Psychologist, 47,* 389–396.

García, M. F., Posthuma, R. A., & Roehling, M. V. (2009). Comparing preferences for employing males and nationals across countries: Extending relational models and social dominance theory. *The International Journal of Human Resource Management, 20,* 2471–2493.

Garcia, S., Tor, A., & Gonzalez, R. (2006). Ranks and rivals: A theory of competition. *Personality and Social Psychology Bulletin, 32,* 970–982.

Garrity, K., & Degelman, D. (1990). Effect of server introduction on restaurant tipping. *Journal of Applied Social Psychology, 20,* 168–172.

Gavin, L. A., & Furman, W. (1989). Age differences in adolescents' perceptions of their peer groups. *Developmental Psychology, 25,* 827–834.

Gawronski, B. (2003a). Implicational schemata and the correspondence bias: On the diagnostic value of situationally constrained behavior. *Journal of Personality and Social Psychology, 84,* 1154–1171.

Gawronski, B. (2003b). On difficult questions and evident answers: Dispositional inference from role-constrained behavior. *Personality and Social Psychology Bulletin, 29,* 1459–1475.

Gee, C.J. & Leith, L. M. (2007). Aggressive behavior in professional ice hockey: A cross-cultural comparison of North American and European born NHL players. *Psychology of Sport & Exercise, 8(4),* 567–583.

Geen, R. G. (1968). Effects of frustration, attack, and prior training in aggressiveness upon aggressive behavior. *Journal of Personality and Social Psychology, 9,* 316–321.

Geen, R. G. (1981). Behavioral and physiological reactions to observed violence: Effects of prior exposure to aggressive stimuli. *Journal of Personality and Social Psychology, 40,* 868–875.

Geertz, C. (1983). *Local Knowledge: Further Essays in Interpretive Anthropology* N.Y.: Basic Books.

Geiselman, R. E., Haight, N. A., & Kimata, L. G. (1984). Context effects on the perceived physical attractiveness of faces. *Journal of Experimental Social Psychology, 20,* 409–424.

Genesee, F., Rogers, P., & Holobow, N. (1983). The social psychology of second language learning: Another point of view. *Language Learning, 33,* 209–224.

Gentzler, A. L., & Kerns, K. A. (2004). Associations between insecure attachment and sexual experiences. *Personal Relationships, 11,* 249–265.

Georgas, J., Berry, J.W., Shaw, A., Christakopoulou, S., & Mylonas, K. (1996). Acculturation of Greek family values. *Journal of Cross-Cultural Psychology , 27,* 329–338.

Gerard, H. B., Wilhelmy, R. A., & Conolley, E. S. (1968). Conformity and group size. *Journal of Personality and Social Psychology, 8,* 79–82.

Gerrard, M., Gibbons, F., Reis-Bergan, M., Trudeau, L., Vande Lune, L., & Buunk, B. (2002). Inhibitory effects of drinker and nondrinker prototypes on adolescent alcohol consumption. *Health Psychology, 21,* 601–609.

Gershoff, E. T. (2002). Corporal punishment by parents and associated child behaviors and experiences: A meta-analytic and theoretical review. *Psychological Bulletin, 128,* 539–579.

Gibbons, F., Eggleston, T., & Benthin, A. (1997). Cognitive reactions to smoking relapse: The reciprocal relation between dissonance and self-esteem. *Journal of Personality and Social Psychology, 72,* 184–195.

Gibbons, F., & Gerrard, M. (1995). Predicting young adults' health risk behavior. *Journal of Personality and Social Psychology, 69,* 505–517.

Gibbons, F., Gerrard, M., Blanton, H., & Russell, D. (1998). Reasoned action and social reaction: Willingness and intention as independent predictors of health risk. *Journal of Personality and Social Psychology, 74,* 1164–1180.

Gibbons, F., Gerrard, M., & McCoy, S. (1995). Prototype perception predicts (lack of) pregnancy prevention. *Personality and Social Psychology Bulletin, 21,* 85–93.

Gibbons, F., & McCoy, S. (1991). Self-esteem, similarity, and reactions to active versus passive downward comparison. *Journal of Personality and Social Psychology, 60,* 414–424.

Gibbons, J., Hamby, B., & Dennis, W. (1997). Researching gender-role ideologies internationally and cross-culturally. *Psychology of Women Quarterly, 21,* 151–170.

Gibbons, F. X., Gerrard, M., Cleveland, M. J., Wills, T. A., & Brody, G. (2004). Perceived discrimination and substance use in African American parents and their children: A panel study. *Journal of Personality and Social Psychology, 86,* 517–529.

Gibson, B., & Maurer, J. (2000). Cigarette smoking in the movies: The influence of product placement on attitudes toward smoking and smokers. *Journal of Applied Social Psychology, 30,* 1457–1473.

Gibson, B., & Sanbonmatsu, D. (2004). Optimism, pessimism, and gambling: The downside of optimism. *Personality and Social Psychology Bulletin, 30,* 149–160.

Gifford, R. (1991). Mapping nonverbal behavior on the interpersonal circle. *Journal of Personality and Social Psychology, 61,* 279–288.

Gigerenzer, G. (2004). Dread risk, September 11, and fatal traffic accidents. *Psychological Science, 15,* 286–287.

Gilbert, D., & Hixon, J. (1991). The trouble of thinking: Activation and application of stereotypic beliefs. *Journal of Personality and Social Psychology, 60,* 509–517.

Gilbert, D., & Osborne, R. (1989). Thinking backward: Some curable and incurable consequences of cognitive busyness. *Journal of Personality and Social Psychology, 57,* 940–949.

Gilbert, D., Pelham, B., & Krull, D. (1988). On cognitive busyness: When person perceivers meet persons perceived. *Journal of Personality and Social Psychology, 54,* 733–740.

Gilbert, D., Pinel, E., Wilson, T., Blumberg, S., & Wheatley, T. (1998). Immune neglect: A source of durability bias in affective forecasting. *Journal of Personality and Social Psychology, 75,* 617–638.

Gilbert, D., & Wilson, T. (2000). Miswanting: Some problems in the forecasting of future affective states. In J. Forgas (Ed.), *Thinking and Feeling: The Role of Affect in Social Cognition* (pp. 178–197). New York: Cambridge University Press.

Gilbert, D. T., Krull, D. S., & Malone, P. S. (1990). Unbelieving the unbelievable: Some problems in the rejection of false information. *Journal of Personality and Social Psychology, 59,* 601–613.

Gilbert, D. T., & Silvera, D. H. (1996). Overhelping. *Journal of Personality and Social Psychology, 70,* 678–690.

Gilbert, D. T., Tafarodi, R. W., & Malone, P. S. (1993). You can't not believe everything you read. *Journal of Personality and Social Psychology, 65,* 221–233.

Gilbert, S. J. (1981). Another look at the Milgram obedience studies: The role of the gradated series of shocks. *Personality and Social Psychology Bulletin, 7,* 690–695.

Gillath, O., Bunge, S. A., Shaver P. R., Wendelken, C., & Mikulincer, M. (2005). Attachment-style differences in the ability to suppress negative thoughts: Exploring the neural correlates. *Neuroimage, 28,* 835–847.

Gilovich, T., Medvec, V., & Savitsky, K. (2000). The spotlight effect in social judgment: An egocentric bias in estimates of the salience of one's own actions and appearance. *Journal of Personality and Social Psychology, 78,* 211–222.

Gilovich, T., Savitsky, K., & Medvec, V. (1997). The illusion of transparency: Biased assessments of others' ability to read our emotional states. *Journal of Personality and Social Psychology, 75,* 332–346.

Giner-Sorolla, R., & Chaiken, S. (1994). The causes of hostile media judgments. *Journal of Experimental Social Psychology, 30,* 165–180.

Giner-Sorolla, R., & Chaiken, S. (1997). Selective use of heuristic and systematic processing under defense motivation. *Personality and Social Psychology Bulletin, 23,* 84–97.

Giumetti, G. W., & Markey, P. M. (2007). Violent video games and anger as predictors of aggression. *Journal of Research in Personality, 41,* 1234–1243.

Gleason, M. E. J., Iida, M., Bolger, N., & Shrout, P. E. (2003). Daily supportive equity in close relationships. *Personality and Social Psychology Bulletin, 29,* 1036–1045.

Glick, P., & Fiske, S. T. (1996). The Ambivalent Sexism Inventory: Differentiating hostile and benevolent sexism. *Journal of Personality and Social Psychology, 70,* 491–512.

Glick, P., & Fiske, S. T. (2001). An ambivalent alliance: Hostile and benevolent sexism as complementary justifications for gender inequality. *American Psychologist, 56,* 109–118.

Glick, P., Fiske, S. T., Mladinic, A., Saiz, J. L., Abrams, D., Masser, B., et al. (2000). Beyond prejudice as simple antipathy: Hostile and benevolent sexism across cultures. *Journal of Personality and Social Psychology, 79,* 763–775.

Glick, P., Gottesman, D., & Jolton, J. (1989). The fault is not in the stars: Susceptibility of skeptics and believers in astrology to the Barnum effect. *Personality and Social Psychology Bulletin, 15,* 572–583.

Glick, P., Lameiras, M., Fiske, S. T., Eckes, T., Masser, B., Volpato, C., et al. (2004). Bad but bold: Ambivalent attitudes toward men predict gender inequality in 16 nations. *Journal of Personality and Social Psychology, 86,* 713–728.

Godfrey, D., Jones, E., & Lord, C. (1986). Self-promotion is not ingratiating. *Journal of Personality and Social Psychology, 50,* 106–115.

Goethals, G., Cooper, J., & Naficy, A. (1979). Role of foreseen, foreseeable, and unforeseeable behavioral consequences in the arousal of cognitive dissonance. *Journal of Personality and Social Psychology, 37,* 1179–1185.

Goff, P. A., Steele, C. M., & Davies, P. G. (2008). The space between us: Stereotype threat and distance in interracial contexts. *Journal of Personality and Social Psychology, 94,* 91– 107.

Goldstein, A. O., Sobel, R. A., & Newman, R. T. (1999). Tobacco and alcohol use in G-rated children's animated films. *Journal of the American Medical Association, 281,* 1131–1136.

Goldstein, N. J., Cialdini, R. B., & Griskevicius, V. (2008). A room with a viewpoint: Using normative appeals to motivate environmental conservation in a hotel setting. *Journal of Consumer Research, 35,* 472–482.

Gonzales, P. M., Blanton, H., & Williams, K. J. (2002). The effects of stereotype threat and double-minority status on the test performance of Latino women. *Personality and Social Psychology Bulletin, 28,* 659–670.

Good, G. E., Dell, D. M., & Mintz, L. B. (1989). Male role and gender role conflict: Relations to help seeking in men. *Journal of Counseling Psychology, 36,* 295–300.

Goodwin, C. J. (1998). *Research in Psychology: Methods and Design.* New York: Wiley.

Goodwin, R., & Findlay, C. (1997). 'We were just fated together'. . . . . Chinese love and the concept of yuan in England and Hong Kong. *Personal Relationships, 4,* 85–92.

Goodyear, R. K. (1990). The endocrinology of transsexualism: A review and commentary. *Psychoneuroendocrinology, 15,* 3–14.

Gorassini, D.R., & Olson, J.M. (1995). Does self-perception change explain the foot-in-the-door effect? *Journal of Personality and Social Psychology. 69(1),* pp. 91–105.

Gordijn, E., Hindriks, I., Koomen, W., Dijksterhuis, A., & Van Knippenberg, A. (2004). Consequences of stereotype suppression and internal suppression motivation: A self-regulation approach. *Personality and Social Psychology Bulletin, 30,* 212–224.

Gordon, R. (1996). Impact of ingratiation on judgments and evaluations: A meta-analytic investigation. *Journal of Personality and Social Psychology, 71,* 54–70.

Gosling, S., Vazire, S., Srivastava, S., & John, O. (2004). Should we trust web-based studies? A comparative analysis of six preconceptions about Internet questionnaires. *American Psychologist, 59,* 93–104.

Gosselin, P., Kirouac, G., & Doré, F. (1995). Components and recognition of facial expression in the communication of emotion by actors. *Journal of Personality and Social Psychology, 68,* 83–96.

Gottman, J., & Levenson, R. W. (2002). A two-factor model for predicting when a couple will divorce: Exploratory analyses using 14-year longitudinal data. *Family Process, 41,* 83–96.

Gottman, J. M., & Krokoff, L. J. (1989). Marital interaction and satisfaction: A longitudinal view. *Journal of Consulting and Clinical Psychology, 57,* 47–52.

Gottman, J. M., & Levenson, R. W. (1992). Marital processes predictive of later dissolution: Behavior, physiology, and health. *Journal of Personality and Social Psychology, 63,* 221–233.

Gottman, J. M., Levenson, R. W., Gross, J., Frederickson, B. L., McCoy, K., Rosenthal, L., et al. (2003). Correlates of gay and lesbian couples' relationship satisfaction and relationship dissolution. *Journal of Homosexuality, 45,* 23–43.

Graham, J. M., & Conoley, C. W. (2006). The role of marital attributions in the relationship between life stressors and marital quality. *Personal Relationships, 13,* 231–241.

Graham, S. (1992). 'Most of the subjects were White and middle class': Trends in published research on African Americans in selected APA journals, 1970–1989. *American Psychologist, 47,* 629–639.

Green, B. L., & Kenrick, D. T. (1994). The attractiveness of gender-typed traits at different relationship levels: Androgynous characteristics may be desirable after all. *Personality and Social Psychology Bulletin, 20,* 244–253.

Green, D. P., Glaser, J., & Rich, A. (1998). From lynching to gay bashing: The elusive connection between economic conditions and hate crime. *Journal of Personality and Social Psychology, 75,* 82–92.

Green, L. R., Richardson, D. S., Lago, T., & Schatten-Jones, E. C. (2001). Network correlates of social and emotional loneliness in young and older adults. *Personality and Social Psychology Bulletin, 27,* 281–288.

Greenwald, A. G., & Banaji, M. R. (1995). Implicit social cognition: Attitudes, self-esteem, and stereotypes. *Psychological Review, 102,* 4–27.

Greenwald, A. G., Spangenberg, E. R., Pratkanis, A. R., & Eskenazi, J. (1991). Double-blind tests of subliminal self-help audiotapes. *Psychological Science, 2,* 119–122.

Greitemeyer, T., & Weiner, B. (2003). Asymmetrical attributions for approach versus avoidance behavior. *Personality and Social Psychology Bulletin, 29,* 1371–1382.

Griffit, W., & Veitch, R. (1971). Hot and crowded: Influence of population density and temperature on interpersonal affective behavior. *Journal of Personality and Social Psychology, 17,* 92–98.

Griffit, W. B. (1970). Environmental effects on interpersonal behavior: Ambient effective temperature and attraction. *Journal of Personality and Social Psychology, 15,* 240–244.

Griskevicius, V., Goldstein, N. J., Mortensen, C. R., Cialdini, R. B., & Kenrick, D. T. (2006). Going along versus going alone: When fundamental motives facilitate strategic (non)conformity. *Journal of Personality and Social Psychology, 91,* 281–294.

Groff, B. D., Baron, R. S., & Moore, D. L. (1983). Distraction, attentional conflict, and drivelike behavior. *Journal of Experimental Social Psychology, 19,* 359–380.

Gronewold, N. (2010, August 17). Western donations lag for Pakistan flood victims. *New York Times.* Retrieved from http://www.nytimes.com/gwire/2010/08/17/17greenwire-western-donations-lag-for-pakistan-flood-victi-56219.html.

Gross, E. F., Juvonen, J., & Gable, S. L. (2002). Internet use and well-being in adolescence. *Journal of Social Issues, 58,* 75–90.

Gross, J. (1998). Antecedent- and response-focused emotion regulation: Divergent consequences for experience, expression, and physiology. *Journal of Personality and Social Psychology, 74,* 224–237.

Gross, J., & Levenson, R. (1993). Emotional suppression: Physiology, self-report, and expressive behavior. *Journal of Personality and Social Psychology, 64,* 970–986.

Grube, J., & Wallach, L. (1994). Television beer advertising and drinking knowledge, beliefs, and intentions among school-children. *American Journal of Public Health, 84,* 254–259.

Grusec, J. E., & Skubiski, S. L. (1970). Model nurturance, demand characteristics of the modeling experiment, and altruism. *Journal of Personality and Social Psychology, 14,* 352–359.

Guéguen, N. (2002). The effects of a joke on tipping when it is delivered at the same time as the bill. *Journal of Applied Social Psychology, 32,* 1955–1963.

Guerin, B. (1986). Mere presence effects in humans: A review. *Journal of Experimental Social Psychology, 22,* 38–77.

Guimond, S. (2000). Group socialization and prejudice: The social transmission of intergroup attitudes and beliefs. *European Journal of Social Psychology, 30,* 335–354.

Guimond, S., & Dambrun, M. (2002). When prosperity breeds intergroup hostility: The effects of relative deprivation and relative gratification on prejudice. *Personality and Social Psychology Bulletin, 28,* 900–912.

Guimond, S., Dambrun, M., Michinov, N., & Duarte, S. (2003). Does social dominance generate prejudice? Integrating individual and contextual determinants of intergroup cognitions. *Journal of Personality and Social Psychology, 84,* 697–721.

Guimond, S., & Dubé-Simard, L. (1983). Relative deprivation theory and the Quebec nationalist movement: The cognition-emotion distinction and the person-group deprivation issue. *Journal of Personality and Social Psychology, 44,* 526–535.

Gump, B. B., & Kulik, J. A. (1997). Stress, affiliation, and emotional contagion. *Journal of Personality and Social Psychology, 72,* 305–319.

Gupta, G.R. (1976). Love, arranged marriage, and the Indian social structure. *Journal of Comparative Family Studies. 7(1),* 75–85.

Gutierres, S., Kenrick, D., & Partch, J. (1999). Beauty, dominance, and the mating game: Contrast effects in self-assessment reflect gender differences in mate selection. *Personality and Social Psychology Bulletin, 25,* 1126–134.

Haberstroh, S., Oyserman, D., Schwarz, N., Kühnen, U., & Ji, L. (2002). Is the interdependent self more sensitive to question context than the independent self? Self-construal and the observation of conversational norms. *Journal of Experimental Social Psychology, 38,* 323–329.

Hafer, C.L., Reynolds, K.L. & Obertynski, M.A. (1996). Message comprehensibility and persuasion: Effects of complex language in counterattitudinal appeals. *Social Cognition. 14(4),* 317–337.

Hagerty, M. R. (2000). Social comparisons of income in one's community: Evidence from national surveys of income and happiness. *Journal of Personality and Social Psychology, 78,* 764–771.

Hahn, J., & Blass, T. (1997). Dating partner preferences: A function of similarity of love styles. *Journal of Social Behavior & Personality, 12,* 595–610.

Halberstadt, J. (2006). The generality and ultimate origins of the attractiveness of prototypes. *Personality and Social Psychology Review, 10,* 166–183.

Halberstadt, J., & Rhodes, G. (2000). The attractiveness of non-face averages: Implications for an evolutionary explanation of the attractiveness of average faces. *Psychological Science, 11,* 285–289.

Halkier, B. (2001). Routinisation or Reflexivity? Consumers and Normative Claims for Environmental Consideration. In J. Gronow & Warde, A. (Eds.), *Ordinary Consumption,* (pp. 25–44.) London, UK: Routledge.

Hamermesh, D. S. & Biddle, J. E. (1994). Beauty and the labor market. *American Economic Review, 4,* 1174–94.

Hamermesh, D. S., & Parker, A. (2005). Beauty in the classroom: Instructors' pulchritude and putative pedagogical productivity. *Economics of Education Review, 24,* 369–76.

Hamilton, D. L., & Gifford, R. K. (1976). Illusory correlation in interpersonal perception: A cognitive basis of stereotypic judgments. *Journal of Experimental Social Psychology, 12,* 392–407.

Hamilton, D. L., & Rose, T. L. (1980). Illusory correlation and the maintenance of stereotypic beliefs. *Journal of Personality and Social Psychology, 39,* 832–845.

Hamilton, M. C. (2001). Sex-related difference research: Personality. In J. Worrell (Ed.), *Encyclopedia of women and gender* (pp. 973–981). San Diego: Academic Press.

Hamilton, V. L., & Sanders, J. (1995). Crimes of obedience and conformity in the workplace: Surveys of Americans, Russians, and Japanese. *Journal of Social Issues, 51,* 67–88.

Hamilton, V. L., Sanders, J., & McKearney, S. J. (1995). Orientations toward authority in an authoritarian state: Moscow in 1990. *Personality and Social Psychology Bulletin, 21,* 356–365.

Hammond, D., Fong, G.T., Borland, R., Cummings, K.M., McNeill, A. & Driezen, P., (2007). Text and Graphic Warnings on Cigarette Packages: Findings from the International Tobacco Control Four Country Study. *American Journal of Preventive Medicine, 32(3),* 202–209.

Han, G., & Park, B. (1995). Children's choice in conflict: Application of the theory of individualism-collectivism. *Journal of Cross-Cultural Psychology, 26*, 298–313.

Han, S., & Shavitt, S. (1994). Persuasion and culture: Advertising appeals in individualistic and collectivistic societies. *Journal of Experimental Social Psychology, 30*, 326–350.

Haney, C., Banks, C., & Zimbardo, P. (1973). Interpersonal dynamics in a simulated prison. *International Journal of Criminology & Penology, 1*, 69–97.

Haney, C., & Zimbardo, P. (1998). The past and future of U.S. prison policy: Twenty-five years after the Stanford Prison Experiment. *American Psychologist, 53*, 709–727.

Hanko, K., Master, S., & Sabini, J. (2004). Some evidence about character and mate selection. *Personality and Social Psychology Bulletin, 30*, 732–742.

Hansen, D. E., Vandenberg, B., & Patterson, M. L. (1995). The effects of religious orientation on spontaneous and nonspontaneous helping behaviors. *Personality and Individual Differences, 19*, 101–104.

Hansen, N., & Sassenberg, K. (2006). Does social identification harm or serve as a buffer? The impact of social identification on anger after experiencing social discrimination. *Personality and Social Psychology Bulletin, 32*, 983–996.

Harasty, A. S. (1997). The interpersonal nature of social stereotypes: Differential discussion patterns about in-groups and out-groups. *Personality and Social Psychology Bulletin, 23*, 270–284.

Harber, K. D. (1998). Feedback to minorities: Evidence of a positive bias. *Journal of Personality and Social Psychology, 74*, 622–628.

Harkins, S. G., & Jackson, J. M. (1985). The role of evaluation in eliminating social loafing. *Personality and Social Psychology Bulletin, 11*, 457–465.

Harkins, S. G., & Petty, R. E. (1981). Effects of source magnification of cognitive effort on attitudes: An information-processing view. *Journal of Personality and Social Psychology, 40*, 401–413.

Harkins, S. G., & Petty, R. E. (1982). Effects of task difficulty and task uniqueness on social loafing. *Journal of Personality and Social Psychology, 43*, 1214–1229.

Harmon-Jones, E. (2000). Cognitive dissonance and experienced negative affect: Evidence that dissonance increases experienced negative affect even in the absence of aversive consequences. *Personality and Social Psychology Bulletin, 26*, 1490–1501.

Harmon-Jones, E., & Allen, J. (2001). The role of affect in the mere exposure effect: Evidence from psychophysiological and individual differences approaches. *Personality and Social Psychology Bulletin, 27*, 889–898.

Harmon-Jones, E., Brehm, J., Greenberg, J., Simon, L., & Nelson, D. (1996). Evidence that the production of aversive consequences is not necessary to create cognitive dissonance. *Journal of Personality and Social Psychology, 70*, 5–16.

Harmon-Jones, E., & Devine, P. (2003). Introduction to the special section on social neuroscience: Promise and caveats. *Journal of Personality and Social Psychology, 85*, 589–593.

Harmon-Jones, E., & Harmon-Jones, C. (2002). Testing the action-based model of cognitive dissonance: The effect of action orientation on postdecisional attitudes. *Personality and Social Psychology Bulletin, 28*, 711–723.

Harper, S. (2008, June 11). Speech to the House of Commons. *Debates (Hansard)*. 39th Parliament, 2nd Session. Vol. 142, no. 110, after 15:20 p.m. Retrieved from http://www.parl.gc.ca/HousePublications/Publication.aspx?Language=E&Mode=1&Parl=39&Ses=2&DocId=3568890.

Harré, N., Brandt, T., & Houkamau, C. (2004). An examination of the actor-observer effect in young drivers' attributions for their own and their friends' risky driving. *Journal of Applied Social Psychology, 34*, 806–824.

Harrell, W. A. (1978). Physical attractiveness, self-disclosure, and helping behavior. *Journal of Social Psychology, 104*, 15–17.

Harris, C. R. (2000). Psychophysiological responses to imagined infidelity: The specific innate modular view of jealousy reconsidered. *Journal of Personality and Social Psychology, 78*, 1082–1091.

Harris, C. R. (2002). Sexual and romantic jealousy in heterosexual and homosexual adults. *Psychological Science, 13*, 7–12.

Harris, C. R., & Christenfeld, N. (1996). Gender, jealousy, and reason. *Psychological Science, 7*, 364–366.

Harris, L. T., & Fiske, S. T. (2006). Dehumanizing the lowest of the low: Neuroimaging responses to extreme out-groups. *Psychological Science, 17*, 847–853.

Harris, P. R., & Napper, L. (2005). Self-affirmation and the biased processing of threatening health-risk information. *Personality and Social Psychology Bulletin, 31*, 1250–1263.

Harrison, K., & Marske, A. (2005). Nutritional content of foods advertised during the television programs children watch most. *American Journal of Public Health, 95*, 1568–1574.

Hart, A. (1995). Naturally occurring expectation effects. *Journal of Personality and Social Psychology, 68*, 109–115.

Hart, A. J., Whalen, P. J., Shin, L. M., McInerney, S. C., Fischer, H., & Rauch, S. L. (2000). Differential response in the human amygdala to racial outgroup vs ingroup face stimuli. *Neuroreport, 11*, 2351–2355.

Harter, P. (2004, Jan. 26). Mauritania's "wife-fattening" farm. *BBC News*. Retrieved from http://news.bbc.co.uk/2/hi/africa/3429903.stm.

Harvey, J. H., & Omarzu, J. (1997). Minding the close relationship. *Personality and Social Psychology Review, 1*, 224–240.

Harwood, J., Hewstone, M., Paolini, S., & Voci, A. (2005). Grandparent-grandchild contact and attitudes toward older adults: Moderator and mediator effects. *Personality and Social Psychology Bulletin, 31*, 393–406.

Hashish, I., Hai, H. K., Harvey, W., Feinmann, C., & Harris, M. (1988). Reduction of postoperative pain and swelling by ultrasound treatment: A placebo effect. *Pain, 33*, 303–311.

Hassin, R., & Trope, Y. (2000). Facing faces: Studies on the cognitive aspects of physiognomy. *Journal of Personality and Social Psychology, 78*, 837–852.

Hastorf, A. H., & Cantril, H. (1954). They saw a game: A case study. *The Journal of Abnormal and Social Psychology, 49*, 129–134.

Hatfield, E., & Sprecher, S. (1986). Measuring passionate love in intimate relationships. *Journal of Adolescence, 9*, 383–410.

Hatfield, E., & Sprecher, S. (1995). Men's and women's preferences in marital partners in the United States, Russia, and Japan. *Journal of Cross-Cultural Psychology, 26*, 728–750.

Hatfield, E., Greenberger, D., Traupmann, J., & Lambert, P. (1982). Equity and sexual satisfaction in recently married couples. *Journal of Sex Research, 18*, 18–32.

Hawkins, S., & Hastie, R. (1990). Hindsight: Biased judgments of past events after the outcomes are known. *Psychological Bulletin, 107*, 311–327.

Hawkley, L. C., Burleson, M. H., Berntson, G. G., & Cacioppo, J. T. (2003). Loneliness in everyday life: Cardiovascular activity, psychosocial context, and health behaviors. *Journal of Personality and Social Psychology, 85*, 105–120.

Hazan, C., & Shaver, P. (1987). Romantic love conceptualized as an attachment process. *Journal of Personality and Social Psychology, 52*, 511–524.

Health Canada. (2006). *2004 Canadian sexually transmitted infections surveillance report: Pre-release*. Public Health Agency of Canada, Retrieved from www.phac-aspc.gc.ca/stds-mts/stddata_pre06_04.

Health Canada. (2009). Childhood immunization. *Health Canada*. http://www.hc-sc.gc.ca/hl-vs/iyh-vsv/med/immuniz-eng.php.

Hearst, P. (1982). *Every Secret Thing*. Garden City, NY: Doubleday & Company, INC.

Heatherton, T., Macrae, C., & Kelley, W. (2004). What the social brain sciences can tell us about the self. *Current Directions in Psychological Science, 13*, 190–193.

Heatherton, T., & Vohs, K. (2000). Interpersonal evaluations following threats to self: Role of self-esteem. *Journal of Personality and Social Psychology, 78*, 725–736.

Hebl, M. R., Foster, J. B., Mannix, L. M., & Dovidio, J. F. (2002). Formal and interpersonal discrimination: A field study of bias toward homosexual applicants. *Personality and Social Psychology Bulletin, 28*, 815–825.

Hedley, A. A., Ogden, C. L., Johnson, C. L., Carroll, M. D., Curtin, L. R., & Flegal, K. M. (2004). Prevalence of over-weight and obesity among US children, adolescents, and adults, 1999–2002. *Journal of the American Medical Association, 291*, 2847–2850.

Heider, F. (1958). *The Psychology of Interpersonal Relations*. Hoboken, NJ: Wiley.

Heilman, M. E., Block, C. J., & Lucas, J. A. (1992). Presumed incompetent? Stigmatization and affirmative action efforts. *Journal of Applied Psychology, 77*, 536–544.

Heine, S., & Lehman, D. (1997). Culture, dissonance, and self-affirmation. *Personality and Social Psychology Bulletin, 23*, 389–400.

Heine, S., & Lehman, D. (1999). Culture, self-discrepancies, and self-satisfaction. *Personality and Social Psychology Bulletin, 25*, 915–925.

Heine, S., Lehman, D., Peng, K., & Greenholtz, J. (2002). What's wrong with cross-cultural comparisons of subjective Likert scales?: The reference-group eff ect. *Journal of Personality and Social Psychology, 82*, 903–918.

Heine, S., Kitayama, S., Lehman, D., Takata, T., Ide, E., Leung, C., & Matsumoto, H. (2001). Divergent consequences of success and failure in Japan and North America: An investigation of self-improving motivations and malleable selves. *Journal of Personality and Social Psychology, 81*, 599–615.

Heine, S. J., & Buchtel, E. E. (2009). Personality: The universal and the culturally specific. *Annual Review of Psychology, 60*, 369–394.

Heine, S. J., & Lehman, D. R. (1995). Cultural variation in unrealistic optimism: Does the West feel more invulnerable than the East? *Journal of Personality and Social Psychology, 68*, 595–607.

Helgeson, V., & Mickelson, K. (1995). Motives for social comparison. *Personality and Social Psychology Bulletin, 21*, 1200–1209.

Henchy, T., & Glass, D. C. (1968). Evaluation apprehension and the social facilitation of dominant and subordinate responses. *Journal of Personality and Social Psychology, 10*, 446–454.

Henderson, M. D., Trope, Y., & Carnevale, P. J. (2006). Negotiation from a near and distant time perspective. *Journal of Personality and Social Psychology, 91*, 712–729.

Hendrick, C., & Hendrick, S. (1986). A theory and method of love. *Journal of Personality and Social Psychology, 50*, 392–402.

Hendrick, S. S., & Hendrick, C. (1993). Lovers as friends. *Journal of Social and Personal Relationships, 10*, 459–466.

Hendrick, S. S., & Hendrick, C. (1995). Gender differences and similarities in sex and love. *Personal Relationships, 2*, 55–65.

Hendrick, S. S., Hendrick, C., & Adler, N. L. (1988). Romantic relationships: Love, satisfaction, and staying together. *Journal of Personality and Social Psychology, 54*, 980–988.

Hennenlotter, A., Dresel, C., Castrop, F., Ceballos, Baumann, A. O., Wohlschlager, A. M., Haslinger, B. (2008). The link between facial feedback and neural activity within central circuitries of emotion - New insights from botulinum toxin-induced denervation of frown muscles. *Cerebral Cortex*, June 17.

Hennigan, K. M., Heath, L., Wharton, J. D., Del Rosario, M. L., Cook, T. D., & Calder, B. J. (1982). Impact of the introduction of television on crime in the United States: Empirical findings and theoretical implications. *Journal of Personality and Social Psychology, 42*, 461–477.

Henry, F., Tator, C., Mattis, W., & Rees, T. (1995). *The colour of democracy: Racism in Canadian society*. Toronto: Harcourt Brace.

Henry, P. J., & Hardin, C. D. (2006). The contact hypothesis revisited: Status bias in the reduction of implicit prejudice in the United States and Lebanon. *Psychological Science, 17*, 862–868.

Hepburn, A. (2001). *An introduction to critical social psychology*. London: Sage.

Hepworth, J. T., & West, S. G. (1988). Lynchings and the economy: A time-series reanalysis of Hovland and Sears (1940). *Journal of Personality and Social Psychology, 55*, 239–247.

Herlocker, C. E., Allison, S. T., Foubert, J. D., & Beggan, J. K. (1997). Intended and unintended overconsumption of physical, spatial, and temporal resources. *Journal of Personality and Social Psychology, 73*, 992–1104.

Hewitt, P., Flett, G., Sherry, S., Habke, M., Parkin, M., Lam, R., et al. (2003). The interpersonal expression of perfection: Perfectionistic self-presentation and psychological distress. *Journal of Personality and Social Psychology, 84*, 1303–1325.

Hewstone, M. (1989). *Causal attribution from cognitive processes to collective beliefs*. Oxford: Blackwell.

Hewstone, M. (1990). The "ultimate attribution error"? A review of the literature on intergroup causal attribution. *European Journal of Social Psychology, 20*, 311–335.

Hewstone, M., Crisp, R. J., Contarello, A., Voci, A., Conway, L., Marletta, G., Willis, H. (2009). Tokens in the tower: Perceptual processes and interaction dynamics in academic settings with "skewed," "tilted" and "balanced" gender ratios. *Group Processes & Intergroup Relations, 9*, 509–532.

Hewstone, M., Hopkins, N., & Routh, D. A. (1992). Cognitive models of stereotype change: I. Generalization and subtyping in young people's views of the police. *European Journal of Social Psychology, 22*, 219–234.

Hewstone, M. & Jaspars, J.M.F. (1982). Intergroup relations and attribution processes. In H. Tajfel (Ed.), *Social identity and attribution processes* (pp. 99–133). Cambridge: Cambridge University press.

Hewstone, M., Macrae, C. N., Griffiths, R., & Milne, A. B. (1994). Cognitive models of stereotype change: 5. Measurement, development, and consequences of subtyping. *Journal of Experimental Social Psychology, 30*, 505–526.

Hewstone, M., & Ward, C. (1985). Ethnocentrism and causal attribution in Southeast Asia. *Journal of Personality and Social Psychology, 48*, 614–623.

Higbee, K. L. (1969). Fifteen years of fear arousal: Research on threat appeals: 1953–1968. *Psychological Bulletin, 72*, 426–444.

Higgins, E. (1996). The 'self digest': Self-knowledge serving self-regulatory functions. *Journal of Personality and Social Psychology, 71*, 1062–1083.

Higgins, N.C & Bhatt, G. (2001). Culture moderates the self-serving bias: Etic and emic features of causal attributions in India and in Canada. *Social Behavior and Personality. 29(1)*, 49–61.

Higgins, R., & Harris, R. (1988). Strategic 'alcohol' use: Drinking to self-handicap. *Journal of Social & Clinical Psychology, 6*, 191–202.

Highhouse, S., Beadle, D., Gallo, A., & Miller, L. (1998). Get em while they last! Effects of scarcity information in job advertisements. *Journal of Applied Social Psychology, 28*, 779–795.

Hill, T., Smith, N., & Lewicki, P. (1989). The development of self-image bias: A real-world demonstration. *Personality and Social Psychology Bulletin, 15*, 205–211.

Hilton, J., & Darley, J. (1985). Constructing other persons: A limit on the effect. *Journal of Experimental Social Psychology, 21*, 1–18.

Hilton, J., Fein, S., & Miller, D. (1993). Suspicion and dispositional inference. *Personality and Social Psychology Bulletin, 19*, 501–512.

Hilton, J. L., & Darley, J. M. (1991). The effects of interaction goals on person perception. In M. P. Zanna (Ed.), *Advances in experimental social psychology*, Vol. 24 (pp. 235–267). New York: Academic Press.

Hilton, J. L., & von Hippel, W. (1990). The role of consistency in the judgment of stereotype-relevant behaviors. *Personality and Social Psychology Bulletin, 16*, 430–448.

Hirt, E., Deppe, R., & Gordon, L. (1991). Self-reported versus behavioral self-handicapping: Empirical evidence for a theoretical distinction. *Journal of Personality and Social Psychology, 61*, 981–991.

Hoeksema-van Orden, C. Y. D., Gaillard, A. W. K., & Buunk, B. P. (1998). Social loafing under fatigue. *Journal of Personality and Social Psychology, 75*, 1179–1190.

Hoffman, M. L. (1981). Is altruism part of human nature? *Journal of Personality and Social Psychology, 40*, 121–137.

Hoffman, M. L. (1994). The contribution of empathy to justice and moral judgment. In B. Puka (Ed.), *Reaching out: Caring, altruism, and prosocial behaviour*, Vol. 7 (pp. 161–194). New York: Garland.

Hofstede, G. (1980). *Culture's consequences: International differences in work-related values.* London: Sage.

Hofstede, G. (1991). *Culture and Organizations: Software of the Mind.* London: McGraw-Hill.

Hofstede, G., (2001). *Culture's Consequences, Comparing Values, Behaviors, Institutions, and Organizations Across Nations.* Thousand Oaks CA: Sage Publications, 2001.

Hogg, M. A. (2006). Intergroup relations. In J. Delamater (Ed.), *Handbook of Social Psychology* (pp. 479–503). New York: Springer.

Hogg, M. A., Hains, S. C., & Mason, I. (1998). Identification and leadership in small groups: Salience, frame of reference, and leader stereotypicality effects on leader evaluations. *Journal of Personality and Social Psychology, 75*, 1248–1263.

Hogg, M. A. & Vaughan, G. M. (2002). *Social Psychology* (3rd ed.). Essex, England: Pearson Prentice Hall.

Holland, R., Verplanken, B., & van Knippenberg, A. (2003). From repetition to conviction: Attitude accessibility as a determinant of attitude certainty. *Journal of Experimental Social Psychology, 39*, 594–601.

Hollander, E. P. (1958). Conformity, status, and idiosyncrasy credit. *Psychological Review, 65*, 117–127.

Hollander, E. P. (1960). Competence and conformity in the acceptance of influence. *The Journal of Abnormal and Social Psychology, 61*, 365–369.

Holloway, S., Tucker, L., & Hornstein, H. A. (1977). The effects of social and nonsocial information on interpersonal behavior of males: The news makes news. *Journal of Personality and Social Psychology, 35*, 514–522.

Holmes, J. G., & Murray, S. L. (1996). *Conflict in close relationships.* In E. T. Higgins & A. W. Kruglanski (Eds.), *Social Psychology: Handbook of Basic Principles* (pp. 622–654). New York: Guilford.

Holtgraves, T. M., & Yang, J. H. (1992). The interpersonal underpinnings of request strategies: General principles and differences due to culture and gender. *Journal of Personality and Social Psychology, 62*, 246–256.

Honeycutt, J. M., Woods, B. L., & Fontenot, K. (1993). The endorsement of communication conflict rules as a function of engagement, marriage and marital ideology. *Journal of Social and Personal Relationships, 10*, 285–304.

Hoorens, V., (1993). Self-enhancement and superiority biases in social comparison. *European Review of Social Psychology, 4*, 113–139.

Hoover, C. W., Wood, E. E., & Knowles, E. S. (1983). Forms of social awareness and helping. *Journal of Experimental Social Psychology, 19*, 577–590.

Horgen, K. B., Choate, M., & Brownell, K. D. (2001). *Television food advertising: Targeting children in a toxic environment.* In D. G. Singer & J. L. Singer (Eds.), *Handbook of Children and the Media* (pp. 447–461). Thousand Oaks, CA: Sage.

Hornsey, M. J., & Hogg, M. A. (2000). Intergroup similarity and subgroup relations: Some implications for assimilation. *Personality and Social Psychology Bulletin, 26*, 948–958.

Hornsey, M. J., & Imani, A. (2004). Criticizing groups from the inside and the outside: An identity perspective on the intergroup sensitivity effect. *Personality and Social Psychology Bulletin, 30*, 365–383.

Hornstein, H. A., Fisch, E., & Holmes, M. (1968). Influence of a model's feeling about his behavior and his relevance as a comparison other on observers' helping behavior. *Journal of Personality and Social Psychology, 10*, 222–226.

Hortacsu, N., & Oral, A. (2001). Comparison of couple- and family-initiated marriages in Turkey. *The Journal of Social Psychology, 134*, 229–239.

Hoshino-Browne, E., Zanna, A., Spencer, S., Zanna, M., Kitayama, S., & Lackenbauer, S. (2005). On the cultural guises of cognitive dissonance: The case of Easterners and Westerners. *Journal of Personality and Social Psychology, 89*, 294–310.

Hosoda, M., Stone-Romero, E. F., & Coats, G. (2003). The effects of physical attractiveness on job related outcomes: A meta-analysis of experimental studies. *Personnel Psychology, 56*, 431–462.

Hovland, C. I., & Sears, R. R. (1940). Minor studies of aggression: VI. Correlation of lynchings with economic indices. *Journal of Psychology: Interdisciplinary and Applied, 9*, 301–310.

Hovland, C. I., & Weiss, W. (1951). The influence of source credibility on communication effectiveness. *Public Opinion Quarterly, 15*, 635–650.

Howard, D. J. (1997). Familiar phrases as peripheral persuasion cues. *Journal of Experimental Social Psychology, 33*, 231–243.

Huesmann, L. R. (1986). Psychological processes promoting the relation between exposure to media violence and aggressive behavior by the viewer. *Journal of Social Issues, 42*, 125–139.

Huesmann, L. R., Eron, L. D., Klein, R., Brice, P., & Fischer, P. (1983). Mitigating the imitation of aggressive behaviors by changing children's attitudes about media violence. *Journal of Personality and Social Psychology, 44*, 899–910.

Huesmann, L. R., Eron, L. D., Lefkowitz, M. M., & Walder, L. O. (1984). Stability of aggression over time and generations. *Developmental Psychology, 20*, 1120–1134.

Huguet, P., Galvaing, M. P., Monteil, J. M., & Dumas, F. (1999). Social presence effects in the Stroop task: Further evidence for an attentional view of social facilitation. *Journal of Personality and Social Psychology, 77*, 1011–1025.

Hull, J., & Young, R. (1983). Self-consciousness, self-esteem, and success-failure as determinants of alcohol consumption in male social drinkers. *Journal of Personality and Social Psychology, 44*, 1097–1109.

Hull, J. G., & Bond, C. F. (1986). Social and behavioral consequences of alcohol consumption and expectancy: A meta-analysis. *Psychological Bulletin, 99*, 347–360.

Huston, T. L., Ruggiero, M., Conner, R., & Geis, G. (1981). Bystander intervention into crime: A study based on naturally-occurring episodes. *Social Psychology Quarterly, 44*, 14–23.

Huston, T. L., & Vangelisti, A. L. (1991). Socioemotional behavior and satisfaction in marital relationships: A longitudinal study. *Journal of Personality and Social Psychology, 61*, 721–733.

Hutchings, C. (2011). *Canada's First Nations: A legacy of institutional racism.* Retrieved from http://www.tolerance.cz/courses/papers/hutchin.htm.

Hyde, J. S. (1984). How large are gender differences in aggression? A developmental meta-analysis. *Developmental Psychology, 20*, 722–736.

Hyman, I., Husband, T., & Billings, F. (1995). False memories of childhood experiences. *Applied Cognitive Psychology, 9*, 181–197.

Hynie, M., & Lydon, J. (1996). The sexual opinion survey and contraceptive behavior revisited: Can there be too much of a good thing? *Journal of Sex Research, 33*, 127–134.

Hynie, M., MacDonald, T.K., & Marques, S., (2006). Self-conscious emotions and self regulation in the promotion of condom use. *Personality and Social Psychology Bulletin,32*(8), 1072–1084.

Ickes, W. (1993). Traditional gender roles: Do they make, and then break, our relationships? *Journal of Social Issues, 49*, 71–86.

Inzlicht, M., & Ben-Zeev, T. (2000). A threatening intellectual environment: Why females are susceptible to experiencing problem-solving deficits in the presence of males. *Psychological Science, 11*, 365–371.

Inzlicht, M., & Ben Zeev, T. (2003). Do high-achieving female students underperform in private? The implications of threatening environments on intellectual processing. *Journal of Educational Psychology, 95*, 796–805.

Isen, A. M., & Levin, P. F. (1972). Effect of feeling good on helping: Cookies and kindness. *Journal of Personality and Social Psychology, 21*, 384–388.

Isenberg, D. J. (1986). Group polarization: A critical review and meta-analysis. *Journal of Personality and Social Psychology, 50*, 1141–1151.

Ishii, K., Reyes, J. A., & Kitayama, S. (2003). Spontaneous attention to word content versus emotional tone: Differences among three cultures. *Psychological Science, 14*, 39–46.

Ito, T., Larsen, J., Smith, N., & Cacioppo, J. (1998). Negative information weighs more heavily on the brain: The negativity bias in evaluative categorizations. *Journal of Personality and Social Psychology, 75*, 887–900.

Ito, T. A., Miller, N., & Pollock, V. E. (1996). Alcohol and aggression: A meta-analysis on the moderating effects of inhibitory cues, triggering events, and self-focused attention. *Psychological Bulletin, 120*, 60–82.

Ito, T. A., & Urland, G. R. (2003). Race and gender on the brain: Electrocortical measures of attention to the race and gender of multiply categorizable individuals. *Journal of Personality and Social Psychology, 85*, 616–626.

Iyengar, S., & Lepper, M. (1999). Rethinking the value of choice: A cultural perspective on intrinsic motivation. *Journal of Personality and Social Psychology, 76*, 349–366.

Izard, C. E. (1971). *The face of emotion*. New York: Appleton-Century-Crofts.

Izard, C. E. (1994). Innate and universal facial expressions: Evidence from developmental and cross-cultural research. *Psychological Bulletin, 115*, 288–299.

Jackiw, L. B., Arbuthnott, K. D., Pfeifer, J. E., Marcon, J. L., & Meissner, C. A. (2008). Examining the cross-race effect in lineup identification using Caucasian and First Nations samples. *Canadian Journal of Behavioural Science, 40*, 52–57.

Jackson, H., Philip, E., Nuttall, R. L., & Diller, L. (2002). Traumatic brain injury: A hidden consequence for battered women. *Professional Psychology: Research and Practice, 33*, 39–45.

Jackson, J. M., & Williams, K. D. (1985). Social loafing on difficult tasks: Working collectively can improve performance. *Journal of Personality and Social Psychology, 49*, 937–942.

Jackson, J. W. (1993). Realistic group conflict theory: A review and evaluation of the theoretical and empirical literature. *Psychological Record, 43*, 395–413.

Jackson, L. M., & Esses, V. M. (1997). Of scripture and ascription: The relation between religious fundamentalism and intergroup helping. *Personality and Social Psychology Bulletin, 23*, 893–906.

James, W. (1890, reprinted 1950). *The principles of psychology*, Vol. 2. New York: Dover Publications.

James, W., & James, H. (1920). *The Letters of William James*. Boston, MA: The Atlantic Monthly Press.

Janes, L. M., & Olson, J. M. (2000). Jeer pressures: The behavioral effects of observing ridicule of others. *Personality and Social Psychology Bulletin, 26*, 474–485.

Janis, I. L. (1972). *Victims of groupthink*. Boston: Houghton-Mifflin.

Janis, I. L., (1982). *Groupthink* (2nd ed.). Boston: Houghton-Mifflin.

Janis, I. L., & Feshbach, S. (1953). Effects of fear-arousing communications. *The Journal of Abnormal and Social Psychology, 48*, 78–92.

Janis, I. L., Kaye, D., & Kirschner, P. (1965). Facilitating effects of 'eating-while-reading' on responsiveness to persuasive communications. *Journal of Personality and Social Psychology, 1*, 181–186.

Janoff-Bulman, R., Timko, C., & Carli, L. L. (1985). Cognitive biases in blaming the victim. *Journal of Experimental Social Psychology, 21*, 161–177.

Jarvis, W. B. G., & Petty, R. E. (1996). The need to evaluate. *Journal of Personality and Social Psychology, 70*, 172–194.

Jemmott, J., & Magloire, K. (1988). Academic stress, social support, and secretory immunoglobulin A. *Journal of Personality and Social Psychology, 55*, 803–810.

Jenkins, S. S., & Aubé, J. (2002). Gender differences and gender-related constructs in dating aggression. *Personality and Social Psychology Bulletin, 28*, 1106–1118.

Jensen-Campbell, L. A., & Graziano, W. G. (2000). Beyond the school yard: Relationships as moderators of daily interpersonal conflict. *Personality and Social Psychology Bulletin, 26*, 923–935.

Jensen-Campbell, L. A., Graziano, W. G., & West, S. G. (1995). Dominance, prosocial orientation, and female preferences: Do nice guys really finish last? *Journal of Personality and Social Psychology, 68*, 427–440.

Jetten, J., Branscombe, N. R., Schmitt, M. T., & Spears, R. (2001). Rebels with a cause: Group identification as a response to perceived discrimination from the mainstream. *Personality and Social Psychology Bulletin, 27*, 1204–1213.

Jewell, L.M. & Wormith, J.S. (2010). Variables associated with attrition from domestic violence treatment programs targeting male batterers: A meta-analysis. *Criminal Justice and Behavior, 37*(10), 1086–1113.

Ji, L., Nisbett, R., & Su, Y. (2001). Culture, change, and prediction. *Psychological Science, 12*, 450–456.

Ji, L., Peng, K., & Nisbett, R. (2000). Culture, control, and perception of relationships in the environment. *Journal of Personality and Social Psychology, 78*, 943–955.

Ji, L., Schwarz, N., & Nisbett, R. E. (2000). Culture, autobiographical memory, and behavioral frequency reports: Measurement issues in cross-cultural studies. *Personality and Social Psychology Bulletin, 26*, 585–593.

Ji, L., Zhang, Z., & Nisbett, R. (2004). Is it culture or is it language? Examination of language effects in cross-cultural research on categorization. *Journal of Personality and Social Psychology, 87*, 57–65.

Johnson, C., & Mullen, B. (1994). Evidence for the accessibility of paired distinctiveness in distinctiveness-based illusory correlation in stereotyping. *Personality and Social Psychology Bulletin, 20*, 65–70.

Johnson, J. (2005). Ascertaining the validity of individual protocols from Web-based personality inventories. *Journal of Research in Personality, 39*, 103–129.

Johnson, R. & Downing, L. (1979). Deindividuation and valence of cues: effects on prosocial and and antisocial behavior. *Journal of Personality and Social Psychology, 37*, 1532–1538.

Johnson, R., Kelly, R., & LeBlanc, B. (1995). Motivational basis of dissonance: Aversive consequences of inconsistency. *Personality and Social Psychology Bulletin, 21*, 850–855.

Johnson, R. C., Danko, G. P., Darvill, T. J., & Bochner, S. (1989). Cross-cultural assessment of altruism and its correlates. *Personality and Individual Differences, 10,* 855–868.

Johnson, T. E., & Rule, B. G. (1986). Mitigating circumstance information, censure, and aggression. *Journal of Personality and Social Psychology, 50,* 537–542.

Johnston, J. (2008). The Citizen-consumer Hybrid: Ideological Tensions and the Case of Whole Foods Market. *Theory and Society, 37,* 229–70.

Joireman, J. A., van Lange, P. A. M., & van Vugt, M. (2004). Who cares about the environmental impact of cars? Those with an eye toward the future. *Environment and Behavior, 36,* 187–206.

Jones, E. (1979). The rocky road from acts to dispositions. *American Psychologist, 34,* 107–117.

Jones, E., Davis, K., & Gergen, K. (1961). Role playing variations and their informational value for person perception. *The Journal of Abnormal and Social Psychology, 63,* 302–310.

Jones, E., & Harris, V. (1967). The attribution of attitudes. *Journal of Experimental Social Psychology, 3,* 1–24.

Jones, E. E., & Davis K. E. *From acts to dispositions: the attribution process in person perception. Advances in experimental social psychology.* (L. Berkowitz, ed.) New York: Academic Press, 1965. (Vol. II, p. 219–266).

Jones, E. E. (1990). *Interpersonal Perception.* New York: WH Freeman.

Jones, E. E., & Nisbett, R. E. (1971). *The Actor and the Observer: Divergent Perceptions of the Causes of Behavior.* New York: General Learning Press.

Jones, J. L., & Leary, M. R. (1994). Effects of appearance-based admonitions against sun exposure on tanning intentions in young adults. *Health Psychology, 13,* 86–90.

Jones, T. F., Craig, A. S., Hoy, D., Gunter, E. W., Ashley, D. L., Barr, D. B., Brock J. W., Schaffner W. (2000). Mass psychogenic illness attributed to toxic exposure at a high school. *New England Journal of Medicine, 342,* 96–100.

Jones, W. H., Carpenter, B. N., & Quintana, D. (1985). Personality and interpersonal predictors of loneliness in two cultures. *Journal of Personality and Social Psychology, 48,* 1503–1511.

Jordan, C. H., Spencer, S. J., & Zanna, M. P. (2003). "I love me . . . I love me not": Implicit self-esteem, explicit self-esteem, and defensiveness. In S. J. Spencer, S. Fein, M. P. Zanna, & J. M. Olson (Eds.), *The Ontario Symposium: Vol. 9. Motivated social perception* (pp. 117–145). Mahwah, NJ: Lawrence Erlbaum.

Jordan, C. H., Spencer S. J., & Zanna, M. P. (2005). Types of high self-esteem and prejudice: How implicit self-esteem relates to ethnic discrimination among high explicit self-esteem individuals. *Personality and Social Psychology Bulletin, 31,* 693–702.

Jordan, C. H., Spencer, S. J., Zanna, M. P., Hoshino-Browne, E., & Correll, J. (2003). Secure and defensive high self-esteem. *Journal of Personality and Social Psychology, 85,* 969–978.

Josephson, W. L. (1987). Television violence and children's aggression: Testing the priming, social script, and disinhibition predictions. *Journal of Personality and Social Psychology, 53,* 882–890.

Judd, C. M., & Park, B. (1988). Out-group homogeneity: Judgments of variability at the individual and group levels. *Journal of Personality and Social Psychology, 54,* 778–788.

Judd, C. M., Ryan, C. S., & Park, B. (1991). Accuracy in the judgment of in-group and out-group variability. *Journal of Personality and Social Psychology, 61,* 366–379.

Julien, D., Chartrand, E., Simard, M., Bouthillier, D., & Bégin, J. (2003). Conflict, social support, and relationship quality: An observational study of heterosexual, gay male, and lesbian couples' communication. *Journal of Family Psychology, 17,* 419–428.

Jussim, L., Coleman, L. M., & Lerch, L. (1987). The nature of stereotypes: A comparison and integration of three theories. *Journal of Personality and Social Psychology, 52,* 536–546.

Jussim, L., & Eccles, J. (1992). Teacher expectations: II. Construction and reflection of student achievement. *Journal of Personality and Social Psychology, 63,* 947–961.

Kachadourian, L. K., Fincham, F., & Davila, J. (2004). The tendency to forgive in dating and married couples: The role of attachment and relationship satisfaction. *Personal Relationships, 11,* 373–393.

Kahneman, D., Knetsch, J. L., & Thaler, R. H. (1986a). Fairness and the assumptions of economics. *Journal of Business, 59,* S285–S300.

Kahneman, D., Knetsch, J. L., & Thaler, R. H. (1986b). Fairness as a constraint on profit seeking: Entitlements in the market. *The American Economic Review, 76,* 728–741.

Kahneman, D., Knetsch, J. L., & Thaler, R. H. (1990). Experimental tests of the endowment effect and the Coase theorem. *Journal of Political Economy, 98,* 1325–1348.

Kahneman, D., & Tversky, A. (1972). Subjective probability: A judgment of representativeness. *Cognitive Psychology, 3,* 430–454.

Kaiser, C. R., & Miller, C. T. (2001). Stop complaining! The social costs of making attributions to discrimination. *Personality and Social Psychology Bulletin, 27,* 254–263.

Kaiser, R. B., Hogan, R., & Craig, S. B. (2008). Leadership and the fate of organizations. *American Psychologist, 63,* 96–110.

Kalichman, S., & Coley, B. (1995). Context framing to enhance HIV-antibody-testing messages targeted to African American women. *Health Psychology, 14,* 247–254.

Kalick, S. M., & Hamilton, T. E. (1986). The matching hypothesis reexamined. *Journal of Personality and Social Psychology, 51,* 673–682.

Kallgren, C. A., Reno, R. R., & Cialdini, R. B. (2000). A focus theory of normative conduct: When norms do and do not affect behavior. *Personality and Social Psychology Bulletin, 26,* 1002–1012.

Kameda, T., & Sugimori, S. (1993). Psychological entrapment in group decision making: An assigned decision rule and a group-think phenomenon. *Journal of Personality and Social Psychology, 65,* 282–292.

Kanagawa, C., Cross, S., & Markus, H. (2001). 'Who am I?' The cultural psychology of the conceptual self. *Personality and Social Psychology Bulletin, 27,* 90–103.

Kanter, R. M. (1977). Some effects of proportions on group life: Skewed gender ratios and responses to token women. *The American Journal of Sociology, 82,* 965–990.

Kaplan, M. F., & Miller, L. E. (1978). Reducing the effects of juror bias. *Journal of Personality and Social Psychology, 36,* 1443–1455.

Kaplan, R. E., & Kaiser, R. B. (2003). Rethinking a classic distinction in leadership: Implications for the assessment and development of executives. *Consulting Psychology Journal: Research and Practice, 55,* 15–25.

Kaptchuk, T. J., Friedlander, E., Kelley, J. M., Sanchez, M. N., Kokkotou, E., Singer, J. P., Kowalczykowski, M., Miller, F. G., Kirsch, I., & Lembo, A. J. (2010). Placebos without deception: A randomized controlled trial in irritable bowel syndrome. *PLoS ONE, 5,* 1–7.

Karau, S. J., & Williams, K. D. (1993). Social loafing: A meta-analytic review and theoretical integration. *Journal of Personality and Social Psychology, 65,* 681–706.

Karnehed, N. (2008). *Socioeconomic consequences of obesity: Population-based longitudinal studies of Swedish men.* Stockholm, Sweden: Department of Public Health Sciences, Karolinska Institute.

Karney, B., & Coombs, R. (2000). Memory bias in long-term close relationships: Consistency or improvement? *Personality and Social Psychology Bulletin, 26,* 959–970.

Karney, B. R., & Bradbury, T. N. (2000). Attributions in marriage: State or trait? A growth curve analysis. *Journal of Personality and Social Psychology, 78,* 295–309.

Karremans, J. C., Stroebe, W., & Claus, J. (2006). Beyond Vicary's fantasies: The impact of subliminal priming and brand choice. *Journal of Experimental Social Psychology, 42,* 792–798.

Kashima, Y., Kokubo, T., Kashima, E., Boxall, D., Yamaguchi, S., & Macrae, K. (2004). Culture and self: Are there within-culture diff erences in self between metropolitan areas and regional cities? *Personality and Social Psychology Bulletin, 30,* 816–823.

Kashima, Y., Siegal, M., Tanaka, K., & Kashima, E. (1992). Do people believe behaviours are consistent with attitudes? Towards a cultural psychology of attribution processes. *British Journal of Social Psychology, 31,* 111–124.

Kassin, S., & Sukel, H. (1997). Coerced confessions and the jury: An experimental test of the 'harmless error' rule. *Law and Human Behavior, 21,* 27–46.

Kassin, S. M. (2005). On the psychology of confessions: Does innocence put innocents at risk? *American Psychologist, 60,* 215–228.

Kassin, S. M., & Kiechel, K. L. (1996). The social psychology of false confessions: Compliance, internalization, and confabulation. *Psychological Science, 7,* 125–128.

Kathryn, G., Bernards, S., Osgood, D.W. & Wells, S. (2006). Bad nights or bad bars? Multi-level analysis of environmental predictors of aggression in late-night large-capacity bars and clubs. *Addiction 101(11),* 1569–1580.

Kathryn, G., Osgood, D.W., Wells, S. & Stockwell, T. (2006). To what extent is intoxication associated with aggression in bars? A multi-level analysis. *Journal of Studies in Alcohol, 67(3),* 382–390.

Kawakami, K., Dovidio, J., & Dijksterhuis, A. (2003). Effect of social category priming on personal attitudes. *Psychological Science, 14,* 315–319.

Kawakami, K., Young, H., & Dovidio, J. F. (2002). Automatic stereotyping: Category, trait, and behavioral activations. *Personality and Social Psychology Bulletin, 28,* 3–15.

Keller, J., & Dauenheimer, D. (2003). Stereotype threat in the classroom: Dejection mediates the disrupting threat effect on women's math performance. *Personality and Social Psychology Bulletin, 29,* 371–381.

Keller, M., Edelstein, W., Schmid, C., Fang, F., & Fang, G. (1998). Reasoning about responsibilities and obligations in close relationships: A comparison across two cultures. *Developmental Psychology, 34,* 731–741.

Kellermann, A. L., Rivara, F. P., Rushforth, N. B., & Banton, J. G. (1993). Gun ownership as a risk factor for homicide in the home. *New England Journal of Medicine, 329,* 1084–1091.

Kelley, H. (1950). The warm-cold variable in first impressions of persons. *Journal of Personality, 18,* 431–439.

Kelley, H. (1967). Attribution theory in social psychology. *Nebraska Symposium on Motivation, 15,* 192–238.

Kelly, D. J., Quinn, P. C., Slater, A. M., Lee, K., Ge, L., & Pascalis, O. (2007). The other-race effect develops during infancy: Evidence of perceptual narrowing. *Psychological Science, 18,* 1084–1089.

Kelly, J. R., Jackson, J. W., & Hutson-Comeaux, S. L. (1997). The effects of time pressure and task differences on influence modes and accuracy in decision-making groups. *Personality and Social Psychology Bulletin, 23,* 10–22.

Kelly, S., & Dunbar, R. I. M. (2001). Who dares, wins: Heroism versus altruism in women's mate choice. *Human Nature, 12,* 89–105.

Kenrick, D. T., & Gutierres, S. E. (1980). Contrast effects and judgments of physical attractiveness: When beauty becomes a social problem. *Journal of Personality and Social Psychology, 38,* 131–140.

Kenrick, D. T., Gutierres, S. E., & Goldberg, L. L. (1989). Influence of popular erotica on judgments of strangers and mates. *Journal of Experimental Social Psychology, 25,* 159–167.

Kenrick, D. T., Groth, G. E., Trost, M. R., & Sadalla, E. K. (1993). Integrating evolutionary and social exchange perspectives on relationships: Effects of gender, self-appraisal, and involvement level on mate selection criteria. *Journal of Personality and Social Psychology, 64,* 951–969.

Kenrick, D. T., Keefe, R. C., Bryan, A., Barr, A., & Brown, S. (1995). Age preferences and mate choice among homosexuals and heterosexuals: A case for modular psychological mechanisms. *Journal of Personality and Social Psychology, 69,* 1166–1172.

Kenrick, D. T., Neuberg, S. L., Zierk, K. L., & Krones, J. M. (1994). Evolution and social cognition: Contrast effects as a function of sex, dominance, and physical attractiveness. *Personality and Social Psychology Bulletin, 20,* 210–217.

Kenrick, D. T., Sadalla, E. K., Groth, G., & Trost, M. R. (1990). Evolution, traits, and the stages of human courtship: Qualifying the parental investment model. *Journal of Personality, Biological foundations of personality: Evolution, behavioral genetics, and psychophysiology, 58,* 97–116.

Kerr, N. L. (1983). Motivation losses in small groups: A social dilemma analysis. *Journal of Personality and Social Psychology, 45,* 819–828.

Kerr, N. L., & Bruun, S. E. (1983). Dispensability of member effort and group motivation losses: Free-rider effects. *Journal of Personality and Social Psychology, 44,* 78–94.

Kerr, N. L., Garst, J., Lewandowski, D. A., & Harris, S. E. (1997). That still, small voice: Commitment to cooperate as an internalized versus a social norm. *Personality and Social Psychology Bulletin, 23,* 1300–1311.

Kerr, N. L., & Kaufman-Gilliland, C. M. (1994). Communication, commitment, and cooperation in social dilemma. *Journal of Personality and Social Psychology, 66,* 513–529.

Kilham, W., & Mann, L. (1974). Level of destructive obedience as a function of transmitter and executant roles in the Milgram obedience paradigm. *Journal of Personality and Social Psychology, 29,* 696–702.

Kim, H., & Markus, H. R. (1999). Deviance or uniqueness, harmony or conformity? A cultural analysis. *Journal of Personality and Social Psychology, 77,* 785–800.

Kim, H. S., Sherman, D. K., Ko, D., & Taylor, S. E. (2006). Pursuit of comfort and pursuit of harmony: Culture, relationships, and social support seeking. *Personality and Social Psychology Bulletin, 32,* 1595–1607.

Kimmel, M. J. (1980). Effects of trust, aspiration, and gender on negotiation tactics. *Journal of Personality and Social Psychology, 38,* 9–22.

Kimmel, P. R. (1994). Cultural perspectives on international negotiations. *Journal of Social Issues, 50,* 179–196.

Kirby, D. (2002). The impact of schools and school programs upon adolescent sexual behavior. *Journal of Sex Research, 39,* 27–33.

Kitayama, S., Markus, H., Matsumoto, H., & Norasakkunkit, V. (1997). Individual and collective processes in the construction of the self: Self-enhancement in the United States and self-criticism in Japan. *Journal of Personality and Social Psychology, 72,* 1245–1267.

Kitayama, S., Mesquita, B., & Karasawa, M. (2006). Cultural affordances and emotional experience: Socially engaging and disengaging emotions in Japan and the United States. *Journal of Personality and Social Psychology, 91,* 890–903.

Kitayama, S., Snibbe, A., Markus, H., & Suzuki, T. (2004). Is there any 'free' choice?: Self and dissonance in two cultures. *Psychological Science, 15,* 527–533.

Kite, M. E., & Deaux, K. (1986). Attitudes toward homosexuality: Assessment and behavioral consequences. *Basic and Applied Social Psychology, 7,* 137–162.

Klassen, R. M., & Krawchuk, L. L. (2009). Collective motivation beliefs of early adolescents working in small groups. *Journal of School Psychology, 47,* 101–120.

Klehe, U., & Anderson, N. (2007). The moderating influence of personality and culture on social loafing in typical versus maximum performance situations. *International Journal of Selection and Assessment, 15,* 250–262.

Klein, J. (1991). Negativity effects in impression formation: A test in the political arena. *Personality and Social Psychology Bulletin, 17,* 412–418.

Klein, W. (1997). Objective standards are not enough: Affective, self-evaluative, and behavioral responses to social comparison information. *Journal of Personality and Social Psychology, 72,* 763–774.

Kleinke, C., Peterson, T., & Rutledge, T. (1998). Effects of self-generated facial expressions on mood. *Journal of Personality and Social Psychology, 74,* 272–279.

Klinesmith, J., Kasser, T., & McAndrew, F. T. (2006). Guns, testosterone, and aggression: An experimental test of a mediational hypothesis. *Psychological Science, 17,* 568–571.

Klofas, J., & Toch, H. (1982). The guard subculture myth. *Journal of Research in Crime and Delinquency, 19,* 238–254.

Klohn, L. S., & Rogers, R. W. (1991). Dimensions of the severity of a health threat: The persuasive effects of visibility, time of onset, and rate of onset on young women's intentions to prevent osteoporosis. *Health Psychology, 10,* 323–329.

Klohnen, E. C., & Mendelsohn, G. A. (1998). Partner selection for personality characteristics: A couple-centered approach. *Personality and Social Psychology Bulletin, 24,* 268–278.

Knafo, A., & Plomin, R. (2006). Prosocial behavior from early to middle childhood: Genetic and environmental influences on stability and change. *Developmental Psychology, 42,* 771–786.

Knafo, A., Schwartz, S. H., & Levine, R. V. (2009). Helping strangers is lower in embedded cultures. *Journal of Cross-Cultural Psychology. 40,* 875–879.

Knight, G. P., Fabes, R. A., & Higgins, D. A. (1996). Concerns about drawing causal inferences from meta-analyses: An example in the study of gender differences in aggression. *Psychological Bulletin, 119,* 410–421.

Knight, G. P., Johnson, L. G., Carlo, G., & Eisenberg, N. (1994). A multiplicative model of the dispositional antecedents of a prosocial behavior: Predicting more of the people more of the time. *Journal of Personality and Social Psychology, 66,* 178–183.

Knowles, E., Morris, M., Chiu, C., & Hong, Y. (2001). Culture and the process of person perception: Evidence for automaticity among East Asians in correcting for situational influences on behavior. *Personality and Social Psychology Bulletin, 27,* 1344–1356.

Knowles, E. S. (1983). Social physics and the effects of others: Tests of the effects of audience size and distance on social judgments and behavior. *Journal of Personality and Social Psychology, 45,* 1263–1279.

Knutson, K. M., Mah, L., Manly, C. F., Grafman, J. (2007). Neural correlates of automatic beliefs about gender and race. *Human Brain Mapping, 28,* 915–930.

Koestner, R., & Wheeler, L. (1988). Self-presentation in personal advertisements: The influence of implicit notions of attraction and role expectations. *Journal of Social and Personal Relationships, 5,* 149–160.

Komorita, S. S., & Barth, J. M. (1985). Components of reward in social dilemmas. *Journal of Personality and Social Psychology, 48,* 364–373.

Komorita, S. S., Chan, D. K., & Parks, C. (1993). The effects of reward structure and reciprocity in social dilemmas. *Journal of Experimental Social Psychology, 29,* 252–267.

Komorita, S. S., & Parks, C. D. (1995). Interpersonal relations: Mixed-motive interaction. *Annual Review of Psychology, 46,* 183–207.

Komorita, S. S., Parks, C. D., & Hulbert, L. G. (1992). Reciprocity and the induction of cooperation in social dilemmas. *Journal of Personality and Social Psychology, 62,* 607–617.

Kong, R., Johnson, H., Beattie, S. & Cardillo, A. (2003). "Sexual offences in Canada." *Juristat.* Vol. 23, no. 6. Statistics Canada Catalogue no. 85-002-XIE. Ottawa.

Kongsompong, K., Powtong, R., & Sen, S. (2010, August 18–20). *Ethnocentrism, materialism, social influence, and collectivism: An inter-and-intra national analysis of the Thais, Chinese, and Indians.* Paper presented at the Third International Conference on Intercultural Collaboration, Copenhagen, Denmark.

Konrath, S., Bushman, B. J., & Campbell, W. K. (2006). Attenuating the link between threatened egotism and aggression. *Psychological Science, 17,* 995–1001.

Korabik, K., Baril, G. L., & Watson, C. (1993). Managers' conflict management style and leadership effectiveness: The moderating effects of gender. *Sex Roles, 29(5/6),* 405–420.

Korchmaros, J. D., & Kenny, D. A. (2006). An evolutionary and close-relationship model of helping. *Journal of Social and Personal Relationships, 23,* 21–43.

Kramer, R. M., & Brewer, M. B. (1984). Effects of group identity on resource use in a simulated commons dilemma. *Journal of Personality and Social Psychology, 46,* 1044–1057.

Kraus, S. (1995). Attitudes and the prediction of behavior: A meta-analysis of the empirical literature. *Personality and Social Psychology Bulletin, 21,* 58–75.

Kraut, R., Kiesler, S., Boneva, B., Cummings, J. N., Helgeson, V., & Crawford, A. M. (2002). Internet paradox revisited. *Journal of Social Issues, 58,* 49–74.

Krebs, D. (1975). Empathy and altruism. *Journal of Personality and Social Psychology, 32,* 1134–1146.

Krebs, D. L. (2008). Morality: An evolutionary account. *Perspectives on Psychological Science, 3,* 149–172.

Kremer, J. F., & Stephens, L. (1983). Attributions and arousal as mediators of mitigation's effect on retaliation. *Journal of Personality and Social Psychology, 45,* 335–343.

Krendl, A. C., Richeson, J. A., Kelley, W. M., & Heatherton, T. F. (2008). The negative consequences of threat: A functional magnetic resonance imaging investigation of the neural mechanisms underlying women's underperformance in math. *Psychological Science, 19,* 168–175.

Krosnick, J. (1989). Attitude importance and attitude accessibility. *Personality and Social Psychology Bulletin, 15,* 297–308.

Krosnick, J., Betz, A., Jussim, L., & Lynn, A. (1992). Subliminal conditioning of attitudes. *Personality and Social Psychology Bulletin, 18,* 152–162.

Krosnick, J., Boninger, D., Chuang, Y., Berent, M., & Carnot, C. (1993). Attitude strength: One construct or many related constructs? *Journal of Personality and Social Psychology, 65,* 1132–1151.

Krosnick, J. A., & Alwin, D. F. (1989). Aging and susceptibility to attitude change. *Journal of Personality and Social Psychology, 57,* 416–425.

Krueger, J., Ham, J., & Linford, K. (1996). Perceptions of behavioral consistency: Are people aware of the actor-observer effect? *Psychological Science, 7,* 259–264.

Krueger, R. F., Hicks, B. M., & McGue, M. (2001). Altruism and antisocial behavior: Independent tendencies, unique personality correlates, distinct etiologies. *Psychological Science, 12,* 397–402.

Kruger, D. J. (2003). Evolution and altruism: Combining psychological mediators with naturally selected tendencies. *Evolution and Human Behavior, 24,* 118–125.

Kruger, J., & Dunning, D. (1999). Unskilled and unaware of it: How difficulties in recognizing one's own incompetence lead to inflated self-assessments. *Journal of Personality and Social Psychology, 77,* 1121–1134.

Kruger, J., & Gilovich, T. (2004). Actions, intentions, and self-assessment: The road to self-enhancement is paved with good intentions. *Personality and Social Psychology Bulletin, 30,* 328–339.

Kruger, J., Wirtz, D., & Miller, D. (2005). Counterfactual thinking and the first instinct fallacy. *Journal of Personality and Social Psychology, 88,* 725–735.

Kruglanski, A. W., & Webster, D. M. (1991). Group members' reactions to opinion deviates and conformists at varying degrees of proximity to decision deadline and of environmental noise. *Journal of Personality and Social Psychology, 61,* 212–225.

Krull, D. (1993). Does the grist change the mill? The effect of the perceiver's inferential goal on the process of social inference. *Personality and Social Psychology Bulletin, 19,* 340–348.

Krull, D., Loy, M., Lin, J., Wang, C., Chen, S., & Zhao, X. (1999). The fundamental attribution error: Correspondence bias in individualist and collectivist cultures. *Personality and Social Psychology Bulletin, 25,* 1208–1219.

Krupp, D. B. (2008). Through Evolution's Eyes: Extracting Mate Preferences by Linking Visual Attention to Adaptive Design. *Archives of Sexual Behavior, 37,* 57–63.

Kubany, E. S., Bauer, G. B., Muraoka, M. Y., & Richard, D. C. (1995). Impact of labeled anger and blame in intimate relationships. *Journal of Social & Clinical Psychology, 14,* 53–60.

Kühen, U., Hannover, B., Roeder, U., Shah, A.A., Schubert, B., Upmeyer, A., Zakaria, S. (2001). Cross-cultural variations in identifying embedded figures: Comparisons from the United States, Germany, Russia, and Malaysia. *Journal of Cross-Cultural Psychology, 32,* 365–71.

Kulik, J. A., & Brown, R. (1979). Frustration, attribution of blame, and aggression. *Journal of Experimental Social Psychology, 15,* 183–194.

Kulik, J. A., & Mahler, H. I. (1989). Social support and recovery from surgery. *Health Psychology, 8,* 221–238.

Kumashiro, M., & Sedikides, C. (2005). Taking on board liability-focused information: Close positive relationships as a self-bolstering resource. *Psychological Science, 16,* 732–739.

Kunda, Z., Davies, P. G., Adams, B. D., & Spencer, S. J. (2002). The dynamic time course of stereotype activation: Activation, dissipation, and resurrection. *Journal of Personality and Social Psychology, 82,* 283–299.

Kunda, Z., & Oleson, K. C. (1995). Maintaining stereotypes in the face of disconfirmation: Constructing grounds for subtyping deviants. *Journal of Personality and Social Psychology, 68,* 565–579.

Kunda, Z., & Oleson, K. C. (1997). When exceptions prove the rule: How extremity of deviance determines the impact of deviant examples on stereotypes. *Journal of Personality and Social Psychology, 72,* 965–979.

Kunda, Z., & Sherman-Williams, B. (1993). Stereotypes and the construal of individuating information. *Personality and Social Psychology Bulletin, 19,* 90–99.

Kunda, Z., Sinclair, L., & Griffin, D. (1997). Equal ratings, but separate meanings: Stereotypes and the construal of traits. *Journal of Personality and Social Psychology, 72,* 720–734.

Kupersmidt, J. B., DeRosier, M. E., & Patterson, C. P. (1995). Similarity as the basis for children's friendships: The roles of sociometric status, aggressive and withdrawn behavior, academic achievement and demographic characteristics. *Journal of Social and Personal Relationships, 12,* 439–452.

Kurdek, L. A. (1992). Relationship stability and relationship satisfaction in cohabiting gay and lesbian couples: A prospective longitudinal test of the contextual and interdependence models. *Journal of Social and Personal Relationships, 9,* 125–142.

Kurdek, L. A. (1999). The nature and predictors of the trajectory of change in marital quality for husbands and wives over the first 10 years of marriage. *Developmental Psychology, 35,* 1283–1296.

Kurdek, L. A. (2000). Attractions and constraints as determinants of relationship commitment: Longitudinal evidence from gay, lesbian, and heterosexual couples. *Personal Relationships, 7,* 245–262.

Kurdek, L. A., & Schmitt, J. P. (1986). Relationship quality of partners in heterosexual married, heterosexual cohabiting, and gay and lesbian relationships. *Journal of Personality and Social Psychology, 51,* 711–720.

LaBrie, J., & Earleywine, M. (2000). Sexual risk behaviors and alcohol: Higher base rates revealed using the unmatched-count technique. *Journal of Sex Research, 37,* 321–326.

Laird, J. (1974). Self-attribution of emotion: The effects of expressive behavior on the quality of emotional experience. *Journal of Personality and Social Psychology, 29,* 475–486.

Lampen, D., & Lampen, J. (2009). Facilitating a mutual deescalation process: Quakers and the Peace and Reconciliation Group in Northern Ireland. In European Centre for Conflict Prevention, *People Building Peace II.* Retrieved from http://www.peoplebuildingpeace.org/thestories/article.php?id=141&typ=theme&pid=32.

Lang, F., & Heckhausen, J. (2001). Perceived control over development and subjective well-being: Differential benefits across adulthood. *Journal of Personality and Social Psychology, 81,* 509–523.

Langer, E. (1975). The illusion of control. *Journal of Personality and Social Psychology, 32,* 311–328.

Langlois, J. H., Kalakanis, L., Rubenstein, A. J., Larson, A., Hallam, M., & Smoot, M. (2000). Maxims or myths of beauty? A meta-analytic and theoretical review. *Psychological Bulletin, 126,* 390–423.

Langlois, J. H., Ritter, J. M., Roggman, L. A., & Vaughn, L. S. (1991). Facial diversity and infant preferences for attractive faces. *Developmental Psychology, 27,* 79–84.

Langlois, J. H., & Roggman, L. A. (1990). Attractive faces are only average. *Psychological Science, 1,* 115–121.

LaPiere, R. T. (1934). Attitudes vs. actions. *Social Forces, 13,* 230–237.

Laplace, A. C., Chermack, S. T., & Taylor, S. P. (1994). Effects of alcohol and drinking experience on human physical aggression. *Personality and Social Psychology Bulletin, 20,* 439–444.

Laroche, M., Kim, C., Hui, M. K., & Tomiuk, M. A. (1998). Test of nonlinear relationships between linguistic acculturation and ethnic identification. *Journal of Cross-Cultural Psychology, 29,* 418–433.

Larson, J. R., Foster-Fishman, P. G., & Keys, C. B. (1994). Discussion of shared and unshared information in decision-making groups. *Journal of Personality and Social Psychology, 67,* 446–461.

Lassiter, G., Geers, A., Handley, I., Weiland, P., & Munhall, P. (2002). Videotaped interrogations and confessions: A simple change in camera perspective alters verdicts in simulated trials. *Journal of Applied Psychology, 87,* 867–874.

Lassiter, G., Geers, A., Munhall, P., Ploutz-Snyder, R., & Breitenbecher, D. (2002). Illusory causation: Why it occurs. *Psychological Science, 13,* 299–305.

Lassiter, G., & Irvine, A. (1986). Videotaped confessions: The impact of camera point on view of judgments of coercion. *Journal of Applied Social Psychology, 16,* 268–276.

Latané, B. (1981). The psychology of social impact. *American Psychologist, 36,* 343–356.

Latané, B., & Darley, J. M. (1968). Group inhibition of bystander intervention in emergencies. *Journal of Personality and Social Psychology, 10,* 215–221.

Latané, B., & Darley, J. M. (1970). *The Unresponsive bystander: Why doesn't he help?* Upper Saddle River, NJ: Prentice-Hall.

Latané, B., & Nida, S. (1981). Ten years of research on group size and helping. *Psychological Bulletin, 89,* 308–324.

Latané, B., Liu, J. H., Nowak, A., Bonevento, M., & Zhang, L. (1995). Distance matters: Physical space and social impact. *Personality and Social Psychology Bulletin, 21,* 795–805.

Latané, B., & Rodin, J. (1969). A lady in distress: Inhibiting effects of friends and strangers on bystander intervention. *Journal of Experimental Social Psychology*, 5, 189–202.

Latané, B., Williams, K., & Harkins, S. (1979). Many hands make light the work: The causes and consequences of social loafing. *Journal of Personality and Social Psychology*, 37, 822–832.

Le Bon, G (1896). The crowd: a study of the popular mind. Retrieved from http://socserv.socsci.mcmaster.ca/~econ/ugcm/3ll3/lebon/Crowds.pdf.

Le, B., & Agnew, C. R. (2003). Commitment and its theorized determinants: A meta-analysis of the investment model. *Personal Relationships*, 10, 37–57.

Leach, C. W., Spears, R., Branscombe, N. R., & Doosje, B. (2003). Malicious pleasure: Schadenfreude at the suffering of another group. *Journal of Personality and Social Psychology*, 84, 932–943.

Leader, T., Mullen, B., & Abrams, D. (2007). Without mercy: The immediate impact of group size on lynch mob atrocity. *Personality and Social Psychology Bulletin*, 33, 1340–1352.

Leahey, T.H. (2004). *A history of psychology: Main currents in psychological thought*, 6th ed. Upper Saddle River, NJ: Prentice-Hall.

Leary, M., Tchividijian, L., & Kraxberger, B. (1994). Self-presentation can be hazardous to your health: Impression management and health risk. *Health Psychology*, 13, 461–470.

Leary, M. R., & Jones, J. L. (1993). The social psychology of tanning and sunscreen use: Self-presentational motives as a predictor of health risk. *Journal of Applied Social Psychology*, 23, 1390–1406.

Ledgerwood, A., & Chaiken, S. (2007). Priming us and them: Automatic assimilation and contrast in group attitudes. *Journal of Personality and Social Psychology*, 93, 940–956.

Lee, F., Hallahan, M., & Herzog, T. (1996). Explaining real-life events: How culture and domain shape attributions. *Personality and Social Psychology Bulletin*, 22, 732–741.

Lee, F., Peterson, C., & Tiedens, L. (2004). Mea culpa: Predicting stock prices from organizational attributions. *Personality and Social Psychology Bulletin*, 30, 1636–1649.

Lee, J. A. (1988). *Love-styles*. In M. H. Barnes & R. J. Sternberg (Eds.). *The Psychology of Love* (pp. 38–67). New Haven, CT: Yale University Press.

Lee, L., & Ward, C. (1998). Ethnicity, idiocentrism-allocentrism, and intergroup attitudes. *Journal of Applied Psychology*, 28, 109–123.

Lee-Baggley, D., Preece, M., DeLongis, A., (2005). Coping with interpersonal stress: Role of big five traits. *Journal of Personality*. 73(5), 1141–1180.

Leets, L. , & Giles, H. (1997). Words as weapons: When do they wound? Investigations of harmful speech. *Human Communication Research* , 24, 260–301.

Legault, L., Green-Demers, I., Grant, P., & Chung, J. (2007). On the self-regulation of implicit and explicit prejudice: A self-determination theory perspective. *Personality and Social Psychology Bulletin*, 33, 732–749.

Leippe, M., & Eisenstadt, D. (1994). Generalization of dissonance reduction: Decreasing prejudice through induced compliance. *Journal of Personality and Social Psychology*, 67, 395–413.

Lemieux, R., & Hale, J. L. (2002). Cross-sectional analysis of intimacy, passion, and commitment: Testing the assumptions of the triangular theory of love. *Psychological Reports*, 90, 1009–1014.

Lepper, M. R., Greene, D., & Nisbett, R. E. (1973). Undermining children's intrinsic interest with extrinsic reward: A test of the 'overjustification' hypothesis. *Journal of Personality and Social Psychology*, 28, 129–137.

Lerner, J., Small, D., & Loewenstein, G. (2004). Heart strings and purse strings: Carryover effects of emotions on economic decisions. *Psychological Science*, 15, 337–341.

Lerner, M. (1980). *The Belief in a Just World*. New York: Plenum Press.

Lerner, M. J., & Miller, D. T. (1978). Just world research and the attribution process: Looking back and ahead. *Psychological Bulletin*, 85, 1030–1051.

Levesque, M., & Kenny, D. (1993). Accuracy of behavioral predictions at zero acquaintance: A social relations analysis. *Journal of Personality and Social Psychology*, 65, 1178–1187.

Levin, S., & Sidanius, J. (1999). Social dominance and social identity in the United States and Israel: Ingroup favoritism or outgroup derogation? *Political Psychology*, 20, 99–126.

Levine, M., Prosser, A., Evans, D., & Reicher, S. (2005). Identity and emergency intervention: How social group membership and inclusiveness of group boundaries shape helping behavior. *Personality and Social Psychology Bulletin*, 31, 443–453.

Levine, R. V., Martinez, T. S., Brase, G., & Sorenson, K. (1994). Helping in 36 U.S. cities. *Journal of Personality and Social Psychology*, 67, 69–82.

Levine, R. V., Norenzayan, A., & Philbrick, K. (2001). Cross-cultural differences in helping strangers. *Journal of Cross-Cultural Psychology*, 32, 543–560.

Levine, R., Sato, S., Hashimoto, T., & Verma, J. (1995). Love and marriage in eleven cultures. *Journal of Cross-Cultural Psychology*, 26, 554–571.

Levy, B., & Langer, E. (1994). Aging free from negative stereotypes: Successful memory in China among the American deaf. *Journal of Personality and Social Psychology*, 66, 989–997.

Lewis, J. R. & Ozaki, R. (2009). *Amae & mardy*: Comparison of two emotion terms. *Journal of Cross-Cultural Psychology, Special Edition on Qualitative Methods*, 40(9), 917–934.

Li, N. P., Bailey, J. M., Kenrick, D. T., & Linsenmeier, J. A. W. (2002). The necessities and luxuries of mate preferences: Testing the tradeoffs. *Journal of Personality and Social Psychology*, 82, 947–955.

Li, N. P., & Kenrick, D. T. (2006). Sex similarities and differences in preferences for short-term mates: What, whether, and why. *Journal of Personality and Social Psychology*, 90, 468–489.

Liberman, A., & Chaiken, S. (1992). Defensive processing of personally relevant health messages. *Personality and Social Psychology Bulletin*, 18, 669–679.

Liberman, N., & Förster, J. (2000). Expression after suppression: A motivational explanation of postsuppressional rebound. *Journal of Personality and Social Psychology*, 79, 190–203.

Liberman, V., Samuels, S. M., & Ross, L. (2004). The name of the game: Predictive power of reputations versus situational labels in determining prisoner's dilemma game moves. *Personality and Social Psychology Bulletin*, 30, 1175–1185.

Lieberman, J., Solomon, S., Greenberg, J., & McGregor, H. (1999). A hot new way to measure aggression: Hot sauce allocation. *Aggressive Behavior*, 25, 331–348.

Lieberman, J. D. (2002). Head over the heart or heart over the head? Cognitive experiential self-theory and extralegal heuristics in juror decision making. *Journal of Applied Social Psychology*, 32, 2526–2553.

Liebkind, K. (2001). Acculturation. In R. Brown & S. L. Gaertner (Eds.), *Blackwell handbook of social psychology: Intergroup processes* (pp. 386–406). Malden, MA: Blackwell.

Lightdale, J. R., & Prentice, D. A. (1994). Rethinking sex differences in aggression: Aggressive behavior in the absence of social roles. *Personality and Social Psychology Bulletin*, 20, 34–44.

Lin, M. H., Kwan, V. S. Y., Cheung, A., & Fiske, S. T. (2005). Stereotype content model explains prejudice for an envied outgroup: Scale of anti–Asian American stereotypes. *Personality and Social Psychology Bulletin*, 31, 34–47.

Lind, E. A., Kanfer, R., & Earley, P. C. (1990).Voice, control, and procedural justice: Instrumental and noninstrumental concerns in fairness judgments. *Journal of Personality and Social Psychology*, 59, 952–959.

Lindsay, J. J., & Anderson, C. A. (2000). From antecedent conditions to violent actions: A general affective aggression model. *Personality and Social Psychology Bulletin, 26*, 533–547.

Lindskold, S., & Han, G. (1988). GRIT as a foundation for integrative bargaining. *Personality and Social Psychology Bulletin, 14*, 335–345.

Lindskold, S., Han, G., & Betz, B. (1986). Repeated persuasion in interpersonal conflict. *Journal of Personality and Social Psychology, 51*, 1183–1188.

Linville, P., Fischer, G., & Fischhoff, B. (1993). AIDS risk perceptions and decision biases. In J. B. Pryor & G. D. Reeder (Eds.), *The social psychology of HIV infection* (pp. 5–38). Hillsdale, NJ: Lawrence Erlbaum Associates.

Linville, P. W., Fischer, G. W., & Salovey, P. (1989). Perceived distributions of the characteristics of in-group and out-group members: Empirical evidence and a computer simulation. *Journal of Personality and Social Psychology, 57*, 165–188.

Linville, P. W., & Jones, E. E. (1980). Polarized appraisals of outgroup members. *Journal of Personality and Social Psychology, 38*, 689–703.

Linz, D. G., Donnerstein, E., & Penrod, S. (1984). The effects of multiple exposures to filmed violence against women. *Journal of Communication, 34*, 130–147.

Linz, D. G., Donnerstein, E., & Penrod, S. (1988). Effects of long-term exposure to violent and sexually degrading depictions of women. *Journal of Personality and Social Psychology, 55*, 758–768.

Lipkus, I. M., Dalbert, C., & Siegler, I. C. (1996). The importance of distinguishing the belief in a just world for self versus for others: Implications for psychological well-being. *Personality and Social Psychology Bulletin, 22*, 666–677.

Lips, H. (2008). *Sex and gender: An introduction* (6th ed). Boston: McGraw-Hill

Locksley, A., Borgida, E., Brekke, N., & Hepburn, C. (1980). Sex stereotypes and social judgment. *Journal of Personality and Social Psychology, 39*, 821–831.

Loeber, R., & Hay, D. (1997). Key issues in the development of aggression and violence from childhood to early adulthood. *Annual Review of Psychology, 48*, 371–410.

Loftin, C., McDowall, D., Wiersema, B., & Cottey, T. J. (1991). Effects of restrictive licensing of handguns on homicide and suicide in the District of Columbia. *New England Journal of Medicine, 325*, 1615–1620.

Loftus, E., & Palmer, J. (1974). Reconstruction of automobile destruction: An example of the interaction between language and memory. *Journal of Verbal Learning & Verbal Behavior, 13*, 585–589.

Loftus, E., & Pickrell, J. (1995). The formation of false memories. *Psychiatric Annals, 25*, 720–725.

Lord, C., Scott, K., Pugh, M., & Desforges, D. (1997). Leakage beliefs and the correspondence bias. *Personality and Social Psychology Bulletin, 23*, 824–836.

Lord, C. G., Ross, L., & Lepper, M. R. (1979). Biased assimilation and attitude polarization: The effects of prior theories on subsequently considered evidence. *Journal of Personality and Social Psychology, 37*, 2098–2109.

Lore, R. K., & Schultz, L. A. (1993). Control of human aggression: A comparative perspective. *American Psychologist, 48*, 16–25.

Lorenz, K. (1966). *On Aggression*. New York: Harcourt, Brace & World.

Lorenz, K. (1974). *Civilized Man's Eight Deadly Sins*. San Diego, CA: Harcourt Brace.

Lott, A. J., & Lott, B. E. (1974). The role of reward in the formation of positive interpersonal attitudes. In T. L. Huston (Ed.), *Foundations of interpersonal attraction* (pp. 171–189). New York: Academic Press.

Lowe, M. D. (1990, October). Alternatives to the automobile: Transport for livable cities. *Worldwatch Paper 98*. Washington, DC: Worldwatch Institute.

Lowery, B. S., Unzueta, M. M., Knowles, E. D., & Goff, P. A. (2006). Concern for the in-group and opposition to affirmative action. *Journal of Personality and Social Psychology, 90*, 961–974.

Lucker, G. W., Rosenfield, D., Sikes, J., & Aronson, E. (1976). Performance in the interdependent classroom: A field study. *American Educational Research Journal, 13*, 115–123.

Luo, S., & Klohnen, E. C. (2005). Assortative mating and marital quality in newlyweds: A couple-centered approach. *Journal of Personality and Social Psychology, 88*, 304–326.

Lupton, D. (1995). *The imperative of health: Public health and the regulated body*. London: Sage.

Luthar, S., & Latendresse, S. (2005). Comparable 'risks' at the socioeconomic status extremes: Preadolescents' perceptions of parenting. *Development and Psychopathology, 17*, 207–230.

Lydon, J. E., Fitzsimons, G. M., & Naidoo, L. (2003). Devaluation versus enhancement of attractive alternatives: A critical test using the calibration paradigm. *Personality and Social Psychology Bulletin, 29*, 349–359.

Lynn, M., & Latané, B. (1984). The psychology of restaurant tipping. *Journal of Applied Social Psychology, 14*, 549–561.

Lynn, M., & Oldenquist, A. (1986). Egoistic and nonegoistic motives in social dilemmas. *American Psychologist, 41*, 529–534.

Lyons, A., & Kashima, Y. (2003). How are stereotypes maintained through communication? The influence of stereotype sharedness. *Journal of Personality and Social Psychology, 85*, 989–1005.

Lyttle, Jim (2001). The effectiveness of humor in persuasion: The case of business ethics training. *Journal of General Psychology. Special Issue: Humor and laughter. 128(2)*, 206–216.

Ma, Z. (2007). Conflict management styles as indicators of behavioral pattern in business negotiation: The impact of contextualism in two countries. *International Journal of Conflict Management, 18*, 260–279.

Maass, A., Cadinu, M., Guarnieri, G., & Grasselli, A. (2003). Sexual harassment under social identity threat: The computer harassment paradigm. *Journal of Personality and Social Psychology, 85*, 853–870.

Maass, A., & Clark, R. D. (1984). Hidden impact of minorities: Fifteen years of minority influence research. *Psychological Bulletin, 95*, 428–450.

MacDonald, G., & Jessica, M. (2006). Family approval as a constraint in dependency regulation: Evidence from Australia and Indonesia. *Personal Relationships, 13*, 183–194.

MacDonald, G., Zanna, M. P., & Holmes, J. G. (2000). An experimental test of the role of alcohol in relationship conflict. *Journal of Experimental Social Psychology, 36*, 182–193.

MacDonald, T., MacDonald, G., Zanna, M., & Fong, G. (2000). Alcohol, sexual arousal, and intentions to use condoms in young men: Applying alcohol myopia theory to risky sexual behavior. *Health Psychology, 19*, 290–298.

MacDonald, T., Zanna, M., & Fong, G. (1995). Decision making in altered states: Effects of alcohol on attitudes toward drinking and driving. *Journal of Personality and Social Psychology, 68*, 973–985.

MacDonald, T. K., Fong, Zanna, & Martineau (2000). Alcohol myopia and condom use: Can alcohol intoxication be associated with more prudent behavior? *Journal of Personality and Social Psychology. 78(4)*, 605–619.

MacDonald, T. K., & Hynie, M. (2008). Ambivalence and unprotected sex: Failure to predict sexual activity and decreased condom use. *Journal of Applied Social Psychology, 38(4)*, 1092–1107.

MacDonald, T. K. & Martineau, A. M. (2002). Self-esteem, mood, and intentions to use condoms: When does low self-esteem lead to risky health behaviors? *Journal of Experimental Social Psychology. 38*(3), 299–306.

MacDonald, T. K. & Ross, M. (1997). Assessing the accuracy of predictions about dating relationships: How and why do lovers' predictions differ from those made by observers? *Personality and Social Psychological Bulletin, 25*, 1417–1429.

MacDonald, T. K., & Ross, M. (1999). Assessing the accuracy of predictions about dating relationships: How and why do lovers' predictions differ from those made by observers? *Personality and Social Psychology Bulletin, 25*, 1417–1429.

MacDonald, T. K., Zanna, M. P., & Fong, G. T. (1996). Why common sense goes out the window: Effects of alcohol on intentions to use condoms.*Personality and Social Psychology Bulletin, 22*, 763–775.

MacIntosh, H., Reissing, E. D., & Andruff, H. (2010). Same-sex marriage in Canada: The impact of legal marriage on the first cohort of gay and lesbian Canadians to wed. *Canadian Journal of Human Sexuality, 19*, 79–90.

Mackie, D. M. (1987). Systematic and nonsystematic processing of majority and minority persuasive communications. *Journal of Personality and Social Psychology, 53*, 41–52.

Mackie, D. M., Gastardo-Conaco, M. C., & Skelly, J. J. (1992). Knowledge of the advocated position and the processing of in-group and out-group persuasive messages. *Personality and Social Psychology Bulletin, 18*, 145–151.

Mackie, D. M., & Worth, L. T. (1989). Processing deficits and the mediation of positive affect in persuasion. *Journal of Personality and Social Psychology, 57*, 27–40.

MacLeod, C., & Campbell, L. (1992). Memory accessibility and probability judgments: An experimental evaluation of the availability heuristic. *Journal of Personality and Social Psychology, 63*, 890–902.

MacNeil, M. and Sherif, M. (1976). Norm change over subject generations as a function of arbitrariness of perceived norms. *Journal of Personality and Social Psychology, 34*, 762–73.

Macrae, C. N., Bodenhausen, G. V., & Milne, A. B. (1998). Saying no to unwanted thoughts: Self-focus and the regulation of mental life. *Journal of Personality and Social Psychology, 74*, 578–589.

Madden, T., Ellen, P., & Ajzen, I. (1992). A comparison of the theory of planned behavior and the theory of reasoned action. *Personality and Social Psychology Bulletin, 18*, 3–9.

Maddux, J. E., & Rogers, R. W. (1980). Effects of source expertness, physical attractiveness, and supporting arguments on persuasion: A case of brains over beauty. *Journal of Personality and Social Psychology, 39*, 235–244.

Maddux, W. W., Galinsky, A. D., Cuddy, A. J. C., & Polifroni, M. (2008). When being a model minority is good . . . and bad: Realistic threat explains negativity toward Asian Americans. *Personality and Social Psychology Bulletin, 34*, 74–89.

Madon, S., Jussim, L., & Eccles, J. (1997). In search of the powerful self-fulfilling prophecy. *Journal of Personality and Social Psychology, 72*, 791–809.

Madon, S., Smith, A., Jussim, L., Russell, D., Eccles, J., Palumbo, P., et al. (2001). Am I as you see me or do you see me as I am? Self-fulfilling prophecies and self-verification. *Personality and Social Psychology Bulletin, 27*, 1214–1224.

Maeda, E., & Ritchie, L. D. (2003). The concept of Shinyuu in Japan: A replication of and comparison to Cole and Bradac's study on U.S. friendship. *Journal of Social and Personal Relationships, 20*, 579–598.

Mael, F. A., & Alderks, C. E. (1993). Leadership team cohesion and subordinate work unit morale and performance. *Military Psychology, 5*, 141–158.

Maheswaran, D., & Chaiken, S. (1991). Promoting systematic processing in low-motivation settings: Effect of incongruent information on processing and judgment. *Journal of Personality and Social Psychology, 61*, 13–25.

Main, M. & Solomon, J. (1986). Discovery of an insecure-disorganized/disoriented attachment pattern. Chapter in T.B. Brazelton & Yogman, M. W. (Eds.), *Affective development in infancy.* (pp. 95–124). Westport, CT, US: Ablex Publishing.

Major, B., Gramzow, R. H., McCoy, S. K., Levin, S., Schmader, T., & Sidanius, J. (2002). Perceiving personal discrimination: The role of group status and legitimizing ideology. *Journal of Personality and Social Psychology, 82*, 269–282.

Major, B., Spencer, S., Schmader, T., Wolfe, C., & Crocker, J. (1998). Coping with negative stereotypes about intellectual performance: The role of psychological disengagement. *Personality and Social Psychology Bulletin, 24*, 34–50.

Malamuth, N. M. (1983). Factors associated with rape as predictors of laboratory aggression against women. *Journal of Personality and Social Psychology, 45*, 432–442.

Malamuth, N. M., & Check, J. V. (1985). The effects of aggressive pornography on beliefs in rape myths: Individual differences. *Journal of Research in Personality, 19*, 299–320.

Malamuth, N. M., Check, J. V., & Briere, J. (1986). Sexual arousal in response to aggression: Ideological, aggressive, and sexual correlates. *Journal of Personality and Social Psychology, 50*, 330–340.

Malamuth, N. M., Linz, D., Heavey, C. L., Barnes, G., & Acker, M. (1995). Using the confluence model of sexual aggression to predict men's conflict with women: A 10-year follow-up study. *Journal of Personality and Social Psychology, 69*, 353–369.

Malinosky-Rummell, R., & Hansen, D. J. (1993). Long-term consequences of childhood physical abuse. *Psychological Bulletin, 114*, 68–79.

Malle, B., & Knobe, J. (1997). Which behaviors do people explain? A basic actor-observer asymmetry. *Journal of Personality and Social Psychology, 72*, 288–304.

Malle, B., & Pearce, G. (2001). Attention to behavioral events during interaction: Two actor-observer gaps and three attempts to close them. *Journal of Personality and Social Psychology, 81*, 278–294.

Malpass, R. S., & Devine, P. G. (1981). Eyewitness identification: Lineup instructions and the absence of the offender. *Journal of Applied Psychology, 66*, 482–489.

Manis, M., Shedler, J., Jonides, J., & Nelson, T. (1993). Availability heuristic in judgments of set size and frequency of occurrence. *Journal of Personality and Social Psychology, 65*, 448–457.

Manly, P.C., McMahon, R. J., Bradley, C. F. & Davidson, P.O. (1982). Depressive Attributional Style and Depression Following Childbirth. *Journal of Abnormal Psychology, 91*(4), pp. 245–254.

Manning, R., Levine, M.,& Collins, A. (2008). The legacy of the 38 witnesses and the importance of getting history right. *American Psychologist, 63*(6), 562–563.

Manucia, G. K., Baumann, D. J., & Cialdini, R. B. (1984). Mood influences on helping: Direct effects or side effects? *Journal of Personality and Social Psychology, 46*, 357–364.

Marcus-Newhall, A., Pedersen, W. C., Carlson, M., & Miller, N. (2000). Displaced aggression is alive and well: A meta-analytic review. *Journal of Personality and Social Psychology, 78*, 670–689.

Mares, M., & Woodard, E. (2005). Positive effects of television on children's social interactions: A meta-analysis. *Media Psychology, 7*, 301–322.

Marin, B. V., Marin, G., Perez-Stable, E. J., Otero-Sabogal, R., & Sabogal, F. (1990). Cultural differences in attitudes toward smoking: Developing messages using the theory of reasoned action. *Journal of Applied Social Psychology, 20*, 478–493.

Marin, G., & Marin, B.V. (1991). Research with Hispanic populations. In *Applied social research methods series* (Vol. 23). Newbury Park, CA: Sage.

Marjanovic, Z., Greenglass, E.R., Struthers, C.W., & Faye, C. (2009). Helping following natural disasters: A social-motivational analysis. *Journal of Applied Social Psychology, 39*, 2604–2625.

Marks, G., Graham, J. W., & Hansen, W. B. (1992). Social projection and social conformity in adolescent alcohol use: A longitudinal analysis. *Personality and Social Psychology Bulletin, 18*, 96–101.

Markus, H. (1977). Self-schemata and processing information about the self. *Journal of Personality and Social Psychology, 35*, 63–78.

Markus, H. (1978). The effect of mere presence on social facilitation: An unobtrusive test. *Journal of Experimental Social Psychology, 14*, 389–397.

Markus, H., Uchida, Y., Omoregie, H., Townsend, S., & Kitayama, S. (2006). Going for the gold: Models of agency in Japanese and American contexts. *Psychological Science, 17*, 103–112.

Markus, H. R., & Kitayama, S. (1991). Culture and the self: Implications for cognition, emotion, and motivation. *Psychological Review, 98*, 224–253.

Markus, H. R., & Kitayama, S. (1994). A collective fear of the collective: Implications for selves and theories of selves. *Personality and Social Psychology Bulletin, 20*, 568–579.

Marlowe, C. M., Schneider, S. L., & Nelson, C. E. (1996). Gender and attractiveness biases in hiring decisions: Are more experienced managers less biased? *Journal of Applied Psychology, 81*, 11–21.

Marques, J., Abrams, D., Paez, D., & Martinez-Taboada, C. (1998). The role of categorization and in-group norms in judgments of groups and their members. *Journal of Personality and Social Psychology, 75*, 976–988.

Marsh, H., Kong, C., & Hau, K. (2000). Longitudinal multilevel models of the big-fish-little-pond effect on academic self-concept: Counterbalancing contrast and reflected-glory effects in Hong Kong schools. *Journal of Personality and Social Psychology, 78*, 337–349.

Marsh, K., Hart-O'Rourke, D., & Julka, D. (1997). The persuasive effects of verbal and nonverbal information in a context of value relevance. *Personality and Social Psychology Bulletin, 23*, 563–579.

Marteau, T. (1989). Framing of information: Its influence upon decisions of doctors and patients. *British Journal of Social Psychology, 28*, 89–94.

Martens, A., Kosloff, S., Greenberg, J., Landau, M. J., & Schmader, T. (2007). Killing begets killing: Evidence from a bug-killing paradigm that initial killing fuels subsequent killing. *Personality and Social Psychology Bulletin, 33*, 1251–1264.

Martin, C. L., & Little, J. K. (1990). The relation of gender understanding to children's sex-typed preferences and gender stereotypes. *Child Development, 61*, 1427–1439.

Martin, G. B., & Clark, R. D. (1982). Distress crying in neonates: Species and peer specificity. *Developmental Psychology, 18*, 3–9.

Martin, K., & Leary, M. (1999). Would you drink after a stranger? The influence of self presentational motives on willingness to take a health risk. *Personality and Social Psychology Bulletin, 25*, 1092–1100.

Martin, P. Y., Laing, J., Martin, R., & Mitchell, M. (2005). Caffeine, cognition, and persuasion: Evidence for caffeine increasing the systematic processing of persuasive messages. *Journal of Applied Social Psychology, 35*, 160–182.

Martin, R. (1996). Minority influence and argument generation. *British Journal of Social Psychology, 35*, 91–103.

Martino, S., Collins, R., Kanouse, D., Elliott, M., & Berry, S. (2005). Social cognitive processes mediating the relationship between exposure to television's sexual content and adolescents' sexual behavior. *Journal of Personality and Social Psychology, 89*, 914–924.

Martz, J. M., Verette, J., Arriaga, X. B., Slovik, L. F., Cox, C. L., & Rusbult, C. E. (1998). Positive illusion in close relationships. *Personal Relationships, 5*, 159–181.

Maruyama, G., Fraser, S. C., & Miller, N. (1982). Personal responsibility and altruism in children. *Journal of Personality and Social Psychology, 42*, 658–664.

Masicampo, E., & Baumeister, R. (2008). Toward a physiology of dual-process reasoning and judgment: Lemonade, willpower, and expensive rule-based analysis. *Psychological Science, 19*, 255–260.

Maslach, C., Santee, R. T., & Wade, C. (1987). Individuation, gender role, and dissent: Personality mediators of situational forces. *Journal of Personality and Social Psychology, 53*, 1088–1093.

Masuda, T., Ellsworth, P., Mesquita, B., Leu, J., Tanida, S., & Veerdonk, E. (2008). Placing the face in context: Cultural differences in the perception of facial emotion. *Journal of Personality and Social Psychology, 94*, 365–381.

Mathews, K. E., & Canon, L. K. (1975). Environmental noise level as a determinant of helping behavior. *Journal of Personality and Social Psychology, 32*, 571–577.

Matsumoto, D., & Juang, L. (2008). *Culture and psychology* (4th ed.). Belmont, CA: Thomson Wadsworth.

Matsumoto, D., & Yoo, S. (2006). Toward a new generation of cross-cultural research. *Perspectives on Psychological Science, 1*, 234–250.

Matthews, K. A., Batson, C. D., Horn, J., & Rosenman, R. H. (1981). "Principles in his nature which interest him in the fortune of others...": The heritability of empathic concern for others. *Journal of Personality, 49*, 237–247.

Mayer, J., & Hanson, E. (1995). Mood-congruent judgment over time. *Personality and Social Psychology Bulletin, 21*, 237–244.

Mazur, A., & Booth, A. (1998). Testosterone and dominance in men. *Behavioral and Brain Sciences, 21*, 353–397.

Mazzella, R., & Feingold, A. (1994). The effects of physical attractiveness, race, socioeconomic status, and gender of defendants and victims on judgments of mock jurors: A meta-analysis. *Journal of Applied Social Psychology, 24*, 1315–1344.

McAndrew, F. T., Akande, A., Bridgstock, R., Mealey, L., Gordon, S. C., Scheib, J. E., et al. (2000). A multicultural study of stereotyping in English-speaking countries. *The Journal of Social Psychology, 140*, 487–502.

McArthur, L. (1980). Illusory causation and illusory correlation: Two epistemological accounts. *Personality and Social Psychology Bulletin, 6*, 507–519.

McArthur, L. Z., & Berry, D. S. (1987). Cross-cultural agreement in perceptions of babyfaced adults. *Journal of Cross-Cultural Psychology, 18*, 165–192.

McAuliffe, T., DiFranceisco, W., & Reed, B. (2007). Effects of question format and collection mode on the accuracy of retrospective surveys of health risk behavior: A comparison with daily sexual activity diaries. *Health Psychology, 26*, 60–67.

McCall, M., & Belmont, H. J. (1996). Credit card insignia and restaurant tipping: Evidence for an associative link. *Journal of Applied Psychology, 81*, 609–613.

McClure, S., Laibson, D., Loewenstein, G., & Cohen, J. (2004). Separate neural systems value immediate and delayed monetary rewards. *Science, 306*, 503–507.

McConahay, J. (1986). *Modern racism, ambivalence, and the Modern Racism Scale. Prejudice, Discrimination, and Racism* (pp. 91–125). San Diego, CA: Academic Press.

McConnell, A. R., Sherman, S. J., & Hamilton, D. L. (1994). Illusory correlation in the perception of groups: An extension of the distinctiveness-based account. *Journal of Personality and Social Psychology, 67*, 414–429.

McCullough, M. E., Rachal, K. C., Sandage, S. J., Worthington, E. L. J., Brown, S. W., & Hight, T. L. (1998). Interpersonal forgiving in close relationships: II. Theoretical elaboration and measurement. *Journal of Personality and Social Psychology, 75*, 1586–1603.

McCullough, M. E., Worthington, E. L. J., & Rachal, K. C. (1997). Interpersonal forgiving in close relationships. *Journal of Personality and Social Psychology, 73*, 321–336.

McDougall, W. (1920). *The group mind.* London: Cambridge University Press.

McGillicuddy, N. B., Welton, G. L., & Pruitt, D. G. (1987). Thirdparty intervention: A field experiment comparing three different models. *Journal of Personality and Social Psychology, 53*, 104–112.

McGonagle, K. A., Kessler, R. C., & Schilling, E. A. (1992). The frequency and determinants of marital disagreements in a community sample. *Journal of Social and Personal Relationships, 9*, 507–524.

McGovern, L. P., Ditzian, J. L., & Taylor, S. P. (1975). The effect of one positive reinforcement on helping with cost. *Bulletin of the Psychonomic Society, 5*, 421–423.

McGuire, W. (1964). *Inducing resistance to persuasion: Some contemporary approaches.* In L. Berkowitz (Ed.), *Advances in Experimental Social Psychology,* Vol. 1 (pp. 191–229). New York: Academic Press.

McKenna, K. Y. A., & Bargh, J. A. (1998). Coming out in the age of the Internet: Identity 'demarginalization' through virtual group participation. *Journal of Personality and Social Psychology, 75*, 681–694.

McKenna, K. Y. A., & Bargh, J. A. (2000). Plan 9 from cyberspace: The implications of the Internet for personality and social psychology. *Personality and Social Psychology Review, 4*, 57–75.

McKenna, K. Y. A., & Green, A. S. (2002). Virtual group dynamics. *Group Dynamics, 6*, 116–127.

McKillip, J., & Reidel, S. L. (1983). External validity of matching on physical attractiveness for same and opposite sex couples. *Journal of Applied Social Psychology, 13*, 328–337.

McNulty, J. K., & Karney, B. R. (2001). Attributions in marriage: Integrating specific and global evaluations of a relationship. *Personality and Social Psychology Bulletin, 27*, 943–955.

McNulty, J. K., & Karney, B. R. (2004). Positive expectations in the early years of marriage: Should couples expect the best or brace for the worst? *Journal of Personality and Social Psychology, 86*, 729–743.

Mealey, L., Bridgstock, R., & Townsend, G. C. (1999). Symmetry and perceived facial attractiveness: A monozygotic co-twin comparison. *Journal of Personality and Social Psychology, 76*, 151–158.

Medvec, V., & Savitsky, K. (1997). When doing better means feeling worse: The effects of categorical cutoff points on counterfactual thinking and satisfaction. *Journal of Personality and Social Psychology, 72*, 1284–1296.

Meeus, W. H. J., & Raaijmakers, Q. A. W. (1995). Obedience in modern society: The Utrecht studies. *Journal of Social Issues, 51*, 155–175.

Meeus, W. H. J. & Raaijmakers, Q. A. W. (1986). Administrative obedience: Carrying out orders to use psychological-administrative violence. *European Journal of Social Psychology, 16*, 311–324.

Mehrabian, A., & Epstein, N. (1972). A measure of emotional empathy. *Journal of Personality, 40*, 525–543.

Meissner, C. A., & Brigham, J. C. (2001). Thirty years of investigating the own-race bias in memory for faces: A meta-analytic review. *Psychology, Public Policy, and Law, 7*, 3–35.

Meleshko, K. G., & Alden, L. E. (1993). Anxiety and self-disclosure: Toward a motivational model. *Journal of Personality and Social Psychology, 64*, 1000–1009.

Mendes, W. B., Major, B., McCoy, S., & Blascovich, J. (2008). How attributional ambiguity shapes physiological and emotional responses to social rejection and acceptance. *Journal of Personality and Social Psychology, 94*, 278–291.

Mendez, L. M. R., & Crawford, K. M. (2002). Gender-role stereotyping and career aspirations: A comparison of gifted early adolescent boys and girls. *Journal of Secondary Gifted Education, 13*, 96–107.

Menon, T., Morris, M., Chiu, C., & Hong, Y. (1999). Culture and the construal of agency: Attribution to individual versus group dispositions. *Journal of Personality and Social Psychology, 76*, 701–717.

Mesquita, B., Frijda, N. H., & Scherer, K. R. (1997). Culture and emotion: Theoretical and methodological issues. In J. W. Berry, M. H. Segall, & C. Kagitçibasi (Eds.), *Handbook of cross-cultural psychology,* Vol. 2 (pp. 255–298). Boston: Allyn & Bacon.

Meyer, J. P., & Mulherin, A. (1980). From attribution to helping: An analysis of the mediating effects of affect and expectancy. *Journal of Personality and Social Psychology, 39*, 201–210.

Meyerowitz, B., & Chaiken, S. (1987). The effect of message framing on breast self-examination attitudes, intentions, and behavior. *Journal of Personality and Social Psychology, 52*, 500–510.

Meyers, S. A., & Berscheid, E. (1997). The language of love: The difference a preposition makes. *Personality and Social Psychology Bulletin, 23*, 347–362.

Mickelson, K. D., Kessler, R. C., & Shaver, P. R. (1997). Adult attachment in a nationally representative sample. *Journal of Personality and Social Psychology, 73*, 1092–1106.

Miles, D. R., & Carey, G. (1997). Genetic and environmental architecture on human aggression. *Journal of Personality and Social Psychology, 72*, 207–217.

Milgram, S. (1963). Behavioral study of obedience. *The Journal of Abnormal and Social Psychology, 67*, 371–378.

Milgram, S. (1970). The experience of living in cities. *Science, 167*, 1461–1468.

Milgram, S. (1974). *Obedience to Authority: An Experimental View.* New York: Harper Collins.

Milhausen, R. R. & Herold, E. S. (2001). Reconceptualizing the sexual double standard. *Journal of Psychology and Human Sexuality, 13(2)*, 63–83.

Millar, M., & Millar, K. (1996). The effects of direct and indirect experience on affective and cognitive responses and the attitude—behavior relation. *Journal of Experimental Social Psychology, 32*, 561–579.

Miller, A., Ashton, W., & Mishal, M. (1990). Beliefs concerning the features of constrained behavior: A basis for the fundamental attribution error. *Journal of Personality and Social Psychology, 59*, 635–650.

Miller, A. G., Collins, B. E., & Brief, D. E. (1995). Perspectives on obedience to authority: The legacy of the Milgram experiments. *Journal of Social Issues, 51*, 1–19.

Miller, A. G., McHoskey, J. W., Bane, C. M., & Dowd, T. G. (1993). The attitude polarization phenomenon: Role of response measure, attitude extremity, and behavioral consequences of reported attitude change. *Journal of Personality and Social Psychology, 64*, 561–574.

Miller, D. T., & McFarland, C. (1987). Pluralistic ignorance: When similarity is interpreted as dissimilarity. *Journal of Personality and Social Psychology, 53*, 298–305.

Miller, D. T., & McFarland, C. (1991). When social comparison goes awry: The case of pluralistic ignorance. In J. Suls & T. A. Wills (Eds.), *Social Comparison: Contemporary Theory and Research* (pp. 287–313). Hillsdale, NJ: Erlbaum.

Miller, D. T., & Prentice, D. A. (1994). Collective errors and errors about the collective. *Personality and Social Psychology Bulletin, 20*, 541–550.

Miller, G., Tybur, J. M., & Jordan, B. D. (2007). Ovulatory cycle effects on tip earnings by lap dancers: Economic evidence for human estrus? *Evolution and Human Behavior, 28*, 375–381.

Miller, J. G. (1984). Culture and the development of everyday social explanation. *Journal of Personality and Social Psychology, 46*, 961–978.

Miller, J. G., & Bersoff, D. M. (1994). Cultural influences on the moral status of reciprocity and the discounting of endogenous motivation. *Personality and Social Psychology Bulletin, 20*, 592–602.

Miller, J. G., Bersoff, D. M., & Harwood, R. L. (1990). Perceptions of social responsibilities in India and in the United States: Moral imperatives or personal decisions? *Journal of Personality and Social Psychology, 58*, 33–47.

Miller, L. C. (1990). Intimacy and liking: Mutual influence and the role of unique relationships. *Journal of Personality and Social Psychology, 59*, 50–60.

Miller, P. A., & Eisenberg, N. (1988). The relation of empathy to aggressive and externalizing/antisocial behavior. *Psychological Bulletin, 103*, 324–344.

Miller, P. A., Eisenberg, N., Fabes, R. A., & Shell, R. (1996). Relations of moral reasoning and vicarious emotion to young children's prosocial behavior toward peers and adults. *Developmental Psychology, 32*, 210–219.

Miller, P. J. E., & Rempel, J. K. (2004). Trust and partner-enhancing attributions in close relationships. *Personality and Social Psychology Bulletin, 30*, 695–705.

Miller, R. S. (1997). Inattentive and contented: Relationship commitment and attention to alternatives. *Journal of Personality and Social Psychology, 73*, 758–766.

Mita, T., Dermer, M., & Knight, J. (1977). Reversed facial images and the mere-exposure hypothesis. *Journal of Personality and Social Psychology, 35*, 597–601.

Mitchell, J., Macrae, C., & Banaji, M. (2004). Encoding-specific effects of social cognition on the neural correlates of subsequent memory. *Journal of Neuroscience, 24*, 4912–4917.

Mitchell, J. P., Ames, D. L., Jenkins, A. C., & Banaji, M. R. (2008). Neural correlates of stereotype application. *Journal of Cognitive Neuroscience, 21*, 594–604.

Mo, F., Wong, T & Merrick, J. (2007). Adolescent lifestyle, sexual behavior and sexually transmitted infections (STI) in Canada. *International Journal on Disability and Human Development, 6(1)*, 53–60.

Modigliani, A., & Rochat, F. (1995). The role of interaction sequences and the timing of resistance in shaping obedience and defiance to authority. *Journal of Social Issues, 51*, 107–123.

Moghaddam, F. M., Ditto, B., & Taylor, D. M. (1990). Attitudes and attributions related to psychological symptomatology in Indian immigrant women. *Journal of Cross-Cultural Psychology, 36*, 380–395.

Mondschein, E. R., Adolph, K. E., & Tamis-LeMonda, C. S. (2000). Gender bias in mothers' expectations about infant crawling. *Journal of Experimental Child Psychology, 77*, 304–316.

Monin, B., & Miller, D. T. (2001). Moral credentials and the expression of prejudice. *Journal of Personality and Social Psychology, 81*, 33–43.

Monin, B., & Norton, M. (2003). Perceptions of a fluid consensus: Uniqueness bias, false consensus, false polarization, and pluralistic ignorance in a water conservation crisis. *Personality and Social Psychology Bulletin, 29*, 559–567.

Monteith, M. J. (1993). Self-regulation of prejudiced responses: Implications for progress in prejudice-reduction efforts. *Journal of Personality and Social Psychology, 65*, 469–485.

Monteith, M. J., Ashburn-Nardo, L., Voils, C. I., & Czopp, A. M. (2002). Putting the brakes on prejudice: On the development and operation of cues for control. *Journal of Personality and Social Psychology, 83*, 1029–1050.

Monteith, M. J., Sherman, J. W., & Devine, P. G. (1998). Suppression as a stereotype control strategy. *Personality and Social Psychology Review, 2*, 63–82.

Moreland, R. L., & Beach, S. R. (1992). Exposure effects in the classroom: The development of affinity among students. *Journal of Experimental Social Psychology, 28*, 255–276.

Moreland, R. L., & Zajonc, R. B. (1982). Exposure effects in person perception: Familiarity, similarity, and attraction. *Journal of Experimental Social Psychology, 18*, 395–415.

Morgan, S. E., Miller, J. K., & Arasaratnam, L. A. (2003). Similarities and differences between African Americans' and European Americans' attitudes, knowledge, and willingness to communicate about organ donation. *Journal of Applied Social Psychology, 33*, 693–715.

Mori, D., Chaiken, S., & Pliner, P. (1987). 'Eating lightly' and the self-presentation of femininity. *Journal of Personality and Social Psychology, 53*, 693–702.

Moriarty, T. (1975). Crime, commitment, and the responsive bystander: Two field experiments. *Journal of Personality and Social Psychology, 31*, 370–376.

Morris, M. W., & Peng, K. (1994). Culture and cause: American and Chinese attributions for social and physical events. *Journal of Personality and Social Psychology, 67*, 949–971.

Morris, M.W., Podolny, J.M., & Ariel, S. (2001). Culture, norms, and obligations: Cross-National differences in patterns of interpersonal norms and felt obligations toward coworkers. In *The Practice of Social Influence in Multiple Cultures*[ST1], 97–124.

Morrison, M., Morrison, T., & Franklin, R. (2009). Modern and old-fashioned homonegativity among samples of Canadian and American university students. *Journal of Cross-Cultural Psychology, 40*, 523–542.

Morrongiello, B., Corbett, M., & Bellissimo, A. (2008). 'Do as I say, not as I do': Family influences on children's safety and risk behaviors. *Health Psychology, 27*, 498–503.

Morrongiello, B.A. & Dawber, T. (2004). Identifying Factors that Relate to Children's Risk-Taking Decisions. *Canadian Journal of Behavioural Science/Revue canadienne des sciences du comportement, 36(4)*, 255–266.

Morry, M. M. (2005). Relationship satisfaction as a predictor of similarity ratings: A test of the attraction-similarity hypothesis. *Journal of Social and Personal Relationships, 22*, 561–584.

Morse, S., & Gergen, K. (1970). Social comparison, self-consistency, and the concept of self. *Journal of Personality and Social Psychology, 16*, 148–156.

Moscovici, S. (1976). *Social Influence and Social Change*. London: Academic Press.

Moscovici, S., Lage, E., & Naffrechoux, M. (1969). Influence of a consistent minority on the responses of a majority in a colour perception task. *Sociometry, 32*, 365–79.

Moscovici, S. & Personnaz, B. (1980). Studies in social influence: V. minority influence and conversion behaviour in a perceptual task. *Journal of Experimental Social Psychology, 16*, 270–82.

Moscovici, S., & Zavalloni, M. (1969). The group as a polarizer of attitudes. *Journal of Personality and Social Psychology, 12*, 125–135.

Moskowitz, G. B., Gollwitzer, P. M., Wasel, W., & Schaal, B. (1999). Preconscious control of stereotype activation through chronic egalitarian goals. *Journal of Personality and Social Psychology, 77*, 167–184.

Moss, M. K., & Page, R. A. (1972). Reinforcement and helping behavior. *Journal of Applied Social Psychology, 2*, 360–371.

Mucchi-Faina, A., Maass, A., & Volpato, C. (1991). Social influence: The role of originality. *European Journal of Social Psychology, 21*, 183–197.

Mueller, C. M., & Dweck, C. S. (1998). Intelligence praise can undermine motivation and performance. *Journal of Personality and Social Psychology, 75*, 33–52.

Mulder, L. B., van Dijk, E., De Cremer, D., & Wilke, H. A. M. (2006). Undermining trust and cooperation: The paradox of sanctioning systems in social dilemmas. *Journal of Experimental Social Psychology, 42*, 147–162.

Mullen, B. (1983). Operationalizing the effect of the group on the individual: A self-attention perspective. *Journal of Experimental Social Psychology, 19,* 295–322.

Mullen, B. (1986). Atrocity as a function of lynch mob composition: A self-attention perspective. *Personality and Social Psychology Bulletin, 12,* 187–197.

Mullen, B., & Copper, C. (1994). The relation between group cohesiveness and performance: An integration. *Psychological Bulletin, 115,* 210–227.

Mullen, B., & Hu, L. (1989). Perceptions of ingroup and outgroup variability: A meta-analytic integration. *Basic and Applied Social Psychology, 10,* 233–252.

Mullin, C. R., & Linz, D. (1995). Desensitization and resensitization to violence against women: Effects of exposure to sexually violent films on judgments of domestic violence victims. *Journal of Personality and Social Psychology, 69,* 449–459.

Munro, G. D., & Ditto, P. H. (1997). Biased assimilation, attitude polarization, and affect in reactions to stereotyped-relevant scientific information. *Personality and Social Psychology Bulletin, 23,* 636–653.

Murphy, C. M., & O'Farrell, T. J. (1996). Marital violence among alcoholics. *Current Directions in Psychological Science, 5,* 183–186.

Murphy, S., & Zajonc, R. (1993). Affect, cognition, and awareness: Affective priming with optimal and suboptimal stimulus exposures. *Journal of Personality and Social Psychology, 64,* 723–739.

Murray, S. L., & Holmes, J. G. (1996). The construction of relationship realities. In G. Fletcher & J. Fitness (Eds.), *Knowledge Structures and Interaction in Close Relationships: A Social Psychological Approach* (pp. 91–120). Hillsdale, NJ: Lawrence Erlbaum Associates, Inc.

Murray, S. L., Holmes, J. G., & Griffin, D. W. (1996). The benefits of positive illusions: Idealization and the construction of satisfaction in close relationships. *Journal of Personality and Social Psychology, 70,* 79–98.

Musick, M. A., & Wilson, J. (2003). Volunteering and depression: The role of psychological and social resources in different age groups. *Social Science and Medicine, 56,* 259–269.

Muskus, J. (2010). Iraq, Afghan veterans call for respect for Muslims: 'America, you gotta have our back.' Huffington Post, September 13, 2010. Retrieved from http://www.huffingtonpost.com/2010/09/13/veterans-muslims-respect-iraq-afghanistan_n_714646.html.

Mussweiler, T. (2006). Doing is for thinking! Stereotype activation by stereotypic movements. *Psychological Science, 17,* 17–21.

Mussweiler, T., & Rüter, K. (2003). What friends are for! The use of routine standards in social comparison. *Journal of Personality and Social Psychology, 85,* 467–481.

Mussweiler, T., & Strack, F. (2000). The use of category and exemplar knowledge in the solution of anchoring tasks. *Journal of Personality and Social Psychology, 78,* 1038–1052.

Mutterperl, J. A., & Sanderson, C. A. (2002). Mind over matter: Internalization of the thinness norm as a moderator of responsiveness to norm misperception education in college women. *Health Psychology, 21,* 519–523.

Myers, D. G., & Kaplan, M. F. (1976). Group-induced polarization in simulated juries. *Personality and Social Psychology Bulletin, 2,* 63–66.

Myers, J. E., Madathil, J., & Tingle, L. R. (2005). Marriage satisfaction and wellness in India and the United States: A preliminary comparison of arranged marriages and marriages of choice. *Journal of Counseling & Development, 83,* 183–190.

Nadler, A. (1987). Determinants of help seeking behaviour: The effects of helper's similarity, task centrality and recipient's self esteem. *European Journal of Social Psychology, 17,* 57–67.

Nadler, A., Altman, A., & Fisher, J. D. (1979). Helping is not enough: Recipient's reactions to aid as a function of positive and negative information about the self. *Journal of Personality, 47,* 615–628.

Nadler, A., & Fisher, J. D. (1986). The role of threat to self-esteem and perceived control in recipient reaction to help: Theory development and empirical validation. In L. Berkowitz (Ed.), *Advances in Experimental Social Psychology* (Vol. 19, pp. 81–121). Orlando, FL: Academic Press.

Nadler, A., Fisher, J. D., & Itzhak, S. B. (1983). With a little help from my friend: Effect of single or multiple act aid as a function of donor and task characteristics. *Journal of Personality and Social Psychology, 44,* 310–321.

Nadler, A., Goldberg, M., & Jaffe, Y. (1982). Effect of self-differentiation and anonymity in group on deindividuation. *Journal of Personality and Social Psychology, 42,* 1127–1136.

Nadler, A., Mayseless, O., Peri, N., & Chemerinski, A. (1985). Effects of opportunity to reciprocate and self-esteem on help-seeking behavior. *Journal of Personality, 53,* 23–35.

Nansel, T. R., Overpeck, M., Pilla, R. S., Ruan, W. J., Simons-Morton, B., & Scheidt, P. (2001). Bullying behaviors among US youth: Prevalence and association with psychosocial adjustment. *Journal of the American Medical Association, 285,* 2094–2100.

Nasco, S., & Marsh, K. (1999). Gaining control through counterfactual thinking. *Personality and Social Psychology Bulletin, 25,* 556–568.

Nattinger, A., Hoffmann, R., Howell-Pelz, A., & Goodwin, J. (1998). Effect of Nancy Reagan's mastectomy on choice of surgery for breast cancer by US women. *Journal of the American Medical Association, 279,* 762–766.

Neff, L. A., & Karney, B. R. (2005). To know you is to love you: The implications of global adoration and specific accuracy for marital relationships. *Journal of Personality and Social Psychology, 88,* 480–497.

Nelson, A. (2010). *Gender in Canada, 4th Ed.* Toronto: Pearson Education Canada.

Nemeth, C., & Chiles, C. (1988). Modelling courage: The role of dissent in fostering independence. *European Journal of Social Psychology, 18,* 275–280.

Nemeth, C., Mayseless, O., Sherman, J., & Brown, Y. (1990). Exposure to dissent and recall of information. *Journal of Personality and Social Psychology, 58,* 429–437.

Neuberg, S. L. (1989). The goal of forming accurate impressions during social interactions: Attenuating the impact of negative expectancies. *Journal of Personality and Social Psychology, 56,* 374–386.

Neuberg, S. L., & Fiske, S. T. (1987). Motivational influences on impression formation: Outcome dependency, accuracy-driven attention, and individuating processes. *Journal of Personality and Social Psychology, 53,* 431–444.

Neuberg, S., Judice, T., Virdin, L., & Carrillo, M. (1993). Perceiver self-presentational goals as moderators of expectancy influences: Ingratiation and the disconfirmation of negative expectancies. *Journal of Personality and Social Psychology, 64,* 409–420.

Newth, S., & DeLongis, A. (2004). Individual differences, mood and coping with chronic pain in rheumatoid arthritis: A daily process analysis. *Psychology and Health, 19,* 283–305.

Ng, W. J., & Lindsay, R. C. L. (1994). Cross-race facial recognition: Failure of the contact hypothesis. *Journal of Cross-Cultural Psychology, 25,* 217–232.

Nguyen, H. H., Messe, L. A., & Strollak, G. E. (1999). Toward a more complex understanding of acculturation and adjustment: Cultural involvements and psychosocial functioning in Vietnames youth. *Journal of Cross-Cultural Psychology, 30,* 5–31.

Nickerson, C., Schwarz, N., Diener, E., & Kahneman, D. (2003). Zeroing in the dark side of the American Dream: A closer look at the negative consequences of the goal for financial success. *Psychological Science, 14,* 531–536.

Nieva, V. F., & Gutek, B. A. (1981). *Women and work: A psychological perspective*. New York: Praeger.

Nisbett, R. E. (1993). Violence and U.S. regional culture. *American Psychologist, 48*, 441–449.

Nisbett, R., Peng, K., Choi, I., & Norenzayan, A. (2001). Culture and systems of thought: Holistic versus analytic cognition. *Psychological Review, 108*, 291–310.

Noel, J. G., Wann, D. L., & Branscombe, N. R. (1995). Peripheral ingroup membership status and public negativity toward outgroups. *Journal of Personality and Social Psychology, 68*, 127–137.

Noels, K. A. & Rollin, E. (1998). *Communicating in a second language: The importance of support from the Latino community for Anglo-Americans' motivation to learn Spanish*. Paper presented at the 1998 Congress of the International Association for Cross-Cultural Psychology, Bellingham, WA.

Nolan, J. M., Schultz, P. W., Cialdini, R. B., Goldstein, N. J., & Griskevicius, V. (2008). Normative social influence is underdetected. *Personality and Social Psychology Bulletin, 34*, 913–923.

Noon, J. M., & Lewis, J. R. (1992). Therapeutic strategies and outcomes: Perspectives from different cultures. *British Journal of Medical Psychology, 65*, 107–117.

Norenzayan, A., Choi, I., & Nisbett, R. (2002). Cultural similarities and differences in social inference: Evidence from behavioral predictions and lay theories of behavior. *Personality and Social Psychology Bulletin, 28*, 109–120.

Norenzayan, A., & Heine, S. J. (2005). Psychological universals: What are they and how can we know? *Psychological Bulletin, 135*, 763–84.

Norenzayan, A., & Nisbett, R. (2000). Culture and causal cognition. *Current Directions in Psychological Science, 9*, 132–135.

Norman, W., & Goldberg, L. (1966). Raters, ratees, and randomness in personality structure. *Journal of Personality and Social Psychology, 4*, 681–691.

North, A. C., Tarrant, M., & Hargreaves, D. J. (2004). The effects of music on helping behavior: A field study. *Environment and Behavior, 36*, 266–275.

Norton, M., Monin, B., Cooper, J., & Hogg, M. (2003). Vicarious dissonance: Attitude change from the inconsistency of others. *Journal of Personality and Social Psychology, 85*, 47–62.

Norton, M. I., Sommers, S. R., Apfelbaum, E. P., Pura, N., & Ariely, D. (2006). Color blindness and interracial interaction: Playing the political correctness game. *Psychological Science, 17*, 949–953.

Nosek, B. A., Greenwald, A. G., & Banaji, M. R. (2005). Understanding and using the Implicit Association Test: II. Method variables and construct validity. *Personality and Social Psychology Bulletin, 31*, 166–180.

Nosek, B. A., Greenwald, A. G., & Banaji, M. R. (2005). Understanding and using the Implicit Association Test: II. Method variables and construct validity. *Personality and Social Psychology Bulletin, 31*, 166–180.

Nsamenang, A. B. (1992). *Human development in cultural context: A third world perspective*. Newbury Park, CA: Sage.

O'Brien, T. B., & DeLongis, A. (1996). The interactional context of problem-, emotion-, and relationship-focused coping: The role of the Big Five personality factors. *Journal of Personality, 64* [Special Issue: Personality and Coping], 775–813.

O'Connor, K. M., & Carnevale, P. J. (1997). A nasty but effective negotiation strategy: Misrepresentation of a commonvalue issue. *Personality and Social Psychology Bulletin, 23*, 504–515.

O'Connor, W.E., Morrison, T.G., McLeod, L.D. and Anderson, D. (1996) A Meta-Analytic Review of the Relationship between Gender and Belief in a Just World. *Journal of Social Behavior & Personality, 11*(1), 141–148.

O'Sullivan, C. S., & Durso, F. T. (1984). Effect of schema-incongruent information on memory for stereotypical attributes. *Journal of Personality and Social Psychology, 47*, 55–70.

O'Sullivan, M. (2003). The fundamental attribution error in detecting deception: The boy-who-cried-wolf effect. *Personality and Social Psychology Bulletin, 29*, 1316–1327.

Ohbuchi, K., Kameda, M., & Agarie, N. (1989). Apology as aggression control: Its role in mediating appraisal of and response to harm. *Journal of Personality and Social Psychology, 56*, 219–227.

Ohbuchi, K., Ohno, T., & Mukai, H. (1993). Empathy and aggression: Effects of self-disclosure and fearful appeal. *Journal of Social Psychology, 133*, 243–253.

Oinonen, K. & Mazmanian, D. (2007). Facial symmetry detection ability changes across the menstrual cycle. *Biological Psychology, 75*(2), 136–145

Oishi, S. (2002). The experiencing and remembering of wellbeing: A cross-cultural analysis. *Personality and Social Psychology Bulletin, 28*, 1398–1406.

Olson, J. M., Herman, C. P., & Zanna, M.P. (1986). Relative deprivation and social comparison: An integrative perspective. In J.M. Olson, C. P. Herman, & M. P. Zanna (Eds.), *Relative Deprivation and Social Comparison: The Ontario Symposium* (Vol. 4., pp. 1–15). Hillsdale, NJ: Erlbaum.

Olson, J., Vernon, P., Harris, J., & Jang, K. (2001). The heritability of attitudes: A study of twins. *Journal of Personality and Social Psychology, 80*, 845–860.

Olweus, D. (1979). Stability of aggressive reaction patterns in males: A review. *Psychological Bulletin, 86*, 852–875.

Olweus, D. (1995). Bullying or peer abuse at school: Facts and interventions. *Current Directions in Psychological Science, 4*, 196–200.

Olweus, D., Mattsson, A., Schalling, D., & Löw, H. (1988). Circulating testosterone levels and aggression in adolescent males: A causal analysis. *Psychosomatic Medicine, 50*, 261–272.

Oman, D., Thoresen, C. E., & McMahon, K. (1999). Volunteerism and mortality among the community-dwelling elderly. *Journal of Health Psychology, 4*, 301–316.

Omoto, A. M., & Snyder, M. (1995). Sustained helping without obligation: Motivation, longevity of service, and perceived attitude change among AIDS volunteers. *Journal of Personality and Social Psychology, 68*, 671–686.

Operario, D., & Fiske, S. T. (2001). Effects of trait dominance on powerholders' judgements of subordinates. *Social Cognition, 19*, 161–180.

Orbell, J. M., van de Kragt, A. J., & Dawes, R. M. (1988). Explaining discussion-induced cooperation. *Journal of Personality and Social Psychology, 54*, 811–819.

Orne, M. (1962). On the social psychology of the psychological experiment: With particular reference to demand characteristics and their implications. *American Psychologist, 17*, 776–783.

Osbourne, J. W. (1995). Academics, self-esteem, and race: A look at the underlying assumptions of the disidentification hypothesis. *Personality and Social Psychology Bulletin, 21*, 449–455.

Osherow, N. (2004). Making sense of the nonsensical: An analysis of Jonestown. In E. Aronson (Ed.), *Readings about the Social Animal* (pp. 80–97). New York: Worth.

Ostrom, T. M., & Sedikides, C. (1992). Out-group homogeneity effects in natural and minimal groups. *Psychological Bulletin, 112*, 536–552.

Ottati, V., Riggle, E., Wyer, R., Schwarz, N., & Kuklinski, J. (1989). Cognitive and affective bases of opinion survey responses. *Journal of Personality and Social Psychology, 57*, 404–415.

Otten, C. A., Penner, L. A., & Altabe, M. N. (1991). An examination of therapists' and college students' willingness to help a psychologically distressed person. *Journal of Social & Clinical Psychology, 10*, 102–120.

Otten, S., & Wentura, D. (1999). About the impact of automaticity in the Minimal Group Paradigm: Evidence from affective priming tasks. *European Journal of Social Psychology, 29*, 1049–1071.

Ouellette, J. A., Hessling, R., Gibbons, F. X., Reis-Bergan, M. J., & Gerrard, M. (2005). Using images to increase exercise behavior: Prototypes vs. possible selves. *Personality and Social Psychology Bulletin, 31*, 610–620.

Paleari, F. G., Regalia, C., & Fincham, F. (2005). Marital quality, forgiveness, empathy, and rumination: A longitudinal analysis. *Personality and Social Psychology Bulletin, 31*, 368–378.

Pallier, G. (2003). Gender differences in the self assessment of accuracy on cognitive tasks. *Sex Roles, 48*, 265–276.

Park, B., Ryan, C. S., & Judd, C. M. (1992). Role of meaningful subgroups in explaining differences in perceived variability for in-groups and out-groups. *Journal of Personality and Social Psychology, 63*, 553–567.

Parks, C. D., Sanna, L. J., & Berel, S. R. (2001). Actions of similar others as inducements to cooperate in social dilemmas. *Personality and Social Psychology Bulletin, 27*, 345–354.

Parks-Stamm, E., Heilman, M., & Hearns, K. (2008). Motivated to penalize: Women's strategic rejection of successful women. *Personality and Social Psychology Bulletin, 34*, 237–247.

Parrot, W. G., & Smith, R. H. (1992). Distinguishing the experiences of envy and jealousy. *Journal of Personality and Social Psychology, 64*, 906–920.

Patrick, H., Neighbors, C., & Knee, C. (2004). Appearance-related social comparisons: The role of contingent self-esteem and self-perceptions of attractiveness. *Personality and Social Psychology Bulletin, 30*, 501–514.

Patterson, M. M., Carron, A. V., & Loughead, T. M. (2005). The influence of team norms on the cohesion–self-reported performance relationship: A multi-level analysis. *Psychology of Sport and Exercise, 6*, 479–493.

Paulhus, D. (1998). Interpersonal and intrapsychic adaptiveness of trait self-enhancement: A mixed blessing? *Journal of Personality and Social Psychology, 74*, 1197–1208.

Paulhus, D., Bruce, M., & Trapnell, P. (1995). Effects of self-presentation strategies on personality profiles and their structure. *Personality and Social Psychology Bulletin, 21*, 100–108.

Paunonen, S.V. (2006). You are honest, therefore I like you and find you attractive. *Journal of Research in Personality. 40(3)*, 237–249.

Peabody, D. (1985). *National characteristics*. Cambridge: Cambridge University Press.

Pearce, P. L. (1980). Strangers, travelers, and Greyhound terminals: A study of small-scale helping behaviors. *Journal of Personality and Social Psychology, 38*, 935–940.

Pearce, Z. J., & Halford, W. K. (2008). Do attributions mediate the association between attachment and negative couple communication? *Personal Relationships, 15*, 155–170.

Pechmann, C. (1997). Do anti-smoking ads combat underage smoking? A review of past practices and research. In M. E. Goldberg, M. Fishbein, & S. Iddlestadt (Eds.), *Social Marketing: Theoretical and Practical Perspectives* (pp. 189–216). Hillsdale, NJ: Lawrence Erlbaum Associates.

Pechmann, C., & Shih, C. (1999). Smoking scenes in movies and antismoking advertisements before movies: Effects on youth. *Journal of Marketing, 63*, 1–13.

Pedersen, W. C., Gonzales, C., & Miller, N. (2000). The moderating effect of trivial triggering provocation on displaced aggression. *Journal of Personality and Social Psychology, 78*, 913–927.

Peled, M. & Moretti, M.M. (2010). Ruminating on rumination: Are rumination on anger and sadness differentially related to aggression and depressed mood? *Journal of Psychopathology and Behavioral Assessment. 32(1)*, 108–117.

Peña, Y., Sidanius, J., & Sawyer, M. (2004). Racial democracy in the Americas: A Latin and U.S. comparison. *Journal of Cross-Cultural Psychology, 35*, 749–762.

Pendry, L. F., & Macrae, C. N. (1994). Stereotypes and mental life: The case of the motivated but thwarted tactician. *Journal of Experimental Social Psychology, 30*, 303–325.

Peng, K., & Nisbett, R. E. (1999). Culture, dialectics, and reasoning about contradiction. *American Psychologist, 54*, 741–754.

Pennebaker, J. W. (1989). Confession, inhibition, and disease. In L. Berkowitz (Ed.), *Advances in Experimental Social Psychology* (Vol. 22, pp. 211–244). New York: Academic Press.

Pennebaker, J. W., & Sanders, D. Y. (1976). American graffiti: Effects of authority and reactance arousal. *Personality and Social Psychology Bulletin, 2*, 264–267.

Pennebaker, J. W., Dyer, M. A., Caulkins, R. S., Litowitz, D. L., Ackreman, P. L., Anderson, D. B., & McGraw, K. (1979). Don't the girls get prettier at closing time? A country and western application to psychology. *Personality and Social Psychology Bulletin, 5*, 122–125.

Pennebaker, J. W., Rimé, B., & Blankenship, V. (1996). Stereotypes of northerners and southerners: A cross-cultural test of Montesqueâs hypothesis. *Journal of Personality and Social Psychology, 70*, 372–380.

Perdue, C. W., Dovidio, J. F., Gurtman, M. B., & Tyler, R. B. (1990). Us and them: Social categorization and the process of intergroup bias. *Journal of Personality and Social Psychology, 59*, 475–486.

Perdue, C. W., & Gurtman, M. B. (1990). Evidence for the automaticity of ageism. *Journal of Experimental Social Psychology, 26*, 199–216.

Peritz, I. (2010, April 14). Moroccan hockey team brings Muslims and Jews together to make peace on ice. *Globe and Mail*, pp. A1, A8.

Perkins, H. W. (2002). Social norms and the prevention of alcohol misuse in collegiate contexts. *Journal of Studies on Alcohol, Supplement 14*, 164–172.

Perkins, H. W., & Craig, D. W. (2006). A successful social norms campaign to reduce alcohol misuse among college student-athletes. *Journal of Studies on Alcohol, 67*, 880–889.

Perlini, A. H. & Hansen, S. D. (2001). Moderating effects of need for cognition on attractiveness stereotyping. *Social Behavior and Personality. 29(4)*, 313–321.

Perrin, S., & Spencer, C. P. (1981). Independence or conformity in the Asch experiment as a reflection of cultural and situational factors. *British Journal of Social Psychology, 20*, 205–209.

Perry, D. G., Perry, L. C., & Rasmussen, P. (1986). Cognitive social learning mediators of aggression. *Child Development, 57*, 700–711.

Peters, L. H., Hartke, D. D., & Pohlmann, J. T. (1985). Fiedler's Contingency Theory of Leadership: An application of the meta-analysis procedures of Schmidt and Hunter. *Psychological Bulletin, 97*, 274–285.

Peterson, A. A., Haynes, G. A., & Olson, J. M. (2008). Self-esteem differences in the effects of hypocrisy induction on behavioral intentions in the health domain. *Journal of Personality, 76*, 305–322.

Peterson, C., & Seligman, M. (1987). Explanatory style and illness. *Journal of Personality, 55*, 237–265.

Peterson, C., & Seligman, M. (2004). *Character strengths and virtues: A handbook and classification*. Oxford: Oxford University Press.

Peterson, C., Seligman, M., Yurko, K., Martin, L., & Friedman, H. (1998). Catastrophizing and untimely death. *Psychological Science, 9*, 127–130.

Peterson, C., Wang, Q., & Hou, Y. (2009). "When I was little": Childhood recollections in Chinese and European Canadian grade school children. *Child Development, 80(2)*, 506–518.

Peterson, L., & Brown, D. (1994). Integrating child injury and abuse-neglect research: Common histories, etiologies, and solutions. *Psychological Bulletin, 116*, 293–315.

Peterson, R. S., & Nemeth, C. J. (1996). Focus versus flexibility: Majority and minority influence can both improve performance. *Personality and Social Psychology Bulletin, 22,* 14–23.

Pettigrew, T. F. (1979). The ultimate attribution error: Extending Allport's cognitive analysis of prejudice. *Personality and Social Psychology Bulletin, 5,* 461–476.

Pettigrew, T. F. (1997). Generalized intergroup contact effects on prejudice. *Personality and Social Psychology Bulletin, 23,* 173–185.

Pettigrew, T. F. (2003). Peoples under threat: Americans, Arabs, and Israelis. *Peace and Conflict: Journal of Peace Psychology, 9,* 69–90.

Petty, R. E., & Cacioppo, J. T. (1984). The effects of involvement on responses to argument quantity and quality: Central and peripheral routes to persuasion. *Journal of Personality and Social Psychology, 46,* 69–81.

Petty, R. E., & Cacioppo, J. T. (1986). *Communication and Persuasion: Central and Peripheral Routes to Attitude Change.* New York: Springer-Verlag.

Petty, R. E., Cacioppo, J. T., & Goldman, R. (1981). Personal involvement as a determinant of argument-based persuasion. *Journal of Personality and Social Psychology, 41,* 847–855.

Petty, R. E., Schumann, D. W., Richman, S. A., & Strathman, A. J. (1993). Positive mood and persuasion: Different roles for affect under high- and low-elaboration conditions. *Journal of Personality and Social Psychology, 64,* 5–20.

Petty, R. E., Wells, G. L., & Brock, T. C. (1976). Distraction can enhance or reduce yielding to propaganda: Thought disruption versus effort justification. *Journal of Personality and Social Psychology, 34,* 874–884.

Petz, S. (2010, Oct 25). Wasn't hazing a thing of past? *Macleans Magazine.* Retrieved from http://oncampus.macleans.ca/education/2010/10/25/wasnt-hazing-a-thing-of-the-past/

Pew Research Center (2009). *Mapping the global Muslim population: A report on the size and distribution of the world's muslim population.* Washington, DC: Pew Research Center.

Phillips, D. (1982). The impact of fictional television stories on U.S. adult fatalities: New evidence on the effect of the mass media on violence. *American Journal of Sociology, 87,* 1340–1359.

Phillips, D. P. (1977). Motor vehicle fatalities increase just after publicized suicide stories. *Science, 196,* 1464–1465.

Phillips, D. P. (1979). Suicide, motor vehicle fatalities, and the mass media: Evidence toward a theory of suggestion. *American Journal of Sociology, 84,* 1150–1174.

Phillips, D. P. (1983). The impact of mass media violence in U.S. homicides. *American Sociological Review, 48,* 560–568.

Phillips, D.P. (1986). Natural experiments on the effects of mass media violence on fatal aggression: Strengths and weaknesses of a new approach. In L. Berkowitz (Ed.), *Advances in Experimental Social Psychology, 19* (pp. 207–250). New York: Academic Press.

Phillips, D. P., & Carstensen, L. L. (1986). Clustering of teenage suicides after television news stories about suicide. *New England Journal of Medicine, 315,* 685–689.

Phinney, J. S., Berry, J. W., Vedder, P., & Liebkind, K. (2006). The Acculturation Experience: Attitudes, Identities, and Behaviors of Immigrant Youth. In J. W. Berry, J. S. Phinney, D. L. Sam & P. Vedder (Eds.), *Immigrant Youth in Cultural Transition* (pp. 71–116). Mahwah, NJ: Lawrence Earlbaum Associates.

Phinney, J. S., Chavira, V., & Williamson, L. (1992). Acculturation attitudes and self-esteem among high school and college students. *Youth and Society, 23,* 299–312.

Pierce, T., & Lydon, J. (1998). Priming relational schemas: Effects of contextually activated and chronically accessible interpersonal expectations on responses to a stressful event. *Journal of Personality and Social Psychology. 75,* 1441–1448.

Piferi, R. L., Jobe, R. L., & Jones, W. H. (2006). Giving to others during national tragedy: The effects of altruistic and egoistic motivations on long-term giving. *Journal of Social and Personal Relationships, 23,* 171–184.

Piliavin, I. M., Piliavin, J. A., & Rodin, J. (1975). Costs, diffusion, and the stigmatized victim. *Journal of Personality and Social Psychology, 32,* 429–438.

Piliavin, I. M., Rodin, J., & Piliavin, J. A. (1969). Good Samaritanism: An underground phenomenon? *Journal of Personality and Social Psychology, 13,* 289–299.

Piliavin, J. A., Dovidio, J. R., Gaertner, S. L. & Clark, R. D., III. (1981). *Emergency Intervention.* New York: Academic Press.

Piliavin, J. A., & Piliavin, I. M. (1972). Effect of blood on reactions to a victim. *Journal of Personality and Social Psychology, 23,* 353–361.

Piliavin, J. A., Piliavin, I. M., & Broll, L. (1976). Time of arrival at an emergency and likelihood of helping. *Personality and Social Psychology Bulletin, 2,* 273–276.

Pinkus, R. T, Lockwood, P. Schimmack, U. & Fournier, M. A. (2008). For Better and for Worse: Everyday Social Comparisons Between Romantic Partners. *Journal of Personality and Social Psychology, 95(5),* 1180–1201.

Pittman, T. (1975). Attribution of arousal as a mediator in dissonance reduction. *Journal of Experimental Social Psychology, 11,* 53–63.

Plaks, J. E., & Higgins, E. T. (2000). Pragmatic use of stereotyping in teamwork: Social loafing and compensation as a function of inferred partner-situation fit. *Journal of Personality and Social Psychology, 79,* 962–974.

Plant, E. A., & Devine, P. G. (1998). Internal and external motivation to respond without prejudice. *Journal of Personality and Social Psychology, 75,* 811–832.

Plant, E. A., Peruche, B. M., & Butz, D. A. (2005). Eliminating automatic racial bias: Making race non-diagnostic for responses to criminal suspects. *Journal of Experimental Social Psychology, 41,* 141–156.

Pliner, P., Hart, H., Kohl, J. & Saari, D. (1974). Compliance without pressure: Some further data on the foot-in-the-door technique. *Journal of Experimental Social Psychology. 10(1),* 17–22.

Pliner, P., Rizvi, S., & Remick, A.K. (2009). Competition affects food choice in women. *International Journal of Eating Disorders, 42(6),* 557–564.

Pollan, M. (2002). An animal's place. *The New York Times Magazine,* 58.

Pollock, C. L., Smith, S. D., Knowles, E. S., & Bruce, H. J. (1998). Mindfulness limits compliance with the that's-not-all technique. *Personality and Social Psychology Bulletin, 24,* 1153–1157.

Pomerantz, E. M., Chaiken, S., & Tordesillas, R. S. (1995). Attitude strength and resistance processes. *Journal of Personality and Social Psychology, 69,* 408–419.

Pope, H., Olivardia, R., Gruber, A., & Borowiecki, J. (1999). Evolving ideals of male body image as seen through action toys. *International Journal of Eating Disorders, 26,* 65–72.

Post, S. G. (2005). Altruism, happiness, and health: It's good to be good. *International Journal of Behavioral Medicine, 12,* 66–77.

Postmes, T., & Spears, R. (1998). Deindividuation and antinormative behavior: A meta-analysis. *Psychological Bulletin, 123,* 238–259.

Postmes, T., & Spears, R. (2002). Behavior online: Does anonymous computer communication reduce gender inequality? *Personality and Social Psychology Bulletin, 28,* 1073–1083.

Postmes, T., Spears, R., & Cihangir, S. (2001). Quality of decision making and group norms. *Journal of Personality and Social Psychology, 80,* 918–930.

Powell, A. A., Branscombe, N. R., & Schmitt, M. T. (2005). Inequality as ingroup privilege or outgroup disadvantage: The impact of group focus on collective guilt and interracial attitudes. *Personality and Social Psychology Bulletin, 31,* 508–521.

Powers, S. I., Pietromonaco, P. R., Gunlicks, M., & Sayer, A. (2006). Dating couples' attachment styles and patterns of cortisol reactivity and recovery in response to a relationship conflict. *Journal of Personality and Social Psychology, 90,* 613–628.

Prati, G., & Pietrantoni, L. (2009). Elaborating the police perspective: The role of perceptions and experience in the explanation of crowd conflict. *European Journal of Social Psychology, 39,* 991–1001.

Pratkanis, A. R., Greenwald, A. G., Leippe, M. R., & Baumgardner, M. H. (1988). In search of reliable persuasion effects: III. The sleeper effect is dead: Long live the sleeper effect. *Journal of Personality and Social Psychology, 54,* 203–218.

Pratto, F., & John, O. (1991). Automatic vigilance: The attention-grabbing power of negative social information. *Journal of Personality and Social Psychology, 61,* 380–391.

Pratto, F., Sidanius, J., Stallworth, L. M., & Malle, B. F. (1994). Social dominance orientation: A personality variable predicting social and political attitudes. *Journal of Personality and Social Psychology, 67,* 741–763.

Prentice, D. A., & Miller, D. T. (1993). Pluralistic ignorance and alcohol use on campus: Some consequences of misperceiving the social norm. *Journal of Personality and Social Psychology, 64,* 243–256.

Prentice-Dunn, S., & Rogers, R. W. (1980). Effects of deindividuating situational cues and aggressive models on subjective deindividuation and aggression. *Journal of Personality and Social Psychology, 39,* 104–113.

Prentice-Dunn, S., & Rogers, R. W. (1982). Effects of public and private self-awareness on deindividuation and aggression. *Journal of Personality and Social Psychology, 43,* 503–513.

Press Association. (2010, Feb. 2). Supermodels including Kate Moss and Naomi Campbell strip off for Love magazine front covers. *The Independent.* Retrieved from http://www.independent.co.uk/news/people/news/supermodels-including-kate-moss-and-naomi-campbell-strip-off-for-love-magazine-front-covers-1886688.html

Pressman, S. D., Cohen, S., Miller, G. E., Barkin, A., Rabin, B. S., & Treanor, J. J. (2005). Loneliness, social network size, and immune response to influenza vaccination in college freshmen. *Health Psychology, 24,* 297–306.

Price, W. F. & Crapo, R. H. (2002). *Cross-cultural perspectives in introductory psychology* (4th ed.). Canada: Wadsworth Cengage Learning.

Priester, J. R., & Petty, R. E. (1995). Source attributions and persuasion: Perceived honesty as a determinant of message scrutiny. *Personality and Social Psychology Bulletin, 21,* 637–654.

Pruitt, D. G., & Kimmel, M. J. (1977). Twenty years of experimental gaming: Critique, synthesis, and suggestions for the future. *Annual Review of Psychology, 28,* 363–392.

Public Health Agency of Canada (2008). *Canadian Incidence Study of Reported Child Abuse and Neglect.* Ottawa: PHAC.

Public Safety Canada (2010). Bullying prevention: Nation and extent of bullying in Canada. Retrieved from http://www.publicsafety.gc.ca/res/cp/res/2008-bp-01-eng.aspx#a4

Punetha, D., Giles, H., & Young, L. (1987). Ethnicity and immigrant values: Religion and language choice. *Journal of Language and Social Psychology, 6,* 229–241.

Quattrone, G., & Jones, E. (1978). Selective self-disclosure with and without correspondent performance. *Journal of Experimental Social Psychology, 14,* 511–526.

Queller, S., & Smith, E. R. (2002). Subtyping versus bookkeeping in stereotype learning and change: Connectionist simulations and empirical findings. *Journal of Personality and Social Psychology, 82,* 300–313.

Radel, R., Sarrazin, P. & Pelletier, L. (2009). Evidence of subliminally primed motivational orientations: The effects of unconscious motivational processes on the performance of a new motor task. *Journal of Sport and Exercise Psychology, 31,* 657–674.

Rajecki, D. W., Bledsoe, S. B., & Rasmussen, J. L. (1991). Successful personal ads: Gender differences and similarities in offers, stipulations, and outcomes. *Basic and Applied Social Psychology, 12,* 457–469.

Ramachandran, V. S. (2009). *Mirror Neurons and imitation learning as the driving force behind 'the great leap forward' in human evolution.* Edge Foundation. Retrieved from http://www.edge.org/3rd_culture/ramachandran/ramachandran_p1.html

Ranganath, K. A. & Nosek, B. A. (2008). Implicit attitude generalization occurs immediately, explicit attitude generalization takes time. *Psychological Science, 19,* 249–254.

Ratcliff, J. J., Lassiter, G. D., Markman, K. D., & Snyder, C. J. (2006). Gender differences in attitudes toward gay men and lesbians: The role of motivation to respond without prejudice. *Personality and Social Psychology Bulletin, 33,* 1325–1338.

Raty, H., Vanska, J., Kasanen, K., & Karkkainen, R. (2002). Parents' explanations of their child's performance in mathematics and reading: A replication and extension of Yee and Eccles. *Sex Roles, 46(314),* 121–128.

Redfield, R., Linton, R., & Herskovits, M. J. (1936). Memorandum on the study of acculturation. *American Anthropologist, 38,* 149–152.

Reeder, G., Vonk, R., Ronk, M., Ham, J., & Lawrence, M. (2004). Dispositional attribution: Multiple inferences about motive-related traits. *Journal of Personality and Social Psychology, 86,* 530–544.

Regan, D., & Fazio, R. (1977). On the consistency between attitudes and behavior: Look to the method of attitude formation. *Journal of Experimental Social Psychology, 13,* 28–45.

Regan, D. T. (1971). Effects of a favor and liking on compliance. *Journal of Experimental Social Psychology, 7,* 627–639.

Regan, D. T., Williams, M., & Sparling, S. (1972). Voluntary expiation of guilt: A field experiment. *Journal of Personality and Social Psychology, 24,* 42–45.

Regan, P. C. (2000). The role of sexual desire and sexual activity in dating relationships. *Social Behavior and Personality, 28,* 51–59.

Rehm, J., Steinleitner, M., & Lilli, W. (1987). Wearing uniforms and aggression: A field experiment. *European Journal of Social Psychology, 17,* 357–360.

Reicher, S. D. (1984). Social influence in the crowd: Attitudinal and behavioural effects of deindividuation in conditions of high and low group salience. *British Journal of Social Psychology, 23,* 341–350.

Reicher, S. D. & Potter, J. (1985). Psychological theory as intergroup perspective: A comparative analysis of "scientific" and "lay" accounts of crowd events. *Human Relations, 38,* 167–189.

Reicher, S., Stott, C., Cronin, P., & Adang, O. (2004). An integrated approach to crowd psychology and public order policing. *Policing: An International Journal of Police Strategies and Management, 27,* 558–572.

Reinhardt, J. P., Boerner, K., & Horowitz, A. (2006). Good to have but not to use: Differential impact of perceived and received support on well-being. *Journal of Social and Personal Relationships, 23,* 117–129.

Reis, H. T., & Aron, A. (2008). Love: What is it, why does it matter, and how does it operate? *Perspectives on Psychological Science, 3,* 80–86.

Reis, H. T., & Collins, W. A. (2004). Relationships, human behavior, and psychological science. *Current Directions in Psychological Science, 13,* 233–237.

Reis, H. T., Collins, W. A., & Berscheid, E. (2000). The relationship context of human behavior and development. *Psychological Bulletin, 126,* 844–872.

Reis, H. T., & Wheeler, L. (1991). Studying social interaction with the Rochester Interaction Record. In M. P. Zanna (Ed.), *Advances in Experimental Social Psychology* (Vol. 24, pp. 270–318). San Diego: Academic Press.

Rennison, C. M., & Welchans, S. (2000). *Intimate Partner Violence Special Report, NCJ 178247.* Washington, DC: US Department of Justice.

Reno, R. R., Cialdini, R. B., & Kallgren, C. A. (1993). The transsituational influence of social norms. *Journal of Personality and Social Psychology, 64,* 104–112.

Reynolds, K. J., Turner, J. C., & Haslam, S. A. (2000). When are we better than them and they worse than us? A closer look at social discrimination in positive and negative domains. *Journal of Personality and Social Psychology, 78,* 64–80.

Rhee, E., Uleman, J., Lee, H., & Roman, R. (1995). Spontaneous self-descriptions and ethnic identities in individualistic and collectivistic cultures. *Journal of Personality and Social Psychology, 69,* 142–152.

Rhodes, G., Halberstadt, J., Jeffery, L., & Palermo, R. (2005). The attractiveness of average faces is not a generalized mere exposure effect. *Social Cognition, 23,* 205–217.

Rhodes, G., Sumich, A., & Byatt, G. (1999). Are average facial configurations attractive only because of their symmetry? *Psychological Science, 10,* 52–58.

Rhodewalt, F., Sanbonmatsu, D., Tschanz, B., Feick, D., & Waller, A. (1995). Self-handicapping and interpersonal trade-offs: The effects of claimed self-handicaps on observers' performance evaluations and feedback. *Personality and Social Psychology Bulletin, 21,* 1042–1050.

Richard, F. D., Bond, C. F. J., & Stokes-Zoota, J. J. (2001). 'That's completely obvious...and important': Lay judgments of social psychological findings. *Personality and Social Psychology Bulletin, 27,* 497–505.

Richards, J., & Gross, J. (1999). Composure at any cost? The cognitive consequences of emotion suppression. *Personality and Social Psychology Bulletin, 25,* 1033–1044.

Rigby, K., Brown, M., Anagnostou, P., Ross, M. W., & Rosser, B. R. S. (1989). Shock tactics to counter AIDS: The Australian experience. *Psychology & Health, 3,* 145–159.

Riggio, H. R. (2004). Parental marital conflict and divorce, parent-child relationships, social support, and relationship anxiety in young adulthood. *Personal Relationships, 11,* 99–114.

Riley, T., & Ungerleider, C. (2008). Preservice Teachers' Discriminatory Judgments. *Alberta Journal Of Educational Research, 54*(4). Retrieved from http://ajer.synergiesprairies.ca/ajer/index.php/ajer/article/view/651

Rilling, J., Gutman, D., Zeh, T., Pagnoni, G., Berns, G., & Kilts, C. (2002). A neural basis for social cooperation. *Neuron, 35,* 395–405.

Risen, J. L., Gilovich, T., & Dunning, D. (2007). One-shot illusory correlations and stereotype formation. *Personality and Social Psychology Bulletin, 33,* 1492–1502.

Rochat, F., & Modigliani, A. (1995). The ordinary quality of resistance: From Milgram's laboratory to the village of Le Chambon. *Journal of Social Issues, 51,* 195–210.

Rodkin, P. C., Farmer, T. W., Pearl, R., & Van Acker, R. (2000). Heterogeneity of popular boys: Antisocial and prosocial configurations. *Developmental Psychology, 36,* 14–24.

Rodrigues, A., & Assmar, E. (1988). On some aspects of distributive justice in Brazil. *Interamerican Journal of Psychology, 22,* 1–20.

Roese, N. (1994). The functional basis of counterfactual thinking. *Journal of Personality and Social Psychology, 66,* 805–818.

Roese, N.J. & Olson, J.M. (1993). Self-esteem and counterfactual thinking. *Journal of Personality and Social Psychology. 65,* 199–206.

Rogers, R. W., & Prentice-Dunn, S. (1981). Deindividuation and anger-mediated interracial aggression: Unmasking regressive racism. *Journal of Personality and Social Psychology, 41,* 63–73.

Rohlen, T. P. (1979). *For Harmony and Strength Japanese White-Collar Organization in Anthropological Perspective.* Berkeley: University of California Press.

Rosenberg, M. (1965). *Society and the Adolescent Self-image.* Princeton, NJ: Princeton University Press.

Rosenfeld, P., Giacalone, R., & Tedeschi, J. (1984). Cognitive dissonance and impression management explanations for effort justification. *Personality and Social Psychology Bulletin, 10,* 394–401.

Rosenhan, D. (1973). On being sane in insane places. *Science, 179,* 250–258.

Rosenhan, D. L., Salovey, P., & Hargis, K. (1981). The joys of helping: Focus of attention mediates the impact of positive affect on altruism. *Journal of Personality and Social Psychology, 40,* 899–905.

Rosenthal, A.M. (1964). *Thirty-Eight Witnesses: The Kitty Genovese Case.* Berkeley, CA: University of California Press.

Rosenthal, R. (1994). Interpersonal expectancy effects: A 30-year perspective. *Current Directions in Psychological Science, 3,* 176–179.

Rosenthal, R., & Fode, K. (1963). The effect of experimenter bias on the performance of the albino rat. *Behavioral Science, 8,* 183–189.

Rosenthal, R., & Jacobson, L. (1968). *Pygmalion in the classroom: Teacher expectation and pupils' intellectual development.* New York: Holt, Rinehart & Winston.

Ross, L., Amabile, T., & Steinmetz, J. (1977). Social roles, social control, and biases in social-perception processes. *Journal of Personality and Social Psychology, 35,* 485–494.

Ross, L., Greene, D., & House, P. (1977). The false consensus effect: An egocentric bias in social perception and attribution processes. *Journal of Experimental Social Psychology, 13,* 279–301.

Ross, L., Lepper, M., & Hubbard, M. (1975). Perseverance in self-perception and social perception: Biased attributional processes in the debriefing paradigm. *Journal of Personality and Social Psychology, 32,* 880–892.

Rosselli, F., Skelly, J., & Mackie, D. (1995). Processing rational and emotional messages: The cognitive and affective mediation of persuasion. *Journal of Experimental Social Psychology, 31,* 163–190.

Roszell, P., Kennedy, D., & Grabb, E. (1989). Physical attractiveness and income attainment among Canadians. *The Journal of Psychology, 123,* 547–559.

Rotenberg, K. J. (1994). Loneliness and interpersonal trust. *Journal of Social & Clinical Psychology, 13,* 152–173.

Rotenberg, K. J. (1997). Loneliness and the perception of the exchange of disclosures. *Journal of Social and Clinical Psychology, 16,* 259–276.

Rothbaum, F., & Tsang, B. Y. (1998). Lovesongs in the United States and China: On the nature of romantic love. *Journal of Cross-Cultural Psychology, 29,* 306–319.

Rothman, A., & Hardin, C. (1997). Differential use of the availability heuristic in social judgment. *Personality and Social Psychology Bulletin, 23,* 123–138.

Rothman, A., & Salovey, P. (1997). Shaping perceptions to motivate healthy behavior: The role of message framing. *Psychological Bulletin, 121,* 3–19.

Rotton, J., & Frey, J. (1985). Air pollution, weather, and violent crimes: Concomitant time-series analysis of archival data. *Journal of Personality and Social Psychology, 49,* 1207–1220.

Rowatt, W., Cunningham, M., & Druen, P. (1998). Deception to get a date. *Personality and Social Psychology Bulletin, 24,* 1228–1242.

Ruback, R. B., & Juieng, D. (1997). Territorial defense in parking lots: Retaliation against waiting drivers. *Journal of Applied Social Psychology, 27,* 821–834.

Rubin, J. M., Hewstone, M., Crisp, R. J., Voci, A., & Richards, Z. (2004). Gender out-group homogeneity: The roles of differential familiarity, gender differences and group size. In V. Yzerbyt, C. M. Judd, & O. Corneille (Eds.), *The psychology of group perception: Perceived variability, entitativity and essentialism*, (pp. 203–220). New York: Psychology Press.

Ruble, D. N., Lurye, L. E., & Zosuls, K. M. (2007). Pink frilly dresses (PFD) and early gender identification. *Princeton Report on Knowledge, 2*(2). Retrieved from http://www.princeton.edu/prok/issues/2-2/pink_frilly.xml

Ruby, P., & Decety, J. (2004). How would you feel versus how do you think she would feel? A neuroimaging study of perspective-taking with social emotions. *Journal of Cognitive Neuroscience, 16*, 988–999.

Ruder, M., & Bless, H. (2003). Mood and the reliance on the ease of retrieval heuristic. *Journal of Personality and Social Psychology, 85*, 20–32.

Rudman, L. (1998). Self-promotion as a risk factor for women: The costs and benefits of counterstereotypical impression management. *Journal of Personality and Social Psychology, 74*, 629–645.

Rudman, L. A., Ashmore, R. D., & Gary, M. L. (2001). "Unlearning" automatic biases: The malleability of implicit prejudice and stereotypes. *Journal of Personality and Social Psychology, 81*, 856–868.

Rudman, L., Phelan, J., & Heppen, J. (2007). Developmental sources of implicit attitudes. *Personality and Social Psychology Bulletin, 33*, 1700–1713.

Rudmin, F. W. (2003). Critical history of the acculturation psychology of assimilation, separation, integration, and marginalization. *Review of General Psychology, 7*, 3–37.

Rule, N., & Ambady, N. (2008). The face of success: Inferences from chief executive officers' appearance predict company profits. *Psychological Science, 19*, 109–111.

Runciman, W. G. (1966). *Relative deprivation and social justice: A study of attitudes to social inequality in twentieth-century England*. Berkeley: Univ. of California Press.

Rupp, H. A., & Wallen, K. (2007). Sex differences in viewing sexual stimuli: An eye-tracking study in men and women. *Hormones and Behavior, 51*, 524–533.

Rusbult, C. E. (1980). Commitment and satisfaction in romantic associations: A test of the investment model. *Journal of Experimental Social Psychology, 16*, 172–186.

Rusbult, C. E. (1983). A longitudinal test of the investment model: The development (and deterioration) of satisfaction and commitment in heterosexual involvements. *Journal of Personality and Social Psychology, 45*, 101–117.

Rusbult, C. E., & Martz, J. M. (1995). Remaining in an abusive relationship: An investment model analysis of nonvoluntary dependence. *Personality and Social Psychology Bulletin, 21*, 558–571.

Rusbult, C. E., Martz, J. M., & Agnew, C. R. (1998). The Investment Model Scale: Measuring commitment level, satisfaction level, quality of alternatives, and investment size. *Personal Relationships, 5*, 357–391.

Rusbult, C. E., Van Lange, P. A. M., Wildschut, T., Yovetich, N. A., & Verette, J. (2000). Perceived superiority in close relationships: Why it exists and persists. *Journal of Personality and Social Psychology, 79*, 521–545.

Rusbult, C. E., & Zembrodt, I. M. (1983). Responses to dissatisfaction in romantic involvements: A multidimensional scaling analysis. *Journal of Experimental Social Psychology, 19*, 274–293.

Rusbult, C. E., Zembrodt, I. M., & Gunn, L. K. (1982). Exit, voice, loyalty, and neglect: Responses to dissatisfaction in romantic involvements. *Journal of Personality and Social Psychology, 43*, 1230–1242.

Rushton, J. P. (1975). Generosity in children: Immediate and long-term effects of modeling, preaching, and moral judgment. *Journal of Personality and Social Psychology, 31*, 459–466.

Rushton, J. P., Chrisjohn, R. D., & Fekken, G. C. (1981). The altruistic personality and the Self-Report Altruism Scale. *Personality and Individual Differences, 2*, 293–302.

Rushton, J. P., Fulker, D. W., Neale, M. C., Nias, D. K. B., & Eysenck, H. J. (1986). Altruism and aggression: The heritability of individual differences. *Journal of Personality and Social Psychology, 50*, 1192–1198.

Rushton, J. P., & Teachman, G. (1978). The effects of positive reinforcement, attributions, and punishment on model induced altruism in children. *Personality and Social Psychology Bulletin, 4*, 322–325.

Russell, D., Peplau, L. A., & Cutrona, C. E. (1980). The revised UCLA Loneliness Scale: Concurrent and discriminant validity evidence. *Journal of Personality and Social Psychology, 39*, 472–480.

Russell, J. (1995). Facial expressions of emotion: What lies beyond minimal universality? *Psychological Bulletin, 118*, 379–391.

Rusting, C. L., & Nolen-Hoeksema, S. (1998). Regulating responses to anger: Effects of rumination and distraction on angry mood. *Journal of Personality and Social Psychology, 74*, 790–803.

Rutkowski, G. K., Gruder, C. L., & Romer, D. (1983). Group cohesiveness, social norms, and bystander intervention. *Journal of Personality and Social Psychology, 44*, 545–552.

Ryan, C., Wapnick, J., Lacaille, N. & Darrow, A. (2006). The effects of various physical characteristics of high-level performers on adjudicators' performance ratings. *Psychology of Music, 34*(4), 559–572.

Ryan, C. S., & Bogart, L. M. (1997). Development of new group members' in-group and out-group stereotypes: Changes in perceived variability and ethnocentrism. *Journal of Personality and Social Psychology, 73*, 719–732.

Ryan, C. S., Judd, C. M., & Park, B. (1996). Effects of racial stereotypes on judgments of individuals: The moderating role of perceived group variability. *Journal of Experimental Social Psychology, 32*, 71–103.

Ryan, R. M., La Guardia, J. G., Solky-Butzel, J., Chirkov, V., & Kim, Y. (2005). On the interpersonal regulation of emotions: Emotional reliance across gender, relationships, and cultures. *Personal Relationships, 12*, 145–163.

Sabini, J., & Green, M. C. (2004). Emotional responses to sexual and emotional infidelity: Constants and differences across genders, samples, and methods. *Personality and Social Psychology Bulletin, 30*, 1375–1388.

Sadalla, E. K., Kenrick, D. T., & Vershure, B. (1987). Dominance and heterosexual attraction. *Journal of Personality and Social Psychology, 52*, 730–738.

Safdar, S, Friedlmeier, W., Matsumoto, D., Yoo, S. H., Kwantes, C. T., Kakai, H. & Shigemasu, E. (2009). Variations of Emotional Display Rules Within and Across Cultures: A Comparison Between Canada, USA, and Japan. *Canadian Journal of Behavioural Science. 41*(1), 1–10.

Safdar, S., Fuller, T., & Lewis, J. R. (2007). Beyond the city limits: An examination of adjustment of immigrants in rural Canada. In A. Chybicka & M. Kazmierczak (Eds.), *The Psychology of Diversity*. Krakow: Impuls.

Safdar, S., Rasmi, S., Dupuis, D., & Lewis, J. R. (2008). An investigation into the cross-cultural adaptation of immigrants to urban and rural Canada using the multidimensional individual difference acculturation (MIDA) model. In A. Chybicka, S. Safdar, & A. Kwiatkowska (Eds.), *Culture and gender an intimate relation*. Gdanskie Wydawnictwo Psychologiczne: Gdansk, Poland.

Safer, M. A. (1980). Attributing evil to the subject, not the situation: Student reaction to Milgram's film on obedience. *Personality and Social Psychology Bulletin, 6*, 205–209.

Sagarin, B. J., Cialdini, R. B., Rice, W. E., & Serna, S. B. (2002). Dispelling the illusion of invulnerability: The motivations and mechanisms of resistance to persuasion. *Journal of Personality and Social Psychology, 83,* 526–541.

Sagrestano, L.M. (1992). The use of power and influence in a gendered world. *Psychology of Women Quarterly, 16*(4), 481–495.

Salganik, M. J., Dodds, P. S., & Watts, D. J. (2006). Experimental study of inequality and unpredictability in an artificial cultural market. *Science, 311,* 854–856.

Salvatore, J., & Shelton, J. N. (2007). Cognitive costs of exposure to racial prejudice. *Psychological Science, 18,* 810–815.

Sanderson, C. A., Darley, J. M., & Messinger, C. S. (2002). 'I'm not as thin as you think I am': The development and consequences of feeling discrepant from the thinness norm. *Personality and Social Psychology Bulletin, 28,* 172–183.

Sanford, A., Fay, N., Stewart, A., & Moxey, L. (2002). Perspective in statements of quantity, with implications for consumer psychology. *Psychological Science, 13,* 130–134.

Sangrigoli, S., Pallier, C., Argenti, A. M., Ventureyra, V. A. G., & de Schonen, S. (2005). Reversibility of the other-race effect in face recognition during childhood. *Psychological Science, 16,* 440–444.

Sanitioso, R., & Wlodarski, R. (2004). In search of information that confirms a desired self perception: Motivated processing of social feedback and choice of social interactions. *Personality and Social Psychology Bulletin, 30,* 412–422.

Sanna, L., & Turley, K. (1996). Antecedents to spontaneous counterfactual thinking: Effects of expectancy violation and outcome valence. *Personality and Social Psychology Bulletin, 22,* 906–919.

Sato, K. (1987). Distribution of the cost of maintaining common resources. *Journal of Experimental Social Psychology, 23,* 19–31.

Saulnier, K., & Perlman, D. (1981). The actor-observer bias is alive and well in prison: A sequel to Wells. *Personality and Social Psychology Bulletin, 7,* 559–564.

Savitsky, K., Epley, N., & Gilovich, T. (2001). Do others judge us as harshly as we think? Overestimating the impact of our failures, shortcomings, and mishaps. *Journal of Personality and Social Psychology, 81,* 44–56.

Sayegh, L., Lasry, J.-C. (1993). Immigrants' adaptation in Canada: Assimilation, acculturation, and orthogonal identification. *Canadian Psychology, 34,* 98–109.

Sbarra, D. A. (2006). Predicting the onset of emotional recovery following nonmarital relationship dissolution: Survival analyses of sadness and anger. *Personality and Social Psychology Bulletin, 32,* 298–312.

Sbarra, D. A., & Emery, R. E. (2005). The emotional sequelae of nonmarital relationship dissolution: Analysis of change and intraindividual variability over time. *Personal Relationships, 12,* 213–232.

Schachter, S., & Singer, J. (1962). Cognitive, social, and physiological determinants of emotional state. *Psychological Review, 69,* 379–399.

Schachner, D. A., & Shaver, P. R. (2004). Attachment dimensions and sexual motives. *Personal Relationships, 11,* 179–195.

Schaller, M., Asp, C. H., Rosell, M. C., & Heim, S. J. (1996). Training in statistical reasoning inhibits the formation of erroneous group stereotypes. *Personality and Social Psychology Bulletin, 22,* 829–844.

Schaller, M., & Cialdini, R. B. (1988). The economics of empathic helping: Support for a mood management motive. *Journal of Experimental Social Psychology, 24,* 163–181.

Scharf, M., & Hertz-Lazarowitz, R. (2003). Social networks in the school context: Effects of culture and gender. *Journal of Personal Relationships, 20,* 843–859.

Scheier, M., & Carver, C. (1993). On the power of positive thinking: The benefits of being optimistic. *Current Directions in Psychological Science, 2,* 26–30.

Scher, S., & Cooper, J. (1989). Motivational basis of dissonance: The singular role of behavioral consequences. *Journal of Personality and Social Psychology, 56,* 899–906.

Scherer, K.R., Abeles, R.P., & Fischer, C.S. (1975). *Human aggression and conflict.* Englewood Cliffs. NJ: Prentice Hall.

Schkade, D., & Kahneman, D. (1998). Does living in California make people happy? A focusing illusion in judgments of life satisfaction. *Psychological Science, 9,* 340–346.

Schleien, S., Ross, H. and Ross, M. (2010), Young Children's Apologies to their Siblings. *Social Development, 19,* 170–186. doi: 10.1111/j.1467–9507.

Schlenker, B., & Trudeau, J. (1990). Impact of self-presentations on private self-beliefs: Effects of prior self-beliefs and misattribution. *Journal of Personality and Social Psychology, 58,* 22–32.

Schlenker, B. R., & Britt, T. W. (1999). Beneficial impression management: Strategically controlling information to help friends. *Journal of Personality and Social Psychology, 76,* 559–573.

Schlenker, B. R., Phillips, S. T., Boniecki, K. A., & Schlenker, D. R. (1995a). Championship pressures: Choking or triumphing in one's own territory? *Journal of Personality and Social Psychology, 68,* 632–643.

Schlenker, B. R., Phillips, S. T., Boniecki, K. A., & Schlenker, D. R. (1995b). Where is the home choke? *Journal of Personality and Social Psychology, 68,* 649–652.

Schmader, T., & Johns, M. (2003). Converging evidence that stereotype threat reduces working memory capacity. *Journal of Personality and Social Psychology, 85,* 440–452.

Schmidt, G., & Weiner, B. (1988). An attribution-affect-action theory of behavior: Replications of judgments of help-giving. *Personality and Social Psychology Bulletin, 14,* 610–621.

Schmitt, B. H., Gilovich, T., Goore, N., & Joseph, L. (1986). Mere presence and social facilitation: One more time. *Journal of Experimental Social Psychology, 22,* 242–248.

Schmitt, D. P. (2005). Is short-term mating the maladaptive result of insecure attachment? A test of competing evolutionary perspectives. *Personality and Social Psychology Bulletin, 31,* 747–768.

Schmitt, D. P., Alcalay, L., Allik, J., Ault, L., Austers, I., Bennett, K. L., et al. (2003). Universal sex differences in the desire for sexual variety: Tests from 52 nations, 6 continents, and 13 islands. *Journal of Personality and Social Psychology, 85,* 85–104.

Schmitt, D. P., Couden, A., & Baker, M. (2001). The effects of sex and temporal context on feelings of romantic desire: An experimental evaluation of sexual strategies theory. *Personality and Social Psychology Bulletin, 27,* 833–847.

Schmitt, M. T., & Branscombe, N. R. (2002). The internal and external causal loci of attributions to prejudice. *Personality and Social Psychology Bulletin, 28,* 620–628.

Schmitt, M. T., Branscombe, N. R., Kobrynowicz, D., & Owen, S. (2002). Perceiving discrimination against one's gender group has different implications for well-being in women and men. *Personality and Social Psychology Bulletin, 28,* 197–210.

Schneider, M. E., Major, B., Luhtanen, R., & Crocker, J. (1996). Social stigma and the potential costs of assumptive help. *Personality and Social Psychology Bulletin, 22,* 201–209.

Schreiber, G., Robins, M., Striegel-Moore, R., Obarzanek, E., Morrison, J.A., & Wright, D.J. (1996). Weight modification efforts reported by black and white preadolescent girls: National Heart, Lung, and Blood Institute Growth and Health Study. *Pediatrics, 98,* 63–70.

Schroeder, C. M., & Prentice, D. A. (1998). Exposing pluralistic ignorance to reduce alcohol use among college students. *Journal of Applied Social Psychology, 28,* 2150–2180.

Schroeder, D. A., Penner, L. A., Dovidio, J. F., & Piliavin, J. A. (1995). *The psychology of helping and altruism: Problems and puzzles.* New York: McGraw-Hill.

Schultz, T., Léveillé, E., & Lepper, M. (1999). Free choice and cognitive dissonance revisited: Choosing 'lesser evils' versus 'greater goods.' *Personality and Social Psychology Bulletin, 25,* 40–48.

Schulz-Hardt, S., Frey, D., Lüthgens, C., & Moscovici, S. (2000). Biased information search in group decision making. *Journal of Personality and Social Psychology, 78,* 655–669.

Schumann, K., & Ross, M.(2010). Why women apologize more than men: gender differences in thresholds for perceiving offensive behavior. *Psychological Science, 21*(11):1649–55.

Schütz, A. (1999). It was your fault! Self-serving biases in autobiographical accounts of conflicts in married couples. *Journal of Social and Personal Relationships, 16,* 193–208.

Schwartz, J. (2003, March 9). The nation: NASA's curse?; 'groupthink' is 30 years old, and still going strong. *The New York Times.* Retrieved from http://www.nytimes.com/2003/03/09/weekinreview/the-nation-nasa-s-curse-groupthink-is-30-years-old-and-still-going-strong.html

Schwartz, S.H. (1994). Beyond individualism/collectivism: New cultural dimensions of values. In U. Kim, H. C. Triandis, C. Kagitcibasi, S. Choi, & G. Yoon, *Cross cultural research and methodology series: Vol. 18. Individualism and collectivism: Theory, method, and applications* (pp. 85-119). Thousand Oaks, CA: Sage.

Schwarz, N. (1998). Accessible content and accessibility experiences: The interplay of declarative and experiential information in judgment. *Personality and Social Psychology Review, 2,* 87–99.

Schwarz, N., Hippler, H., Deutsch, B., & Strack, F. (1985). Response scales: Effects of category range on reported behavior and comparative judgments. *Public Opinion Quarterly, 49,* 388–395.

Schwarz, N., Strack, F., & Mai, H. (1991). Assimilation and contrast effects in part-whole question sequences: A conversational logic analysis. *Public Opinion Quarterly, 55,* 3–23.

Schwarzwald, J., Bizman, A., & Raz, M. (1983). The foot-in-the-door paradigm: Effects of second request size on donation probability and donor generosity. *Personality and Social Psychology Bulletin, 9,* 443–450.

Schweitzer, M. E., DeChurch, L. A., & Gibson, D. E. (2005). Conflict frames and the use of deception: Are competitive negotiators less ethical? *Journal of Applied Social Psychology, 35,* 2123–2149.

Scottham, K. M., & Dias, R. H. (2010). Acculturative strategies and the psychological adaptation of Brazilian migrants to Japan. *Identity: An International Journal of Theory and Research, 10,* 284–303.

Searcy, E., & Eisenberg, N. (1992). Defensiveness in response to aid from a sibling. *Journal of Personality and Social Psychology, 62,* 422–433.

Sears, D. O. (1986). College sophomores in the laboratory: Influences of a narrow data base on social psychology's view of human nature. *Journal of Personality and Social Psychology, 51,* 515–530.

Sechrist, G. B., & Stangor, C. (2001). Perceived consensus influences intergroup behavior and stereotype accessibility. *Journal of Personality and Social Psychology, 80,* 645–654.

Sedikides, C. (1993). Assessment, enhancement, and verification determinants of the self-evaluation process. *Journal of Personality and Social Psychology, 65,* 317–338.

Sedikides, C., & Anderson, C. (1994). Causal perceptions of intertrait relations: The glue that holds person types together. *Personality and Social Psychology Bulletin, 20,* 294–302.

Sedikides, C., Oliver, M. B., & Campbell, W. K. (1994). Perceived benefits and costs of romantic relationships for women and men: Implications for exchange theory. *Personal Relationships, 1,* 5–21.

Segal, N. L. (1993). Twin, sibling, and adoption methods: Tests of evolutionary hypotheses. *American Psychologist, 48,* 943–956.

Segrin, C., Taylor, M. E., & Altman, J. (2005). Social cognitive mediators and relational outcomes associated with parental divorce. *Journal of Social and Personal Relationships, 22,* 361–377.

Seidman, G., Shrout, P. E., & Bolger, N. (2006). Why is enacted social support associated with increased distress?: Using simulation to test two possible sources of spuriousness. *Personality and Social Psychology Bulletin, 32,* 52–65.

Seijts, G. H., & Latham, G. P. (2011). The effect of commitment to a learning goal, self-efficacy, and the interaction between learning goal difficulty and commitment on performance in a business simulation. *Human Performance, 24,* 189–204.

Seiter, J. S., & Gass, R. H. (2005). The effect of patriotic messages on restaurant tipping. *Journal of Applied Social Psychology, 35,* 1197–1205.

Sekaquaptewa, D., & Thompson, M. (2002). The differential effects of solo status on members of high- and low-status groups. *Personality and Social Psychology Bulletin, 28,* 694–707.

Seligman, M.E.P., Abramson, L.Y., Semmel, A. & von Baeyer, C. (1979). Depressive Attributional Style. *Journal of Abnormal Psychology, 88*(3), 242–247.

Sellers, R. M., & Shelton, J. N. (2003). The role of racial identity in perceived racial discrimination. *Journal of Personality and Social Psychology, 84,* 1079–1092.

Seta, C., Hayes, N., & Seta, J. (1994). Mood, memory, and vigilance: The influence of distraction on recall and impression formation. *Personality and Social Psychology Bulletin, 20,* 170–177.

Shackelford, T. K., & Larsen, R. J. (1997). Facial asymmetry as an indicator of psychological, emotional, and physiological distress. *Journal of Personality and Social Psychology, 72,* 456–466.

Shamir, J. & Shikak, K. (2002). Determinants of reconciliation and compromise among Israelis and Palestinians. *Journal of Peace Research, 39*(2), 185–202.

Shapiro, D. L., & Brett, J. M. (1993). Comparing three processes underlying judgments of procedural justice: A field study of mediation and arbitration. *Journal of Personality and Social Psychology, 65,* 1167–1177.

Shapka, J. D., & Keating, D. P. (2005). Structure and change in self-concept during adolescence. *Canadian Journal of Behavioural Sciences, 37,* 83–96.

Shariff, A. F., & Norenzayan, A. (2007). God is watching you: Priming God concepts increases prosocial behavior in an anonymous economic game. *Psychological Science, 18,* 803–809.

Sharp, F. C. (1928). *Ethics.* New York: Century Company.

Sharp, M., & Getz, J. (1996). Substance use as impression management. *Personality and Social Psychology Bulletin, 22,* 60–67.

Sharpsteen, D. J. (1995). The effects of relationship and self-esteem threats on the likelihood of romantic jealousy. *Journal of Social and Personal Relationships, 12,* 89–101.

Sheeran, P., Abraham, C., & Orbell, S. (1999). Psychosocial correlates of heterosexual condom use: A meta-analysis. *Psychological Bulletin. 125,* 90–132.

Sheese, B. E., & Graziano, W. G. (2005). Deciding to defect: The effects of video-game violence on cooperative behavior. *Psychological Science, 16,* 354–357.

Sheldon, K. (1996). The Social Awareness Inventory: Development and applications. *Personality and Social Psychology Bulletin, 22,* 620–634.

Sheldon, K. (2005). Positive value change during college: Normative trends and individual differences. *Journal of Research in Personality, 39,* 209–223.

Sheldon, K., Ryan, R., Deci, E., & Kasser, T. (2004). The independent effects of goal contents and motives on well-being: It's both what you pursue and why you pursue it. *Personality and Social Psychology Bulletin, 30,* 475–486.

Sheldon, K. M. (1999). Learning the lessons of tit-for-tat: Even competitors can get the message. *Journal of Personality and Social Psychology, 77,* 1245–1253.

Shell, R. M., & Eisenberg, N. (1992). A developmental model of recipients' reactions to aid. *Psychological Bulletin, 111,* 413–433.

Shelton, J. N., & Richeson, J. A. (2005). Intergroup contact and pluralistic ignorance. *Journal of Personality and Social Psychology, 88,* 91–107.

Shepperd, J. (1993). Student derogation of the Scholastic Aptitude Test: Biases in perceptions and presentations of college board scores. *Basic and Applied Social Psychology, 14,* 455–473.

Shepperd, J., & Taylor, K. (1999). Ascribing advantages to social comparison targets. *Basic and Applied Social Psychology, 21,* 103–117.

Shepperd, J. A. (1993a). Student derogation of the Scholastic Aptitude Test: Biases in perceptions and presentations of college board scores. *Basic and Applied Social Psychology, 14,* 455–473.

Shepperd, J. A. (1993b). Productivity loss in performance groups: A motivation analysis. *Psychological Bulletin, 113,* 67–81.

Shepperd, J. A., & Taylor, K. M. (1999). Social loafing and expectancy-value theory. *Personality and Social Psychology Bulletin, 25,* 1147–1158.

Sherif, M. (1936). *The psychology of social norms.* New York: Harper.

Sherif, M. (1966). *In common predicament: social psychology of intergroup conflict and cooperation.* Boston: Houghton Mifflin.

Sherif, M., & Sherif, C. W. (1969). *Social psychology.* New York: Harper & Row.

Sherman, D. A. K., Nelson, L. D., & Steele, C. M. (2000). Do messages about health risks threaten the self? Increasing the acceptance of threatening health messages via self-affirmation. *Personality and Social Psychology Bulletin, 26,* 1046–1058.

Sherman, M. D., & Thelen, M. H. (1996). Fear of intimacy scale: Validation and extension with adolescents. *Journal of Social and Personal Relationships, 13,* 507–521.

Sherman, R., Buddie, A., Dragan, K., End, C., & Finney, L. (1999). Twenty years of PSPB: Trends in content, design, and analysis. *Personality and Social Psychology Bulletin, 25,* 177–187.

Sherr, L. (1990). Fear arousal and AIDS: Do shock tactics work? *AIDS, 4,* 361–364.

Shih, M., Pittinsky, T. L., & Ambady, N. (1999). Stereotype susceptibility: Identity salience and shifts in quantitative performance. *Psychological Science, 10,* 80–83.

Shook, N. J., & Fazio, R. H. (2008). Interracial roommate relationships: An experimental field test of the contact hypothesis. *Psychological Science, 19,* 717–723.

Shotland, R. L., & Heinold, W. D. (1985). Bystander response to arterial bleeding: Helping skills, the decision-making process, and differentiating the helping response. *Journal of Personality and Social Psychology, 49,* 347–356.

Shotland, R. L., & Straw, M. K. (1976). Bystander response to an assault: When a man attacks a woman. *Journal of Personality and Social Psychology, 34,* 990–999.

Sidanius, J., & Pratto, F. (2001). *Social dominance: An intergroup theory of social hierarchy and oppression.* New York: Cambridge University Press.

Siegel, J. M. (1990). Stressful life events and use of physician services among the elderly: The moderating role of pet ownership. *Journal of Personality and Social Psychology, 58,* 1081–1086.

Siegel, J. T., Alvaro, E. M., Crano, W. D., Lac, A., Ting, S., & Jones, S. P. (2008). A quasi-experimental investigation of message appeal variations on organ donor registration rates. *Health Psychology, 27,* 170–178.

Sigall, H. & Landy, D. (1973). Radiating beauty: Effects of having a physically attractive partner on person perception. *Journal of Personality and Social Psychology, 28,* 218–224.

Silvia, P. J. (2005). Deflecting reactance: The role of similarity in increasing compliance and reducing resistance. *Basic and Applied Social Psychology, 27,* 277–284.

Simmons, C. H., vom Kolke, A., & Shimizu, H. (1986). Attitudes toward romantic love among American, German, and Japanese students. *Journal of Social Psychology, 126,* 327–336.

Simon, D., Krawczyk, D., & Holyoak, K. (2004). Construction of preferences by constraint satisfaction. *Psychological Science, 15,* 331–336.

Simon, L., Greenberg, J., & Brehm, J. (1995). Trivialization: The forgotten mode of dissonance reduction. *Journal of Personality and Social Psychology, 68,* 247–260.

Simpson, D., & Ostrom, T. (1976). Contrast effects in impression formation. *Journal of Personality and Social Psychology, 34,* 625–629.

Simpson, J. A., Gangestad, S. W., & Lerman, M. (1990). Perception of physical attractiveness: Mechanisms involved in the maintenance of romantic relationships. *Journal of Personality and Social Psychology, 59,* 1192–1201.

Simpson, J. A., Ickes, W., & Blackstone, T. (1995). When the head protects the heart: Empathic accuracy in dating relationships. *Journal of Personality and Social Psychology, 69,* 629–641.

Simpson, J. A., Rholes, W. S., & Nelligan, J. S. (1992). Support seeking and support giving within couples in an anxiety-provoking situation: The role of attachment styles. *Journal of Personality and Social Psychology, 62,* 434–446.

Simpson, J. A., Rholes, W. S., & Phillips, D. (1996). Conflict in close relationships: An attachment perspective. *Journal of Personality and Social Psychology, 71,* 899–914.

Singelis, T., Choo, P., & Hatfield, E. (1995). Love Schemas and romantic love. *Journal of Social Behavior and Personality, 10,* 15–36.

Singer, A. R., Cassin, S. E., & Dobson, K. S. (2005). The role of gender in the career aspirations of professional psychology graduates: Are there more similarities than differences? *Canadian Psychology, 46,* 215–222.

Singh, D. (1993). Body shape and women's attractiveness: The critical role of waist-to-hip ratio. *Human Nature, 4,* 297–321.

Singh, D. (1995). Female judgment of male attractiveness and desirability for relationships: Role of waist-to-hip ratio and financial status. *Journal of Personality and Social Psychology, 69,* 1089–1101.

Skelton, J. A. & Pennebaker, J. W. (1982). *The psychology of physical symptoms and sensations.* In G. S. Sanders & J. Suls (Eds.), *Social psychology of health and illness* (pp. 99–128). Hillsdale, NJ: Lawrence Erlbaum Associates.

Skinner, B. (1938). *The Behavior of Organisms: An Experimental Analysis.* Oxford, England: Appleton-Century.

Skitka, L. J. (1999). Ideological and attributional boundaries on public compassion: Reactions to individuals and communities affected by a natural disaster. *Personality and Social Psychology Bulletin, 25,* 793–808.

Skitka, L. J., Bauman, C. W., & Sargis, E. G. (2005). Moral conviction: Another contributor to attitude strength or something more? *Journal of Personality and Social Psychology, 88,* 895–917.

Skitka, L. J., & Tetlock, P. E. (1993). Providing public assistance: Cognitive and motivational processes underlying liberal and conservative policy preferences. *Journal of Personality and Social Psychology, 65,* 1205–1223.

Slavin, R. E., & Cooper, R. (1999). Improving intergroup relations: Lessons learned from cooperative learning programs. *Journal of Social Issues, 55,* 647–663.

Slavin, R. E., & Madden, N. A. (1979). School practices that improve race relations. *American Educational Research Journal, 16,* 169–180.

Sloan, J. H., Kellermann, A. L., Reay, D. T., & Ferris, J. A. (1988). Handgun regulations, crime, assaults, and homicide: A tale of two cities. *New England Journal of Medicine, 319*, 1256–1262.

Slone, A. E., Brigham, J. C., & Meissner, C. A. (2000). Social and cognitive factors affecting the own-race bias in Whites. *Basic and Applied Social Psychology, 22*, 71–84.

Slovic, P., & Fischhoff, B. (1977). On the psychology of experimental surprise. *Journal of Experimental Psychology: Human Perception and Performance, 3*, 544–551.

Smith, A., Jussim, L., & Eccles, J. (1999). Do self-fulfilling prophecies accumulate, dissipate, or remain stable over time? *Journal of Personality and Social Psychology, 77*, 548–565.

Smith, C. L., Gelfand, D. M., Hartmann, D. P., & Partlow, M. E. (1979). Children's causal attributions regarding help giving. *Child Development, 50*, 203–210.

Smith, E. R., & Henry, S. (1996). An in-group becomes part of the self: Response time evidence. *Personality and Social Psychology Bulletin, 22*, 635–642.

Smith, H. J., & Tyler, T. R. (1997). Choosing the right pond: The impact of group membership on self-esteem and group-oriented behavior. *Journal of Experimental Social Psychology, 33*, 146–170.

Smith, P. B., Bond, M. H., & Kagitcibasi, C. (2006). Understanding social psychology across cultures: Living and working in a changing world. London: Sage.

Smith, S. M., & Shaffer, D. R. (1991). Celerity and cajolery: Rapid speech may promote or inhibit persuasion through its impact on message elaboration. *Personality and Social Psychology Bulletin, 17*, 663–669.

Smith, S. M., & Shaffer, D. R. (1995). Speed of speech and persuasion: Evidence for multiple effects. *Personality and Social Psychology Bulletin, 21*, 1051–1060.

Snyder, C. R., Lassegard, M., & Ford, C. E. (1986). Distancing after group success and failure: Basking in reflected glory and cutting off reflected failure. *Journal of Personality and Social Psychology, 51*, 382–388.

Snyder, M. (1974). Self-monitoring of expressive behavior. *Journal of Personality and Social Psychology, 30*, 526–537.

Snyder, M., Berscheid, E., & Glick, P. (1985). Focusing on the exterior and the interior: Two investigations of the initiation of personal relationships. *Journal of Personality and Social Psychology, 48*, 1427–1439.

Snyder, M., & DeBono, K. G. (1985). Appeals to image and claims about quality: Understanding the psychology of advertising. *Journal of Personality and Social Psychology, 49*, 586–597.

Snyder, M., & Gangestad, S. (1986). On the nature of self-monitoring: Matters of assessment, matters of validity. *Journal of Personality and Social Psychology, 51*, 125–139.

Snyder, M., & Haugen, J. (1994). Why does behavioral confirmation occur? A functional perspective on the role of the perceiver. *Journal of Experimental Social Psychology, 30*, 218–246.

Snyder, M., & Swann, W. (1978). Behavioral confirmation in social interaction: From social perception to social reality. *Journal of Experimental Social Psychology, 14*, 148–162.

Snyder, M., Tanke, E., & Berscheid, E. (1977). Social perception and interpersonal behavior: On the self-fulfilling nature of social stereotypes. *Journal of Personality and Social Psychology, 35*, 656–666.

Zimbardo, P. (2011). The Stanford Prison Experiment. Retrieved from http://www.prisonexp.org/psychology/4

Solano, C. H., Batten, P. G., & Parish, E. A. (1982). Loneliness and patterns of self-disclosure. *Journal of Personality and Social Psychology, 43*, 524–531.

Sommer, K. L., Horowitz, I. A., & Bourgeois, M. J. (2001). When juries fail to comply with the law: Biased evidence processing in individual and group decision making. *Personality and Social Psychology Bulletin, 27*, 309–320.

Sommers, S. R. (2006). On racial diversity and group decision making: Identifying multiple effects of racial composition on jury deliberations. *Journal of Personality and Social Psychology, 90*, 597–612.

Sommers, S. R., & Ellsworth, P. C. (2000). Race in the courtroom: Perceptions of guilt and dispositional attributions. *Personality and Social Psychology Bulletin, 26*, 1367–1379.

Son Hing, L. S., Bobocel, D. R., & Zanna, M. P. (2002). Meritocracy and opposition to affirmative action: Making concessions in the face of discrimination. *Journal of Personality and Social Psychology, 83*, 493–509.

Song Hing, L. S., Bobocel, D. R., Zanna, M. P., & McBride, M. V. (2007). Authoritarian dynamics and unethical decision making: High social dominance orientation leaders and high right-wing authoritarianism followers. *Journal of Personality and Social Psychology, 92*, 67–81.

Son Hing, L. S., Li, W., & Zanna, M. P. (2002). Inducing hypocrisy to reduce prejudicial responses among aversive racists. *Journal of Experimental Social Psychology, 38*, 71–78.

Sorrentino, R. M., & Field, N. (1986). Emergent leadership over time: The functional value of positive motivation. *Journal of Personality and Social Psychology, 50*, 1091–1099.

Sourander, A., Helstela, L., Helenius, H., & Piha, J. (2000). Persistence of bullying from childhood to adolescence – a longitudinal 8 year follow-up study. *Child Abuse and Neglect, 24*(7), 873–881.

Spears, G. & Seydegart, K. (2004). Kids' Views on Violence in the Media. *Canadian Child and Adolescent Psychiatry Review. 13*(1), 7–12.

Spencer, S. J., Steele, C. M., & Quinn, D. M. (1999). Stereotype threat and women's math performance. *Journal of Experimental Social Psychology, 35*, 4–28.

Spielmann, S. S., MacDonald, G., & Wilson, A. E. (2009). On the rebound: Focusing on someone new helps anxiously attached individuals let go of ex-partners. *Personality & Social Psychology Bulletin, 35*, 1382–1394.

Sporer, S. L. (2001). Recognizing faces of other ethnic groups: An integration of theories. *Psychology, Public Policy, and Law, 7*, 36–97.

Sprafkin, J. N., Liebert, R. M., & Poulos, R. W. (1975). Effects of a prosocial televised example on children's helping. *Journal of Experimental Child Psychology, 20*, 119–126.

Sprecher, S. (1999). 'I love you more today than yesterday': Romantic partners' perceptions of changes in love and related affect over time. *Journal of Personality and Social Psychology, 76*, 46–53.

Sprecher, S., McKinney, K., & Crown, T. L. (1991). The effect of current sexual behavior on friendship, dating, and marriage desirability. *Journal of Sex Research, 28*, 387–408.

Sprecher, S. & Regan, P. C. (1996). College virgins: How men and women perceive their sexual status. *Journal of Sex Research, 33*(1), 3–15.

Sprecher, S., Sullivan, Q., & Hatfield, E. (1994). Mate selection preferences: Gender differences examined in a national sample. *Journal of Personality and Social Psychology, 66*, 1074–1080.

Stangor, C., Sechrist, G. B., & Jost, J. T. (2001). Changing racial beliefs by providing consensus information. *Personality and Social Psychology Bulletin, 27*, 486–496.

Stangor, C., Swim, J. K., Van Allen, K. L., & Sechrist, G. B. (2002). Reporting discrimination in public and private contexts. *Journal of Personality and Social Psychology, 82*, 69–74.

Stapel, D., & Blanton, H. (2004). From seeing to being: Subliminal social comparisons affect implicit and explicit self-evaluations. *Journal of Personality and Social Psychology, 87*, 468–481.

Stapel, D., & Suls, J. (2004). Method matters: Effects of explicit versus implicit social comparisons on activation, behavior, and self-views. *Journal of Personality and Social Psychology, 87*, 860–875.

Stasser, G., Stewart, D. D., & Wittenbaum, G. M. (1995). Expert roles and information exchange during discussion: The importance of knowing who knows what. *Journal of Experimental Social Psychology, 31*, 244–265.

Stasser, G., & Titus, W. (1985). Pooling of unshared information in group decision making: Biased information sampling during discussion. *Journal of Personality and Social Psychology, 48*, 1467–1478.

Statistics Canada. (2005). *Women in Canada 2005: A Gender-based statistical report* (5th ed.), Catalogue no. 89-503-XIE, Table 6.11, p. 155. Retrieved from http://dsp-psd.pwgsc.gc.ca/Collection-R/Statcan/89-503-X/0010589-503-XIE.pdf

Statistics Canada (2006). Immigrant population by place of birth, by province and territory (2006 Census). Ottawa, Canada: Minister of Industry. Retrieved from http://www40.statcan.gc.ca/l01/cst01/demo34a-eng.htm

Statistics Canada (2006). *Violence against women in Canada... by the numbers*. Retrieved from http://www42.statcan.ca/smr08/2006/smr08_012_2006-eng.htm

Statistics Canada (2007). *Family violence in Canada: A statistical profile 2007.* Catalogue no. 85-2240XIE, October. Ottawa: Minister of Industry.

Statistics Canada (2007). *Youth self-reported delinquency, Toronto 2006.* Juristat (27): 6. Ottawa: Canadian Centre of Justice Statistics, Statistics Canada.

Stattin, H., & Magnusson, D. (1989). The role of early aggressive behavior in the frequency, seriousness, and types of later crime. *Journal of Consulting and Clinical Psychology, 57*, 710–718.

Staub, E. (1996). Preventing genocide: Activating bystanders, helping victims, and the creation of caring. *Peace and Conflict: Journal of Peace Psychology, 2*, 189–200.

Steblay, N. M. (1987). Helping behavior in rural and urban environments: A meta-analysis. *Psychological Bulletin, 102*, 346–356.

Steele, C., & Josephs, R. (1990). Alcohol myopia: Its prized and dangerous effects. *American Psychologist, 45*, 921–933.

Steele, C., & Liu, T. (1983). Dissonance processes as self-affirmation. *Journal of Personality and Social Psychology, 45*, 5–19.

Steele, C., Spencer, S., & Lynch, M. (1993). Self-image resilience and dissonance: The role of affirmational resources. *Journal of Personality and Social Psychology, 64*, 885–896.

Steele, C. M. (1997). A threat in the air: How stereotypes shape intellectual identity and performance. *American Psychologist, 52*, 613–629.

Steele, C. M., & Aronson, J. (1995). Stereotype threat and the intellectual test performance of African Americans. *Journal of Personality and Social Psychology, 69*, 797–811.

Steele, C. M., & Josephs, R. A. (1988). Drinking your troubles away: II. An attention-allocation model of alcohol's effect on psychological stress. *Journal of Abnormal Psychology, 97*, 196–205.

Steele, C. M., & Southwick, L. (1985). Alcohol and social behavior: I. The psychology of drunken excess. *Journal of Personality and Social Psychology, 48*, 18–34.

Steele, C. M., Southwick, L., & Critchlow, B. (1981). Dissonance and alcohol: Drinking your troubles away. *Journal of Personality and Social Psychology, 4*, 831–846.

Steinberg, L. D., Catalano, R., & Dooley, D. (1981). Economic antecedents of child abuse and neglect. *Child Development, 52*, 975–985.

Steinel, W., & De Dreu, C. K. W. (2004). Social motives and strategic misrepresentation in social decision making. *Journal of Personality and Social Psychology, 86*, 419–434.

Stephan, C., Presser, N. R., Kennedy, J. C., & Aronson, E. (1978). Attributions to success and failure after cooperative or competitive interaction. *European Journal of Social Psychology, 8*, 269–274.

Stepper, S., & Strack, F. (1993). Proprioceptive determinants of emotional and nonemotional feelings. *Journal of Personality and Social Psychology, 64*, 211–220.

Sternberg, R. J. (1986). A triangular theory of love. *Psychological Review, 93*, 119–135.

Sternberg, R. J. (1997). Construct validation of a triangular love scale. European Journal of Social Psychology, 27, 313–335.

Stevahn, L., Munger, L. & Kealey, K. (2005). Conflict Resolution in a French Immersion Elementary School. *Journal of Educational Research, 99(1)*, 3–18.

Stewart, D. D., & Stasser, G. (1995). Expert role assignment and information sampling during collective recall and decision making. *Journal of Personality and Social Psychology, 69*, 619–628.

Stewart, J. E. (1980). Defendant's attractiveness as a factor in the outcome of criminal trials: An observational study. *Journal of Applied Social Psychology, 10*, 348–361.

Stewart, J. E. (1985). Appearance and punishment: The attraction-leniency effect in the courtroom. *Journal of Social Psychology, 125*, 373–378.

Stewart, S., Stinnett, H., & Rosenfeld, L. B. (2000). Sex differences in desired characteristics of short-term and long-term relationship partners. *Journal of Social and Personal Relationships, 17*, 843–853.

Stewart, T., Vassar, P., Sanchez, D., & David, S. (2000). Attitude toward women's societal roles moderates the effect of gender cues on target individuation. *Journal of Personality and Social Psychology, 79*, 143–157.

Stice, E., Chase, A., Stormer, S., & Appel, A. (2001). A randomized trial of a dissonance-based eating disorder prevention program. *International Journal of Eating Disorders, 29*, 247–262.

Stice, E., Mazotti, L., Weibel, D., & Agras, W. (2000). Dissonance prevention program decreases thin-ideal internalization, body dissatisfaction, dieting, negative affect, and bulimic symptoms: A preliminary experiment. *International Journal of Eating Disorders, 27*, 206–217.

Stice, E., Trost, A., & Chase, A. (2003). Healthy weight control and dissonance-based eating disorder prevention programs: Results from a controlled trial. *International Journal of Eating Disorders, 33*, 10–21.

Stigler, J., Smith, S., & Mao, L. (1985). The self-perception of competence by Chinese children. *Child Development, 56*, 1259–1270.

Stiles, W. B., Walz, N. C., Schroeder, M. A. B., & Williams, L. L. (1996). Attractiveness and disclosure in initial encounters of mixed-sex dyads. *Journal of Social and Personal Relationships, 13*, 303–312.

Stinson, D. A., Cameron, J. J., Wood, J. V., Gaucher, D., & Holmes, J. G. (2009). Deconstructing the "Reign of Error": Interpersonal warmth explains the self-fulfilling prophecy of anticipated acceptance. *Personality and Social Psychology Bulletin, 35*, 1165–1178.

Stipek, D., & Gralinski, J. (1991). Gender differences in children's achievement-related beliefs and emotional responses to success and failure in mathematics. *Journal of Educational Psychology, 83*, 361–371.

Stone, A., Hedges, S., Neale, J., & Satin, M. (1985). Prospective and cross-sectional mood reports offer no evidence of a 'blue Monday' phenomenon. *Journal of Personality and Social Psychology, 49*, 129–134.

Stone, J. (2003). Self-consistency for low self-esteem in dissonance processes: The role of self-standards. *Personality and Social Psychology Bulletin, 29*, 846–858.

Stone, J., Aronson, E., Crain, A. L., Winslow, M. P. & Fried, C. B., (1994). Inducing hypocrisy as a means of encouraging young adults to use condoms. *Personality and Social Psychology Bulletin*, 20, 116–128.

Stone, J., & Cooper, J. (2001). A self-standards model of cognitive dissonance. *Journal of Experimental Social Psychology*, 37, 228–243.

Stone, J., Wiegand, A., Cooper, J., & Aronson, E. (1997). When exemplification fails: Hypocrisy and the motive for self-integrity. *Journal of Personality and Social Psychology*, 72, 54–65.

Storms, M. (1973). Videotape and the attribution process: Reversing actors' and observers' points of view. *Journal of Personality and Social Psychology*, 27, 165–175.

Story, M., & Faulkner, P. (1990). The prime time diet: A content analysis of eating behavior and food messages in television program content and commercials. *American Journal of Public Health*, 80, 738–740.

Stott, C., & Reicher, S. D. (1998). Crowd action as intergroup process: Introducing the police perspective. *European Journal of Social Psychology*, 28, 509–529.

Stouffer, S. A., Suchman, E. A., DeVinney, L. C., Star, S. A., & Williams, R. M. (1949). *The American soldier: Adjustment during army life* (Vol. 1). Princeton: Princeton Univ. Press.

Strack, F., & Mussweiler, T. (1997). Explaining the enigmatic anchoring effect: Mechanisms of selective accessibility. *Journal of Personality and Social Psychology*, 73, 437–446.

Strahan, E. J., Spencer, S. J., & Zanna, M. P. (2002). Subliminal priming and persuasion: Striking while the iron is hot. *Journal of Experimental Social Psychology*, 38, 556–568.

Strauman, T., Lemieux, A., & Coe, C. (1993). Self-discrepancy and natural killer cell activity: Immunological consequences of negative self-evaluation. *Journal of Personality and Social Psychology*, 64, 1042–1052.

Stroebe, W., & Stroebe, M. (1996). The social psychology of social support. In E. T. Higgins & A. W. Kruglanski (Eds.), *Social Psychology: Handbook of Basic Principles* (pp. 597–621). New York: Guilford Press.

Strohmetz, D. B., Rind, B., Fisher, R., & Lynn, M. (2002). Sweetening the till: The use of candy to increase restaurant tipping. *Journal of Applied Social Psychology*, 32, 300–309.

Strube, M. J., & Rahimi, A. M. (2006). "Everybody knows it's true": Social dominance orientation and right-wing authoritarianism moderate false consensus for stereotypic beliefs. *Journal of Research in Personality*, 40, 1038–1053.

Stukas, A., Snyder, M., & Clary, E. (1999). The effects of 'mandatory volunteerism' on intentions to volunteer. *Psychological Science*, 10, 59–64.

Stürmer, S., Snyder, M., Kropp, A., & Siem, B. (2006). Empathy-motivated helping: The moderating role of group membership. *Personality and Social Psychology Bulletin*, 32, 943–956.

Stürmer, S., Snyder, M., & Omoto, A. M. (2005). Prosocial emotions and helping: The moderating role of group membership. *Journal of Personality and Social Psychology*, 88, 532–546.

Suh, E. (2002). Culture, identity consistency, and subjective well-being. *Journal of Personality and Social Psychology*, 83, 1378–1391.

Suls, J., & Wan, C. (1987). In search of the false-uniqueness phenomenon: Fear and estimates of social consensus. *Journal of Personality and Social Psychology*, 52, 211–217.

Susman, E. J., Inoff-Germain, G., Nottelmann, E. D., & Loriaux, D. L. (1987). Hormones, emotional dispositions, and aggressive attributes in young adolescents. *Child Development*, 58, 1114–1134.

Sutton, S. R., & Eiser, J. R. (1984). The effect of fear-arousing communications on cigarette smoking: An expectancy-value approach. *Journal of Behavioral Medicine*, 7, 13–33.

Swaab, R., Postmes, T., Van Beest, I., & Spears, R. (2007). Shared cognition as a product of, and precursor to, shared identity in negotiations. *Personality and Social Psychology Bulletin*, 33, 187–199.

Swann, W. (1987). Identity negotiation: Where two roads meet. *Journal of Personality and Social Psychology*, 53, 1038–1051.

Swann, W., & Ely, R. (1984). A battle of wills: Self-verification versus behavioral confirmation. *Journal of Personality and Social Psychology*, 46, 1287–1302.

Swann, W., & Hill, C. (1982). When our identities are mistaken: Reaffirming self-conceptions through social interaction. *Journal of Personality and Social Psychology*, 43, 59–66.

Swann, W., Hixon, J., & de la Ronde, C. (1992). Embracing the bitter 'truth': Negative self-concepts and marital commitment. *Psychological Science*, 3, 118–121.

Swann, W., Pelham, B., & Krull, D. (1989). Agreeable fancy or disagreeable truth? Reconciling self-enhancement and self-verification. *Journal of Personality and Social Psychology*, 57, 782–791.

Swann, W. B., de la Ronde, C., & Hixon, J. G. (1994). Authenticity and positivity strivings in marriage and courtship. *Journal of Personality and Social Psychology*, 66, 857–869.

Swim, J. K. (1994). Perceived versus meta-analytic effect sizes: An assessment of the accuracy of gender stereotypes. *Journal of Personality and Social Psychology*, 66, 21–36.

Swim, J. K., Aikin, K. J., Hall, W. S., & Hunter, B. A. (1995). Sexism and racism: Old-fashioned and modern prejudices. *Journal of Personality and Social Psychology*, 68, 199–214.

Swim, J. K., & Hyers, L. L. (1999). Excuse me—What did you just say?!: Women's public and private responses to sexist remarks. *Journal of Experimental Social Psychology*, 35, 68–88.

Swim, J., & Sanna, L. (1996). He's skilled, she's lucky: A meta-analysis of observers' attributions for women's and men's successes and failures. *Personality and Social Psychology Bulletin*, 22, 507–519.

Tafarodi, R. W., Kang, S., & Milne, A. B. (2002). When different becomes similar: Compensatory conformity in bicultural visible minorities. *Personality and Social Psychology Bulletin*, 28, 1131–1142.

Tafarodi, R. W., Lo, C., Yamaguchi, S., Lee, W. W.-S., & Katsura, H. (2004). The inner self in three countries. *Journal of Cross-Cultural Psychology*, 35, 97–117.

Tajfel, H. (1982). Social psychology of intergroup relations. *Annual Review of Psychology*, 33, 1–39.

Tajfel, H., & Turner, J. C. (1979). An integrative theory of intergroup conflict. In W. G. Austin, & S. Worchel (Eds.), *The social psychology of intergroup relations*. Montery, CA: Brooks Cole.

Tanford, S., & Penrod, S. (1984). Social influence model: A formal integration of research on majority and minority influence processes. *Psychological Bulletin*, 95, 189–225.

Tashiro, T., & Frazier, P. (2003). 'I'll never be in a relationship like that again': Personal growth following romantic relationship breakups. *Personal Relationships*, 10, 113–128.

Taylor, D. A., Gould, R. J., & Brounstein, P. J. (1981). Effects of personalistic self-disclosure. *Personality and Social Psychology Bulletin*, 7, 487–492.

Taylor, D. M. & Moghaddam, F. M. (1994). *Theories of intergroup relations: International social psychological perspectives* (2nd ed.). Westport, Connecticut: Praeger.

Taylor, S. (1989). *Positive Illusions: Creative Self-deception and the Healthy Mind*. New York: Basic Books.

Taylor, S., & Brown, J. (1988). Illusion and well-being: A social psychological perspective on mental health. *Psychological Bulletin*, 103, 193–210.

Taylor, S., & Fiske, S. (1975). Point of view and perceptions of causality. *Journal of Personality and Social Psychology*, 32, 439–445.

Taylor, S. E., & Brown, J. D., (1988). Illusion and well-being: A social psychological perspective on mental health. *Psychological Bulletin*, 103, 193–210.

Taylor, S. E., (1991). *Positive illusions*. New York: Basic.

Taylor, S. E., & Brown, J. D. (1994). Positive illusions and well-being revisited: Separating fact from fiction. *Psychological Bulletin, 116*, 21–27

Taylor, S. E., Sherman, D. K., Kim, H. S., Jarcho, J., Takagi, K., & Dunagan, M. S. (2004). Culture and social support: Who seeks it and why? *Journal of Personality and Social Psychology, 87*, 354–362.

Tazelaar, M. J. A., van Lange, P. A. M., & Ouwerkerk, J. W. (2004). How to cope with "noise" in social dilemmas: The benefits of communication. *Journal of Personality and Social Psychology, 87*, 845–859.

Teger, A. I., & Pruitt, D. G. (1967). Components of group risk taking. *Journal of Experimental Social Psychology, 3*, 189–205.

Tesser, A. (1980). Self-esteem maintenance in family dynamics. *Journal of Personality and Social Psychology, 39*, 77–91.

Tesser, A. (1993). The importance of heritability in psychological research: The case of attitudes. *Psychological Review, 100*, 129–142.

Tesser, A., & Smith, J. (1980). Some effects of task relevance and friendship on helping: You don't always help the one you like. *Journal of Experimental Social Psychology, 16*, 582–590.

Tetlock, P. (2005). *Expert political judgment: How good is it? How can we know?* Princeton, NJ: Princeton University Press.

Tetlock, P. E., Peterson, R. S., McGuire, C., Chang, S., & Feld, P. (1992). Assessing political group dynamics: A test of the groupthink model. *Journal of Personality and Social Psychology, 63*, 403–425.

Thaler, R. (1980). Towards a positive theory of consumer choice. *Journal of Economic Behavior and Organization, 1*, 39–60.

The Daily Telegraph. (2009, December 21). Facebook fuelling divorce, research claims. *The Daily Telegraph*. Retrieved from www.telegraph.co.uk/technology/facebook/6857918/Facebook-fuelling-divorce-research-claims.html

Thibaut, J. W., & Kelley, H. H. (1959). *The Social Psychology of Groups*. New York: Wiley.

Thomas, G. C., Batson, C. D., & Coke, J. S. (1981). Do good samaritans discourage helpfulness? Self-perceived altruism after exposure to highly helpful others. *Journal of Personality and Social Psychology, 40*, 194–200.

Thomas, M. H. (1982). Physiological arousal, exposure to a relatively lengthy aggressive film, and aggressive behavior. *Journal of Research in Personality, 16*, 72–81.

Thomas, M. H., & Drabman, R. S. (1978). Effects of television violence on expectations of other's aggression. *Personality and Social Psychology Bulletin, 4*, 73–76.

Thompson, L., & Hrebec, D. (1996). Lose-lose agreements in interdependent decision making. *Psychological Bulletin, 120*, 396–409.

Thompson, L., Peterson, E., & Brodt, S. E. (1996). Team negotiation: An examination of integrative and distributive bargaining. *Journal of Personality and Social Psychology, 70*, 66–78.

Thompson, S. (1999). Illusions of control: How we overestimate our personal influence. *Current Directions in Psychological Science, 8*, 187–190.

Thompson, W. C., Cowan, C. L., & Rosenhan, D. L. (1980). Focus of attention mediates the impact of negative affect on altruism. *Journal of Personality and Social Psychology, 38*, 291–300.

Tilker, H. A. (1970). Socially responsible behavior as a function of observer responsibility and victim feedback. *Journal of Personality and Social Psychology, 14*, 95–100.

Tishkoff, S. A., & Kidd, K. K. (2004). Implications of biogeography of human populations for "race" and medicine. *Nature Genetics, 36*, S21–27.

Tobin, R. J., & Eagles, M. (1992). U.S. and Canadian attitudes toward international interactions: A cross-national test of the double-standard hypothesis. *Basic and Applied Social Psychology, 13*, 447–459.

Todorov, A., Mandisodza, A., Goren, A., & Hall, C. (2005). Inferences of competence from faces predict election outcomes. *Science, 308*, 1623–1626.

Toi, M., & Batson, C. D. (1982). More evidence that empathy is a source of altruistic motivation. *Journal of Personality and Social Psychology, 43*, 281–292.

Tolstoy, L. N. (1978). *Anna Karenin* (R. Edmonds, Trans.). London: Penguin. (Original work published 1878).

Tormala, Z. L., & Clarkson, J. J. (2007). Assimilation and contrast in persuasion: The effects of source credibility in multiple message situations. *Personality and Social Psychology Bulletin, 33*, 559–571.

Tormala, Z. L., & Petty, R. E. (2004). Resistance to persuasion and attitude certainty: The moderating role of elaboration. *Personality and Social Psychology Bulletin, 30*, 1446–1457.

Towles-Schwen, T., & Fazio, R. H. (2001). On the origins of racial attitudes: Correlates of childhood experiences. *Personality and Social Psychology Bulletin, 27*, 162–175.

Trafimow, D., & Finlay, K. (1996). The importance of subjective norms for a minority of people: Between-subjects and within-subjects analyses. *Personality and Social Psychology Bulletin, 22*, 820–828.

Trafimow, D., Silverman, E., Fan, R., & Law, J. (1997). The effects of language and priming on the relative accessibility of the private self and the collective self. *Journal of Cross-Cultural Psychology, 28*, 107–123.

Tremblay, P. F., Graham, K., & Wells, S. (2008). Severity of physical aggression reported by university students: A test of the interaction between trait aggression and alcohol consumption. *Personality and Individual Differences, 45*, 3–9.

Trenholm, C., Devaney, B., Fortson, K., Clark, M., Bridgespan, L. Q., & Wheeler, J. (2007). Impacts of abstinence education on teen sexual activity, risk of pregnancy, and risk of sexually transmitted diseases. *Journal of Policy Analysis and Management, 27*, 255–276.

Triandis, H. (1989). The self and social behavior in differing cultural contexts. *Psychological Review, 96*, 506–520.

Triandis, H. C. (1972). *The Analysis of Subjective Culture*. New York: Wiley.

Triandis, H. C., & Trafimow, D. (2001). Culture and its implications for intergroup behaviour. In R. Brown & S. L. Gaertner (Eds.), *Blackwell handbook of social psychology: Intergroup processes* (pp. 367–385). Malden, MA: Blackwell.

Triandis, H. C., Chen, X. P., & Chan, D. K. (1998). Scenarios for the measurement of collectivism and individualism. *Journal of Cross-Cultural Psychology, 29*, 275–289.

Triandis, H.C., Marin, G., Lisansky, J., & Betancourt, H. H. (1984). Simpatia as a cultural script of Hispanics. *Journal of Personality and Social Psychology, 47*, 1363–1375.

Triandis, H. C., McCusker, C., & Hui, C. H. (1990). Multimethod probes of individualism and collectivisim. *Journal of Personality and Social Psychology, 59*, 1006–1020.

Triandis, H. C., & Triandis, L. M. (1962). A cross-cultural study of social distance. *Psychological Monographs, 76*(21), no. 540. Washington: APA.

Tripathi, R. C., & Srivastava, R. (1981). Relative deprivation and intergroup attitudes. *European Journal of Social Psychology, 11*, 313–318.

Triplett, N. (1898). The dynamogenic factors in pacemaking and competition. *American Journal of Psychology, 9*, 507–533.

Trivers, R. L. (1971). The evolution of reciprocal altruism. *The Quarterly Review of Biology, 46*, 35–57.

Trivers, R. L. (1985). *Social Evolution*. Menlo Park, CA: Benjamin/Cummings.

Trope, Y., & Thompson, E. P. (1997). Looking for truth in all the wrong places? Asymmetric search of individuating information about stereotyped group members. *Journal of Personality and Social Psychology, 73*, 229–241.

Tsai, J., Simeonova, D., & Watanabe, J. (2004). Somatic and social: Chinese Americans talk about emotion. *Personality and Social Psychology Bulletin, 30*, 1226–1238.

Tupperware Brands: The Company (2008). Retrieved from http://www.tupperwarebrands.com/company.html

Turner, J. C. (1982). Towards a cognitive redefinition of the social group. In H. Tajfel (Ed.), *Social identity and intergroup relations.* Cambridge: Cambridge University Press.

Turner, J. C. (1987). Introducing the problem: Individual and group. In J. C. Turner, M. A. Hogg, P. J. Oakes, S. D. Reicher, & M. S. Wetherell (Eds.), *Rediscovering the social group: A self-categorization theory.* Oxford: Basil Blackwell.

Turner, L. (2005). Is cultural sensitivity sometimes insensitive? *Canadian Family Physician, 5*, 478–480.

Turner, M. E., Pratkanis, A. R., Probasco, P., & Leve, C. (1992). Threat, cohesion, and group effectiveness: Testing a social identity maintenance perspective on groupthink. *Journal of Personality and Social Psychology, 63*, 781–796.

Tversky, A., & Kahneman, D. (1973). Availability: A heuristic for judging frequency and probability. *Cognitive Psychology, 5*, 207–232.

Tversky, A., & Kahneman, D. (1974). Judgment under uncertainty: Heuristics and biases. *Science, 185*, 1124–1131.

Tversky, A., & Kahneman, D. (1981). The framing of decisions and the psychology of choice. *Science, 211*, 453–458.

Twenge, J. M., Baumeister, R. F., DeWall, C. N., Ciarocco, N. J., & Bartels, J. M. (2007). Social exclusion decreases prosocial behavior. *Journal of Personality and Social Psychology, 92*, 56–66.

Twenge, J. M., Baumeister, R. F., Tice, D. M., & Stucke, T. S. (2001). If you can't join them, beat them: Effects of social exclusion on aggressive behavior. *Journal of Personality and Social Psychology, 81*, 1058–1069.

Tykocinski, O., & Pittman, T. (1998). The consequences of doing nothing: Inaction inertia as avoidance of anticipated counterfactual regret. *Journal of Personality and Social Psychology, 75*, 607–616.

Tykocinski, O., Pittman, T., & Tuttle, E. (1995). Inaction inertia: Foregoing future benefits as a result of an initial failure to act. *Journal of Personality and Social Psychology, 68*, 793–803.

Uchida, Y., Norasakkunkit, V., & Kitayama, S. (2004). Cultural constructions of happiness: Theory and empirical evidence. *Journal of Happiness Studies, 5*(3), 223–239.

Uchino, B. N., Cacioppo, J. T., & Kiecolt-Glaser, J. K. (1996). The relationship between social support and physiological processes: A review with emphasis on underlying mechanisms and implications for health. *Psychological Bulletin, 119*, 488–531.

Uehara, E. S. (1995). Reciprocity reconsidered: Gouldner's 'moral norm of reciprocity' and social support. *Journal of Social and Personal Relationships, 12*, 483–502.

Uhlmann, E. L., & Cohen, G. L. (2005). Constructed criteria: Redefining merit to justify discrimination. *Psychological Science, 16*, 474–480.

United Nations (2009). Field update on Gaza from the humanitarian coordinator 24–26 January 2009, 1700 hours. Report prepared by the Office for the Coordination of Humanitarian Affairs. Retrieved from http://www.ochaopt.org/documents/ocha_opt_gaza_humanitarian_situation_report_2009_01_26_english.pdf

United Nations Office on Drugs and Crimes (2010). Retrieved from http://www.unodc.org/unodc/en/data-and-analysis/homicide.html

Väänänen, A., Buunk, B. P., Kivimäki, M., Pentti, J., & Vahtera, J. (2005). When it is better to give than to receive: Long-term health effects of perceived reciprocity in support exchange. *Journal of Personality and Social Psychology, 89*, 176–193.

Valins, S. (1966). Cognitive effects of false heart-rate feedback. *Journal of Personality and Social Psychology, 4*, 400–408.

Vallone, R., Griffin, D., Lin, S., & Ross, L. (1990). Overconfident prediction of future actions and outcomes by self and others. *Journal of Personality and Social Psychology, 58*, 582–592.

Van Boven, L., White, K., Kamada, A., & Gilovich, T. (2003). Intuitions about situational correction in self and others. *Journal of Personality and Social Psychology, 85*, 249–258.

van Dick, R., Wagner, U., Pettigrew, T. F., Christ, O., Wolf, C., Petzel, T., et al. (2004). Role of perceived importance in intergroup contact. *Journal of Personality and Social Psychology, 87*, 211–227.

van Dijk, E., Wilke, H., & Wit, A. (2003). Preferences for leadership in social dilemmas: Public good dilemmas versus common resource dilemmas. *Journal of Experimental Social Psychology, 39*, 170–176.

van Engen, M. L., & Willemsen, T. M. (2004). Sex and leadership styles: A meta-analysis of research published in the 1990s. *Psychological Reports, 94*, 3–18.

van Kleef, G. A., De Dreu, C. K. W., & Manstead, A. S. R. (2004). The interpersonal effects of emotions in negotiations: A motivated information processing approach. *Journal of Personality and Social Psychology, 87*, 510–528.

van Lange, P. A. M., van Vugt, M., Meertens, R. M., & Ruiter, R. A. C. (1998). A social dilemma analysis of commuting preferences: The roles of social value orientation and trust. *Journal of Applied Social Psychology, 28*, 796–820.

van Vugt, M. (2001). Community identification moderating the impact of financial incentives in a natural social dilemma: Water conservation. *Personality and Social Psychology Bulletin, 27*, 1440–1449.

Van Yperen, N. W., & Buunk, B. P. (1990). A longitudinal study of equity and satisfaction in intimate relationships. *European Journal of Social Psychology, 20*, 287–309.

Van Boven, L., Kamada, A., & Gilovich, T. (1999). The perceiver as perceived: Everyday intuitions about the correspondence bias. *Journal of Personality and Social Psychology, 77*, 1188–1199.

Vandello, J. A., & Cohen, D. (2003). Male honor and female fidelity: Implicit cultural scripts that perpetuate domestic violence. *Journal of Personality and Social Psychology, 84*, 997–1010.

Vandello, J. A., Cohen, D., Grandon, R., & Franiuk, R. (2009). Stand by your man: Indirect prescriptions for honorable violence and feminine loyalty in Canada, Chile, and the United States. *Journal of Cross-Cultural Psychology, 40*, 81–104.

Vanneman, R. D., & Pettigrew, T. F. (1972). Race and relative deprivation in the United States. *Race, 13*, 461–486.

Vedder, P., van de Vijver, F. J. R., & Liebkind, K. (2006). Predicting immigrant youths' adaptation across countries and ethnocultural groups. In J. W. Berry, J. S. Phinney, D. L. Sam, & P. Vedder (Eds.), *Immigrant youth in cultural transition: Acculturation, identity, and adaptation across national contexts.* Mahwah, NJ: Lawrence Erlbaum Associates.

Velasquez, A.M., Santo, J.B., Saldarriaga, L.M., Lopez, L.H., & Bukowski, W.M. (2010). Context-dependent victimization and aggression differences between all-girl and mixed-sex schools. *Merrill-Palmer Quarterly, 56*(3),283–302.

Verhofstadt, L. L., Buysee, A., De Clercq, A., & Goodwin, R. (2005). Emotional arousal and negative affect in marital conflict: The influence of gender, conflict structure, and demand-withdrawal. *European Journal of Social Psychology, 35*, 449–467.

Verplanken, B. (1991). Persuasive communication of risk information: A test of cue versus message processing effects in a field experiment. *Personality and Social Psychology Bulletin, 17*, 188–193.

Villeneuve, P. J., Holowaty, E. J., Brisson, J., Xie, L., Ugnat, A-M., Latulippe, L., & Mao, Y. (2006). Mortality among Canadian women with cosmetic breast implants. *American Journal of Epidemiology, 164* (4), 334–341.

Visser, P., & Mirabile, R. (2004). Attitudes in the social context: The impact of social network composition on individual-level attitude strength. *Journal of Personality and Social Psychology, 87*, 779–795.

Visser, P., Krosnick, J., & Simmons, J. (2003). Distinguishing the cognitive and behavioral consequences of attitude and certainty: A new approach to testing the common-factor hypothesis. *Journal of Experimental Social Psychology, 39*, 118–141.

Visser, P. S., & Krosnick, J. A. (1998). Development of attitude strength over the life cycle: Surge and decline. *Journal of Personality and Social Psychology, 75*, 1389–1410.

Vittengl, J. R., & Holt, C. S. (2000). Getting acquainted: The relationship of self-disclosure and social attraction to positive affect. *Journal of Social and Personal Relationships, 17*, 53–66.

Vivian, J. E., & Berkowitz, N. H. (1992). Anticipated bias from an outgroup: An attributional analysis. *European Journal of Social Psychology, 22*, 415–424.

Vivian, J. E., & Berkowitz, N. H. (1993). Anticipated outgroup evaluations and intergroup bias. *European Journal of Social Psychology, 23*, 513–524.

Von Arnim, E. (1922). *The enchanted April.* London: Virago Press.

von Hippel, W., Silver, L. A., & Lynch, M. E. (2000). Stereotyping against your will: The role of inhibitory ability in stereotyping and prejudice among the elderly. *Personality and Social Psychology Bulletin, 26*, 523–532.

Vonk, R. (1993). The negativity effect in trait ratings and in open-ended descriptions of persons. *Personality and Social Psychology Bulletin, 19*, 269–278.

Vonk, R. (1998). The slime effect: Suspicion and dislike of likeable behavior toward superiors. *Journal of Personality and Social Psychology, 74*, 849–864.

Vonk, R. (1999). Differential evaluations of likeable and dislikeable behaviours enacted towards superiors and subordinates. *European Journal of Social Psychology, 29*, 139–146.

Vonofakou, C., Hewstone, M., & Voci, A. (2007). Contact with out-group friends as a predictor of meta-attitudinal strength and accessibility of attitudes toward gay men. *Journal of Personality and Social Psychology, 92*, 804–820.

Vorauer, J. D. (2005). Miscommunications surrounding efforts to reach out across group boundaries. *Personality and Social Psychology Bulletin, 31*, 1653–1664.

Vorauer, J. D., Cameron, J. J., Holmes, J. G., & Pearce, D. G. (2003). Invisible overtures: Fears of rejection and the signal amplification bias. *Journal of Personality and Social Psychology, 84*, 793–812.

Vorauer, J. D., & Claude, S. D. (1998). Perceived versus actual transparency of goals in negotiation. *Personality and Social Psychology Bulletin, 24*, 371–385.

Vorauer, J. D., Main, K. J., & O'Connell, G. B. (1998). How do individuals expect to be viewed by members of lower status groups? Content and implications of meta-stereotypes. *Journal of Personality and Social Psychology, 75*, 917–937.

Vorauer, J. D., & Ratner, R. K. (1996). Who's going to make the first move? Pluralistic ignorance as an impediment to relationship formation. *Journal of Social and Personal Relationships, 13*, 483–506.

Vorauer, J., & Ross, M. (1999). Self-awareness and feeling transparent: Failing to suppress one's self. *Journal of Experimental Social Psychology, 35*, 415–440.

Vorauer, J. D., & Sasaki, S. J. (2010). In need of liberation or constraint? How intergroup attitudes moderate the behavioral

implications of intergroup ideologies. *Journal of Experimental Social Psychology, 46*, 133–138.

Vorauer, J. D., & Turpie, C. A. (2004). Disruptive effects of vigilance on dominant group members' treatment of outgroup members: Choking versus shining under pressure. *Journal of Personality and Social Psychology, 87*, 384–399.

Vroom, V. H., & Jago, A. G. (2007). The role of the situation in leadership. *American Psychologist, 62*, 17–24.

Wade-Benzoni, K. A., Okumura, T., Brett, J. M., Moore, D. A., Tenbrunsel, A. E., & Bazerman, M. H. (2002). Cognitions and behavior in asymmetric social dilemmas: A comparison of two cultures. *Journal of Applied Psychology, 87*, 87–95.

Wagner, C., & Wheeler, L. (1969). Model, need, and cost effects in helping behavior. *Journal of Personality and Social Psychology, 12*, 111–116.

Wallach, M. A., Kogan, N., & Bem, D. J. (1962). Group influence on individual risk taking. *The Journal of Abnormal and Social Psychology, 65*, 75–86.

Walster, E., Walster, G. W., & Traupmann, J. (1978). Equity and premarital sex. *Journal of Personality and Social Psychology, 36*, 82–92.

Walster, E., Walster, G. W., Piliavin, J., & Schmidt, L. (1973). 'Playing hard to get': Understanding an elusive phenomenon. *Journal of Personality and Social Psychology, 26*, 113–121.

Walther, E. (2002). Guilty by mere association: Evaluative conditioning and the spreading attitude effect. *Journal of Personality and Social Psychology, 82*, 919–934.

Wang, C. L., Bristol, T., Mowen, J. C., & Chakraborty, G. (2000). Alternative modes of self-construal: Dimensions of connectedness-separateness and advertising appeals to the cultural and gender-specific self. *Journal of Consumer Psychology, 9*, 107–115.

Wang, Q. (2001). Culture effects on adults' earliest childhood recollection and self-description: Implications for the relation between memory and the self. *Journal of Personality and Social Psychology, 81*, 220–233.

Wansink, B., van Ittersum, K., & Painter, J. (2006). Ice cream illusions: Bowls, spoons, and self-served portion sizes. *American Journal of Preventive Medicine, 31*, 240–243.

Wapnick, J., Mazza, J. K. & Darrow, A., (2000). Effects of Performer Attractiveness, Stage Behavior, and Dress on Evaluation of Children's Piano Performances. *Journal of Research in Music Education, 48*(4), 323–335.

Watson, R. I. (1973). Investigation into deindividuation using a cross-cultural survey technique. *Journal of Personality and Social Psychology, 25*, 342–345.

Weary, G., Jacobson, J. A., Edwards, J. A., & Tobin, S. J. (2001). Chronic and temporarily activated causal uncertainty beliefs and stereotype usage. *Journal of Personality and Social Psychology, 81*, 206–219.

Weber, R., & Crocker, J. (1983). Cognitive processes in the revision of stereotypic beliefs. *Journal of Personality and Social Psychology, 45*, 961–977.

Weber, R., Ritterfeld, U., & Mathiak, K. (2006). Does playing violent video games induce aggression? Empirical evidence of a functional magnetic resonance imaging study. *Media Psychology, 8*, 39–60.

Webster, D. (1993). Motivated augmentation and reduction of the overattribution bias. *Journal of Personality and Social Psychology, 65*, 261–271.

Webster, D., & Kruglanski, A. (1994). Individual differences in need for cognitive closure. *Journal of Personality and Social Psychology, 67*, 1049–1062.

Webster, D., Richter, L., & Kruglanski, A. (1996). On leaping to conclusions when feeling tired: Mental fatigue effects on impressional primacy. *Journal of Experimental Social Psychology, 32*, 181–195.

Wechsler, H., Dowdall, G., Davenport, A., & Castillo, S. (1995). Correlates of college student binge drinking. *American Journal of Public Health, 85,* 921–926.

Wegener, D. T., & Petty, R. E. (1994). Mood management across affective states: The hedonic contingency hypothesis. *Journal of Personality and Social Psychology, 66,* 1034–1048.

Wegener, D., & Petty, R. (1995). Flexible correction processes in social judgment: The role of naive theories in corrections for perceived bias. *Journal of Personality and Social Psychology, 68,* 36–51.

Wegener, D. T., Petty, R. E., Detweiler-Bedell, B. T., & Jarvis, W. B. G. (2001). Implications of attitude change theories for numerical anchoring: Anchor plausibility and the limits of anchor effectiveness. *Journal of Experimental Social Psychology, 37,* 62–69.

Wegener, D. T., Petty, R. E., & Smith, S. M. (1995). Positive mood can increase or decrease message scrutiny: The hedonic contingency view of mood and message processing. *Journal of Personality and Social Psychology, 69,* 5–15.

Weger, H. Jr., (2005). Disconfirming communication and self-verification in marriage: Associations among the demand/withdraw interaction pattern, feeling understood, and marital satisfaction. *Journal of Social and Personal Relationships, 22,* 19–31.

Wegner, D. (1994). Ironic processes of mental control. *Psychological Review, 101,* 34–52.

Wegner, D., & Gold, D. (1995). Fanning old flames: Emotional and cognitive effects of suppressing thoughts of a past relationship. *Journal of Personality and Social Psychology, 68,* 782–792.

Wegner, D., Shortt, J., Blake, A., & Page, M. (1990). The suppression of exciting thoughts. *Journal of Personality and Social Psychology, 58,* 409–418.

Wegner, D. M. (1997). When the antidote is the poison: Ironic mental control processes. *Psychological Science, 8,* 148–150.

Wegner, D. M., Lane, J. D., & Dimitri, S. (1994). The allure of secret relationships. *Journal of Personality and Social Psychology, 66,* 287–300.

Wehrle, T., Kaiser, S., Schmidt, S., & Scherer, K. (2000). Studying the dynamics of emotional expression using synthesized facial muscle movements. *Journal of Personality and Social Psychology, 78,* 105–119.

Weigel, R. H., Wiser, P. L., & Cook, S. W. (1975). The impact of cooperative learning experiences on cross-ethnic relations and attitudes. *Journal of Social Issues, 31,* 219–244.

Weiner, B. (1979). A theory of motivation for some classroom experiences. *Journal of Educational Psychology, 71,* 3–25.

Weiner, B. (1980). May I borrow your class notes? An attributional analysis of judgments of help giving in an achievement-related context. *Journal of Educational Psychology, 72,* 676–681.

Weiner, B. (1986). Attribution, emotion, and action. In R. M. Sorrentino & E. T. Higgins (Eds.), *Handbook of Motivation and Cognition: Foundations of Social Behavior* (pp. 281–312). New York: Guilford.

Weiner, B., Amirkhan, J., Folkes, V. S., & Verette, J. A. (1987). An attributional analysis of excuse giving: Studies of a naive theory of emotion. *Journal of Personality and Social Psychology, 52,* 316–324.

Weiner, B., Perry, R. P., & Magnusson, J. (1988). An attributional analysis of reactions to stigmas. *Journal of Personality and Social Psychology, 55,* 738–748.

Weinstein, N. (1980). Unrealistic optimism about future life events. *Journal of Personality and Social Psychology, 39,* 806–820.

Weinstein, N. (1984). Why it won't happen to me: Perceptions of risk factors and susceptibility. *Health Psychology, 3,* 431–457.

Weinstein, N. (1987). Unrealistic optimism about susceptibility to health problems: Conclusions from a community-wide sample. *Journal of Behavioral Medicine, 10,* 481–500.

Weinstein, N. D., (1980). Unrealistic optimism about future life events. *Journal of Personality and Social Psychology, 39,* 806–820.

Weiss, B., Dodge, K. A., Bates, J. E., & Pettit, G. S. (1992). Some consequences of early harsh discipline: Child aggression and a maladaptive social information processing style. *Child Development, 63,* 1321–1335.

Weldon, E., & Gargano, G. M. (1988). Cognitive loafing: The effects of accountability and shared responsibility on cognitive effort. *Personality and Social Psychology Bulletin, 14,* 159–171.

Wells, G., & Bradfield, A. (1999). Distortions in eyewitnesses' recollections: Can the postidentification-feedback effect be moderated? *Psychological Science, 10,* 138–144.

Wells, G. L., & Gavanski. I. (1989). Mental simulation of causality. *Journal of Personality and Social Psychology, 56,* 161–169.

Wells, G. L., Olson, E. A., & Charman, S. D. (2003). Distorted retrospective eyewitness reports as functions of feedback and delay. *Journal of Experimental Psychology: Applied, 9,* 42–52.

Werhun, C. G., & Penner, A. J. (2010). The effects of stereotyping and implicit theory on benevolent prejudice toward Aboriginal Canadians. *Journal of Applied Social Psychology, 40,* 899–916.

Werner, C. M., Byerly, S., White, P. H., & Kieffer, M. (2004). Validation, persuasion and recycling: Capitalizing on the social ecology of newspaper use. *Basic and Applied Social Psychology, 26,* 183–198.

Werner, C. M., Stoll, R., Birch, P., & White, P. H. (2002). Clinical validation and cognitive elaboration: Signs that encourage sustained recycling. *Basic and Applied Social Psychology, 24,* 185–203.

Westen, D., Blagov, P. S., Harenski, K., Kilts, C., & Hamann, S. (2006). Neural bases of motivated reasoning: An fMRI study of emotional constraints on partisan political judgment in the 2004 U.S. presidential election. *Journal of Cognitive Neuroscience, 18,* 1947–1958.

Westmaas, J. L., & Silver, R. C. (2006). The role of perceived similarity in supportive responses to victims of negative life events. *Personality and Social Psychology Bulletin, 32,* 1537–1546.

Weyant, J. M. (1978). Effects of mood states, costs, and benefits on helping. *Journal of Personality and Social Psychology, 36,* 1169–1176.

Wheeler, L., & Kim, Y. (1997). What is beautiful is culturally good: The physical attractiveness stereotype has different content in collectivistic cultures. *Personality and Social Psychology Bulletin, 23,* 795–800.

White, G. L., Fishbein, S., & Rutsein, J. (1981). Passionate love and the misattribution of arousal. *Journal of Personality and Social Psychology, 41,* 56–62.

White, J. W., & Roufail, M. (1989). Gender and influence strategies of first choice and last resort. *Psychology of Women Quarterly, 13*(2), 175–189.

White, K., & Lehman, D. (2005). Culture and social comparison seeking: The role of self-motives. *Personality and Social Psychology Bulletin, 31,* 232–242.

Whitley, B. E. (1993). Reliability and aspects of the construct validity of Sternberg's Triangular Love Scale. *Journal of Social and Personal Relationships, 10,* 475–480.

Whitley, B. E. J. (1999). Right-wing authoritarianism, social dominance orientation, and prejudice. *Journal of Personality and Social Psychology, 77,* 126–134.

Whyte, G. (1998). Recasting Janis's groupthink model: The key role of collective efficacy in decision fiascoes. *Organizational Behavior and Human Decision Processes, 73,* 185–209.

Wicklund, R. A., & Frey, D. (1980). Self-awareness theory: When the self makes a difference. In D. M. Wegner, & R. R. Vallacher (Eds.), *The self in social psychology* (pp. 31–54). New York: Oxford University Press.

Wilder, D. A. (1990). Some determinants of the persuasive power of in-groups and out-groups: Organization of information and attribution of independence. *Journal of Personality and Social Psychology, 59*, 1202–1213.

Wilder, D. A., Simon, A. F., & Faith, M. (1996). Enhancing the impact of counterstereotypic information: Dispositional attributions for deviance. *Journal of Personality and Social Psychology, 71*, 276–287.

Wilke, H., & Lanzetta, J. T. (1970). The obligation to help: The effects of amount of prior help on subsequent helping behavior. *Journal of Experimental Social Psychology, 6*, 488–493.

Wilke, H., & Lanzetta, J. T. (1982). The obligation to help: Factors affecting response to help received. *European Journal of Social Psychology, 12*, 315–319.

Williams, J. E., & Best, D. L. (1990). *Measuring sex stereotypes: A multi-nation study* (Rev. ed.). Newbury Park, CA: Sage.

Williams, K. D., & Karau, S. J. (1991). Social loafing and social compensation: The effects of expectations of co-worker performance. *Journal of Personality and Social Psychology, 61*, 570–581.

Williams, K. D., Bourgeois, M. J., & Croyle, R. T. (1993). The effects of stealing thunder in criminal and civil trials. *Law and Human Behavior, 17*, 597–609.

Williams, K. D., Nida, S. A., Baca, L. D., & Latané, B. (1989). Social loafing and swimming: Effects of identifiability on individual and relay performance of intercollegiate swimmers. *Basic and Applied Social Psychology, 10*, 73–81.

Williams, K., Harkins, S. G., & Latané, B. (1981). Identifiability as a deterrent to social loafing: Two cheering experiments. *Journal of Personality and Social Psychology, 40*, 303–311.

Williams, S., Kimble, D., Covell, N., & Weiss, L. (1992). College students use implicit personality theory instead of safer sex. *Journal of Applied Social Psychology, 22*, 921–933.

Williams, W. (1991). *Javanese lives: Men and women in modern Indonesian society*. New Brunswick, NJ: Rutgers University Press.

Wilson, D. W. (1978). Helping behavior and physical attractiveness. *Journal of Social Psychology, 104*, 313–314.

Wilson, D., Kaplan, R., & Schneiderman, L. (1987). Framing of decisions and selections of alternatives in health care. *Social Behaviour, 2*, 51–59.

Wilson, M., & Dovidio, J. F. (1985). Effects of perceived attractiveness and feminist orientation on helping behavior. *Journal of Social Psychology, 125*, 415–420.

Wilson, M. I., & Daly, M. (1996). Male sexual proprietariness and violence against wives. *Current Directions in Psychological Science, 5*, 2–7.

Wilson, T. D., Dunn, D. S., Bybee, J. A., Hyman, D. B., & Rotondo, J. A. (1984). Effects of analyzing reasons on attitude–behavior consistency. *Journal of Personality and Social Psychology, 47*, 5–16.

Wilson, T., & LaFleur, S. (1995). Knowing what you'll do: Effects of analyzing reasons on self-prediction. *Journal of Personality and Social Psychology, 68*, 21–35.

Wilson, T., Laser, P., & Stone, J. (1982). Judging the predictors of one's own mood: Accuracy and the use of shared theories. *Journal of Experimental Social Psychology, 18*, 537–556.

Wilson, T., Lisle, D., Schooler, J., Hodges, S., Klaaren, K. J., & LaFleur, S. J. (1993). Introspecting about reasons can reduce post-choice satisfaction. *Personality and Social Psychology Bulletin, 19*, 331–339.

Wilson, T., Wheatley, T., Meyers, J., Gilbert, D., & Axsom, D. (2000). Focalism: A source of durability bias in affective forecasting. *Journal of Personality and Social Psychology, 78*, 821–836.

Windschitl, P., Kruger, J., & Simms, E. (2003). The influence of egocentrism and focalism on people's optimism in competitions: When what affects us equally affects me more. *Journal of Personality and Social Psychology, 85*, 389–408.

Winnipeg Free Press, (2011, March 31). Japanese quake: Rising radiation stirs concern about food safety and evacuations. *Winnipeg Free Press*. Retrieved from http://www.winnipegfreepress.com/world/japanese-quake-rising-radiation-stirs-concern-about-food-safety-and-evacuations-118974149.html

Wintemute, G. J., Parham, C. A., Beaumont, J. J., Wright, M., & Drake, C. (1999). Mortality among recent purchasers of handguns. *New England Journal of Medicine, 341*, 1583–1589.

Witkin, H. A., & Berry, J. W. (1975). Psychological differentiation in cross-cultural perspective. *Journal of Cross-Cultural Psychology, 19*, 1–15.

Witkin, H. A., Moore, C. A., Goodenough, D. R., & Cox, P. W. (1977). Field-dependent and field-independent cognitive styles and their educational implications. *Review of Educational Research, 47*, 1–64.

Wittenbrink, B., & Henly, J. R. (1996). Creating social reality: Informational social influence and the content of stereotypic beliefs. *Personality and Social Psychology Bulletin, 22*, 598–610.

Wittenbrink, B., Judd, C. M., & Park, B. (2001). Spontaneous prejudice in context: Variability in automatically activated attitudes. *Journal of Personality and Social Psychology, 81*, 815–827.

Witvliet, C. V., Ludwig, T. E., & Vander Laan, K. L. (2001). Granting forgiveness or harboring grudges: Implications for emotion, physiology, and health. *Psychological Science, 12*, 117–123.

Wohl, M. J. A., & Branscombe, N. R. (2005). Forgiveness and collective guilt assignment to historical perpetrator groups depend on level of social category inclusiveness. *Journal of Personality and Social Psychology, 88*, 288–303.

Wolsko, C., Park, B., Judd, C. M., & Wittenbrink, B. (2000). Framing interethnic ideology: Effects of multicultural and color-blind perspectives on judgments of groups and individuals. *Journal of Personality and Social Psychology, 78*, 635–654.

Wong, R. Y., & Hong, Y. (2005). Dynamic influences of culture on cooperation in the prisoner's dilemma. *Psychological Science, 16*, 429–434.

Wood, J. V., Giordano-Beech, M., & Ducharme, M. J. (1999). Compensating for failure through social comparison. *Personality and Social Psychology Bulletin, 25*, 1370–1386.

Wood, W. (1982). Retrieval of attitude-relevant information from memory: Effects on susceptibility to persuasion and on intrinsic motivation. *Journal of Personality and Social Psychology, 42*, 798–810.

Wood, W., & Eagly, A. H. (1981). Stages in the analysis of persuasive messages: The role of causal attributions and message comprehension. *Journal of Personality and Social Psychology, 40*, 246–259.

Wood, W., Kallgren, C. A., & Preisler, R. M. (1985). Access to attitude-relevant information in memory as a determinant of persuasion: The role of message attributes. *Journal of Experimental Social Psychology, 21*, 73–85.

Wood, W., Lundgren, S., Ouellette, J. A., Busceme, S., & Blackstone, T. (1994). Minority influence: A meta-analytic review of social influence processes. *Psychological Bulletin, 115*, 323–345.

Wood, W., Pool, G. J., Leck, K., & Purvis, D. (1996). Self-definition, defensive processing, and influence: The normative impact of majority and minority groups. *Journal of Personality and Social Psychology, 71*, 1181–1193.

Wood, W., Wong, F. Y., & Chachere, J. G. (1991). Effects of media violence on viewers' aggression in unconstrained social interaction. *Psychological Bulletin, 109*, 371–383.

Worchel, S., Lee, J., & Adewole, A. (1975). Effects of supply and demand on ratings of object value. *Journal of Personality and Social Psychology, 32*, 906–914.

Word, C. O., Zanna, M. P., & Cooper, J. (1974). The nonverbal mediation of self-fulfilling prophecies in interracial interaction. *Journal of Experimental Social Psychology, 10*, 109–120.

Wright, A. F. (1960) *The Confucian persuasion*. Stanford, CA: Stanford University Press.

Wright, S. C., Aron, A., McLaughlin-Volpe, T., & Ropp, S. A. (1997). The extended contact effect: Knowledge of crossgroup friendships and prejudice. *Journal of Personality and Social Psychology, 73*, 73–90.

Wyer, N. A. (2004). Not all stereotypic biases are created equal: Evidence for a stereotype-disconfirming bias. *Personality and Social Psychology Bulletin, 30*, 706–720.

Wyer, N. A., Sherman, J. W., & Stroessner, S. J. (2000). The roles of motivation and ability in controlling the consequences of stereotype suppression. *Personality and Social Psychology Bulletin, 26*, 13–25.

Xiaohe, X., & Whyte, M. K. (1990). Love matches and arranged marriages: A Chinese replication. *Journal of Marriage & the Family, 52*, 709–722.

Yagi, Y., & Shimizu, T. (1996). Helping behavior following a failure experience. *Japanese Psychological Research, 38*, 53–65.

Yakimovich, D., & Saltz, E. (1971). Helping behavior: The cry for help. *Psychonomic Science, 23*, 427–428.

Ybarra, M. L., Mitchell, K. J., Wolak, J., & Finkelhor, D. (2006). Examining characteristics and associated distress related to Internet harassment: Findings from the Second Youth Internet Safety Survey. *Pediatrics, 118*, 1169–1177.

Yi, S. & Baumgartner, H. (2009). Regulatory focus and message framing: A test of three accounts. *Motivation and Emotion. 33(4)*, 435–443.

Yik, M., Bond, M., & Paulhus, D. (1998). Do Chinese self-enhance or self-efface? It's a matter of domain. *Personality and Social Psychology Bulletin, 24*, 399–406.

Yim, H.Y.B., & Ebbeck, M. (2009). Children's preferences for group musical activities in child care centres: A cross-cultural study. *Early Childhood Education Journal, 37(4)*, 103–111.

Yoo, B., & Donthu, N. (2005). The effect of personal cultural orientation on consumer ethnocentrism: Evaluations and behaviors of U.S. consumers toward Japanese products. *Journal of International Consumer Marketing, 18*, 7–44.

Young, J. E. Klosko, J. S., & Weishaar, M. E. (2003). *Schema therapy: A practitioner's guide*. New York: Guilford Press.

Yum, Y. (2004). Culture and self-construal as predictors of responses to accommodative dilemmas in dating relationships. *Journal of Social and Personal Relationships, 21*, 817–835.

Zaccaro, S. J. (2007). Trait-based perspectives of leadership. *American Psychologist, 62*, 6–16.

Zahn-Waxler, C., Radke-Yarrow, M., Wagner, E., & Chapman, M. (1992). Development of concern for others. *Developmental Psychology, 28*, 126–136.

Zajonc, R. (1968). Attitudinal effects of mere exposure. *Journal of Personality and Social Psychology, 9*, 1–27.

Zajonc, R. B. (1965). Social facilitation. *Science, 149*, 269–274.

Zajonc, R. B. (2001). Mere exposure: A gateway to the subliminal. *Current Directions in Psychological Science, 10*, 224–228. Retrieved from http://www.ideal.forestry.ubc.ca/frst524/Mere_exposure_gate_way_to_the_subliminal.pdf

Zajonc, R. B., Heingartner, A., & Herman, E. M. (1969). Social enhancement and impairment of performance in the cockroach. *Journal of Personality and Social Psychology, 13*, 83–92.

Zajonc, R. B., & Sales, S. M. (1966). Social facilitation of dominant and subordinate responses. *Journal of Experimental Social Psychology, 2*, 160–168.

Zajonc, R., Murphy, S., & Inglehart, M. (1989). Feeling and facial efference: Implications of the vascular theory of emotion. *Psychological Review, 96*, 395–416.

Zanna, M. P., & Cooper J. (1974). Dissonance and the pill: An attribution approach to studying the arousal properties of dissonance. *Journal of Personality Social Psychology, 29*, 703–709.

Zanna, M., Olson, J., & Fazio, R. (1981). Self-perception and attitude-behavior consistency. *Personality and Social Psychology Bulletin, 7*, 252–256.

Zárate, M., Uleman, J., & Voils, C. (2001). Effects of culture and processing goals on the activation and binding of trait concepts. *Social Cognition, 19*, 295–323.

Zebrowitz, L. A., Collins, M. A., & Dutta, R. (1998). The relationship between appearance and personality across the life span. *Personality and Social Psychology Bulletin, 24*, 736–749.

Zemack-Rugar, Y., Bettman, J., & Fitzsimons, G. (2007). The effects of nonconsciously priming emotion concepts on behavior. *Journal of Personality and Social Psychology, 93*, 927–939.

Zillman, D. (1983). *Transfer of excitation in emotional behavior*. In J. T. Caccioppo & R. E. Petty (Eds.), *Social Psychophysiology* (pp. 214–240). New York: Guilford Press.

Zillman, D., Baron, R. A., & Tamborini, R. (1981). Social costs of smoking: Effects of tobacco smoke on hostile behavior. *Journal of Applied Social Psychology, 11*, 548–561.

Zillman, D., Katcher, A. H., Milavsky, B. (1972). Excitation transfer from physical exercise to subsequent aggressive behavior. *Journal of Experimental Social Psychology, 8*, 247–259.

Zillman, D., & Weaver, J. B. I. (1999). Effects of prolonged exposure to gratuitous media violence on provoked and unprovoked hostile behavior. *Journal of Applied Social Psychology, 29*, 145–165.

Zimbardo, P. G. (1969). The human choice: Individuation, reason, and order vs. deindividuation, impulse and chaos. In W. J. Arnold & D. Levine (Eds.), *Nebraska Symposium on Motivation* (Vol. 17, pp. 237–307). Lincoln, NE: Univ. of Nebraska Press.

Zuckerman, M., Kieffer, S., & Knee, C. (1998). Consequences of self-handicapping: Effects on coping, academic performance, and adjustment. *Journal of Personality and Social Psychology, 74*, 1619–1628.

Zuckerman, M., Knee, C., Hodgins, H., & Miyake, K. (1995). Hypothesis confirmation: The joint effect of positive test strategy and acquiescence response set. *Journal of Personality and Social Psychology, 68*, 52–60.

Zuwerink, J. R., & Devine, P. G. (1996). Attitude importance and resistance to persuasion: It's not just the thought that counts. *Journal of Personality and Social Psychology, 70*, 931–944.

NAME INDEX

SUBJECT INDEX